FINANCIAL & MANAGERIAL ACCOUNTING

Houghton Mifflin Company   Boston

Dallas   Geneva, Illinois   Palo Alto   Princeton, New Jersey

FINANCIAL & MANAGERIAL ACCOUNTING

Belverd E. Needles, Jr.
Ph.D., CPA, CMA
Professor of Accounting
DePaul University

Henry R. Anderson
Ph.D., CPA, CMA
Professor of Accounting
Director, School of Accounting
University of Central Florida

James C. Caldwell
Ph.D., CPA
Partner, Educational Consulting Services
Arthur Andersen & Co.
Dallas/Fort Worth

To: **Professor Reginald R. Rushing**
Texas Tech University

Professor S. James Galley
Augustana College (Illinois)

Professor W. Baker Flowers
University of Alabama

For motivating and guiding us through our undergraduate accounting programs and inspiring us to become accounting educators.

Cover photograph by Gorchev & Gorchev

Printed in the U.S.A.

Library of Congress Catalog Card Number: 87-80110

ISBN: 0-395-43348-7

BCDEFGHIJ-VH-9543210-898

CONTENTS

Note: The topic of income tax is integrated throughout the book at those points where it is relevant to the discussion. Appendix F covers personal income taxes.

LOTUS® Problems for Accounting workbooks and accompanying LOTUS® template diskettes can be used to solve the end of chapter problems.

PREFACE

FINANCIAL & MANAGERIAL ACCOUNTING is a comprehensive first course in accounting for students with no previous training in accounting or business. Designed for both majors and non-majors, it is intended for use in two-semester, two-quarter, or three-quarter sequences in which there is an equal emphasis of financial and managerial accounting. The textbook is part of a well-integrated package of materials for students and instructors, including both manual and computer ancillaries.

Objectives of This Textbook

Our discussions with college and university instructors throughout the country lead us to believe that in today's environment there is a desire on the part of many of our colleagues for a new organization to the principles of accounting course, one that devotes approximately the same amount of time to managerial accounting as it does to financial accounting while maintaining the same pedagogical method that has been used successfully in the principles course for many years. Specifically, our objectives in writing this textbook are:

1. To provide equal coverage of financial accounting and managerial accounting;
2. To provide more coverage of managerial accounting than is found in the typical principles of accounting textbook;
3. To cover both topics at a level suitable for freshman and sophomore students.

Equal Coverage of Financial and Managerial Accounting

This text contains twenty-eight chapters. Chapters 1–14 are financial accounting topics, and chapters 15–28 are managerial accounting topics. Sometimes considered to be financial accounting topics, the statement of cash flows and financial statement analysis, Chapters 27 and 28, respectively, may be inserted immediately after Chapter 14, if desired.

Increased Coverage of Managerial Accounting

With twelve chapters devoted to managerial accounting, our text provides the most complete coverage of managerial accounting of any principles textbook. This coverage is equivalent to that found in single volume managerial accounting books and means that students are introduced to the field of management accounting in a patient, pedagogically sound way and that the topics are covered thoroughly enough to give students an understanding of the topics that they can use throughout their future business and accounting careers.

Coverage at the Principles Level

Using the time-tested approach to the principles course, this text presents the accounting cycle and merchandising accounting (Chapters 1–5) based on the sole proprietorship. The approach used in Chapter 6 and following chapters is the same type as that used in single-volume accounting texts based on the corporate approach. Thus, freshmen and sophomore students are introduced to accounting in a way they can understand. At the same time, they are introduced to all the topics necessary to understand at this level the financial reporting of modern corporations. We have judiciously chosen the topics to be covered so that they can be presented with the same readability, pacing of topics, clarity of presentation, and balance of concepts and practices that appears in an optimally organized principles textbook. To provide maximum flexibility, we have also provided a series of six appendixes of optional topics, each presented in a mini-chapter format with exercises and problems.

Features of This Textbook

In writing FINANCIAL & MANAGERIAL ACCOUNTING we have included the same features that have made our previous textbooks among the most widely-used textbooks in accounting education. These features include:

1. Readability and clarity of presentation
2. Integrated learning objectives throughout the package
3. Authoritative, practical, and contemporary content
4. Decision-making emphasis
5. Strict system of quality control
6. Most complete and flexible package.

Readability and Clarity of Presentation

The text's intended audience, the freshman or sophomore student, has influenced the organization of the book in several ways. First, we have carefully planned the timing of new concepts and techniques to facilitate learning. The pace enables the student to grasp and retain the material. Second, we have taken special care, particularly in the early part of the book, to limit the number of difficult concepts or practices in each chapter. Third, clarity of presentation, consistent reading level, and uniform terminology have been rigorously applied throughout the text, including the chapter assignment material. Fourth, we focus throughout on understanding, rather than mere memorization. We believe that concepts take on meaning when applied, and practices are most easily understood if related to a conceptual foundation. Fifth, we emphasize concepts and practices that will be useful to students throughout their careers, whether they are accounting majors or not.

Learning by Objectives

We take a definite pedagogical approach to writing FINANCIAL & MANAGERIAL ACCOUNTING. We have made extensive use of integrated learning objectives and learning theory. Learning objectives are integrated throughout the text and package, from the preview and presentation of the chapters to the assignment material, chapter reviews, study aids, and the testing and evaluation materials.

Authoritative, Practical, and Contemporary

This book presents accounting as it is practiced, but the concepts underlying each accounting practice are also carefully explained. Accounting terms and concepts are defined according to current pronouncements of the AICPA, APB, and FASB. The Statement of Financial Accounting Concepts of the FASB's Conceptual Framework Study form the theoretical underpinning of the book and are used to assess various accounting situations and controversies. In addition, we have taken steps to assure that, to the extent possible within the framework of introductory accounting, the practical material is realistic in terms of how accounting is practiced today.

Decision-Making Emphasis

Another objective has been to present the contemporary business world and the real-life complexities of accounting in a clear, concise, easy-to-understand manner. Accounting is treated as an information system that helps management, investors, and creditors make economic decisions. In addition to other questions, exercises, and problems, the chapter assignments include two decision-oriented features in each chapter—an exercise on "Interpreting Accounting Information" and a "Financial or Management Decision Case." In each situation the student is required to extract quantitative information from the exercise or case and make an interpretation or a decision.

Quality Control

We have developed, together with our publisher, a system of quality control that has been applied to all parts of the package to assure the most technically and conceptually accurate textbook and package possible. Among many other steps, this system involves thorough reviews by users, visits to and discussion with users by the authors, extensive in-house editorial review and accuracy checking, and class testing.

Complete and Flexible Learning System

Finally, we believe that FINANCIAL & MANAGERIAL ACCOUNTING is the most complete and flexible package for a first-year accounting course that places equal emphasis on financial and managerial accounting. All parts of the system fit within the pedagogical system of learning by objectives established by the authors. This comprehensive learning is described in the following sections.

Pedagogical Features

Learning Objectives Action-oriented objectives at the beginning of each chapter indicate in precise terms what the students should be able to do when they complete the chapter. The objectives are stated again in the margins beside pertinent text discussion. Then, the end-of-chapter review clearly relates each objective to the content of the chapter. The end-of-chapter assignments are also keyed to specific learning objectives.

Real-World Applications Many chapters include graphs or tables illustrating the practice of actual businesses in relation to the topics of the chapter. In addition, most of the exercises on Interpreting Accounting Information are based on the published financial reports of real companies.

Key Terms and Glossary Throughout the book, key accounting terms are emphasized with bold color type and clearly defined in context. These terms are also assembled in a comprehensive glossary for easy reference.

Chapter Review A unique feature of each chapter is a special review section comprising (1) a Review of Learning Objectives that summarizes the main points of the chapter in relation to the objectives; (2) a Review Problem with complete solution to demonstrate the Chapter's major procedures before students tackle the exercises and problems; and (3) a Self-Test in Chapters 1 through 7 that reviews the basic concepts of these crucial early chapters, with end-of-chapter answers that provide immediate feedback to the students.

Questions Discussion questions at the end of each chapter focus, for the most part, on major concepts and terms.

Classroom Exercises Classroom Exercises provide practice in applying concepts taught in the chapter and are very effective in illustrating lecture points. Each exercise is keyed to the learning objectives. In addition, transparencies are available for all exercise solutions.

Interpreting Accounting Information This feature asks the student to interpret published financial information (in Chapters 1–14 and 27–28) or internal management reports (in Chapters 15–26). Most are based on excerpts from actual annual reports or on published articles about well-known corporations or organizations. Among the companies included are K Mart, Sears, U.S. Steel, Marathon Oil, Chrysler, Lockheed, and Airborne Express. Each of these exercises required students to demonstrate their ability to interpret published information by extracting data from what they read and by making a computation and interpretation.

A and B Problems We have included two sets of problems to provide maximum flexibility in homework assignments. In general the problems are arranged in order of difficulty, with Problems A-1 or B-1 for each chapter being the simplest and the last in the series the most comprehensive. A and B problems have been matched by topic so that A-1 and B-1, for example, are equivalent in content and level of difficulty. In addition, all problems are keyed to the learning objectives. Difficulty ratings, time estimates, and solutions are available to the instructor. Transparencies of all solutions are also available.

Financial and Management Decision Cases Each chapter contains a case that emphasizes the usefulness of accounting information in making decisions. The business background and financial information for each case are presented in a decision context. The decision maker may be a manager, an investor, an analyst, or a creditor. In the role of decision maker the student is asked to extract the relevant data from the case, make computations as necessary, and make a decision.

Appendixes To provide the maximum flexibility, we have included six appendixes at the end of the book on optional topics that may be inserted as desired by the school or faculty. Each appendix is in mini-chapter format with questions, exercises, and problems. The topics of these appendixes are:

Appendix A: Special-Purpose Journals

Appendix B: Financial Accounting Concepts

Appendix C: The Use of Future Value and Present Value in Accounting

Appendix D: Compound Interest and Present Value Tables

Appendix E: International Accounting

Appendix F: Overview of Income Taxes for Individuals

Supplementary Learning Materials

Study Guide with Selected Readings

This learning aid is a chapter-by-chapter guide to help the student understand the main points of the chapter. Each chapter begins with a summary, organized by learning objective, of the major concepts and applications in the chapter. Next, to test the student's basic knowledge of the chapter content, there are matching, completion, true-false, and multiple choice exercises. Finally, students are asked to apply their knowledge in short exercises. All answers are provided at the end of the Study Guide.

The Study Guide also contains readings selected from professional journals and the popular press to provide broader understanding of the topics in the chapters. A summary of financial accounting theory is also provided. In addition, the complete financial statements with all footnotes, supplementary disclosures, management commentary, and auditor's report for the Coca-Cola Bottling Company are provided for additional student analysis.

Working Papers 1 and 2

Working Papers are designed to accompany all the A & B problems in the text. Forms are provided for each problem with column headings and company names preprinted for easy identification. Working papers for Chapter 27, "The Statement of Cash Flows" and Chapter 28, "Financial Statement Analysis" are included in both volumes to allow for flexible coverage of these chapters during the course.

Traditional Practice Sets

With the exception of *Sailsports* and *The Windham Company,* the following practice sets require a knowledge of special journals and subsidiary ledgers, covered in Appendix A.

Sailsports: Cumulative Practice Set Covers seven months' worth of business transactions for a sole-proprietorship rental company. Provides hands-on training in accounting procedures. (After Chapter 2)

Micro-Tec, 2nd Edition This practice set covers a one-month accounting cycle for a sole-proprietorship merchandising company. It is available in both workbook and business papers formats, and requires about 12 hours to complete. (Chapter 5)

Oak Shoppe: Audit Problem Requires students to use source documents to trace and correct errors in one month's transactions, and then generate an accurate set of financial statements for the company. It requires 10–12 hours to complete. (Chapter 5)

The Book Loft: Shoebox Practice Set This unique practice set requires students to organize a disordered set of documents covering one month's transactions for a retail bookstore, and establish a complete set of accounting records for the company. It requires 10–12 hours to complete. (Chapter 5)

College Words and Sounds Store, 2nd Edition This practice set covers a two-month accounting cycle for a small merchandising concern. In addition to special journals, it deals with credit card sales, petty cash, vouchers, and payroll. This practice set is available in workbook format and requires 12–15 hours. (Chapter 9)

The Windham Company This practice set is really two sets in one. The first (used after Chapter 16) requires students to prepare the worksheet and financial statements for a manufacturer using a periodic inventory system. The second (used after Chapter 17) covers the same tasks for a manufacturing firm using a perpetual inventory system. The practice set has been formatted in such a way that it can be easily solved using the LOTUS® 1-2-3 spreadsheet. This practice set is available in workbook format, requiring about 10 hours.

Financial Analysis Cases

Three financial analysis cases are available to realistically introduce students to the interpretation and analysis of the information contained in a company's annual report. Although both cases are comprehensive in nature, *Heartland Airways* places more emphasis on such issues as debt equity and long-term solvency and *Richland Home Centers, Inc.* places more emphasis on short-term liquidity, inventory management, and accounts receivable. Both cases require students to perform ratio and trend analysis and to prepare a statement of cash flows.

General Mills involves the broad analysis of consolidated financial statements for a major corporation.

All three cases may be introduced after covering the chapters in Part Eight, Analyses of Accounting Information, wherever they may appear in the course.

Management Decision Case

McHenry Hotels, Inc. involves the systematic analysis of the Dallas branch of McHenry Hotels, Inc., a chain of luxury hotels. Students are required to evaluate all major aspects of the hotel's operations, including its accounting system, past and future profitability, and budget, while preparing a comprehensive report for the Board of Directors. (This case may be started after Chapter 21).

Computerized Financial Practice Sets

Instructors may choose among six computer-assisted, interactive practice sets covering a broad range of business organizations and accounting tasks. These practice sets require no prior computer knowledge. They do, however, with the exception of *Sounds Abound* and *Cook's Solar Energy*, require a knowledge of special journals, covered in Appendix A.

Berger Automotive Company and Stormer Painting Company These are computer-assisted, interactive practice sets that can actually be done manually if the instructor wishes. Each covers twelve months' activity, during which time the company evolves from a sole proprietorship service business to a corporation. Transaction analysis is stressed and the speed with which a computer can speed the flow of accounting data is demonstrated. The practice sets require only 40 to 90 minutes a week and can be handled as a laboratory or as a test. (These sets may be begun after Chapter 2.)

Parks Computer Company and Matthew Sports Company Each covers twelve months' financial activity. During this time, each evolves from (1) a sole proprietorship service business to (2) a sole proprietorship merchandising business to (3) a corporation merchandising business to (4) a corporation manufacturing business. Most of the major transactions specific to each form of business organization are covered—from simple sales and purchase transactions, through accounting for cost of goods sold to various stock transactions through such manufacturing accounting procedures as applying factory overhead and accounting for raw materials, work in process, and finished goods inventories. Work sheets and financial statements for a manufacturing business are also covered. (These may be begun after Chapter 2, but a knowledge of special journals, covered in Appendix A, is necessary to begin the fourth month's transactions.)

Cook's Solar Energy Systems, 2nd Ed. Covers a one-month accounting cycle for a sole proprietorship merchandising company. This program covers 50 transactions and requires only 75 minutes of computer time to complete. (Chapter 5)

Sounds Abound This covers 39 transactions comprising a one-month accounting cycle for a sole proprietorship service company. It shows students how to record transactions using a computer and enables them to prepare financial statements automatically. It is easy to use and can be completed in two hours on the computer.

Computerized Managerial Decision Case

Polyform, Inc. is a plastics manufacturing firm. Students are required to evaluate data, make decisions, and analyze those decisions using the microcomputer. A cost and/or managerial emphasis is possible by selecting units from the case's modular organization. (After Chapter 17)

Microcomputer Business Simulations

Lawson's Supply Center, Inc. introduces students to computerized procedures used by a building supplies company to carry out five accounting tasks. Each stand-alone simulation—General Ledger (Chapter 4), Accounts Receivable (Chapter 7), Cash (Chapter 7), Payroll (Chapter 9), and Accounts Payable (Chapter 9)—cover one month's business transactions.

LOTUS® Problems for Accounting Software and Workbook

This disk-based program, when used with the LOTUS® spreadsheet software allows students to select pre-programmed worksheets and use them to solve problems from the text. The workbook contains instructions for using the program. A guide to the templates is available.

TRICALC™ Integrated Software for Accounting and Workbook

This teaches students how to build spreadsheets using approximately 40 problems, similar to those in the text, using the TRICALC™ software program. TRICALC™ software also includes word processing and data base applications.

Instructor's Resource Materials

Instructor's Handbook with Achievement Tests The Instructor's Handbook provides for each chapter a list of the topic headings in the text; a learning objectives chart for the end-of-chapter assignments; an analysis of the time and difficulty involved to solve each problem; lecture resource materials that provide, for each learning objective, a summary statement, a list of new words, terms, and related text illustrations, and a suggested lecture outline. Also included are Achievement Tests. Each test covers two or three chapters.

Instructor's Solutions Manual The Instructor's Solutions Manual contains solutions to all questions, exercises, and problems in the text. Each problem is rated by level of difficulty (easy, medium, or difficult) and time needed to solve it. Charts indicate the learning objectives covered by each question, exercise, and problem.

Check List of Key Figures This item is available in quantity to instructors.

Test Bank Contains more than 2,800 items with about 30 true-false questions, 55 multiple-choice questions, ten exercises, and five problems per chapter. Every question is carefully matched to a specific learning objective in the text, and is classified according to one of four levels of student mastery: recall, comprehension and understanding, applications, and analysis.

Microtest and Call-in Testing Service Computer version of the *Test Bank.*

Boxed Solutions Transparencies and Lecture Outlines Over 950 flexible mylar transparencies (printed in oversize, clear, 11-point bold type) provide instructors with solutions to every question, exercise and problem in the text. A nine- to ten-page lecture outline for each chapter is included.

Teaching Transparencies About 100 two-color teaching transparencies are supplied in a convenient three-ring binder for instructors' use.

Grade Performance Analyzer This computerized gradebook program for microcomputers facilitates orderly recordkeeping, calculating, and posting of student grades.

ACKNOWLEDGMENTS

An introductory accounting text is a long and demanding project that cannot succeed without the help of one's colleagues. We are grateful to a large number of professors and other professional colleagues as well as students for constructive comments that have led to improvements in the text. Unfortunately, space does not permit us to mention all those who have contributed to this volume.

Some of those who have been supportive and who have had an impact on the text are:

Professor John Aheto
Pace University

Professor Albert Arsenault
Hillsborough Community College

Professor Joseph Aubert
Bemidji State University

Professor D. Dale Bandy
University of Central Florida

Professor Anne C. Baucom
University of North Carolina—Charlotte

Professor Wilfred Beaupre
San Juan College

Professor Linda Benz
Jefferson Community College

Professor Gregory Bischoff
Houston Community College

Professor Martin J. Canavan
Skidmore College

Professor Kenneth L. Coffey
Johnson County Community College

Professor William Costello
Harcum Junior College

Professor Richard Cross
Bentley College

Professor Jarvis Dean
Chattanooga State Technical Community College

Professor Joseph Doser
Truckee Meadows Community College

Professor William Evans
Cerritos College

Professor Frank Falcetta
Middlesex Community College

Professor Thomas Forsythe
Brown University

Professor Esther Grant
Hillsborough Community College

Professor Raymond Green
Texas Tech University

Ms. Margaret Griffith

Professor Judy Hansen
Waukesha County Technical Institute

Professor Kenneth Hart
Ricks College

Professor Roger Hehman
Raymond Walters College of University of Cincinnati

Professor Arthur Hirschfield
Bronx Community College

Professor George Holdren
University of Nebraska—Lincoln

Professor Bonnie Jack-Givens
Avila College

Professor Alice James
Meridian Junior College

Professor Mark Kiel
North Carolina Agricultural and Technical State University

Professor Rhonda Kodjayan
Mundelein College

Ms. Donna Randall Lacey

Ms. Kim Lazar

Professor Nancy Magrone
Delaware Technical and Community College

Professor William McClung
Tarrant County Junior College

Professor Greg Merrill
University of San Diego

Professor Jean Redfern
Golden West College

Professor Juan Rivera
University of Notre Dame

Professor Harold L. Royer
Miami-Dade Community College

Professor Ronald N. Savey
Western Washington University

Professor Joseph Schliep
Normandale Community College

Professor Nathan Schmukler
Long Island University

Professor Donald L. Seat
Valdosta State College

Professor David A. Skougstad
Metropolitan State College

Professor John R. Stewart
University of Northern Colorado

Dr. DuWayne Wacker
University of North Dakota

Professor Loren K. Waldman
Franklin University

Dr. Richard B. Watson
University of California—Santa Barbara

Professor Robert Wennagel
College of the Mainland

Professor Kenneth Winter
University of Wisconsin—Whitewater

Professor Gilroy J. Zuckerman
North Carolina State University

Substantial portions of the manuscript have been reviewed for technical accuracy by Professors Judy Harris; Michael Haselkorn, Bently College; Robert Landry; Massasoit Community College; S. Murray Simons; and the accounting firm of Arthur Young & Company.

Without the help of these and others, this book would not be possible.

Permission has been received from the Institute of Certified Management Accountants of the National Association of Accountants to use questions and/or unofficial answers from past CMA examinations.

B.E.N. H.R.A. J.C.C.

FINANCIAL & MANAGERIAL ACCOUNTING

CALDWELL NEEDLES ANDERSON

PART ONE THE BASIC ACCOUNTING MODEL

Accounting is an information system for measuring, processing, and communicating information that is useful in making economic decisions. Part One presents the fundamental concepts and techniques of the basic accounting system, including accounting for a complete cycle of business activities for a service enterprise.

Chapter 1 explores the nature and environment of accounting, with special emphasis on the users of accounting information, the roles of accountants in society, and the organizations that influence accounting practice. It also introduces the four basic financial statements, the concept of accounting measurement, and the effects of business transactions on financial position.

Chapter 2 continues the discussion of accounting measurement by focusing on the problems of recognition, valuation, and classification and how they are solved in the recording of business transactions.

Chapter 3 defines the accounting concept of business income and discusses the role of adjusting entries in its measurement.

Chapter 4 completes the accounting system with a presentation of the work sheet and closing entries.

CHAPTER 1 ACCOUNTING AS AN INFORMATION SYSTEM

LEARNING OBJECTIVES

1. Define accounting and describe its role in making informed decisions.
2. Identify the many users of accounting information in society.
3. Distinguish financial and management accounting, define generally accepted accounting principles (GAAP), and identify the organizations that influence GAAP.
4. Explain the importance of separate entity, business transactions, and money measure to accounting measurement.
5. Identify the three basic forms of business organization.
6. Define financial position and show how it is affected by simple transactions.
7. Identify the four basic financial statements.
8. Recognize accounting as a profession with a wide career choice.

Your first accounting course begins with a general view of the accounting discipline and profession. In this chapter, you will begin the study of accounting measurement of business transactions and accounting communication through financial statements. You will also learn about the important roles that accountants play in society and about the organizations where they work. After studying this chapter, you should be able to meet the learning objectives listed on the left.

Every individual or group in society must make economic decisions about the future. For example, the manager of a company needs to know which products have been unsuccessful. With this information, the manager can decide whether to stop selling them or to do something that will increase their appeal to customers. Other persons will want to find out if a firm is financially sound before accepting a job or investing money in the company. Similarly, nonprofit organizations need financial information. Federal, state, and local government units, for example, need financial information to levy taxes. Other nonprofit institutions such as churches and charities need meaningful and easily understood economic information before planning their social programs. Because of their financial knowledge, accountants are often asked to search through the available financial data for clues that will serve as guides to the future.

Accounting Defined

Early definitions of accounting generally focused on the traditional recordkeeping functions of the accountant. In 1941, the American Institute of Certified Public Accountants (AICPA) defined accounting as "the art of recording, classifying, and summarizing in a significant manner and in terms of money, transactions and events which are, in part at least, of a financial character, and interpreting the results thereof."[1] The modern definition of accounting, however, is much broader. In 1970, the AICPA stated that the function of accountancy

1. Committee on Accounting Terminology, *Accounting Terminology Bulletin, Number 2* (New York: American Institute of Certified Public Accountants, 1953), p. 9.

OBJECTIVE 1
Define accounting and describe its role in making informed decisions

is "to provide quantitative information, primarily financial in nature, about economic entities that is intended to be useful in making economic decisions."[2] (An economic entity is a unit such as a business that has an independent existence.)

The modern accountant, therefore, is concerned not only with record keeping but also with a whole range of activities involving planning and problem solving; control and attention directing; and evaluation, review, and auditing. Today's accountant focuses on the ultimate needs of those who use accounting information, whether these users are inside or outside the business itself. So **accounting** "is not an end in itself."[3] Instead it is defined as **an information system that measures, processes, and communicates financial information about an identifiable economic entity.** This information allows users to make "reasoned choices among alternative uses of scarce resources in the conduct of business and economic activities."[4]

This modern view of accounting is shown in Figure 1-1. In this view, accounting is seen as a service activity. It is a link between business activities and decision makers. First, accounting measures business activities by recording data about them for future use. Second, through data processing, the data are stored until needed, then processed in such a way as to become useful information. Third, the information is

Figure 1-1. Accounting as an Information System for Business Decisions

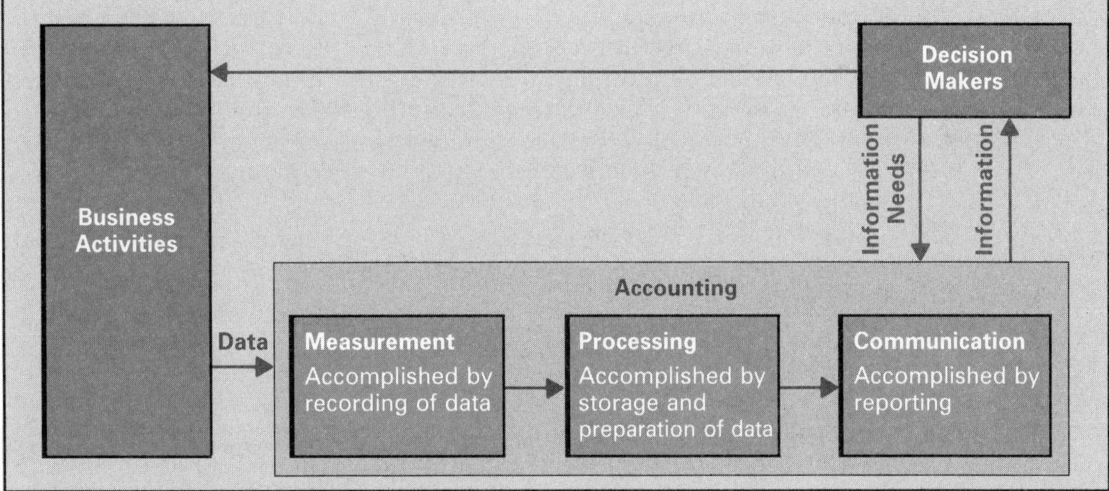

2. *Statement of the Accounting Principles Board, No. 4,* "Basic Concepts and Accounting Principles Underlying Financial Statements of Business Enterprises" (New York: American Institute of Certified Public Accountants, 1970), par. 40.
3. *Statement of Financial Accounting Concepts, No. 1,* p. 5.
4. Ibid.

communicated, through reports, to those who can use it in making decisions. One might say that data about business activities are the input to the accounting system, and useful information for decision makers is the output.

To avoid certain misunderstandings about accounting, it is important to clarify its relationship with bookkeeping, the computer, and management information systems.

People often fail to understand the difference between accounting and bookkeeping. **Bookkeeping,** which is a process of accounting, is the means of recording transactions and keeping records. Mechanical and repetitive, bookkeeping is only a small, simple part of accounting. Accounting, on the other hand, includes the design of an information system that meets user needs, as described earlier. The major goal of accounting is the analysis, interpretation, and use of information. Accountants look for important relationships in the information they produce. They are interested in finding trends and studying the effects of different alternatives. Accounting includes systems design, budgeting, cost analysis, auditing, and income tax preparation or planning.

The **computer** is an electronic tool that is used to collect, organize, and communicate vast amounts of information with great speed. Accountants were among the earliest and most enthusiastic users of computers, and today they use microcomputers in all aspects of their work. Before the age of computers, the millions of transactions of large organizations had to be recorded by hand. It often took months to produce financial reports that now take days or hours. Although it may appear that the computer is doing the accountant's job, it is in fact only a tool that is instructed to do the routine bookkeeping operations and to perform complex analyses for decision-making purposes in a more time-efficient way. It is important that the user of accounting information and the new accountant understand the processes underlying accounting. For this reason, most examples in this book are treated from the standpoint of manual accounting. You should remember, however, that most accounting operations are now computerized.

Most businesses use a large amount of nonfinancial information. Their marketing departments, for example, are interested in the style or packaging of competitors' products. Personnel departments keep health and employment records of employees. With the widespread use of the computer today, many of these varied information needs are being organized into what might be called a **management information system (MIS).** The management information system consists of the interconnected subsystems that provide the information needed to run a business. The accounting information system is the most important subsystem because it plays the primary role of managing the flow of economic data to all parts of a business and to interested parties outside the business. Accounting is the financial hub of the management information system. It gives both management and outsiders a complete view of the business organization.

Accounting Information and Decision Making

The major reason for studying accounting is to acquire the knowledge and skills to participate in important economic decisions. The information that accounting provides is the basis for such decisions both inside and outside the business enterprise.

Thus accounting information

> is a tool and, like most tools, cannot be of much direct help to those who are unable or unwilling to use it or who misuse it. Its use can be learned, however, and [accounting] should provide information that can be used by all—nonprofessionals as well as professionals—who are willing to use it properly.[5]

The first step in this learning process is to understand how decisions are made and how accountants can contribute to the process.

To make a wise decision and carry it out effectively, the decision maker must answer the following questions:

What is the goal to be achieved? (Step 1)
What different ways are available to reach the goal? (Step 2)
Which alternative provides the best way to achieve the goal? (Step 3)
What action should be taken? (Step 4)
Was the goal achieved? (Step 5)

Figure 1-2 shows the steps that an individual or an institution follows in making a decision.

When the decision involves business and economic questions, accounting information is essential to the decision-making system because it

Figure 1-2. A Decision System

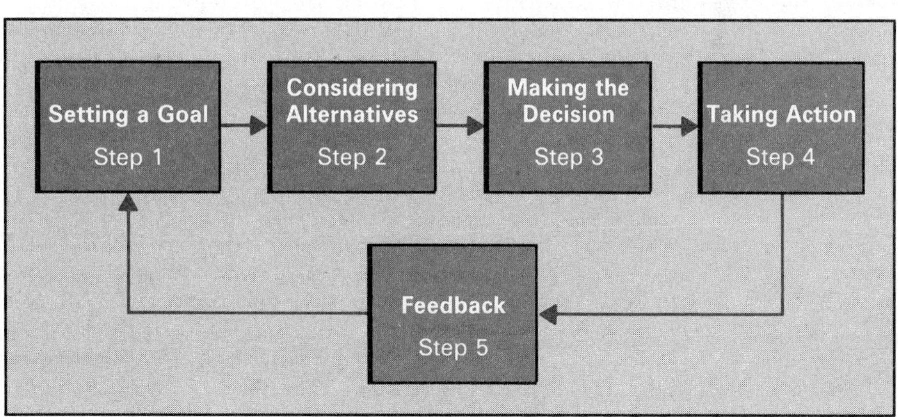

5. *Statement of Financial Accounting Concepts, No. 1,* "Objectives of Financial Reporting by Business Enterprises" (Stamford, Conn.: Financial Accounting Standards Board, 1978), p. 17.

provides quantitative information for three functions: planning, control, and evaluation.

Planning is the process of formulating a course of action. It includes setting a goal, finding alternative ways of accomplishing the goal, and deciding which alternative is the best course of action. At this stage, the accountant should be able to present a clear statement of the financial alternatives. Accounting information dealing with projections of income and budgets of cash requirements would also be important in planning for the future.

Control is the process of seeing that plans are, in fact, carried out. In other words, do actions agree with plans? At this point, the accountant might be expected to present information that compares actual costs with costs planned earlier.

Evaluation, which involves the whole decision system, is the process of studying the decision system to improve it. It asks the question, Was the original goal met (feedback)? If not, the reason could have been poor planning or control, or perhaps the wrong goal was chosen. Evaluation information may be given in annual reports and other financial statements based on accounting information.

Decision Makers: The Users of Accounting Information

OBJECTIVE 2
Identify the many users of accounting information in society

Accounting and accounting information are used more than commonly realized. The users of accounting information can be divided roughly into three groups: (1) those who manage a business; (2) those outside a business enterprise who have a direct financial interest in the business; and (3) those persons, groups, or agencies that have an indirect financial interest in the business. These groups are shown in Figure 1-3.

Management

Management is the group of people in a business who have overall responsibility for operating the business and for achieving the company's goals. Business enterprises have many goals. These goals include providing quality goods and services at low cost, creating new and improved products, increasing the number of jobs available, improving the environment, and accomplishing many other social tasks. To achieve these goals, of course, the company must be successful. Success and survival in a tough, competitive business environment require that management concentrate much of its effort on two important goals: profitability and liquidity. **Profitability** is the ability to make enough profit to attract and hold investment capital. **Liquidity** means having enough funds on hand to pay debts when they fall due.

Managers must constantly decide what to do, how to do it, and whether the results match the original plans. Successful managers consistently make the right decisions on the basis of timely and valid information. Many of these decisions are based on the flow of accounting data and their analysis. For this reason, management is one of the most important users of accounting information, and a major function of accounting is to provide management with relevant and useful information. For example, some typical questions that a manager might ask include: What was the company's net income during the past quarter? Is the rate of return to the owners adequate? Does the company have enough cash? What products are most profitable? What is the cost of manufacturing each product?

Users with a Direct Financial Interest

A major function of accounting is to measure and report information about how a business has performed. Most businesses periodically publish a set of general-purpose financial statements that report on their success in meeting objectives of profitability and liquidity. Though these statements show what has happened in the past, they are important guides to future success. Today there are many people outside the company who carefully study these financial reports.

Present or Potential Investors. Those who are thinking of investing in a company and those such as financial analysts who advise investors are interested in the past success of the business and its potential earnings in the future. A thorough study of the company's financial statements will help potential investors judge the prospects for a profitable investment. After investing in a company, investors must continually review their commitment.

Present or Potential Creditors. Most companies must borrow money for both long- and short-term operating needs. The creditors, who lend the money, are interested mainly in whether the company will have the cash to pay the interest charges and repay the debt at the appropriate time. They will study the company's liquidity and cash flow as well as its profitability. Banks, finance companies, mortgage companies, securities firms, insurance firms, individuals, and others who lend money expect to analyze a company's financial position before making a loan to that company.

Users with an Indirect Financial Interest

Society as a whole, through its government officials and public groups, has in recent years become one of the biggest and most important users of accounting information. Some of the users who need accounting information to make decisions on public issues include (1) taxing authorities, (2) regulatory agencies, (3) economic planners, and (4) other groups.

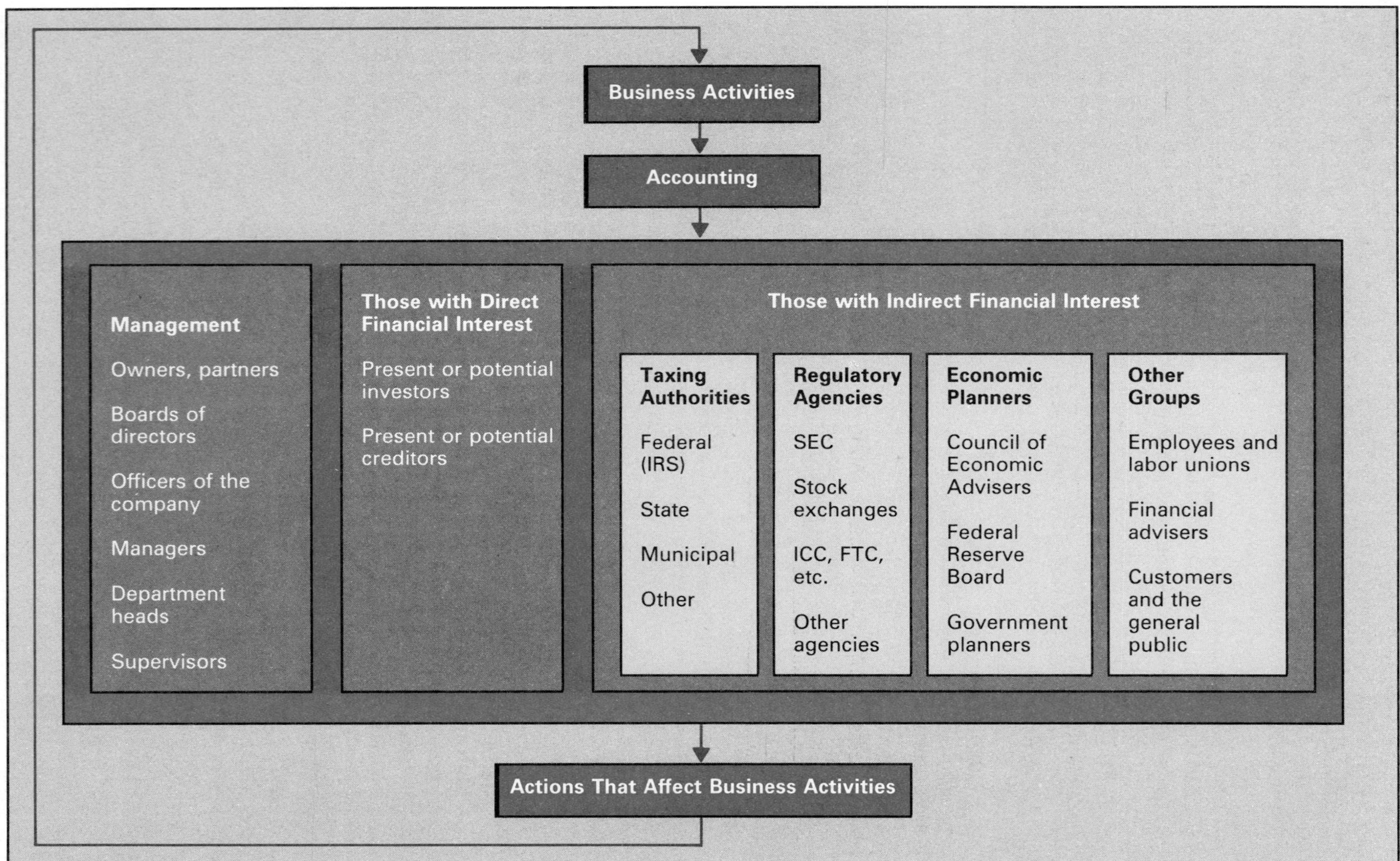

Figure 1-3. The Users of Accounting Information

Taxing Authorities. Our governments are financed through the payment of taxes. Under federal, state, and local laws, companies and individuals pay many kinds of taxes. Among these levies are federal, state, and city income taxes, social security and other payroll taxes, excise taxes, and sales taxes. Each tax requires special tax returns and often a complex set of records as well. Proper reporting is generally a matter of law and can be very complicated. The Internal Revenue Code of the federal government, for instance, contains thousands of rules governing preparation of the financial statements used in computing federal income taxes.

Regulatory Agencies. Most companies must report to one or more regulatory agencies at the federal, state, and local levels. All public corporations must report periodically to the Securities and Exchange Commission. This body was set up by Congress to protect the public and therefore regulates the issuing, buying, and selling of stocks in the United States. Companies that are listed on stock exchanges, such as the New York Stock Exchange, must also meet the special reporting requirements of their exchange. The Interstate Commerce Commission regulates industries such as trucking and railroads, and the Federal Aviation Administration regulates airlines. All public utilities, such as electric, gas, and telephone companies, are regulated and must defend their rates with accounting reports. Accounting is also involved in the new and broader regulations like those of the Environmental Protection Agency, which is concerned with the cost and speed of reducing environmental pollution.

Economic Planners. Since the 1930s, the government's wish to take a more active part in planning and forecasting economic activity has led to greater use of accounting and accounting information. A system of accounting called national income accounting has been developed for the whole economy. It deals with the total production, inventories, income, dividends, taxes, and so forth of our economy. Planners who are members of the President's Council of Economic Advisers or are connected with the Federal Reserve System use this information to set economic policies and judge economic programs.

Other Groups. Labor unions study the financial statements of corporations as part of their task of preparing for important labor negotiations. The amount and computation of income and costs are often important in these negotiations. Those who advise investors and creditors also have an indirect interest in the financial performance and prospects of a business. In this group are financial analysts and advisers, brokers, underwriters, lawyers, economists, and the financial press. Consumers' groups, customers, and the general public have become more concerned about the financing and earnings of corporations as well as with the effects that corporations have on inflation, the environment, social problems, and the quality of life.

Financial and Management Accounting

OBJECTIVE 3
Distinguish financial and management accounting, define generally accepted accounting principles (GAAP), and identify the organizations that influence GAAP

Accounting was defined earlier as an information system that measures, processes, and communicates information that is useful for decision making. A distinction is commonly made between the concepts of management accounting and financial accounting. **Management accounting** refers to all types of accounting information that are measured, processed, and communicated for the internal use of management. **Financial accounting** refers to accounting information that, in addition to being used internally by management, is communicated to those outside the organization. Chapters 1–14 of this book focus on financial accounting. Chapters 15–28 concern management accounting.

Generally Accepted Accounting Principles

Because it is important that all who receive accounting reports be able to interpret them, a set of practices has developed that provides guidelines as to how financial accounting should be done. The term used to describe these practices is **generally accepted accounting principles (GAAP).** Although the term has several meanings in the literature, perhaps the best definition is the following: "Generally accepted accounting principles encompass the conventions, rules, and procedures necessary to define accepted accounting practice at a particular time."[6] In other words, GAAP arise from wide agreement on the theory and practice of accounting at a particular time. These "principles" are not like the unchangeable laws of nature found in chemistry or physics. They are developed by accountants and businesses to serve the needs of decision makers, and they can be altered as better methods are developed or as circumstances change.

In this book, we present accounting practice, or GAAP, as it is today. We have also tried to explain the reasons or theory on which the practice is based. The two—theory and practice—are part and parcel of the study of accounting. However, you should realize that accounting is a discipline that is always growing, changing, and improving. Just as years of research may be necessary before a new surgical method or lifesaving drug can be introduced into medical practice, research and new discoveries in accounting frequently take years to become common practice. As a result, you may sometimes hear of practices that seem inconsistent. In some cases, we have pointed toward new directions in accounting. Your instructor may mention certain weaknesses in current theory or practice as well.

Organizations That Influence Current Practice

Many organizations directly or indirectly influence current GAAP and thus influence much of what is in this book. The most important of these or-

6. *Statement of the Accounting Principles Board, No. 4,* par. 138.

ganizations are the American Institute of Certified Public Accountants, the Financial Accounting Standards Board, the Securities and Exchange Commission, the Internal Revenue Service, and the Government Accounting Standards Board. There are international and other groups as well.

American Institute of Certified Public Accountants. The **American Institute of Certified Public Accountants (AICPA)** has been concerned with accounting practice longer than most groups. From 1938 to 1958 the AICPA's Committee on Accounting Procedures issued a series of pronouncements dealing with accounting principles, procedures, and terms. In 1959 the AICPA organized the Accounting Principles Board (APB) to replace the Committee on Accounting Procedures. The board published a number of APB Opinions on accounting practice. APB Opinions carry so much weight that since December 31, 1965, departures from them in accounting practice must be justified and reported along with a company's financial statements.

Financial Accounting Standards Board. Many APB Opinions are still in effect and will be referred to often in this book. However, in 1973 the responsibility for developing and issuing rules on accounting practice was given to a new body called the Financial Accounting Foundation and, in particular, to an arm of the foundation called the **Financial Accounting Standards Board (FASB).** This group is separate from the AICPA and issues Statements of Financial Accounting Standards. The group is governed by a board of trustees that includes the president of the AICPA and eight others elected by the AICPA.

Securities and Exchange Commission. The **Securities and Exchange Commission (SEC)** is an agency of the U.S. government that has the legal power to set and enforce accounting practices for companies whose securities are offered for sale to the general public. As such, it has great influence on accounting practice. Because the APB failed to solve some of the major problems in accounting practice, the SEC began to play a larger and more aggressive part in deciding rules of accounting. The FASB represents a major effort on the part of accountants to keep control over their profession and to limit the SEC to its traditional role of allowing the accounting profession to regulate itself. It appears certain that during the coming years, the SEC will keep putting pressure on the accounting profession to improve its accounting practice. The success or failure of the FASB will be important in determining how much influence the SEC will have on accounting in the future.

Internal Revenue Service. The U.S. tax laws govern the assessment and collection of revenue for operating the government. Because a major source of the government's revenue is the income tax, the law specifies the rules for determining taxable income. These rules are interpreted and enforced by the **Internal Revenue Service (IRS).** In some cases, these rules may be in conflict with good accounting practice, but they are an important influence on practice. Income tax is a major cost of most profitable businesses and must be shown in the records. Businesses must use certain accounting practices simply because they are required by the tax law. Sometimes companies follow an accounting practice specified in the tax law to take advantage of rules that will help them financially. Cases where the tax law may affect accounting practice are noted throughout this book.

Government Accounting Standards Board. Concern over the financial reporting of government units has resulted in increased attention to the development of accounting principles for these units. The **Government Accounting Standards Board (GASB),** which was established in 1984 under the same governing body as the Financial Accounting Standards Board, is responsible for issuing accounting standards for state and local governments. The GASB will undoubtedly have a great influence on financial reporting by these units.

International Organizations. Worldwide cooperation in the development of accounting principles has made great strides in recent years. The International Accounting Standards Committee (IASC) has approved more than twenty international standards; these have been translated into six languages. In 1977, the International Federation of Accountants (IFAC), now made up of professional accounting bodies from more than fifty countries, was founded to promote international agreement on accounting questions.

Other Organizations Concerned with Accounting. The National Association of Accountants (NAA) is composed mainly of industrial accountants. This organization is engaged in education and research, with an emphasis on management accounting and accounting for management decisions. The Financial Executives Institute (FEI) is made up of persons who hold the highest financial positions in large businesses. It is most interested in standards and research in financial accounting.

The American Accounting Association (AAA) was founded in 1935, succeeding the American Association of University Instructors in Accounting, which was started in 1916. This group has an academic and theoretical point of view. Its members have contributed greatly to the development of accounting theory.

Accounting Measurement

Accounting has been defined thus far as an information system that measures, processes, and communicates financial information. This section begins the study of the measurement aspects of accounting. You will learn what accounting actually measures and study the effects of certain transactions on a company's financial position.

The accountant must answer four basic questions to make an accounting measurement:

OBJECTIVE 4
Explain the importance of separate entity, business transactions, and money measure to accounting measurement

1. What is to be measured?
2. When should the measurement occur?
3. What value should be placed on what is measured?
4. How is what is measured to be classified?

All the questions deal with basic underlying assumptions and generally accepted accounting principles, and their answers establish what accounting is and what it is not. Accountants in industry, professional associations, public accounting, government, and academic circles debate the answers to these questions constantly. As explained earlier, the answers change as new knowledge and practice require, but the basis of today's accounting practice rests on a number of widely accepted concepts and conventions, which are described in this book.

What Is to Be Measured?

The world contains an unlimited number of things to measure. For example, consider a machine that makes bottle caps. How many measurements of this machine could be made? They might include size, location, weight, cost, and many others. Some attributes of this machine are relevant to accounting; some are not. Every system must define what it measures, and accounting is no exception. Basically, **financial accounting is concerned with measuring business transactions of specific business entities in terms of money measures.** The concepts of separate entity, business transaction, and money measure are discussed below.

The Concept of Separate Entity

For accounting purposes, a business is treated as a **separate entity** that is distinct not only from its creditors and customers but also from its owner or owners. It should have a completely separate set of records. Its financial records and reports refer only to its own financial affairs. The business owns assets and owes creditors and owners in the amount of their claims.

For example, the Jones Florist Company should have a bank account that is separate from the account of Kay Jones, the owner. Kay Jones may own a home, a car, and other property, and she may have personal debts, but these are not the Jones Florist Company's assets or debts. Kay Jones may own another business such as a stationery shop. If so, she should have a completely separate set of records for each business.

Business Transactions as the Object of Measurement

Business transactions are economic events that affect the financial position of a business entity. Business entities may have hundreds or even thousands of transactions every day. These transactions are the raw material of accounting reports.

A transaction may involve an exchange of value (such as a purchase, sale, payment, collection, or borrowing) between two or more independent parties. A transaction may also involve a nonexchange economic event that has the same effect as an exchange transaction. Some examples of nonexchange transactions are losses from fire, flood, explosion, and theft; physical wear and tear on machinery and equipment; and day-by-day accumulation of interest.

In any case, to be recorded the transaction must relate directly to the business entity. For example, a customer buys a shovel from Ace Hardware but must buy a hoe from a competing store because Ace is out of hoes. The transaction for selling the shovel must be recorded in Ace's records. However, the purchase of a hoe from a competitor is not recorded in Ace's records because, even though it indirectly affects Ace economically, it does not directly involve an exchange of value between Ace and the customer.

Money Measure

All business transactions are recorded in terms of money; this concept is termed the **money measure**. In the United States, the basic unit of money measure is dollars. Of course, information of a nonfinancial nature may be recorded, but it is only through the recording of dollar amounts that the diverse transactions and activities of a business are measured. Money is the only factor common to all business transactions, and thus it is the only practical unit of measure that can produce financial data that are alike and can be compared.

Forms of Business Organization

OBJECTIVE 5
Identify the three basic forms of business organization

Accountants need to understand the three basic forms of business organization: sole proprietorships, partnerships, and corporations. Accountants recognize each form as an economic unit separate from its owners, although legally only the corporation is considered separate from its owners. Other legal differences among the three forms are summarized in Table 1-1 and discussed briefly below. In this book, we first show accounting for the sole proprietorship because it is the simplest form of accounting. At critical points, however, we call attention to its essential differences from accounting for corporations and partnerships. Later, in Part Four, we deal specifically with partnership accounting and corporation accounting.

Sole Proprietorships

A **sole proprietorship** is a business formed by one person. This form of business gives the individual a means of controlling the business apart from his or her personal interests. Legally, however, the proprietorship is the same economic unit as the individual. The individual receives all profits or losses and is liable for all obligations of the proprietorship. Proprietorships represent the largest number of businesses in the United States, but typically they are the smallest in size. The life of a proprie-

Table 1-1. Comparative Features of the Forms of Business Organization

	Sole Proprietorship	Partnership	Corporation
1. Legal status	Not a separate legal entity	Not a separate legal entity	Separate legal entity
2. Risk of ownership	Owner's personal resources at stake	Partners' resources at stake	Limited to investment in corporation
3. Duration or life	Limited by desire or death of owner	Limited by desire or death of each partner	Indefinite, possibly unlimited
4. Transferability of ownership	Sale by owner establishes new company	Changes in any partner's percentage of interest requires new partnership	Transferable by sale of stock
5. Accounting treatment	Separate economic unit	Separate economic unit	Separate economic unit

torship ends when the owner wishes it to, or at the owner's death or incapacity.

Partnerships

A **partnership** is like a proprietorship in most ways except that it has more than one owner. A partnership is not a legal economic unit separate from the owners but an unincorporated association that brings together the talents and resources of two or more people. The partners share profits and losses of the partnership according to an agreed-upon formula. Generally, any partner can bind the partnership to another party and, if necessary, the personal resources of each partner can be called on to pay obligations of the partnership. In some cases, one or more partners may limit their liability, but at least one partner must have unlimited liability. A partnership must be dissolved if the ownership changes, as when a partner leaves or dies. If the business continues, a new proprietorship or partnership must be formed.

Corporations

A **corporation** is a business unit that is legally separate from its owners. The owners, whose ownership is represented by shares of stock in the corporation, do not directly control the operations of the corporation. Instead they elect a board of directors who run the corporation for the benefit of the stockholders. In exchange for limited involvement in the corporation's actual operations, stockholders enjoy limited liability. That is, their risk of loss is limited to the amount paid for their shares. If they wish, stockholders can sell their shares to other persons without affecting corporate operations. Because of this limited liability, stockholders are often willing to invest in riskier, but potentially profitable, activities. Also, because ownership can be transferred without dissolving the corporation, the life of the corporation is unlimited and not subject to the whims or health of a proprietor or partner.

Corporations have several important advantages over proprietorships and partnerships (see Chapter 12) that make them very efficient in amassing capital for the formation and growth of very large companies. Even though corporations are fewer in number than the proprietorships and partnerships, they contribute much more to the U.S. economy in monetary terms. For example, in 1986, General Motors generated more revenues than all but thirteen of the world's countries.

Financial Position and the Accounting Equation

OBJECTIVE 6 Define financial position and show how it is affected by simple transactions

Financial position refers to the economic resources belonging to a company and the claims against those resources at a point in time. Another term for claims is equities. Thus, a company can be viewed as economic resources and equities,

$$\text{economic resources} = \text{equities}$$

Every company has two types of equities, creditors' equity and owner's equity. Thus,

$$\text{economic resources} = \text{creditors' equity} + \text{owner's equity}$$

Since in accounting terminology, Economic Resources are referred to as Assets and Creditors' Equities are referred to as Liabilities, this equation may be presented as follows:

Balance Sheet equation:

$$\text{assets} = \text{liabilities} + \text{owner's equity}$$

This equation is known as the **balance sheet equation**, because the two sides of the equation represent the two sides of the balance sheet and must always be equal or "in balance." The components of this equation will now be defined.

Assets

Assets are "probable future economic benefits obtained or controlled by a particular entity as a result of past transactions or events."[7] In other words, they are economic resources owned by a business that are expected

7. *Statement of Financial Accounting Concepts No. 6,* "Elements of Financial Statements" (Stamford, Conn.: Financial Accounting Standards Board, December, 1985), par. 25.

to benefit future operations. Certain kinds of assets are monetary items such as receivables (money owed to the company) from customers and cash, and others are nonmonetary physical things such as inventories (goods held for sale), land, buildings, and equipment. Still other assets are nonphysical rights such as those granted by patent, trademark, or copyright.

Liabilities

Liabilities are "probable future sacrifices of economic benefits arising from present obligations of a particular entity to transfer assets or provide services to other entities in the future as a result of past transactions or events."[8] Among these are debts of the business, amounts owed to creditors for goods or services bought on credit (called *Accounts Payable*), borrowed money such as notes payable, salaries and wages owed to employees, and taxes owed to the government.

As debts, liabilities are a claim recognized by law. That is, the law gives to creditors the right to force the sale of a company's assets to pay debts if the company fails to pay. Creditors have rights over owners and must be paid in full before the owners may receive anything, even if payment of the debt uses up all assets of the business.

Owner's Equity

Equity is "the residual interest in the assets of an entity that remains after deducting its liabilities."[9] In a business, the equity is called the ownership interest or **owner's equity.** The owner's equity is the resources invested in the business by the owner. It is also known as the residual equity because it is what would be left over if all the liabilities were paid. Transposing the balance sheet equation, we can state owner's equity as follows:

$$\text{assets} - \text{liabilities} = \text{owner's equity}$$

Because it equals the assets after deducting the liabilities, owner's equity is sometimes said to equal **net assets.**

The four types of transactions that affect owner's equity are shown in Figure 1-4. Two of these transactions, **owner's investments** and **owner's withdrawals,** designate assets that the owner either puts in the business or takes out of the business. For instance, if the owner of Shannon Realty, John Shannon, takes cash out of his personal bank account and places it in the business bank account, it is an owner's investment. The assets (cash) of the business increased, and John Shannon's equity in those assets also increased. Conversely, if John Shannon takes cash out of the business bank account and places it in his personal bank account, he has made a withdrawal from the business. The assets of the business have decreased, and John Shannon's equity in the business has also decreased.

8. Ibid., par. 35.
9. Ibid., par. 49.

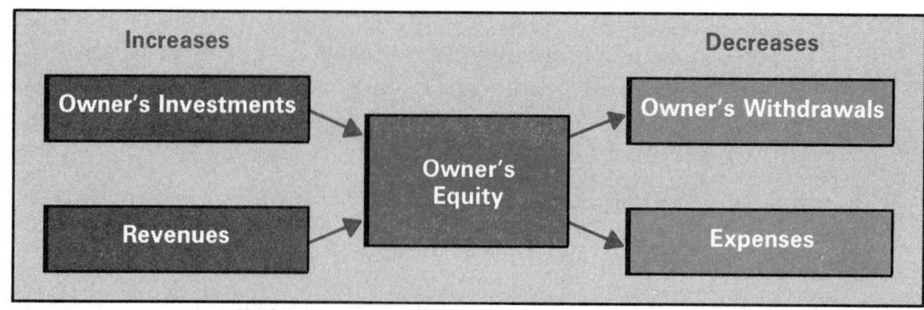

Figure 1-4. Four Types of Transactions That Affect Owner's Equity

The other two types of transactions that affect owner's equity are revenues and expenses. Simply stated, **revenues** and **expenses** are the increases and decreases in owner's equity that result from operating the business. For example, if a customer pays cash to Shannon Realty in return for a service provided by the company, a revenue results. Assets (cash) of Shannon Realty have increased, and the owner's equity in those assets has also increased. On the other hand, if Shannon Realty pays out cash in the process of providing the service, an expense results and is represented by a decrease in assets (cash) and a decrease in the owner's equity in those assets. Generally speaking, a company is successful if its revenues exceed its expenses. When revenues exceed expenses, the difference is called **net income**, and when expenses exceed revenues, the difference is called **net loss.**

Some Illustrative Transactions

Let us now examine the effect of some of the most common business transactions on the balance sheet equation. Suppose that John Shannon opens a real estate agency called Shannon Realty on December 1. During December, he conducts his business by engaging in the transactions described in the following paragraphs.

Owner's Investment. John begins his business by depositing $50,000 in a bank account in the name of Shannon Realty. The transfer of cash from his personal account to the business account is an owner's investment and increases the assets (Cash) and the owner's equity (John Shannon, Capital) of Shannon Realty:

	Assets	=	Owner's Equity	
	Cash		John Shannon, Capital	Type of OE Transaction
1.	$50,000		$50,000	Owner's Investment

At this point, the company has no liabilities, and assets equal owner's equity. The labels Cash and John Shannon, Capital are called accounts and are used by accountants to accumulate amounts that result from similar transactions. Transactions that affect owner's equity are identified by type so that similar types may later be grouped together on accounting reports.

Purchase of Assets With Cash. John finds a good location and purchases with cash a lot for $10,000 and a small building on the lot for $25,000. This transaction does not change the total assets, liabilities, or owner's equity of Shannon Realty, but it does change the composition of the assets—decreasing Cash and increasing Land and Building:

	Assets			=	Owner's Equity	
	Cash	**Land**	**Building**		**John Shannon, Capital**	**Type of OE Transaction**
bal.	$50,000				$50,000	
2.	−35,000	+$10,000	+$25,000			
bal.	$15,000	$10,000	$25,000		$50,000	
	$50,000					

Purchase of Asset by Incurring a Liability. Assets do not always have to be purchased with cash. They may also be purchased on credit, that is, on the basis of an agreement to pay for them later. Suppose John buys some supplies for the office for $500 on credit. This transaction increases the assets (Supplies) and increases the liabilities of Shannon Realty. This liability is designated by an account called Accounts Payable:

	Assets				=	Liabilities +	Owner's Equity	
	Cash	**Supplies**	**Land**	**Building**		**Accounts Payable**	**John Shannon, Capital**	**Type of OE Transaction**
bal.	$15,000		$10,000	$25,000			$50,000	
3.		+$500				+$500		
bal.	$15,000	$500	$10,000	$25,000		$500	$50,000	
	$50,500					$50,500		

Note that this transaction increases both sides of the balance sheet equation to $50,500.

Payment of a Liability. If John later pays $200 of the $500 owed for the supplies, both assets (Cash) and liabilities (Accounts Payable) will decrease, but Supplies will be unaffected:

	Assets				= Liabilities +	Owner's Equity	
	Cash	Supplies	Land	Building	Accounts Payable	John Shannon, Capital	Type of OE Transaction
bal.	$15,000	$500	$10,000	$25,000	$500	$50,000	
4.	−200				−200		
bal.	$14,800	$500	$10,000	$25,000	$300	$50,000	
	$50,300				$50,300		

Note that the balance sheet equation is still equal on both sides of the equation, although now at a total of $50,300.

Revenues. Shannon Realty earns revenues in the form of commissions received from selling houses for clients. Sometimes these commissions are paid to Shannon Realty immediately in the form of cash, and sometimes the client agrees to pay the commission later. In either case, the commission is recorded when it is earned. First, assume Shannon Realty sells a house and receives a commission in cash of $1,500. This transaction increases assets (Cash) and owner's equity (John Shannon, Capital):

	Assets				= Liabilities +	Owner's Equity	
	Cash	Supplies	Land	Building	Accounts Payable	John Shannon, Capital	Type of OE Transaction
bal.	$14,800	$500	$10,000	$25,000	$300	$50,000	
5.	+1,500					+1,500	Commissions Earned
bal.	$16,300	$500	$10,000	$25,000	$300	$51,500	
	$51,800				$51,800		

Now assume John sells a house calling for a commission of $2,000 for which John agrees to wait for payment. Since the commission is earned now, it is recorded now. This revenue transaction increases both assets and owner's equity as before, but a new asset account, Accounts Receivable, shows that Shannon Realty is awaiting receipt of the commission:

	Assets					= Liabilities +	Owner's Equity	
	Cash	Accounts Receiv-able	Supplies	Land	Building	Accounts Payable	John Shannon, Capital	Type of OE Transaction
bal.	$16,300		$500	$10,000	$25,000	$300	$51,500	
6.		+$2,000					+2,000	Commissions Earned
bal.	$16,300	$2,000	$500	$10,000	$25,000	$300	$53,500	
	$53,800					$53,800		

Collection of Accounts Receivable. If it is assumed that a few days later Shannon receives $1,000 from the client in transaction (6), the asset Cash is increased and the asset Accounts Receivable is decreased:

	Assets					= Liabilities +	Owner's Equity	
	Cash	Accounts Receivable	Supplies	Land	Building	Accounts Payable	John Shannon, Capital	Type of OE Transaction
bal.	$16,300	$2,000	$500	$10,000	$25,000	$300	$53,500	
7.	+1,000	−1,000						
bal.	$17,300	$1,000	$500	$10,000	$25,000	$300	$53,500	
	$53,800					$53,800		

Note that this transaction does not affect owner's equity because the commission revenue has already been recorded in transaction (6). Also, note that the balance of Accounts Receivable is $1,000, indicating that $1,000 is still to be collected.

Expenses. Just as revenues are recorded when they are earned, expenses are recorded when they are incurred. Expenses may be paid in cash when they occur or if payment is to be made later, a liability such as Accounts Payable or Wages Payable is increased. In both cases, owner's equity is decreased. Assume that John Shannon pays $1,000 to rent some equipment for the office and $400 in wages to a part-time helper during December. These transactions reduce assets (Cash) and owner's equity (John Shannon, Capital):

	Assets					= Liabilities +	Owner's Equity	
	Cash	Accounts Receivable	Supplies	Land	Building	Accounts Payable	John Shannon, Capital	Type of OE Transaction
bal.	$17,300	$1,000	$500	$10,000	$25,000	$300	$53,500	
8.	−1,000						−1,000	Equip. Rental Expense
9.	− 400						− 400	Wages Expense
bal.	$15,900	$1,000	$500	$10,000	$25,000	$300	$52,100	
	$52,400					$52,400		

Also, John has not paid the bill for utilities expense of $300 that was incurred by Shannon Realty for December. In this case, the effect on owner's equity is the same as when the expense is paid in cash, but instead of a reduction in assets, there is an increase in liabilities (Accounts Payable), as follows:

	Assets					= Liabilities +	Owner's Equity	
	Cash	Accounts Receiv-able	Supplies	Land	Building	Accounts Payable	John Shannon, Capital	Type of OE Transaction
bal.	$15,900	$1,000	$500	$10,000	$25,000	$300	$52,100	
10.						+300	−300	Utilities Expense
bal.	$15,900	$1,000	$500	$10,000	$25,000	$600	$51,800	
			$52,400			$52,400		

Owner's Withdrawals. John now withdraws $600 in cash from Shannon Realty and deposits it in his personal account for his personal use. The effect of this transaction is to reduce assets (Cash) and owner's equity (John Shannon, Capital). Although, as can be seen below, withdrawals have the same effect on the balance sheet equation as expenses (see transactions 8 and 9), it is important not to confuse them. Withdrawals are personal to the owner whereas expenses are incurred by the business in the operation of the business.

	Assets					= Liabilities +	Owner's Equity	
	Cash	Accounts Receiv-able	Supplies	Land	Building	Accounts Payable	John Shannon, Capital	Type of OE Transaction
bal.	$15,900	$1,000	$500	$10,000	$25,000	$600	$51,800	
11.	−600						−600	Withdrawal
bal.	$15,300	$1,000	$500	$10,000	$25,000	$600	$51,200	
			$51,800			$51,800		

Summary. A summary of these eleven illustrative transactions is presented in Exhibit 1-1.

Accounting Communication Through Financial Statements

Financial statements are a central feature of accounting because they are the primary means of communicating important accounting information to users. It is helpful to think of these statements as models of the business enterprise, because they are attempts to show the business in

Exhibit 1-1. Summary of Effects of Illustrative Transactions on Financial Position

	Assets					= Liabilities +	Owner's Equity	
	Cash	Accounts Receiv-able	Supplies	Land	Building	Accounts Payable	John Shannon, Capital	Type of Owner's Equity Transaction
1.	$50,000						$50,000	Owner's Investment
2.	−35,000			+$10,000	+$25,000			
bal.	$15,000			$10,000	$25,000		$50,000	
3.			$500			+$500		
bal.	$15,000		$500	$10,000	$25,000	$500	$50,000	
4.	−200					−200		
bal.	$14,800		$500	$10,000	$25,000	$300	$50,000	
5.	+1,500						+1,500	Commissions Earned
bal.	$16,300		$500	$10,000	$25,000	$300	$51,500	
6.		+$2,000					+2,000	Commissions Earned
bal.	$16,300	$2,000	$500	$10,000	$25,000	$300	$53,500	
7.	+1,000	−1,000						
bal.	$17,300	$1,000	$500	$10,000	$25,000	$300	$53,500	
8.	−1,000						−1,000	Equip. Rental Expense
9.	−400						−400	Wages Expense
bal.	$15,900	$1,000	$500	$10,000	$25,000	$300	$52,100	
10.						+300	−300	Utilities Expense
bal.	$15,900	$1,000	$500	$10,000	$25,000	$600	$51,800	
11.	−600						−600	Withdrawal
bal.	$15,300	$1,000	$500	$10,000	$25,000	$600	$51,200	
			$51,800			$51,800		

financial terms. As is true of all models, however, financial statements are not perfect pictures of the real thing but the accountant's best effort to represent what is real.

OBJECTIVE 7
Identify the four basic financial statements

Four major financial statements are used to communicate the required information about a business. One is the income statement, which reports income-generating activities or earnings of a business during the period. A second statement, called the statement of owner's equity, shows the changes in the owner's interest in the business. Both of these statements are prepared from the four types of transactions that affect owner's equity. This is why in Exhibit 1-2 and prior examples, these transactions were identified by type.

A third is the balance sheet. The balance sheet shows the financial position of the business at a particular date, such as at the end of the accounting period. A fourth statement, called the statement of cash flows, is used to summarize all the changes in cash that result from operating activities, investment activities, and financing activities. Exhibit 1-2 illustrates the relationships of the first three statements by showing how they would appear for Shannon Realty after the eleven illustrative transactions shown in Exhibit 1-1. It is assumed that these transactions took place during the month of December 19xx.

Note that each statement is headed in a similar way. Each identifies the company and the kind of statement for the user. The balance sheet gives the specific date to which it applies, and the income statement and statement of owner's equity give the time period to which they apply. These statements are typical ones for proprietorships. Statements for partnerships and corporations, which are similar, are discussed in Chapter 11 and later chapters.

The Income Statement

The **income statement** is a financial statement that summarizes the amount of revenues earned and expenses incurred by a business over a period of time. Many people consider it the most important financial report because its purpose is to measure whether or not the business achieved or failed to achieve its primary objective of earning an acceptable income. In Exhibit 1-2, Shannon Realty had revenues in the form of commissions earned of $3,500. From this amount total expenses of $1,700 were deducted, consisting of equipment rental expense of $1,000, wages expense of $400, and utilities expense of $300 to arrive at a net income of $1,800. To show that it applies to a period of time, the statement is dated, "For the month ended December 31, 19xx."

The Statement of Owner's Equity

The **statement of owner's equity** shows the changes in the owner's capital account over a period of time. In Exhibit 1-2, the beginning capital is zero because the company was started in this accounting period. During the month John Shannon made an investment in the business of $50,000, and the company earned an income (as shown in the income statement) of $1,800, for a total increase of $51,800. Deducted from this amount are the withdrawals for the month of $600, leaving an ending balance of $51,200 in Shannon's capital account.

Exhibit 1-2. Income Statement, Statement of Owner's Equity, and Balance Sheet for Shannon Realty

Shannon Realty
Income Statement
For the Month Ended December 31, 19xx

Revenues		
Commissions Earned		$3,500
Expenses		
Equipment Rental Expense	$1,000	
Wages Expense	400	
Utilities Expense	300	
Total Expenses		1,700
Net Income		$1,800

Shannon Realty
Statement of Owner's Equity
For the Month Ended December 31, 19xx

John Shannon, Capital, December 1, 19xx		$ 0
Add: Investments by John Shannon	$50,000	
Net Income for the Month	1,800	51,800
Subtotal		$51,800
Less: Withdrawals by John Shannon		600
John Shannon, Capital, December 31, 19xx		$51,200

Shannon Realty
Balance Sheet
December 31, 19xx

Assets		Liabilities	
Cash	$15,300	Accounts Payable	$ 600
Accounts Receivable	1,000	**Owner's Equity**	
Supplies	500		
Land	10,000	John Shannon, Capital	51,200
Building	25,000	Total Liabilities and	
Total Assets	$51,800	Owner's Equity	$51,800

The Balance Sheet

The purpose of the **balance sheet** is to show the financial position of a business on a certain date. For this reason, it is often called the statement of financial position and is dated as of a certain date. The balance sheet presents a view of the business as the holder of resources or assets that are equal to the sources of or claims against those assets. The sources or claims consist of the company's liabilities and the owner's equity in the company. In Exhibit 1-2, Shannon Realty has several categories of assets that total $51,800. These assets equal the total liabilities of $600 (accounts payable) plus the ending balance of owner's equity of $51,200 (John Shannon's capital account). Note that the capital account on the balance sheet comes from the ending balance as shown on the statement of owner's equity.

The Statement of Cash Flows

During the past three decades it has become clear that the income statement has one major deficiency. It only shows the changes in financial position caused by those operations that produced an operating income or loss. Many important events, especially those relating to

Exhibit 1-3. Statement of Cash Flows for Shannon Realty

Shannon Realty Statement of Cash Flows For the Month Ended December 31, 19xx		
Cash Flows from Operating Activities		
Net Income		$ 1,800
Noncash Expenses and Revenues Not Included in Income		
Increase in Accounts Receivable	$ (1,000)	
Increase in Supplies	(500)	
Increase in Accounts Payable	600	(900)
Net Cash Flows from Operating Activities		$ 900
Cash Flows from Investing Activities		
Purchase of Land	$(10,000)	
Purchase of Building	(25,000)	
Net Cash Flows Used by Investment Activities		(35,000)
Cash Flows from Financing Activities		
Investment by John Shannon	$ 50,000	
Withdrawals by John Shannon	(600)	
Net Cash Flows Provided by Financing Activities		$49,400
Net Increase (Decrease) in Cash		$15,300

investing and financing activities, can take place during an accounting period and not appear on the income statement. For example, the owner may put more money into the business or take it out. Buildings, equipment, or other assets may be bought or sold. New liabilities can be incurred or old ones paid off. For this reason, the **statement of cash flows** is now widely used to show all changes in financial position and cash that take place during an accounting period.

Exhibit 1-3 is an example of the statement of cash flows for Shannon Realty. Note that the name of the company, the title of the statement, and the period covered by the statement are identified. Also note that the statement explains how Cash changed during the period. Cash increased by $15,300. Operating activities produced net cash flows of $900 and financing activities produced net cash flows of $49,400. Investment activities used cash flows of $35,000.

This statement is directly related to the other three statements. Notice that net income comes from the income statement and that investments by John Shannon and withdrawals by John Shannon come from the statement of owner's equity. The other items in the statement represent changes in the balance sheet accounts of Accounts Receivable, Supplies, Accounts Payable, Land, and Buildings. The construction and use of the statement of cash flows is discussed in detail in Chapter 27.

Relationships Among the Four Statements

You are not expected to understand all the fine points and terminology of these statements at this stage. They are presented to show that accounting tries to sum up in a meaningful and useful way the financial history of a business, no matter how large and complex, in four relatively simple financial statements—an amazing feat. Two of the statements—the income statement and the statement of cash flows—deal with the activities of the business system over time. One statement—the balance sheet—shows the state of the system at a particular point in time. Another statement—the statement of owner's equity—ties the balance sheet and income statement together over a period of time. Much of the rest of this book deals with how to develop, use, and interpret these four statements.

The Accounting Profession

OBJECTIVE 8 Recognize accounting as a profession with a wide career choice

The accounting function is as old as the need to exchange things of value and keep track of the wealth. The commercial and trading revolution of the Renaissance was a great impetus to accounting, as was the Industrial Revolution later. The enormous growth of industry and government in the twentieth century has expanded the need for accountants even further.

Today, accounting offers interesting, challenging, well-paid, and socially satisfying careers. The profession can be divided into four broad fields: (1) management accounting, (2) public accounting, (3) government and other nonprofit accounting, and (4) accounting education.

Management Accounting

An accountant who is employed by a business is said to be in **management accounting.** A small business may have only one or a few people doing this work, though a medium-size or large company may have hundreds of accountants working under a chief accounting officer called a controller, treasurer, or financial vice president. Other positions that may be held by accountants at lower managerial levels are assistant controller, chief accountant, internal auditor, plant accountant, systems analyst, financial accountant, and cost accountant.

Because of their broad and intimate view of all aspects of a company's operations, management accountants often have an important effect on management decision making. According to most recent surveys, more top-level business executives have backgrounds in accounting and finance than in any other field. Just a few of the well-known companies whose presidents or chairmen of the board are (or have been) accountants are American Airlines, General Foods, International Business Machines, Caterpillar Tractor, General Motors, Kennecott Copper, Ford, General Electric, General Telephone and Electronics, Consolidated Edison, International Telephone and Telegraph, and 3M.

The main task of management accountants is to give management the information it needs to make wise decisions. Management accountants also set up a system of internal control to increase efficiency and prevent fraud in their companies. They aid in profit planning, budgeting, and cost control. It is their duty to see that a company has good records, prepares proper financial reports, and complies with tax laws and government regulations. Management accountants also need to keep up with the latest developments in the uses of computers and in computer systems design.

Management accountants may certify their professional competence and training by qualifying for the status of **Certified Management Accountants (CMA),** which is awarded by the Institute of Certified Management Accountants of the National Association of Accountants. Under the CMA program, candidates must pass a number of examinations and meet educational and professional standards.

Public Accounting

The field of **public accounting** offers services in auditing, taxes, and management consulting to the public for a fee. In the short time since about 1900, public accounting in this country has gained a stature similar to that of the older professions of law and medicine. **Certified public accountants (CPAs)** are licensed by all states for the same reason that lawyers and doctors are—to protect the public by ensuring a high quality of professional service.

To become a CPA, the applicant must meet rigorous requirements. These requirements vary from state to state but have certain characteristics in common. An applicant must be a person of integrity and have at least a high school education. Most states require four years of college (a few require five years) with a major in accounting. Further, the applicant must pass a difficult and comprehensive two-and-one-half-day examination in accounting practice, accounting theory, auditing, and business law. Although the examination is uniform in all states, some states also require an examination in such areas as economics or professional ethics. The examination is prepared by the American Institute of Certified Public Accountants and is given twice a year. Most states also require from one to five years' experience in the office of a certified public accountant or acceptable equivalent experience. In some cases, additional education can be substituted for one or more years of accounting experience.

Certified public accountants offer their services to the public for a fee, just as doctors or lawyers do. Accounting firms are made up of partners, who must be CPAs, and staff accountants, many of whom are CPAs and hope to become partners someday. Accounting firms vary in size from large international firms with hundreds of partners and thousands of employees (see Table 1-2) to small one- or two-person firms.

The work of the public accountant is varied, complex, and interesting. Most accounting firms organize themselves into several principal areas of specialization, which may include (1) auditing, (2) tax services, (3) management advisory services, and (4) small business services.

Auditing. The most important and distinctive function of a certified public accountant is **auditing** (also called the **attest** function), which is the examination and testing of financial statements. Society relies heavily on the auditing function for credible financial reports. All public corporations and many companies that apply for sizable loans must have their financial statements and records audited by an independent certified public accountant.

An audit's purpose is to give the auditor's professional opinion as to whether the company's financial reports fairly present its financial position and operating results. Auditors check and test the accounting records

Table 1-2. Accounting's "Big Eight" Certified Public Accounting Firms

Firm	Home Office	Some Major Clients
Arthur Andersen & Co.	Chicago	ITT, Texaco, United Airlines
Arthur Young & Co.	New York	Mobil, Beatrice, McDonald's
Coopers & Lybrand	New York	AT&T, Ford, Firestone
Deloitte, Haskins & Sells	New York	General Motors, Procter & Gamble
Ernst & Whinney	Cleveland	McDonnell Douglas, Coca-Cola
Peat, Marwick, Main & Co.	New York	General Electric, Xerox
Price Waterhouse	New York	IBM, Exxon, DuPont
Touche Ross & Co.	New York	Chrysler, Boeing, Sears

and controls as necessary to satisfy themselves about the quality of the financial statements. Auditors must prove cash balances, confirm physical inventories, and verify the amounts owed by customers. They must also decide if there are adequate controls and if the company's records are kept in accordance with accepted accounting practices. In the end, auditors must depend on their own judgment to reach an opinion about a company's financial reports. Their professional reputation is at stake because banks, investors, and creditors depend on the financial statements bearing the auditor's opinions in buying and selling the company's stocks, making loans, and giving credit.

Tax Services. In the area of **tax services**, public accountants assist businesses and individuals in preparing tax returns and complying with tax laws. They also help plan business decisions to reduce taxes in the future. Tax accounting work calls for much knowledge and skill regardless of the size of a business. Few business decisions are without tax effects.

Management Advisory Services. A growing and important part of most public accounting firms' practice is **management advisory services**, or consulting. With their intimate knowledge of a business's operations, auditors can make important suggestions for improvements and, as a matter of course, usually do. In the past, these recommendations have dealt mainly with accounting records, budgeting, and cost accounting. But in the last few years they have expanded into marketing, organizational planning, personnel and recruiting, production, systems, and many other business areas. The wide use of computers has led to the offering of services in systems design and control and to the use of mathematical and statistical decision models. All these different services combined make up management advisory services.

Small Business Services. Many small businesses look to their CPA for advice on operating their businesses and keeping their accounting records. Although small CPA firms have traditionally performed these functions, large firms are also establishing small business practice units. Among the types of services a CPA might provide are setting up or revising an accounting system, compiling monthly financial statements, preparing a budget of cash needs over the next year, and assisting the client in obtaining a bank loan.

Government and Other Nonprofit Accounting

Agencies and departments at all levels of government hire accountants to prepare reports so that officials can responsibly carry out their duties. Millions of income, payroll, and sales tax returns must be checked and audited. In the federal government, the Federal Bureau of Investigation and the Internal Revenue Service use thousands of accountants. The General Accounting Office audits government activities for Congress, using many auditors and other accounting specialists all over the world. Federal agencies such as the Securities and Exchange Commission,

Interstate Commerce Commission, and Federal Communications Commission hire accountants, as do state agencies such as those dealing with public utilities regulation or tax collection.

Many other nonprofit enterprises besides the government employ accountants. Some of these organizations are hospitals, colleges, universities, and foundations. These institutions, like the government, are interested in compliance with the law and efficient use of public resources. They account for over 25 percent of the gross output of our economy. Clearly, the role of accountants in helping these organizations use their resources wisely is important to our society.

Accounting Education

Training new accountants is a challenging and rewarding career, and today instructors of accounting are in great demand. Accounting instructors at the secondary level must have a college degree with a major in accounting and must meet state teacher certification requirements. One entry-level requirement for teaching at the smaller and two-year college level is the master's degree. Faculty members at most larger universities must have their Ph.D. degree and engage in research. In many schools, holding the CPA, CMA, or **CIA (Certified Internal Auditor)** certificate will help an instructor to advance professionally.

Chapter Review

Review of Learning Objectives

1. **Define accounting and describe its role in making informed decisions.**
   Accounting is an information system that measures, processes, and communicates information, primarily financial in nature, about an identifiable entity for the purpose of making economic decisions. It is not an end in itself but is a tool to be used in providing information that is useful in making reasoned choices among alternative uses of scarce resources in the conduct of business and economic activities.

2. **Identify the many users of accounting information in society.**
   Accounting plays a significant role in society by providing information to managers of all institutions and to those with direct financial interest in those institutions, such as present or potential investors or creditors. Accounting information is also important to those with indirect financial interest, such as taxing authorities, regulatory agencies, economic planners, and other groups.

3. **Distinguish financial and management accounting, define generally accepted accounting principles (GAAP), and identify the organizations that influence GAAP.**
   Financial accounting refers to the development and use of accounting reports that are communicated to those external to the business organization whereas management accounting refers to the preparation of information for the internal use of management. Acceptable accounting practice at a particular time consists of those conventions, rules, and procedures that make up

generally accepted accounting principles. GAAP are essential to the preparation and interpretation of financial accounting reports.

Among the organizations that influence the formulation of GAAP are the American Institute of Certified Public Accountants, the Financial Accounting Standards Board, the Securities and Exchange Commission, and the Internal Revenue Service. Other organizations with an interest in accounting are the National Association of Accountants, the Financial Executives Institute, and the American Accounting Association.

4. **Explain the importance of separate entity, business transactions, and money measure to accounting measurement.**
To make an accounting measurement, the accountant must determine what is to be measured, when the measurement should occur, what value should be placed on what is measured, and how what is measured should be classified. Generally accepted accounting principles define the objects of accounting measurement as separate entities, business transactions, and money measures. Relating these three concepts, financial accounting measures business transactions of separate business entities in terms of money measures.

5. **Identify the three basic forms of business organization.**
The three basic forms of business organization are sole proprietorships, partnerships, and corporations. Sole proprietorships, which are formed by one individual, and partnerships, which are formed by more than one individual, are not separate economic units from the legal standpoint. In accounting, however, they are treated separately. Corporations, whose ownership is represented by shares of stock, are separate entities for both legal and accounting purposes.

6. **Define financial position and show how it is affected by simple transactions.**
Business transactions affect financial position by decreasing or increasing assets, liabilities, and/or owner's equity in such a way that the basic balance sheet equation (assets = liabilities + owner's equity) is always in balance.

7. **Identify the four basic financial statements.**
Financial statements are the means by which accountants communicate the financial condition and activities of a business to those who have an interest in the business. The four basic financial statements are the balance sheet, the income statement, the statement of owner's equity, and the statement of cash flows.

8. **Recognize accounting as a profession with a wide career choice.**
The people who provide accounting information to users make up the accounting profession. They may be management accountants, public accountants, or government or other nonprofit accountants. Accounting educators provide still another career choice. Each type of accounting work is an important specialization and represents a challenging career.

Self-Test

Test your knowledge of the chapter by choosing the best answer for each item below.

1. Which of the following is an important reason for studying accounting?
   a. The information provided by accounting and accountants is useful in making many economic decisions.

b. Accounting plays an important role in society.
c. The study of accounting could lead to a challenging career.
d. All of the above are important reasons.

2. Which of the following groups uses accounting information for planning a company's profitability and liquidity?
   a. Management
   b. Investors
   c. Creditors
   d. Economic planners
3. Which of the following forms of organization is not treated as a separate economic unit in accounting?
   a. Sole proprietorship
   b. Committee
   c. Partnership
   d. Corporation
4. Generally accepted accounting principles
   a. define accounting practice at a point in time.
   b. are similar in nature to the principles of chemistry or physics.
   c. are rarely changed.
   d. are not affected by changes in the ways businesses operate.
5. Economic events that affect the financial position of a business are called
   a. separate entities.
   b. business transactions.
   c. money measures.
   d. financial actions.
6. If a company has liabilities of $19,000 and owner's equity of $57,000, the assets of the company are
   a. $38,000.
   b. $76,000.
   c. $57,000.
   d. $19,000.
7. The payment of a liability will
   a. increase both assets and liabilities.
   b. increase assets and decrease liabilities.
   c. decrease assets and increase liabilities.
   d. decrease assets and decrease liabilities.
8. The purchase of an asset for cash will
   a. increase and decrease assets at the same time.
   b. increase both assets and liabilities.
   c. increase assets and owner's equity.
   d. increase assets and decrease liabilities.
9. The balance sheet is related to the income statement in the same way that
   a. a point in time is related to a period of time.
   b. a period of time is related to a point in time.
   c. a point in time is related to another point in time.
   d. a period of time is related to another period of time.
10. Expenses and withdrawals appear, respectively, on which of the following financial statements?
   a. Balance sheet and income statement
   b. Income statement and balance sheet
   c. Statement of owner's equity and balance sheet
   d. Income statement and statement of owner's equity

Review Problem
Effect of Transactions on the Accounting Equation

Charlene Rudek finished law school in June and immediately set up her own law practice. During the first month she completed the following transactions:

a. Invested in the practice by placing $2,000 in a bank account established for the business.
b. Purchased a law library for $900 cash.
c. Purchased office supplies for $400 on credit.
d. Accepted $500 in cash for completing a contract.
e. Billed clients $1,950 for services rendered during the month.
f. Paid $200 of the amount owed for office supplies.
g. Received $1,250 in cash from one client previously billed for services rendered.
h. Paid for rent, utilities, secretarial services, and other expenses during the month in the amount of $1,200.
i. Withdrew $400 from the practice for personal use.

Required

Show the effect of each of these transactions on the balance sheet equation by completing a table similar to Exhibit 1-1. Identify each owner's equity transaction.

Answer to Review Problem

	Assets				= Liabilities +	Owner's Equity	
	Cash	Accounts Receivable	Office Supplies	Law Library	Accounts Payable	Charlene Rudek, Capital	Type of OE Transaction
a.	$2,000					$2,000	Owner's Investment
b.	−900			+$900			
bal.	$1,100			$900		$2,000	
c.			+$400		+$400		
bal.	$1,100		$400	$900	$400	$2,000	
d.	+500					+500	Service Revenue
bal.	$1,600		$400	$900	$400	$2,500	
e.		+$1,950				+$1,950	Service Revenue
bal.	$1,600	$1,950	$400	$900	$400	$4,450	
f.	−200				−200		
bal.	$1,400	$1,950	$400	$900	$200	$4,450	
g.	+1,250	−1,250					
bal.	$2,650	$ 700	$400	$900	$200	$4,450	
h.	−1,200					−1,200	Expenses
bal.	$1,450	$ 700	$400	$900	$200	$3,250	
i.	−400					−400	Owner's Withdrawal
bal.	$1,050	$ 700	$400	$900	$200	$2,850	

$3,050 = $3,050

Chapter Assignments

Questions

1. What is the new focus of accounting?
2. Distinguish among these terms: accounting, bookkeeping, and management information systems.
3. How are decisions made, and what is the role of accounting in the decision system?
4. What decision makers use accounting information?
5. What objectives does management seek to achieve by using accounting information?
6. Why are investors and creditors interested in the financial statements of a company?
7. Why has society as a whole become one of the biggest users of accounting information? What groups besides business managers, investors, and creditors use accounting information?
8. What are some of the fields encompassed by the accounting profession?
9. What are some activities the management accountant might participate in?
10. How is a public accountant different from a management accountant?
11. Describe in general terms the requirements that an individual must meet to become a CPA and the four major activities of CPAs.
12. In what important ways do sole proprietorships, partnerships, and corporations differ?
13. Define assets, liabilities, and owner's equity.
14. What four items affect owner's equity, and how?
15. Arnold Smith's company has assets of $22,000 and liabilities of $10,000. What is the amount of his owner's equity?

16. Give examples of the types of transactions that will (a) increase assets, and (b) increase liabilities.
17. Why is the balance sheet sometimes called the statement of financial position?
18. Contrast the purposes of the balance sheet and those of the income statement.
19. How does the income statement differ from the statement of cash flows?
20. A statement for an accounting period that ends in June may have either (1) June 30, 19xx, or (2) For the Year Ended June 30, 19xx, as part of its identification. State which would be appropriate with (a) a balance sheet, and (b) an income statement.
21. Accounting can be viewed as (1) an intellectual discipline, (2) a profession, or (3) a social force. In what sense is it each of these?

Classroom Exercises

Exercise 1-1. Role of Computer, Bookkeeper, and Accountant (L.O. 1)

Tom, Tina, and Ted opened a clothing store earlier this year called The 3 Ts. They began by opening a checking account in the name of the business, renting a store, and buying some clothes to sell. They paid for the purchases and expenses out of the checking account and deposited cash in the account when they sold the clothes. At this point, they are arguing over how their business is doing and how much each of them should be paid. They also realize that they are supposed to make certain tax reports and payments, but they know very little about them. The following statements are excerpts from their conversation:

Tom: If we just had a computer, we wouldn't have had this argument.
Tina: No, what we need is a bookkeeper.
Ted: I don't know, but maybe we need an accountant.

Distinguish among a computer, a bookkeeper, and an accountant and comment on how each might help the operations of The 3 Ts.

Exercise 1-2. Users of Accounting Information (L.O. 2)

Public companies report each year on their success or failure in making a profit. Suppose that the following item appeared in the newspaper:

New York. Commonwealth Power Company, a major electric utility, reported yesterday that its net income for the year just ended represented a 50 percent increase over the previous year. . . .

Explain why each of the following individuals or groups may be interested in seeing the accounting reports that support the above statement.

1. The management of Commonwealth Power
2. The stockholders of Commonwealth Power
3. The creditors of Commonwealth Power
4. Potential stockholders of Commonwealth Power
5. The Internal Revenue Service
6. The Securities and Exchange Commission
7. The electrical workers' union
8. A consumers' group called the Public Cause
9. An economic adviser to the president

Exercise 1-3. The Accounting Equation (L.O. 6)

Use the accounting equation to answer each question below, and show your calculations.

1. The assets of Cruse Company are $480,000, and the owner's equity is $360,000. What is the amount of the liabilities?
2. The liabilities of Nabors Company equal one-third of the total assets. The firm's owner's equity is $80,000. What is the amount of the liabilities?
3. At the beginning of the year, Gilbert Company's assets were $180,000, and its owner's equity was $100,000. During the year, assets increased $60,000, and liabilities decreased $10,000. What was the owner's equity at the end of the year?

Exercise 1-4. Owner's Equity Transactions (L.O. 6)

Identify each of the following transactions by type of owner's equity transaction by marking each as either an owner's investment (I), owner's withdrawal (W), revenue (R), expense (E), or not an owner's equity transaction (NOE).

_____ a. Received cash for providing a service.
_____ b. Took assets out of business for personal use.
_____ c. Received cash from customer who had been previously billed for a service.
_____ d. Transferred assets to the business from a personal account.
_____ e. Paid service station for gasoline.
_____ f. Performed a service and received a promise of payment.
_____ g. Paid cash to purchase equipment.
_____ h. Paid cash to employee for services performed.

Exercise 1-5. Effect of Transactions on Accounting Equation
(L.O. 6)

During the month of April, the Ackley Company had the following transactions:

a. Paid salaries for April, $1,800.
b. Purchased equipment on account, $3,000.
c. Purchased supplies with cash, $100.
d. Additional investment by owner, $4,000.
e. Received payment for services performed, $600.
f. Paid for part of equipment previously purchased on credit, $1,000.
g. Billed customers for services performed, $1,600.
h. Withdrew cash, $1,500.
i. Received payment from customers billed previously, $300.
j. Received utility bill, $70.

On a sheet of paper, list the letters a through j, with columns for Assets, Liabilities, and Owner's Equity. In the columns, indicate whether each transaction caused an increase (+), a decrease (−), or no change (NC) in assets, liabilities, and owner's equity.

Exercise 1-6. Examples of Transactions
(L.O. 6)

For each of the following categories, describe a transaction that will have the required effect on the elements of the accounting equation.

1. Increase one asset and decrease another asset.
2. Decrease an asset and decrease a liability.
3. Increase an asset and increase a liability.
4. Increase an asset and increase owner's equity.
5. Decrease an asset and decrease owner's equity.

Exercise 1-7. Accounting Equation and Determination of Net Income
(L.O. 6)

The total assets and liabilities at the beginning and end of the year for Murillo Company are listed below.

	Assets	Liabilities
Beginning of the year	$ 70,000	$30,000
End of the year	100,000	50,000

Determine the net income for the year under each of the following alternatives:

1. The owner made no investments in the business or withdrawals from the business during the year.
2. The owner made no investments in the business, but the owner withdrew $22,000 during the year.
3. The owner made an investment of $10,000, but made no withdrawals during the year.
4. The owner made an investment of $10,000, and withdrew $22,000 during the year.

Exercise 1-8. Balance Sheet Preparation
(L.O. 7)

Appearing in random order below are the balance sheet balances for Bender Company as of December 31, 19xx.

Accounts Payable	$ 40,000	Accounts Receivable	$50,000
Building	80,000	Cash	20,000
Leon Bender, Capital	160,000	Equipment	40,000
Supplies	10,000		

Sort out the balances on page 37 and prepare a balance sheet similar to the one in Exhibit 1-2.

Interpreting Accounting Information

Merrill Lynch & Co.
(L.O. 6)

Merrill Lynch & Co. is the largest investment services company in the United States. Condensed balance sheets for 1983 and 1982 from the company's annual report are presented below. (All numbers represent thousands.) The owner's equity section has been adapted for use in this case.

	December 31	
	1983	1982
Assets		
Cash	$ 1,158,834	$ 1,259,829
Marketable Securities	6,828,083	5,371,482
Accounts Receivable	15,699,605	11,921,212
Property and Equipment	615,699	443,738
Other Assets	1,836,863	1,700,978
Total Assets	$26,139,084	$20,697,239
Liabilities		
Short-Term Liabilities	$14,996,339	$11,229,549
Long-Term Liabilities	1,264,096	756,869
Other Liabilities	7,990,630	7,277,939
Owner's Equity		
Merrill Lynch, Capital	1,888,019	1,432,882
Total Liabilities and Owner's Equity	$26,139,084	$20,697,239

Three students who were looking at Merrill Lynch's annual report were overheard to make the following comments:

Student A: What a superb year the company had in 1983! It earned a net income of $5,441,845,000, because total assets increased by that amount ($26,139,084,000 – $20,697,239,000).

Student B: Merrill Lynch had a terrible year in 1983! It had a net loss of $100,995,000, because cash decreased by that amount ($1,259,829,000 – $1,158,834,000).

Student C: I see from the annual report that Merrill Lynch paid cash dividends of $66,284,000 in 1983. Don't you have to take this fact into consideration? (Note: For a corporation, cash dividends are similar to withdrawals in a sole proprietorship.)

Required

1. Comment on the interpretations of Students A and B and answer Student C's question.
2. Calculate the 1983 net income from the information given.

Problem Set A

Problem 1A-1. Effect of Transactions on the Balance Sheet Equation (L.O. 6)

The Ryan Message Delivery Company was founded by L. V. Ryan on December 1 and engaged in the following transactions:

a. L. V. Ryan began the business by placing $8,000 cash in a bank account established in the name of Ryan Message Delivery Company.
b. Purchased a motor bike on credit, $2,800.
c. Purchased delivery supplies for cash, $200.
d. Billed customer for delivery fee, $100.
e. Received delivery fees in cash, $300.
f. Made payment on motor bike, $700.
g. Paid expenses, $120.
h. Received payment from customer billed in **d,** $50.
i. Withdrew cash for personal expenses, $150.

Required

1. Arrange the following assets, liabilities, and owner's equity accounts in an equation similar to Exhibit 1-1: Cash; Accounts Receivable; Delivery Supplies; Motor Bike; Accounts Payable; and L. V. Ryan, Capital.
2. Show by addition and subtraction, as in Exhibit 1-1, the effects of the transactions on the balance sheet equation. Show new balances after each transaction and identify each owner's equity transaction by type.

Problem 1A-2. Effect of Transactions on the Balance Sheet Equation (L.O. 6)

Quality Framing Boutique was started by Mary Kline in a small shopping center. After starting the business, she completed the following transactions:

a. Deposited $6,500 in a bank account in the company's name to start business.
b. Paid two months' rent in advance, $600.
c. Purchased store equipment on credit, $3,600.
d. Purchased framing supplies for cash, $1,700.
e. Received framing revenues, $800.
f. Billed customers for framing services, $700.
g. Paid expenses, $310.
h. Received payment from customers in **f,** $200.
i. Made payment on store equipment, $1,800.
j. Withdrew cash for personal expenses, $400.

Required

1. Arrange the following assets, liabilities, and owner's equity accounts in an equation similar to Exhibit 1-1: Cash; Accounts Receivable; Prepaid Rent; Framing Supplies; Store Equipment; Accounts Payable; and Mary Kline, Capital.
2. Show by addition and subtraction, as in Exhibit 1-1, the effects of the transactions on the balance sheet equation. Show new balances after each transaction and identify each owner's equity transaction by type.

Problem 1A-3. Effect of Transactions on the Balance Sheet Equation
(L.O. 6)

After completing her Ph.D. in management, Meredith Lacey set up a consulting practice. At the end of her first month of operation Dr. Lacey had the following account balances: Cash, $2,800; Accounts Receivable, $1,400; Office Supplies, $270; Office Equipment, $4,200; Accounts Payable, $1,900; Meredith Lacey, Capital, $6,770. Shortly thereafter the following transactions were completed:

a. Paid one month's rent, $300.
b. Made payment toward accounts payable, $500.
c. Billed clients for services performed, $800.
d. Received amount from clients billed last month, $1,000.
e. Purchased office supplies for cash, $80.
f. Paid secretary's salary, $850.
g. Paid utility expense, $90.
h. Paid telephone expense, $50.
i. Purchased additional office equipment for cash, $400.
j. Received cash from clients for services performed, $1,200.
k. Withdrew cash for personal expense, $500.

Required

1. Arrange the following assets, liabilities, and owner's equity accounts in an equation similar to Exhibit 1-1: Cash; Accounts Receivable; Office Supplies; Office Equipment; Accounts Payable; and Meredith Lacey, Capital.
2. Enter the beginning balances of the assets, liabilities, and owner's equity.
3. Show by addition and subtraction, as in Exhibit 1-1, the effects of the transactions on the balance sheet equation. Show new balances after each transaction and identify each owner's equity transaction by type.

Problem 1A-4. Preparation of Financial Statements
(L.O. 7)

At the end of its first month of operation, June 19xx, Branchi Plumbing Company had the following account balances:

Cash	$28,200
Accounts Receivable	5,400
Delivery Truck	19,000
Tools	3,800
Accounts Payable	4,300

In addition, the following transactions affected owner's equity:

Investment by L. Branchi	$30,000
Withdrawal by L. Branchi	2,000
Further investment by L. Branchi	20,000
Contract Revenue	11,100
Repair Revenue	2,200
Salaries Expense	8,300
Rent Expense	700
Fuel Expense	200

Required

Using Exhibit 1-2 as a model, prepare an income statement, a statement of owner's equity, and a balance sheet for Branchi Plumbing Company. (Hint: The final balance of L. Branchi, Capital is $52,100.)

Problem 1A-5. Effect of Transactions on the Balance Sheet Equation and Preparation of Financial Statements
(L.O. 6, 7)

The Campus Copy Service began operation and engaged in the following transactions during July 19xx:

a. Investment by owner, Ann Woodberry, $4,500.
b. Paid one month's rent, $400.
c. Purchased copier, $2,300.
d. Copying job received in cash, $950.
e. Copying job billed to major customer, $570.
f. Paid for paper used for previous two jobs, $240.
g. Paid wages to part-time employees, $280.
h. Purchased copier supplies on credit (none of these supplies are expected to be used this month), $140.
i. Received partial payment from customer in **e,** $300.
j. Paid utility bill, $90.
k. Made partial payment on supplies purchased in **h,** $70.
l. Withdrew cash for personal use, $800.

Required

1. Arrange the assets, liabilities, and owner's equity accounts in an equation similar to Exhibit 1-1, using the following account titles: Cash; Accounts Receivable; Supplies; Copier; Accounts Payable; and Ann Woodberry, Capital.
2. Show by addition and subtraction, as in Exhibit 1-1, the effects of the transactions on the balance sheet equation. Show new balances after each transaction and identify each owner's equity transaction by type.
3. Prepare an income statement, a statement of owner's equity, and a balance sheet.

Problem Set B

Problem 1B-1. Effect of Transactions on the Balance Sheet Equation
(L.O. 6)

Selected transactions for the Harding Carriage Company, begun on June 1 by Raymond Harding, are as follows:

a. Raymond Harding invests $57,000 cash in a new business called Harding Carriage Company.
b. A truck is purchased by the business for $36,000.
c. Equipment is purchased on credit for $9,000.
d. A fee of $1,200 for hauling goods is billed to a customer.
e. A fee of $2,300 for hauling goods is received in cash.
f. Cash of $600 is received from the customer who was billed in (**d**).
g. A payment of $5,000 is made on the equipment purchased in (**c**).
h. Expenses of $1,700 are paid in cash.
i. Cash of $1,200 is withdrawn for the business for Raymond Harding's personal use.

Required

1. Arrange the assets, liabilities, and owner's equity accounts in equation form similar to Exhibit 1-1, using the following account titles: Cash; Accounts Receivable; Truck; Equipment; Accounts Payable; and Raymond Harding, Capital.
2. Show by addition and subtraction as in Exhibit 1-1, the effects of the transactions on the balance sheet equation. Show new balances after each transaction and identify each owner's equity transaction by type.

Problem 1B-2. Effect of Transactions on the Balance Sheet Equation (L.O. 6)

Rita Nakawa, after receiving her degree in computer science, began her own practice called Programming Services Company. She completed the following transactions soon after starting the business:

a. Rita began her practice with a $10,000 cash investment, which she deposited in the bank, and a systems library, which cost $800.
b. Paid one month's rent on an office for her practice. Rent is $360 per month.
c. Purchased a minicomputer for $7,000 cash.
d. Purchased computer supplies on credit, $600.
e. Collected revenue from a client, $800.
f. Billed a client $110 upon completion of a short project.
g. Paid expenses of $400.
h. Received $80 from the client billed previously.
i. Withdrew $250 in cash for personal expenses.

Required

1. Arrange the assets, liabilities, and owner's equity accounts in an equation similar to Exhibit 1-1, using the following account titles: Cash; Accounts Receivable; Supplies; Equipment; Systems Library; Accounts Payable; and Rita Nakawa, Capital.
2. Show by additions and subtractions, as in Exhibit 1-1, the effects of the transactions on the balance sheet equation. Show new totals after each transaction and identify each owner's equity transaction by type.

Problem 1B-3. Effect of Transactions on the Balance Sheet Equation (L.O. 6)

Dr. Ted Pomeroy, psychologist, moved from his home town to set up an office in Cincinnati. After one month, the business had the following assets: Cash, $1,900; Accounts Receivable, $680; Office Supplies, $300; Office Equipment, $1,500; and Car, $6,000. Owner's Equity consisted of $7,780 of Capital. The debts were $2,600 for purchases of a car and office equipment on credit. During a short period of time, the following transactions were completed:

a. Paid one month's rent, $350.
b. Billed patient $60 for services rendered.
c. Paid $300 on office equipment previously purchased.
d. Paid for office supplies, $100.
e. Paid secretary's salary, $300.
f. Received $800 from patients not previously billed.
g. Made car payment, $360.
h. Withdrew $500 for living expenses.
i. Paid telephone bill, $70.
j. Received $290 from patients previously billed.
k. Purchased additional office equipment on credit, $300.

Required

1. Arrange the assets, liabilities, and owner's equity accounts in an equation similar to Exhibit 1-1, using the following account titles: Cash; Accounts Receivable; Office Supplies; Office Equipment; Car; Accounts Payable; and Ted Pomeroy, Capital.
2. Enter the beginning balances of the assets, liabilities, and owner's equity.
3. Show by additions and subtractions, as in Exhibit 1-1, the effect of the transactions on the balance sheet equation. Show new totals after each transaction and identify each owner's equity transaction by type.

Problem 1B-4. Preparation of Financial Statements (L.O. 7)

At the end of October, 19xx, the Mark Ratner, Capital account had a balance of $50,000. After operating during November, his Holiday Riding Club had the following account balances:

Cash	$16,600
Accounts Receivable	1,200
Supplies	1,000
Land	21,000
Building	30,000
Horses	10,000
Accounts Payable	17,800

In addition, the following transactions affected Owner's Equity:

Withdrawal by Mark Ratner	$ 6,400
Investment by Mark Ratner	16,000
Riding Lesson Revenue	4,800
Locker Rental Revenue	1,500
Salaries Expense	2,300
Feed Expense	1,000
Utilities Expense	600

Required

Using Exhibit 1-2 as a model, prepare an income statement, a statement of owner's equity, and a balance sheet for Holiday Riding Club (Hint: The final balance of Mark Ratner, Capital is $62,000).

Problem 1B-5. Effect of Transactions on the Balance Sheet Equation and Preparation of Financial Statements (L.O. 6, 7)

On April 1, 19xx, Turnbow Taxi Service began operation and engaged in the following transactions during April:

a. Investment by owner, Sara Turnbow, $35,000.
b. Purchase of taxi for cash, $19,000.
c. Purchase of uniforms on credit, $400.
d. Taxi fares received in cash, $2,500.
e. Paid wages to part-time drivers, $500.
f. Purchased gasoline during month for cash, $800.
g. Purchased car washes during month on credit, $120.
h. Further investment by owner, $5,000.
i. Paid part of the amount owed for the uniforms purchased in **c**, $200.
j. Billed major client for fares, $900.
k. Paid for automobile repairs, $250.
l. Withdrew cash from business for personal use, $1,000.

Required

1. Arrange the assets, liabilities, and owner's equity accounts in equation form similar to Exhibit 1-1, using the following account titles: Cash; Accounts Receivable; Uniforms; Taxi; Accounts Payable; and Sara Turnbow, Capital.
2. Show by addition and subtraction, as in Exhibit 1-1, the effects of the transactions on the balance sheet equation. Identify each owner's equity transaction by type.
3. Using Exhibit 1-2 as a guide, prepare an income statement, a statement of owner's equity, and a balance sheet for Turnbow Taxi Service.

Financial Decision Case

Murphy Lawn Services Company
(L.O. 6, 7)

Instead of hunting for a summer job after completing her junior year in college, Beth Murphy organized a lawn service company in her neighborhood. To start her business on June 1, she deposited $2,500 in a new bank account in the name of her company. The $2,500 consisted of a $1,000 loan from her father and $1,500 of her own money.

Using the money in this checking account, she rented lawn equipment, purchased supplies, and hired neighborhood high school students to mow and trim lawns of neighbors who had agreed to pay her for the service. At the end of each month, she mailed out bills to her customers.

On September 30, Beth was ready to dissolve her business and go back to school for the fall quarter. Because she had been so busy, she had not kept any records other than her checkbook and a list of amounts owed to her by customers. Her checkbook had a balance of $3,250, and the amount owed to her by the customers totaled $875. She expected these customers to pay her during October. She remembered that she could return unused supplies to the Lawn Care Center for a full credit of $50. When she brought back the rented lawn equipment, the Lawn Care Center would also return a deposit of $200 she had made in June. She owed the Lawn Care Center $475 for equipment rentals and supplies. In addition, she owed the students who had worked for her $100, and she still owed her father $600. Though Beth feels she did quite well, she is not sure just how successful she was.

Required

1. Prepare a balance sheet dated June 1 and one dated September 30 for Murphy Lawn Services Company.
2. Comment on the performance of Murphy Lawn Services Company by comparing the two balance sheets. Did the company have a profit or loss? (Assume that Beth used none of the company's assets for personal purposes.)
3. If Beth is to continue her business next summer, what kind of information from her recordkeeping system would help make it easier to tell whether she is earning a profit or losing money?

Answers to Self-Test

1. d	3. b	5. b	7. d	9. a
2. a	4. a	6. b	8. a	10. d

CHAPTER 2 THE DOUBLE-ENTRY SYSTEM

LEARNING OBJECTIVES

1. Explain in simple terms the generally accepted ways of solving the measurement problems of recognition, valuation, and classification.
2. Define and use the terms *account* and *ledger*.
3. Recognize commonly used asset, liability, and owner's equity accounts.
4. State the rules for debit and credit.
5. Apply the procedure for transaction analysis to simple transactions.
6. Record transactions in the general journal.
7. Explain the relationship of the journal to the ledger.
8. Prepare a trial balance and recognize its value and limitations.

In the last chapter you learned the answer to the question, What is to be measured? Chapter 2 opens with a discussion of these questions: When should the measurement occur? What value should be placed on the measurement? and How is the measurement to be classified? Then, as the focus shifts from accounting concepts to actual practice, you begin working with the double-entry system and applying it to the analysis and recording of business transactions. After studying this chapter, you should be able to meet the learning objectives listed on the left.

Measurement Problems

Business transactions were defined earlier as economic events that affect the financial position of a business entity. To measure a business transaction, the accountant must decide when the transaction occurred (the recognition problem), what value should be placed on the transaction (the valuation problem), and how the components of the transaction should be categorized (the classification problem).

These three problems—recognition, valuation, and classification—are the basis of almost every major issue in financial accounting today. They lie at the heart of such complex issues as accounting for pension plans, mergers of giant companies, international transactions, and the effects of inflation. In discussing the three basic problems, we follow generally accepted accounting principles and use an approach that promotes the understanding of the basic ideas of accounting. Keep in mind that controversy does exist, however, and some solutions to the problems are not as cut and dried or generally agreed upon as they may appear.

The Recognition Problem

The **recognition problem** refers to the difficulty of deciding when a business transaction should be recorded. Often the facts of a situation are known, but there is disagreement as to *when* the events should be recorded. For instance, consider the problem of when to recognize or first record a simple purchase. A company orders, receives, and pays for an office desk. Which of the following actions constitutes a recordable event?

1. An employee sends a purchase requisition to the purchasing department.
2. The purchasing department sends a purchase order to the supplier.
3. The supplier ships the desk.
4. The company receives the desk.
5. The company receives the bill from the supplier.
6. The company pays the bill.

OBJECTIVE 1
Explain in simple terms the generally accepted ways of solving the measurement problems of recognition, valuation, and classification

The answer to this question is important, because the amounts in the financial statements are affected by the date on which the purchase is recorded. Accounting tradition provides a guideline or generally accepted accounting principle stating that the transaction will be recorded when the title to the desk passes from supplier to purchaser and an obligation to pay results. Thus, depending on the details of the shipping agreement, the transaction is recognized at the time of either action 3 or action 4. This is the guideline that we will use generally in this book. However, in many small businesses that use simple business systems, the initial recording of the transaction occurs when the bill is received (action 5) or when the transfer of cash occurs (action 6), because these are the implied points of transfer of title.

Such problems are not always solved easily. Consider the case of an automobile manufacturer who builds a car. The finished car will be worth substantially more than the parts and labor that went into it. Should the amount of value added be recognized as the automobile is being produced or at the time it is completed? According to the above guideline, the increase in value is recorded at the time the automobile is sold. Normally, legal title passes from the automobile manufacturer to the dealer at the point of sale.

The Valuation Problem

The **valuation problem** is perhaps the most controversial issue in accounting. It has to do with the difficulty of assigning a value to a business transaction. Generally accepted accounting principles state that, in general, the appropriate valuation to assign to all business transactions, and therefore to all assets, liabilities, owner's equity, revenues, and expenses acquired by a business, is the original cost (often called historical cost). **Cost** is defined here as the exchange price associated with a business transaction at the point of recognition. According to this guideline, the purpose of accounting is not to account for "value," which may change after a transaction occurs, but to account for the cost or value at the time of the transaction. For example, the cost of assets is recorded when they are acquired, and their "value" is also held at that level until they are sold, expire, or are consumed. In this context, value in accounting means the cost at the time of the transaction that brought the item into or took it out of the business entity. This practice is referred to by accountants as the **cost principle**.

Suppose that a person offers a building for sale at $120,000. It may be valued for real estate taxes at $75,000, and it may be insured for $90,000. One prospective buyer may offer $100,000 for the building, and another may offer $105,000. At this point, several different, unverifiable opinions of value have been expressed. Finally, the seller and a buyer may settle on a price and complete a sale for $110,000. All these figures are values of one kind or another, but only the last figure is sufficiently reliable to be used in the records. The market value of this building may vary over the years, but it will remain on the new buyer's records at $110,000 until it is sold again. At that point, the accountant would record the new transaction at the new exchange price, and a profit or loss on the sale would be recognized.

The cost guideline is used because it meets the standard of verifiability. Cost is verifiable because it results from the actions of independent buyers and sellers who come to an agreement about price. This exchange price is an objective price that can be verified by evidence created at the time of the transaction. Both the buyer and the seller may have thought they got the better deal, but their opinions are irrelevant in recording cost. The final price of $110,000, verified by agreement of the two parties, is the price at which the transaction is recorded.

The Classification Problem

The **classification problem** is that of assigning all the transactions in which a business will engage to the appropriate accounts. For example, a company's ability to borrow money may be affected by the way in which some of its debts are categorized. Or a company's income may be affected by whether a purchase of a small item such as a tool is considered an item of repair expense or an item of equipment (an asset). Proper classification depends not only on the correct analysis of the effect of each transaction on the business enterprise but also on the maintenance of a system of accounts that will reflect that effect. The rest of this chapter explains the classification of accounts and the analysis and recording of transactions.

Accounts

OBJECTIVE 2
Define and use the terms *account* and *ledger*

When large amounts of data are gathered in the measurement of business transactions, a method of storage is required. Business people should be able to retrieve transaction data quickly and in the form desired. In other words, there should be a filing system to sort out or classify all the transactions that occur in a business. Only in this way can financial statements and other reports be prepared quickly and easily. This filing system consists of accounts. An **account** is the basic storage unit for data in accounting. An accounting system has separate accounts for each asset, each liability, and each component of owner's equity, including revenues and expenses. Whether a company keeps records by hand or by computer, management must be able to refer to these accounts so that it can study the company's financial history and plan for the future. A very small company may need only a few dozen accounts, whereas a multinational corporation will have thousands.

Management's Use of Accounts

The accumulation of information in account form is useful to management in running a business. In the example of Shannon Realty from Chapter 1, for instance, John Shannon can keep a running balance of cash receipts and payments so that he knows how much cash is on hand at any one time. He can plan ahead to have enough funds to pay salaries and various bills when they are due. He can foresee the need to borrow money from the bank by estimating future cash payments and cash receipts. Good planning for future cash needs requires that he have a record of past receipts and expenditures as well as of his current cash balance. The Cash account gives him this information.

The Ledger

In a manual accounting system, each account is kept on a separate page or card. These pages or cards are placed together in a book or file. This book or file, which contains all or groups of the company's accounts, is called a **ledger.** In a computer system, which most companies have today, the accounts are maintained on magnetic tapes or disks. However, as a matter of convenience, the accountant still refers to the group of company accounts as the ledger.

To be able to find an account in the ledger easily and to identify accounts when working with the accounting records, an accountant often numbers the accounts. A list of these numbers with the corresponding account names is usually called a **chart of accounts**. A very simple chart of accounts appears on the next page. Note that the first digit refers to the major financial statement classifications. An account number beginning with the digit 1 is an asset, an account number beginning with a 2 is a liability, and so forth.

You will be introduced to these accounts in the following section and over the next two-and-a-half chapters through the illustrative case of the Joan Miller Advertising Agency. At this time, notice the gaps in the sequence of numbers. These gaps allow for expansion in the number of accounts. Of course, every company develops a chart of accounts for its own needs. Seldom will two companies have exactly the same chart of accounts and larger companies will require more digits to accommodate all of their accounts.

Types of Commonly Used Accounts

OBJECTIVE 3 Recognize commonly used asset, liability, and owner's equity accounts

The specific accounts used by a company depend on the nature of the company's business. A steel company will have many equipment and inventory accounts, whereas an advertising agency may have few. Each company must design its accounts in a way that will reflect the nature of its business and the needs of its management in directing that business. There are, however, accounts that are common to most businesses. Some important ones are described in the following paragraphs.

Assets		Liabilities	
Cash	111	Notes Payable	211
Notes Receivable	112	Accounts Payable	212
Accounts Receivable	113	Unearned Art Fees	213
Accrued Fees Receivable	114	Wages Payable	214
Art Supplies	115	Mortgage Payable	221
Office Supplies	116		
Prepaid Rent	117	**Owner's Equity**	
Prepaid Insurance	118	Joan Miller, Capital	311
Land	141	Joan Miller, Withdrawals	312
Buildings	142	Income Summary	313
Accumulated Depreciation, Buildings	143	**Revenues**	
Art Equipment	144	Advertising Fees Earned	411
Accumulated Depreciation, Art Equipment	145	Art Fees Earned	412
Office Equipment	146	**Expenses**	
Accumulated Depreciation, Office Equipment	147	Office Wages Expense	511
		Utility Expense	512
		Telephone Expense	513
		Rent Expense	514
		Insurance Expense	515
		Art Supplies Expense	516
		Office Supplies Expense	517
		Depreciation Expense, Buildings	518
		Depreciation Expense, Art Equipment	519
		Depreciation Expense, Office Equipment	520

Asset Accounts. A company must keep records of the increases and decreases in each asset that it owns. Some of the more common asset accounts are as follows:

Cash "Cash" is the title of the account used to record increases and decreases in cash. Cash consists of money or any medium of exchange that a bank will accept at face value for deposit. Included are coins, currency, checks, postal and express money orders, certificates of deposit, and money deposited in a bank or banks. The Cash account also includes cash on hand such as that in a cash register or a safe.

Notes Receivable A promissory note is a written promise to pay a definite sum of money at a fixed future date. Amounts due from others in the form of promissory notes are recorded in an account called Notes Receivable.

Accounts Receivable Companies often sell goods and services to customers on the basis of the customers' oral or implied promises to pay in the future, such as in thirty days or at the first of the month. These sales are called Credit Sales, or Sales on Account, and the promises to pay are known as Accounts Receivable. Credit sales increase Accounts Receivable, and collections from customers decrease Accounts Receivable. Of course, it is necessary to keep a record of how much each customer owes the company. How these records are kept is explained in Appendix A.

Prepaid Expenses Companies often pay for goods and services before they receive or use them. These prepaid expenses are considered assets until they are used, at which time they become expenses. There should be a separate account for each prepaid expense. An example of a prepaid expense is Prepaid Insurance (or Unexpired Insurance). Insurance protection against fire, theft, and other hazards is usually paid in advance for a period of from one to five years. When the premiums are paid, the Prepaid Insurance account is increased. These premiums expire day by day and month by month. Therefore, at intervals, usually at the end of the accounting period, the Prepaid Insurance must be reduced by the amount of insurance that has expired. Another common type of prepaid expense is Office Supplies. Stamps, stationery, pencils, pens, paper, and other office supplies are assets when they are purchased and are recorded as an increase in Office Supplies. As the office supplies are used, the account is reduced. Other typical prepaid expenses that are assets when they are purchased and become expenses through use or the passage of time are prepaid rent, store supplies, and prepaid taxes.

Land An account called Land is used to record purchases of property to be used in the ordinary operations of the business.

Buildings Purchases of structures to be used in the business are recorded in an account called Buildings. Although a building cannot be separated from the land it occupies, it is important to maintain separate accounts for the land and the building. The reason for doing so is that the building is subject to wear and tear, but the land is not. Later in the book the subject of depreciation will be introduced. Wear and tear is an important aspect of depreciation.

Equipment A company may own many different types of equipment. Usually there is a separate account for each type. Changes in amounts representing the cost of desks, chairs, office machines, filing cabinets, and typewriters are recorded in an account called Office Equipment. Increases and decreases in cash registers, counters, showcases, shelves, and similar items are recorded in the Store Equipment account. When a company has a factory, it may own lathes, drill presses, and other factory equipment and would record changes in such items in an account titled Machinery and Equipment. Some companies may have use for a Trucks and Automobiles account.

Liability Accounts. Another word for *liabilities* is *debt*. Most companies have fewer liability accounts than asset accounts. But it is just as important to keep records of what the company owes as it is to keep asset accounts. There are two types of liabilities: short-term and long-term. The distinction between them is introduced in Chapter 5. The following accounts are short-term liabilities:

Notes Payable The account called Notes Payable is the opposite of Notes Receivable. It is used to record increases and decreases in promissory notes owed to creditors within the next year or operating cycle.

Accounts Payable Similarly, Accounts Payable is the opposite of Accounts Receivable. It represents amounts owed to creditors on the basis of an oral or implied promise to pay. Accounts payable usually arise as the result of the purchase of merchandise, services, supplies, or equipment on credit. When Company A buys an item from Company B and promises to pay at the beginning of the month, the amount of the transaction is an Account Payable on Company A's books and an Account Receivable on Company B's books. As with Accounts Receivable, records of amounts owed to individual creditors must be known. Appendix A covers the method of accomplishing this task.

Other Short-Term Liabilities A few other liabilities and liability accounts are Wages Payable, Taxes Payable, Rent Payable, and Interest Payable. Often customers make deposits on, or pay in advance for, goods and services to be delivered in the future. Such customers' deposits are also recorded as liabilities. They are liabilities because the money must be returned to the customer if the goods or services are not delivered. These kinds of liability accounts are often called Unearned Fees, Customer Deposits, Advances from Customers, or, more commonly, Unearned Revenues.

Long-Term Liabilities The most common type of long-term liabilities are bonds or property mortgages. Because a wide variety of bonds and mortgages have been developed for special financing needs, it is difficult to classify them. They may or may not require the backing of certain of the company's assets for security. For example, a mortgage holder may have the right to force the sale of certain assets if the mortgage debt is not paid when due. For now, however, it will suffice to record increases and decreases in long-term debt in an account called Bonds Payable or Mortgage Payable.

Owner's Equity Accounts. In Chapter 1, several transactions affected owner's equity. The effects of all these transactions were shown by the increases or decreases in the single column representing owner's equity (see Exhibit 1-1) with an indication of the type of each transaction. For legal and managerial reasons, it is important to sort these transactions into separate owner's equity accounts. Among the most important information that management receives for business planning is a detailed breakdown of revenues and expenses. For income tax reporting, financial reporting, and other reasons, the law requires that capital contributions and withdrawals be separated from revenues and expenses. Ownership and equity accounts, especially those for partnerships and corporations, are covered in much more detail in Part Four, but for now the following accounts, whose relationships are shown in Figure 2-1, are important to the study of sole proprietorships.

Capital Account When someone invests in his or her own company, the amount of the investment is recorded in a capital account. For instance, in Chapter 1 when John Shannon invested his personal resources in his

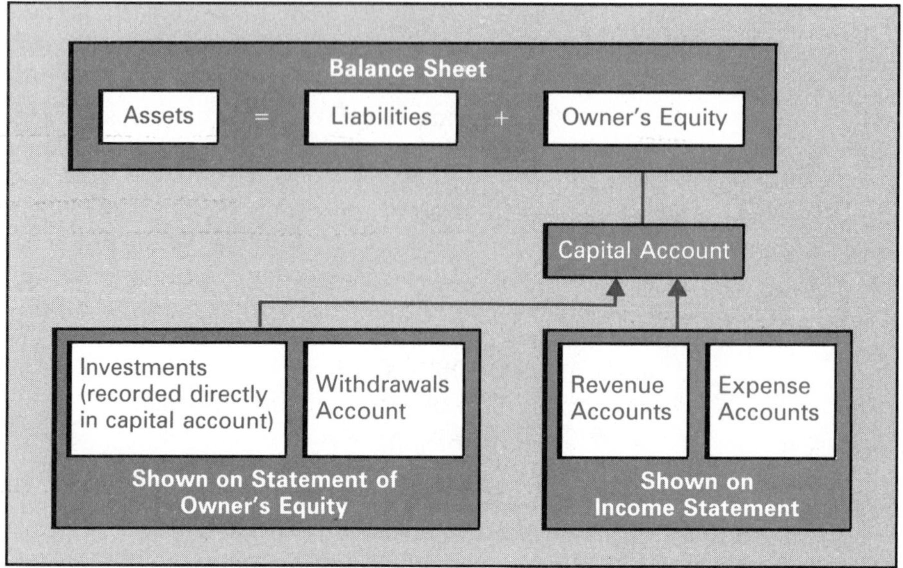

Figure 2-1. Relationships of Owner's Equity Accounts

firm, he recorded the amount in the owner's equity account titled John Shannon, Capital. Any additional investments by John Shannon in his firm would be recorded in this account. The capital accounts for corporations are discussed in Part Four.

Withdrawals Account A person who invests in a business usually expects to earn an income and to use at least part of the assets earned from profitable operations to pay personal living expenses. Since the income for a business is determined at the end of the accounting period, the owner often finds it necessary to withdraw assets from the business for living expenses long before income has been determined. We do not describe these withdrawals as salary, although the owner might think of them as such, because there is no change in the ownership of the money withdrawn; we say, simply, that the owner has withdrawn assets for personal use. As a result, it has become common practice to set up a withdrawals account to record these payments, which are made with the expectation of earning an income. For example, an account called John Shannon, Withdrawals, would be used to record John Shannon's withdrawals from his firm. In practice, the withdrawals account often goes by several other names. Among these other titles are Personal and Drawing. This account is not used by corporations.

Revenue and Expense Accounts Revenues increase owner's equity, and expenses decrease owner's equity. The greater the revenues, the more the owner's equity is increased. The greater the expenses, the more the owner's equity is decreased. Of course, when revenues are greater than expenses, the company has earned a profit or net income. When expenses are more than revenues, the company has suffered a loss or net loss. Management's major goal is to earn an income, and an important function of accounting is to give management the information that will help it meet this goal. One way of doing this is by having a ledger account for every revenue and expense item. From these accounts, which are identified on the income statement, management can identify exactly the source of all revenues and the nature of all expenses. A particular company's revenue and expense accounts will depend on its kind of business and the nature of its operations. A few of the revenue accounts used in this book are Commissions Earned, Advertising Fees Earned, and Sales. Some of the expense accounts are Wages Expense, Supplies Expense, Rent Expense, and Advertising Expense.

Titles of Accounts

The names of accounts are often confusing to beginning accounting students because some of the words are new or have special technical meanings. It is also true that the same asset, liability, or owner's equity account may be called by different names in different companies. This fact is not so strange. People too are often called different names by their friends, families, and associates.

Similarly, long-term assets may be known in various contexts as Fixed Assets, Plant and Equipment, Capital Assets, Long-Lived Assets, and so forth. Even the most acceptable names change over a period of time in accounting, and by habit some companies may use names that are out of date. In general, the account title should describe what is recorded in the account. When you encounter an account title that you do not recognize, you should examine the context of the name—that is, whether it is classified as asset, liability, owner's equity, revenue, or expense on the financial statement—and look for the kind of transaction that gave rise to the account.

The Double-Entry System: The Basic Method of Accounting

The double-entry system, the backbone of accounting, evolved during the Renaissance. The first systematic presentation of double-entry bookkeeping appeared in 1494, two years after Columbus discovered America. It was described in a mathematics book written by Fra Luca Pacioli, a Franciscan monk who was a friend of Leonardo da Vinci. Goethe, the famous German poet and dramatist, referred to double-entry bookkeeping as "one of the finest discoveries of the human intellect." Werner Sombart, an eminent economist-sociologist, expressed the belief that "double-entry bookkeeping is born of the same spirit as the system of Galileo and Newton."

What is the significance of the double-entry system for accounting? The double-entry system is based on the principle of duality, which means that all events of economic importance have two aspects—effort and reward, sacrifice and benefit, sources and uses—that offset or balance each other. In the **double-entry system** each transaction must be recorded with at least one debit and one credit, in such a way that the total dollar amount of debits and the total dollar amount of credits equal each other.

Because of the way it is designed, the system as a whole is always in balance. All accounting systems, no matter how sophisticated, are based on this principle of duality. The T account is a helpful place to begin the study of the double-entry system.

The T Account

In its simplest form, an account has three parts: (1) a title that describes the asset, liability, or owner's equity account; (2) a left side, which is called the **debit** side; and (3) a right side, which is called the **credit** side. This form of the account, called a **T account** because of its resemblance to the letter *T*, is used to analyze transactions. It appears as follows:

Title of Account	
Left or Debit Side	Right or Credit Side

Thus any entry made on the left side of the account is a debit, or debit entry, and any entry made on the right side of the account is a credit, or credit entry. The terms *debit* (abbreviated Dr., from the Latin *debere*) and *credit* (abbreviated Cr., from the Latin *credere*) are simply the accountant's words for "left" and "right" (not for "increase" or "decrease"). A more formal version of the T account will be presented later in this chapter.

The T Account Illustrated

In Chapter 1, Shannon Realty had several transactions that involved the receipt or payment of cash. (See Exhibit 1-1 for a summary of the numbered transactions given below.) These transactions can be summarized in the Cash account by recording receipts on the left or debit side of the account and payments on the right or credit side of the account as follows:

Cash			
(1)	50,000	(2)	35,000
(5)	1,500	(4)	200
(7)	1,000	(8)	1,000
		(9)	400
		(11)	600
	52,500		37,200
Bal.	15,300		

The cash receipts have been totaled on the left as $52,500, and this total is written in small-size figures so that it will not be confused with an actual debit entry. The cash payments are totaled in a similar way on the right side. These figures are simply working totals called **footings**. Footings are calculated at the end of the month as an easy way to determine cash on hand. The difference in total dollars between the total debit footings and the total credit footings is called the **balance** or **account balance**. If the balance is a debit, it is written on the left side.

If it is a credit, it is written on the right. Notice that Shannon Realty's Cash account has a debit balance of $15,300 ($52,500 − $37,200). This represents Shannon's cash on hand at the end of the month.

Analysis of Transactions

OBJECTIVE 4
State the rules for debit and credit

The rules of double-entry bookkeeping are that every transaction affects at least two accounts. In other words, there must be one or more accounts debited and one or more accounts credited, and the total debits must equal the total credits.

When we look at the accounting equation

assets = liabilities + owner's equity

we can see that if a debit increases assets, then a credit must be used to increase liabilities or owner's equity. On the other hand, if a credit decreases assets, then a debit must be used to show a decrease in liabilities or owner's equity. These are the rules because assets are on the opposite side of the equation from liabilities and owner's equity. These rules can be shown as follows:

Assets		=	Liabilities		+	Owner's Equity	
Debit for Increases	Credit for Decreases		Debit for Decreases	Credit for Increases		Debit for Decreases	Credit for Increases

1. Increases in assets are debited to asset accounts. Decreases in assets are credited to asset accounts.
2. Increases in liabilities and owner's equity are credited to liability and owner's equity accounts. Decreases in liabilities and owner's equity are debited to liability and owner's equity accounts.

One of the more difficult points to understand is the application of these rules to the owner's equity components of revenues, expenses, and withdrawals. Since revenues increase owner's equity and expenses and withdrawals decrease it, the following relationships hold:

Owner's Equity	
Decreases (Debits)	Increases (Credits)

Expenses	
Increases (Debits)	Decreases (Credits)

Revenues	
Decreases (Debits)	Increases (Credits)

Withdrawals	
Increases (Debits)	Decreases (Credits)

Thus, a transaction that increases revenues by a credit also increases owner's equity by a credit. However, expenses and withdrawals that are *increased* by debits *decrease* owner's equity. In other words, the more expenses and withdrawals are *increased* by debits, the more these debits *decrease* owner's equity, and the more expenses and withdrawals are *decreased* by credits, the more these credits *increase* owner's equity.

At this point we can explain how to analyze transactions. Transactions are usually supported by some kind of document, such as an invoice, a receipt, a check, or a contract. These source documents provide the basis for analyzing each transaction. As an example, let us suppose that Jones Company borrows $1,000 from its bank on a promissory note. The procedure is as follows:

1. Analyze the effect of the transaction on assets, liabilities, and owner's equity. In this case, both an asset (Cash) and a liability (Notes Payable) were increased.
2. Apply the correct double-entry rule. Increases in assets are recorded by debits. Increases in liabilities are recorded by credits.
3. Make the entry. The increase in assets is recorded by a debit to the Cash account, and the increase in liabilities is recorded by a credit to the Notes Payable account.

Cash	
1,000	

Notes Payable	
	1,000

The debit to Cash of $1,000 equals the credit to Notes Payable of $1,000.

Another form of this entry, which will be explained later in this chapter, is as follows:

	Dr.	**Cr.**
Cash	1,000	
Notes Payable		1,000

Transaction Analysis Illustrated

OBJECTIVE 5
Apply the procedure for transaction analysis to simple transactions

The next few pages consist of the transactions for the Joan Miller Advertising Agency during the month of January. We will use the transactions to illustrate the application of the principle of duality and to show how transactions are recorded in the accounts.

January 1: Joan Miller invested $10,000 in her own advertising agency.

Cash	
Jan. 1 10,000	

Joan Miller, Capital	
	Jan. 1 10,000

Transaction: Investment in business.
Analysis: Assets increased. Owner's equity increased.
Rules: Increases in assets are recorded by debits. Increases in owner's equity are recorded by credits.
Entry: Increase in assets is recorded by a debit to Cash. Increase in owner's equity is recorded by a credit to Joan Miller, Capital.

	Dr.	Cr.
Cash	10,000	
Joan Miller, Capital		10,000

January 2: Rented an office, paying two months' rent in advance, $800.

Cash

Jan. 1	10,000	Jan. 2	800

Prepaid Rent

Jan. 2	800		

Transaction: Expense paid in advance.
Analysis: Assets increased. Assets decreased.
Rules: Increases in assets are recorded by debits. Decreases in assets are recorded by credits.
Entry: Increase in assets is recorded by a debit to Prepaid Rent. Decrease in assets is recorded by a credit to Cash.

	Dr.	Cr.
Prepaid Rent	800	
Cash		800

January 3: Ordered art supplies, $1,800 and office supplies, $800.

Analysis: No entry is made because no transaction has occurred. There is no liability until the supplies are received and there is an obligation to pay for them.

January 4: Purchased art equipment for $4,200 cash.

Cash

Jan. 1	10,000	Jan. 2	800
		4	4,200

Art Equipment

Jan. 4	4,200		

Transaction: Purchase of equipment.
Analysis: Assets increased. Assets decreased.
Rules: Increases in assets are recorded by debits. Decreases in assets are recorded by credits.
Entry: Increase in assets is recorded by a debit to Art Equipment. Decrease in assets is recorded by a credit to Cash.

	Dr.	Cr.
Art Equipment	4,200	
Cash		4,200

January 5: Purchased office equipment from Morgan Equipment for $3,000, paying $1,500 in cash and agreeing to pay the rest next month.

Cash

Jan. 1	10,000	Jan. 2	800
		4	4,200
		5	1,500

Office Equipment

Jan. 5	3,000		

Accounts Payable

		Jan. 5	1,500

Transaction: Purchase of equipment, partial payment.
Analysis: Assets increased. Assets decreased. Liabilities increased.
Rules: Increases in assets are recorded by debits. Decreases in assets are recorded by credits. Increases in liabilities are recorded by credits.
Entry: Increase in assets is recorded by a debit to Office Equipment. Decrease in assets is recorded by a credit to Cash. Increase in liabilities is recorded by a credit to Accounts Payable.

	Dr.	Cr.
Office Equipment	3,000	
Cash		1,500
Accounts Payable		1,500

January 6: Purchased on credit art supplies for $1,800 and office supplies for $800 from Taylor Supply Company.

Art Supplies

Jan. 6	1,800		

Office Supplies

Jan. 6	800		

Accounts Payable

		Jan. 5	1,500
		6	2,600

Transaction: Purchase of supplies on credit.
Analysis: Assets increased. Liabilities increased.
Rules: Increases in assets are recorded by debits. Increases in liabilities are recorded by credits.
Entry: Increase in assets is recorded by debits to Art Supplies and Office Supplies. Increase in liabilities is recorded by a credit to Accounts Payable.

	Dr.	Cr.
Art Supplies	1,800	
Office Supplies	800	
Accounts Payable		2,600

January 8: Paid $480 for a one-year insurance policy with coverage effective January 1.

Cash

Jan. 1	10,000	Jan. 2	800
		4	4,200
		5	1,500
		8	480

Prepaid Insurance

Jan. 8	480		

Transaction: Paid for insurance coverage in advance.
Analysis: One asset increased. Another asset decreased.
Rules: Increases in assets are recorded by debits. Decreases in assets are recorded by credits.
Entry: Increase in assets is recorded by a debit to Prepaid Insurance. Decrease in assets is recorded by a credit to Cash.

	Dr.	Cr.
Prepaid Insurance	480	
Cash		480

January 9: Paid Taylor Supply Company $1,000 of the amount owed.

Cash

Jan. 1	10,000	Jan. 2	800
		4	4,200
		5	1,500
		8	480
		9	1,000

Accounts Payable

Jan. 9	1,000	Jan. 5	1,500
		6	2,600

Transaction: Partial payment on a liability.
Analysis: Assets decreased. Liabilities decreased.
Rules: Decreases in assets are recorded by credits. Decreases in liabilities are recorded by debits.
Entry: Decrease in liabilities is recorded by a debit to Accounts Payable. Decrease in assets is recorded by a credit to Cash.

	Dr.	Cr.
Accounts Payable	1,000	
Cash		1,000

January 10: Performed a service by placing advertisements for an automobile dealer in the newspaper and collected a fee of $1,400.

Cash

Jan. 1	10,000	Jan. 2	800
10	1,400	4	4,200
		5	1,500
		8	480
		9	1,000

Advertising Fees Earned

		Jan. 10	1,400

Transaction: Revenue earned and collected.
Analysis: Assets increased. Owner's equity increased.
Rules: Increases in assets are recorded by debits. Increases in owner's equity are recorded by credits.
Entry: Increase in assets is recorded by debit to Cash. Increase in owner's equity is recorded by credit to Advertising Fees Earned.

	Dr.	Cr.
Cash	1,400	
Advertising Fees Earned		1,400

January 12: Paid the secretary two weeks' salary, $600.

Cash

Jan. 1	10,000	Jan. 2	800
10	1,400	4	4,200
		5	1,500
		8	480
		9	1,000
		12	600

Office Wages Expense

Jan. 12	600		

Transaction: Payment of wages expense.
Analysis: Assets decreased. Owner's equity decreased.
Rules: Decreases in assets are recorded by credits. Decreases in owner's equity are recorded by debits.
Entry: Decrease in owner's equity is recorded by a debit to Office Wages Expense. Decrease in assets is recorded by a credit to Cash.

	Dr.	Cr.
Office Wages Expense	600	
Cash		600

January 15: Accepted $1,000 as an advance fee for art work to be done for another agency.

Cash

Jan. 1	10,000	Jan. 2	800
10	1,400	4	4,200
15	1,000	5	1,500
		8	480
		9	1,000
		12	600

Unearned Art Fees

		Jan. 15	1,000

Transaction: Accepted payment for services to be performed.
Analysis: Assets increased. Liabilities increased.
Rules: Increases in assets are recorded by debits. Increases in liabilities are recorded by credits.
Entry: Increase in assets is recorded by a debit to Cash. Increase in liabilities is recorded by a credit to Unearned Art Fees.

	Dr.	Cr.
Cash	1,000	
Unearned Art Fees		1,000

January 19: Performed a service by placing several major advertisements for Ward Department Stores. The earned fees of $2,800 will be collected next month.

Accounts Receivable

Jan. 19 2,800	

Advertising Fees Earned

	Jan. 10 1,400
	19 2,800

Transaction: Revenue earned, to be received later.
Analysis: Assets increased. Owner's equity increased.
Rules: Increases in assets are recorded by debits. Increases in owner's equity are recorded by credits.
Entry: Increase in assets is recorded by a debit to Accounts Receivable. Increase in owner's equity is recorded by a credit to Advertising Fees Earned.

	Dr.	Cr.
Accounts Receivable	2,800	
Advertising Fees Earned		2,800

January 25: Joan Miller withdrew $1,400 from the business for personal living expenses.

Cash

Jan. 1 10,000	Jan. 2 800
10 1,400	4 4,200
15 1,000	5 1,500
	8 480
	9 1,000
	12 600
	25 1,400

Joan Miller, Withdrawals

Jan. 25 1,400	

Transaction: Withdrawal of assets for personal use.
Analysis: Assets decreased. Owner's equity decreased.
Rules: Decreases in assets are recorded by credits. Decreases in owner's equity are recorded by debits.
Entry: Decrease in owner's equity is recorded by a debit to Joan Miller, Withdrawals. Decrease in assets is recorded by a credit to Cash.

	Dr.	Cr.
Joan Miller, Withdrawals	1,400	
Cash		1,400

January 26: Paid the secretary two more weeks' salary, $600.

Cash

Jan. 1 10,000	Jan. 2 800
10 1,400	4 4,200
15 1,000	5 1,500
	8 480
	9 1,000
	12 600
	25 1,400
	26 600

Office Wages Expense

Jan. 12 600	
26 600	

Transaction: Payment of wages expense.
Analysis: Assets decreased. Owner's equity decreased.
Rules: Decreases in assets are recorded by credits. Decreases in owner's equity are recorded by debits.
Entry: Decrease in owner's equity is recorded by a debit to Office Wages Expense. Decrease in assets is recorded by a credit to Cash.

	Dr.	Cr.
Office Wages Expense	600	
Cash		600

January 29: Received and paid the utility bill of $100.

Cash

Jan. 1	10,000	Jan. 2	800
10	1,400	4	4,200
15	1,000	5	1,500
		8	480
		9	1,000
		12	600
		25	1,400
		26	600
		29	100

Utility Expense

Jan. 29	100		

Transaction: Payment of expenses.
Analysis: Assets decreased. Owner's equity decreased.
Rules: Decreases in assets are recorded by credits. Decreases in owner's equity are recorded by debits.
Entry: Decrease in owner's equity is recorded by a debit to Utility Expense. Decrease in assets is recorded by a credit to Cash.

	Dr.	Cr.
Utility Expense	100	
Cash		100

January 30: Received (but did not pay) a telephone bill, $70.

Accounts Payable

Jan. 9	1,000	Jan. 5	1,500
		6	2,600
		30	70

Telephone Expense

Jan. 30	70		

Transaction: Expense incurred, payment deferred.
Analysis: Liabilities increased. Owner's equity decreased.
Rules: Increases in liabilities are recorded by credits. Decreases in owner's equity are recorded by debits.
Entry: Decrease in owner's equity is recorded by a debit to Telephone Expense. Increase in liabilities is recorded by a credit to Accounts Payable.

	Dr.	Cr.
Telephone Expense	70	
Accounts Payable		70

Summary of Transactions

As you may have discovered from the examples, there are only a few ways in which transactions can affect the accounting equation, as follows:

Effect	Example Transactions
1. Increase both assets and liabilities	Jan. 6, 15
2. Increase both assets and owner's equity	Jan. 1, 10, 19
3. Decrease both assets and liabilities	Jan. 9
4. Decrease both assets and owner's equity	Jan. 12, 25, 26, 29
5. Increase one asset and decrease another	Jan. 2, 4, 8
6. Increase one liability or owner's equity and decrease another liability or owner's equity	Jan. 30
7. No effect	Jan. 3

The January 5 transaction is a more complex transaction; it increases one asset (Office Equipment), decreases another asset (Cash), and increases a liability (Accounts Payable). All the transactions above are presented in Exhibit 2-1 in their correct accounts, and their relation to the accounting equation is shown.

Recording Transactions

OBJECTIVE 6
Record transactions in the general journal

So far, the analysis of transactions has been illustrated by entering the transactions directly into the T accounts. This method was used because it is a very simple and useful way of analyzing the effect of transactions. Advanced accounting students and professional accountants often use T accounts to analyze very complicated transactions. However, there are in fact three steps to be followed in the recording process.

Steps in the Recording Process

1. Analyze the transactions from the source documents.
2. Enter the transactions into the journal (a procedure usually called journalizing).
3. Post the entries to the ledger (a procedure usually called posting).

The Journal

As illustrated in this chapter, transactions can be recorded directly into the accounts. When this method is used, however, it is very difficult to follow individual transactions with the debit recorded in one account and the credit in another. When a large number of transactions are involved, errors in analyzing or recording transactions are very difficult to find. The solution to this problem is to make a chronological record of all transactions by recording them in a **journal**. The journal is sometimes called the book of original entry, because this is where transactions are first recorded. The journal shows the transactions for each day and may contain explanatory information concerning the transactions. The debits and credits of the transactions can then be transferred to the appropriate accounts.

A separate **journal entry** is used to record each transaction, and the process of recording transactions is called **journalizing**.

The General Journal

It is common for a business to have more than one kind of journal. Several types of journals are discussed in Appendix A. The simplest and most flexible type is the **general journal**, which is used in the rest of this chapter. The general journal provides for recording the following information about each transaction:

1. The date
2. The names of the accounts debited and credited

Exhibit 2-1. Summary of Illustrative Accounts and Transactions for Joan Miller Advertising Agency

Assets = Liabilities + Owner's Equity

Assets

Cash

Date	Debit	Date	Credit
Jan. 1	10,000	Jan. 2	800
10	1,400	4	4,200
15	1,000	5	1,500
		8	480
		9	1,000
		12	600
		25	1,400
		26	600
		29	100
	12,400		**10,680**
Bal.	**1,720**		

Accounts Receivable

Date	Debit	Date	Credit
Jan. 19	2,800		

Art Supplies

Date	Debit	Date	Credit
Jan. 6	1,800		

Office Supplies

Date	Debit	Date	Credit
Jan. 6	800		

Prepaid Rent

Date	Debit	Date	Credit
Jan. 2	800		

Prepaid Insurance

Date	Debit	Date	Credit
Jan. 8	480		

Art Equipment

Date	Debit	Date	Credit
Jan. 4	4,200		

Office Equipment

Date	Debit	Date	Credit
Jan. 5	3,000		

Liabilities

Accounts Payable

Date	Debit	Date	Credit
Jan. 9	1,000	Jan. 5	1,500
		6	2,600
		30	70
	1,000		**4,170**
		Bal.	**3,170**

Unearned Art Fees

Date	Debit	Date	Credit
		Jan. 15	1,000

Owner's Equity

Joan Miller, Capital

Date	Debit	Date	Credit
		Jan. 1	10,000

Joan Miller, Withdrawals

Date	Debit	Date	Credit
Jan. 25	1,400		

Advertising Fees Earned

Date	Debit	Date	Credit
		Jan. 10	1,400
		19	2,800
		Bal.	**4,200**

Office Wages Expense

Date	Debit	Date	Credit
Jan. 12	600		
26	600		
Bal.	**1,200**		

Utility Expense

Date	Debit	Date	Credit
Jan. 29	100		

Telephone Expense

Date	Debit	Date	Credit
Jan. 30	70		

3. The dollar amounts debited or credited to each account
4. An explanation of the transaction
5. The account identification numbers, if appropriate

Two transactions for the Joan Miller Advertising Agency are recorded in Exhibit 2-2.

The procedures for recording transactions in the general journal can be summarized as follows:

1. Record the date by writing the year in small figures at the top of the first column, the month on the first line of the first column, and the day in the second column of the first line. For subsequent entries on the same page for the same month and year, the month and year can be omitted.
2. Write the exact names of the accounts debited and credited under the heading "Description." Write the name of the account debited next to the left margin of the first line, and indent the name of the account credited. The explanation is placed on the next line and further indented. It should be brief but sufficient to explain and identify the transaction. A transaction can have more than one debit and/or credit entry; in such a case it is called a **compound entry.** In a compound entry, all debit accounts involved are listed before any credit accounts.
3. Write the debit amounts in the appropriate column opposite the accounts to be debited, and write the credit amounts opposite the accounts to be credited.
4. At the time of recording the transactions, nothing is placed in the Post. Ref. (posting reference) column. (This column is sometimes called LP or Folio.) Later, if the company uses account numbers to identify accounts in the ledger, fill in the account numbers to provide a convenient cross-reference from general journal to ledger and to indicate that posting to the ledger has been completed. If account numbers are not used, a check (✔) is used.
5. It is customary to skip a line after each journal entry.

Exhibit 2-2. The General Journal

General Journal					Page 1
Date		Description	Post. Ref.	Debit	Credit
19xx					
Jan.	6	Art Supplies		1,800	
		Office Supplies		800	
		Accounts Payable			2,600
		Purchase of art and office			
		supplies on credit			
	8	Prepaid Insurance		480	
		Cash			480
		Paid one-year life			
		insurance premium			

The Ledger Account Form

So far, the T form of account has been used as a simple and direct means of recording transactions. In practice, a somewhat more complicated form of the account is needed to record more information. The **ledger account form**, with four columns for dollar amounts, is illustrated in Exhibit 2-3.

The *account title* and *number* appear at the top of the account form. The *date* of the transaction appears in the first two columns as it does in the journal. The Item column is used only rarely, because an explanation already appears in the journal. The Post. Ref. column is used to note the journal page number where the journal entry for the transaction can be found. The dollar amount of the entry is entered in the appropriate Debit or Credit column, and a new account balance is computed in the final two columns after each entry. The advantage of this form of account over the T account is that the current balance of the account is always easily available.

Relationship Between the Journal and the Ledger

OBJECTIVE 7
Explain the relationship of the journal to the ledger

After the transactions have been entered in the journal, they must be transferred to the ledger. This process of transferring journal entry information from the journal to the ledger is called **posting**. Posting is usually done, not after each journal entry, but after several entries have been made—for example, at the end of each day or less frequently, depending on the number of transactions.

Posting consists of transferring each amount in the Debit column of the journal into the Debit column of the appropriate account in the ledger and copying each amount in the Credit column of the journal into the Credit column of the appropriate account in the ledger. This procedure is keyed to Exhibit 2-4. The steps in posting are at the bottom of page 66.

Exhibit 2-3. Accounts Payable in the General Ledger

General Ledger

Accounts Payable Account No. *212*

Date		Item	Post. Ref.	Debit	Credit	Balance Debit	Balance Credit
19xx							
Jan.	5		J1		1,500		1,500
	6		J1		2,600		4,100
	9		J1	1,000			3,100
	30		J2		70		3,170

Exhibit 2-4. Posting from the General Journal to the Ledger

General Journal — (2) Page 2

Date		Description	Post. Ref.	Debit	Credit
19xx	(2)	(1)	(4)	(3)	
Jan.	30	Telephone Expense	513	70	
		Accounts Payable	212		70
		Received bill for			
		telephone expense			

General Ledger

Accounts Payable — Account No. *212*

Date		Item	Post. Ref.	Debit	Credit	Balance Debit	Balance Credit
19xx							
Jan.	5		J1		1,500		1,500
	6		J1		2,600		4,100
	9		J1	1,000			3,100
	30		J2		70		3,170

Telephone Expense — Account No. *513*

Date		Item	Post. Ref.	Debit	Credit	Balance Debit	Balance Credit
19xx							
Jan.	30		J2	70		70	

1. Locate in the ledger the debit account named in the journal entry.
2. Enter the date of the transaction and, in the Post. Ref. column of the ledger, the journal page number from which the entry comes.
3. Enter in the Debit column of the ledger account the amount of the debit as it appears in the journal.
4. Enter in the Post. Ref. column of the journal the account number of the account to which the amount was posted.
5. Repeat the preceding four steps for the credit side of the journal entry.

Note that Step 4 is the last step in the posting process for each debit and credit. In addition to serving as an easy reference between journal entry and ledger account, this entry in the Post. Ref. column of the journal serves as a check, indicating that all steps for the item are completed. For example, when accountants are called away from their work by telephone calls or other interruptions, they can easily find where they were before the interruption.

In a microcomputer accounting system such as many small businesses have today, the posting is done automatically by the computer after the transactions have been entered on the computer. The computer will also do the next step in the accounting cycle, which is to prepare a trial balance.

The Trial Balance

OBJECTIVE 8
Prepare a trial balance and recognize its value and limitations

The equality of debit and credit balances in the ledger can be tested periodically by preparing a **trial balance**. Exhibit 2-5 shows a trial balance for the Joan Miller Advertising Agency. It was prepared from the accounts in Exhibit 2-1. The steps to follow in preparing a trial balance follow.

1. Determine the balance of each account in the ledger.
2. List each account in the ledger that has a balance, with the debit balances in one column and the credit balances in another. Accounts are listed in the order they appear in the ledger.
3. Add each column.
4. Compare the totals of each column.

Exhibit 2-5. Trial Balance

Joan Miller Advertising Agency
Trial Balance
January 31, 19xx

Cash	$1,720	
Accounts Receivable	2,800	
Art Supplies	1,800	
Office Supplies	800	
Prepaid Rent	800	
Prepaid Insurance	480	
Art Equipment	4,200	
Office Equipment	3,000	
Accounts Payable		$ 3,170
Unearned Art Fees		1,000
Joan Miller, Capital		10,000
Joan Miller, Withdrawals	1,400	
Advertising Fees Earned		4,200
Office Wages Expense	1,200	
Utility Expense	100	
Telephone Expense	70	
	$18,370	$18,370

In performing steps 1 and 2, recall that the account form in the ledger has two balance columns, one for debit balances and one for credit balances. The usual balance for an account is known as the **normal balance**. Consequently, if increases are recorded by debits, the normal balance is a debit balance; if increases are recorded by credits, the normal balance is a credit balance. The table below summarizes the normal account balances of the major account categories.

Account Category	Increases Recorded by Debit	Increases Recorded by Credit	Normal Balance Debit	Normal Balance Credit
Asset	×		×	
Liability		×		×
Owner's Equity:				
Capital		×		×
Withdrawals	×		×	
Revenues		×		×
Expenses	×		×	

According to the table, the ledger account for Accounts Payable will typically have a credit balance and can be copied into the Trial Balance columns as a credit balance.

Once in a while, a transaction will cause an account to have a balance opposite from its normal account balance. Examples are when a customer overpays a bill or when a company overdraws its account at the bank by writing a check for more money than it has in its balance. If this happens, the abnormal balance should be copied into the Trial Balance columns.

The significance of the trial balance is that it proves whether or not the ledger is in balance. "In balance" means that equal debits and credits have been recorded for all transactions.

If the debit and credit columns of the trial balance do not equal each other, it may be the result of one or more of the following errors: (1) a debit was entered in an account as a credit, or vice versa, (2) the balance of an account was incorrectly computed, (3) an error was made in carrying the account balance to the trial balance, or (4) the trial balance was incorrectly summed.

The trial balance proof does not mean that transactions were analyzed correctly or recorded in the proper accounts. For example, there would be no way of determining from the trial balance that a debit should have been made in the Art Equipment account rather than the Office Equipment account. Further, if a transaction that should be recorded is omitted, it will not be detected by a trial balance proof because equal credits and debits will have been omitted. Also, if an error of the same amount is made both as a credit and as a debit, it will not be discovered by the trial balance. The trial balance proves only the equality of the debits and credits in the accounts.

Other than simply adding the columns wrong, the two most common mistakes in preparing a trial balance are (1) recording an account with a debit balance as a credit, or vice versa, and (2) transposing two numbers in an amount when transferring it to the trial balance (for example, transferring $23,459 as $23,549). The first of these mistakes will cause the trial balance to be out of balance by an amount divisible by 2. The second will cause the trial balance to be out of balance by a number divisible by 9. Thus if a trial balance is out of balance and the addition has been verified, determine the amount by which the trial balance is out of balance and divide it first by 2 and then by 9. If the amount is divisible by 2, look in the trial balance for an amount equal to the quotient. If such a number exists, it is likely that this amount is in the wrong column. If the amount is divisible by 9, trace each amount to the ledger account balance, checking carefully for a transposition error. If neither of these techniques identifies the error, it is necessary first to recompute the balance of each account in the ledger and, if the error still has not been found, then retrace each posting from the journal to the ledger.

Some Notes on Bookkeeping Techniques

Ruled lines appear in financial reports before each subtotal or total to indicate that the amounts above are to be added or subtracted. It is common practice to use a double line under a final total.

Dollars signs ($) are required in all financial statements including the balance sheet and income statement and in schedules such as the trial balance. On these statements, a dollar sign should be placed before the first amount in each column and before the first amount in a column following a ruled line. Dollar signs are *not* used in journals or ledgers.

On unruled paper, commas and periods are used in representing dollar amounts, but when paper with ruled columns is used in journals and ledgers, commas and periods are not needed. In this book, because most problems and illustrations are in whole dollar amounts, the cents column is usually omitted. When professional accountants deal with whole dollars, they will often use a dash in the cents column to indicate whole dollars rather than take the time to write zeros.

Chapter Review

Review of Learning Objectives

1. **Explain in simple terms the generally accepted ways of solving the measurement problems of recognition, valuation, and classification.**
   To measure a business transaction, the accountant must determine when the transaction occurred (the recognition problem), what value should be placed on the transaction (the valuation problem), and how the components of the transaction should be categorized (the classification problem). In general, recognition occurs when title passes, and a transaction is valued at the cost

or exchange price when the transaction is recognized. Classification refers to the categorizing of transactions according to a system of accounts.

2. **Define and use the terms *account* and *ledger*.**
   An account is a device for storing data from transactions. There is one account for each asset, liability, and component of owner's equity, including revenues and expenses. The ledger is a book or file consisting of all of a company's accounts arranged according to a chart of accounts.

3. **Recognize commonly used asset, liability, and owner's equity accounts.**
   Commonly used asset accounts are Cash, Notes Receivable, Accounts Receivable, Prepaid Expenses, Land, Buildings, and Equipment. Common liability accounts are Notes Payable, Accounts Payable, and Bonds or Mortgages Payable. Common owner's equity accounts are Capital, Withdrawals, Revenues, and Expenses.

4. **State the rules for debit and credit.**
   The rules for debit and credit are (1) increases in assets are debited to asset accounts; decreases in assets are credited to asset accounts; (2) increases in liabilities and owner's equity are credited to liability and owner's equity accounts; decreases in liabilities and owner's equity are debited to liability and owner's equity accounts.

5. **Apply the procedure for transaction analysis to simple transactions.**
   The procedures for analyzing transactions are to (1) analyze the effect of the transaction on assets, liabilities, and owner's equity; (2) apply the appropriate double-entry rule; and (3) make the entry.

6. **Record transactions in the general journal.**
   The general journal is a chronological record of all transactions. The record of a transaction in the general journal contains the date of the transaction, the names of the accounts and dollar amounts debited and credited, an explanation of the journal entries, and the account numbers to which postings have been made.

7. **Explain the relationship of the journal to the ledger.**
   After the transactions have been entered in the journal, they must be posted to the ledger. Posting is done by transferring each amount in the debit column of the journal to the debit column of the appropriate account in the ledger and transferring each amount in the credit column of the journal to the credit column of the appropriate account in the ledger.

8. **Prepare a trial balance and recognize its value and limitations.**
   A trial balance is used to test the equality of the debit and credit balances in the ledger. It is prepared by listing each account with its balance in the appropriate debit or credit column. The two columns are added and compared to test their balances. The major limitation of the trial balance is that the equality of debit and credit balances does not mean that transactions were analyzed correctly or recorded in the proper accounts.

Self-Test

Test your knowledge of the chapter by choosing the best answer for each item on the next page.

1. Deciding whether an expenditure for a desk is properly recorded as store equipment or office equipment is an example of
   a. a recognition problem.
   b. a valuation problem.
   c. a classification problem.
   d. a communication problem.
2. Deciding whether to record a sale when the order for services is received or when the services are performed is an example of
   a. a recognition problem.
   b. a valuation problem.
   c. a classification problem.
   d. a communication problem.
3. Recording an asset at its exchange price is an example of the accounting solution to the
   a. recognition problem.
   b. valuation problem.
   c. classification problem.
   d. communication problem.
4. The left side of an account is referred to as
   a. the balance.
   b. a debit.
   c. a credit.
   d. a footing.
5. Which of the following is a liability account?
   a. Accounts Receivable
   b. Withdrawals
   c. Rent Expense
   d. Accounts Payable
6. A purchase of office equipment on credit requires a credit to
   a. Office Equipment.
   b. Cash.
   c. Accounts Payable.
   d. Equipment Expense.
7. Payment for a two-year insurance policy requires a debit to
   a. Prepaid Insurance.
   b. Insurance Expense.
   c. Cash.
   d. Accounts Payable.
8. An agreement to spend $100 a month on advertising beginning next month requires
   a. a debit to Advertising Expense.
   b. a credit to Cash.
   c. no entry.
   d. a debit to Prepaid Advertising.
9. Transactions are initially recorded in the
   a. trial balance.
   b. T account.
   c. general journal.
   d. ledger.
10. The equality of debits and credits can be tested periodically by preparing a
    a. trial balance.
    b. T account.
    c. general journal.
    d. ledger.

Answers to Self-Test are at the end of this chapter.

Review Problem
Journal Entries, Ledger Accounts, and Trial Balance

After graduation from veterinary school, Laura Cox entered private practice. The transactions of the business through May 27 are as follows:

19xx

May	1	Laura Cox deposited $2,000 in her business bank account.
	3	Paid $300 for two months' rent in advance for an office.
	9	Purchased medical supplies for $200 in cash.
	12	Purchased $400 of equipment on credit, making a one-fourth down payment.
	15	Delivered a calf for a fee of $35.
	18	Made a partial payment of $50 on the equipment purchased on May 12.
	27	Paid a utility bill for $40.

Required

1. Record the above entries in the general journal.
2. Post the entries from the journal to the following ledger accounts in the ledger: Cash (111), Medical Supplies (115), Prepaid Rent (116), Equipment (141), Accounts Payable (211), Laura Cox, Capital (311), Veterinary Fees Earned (411), Utility Expense (511).
3. Prepare a trial balance.

Answer to Review Problem

1. Recording journal entries

General Journal **Page 1**

Date		Description	Post. Ref.	Debit	Credit
19xx					
May	1	Cash	111	2,000	
		Laura Cox, Capital	311		2,000
		Laura Cox deposited $2,000 in her business bank account			
	3	Prepaid Rent	116	300	
		Cash	111		300
		Paid two months' rent in advance for an office			
	9	Medical Supplies	115	200	
		Cash	111		200
		Purchased medical supplies for cash			
	12	Equipment	141	400	
		Accounts Payable	211		300
		Cash	111		100
		Purchased equipment on credit, paying 25 percent down			
	15	Cash	111	35	
		Veterinary Fees Earned	411		35
		Collected fee for delivering a calf			
	18	Accounts Payable	211	50	
		Cash	111		50
		Made partial payment for the equipment purchased on May 12			
	27	Utility Expense	511	40	
		Cash	111		40
		Paid utility bill			

2. Posting transactions to the ledger accounts

General Ledger

Cash — Account No. *111*

Date		Item	Post. Ref.	Debit	Credit	Balance Debit	Balance Credit
19xx							
May	*1*		*J1*	*2,000*		*2,000*	
	3		*J1*		*300*	*1,700*	
	9		*J1*		*200*	*1,500*	
	12		*J1*		*100*	*1,400*	
	15		*J1*	*35*		*1,435*	
	18		*J1*		*50*	*1,385*	
	27		*J1*		*40*	*1,345*	

Medical Supplies — Account No. *115*

Date	Item	Post. Ref.	Debit	Credit	Balance Debit	Balance Credit
19xx						
May 9		*J1*	*200*		*200*	

Prepaid Rent — Account No. *116*

Date	Item	Post. Ref.	Debit	Credit	Balance Debit	Balance Credit
19xx						
May 3		*J1*	*300*		*300*	

Equipment — Account No. *141*

Date	Item	Post. Ref.	Debit	Credit	Balance Debit	Balance Credit
19xx						
May 12		*J1*	*400*		*400*	

Accounts Payable — Account No. *211*

Date	Item	Post. Ref.	Debit	Credit	Balance Debit	Balance Credit
19xx						
May 12		*J1*		*300*		*300*
18		*J1*	*50*			*250*

Laura Cox, Capital — Account No. *311*

Date	Item	Post. Ref.	Debit	Credit	Balance Debit	Balance Credit
19xx						
May 1		*J1*		*2,000*		*2,000*

Veterinary Fees Earned — Account No. *411*

Date	Item	Post. Ref.	Debit	Credit	Balance Debit	Balance Credit
19xx						
May 15		*J1*		*35*		*35*

Utility Expense — Account No. *511*

Date	Item	Post. Ref.	Debit	Credit	Balance Debit	Balance Credit
19xx						
May 27		*J1*	*40*		*40*	

3. Completion of trial balance

Laura Cox, Veterinarian
Trial Balance
May 31, 19xx

Cash	*$1,345*	
Medical Supplies	*200*	
Prepaid Rent	*300*	
Equipment	*400*	
Accounts Payable		*$ 250*
Laura Cox, Capital		*2,000*
Veterinary Fees Earned		*35*
Utility Expense	*40*	
	$2,285	*$2,285*

Chapter Assignments

Questions

1. What three problems underlie most accounting issues?
2. Why is recognition a problem to accountants?
3. A customer asks the owner of a store to save an item for him and says that he will pick it up and pay for it next week. The owner agrees to hold it. Should this transaction be recorded as a sale? Explain.
4. Why is it practical for the accountant to rely on original cost for valuation purposes?
5. What is the basic limitation of using original cost in accounting measurements?
6. What is an account, and how is it related to the ledger?
7. "Debits are bad; credits are good." Comment on this statement.
8. Why is the system of recording entries called the double-entry system? What is so special about it?
9. Suppose that a system of double-entry bookkeeping were developed in which credits increased assets and debits decreased assets. How would accounting for liabilities and owner's equity be affected under that system?
10. Give the rules of debits and credits for (a) assets, (b) liabilities, and (c) owner's equity.
11. Why are the rules the same for liabilities and owner's equity?
12. What is the meaning of the statement "The Cash account has a debit balance of $500"?
13. What are the three steps in transaction analysis?
14. Tell whether each of the following accounts is an asset account, a liability account, or an owner's equity account:
    a. Notes Receivable
    b. Land
    c. Withdrawals
    d. Bonds Payable
    e. Prepaid Expense
    f. Expense
    g. Revenue
15. List the following six items in a logical sequence to illustrate the flow of events through the accounting system:
    a. Analysis of transaction
    b. Debits and credits posted from the journal to the ledger
    c. Occurrence of business transaction
    d. Preparation of financial statements
    e. Entry made in a journal
    f. Preparation of trial balance
16. What purposes are served by a trial balance?
17. Can errors be present even though the trial balance balances? Comment.
18. In recording entries in a journal, which is written first, the debit or the credit? How is indentation used in the general journal?
19. What is the relationship between the journal and the ledger?
20. Describe each of the following:
    a. Account
    b. Journal
    c. Ledger
    d. Book of original entry
    e. Post. Ref. column
    f. Journalizing
    g. Posting
    h. Footings
    i. Compound entry
21. Does double-entry accounting refer to entering a transaction in both the journal and the ledger? Comment.
22. Is it possible or desirable to forgo the journal and enter the transaction directly into the ledger? Comment.
23. What is the normal balance of Accounts Payable? Under what conditions could an Accounts Payable account have a debit balance?

Classroom Exercises

Exercise 2-1. Transaction Analysis (L.O. 5)

Analyze each of the following transactions, using the form shown in the example below the list.

a. Henry Sellers established Sellers Barber Shop by placing $1,000 in a bank account.
b. Paid two months' rent in advance, $420.
c. Purchased supplies on credit, $60.
d. Received cash for barbering services, $50.
e. Paid for supplies purchased in **c**.
f. Paid utility bill, $36.

Example

a. The asset Cash was increased. Increases in assets are recorded by debits. Debit Cash, $1,000.

The owner's equity Henry Sellers, Capital, was increased. Increases in owner's equity are recorded by credits. Credit Henry Sellers, Capital, $1,000.

Exercise 2-2. Recording Transactions in T Accounts (L.O. 5)

Place the following T accounts on a sheet of paper: Cash; Repair Supplies; Repair Equipment; Accounts Payable; Marjorie Barnes, Capital; Marjorie Barnes, Withdrawals; Repair Fees Earned; Salary Expense; and Rent Expense. Record the following transactions for the month of June directly in the T accounts using the letters to identify the transactions.

a. Marjorie Barnes opened the Suburban Fix-it Service by investing $3,200 in cash and $1,200 in repair equipment.
b. Paid $300 for one month's rent.
c. Purchased repair supplies on credit, $400.
d. Purchased additional repair equipment, $300.
e. Paid salary of $450.
f. Paid $200 of amount purchased on credit in **c**.
g. Withdrew $600 from business for living expenses.
h. Accepted cash for repairs completed, $860.

Exercise 2-3. Trial Balance (L.O. 8)

After recording the transactions in Exercise 2-2, prepare a trial balance for Suburban Fix-it Service.

Exercise 2-4. Application of Recognition Point (L.O. 1)

Mantilla's Body Shop uses a large amount of supplies in its business. The following table summarizes selected transaction data for orders of supplies purchased.

Order	Date Shipped	Date Received	Amount
a	April 25	May 5	$ 700
b	May 10	15	1,400
c	16	22	800
d	23	30	1,200
e	27	June 2	1,500
f	June 1	5	1,000

Determine the total purchases of supplies for May alone under each of the following assumptions:

1. Mantilla's Body Shop recognizes purchases when orders are shipped.
2. Mantilla's Body Shop recognizes purchases when orders are received.

Exercise 2-5. Preparation of Trial Balance (L.O. 8)

The following accounts of the Radatz Service Company as of January 31, 19xx, are listed in alphabetical order. The amount of Accounts Payable is omitted.

Accounts Payable	?	Equipment	$12,000
Accounts Receivable	$ 2,000	Bill Radatz, Capital	30,760
Building	34,000	Land	5,200
Cash	9,000	Notes Payable	20,000
		Prepaid Insurance	1,100

Prepare a trial balance with the proper heading and with the accounts listed in the balance sheet sequence (see Exhibit 2-5). Compute the balance of Accounts Payable.

Exercise 2-6. Effect of Errors on Trial Balance (L.O. 8)

Which of the following errors would cause a trial balance to have unequal totals? Explain your answers.

a. A payment to a creditor was recorded as a debit to Accounts Payable for $75 and a credit to Cash for $57.
b. A payment of $100 to a creditor for an account payable was debited to Accounts Receivable and credited to Cash.
c. A purchase of office supplies of $280 was recorded as a debit to Office Supplies for $28 and a credit to Cash for $28.
d. A purchase of equipment of $300 was recorded as a debit to Supplies for $300 and a credit to Cash for $300.

Exercise 2-7. Preparation of Ledger Account (L.O. 7)

A T account showing the cash transactions for a month follows:

Cash

3/1	10,000	3/2	900
3/7	1,200	3/4	200
3/14	4,000	3/8	1,700
3/21	200	3/9	5,000
3/28	6,400	3/23	600

Prepare the account in ledger account form for Cash (Account 111) in a manner similar to the example in Exhibit 2-3.

Exercise 2-8. Recording Transactions in General Journal and Posting to Ledger Accounts (L.O. 6, 7)

On a sheet of notebook paper, draw a general journal form like the one in Exhibit 2-2, and label it page 10. After completing the form, record the following transactions in the journal.

Dec. 14 Purchased an item of equipment for $3,000, paying $1,000 as a cash down payment.

28 Paid $1,000 of the amount owed on the equipment.

On a sheet of notebook paper, draw three ledger account forms like those shown in Exhibit 2-3. Use the following account numbers: Cash, 111; Equipment, 143; and Accounts Payable, 212. After completing the forms, post the two transactions from the general journal to the ledger accounts, at the same time making proper posting references in the general journal.

Exercise 2-9. Correcting Errors in Trial Balance
(L.O. 8)

The following trial balance for Blosten Services at the end of July does not balance because of a number of errors.

Blosten Services
Trial Balance
July 31, 19xx

Cash	$ 1,730	
Accounts Receivable	2,830	
Supplies	60	
Prepaid Insurance	90	
Equipment	4,200	
Accounts Payable		$ 2,080
L. Blosten, Capital		5,780
L. Blosten, Withdrawals		350
Revenues		2,960
Salary Expense	1,300	
Rent Expense	300	
Advertising Expense	170	
Utility Expense	13	
	$10,693	$11,170

The accountant for Blosten has compared the amounts in the trial balance with the ledger, recomputed the account balances, and compared the postings. He found the following errors:

a. The pencil footing of the credits to Cash was overstated by $200.
b. A cash payment of $210 was credited to Cash for $120.
c. A debit of $60 to Accounts Receivable was not posted.
d. Supplies purchased for $30 were posted as a credit to Supplies.
e. A debit of $90 to Prepaid Insurance was overlooked and not posted.
f. The pencil footings for the Accounts Payable account were debits of $2,660 and credits of $4,400.
g. A Notes Payable account with a credit balance of $1,200 was not included in the trial balance.
h. The debit balance of L. Blosten, Withdrawals, was listed in the trial balance as a credit.
i. A $100 debit to L. Blosten, Withdrawals, was posted as a credit.
j. The Utility Expense of $130 was listed as $13 in the trial balance.

Prepare a correct trial balance.

Exercise 2-10. Preparation of Trial Balance
(L.O. 8)

The Ungar Construction Company builds foundations for buildings and parking lots. Following is an alphabetical list of account balances on April 30, 19xx:

Accounts Payable	$ 4,400
Accounts Receivable	9,460
Cash	?
Construction Supplies	1,900
Equipment	24,500
Notes Payable	20,000
Office Trailer	2,200
Prepaid Insurance	4,600
Revenue Earned	17,400
Supplies Expense	7,200
Utility Expense	420
Ray Ungar, Capital	40,000
Ray Ungar, Withdrawals	7,800
Wages Expense	8,800

Prepare a trial balance for the company with the proper heading. Determine the correct balance for the Cash account on April 30, 19xx.

Interpreting Accounting Information

Zenith Radio Corporation[1]
(L.O. 3, 4, 6)

The condensed data below are adapted from the annual report of Zenith Radio Corporation, one of the world's largest manufacturers of television sets and other electronic entertainment products. All amounts are in millions of dollars.

	December 31,1980
Accounts Payable	$ 59.1
Accounts Receivable	166.8
Buildings and Equipment	138.1
Cash	11.7
Inventories	235.8
Land	13.0
Long-Term Debt	160.0
Marketable Securities	51.6
Other Assets	9.5
Other Liabilities	145.3
Owners' Equity	291.0
Prepaid Expenses	28.9

The following quotations were also taken from the annual report:

Long-Term Obligations
"Total long-term debt increased to $160 million at December 31, 1980, from $110 million at year-end 1979. In 1980, $50 million of long-term debt due 2005, . . . , [was] sold to the public."
Capital Expenditures
"Zenith plans to use the [$50 million in proceeds] from the sales of the long-term debt, described previously, largely for investments in Buildings and

1. Figures reprinted by permission from the 1980 Annual Report of Zenith Electronics Corporation, 1000 Milwaukee Avenue, Glenview, Illinois 60025.

Equipment related to color television assembly and picture tube manufacturing. Pending such use, at year-end 1980, the debt proceeds were invested in marketable securities."

Required

1. Using the data provided, prepare a balance sheet for Zenith at December 31, 1980.
2. What effect did the transaction described under "Long-Term Obligations" have on Zenith's balance sheet? Prepare the entry in general journal form to record the transaction.
3. From reading the information under "Capital Expenditures," you know what Zenith did with the proceeds of the sales of long-term debt in 1980 and what the company plans to do with the proceeds in 1981. Before it can carry out these plans, what transaction must occur? Prepare three entries in general journal form to record the one completed and two planned transactions. Use the account Marketable Securities to record entries related to the investments.

Problem Set A

Problem 2A-1. Transaction Analysis, T Accounts, and Trial Balance
(L.O. 5, 8)

Sandy Kim established a small business, Kim Training Center, to teach individuals how to use spreadsheet analysis, word processing, and other techniques on microcomputers.

a. Kim began by transferring the following assets to the business:

Cash	$8,000
Furniture	2,400
Microcomputer	5,200

b. Paid the first month's rent on a small storefront, $280.
c. Purchased computer software on credit, $750.
d. Paid for an advertisement in the school newspaper, $100.
e. Received enrollment applications from five students for a five-day course, costing $200 per student, to start next week.
f. Paid wages to a part-time helper, $150.
g. Received cash payment from three of the students enrolled in **e**, $600.
h. Billed the other students in **e**, $400.
i. Paid utility bill, $110.
j. Made payment toward software purchased in **c**, $250.
k. Received payment from one student billed in **h**, $200.
l. Purchased a second microcomputer, $4,700.
m. Transferred cash to personal checking account, $300.

Required

1. Set up the following T accounts: Cash; Accounts Receivable; Software; Furniture; Microcomputer; Accounts Payable; Sandy Kim, Capital; Sandy Kim, Withdrawals; Tuition Revenue; Rent Expense; Wages Expense; Advertising Expense; Utility Expense.
2. Record transactions by entering debits and credits directly in the T accounts using the transaction letter to identify each debit and credit.
3. Prepare a trial balance using the current date.

Problem 2A-2. Transaction Analysis, General Journal, T Accounts, and Trial Balance
(L.O. 5, 6, 8)

Sal Prado won a concession to rent bicycles in the local park during the summer. During the month of June, Sal completed the following transactions for his bicycle rental business:

June 2 Began business by placing $6,000 in a business checking account.
3 Purchased supplies on account, $150.
4 Purchased 10 bicycles for $2,000, paying $1,000 down and agreeing to pay the rest in 30 days.
5 Purchased for cash a small shed to hold his bicycles and to use for other operations, $2,500.
6 Paid a mover to place the shed at the park entrance, $200. (Debit to Shed account.)
8 Received cash for rentals of $220 during the first week of operation.
13 Hired a part-time assistant to help out on weekends at $4 per hour.
14 Paid a maintenance person to clean the grounds around the shed, $75.
15 Received cash for rentals of $300 during the second week of operation.
16 Paid the assistant for a weekend's work, $80.
20 Paid for the supplies purchased on June 3, $150.
21 Paid repair bill on bicycles, $55.
22 Received cash for rentals during the third week of operation, $400.
23 Paid the assistant for a weekend's work, $80.
26 Agreed to bill a company for bicycle rentals for an employee outing and did so, $110.
27 Paid the fee for June to the Park District for the right to the rental concession, $100.
28 Received cash for rentals during the week, $410.
29 Paid the assistant for a weekend's work, $80.
30 Transferred $500 to personal checking account.

Required

1. Prepare journal entries to record the above transactions in the general journal.
2. Set up the following T accounts and post all the journal entries: Cash; Accounts Receivable; Supplies; Shed; Bicycles; Accounts Payable; Sal Prado, Capital; Sal Prado, Withdrawals; Rental Income; Wages Expense; Maintenance Expense; Repair Expense; Concession Fee Expense.
3. Prepare a trial balance for Prado Rentals as of June 30, 19xx.
4. Compare how recognition applies to the transactions of June 26 and 28 and how classification applies to the transactions of June 6 and 14.

Problem 2A-3. Transaction Analysis, General Journal, Ledger Accounts, and Trial Balance
(L.O. 5, 6, 8)

Coleman Turner opened a photography and portrait studio on March 1 and completed the following transactions during March:

Mar. 1 Began business by depositing $18,000 in the business bank account.
2 Paid two months' rent in advance for a studio, $800.
3 Transferred personal photography equipment to the business valued at $3,500.
4 Ordered additional photography equipment, $2,500.
5 Purchased office equipment for cash, $1,800.
8 Received and paid for the photography equipment ordered on March 4, $2,500.
10 Purchased photography supplies on credit, $700.
15 Received cash for portraits, $300.
16 Billed customers for portraits, $750.

21 Paid for one-half the supplies purchased on March 10, $350.
24 Paid utility bill for March, $120.
25 Paid telephone bill for March, $70.
29 Received payment from customers billed on March 16, $250.
30 Paid wages to assistant, $400.
31 Withdrew cash for personal expenses, $900.

Required

1. Prepare journal entries to record the above transactions in the general journal (pages 1 and 2).
2. Set up the following ledger accounts and post the journal entries: Cash (111); Accounts Receivable (112); Photography Supplies (115); Prepaid Rent (116); Photography Equipment (141); Office Equipment (143); Accounts Payable (211); Coleman Turner, Capital (311); Coleman Turner, Withdrawals (312); Portrait Income (411); Wages Expense (511); Utility Expense (512); and Telephone Expense (513).
3. Prepare a trial balance for Turner Portrait Studio as of March 31, 19xx.

Problem 2A-4. Transaction Analysis, General Journal, Ledger Accounts, and Trial Balance (L.O. 5, 6, 8)

Reliable Security Service provides ushers and security personnel at athletic events and other functions. Reliable's trial balance at the end of April was as follows:

Reliable Security Service
Trial Balance
April 30, 19xx

Cash (111)	$12,200	
Accounts Receivable (112)	8,700	
Supplies (115)	560	
Prepaid Insurance (116)	600	
Equipment (141)	7,800	
Accounts Payable (211)		$ 4,200
Gabe Borelli, Capital (311)		20,460
Gabe Borelli, Withdrawals (312)	2,000	
Security Services Revenue (411)		28,000
Wages Expense (412)	16,000	
Rent Expense (413)	3,200	
Utilities Expense (414)	1,600	
	$52,660	$52,660

During May, Reliable engaged in the following transactions:

May 1 Received cash from customers billed last month, $3,800.
2 Made payment on accounts payable, $2,600.
3 Purchased new one-year insurance policy in advance, $3,600.
5 Purchased supplies on credit, $430.
6 Billed client for security services, $2,200.
7 Made rent payment for May, $800.
9 Received cash from customers for security services, $1,600.

14 Paid wages in connection with services provided, $1,400.
16 Ordered equipment, $800.
17 Paid monthly utility bill, $400.
18 Received and paid for equipment ordered on May 16, $800.
19 Returned for full credit some of the supplies purchased on May 5 because they were defective, $120.
24 Withdrew cash for personal expenses, $1,000.
28 Paid for supplies purchased on May 5 less return on May 19, $310.
30 Billed customer for security services performed, $1,800.
31 Paid wages in connection with security services, $1,050.

Required

1. Prepare journal entries to record the above transactions in the general journal (pages 26 and 27).
2. Open ledger accounts for the accounts shown in the trial balance. Enter the April 30 trial balance amounts in the ledger accounts.
3. Post the entries to the ledger accounts.
4. Prepare a trial balance as of May 31, 19xx.

Problem 2A-5. Relationship of General Journal, Ledger, and Trial Balance (L.O. 6, 7, 8)

Sinclair Services Company is a public relations firm. On July 31, 19xx, the company had a trial balance (account numbers) as follows:

Sinclair Services Company
Trial Balance
July 31, 19xx

Cash (111)	$ 9,400	
Accounts Receivable (112)	4,300	
Supplies (115)	450	
Office Equipment (141)	3,600	
Accounts Payable (211)		$ 1,900
Samuel Sinclair, Capital (311)		15,850
	$17,750	$17,750

During the month of August, the company completed the following transactions:

Aug. 2 Paid rent for August, $650.
3 Received payments from customers on account, $2,300.
5 Paid telephone bill for August, $120.
7 Ordered supplies, $380.
10 Billed customers for services provided, $2,800.
12 Made payment on accounts payable, $1,100.
15 Paid salaries for first half of August, $1,900.
16 Received the supplies ordered on August 7 and agreed to pay for them in 30 days, $380.
17 Discovered some of the supplies were not as ordered and returned them for full credit, $80.
19 Received cash from a customer for services provided, $4,800.
20 Took some supplies out of the business for personal use, $150.

24 Paid utility bill for August, $160.
26 Received a bill, to be paid in September, for advertisements placed during August in the local newspaper to promote Sinclair Services, $700.
29 Billed customer for services provided, $2,700.
30 Paid salaries for last half of August, $1,900.
31 Withdrew cash for personal use, $1,200.

Required

1. Enter the above transactions in the general journal (pages 22 and 23).
2. Open accounts in the ledger for the accounts in the trial balance plus the following accounts: Samuel Sinclair, Withdrawals (312); Public Relations Fees (411); Salaries Expense (511); Rent Expense (512); Utility Expense (513); Telephone Expense (514); Advertising Expense (515).
3. Enter the July 31 account balances in the appropriate ledger account forms from the trial balance.
4. Post the entries to the ledger accounts. Be sure to insert the appropriate posting references in the journal and ledger as you post.
5. Prepare a trial balance as of August 31, 19xx.

Problem Set B

Problem 2B-1. Transaction Analysis, T Accounts, and Trial Balance (L.O. 5, 8)

Betty Allegretti opened a secretarial school called Modern Secretary Training.

a. As an individual, she contributed the following assets to the business:

Cash	$4,600
Typewriters	2,800
Office Equipment	2,000

b. Found a storefront for her business and paid the first month's rent, $260.
c. Paid $190 for advertisement announcing the opening of the school.
d. Enrolled three students in four-week secretarial program and two students in ten-day typing course.
e. Purchased supplies on credit, $330.
f. Billed enrolled students, $1,300.
g. Paid assistant one week's salary, $220.
h. Purchased a typewriter, $480, and office equipment, $380, on credit.
i. Paid for supplies purchased on credit in **e** above.
j. Repaired broken typewriter, $40.
k. Billed new students, $440.
l. Transferred $300 to personal checking account.
m. Received payment from students previously billed, $1,080.
n. Paid utility bill, $90.
o. Paid assistant one week's salary, $220.
p. Received cash revenue from another new student, $250.

Required

1. Set up the following T accounts: Cash; Accounts Receivable; Supplies; Typewriters; Office Equipment; Accounts Payable; Betty Allegretti, Capital; Betty Allegretti, Withdrawals; Revenue from Business; Rent Expense; Advertising Expense; Salary Expense; Repair Expense; Utility Expense.

2. Record transactions by entering debits and credits directly in the T accounts, using the transaction letters to identify each debit and credit.
3. Prepare a trial balance using the current date.

Problem 2B-2. Transaction Analysis, General Journal, T Accounts, and Trial Balance
(L.O. 5, 6, 8)

Tyrone Lewis is a house painter. During the month of April, he completed the following transactions:

April 2 Began his business with equipment valued at $970 and placed $6,200 in a business checking account.
3 Purchased a used truck costing $1,100. Paid $400 cash and signed a note for the balance.
4 Purchased supplies on account, $320.
5 Completed painting two-story house and billed customer, $480.
7 Received cash for painting two rooms, $150.
8 Hired assistant to work with him, to be paid $6 an hour.
10 Purchased supplies, $160.
11 Received check from customer previously billed, $480.
12 Paid $400 on insurance policy for 18 months' coverage.
13 Billed customer for painting job, $620.
14 Paid assistant for 25 hours' work, $150.
15 Gasoline and oil for truck, $40.
18 Paid for supplies purchased on April 4.
20 Purchased new ladder (equipment) for $60 and supplies for $290 on account.
22 Received telephone bill to be paid next month, $60.
23 Received cash from customer previously billed, $330.
24 Transferred $300 to personal checking account.
25 Received cash for painting five-room apartment, $360.
27 Paid $200 on note signed for truck.
29 Paid assistant for 30 hours' work, $180.

Required

1. Prepare journal entries to record the above transactions in the general journal.
2. Set up the following T accounts and post all the journal entries: Cash; Accounts Receivable; Supplies; Prepaid Insurance; Equipment; Truck; Notes Payable; Accounts Payable; Tyrone Lewis, Capital; Tyrone Lewis, Withdrawals; Painting Fees Earned; Wages Expense; Telephone Expense; Truck Expense.
3. Prepare a trial balance for Tyrone Lewis Painting Service as of April 30, 19xx.
4. Compare how recognition applies to the transactions of April 5 and 7 and how classification applies to the transactions of April 12 and 14.

Problem 2B-3. Transaction Analysis, General Journal, Ledger Accounts, and Trial Balance
(L.O. 5, 6, 8)

Sheldon Thomas began his rug cleaning business on October 1 and engaged in the following transactions during October:

Oct. 1 Began business by transferring $5,000 from his personal bank account to the business bank account.
2 Ordered cleaning supplies, $500.
3 Purchased cleaning equipment, $1,200.
4 Leased a van by making two month's lease payments in advance, $600.
7 Received the cleaning supplies ordered on October 2 by agreeing to pay half in 10 days and the rest in 30 days, $500.

9 Purchased gasoline for the van, $40.
12 Received cash for cleaning carpets, $360.
17 Paid half of the amount owed on supplies purchased on October 7, $250.
21 Billed customers for cleaning carpets, $670.
24 Purchased gasoline for the van, $40.
27 Received $300 from the customers billed on October 21.
31 Withdrew $200 from the business for personal use.

Required

1. Prepare journal entries to record the above transactions in the general journal (pages 1 and 2).
2. Set up the following ledger accounts and post the journal entries: Cash (111), Accounts Receivable (112), Cleaning Supplies (115), Prepaid Lease (116), Cleaning Equipment (141), Accounts Payable (211), Sheldon Thomas, Capital (311), Sheldon Thomas, Withdrawals (312), Cleaning Revenues (411), Gasoline Expense (511).
3. Prepare a trial balance for Thomas Carpet Cleaning Service as of October 31, 19xx.

Problem 2B-4. Transaction Analysis, General Journal, Ledger Accounts, and Trial Balance
(L.O. 5, 6, 8)

The account balances for Chuck's Barber Shop at the end of July are presented in the trial balance shown on the next page.

During August, Mr. Hudson completed the following transactions:

Aug. 1 Paid for supplies purchased on credit last month, $220.
2 Billed customers for services, $360.
3 Paid rent for August, $180.
5 Purchased supplies on credit, $150.
7 Received cash from customers not previously billed, $290.
8 Purchased new equipment from Pendleton Manufacturing Company on account, $1,300.
9 Received telephone bill for last month, $40.
12 Returned a portion of equipment which was defective. Purchase was made August 8, $320.
13 Received payment from customers previously billed, $190.
14 Paid telephone bill received August 9.
16 Took $110 from business for personal use.
19 Paid for supplies purchased on August 5.
20 Billed customers for services, $270.
23 Purchased equipment from a friend who is retiring, $280. Payment was made from personal checking account but equipment will be used in the business.
25 Received payment from customers previously billed, $390.
27 Paid electric bill, $30.
29 Paid $600 on note.

Required

1. Prepare journal entries to record the next transactions in the general journal (pages 11 and 12).
2. Open ledger accounts for the accounts shown in the trial balance. Enter the July 31 trial balance amounts in the ledger accounts.
3. Post the entries to the ledger accounts.
4. Prepare a trial balance as of August 31, 19xx.

Chuck's Barber Shop Trial Balance July 31, 19xx		
Cash (111)	$2,700	
Accounts Receivable (112)	220	
Supplies (115)	460	
Prepaid Insurance (116)	400	
Equipment (141)	4,400	
Notes Payable (211)		$3,000
Accounts Payable (212)		300
Chuck Hudson, Capital (311)		4,200
Chuck Hudson, Withdrawals (312)	420	
Service Revenue (411)		1,380
Rent Expense (412)	180	
Utilities Expense (413)	100	
	$8,880	$8,880

Problem 2B-5. Relationship of General Journal, Ledger Accounts, and Trial Balance (L.O. 6, 7, 8)

The Child-watch Services Company provides babysitting and child-care programs. On January 31, 19xx, the company had a trial balance (account numbers) as follows:

Child-watch Services Company Trial Balance January 31, 19xx		
Cash (111)	$ 1,780	
Accounts Receivable (112)	1,600	
Equipment (141)	990	
Buses (143)	7,400	
Notes Payable (211)		$ 7,000
Accounts Payable (212)		1,470
Janet Escamilla, Capital (311)		3,300
	$11,770	$11,770

During the month of February, the company completed the following transactions:

Feb. 2 Paid one month's rent, $140.
3 Received fees for one month's services, $400.
4 Purchased supplies on account, $85.
5 Reimbursed bus driver for gas expenses, $20.
6 Ordered playground equipment, $1,000.
7 Paid assistants for two weeks' services, $230.
8 Paid $170 on account.
9 Received $1,200 from customers on account.
10 Billed customers who had not yet paid for this month's services, $700.
11 Paid for supplies purchased on February 4.
13 Purchased playground equipment, $1,000.

14 Withdrew $110 for personal expenses.
17 Equipment contributed to business by owner, $90.
19 Paid utility bill, $45.
22 Received $500 for one month's services from customers previously billed.
25 Paid assistants for two weeks' services, $320.
27 Purchased gas and oil for bus on account, $35.
28 Paid $290 for a one-year insurance policy.

Required

1. Enter the above transactions in the general journal (pages 17 and 18).
2. Open accounts in the ledger account form for the accounts in the trial balance plus the following accounts: Supplies (115), Prepaid Insurance (116), Janet Escamilla, Withdrawals (312), Service Revenue (411), Rent Expense (511), Bus Expense (512), Wages Expense (513), Utility Expense (514).
3. Enter the February 1 account balances in the appropriate ledger account forms from the trial balance.
4. Post the entries to the ledger accounts. Be sure to insert the appropriate posting references in the journal and ledger as you post.
5. Prepare a trial balance as of February 29, 19xx.

Financial Decision Case

Ruiz Repair Service Company
(L.O. 1, 3, 5, 8)

Luis Ruiz engaged an attorney to help him start Ruiz Repair Service Company. On March 1, Luis invested $8,000 cash in the business. When he paid the attorney's bill of $500, the attorney advised him to hire an accountant to keep his records. However, Luis was so busy that it was March 31 before he asked you to straighten out his records. Your first task is to develop a trial balance based on the March transactions. You discover the following information.

After the investment and payment to the attorney, Mr. Ruiz borrowed $4,000 from the bank. He later paid $140, including interest of $40 on this loan. He also purchased a pickup truck in the company name, paying $1,500 down and financing $7,400. The first payment on the truck is due April 15. Luis then rented an office and paid three months' rent of $900 in advance. Credit purchases of office equipment of $700 and repair tools of $500 must be paid by April 10.

In March, Ruiz Repair Service completed repairs of $1,300—$400 were cash transactions. Of the credit transactions, $300 was collected during March, and $600 remained to be collected at the end of March. Wages of $400 were paid to employees. On March 31, the company received a $75 bill for March utility expenses and a $50 check from a customer for work to be completed in April.

Required

1. Prepare a March 31 trial balance for Ruiz Repair Service Company. First you must record the March transactions and determine the balance of each T account.
2. Luis Ruiz is unsure how to evaluate the trial balance. His Cash account balance is $9,310, which exceeds his original investment of $8,000 by $1,310. Did he make a profit of $1,310? Explain why the Cash account is not an indicator of business earnings. Cite specific examples to show why it is difficult to determine net income by looking solely at figures in the trial balance.

Answers to Self-Test

1. c	3. b	5. d	7. a	9. c
2. a	4. b	6. c	8. c	10. a

CHAPTER 3 BUSINESS INCOME AND ADJUSTING ENTRIES

LEARNING OBJECTIVES

1. Define *net income* and its components, revenues and expenses.
2. Recognize the difficulties of income measurement caused by (a) the accounting period problem, (b) the continuity problem, and (c) the matching problem.
3. Define accrual accounting and explain two broad ways of accomplishing it.
4. State the four principal situations that require adjusting entries.
5. Prepare typical adjusting entries.
6. Prepare an adjusted trial balance.
7. Relate the need for adjusting entries to the usefulness of accounting information.
8. Prepare correcting entries.

In this chapter you will learn how accountants define business income. The chapter should also help you recognize the problems of assigning income to specific time periods. Then, through a realistic example, you can gain an understanding of the adjustment process necessary for measuring periodic business income. After studying this chapter, you should be able to meet the learning objectives listed on the left.

Profitable operation is essential for a business to succeed or even to survive. So earning a profit is an important goal of most businesses. A major function of accounting, of course, is to measure and report the success or failure of a company in achieving this goal.

Profit has many meanings. One definition is the increase in owner's equity resulting from business operations. However, even this definition can be interpreted differently by economists, lawyers, business people, and the public. Because the word *profit* has more than one meaning, accountants prefer to use the term *net income,* which from an accounting point of view has a precise definition. To the accountant, net income equals revenues minus expenses.

The Measurement of Business Income

Business enterprises are engaged at all times in activities aimed at earning income. As mentioned in Chapter 1, it would be fairly easy to determine the income of a company if we could wait until the business ceased to exist. However, the business environment requires a firm to report income or loss regularly for short and equal periods of time. For example, owners must receive income reports every year, and the government requires the company to pay taxes on annual income. Within the business, management often wants financial statements prepared every month, or more often, so that it can monitor performance.

Faced with these demands, the accountant measures net income in accordance with generally accepted accounting principles. Readers of financial reports who are familiar with these principles can understand how the accountant is defining net income and will be aware of its strengths and weaknesses as a measurement. The following paragraphs present the accounting definition of net income and explain the problems of implementing it.

Net Income

OBJECTIVE 1 Define net income and its components, revenues and expenses

Net income is the net increase in owner's equity resulting from the operations of the company. Net income is measured by the difference between revenues and expenses:

net income = revenues − expenses

If expenses exceed revenues, a **net loss** occurs.

Revenues. **Revenues** "are inflows or other enhancements of assets of an entity or settlement of its liabilities (or a combination of both) during a period from delivering or producing goods, rendering services, or other activities that constitute the entity's major or central operations."[1] In the simplest case, they equal the price of goods sold and services rendered during that time. When a business provides a service or delivers a product to a customer, it usually receives either cash or a promise to pay cash in the near future. The promise to pay is recorded in either Accounts Receivable or Notes Receivable. The revenue for a given period of time equals the total of cash and receivables from goods and services provided to customers during that period.

As shown in Chapter 1, revenues are reflected by a rise in owner's equity. Note that liabilities are not generally affected and that there are transactions that increase cash and other assets but are not revenues. For example, borrowing money from a bank increases cash and liabilities but does not result in revenue. The collection of accounts receivable, which increases cash and decreases accounts receivable, does not result in revenue either. Remember that when a sale on credit took place, an asset called Accounts Receivable was increased, and at the same time an owner's equity revenue account was increased. So counting the collection of the receivable as revenue later would be counting the same sales event twice.

Not all increases in owner's equity arise from revenues. The investment in the company by an owner increases owner's equity, but it is not revenue.

Expenses. **Expenses** are "outflows or other using up of assets or incurrences of liabilities (or a combination of both) during a period from delivering or producing goods, rendering services, or carrying out other activities that constitute the entity's ongoing major or central operations."[2] In other words, expenses are the costs of the goods and services used up in the course of gaining revenues. Often called the cost of doing business, expenses include the costs of goods sold, the costs of activities necessary to carry on the business, and the costs of attracting and serving customers. Examples are salaries, rent, advertising, telephone service, and the depreciation (allocation of the cost) of the building and office equipment.

1. *Statement of Financial Accounting Concepts No. 6*, "Elements of Financial Statements" (Stamford, Conn.: Financial Accounting Standards Board, December, 1985), par. 78.
2. Ibid., par. 80.

Expenses are the opposite of revenues in that they result in a decrease in owner's equity. They also result in a decrease in assets or an increase in liabilities. Just as not all cash receipts are revenues, not all cash payments are expenses. A cash payment to reduce a liability does not result in an expense. The liability may have come from incurring an expense, such as for advertising, that is to be paid later. There may be two steps before an expenditure of cash becomes an expense. For example, prepaid expenses or plant assets (such as machinery and equipment) are recorded as assets when they are acquired. Later, as their usefulness expires in the operation of the business, their cost is transformed into expenses. In fact, expenses are sometimes called expired costs. Later in this chapter, we shall explain these terms and processes further.

Not all decreases in owner's equity arise from expenses. Withdrawals from the company by the owner decrease owner's equity, but they are not expenses.

Temporary and Permanent Accounts. As you saw in Chapter 1, revenues and expenses can be recorded directly as increases and decreases in owner's equity. In practice, management and others want to know the details of the increases and decreases in owner's equity caused by revenues and expenses. For this reason, separate accounts for each revenue and expense are needed to accumulate these amounts each accounting period. Because the amounts in these accounts apply only to the current accounting period, they are sometimes called **temporary** or **nominal** accounts. Temporary accounts show the accumulation of revenues and expenses during the accounting period. At the end of the period, their account balances are transferred to owner's equity. Thus, these nominal accounts start the next accounting period with zero balances and are ready to accumulate the specific revenues and expenses of that period. On the other hand, the balance sheet accounts, such as specific assets and liabilities, are called **permanent** or **real accounts** because their balances can extend past the end of an accounting period. The process of transferring the totals from the temporary revenue and expense accounts to the permanent owner's equity accounts is presented in Chapter 4.

The Accounting Period Problem

OBJECTIVE 2a Recognize the difficulties of income measurement caused by the accounting period problem

The **accounting period problem** recognizes the difficulty of assigning revenues and expenses to a short period of time such as a month or year. Not all transactions can be easily assigned to specific periods of time. Purchases of buildings and equipment, for example, have an effect that extends over many years of a company's life. How many years the buildings or equipment will be in use and how much of the cost should be assigned to each year must of course be an estimate. Accountants solve this problem with an assumption about **periodicity**. The assumption is that the net income for any period of time less than the life of the business must be regarded as tentative but still is a useful estimate of the net income for the period. Generally the time periods are of equal length to make comparisons easier. The time period should be noted in the financial statements.

Any twelve-month accounting period used by a company is called its **fiscal year**. Many companies use the calendar year, ending December 31, for their fiscal year. Many other companies find it convenient to choose a fiscal year that ends during a slack season rather than a peak season. In this case, the fiscal year would correspond to the natural yearly cycle of business activity for the company. The list below shows the diverse fiscal years used by some well-known companies in the leisure time business:

Company	Last Month of Fiscal Year
American Greetings	February
Caesar's World	July
Coleco Industries	December
Walt Disney Productions	September
Eastman Kodak	December
Fleetwood Enterprises	April
Lorimar	July
MGM/UA Entertainment	August
Mattel	January
Polaroid	December

Many government and educational units use fiscal years that end September 30 or June 30.

The Continuity Problem

OBJECTIVE 2b
Recognize the difficulties of income measurement caused by the continuity problem

Income measurement, as noted above, requires that certain expense transactions and revenue transactions be allocated over several accounting periods. This creates another problem for the accountant, who of course does not know how long the business will last. Many businesses last less than five years and, in any given year, thousands will go bankrupt. This dilemma is called the **continuity problem**. To prepare financial statements for an accounting period, the accountant must make an assumption about the ability of the business to continue. Specifically, the accountant assumes that unless there is evidence to the contrary, the business will continue to operate for an indefinite period. This method of dealing with the problem is sometimes called the **going concern** or continuity assumption.

In measuring net income, the accountant must make assumptions regarding the life expectancy of most assets. It is a well-known fact that the value of assets often is much less if a company is not expected to continue in existence than if it is a going concern. However, we have already pointed out in Chapter 2 that the accountant, after recording assets at cost, does not record subsequent changes in their value. Assets become expenses as they are used up. The justification for all of the techniques of income measurement rests on this assumption of continuity.

If accountants have evidence that a company will not continue, of course, then their procedures must change. Sometimes accountants are asked, in bankruptcy cases, to drop the continuity assumption and prepare statements based on the assumption that the firm will go out of business and sell all its assets at liquidation values—that is, for what they will bring in cash.

The Matching Problem

OBJECTIVE 2c
Recognize the difficulties of income measurement caused by the matching problem

Revenues and expenses may be accounted for on a cash received and cash paid basis. This is known as the **cash basis of accounting.** In certain cases, an individual or business may use the cash basis of accounting for income tax purposes. When this method is used, revenues are reported as earned in the period in which cash is received, and expenses are reported in periods in which cash is paid. Taxable income is therefore calculated as the difference between cash receipts from revenues and cash payments for expenses.

Even though the cash basis of accounting works well for some small businesses and many individuals, it does not meet the needs of most businesses. As explained above, revenues can be earned in a period other than when cash is received, and expenses can be incurred in a period other than when cash is paid. If net income is going to be measured adequately, revenues and expenses must be assigned to the appropriate accounting period. The accountant solves this problem by applying the **matching rule:**

Revenues must be assigned to the accounting period in which the goods were sold or the services performed, and expenses must be assigned to the accounting period in which they were used to produce revenue.

Though direct cause-and-effect relationships can seldom be demonstrated for certain, many costs appear to be related to particular revenue. The accountant will recognize such expenses and related revenue in the same accounting period. Examples are the costs of goods sold and sales commissions. When there is no direct means of connecting cause and effect, the accountant tries to allocate costs in a systematic and rational way among the accounting periods that benefit from the cost. For example, a building is converted from an asset to an expense by allocating its cost over the years that benefit from its use.

Accrual Accounting

OBJECTIVE 3
Define accrual accounting and explain two broad ways of accomplishing it

To apply the matching rule stated above, accountants have developed accrual accounting. **Accrual accounting** "attempts to record the financial effects on an enterprise of transactions and other events and circumstances . . . in the periods in which those transactions, events, and circumstances occur rather than only in the periods in which cash is received or paid by the enterprise."[3] In other words, accrual accounting consists of all the techniques developed by accountants to apply the matching rule. It is done in two general ways: (1) by recognizing revenues when earned and expenses when incurred and (2) by adjusting the accounts.

3. *Statement of Financial Accounting Concepts No. 1,* "Objectives of Financial Reporting by Business Enterprises" (Stamford, Conn.: Financial Accounting Standards Board, 1978), par. 44.

Recognizing Revenues When Earned and Expenses When Incurred. The first method has already been illustrated several times in Chapter 2. For example, when the Joan Miller Advertising Agency made sales on credit by placing the advertisements for clients (in the January 19 transaction), revenue was immediately recorded by debiting (increasing) Accounts Receivable and crediting the revenue account Advertising Fees Earned at the time of the sale. In this way, the credit sale is recognized before the collection of cash. Accounts Receivable, then, serves as a holding account until the payment is received. This process of determining when a sale takes place is known as **revenue recognition**. When the Joan Miller Advertising Agency received the telephone bill on January 30, the expense was recognized both as having been incurred and as helping to produce revenue in the current month. The transaction was recorded by debiting Telephone Expense and crediting Accounts Payable. Until the bill is paid, Accounts Payable serves as a holding account. Recognition of the expense does *not* depend on payment of cash.

Adjusting the Accounts. An accounting period by definition must end on a particular day. On that day, the balance sheet must contain all assets and liabilities as of the end of that day. The income statement must contain all revenues and expenses applicable to the period ending on that day. Although a business is recognized as a continuous process, there must be a cutoff point. Some transactions invariably span the cutoff point, and as a result some of the accounts need adjustment.

Exhibit 3-1. Trial Balance for the Joan Miller Advertising Agency

Joan Miller Advertising Agency
Trial Balance
January 31, 19xx

Cash	$ 1,720	
Accounts Receivable	2,800	
Art Supplies	1,800	
Office Supplies	800	
Prepaid Rent	800	
Prepaid Insurance	480	
Art Equipment	4,200	
Office Equipment	3,000	
Accounts Payable		$ 3,170
Unearned Art Fees		1,000
Joan Miller, Capital		10,000
Joan Miller, Withdrawals	1,400	
Advertising Fees Earned		4,200
Office Wages Expense	1,200	
Utility Expense	100	
Telephone Expense	70	
	$18,370	$18,370

For example, some of the accounts in the end-of-the-period trial balance for the Joan Miller Advertising Agency from Chapter 2 (also shown in Exhibit 3-1) do not show the proper balances for preparing financial statements. On January 31, the trial balance contains prepaid rent of $800. At $400 per month, this represented rent paid in advance for the months of January and February. So at January 31, one-half of the $800, or $400, represents rent expense for January, and the remaining $400 represents the cost of asset services to be used up in February. An adjustment is needed to reflect the $400 balance of the Prepaid Rent account on the balance sheet and the $400 rent expense on the income statement. As you will see, several other accounts of the Joan Miller Advertising Agency do not reflect their proper balances. Like the Prepaid Rent account, they also need adjusting entries.

The Adjustment Process

OBJECTIVE 4
State the four principal situations that require adjusting entries

Accountants use **adjusting entries** to apply accrual accounting to transactions that span more than one accounting period. Adjusting entries are journal entries that have at least one balance sheet (or permanent) account entry and at least one income statement (or temporary) account entry. Adjusting entries will never involve the Cash account. They are needed when deferrals or accruals exist. A **deferral** is the postponement of the recognition of an expense already paid or incurred or of a revenue already received. Deferrals would be needed in the following two cases:

1. There are costs recorded that must be apportioned between two or more accounting periods. Examples are the cost of a building, prepaid insurance, and supplies. The adjusting entry will involve an asset account and an expense account.
2. There are revenues recorded that must be apportioned between two or more accounting periods. An example is commissions collected in advance for services to be rendered in later periods. The adjusting entry will involve a liability account and a revenue account.

An **accrual** is the recognition of an expense or revenue that has arisen but has not yet been recorded. Accruals would be required in the following two cases:

1. There are unrecorded revenues. An example is commissions earned but not yet collected or billed to customers. The adjusting entry will involve an asset account and a revenue account and the estimated income taxes that are applicable to the period.
2. There are unrecorded expenses. Examples are the wages earned by employees in the current accounting period but after the last pay period. The adjusting entry will involve an expense account and a liability account.

Once again the Joan Miller Advertising Agency will be used to illustrate the kinds of adjusting entries that most businesses will have.

Apportioning Recorded Expenses Between Two or More Accounting Periods (Deferrals)

OBJECTIVE 5
Prepare typical adjusting entries

Companies often make expenditures that benefit more than one period. These expenditures are generally debited to an asset account. At the end of the accounting period, the amount that has been used up in the period is transferred from the asset account to an expense account. Two of the more important kinds of adjustments are prepaid expenses and depreciation of plant and equipment.

Prepaid Expenses. Some expenses are customarily paid in advance. These expenditures are called **prepaid expenses.** Among these items are rent, insurance, and supplies. At the end of an accounting period, a portion (or all) of these goods or services most likely will have been used up or will have expired. The part of the expenditure that has benefited current operations is treated as an expense of the period. On the other hand, the part not consumed or expired is treated as an asset applicable to future operations of the company. If adjusting entries for prepaid expenses are not made at the end of the month, both the balance sheet and income statement will be stated wrong. First, the assets of the company will be overstated. Second, the expenses of the company will be understated. For this reason, owner's equity on the balance sheet and net income on the income statement will be overstated. Besides prepaid rent, the Joan Miller Advertising Agency has prepaid expenses for prepaid insurance, art supplies, and office supplies, all of which call for adjusting entries.

At the beginning of the month, the Joan Miller Advertising Agency paid two months' rent in advance. This expenditure resulted in an asset consisting of the right to occupy the office for two months. As each day in the month passed, part of the asset's costs expired and became an expense. By January 31, one-half had expired, and should be treated as an expense. The analysis of this economic event is shown below.

Prepaid Rent (Adjustment a)

Prepaid Rent			
Jan. 2	800	Jan. 31	400

Rent Expense			
Jan. 31	400		

Transaction: Expiration of one month's rent.
Analysis: Assets decreased. Owner's equity decreased.
Rules: Decreases in assets are recorded by credits. Decreases in owner's equity are recorded by debits.
Entries: Decrease in owner's equity is recorded by a debit to Rent Expense. Decrease in assets is recorded by a credit to Prepaid Rent.

	Dr.	Cr.
Rent Expense	400	
Prepaid Rent		400

The Prepaid Rent account now has a balance of $400, which represents one month's rent paid in advance. The Rent Expense account reflects the $400 expense for the month.

The Joan Miller Advertising Agency also purchased a one-year insurance policy, paying for it in advance. In a manner similar to prepaid rent, prepaid insurance offers protection that expires day by day. By the end of the month, one-twelfth of the protection had expired. The adjustment is analyzed and recorded as shown below.

Prepaid Insurance (Adjustment b)

Prepaid Insurance

Jan. 8	480	Jan. 31	40

Insurance Expense

Jan. 31	40		

Transaction: Expiration of one month's insurance.
Analysis: Assets decreased. Owner's equity decreased.
Rules: Decreases in assets are recorded by credits. Decreases in owner's equity are recorded by debits.
Entries: Decrease in owner's equity is recorded by a debit to Insurance Expense. Decrease in assets is recorded by a credit to Prepaid Insurance.

	Dr.	Cr.
Insurance Expense	40	
Prepaid Insurance		40

The Prepaid Insurance account now has the proper balance of $440, and Insurance Expense reflects the expired cost of $40 for the month.

Early in the month, the Joan Miller Advertising Agency purchased art supplies and office supplies. As Joan Miller did art work for various clients during the month, art supplies were consumed. Her secretary also used up office supplies. There is no need to account for these supplies every day, because the financial statements are not prepared until the end of the month, and the record keeping would involve too much work.

Instead, Joan Miller makes a careful inventory of the art and office supplies at the end of the month. This inventory records the number and cost of those supplies that are still assets of the company—yet to be consumed. The inventory shows that art supplies costing $1,300 and office supplies costing $600 are still on hand. This means that of the art supplies originally purchased for $1,800, $500 worth were used up or became an expense. Of the office supplies originally costing $800, $200 worth were consumed. These transactions are analyzed and recorded as follows:

Art Supplies and Office Supplies (Adjustments c and d)

Art Supplies

Jan. 6	1,800	Jan. 31	500

Art Supplies Expense

Jan. 31	500		

Transaction: Consumption of supplies.
Analysis: Assets decreased. Owner's equity decreased.
Rules: Decreases in assets are recorded by credits. Decreases in owner's equity are recorded by debits.

Office Supplies

Jan. 6	800	Jan. 31	200

Office Supplies Expense

Jan. 31	200		

Entries: Decreases in owner's equity are recorded by debits to Art Supplies Expense and Office Supplies Expense. Decreases in assets are recorded by credits to Art Supplies and Office Supplies.

	Dr.	Cr.
Art Supplies Expense	500	
Art Supplies		500
Office Supplies Expense	200	
Office Supplies		200

The asset accounts of Art Supplies and Office Supplies now reflect the proper amounts of $1,300 and $600, respectively, yet to be consumed. In addition, the amounts of art and office supplies used up during the accounting period are reflected as $500 and $200, respectively.

Depreciation of Plant and Equipment. When a company buys a long-lived asset such as a building, equipment, trucks, automobiles, a computer, store fixtures, or office furniture, it is basically buying or prepaying for the usefulness of that asset for as long as the asset provides a benefit to the company. In other words, the asset is a deferral of an expense. Proper accounting therefore requires the allocation of the cost of the asset over its estimated useful life. The amount allocated to any one accounting period is called **depreciation** or **depreciation expense.** Depreciation is an expense just like any other incurred during an accounting period to obtain revenue.

It is often impossible to tell how long an asset will last or how much of the asset is used in any one period. For this reason, depreciation must be estimated. Accountants have developed a number of methods for estimating depreciation and for dealing with other complex problems concerning it. Only the simplest case is presented here as an illustration.

Suppose that the Joan Miller Advertising Agency estimates that the art equipment and office equipment will last five years (sixty months) and will be worthless at the end of that time. The depreciation of art equipment and office equipment for the month is computed as $70 ($4,200 ÷ 60 months) and $50 ($3,000 ÷ 60 months), respectively. These amounts represent the cost allocated to the month, thus reducing the asset accounts and increasing the expense accounts (reducing owner's equity). These transactions can be analyzed as shown below. The use of the contra-asset account called Accumulated Depreciation is described in the next section.

Art Equipment and Office Equipment (Adjustments e and f)

Art Equipment

Jan. 4	4,200		

Transaction: Recording depreciation expense.
Analysis: Assets decreased. Owner's equity decreased.

Accumulated Depreciation, Art Equipment

	Jan. 31 70

Office Equipment

Jan. 5 3,000	

Accumulated Depreciation, Office Equipment

	Jan. 31 50

Depreciation Expense, Art Equipment

Jan. 31 70	

Depreciation Expense, Office Equipment

Jan. 31 50	

Rules: Decreases in assets are recorded by credits. Decreases in owner's equity are recorded by debits.
Entries: Owner's equity is decreased by debits to Depreciation Expense, Art Equipment, and Depreciation Expense, Office Equipment. Assets are decreased by credits to contra-asset accounts Accumulated Depreciation, Art Equipment, and Accumulated Depreciation, Office Equipment.

	Dr.	Cr.
Depreciation Expense, Art Equipment	70	
Accumulated Depreciation, Art Equipment		70
Depreciation Expense, Office Equipment	50	
Accumulated Depreciation, Office Equipment		50

Accumulated Depreciation—A Contra Account. Note that in the analysis of the case above, the asset accounts were not credited directly. Instead, new accounts—Accumulated Depreciation, Art Equipment, and Accumulated Depreciation, Office Equipment—were credited. These **accumulated depreciation** accounts are contra-asset accounts used to accumulate the total past depreciation expense on a specific long-lived asset. A **contra account** is an account that is paired with and deducted from another related account in the financial statements. There are several types of contra accounts. In this case, the balance of Accumulated Depreciation, Art Equipment, is a deduction from the associated account Art Equipment. Likewise, Accumulated Depreciation, Office Equipment, is a deduction from Office Equipment. After these adjusting entries have been made, the plant and equipment section of the balance sheet for the Joan Miller Advertising Agency appears as in Exhibit 3-2.

The contra account is used for two very good reasons. First, it recognizes that depreciation is an estimate. Second, the use of the contra account preserves the fact of original cost of the asset and shows how much of the asset has been allocated to expense as well as the balance left to be depreciated. As the months pass, the amount of the accumulated depreciation will grow, and so the net amount shown as an asset will be reduced. In six months, for instance, Accumulated Depreciation, Art Equipment, will have a total of $420; when this amount is subtracted from Art Equipment, a net amount of $3,780 will remain. This net amount is referred to as the **carrying value**.

Other names are sometimes used for accumulated depreciation, such as "allowance for depreciation," or the wholly unacceptable term "reserve for depreciation." Accumulated depreciation is the newer, better term.

Exhibit 3-2. Plant and Equipment Section of Balance Sheet

Joan Miller Advertising Agency
Partial Balance Sheet
January 31, 19xx

Plant and Equipment		
Art Equipment	$4,200	
Less Accumulated Depreciation	70	$4,130
Office Equipment	$3,000	
Less Accumulated Depreciation	50	2,950
Total Plant and Equipment		$7,080

Apportioning Recorded Revenues Between Two or More Accounting Periods (Deferrals)

Just as costs may be paid and recorded before they are used up, revenues may be received before they are earned. When such revenues are received in advance, the company has an obligation to deliver goods or perform services. Therefore, **unearned revenues** would be a liability account. For example, publishing companies usually receive payment for magazine subscriptions in advance. These receipts must be recorded in a liability account. If the company fails to deliver the magazines for the subscription period, subscribers are entitled to their money back. As the company delivers each issue of the magazine, it earns a part of the advance payments. This earned portion must be transferred from the Unearned Subscription account to the Subscription Revenue account.

During the month, the Joan Miller Advertising Agency received $1,000 as an advance payment for art work to be done for another agency. Assume that by the end of the month, $400 of the art work was done and accepted by the other agency. This transaction is analyzed as follows:

Unearned Art Fees (Adjustment g)

Unearned Art Fees

Jan. 31	400	Jan. 15	1,000

Art Fees Earned

		Jan. 31	400

Transaction: Performance of services received in advance.
Analysis: Liabilities decreased. Owner's equity increased.
Rules: Decreases in liabilities are recorded by debits. Increases in owner's equity are recorded by credits.
Entries: Decrease in liabilities is recorded by a debit to Unearned Art Fees. Increase in owner's equity is recorded by a credit to Art Fees Earned.

	Dr.	**Cr.**
Unearned Art Fees	400	
Art Fees Earned		400

The liability account Unearned Art Fees now reflects the amount of work to be performed, or $600. The revenue account Art Fees Earned reflects the amount of services performed and earned during the month, or $400.

Unrecorded or Accrued Revenues

Unrecorded or **accrued revenues** are revenues for which the service has been performed or the goods delivered but for which no entry has been recorded in the accounts. Any revenues that have been earned but not recorded during the accounting period call for an adjusting entry that debits an asset account and credits a revenue account. For example, the interest on a note receivable is earned day by day but may not in fact be received until another accounting period. Interest Revenue should be credited and Interest Receivable debited for the interest accrued at the end of the current period.

Suppose that the Joan Miller Advertising Agency has agreed to place a series of advertisements for Marsh Tire Company and that the first appears on January 31, the last day of the month. The fee of $200 for this advertisement, which has now been earned but has not been recorded, should be recorded as shown below. Marsh will be billed for the series of advertisements when they are completed. At that time, Accounts Receivable will be debited and Accrued Fees Receivable will be credited.

Unrecorded or Accrued Advertising Fees (Adjustment h)

Accrued Fees Receivable

Debit		Credit	
Jan. 31	200		

Advertising Fees Earned

Debit		Credit	
		Jan. 10	1,400
		19	2,800
		31	200

Transaction: Accrual of unrecorded revenue.
Analysis: Assets increased. Owner's equity increased.
Rules: Increases in assets are recorded by debits. Increases in owner's equity are recorded by credits.
Entries: Increase in assets is recorded by debit to Accrued Fees Receivable. Increase in owner's equity is recorded by credit to Advertising Fees Earned.

	Dr.	Cr.
Accrued Fees Receivable	200	
Advertising Fees Earned		200

Asset and revenue accounts now both show the proper balance: $200 in accrued fees receivable is owed to the company, and $4,400 in advertising fees has been earned by the company during the month.

Unrecorded or Accrued Expenses

At the end of an accounting period, there are usually expenses that have been incurred but not recorded in the accounts. These expenses require adjusting entries. One such case is borrowed money. Each day interest accumulates on the debt, and it is necessary to use an adjusting entry at the end of each accounting period to record this accumulated interest, which is an expense to the period, and the corresponding liability to pay the interest. Other comparable expenses are taxes, wages, and salaries. As the expense and the corresponding liability accumulate, they are said to accrue—hence the term **accrued expenses.**

Suppose that the calendar for January appears as shown in the following illustration:

January

Su	M	T	W	Th	F	Sa
	1	2	3	4	5	6
7	8	9	10	11	12	13
14	15	16	17	18	19	20
21	22	23	24	25	26	27
28	29	30	31			

By the end of business on January 31, the Joan Miller Advertising Agency's secretary will have worked three days (Monday, Tuesday, and Wednesday) beyond the last biweekly pay period, which ended on January 26. The employee has earned the salary for these days, but it is not due to be paid until the regular payday in February. The salary for these three days is rightfully an expense for January, and the liabilities should reflect the fact that the company does owe the secretary for those days. Because the secretary's salary rate is $600 every two weeks or $60 per day ($600 ÷ 10 working days), the expense is $180 ($60 × 3 days). This unrecorded or accrued expense can be analyzed as shown below.

Unrecorded or Accrued Wages (Adjustment i)

Accrued Wages Payable

		Jan. 31	180

Office Wages Expense

Jan. 12	600		
26	600		
31	180		

Transaction: Accrual of unrecorded expense.
Analysis: Liabilities increased. Owner's equity decreased.
Rules: Increases in liabilities are recorded by credits. Decreases in owner's equity are recorded by debits.
Entries: Decrease in owner's equity is recorded by debit to Office Wages Expense. Increase in liabilities is recorded by credit to Accrued Wages Payable.

	Dr.	Cr.
Office Wages Expense	180	
Accrued Wages Payable		180

The liability of $180 is now correctly reflected in the Accrued Wages Payable account. The actual expense incurred for office wages during the month is also correct at $1,380.

The Adjusted Trial Balance

OBJECTIVE 6
Prepare an adjusted trial balance

In Chapter 2, a trial balance was prepared before any adjusting entries were recorded. After recording the adjusting entries in the general journal and posting them to the general ledger, it is desirable to prepare an **adjusted trial balance,** which is a list of the accounts and balances after the recording and posting of the adjusting entries. Exhibit 3-3 shows the trial balance from Chapter 2, along with the adjusting entries and the resulting adjusted trial balance. If the adjusting entries have been posted correctly to the accounts, the adjusted trial balance must have equal debit and credit totals.

Using the Adjusted Trial Balance to Prepare Financial Statements

The adjusted trial balance for the Joan Miller Advertising Agency now shows the correct balances for all the accounts. From this adjusted trial balance, the financial statements can be easily prepared. The income statement can be prepared from the revenue and expense accounts, as shown in Exhibit 3-4. Then, in Exhibit 3-5, the balance sheet has been prepared from the balance sheet accounts, except for Joan Miller, Capital, which must come from the statement of owner's equity. Notice that the net income from the income statement is combined with withdrawals on the statement of owner's equity to give the net increase in Joan Miller's capital account of $590.

The Importance of Adjustments in Accounting

OBJECTIVE 7
Relate the need for adjusting entries to the usefulness of accounting information

One might ask, Why worry about adjustments? Doesn't everything come out all right in the end? The main reason for making adjustments is that they help accountants give accounting information that is useful to decision makers. For example, adjusting entries are necessary to measure income and financial position in a relevant and useful way. The management of a company wants to know how much it has earned during the last month, quarter, or year and what its liabilities and assets are at a certain date. This need is an important reason for making the adjusting entries. For instance, if the three days' accrued salary for Joan Miller's secretary is not recorded, the income of the agency will be overstated by $180 and the liabilities understated by $180.

Another important reason for the use of adjusting entries is that they allow financial statements to be compared from one period to the next. Management can see if the company is making progress toward earning a profit or if the company has improved its financial position. To return to our example, if the three days' accrued salary for Joan Miller's secretary is not recorded, not only will the income for January be overstated by

Exhibit 3-3. Determination of the Adjusted Trial Balance

Joan Miller Advertising Agency
Preparation of Adjusted Trial Balance
January 31, 19xx

Accounts	Trial Balance Debit	Trial Balance Credit	Adjustments Debit	Adjustments Credit	Adjusted Trial Balance Debit	Adjusted Trial Balance Credit
Cash	$ 1,720				$ 1,720	
Accounts Receivable	2,800				2,800	
Art Supplies	1,800			(c) $500	1,300	
Office Supplies	800			(d) 200	600	
Prepaid Rent	800			(a) 400	400	
Prepaid Insurance	480			(b) 40	440	
Art Equipment	4,200				4,200	
Accumulated Depreciation, Art Equipment				(e) 70		$ 70
Office Equipment	3,000				3,000	
Accumulated Depreciation, Office Equipment				(f) 50		50
Accounts Payable		$ 3,170				3,170
Unearned Art Fees		1,000	(g) $400			600
Joan Miller, Capital		10,000				10,000
Joan Miller, Withdrawals	1,400				1,400	
Advertising Fees Earned		4,200		(h) 200		4,400
Office Wages Expense	1,200		(i) 180		1,380	
Utility Expense	100				100	
Telephone Expense	70				70	
	$18,370	$18,370				
Rent Expense			(a) 400		400	
Insurance Expense			(b) 40		40	
Art Supplies Expense			(c) 500		500	
Office Supplies Expense			(d) 200		200	
Depreciation Expense, Art Equipment			(e) 70		70	
Depreciation Expense, Office Equipment			(f) 50		50	
Art Fees Earned				(g) 400		400
Accrued Fees Receivable			(h) 200		200	
Accrued Wages Payable				(i) 180		180
			$2,040	$2,040	$18,870	$18,870

Exhibit 3-4. Relationship of Adjusted Trial Balance to Income Statement

Joan Miller Advertising Agency
Adjusted Trial Balance
January 31, 19xx

Cash	$ 1,720	
Accounts Receivable	2,800	
Art Supplies	1,300	
Office Supplies	600	
Prepaid Rent	400	
Prepaid Insurance	440	
Art Equipment	4,200	
Accumulated Depreciation, Art Equipment		$ 70
Office Equipment	3,000	
Accumulated Depreciation, Office Equipment		50
Accounts Payable		3,170
Unearned Art Fees		600
Joan Miller, Capital		10,000
Joan Miller, Withdrawals	1,400	
Advertising Fees Earned		4,400
Office Wages Expense	1,380	
Utility Expense	100	
Telephone Expense	70	
Rent Expense	400	
Insurance Expense	40	
Art Supplies Expense	500	
Office Supplies Expense	200	
Depreciation Expense, Art Equipment	70	
Depreciation Expense, Office Equipment	50	
Art Fees Earned		400
Accrued Fees Receivable	200	
Accrued Wages Payable		180
	$18,870	$18,870

Joan Miller Advertising Agency
Income Statement
For the Month Ended January 31, 19xx

Revenues		
Advertising Fees Earned	$4,400	
Art Fees Earned	400	
Total Revenue		$4,800
Expenses		
Office Wages Expense	$1,380	
Utility Expense	100	
Telephone Expense	70	
Rent Expense	400	
Insurance Expense	40	
Art Supplies Expense	500	
Office Supplies Expense	200	
Depreciation Expense, Art Equipment	70	
Depreciation Expense, Office Equipment	50	
Total Expenses		2,810
Net Income		$1,990

Exhibit 3-5. Relationship of Adjusted Trial Balance to Balance Sheet

Joan Miller Advertising Agency
Adjusted Trial Balance
January 31, 19xx

Cash	$ 1,720	
Accounts Receivable	2,800	
Art Supplies	1,300	
Office Supplies	600	
Prepaid Rent	400	
Prepaid Insurance	440	
Art Equipment	4,200	
Accumulated Depreciation, Art Equipment		$ 70
Office Equipment	3,000	
Accumulated Depreciation, Office Equipment		50
Accounts Payable		3,170
Unearned Art Fees		600
Joan Miller, Capital		10,000
Joan Miller, Withdrawals	1,400	
Advertising Fees Earned		4,400
Office Wages Expense	1,380	
Utility Expense	100	
Telephone Expense	70	
Rent Expense	400	
Insurance Expense	40	
Art Supplies Expense	500	
Office Supplies Expense	200	
Depreciation Expense, Art Equipment	70	
Depreciation Expense, Office Equipment	50	
Art Fees Earned		400
Accrued Fees Receivable	200	
Accrued Wages Payable		180
	$18,870	$18,870

Joan Miller Advertising Agency
Balance Sheet
January 31, 19xx

Assets		
Cash		$ 1,720
Accounts Receivable		2,800
Accrued Fees Receivable		200
Art Supplies		1,300
Office Supplies		600
Prepaid Rent		400
Prepaid Insurance		440
Art Equipment	$4,200	
Less Accumulated Depreciation	70	4,130
Office Equipment	$3,000	
Less Accumulated Depreciation	50	2,950
Total Assets		$14,540
Liabilities		
Accounts Payable	$3,170	
Unearned Art Fees	600	
Accrued Wages Payable	180	
Total Liabilities		$ 3,950
Owner's Equity		
Joan Miller, Capital, January 31, 19xx		10,590
Total Liabilities and Owner's Equity		$14,540

Joan Miller Advertising Agency
Statement of Owner's Equity
For the Month Ended January 31, 19xx

Joan Miller, Capital, January 1, 19xx		$ —
Add: Investment by Joan Miller	$10,000	
Net Income	1,990	11,990
Subtotal		$11,990
Less Withdrawals		1,400
Joan Miller, Capital, January 31, 19xx		$10,590

$180, but the net income for February (the month when payment is made) will be understated by $180. This error will make the February earnings, whatever they may be, appear worse than they actually are. Look back over all the adjustments for the Joan Miller Advertising Agency for prepaid rent and insurance, art and office supplies, depreciation of office and art equipment, unearned art fees, accrued wages and expenses, and accrued advertising fees. These are all normal and usual adjustments; the combined effect of all of them on net income is significant.

Accountants also insist that adjusting procedures and entries be complete and consistent at the end of every accounting period because there is often more than one acceptable way to apply the matching rule in a given case. For example, there are several methods of determining the amount of depreciation expense for a given accounting period. Consequently, there is a need for the consistent application of accounting practice from one period to the next so that the financial statements of successive periods can be compared and understood. Accounting methods can be changed if new circumstances or other logical reasons require that they be changed. Since a change would make it hard to compare the financial statements of different periods, however, the company must explain in the financial statements the nature and effect of the change. Without such a disclosure, the statement reader can assume that accounting methods have been consistently applied from one period to the next.

The adjustment process can also be related to the characteristic of verifiability. To the fullest extent possible, accounting practice should be based on objective, verifiable evidence. For example, transactions are recorded at cost because two independent parties have produced objective and verifiable evidence as to the value of the transactions. Accounting transactions should be supported by verifiable business documents. In making adjustments, a problem arises because estimates often must be used. Estimates, however, can be supported by objective evidence. For example, in estimating how long buildings or equipment may last, the accountant can rely on objective studies of past experience.

Correcting Errors

OBJECTIVE 8
Prepare correcting entries

When an error is discovered in either the journal or the ledger, it must be corrected. The method of correction will depend on the kind of error. However, the error must *never* be erased, because this action would seem to indicate an effort to hide something. If an error is discovered in a journal entry before it is posted to the ledger, a line drawn through the incorrect item and the correct item written above will suffice. Similarly, when a posting error involves entering an incorrect amount in the ledger, it is acceptable to draw a line through the wrong amount and write in the correct amount.

However, if a journal entry has been posted to the wrong account in the ledger, then it is necessary to prepare another journal entry to correct the error. For example, suppose that a purchase of art equipment was recorded as follows:

		Debit	Credit
Feb. 20	Art Supplies	100	
	Cash		100
	To record purchase of art equipment		

It is clear that the debit should be to Art Equipment, not to Art Supplies. Therefore, the following entry is needed to correct the error:

		Debit	Credit
Feb. 24	Art Equipment	100	
	Art Supplies		100
	To correct error of Feb. 20, when Art Supplies was debited in error for the purchase of art equipment		

The full explanation provides a record for those who might later question the entry. The Cash account is not involved in the correction, because it was correct originally. The effect of the correction is to reduce Art Supplies by $100 and increase Art Equipment by $100.

A Note About Journal Entries

Throughout Chapters 2 and 3, except in the above section, all journal entries have been presented with a full analysis of the transaction. This complete analysis was given to show you the thought process behind each entry. By now, you should be fully aware of the effects of transactions on the balance sheet equation and the rules of debit and credit. For this reason, journal entries will be presented in the rest of the book with explanations as shown in the section above.

Chapter Review

Review of Learning Objectives

1. **Define *net income* and its components, revenues and expenses.**
   Net income is the net increase in owner's equity resulting from the profit-seeking operations of a company. Net income equals revenues minus expenses. Revenues are a measure of the asset values received from customers as a result of income-earning activity during a specific period of time. Expenses are the costs of goods and services used up in the process of obtaining revenues.

2. **Recognize the difficulties of income measurement caused by (a) the accounting period problem, (b) the continuity problem, and (c) the matching problem.**
   The accounting period problem recognizes that net income measurements for short periods of time are necessarily tentative. The continuity problem recognizes that even though businesses face an uncertain future, accountants must assume that without evidence to the contrary, a business will continue

indefinitely. The matching problem results from the difficulty of assigning revenue and expenses to a period of time and is solved by application of the matching rule.

3. **Define accrual accounting and explain two broad ways of accomplishing it.**
   Accrual accounting consists of all the techniques developed by accountants to apply the matching rule. The two general ways of accomplishing it are (1) by recognizing revenue when earned and expenses when incurred and (2) by adjusting the accounts.

4. **State the four principal situations that require adjusting entries.**
   Adjusting entries are required (1) when recorded expenses are to be apportioned between two or more accounting periods, (2) when recorded revenues are to be apportioned between two or more accounting periods, (3) when unrecorded expenses exist, and (4) when unrecorded revenues exist.

5. **Prepare typical adjusting entries.**
   The preparation of adjusting entries is summarized in the following table:

Type of Adjusting Entry	Type of Account: Debited	Type of Account: Credited	Examples
Deferrals			
1. Apportioning Recorded Expenses	Expense	Asset	Prepaid Rent Prepaid Insurance Supplies Buildings Equipment
2. Apportioning Recorded Revenues	Liability	Revenue	Commissions Received in Advance
Accruals			
1. Unrecorded Revenues (Earned, not received)	Asset	Revenue	Commissions Receivable Accrued Interest Receivable
2. Unrecorded Expenses (Incurred, not paid)	Expense	Liability	Accrued Wages Payable Accrued Interest Payable

6. **Prepare an adjusted trial balance.**
   An adjusted trial balance is a trial balance that is prepared after adjusting entries have been posted to the accounts in the ledger. Its purpose is to test the balance of the ledger after the adjusting entries are made and before financial statements are prepared.

7. **Relate the need for adjusting entries to the usefulness of accounting information.**
   Adjusting entries are a means of implementing accrual accounting and thereby aid in producing financial statements that are comparable from period to period and relevant to the needs of users. Although adjusting entries often require estimates, the estimates are usually based on verifiable formulas or facts.

8. **Prepare correcting entries.**
When a correcting entry is required, it should be made in such a way as to adjust the appropriate accounts to the correct balances. A full explanation should accompany each correcting entry.

Self-Test

Test your knowledge of the chapter by choosing the best answer for each item below.

1. The net increase in owner's equity resulting from business operations is called
   a. net income.
   b. revenue.
   c. expense.
   d. asset.
2. The costs of the goods and services used up in the process of obtaining revenue are called
   a. net income.
   b. revenues.
   c. expenses.
   d. liabilities.
3. In general, the accounts in the income statement are known as
   a. permanent accounts.
   b. temporary accounts.
   c. unearned revenue accounts.
   d. contra-asset accounts.
4. A business may choose a fiscal year that corresponds to
   a. the calendar year.
   b. the natural business year.
   c. any twelve-month period.
   d. Any of the above.
5. Assigning revenues to the accounting period in which the goods were delivered or the services performed and expenses to the accounting period in which they were used to produce revenues is known as the
   a. accounting period problem.
   b. continuity assumption.
   c. matching rule.
   d. recognition rule.
6. Adjusting entries are essential to
   a. the matching rule.
   b. accrual accounting.
   c. a proper determination of net income.
   d. All of the above.
7. The adjustment for depreciation is an example of
   a. apportioning costs between two or more periods.
   b. apportioning revenues between two or more periods.
   c. recognizing an accrued expense.
   d. recognizing an unrecorded revenue.
8. Accumulated depreciation is an example of
   a. an expense.
   b. an unrecorded revenue.
   c. a liability.
   d. a contra account.
9. The recording of wages earned but not yet paid is an example of an adjustment that
   a. apportions revenues between two or more periods.
   b. recognizes an accrued expense.
   c. recognizes an unrecorded revenue.
   d. None of the above.
10. Prepaid Insurance has an ending balance of $2,300. During the period, insurance in the amount of $1,200 expired. The adjusting entry would contain a debit

a. to Prepaid Insurance for $1,200.
b. to Insurance Expense for $1,200.
c. to Unexpired Insurance for $1,100.
d. to Insurance Expense for $1,100.

Answers to Self-Test are at the end of this chapter.

Review Problem
Adjusting Entries, T Accounts, and Adjusted Trial Balance

The unadjusted trial balance for Certified Answering Service appears as follows on December 31, 19xx:

Certified Answering Service
Trial Balance
December 31, 19xx

Cash	$2,160	
Accounts Receivable	1,250	
Office Supplies	180	
Prepaid Insurance	240	
Office Equipment	3,400	
Accumulated Depreciation, Office Equipment		$ 600
Accounts Payable		700
Revenue Received in Advance		460
James Neal, Capital		4,470
Answering Service Revenue		2,900
Wages Expense	1,500	
Rent Expense	400	
	$9,130	$9,130

The following information is also available:

a. Insurance that expired during December amounted to $40.
b. Office supplies on hand at the end of December totaled $75.
c. Depreciation for the month of December totaled $100.
d. Accrued wages at the end of December totaled $120.
e. Revenues earned for services performed but not yet billed on December 31 totaled $300.
f. Revenues earned for services performed that were paid in advance totaled $160.

Required

1. Prepare T accounts for the accounts in the trial balance.
2. Determine the required adjusting entries, and record them directly in the T accounts. Open any new T accounts as needed.
3. Prepare an adjusted trial balance.

Answer to Review Problem

1. T accounts set up and amounts from trial balance entered.
2. Adjusting entries recorded.

Cash

Bal.	2,160		

Accounts Receivable

Bal.	1,250		

Accrued Service Revenue Receivable

(e)	300		

Office Supplies

Bal.	180	(b)	105
Bal.	75		

Prepaid Insurance

Bal.	240	(a)	40
Bal.	200		

Office Equipment

Bal.	3,400		

Accumulated Depreciation, Office Equipment

		Bal.	600
		(c)	100
		Bal.	700

Accounts Payable

		Bal.	700

Revenue Received in Advance

(f)	160	Bal.	460
		Bal.	300

Accrued Wages Payable

		(d)	120

James Neal, Capital

		Bal.	4,470

Answering Service Revenue

		Bal.	2,900
		(e)	300
		(f)	160
		Bal.	3,360

Wages Expense

Bal.	1,500		
(d)	120		
Bal.	1,620		

Rent Expense

Bal.	400		

Insurance Expense

(a)	40		

Office Supplies Expense

(b)	105		

Depreciation Expense, Office Equipment

(c)	100		

3. Adjusted trial balance prepared.

Certified Answering Service
Adjusted Trial Balance
December 31, 19xx

Cash	$2,160	
Accounts Receivable	1,250	
Accrued Service Revenue Receivable	300	
Office Supplies	75	
Prepaid Insurance	200	
Office Equipment	3,400	
Accumulated Depreciation, Office Equipment		$ 700
Accounts Payable		700
Revenue Received in Advance		300
Accrued Wages Payable		120
James Neal, Capital		4,470
Answering Service Revenue		3,360
Wages Expense	1,620	
Rent Expense	400	
Insurance Expense	40	
Office Supplies Expense	105	
Depreciation Expense, Office Equipment	100	
	$9,650	$9,650

Chapter Assignments

Questions

1. Why does the accountant use the term *net income* instead of *profit?*
2. Define the terms *revenues* and *expenses*.
3. Why are income statement accounts called nominal accounts?
4. Why does the need for the accounting period cause problems?
5. What is the significance of the continuity assumption?
6. "The matching rule is the most significant concept in accounting." Do you agree with this statement? Explain.
7. What is the difference between the cash basis and the accrual basis of accounting?
8. In what two ways is accrual accounting accomplished?
9. Why do adjusting entries need to be made?
10. What are the four situations that require adjusting entries? Give an example of each.
11. Explain the statement, "Some assets are expenses that have not expired."
12. What is a contra account? Give an example.
13. What do plant and equipment, office supplies, and prepaid insurance have in common?

14. What is the difference between accumulated depreciation and depreciation expense?
15. Why are contra accounts used in recording depreciation?
16. How does unearned revenue arise? Give an example.
17. Where does unearned revenue appear on the balance sheet?
18. What accounting problem does a magazine publisher who sells three-year subscriptions have?
19. What is an accrued expense? Give three examples.
20. Under what circumstances might a company have unrecorded revenue? Give an example.
21. Why is the income statement usually the first statement prepared from the trial balance?
22. "Why worry about adjustments? Doesn't it all come out in the wash?" Discuss.
23. What is the difference between a correcting entry and an adjusting entry?

Classroom Exercises

Exercise 3-1. Adjusting Entries for Prepaid Insurance
(L.O. 5)

An examination of the Prepaid Insurance account shows a balance of $1,827 at the end of an accounting period before adjustments.

Prepare journal entries to record the insurance expense for the period under each of the following independent assumptions:

1. An examination of insurance policies shows unexpired insurance that cost $987 at the end of the period.
2. An examination of insurance policies shows insurance that cost $347 has expired during the period.

Exercise 3-2. Supplies Account: Missing Data
(L.O. 5)

Determine the amounts indicated by question marks in the columns below. Consider each column a separate problem.

	a	b	c	d
Supplies on hand July 1	127	224	84	?
Supplies purchased during month	26	?	87	746
Supplies consumed during month	97	486	?	816
Supplies remaining on July 31	?	218	28	594

Exercise 3-3. Adjusting Entry for Accrued Salaries
(L.O. 5)

Dialcom pays salaries of $35,000 each Friday.

1. Make the adjusting entry required on May 31, assuming that June 1 falls on a Wednesday.
2. Make the entry to pay the salaries on June 3.

Exercise 3-4. Adjusting Entries
(L.O. 5)

Prepare year-end adjusting entries for each of the following:

a. Office Supplies had a balance of $75 on January 1. Purchases debited to Office Supplies during the year amount to $415. A year-end inventory reveals supplies of $285 on hand.
b. Depreciation of office equipment is estimated to be $1,450 for the year.

c. Property taxes for six months, estimated to total $750, have accrued but are unrecorded.
d. Unrecorded interest receivable on U.S. government bonds is $900.
e. Unearned Revenue has a balance of $900. The services for $300 of these revenues received in advance have now been performed.
f. Services totaling $200 have been performed for which the customer has not yet been billed.

Exercise 3-5. Relationship of Expenses to Cash Paid
(L.O. 5)

The income statement for Ideal Company included the following expenses for 19xx:

Rent Expense	$ 2,400
Interest Expense	4,200
Salaries Expense	38,500

Listed below are the related balance sheet account balances at year-end for last year and this year:

	Last Year	This Year
Prepaid Rent	—	$ 400
Accrued Interest Payable	$ 600	—
Accrued Salaries Payable	2,500	5,000

1. Compute cash paid for rent during the year.
2. Compute cash paid for interest during the year.
3. Compute cash paid for salaries during the year.

Exercise 3-6. Accounting for Revenue Received in Advance
(L.O. 5, 7)

Holly Iglesias, a lawyer, was paid $24,000 on September 1 to represent a client in certain real estate negotiations during the next twelve months.

Give the entries required on September 1 and at the end of the year, December 31. How would this transaction affect the balance sheet and income statement on December 31?

Exercise 3-7. Correction of Errors
(L.O. 8)

A number of errors in journalizing and posting transactions are described below. Prepare the journal entries to correct the errors.

1. Rent payment of $500 for the current month was recorded as a debit to Prepaid Rent and a credit to Cash.
2. Payment of $340 to a creditor was recorded in the amount of $430 as a debit to Accounts Payable and a credit to Cash.
3. A $100 cash payment for equipment repair expense was recorded as a debit to Equipment.
4. Payment of the gas and oil bill of $80 for the owner's personal car was recorded as a debit to Delivery Truck Expense and a credit to Cash.
5. A cash receipt of $100 for services yet to be performed was debited to Cash and credited to Revenue.

Exercise 3-8. Relationship of Cash to Expenses Paid
(L.O. 5)

The 19x1 and 19x2 balance sheets of Reliable Company showed the following asset and liability amounts at the end of each year:

	19x1	19x2
Prepaid Insurance	$3,000	$2,400
Accrued Wages Payable	1,900	1,200
Unearned Fees	2,200	4,200

From the accounting records the following amounts of cash disbursements and cash receipts for 19x2 were determined:

Cash disbursed to pay insurance premiums	$ 3,700
Cash disbursed to pay wages	21,500
Cash received for fees	9,200

Calculate the amount of insurance expense, wages expense, and fees earned to be reported on the 19x2 income statement.

Interpreting Accounting Information

City of Chicago
(L.O. 2, 3)

In 1979, Mayor Jane Byrne won the election in the city of Chicago partly on the basis of her charge that Michael Bilandic, the former mayor, had caused a budget deficit. Taking office in 1980, she hired a major international accounting firm, Peat, Marwick, Mitchell & Co., to straighten things out. The following excerpt appeared in an article from a leading Chicago business publication:

> [A riddle]
> Q: When is a budget deficit not a deficit?
> A: When it is a surplus, of course.
>
> Chicago Mayor Jane Byrne was once again caught with egg on her face last week as she and her financial advisers tried to defend that riddle. On one hand, Comptroller Daniel J. Grim [Byrne appointee], explaining $75 million in assets the mayor [Byrne] hopes to hold in reserve in the 1981 Chicago city budget, testified in hearings that the city had actually ended 1979 with a $6 million surplus, not the much-reported deficit. He said further that the modest surplus grew to $54 million as a result of tax-enrichment supplements to the 1979 balance sheet.
>
> On the other hand, the mayor stuck by the same guns she used last year on her predecessor: The city had ended 1979, under the Michael Bilandic Administration, not merely without a surplus, but with a deficit. The apparent discrepancy can be explained.[4]
>
> Like most U.S. cities, Chicago operates under the modified accrual accounting basis. This is a combination of the straight cash basis and the accrual basis. The modified accrual basis differs from the accrual method in that an account receivable is recorded only when it is collected in the next accounting period. The collection of Chicago's parking tax, which is assessed on all city parking lots and garages, is an example:
>
> The tax is assessed and collected on a quarterly basis but the city doesn't collect the amount due for the last quarter of 1980 until the first quarter of 1981. Under ideal

4. Reprinted with permission from the December 8, 1980, issue of *Crain's Chicago Business*. Copyright 1980 by Crain Communications, Inc.

accrual methods, the parking revenues should be recorded in the 1980 financial statement. Under a cash approach, the revenues would be recorded in the 1981 budget. What the city did before was to record the money whenever it was advantageous politically. That, combined with the infamous revolving funds, allowed the city to hide the fact it was running large deficits under [former] Mayor Bilandic. That also means that no one really knew where the city stood.[5]

The auditors are now reallocating the parking revenues to the 1981 budget but are accruing other revenues by shifting the period of collection from a year in the past. Overall, more revenues were moved into earlier fiscal years than into later years, inflating those budgets. Thus, the 1979 deficit is a surplus.

The upshot is that both Mayor Byrne and Mr. Grim [the comptroller] were correct. There was a deficit in the 1979 corporate or checkbook fund, but because of corrections taking place now, a surplus exists.[6]

Required

1. Do you agree with how the auditors handled parking revenues? Support your answer by explaining which method of accounting you think a city should use.
2. Comment on the statement, "Systematically applied accounting principles will allow all to know exactly where the city stands," made by the author in another part of the same article that was quoted above.

Problem Set A

Problem 3A-1. Preparation of Adjusting Entries (L.O. 5)

On November 30, the end of the current year, the following information was to assist Stull Company's accountants in making adjusting entries:

a. The Supplies account showed a beginning balance of $2,714. Purchases during the year were $4,256. The end-of-year inventory revealed supplies on hand that cost $1,937.

b. The Prepaid Insurance account showed the following entries at November 30:

Beginning Balance	$3,850
July 1	4,200
October 1	7,272

The beginning balance represents the unexpired portion of a one-year policy purchased the previous year. The July 1 entry represents a new one-year policy, and the October 1 entry represents additional coverage in the form of a three-year policy.

c. The table below contains the cost and annual depreciation for buildings and equipment, all of which were purchased before the current year:

Account	Cost	Annual Depreciation
Buildings	$286,000	$15,400
Equipment	374,000	34,500

d. On September 1, the company completed negotiations with a client and accepted a payment of $14,400, which represented one year's services paid in advance. The $14,400 was credited to Unearned Services Revenue.

5. Ibid.
6. Ibid.

e. The company calculated that as of November 30 it had earned $3,000 on a $9,000 contract that would be completed and billed in January.
f. Among the liabilities of the company is a note payable in the amount of $200,000. On November 30, the accrued interest on this mortgage amounted to $12,000.
g. On Friday, December 2, the company will pay its regular weekly employees $11,200.
h. On November 29, the company completed negotiations and signed a contract to provide services to a new client at an annual rate of $21,500.

Required

Prepare adjusting entries for each item listed above.

Problem 3A-2. Determining Adjusting Entries from Changes in Trial Balance (L.O. 5)

The schedule below presents the trial balance and adjusted trial balance for the Personal Financial Planning Service on December 31.

Personal Financial Planning Service
Adjusted Trial Balance
December 31, 19xx

	Trial Balance		Adjusted Trial Balance	
	Debit	**Credit**	**Debit**	**Credit**
Cash	$ 16,500		$ 16,500	
Accounts Receivable	8,250		8,250	
Office Supplies	2,662		264	
Prepaid Rent	1,320		440	
Office Equipment	9,240		9,240	
Accumulated Depreciation, Office Equipment		$ 1,540		$ 1,760
Accounts Payable		5,940		6,270
Notes Payable		11,000		11,000
Accrued Interest Payable				550
Unearned Fees		2,970		1,166
Sylvia Jarvis, Capital		24,002		24,002
Sylvia Jarvis, Withdrawals	22,000		22,000	
Fees Revenue		72,600		76,604
Salaries Expense	48,400		48,400	
Utility Expense	5,280		5,610	
Rent Expense	4,400		5,280	
Office Supplies Expense			2,398	
Depreciation Expense, Office Equipment			220	
Interest Expense			550	
Accrued Fees Receivable			2,200	
	$118,052	$118,052	$121,352	$121,352

Required

Prepare in journal form, with explanations, the seven adjusting entries that explain the changes in the account balances from the trial balance to the adjusted trial balance.

Problem 3A-3. Determining Adjusting Entries and Tracing Their Effects to Financial Statements (L.O. 5, 6)

The Master Janitorial Service is owned by Ray Rybac. After six months of operation the June 30, 19xx, trial balance for the company is presented below:

Master Janitorial Service
Trial Balance
June 30, 19xx

Cash	$ 695	
Accounts Receivable	856	
Prepaid Insurance	380	
Prepaid Rent	700	
Cleaning Supplies	1,396	
Cleaning Equipment	1,740	
Truck	3,600	
Accounts Payable		$ 170
Unearned Janitorial Fees		480
Ray Rybac, Capital		7,037
Ray Rybac, Withdrawals	3,000	
Janitorial Fees		7,420
Wages Expense	2,400	
Gas, Oil, and Other Truck Expense	340	
	$15,107	$15,107

The following information is also available:

a. Cleaning supplies on hand, $76.
b. Prepaid insurance is the cost of a one-year policy purchased on January 1.
c. Prepaid rent represents a $100 payment made on January 1 toward the last month's rent of a three-year lease plus $100 rent per month for each of the past six months.
d. The cleaning equipment and trucks are depreciated at the rate of 20 percent per year (10 percent for each six months).
e. The unearned revenue represents a six-month payment in advance made by a customer on May 1.
f. During the last week of June, Ray completed the first stage of work on a contract that will not be billed until the contract is completed. The price of this stage is $400.
g. On Saturday, July 3, Ray will owe his employees $300 for one week's work (six day work week).

The balance of the capital account represents the investments made by Ray Rybac.

Required

1. Open T accounts for the accounts of the trial balance plus the following: Accrued Fees Receivable; Accumulated Depreciation, Cleaning Equipment;

Accumulated Depreciation, Truck; Accrued Wages Payable; Rent Expense; Insurance Expense; Cleaning Supplies Expense; Depreciation Expense, Cleaning Equipment; Depreciation Expense, Truck.
2. Determine adjusting entries and post them directly to the T accounts.
3. Prepare an adjusted trial balance, an income statement, a statement of owner's equity, and a balance sheet.

Problem 3A-4. Determining Adjusting Entries and Tracing Their Effects to Financial Statements (L.O. 5, 6)

The trial balance for Classical Dance Studio at the end of the current fiscal year appeared as follows:

Classical Dance Studio
Trial Balance
October 31, 19x2

Cash (111)	$ 827	
Accounts Receivable (112)	422	
Supplies (115)	170	
Prepaid Rent (116)	400	
Prepaid Insurance (117)	360	
Equipment (141)	4,100	
Accumulated Depreciation, Equipment (142)		$ 400
Accounts Payable (211)		380
Unearned Dance Fees (213)		900
Florence Powers, Capital (311)		2,299
Florence Powers, Withdrawals (312)	12,000	
Dance Fees (411)		20,900
Wages Expense (511)	3,200	
Rent Expense (512)	2,200	
Utility Expense (515)	1,200	
	$24,879	$24,879

Florence Powers made no investments in the business during the year. The following information is available to assist in the preparation of adjusting entries:

a. An inventory of supplies reveals $65 still on hand.
b. The prepaid rent reflects the rent for October plus the rent for the last month of the lease.
c. Prepaid insurance consists of a two-year policy purchased on May 2, 19x2.
d. Depreciation on equipment is estimated to be $800.
e. Accrued wages are $50 on October 31.
f. Two-thirds of the unearned dance fees have been earned by October 31.

Required

1. Open ledger accounts for the accounts on the trial balance plus the following: Accrued Wages Payable (212); Supplies Expense (513); Insurance Expense (514); and Depreciation Expense, Equipment (516).
2. Record the adjusting entries in the general journal (page 53).

3. Post the adjusting entries from the general journal to the ledger accounts, showing proper references.
4. Prepare an adjusted trial balance, an income statement, a statement of owner's equity, and a balance sheet.

Problem 3A-5. Determining Adjusting Entries and Tracing Their Effects to Financial Statements (L.O. 3, 5, 6)

At the end of the first three months of operations, the trial balance of the Executive Answering Service appeared as follows:

Executive Answering Service
Trial Balance
March 31, 19x2

Cash (111)	$ 2,014	
Accounts Receivable (112)	3,932	
Office Supplies (115)	816	
Prepaid Rent (116)	800	
Prepaid Insurance (117)	720	
Office Equipment (141)	2,300	
Communication Equipment (143)	2,400	
Accounts Payable (211)		$ 1,925
Unearned Answering Service Revenue (213)		888
Leon Burr, Capital (311)		5,629
Leon Burr, Withdrawals (312)	2,130	
Answering Service Revenue (411)		8,915
Wages Expense (511)	1,900	
Office Cleaning Expense (513)	345	
	$17,357	$17,357

Leon engaged an accountant to prepare financial statements for the company in order to determine how well the company was doing after three months. Upon examining the accounting records, the accountant found the following items of interest:

a. An inventory of office supplies revealed supplies on hand of $119.
b. The Prepaid Rent account includes the rent for the first three months plus a deposit for the last month's rent.
c. The Prepaid Insurance account reflects a one-year policy purchased on January 4.
d. Depreciation is computed to be $92 on the office equipment and $96 on the communications equipment for the first three months.
e. The balance of the Unearned Answering Service Revenue account represents a 12-month service contract paid in advance on February 1.
f. On March 31, accrued salaries totaled $60.

The balance of the capital account represents investments by Leon Burr.

Required

1. Open ledger accounts for the accounts in the trial balance plus the following: Accumulated Depreciation, Office Equipment (142); Accumulated Deprecia-

tion, Communications Equipment (144); Accrued Wages Payable (212); Rent Expense (512); Insurance Expense (514); Office Supplies Expense (515); Depreciation Expense, Office Equipment (516); Depreciation Expense, Communication Equipment (517).

2. Record the appropriate adjusting entries in the general journal (page 12).
3. Post the adjusting entries from the general journal to the ledger accounts showing proper references.
4. Prepare an adjusted trial balance.
5. Prepare an income statement, a statement of owner's equity, and a balance sheet.
6. Give examples of how the techniques of accrual accounting affect the income statement in **5**.

Problem Set B

Problem 3B-1. Preparation of Adjusting Entries
(L.O. 5)

On June 30, the end of the current year, the following information was available to aid the Peninsula Company accountants in making adjusting entries.

a. Among the liabilities of the company is a mortgage payable in the amount of $200,000. On June 30, the accrued interest on this mortgage amounted to $9,000.
b. On Friday, July 2, the company will pay its regular weekly employees $15,600.
c. On June 29, the company completed negotiations and signed a contract to provide services to a new client at an annual rate of $2,000.
d. The Supplies account showed a beginning balance of $1,516 and purchases during the year of $3,667. The end-of-year inventory revealed supplies on hand that cost $1,186.
e. The Prepaid Insurance account showed the following entries at June 30:

Beginning balance	$1,350
January 1	2,800
May 1	3,636

The beginning balance represents the unexpired portion of a one-year policy purchased the previous year. The January 1 entry represents a new one-year policy, and the May 1 entry represents additional coverage in the form of a three-year policy.

f. The table below contains the cost and annual depreciation for buildings and equipment, all of which were purchased before the current year:

Account	Cost	Annual Depreciation
Buildings	$175,000	$ 7,000
Equipment	218,000	21,800

g. On June 1, the company completed negotiations with another client and accepted a payment of $18,000, which represented one year's services paid in advance. The $18,000 was credited to Services Collected in Advance.
h. The company calculated that as of June 30, it had earned $2,500 on a $7,500 contract that would be completed and billed in August.

Required

Prepare adjusting entries for each item listed above.

Problem 3B-2. Determining Adjusting Entries from Changes in Trial Balance (L.O. 5)

The schedule below presents the trial balance and adjusted trial balance for the Northwest Consultants Company on December 31.

Northwest Consultants Company
Adjusted Trial Balance
December 31, 19xx

	Trial Balance		Adjusted Trial Balance	
	Debit	Credit	Debit	Credit
Cash	$ 12,786		$ 12,786	
Accounts Receivable	24,840		24,840	
Accrued Fees Receivable			600	
Office Supplies	991		86	
Prepaid Rent	1,400		700	
Office Equipment	6,700		6,700	
Accumulated Depreciation, Office Equipment		$ 1,600		$ 2,200
Accounts Payable		1,820		2,020
Notes Payable		10,000		10,000
Accrued Interest Payable				600
Accrued Salaries Payable				200
Unearned Fees		2,860		1,410
Dong Kim, Capital		29,387		29,387
Dong Kim, Withdrawals	15,000		15,000	
Fees Revenue		58,500		60,550
Salary Expense	33,000		33,200	
Utility Expense	1,750		1,950	
Rent Expense	7,700		8,400	
Office Supplies Expense			905	
Depreciation Expense, Office Equipment			600	
Interest Expense			600	
	$104,167	$104,167	$106,367	$106,367

Required

Prepare in journal form, with explanations, the eight adjusting entries that explain the changes in the account balances from the trial balance to the adjusted trial balance.

Problem 3B-3. Determining Adjusting Entries and Tracing Their Effects to Financial Statements (L.O. 5, 6)

Having graduated from college with a degree in accounting, Dorothy Sawyer opened a small tax preparation service. At the end of its second year of operation, the Sawyer Tax Service has the following trial balance:

Sawyer Tax Service
Trial Balance
December 31, 19xx

Cash	$ 1,628	
Accounts Receivable	986	
Prepaid Insurance	240	
Office Supplies	782	
Office Equipment	4,100	
Accumulated Depreciation, Office Equipment		$ 210
Copier	2,800	
Accumulated Depreciation, Copier		360
Accounts Payable		635
Unearned Tax Fees		219
Dorothy Sawyer, Capital		5,394
Dorothy Sawyer, Withdrawals	6,000	
Fees Revenue		21,286
Office Salaries Expense	8,300	
Advertising Expense	650	
Rent Expense	2,400	
Telephone Expense	218	
	$28,104	$28,104

Dorothy Sawyer made no investments in her business during the year. The following information was also available:

a. Supplies on hand, December 31, 19xx, were $212.
b. Insurance still unexpired amounted to $120.
c. Estimated depreciation of office equipment was $210.
d. Estimated depreciation of copier was $360.
e. The telephone expense for December is $19. This bill has been received but not recorded.
f. The services for all unearned tax fees had been performed by the end of the year.

Required

1. Open T accounts for the accounts of the trial balance plus the following: Insurance Expense; Office Supplies Expense; Depreciation Expense, Office Equipment; Depreciation Expense, Copier. Record the balances as shown in the trial balance.
2. Determine adjusting entries, and post them directly to the T accounts.
3. Prepare an adjusted trial balance, an income statement, a statement of owner's equity, and a balance sheet.

Problem 3B-4. Determining Adjusting Entries and Tracing Their Effects to Financial Statements (L.O. 5, 6)

The Swank Limo Service was organized to provide limousine service between the airport and various suburban locations. It has just completed its second year of business. Its trial balance appeared as follows:

Swank Limo Service
Trial Balance
June 30, 19xx

Cash (111)	$ 10,414	
Accounts Receivable (112)	12,655	
Prepaid Rent (117)	12,000	
Prepaid Insurance (118)	4,900	
Prepaid Maintenance (119)	12,000	
Spare Parts (141)	11,310	
Limousines (142)	200,000	
Accumulated Depreciation, Limousines (143)		$ 25,000
Notes Payable (211)		45,000
Unearned Passenger Service Revenue (212)		30,000
Dexter Brown, Capital (311)		78,813
Dexter Brown, Withdrawals (312)	20,000	
Passenger Service Revenue (411)		426,926
Gas and Oil Expense (511)	89,300	
Salaries Expense (512)	206,360	
Advertising Expense (513)	26,800	
	$605,739	$605,739

Dexter Brown made no investments during the year. The following information is also available:

a. To obtain space at the airport, Swank paid two years' rent in advance when it began business.
b. An examination of insurance policies reveals that $3,600 expired during the year.
c. To provide regular maintenance for the vehicles, a deposit of $12,000 was made with a local garage. Examination of maintenance invoices reveals that there are $11,277 in charges against the deposit.
d. An inventory of spare parts shows $2,110 on hand.
e. Limousines are to be depreciated at the rate of 12.5 percent a year.
f. A payment of $10,500 for one year's interest on notes payable is now due.
g. Unearned Passenger Service Revenue on June 30 includes $17,815 in tickets that were purchased by employers for use by their executives and that have not been redeemed.

Required

1. Open ledger accounts for the accounts in the trial balance plus the following ones: Accrued Interest Payable (213); Rent Expense (514); Insurance Expense (515); Spare Parts Expense (516); Depreciation Expense, Limousines (517); Maintenance Expense (518); Interest Expense (519). Record the balances as shown in the trial balance.

2. Record the appropriate adjusting entries in the general journal (page 14).
3. Post the adjusting entries from the general journal to the ledger accounts, showing proper references.
4. Prepare an adjusted trial balance, an income statement, a statement of owner's equity, and a balance sheet.

Problem 3B-5. Determining Adjusting Entries and Tracing Their Effects to Financial Statements
(L.O. 3, 5, 6)

At the end of its accounting period, the trial balance for Taber Dry Cleaning appeared as follows:

Taber Dry Cleaning
Trial Balance
September 30, 19xx

Cash (111)	$ 1,256	
Accounts Receivable (112)	10,280	
Prepaid Insurance (115)	1,700	
Cleaning Supplies (116)	3,687	
Land (141)	9,000	
Building (142)	75,000	
Accumulated Depreciation, Building (143)		$ 14,200
Delivery Truck (144)	11,500	
Accumulated Depreciation, Delivery Truck (145)		2,600
Accounts Payable (212)		10,200
Unearned Dry Cleaning Revenue (215)		800
Mortgage Payable (221)		60,000
Wesley Taber, Capital (311)		23,642
Wesley Taber, Withdrawals (312)	10,000	
Dry Cleaning Revenue (411)		57,200
Laundry Revenue (412)		18,650
Plant Wages Expense (511)	32,560	
Sales and Delivery Wages Expense (512)	18,105	
Cleaning Equipment Rent Expense (513)	3,000	
Delivery Truck Expense (514)	2,187	
Interest Expense (519)	5,500	
Other Expenses (520)	3,517	
	$187,292	$187,292

The following information is also available:

a. A study of insurance policies shows that $170 is unexpired at the end of the year.
b. An inventory of cleaning supplies shows $414 on hand.
c. Estimated depreciation for the year was $4,300 on the building and $1,300 on the delivery truck.
d. Accrued interest on the mortgage payable amounted to $500.
e. On August 1, the company signed a contract effective immediately with Delaware County Hospital to dry clean, for a fixed monthly charge of $200, the uniforms used by doctors in surgery. The hospital paid for four months of service in advance.

f. Unrecorded plant wages totaled $982.
g. Sales and delivery wages are paid on Friday. The weekly payroll is $350. September 30 falls on a Thursday.

Required

1. Open Ledger accounts for each account in the trial balance plus the following: Accrued Wages Payable (213); Accrued Interest Payable (214); Insurance Expense (515); Cleaning Supplies Expense (516); Depreciation Expense, Building (517); Depreciation Expense, Delivery Truck (518). Record the balances as shown in the trial balance.
2. Determine adjusting entries, and enter each in the general journal (page 42).
3. Post the adjusting entries to the ledger accounts, showing proper references.
4. Prepare an adjusted trial balance.
5. Prepare an income statement, a statement of owner's equity, and a balance sheet.
6. Give examples of how the techniques of accrual accounting affect the income statement in **5.**

Financial Decision Case

Lockyer Systems Company
(L.O. 5, 7)

Tim Lockyer began his new business, called Lockyer Systems Company, on July 1, 19xx. The company is engaged in writing computer programs with special applications for businesses that own small computers. During the first six months of operation, the business was so successful that Tim had to hire new employees on several occasions. Yet he continually had to put off creditors because he lacked the funds to pay them. He wants to apply for a bank loan, but after preparing a statement showing the totals of receipts of cash and payments of cash, he wonders whether a bank will make a loan to him on the basis of such apparently poor results. Deciding that he needs some accounting help, Tim asks you to review the statement and the company's operating results.

After verifying the information in Tim's statement, you assemble the following additional facts about Lockyer Systems Company:

a. In addition to the amount received from customers, programming services totaling $9,700 had been performed but were not yet paid for.
b. Employees have been paid all the wages owed to them except for $350 earned since the last payday. The next regular payday is January 3.
c. The insurance expense represents a two-year policy purchased on July 1.
d. The rent expense represents $600 per month, including the rent for January.
e. In examining the expenditures for supplies, you find invoices for $650 that have not been recorded or paid, and an inventory reveals $875 of unused supplies still on hand.
f. The office equipment is fully paid for and it is estimated it will last 5 years and be worthless at the end of that time.
g. The computer rental agreement provides for a security deposit of $2,000 plus monthly payments of $1,000.
h. The maintenance expense represents a one-year maintenance agreement, paid in advance on July 1.
i. The service van expense represents the down payment on a van purchased on December 30 for $15,000. Prior to this purchase, the company had reimbursed employees for oil and gas when using their own cars for business. A study of the documents shows that $120 in employee oil and gas receipts must still be reimbursed.

Lockyer Systems Company
Statement of Cash Receipts and Payments
For the Six Months Ended December 31, 19xx

Receipts from		
Investment by Tim Lockyer		$15,000
Customers for Programming Services Provided		24,600
Total Cash Receipts		$39,600
Payments for		
Wages	$9,800	
Insurance	2,400	
Rent	4,200	
Supplies	1,900	
Office Equipment	6,200	
Computer Rental	8,000	
Maintenance	900	
Service Van	5,000	
Oil and Gas Reimbursements	690	
Utility	540	
Telephone	300	
Total Cash Payments		$39,930
Bank Overdraft		$(330)

Required

1. From the information given, prepare an income statement and a balance sheet for Lockyer Systems Company.
2. What is your assessment of the company's performance? If you were a bank loan officer, would you look favorably on a loan application from Lockyer Systems Company?

Answers to Self-Test

1. a	3. b	5. c	7. a	9. b
2. c	4. d	6. d	8. d	10. b

CHAPTER 4 COMPLETING THE ACCOUNTING CYCLE

LEARNING OBJECTIVES

1. State all the steps in the accounting cycle.
2. Prepare a work sheet.
3. Identify the three principal uses of a work sheet.
4. Prepare financial statements from a work sheet.
5. Record the adjusting entries from a work sheet.
6. Explain the purposes of closing entries.
7. Prepare the required closing entries.
8. Prepare the post-closing trial balance.
9. Prepare reversing entries as appropriate.

You will see the accounting cycle completed in this chapter. First you study the uses and preparation of the work sheet, an important tool for accountants. Then, as the final step in the accounting cycle, you learn how to prepare closing entries. After studying this chapter, you should be able to meet the learning objectives listed on the left.

In previous chapters, the main focus was on the measurement process in accounting. In this chapter, the emphasis is on the accounting system itself and the sequence of steps used by the accountant in completing the accounting cycle. An important part of the accounting system involves the preparation of a work sheet, so we present in detail each step in its preparation. This chapter also explains the uses of the work sheet in accomplishing the end-of-period procedures of recording the adjusting entries, preparing financial statements, and closing the accounts. The optional first step of the next accounting period, preparation of reversing entries, is also discussed.

Overview of the Accounting System

The **accounting system** encompasses the sequence of steps followed in the accounting process, from analyzing transactions to preparing financial statements and closing the accounts. This system is sometimes called the **accounting cycle**. The purpose of the system, as illustrated in Figure 4-1, is to treat the business transactions as raw material and develop the finished product of accounting—the financial statements—in a systematic way. The steps in this system are as follows:

1. The transactions are *analyzed* from the *source documents*.
2. The transactions are *recorded* in the *journal*.
3. The entries are *posted* to the *ledger*.
4. The accounts are *adjusted* at the end of the period with the aid of a *work sheet*.
5. *Financial statements* are *prepared* from the work sheet.
6. The accounts are *closed* to conclude the current accounting period and prepare for the beginning of the new accounting period.

OBJECTIVE 1
State all the steps in the accounting cycle

The first four steps were introduced in Chapters 2 and 3. In this chapter, they are reviewed in conjunction with the use of the work sheet. The use of the work sheet and the final two steps are the major topics of this chapter.

The Work Sheet: A Tool of Accountants

OBJECTIVE 2
Prepare a work sheet

The flow of information affecting a business does not arbitrarily stop at the end of an accounting period. In order to prepare the financial reports, accountants must collect relevant data to determine what should go into the financial reports. For example, accountants must examine insurance policies to see how much prepaid insurance has expired, examine plant and equipment records to determine depreciation, take an inventory of supplies on hand, and calculate the amount of accrued wages. These calculations, together with the other computations, analyses, and preliminary drafts of statements, make up the accountants' **working papers.** Working papers are important for two reasons. First, they aid accountants in organizing their work so that they do not omit important data or steps that affect the accounting statements. Second, they provide evidence of what has been done so that accountants or auditors can retrace their steps and support the basis of the financial statements.

A special kind of working paper is the **work sheet.** The work sheet is used frequently as a preliminary step in the preparation of financial statements. Using a work sheet lessens the possibility of ignoring an adjustment, aids in checking the arithmetical accuracy of the accounts, and facilitates the preparation of financial statements. The work sheet is never published and is rarely seen by management. Nevertheless, it is a useful tool for the accountant. Because preparation of the work sheet is a very mechanical process, accountants often use a microcomputer to assist in its preparation.

Figure 4-1. An Overview of the Accounting System

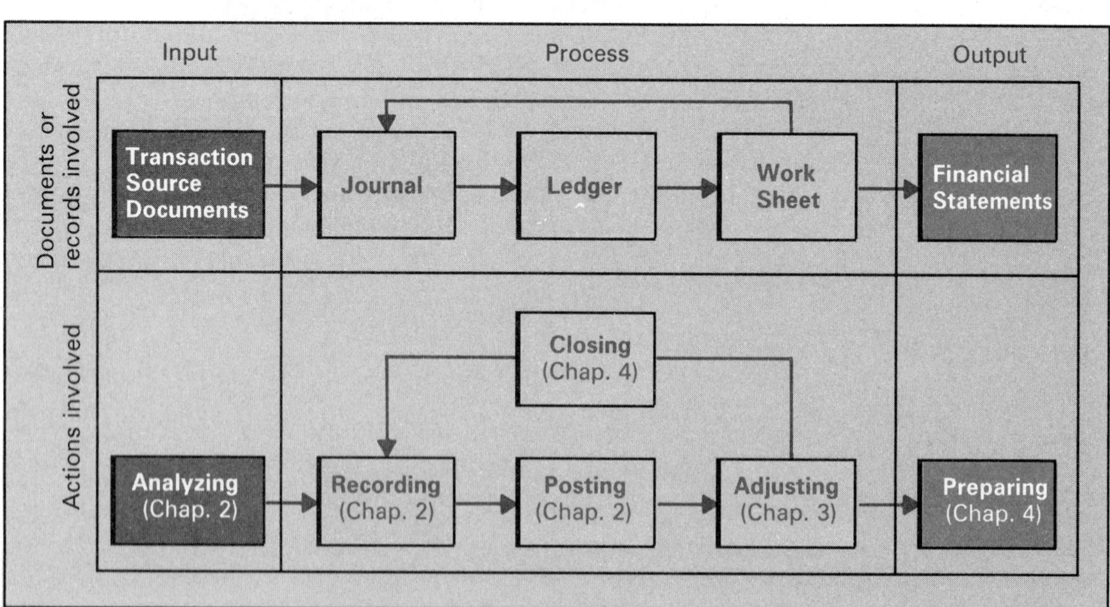

Steps in Preparing the Work Sheet

In Chapter 3, the adjustments were entered directly in the journal and posted to the ledger, and the financial statements were prepared from the adjusted trial balance. These steps were done rather easily for the Joan Miller Advertising Agency because it is a small company. For larger companies, however, which may require many adjusting entries, a work sheet is essential. To illustrate the preparation of the work sheet, the Joan Miller Advertising Agency case will be continued.

A commonly used form of work sheet has one column for account names and/or numbers and ten more columns with appropriate headings, as shown in Exhibit 4-1. Note that the work sheet is identified by a heading that consists of (1) the name of the company, (2) the title "Work Sheet," and (3) the period of time covered (as on the income statement).

There are five steps in the preparation of a work sheet, as follows:

1. Enter and total the account balances in the Trial Balance columns.
2. Enter and total the adjustments in the Adjustments columns.
3. Enter and total the account balances as adjusted in the Adjusted Trial Balance columns.
4. Extend the account balances from the Adjusted Trial Balance columns to the Income Statement columns or the Balance Sheet columns.
5. Total the Income Statement columns and the Balance Sheet columns. Enter the net income or net loss in both pairs of columns as a balancing figure, and recompute column totals.

1. Enter and total the account balances in the Trial Balance columns The titles and balances of the accounts as of January 31 are copied directly from the ledger into the Trial Balance columns, as shown in Exhibit 4-1. When a work sheet is prepared, a separate trial balance is not required.

2. Enter and total the adjustments in the Adjustments columns The required adjustments for the Joan Miller Advertising Agency were explained in Chapter 3. The same adjustments are entered in the Adjustments columns of the work sheet in Exhibit 4-2. As each adjustment is entered, a letter is used to identify the debit and credit parts of the same entry. The first adjustment, identified by the letter *a*, is for recognition of rent expense, which results in a debit to Rent Expense and a credit to Prepaid Rent. In practice, this letter may be used to reference supporting computations or documentation underlying the adjusting entry.

If the adjustment calls for an account that has not already been used in the trial balance, the new account is added below the accounts listed for the trial balance because the trial balance only includes those accounts that have balances. For example, Rent Expense has been added in Exhibit 4-2. The only exception to this is the Accumulated Depreciation accounts, which will have a zero balance only in the initial period of operation.

When all the adjustments have been made, the pair of Adjustments columns must be added. This step proves that the debits and credits of the adjustments are equal and generally reduces errors in the preparation of the work sheet.

Exhibit 4-1. Entering the Account Balances in the Trial Balance Columns

Joan Miller Advertising Agency
Work Sheet
For the Month Ended January 31, 19xx

Account Name	Trial Balance		Adjustments		Adjusted Trial Balance		Income Statement		Balance Sheet	
	Debit	Credit	Debit	Credit	Debit	Credit	Debit	Credit	Debit	Credit
Cash	1,720									
Accounts Receivable	2,800									
Art Supplies	1,800									
Office Supplies	800									
Prepaid Rent	800									
Prepaid Insurance	480									
Art Equipment	4,200									
Accumulated Depreciation, Art Equipment										
Office Equipment	3,000									
Accumulated Depreciation, Office Equipment										
Accounts Payable		3,170								
Unearned Art Fees		1,000								
Joan Miller, Capital		10,000								
Joan Miller, Withdrawals	1,400									
Advertising Fees Earned		4,200								
Office Wages Expense	1,200									
Utility Expense	100									
Telephone Expense	70									
	18,370	18,370								

3. Enter and total the account balances as adjusted in the Adjusted Trial Balance columns Exhibit 4-3 (page 134) shows the adjusted trial balance, prepared by combining the amount of each account in the original Trial Balance columns with the corresponding amounts in the Adjustments columns and entering the combined amounts on a line-by-line basis in the Adjusted Trial Balance columns.

Some examples from Exhibit 4-3 will illustrate **crossfooting.** The first line shows Cash with a debit balance of $1,720. Because there are no adjustments to the Cash account, $1,720 is entered in the debit column of the Adjusted Trial Balance. The second line is Accounts Receivable, which shows a debit of $2,800 in the Trial Balance columns. Because there are no adjustments to Accounts Receivable, the $2,800 balance is carried over to the debit column of the Adjusted Trial Balance. The next line is Art Supplies, which shows a debit of $1,800 in the Trial Balance columns and a credit from adjustment **c** in the Adjustments columns. Subtracting $500 from $1,800 therefore results in a $1,300 debit balance in the Adjusted Trial Balance. This process is followed through all the accounts, including those added below the accounts listed for the trial balance. The Adjusted Trial Balance columns are then footed, that is, totaled, to check the arithmetical accuracy of the crossfooting.

Exhibit 4-2. Entries in the Adjustments Columns

Joan Miller Advertising Agency
Work Sheet
For the Month Ended January 31, 19xx

Account Name	Trial Balance		Adjustments		Adjusted Trial Balance		Income Statement		Balance Sheet	
	Debit	Credit	Debit	Credit	Debit	Credit	Debit	Credit	Debit	Credit
Cash	1,720									
Accounts Receivable	2,800									
Art Supplies	1,800			(c) 500						
Office Supplies	800			(d) 200						
Prepaid Rent	800			(a) 400						
Prepaid Insurance	480			(b) 40						
Art Equipment	4,200									
Accumulated Depreciation, Art Equipment				(e) 70						
Office Equipment	3,000									
Accumulated Depreciation, Office Equipment				(f) 50						
Accounts Payable		3,170								
Unearned Art Fees		1,000	(g) 400							
Joan Miller, Capital		10,000								
Joan Miller, Withdrawals	1,400									
Advertising Fees Earned		4,200		(h) 200						
Office Wages Expense	1,200		(i) 180							
Utility Expense	100									
Telephone Expense	70									
	18,370	18,370								
Rent Expense			(a) 400							
Insurance Expense			(b) 40							
Art Supplies Expense			(c) 500							
Office Supplies Expense			(d) 200							
Depreciation Expense, Art Equipment			(e) 70							
Depreciation Expense, Office Equipment			(f) 50							
Art Fees Earned				(g) 400						
Accrued Fees Receivable			(h) 200							
Accrued Wages Payable				(i) 180						
			2,040	2,040						

4. Extend the account balances from the Adjusted Trial Balance columns to the Income Statement columns or the Balance Sheet columns Every account in the adjusted trial balance is either a balance sheet account or an income statement account. The accounts are sorted, and each account is extended to its proper place as a debit or credit in either the Balance Sheet columns or the Income Statement columns. The result of extending the accounts is shown in Exhibit 4-4. Revenue and expense accounts are moved to the Income Statement columns. Assets and liabilities as well as the capital and withdrawal accounts are then extended to the Balance Sheet columns. To avoid overlooking an account, extend the accounts line by line, beginning with the first line (which is Cash) and not omitting

Exhibit 4-3. Entries in the Adjusted Trial Balance Columns

Joan Miller Advertising Agency
Work Sheet
For the Month Ended January 31, 19xx

	Trial Balance		Adjustments		Adjusted Trial Balance		Income Statement		Balance Sheet	
Account Name	Debit	Credit	Debit	Credit	Debit	Credit	Debit	Credit	Debit	Credit
Cash	1,720				1,720					
Accounts Receivable	2,800				2,800					
Art Supplies	1,800			(c) 500	1,300					
Office Supplies	800			(d) 200	600					
Prepaid Rent	800			(a) 400	400					
Prepaid Insurance	480			(b) 40	440					
Art Equipment	4,200				4,200					
Accumulated Depreciation, Art Equipment				(e) 70		70				
Office Equipment	3,000				3,000					
Accumulated Depreciation, Office Equipment				(f) 50		50				
Accounts Payable		3,170				3,170				
Unearned Art Fees		1,000	(g) 400			600				
Joan Miller, Capital		10,000				10,000				
Joan Miller, Withdrawals	1,400				1,400					
Advertising Fees Earned		4,200		(h) 200		4,400				
Office Wages Expense	1,200		(i) 180		1,380					
Utility Expense	100				100					
Telephone Expense	70				70					
	18,370	18,370								
Rent Expense			(a) 400		400					
Insurance Expense			(b) 40		40					
Art Supplies Expense			(c) 500		500					
Office Supplies Expense			(d) 200		200					
Depreciation Expense, Art Equipment			(e) 70		70					
Depreciation Expense, Office Equipment			(f) 50		50					
Art Fees Earned				(g) 400		400				
Accrued Fees Receivable			(h) 200		200					
Accrued Wages Payable				(i) 180		180				
			2,040	2,040	18,870	18,870				

any subsequent lines. For instance, the Cash debit balance of $1,720 is extended to the debit column of the balance sheet; the Accounts Receivable debit balance of $2,800 is extended to the same debit column, and so forth. Each amount is carried forward to only one column.

5. Total the Income Statement columns and the Balance Sheet columns. Enter the net income or net loss in both pairs of columns as a balancing figure, and recompute column totals This last step, as shown in Exhibit 4-5, is necessary to compute net income or net loss and to prove the arithmetical accuracy of the work sheet.

Exhibit 4-4. Entries in the Income Statement and Balance Sheet Columns

Joan Miller Advertising Agency
Work Sheet
For the Month Ended January 31, 19xx

	Trial Balance		Adjustments		Adjusted Trial Balance		Income Statement		Balance Sheet	
Account Name	Debit	Credit	Debit	Credit	Debit	Credit	Debit	Credit	Debit	Credit
Cash	1,720				1,720				1,720	
Accounts Receivable	2,800				2,800				2,800	
Art Supplies	1,800			(c) 500	1,300				1,300	
Office Supplies	800			(d) 200	600				600	
Prepaid Rent	800			(a) 400	400				400	
Prepaid Insurance	480			(b) 40	440				440	
Art Equipment	4,200				4,200				4,200	
Accumulated Deprecia-tion, Art Equipment				(e) 70		70				70
Office Equipment	3,000				3,000				3,000	
Accumulated Deprecia-tion, Office Equipment				(f) 50		50				50
Accounts Payable		3,170				3,170				3,170
Unearned Art Fees		1,000	(g) 400			600				600
Joan Miller, Capital		10,000				10,000				10,000
Joan Miller, Withdrawals	1,400				1,400				1,400	
Advertising Fees Earned		4,200		(h) 200		4,400		4,400		
Office Wages Expense	1,200		(i) 180		1,380		1,380			
Utility Expense	100				100		100			
Telephone Expense	70				70		70			
	18,370	18,370								
Rent Expense			(a) 400		400		400			
Insurance Expense			(b) 40		40		40			
Art Supplies Expense			(c) 500		500		500			
Office Supplies Expense			(d) 200		200		200			
Depreciation Expense, Art Equipment			(e) 70		70		70			
Depreciation Expense, Office Equipment			(f) 50		50		50			
Art Fees Earned				(g) 400		400		400		
Accrued Fees Receivable			(h) 200		200				200	
Accrued Wages Payable				(i) 180		180				180
			2,040	2,040	18,870	18,870				

Net income or net loss is equal to the difference between the debit and credit columns of the income statement and the debit and credit columns of the balance sheet.

Revenue (Income Statement credit column total)	$4,800
Expenses (Income Statement debit column total)	2,810
Net Income	$1,990

In this case, the revenue (credit column) has exceeded the expenses (debit column). Consequently, the company has a net income of $1,990.

Exhibit 4-5. Entries in the Balance Sheet Columns and Totals

Joan Miller Advertising Agency
Work Sheet
For the Month Ended January 31, 19xx

	Trial Balance		Adjustments		Adjusted Trial Balance		Income Statement		Balance Sheet	
Account Name	**Debit**	**Credit**	**Debit**	**Credit**	**Debit**	**Credit**	**Debit**	**Credit**	**Debit**	**Credit**
Cash	1,720				1,720				1,720	
Accounts Receivable	2,800				2,800				2,800	
Art Supplies	1,800			(c) 500	1,300				1,300	
Office Supplies	800			(d) 200	600				600	
Prepaid Rent	800			(a) 400	400				400	
Prepaid Insurance	480			(b) 40	440				440	
Art Equipment	4,200				4,200				4,200	
Accumulated Deprecia-tion, Art Equipment				(e) 70		70				70
Office Equipment	3,000				3,000				3,000	
Accumulated Deprecia-tion, Office Equipment				(f) 50		50				50
Accounts Payable		3,170				3,170				3,170
Unearned Art Fees		1,000	(g) 400			600				600
Joan Miller, Capital		10,000				10,000				10,000
Joan Miller, Withdrawals	1,400				1,400				1,400	
Advertising Fees Earned		4,200		(h) 200		4,400		4,400		
Office Wages Expense	1,200		(i) 180		1,380		1,380			
Utility Expense	100				100		100			
Telephone Expense	70				70		70			
	18,370	18,370								
Rent Expense			(a) 400		400		400			
Insurance Expense			(b) 40		40		40			
Art Supplies Expense			(c) 500		500		500			
Office Supplies Expense			(d) 200		200		200			
Depreciation Expense, Art Equipment			(e) 70		70		70			
Depreciation Expense, Office Equipment			(f) 50		50		50			
Art Fees Earned				(g) 400		400		400		
Accrued Fees Receivable			(h) 200		200				200	
Accrued Wages Payable				(i) 180		180				180
			2,040	2,040	18,870	18,870	2,810	4,800	16,060	14,070
Net Income							1,990			1,990
							4,800	4,800	16,060	16,060

The $1,990 is entered in the debit side of the Income Statement columns to balance the columns, and it is entered on the credit side of the Balance Sheet columns. This is done because excess revenue (net income) increases owner's equity, and increases in owner's equity are recorded by credits.

If a net loss had occurred, the opposite rule would apply. The excess of expenses (net loss) would be placed in the credit side of the Income Statement columns as a balancing figure and extended to the debit side of the Balance Sheet columns, because a net loss causes a decrease in owner's equity, which would be shown by a debit.

As a final check, the four columns are totaled again. If the Income Statement columns and the Balance Sheet columns do not balance, there may be an account extended or sorted to the wrong column, or an error may have been made in adding the columns. Equal totals in the Balance Sheet columns, however, are not absolute proof of accuracy. If an asset has been carried to the debit column of the income statement and if a similar error involving revenues or liabilities has been made, the work sheet will still balance, but the net income figure will be wrong.

Uses of the Work Sheet

OBJECTIVE 3
Identify the three principal uses of a work sheet

The work sheet, a basic tool of the accountant, assists the accountant in three principal ways: (1) in preparing the financial statements, (2) in recording the adjusting entries, and (3) in recording the closing entries, which prepare the records for the beginning of the next period.

Preparing the Financial Statements

OBJECTIVE 4
Prepare financial statements from a work sheet

After completion of the work sheet, it is a simple step to prepare the financial statements because the account balances have been sorted into Income Statement and Balance Sheet columns. The income statement shown in Exhibit 4-6 is prepared from the accounts in the Income Statement columns in Exhibit 4-5.

The statement of owner's equity and the balance sheet of Joan Miller Advertising Agency are presented in Exhibits 4-7 and 4-8. The account balances for these statements are drawn from the Balance Sheet columns of the work sheet shown in Exhibit 4-5. The totals of the assets and liabilities and owner's equity in the balance sheet do not agree with the totals of the Balance Sheet columns of the work sheet because contra accounts such as Accumulated Depreciation and withdrawals are deducted from the side of the balance sheet opposite the balance of the account. In addition, the capital account on the balance sheet is the amount determined on the statement of owner's equity.

Recording the Adjusting Entries

OBJECTIVE 5
Record the adjusting entries from a work sheet

It was necessary to determine the adjusting entries for Joan Miller Advertising Agency in the step just before the preparation of the adjusted trial balance on the work sheet. They are essential to the preparation of the financial statements. The adjusting entries could have been recorded in the general journal at that point. However, it is usually convenient to delay recording them until after the work sheet and the financial statements have been prepared because this task can be done at the same time as the recording of the closing entries described in the next section. Recording the adjusting entries with appropriate explanations in the general journal, as shown in Exhibit 4-9 (page 140), is an easy step because they may simply be copied from the work sheet. They are then posted to the general ledger.

Exhibit 4-6. Income Statement for the Joan Miller Advertising Agency

Joan Miller Advertising Agency Income Statement For the Month Ended January 31, 19xx		
Revenues		
Advertising Fees Earned	$4,400	
Art Fees Earned	400	
Total Revenues		$4,800
Expenses		
Office Wages Expense	$1,380	
Utility Expense	100	
Telephone Expense	70	
Rent Expense	400	
Insurance Expense	40	
Art Supplies Expense	500	
Office Supplies Expense	200	
Depreciation Expense, Art Equipment	70	
Depreciation Expense, Office Equipment	50	
Total Expenses		2,810
Net Income		**$1,990**

Recording the Closing Entries

OBJECTIVE 6 Explain the purposes of closing entries

Closing entries, which are journal entries made at the end of the accounting period, accomplish two purposes. First, at the end of an accounting period, closing entries set the stage for the next accounting period by closing or clearing the expense and revenue accounts of their balances. This step must be carried out because an income statement reports the net income for a single accounting period and shows the expenses and revenues only for that period. For this reason, the expense and revenue accounts must be closed or cleared of their balances at the end of the period so that the next period begins with a zero balance in those accounts. The Withdrawals account is closed in a similar manner.

The second aim of closing entries is to summarize a period's revenues and expenses. This is done by transferring the balances of revenues and expenses to the Income Summary account to record the net profit or loss in that account. **Income Summary**, a new temporary account, appears in the chart of accounts between the withdrawals account and the first revenue account. This account gives us a place to summarize all revenues and expenses in a single net figure before transferring the result to the capital account. Also, it is used only in the closing process and never appears in the financial statements.

Exhibit 4-7. Statement of Owner's Equity for the Joan Miller Advertising Agency

Joan Miller Advertising Agency
Statement of Owner's Equity
For the Month Ended January 31, 19xx

Joan Miller, Capital, January 1, 19xx		$ —
Add: Investments by Joan Miller	$10,000	
Net Income	1,990	11,990
Subtotal		$11,990
Less Withdrawals		1,400
Joan Miller, Capital, January 31, 19xx		$10,590

Exhibit 4-8. Balance Sheet for the Joan Miller Advertising Agency

Joan Miller Advertising Agency
Balance Sheet
January 31, 19xx

Assets		
Cash		$ 1,720
Accounts Receivable		2,800
Accrued Fees Receivable		200
Art Supplies		1,300
Office Supplies		600
Prepaid Rent		400
Prepaid Insurance		440
Art Equipment	$4,200	
Less Accumulated Depreciation	70	4,130
Office Equipment	$3,000	
Less Accumulated Depreciation	50	2,950
Total Assets		$14,540
Liabilities		
Accounts Payable	$3,170	
Unearned Art Fees	600	
Accrued Wages Payable	180	
Total Liabilities		$ 3,950
Owner's Equity		
Joan Miller, Capital		10,590
Total Liabilities and Owner's Equity		$14,540

Exhibit 4-9. Adjustments on Work Sheet Entered in the General Journal

General Journal — Page 3

Date		Description	Post. Ref.	Debit	Credit
Jan.	31	Rent Expense	514	400	
		Prepaid Rent	117		400
		To recognize expiration of one month's rent			
	31	Insurance Expense	515	40	
		Prepaid Insurance	118		40
		To recognize expiration of one month's insurance			
	31	Art Supplies Expense	516	500	
		Art Supplies	115		500
		To recognize art supplies used during the month			
	31	Office Supplies Expense	517	200	
		Office Supplies	116		200
		To recognize office supplies used during the month			
	31	Depreciation Expense, Art Equipment	519	70	
		Accumulated Depreciation, Art Equipment	145		70
		To record depreciation of art equipment for a month			
	31	Depreciation Expense, Office Equipment	520	50	
		Accumulated Depreciation, Office Equipment	147		50
		To record depreciation of office equipment for a month			
	31	Unearned Art Fees	213	400	
		Art Fees Earned	412		400
		To recognize performance of services paid in advance			
	31	Accrued Fees Receivable	114	200	
		Advertising Fees Earned	411		200
		To accrue advertising fees earned but unrecorded			
	31	Office Wages Expense	511	180	
		Accrued Wages Payable	214		180
		To accrue unrecorded wages			

The balance of Income Summary equals the net income or loss reported on the income statement. The net income or loss is then transferred to the owner's Capital account. This step is needed because, even though expenses and revenues are recorded in expense and revenue accounts, they actually represent decreases and increases in owner's equity. Thus closing entries must transfer the net effect of increases (revenues) and decreases (expenses) to the owner's Capital account.

Closing entries are sometimes called **clearing entries** because one of their functions is to clear the revenue and expense accounts and leave them with zero balances.

As stated in Chapter 3, revenue and expense accounts are called temporary accounts. Nominal accounts begin each period at zero, accumulate a balance during the period, and return to zero by means of closing entries when the balance is transferred to the owner's Capital account. The accountant uses these accounts to keep track of the increases and decreases in owner's equity in a way that is helpful to management and others interested in the success or progress of the company. However, temporary accounts are different from balance sheet accounts. Balance sheet, or permanent, accounts often begin with a balance, increase or decrease during the period, and carry the end-of-period balance into the next accounting period.

Required Closing Entries

OBJECTIVE 7
Prepare the required closing entries

Closing entries are needed for four important tasks:

1. Transferring the revenue account balances to Income Summary
2. Transferring the expense account balances to Income Summary
3. Transferring the Income Summary balance to the Capital account
4. Transferring the Withdrawals account balance to the Capital account

Closing the Revenue Accounts to the Income Summary

Revenue accounts have credit balances before the closing entries are posted. For this reason, an entry debiting each revenue account in the amount of its balance is needed to close the account. The credit part of the entry is made to the Income Summary account. The compound entry that closes the two revenue accounts for the Joan Miller Advertising Agency is as follows:

Jan. 31	Advertising Fees Earned	411	4,400	
	Art Fees Earned	412	400	
	Income Summary	313		4,800
	To close revenue accounts			

The effect of posting the entry is shown in Exhibit 4-10. Note that the dual effect of the entry is to (1) set the balances of the revenue accounts

Exhibit 4-10. Posting the Closing Entry of the Revenue Accounts to the Income Summary Account

Advertising Fees Earned — Account No. 411

Date	Item	Post. Ref.	Debit	Credit	Balance Debit	Balance Credit
Jan. 10		J2		1,400		1,400
19		J2		2,800		4,200
31	Adj. (h)	J3		200		4,400
31	Closing	J4	4,400			—

Income Summary — Account No. 313

Date	Item	Post. Ref.	Debit	Credit	Balance Debit	Balance Credit
Jan. 31	Closing	J4		4,800		4,800

4,400
400
4,800

Art Fees Earned — Account No. 412

Date	Item	Post. Ref.	Debit	Credit	Balance Debit	Balance Credit
Jan. 31	Adj. (g)	J3		400		400
31	Closing	J4	400			—

equal to zero, and (2) transfer the balances in total to the credit side of the Income Summary account. Also note that the data for closing the revenue accounts can be found in the credit side of the Income Statement columns in the work sheet illustrated in Exhibit 4-5. If a work sheet is not used, the data may also be found in the appropriate general ledger accounts after the adjusting entries have been posted.

Closing the Expense Accounts to the Income Summary

Expense accounts have debit balances before the closing entries are posted. For this reason, a compound entry is needed crediting each expense account for its balance and debiting the Income Summary for the total (which can be found in the debit side of the Income Statement columns):

Date	Account	Ref.	Debit	Credit
Jan. 31	Income Summary	313	2,810	
	Office Wages Expense	511		1,380
	Utility Expense	512		100
	Telephone Expense	513		70
	Rent Expense	514		400
	Insurance Expense	515		40
	Art Supplies Expense	516		500
	Office Supplies Expense	517		200
	Depreciation Expense, Art Equipment	519		70
	Depreciation Expense, Office Equipment	520		50
	To close the expense accounts			

The effect of posting the closing entries to the ledger accounts is shown in Exhibit 4-11. Note again the double effect of (1) reducing expense account balances to zero and (2) transferring the total of the account balances to the debit side of the Income Summary account. Note also that data for closing the expense accounts are on the debit side of the Income Statement columns of the work sheet (Exhibit 4-5).

Exhibit 4-11. Posting the Closing Entry of the Expense Accounts to the Income Summary Account

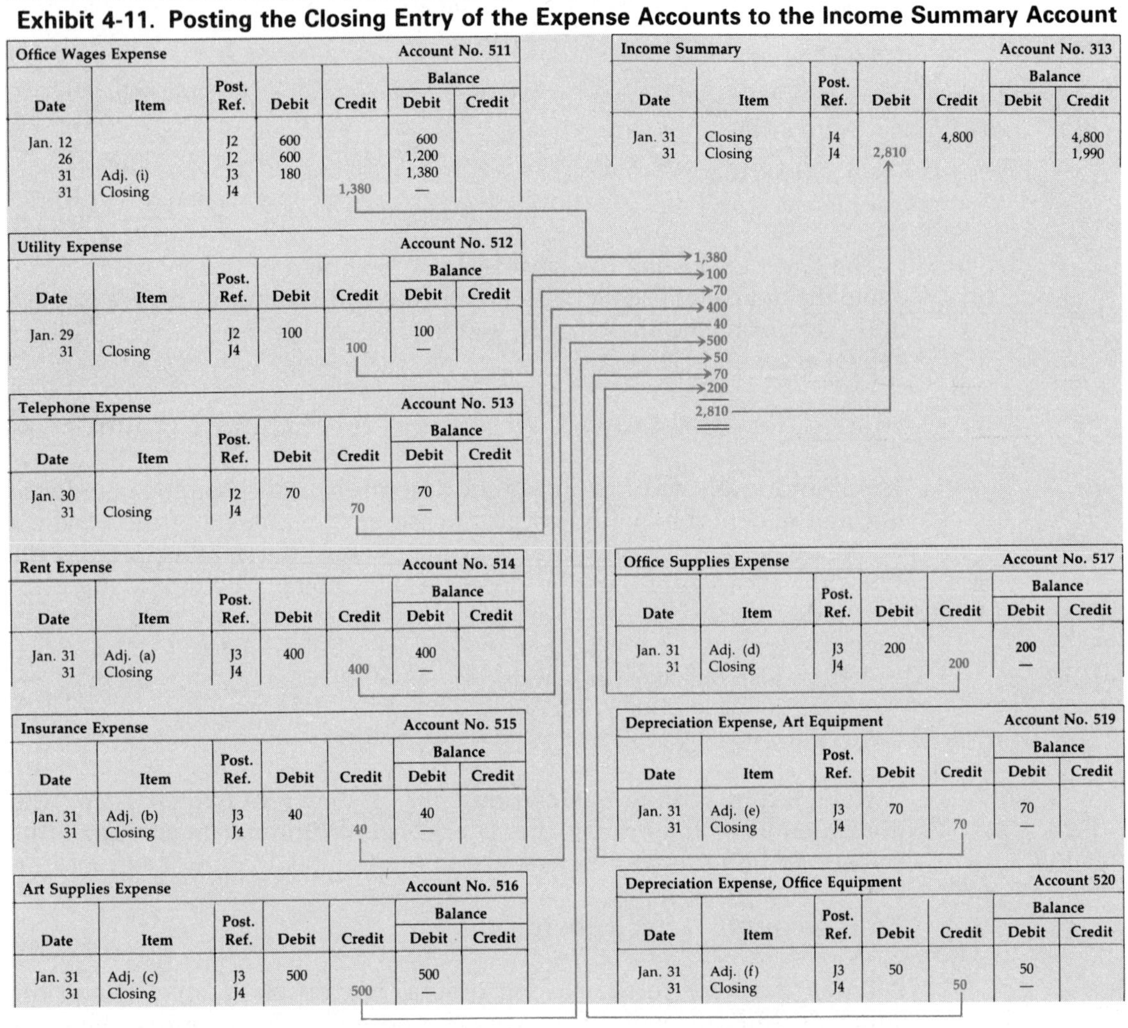

Office Wages Expense — Account No. 511

Date	Item	Post. Ref.	Debit	Credit	Balance Debit	Balance Credit
Jan. 12		J2	600		600	
26		J2	600		1,200	
31	Adj. (i)	J3	180		1,380	
31	Closing	J4		1,380	—	

Utility Expense — Account No. 512

Date	Item	Post. Ref.	Debit	Credit	Balance Debit	Balance Credit
Jan. 29		J2	100		100	
31	Closing	J4		100	—	

Telephone Expense — Account No. 513

Date	Item	Post. Ref.	Debit	Credit	Balance Debit	Balance Credit
Jan. 30		J2	70		70	
31	Closing	J4		70	—	

Rent Expense — Account No. 514

Date	Item	Post. Ref.	Debit	Credit	Balance Debit	Balance Credit
Jan. 31	Adj. (a)	J3	400		400	
31	Closing	J4		400	—	

Insurance Expense — Account No. 515

Date	Item	Post. Ref.	Debit	Credit	Balance Debit	Balance Credit
Jan. 31	Adj. (b)	J3	40		40	
31	Closing	J4		40	—	

Art Supplies Expense — Account No. 516

Date	Item	Post. Ref.	Debit	Credit	Balance Debit	Balance Credit
Jan. 31	Adj. (c)	J3	500		500	
31	Closing	J4		500	—	

Income Summary — Account No. 313

Date	Item	Post. Ref.	Debit	Credit	Balance Debit	Balance Credit
Jan. 31	Closing	J4		4,800		4,800
31	Closing	J4	2,810			1,990

1,380
100
70
400
40
500
50
70
200
2,810

Office Supplies Expense — Account No. 517

Date	Item	Post. Ref.	Debit	Credit	Balance Debit	Balance Credit
Jan. 31	Adj. (d)	J3	200		200	
31	Closing	J4		200	—	

Depreciation Expense, Art Equipment — Account No. 519

Date	Item	Post. Ref.	Debit	Credit	Balance Debit	Balance Credit
Jan. 31	Adj. (e)	J3	70		70	
31	Closing	J4		70	—	

Depreciation Expense, Office Equipment — Account 520

Date	Item	Post. Ref.	Debit	Credit	Balance Debit	Balance Credit
Jan. 31	Adj. (f)	J3	50		50	
31	Closing	J4		50	—	

Closing the Income Summary Account to the Capital Account

After the entries closing the revenue and expense accounts have been posted, the balance of the Income Summary account is equal to the net income or loss for the period. A net income will be indicated by a credit balance and a net loss by a debit balance. At this point, the Income Summary balance, regardless of its nature, must be closed to the Capital account. For the Joan Miller Advertising Agency the entry is as follows:

Jan. 31	Income Summary	313	1,990	
	Joan Miller, Capital	311		1,990
	To close the Income Summary account			

Exhibit 4-12. Posting the Closing Entry of the Income Summary Account to the Capital Account

Income Summary					Account No. 313	
					Balance	
Date	Item	Post. Ref.	Debit	Credit	Debit	Credit
Jan. 31	Closing	J4		4,800		4,800
31	Closing	J4	2,810			1,990
31	Closing	J4	1,990			—

Joan Miller, Capital					Account No. 311	
					Balance	
Date	Item	Post. Ref.	Debit	Credit	Debit	Credit
Jan. 1		J1		10,000		10,000
31	Closing	J4		1,990		11,990

The effect of posting the closing entry is shown in Exhibit 4-12. Note again the double effect of (1) closing the Income Summary account balance and (2) transferring the balance, net income in this case, to Joan Miller's capital account.

Closing the Withdrawals Account to the Capital Account

The Withdrawals account shows the amount by which capital is reduced during the period by withdrawals of cash or other assets of the business by the owner for personal use. For this reason, the debit balance of the Withdrawals account must be closed to the Capital account, as follows:

Jan. 31	Joan Miller, Capital	311	1,400	
	Joan Miller, Withdrawals	312		1,400
	To close the Withdrawals account			

The effect of posting this closing entry is shown in Exhibit 4-13. The double effect of the entry is to (1) close the Withdrawals account of its balance and (2) transfer the balance to the Capital account.

The Accounts After Closing

After all the steps in the closing process have been completed and the adjusting and closing entries have been posted to the accounts, the stage is set for the next accounting period. The ledger accounts of the Joan Miller Advertising Agency as they appear at this point are shown in Exhibit 4-14. The revenue, expense, and withdrawals accounts (temporary accounts) have zero balances. The Capital account has been increased or decreased depending on net income or loss and withdrawals. The balance sheet accounts (permanent accounts) have the appropriate balances, which are carried forward to the next period.

Exhibit 4-13. Posting the Closing Entry of the Withdrawals Account to the Capital Account

Joan Miller, Withdrawals					Account No. 312	
					Balance	
Date	Item	Post. Ref.	Debit	Credit	Debit	Credit
Jan. 25		J2	1,400		1,400	
31	Closing	J4		1,400	—	

Joan Miller, Capital					Account No. 311	
					Balance	
Date	Item	Post. Ref.	Debit	Credit	Debit	Credit
Jan. 1		J1		10,000		10,000
31	Closing	J4		1,990		11,990
31	Closing	J4	1,400			10,590

Exhibit 4-14. The Accounts After Closing Entries Are Posted

Cash — Account No. 111

Date		Item	Post. Ref.	Debit	Credit	Balance Debit	Balance Credit
Jan.	1		J1	10,000		10,000	
	2		J1		800	9,200	
	4		J1		4,200	5,000	
	5		J1		1,500	3,500	
	8		J1		480	3,020	
	9		J1		1,000	2,020	
	10		J2	1,400		3,420	
	12		J2		600	2,820	
	15		J2	1,000		3,820	
	25		J2		1,400	2,420	
	26		J2		600	1,820	
	29		J2		100	1,720	

Accounts Receivable — Account No. 113

Date		Item	Post. Ref.	Debit	Credit	Balance Debit	Balance Credit
Jan.	19		J2	2,800		2,800	

Accrued Fees Receivable — Account No. 114

Date		Item	Post. Ref.	Debit	Credit	Balance Debit	Balance Credit
Jan.	31	Adj. (h)	J3	200		200	

Art Supplies — Account No. 115

Date		Item	Post. Ref.	Debit	Credit	Balance Debit	Balance Credit
Jan.	6		J1	1,800		1,800	
	31	Adj. (c)	J3		500	1,300	

Office Supplies — Account No. 116

Date		Item	Post. Ref.	Debit	Credit	Balance Debit	Balance Credit
Jan.	6		J1	800		800	
	31	Adj. (d)	J3		200	600	

Prepaid Rent — Account No. 117

Date		Item	Post. Ref.	Debit	Credit	Balance Debit	Balance Credit
Jan.	2		J1	800		800	
	31	Adj. (a)	J3		400	400	

Prepaid Insurance — Account No. 118

Date		Item	Post. Ref.	Debit	Credit	Balance Debit	Balance Credit
Jan.	8		J1	480		480	
	31	Adj. (b)	J3		40	440	

Art Equipment — Account No. 144

Date		Item	Post. Ref.	Debit	Credit	Balance Debit	Balance Credit
Jan.	4		J1	4,200		4,200	

Accumulated Depreciation, Art Equipment — Account No. 145

Date		Item	Post. Ref.	Debit	Credit	Balance Debit	Balance Credit
Jan.	31	Adj. (e)	J3		70		70

Office Equipment — Account No. 146

Date		Item	Post. Ref.	Debit	Credit	Balance Debit	Balance Credit
Jan.	5		J1	3,000		3,000	

Accumulated Depreciation, Office Equipment — Account No. 147

Date		Item	Post. Ref.	Debit	Credit	Balance Debit	Balance Credit
Jan.	31	Adj. (f)	J3		50		50

Accounts Payable — Account No. 212

Date		Item	Post. Ref.	Debit	Credit	Balance Debit	Balance Credit
Jan.	5		J1		1,500		1,500
	6		J1		2,600		4,100
	9		J1	1,000			3,100
	30		J2		70		3,170

Unearned Art Fees — Account No. 213

Date		Item	Post. Ref.	Debit	Credit	Balance Debit	Balance Credit
Jan.	15		J2		1,000		1,000
	31	Adj. (g)	J3	400			600

Accrued Wages Payable — Account No. 214

Date		Item	Post. Ref.	Debit	Credit	Balance Debit	Balance Credit
Jan.	31	Adj. (i)	J3		180		180

Exhibit 4-14 (*continued*)

Joan Miller, Capital — Account No. 311

Date		Item	Post. Ref.	Debit	Credit	Balance Debit	Balance Credit
Jan.	1		J1		10,000		10,000
	31	Closing	J4		1,990		11,990
	31	Closing	J4	1,400			10,590

Joan Miller, Withdrawals — Account No. 312

Date		Item	Post. Ref.	Debit	Credit	Balance Debit	Balance Credit
Jan.	25		J2	1,400		1,400	
	31	Closing	J4		1,400	—	

Income Summary — Account No. 313

Date		Item	Post. Ref.	Debit	Credit	Balance Debit	Balance Credit
Jan.	31	Closing	J4		4,800		4,800
	31	Closing	J4	2,810			1,990
	31	Closing	J4	1,990			—

Advertising Fees Earned — Account No. 411

Date		Item	Post. Ref.	Debit	Credit	Balance Debit	Balance Credit
Jan.	10		J2		1,400		1,400
	19		J2		2,800		4,200
	31	Adj. (h)	J3		200		4,400
	31	Closing	J4	4,400			—

Art Fees Earned — Account No. 412

Date		Item	Post. Ref.	Debit	Credit	Balance Debit	Balance Credit
Jan.	31	Adj. (g)	J3		400		400
	31	Closing	J4	400			—

Office Wages Expense — Account No. 511

Date		Item	Post. Ref.	Debit	Credit	Balance Debit	Balance Credit
Jan.	12		J2	600		600	
	26		J2	600		1,200	
	31	Adj. (i)	J3	180		1,380	
	31	Closing	J4		1,380	—	

Utility Expense — Account No. 512

Date			Post. Ref.	Debit	Credit	Balance Debit	Balance Credit
Jan.	29		J2	100		100	
	31	Closing	J4		100	—	

Telephone Expense — Account No. 513

Date		Item	Post. Ref.	Debit	Credit	Balance Debit	Balance Credit
Jan.	30		J2	70		70	
	31	Closing	J4		70	—	

Rent Expense — Account No. 514

Date		Item	Post. Ref.	Debit	Credit	Balance Debit	Balance Credit
Jan.	31	Adj. (a)	J3	400		400	
	31	Closing	J4		400	—	

Insurance Expense — Account No. 515

Date		Item	Post. Ref.	Debit	Credit	Balance Debit	Balance Credit
Jan.	31	Adj. (b)	J3	40		40	
	31	Closing	J4		40	—	

Art Supplies Expense — Account No. 516

Date		Item	Post. Ref.	Debit	Credit	Balance Debit	Balance Credit
Jan.	31	Adj. (c)	J3	500		500	
	31	Closing	J4		500	—	

Office Supplies Expense — Account No. 517

Date		Item	Post. Ref.	Debit	Credit	Balance Debit	Balance Credit
Jan.	31	Adj. (d)	J3	200		200	
	31	Closing	J4		200	—	

Depreciation Expense, Art Equipment — Account No. 519

Date		Item	Post. Ref.	Debit	Credit	Balance Debit	Balance Credit
Jan.	31	Adj. (e)	J3	70		70	
	31	Closing	J4		70	—	

Depreciation Expense, Office Equipment — Account No. 520

Date		Item	Post. Ref.	Debit	Credit	Balance Debit	Balance Credit
Jan.	31	Adj. (f)	J3	50		50	
	31	Closing	J4		50	—	

The Post-Closing Trial Balance

OBJECTIVE 8
Prepare the post-closing trial balance

Because it is possible to make an error in posting the adjustments and closing entries to the ledger accounts, it is necessary to retest the equality of the accounts by preparing a new trial balance. This final trial balance, called a **post-closing trial balance**, is shown in Exhibit 4-15 for the Joan Miller Advertising Agency. Notice that only balance sheet accounts have balances since the income statement accounts have all been closed.

The income summary and post-closing trial balance are used in preparing financial statements. These statements often *summarize* certain groups of accounts, rather than list them separately, such as a depreciable asset and its related accumulated depreciation account:

Office Equipment	2,950

rather than

Office Equipment	3,000
Accumulated Depreciation, Office Equipment	(50)

It is important to be aware that summarizing will cause some account balances in the final balance sheet to differ from the detail account balances in the adjusted trial balance.

Reversing Entries: Optional First Step of the Next Accounting Period

OBJECTIVE 9
Prepare reversing entries as appropriate

At the end of each accounting period, adjusting entries are made to bring revenues and expenses into conformity with the matching rule. A **reversing entry** is a general journal entry made on the first day of an

Exhibit 4-15. Post-Closing Trial Balance

Joan Miller Advertising Agency
Post-Closing Trial Balance
January 31, 19xx

Cash	$ 1,720	
Accounts Receivable	2,800	
Accrued Fees Receivable	200	
Art Supplies	1,300	
Office Supplies	600	
Prepaid Rent	400	
Prepaid Insurance	440	
Art Equipment	4,200	
Accumulated Depreciation, Art Equipment		$ 70
Office Equipment	3,000	
Accumulated Depreciation, Office Equipment		50
Accounts Payable		3,170
Unearned Art Fees		600
Accrued Wages Payable		180
Joan Miller, Capital		10,590
	$14,660	$14,660

accounting period that is the exact reverse of an adjusting entry made in the previous period. Reversing entries are optional journal entries that are intended to simplify the bookkeeping process for transactions involving certain types of adjustments. Not all adjusting entries are reversed. For the system of recording used in this book, only adjustments for accruals (accrued revenues and accrued expenses) need to be reversed. Deferrals do not need to be reversed.

To show how reversing entries can be helpful, consider the adjusting entry made in the records of Joan Miller Advertising Agency to accrue office wages expense:

Jan. 31	Office Wages Expense	180	
	Accrued Wages Payable		180
	To accrue unrecorded wages		

When the secretary is paid on the next regular payday, the accountant would make the following entry, using the accounting procedure that you know to this point:

Feb. 9	Accrued Wages Payable	180	
	Office Wages Expense	420	
	Cash		600
	To record payment of two weeks' wages to secretary, $180 of which was accrued in the previous period		

Note that when the payment is made, without a prior reversing entry, the accountant must look in the records to find out how much of the $600 applied to the current accounting period and how much was accrued at the beginning of the period. This step may appear easy in this simple case, but think of the problems if the company had many employees, especially if some of them are paid on different time schedules such as weekly or monthly. A reversing entry is an accounting procedure that helps to solve this difficult problem. As noted above, a reversing entry is exactly what its name implies. It is a reversal of the adjusting entry made by debiting the credits and crediting the debits of the adjusting entry. For example, note the following sequence of transactions and their effects on the ledger account for Office Wages Expense:

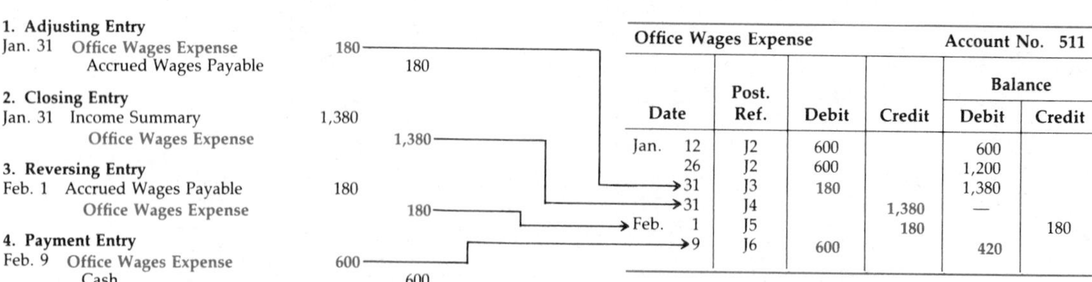

1. Adjusting Entry

Jan. 31	Office Wages Expense	180	
	Accrued Wages Payable		180

2. Closing Entry

Jan. 31	Income Summary	1,380	
	Office Wages Expense		1,380

3. Reversing Entry

Feb. 1	Accrued Wages Payable	180	
	Office Wages Expense		180

4. Payment Entry

Feb. 9	Office Wages Expense	600	
	Cash		600

Office Wages Expense — Account No. 511

Date		Post. Ref.	Debit	Credit	Balance Debit	Balance Credit
Jan.	12	J2	600		600	
	26	J2	600		1,200	
	31	J3	180		1,380	
	31	J4		1,380	—	
Feb.	1	J5		180		180
	9	J6	600		420	

These transactions had the following effects on Office Wages Expense:

1. Adjusted Office Wages Expense to accrue $180 in the proper accounting period.
2. Closed the $1,380 in total Office Wages Expense for January to Income Summary, leaving a zero balance.
3. Set up a credit balance of $180 on February 1 in Office Wages Expense equal to the expense recognized through the adjusting entry in January (and also reduced the liability account Accrued Wages Payable to a zero balance).
4. Recorded the $600 payment of two weeks' wages, as a debit to Office Wages Expense, automatically leaving a balance of $420, which represents the correct wages expense so far for February.

Making the February 9 payment entry was simplified by the reversing entry. Reversing entries apply to any accrued expenses or revenues. In the case of the Joan Miller Advertising Agency, Office Wages Expense was the only accrued expense. However, the asset Accrued Fees Receivable was created as a result of the adjusting entry made to accrue fees earned but not yet billed. The adjusting entry for this accrued revenue would therefore require a reversing entry, as follows:

Feb. 1	Advertising Fees Earned	200	
	Accrued Fees Receivable		200
	To reverse adjusting entry for accrued fees receivable		

When the series of advertisements is finished, the company can credit the entire proceeds to Advertising Fees Earned without regard to the amount accrued in the previous period. The credit will automatically be reduced to the amount earned during February by the $200 debit in the account.

As noted above, under the system of recording used in this book, reversing entries apply only to accruals. For this reason, reversing entries do not apply to deferrals such as those that involve supplies, prepaid rent, prepaid insurance, depreciation, and unearned art fees.

Chapter Review

Review of Learning Objectives

1. **State all the steps in the accounting cycle.**
   The steps in the accounting cycle are to (1) analyze the transactions from the source documents, (2) record the transactions in the journal, (3) post the entries to the ledger, (4) adjust the accounts at the end of the period, (5) prepare the financial statements, and (6) close the accounts.

2. **Prepare a work sheet.**
   A work sheet is prepared by first entering the account balances in the Trial Balance columns, the adjustments in the Adjustments columns, and the adjusted account balances in the Adjusted Trial Balance columns. Then the

amounts from the Adjusted Trial Balance columns are extended to the Income Statement or Balance Sheet columns as appropriate. Next, the Income Statement and Balance Sheet columns are totaled. Finally, net income or net loss is determined from the Income Statement columns and extended to the Balance Sheet columns. The statement columns should now be in balance.

3. **Identify the three principal uses of a work sheet.**
   A work sheet is useful in (1) preparing the financial statements, (2) recording the adjusting entries, and (3) recording the closing entries.

4. **Prepare financial statements from a work sheet.**
   The balance sheet and income statements can be prepared directly from the Balance Sheet and Income Statement columns of a completed work sheet. It is common practice to prepare a separate statement of owner's equity from the work sheet. When this is done, the balance sheet contains only the ending balance of owner's equity.

5. **Record the adjusting entries from a work sheet.**
   Adjusting entries can be recorded in the general journal directly from the Adjustments columns of the work sheet.

6. **Explain the purposes of closing entries.**
   Closing entries have two objectives. First, they close the balances from the revenue and expense accounts in preparation for the next accounting period. Second, they summarize a period's revenues and expenses in the Income Summary so that the net income or net loss for the period may be transferred as a total to owner's equity.

7. **Prepare the required closing entries.**
   Closing entries are prepared by first transferring the revenue and expense account balances to the Income Summary. Then the balance of the Income Summary account is transferred to the Capital account. Finally, the balance of the Withdrawals account is transferred to the Capital account.

8. **Prepare the post-closing trial balance.**
   As a final check on the balance of the ledger, a post-closing trial balance is prepared after the closing entries have been posted to the ledger accounts.

9. **Prepare reversing entries as appropriate.**
   Reversing entries are optional general journal entries made on the first day of a new accounting period that exactly reverse certain adjusting entries made in the prior period. They apply only to accruals and facilitate routine bookkeeping procedures.

Self-Test

Test your knowledge of the chapter by choosing the best answer for each item below.

1. Which of the following sequences of actions describes the proper sequence in the accounting cycle?
   a. Post, enter, analyze, prepare, close, adjust
   b. Analyze, enter, post, adjust, prepare, close
   c. Prepare, enter, post, adjust, analyze, close
   d. Enter, post, close, prepare, adjust, analyze

2. The work sheet is a type of
   a. ledger.
   b. journal.
   c. working paper.
   d. financial statement.
3. The normal account balances for Equipment and Accumulated Depreciation, Equipment, are
   a. debit and credit, respectively.
   b. credit and debit, respectively.
   c. debits.
   d. credits.
4. The work sheet is useful in
   a. preparing financial statements.
   b. recording adjusting entries.
   c. recording closing entries.
   d. All of the above.
5. An important purpose of closing entries is
   a. to adjust the accounts in the ledger.
   b. to set balance sheet accounts to zero in order to begin the next period.
   c. to set income statement accounts to zero in order to begin the next period.
   d. None of the above.
6. In preparing closing entries, it is helpful to refer first to
   a. the Adjustments columns of the work sheet.
   b. the Adjusted Trial Balance columns of the work sheet.
   c. the Income Statement columns of the work sheet.
   d. the general journal.
7. After all closing entries have been posted, the balance of the Income Summary account will be
   a. a debit if a net income has been earned.
   b. a debit if a net loss has been incurred.
   c. a credit if a net loss has been incurred.
   d. zero.
8. After closing entries have been posted, which of the following accounts would have a nonzero balance?
   a. Service Revenue Earned
   b. Depreciation Expense
   c. Unearned Service Revenue
   d. Service Wages Expense
9. The post-closing trial balance will
   a. contain only income statement accounts.
   b. contain only balance sheet accounts.
   c. contain both income statement and balance sheet accounts.
   d. be prepared before closing entries are posted to the ledger.
10. For which of the following adjustments would a reversing entry facilitate bookkeeping procedures?
    a. Adjustment for depreciation expense
    b. Adjustment to allocate prepaid insurance to the current period
    c. Adjustment made as a result of inventory of supplies
    d. Adjustment for wages earned by employees but not yet paid

Answers to Self-Test are at the end of this chapter.

Review Problem
Completion of Work Sheet; Preparation of Financial Statements, Adjusting Entries, and Closing Entries

This chapter contains an extended example of the preparation of a work sheet and the last two steps of the accounting cycle for the Joan Miller Advertising Agency. Instead of studying a demonstration problem, you should carefully review and retrace the steps through the illustrations in the chapter.

Required

1. In Exhibit 4-5, what is the source of the trial balance figures?
2. Trace the entries in the Adjustments column of Exhibit 4-5 to the journal entries in Exhibit 4-9.
3. Trace the journal entries in Exhibit 4-9 to the ledger accounts in Exhibit 4-14.
4. Trace the amounts in the Income Statement and Balance Sheet columns of Exhibit 4-5 to the income statement in Exhibit 4-6, the statement of owner's equity in Exhibit 4-7, and the balance sheet in Exhibit 4-8.
5. Trace the amounts in the Income Statement columns and the withdrawals account balance of Exhibit 4-5 to the closing entries on pages 141–144.
6. Trace the closing entries on pages 141–144 to the ledger accounts in Exhibit 4-14.
7. Trace the balances of the ledger accounts in Exhibit 4-14 to the post-closing trial balance in Exhibit 4-15.

Chapter Assignments

Questions

1. Arrange the following activities in proper order by placing the numbers 1 through 6 in the blanks:

   _____ a. The transactions are entered in the journal.
   _____ b. Financial statements are prepared.
   _____ c. The transactions are analyzed from the source documents.
   _____ d. The accounts are adjusted with the aid of a work sheet.
   _____ e. Closing entries are prepared.
   _____ f. The transactions are posted to the ledger.

2. Why are working papers important to the accountant?
3. Why are work sheets never published and rarely seen by management?
4. Is the work sheet a substitute for the financial statements? Discuss.
5. At the end of the accounting period, does the posting of adjusting entries to the ledger precede or follow the preparation of the work sheet?
6. What is the normal balance of the following accounts, in terms of debit and credit? Cash; Accounts Payable; Prepaid Rent; Sam Jones, Capital; Commission Revenue; Sam Jones, Withdrawals; Rent Expense; Accumulated Depreciation, Office Equipment; Office Equipment.
7. What is the probable cause of a credit balance in the Cash account?
8. Should the Adjusted Trial Balance columns of the work sheet be totaled before or after the adjusted amounts are carried to the Income Statement and Balance Sheet columns? Discuss.
9. What sequence should be followed in extending the Adjusted Trial Balance columns to the Income Statement and Balance Sheet columns? Discuss.
10. Do the totals of the Balance Sheet columns of the work sheet usually agree with the totals on the balance sheet? Explain.
11. Do the Income Statement columns and Balance Sheet columns balance after the adjusted amounts from the Adjusted Trial Balance columns are extended?
12. What is the purpose of the Income Summary account?
13. Are adjusting entries posted to the ledger accounts at the same time as the closing entries? Explain.

14. What is the difference between adjusting and closing entries?
15. What are the four basic tasks of closing entries?
16. Which of the following accounts will not have a balance after closing entries are prepared and posted? Insurance Expense; Accounts Receivable; Commission Revenue; Prepaid Insurance; Withdrawals; Supplies; Supplies Expense.
17. What is the significance of the post-closing trial balance?
18. Which of the following accounts will appear on the post-closing trial balance? Insurance Expense; Accounts Receivable; Commission Revenue; Prepaid Insurance; Withdrawals; Supplies; Supplies Expense; Capital.
19. How can reversing entries aid in the bookkeeping process?
20. To what types of adjustments do reversing entries apply? To what types do they not apply?

Classroom Exercises

Exercise 4-1. Preparation of Trial Balance (L.O. 2)

The following alphabetical list represents the accounts and balances for Lemon Realty on December 31, 19xx. All accounts have normal balances.

Accounts Payable	$ 4,340
Accounts Receivable	1,750
Accumulated Depreciation, Office Equipment	450
Advertising Expense	600
Cash	2,545
Office Equipment	5,170
Prepaid Insurance	560
Rent Expense	2,400
Revenue from Commissions	19,300
Supplies	275
Wages Expense	12,000
Lemon, Capital	10,210
Lemon, Withdrawals	9,000

Prepare a trial balance by listing the accounts on a sheet of accounting paper in the same order, with the balances in the appropriate debit or credit column.

Exercise 4-2. Preparing a Statement of Owner's Equity (L.O. 4)

The Capital, Withdrawal, and Income Summary accounts for Wayne's Barber Shop for the year ended December 31, after recording of closing entries, are presented in T account form below.

Wayne Hall, Capital

12/31	12,000	1/1	26,000
		12/31	13,000
		Bal.	27,000

Wayne Hall, Withdrawals

4/1	4,000	12/31	12,000
7/1	4,000		
10/1	4,000		
Bal.	—		

Income Summary

12/31	39,000	12/31	52,000
12/31	13,000		
Bal.	—		

Prepare a statement of owner's equity for Wayne's Barber Shop.

Exercise 4-3. Preparation of Adjusting and Reversing Entries from Work Sheet Columns
(L.O. 5, 9)

The items listed below are from the Adjustments columns of a work sheet as of December 31.

1. Prepare the adjusting entries from the information.
2. If required, prepare reversing entries as appropriate.

	Adjustments			
	Debit		Credit	
Prepaid Insurance			(a)	120
Office Supplies			(b)	315
Accumulated Depreciation, Office Equipment			(c)	700
Accumulated Depreciation, Store Equipment			(d)	1,100
Office Salaries Expense	(e)	120		
Store Salaries Expense	(e)	240		
Insurance Expense	(a)	120		
Office Supplies Expense	(b)	315		
Depreciation Expense, Office Equipment	(c)	700		
Depreciation Expense, Store Equipment	(d)	1,100		
Accrued Salaries Payable			(e)	360
		2,595		2,595

Exercise 4-4. Preparation of Closing Entries from Work Sheet
(L.O. 7)

The following items are from the Income Statement columns of the work sheet of the Dexter James Repair Shop for the year ended December 31.

	Income Statement	
	Debit	Credit
Repair Revenue		24,240
Wages Expense	7,840	
Rent Expense	1,200	
Supplies Expense	4,260	
Insurance Expense	915	
Depreciation Expense, Repair Equipment	1,345	
	15,560	24,240
Net Income	8,680	
	24,240	24,240

Prepare entries to close the revenue, expense, Income Summary, and Withdrawals accounts. Mr. James withdrew $10,000 during the year.

Exercise 4-5. Completion of Work Sheet (L.O. 2)

The following list of alphabetically arranged accounts and balances represents a trial balance in highly simplified form for the month ended October 31, 19xx.

Trial Balance Accounts and Balances

Accounts Payable	$ 3	Office Equipment	$ 6
Accounts Receivable	6	Prepaid Insurance	2
Accumulated Depreciation, Office Equipment	1	Service Revenue	21
Julio Lopez, Capital	12	Supplies	4
Julio Lopez, Withdrawals	6	Unearned Revenue	3
Cash	4	Utilities Expense	2
		Wages Expense	10

1. On accounting paper, prepare a work sheet form, entering the trial balance accounts in the order in which they would normally appear, and arranging the balances in the correct debit or credit column.
2. Complete the work sheet using the following information:
   a. Expired insurance, $1.
   b. Of the unearned revenue, $2 has been earned by the balance sheet date.
   c. Estimated depreciation on office equipment, $1.
   d. Accrued wages, $1.
   e. Unused supplies on hand, $1.

Exercise 4-6. Deriving Adjusting Entries from Trial Balance and Income Statement Columns (L.O. 5)

Presented below is a partial work sheet in which the Trial Balance and Income Statement columns have been completed. All amounts are in dollars.

Accounts	Trial Balance		Income Statement	
Cash	5			
Accounts Receivable	10			
Supplies	11			
Prepaid Insurance	8			
Building	25			
Accumulated Depreciation, Building		8		
Accounts Payable		4		
Unearned Revenue		2		
R. L., Capital		32		
Revenue		40		42
Wages Expense	27	—	30	
	86	86		
Insurance Expense			4	
Supplies Expense			8	
Depreciation Expense, Building			2	—
			44	42
Net Loss			—	2
			44	44

1. Determine the adjusting entries that have been made. Assume that no adjustments are made to Accounts Receivable or Accounts Payable.
2. Prepare a balance sheet.

Exercise 4-7. Reversing Entries
(L.O. 9)

Selected T accounts for Winters Company are presented below for December:

1. In which case below is a reversing entry helpful? Why?
2. Prepare the appropriate reversing entry.
3. Prepare the entry to record payments for wages totaling $1,570 in January. How much is Wages Expense for January?

Supplies

12/1 Bal.	430	12/31 Adjust.	640
Dec. purchases	470		
Bal.	260		

Supplies Expense

12/31 Adjust.	640	12/31 Closing	640
Bal.	—		

Accrued Wages Payable

		12/31 Adjust.	320
		Bal.	320

Wages Expense

Dec. Wages	1,970	12/31 Closing	2,290
12/31 Adjust.	320		
Bal.	—		

Interpreting Accounting Information

Sperry & Hutchinson
(L.O. 1, 5, 7)

Sperry & Hutchinson is known as "The Green Stamp Company" because its principal business is selling S & H Green Stamps to merchants who give them to customers who, in turn, may redeem them for merchandise. When S & H sells green stamps, it incurs a liability to redeem the stamps. It makes a profit to the extent that people do not redeem the stamps. In the past, S & H has assumed that 95 percent of all stamps will be redeemed. Thus a sale of $1,000 worth of stamps would be recorded as follows:

Cash	1,000	
Liability to Redeem Stamps		950
Stamp Revenue		50

Since it may be years before some stamps are redeemed, the company keeps the liability on its balance sheet indefinitely. An article in *Forbes*, a leading business weekly magazine, commented on S & H's situation as follows:

> The company [S & H] is sitting on a mountain of money held in reserve to redeem stamps already issued but not yet cashed in. How many of these stamps will ultimately be redeemed? Nobody knows for sure. But Sperry [S & H] has made some assumptions in drawing up its financial statements, and at last count it had stashed away no less than $308 million to match unredeemed stamps. That's more than last year's stamp sales. It's one-third more than the company's total [owners'] equity of $231 million. What's more, to the extent that the company has overestimated the need for that liability—setting aside cash for Green Stamps that have been thrown into the garbage—some of the cash is clearly equity in all but name.

The Liability for Redemption of Stamps became so large that in 1979 S & H began setting aside only 90 percent (instead of 95 percent) of stamp sales for redemption. The immediate effect of this change was to boost profits. The reason for this effect is, as stated in *Forbes*, "the extra 5 percent of stamps now assumed to be lost forever goes straight through as pure profit." [1]

1. *Forbes*, October 12, 1981, pages 72, 74.

Required

1. Assume that S & H has an asset account called Merchandise that represents the goods that can be purchased. What entry would be made if $700 worth of stamps were redeemed for merchandise?
2. What does *Forbes* mean when it says that "some of the cash is clearly equity in all but name"? Is the word "cash" used properly? Show that you know what *Forbes* means by presenting the adjusting entry and closing entries that would be made if S & H decided to reduce the liability for redemption of stamps.
3. Explain *Forbes*'s comment that the extra 5 percent "goes straight through as pure profit."

Problem Set A

Problem 4A-1. Preparation of Financial Statements and End-of-Period Entries
(L.O. 4, 5, 7, 9)

Longbow Campgrounds rents one hundred campsites in a wooded park to campers. The Trial Balance and Adjusted Trial Balance columns of the work sheet for Longbow Campgrounds on May 31, the end of the current fiscal year, are presented below.

Longbow Campgrounds
Trial Balance and Adjusted Trial Balance
For the Year Ended May 31, 19xx

Account Name	Trial Balance Debit	Trial Balance Credit	Adjusted Trial Balance Debit	Adjusted Trial Balance Credit
Cash	2,040		2,040	
Accounts Receivable	3,660		3,660	
Supplies	774		114	
Prepaid Insurance	1,113		594	
Building	45,900		45,900	
Accumulated Depreciation, Building		7,500		10,500
Accounts Payable		1,650		1,725
Bonnie Higgins, Capital		46,535		46,535
Bonnie Higgins, Withdrawals	18,000		18,000	
Campsite Rentals		29,100		29,100
Wages Expense	11,100		11,100	
Insurance Expense	1,373		1,892	
Utility Expense	825		900	
	84,785	84,785		
Supplies Expense			660	
Depreciation Expense, Building			3,000	
			87,860	87,860

Required

1. From the information given, prepare an income statement, a statement of owner's equity, and a balance sheet.
2. From the information given, record the adjusting, closing, and, if required, reversing entries in the general journal.

Problem 4A-2. Preparation of Work Sheet, Adjusting, Closing, and Reversing Entries
(L.O. 2, 4, 5, 7, 9)

Ray Griffin opened his executive search service on April 1, 19xx. Some customers paid for his services after they were rendered, and others paid in advance for one year of service. After six months of operation, Ray wanted to know how he stood. The trial balance on September 30 appears below.

Griffin Executive Search Service
Trial Balance
September 30, 19xx

Cash	$ 713	
Prepaid Rent	1,800	
Office Supplies	413	
Office Equipment	3,750	
Accounts Payable		$ 2,513
Unearned Revenue		1,823
Ray Griffin, Capital		6,000
Ray Griffin, Withdrawals	3,600	
Search Revenue		5,070
Telephone and Utility Expense	630	
Wages Expense	4,500	
	$15,406	$15,406

Required

1. Enter the trial balance amounts in the Trial Balance columns of a work sheet and complete the work sheet using the following information:
   a. One year's rent was paid in advance when Ray began business.
   b. Inventory of unused supplies, $75.
   c. One-half year's depreciation on office equipment, $300.
   d. Service rendered that had been paid for in advance, $863.
   e. Executive search services rendered during the month but not yet billed, $270.
   f. Wages earned by employees but not yet paid, $188.
2. From the work sheet, prepare an income statement, a statement of owner's equity, and a balance sheet.
3. From the work sheet, prepare adjusting, closing, and, if required, reversing entries.
4. What is your evaluation of Ray's first six months in business?

Problem 4A-3. Completion of Work Sheet, Preparation of Financial Statements, Adjusting, Closing, and Reversing Entries
(L.O. 2, 4, 5, 7, 9)

The trial balance below was taken from the ledger of Farwell Package Delivery Company on August 31, the end of the company's accounting period.

Required

1. Enter the trial balance amounts in the Trial Balance columns of a work sheet and complete the work sheet using the following information:
   a. Expired insurance, $1,455.
   b. Inventory of unused delivery supplies, $675.
   c. Inventory of unused office supplies, $105.
   d. Estimated depreciation, building, $7,200.
   e. Estimated depreciation, trucks, $7,725.
   f. Estimated depreciation, office equipment, $1,350.
   g. The company credits the lockbox fees of customers who pay in advance to the Unearned Lockbox Fees account. Of the amount credited to this account during the year, $2,775 has been earned by August 31.
   h. There are $397 worth of accrued lockbox fees earned but unrecorded and uncollected at the end of the accounting period.
   i. There are $960 worth of accrued but unpaid truck drivers' wages at the end of the year.
2. Prepare an income statement, a statement of owner's equity, and a balance sheet.
3. Prepare adjusting, closing, and, if required, reversing entries from the work sheet.

Farwell Package Delivery Company
Trial Balance
August 31, 19xx

Cash	$ 4,028	
Accounts Receivable	14,122	
Prepaid Insurance	2,670	
Delivery Supplies	7,350	
Office Supplies	1,230	
Land	7,500	
Building	78,000	
Accumulated Depreciation, Building		$ 26,700
Trucks	51,900	
Accumulated Depreciation, Trucks		15,450
Office Equipment	7,950	
Accumulated Depreciation, Office Equipment		5,400
Accounts Payable		3,690
Unearned Lockbox Fees		4,170
Mortgage Payable		36,000
Louis Farwell, Capital		64,365
Louis Farwell, Withdrawals	15,000	
Delivery Services Revenue		121,200
Lockbox Fees Earned		14,400
Truck Drivers' Wages Expense	63,900	
Office Salaries Expense	22,200	
Gas, Oil, and Truck Repairs Expense	15,525	
	$291,375	$291,375

Problem 4A-4. The Complete Accounting Cycle: Two Months
(L.O. 1, 2, 4, 5, 7, 8)

On October 1, 19xx, Ruben Amoros opened Amoros Appliance Service and during the month completed the following transactions for the new company:

October 1 Deposited $3,000 of his savings in a bank account in the name of the company.
1 Paid the rent for a store for one month, $225.
1 Paid the premium on a one-year insurance policy, $360.
2 Purchased repair equipment from Hulett Company for $4,200 on the basis of $600 down payment and $300 per month for one year. The first payment is due November 1.
5 Purchased repair supplies from Fisk Company for $412 on credit.
8 Purchased an advertisement in a local newspaper for $60.
15 Cash repair revenue for the first half of the month, $300.
21 Paid $225 of the amount owed to Fisk Company.
25 Ruben Amoros withdrew $450 from the company bank account to pay living expenses.
31 Cash repair revenue for the second half of October, $675.

Required for October

1. Prepare journal entries to record the October transactions.
2. Open the following accounts: Cash (111); Prepaid Insurance (117); Repair Supplies (119); Repair Equipment (144); Accumulated Depreciation, Repair Equipment (145); Accounts Payable (212); Ruben Amoros, Capital (311); Ruben Amoros, Withdrawals (312); Income Summary (313); Repair Revenue (411); Store Rent Expense (511); Advertising Expense (512); Insurance Expense (513); Repair Supplies Expense (514); Depreciation Expense, Repair Equipment (515). Post the October journal entries to ledger accounts.
3. Prepare a trial balance in the Trial Balance columns of a work sheet, and complete the work sheet using the following information:
   a. One month's insurance has expired.
   b. Remaining inventory of unused repair supplies, $157.
   c. Estimated depreciation on repair equipment, $60.
4. From the work sheet, prepare an income statement, a statement of owner's equity, and a balance sheet for October.
5. From the work sheet, prepare and post adjusting and closing entries.
6. Prepare a post-closing trial balance.

During November Ruben Amoros completed the following transactions for the Amoros Appliance Service:

Nov. 1 Paid the monthly rent, $225.
1 Made monthly payment to Hulett Company, $300.
6 Purchased additional repair supplies on credit from Fisk Company, $863.
15 Cash repair revenue for the first half of the month, $863.
20 Purchased an additional advertisement in local newspaper, $60.
23 Paid Fisk Company on account, $600.
25 Ruben Amoros withdrew $450 from the company for living expenses.
30 Cash repair revenue for the last half of the month, $817.

Required for November

7. Prepare and post journal entries to record November transactions.
8. Prepare a trial balance in the Trial Balance columns of a work sheet and complete the work sheet based on the following information:

   a. One month's insurance has expired.
   b. Inventory of unused repair supplies, $413.
   c. Estimated depreciation on repair equipment, $60.
9. From the work sheet, prepare the November income statement, statement of owner's equity, and balance sheet.
10. From the work sheet, prepare and post adjusting and closing entries.
11. Prepare a post-closing trial balance.

Problem 4A-5. Preparation of Work Sheet from Limited Data
(L.O. 2, 4, 5)

Paul Matushek started work as an accountant with the Marysville Tennis Club on April 30, the end of the accounting period. His boss tells him that he must have an income statement and a balance sheet by 9:00 A.M. the next day in order to obtain a renewal of the bank loan. Paul takes home the general ledger and supporting data for adjusting entries. At 3:00 A.M., after completing the statements, he lights a cigarette and falls asleep. A few minutes later he awakes to find the papers on fire. He quickly puts out the fire but is horrified to discover that except for the general ledger and the income statement everything else, including the work sheet, supporting data, and balance sheet, is destroyed. He decides that he should be able to reconstruct the balance sheet and adjusting entries from the general ledger and the income statement, even though he had not yet recorded and posted the adjusting and closing entries. The information available is as follows:

General Ledger

Account	Debit	Credit
Cash	Bal. 10,800	
Supplies	Bal. 3,600	
Equipment	Bal. 78,000	
Accounts Payable		Bal. 150,000
Roger Dean, Capital		Bal. 235,575
Revenue from Court Fees		Bal. 336,750
Maintenance Expense	Bal. 25,800	
Water and Utility Expense	Bal. 30,900	
Prepaid Advertising	Bal. 2,550	
Land	Bal. 372,600	
Accumulated Depreciation, Equipment		Bal. 19,200
Unearned Revenue Locker Fees		Bal. 6,300
Roger Dean, Withdrawals	Bal. 27,000	
Wages Expense	Bal. 171,000	
Advertising Expense	Bal. 22,125	
Miscellaneous Expense	Bal. 3,450	

Required

1. Using the information above, fill in the Trial Balance and Income Statement columns of a work sheet.
2. Reconstruct the adjusting entries and complete the work sheet. Then record the adjusting entries in the general journal with explanations.
3. Prepare the statement of owner's equity and the balance sheet for April 30, 19xx.

Marysville Tennis Club
Income Statement
For the Period Ended April 30, 19xx

Revenues		
Revenue from Court Fees	$336,750	
Revenue from Locker Fees	4,800	
Total Revenues		$341,550
Expenses		
Wages Expense	$175,500	
Maintenance Expense	25,800	
Advertising Expense	19,875	
Water and Utility Expense	32,400	
Miscellaneous Expense	3,450	
Property Taxes Expense	11,250	
Supplies Expense	3,000	
Depreciation Expense, Equipment	6,000	
Total Expenses		277,275
Net Income		$ 64,275

Problem Set B

Problem 4B-1. Preparation of Work Sheet, Adjusting Entries, and Closing Entries (L.O. 2, 4, 5, 7, 9)

Arthur Hong began his law practice immediately after graduation from law school. To help him get started, several clients paid him retainers (payment in advance) for future services. Other clients paid when service was provided. After one year in practice, the law firm had the trial balance shown below.

Arthur Hong, Attorney
Trial Balance
December 31, 19xx

Cash	$ 2,750	
Accounts Receivable	2,109	
Office Supplies	382	
Office Equipment	3,755	
Accounts Payable		$ 796
Unearned Retainers		5,000
Arthur Hong, Capital		4,000
Arthur Hong, Withdrawals	6,000	
Legal Fees		17,575
Rent Expense	1,800	
Utility Expense	717	
Wages Expense	9,858	
	$27,371	$27,371

Required

1. Enter the trial balance amounts in the Trial Balance columns of a work sheet, and complete the work sheet using the following information:
   a. Inventory of unused supplies, $91.
   b. Estimated depreciation on equipment, $600.
   c. Services rendered during the month but not yet billed, $650.
   d. Services rendered to clients who paid in advance that should be applied against retainers, $2,900.
   e. Salaries earned by employees but not yet paid, $60.
2. Prepare an income statement, statement of owner's equity, and balance sheet.
3. Prepare adjusting, closing, and, if required, reversing entries.
4. How would you evaluate the first year of Mr. Hong's law practice?

Problem 4B-2. Preparation of Financial Statements and End-of-Period Entries
(L.O. 4, 5, 7, 9)

Harbor Trailer Rental owns thirty small trailers that are rented by the day for local moving jobs. The Trial Balance and Adjusted Trial Balance columns of the work sheet for Harbor Trailer Rental on June 30, 19xx, which is the end of the current fiscal year, appear below.

Harbor Trailer Rental
Trial Balance and Adjusted Trial Balance
For Year Ended June 30, 19xx

Account Name	Trial Balance Debit	Trial Balance Credit	Adjusted Trial Balance Debit	Adjusted Trial Balance Credit
Cash	692		692	
Accounts Receivable	972		972	
Supplies	385		119	
Prepaid Insurance	720		360	
Trailers	12,000		12,000	
Accumulated Depreciation, Trailers		4,800		7,200
Accounts Payable		271		271
Amy Rozema, Capital		5,694		5,694
Amy Rozema, Withdrawals	7,200		7,200	
Trailer Rentals		45,546		45,546
Wages Expense	23,200		23,400	
Insurance Expense	360		720	
Other Expenses	10,782		10,782	
	56,311	56,311		
Supplies Expense			266	
Depreciation Expense, Trailers			2,400	
Accrued Wages Payable				200
			58,911	58,911

Required

1. Prepare an income statement, statement of owner's equity, and balance sheet.
2. From the information given, record adjusting entries, closing entries, and, if required, reversing entries in the general journal.

Problem 4B-3. Completion of Work Sheet, Preparation of Financial Statements, Adjusting, Closing, and Reversing Entries
(L.O. 2, 4, 5, 7, 9)

At the end of the current fiscal year, the trial balance of the Fountain Theater appeared as follows:

Fountain Theater
Trial Balance
September 30, 19xx

Cash	$ 14,700	
Accounts Receivable	8,472	
Prepaid Insurance	9,800	
Office Supplies	280	
Cleaning Supplies	1,795	
Land	10,000	
Building	200,000	
Accumulated Depreciation, Building		$ 18,500
Theater Furnishings	185,000	
Accumulated Depreciation, Theater Furnishings		32,500
Office Equipment	15,800	
Accumulated Depreciation, Office Equipment		7,780
Accounts Payable		22,643
Gift Books Liability		20,950
Mortgage Payable		150,000
Judy Larson, Capital		156,324
Judy Larson, Withdrawals	30,000	
Ticket Sales		204,900
Theater Rental		22,600
Usher Wages Expense	92,000	
Office Wages Expense	12,000	
Utilities Expense	56,350	
	$636,197	$636,197

Required

1. Enter the trial balance amounts in the Trial Balance columns of a work sheet and complete the work sheet using the following information:
   a. Expired insurance, $8,900.
   b. Inventory of unused office supplies, $88.
   c. Inventory of unused cleaning supplies, $173.
   d. Estimated depreciation on building, $5,000.
   e. Estimated depreciation on theater furnishings, $18,000.
   f. Estimated depreciation on office equipment, $1,580.
   g. The company credits all gift books sold during the year to a Gift Books Liability account. Gift books are booklets of ticket coupons that are purchased in advance to give to someone. The recipient may then use the coupons to attend future movies. On September 30, it was estimated that $18,500 worth of the gift books had been redeemed.
   h. There are $410 worth of accrued but unpaid usher wages at the end of the year.
2. Prepare an income statement, a statement of owner's equity, and a balance sheet.
3. Prepare adjusting, closing, and, if required, reversing entries from the work sheet.

Problem 4B-4. The Complete Accounting Cycle: Two Months
(L.O. 1, 2, 4, 5, 7, 8)

During the two months of operation, the Santiago Bicycle Repair Store completed the following transactions:

May 1 Began business by depositing $5,000 in a company bank account.
1 Paid the premium on a one-year insurance policy, $360.
1 Paid one month's rent, $320.
2 Purchased repair equipment from Huleff Company for $1,900. The terms were $300 down payment and $100 per month for sixteen months. The first payment is due June 1.
5 Purchased repair supplies from Moreland Company for $195 on credit.
14 Paid utility expense for the month of May, $77.
15 Cash bicycle repair revenue for the first half of May, $481.
20 Paid $100 of the amount owed to Moreland Company.
29 Owner withdrew $400 from the company for personal living expenses.
31 Cash bicycle repair revenue for the last half of May, $566.

June 1 Paid the monthly rent, $320.
1 Made the monthly payment to Huleff Company, $100.
9 Purchased repair supplies on credit from Moreland Company, $447.
15 Cash bicycle repair revenue for the first half of June, $525.
18 Paid utility expense for June, $83.
19 Paid Moreland Company on account, $200.
28 Withdrew $400 from the company for personal living expenses.
30 Cash bicycle repair revenue for the last half of June, $436.

Required

1. Prepare journal entries to record the May transactions.
2. Open the following accounts: Cash (111); Prepaid Insurance (117); Repair Supplies (119); Repair Equipment (144); Accumulated Depreciation, Repair Equipment (145); Accounts Payable (212); Juan Santiago, Capital (311); Juan Santiago, Withdrawals (312); Income Summary (313); Bicycle Repair Revenue (411); Store Rent Expense (511); Utility Expense (512); Insurance Expense (513); Repair Supplies Expense (514); Depreciation Expense, Repair Equipment (515). Post the May journal entries to ledger accounts.
3. Prepare a trial balance for May in the Trial Balance columns of a work sheet, and complete the work sheet using the following information:
   a. One month's insurance has expired.
   b. Inventory of unused repair supplies, $86.
   c. Estimated depreciation on repair equipment, $25.
4. From the work sheet, prepare an income statement, a statement of owner's equity, and a balance sheet for May.
5. From the work sheet, prepare and post adjusting and closing entries for May.
6. Prepare a post-closing trial balance for May.
7. Prepare and post journal entries to record June transactions.
8. Prepare a trial balance for June in the Trial Balance columns of a work sheet, and complete the work sheet based on the following information:
   a. One month's insurance has expired.
   b. Inventory of unused repair supplies, $191.
   c. Estimated depreciation on repair equipment, $25.
9. From the work sheet, prepare the June income statement, statement of owner's equity, and balance sheet.
10. From the work sheet, prepare and post adjusting and closing entries for June.
11. Prepare a post-closing trial balance for June.

Problem 4B-5. Preparation of Work Sheet from Limited Data
(L.O. 2, 4, 5)

Presented below are the income statement and trial balance for Parkside Bowling Lanes for the year ending December 31, 19xx:

Parkside Bowling Lanes
Income Statement
For the Year Ended December 31, 19xx

Revenues		$618,263
Expenses		
Wages Expense	$381,076	
Advertising Expense	15,200	
Utility Expense	42,900	
Maintenance Expense	81,300	
Miscellaneous Expense	10,200	
Supplies Expense	1,148	
Insurance Expense	1,500	
Depreciation Expense, Building	4,800	
Depreciation Expense, Equipment	11,000	
Property Taxes Expense	10,000	
Total Expenses		559,124
Net Income		$ 59,139

Parkside Bowling Lanes
Trial Balance
December 31, 19xx

Cash	$ 14,187	
Accounts Receivable	7,388	
Supplies	1,304	
Unexpired Insurance	1,800	
Prepaid Advertising	900	
Land	5,000	
Building	100,000	
Accumulated Depreciation, Building		$ 19,000
Equipment	125,000	
Accumulated Depreciation, Equipment		22,000
Accounts Payable		14,317
Notes Payable		70,000
Unearned Revenues		2,300
Brad Holland, Capital		60,813
Brad Holland, Withdrawals	24,000	
Revenues		616,263
Wages Expense	377,114	
Advertising Expense	14,300	
Utility Expense	42,200	
Maintenance Expense	81,300	
Miscellaneous Expense	10,200	
	$804,693	$804,693

Required

1. Fill in the Trial Balance and Income Statement columns of a work sheet.
2. Reconstruct the adjusting entries and complete the work sheet. Assume that there is no adjustment to Accounts Receivable. Then record the adjusting entries in the general journal with explanations.
3. Prepare the statement of owner's equity and the balance sheet as of December 31, 19xx.

Financial Decision Case

Donna's Quik-Type
(L.O. 4)

Donna's Quik-Type is a very simple business. Donna provides typing services for students at the local university. Her accountant prepared the income statement below for the year ended August 31, 19x2.

In reviewing this statement, Donna is puzzled since she knows that she withdrew $8,400 in cash for personal expenses, and yet the cash balance in the company's bank account increased from $230 to $950 from last August 31 to this August 31. She wants to know how her net income could be less than the cash she took out of the business if there is an increase in the cash balance.

Her accountant shows her the balance sheet for August 31, 19x2, and compares it to the one for August 31, 19x1. He explains that besides the change in the cash balance, accounts receivable from customers decreased by $740, and accounts payable increased by $190 (supplies are the only items Donna buys on credit). The only other asset or liability account that changed during the year was accumulated depreciation on office equipment, which increased by $900.

Donna's Quik-Type
Income Statement
For the Year Ended August 31, 19x2

Revenues		
Typing Services		$10,490
Expenses		
Rent Expense	$1,200	
Depreciation Expense, Office Equipment	900	
Supplies Expense	480	
Other Expenses	620	
Total Expenses		3,200
Net Income		$ 7,290

Required

Explain to Donna why the accountant is answering Donna's question by pointing out year-to-year changes in the balance sheet. Verify the cash balance increase by preparing a statement that lists the receipts of cash and the expenditures of cash during the year. How did you treat depreciation expense? Why?

Answers to Self-Test

1. b	3. a	5. c	7. d	9. b
2. c	4. d	6. c	8. c	10. d

CALDWELL NEEDLES ANDERSON

PART TWO EXTENSIONS OF THE BASIC ACCOUNTING MODEL

Accounting, as you have seen, is an information system that measures, processes, and communicates information, primarily financial in nature, for decision making. Part One presented the principles and practices of the basic accounting system. In Part Two, the basic accounting system is extended to more complex applications.

Chapter 5 deals with accounting for merchandising companies, which is different in certain ways from the accounting for service companies you studied earlier.

Chapter 6 first describes the basic principles of internal control and then applies these principles to merchandising transactions.

CHAPTER 5 ACCOUNTING FOR MERCHANDISING OPERATIONS

LEARNING OBJECTIVES

1. Identify the components of merchandising income statement.
2. Journalize revenue transactions for merchandising concerns.
3. Calculate cost of goods sold.
4. Differentiate the perpetual and periodic inventory methods.
5. Journalize purchase transactions for merchandise.
6. Explain the objectives of handling merchandise inventory at the end of the accounting period and how they are achieved.
7. Prepare a work sheet for a merchandising concern under one of two alternative methods.
8. Prepare adjusting and closing entries for a merchandising concern.
9. Prepare a merchandising income statement and distinguish between multistep and single-step classified income statements.
10. Identify and describe the basic components of a classified balance sheet.

Up to this point, you have studied the accounting records and reports for the simplest type of business—the service company. In this chapter, you will study a more complex type of business—the merchandising company. This chapter focuses on the merchandising company's special buying and selling transactions and their effects on the income statement. After studying this chapter, you should be able to meet the learning objectives listed on the left.

Service companies such as advertising agencies or law firms perform a service for a fee or commission. In determining net income, a very simple income statement is all that is needed. Net income is measured as the difference between revenues and expenses.

In contrast, many other companies attempt to earn an income by buying and selling merchandise. Merchandising companies, whether wholesale or retail, use the same basic accounting methods as service companies, but the process of buying and selling merchandise requires some additional accounts and concepts. This process results in a more complicated income statement than that for a service business.

Income Statement for a Merchandising Concern

Exhibit 5-1 highlights the three major parts of the income statement for a merchandising concern: (1) revenues from sales, (2) cost of goods sold, and (3) operating expenses. Such an income statement differs from the income statement for a service firm in that gross margin from sales must be computed before operating expenses are deducted to arrive at net income.

Revenues from sales arise from sales of goods by the merchandising company and the **cost of goods sold** tells how much the merchant paid for the goods that were sold. The difference between revenues from sales and cost of goods sold is known as **gross margin from sales**, or simply **gross margin** To be successful, the merchant must sell the goods for enough more than cost—that is, gross margin from sales must be great enough—to pay operating expenses and have an adequate income left over. **Operating expenses** are those expenses, other than cost of goods sold, that are incurred in running the business. In a merchandising company, operating expenses are

Exhibit 5-1. The Parts of an Income Statement for a Merchandising Concern

Fenwick Fashions Company
Income Statement
For the Year Ended December 31, 19xx

Revenues from Sales	$239,325
Cost of Goods Sold	131,360
Gross Margin from Sales	$107,965
Operating Expenses	78,484
Net Income	$ 29,481

OBJECTIVE 1
Identify the components of income statements for merchandising concerns

similar to the expenses you have seen in a service company. **Net income** for merchandising companies is what is left after deducting operating expenses from gross margin. Note that Fenwick Fashions Company had a gross margin from sales of $107,965 ($239,325 – $131,360) and net income of $29,481 ($107,965 – $78,484).

All three parts of the merchandising income statement are important to a company's management. Management is interested both in the percentage of gross margin from sales and in the amount of gross margin (45 percent and $107,965, respectively, for the Fenwick Fashions Company). This information is helpful in planning business operations. For instance, management may try to increase total sales dollars by reducing the selling price. This strategy results in a reduction in the percentage of gross margin. It will work if total items sold increase enough to raise gross margin (which raises income from operations). On the other hand, management may increase operating expenses (such as advertising expense) in an effort to increase sales dollars and the amount of gross margin. If the increase in gross margin is greater than the increase in advertising, net income will improve. Other strategies, such as reducing cost of goods sold or operating expenses, may also be examined.

In this chapter, we discuss the three parts of the merchandising income statement and the transactions that give rise to the amounts in each part. Then we present two alternative methods for preparing the work sheet for a merchandising company. The chapter ends with a comprehensive illustration of the merchandising income statement.

Revenues from Sales

OBJECTIVE 2
Journalize transactions involving revenues for merchandising concerns

The first part of the merchandising income statement is revenues from sales, as presented in Exhibit 5-2. This section requires the computation of **net sales,** which consist of gross proceeds from sales of merchandise less sales returns and allowances and sales discounts. If a business is to

Exhibit 5-2. Partial Income Statement: Revenues from Sales

Fenwick Fashions Company
Partial Income Statement
For the Year Ended December 31, 19xx

Revenues from Sales		
Gross Sales		$246,350
Less: Sales Returns and Allowances	$2,750	
Sales Discounts	4,275	7,025
Net Sales		$239,325

succeed or even survive, net sales must be great enough to pay for cost of goods sold and operating expenses and to provide an adequate net income.

Management, investors, and others often consider the amount and trend of sales to be important indicators of a firm's progress. Increasing sales suggest growth, whereas decreasing sales indicate the possibility of decreased earnings and other financial problems in the future. Thus, to detect trends, comparisons are frequently made between net sales of different periods.

Gross Sales

Under accrual accounting, revenues from the sale of merchandise are considered to be earned in the accounting period in which the goods are delivered to the customer. **Gross sales** consist of total sales for cash and total sales on credit during a given accounting period. Even though the cash for the sale may not be collected until the following period, the revenue is recognized as being earned at the time of the sale. For this reason, there is likely to be a difference between revenues from sales and cash collected from those sales in a given period.

The Sales account is used only for recording sales of merchandise, whether the sale is made for cash or for credit. The journal entry to record a sale of merchandise for cash is as follows:

Sept. 16	Cash	1,286	
	Sales		1,286
	To record the sale of merchandise for cash		

If the sale of merchandise is made on credit, the entry is as follows:

Sept. 16	Accounts Receivable	746	
	Sales		746
	To record the sale of merchandise on credit		

Trade Discounts

In order to avoid reprinting catalogues and price lists every time there is a price change, some manufacturers and wholesalers quote prices of merchandise at a discount (usually 30 percent or more) off the list or catalogue price. Such discounts are called **trade discounts.** For example, the seller of an article listed at $1,000 with a trade discount of 40 percent, or $400, would record the sale at $600. The buyer would also record the transaction as a purchase of $600. The list price and related trade discounts are used only for the convenience of arriving at the agreed upon price and do not appear in the accounting records.

Sales Returns and Allowances

If a customer receives a defective or otherwise unsatisfactory product, the seller will usually try to accommodate the customer. The business may allow the customer to return the item for a cash refund or credit on account, or it may give the customer an allowance off the sales price. A good accounting system will provide management with information for determining the reason for sales returns and allowances because such transactions may reveal dissatisfied customers. Each return or allowance is recorded as a debit to an account called **Sales Returns and Allowances.** An example of such a transaction follows:

Sept. 17	Sales Returns and Allowances	76	
	Accounts Receivable (or Cash)		76
	To record return or allowance on unsatisfactory merchandise		

Sales Returns and Allowances is a contra account and is accordingly deducted from gross sales in the income statement (see Exhibit 5-2).

Sales Discounts

When goods are sold on credit, both parties should always have a definite understanding as to the amount and time of payment. These terms are usually printed on the sales invoice and constitute part of the sales agreement. Customary terms differ from industry to industry. In some industries, payment is expected in a short period of time such as ten days or thirty days. In these cases, the invoice may be marked "n/10" or "n/30" meaning that the amount of the invoice is due ten days or thirty days, respectively, after the invoice date. If the invoice is due ten days after the end of the month, it may be marked "n/10 eom."

Some industries give discounts for early payment, called **sales discounts.** This practice increases the seller's liquidity by reducing the amount of money tied up in accounts receivable. These terms may be stated on the invoice as 2/10, n/30 or 2/10, n/60. Terms of **2/10, n/30** mean the debtor may take a 2 percent discount if the invoice is paid within ten days of the invoice date. Otherwise, the debtor may wait thirty days and pay the full amount of the invoice without the discount.

Because it is not usually possible to know at the time of sale whether the customer will take advantage of the discount by paying within the discount period, sales discounts are recorded only at the time the customer pays. For example, assume that Fenwick Fashions Company sells merchandise to a customer on September 20 for $300 on terms of 2/10, n/60. At the time of sale the entry would be:

Sept. 20	Accounts Receivable	300	
	Sales		300
	To record sale of merchandise on credit, terms 2/10, n/60		

The customer may take advantage of the sales discount any time on or before September 30, which is 10 days after the date of the invoice. If he or she pays on September 29, the entry in Fenwick's records is:

Sept. 29	Cash	294	
	Sales Discounts	6	
	Accounts Receivable		300
	To record payment for Sept. 20 sale; discount taken		

At the end of the accounting period, the Sales Discounts account has accumulated all the sales discounts for the period. Because sales discounts reduce revenues from sales, they are considered a contra account and deducted from gross sales in the income statement (see Exhibit 5-2).

Cost of Goods Sold

OBJECTIVE 3
Calculate cost of goods sold

Cost of goods sold is an important concept. Every merchandising business has goods on hand that it holds for sale to customers. The amount of goods on hand at any one time is known as **merchandise inventory.** The cost of **goods available for sale** during the year is the sum of two factors—merchandise inventory at the beginning of the year plus net purchases during the year.

If a company were to sell all the goods available for sale during a given accounting period or year, the cost of goods sold would then equal goods that had been available for sale. In most cases, however, the business will have goods still unsold and on hand at the end of the year. To find the actual cost of goods sold, therefore, we must subtract the merchandise inventory at the end of the year from the goods available for sale.

The partial income statement in Exhibit 5-3 shows the cost of goods sold section for Fenwick Fashions Company. In this case, goods costing $179,660 were available and could have been sold because Fenwick started with $52,800 in merchandise inventory at the beginning of the year and purchased $126,860 in goods during the year. At the end of the year, $48,300 in goods were left unsold and should appear as merchandise

Exhibit 5-3. Partial Income Statement: Cost of Goods Sold

Fenwick Fashions Company
Partial Income Statement
For the Year Ended December 31, 19xx

Cost of Goods Sold				
Merchandise Inventory, January 1, 19xx			$ 52,800	
Purchases		$126,400		
Less: Purchases Returns and Allowances	$5,640			
Purchases Discounts	2,136	7,776		
		$118,624		
Freight In		8,236		
Net Purchases			126,860	
Goods Available for Sale			$179,660	
Less Merchandise Inventory, December 31, 19xx			48,300	
Cost of Goods Sold				$131,360

inventory on the balance sheet. When this unsold merchandise inventory is subtracted from the total available goods that could have been sold, the resulting cost of goods sold is $131,360, which should appear on the income statement.

To understand fully the concept of the cost of goods sold, it is necessary to examine merchandise inventory and net purchases.

Merchandise Inventory

The inventory of a merchandising concern consists of the goods on hand and available for sale to customers. For a grocery store, inventory would be made up of meats, vegetables, canned goods, and the other items a store of this type might have for sale. For a service station, it would be gasoline, oil, and automobile parts. Merchandising concerns purchase their inventories from wholesalers, manufacturers, and other suppliers.

The merchandise inventory on hand at the beginning of the accounting period is called the **beginning inventory**. Conversely, the merchandise inventory on hand at the end of the accounting period is called the **ending inventory**. As we have seen, beginning and ending inventories are used in calculating cost of goods sold on the income statement. Ending inventory appears on the balance sheet as an asset. It will become a part of cost of goods sold in a later period when it is sold. This year's beginning inventory, you will notice, was last year's ending inventory and appeared on last year's balance sheet.

Measuring Merchandise Inventory. Merchandise inventory is a key factor in determining cost of goods sold. Because merchandise inventory represents goods available for sale that are still unsold, there must be a method for determining both the quantity and the cost of these goods on hand. The two basic methods of accounting for the number of items in the merchandise inventory are the periodic inventory method and the perpetual inventory method.

OBJECTIVE 4
Differentiate the perpetual inventory method from the periodic inventory method

Under the **periodic inventory method**, the count of the physical inventory takes place periodically, usually at the end of the accounting period, and no detailed records of the physical inventory on hand are maintained during the period. Under the **perpetual inventory method**, records are kept of the quantity and, usually, the cost of individual items of inventory as they are bought and sold.

Cost of goods sold under the periodic inventory method is determined at the end of the accounting period in a manner similar to the method of accounting for supplies expense, with which you are already familiar. In the simplest case, the cost of inventory purchased is accumulated in a Purchases account. Then, at the end of the accounting period, the actual count of the physical inventory is deducted from the total of purchases plus beginning merchandise inventory to determine cost of goods sold. Under the perpetual inventory method, on the other hand, the cost of each item is debited to the Merchandise Inventory account as it is purchased. As items are sold, the Merchandise Inventory account is credited and the Cost of Goods Sold account is debited for the cost of the items sold. In this way the balance of the Merchandise Inventory account always equals the cost of goods on hand at a point in time, and the Cost of Goods Sold account equals total cost associated with items sold to that point in time.

Traditionally, the periodic inventory method has been used by companies that sell items of low value and high volume because of the difficulty and expense of accounting for the purchase and sale of each item. Examples of such companies are drugstores, automobile parts stores, department stores, discount companies, and grain companies. In contrast, companies that sell items of high unit value, such as appliances or automobiles, have tended to use the perpetual inventory method. This distinction between high and low unit value for inventory methods has blurred considerably in recent years because of the widespread use of the computer. Although the periodic inventory method is still widely used, use of the perpetual inventory method has increased greatly. For example, many grocery stores, which traditionally used the periodic inventory method, can now, through the use of electronic markings on each product, update the physical inventory as items are sold by linking their cash registers to a computer. This trend is evident in most industries.

The periodic inventory method for determining cost of goods sold is described in this chapter. The perpetual inventory method is discussed further in Chapter 8.

The Periodic Inventory Method. Most companies rely on an actual count of goods on hand at the end of an accounting period to determine ending inventory and, indirectly, the cost of goods sold. The procedure for determining the merchandise inventory under the periodic inventory method, can be summarized as follows:

1. Make a physical count of the merchandise on hand at the end of the accounting period.
2. Multiply the quantity of each type of merchandise by its unit cost.
3. Add the resulting costs of each type of merchandise together to obtain a total. This total is the ending merchandise inventory.

The cost of the ending merchandise inventory is deducted from goods available for sale to determine cost of goods sold. The ending inventory of one period is the beginning inventory of the next period. Entries are made as part of the closing process at the end of the period—to remove the beginning inventory (the last period's ending inventory) and to enter the ending inventory of the current period. These entries are the only ones made to the Inventory account during the period. Consequently, only on the balance sheet date and after the closing entries does the Inventory account represent the actual amount on hand. As soon as purchases or sales are made, the inventory figure becomes a historical amount and remains so until the new inventory is entered at the end of the next accounting period.

Taking the Physical Inventory. Making a physical count of all merchandise on hand at the end of an accounting period is referred to as **taking a physical inventory.** It can be a difficult task, since it is easy to omit items or to count them twice.

Merchandise inventory includes all salable goods owned by the concern regardless of where they are located. It includes all goods on shelves, in storerooms, in warehouses, and in trucks en route between warehouses and stores. It includes goods in transit from suppliers if title to the goods has passed to the merchant. Ending inventory does not include merchandise sold to customers but not delivered or goods that cannot be sold because they are damaged or obsolete. If the damaged or obsolete goods can be sold at a reduced price, they may be included in ending inventory at the reduced value.

The actual count is usually taken after the close of business on the last day of the fiscal year. Many companies end their fiscal year in a slow season to facilitate the taking of physical inventory. Retail department stores often end their fiscal year in January or February, for example. After hours, at night or on the weekend, employees count and record all items on numbered inventory tickets or sheets. Sometimes a store will close for all or part of a day for inventory taking. They follow established procedures to make sure that no items are missed. When the inventory tickets or sheets are completed, they are forwarded to the accounting office.

The accounting office checks to see that all numbered tickets and sheets are accounted for, and copies the information onto inventory ledgers. The appropriate unit costs are then entered and the computations made to determine ending merchandise inventory.

Net Purchases

Under the periodic inventory method, the **net purchases** consists of gross purchases less purchases discounts and purchases returns and allowances plus any freight charges on the purchases.

OBJECTIVE 5 Journalize transactions involving purchases of merchandise

Purchases. When the periodic inventory method is used, all purchases of merchandise for resale are debited to the Purchases account at the gross purchase price, as shown below.

Nov. 12	Purchases	1,500	
	Accounts Payable		1,500
	To record purchases of merchandise, terms 2/10, n/30		

The **Purchases** account, a temporary or nominal account, is used only for merchandise purchased for resale. Its sole purpose is to accumulate the total cost of merchandise purchased during an accounting period. Inspection of the Purchases account alone does not indicate whether the merchandise has been sold or is still on hand. Purchases of other assets such as equipment should be recorded in the appropriate asset account.

Purchases Returns and Allowances. For various reasons, a company may need to return merchandise acquired for resale. The firm may not have been able to sell the merchandise and may ask to return it to the original supplier. Or the merchandise may be defective or damaged in some way and may have to be returned. In some cases, the supplier may suggest that an allowance be given as an alternative to returning the goods for full credit. In any event, **purchases returns and allowances** form a separate account and should be recorded in the journal as follows:

Nov. 14	Accounts Payable	200	
	Purchases Returns and Allowances		200
	Return of damaged merchandise purchased on November 12		

Here, the purchaser receives "credit" (in the seller's accounts receivable) for the returned merchandise. Purchases Returns and Allowances is a contra account and is accordingly deducted from purchases in the income statement (see Exhibit 5-3). It is important that a separate account be used to record purchases returns and allowances because management needs the resulting information for decision-making purposes. It can be very costly to return merchandise for credit. There are many costs that cannot be recovered, such as ordering costs, accounting costs, sometimes freight costs, and interest on the money invested in the goods. Sometimes there are lost sales resulting from poor ordering or unusable goods. Excessive returns may call for new purchasing procedures or new suppliers.

Purchases Discounts. Merchandise purchases are usually made on credit and commonly involve **purchases discounts** for early payment. It is almost always worthwhile for the company to take a discount if offered. For example, the terms 2/10, n/30 offer a 2 percent discount for paying only twenty days early (the period including the eleventh and the thirtieth days). This is an effective interest rate of 36 percent (there are 18 twenty-day periods in a year) on a yearly basis. Most companies can borrow money for less than this rate. For this reason, management wants to know the amount of discounts taken, which form a separate account and are recorded as follows when the payment is made:

Nov. 22	Accounts Payable		1,300	
	Purchases Discounts			26
	Cash			1,274
	Paid the invoice of Nov. 12			
	Purchase Nov. 12	$1,500		
	Less return	200		
	Net purchase	$1,300		
	Discount: 2%	26		
	Cash	$1,274		

Like Purchases Returns and Allowances, Purchases Discounts is a contra account that is deducted from Purchases on the income statement. If a company is able to make only a partial payment on an invoice, most creditors will allow the company to take the discount applicable to the partial payment. The discount usually does not apply to freight, postage, or other charges that might appear on the invoice.

Good management of cash resources calls for both taking the discount and waiting as long as possible to pay. To accomplish these two objectives, some companies file invoices according to their due dates as they get them. Each day, the invoices due on that day are pulled from the file and paid. In this manner, the company uses cash as long as possible and also takes advantage of the discounts. A method commonly used to control these discounts is illustrated on pages 180–181.

Freight In. In some industries, it is customary for the supplier (seller) to pay transportation costs, charging a higher price to include them. In other industries, it is customary for the purchaser to pay transportation charges on merchandise. These charges, called **freight in** or **transportation in** should logically be included as an addition to purchases, but as in the case of purchases discounts, they should be accumulated in the Freight In account so that management can monitor this cost. The entry for the purchaser is as follows:

Nov. 12	Freight In	134	
	Cash (or Accounts Payable)		134
	Incurred freight charges on merchandise purchased		

Special terms designate whether the supplier or the purchaser is to pay the freight or transportation charges. **FOB shipping point** means that the supplier will place the merchandise "free on board" at the point of origin, and the buyer is responsible for paying the charges from that point. In addition, the title to the merchandise passes to the buyer at that point. If you have purchased a car, you know that if the sales agreement says "FOB Detroit," you must pay the freight from that point to where you are.

On the other hand, **FOB destination** means that the supplier is bearing the transportation costs to the destination. In this case, title remains with the supplier until the merchandise reaches its destination. The supplier normally prepays the amount. In rare cases, the buyer may pay the charges and deduct them from the invoice.

The effects of these special shipping terms are summarized below.

Shipping Term	Where Title Passes	Who Bears Cost of Transportation
FOB shipping point	At origin	Buyer
FOB destination	At destination	Seller

In some cases, the supplier pays the freight charges but bills the buyer for them by including them as a separate item on the sales invoice. When this occurs the buyer should still record the purchases and the Freight In in separate accounts. For example, assume an invoice for purchase of merchandise inventory totaling $1,890 included the cost of merchandise of $1,600, freight charges of $290, and terms of 2/10, n/30. The entry to record this transaction would be:

Nov. 25	Purchases	1,600	
	Freight In	290	
	Accounts Payable		1,890
	Purchased merchandise for $1,600; included in the invoice were freight charges of $290 and terms of 2/10, n/30		

If this invoice is paid within ten days, the purchases discount will be $32 ($1,600 × 2%), because the discount would not apply to the freight charges.

It is important not to confuse freight-in costs with freight-out or delivery costs. If you, as seller, agree to pay transportation charges on goods you have sold, this expense is a cost of selling merchandise, not a cost of purchasing merchandise, and is shown as an operating expense on the income statement.

Control of Purchases Discounts Using the Net Method

As noted in the earlier discussion of purchases discounts, it is usually worthwhile to pay invoices in time to qualify for the cash discount allowed for prompt payment. In fact, it is bad management not to take advantage of such discounts. The system of recording purchases initially at the gross purchase price, called the **gross method** and described on pages 178–179, has the disadvantage of telling management only about what discounts were taken, but not about the discounts that were not taken or, in other words, were "lost."

A procedure called the **net method** of recording purchases, which will identify the discounts that are lost, requires that purchases be recorded initially at the net price. Then, if the discount is not taken, a special account is debited for the amount of the lost discount. For example, suppose that a company purchases goods on November 12 for $1,500 with terms of 2/10, n/30 and that it returns $200 worth of merchandise on November 14. Suppose also that payment is not made until December 12, so the company is not eligible for the 2 percent discount. The entries to record these three transactions are as follows:

Date	Account	Debit	Credit
Nov. 12	Purchases	1,470	
	Accounts Payable		1,470
	To record purchases of merchandise at net price, terms 2/10, n/30; $1,500 − (.02 × $1,500) = $1,470		
Nov. 14	Accounts Payable	196	
	Purchases Returns and Allowances		196
	Return of damaged merchandise purchased on November 12; recorded at net price: $200 − (.02 × $200) = $196		
Dec. 12	Accounts Payable	1,274	
	Discounts Lost	26	
	Cash		1,300
	Paid invoice of Nov. 12		
	Purchase Nov. 12 $1,500		
	Less return Nov. 14 200		
	Net purchase $1,300		
	Discount lost: .02 × $1,300 = $26		

If the company pays by November 22 and uses the net method of recording purchases, it will make a payment of $1,274. Since purchases were recorded at net prices, no Discounts Lost account would be required. However, if the company makes the payment after the discount period, as illustrated, management learns of the failure to take the discount by examining the Discounts Lost account. The amount of discounts lost is shown as an operating expense on the income statement.

Inventory Losses

Many companies have substantial losses in merchandise inventory from spoilage, shoplifting, and employee pilferage. Management will, of course, want to take steps to prevent such losses from occurring, but if they do occur, under the periodic inventory method, these costs are automatically included in the cost of goods sold. For example, assume that a company lost $1,250 during an accounting period because merchandise had been stolen or spoiled. Thus, when the physical inventory is taken, the missing items will not be in stock and cannot be counted. Because the ending inventory will not contain these items, the amount subtracted from goods available for sale is less than it would be if the goods were in stock. Cost of goods sold, therefore, is greater by $1,250. In a sense, cost of goods sold is inflated by the amount of merchandise that has been stolen or spoiled. If the perpetual inventory method is used, it is easier to identify these types of losses because the loss then shows up as the difference between the inventory records and the physical inventory.

Operating Expenses

Operating expenses make up the third major part of the income statement for a merchandising concern. As noted earlier, they are the expenses, other than the cost of goods sold, that are necessary to run the business. It is customary to group operating expenses into useful categories. Selling expenses and general and administrative expenses are common categories. Selling expenses include all expenses of storing and preparing goods for sale; displaying, advertising, and otherwise promoting sales; making the sales; and delivering the goods to the buyer if the seller bears the cost of delivery. Among the general and administrative expenses are general office expenses, those for accounting, personnel, and credit and collections, and any other expenses that apply to the overall operation of the company. Although general occupancy expenses, such as rent expense and utilities expenses, are often classified as general and administrative, they are sometimes allocated or divided between the selling and the general and administrative categories on a basis determined by management.

Handling Merchandise Inventory at the End of the Accounting Period

OBJECTIVE 6
Explain the objectives of handling merchandise inventory at the end of the accounting period and how they are achieved

Recall that under the periodic inventory system, purchases of inventory are accumulated in the Purchases account. During the accounting period, no entries are made to the Merchandise Inventory account. Its balance at the end of the period, before adjusting and closing entries, is the same as it was at the beginning of the period. Thus its balance at this point represents beginning merchandise inventory. Recall also that the cost of goods sold is determined by adding beginning merchandise inventory to net purchases and then subtracting ending merchandising inventory. The objectives of handling merchandise inventory at the end of the period are to (1) remove the beginning balance from the Merchandise Inventory account, (2) enter the ending balance in the Merchandise Inventory account, and (3) enter these two amounts in the Income Summary account in such a way as to result in the proper calculation of net income. Using the figures for Fenwick Fashions, these objectives can be accomplished if the following effects on the Merchandise Inventory and Income Summary accounts are achieved:

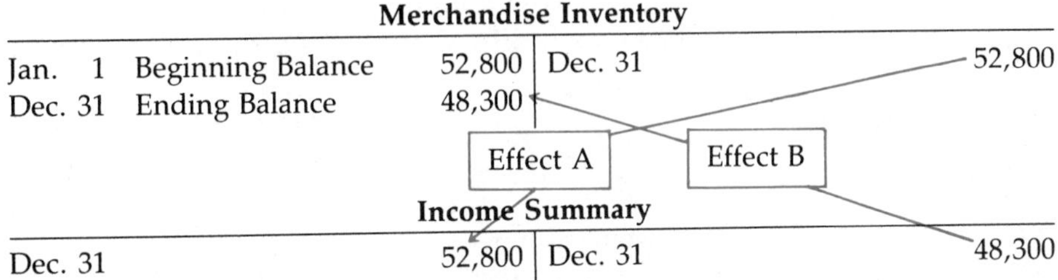

Merchandise Inventory
Jan. 1 Beginning Balance 52,800
Dec. 31 Ending Balance 48,300
Dec. 31 52,800
Effect A
Effect B
Income Summary
Dec. 31 52,800
Dec. 31 48,300

In this example, merchandise inventory was $52,800 at the beginning of the year and $48,300 at the end of the year. Effect A removes the $52,800 from Merchandise Inventory, leaving a zero balance, and transfers it to Income Summary. In Income Summary, the $52,800 is in effect added to net purchases because, like expenses, the balance of the Purchases account is debited to Income Summary by a closing entry. Effect B establishes the ending balance of Merchandise Inventory of $48,300 and enters it as a credit in the Income Summary account. The credit entry in Income Summary has the effect of deducting the ending inventory from goods available for sale because both purchases and beginning inventory are entered on the debit side. In other words, beginning merchandise inventory and purchases are debits to Income Summary and ending merchandise inventory is a credit to Income Summary.

Thus the objectives stated above are accomplished if effects A and B both occur. The question then arises as to how to achieve the effects. Two acceptable methods are available. They are the adjusting entry method and the closing entry method. Each method produces exactly the same result and only one of them would be used by a company. However, since practice varies in different regions of the country as to which method is most used, both are described here. The student should realize that both methods are simply bookkeeping techniques designed to deal with the Merchandise Inventory account under the periodic inventory system.

Using the adjusting entry method, the two entries indicated by effects A and B are prepared at the time the other adjusting entries are made, as follows:

Adjusting Entries

Dec. 31	Income Summary	52,800	
	Merchandise Inventory		52,800
	To remove beginning balance of Merchandise Inventory and transfer it to Income Summary		

Dec. 31	**Merchandise Inventory**	48,300	
	Income Summary		48,300
	To establish ending balance of Merchandise Inventory and deduct it from goods available for sale in Income Summary		

The closing entry method makes the debit and the credit to Merchandise Inventory by including them among the closing entries, as follows:

Closing Entries

Dec. 31	Income Summary	Total of credits	
	Merchandise Inventory		52,800
	Expenses and Other Income Statement Accounts with Debit Balances		Various amounts
	To close temporary expense and revenue accounts having debit balances and to remove beginning inventory		
Dec. 31	**Merchandise Inventory**	48,300	
	Revenues and Other Income Statement Accounts with Credit Balances	Various amounts	
	Income Summary		Total of debits
	To close temporary expense and revenue accounts having credit balances and to establish the ending merchandise inventory		

Notice that under both methods, Merchandise Inventory is credited for the beginning balance and debited for the ending balance and that the opposite entries are made to Income Summary.

Work Sheet of a Merchandising Concern

OBJECTIVE 7 Prepare a work sheet for a merchandising concern under one of two alternative methods

In Chapter 4, the work sheet was presented as a useful tool in preparing adjusting entries, closing entries, and financial statements. The work sheet of a merchandising business is basically the same as that of a service business except that it has to deal with the new accounts that are needed to handle merchandising transactions. These accounts include Sales, Sales Returns and Allowances, Sales Discounts, Purchases, Purchases Returns and Allowances, Purchases Discounts, Freight In, and Merchandise Inventory. Except for Merchandise Inventory, these accounts are treated in the records and on the work sheet much as revenue and expense accounts are for a service company. In the records, they are transferred to the Income Summary account in the closing process. On the work sheet, they are extended to the Income Statement columns.

The handling of merchandise inventory, however, depends on whether the adjusting entry method or the closing entry method is to be used. The student needs to learn only one of these methods because, as already noted, they are both acceptable and they accomplish the same objectives. The student should ask the instructor which method is to be used in this course.

The Adjusting Entry Method

The work sheet for Fenwick Fashions using the adjusting entry method is presented in Exhibit 5-4. Each pair of columns in the work sheet and the adjusting and closing entries are discussed below.

Trial Balance Columns. The first step in preparing the work sheet is to enter the balances from the ledger accounts into the Trial Balance columns. You are already familiar with this procedure.

Adjustments Columns. Under the adjusting entry method of handling merchandise inventory, the first two adjusting entries to be entered in the work sheet were explained in the previous section. The first entry transfers beginning merchandise inventory to the Income Summary account by crediting Merchandise Inventory and debiting Income Summary for $52,800 (adjustment a). The second entry establishes the ending merchandise inventory by debiting Merchandise Inventory and crediting Income Summary for $48,300 (adjustment b). Note that the Income Summary account is listed immediately below the trial balance totals. The remaining adjustments for Fenwick Fashions are familiar to you. They involve insurance expired during the period (adjustment c), store and office supplies used (adjustments d and e), and depreciation of building and office equipment (adjustments f and g). After the adjusting entries are entered on the work sheet, the Trial Balance columns are totaled to prove the equality of the debits and credits.

Omission of Adjusted Trial Balance Columns. Note that the two columns for the adjusted trial balance do not appear on the work sheet as they did when the work sheet for a service company was illustrated in Chapter 4. These columns are optional and are used when there are many adjusting entries to record. When only a few adjusting entries are required, as is the case for Fenwick Fashions, these columns are not necessary and may be omitted to save time.

Income Statement and Balance Sheet Columns. After the Trial Balance columns have been totaled, the adjustments entered, and the equality of the columns proved, the balances are extended to the statement columns. This process is accomplished most efficiently by beginning with the Cash account at the top of the work sheet and moving sequentially down the work sheet one account at a time. Each account balance is entered in the proper column of the income statement or balance sheet. The only exception to this rule is that both the debit (beginning merchandise inventory of $52,800) and the credit (ending merchandise inventory of

Exhibit 5-4. Work Sheet for Fenwick Fashions Company: Adjusting Entry Method

Fenwick Fashions Company
Work Sheet
For the Year Ended December 31, 19xx

Account Name	Trial Balance		Adjustments		Income Statement		Balance Sheet	
	Debit	Credit	Debit	Credit	Debit	Credit	Debit	Credit
Cash	29,410						29,410	
Accounts Receivable	42,400						42,400	
Merchandise Inventory	52,800		(b) 48,300	(a) 52,800			48,300	
Prepaid Insurance	17,400			(c) 5,800			11,600	
Store Supplies	2,600			(d) 1,540			1,060	
Office Supplies	1,840			(e) 1,204			636	
Land	4,500						4,500	
Building	20,260						20,260	
Accumulated Depreciation, Building		5,650		(f) 2,600				8,250
Office Equipment	8,600						8,600	
Accumulated Depreciation, Office Equipment		2,800		(g) 2,200				5,000
Accounts Payable		25,683						25,683
Joseph Fenwick, Capital		118,352						118,352
Joseph Fenwick, Withdrawals	20,000						20,000	
Sales		246,350				246,350		
Sales Returns and Allowances	2,750				2,750			
Sales Discounts	4,275				4,275			
Purchases	126,400				126,400			
Purchases Returns and Allowances		5,640				5,640		
Purchases Discounts		2,136				2,136		
Freight In	8,236				8,236			
Sales Salaries Expense	22,500				22,500			
Freight Out Expense	5,740				5,740			
Advertising Expense	10,000				10,000			
Office Salaries Expense	26,900				26,900			
	406,611	406,611						
Income Summary			(a) 52,800	(b) 48,300	52,800	48,300		
Insurance Expense, Selling			(c) 1,600		1,600			
Insurance Expense, General			(c) 4,200		4,200			
Store Supplies Expense			(d) 1,540		1,540			
Office Supplies Expense			(e) 1,204		1,204			
Depreciation Expense, Building			(f) 2,600		2,600			
Depreciation Expense, Office Equipment			(g) 2,200		2,200			
			114,444	114,444	272,945	302,426	186,766	157,285
Net Income					29,481			29,481
					302,426	302,426	186,766	186,766

$48,300) to Income Summary are extended to the corresponding columns of the income statement. The reason for this procedure is that both the beginning and ending inventory figures are needed to prepare the cost of goods sold section of the income statement.

After all the items have been extended into the proper statement columns, the four columns are totaled. The net income or net loss is determined as the difference in the debit and credit columns of the income statement. In this case, Fenwick Fashions has earned a net income of $29,481, which is extended to the credit column of the balance sheet. The four columns are then added to prove the equality of the debits and credits for the two pairs of columns.

OBJECTIVE 8
Prepare adjusting and closing entries for a merchandising concern

Adjusting Entries. The adjusting entries are now entered from the work sheet into the general journal and posted to the ledger as they would be in a service company. The only difference is that under the adjusting entry method, the two adjustments involving Merchandise Inventory and Income Summary, already illustrated on pages 183–184, appear among the adjusting entries.

Closing Entries. The closing entries for Fenwick Fashions under the adjusting entry method appear in Exhibit 5-5. These closing entries are very similar to those for a service company except that the new accounts for merchandising companies introduced in this chapter must also be closed to Income Summary. All income statement accounts with debit balances, including Sales Returns and Allowances, Sales Discounts, Purchases, and Freight In, are credited in the first entry. All income statement accounts with credit balances, including Sales, Purchases Returns and Allowances, and Purchases Discounts, are debited in the second entry. When copying the accounts and their balances out of the Income Statement columns of the work sheet, do not include the debit and credit to Income Summary, because these amounts are already in the Income Summary account as a result of the adjusting entries. The third and fourth entries are used to close the Income Summary account and transfer net income to the Capital account, and to close the Withdrawals account to the Capital account.

The Closing Entry Method

The work sheet for Fenwick Fashions using the closing entry method is presented in Exhibit 5-6. Each pair of columns in the work sheet and the adjusting and closing entries are discussed on the following pages.

Trial Balance Columns. The first step in the preparation of the work sheet is to enter the balances from the ledger accounts into the Trial Balance columns. You are already familiar with this procedure.

Adjustments Columns. Under the closing entry method of handling merchandise inventory, the adjusting entries for Fenwick Fashions are entered in the adjustments columns in the same way that they were for service companies. They involve insurance expired during the period

Exhibit 5-5. Closing Entries for a Merchandising Concern: Adjusting Entry Method

General Journal — Page 1

Date		Description	Post. Ref.	Debit	Credit
Dec.	31	Income Summary		220,145	
		Sales Returns and Allowances			2,750
		Sales Discounts			4,275
		Purchases			126,400
		Freight In			8,236
		Sales Salaries Expense			22,500
		Freight Out Expense			5,740
		Advertising Expense			10,000
		Office Salaries Expense			26,900
		Insurance Expense, Selling			1,600
		Insurance Expense, General			4,200
		Store Supplies Expense			1,540
		Office Supplies Expense			1,204
		Depreciation Expense, Building			2,600
		Depreciation Expense, Office Equipment			2,200
		To close temporary expense and revenue accounts having debit balances			
	31	Sales		246,350	
		Purchases Returns and Allowances		5,640	
		Purchases Discounts		2,136	
		Income Summary			254,126
		To close temporary expense and revenue accounts having credit balances			
	31	Income Summary		29,481	
		Joseph Fenwick, Capital			29,481
		To close the Income Summary account			
	31	Joseph Fenwick, Capital		20,000	
		Joseph Fenwick, Withdrawals			20,000
		To close the Withdrawals account			

Exhibit 5-6. Work Sheet for Fenwick Fashions Company: Closing Entry Method

Fenwick Fashions Company
Work Sheet
For the Year Ended December 31, 19xx

Account Name	Trial Balance		Adjustments		Income Statement		Balance Sheet	
	Debit	Credit	Debit	Credit	Debit	Credit	Debit	Credit
Cash	29,410						29,410	
Accounts Receivable	42,400						42,400	
Merchandise Inventory	52,800				52,800	48,300	48,300	
Prepaid Insurance	17,400			(a) 5,800			11,600	
Store Supplies	2,600			(b) 1,540			1,060	
Office Supplies	1,840			(c) 1,204			636	
Land	4,500						4,500	
Building	20,260						20,260	
Accumulated Depreciation, Building		5,650		(d) 2,600				8,250
Office Equipment	8,600						8,600	
Accumulated Depreciation, Office Equipment		2,800		(e) 2,200				5,000
Accounts Payable		25,683						25,683
Joseph Fenwick, Capital		118,352						118,352
Joseph Fenwick, Withdrawals	20,000						20,000	
Sales		246,350				246,350		
Sales Returns and Allowances	2,750				2,750			
Sales Discounts	4,275				4,275			
Purchases	126,400				126,400			
Purchases Returns and Allowances		5,640				5,640		
Purchases Discounts		2,136				2,136		
Freight In	8,236				8,236			
Sales Salaries Expense	22,500				22,500			
Freight Out Expense	5,740				5,740			
Advertising Expense	10,000				10,000			
Office Salaries Expense	26,900				26,900			
	406,611	406,611						
Insurance Expense, Selling			(a) 1,600		1,600			
Insurance Expense, General			(a) 4,200		4,200			
Store Supplies Expense			(b) 1,540		1,540			
Office Supplies Expense			(c) 1,204		1,204			
Depreciation Expense, Building			(d) 2,600		2,600			
Depreciation Expense, Office Equipment			(e) 2,200		2,200			
			13,344	13,344	272,945	302,426	186,766	157,285
Net Income					29,481			29,481
					302,426	302,426	186,766	186,766

(adjustment a), store and office supplies used (adjustments b and c), and depreciation of building and office equipment (adjustments d and e). No adjusting entry is made for merchandise inventory. After the adjusting entries are entered on the work sheet, the Trial Balance columns are totaled to prove the equality of the debits and credits.

Omission of Adjusted Trial Balance Columns. These two columns may be omitted from the work sheet. See the discussion under the adjusting entry method.

Income Statement and Balance Sheet Columns. After the Trial Balance columns have been totaled, the adjustments entered, and the equality of the columns proved, the balances are extended to the statement columns. This process is accomplished most efficiently by beginning with the Cash account at the top of the work sheet and moving sequentially down the work sheet one account at a time. Each account balance is entered in the proper column of the income statement or balance sheet.

The extension that may not be obvious is in the Merchandise Inventory row. The beginning inventory balance of $52,800 (which is already in the trial balance) is first extended to the debit column of the income statement, as illustrated in Exhibit 5-6. This procedure has the effect of adding beginning inventory to net purchases because the Purchases account is also in the debit column of the income statement. The ending inventory balance of $48,300 (which is determined by the physical inventory and is not in the trial balance) is then inserted in the credit column of the income statement. This procedure has the effect of subtracting the ending inventory from goods available for sale. Finally, the ending merchandise inventory ($48,300) is then inserted in the debit column of the balance sheet because it will appear on the balance sheet.

After all the items have been extended into the proper statement columns, the four columns are totaled. The net income or net loss is determined as the difference in the debit and credit columns of the income statement. In this case, Fenwick Fashions has earned a net income of $29,481, which is extended to the credit column of the balance sheet. The four columns are then added to prove the equality of the debits and credits for the two pairs of columns.

Adjusting Entries. The adjusting entries are now entered from the work sheet into the general journal and posted to the ledger as they would be in a service company. Under the closing entry method, there is no difference in this procedure between a service company and a merchandising company.

Closing Entries. The closing entries for Fenwick Fashions under the closing entry method appear in Exhibit 5-7. Note that Merchandise Inventory is credited in the first entry for the amount of beginning inventory ($52,800) and debited in the second entry for the amount of the ending inventory ($48,300), as shown on pages 183–184. Otherwise, these closing entries are very similar to those for a service company

Exhibit 5-7. Closing Entries for a Merchandising Concern: Closing Entry Method

General Journal — Page 1

Date		Description	Post. Ref.	Debit	Credit
Dec.	31	Income Summary		272,945	
		Merchandise Inventory			52,800
		Sales Returns and Allowances			2,750
		Sales Discounts			4,275
		Purchases			126,400
		Freight In			8,236
		Sales Salaries Expense			22,500
		Freight Out Expense			5,740
		Advertising Expense			10,000
		Office Salaries Expense			26,900
		Insurance Expense, Selling			1,600
		Insurance Expense, General			4,200
		Store Supplies Expense			1,540
		Office Supplies Expense			1,204
		Depreciation Expense, Building			2,600
		Depreciation Expense, Office Equipment			2,200
		To close temporary expense and revenue accounts having debit balances and to remove beginning inventory			
	31	Merchandise Inventory		48,300	
		Sales		246,350	
		Purchases Returns and Allowances		5,640	
		Purchases Discounts		2,136	
		Income Summary			302,426
		To close temporary expense and revenue accounts having credit balances and to establish the ending merchandise inventory			
	31	Income Summary		29,481	
		Joseph Fenwick, Capital			29,481
		To close the Income Summary account			
	31	Joseph Fenwick, Capital		20,000	
		Joseph Fenwick, Withdrawals			20,000
		To close the Withdrawals account			

except that the new accounts for merchandising companies introduced in this chapter must also be closed to Income Summary. All income statement accounts with debit balances, for instance, Sales Returns and Allowances, Sales Discounts, Purchases, and Freight In, are credited in the first entry. All income statement accounts with credit balances, namely, Sales, Purchases Returns and Allowances, and Purchases Discounts, are debited in the second entry. The third and fourth entries are used to close the Income Summary account and transfer net income to the Capital account and to close the Withdrawals account to the Capital account.

Income Statement Illustrated

OBJECTIVE 9
Prepare an income statement for a merchandising concern and distinguish between multistep and single-step classified income statements.

Earlier in this chapter, the parts of the income statement for a merchandising concern were presented and the transactions pertaining to each part were discussed. Exhibit 5-8 (page 193) pulls the parts together and shows the complete income statement for Fenwick Fashions Company. The statement may be prepared by referring to the accounts in the ledger that pertain to the income statement, or when a work sheet is prepared, the accounts and their balances may be taken from the Income Statement columns of the work sheet. For external reporting purposes, the income statement is usually presented in condensed form. **Condensed financial statements** present only the major categories of the financial statement. There are two common forms of the condensed income statement, the multistep form and the single-step form. The **multistep form**, illustrated in Exhibit 5-9, derives net income in the same step-by-step fashion as the detailed income statement for Fenwick Fashions Company in Exhibit 5-8 except that only the totals of significant categories are given. Usually some breakdown is shown for operating expenses such as the totals for selling expenses and for general and administrative expenses. Other revenues and expenses are also usually broken down. The **single-step form**, illustrated in Exhibit 5-10, derives net income in a single step by putting the major categories of revenues in the first part of the statement and the major categories of costs and expenses in the second part. Each of these forms has its advantages. The multistep form shows the components used in deriving net income, while the single-step form has the advantage of simplicity. About an equal number of large U.S. companies use each form in their public reports.

Classified Balance Sheet

So far in this book, balance sheets have listed the balances of accounts that fell in the categories of assets, liabilities, and owner's equity. Because even a fairly small company may have hundreds of accounts, simply

Exhibit 5-8. Income Statement for Fenwick Fashions Company

Fenwick Fashions Company
Income Statement
For the Year Ended December 31, 19xx

Revenues from Sales				
Gross Sales				$246,350
Less: Sales Returns and Allowances			$ 2,750	
Sales Discounts			4,275	7,025
Net Sales				$239,325
Cost of Goods Sold				
Merchandise Inventory, Jan. 1, 19xx			$ 52,800	
Purchases		$126,400		
Less: Purchases Returns and Allowances	$5,640			
Purchases Discounts	2,136	7,776		
		$118,624		
Freight In		8,236		
Net Purchases			126,860	
Goods Available for Sale			$179,660	
Less: Merchandise Inventory, Dec. 31, 19xx			48,300	
Cost of Goods Sold				131,360
Gross Margin from Sales				$107,965
Operating Expenses				
Selling Expenses				
Sales Salaries		$ 22,500		
Freight Out		5,740		
Advertising Expense		10,000		
Insurance Expense, Selling		1,600		
Store Supplies Expense		1,540		
Total Selling Expenses			$ 41,380	
General and Administrative Expenses				
Office Salaries Expense		$ 26,900		
Insurance Expense, General		4,200		
Office Supplies Expense		1,204		
Depreciation Expense, Building		2,600		
Depreciation Expense, Office Equipment		2,200		
Total General and Administrative Expenses			37,104	
Total Operating Expenses				78,484
Net Income				$ 29,481

Exhibit 5-9. Condensed Multistep Income Statement for Fenwick Fashions Company

Fenwick Fashions Company Income Statement For the Year Ended December 31, 19xx		
Revenues from Sales		$239,325
Cost of Goods Sold		131,360
Gross Margin from Sales		$107,965
Operating Expenses		
Selling Expenses	$41,380	
General and Administrative Expenses	37,104	
Total Operating Expenses		78,484
Net Income		$ 29,481

Exhibit 5-10. Condensed Single-Step Income Statement for Fenwick Fashions Company

Fenwick Fashions Company Income Statement For the Year Ended December 31, 19xx		
Revenues		
Net Sales		$239,325
Costs and Expenses		
Cost of Goods Sold	$131,360	
Selling Expenses	41,380	
General and Administrative Expenses	37,104	
Total Costs and Expenses		209,844
Net Income		$ 29,481

OBJECTIVE 10
Identify and describe the basic components of a classified balance sheet

listing these accounts by broad categories is not very helpful to a statement user. Setting up subcategories within the major categories will often make the financial statements much more useful. Investors and creditors often study and evaluate the relationships among the subcategories. When general-purpose external financial statements are divided into useful subcategories, they are called **classified financial statements.**

The balance sheet presents the financial position of a company at a particular time. The permanent accounts used by Fenwick Fashions Company are not diverse enough to merit a classified balance sheet. Consequently, in Exhibit 5-11, the classified balance sheet for another merchandising concern, Shafer Auto Parts Company, is shown. It has subdivisions that are typical of most companies in the United States. The subdivisions under owner's equity, of course, depend on the form of business.

Assets

The assets of a company are often divided into four categories: (1) current assets; (2) investments; (3) property, plant, and equipment; and (4) intangible assets. Some companies use a fifth category called other assets if there are miscellaneous assets that do not fall into any of the other groups. These categories are listed in the order of their presumed liquidity (the ease with which an asset can be converted into cash). For example, current assets are said to be more liquid than property, plant, and equipment.

Current Assets. The Accounting Principles Board has defined **current assets** in the following way:

> Current assets are defined as . . . cash or other assets that are reasonably expected to be realized in cash or sold during a normal operating cycle of a business or within one year if the operating cycle is shorter than one year.[1]

The normal operating cycle of a company is the average time that is needed to go from cash to cash. Cash is used to buy merchandise inventory, which is sold for cash or for a promise of cash (a receivable) if the sale is made on account (for credit). If the sales are on account, the resulting receivables must be collected before the cycle is completed.

The normal operating cycle for most companies is less than one year, but there are exceptions. Tobacco companies, for example, must cure the tobacco for two or three years before their inventory can be sold. The tobacco inventory is still considered a current asset because it will be sold within the normal operating cycle. Another example is a company that sells on the installment basis. The collection payments for a television set or stove may be as long as twenty-four or thirty-six months, but these receivables are still considered current assets.

Cash is obviously a current asset. Temporary investments, accounts and notes receivable, and inventory are also current assets because they are expected to be converted to cash within the next year or during the normal operating cycle of most firms. They are listed in the order of the ease of their conversion into cash. Accounting for these short-term assets is presented in Chapter 7.

Prepaid expenses, such as rent and insurance paid for in advance, and

1. Accounting Principles Board, *Statement of the Accounting Principles Board, No. 4* (New York: American Institute of Certified Public Accountants, 1970), par. 198.

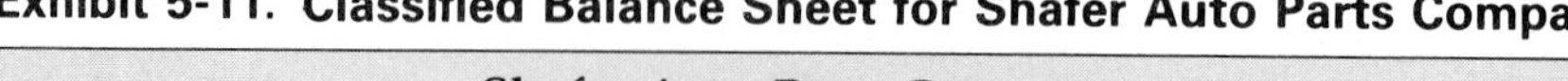

Exhibit 5-11. Classified Balance Sheet for Shafer Auto Parts Company

Shafer Auto Parts Company
Balance Sheet
December 31, 19xx

Assets			
Current Assets			
Cash		$10,360	
Short-Term Investments		2,000	
Notes Receivable		8,000	
Accounts Receivable		35,300	
Merchandise Inventory		60,400	
Prepaid Insurance		6,600	
Store Supplies		1,060	
Office Supplies		636	
Total Current Assets			$124,356
Investments			
Land Held for Future Use			5,000
Property, Plant, and Equipment			
Land		$ 4,500	
Building	$20,650		
Less Accumulated Depreciation	8,640	12,010	
Delivery Equipment	$18,400		
Less Accumulated Depreciation	9,450	8,950	
Office Equipment	$ 8,600		
Less Accumulated Depreciation	5,000	3,600	
Total Property, Plant, and Equipment			29,060
Intangible Assets			
Trademark			500
Total Assets			$158,916
Liabilities			
Current Liabilities			
Notes Payable	$15,000		
Accounts Payable	25,683		
Salaries Payable	2,000		
Total Current Liabilities		$42,683	
Long-Term Liabilities			
Mortgage Payable		17,800	
Total Liabilities			$ 60,483
Owner's Equity			
Fred Shafer, Capital			98,433
Total Liabilities and Owner's Equity			$158,916

inventories of various supplies bought for use rather than for sale should also be classified as current assets. These kinds of assets are current in the sense that, if they had not been bought earlier, a current outlay of cash would be needed to obtain them. They are an exception to the current asset definition presented earlier.[2]

In deciding whether or not an asset is current or noncurrent, the idea of "reasonable expectation" is important. For example, short-term investments represent an account used for temporary investments of idle cash or cash not immediately required for operating purposes. Management can reasonably expect to sell these securities as cash needs arise over the next year or operating cycle. Investments in securities that management does not expect to sell within the next year and that do not involve the temporary use of idle cash should be shown in the investments category of a classified balance sheet.

Investments. The **investments** category includes assets, generally of a long-term nature, that are not used in the normal operation of a business and that management does not plan to convert to cash within the next year. Items in this category are securities held for long-term investment, long-term notes receivable, land held for future use, plant or equipment not used in the business, and special funds such as a fund to be used to pay off a debt or buy a building. Also in this category are large permanent investments in another company for the purpose of controlling that company.

Property, Plant, and Equipment. The **property, plant, and equipment** category includes long-term assets that are used in the continuing operation of the business. They represent a place to operate (land and buildings) and equipment to produce, sell, deliver, and service its goods. For this reason, they are often called operating assets or sometimes fixed assets, tangible assets, or long-lived assets. We have seen earlier in the book that, through depreciation, the cost of these assets (except land) is spread over the periods they benefit. Past depreciation is recorded in the accumulated depreciation accounts. The exact order in which property, plant, and equipment are listed is not the same everywhere in practice. Assets not used in the regular course of business should be listed in the investments category, as noted above. Chapter 10 is devoted largely to property, plant, and equipment.

Intangible Assets. **Intangible assets** are long-term assets that have no physical substance but have a value based on rights or privileges that belong to the owner. Examples are patents, copyrights, goodwill, franchises, and trademarks. These assets are recorded at cost, which is spread over the expected life of the right or privilege. These assets are explained further in Chapter 10.

2. *Accounting Research and Terminology Bulletin,* Final Edition (New York: American Institute of Certified Public Accountants, 1961), p. 20.

Liabilities

Liabilities are divided into two categories: current liabilities and long-term liabilities.

Current Liabilities. The category called **current liabilities** is made up of obligations due within the normal operating cycle of the business or within a year, whichever is longer. They are generally paid from current assets or by incurring new short-term liabilities. Under this heading are notes payable, accounts payable, current portion of long-term debt, wages payable, taxes payable, and customer advances (unearned revenues). Current liabilities are presented in more detail in Chapter 9.

Long-Term Liabilities. Debts of a business that fall due more than one year ahead or beyond the normal operating cycle, or that are to be paid out of noncurrent assets are **long-term liabilities.** Mortgages payable, long-term notes, bonds payable, employee pension obligations, and long-term lease liabilities generally fall in this category. Long-term liabilities are presented in Chapter 14.

Owner's Equity

The terms *owner's equity, proprietorship, capital,* and *net worth* are used interchangeably. They all stand for the owner's interest in the company. The first three terms are felt to be better usage than *net worth* because most assets are recorded at original cost rather than at current value. For this reason, the ownership section will not represent "worth." It is really a claim against the assets.

The accounting treatment of assets and liabilities is not generally affected by the form of business organization. However, the owner's equity section of the balance sheet will be different depending on whether the business is a sole proprietorship, a partnership, or a corporation. The owners' equity accounts for partnerships are presented in Chapter 11 and those for corporations in Chapters 12 and 13.

Chapter Review

Review of Learning Objectives

1. **Identify the components of merchandising income statements.**
The merchandising company differs from the service company in that it attempts to earn a profit by buying and selling merchandise rather than by offering services. The income statement for a merchandising company has three major parts: (1) revenues from sales, (2) cost of goods sold, and (3) operating expenses. The cost of goods sold section is necessary for the computation of gross margin from sales made on the merchandise that has been sold. Merchandisers must sell their merchandise for more than cost to pay operating expenses and have an adequate profit left over.

2. **Journalize revenue transactions for merchandising concerns.**
Revenues from sales consist of gross sales less sales returns and allowances and sales discounts. The amount of the sales discount can be determined from the terms of the sale. Revenue transactions for merchandising firms may be summarized as follows:

	Related Accounting Entries	
Transaction	**Debit**	**Credit**
Sell merchandise to customer.	Cash (or Accounts Receivable)	Sales
Collect for merchandise sold on credit.	Cash (and Sales Discounts, if applicable)	Accounts Receivable
Permit customers to return merchandise or grant a reduction on original price.	Sales Returns and Allowances	Cash (or Accounts Receivable)

3. **Calculate cost of goods sold.**
To compute cost of goods sold, add beginning merchandise inventory to the net purchases to determine goods available for sale and then subtract ending merchandise inventory from the total.
Net Purchases are calculated by subtracting the purchases discounts and purchases returns and allowances from gross purchases and then adding any freight-in charges on the purchases. The Purchases account, which is used under a periodic inventory method, is debited only for merchandise purchased for resale. Its sole purpose is to accumulate the total cost of merchandise purchased during an accounting period.

4. **Differentiate the perpetual and periodic inventory methods.**
Merchandise inventory may be determined by one of two methods. (1) Under the perpetual inventory method, the balance of the inventory account is kept current throughout the year or as items are bought and sold. (2) Under the periodic inventory method, the company waits until the end of the accounting

period to take a physical inventory. Merchandise inventory includes all salable goods owned by the concern regardless of where they are located.

5. **Journalize purchase transactions for merchandise.**
   The transactions involving purchases under a periodic inventory method may be summarized as follows:

Transaction	Related Accounting Entries	
	Debit	Credit
Purchase merchandise for resale.	Purchases	Cash (or Accounts Payable)
Incur transportation charges on merchandise purchased for resale.	Freight In	Cash (or Accounts Payable)
Return unsatisfactory merchandise to supplier, or obtain a reduction from original price.	Cash (or Accounts Payable)	Purchases Returns and Allowances
Pay for merchandise purchased on credit.	Accounts Payable	Cash (and Purchases Discounts, if applicable)

6. **Explain the objectives of handling merchandise inventory at the end of the accounting period and how they are achieved.**
   At the end of the accounting period under a periodic inventory method, it is necessary to (1) remove the beginning balance from the Merchandise Inventory account, (2) enter the ending balance in the Merchandise Inventory account, and (3) enter these two amounts in the Income Summary account so the proper calculation of net income results. These objectives are accomplished by crediting Merchandise Inventory and debiting Income Summary for the beginning balance and debiting Merchandise Inventory and crediting Income Summary for the ending balance, as shown:

Inventory Procedures at End of Period	Related Accounting Entries	
	Debit	Credit
Transfer the balance of the beginning inventory to the Income Summary account.	Income Summary	Merchandise Inventory
Take a physical inventory of goods on hand at the end of the period, and establish the balance of ending inventory.	Merchandise Inventory	Income Summary

There are two ways of accomplishing these effects. Under the adjusting entry method, the entries are included among the adjusting entries. Under the closing entry method, the entries are included among the closing entries.

7. **Prepare a work sheet for a merchandising concern under one of two alternative methods.**
The major difference between preparing a work sheet for a merchandising concern and preparing one for a service company are the acccounts relating to merchandising transactions. The accounts necessary to compute cost of goods sold appear in the Income Statement columns. Merchandise inventory is treated differently under each of the following two methods:

Adjusting entry method: Under this method, Merchandise Inventory and Income Summary are adjusted in the Adjustments columns, the ending inventory is extended to the Balance Sheet debit column, and the two adjustments to Income Summary are extended to the Income Statement columns.

Closing entry method: Under this method, the beginning inventory from the trial balance is extended to the debit column of the Income Statement and the ending balance of Merchandise Inventory is inserted in the credit column of the Income Statement and the debit column of the Balance Sheet.

8. **Prepare adjusting and closing entries for a merchandising concern.**
The adjusting and closing entries for a merchandising concern are similar to those for a service business. The most unique feature is the handling of merchandise inventory, which is summarized under each of the two methods in the following table:

Method	Adjusting Entries	Closing Entries
Adjusting entry method	Dr. Income Summary Cr. Merchandise Inventory for amount of beginning inventory Dr. Merchandise Inventory Cr. Income Summary for the amount of ending inventory	Follow procedures for service companies
Closing entry method	Follow procedures for service companies	Include among closing entries the following: Dr. Income Summary Cr. Merchandise Inventory for amount of beginning inventory Dr. Merchandise Inventory for amount of ending inventory Cr. Income Summary

9. **Prepare a merchandising income statement and distinguish between multi-step and single-step classified income statements.**
The income statement of a merchandising company is constructed by displaying in each major section the individual parts of that section. The revenues from sales section will show gross sales, with contra sales accounts

deducted from them to arrive at net sales. The cost of goods sold section will show the accounts that make up goods available for sale. The operating expenses section will divide the expenses into useful categories such as selling expenses and general and administrative expenses. On the other hand, condensed multistep or single-step income statements may be used for external reporting purposes. The multistep form arrives at net income through a series of steps, whereas the single-step form arrives at net income in a single step. There is usually a separate section in the multistep form for other revenues and expenses.

10. **Identify and describe the basic components of a classified balance sheet.** The classified balance sheet is subdivided as follows:

Assets

Current Assets
Investments
Property, Plant, and Equipment
Intangible Assets

Liabilities

Current Liabilities
Long-Term Liabilities

Owner's Equity

(category depends on form of business)

Self-Test

Test your knowledge of the chapter by choosing the best answer for each item below.

1. A net income will always result if
   a. cost of goods sold exceeds operating expenses.
   b. revenues exceed cost of goods sold.
   c. revenues exceed operating expenses.
   d. gross margin from sales exceeds operating expenses.
2. A sale is made on June 1 for $200 on terms of 2/10, n/30 on which a sales return of $50 is granted on June 7. The dollar amount received for payment in full on June 9 is
   a. $200. b. $150. c. $147. d. $144.
3. If beginning and ending merchandise inventories are $400 and $700, respectively, and cost of goods sold is $3,400, net purchases are
   a. $3,700. b. $3,400. c. $3,100. d. Cannot be determined.
4. Under which of the following inventory methods would a wholesaler most likely know the exact quantity in inventory of a particular item on hand in the middle of a month?
   a. Periodic inventory method.
   b. Perpetual inventory method.
   c. Either the periodic or perpetual inventory method.
   d. Neither the periodic nor perpetual inventory method.
5. The entry to record the payment for a purchase of $1,000 under terms of 2/10, n/30 within the discount period on which a purchase return of $300 was made would include a credit to Cash for
   a. $980. b. $700. c. $686. d. $680.
6. A purchase of merchandise for $750 including freight of $50 under terms of 2/10, n/30, FOB shipping point would include
   a. a debit to Freight In of $50.
   b. a debit to Purchases of $750.
   c. a credit to Accounts Payable of $700.
   d. a credit to Freight Payable of $50.

7. Which of the following accounts can only result from using the net method of recorded purchases?
   a. Purchases Returns and Allowances.
   b. Discounts Lost.
   c. Purchase.
   d. Purchases Discounts.
8. Samuel's Company has beginning merchandise inventory of $12,000 and ending merchandise inventory of $14,000. Under the periodic inventory method the Merchandise Inventory account at the end of the accounting period would have the following balances, respectively, before and after adjusting and closing entries:
   a. $12,000 and $14,000.
   b. $14,000 and $12,000.
   c. $14,000 and $14,000.
   d. $12,000 and $12,000.
9. The closing entries for a merchandising concern would contain a debit to
   a. Sales Discounts.
   b. Purchases.
   c. Freight In.
   d. Purchases Discounts.
10. Which of the following would appear as an operating expense on the income statement of a merchandising concern?
   a. Freight In.
   b. Freight Out.
   c. Sales Returns and Allowances.
   d. Purchases Returns and Allowances.

Answers to Self-Test are at the end of this chapter.

Review Problem
Completion of Work Sheet, Preparation of Income Statement and Closing Entries for a Merchandising Concern

This chapter extends the basic accounting system to include the transactions necessary to handle merchandising transactions. The chapter contains a comprehensive illustration of the accounting for Fenwick Fashions Company. Instead of studying a review problem, you should carefully review and retrace the steps through the illustrations in the chapter. You need to focus only on the adjusting entry method or the closing entry method, depending on which method your school or instructor has chosen to follow.

Required

1. In Exhibit 5-4 (adjusting entry method) or Exhibit 5-6 (closing entry method), how are the merchandising accounts and merchandise inventory treated in the Adjustments columns and the Income Statement columns?
2. In Exhibit 5-5 (adjusting entry method) or Exhibit 5-7 (closing entry method), how do the closing entries relate back to the work sheet?
3. Trace the amounts in the detailed income statement in Exhibit 5-8 back to the Income Statement columns of the work sheet in Exhibit 5-6.

Chapter Assignments

Questions

1. What is the source of revenues for a merchandising concern?
2. Define gross margin from sales.
3. Kumler Nursery had a cost of goods sold during its first year of $64,000 and a gross margin from sales equal to 40 percent of sales. What was the dollar amount of the company's sales?
4. Could Kumler Nursery (in question **3**) have a net loss for the year? Explain.

5. Why is it advisable to maintain an account for sales returns and allowances when the same result could be obtained by debiting each return or allowance to the Sales account?
6. What is a sales discount? If the terms are 2/10, n/30, what is the length of the credit period? What is the length of the discount period?
7. What two related transactions are reflected in the T accounts below?

Cash

(b)	980		

Accounts Receivable

(a)	1,000	(b)	1,000

Sales

		(a)	1,000

Sales Discounts

(b)	20		

8. How much is the cash discount on a sale of $2,250 with terms of 2/10, n/60, on which a credit memo for $250 is issued prior to payment?
9. What is the normal balance of the Sales Discounts account? Is it an asset, liability, expense, or contra revenue account?
10. During the current year, Pruitt Corporation purchased $100,000 in merchandise. Compute the cost of goods sold under each of the following conditions.

	Beginning Inventory	Ending Inventory
a.	—	—
b.	—	$30,000
c.	$30,000	—
d.	28,000	35,000
e.	35,000	28,000

11. Compute cost of goods sold, given the following account balances: Beginning Inventory, $30,000; Purchases, $160,000; Purchases Returns and Allowances, $4,000; Purchases Discounts, $1,600; Freight In, $3,000; Ending Inventory, $25,000.
12. In counting the ending inventory, a clerk counts a $200 item of inventory twice. What effect does this error have on the balance sheet and income statement?
13. Hornberger Hardware purchased the following items: (a) a delivery truck, (b) two dozen hammers, (c) supplies for office workers, (d) a broom for the janitor. Which item(s) should be debited to the Purchases account?
14. What three related transactions are reflected in the T accounts below?

Cash

		(c)	441

Accounts Payable

(b)	50	(a)	500
(c)	450		

Purchases

(a)	500		

Purchases Returns and Allowances

		(b)	50

Purchases Discounts

		(c)	9

How would these transactions differ if the net method of recording purchases were used?

15. Is Freight In an operating expense? Explain.
16. Prices and terms are quoted from two companies on fifty units of product, as follows: Supplier A—50 at $20 per unit, FOB shipping point; Supplier B—50 at $21 per unit, FOB destination. Which supplier has quoted the best deal? Explain.
17. Does the beginning or ending inventory appear in the year-end unadjusted trial balance prepared by a company that uses the periodic inventory method?
18. Under the periodic inventory method, how is the amount of inventory at the end of the year determined?
19. What is your assessment of the following statement: "The perpetual inventory method is the best method because management always needs to know how much inventory it has"?
20. Why is the handling of merchandise inventory at the end of the accounting period of special importance to the determination of net income? What must be achieved in the accounting records in this regard for net income to be properly determined?
21. Explain how the multistep form of the income statement differs from the single-step form. What are the relative merits of each?
22. Name the two major categories of liabilities.

Classroom Exercises

Exercise 5-1. Computation of Net Sales (L.O. 2)

During 19xx, the Tri-City Corporation had total sales on credit of $160,000. Of this amount, $120,000 was collected during the year. In addition, the corporation had cash sales of $60,000. Furthermore, customers returned merchandise for credit of $4,000, and cash discounts of $2,000 were allowed. How much would net sales be for the Tri-City Corporation for 19xx?

Exercise 5-2. Parts of the Income Statement: Missing Data (L.O. 3, 9)

Compute the dollar amount of each item indicated by a letter in the table below. Treat each horizontal row of numbers as a separate problem.

Sales	Beginning Inventory	Net Purchases	Ending Inventory	Cost of Goods Sold	Gross Margin	Operating Expenses	Net Income (or Loss)
85,000	a	35,000	10,000	b	40,000	c	10,000
d	12,000	e	18,000	94,000	60,000	40,000	20,000
210,000	22,000	167,000	f	g	50,000	h	(1,000)
360,000	40,000	i	60,000	j	k	120,000	50,000

Exercise 5-3. Gross Margin from Sales Computation: Missing Data (L.O. 3)

Determine the amount of gross purchases by preparing a partial income statement showing the calculation of gross margin from sales, from the following data: Purchases Discounts, $2,500; Freight In, $11,000; Cost of Goods Sold, $175,000; Sales, $255,000; Beginning Inventory, $15,000; Purchases Returns and Allowances, $4,000; Ending Inventory, $10,000.

Exercise 5-4. Purchases and Sales Involving Discounts (L.O. 2, 5)

The Andujar Company purchased $3,400 of merchandise, terms 2/10, n/30, from the Bowa Company and paid for the merchandise within the discount period.

Give the entries (1) by the Andujar Company to record purchase and payment, assuming purchases are recorded at gross purchase price, and (2) by the Bowa Company to record the sale and receipt.

Exercise 5-5. Gross and Net Methods of Recording Purchases Contrasted (L.O. 5)

Empire Corporation purchases $7,800 of merchandise, terms 2/10, n/30, on June 10. Give the entries to record purchase and payment under each of the four assumptions below.

1. Purchases are recorded at gross amount, and payment is made June 20.
2. Purchases are recorded at gross amount, and payment is made July 10.
3. Purchases are recorded at net amount, and payment is made June 20.
4. Purchases are recorded at net amount, and payment is made July 10.

Exercise 5-6. Recording Purchases: Gross and Net Methods (L.O. 5)

Give the entries to record each of the following transactions first using the gross method and then using the net method:

1. Purchased merchandise on credit, terms, 2/10, n/30, FOB shipping point, $2,000.
2. Paid freight on shipment in transaction **1**, $50.
3. Purchased merchandise on credit, $1,200, terms 2/10, n/30 FOB destination.
4. Purchased merchandise on credit, terms 2/10, n/30, FOB shipping point, $2,600, including freight paid by supplier of $200.
5. Returned merchandise pertaining to transaction **3**, $500.
6. Paid the amount owed on the purchases in transactions **1** and **4**, respectively, within the discount periods.
7. Paid the amount owed on the purchase in transaction **3**, but not within the discount period.

Exercise 5-7. Preparation of Income Statement from Work Sheet (L.O. 9)

Selected items from the Income Statement columns of the December 31, 19xx, work sheet for Old Fort General Store appear below.

Account Name	Income Statement	
	Debit	**Credit**
Sales		304,000
Sales Returns and Allowances	11,000	
Sales Discounts	4,200	
Purchases	117,300	
Purchases Returns and Allowances		1,800
Purchases Discounts		2,200
Freight In	5,600	
Selling Expenses	48,500	
General and Administrative Expenses	37,200	

Beginning merchandise inventory was $26,000 and ending merchandise inventory is $22,000. Prepare a multistep income statement for the company. Then, prepare the income statement in condensed, single-step form.

Exercise 5-8. Preparation of Closing Entries (L.O. 8)

Using either the adjusting entry method or the closing entry method, prepare closing entries from the information given in Exercise 5-7, assuming that Old Fort General Store is owned by Clyde Silver and that he made withdrawals of $20,000 during the year.

Exercise 5-9. Preparation of Work Sheet (L.O. 7)

Simplified trial balance accounts and their balances follow in alphabetical order: Accounts Payable, $3; Accounts Receivable, $5; Accumulated Depreciation, Store Equipment, $6; Cash, $12; Freight In, $2; General Expense, $15; Merchandise Inventory (Beginning), $8; Doris Pran, Capital, $67; Doris Pran, Withdrawals, $12; Prepaid Insurance, $2; Purchases, $35; Purchases Returns and Allowances, $2; Sales, $77; Sales Discounts, $3; Selling Expenses, $22; Store Equipment, $30; Store Supplies, $9.

Prepare a work sheet form on accounting paper, and copy the trial balance accounts and amounts onto it in the same order as they appear above. Complete the work sheet, using either the adjusting entry method or the closing entry method and the following information: (a) estimated depreciation on store equipment, $3; (b) ending inventory of store supplies, $2; (c) expired insurance, $1; (d) ending merchandise inventory, $7.

Exercise 5-10. Classification of Accounts: Balance Sheet (L.O. 10)

The lettered items below represent a classification scheme for a balance sheet, and the numbered items are account titles. In the blank next to each account, write the letter indicating in which category it belongs.

a. Current assets
b. Investments
c. Property, plant, and equipment
d. Intangible assets
e. Current liabilities
f. Long-term liabilities
g. Owner's equity
h. Not on balance sheet

____ 1. Patent
____ 2. Building Held for Sale
____ 3. Prepaid Rent
____ 4. Wages Payable
____ 5. Note Payable in Five Years
____ 6. Building Used in Operations
____ 7. Fund Held to Pay Off Long-Term Debt
____ 8. Inventory
____ 9. Prepaid Insurance
____ 10. Depreciation Expense
____ 11. Accounts Receivable
____ 12. Interest Expense
____ 13. Revenue Received in Advance
____ 14. Short-Term Investments
____ 15. Accumulated Depreciation
____ 16. T. Parker, Capital

Exercise 5-11. Classified Balance Sheet Preparation (L.O. 10)

The following data pertain to a corporation: Cash, $22,500; Investment in Six-Month Government Securities, $14,600; Accounts Receivable, $38,000; Inventory, $40,000; Prepaid Rent, $1,200; Investment in Corporate Securities (long-term), $20,000; Land, $8,000; Building, $70,000; Accumulated Depreciation, Building, $14,000; Equipment, $152,000; Accumulated Depreciation, Equipment, $17,000; Copyright, $6,200; Accounts Payable, $51,000; Revenue Received in Advance, $2,800; Bonds Payable, $60,000; Common Stock—$10 par, 10,000 shares issued and outstanding, $100,000; Contributed Capital in Excess of Par Value, $50,000; Retained Earnings, $77,700.

Prepare a classified balance sheet.

Interpreting Accounting Information

Sears vs. K mart
(L.O. 1)

Sears, Roebuck and Company and K mart Corporation, the two largest retailers in the United States, have very different approaches to retailing. Sears operates a chain of full-service department stores, whereas K mart is known as a discounter. Selected information from their annual reports for the year ended in January 1983 is presented below. (All amounts are in millions and for Sears, only data for the Merchandise Group is shown.)

Sears: Net Sales, $25,089; Cost of Goods Sold, $15,692; Operating Expenses, $7,948; Ending Inventory, $3,617
K mart: Net Sales, $18,598; Cost of Goods Sold, $12,447; Operating Expenses, $4,578; Ending Inventory, $3,582

Required

1. Prepare a schedule computing gross margin from sales and net income (ignore income taxes) for both companies as dollar amounts and as percentages of net sales. Also, compute inventory as a percentage of cost of goods sold.
2. From what you know about the different retailing approaches of these two companies, do the gross margin and net income computations from **1** seem compatible with these approaches? What is it about the nature of K mart's operations that allows the company to earn less gross margin from sales and more net income in dollar amounts and in percentages than Sears?
3. Both Sears and K mart chose a fiscal year that ends on January 31. Why do you suppose they made this choice? How realistic do you think the inventory figures are as indicators of inventory levels during the rest of the year?

Problem Set A

Note: For Problems 5A-3 and 5A-5, the instructor should indicate whether students are to use the adjusting entry method or the closing entry method.

Problem 5A-1. Merchandising Transactions
(L.O. 2, 5)

Horner Company, which uses the periodic inventory method, engaged in the following transactions:

March 1 Purchased merchandise on credit from Jet Company, terms 2/10, n/30, FOB shipping point, $2,250.
1 Paid Baird Company $112 for shipping charges on merchandise received.
3 Sold merchandise on credit to Mark Ford, terms 2/10, n/60, $1,500.
6 Purchased merchandise on credit from Bell Company, terms 2/10, n/30, FOB shipping point, $4,800, including $300 freight costs paid by Bell.
7 Purchased merchandise on credit from Star Company, terms 1/10, n/30, FOB shipping point, $3,000.
7 Paid Baird Company $127 for shipping charges on merchandise received.
8 Purchased office supplies on credit from Hart Company, terms n/10, $1,200.
10 Sold merchandise on credit to Tony Pasqua, terms 2/10, n/30, $1,200.

11 Paid Jet Company for purchase of March 1.
12 Returned for credit $300 of damaged merchandise received from Star Company on March 7.
13 Received check from Mark Ford for his purchase of March 3.
16 Paid Bell Company for purchase of March 6.
19 Paid Star Company balance from transactions of March 7 and 12.
20 Received payment in full from Tony Pasqua for sale of March 10.
23 Paid Hart Company for purchase of March 8.
31 Sold merchandise for cash, $750.

Required

1. Prepare general journal entries to record the transactions, assuming purchases are recorded initially at the gross purchase price.
2. Which entries would differ if the purchases were recorded initially at net purchase price and discounts lost were recognized? What advantages does this method have?

Problem 5A-2. Income Statement for a Merchandising Concern
(L.O. 9)

At the end of the fiscal year, August 31, 19x2, selected accounts from the adjusted trial balance for Polly's Fashion Shop appeared as follows:

Sales		154,000
Sales Returns and Allowances	2,000	
Purchases	61,400	
Purchases Returns and Allowances		1,400
Purchases Discounts		1,200
Freight In	2,300	
Store Salaries Expense	32,625	
Office Salaries Expense	12,875	
Advertising Expense	24,300	
Rent Expense	2,400	
Insurance Expense	1,200	
Utility Expense	1,560	
Store Supplies Expense	2,880	
Office Supplies Expense	1,175	
Depreciation Expense, Store Equipment	1,050	
Depreciation Expense, Office Equipment	800	

In addition, merchandise inventory was $34,200 at the beginning of the year and $26,400 at the end of the year.

Required

1. Prepare a multistep income statement for Polly's Fashion Shop. Store Salaries Expense; Advertising Expense; Store Supplies Expense; and Depreciation Expense, Store Equipment, are considered to be selling expenses. The other expenses are considered to be general and administrative expenses.
2. Prepare the same income statement in condensed multistep form and in condensed single-step form.
3. Based on your knowledge at this point in the course, how might you use Polly's income statement to evaluate the company's profitability?

Problem 5A-3. Work Sheet, Income Statement, Balance Sheet, and Closing Entries for Merchandising Company
(L.O. 7, 8, 9)

The year-end trial balance below was taken from the ledger of Fontes Party Costumes Company at the end of its annual accounting period at June 30 19xx.

Cash	$ 5,050	
Accounts Receivable	24,830	
Merchandise Inventory	71,400	
Store Supplies	3,800	
Prepaid Insurance	4,800	
Store Equipment	51,300	
Accumulated Depreciation, Store Equipment		$ 24,300
Accounts Payable		38,950
Emilio Fontes, Capital		161,350
Emilio Fontes, Withdrawals	24,000	
Sales		373,250
Sales Returns and Allowances	4,690	
Sales Discounts	3,790	
Purchases	250,400	
Purchases Returns and Allowances		3,150
Purchases Discounts		2,900
Freight In	10,400	
Sales Salaries Expense	64,600	
Rent Expense	48,000	
Other Selling Expense	32,910	
Utilities Expense	3,930	
	$603,900	$603,900

Required

1. Enter the trial balance on a work sheet, and complete the work sheet using the following information: (a) ending merchandise inventory, $85,200; (b) ending store supplies inventory, $550; (c) expired insurance, $2,400; (d) estimated depreciation on store equipment, $5,000; (e) accrued sales salaries payable, $650; (f) accrued utilities expense, $100.
2. Prepare a multistep income statement and a classified balance sheet. Sales Salaries Expense; Other Selling Expense; Store Supplies Expense; and Depreciation Expense, Store Equipment, are to be considered selling expenses. The other expenses are to be considered general and administrative expenses.
3. From the work sheet, prepare closing entries.

Problem 5A-4. Journalizing Transactions of a Merchandising Company
(L.O. 2, 5)

Prepare general journal entries to record the following transactions, assuming that the periodic inventory method is used and that purchases are recorded initially at gross purchase price. Also, tell how the entries would differ if the net method of recording purchases were used.

June 1 Sold merchandise on credit to T. Linder, terms 2/10, n/60, FOB shipping point, $800.

2 Purchased merchandise on credit from World Company, terms 2/10, n/30, FOB shipping point, $6,400.

3 Received freight bill for shipment received on June 2, $450.

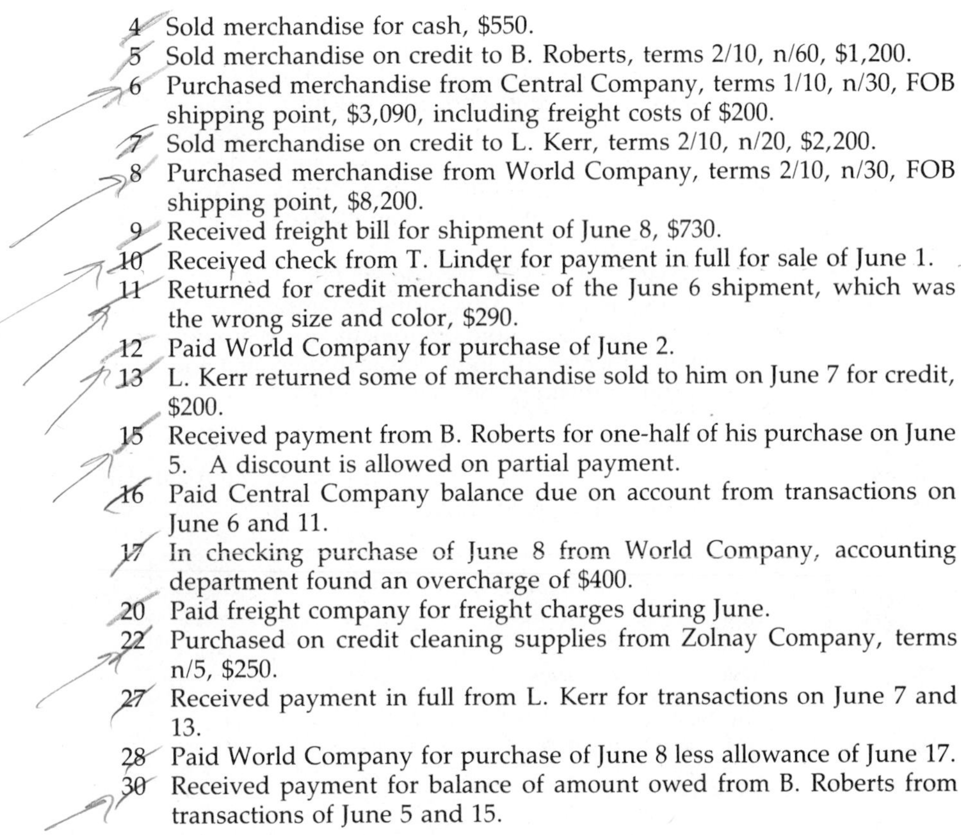

4 Sold merchandise for cash, $550.
5 Sold merchandise on credit to B. Roberts, terms 2/10, n/60, $1,200.
6 Purchased merchandise from Central Company, terms 1/10, n/30, FOB shipping point, $3,090, including freight costs of $200.
7 Sold merchandise on credit to L. Kerr, terms 2/10, n/20, $2,200.
8 Purchased merchandise from World Company, terms 2/10, n/30, FOB shipping point, $8,200.
9 Received freight bill for shipment of June 8, $730.
10 Received check from T. Linder for payment in full for sale of June 1.
11 Returned for credit merchandise of the June 6 shipment, which was the wrong size and color, $290.
12 Paid World Company for purchase of June 2.
13 L. Kerr returned some of merchandise sold to him on June 7 for credit, $200.
15 Received payment from B. Roberts for one-half of his purchase on June 5. A discount is allowed on partial payment.
16 Paid Central Company balance due on account from transactions on June 6 and 11.
17 In checking purchase of June 8 from World Company, accounting department found an overcharge of $400.
20 Paid freight company for freight charges during June.
22 Purchased on credit cleaning supplies from Zolnay Company, terms n/5, $250.
27 Received payment in full from L. Kerr for transactions on June 7 and 13.
28 Paid World Company for purchase of June 8 less allowance of June 17.
30 Received payment for balance of amount owed from B. Roberts from transactions of June 5 and 15.

Problem 5A-5. Work Sheet, Income Statement, and Closing Entries for a Merchandising Concern (L.O. 7, 8, 9)

A year-end trial balance for Hairston Sporting Goods Store appears below.

Hairston Sporting Goods Store
Trial Balance
May 31, 19xx

Cash	$ 5,340	
Accounts Receivable	6,322	
Merchandise Inventory	93,750	
Store Supplies	7,170	
Prepaid Insurance	5,400	
Store Equipment	151,800	
Accumulated Depreciation, Store Equipment		$ 41,100
Accounts Payable		53,670
Eddie Hairston, Capital		126,337
Eddie Hairston, Withdrawals	27,000	
Sales		984,600
Sales Returns and Allowances	8,100	
Purchases	702,375	
Purchases Returns and Allowances		12,375
Purchases Discounts		11,850
Freight In	4,800	
Rent Expense	39,000	
Store Salaries Expense	113,250	
Advertising Expense	56,655	
Utility Expense	8,970	
	$1,229,932	$1,229,932

Required

1. Copy the trial balance amounts into the Trial Balance columns of a work sheet, and complete the work sheet using the following information: (a) ending merchandise inventory, $85,170; (b) ending store supplies inventory, $870; (c) expired insurance, $2,700; (d) estimated depreciation on store equipment, $15,900; (e) during current year, rent paid through June of next year; amount debited to rent expense and applicable to June of next year, $1,800; (f) accrued store salaries, $375.
2. Prepare a multistep income statement for the sporting goods store. Store Salaries Expense; Advertising Expense; Store Supplies Expense; and Depreciation Expense, Store Equipment, are to be considered selling expenses. The other expenses are to be considered general and administrative expenses.
3. Prepare adjusting and closing entries.

Problem 5A-6. Classified Balance Sheet (L.O. 10)

Accounts from the March 31, 19xx post-closing trial balance of Ramos Hardware Company appear below.

Account Name	Debit	Credit
Cash	14,400	
Short-Term Investments	15,600	
Notes Receivable	4,000	
Accounts Receivable	138,000	
Merchandise Inventory	75,200	
Prepaid Rent	800	
Unexpired Insurance	2,400	
Sales Supplies	640	
Office Supplies	220	
Deposit for Future Advertising	1,840	
Building, Not in Use	24,800	
Land	11,200	
Delivery Equipment	20,600	
Accumulated Depreciation, Delivery Equipment		12,400
Franchise Fee	2,000	
Accounts Payable		53,720
Salaries Payable		2,600
Interest Payable		420
Long-Term Notes Payable		40,000
Carlos Ramos, Capital		202,560

Required

From the information provided, prepare a classified balance sheet.

Problem Set B

Note: For Problems 5B-3 and 5B-5, the instructor should indicate whether students are to use the adjusting entry method or the closing entry method.

Problem 5B-1. Merchandising Transactions (L.O. 2, 5)

Baines Company, which uses the periodic inventory method, engaged in the following transactions:

Oct. 1 Sold merchandise to Manuel Cruz on credit, terms 2/10, n/30, $800.

2 Purchased merchandise on credit from Driessen Company, terms 2/10, n/30, FOB shipping point, $1,800.
2 Paid Fast Freight $145 for freight charges on merchandise received.
6 Purchased store supplies on credit from Furillo Supply House, terms n/20, $318.
8 Purchased merchandise on credit from GR Company, terms 2/10, n/30, FOB shipping point, $1,200.
8 Paid Fast Freight $97 for freight charges on merchandise received.
9 Purchased merchandise on credit from BEZ Company, terms 2/10, n/30, FOB shipping point, $1,800, including $100 freight costs paid by BEZ.
11 Received full payment from Manuel Cruz for his October 1 purchase.
12 Paid Driessen Company for purchase of October 2.
13 Sold merchandise on credit to Archie Brown, terms 2/10, n/30, $600.
14 Returned for credit $300 of merchandise received on October 8.
19 Paid BEZ Company for purchase of October 9.
22 Paid GR Company for purchase of October 8 less return of October 14.
23 Received full payment from Archie Brown for his October 13 purchase.
26 Paid Furillo Supply House for purchase of October 6.

Required

1. Prepare general journal entries to record the transactions, assuming purchases are recorded initially at the gross purchase price.
2. Which entries would differ if the purchases were recorded initially at net purchase price and discounts lost were recognized? What advantages does this method have?

Problem 5B-2. Income Statement for a Merchandising Concern (L.O. 6)

The following data comes from Gene's Camera Store's adjusted trial balance at June 30, 19x3:

Sales		426,457
Sales Returns and Allowances	11,250	
Purchases	218,350	
Purchases Returns and Allowances		26,450
Purchases Discounts		3,788
Freight In	10,078	
Store Salaries Expense	107,550	
Office Salaries Expense	26,500	
Advertising Expense	18,200	
Rent Expense	14,400	
Insurance Expense	2,800	
Utility Expense	18,760	
Selling Supplies Expense	464	
Office Supplies Expense	814	
Depreciation Expense, Store Equipment	1,800	
Depreciation Expense, Office Equipment	1,850	

Gene's beginning merchandise inventory was $176,551, and the ending merchandise inventory is $182,657.

Required

1. Prepare a multistep income statement for Gene's Camera. Store Salaries Expense, Advertising Expense, Selling Supplies Expense, and Depreciation Expense, Store Equipment, are considered to be selling expenses. The other expenses are considered to be general and administrative.
2. Prepare the same income statement in condensed multistep form and in condensed single-step form.
3. Based on your knowledge at this point in the course, how might you use Gene's income statement to evaluate the company's profitability?

Problem 5B-3. Work Sheet, Income Statement, Balance Sheet, and Closing Entries for Merchandising Company (L.O. 7, 8, 9)

The following trial balance was taken from the ledger of Santo Book Store at the end of its annual accounting period:

Santo Book Store
Trial Balance
June 30, 19x2

Cash	$ 4,075	
Accounts Receivable	9,280	
Merchandise Inventory	29,450	
Store Supplies	1,911	
Prepaid Insurance	1,600	
Store Equipment	37,200	
Accumulated Depreciation, Store Equipment		$ 14,700
Accounts Payable		12,300
Ted Santo, Capital		41,994
Ted Santo, Withdrawals	12,000	
Sales		100,300
Sales Returns and Allowances	987	
Purchases	62,300	
Purchases Returns and Allowances		19,655
Purchases Discounts		1,356
Freight In	2,261	
Sales Salaries Expense	21,350	
Rent Expense	3,600	
Other Selling Expense	2,614	
Utilities Expense	1,677	
	$190,305	$190,305

Required

1. Enter the trial balance on a work sheet, and complete the work sheet using the following information: (a) ending merchandise inventory, $31,772; (b) ending store supplies inventory, $304; (c) unexpired insurance, $200; (d) estimated depreciation on store equipment, $4,300; (e) accrued sales salaries payable, $80; (f) accrued utilities expense, $150.
2. Prepare a multistep income statement and a classified balance sheet. Sales Salaries Expense; Other Selling Expense; Store Supplies Expense; and Depre-

ciation Expense, Store Equipment are to be considered selling expenses. The other expenses are to be considered general and administrative expenses.

3. From the work sheet, prepare closing entries.

Problem 5B-4. Journalizing Transactions of a Merchandising Company
(L.O. 2, 5)

Prepare general journal entries to record the following transactions, assuming that the periodic inventory method is used and that purchases are recorded at gross purchase price. Also, tell how the entries would differ if the net method of recording purchases were used.

Jan. 2 Purchased merchandise on credit from TEL Company, terms 2/10, n/30, FOB destination, $6,800.
3 Sold merchandise on credit to D. Thon, terms 1/10, n/30, FOB shipping point, $1,000.
5 Sold merchandise for cash, $700.
6 Purchased merchandise on credit from Reyes Company, terms 2/10, n/30, FOB shipping point, $4,200.
7 Received freight bill from Central Express for shipment received on January 6, $570.
9 Sold merchandise on credit to T. Bronson, terms 1/10, n/30, FOB destination, $3,800.
10 Purchased merchandise from TEL Company, terms 2/10, n/30, FOB shipping point, $2,650, including freight costs of $150.
11 Received freight bill from Central Express for sale to T. Bronson on January 9, $291.
12 Paid TEL Company for purchase of January 2.
13 Received payment in full for D. Thon purchase of January 3.
14 Returned faulty merchandise worth $300 to TEL Company for credit against purchase of January 10.
16 Paid Reyes Company one-half of the amount owed from purchase of January 6.
17 Sold merchandise to R. Chin on credit, terms 2/10, n/30, FOB shipping point, $780.
19 Received payment from T. Bronson for one-half of the purchase of January 9.
20 Paid TEL Company in full for amount owed on purchase of January 10 less return on January 14.
22 Gave credit to R. Chin for returned merchandise, $180.
26 Paid freight company for freight charges during January.
27 Received payment of amount owed by R. Chin from purchase of January 17 less credit of January 22.
28 Paid Reyes Company for balance of January 6 purchase.

Problem 5B-5. Work Sheet, Income Statement, and Closing Entries for a Merchandising Concern
(L.O. 7, 8, 9)

The year-end trial balance for Advincula's Shoe Store appears on page 216.

Required

1. Copy the trial balance amounts into the Trial Balance columns of a work sheet, and complete the work sheet using the following information: (a) ending merchandise inventory, $29,350; (b) ending store supplies inventory, $288; (c) expired insurance, $2,400; (d) estimated depreciation on store equipment, $8,800; (e) advertising expense includes $1,470 for January clearance sale

advertisements, which will begin appearing on January 2; (f) accrued store salaries, $320.

2. Prepare a multistep income statement for the shoe store. Store Salaries Expense, Advertising Expense, Store Supplies Expense, and Depreciation Expense, Store Equipment, are to be considered selling expenses. The other expenses are to be considered general and administrative expenses.
3. Prepare adjusting and closing entries.

Advincula's Shoe Store
Trial Balance
December 31, 19xx

Cash	$ 3,775	
Accounts Receivable	19,307	
Merchandise Inventory	26,500	
Store Supplies	951	
Prepaid Insurance	2,600	
Store Equipment	32,000	
Accumulated Depreciation, Store Equipment		$ 19,500
Accounts Payable		22,366
Cora Advincula, Capital		63,601
Cora Advincula, Withdrawals	15,000	
Sales		104,100
Sales Returns and Allowances	2,150	
Purchases	61,115	
Purchases Returns and Allowances		17,310
Purchases Discounts		1,300
Freight In	2,144	
Rent Expense	4,800	
Store Salaries Expense	41,600	
Advertising Expense	14,056	
Utility Expense	2,179	
	$228,177	$228,177

Problem 5B-6. Classified Balance Sheet (L.O. 10)

Accounts from the June 30, 19xx, post-closing trial balance of Bowie Hardware Company appear on page 217.

Required

From the information provided, prepare a classified balance sheet.

Account Name	Debit	Credit
Cash	20,400	
Short-Term Investments	11,350	
Notes Receivable	40,500	
Accounts Receivable	76,570	
Merchandise Inventory	156,750	
Prepaid Rent	2,000	
Prepaid Insurance	1,200	
Sales Supplies	426	
Office Supplies	97	
Land Held for Future Expansion	11,500	
Fixtures	72,400	
Accumulated Depreciation, Fixtures		21,000
Office Equipment	24,100	
Accumulated Depreciation, Office Equipment		10,250
Trademark	4,000	
Accounts Payable		107,945
Salaries Payable		787
Interest Payable		600
Notes Payable (due in three years)		36,000
Walter Bowie, Capital		244,711

Financial Decision Case

Jefferson Jeans Company
(L.O. 3)

In 19x1, Joseph "JJ" Jefferson opened a small retail store in a suburban mall. Called Jefferson Jeans Company, the shop sold designer jeans to rather well-to-do customers. JJ worked fourteen hours a day and was in control of all aspects of the operation. All sales were made for cash or bank credit card. The business was such a success that in 19x2, JJ decided to expand by opening a second outlet in another mall. Since the new shop needed his attention, he hired a manager for the original store to work with the two sales clerks who had been helping JJ in the store.

During 19x2, the new store was successful, but the operations of the original store did not match the first year's performance. Concerned about this turn of events, JJ compared the two years' results for the original store. The figures are as follows:

	19x1	19x2
Net Sales	$350,000	$325,000
Cost of Goods Sold	225,000	225,000
Gross Margin from Sales	$125,000	$100,000
Operating Expenses	50,000	75,000
Net Income	$ 75,000	$ 25,000

In addition, JJ's analysis revealed that the cost and selling price of jeans were about the same in both years and that the level of operating expenses was roughly the same in both years except for the $25,000 salary of the new manager. Sales returns and allowances were insignificant amounts in both years.

Studying the situation further, JJ discovered the following facts about cost of goods sold:

a. Gross purchases were $271,000 in 19x1 and $200,000 in 19x2.
b. Total purchases returns and allowances and purchases discounts were $20,000 in 19x1 and $15,000 in 19x2.
c. Freight in was $27,000 in 19x1 and $19,000 in 19x2.
d. The physical inventory for 19x1 revealed $53,000 on hand at the end of 19x1 and $32,000 on hand at the end of 19x2.

Still not satisfied, JJ went through all the individual sales and purchase records for the year. Both sales and purchases were verified. However, the 19x2 ending inventory should have been $57,000, given the unit purchases and sales during the year. After puzzling over all this information, JJ comes to you for accounting help.

Required

1. Using JJ's new information, recompute cost of goods sold for 19x1 and 19x2, and account for the difference in net income between 19x1 and 19x2.
2. Suggest at least two reasons that might have caused the difference. (Assume that the new manager's salary is proper.) How might JJ improve his management of the original store?

Answers to Self-Test

1. d	3. a	5. c	7. b	9. d
2. c	4. b	6. a	8. a	10. b

CHAPTER 6 INTERNAL CONTROL AND MERCHANDISING TRANSACTIONS

LEARNING OBJECTIVES

1. Define internal accounting control and state its four objectives.
2. State five attributes of an effective system of internal control.
3. Describe the inherent limitations of internal control.
4. Apply the attributes of internal control to the control of certain merchandising transactions.
5. Describe a bank account and prepare a bank reconciliation.
6. Describe and record the related entries for a simple petty cash system.
7. Describe the components of a voucher system.
8. State and perform the five steps in operating a voucher system.

Effective control is maintained in an accounting system through a network of checks and procedures known as internal control. This chapter is an introduction to the concept of internal control and its application to certain merchandising transactions including banking transactions and voucher system transactions. After studying this chapter, you should be able to meet the learning objectives listed on the left.

This chapter has five main parts. The first part presents the general principles and characteristics of internal control. In the second part, these principles are applied to certain merchandising transactions. The third and fourth parts explain the role of banking transactions and petty cash procedures in the control of cash. The fifth part describes the voucher system, a common means of controlling purchases and cash disbursements.

Internal Control: Basic Principles and Policies

Accounting for merchandising companies, as you have seen, focuses on buying and selling. These transactions involve asset accounts—cash, accounts receivable, and merchandise inventory—that are very vulnerable to theft and embezzlement. There are two reasons for this vulnerability. One is that cash and inventory are fairly easy to steal. The other is that these assets involve a large number of transactions—cash sales, receipts on account, payments for purchases, receipts and shipments of inventory, and so on. A merchandising company can have high losses of cash and inventory if it does not take steps to prevent them. The best way to do so is to set up and maintain a good system of internal control.

Internal Control Defined

Internal control is defined by the AICPA as

the plan of organization and all of the co-ordinate methods and measures adopted within a business to safeguard its assets, check the accuracy and reliability of its accounting data, promote operational efficiency, and encourage adherence to prescribed managerial policies.[1]

This is a broad definition. Clearly, a system of internal control goes beyond the matters directly related to the accounting function. In fact, there are two kinds of internal controls: internal accounting controls and internal administrative controls.

OBJECTIVE 1
Define internal accounting control and state its four objectives

Internal accounting controls are used mainly to protect assets and make sure of the accuracy and reliability of the accounting records. They include systems of authorization and the separation of recordkeeping duties from the duties of running a department or being the custodian of assets. They are aimed at helping to ensure that the following conditions are maintained:

a. Transactions are executed in accordance with management's general or specific authorization.
b. Transactions are recorded as necessary (1) to permit preparation of financial statements in conformity with generally accepted accounting principles . . . and (2) to maintain accountability for assets.
c. Access to assets is permitted only in accordance with management's authorization.
d. The recorded accountability for assets is compared with the existing assets at reasonable intervals and appropriate action is taken with respect to any differences.[2]

Internal administrative controls are controls that deal mainly with efficient operation and adherence to managerial policies. They are related to accounting controls in that they have to do with the decision processes leading to management's authorization of transactions. One form of internal administrative control is employee training programs that are intended to teach new employees the proper methods of authorization for handling purchases, sales, and so forth. Sometimes administrative and accounting controls overlap. That is, sales and cost records broken down by departments may be used in making management decisions as well as for accounting control. In the study of internal control, any control—either administrative or accounting—that is connected with transactions involving assets or accounting records is important.

Attributes of Internal Control

OBJECTIVE 2
State five attributes of an effective system of internal control

An effective system of internal control will have certain important attributes or qualities. These attributes are explained below.

Separation of Duties. The plan of organization should describe proper separation of functional responsibilities. Authorizing transactions, running a department, handling assets, and keeping the records of assets for the department should not be the responsibility of one person. In other words, separation of duties should mean that a mistake, honest or not, cannot be made without being seen by at least one other person.

1. *Professional Standards* (New York: American Institute of Certified Public Accountants, June 1, 1982), Vol. I, Sec. AU 320.09.
2. Ibid., Sec. AU 320.28.

Sound Accounting System. The systems of authorization and record keeping should offer good accounting control over assets, liabilities, revenues, and expenses. For records and procedures, there should be a system of routine and automatic checks and balances that should always be done exactly as prescribed. Independent checks should be made, and physical safeguards of assets should be used where possible.

Sound Personnel Policies. Sound practices should be followed in managing the people who carry out the duties and functions of each department. Among these practices are good supervision, rotation of key people in different jobs, insistence that employees take earned vacations, and bonding of personnel who handle cash or inventories. **Bonding** means carefully checking on an employee's background and insuring the company against any theft by that person.

Reliable Personnel. Personnel should be qualified to handle responsibilities, which means that employees must be well trained and well informed. It is clear that an accounting system, no matter how well designed, is only as good as the people who run it.

Regular Internal Review. The system should come under regular review. Large companies often have a staff of internal auditors who regularly review their company's system of internal control to see that it is working properly and that its procedures are being followed.

Limitations of Internal Control

OBJECTIVE 3
Describe the inherent limitations of internal control

No system of internal control is without certain weaknesses. As long as people must carry out control procedures, the internal control system is open to human error. Errors may arise because of misunderstanding of instructions, mistakes of judgment, carelessness, distraction, or fatigue. The separation of duties can be defeated through collusion—that is, when employees secretly agree to deceive the company. Also, procedures designed by management may be ineffective against management errors or dishonesty. In addition, controls that may have been effective at first may become ineffective because of changes in conditions.[3] In some cases, the costs of establishing and maintaining elaborate systems may exceed the benefits. In a small business, for example, active involvement by the owner may be a practical substitute for certain separation of duties.

Internal Control over Merchandising Transactions

Sound internal control procedures are needed in all aspects of a business, but particularly where assets are involved. Assets are especially vulnerable where they enter or leave the business. When sales are made, for example, cash or other assets enter the business, and goods or services

3. Ibid., Sec. AU 320.34.

OBJECTIVE 4 Apply the attributes of internal control to the control of certain merchandising transactions

leave the business. Procedures must be set up to prevent theft during these transactions. Likewise, purchases and payments of assets and liabilities must be controlled. The majority of these transactions can be safeguarded by adequate purchasing and payroll systems. In addition, assets on hand such as cash, investments, inventory, plant, and equipment must be protected.

In this and the following sections, internal control procedures will be applied to such merchandising transactions as sales, cash receipts, purchases, and cash payments. Internal control for other kinds of transactions will be covered at several points later in the book.

When a system of internal control is applied effectively to merchandising transactions, it can achieve some very important goals for both accounting and administrative controls. The accounting controls have two aims. They are

1. to prevent losses of cash or inventory from theft or fraud, and
2. to provide accurate records of merchandising transactions and account balances.

The administrative controls over merchandising transactions have three goals. They are

1. to keep just enough inventory on hand to sell to customers without overstocking,
2. to keep enough cash on hand to pay for purchases in time to receive purchases discounts, and
3. to keep credit losses as low as possible by restricting credit sales to those customers who are likely to pay on time.

An example of an administrative control is the cash budget, which projects future cash receipts and disbursements. By maintaining adequate cash balances, the company is able to take advantage of discounts on purchases, prepare for borrowing money when necessary, and avoid the embarrassing and possibly damaging effects of not being able to pay bills when they are due. On the other hand, if the company has more cash at a particular time than it needs, this cash can be invested, earning interest, until it is needed.

An example of an accounting control is the separation of duties involving the control of cash. This separation means that theft without detection is impossible except through the collusion of two or more employees. The subdivision of duties is easier in large businesses than in small ones, where one person may have to carry out several duties. The effectiveness of internal control over cash will vary depending on the size and nature of the company. Most firms, however, should use the following procedures:

1. The functions of recordkeeping and the custodianship of cash should be kept separate.
2. The number of persons who have access to cash should be limited.
3. Persons who are to have responsibility for handling cash should be specifically designated.
4. Banking facilities should be used as much as possible, and the amount of cash on hand should be kept to a minimum.

5. All employees having access to cash should be bonded.
6. Cash on hand should be protected physically by the use of such devices as cash registers, cashiers' cages, and safes.
7. Surprise audits of cash on hand should be made by a person who does not handle or record cash.
8. All cash receipts should be recorded promptly.
9. All cash receipts should be deposited promptly.
10. All cash payments should be made by check.

Note that each of the above procedures helps to safeguard cash by making it more difficult for any one person to have access to cash and to steal or misuse it undetected. These procedures may be specifically related to the control of cash receipts and cash disbursements.

Control of Cash Sales Receipts

Cash receipts for sales of goods and services may be received by mail or over the counter in the form of checks or currency. Whatever the source, cash receipts should be recorded immediately upon receipt. This is generally done by making an entry in a cash receipts journal. As shown in the last chapter, this step establishes a written record of the receipt of cash and should prevent errors and make theft more difficult.

Control of Cash Receipts Received Through the Mail. Cash that comes in through the mail should be handled by two or more employees. The employee who opens the mail should make a list in triplicate of the money received. This list should contain each sender's name, the purpose for which the money was sent, and the amount. One copy goes with the cash to the cashier, who deposits the money. The second copy goes to the accounting department to be recorded in the cash receipts journal. The person who opens the mail keeps the third copy of the list. Errors can be caught easily because the amount deposited by the cashier must agree with the amount received and the amount recorded in the cash receipts journal.

Control of Cash Sales Received over the Counter. Two common means of controlling cash sales are through the use of cash registers and prenumbered sales tickets. Amounts from cash sales should be rung up on a cash register at the time of each sale. The cash register should be placed so that the customer can see the amount recorded. Each cash register should have a locked-in tape on which it prints the day's transactions. At the end of the day, the cashier counts the cash in the cash register and turns it in to the cashier's office. Another employee takes the tape out of the cash register and records the cash receipts for the day in the cash receipts journal. The amount of cash turned in and the amount recorded on the tape should be in agreement; if not, any differences should be accounted for. Large retail chains commonly perform this function by having each cash register tied directly into a computer. In this way each transaction is recorded as it occurs. The separation of duties involving cash receipts, cash deposits, and record keeping is thus achieved, ensuring good internal control.

In some stores, internal control is strengthened further by the use of prenumbered sales tickets and a central cash register or cashier's office, where all sales are rung up and collected by a person who does not participate in the sale. Under this procedure, the salesperson completes a prenumbered sales ticket at the time of sale, giving one copy to the customer and keeping a copy. At the end of the day, all sales tickets must be accounted for, and the sales total computed from the sales tickets should equal the total sales recorded on the cash register.

Cash Short or Over. When there are numerous transactions involving cash receipts, small mistakes are bound to occur. For example, cash registers in grocery and retail stores will often have a cash shortage or overage at the end of the day. When the shortages are consistent or large, they should, of course, be investigated. If at the end of a day a cash register shows recorded cash sales of $675 but contains only $670 in cash, the following entry would record the sales:

Cash	670	
Cash Short or Over	5	
Sales		675
To record cash sales; a cash shortage of $5 was found		

The **Cash Short or Over** account is debited with shortages and credited with overages. The use of a separate account to record cash short or over calls management's attention to irregular activity. If at the end of an accounting period a debit balance appears in Cash Short or Over, it would be reported as a general operating expense on the income statement. A credit balance would be reported as other revenue.

Control of Purchases and Cash Disbursements

Cash disbursements are very vulnerable to fraud and embezzlement. In a recent and notable case, the treasurer of one of the nation's largest jewelry retailers was charged with having stolen over one-half million dollars by systematically overpaying federal income taxes and pocketing the refund checks as they came back to the company.

To avoid this kind of theft, cash should be paid only on the basis of specific authorization that is supported by documents establishing the validity and amount of the claim. In addition, maximum possible use should be made of the principle of separation of duties in the purchase of goods and services and the payments for them. Figure 6-1 shows how this kind of control can be achieved. In this example, five internal units (the requesting department, the purchasing department, the accounting department, the receiving department, and the treasurer) and two external companies (the supplier and the bank) all play a role in the internal control plan. Note that business documents also play an important role in the plan. The plan is summarized in Table 6-1. Under this plan, every action is documented and subject to verification

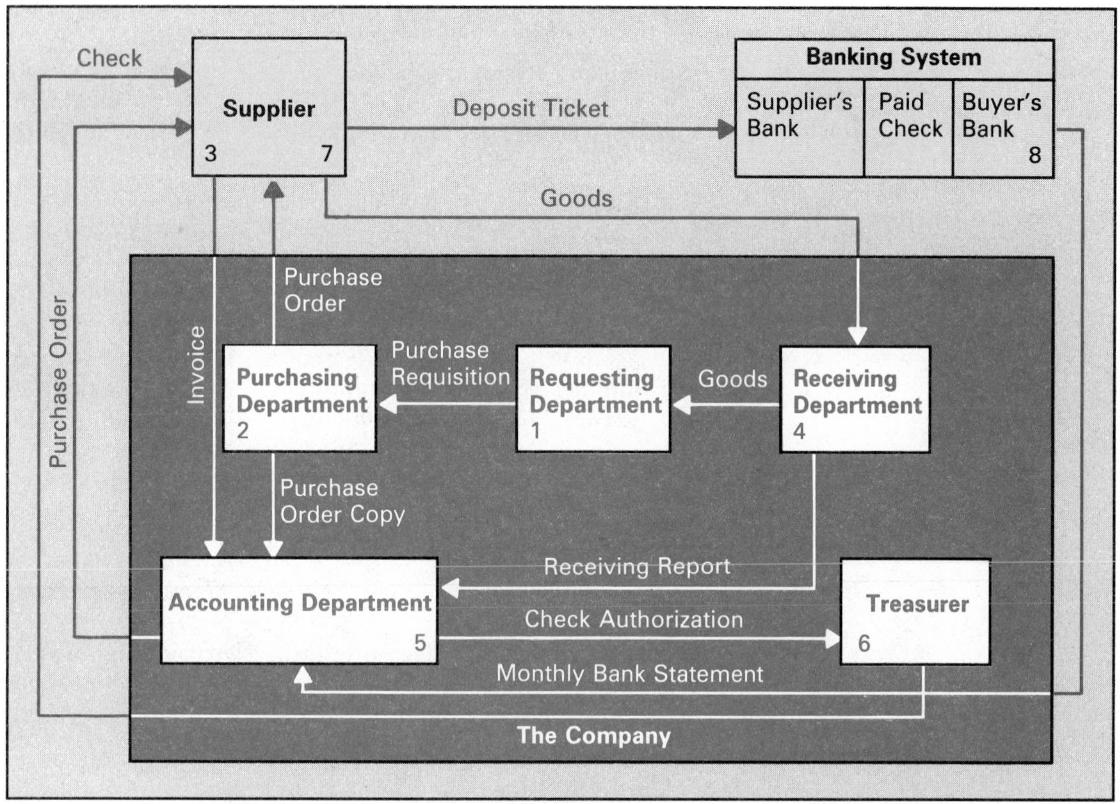

Figure 6-1. Internal Control for Purchasing and Paying for Goods and Services

by at least one other person. For instance, the requesting department cannot work out a kickback scheme with the supplier because the receiving department independently records receipts and the accounting department verifies prices. The receiving department cannot steal goods because the receiving report must equal the invoices. For the same reason, the supplier cannot bill for more goods than were shipped. The accounting department's work is verified by the treasurer, and the treasurer is ultimately checked by the accounting department.

Figures 6-2 through 6-6, which show typical documents used in this plan, serve as a concrete example involving the purchase of twenty boxes of typewriter ribbons. In Figure 6-2 (page 227) the credit office of Martin Maintenance fills out a **purchase requisition** for twenty boxes of typewriter ribbons. The department head approves it and forwards it to the purchasing department. The people in the purchasing department who carry out the purchasing activity prepare a **purchase order** as illustrated in Figure 6-3 (page 227). The purchase order is addressed to the vendor (seller) and contains a description of the items ordered; their expected price, terms, and shipping date; and other shipping instructions. Martin will not pay any bill that is not accompanied by a purchase order.

Table 6-1. Internal Control Plan for Cash Disbursements

Business Document	Prepared by	Sent to	Verifications and Related Procedures
1. Purchase requisition	Requesting department	Purchasing department	Purchasing verifies authorization.
2. Purchase order	Purchasing department	Supplier	Supplier sends goods or services in accordance with purchase order.
3. Invoice	Supplier	Accounting department	Accounting receives invoice from supplier.
4. Receiving report	Receiving department	Accounting department	Accounting compares invoice, purchase order, and receiving report. Accounting verifies prices.
5. Check authorization (or voucher)	Accounting department	Treasurer	Accounting staples check authorization to top of invoice, purchase order, and receiving report.
6. Check	Treasurer	Supplier	Treasurer verifies all documents before preparing check.
7. Deposit ticket	Supplier	Supplier's bank	Supplier compares check with invoice. Bank deducts check from buyer's account.
8. Bank statement	Buyer's bank	Accounting department	Accounting compares amount and payee's name on returned check with check authorization.

After receiving the purchase order, the vendor, Henderson Supply Company, ships the goods (in this case delivers them) and sends an **invoice**, or bill (Figure 6-4, page 228) to Martin Maintenance. The invoice gives the quantity and a description of the goods delivered and the terms of payment. If all goods cannot be shipped immediately, the estimated date for shipment of the remainder is indicated.

When the goods reach the receiving department of Martin Maintenance Company, an employee of this department writes the description, quantity, and condition of the goods on the **receiving report**. The receiving department does not get the purchase order or invoice, so that the people in this department will not know what is to be received. Thus, because

Figure 6-2. Purchase Requisition

PURCHASE REQUISITION No. 7077

Martin Maintenance Company

From: Credit Office Date September 6, 19xx

To: Accounting Department Suggested Vendor: Henderson Supply Company

Please purchase the following items:

Quantity	Number	Description
20 boxes	X 144	Typewriter ribbons
Reason for Request Six months' supply for office Approved B.M.		To be filled in by Accounting Department Date ordered 9/8/xx P.O. No. J 102

Figure 6-3. Purchase Order

PURCHASE ORDER No. J 102

Martin Maintenance Company
8428 Rocky Island Avenue
Chicago, Illinois 60643

To: Henderson Supply Company
2525 25th Street
Mesa, Illinois 61611

Date September 8, 19xx

FOB Destination

Ship by September 12, 19xx

Ship to: Martin Maintenance Company
Above Address

Terms 2/10, n/30

Please ship the following:

Quantity	✓	Number	Description	Price	Per	Amount
20 boxes		X 144	Typewriter ribbons	12.00	box	$240.00
Purchase order number must appear on all shipments and invoices.				Ordered by Marsha Owen		

Figure 6-4. Invoice

INVOICE No. 0468

Henderson Supply Company
2525 25th Street
Mesa, Illinois 61611

Date September 12, 19xx

Your Order No. J 102

Sold to:

Martin Maintenance Company
8428 Rocky Island Avenue
Chicago, Illinois 60643

Ship to:
Same

Sales Representative: Joe Jacobs

Quantity		Description	Price	Per	Amount
Ordered	Shipped				
20	20	X 144 Typewriter ribbons	12.00	box	$240.00

FOB Delivered | Terms: 2/10, n/30 | Date Shipped: 9/12/xx Via: Self

Figure 6-5. Check Authorization

CHECK AUTHORIZATION

	NO.	CHECK
Requisition	7077	
Purchase Order	J 102	
Receiving Report	JR 065	
INVOICE	0468	
Price		
Calculations		
Terms		

Approved for Payment J. Joseph

they do not know if they have received a larger quantity than ordered, they are not tempted to steal the excess.

The receiving report is sent to the accounting department, where it is compared with the purchase order and the invoice. If all is correct, the accounting department completes a **check authorization** and attaches it to the three supporting documents. The check authorization form shown in Figure 6-5 has a space for each item to be checked off as it is examined.

Figure 6-6. Check with Attached Remittance Advice

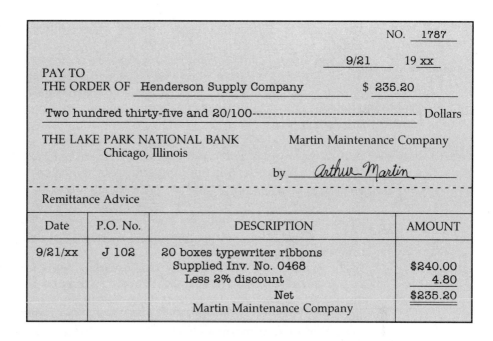

NO. 1787

9/21 19 xx

PAY TO
THE ORDER OF Henderson Supply Company $ 235.20

Two hundred thirty-five and 20/100-- Dollars

THE LAKE PARK NATIONAL BANK
Chicago, Illinois

Martin Maintenance Company

by Arthur Martin

Remittance Advice

Date	P.O. No.	DESCRIPTION	AMOUNT
9/21/xx	J 102	20 boxes typewriter ribbons	
		Supplied Inv. No. 0468	$240.00
		Less 2% discount	4.80
		Net	$235.20
		Martin Maintenance Company	

Note that the accounting department has all the documentary evidence for the transaction but does not have access to the assets purchased. Nor does it write the checks for payment. For this reason, the people performing the accounting function cannot gain by falsifying the documents in an effort to conceal a fraud.

Finally, the treasurer again examines all the evidence and issues a **check** (Figure 6-6) for the amount of the invoice less the appropriate discount. In some systems, the accounting department fills out the check so that all the treasurer has to do is inspect and sign it. The check is then sent to the supplier, with remittance advice attached to the bottom, which shows what the check is paying. A supplier who is not paid the proper amount will complain, of course, thus providing a form of outside control over the payment. The supplier will deposit the check in the bank, which will return the canceled check with Martin's next monthly bank statement. If the treasurer has made the check for an incorrect amount (or altered a prefilled-in check), it will show up at this point.

There are many variations of the system just described. This example is offered as a simple system that provides adequate internal control.

Banking Transactions

Banking facilities are also an important aid to merchandising businesses (and other types of business) in controlling both cash receipts and cash disbursements. Banks are safe depositories of cash, negotiable instruments, and other valuable business documents such as stocks and bonds.

The use of checks for disbursements improves control by minimizing the amount of currency on hand and by providing a permanent record of all cash payments. Furthermore, banks can serve as agents for a company in a variety of important transactions such as the collection and payment of certain kinds of debts and the exchange of foreign currencies.

Bank Account

OBJECTIVE 5
Describe a bank account and prepare a bank reconciliation

A bank account is an account a person opens with a bank, into which cash is deposited for safekeeping and from which cash is withdrawn by writing checks. The procedure for establishing a bank account varies. In some small towns where the bank personnel are familiar with townspeople's activities, it may be very easy to open an account. In other cases, particularly in large metropolitan areas, the bank may require a financial statement and references.

The evidence used for the bank account is a **signature card.** When a person opens an account, this card must be signed by the depositor in exactly the same way that he or she expects to sign the checks. This signature card is required so that a bank teller can authenticate the depositor's signature on a check. When a corporation opens an account, the board of directors must sign an authorization giving a particular official or officials the right to sign checks. The bank receives a copy of the authorization.

Deposits

When making a deposit, the depositor fills out a **deposit ticket** (usually in duplicate), as illustrated in Figure 6-7. Space is provided for listing each check and the amounts of coin and currency deposited.

Bank Statement

Once a month the bank will send a statement to the depositor and return the canceled checks that it has paid and charged to the depositor's account. The returned checks are called "canceled" because the bank stamps, or cancels, them to show that they have been paid. The **bank statement** shows the balance at the beginning of the month, the deposits, the checks paid, other debits and credits during the month, and the balance at the end of the month. A bank statement is illustrated in Figure 6-8 (page 232).

Preparing a Bank Reconciliation

Rarely will the balance of a company's Cash account exactly equal the cash balance as shown on the bank statement when it is received. Certain transactions shown in the company's records may not be recorded by the bank, and certain bank transactions may not appear in the company's records. Therefore, a necessary step in internal control is to prove both the balance of the bank and the balance of Cash in the accounting records. The term **bank reconciliation** means accounting for the differences

Figure 6-7.
Deposit Ticket

DEPOSIT TICKET
THE LAKE PARK NATIONAL BANK
Chicago, Illinois

Date 10/6/xx

Name Martin Maintenance Company
Address 8428 Rocky Island Avenue
Chicago, Illinois

CASH	CURRENCY	22	00
	COIN	2	50
CHECKS—LIST SINGLY	G. Mason	30	00
	R Enterprises	39	00
	Preston Company	206	50
TOTAL		300	00
Less Cash Received			—
NET DEPOSIT		300	00

between the balance appearing on the bank statement and the balance of Cash according to the depositor's records. This process involves adjusting both balances to the adjusted cash balance.

The most common examples of transactions shown in the company's records but not entered in the bank's records are the following:

1. *Outstanding checks* These are checks issued and recorded by the company, but not yet presented to the bank for payment.
2. *Deposits in transit* These are deposits mailed or taken to the bank but not received by the bank in time to be recorded before preparation of the monthly statement.

Transactions that may appear on the bank statement but have not yet been recorded by the company include the following:

1. *Service Charge (SC)* Banks cannot profitably handle small accounts without making a service charge. Many banks base the service charge on a number of factors, such as the average balance of the account during the month or the number of checks drawn.

Figure 6-8.
Bank Statement

Statement of Account with
THE LAKE PARK NATIONAL BANK
Chicago, Illinois

Martin Maintenance Company
8428 Rocky Island Avenue
Chicago, Illinois 60643

Checking Acct No
66-66183
Period covered
Sept. 30-Oct. 31, 19xx

Previous Balance	Checks/Debits—No.	Deposits/Credits—No.	S.C.	Current Balance
$2,645.78	$4,319.33 --15	$5,157.12 --6	$12.50	$3,471.07

CHECKS/DEBITS			DEPOSITS/CREDITS		DAILY BALANCES	
Posting Date	Check No.	Amount	Posting Date	Amount	Date	Amount
					09/30	2,645.78
10/01	564	100.00	10/01	586.00	10/01	2,881.78
10/01	565	250.00	10/05	1,500.00	10/04	2,825.60
10/04	567	56.18	10/06	300.00	10/05	3,900.46
10/05	566	425.14	10/16	1,845.50	10/06	4,183.34
10/06	568	17.12	10/21	600.00	10/12	2,242.34
10/12	569	1,705.80	10/24	300.00CM	10/16	3,687.84
10/12	570	235.20	10/31	25.62IN	10/17	3,589.09
10/16	571	400.00			10/21	4,189.09
10/17	572	29.75			10/24	3,745.59
10/17	573	69.00			10/25	3,586.09
10/24	574	738.50			10/28	3,457.95
10/24		5.00DM			10/31	3,471.07
10/25	575	7.50				
10/25	577	152.00				
10/28		128.14NSF				
10/31		12.50SC				

Explanation of Symbols:

CM —Credit Memo
DM —Debit Memo
NSF—Non-Sufficient Funds

SC —Service Charge
EC —Error Correction
OD—Overdraft
IN —Interest on Average Balance

The last amount in this column is your balance.

Please examine; if no errors are reported within ten (10) days, the account will be considered to be correct.

2. *NSF (non-sufficient funds) checks* An NSF check is a check deposited by the company that is not paid when the company's bank presents it for payment to the maker's bank. The bank charges the company's account and returns the check so that the company can try to collect the amount due. If the bank has deducted the NSF check from the bank statement but the company has not deducted it from its book balance, an adjustment must be made in the bank reconciliation. The depositor usually reclassifies the NSF check from Cash to Accounts Receivable because the company must now collect from the person or company that wrote the check.

3. *Interest earned* It is very common for banks to pay interest on a company's average balance. These accounts are sometimes called N.O.W. accounts but can take other forms. Interest earned in this way is reported by the bank on the bank statement.
4. *Miscellaneous charges and credits* Banks also charge for other services such as collection and payment of promissory notes, stopping payment on checks, and printing checks. The bank notifies the depositor of each deduction by including a debit memorandum with the monthly statement. A bank will sometimes serve as an agent in collecting on promissory notes for the depositor. In such a case, a credit memorandum will be included.

An error by either the bank or the depositor will, of course, require correction.

Steps in Reconciling the Bank Balance. The steps to be followed in achieving a bank reconciliation are as follows:

1. Compare the deposits listed on the bank statement with deposits shown in the accounting records. Any deposits in transit should be added to the bank balance. (Any deposits in transit from last month still not listed on the bank statement should be immediately investigated.)
2. Trace returned checks to the bank statement, making sure that all checks are issued by the company, properly charged to the company's account, and properly signed.
3. Arrange the canceled checks returned with the bank statement in numerical order, and compare them with the record of checks issued. List checks issued but not on the bank statement. (Be sure to include any checks still outstanding from last month.) Deduct outstanding checks from the bank balance.
4. Prepare a bank reconciliation similar to the one shown on page 234.
5. Deduct from the balance per books any debit memoranda issued by the bank such as NSF checks and service charges that are not yet recorded on the company's records.
6. Add to the balance per books any interest earned or credit memoranda issued by the bank such as collection of a promissory note that is not yet recorded on the company's books.
7. Make journal entries for any items on the bank statement that have not been recorded in the company's books.

Illustration of a Bank Reconciliation. The October bank statement for Martin Maintenance Company, as shown in Figure 6-8, indicates a balance on October 31 of $3,471.07. We shall assume that Martin Maintenance Company has a cash balance in its records on October 31 of $2,405.91. The purpose of a bank reconciliation is to identify the items that make up this difference and to determine the correct cash balance.

The bank reconciliation for Martin Maintenance is given in Exhibit 6-1. The numbered items there refer to the following:

1. A deposit in the amount of $276.00 was mailed to the bank on October 31 and was unrecorded by the bank.

Exhibit 6-1. Bank Reconciliation

Martin Maintenance Company
Bank Reconciliation
October 31, 19xx

Balance per bank, October 31		$3,471.07
① Add deposit of October 31 in transit		276.00
		$3,747.07
② Less outstanding checks:		
No. 551	$150.00	
No. 576	40.68	
No. 578	500.00	
No. 579	370.00	
No. 580	130.50	1,191.18
Adjusted cash balance, October 31		$2,555.89
Balance per books, October 31		$2,405.91
Add:		
④ Notes receivable collected by bank, including $20.00 of interest earned	$300.00	
⑦ Interest earned	25.62	325.62
		$2,731.53
Less:		
③ Overstatement of deposit of October 6	$ 30.00	
④ Collection fee	5.00	
⑤ NSF check of Arthur Clubb	128.14	
⑥ Service charge	12.50	175.64
Adjusted cash balance, October 31		$2,555.89

Note: The circled numbers refer to the items listed in the text.

2. Five checks issued in October or prior months have not yet been paid by the bank, as follows:

Check No.	Date	Amount
551	Sept. 14	$150.00
576	Oct. 30	40.68
578	Oct. 31	500.00
579	Oct. 31	370.00
580	Oct. 31	130.50

3. The deposit for cash sales of October 6 was incorrectly recorded in Martin's records as $330.00. The bank recorded the deposit on Martin's bank statement correctly as $300.00.
4. Among the returned checks was a credit memorandum showing that the bank had collected a promissory note from A. Jacobs in the amount

of $280.00 plus $20.00 in interest on the note. A debit memorandum was also enclosed for the $5.00 collection fee. No entry had been made on Martin's records.

5. Also returned with the bank statement was an NSF check for $128.14. This check had been received from a customer named Arthur Clubb. The NSF check was not reflected in Martin's accounting records.
6. A debit memorandum was enclosed for the regular monthly service charge of $12.50. This charge was not yet recorded by Martin Maintenance Company.
7. Interest earned by the company on the average balance was reported as $25.62.

Note in Exhibit 6-1 that, starting from their separate balances, the bank and book amounts are adjusted to the amount of $2,555.89. This adjusted balance is the amount of cash owned by the company on October 31 and thus is the amount that should appear on its October 31 balance sheet.

Adjusting the Records After Reconciliation. The adjusted balance of cash differs from both the bank statement and the Martin Maintenance Company's records. The bank balance will automatically become correct when outstanding checks are presented for payment and when the deposit in transit is received and recorded by the bank. Entries are necessary, however, to adjust the company's records to the correct balance. All the items reported by the bank but not yet recorded by the company must be entered into the records by means of the following adjustments:

Date	Account	Debit	Credit
Oct. 31	Cash	300.00	
	Notes Receivable		280.00
	Interest Income		20.00
	Note receivable of $280.00 and interest of $20.00 collected by bank from A. Jacobs		
31	Cash	25.62	
	Interest Income		25.62
	Interest earned on average bank account balance		
31	Sales	30.00	
	Cash		30.00
	Correction of error in recording a $300.00 deposit as $330.00		
31	Accounts Receivable, Arthur Clubb	128.14	
	Cash		128.14
	NSF check of Arthur Clubb returned by bank		
31	Bank Service Charges Expense	17.50	
	Cash		17.50
	Bank service charge ($12.50) and collection fee ($5.00) for October		

It is acceptable to record these entries in one or two compound entries to save time and space.

Petty Cash Procedures

OBJECTIVE 6
Describe and record the related entries for a simple petty cash system

Under some circumstances, it is not practical to make all disbursements by check. In most businesses, for example, it is sometimes necessary to make small payments of cash for such things as a few postage stamps, incoming postage or shipping charges due, or minor purchases of supplies.

For situations when it is inconvenient to pay with a check, most companies set up a **petty cash fund**. One of the best methods to use is the **imprest system**. Under this system, a petty cash fund is established for a fixed amount and is periodically reimbursed for the exact amount necessary to bring it back to the fixed amount.

Establishing the Petty Cash Fund

For purposes of control, companies should have a regular cashier, secretary, or receptionist to administer and be responsible for the petty cash fund. To establish the petty cash fund, the company issues a check to the person responsible for the fund for an amount that is intended to cover two to four weeks of small expenditures. The check is cashed, and the money is placed in the petty cash box, drawer, or envelope.

The only entry required when the fund is established is one to record the issuance of the check, as follows:

Oct. 14	Petty Cash	100.00	
	Cash		100.00
	To establish petty cash fund		

Making Disbursements from the Petty Cash Fund

The custodian of the petty cash fund should prepare a **petty cash voucher** for each expenditure, as illustrated in Figure 6-9. On each petty cash voucher the custodian enters the date, amount, and purpose of the expenditure. The voucher is signed by the person receiving the payment.

The custodian should be informed that surprise audits of the fund will be made occasionally. The cash in the fund plus the sum of the petty cash vouchers should equal the fixed amount of the fund at all times.

Figure 6-9. Petty Cash Voucher

PETTY CASH VOUCHER

No. X 744

Date Oct. 23, 19xx

For Postage due

Charge to Postage Expense

Amount $2.86

W.S. — Approved by

Tom L. — Received by

Reimbursing the Petty Cash Fund

At specified intervals or when the petty cash fund becomes low and always on the balance sheet date, it is replenished by a check issued to the custodian for the exact amount of the expenditures. From time to time there may be minor discrepancies in the amount of cash left in the fund at the time of reimbursement. In these cases, the amount of the discrepancy should be recorded in Cash Short or Over as a debit if short or as a credit if over.

Assume that after two weeks the petty cash fund established earlier had a cash balance of $14.27 and petty cash vouchers as follows: postage, $25.00; supplies, $30.55; freight in, $30.00. The entry to replenish, or replace, the fund is as follows:

Oct. 28	Postage Expense	25.00	
	Supplies	30.55	
	Freight In	30.00	
	Cash Short or Over	.18	
	Cash		85.73
	To replenish petty cash fund		

Note that the Petty Cash account is debited only when the fund is first established. Expense or asset accounts will be debited each time the fund is replenished. In most cases, no further entries to the Petty Cash account are needed unless there is a desire to increase or decrease the original fixed amount of the fund.

The petty cash fund should be replenished at the end of an accounting period to bring it up to its fixed amount and ensure that the other accounts involved will be properly reflected in the current period's financial statements. If through an oversight the petty cash fund is not replenished at year end, expenditures must still appear on the income statement. They are shown by an entry debiting the expense or assets accounts and crediting Petty Cash. Since the fund was not replenished at this time, the result is an unintentional reduction in the petty cash fund.

The Voucher System

OBJECTIVE 7 Describe the components of a voucher system

A **voucher system** is any system giving documentary proof of and written authorization for business transactions. Here, a voucher system for a company's expenditures is presented. It consists of records and procedures for systematically gathering, recording, and paying a company's expenditures. It is much like the control of cash because its goal is to keep the tightest possible control over expenditures. Under this system there is strong internal control because duties and responsibilities in the following functions are separated:

1. Authorization of expenditures
2. Receipt of goods and services

Figure 6-10. Front and Back of a Typical Voucher Form

FACE OF VOUCHER

Thomas Appliance Company

Payee Belmont Products — Voucher No. 704

Address Gary, Indiana — Date Due 7/13

Date Paid 7/13

Terms 2/10, n/30 — Check No. 205

Date	Invoice No.	Description	Amount
7/12	XL1066	10 cases Model 70X14	1,200--

Approved M.N. (Controller) — Approved A. Thomas (Treasurer)

Exhibit 6-2. Voucher Register

Voucher Register									
				Payment		Credit	Debits		
Date		Voucher No.	Payee	Date	Check No.	Vouchers Payable	Purchases	Freight In	Store Supplies
July	1	701	Common Utility	7/6	203	75			
	2	702	Ade Realty	7/2	201	400			
	2	703	Buy Rite Supplies	7/6	202	25			
	3	704	Belmont Products	7/13	205	1,200	1,200		
	6	705	M & M Freight			60		60	
	7	706	Petty Cash	7/7	204	50			
	8	707	Belmont Products	7/18	208	600	600		
	11	708	M & M Freight			30		30	
	11	709	Mack Truck			5,600			
	12	710	Livingstone Wholesale	7/22	209	785	750	35	
	14	711	Payroll	7/14	206	2,200			
	17	712	First National Bank	7/17	207	4,250			
	20	713	Livingstone Wholesale			525	500	25	
	21	714	Belmont Products			400	400		
	24	715	M & M Freight			18		18	
	30	716	Payroll	7/30	210	2,200			
	31	717	Petty Cash	7/31	211	47		17	
	31	718	Maintenance Company			175			
	31	719	Store Supply Company			350			350
						18,990	3,450	185	350
						211	511	512	116

BACK OF VOUCHER

Account Debited	Acct. No.	Amount
Purchases	511	1,200.00
Freight In	512	
Rent Expense	631	
Salary Expense	611	
Utility Expense	635	
Total		$1,200.00

Voucher No. 704
Payee Belmont Products
Address Gary, Indiana

Invoice Amount	1,200.00
Less Discount	24.00
Net	1,176.00
Date Due	7/13
Date Paid	7/13
Check No.	205

Exhibit 6-2. ***(continued)***

Page 1

Debits								
						Other Accounts		
Office Supplies	Sales Salaries Expense	Office Salaries Expense	Mainte-nance, Selling	Mainte-nance, Office	Utilities Expense	Name	No.	Amount
					75			
						Rent Expense	631	400
25								
						Petty Cash	121	50
						Trucks	148	5,600
	1,400	800						
						Notes Payable	212	4,000
						Interest Exp.	645	250
	1,400	800						
20						Misc. Exp.	649	10
			100	75				
45	2,800	1,600	100	75	75			10,310
117	611	612	621	622	635			✓

3. Validation of liability by examination of invoices from suppliers for correctness of prices, extensions, shipping costs, and credit terms
4. Payment of expenditure by check, taking discounts when possible

Under the voucher system, every liability must be recorded as soon as it is incurred. A written authorization, called a **voucher,** is prepared for each expenditure, and checks are written only when an approved voucher is shown. No one person has authority both to incur expenses and to issue checks. In large companies, the duties of authorizing expenditures, verifying receipt of goods and services, checking invoices, recording liabilities, and issuing checks are divided among different people. So for both accounting and administrative control, every expenditure must be carefully and routinely reviewed and verified before payment. For each transaction, the written approval of key people leaves a trail of documentary evidence, or an **audit trail.**

Though there is more than one way to set up a voucher system, most systems would use (1) vouchers, (2) voucher checks, (3) a voucher register, and (4) a check register.

Vouchers

A voucher is a written authorization for each expenditure, and serves as the basis of an accounting entry. A separate voucher is attached to each bill as it comes in, and it is given a number. Vouchers are prenumbered in order. In the illustration of a cash disbursement system earlier in this chapter, the voucher would take the place of the check authorization form. On the face of a typical voucher (see Figure 6-10), there is important information about the expenditure. The voucher must be signed by authorized individuals before payment is made. On the reverse side of the voucher is information about the accounts and amounts to be debited and credited. The voucher shown identifies the transaction by voucher number and check number and is recorded in the voucher register and check register, as described below.

Voucher Checks

Although regular checks can be used effectively with a voucher system, many businesses use a form of **voucher check** that tells the payee the reason for issuing the check. This information may be written either on the check itself or on a detachable stub.

Voucher Register

The **voucher register** is the book of original entry in which vouchers are recorded after they have been properly approved. The voucher register takes the place of the purchases journal shown in the preceding chapter.

A voucher register appears in Exhibit 6-2. Note that in a voucher system, instead of the Accounts Payable account column there is a new account column called Vouchers Payable. As you can see, the first entry in the voucher register records the receipt of a utility bill. It is recorded as a debit to utilities expense and a credit to Vouchers Payable (not Accounts Payable). Note that the utility bill was later paid by check number 203 on July 6.

Check Register

In a voucher system, the **check register** replaces the cash payments journal in the sense that it is the journal in which the checks are listed as they are written, as shown in Exhibit 6-3. Study carefully the connection between the voucher register and the check register. The incurring of a liability is recorded in the voucher register; its payment is recorded in the check register.

Operation of a Voucher System

OBJECTIVE 8
State and perform the five steps in operating a voucher system

There are five steps in the operation of a voucher system, as follows:

1. Preparing the voucher
2. Recording the voucher
3. Paying the voucher
4. Posting the voucher and check registers
5. Summarizing unpaid vouchers

Exhibit 6-3. Check Register

Check Register

Check No.	Date		Payee	Debit		Credits	
				Voucher No.	Vouchers Payable	Purchases Discounts	Cash
201	July	2	Ade Realty	702	400		400
202		6	Buy Rite Supplies	703	25		25
203		6	Common Utility	701	75		75
204		7	Petty Cash	706	50		50
205		**13**	**Belmont Products**	**704**	**1,200**	**24**	**1,176**
206		14	Payroll	711	2,200		2,200
207		17	First National Bank	712	4,250		4,250
208		18	Belmont Products	707	600	12	588
209		22	Livingstone Wholesale	710	785	15	770
210		30	Payroll	716	2,200		2,200
211		31	Petty Cash	717	47		47
					11,832	51	11,781
					211	513	111

1. Preparing the Voucher. A voucher is prepared for each expenditure. All evidence such as purchase orders, invoices, receiving reports, and/or authorization statements should be attached to the voucher when it is submitted for approval.

Many companies pay their employees out of a separate bank account or Payroll account. In this case, a voucher is prepared to cover the total payroll. The check for this voucher is then deposited in the special Payroll account, and individual payroll checks are drawn on that bank account.

2. Recording the Voucher. All approved vouchers should be recorded in the voucher register, as shown in Exhibit 6-2. Vouchers that do not have appropriate approvals or support documents should be investigated immediately. In this illustration, all purchases are recorded at gross purchase price. If the net method were used, the purchases would be recorded at the net purchase price after deducting the anticipated purchases discount.

3. Paying the Voucher. After a voucher has been recorded, it is placed in an unpaid voucher file. Many companies file the vouchers by due date so that checks can be drawn each day to cover all vouchers due on that day. In this way, all discounts for prompt payment can be taken without risk of missing the discount date.

On the date the voucher is due, a check for the correct amount, accompanied by the voucher and supporting documents, is presented to the individual authorized to sign checks. The check is then entered in the check register, as shown in Exhibit 6-3. The date of payment and the check number are then entered in the voucher register on the same line as the corresponding voucher. This procedure aids in the preparation of a schedule of unpaid vouchers, as explained below. However, if the net method of recording purchases were illustrated instead of the gross method, a Purchases Discounts Lost (Debit) column would replace the Purchases Discounts (Credit) column.

A problem arises in paying a voucher when there has been a purchase return or allowance that applies to the voucher. For example, suppose a part of a shipment of merchandise is defective and is returned to the supplier for credit. At the time the merchandise is returned or the allowance is given, an entry should be made in the general journal debiting Vouchers Payable and crediting Purchases Returns and Allowances, and a notation should be made on the voucher in the voucher file. At the time of payment, only the net amount of the voucher (original amount less return or allowance and any applicable discount) should be paid and recorded in the check register. Rather than noting the change on the voucher, some companies follow the practice of cancelling the original voucher and preparing a new one for the amount to be paid.

4. Posting the Voucher and Check Registers. Posting of the voucher and check registers is very similar to the posting of the purchases journal

Exhibit 6-4. Schedule of Unpaid Vouchers

Thomas Appliance Company
Schedule of Unpaid Vouchers
July 31, 19xx

Payee	Voucher Number	Amount
M & M Freight	705	$ 60
M & M Freight	708	30
Mack Truck	709	5,600
Livingstone Wholesale	713	525
Belmont Products	714	400
M & M Freight	715	18
Maintenance Company	718	175
Store Supply Company	719	350
Total Unpaid Vouchers		$7,158

and of the cash payments journal, as illustrated in Appendix A. The only exception is that the Vouchers Payable account is substituted for the Accounts Payable account.

5. Summarizing Unpaid Vouchers. At any particular time, the sum of the vouchers in the unpaid vouchers file equals the credit balance of the Vouchers Payable account. So an accounts payable subsidiary ledger like that described in Appendix A is unnecessary. At the end of each accounting period, the unpaid voucher file should be totaled to prove the balance of the Vouchers Payable account. Exhibit 6-4, a schedule of unpaid vouchers, is prepared by listing all unpaid vouchers shown in Exhibit 6-2. A reconciliation of the voucher register (Exhibit 6-2) and check register (Exhibit 6-3) can be accomplished by simple subtraction:

Vouchers Payable credit from voucher register	$18,990
Vouchers Payable debit from check register	11,832
Vouchers Payable credit balance from schedule of unpaid vouchers	$ 7,158

Sometimes the account title Vouchers Payable appears on the liability side of the balance sheet. However, it is preferred practice to use the more widely known term Accounts Payable, even when a voucher system is in use.

Chapter Review

Review of Learning Objectives

1. **Define internal accounting control and state its four objectives.**
   Internal accounting controls are the methods and procedures employed primarily to protect assets and ensure the accuracy and reliability of the accounting records. The objectives of internal accounting control are to provide reasonable assurance that (1) transactions are executed in accordance with management's general or specific authorization, (2) transactions are recorded to permit preparation of the financial statements in accordance with generally accepted accounting principles and to maintain accountability for assets, (3) access to assets is permitted only in accordance with management's authorization, and (4) recorded accountability is compared with existing assets at reasonable intervals.

2. **State five attributes of an effective system of internal control.**
   Five attributes of an effective system of internal control are (1) separation of duties, (2) a sound accounting system, (3) sound personnel policies, (4) reliable personnel, and (5) regular internal review.

3. **Describe the inherent limitations of internal control.**
   To be effective, a system of internal control must rely on the people who perform the duties assigned. Thus, the effectiveness of internal control is limited by the people involved. Human errors, collusion, management interference, and failure to recognize changed conditions can all contribute to a system failure.

4. **Apply the attributes of internal control to the control of certain merchandising transactions.**
   Internal control over sales, cash receipts, purchases, and cash disbursements is strengthened if the five attributes of effective internal control are applied. First, the functions of authorization, record keeping, and custody should be kept separate. Second, the accounting system should provide for physical protection of assets (especially cash and merchandise inventory), prompt recording and depositing of cash receipts, and payment by check only on the basis of documentary support. Third, persons who have access to cash and merchandise inventory should be specifically designated and their number limited. Fourth, personnel should be trained and bonded. Fifth, the Cash account should be reconciled monthly, and surprise audits of cash on hand should be made by an individual who does not handle or record cash.

5. **Describe a bank account and prepare a bank reconciliation.**
   A bank account is an account a person opens with a bank, into which cash is deposited for safekeeping and from which cash is withdrawn by writing checks. The term *bank reconciliation* means accounting for the differences between the balance appearing on the bank statement and the balance of cash according to the depositor's records. It involves adjusting both balances to arrive at the adjusted cash balance. The bank balance is adjusted for outstanding checks and deposits in transit. The depositor's book balance is adjusted for service charges, NSF checks, interest earned, and miscellaneous charges and credits.

6. **Describe and record the related entries for a simple petty cash system.**
   A petty cash system is established by a debit to Petty Cash and a credit to Cash. It is replenished by debits to various expense or asset accounts and a credit to Cash. Each expenditure should be supported by a petty cash voucher.

7. **Describe the components of a voucher system.**
A voucher system consists of written authorizations called vouchers; voucher checks; a special journal to record the vouchers, called the voucher register; and a special journal to record the voucher checks, called the check register.

8. **State and perform the five steps in operating a voucher system.**
The five steps in operating a voucher system are (1) preparing the voucher, (2) recording the voucher, (3) paying the voucher, (4) posting the voucher and check registers, and (5) summarizing unpaid vouchers.

Self-Test

Test your knowledge of the chapter by choosing the best answer for each item below.

1. Internal accounting control encompasses all the following except the
   a. system for safeguarding assets.
   b. accuracy of the accounting records.
   c. system of authorization of transactions.
   d. measurement of compliance with organizational goals.
2. The separation of duties means that with regard to a particular asset or transaction separate individuals should be responsible for authorization, custody, and
   a. approval.
   b. recordkeeping.
   c. control.
   d. protection.
3. All of the following are examples of internal accounting controls except
   a. monthly bank reconciliations.
   b. rotation of key accounting personnel.
   c. customer satisfaction surveys.
   d. use of internal auditing.
4. Which of the following documents should be presented and agreed upon before a check authorization is prepared?
   a. Purchase requisition and purchase order.
   b. Purchase order and receiving report.
   c. Purchase requisition, purchase order, and invoice.
   d. Purchase order, invoice, and receiving report.
5. On a bank reconciliation which of the following would be added to the balance per bank?
   a. Outstanding checks.
   b. Deposits in transit.
   c. Service charge.
   d. Interest on balance.
6. Which of the following items appearing on a bank reconciliation would require an adjusting entry?
   a. Outstanding checks.
   b. Deposits in transit.
   c. Interest on balance.
   d. Adjusted cash balance.
7. The entry to replenish a $50 petty cash fund that has $20 cash and a receipt for $30 of postage would include a credit to
   a. Cash.
   b. Petty Cash.
   c. Postage Expense.
   d. Prepaid Postage.
8. The voucher system strengthens internal accounting control by requiring that a voucher be prepared to authorize payment of the liability at the time the liability is
   a. paid.
   b. incurred.
   c. planned.
   d. audited.

9. To assist in making timely payment the file of unpaid vouchers is filed by
   a. voucher number.
   b. date of authorization.
   c. due date.
   d. check number.
10. Under the voucher system, at the end of the accounting period the amount of accounts payable on the balance sheet would equal the
    a. Total of the schedule of unpaid vouchers.
    b. Amounts paid to creditors during the accounting period.
    c. The total of the subsidiary accounts payable file.
    d. None of the above.

Answers to Self-Test are at the end of this chapter.

Review Problem
Bank Reconciliation

The information below and on the next page comes from the records of Maynard Company:

From the Cash Receipts Journal p. 14

Date	Debit Cash
Apr. 1	560
10	1,440
17	780
30	2,900
	5,680

From the Cash Payments Journal p. 18

Date	Check Number	Credit Cash
Apr. 4	1716	580
6	1717	800
17	1718	1,050
25	1719	110
		2,540

From the General Ledger

Cash **Account No. 111**

Date	Item	Post. Ref.	Debit	Credit	Balance Debit	Balance Credit
Mar. 31	Balance				4,200	
Apr. 30		CR14	5,680		9,880	
30		CP18		2,540	7,340	

Required

1. Prepare a bank reconciliation as of April 30, 19xx.
2. Prepare adjusting entries in general journal form.

From the Company's Bank Statements

Checks and Other Debits			Deposits		Balance	
Date	Check Number	Balance				
					4/1	4,480
4/5	1714	210	4/2	560	4/2	5,040
4/15	1716	580	4/11	1,440	4/5	4,250
4/12	1717	800	4/15	1,500CM	4/11	5,640
4/28		20SC	4/17	780	4/12	4,890
			4/28	220IN	4/15	6,380
					4/17	7,170
					4/28	7,370

CM—Credit Memo SC—Service Charge IN—Interest

The credit memo on April 15 is for the collection of a note including $100 in interest. Checks No. 1714 for $210 and No. 1715 for $70 were outstanding on April 1.

Answer to Review Problem

1. Bank reconciliation prepared

Maynard Company
Bank Reconciliation
April 30, 19xx

Balance Per Bank, April 30, 19xx		$ 7,370
Add Deposit of April 30 in Transit		2,900
		$10,270
Less Outstanding Checks		
No. 1715	$ 70	
1718	1,050	
1719	110	1,230
Adjusted Cash Balance, April 30, 19xx		$ 9,040
Balance Per Books, April 30, 19xx		$ 7,340
Add		
Note collected by bank including $100 of interest earned	$1,500	
Interest earned	220	$ 1,720
		$ 9,060
Less		
Service Charge		20
Adjusted Cash Balance, April 30, 19xx		$ 9,040

2. Adjusting entries prepared

April 30	Cash	1,500	
	Notes Receivable		1,400
	Interest Earned		100
	Collection of note by bank		
30	Cash	220	
	Interest Earned		220
	Interest earned on bank account		
30	Bank Service Charges Expense	20	
	Cash		20
	Service charge from bank statement		

Chapter Assignments

Questions

1. Most people think of internal control as making fraud harder to commit and easier to detect. What are some other important purposes of internal control?
2. What are the attributes of an effective system of internal control?
3. Why is a separation of duties necessary to ensure sound internal control?
4. Should the bookkeeper have responsibility for determining the accounts receivable to be written off? Explain.
5. At Thrifty Variety Store, each sales clerk counts the cash in his or her cash drawer at the end of the day and then removes the cash register tape and prepares the daily cash form, noting any discrepancies. This information is checked by an employee of the cashier's office, who counts the cash, compares the total with the form, and takes the cash to the cashier's office. What is the weakness in this system of internal control?
6. How does a movie theater control cash receipts?
7. What is the difference between internal accounting controls and internal administrative controls?
8. What does a credit balance in the Cash Short or Over account indicate?
9. One of the basic principles of internal control is separation of duties. What does this principle assume about the relationships of employees in a company and the possibility of two or more of them stealing from the company?
10. Why is a bank reconciliation prepared?
11. Assume that each of the numbered items below appeared on a bank reconciliation. Which item would be (a) an addition to the balance on the bank statement? (b) a deduction from the balance on the bank statement? (c) an addition to the balance on the books? (d) a deduction from the balance on the books? Write the correct letter after each numbered item.
    (1) Outstanding checks
    (2) Deposits in transit
    (3) Bank service charge
    (4) NSF check returned with statement
    (5) Note collected by bank
    Which of the above items require an adjusting entry?

12. In a small business, it is sometimes impossible to obtain complete separation of duties. What are three other practices that a small business can follow to achieve the objectives of internal control over cash?
13. Explain how each of the following can contribute to internal control over cash: (a) a bank reconciliation, (b) a petty cash fund, (c) a cash register with printed receipts, (d) printed, prenumbered cash sales receipts, (e) a regular vacation for the cashier, (f) two signatures on checks, and (g) prenumbered checks.
14. At the end of the day, the combined count of cash for all cash registers in a store reveals a cash shortage of $17.20. In what account would this cash shortage be recorded? Would the account be debited or credited?
15. What is the purpose of a petty cash fund, and what is the significance of the total of the fund (the level at which the fund is established)?
16. What account or accounts are debited when a petty cash fund is established? What account or accounts are debited when a petty cash fund is replenished?
17. Should a petty cash fund be replenished as of the last day of the accounting period? Explain.
18. What is the greatest advantage of the voucher system?
19. Before a voucher for the purchase of merchandise is approved for payment, three documents should be compared to verify the amount of the liability. What are the three documents?
20. When the voucher system is used, is there an Accounts Payable controlling account and a subsidiary accounts payable ledger?
21. A company that presently uses a general journal, a sales journal, a cash receipts journal, a cash payments journal, and a purchases journal decides to adopt the voucher system. Which of the five journals would be changed or replaced? What would replace them?
22. What is the correct order for filing (a) unpaid vouchers? (b) paid vouchers?

Classroom Exercises

Exercise 6-1. Petty Cash Entries
(L.O. 6)

The petty cash fund of Chong Company appeared as follows on December 31, 19xx:

Cash on Hand		$ 66.97
Petty Cash vouchers		
Freight In	$18.47	
Postage	20.84	
Flowers for a sick employee	17.50	
Office Supplies	26.22	83.03
Total		$150.00

1. Because there is cash on hand, is there a need to replenish the petty cash fund on December 31? Explain.
2. Prepare in general journal form an entry to replenish the fund.

Exercise 6-2. Bank Reconciliation
(L.O. 5)

Prepare a bank reconciliation from the following information: (a) balance per bank statement as of May 31, $3,944.65; (b) balance per books as of May 31, $2,786.40; (c) deposits in transit, $567.21; (d) outstanding checks, $1,727.96; (e) bank service charge, $2.50.

Exercise 6-3. Bank Reconciliation: Missing Data
(L.O. 5)

Compute the correct amounts to replace each letter in the following table:

Balance per bank statement	a	$9,200	$275	$2,200
Deposits in transit	$ 600	b	50	125
Outstanding checks	1,500	1,000	c	75
Balance per books	3,600	9,400	225	d

Exercise 6-4. Voucher System Entries
(L.O. 8)

Marino Company uses a voucher system. The following transactions occurred recently: (a) voucher no. 700 prepared to purchase merchandise from Blue Corp., $600; (b) check no. 401 issued in payment of voucher no. 700; (c) voucher no. 701 prepared to establish petty cash fund of $100; (d) check no. 402 issued in payment of voucher no. 701; (e) voucher no. 702 prepared to replenish the petty cash fund, which contains cash of $30 and the following receipts: supplies, $27; postage, $36; and miscellaneous expense, $7; (f) check no. 403 issued in payment of voucher no. 702.

Draw a Voucher Register and Check Register similar to the illustrations in Exhibits 6-2 and 6-3. Record each of the above transactions and foot and crossfoot the journals.

Exercise 6-5. Voucher System Entries
(L.O. 8)

Rosenthal Company uses a voucher system. Some related transactions are as follows:

Aug. 1 Voucher no. 352 prepared to purchase office equipment from Farrar Equipment Company, $640, terms n/30.
4 Voucher no. 353 prepared to purchase merchandise from Halsted Corporation, $1,200, terms 2/10, n/30, FOB shipping point.
5 Voucher no. 354 prepared to pay freight charge to Jartran Freight for August 4 shipment, $175, terms n/10.
14 Issued check no. 846 to pay voucher no. 353.
15 Issued check no. 847 to pay voucher no. 354.
30 Issued check no. 848 to pay voucher no. 352.

Draw a Voucher Register and a Check Register similar to the illustrations in Exhibits 6-2 and 6-3. Record each of the preceding transactions and foot and crossfoot the journals.

Exercise 6-6. Internal Control Evaluation
(L.O. 4)

Developing a convenient means of providing sales representatives with cash for their incidental expenses, such as entertaining a client at lunch, is a problem many companies face. One company has a plan whereby the sales representatives receive advances in cash from the petty cash fund. Each advance is supported by an authorization from the sales manager. The representative returns the receipt for the expenditure and any unused cash, which is replaced in the petty cash fund. The cashier of the petty cash fund is responsible for seeing that the receipt and the cash returned equal the advance. At the time that the petty cash fund is reimbursed, the amount of the representative's expenditure is debited to Direct Sales Expense.

1. What is the weak point of the procedure, and what fundamental principle of internal control has been ignored?
2. What improvement in the procedure can you suggest?

Exercise 6-7. Collection of Note by Bank (L.O. 5)

Ries Corporation received a notice with its bank statement that the bank had collected a note for $1,500.00 plus $7.50 interest from R. Wexler and credited Ries Corporation's account for the total less a collection charge of $3.50.

1. Explain the effect that these items have on the bank reconciliation.
2. Prepare a general journal entry to record the information.

Exercise 6-8. Internal Control Evaluation (L.O. 4)

An accountant and his assistants are responsible for the following procedures: (a) receipt of all cash; (b) maintenance of the general ledger; (c) maintenance of the accounts receivable ledger; (d) maintenance of the journals for recording sales, cash receipts, and purchases; and (e) preparation of monthly statements to be sent to customers. As a service to customers and employees, the company allows the accountant to cash checks of up to $50 with money from the cash receipts. The accountant may approve the cashing of such a check for current employees and customers. When the deposits are made, the checks are included in place of the cash receipts.

What weakness in internal control exists in this system?

Interpreting Accounting Information

J. Walter Thompson (L.O. 4)

J. Walter Thompson Co. (JWT) is one of the world's largest advertising agencies, with more than $1 billion in billings per year. One of its smaller units is a television syndication unit that acquires rights to distribute television programming and sells those rights to local television stations, receiving in exchange advertising time that is sold to the agency's clients. Cash rarely changes hands between the unit and the television station, but the unit is supposed to recognize revenue when the television programs are exchanged for advertising time that will be used by clients at a later date.

The *Wall Street Journal* reported on February 17, 1982, that the company "had discovered 'fictitious' accounting entries that inflated revenue at the television program syndication unit." The article went on to say that "the syndication unit booked revenue of $29.3 million over a five-year period, but that $24.5 million of that amount was fictitious" and that "the accounting irregularities didn't involve an outlay of cash . . . and its (JWT's) advertising clients weren't improperly billed. . . . The fictitious sales were recorded in such a manner as to prevent the issuance of billings to advertising clients. The sole effect of these transactions was to overstate the degree to which the unit was achieving its revenue and profit objectives."

The chief financial officer of JWT indicated that "the discrepancies began to surface . . . when the company reorganized so that all accounting functions reported to the chief financial officer's central office. Previously, he said, 'we had been decentralized in accounting,' with the unit keeping its own books."[4]

Required

1. Show an example entry to recognize revenue from the exchange of the right to televise a show for advertising time and an example entry to bill a client for using the advertising time. Explain how the fraud was accomplished.
2. What would motivate the head of the syndication unit to perpetrate this fraud if no cash or other assets were stolen?
3. What principles of internal control were violated that would allow this fraud to exist for five years, and how did correction of the weaknesses in internal control allow the fraud to be discovered?

4. Blustein, Paul, "JWT Sees Pretax Write-Off of $18 Million, Fictitious Accounting Entries . . . ," reprinted by permission of *The Wall Street Journal,* © Dow Jones & Company, Inc., 1982. All rights reserved.

Problem Set A

Problem 6A-1. Petty Cash Transactions (L.O. 6)

A small company maintains a petty cash fund in its office for small expenditures. The following transactions occurred:

a. The fund was established in the amount of $80.00 on September 1 from the proceeds of check no. 2707.
b. On September 30, the petty cash fund had cash of $3.46 and the following receipts on hand: postage, $35.00; supplies, $24.94; delivery service, $12.40; and a rubber stamp, $4.20. Check no. 2778 was drawn to replenish the fund.
c. On October 31, the petty cash fund had cash of $5.06 and the following receipts on hand: postage, $31.20; supplies, $32.84; and delivery service, $6.40. The petty cash custodian could not account for the shortage of $4.50. Check no. 2847 was written to replenish the fund.

Required

Prepare in general journal form the entries necessary to record each of the above transactions.

Problem 6A-2. Bank Reconciliation (L.O. 5)

Use the following information to prepare a bank reconciliation for Durham Company as of June 30, 19xx:

a. Cash on the books as of June 30 amounted to $54,492.52. Cash on the bank statement for the same date was $68,513.42.
b. A deposit of $7,124.92, representing cash receipts of June 30, did not appear on the bank statement.
c. Outstanding checks totaled $3,646.82.
d. A check for $1,210.00 returned with the statement was recorded in the cash payments journal as $1,012.00. The check was made in payment for advertising.
e. Bank service charges for June amounted to $13.00.
f. The bank collected for Durham Company $18,200.00 note left for collection. The face value of the note was $18,000.00.
g. An NSF check for $570.00 from a customer, Leon Booker, was returned with the statement.
h. The bank mistakenly deducted a check for $400.00 drawn by Eckersley Corporation.
i. The bank reported a credit to the account of $480.00 for interest earned on the average balance.

Required

1. Prepare a bank reconciliation for Durham Company as of June 30, 19xx.
2. Prepare the journal entries necessary to adjust the accounts.
3. State the amount of cash that should appear on the balance sheet as of June 30.

Problem 6A-3. Internal Control (L.O. 4)

Marmon Company, a small concern, is attempting to organize its accounting department to achieve maximum internal control, subject to the constraint of limited resources. There are three employees (1, 2, and 3) in the accounting department, each of whom has had accounting courses and some accounting experience. The accounting department must accomplish the following functions: (a) maintain the general ledger, (b) maintain the accounts payable ledger,

(c) maintain the accounts receivable ledger, (d) prepare checks for signature, (e) maintain the cash payments journal, (f) issue credits on returns and allowances, (g) reconcile the bank account, and (h) handle and deposit cash receipts.

Required

1. Assuming that each employee will do only the jobs assigned, assign the functions to the three employees in a way that will ensure the highest degree of internal control possible.
2. Identify four possible unsatisfactory combinations of functions.

Problem 6A-4. Voucher System Transactions
(L.O. 8)

During the month of March, Deluxe Video Center had the following transactions affecting vouchers payable:

1 Prepared voucher no. 125, payable to Petty Cash Cashier, to establish a petty cash fund, $200.
1 Issued check no. 262 for voucher no. 125.
2 Prepared voucher no. 126, payable to Mellon Distributing, for a shipment of merchandise, $700, invoice dated March 1, terms 2/10, n/60, FOB shipping point. Mellon prepaid freight of $40 and added it to the invoice, for a total of $740.
3 Prepared voucher no. 127, payable to Berkow Realty, for March rent, $1,000.
3 Issued check no. 263 for voucher no. 127.
5 Prepared voucher no. 128, payable to Welles Distributors, for merchandise, $1,000, invoice dated March 3, terms 2/10, n/60, FOB shipping point.
6 Prepared voucher no. 129, payable to Rapid Express, for freight in on March 5 shipment, $64, terms n/10.
7 Prepared voucher no. 130, payable to Handy Hardware, for office equipment, $400, terms n/30.
8 Received credit memorandum from Welles Distributors for damaged records returned, $100.
9 Prepared voucher no. 131, payable to Welles Distributors, for merchandise, $1,300, invoice dated March 8, terms 2/10, n/60, FOB shipping point.
10 Prepared voucher no. 132, payable to Rapid Express, for freight in on March 9, $94, terms n/10.
11 Issued check no. 264 for voucher no. 126.
12 Prepared voucher no. 133, payable to Marty Becker, for his personal expenses, $1,000.
12 Issued check no. 265 for voucher no. 133.
13 Issued check no. 266 for voucher no. 128. There was a return on this March 8.
15 Issued check no. 267 for voucher no. 129.
17 Prepared vouchers no. 134, 135, 136, and 137, payable to Broyard Furniture, for office furniture having an invoice price of $2,400, terms one-fourth down and one-fourth each month for three months.
17 Issued check no. 268 for voucher no. 134.
18 Issued check no. 269 for voucher no. 131.
19 Issued check no. 270 for voucher no. 132.
20 Prepared voucher no. 138, payable to Soriano Supply, $270 ($190 to be charged to Store Supplies and $80 to Office Supplies), terms n/10th of next month.
22 Prepared voucher no. 139, payable to Breslin Videocassettes, for merchandise, $330, invoice dated March 19, terms 2/10, n/30, FOB shipping point. Freight paid by shipper and included in invoice total, $30.

23 Prepared voucher no. 140, payable to Boundary National Bank, in payment of a $4,000 note plus interest, $100, total $4,100.
23 Issued check no. 271 for voucher no. 140.
24 Prepared voucher no. 141, payable to Clifton Insurance Company, for a one-year policy, $480.
24 Issued check no. 272 for voucher no. 141.
26 Prepared voucher no. 142, payable to Welles Distributors, for merchandise, $600, invoice dated March 25, terms 2/10, n/60, FOB shipping point.
27 Prepared voucher no. 143, payable to Rapid Express, for freight in on shipment of March 26, $38.
28 Prepared voucher no. 144, payable to Payroll Account, for monthly salaries, $7,900 (to be divided as follows: sales salaries, $4,400, and office salaries, $3,500).
28 Issued check no. 273 for voucher no. 144.
29 Issued check no. 274 for voucher no. 139.
31 Prepared voucher no. 145 to reimburse the petty cash fund. A count of the fund revealed cash on hand, $30, and the following receipts: postage, $44; office supplies, $34; collect telegram, $6; flowers for sick employee, $20; delivery service, $54. The total of cash on hand and receipts was $12 less than the book balance of Petty Cash.
31 Issued check no. 275 for voucher no. 145.

Required

1. Prepare a voucher register, a check register, and a general journal similar to those illustrated in this chapter and record the transactions.
2. Prepare a Vouchers Payable account (number 211) and post those portions of the journal and register entries that affect this account. Assume the Vouchers Payable account had a zero balance on March 30.
3. Prove the balance of the Vouchers Payable account by preparing a schedule of unpaid vouchers.

Problem 6A-5. Bank Reconciliation (L.O. 5)

The following information comes from the records of Canseco Company:

From the Cash Receipts Journal — Page 9

Date	Debit Cash
Nov. 1	1,828
7	2,024
14	6,480
21	5,292
30	3,884
	19,508

From the Cash Payments Journal — Page 12

Date	Check Number	Credit Cash
Nov. 1	721	28
2	722	566
3	723	832
4	724	54
5	726	10
10	727	11,492
11	728	1,418
20	729	2,492
21	730	152
		17,044

From the General Ledger

Cash — **Account No. 111**

Date		Item	Post. Ref.	Debit	Credit	Balance Debit	Balance Credit
Oct.	31	Balance				4,930	
Nov.	30		CR9	19,508		24,438	
	30		CP12		17,044	7,394	

The bank statement for Canseco Company appears as follows:

LAKE NATIONAL BANK — **Statement of Canseco Company, Oak and Foster Streets**

Checks/Debits Posting Date	Check No.	Amount	Deposits/Credits Posting Date	Amount	Daily Balances Date	Amount
11/02	700	200.00	11/02	1,828.00	11/01	7,570.00
11/02	707	1,000.00	11/08	2,024.00	11/02	8,198.00
11/04	720	920.00	11/15	6,480.00	11/04	7,250.00
11/04	721	28.00	11/22	5,292.00	11/06	6,418.00
11/06	723	832.00	11/26	816.00 CM	11/08	8,388.00
11/08	724	54.00	11/30	84.00 IN	11/12	8,348.00
11/12	726	10.00			11/14	6,534.00
11/12		30.00 NSF			11/15	13,014.00
11/14	728	1,814.00			11/22	18,306.00
11/24	727	11,492.00			11/24	6,814.00
11/26	730	152.00			11/26	7,478.00
11/30		8.00 SC			11/30	7,554.00

Code: CM—Credit Memo; DM—Debit Memo; IN—Interest; SC—Service Charge; NSF—Non-Sufficient Funds

The NSF check was received from J. Pindar, a customer, for merchandise. The credit memorandum represents an $800 note collected by the bank plus interest. Check number 728 for a purchase of merchandise was incorrectly recorded in the cash payments journal as $1,418 instead of $1,814. On November 1, there were only the following outstanding checks as reconciling items: number 700 at $200, number 707 at $1000, number 719 at $520, and number 720 at $920.

Required

1. Prepare a bank reconciliation as of November 30, 19xx.
2. Prepare adjusting entries in general journal form.
3. What amount should appear on the balance sheet for cash as of Nov. 30?

Problem Set B

Problem 6B-1. Petty Cash Transactions (L.O. 6)

The Eastland Theater Company established a petty cash fund in its snack bar so that payment can be made for small deliveries upon receipt. The following transactions occurred:

Oct. 1 The fund was established in the amount of $250.00 from the proceeds of a check drawn for that purpose.

31 The petty cash fund has cash of $60.71 and the following receipts on hand: for merchandise received, $110.15; delivery charges, $32.87; laundry service, $42.00; miscellaneous expense, $4.27. A check was drawn to replenish the fund.

Nov. 30 The petty cash fund has cash of $72.50 and the following receipts on hand: merchandise, $98.42; delivery charges, $38.15; laundry service, $42.00; miscellaneous expense, $3.93. The petty cash custodian cannot account for the fact that there is an excess of $5.00 in the fund. A check is drawn to replenish the fund.

Required

In general journal form, prepare the entries necessary to record each of the above transactions.

Problem 6B-2. Bank Reconciliation (L.O. 5)

Use the following information to prepare a bank reconciliation for Jorge Mendoza Company as of October 31, 19xx.

a. Cash on the books as of October 31 amounted to $21,327.08. Cash on the bank statement for the same date was $26,175.73.
b. A deposit of $2,610.47, representing cash receipts of October 31, did not appear on the bank statement.
c. Outstanding checks totaled $1,968.40.
d. A check for $960.00 returned with the statement was recorded incorrectly in the check register as $690.00. The check was made for a purchase of merchandise.
e. Bank service charges for October amounted to $12.50.
f. The bank collected for Jorge Mendoza Company $6,120.00 on a note left for collection. The face value of the note was $6,000.00
g. A NSF check for $91.78 from a customer, Beth Franco, was returned with the statement.
h. The bank mistakenly charged to the company account a check for $425.00 drawn by Jorge Mendoza on his personal checking account.
i. The bank reported that it had credited the account with $170.00 in interest on the average balance for October.

Required

1. Prepare a bank reconciliation for Jorge Mendoza Company as of October 31, 19xx.
2. Prepare the journal entries necessary to adjust the accounts.
3. State the amount that should appear on the balance sheet as of October 31.

Problem 6B-3. Internal Control
(L.O. 4)

Jablonski Company, a large merchandising concern that stocks over 85,000 different items in inventory, has just installed a sophisticated computer system for inventory control. The computer's data storage system has random access processing and carries all pertinent data relating to individual items of inventory. The system is equipped with fifteen remote computer terminals, distributed at various locations throughout the warehouse and sales areas. Using these terminals, employees can obtain information from the computer system about the status of any inventory item. To make an inquiry, they use a keyboard, similar to a typewriter's, that forms part of the remote terminal. The answer is relayed back instantaneously on a screen, which is also part of the terminal. As inventory is received, shipped, or transferred, employees update the inventory records in the computer system by means of the remote terminals.

Required

1. What potential weakness in internal control exists in the system?
2. What suggestions do you have for improving the internal control?

Problem 6B-4. Voucher System Transactions
(L.O. 8)

In January, M and S Company had these transactions affecting vouchers payable:

Jan. 2 Prepared voucher no. 7901, payable to Banyan Realty, for January rent, $700.

2 Issued check no. 5501 for voucher no 7901.

3 Prepared voucher no. 7902, payable to Fishman Company, for merchandise, $4,200, invoice dated January 2, terms 2/10, n/30, FOB destination.

5 Prepared voucher no. 7903, payable to Holiday Supply House, for supplies, $650, to be allocated $450 to Store Supplies and $200 to Office Supplies, terms n/10.

6 Prepared voucher no. 7904, payable to City Power and Light, for monthly utilities, $314.

6 Issued check no. 5502 for voucher no. 7904.

9 Prepared voucher no. 7905, payable to Crandall Company, for merchandise, $1,700, invoice dated January 7, terms 2/10, n/30, FOB shipping point. Crandall Company prepaid freight charges of $146 and added them to the invoice, for a total of $1,846.

12 Issued check no. 5503 for voucher no. 7902.

15 Issued check no. 5504 for voucher no. 7903.

16 Prepared voucher no. 7906, payable to Lopez Company, for merchandise, $970, invoice dated January 14, terms 2/10, n/30, FOB shipping point.

16 Prepared voucher no. 7907, payable to Kidd Freight Company, for freight shipment from Lopez Company, $118, terms n/10th of next month.

17 Issued check no. 5505 for voucher no. 7905.

18 Returned $220 in defective merchandise to Lopez Company for credit.

22 Prepared voucher no. 7908, payable to Holiday Supply House, for supplies, $375, to be allocated $200 to Store Supplies and $175 to Office Supplies, terms n/10.

23 Prepared voucher no. 7909, payable to Expo National Bank, for 90-day note, which is due, $5,000 plus $150 interest.

23 Issued check no. 5506 for voucher no. 7909.

24 Issued check no. 5507 for voucher no. 7906. There was a return on January 18.

26 Prepared voucher no. 7910, payable to Crandall Company, for merchandise, $2,100, invoice dated January 24, terms 2/10, n/30, FOB shipping point. Crandall Company prepaid freight charges of $206 and added them to the invoice, for a total of $2,306.

27 Prepared voucher no. 7911, payable to Telephone Company, $37. Payments for telephone are considered a utility expense.

27 Issued check no. 5508 for voucher no. 7911.

30 Prepared voucher no. 7912, payable to Payroll account, for monthly payroll, $17,200, to be allocated $13,300 to Sales Salaries and $3,900 to Office Salaries.

30 Issued check no. 5509 for voucher no. 7912.

31 Prepared voucher no. 7913, payable to Maintenance Company, $360, to be allocated two-thirds to Selling Maintenance and one-third to Office Maintenance.

Required

1. Prepare a voucher register and a check register similar to those illustrated in this chapter, and prepare a general journal. Record the transactions.
2. Prepare a Vouchers Payable account (number 211), and post the appropriate portions of the journal and register entries. Assume that the December 31 balance of Vouchers Payable was zero.
3. Prove the balance of the Vouchers Payable account by preparing a schedule of unpaid vouchers.

Problem 6B-5. Bank Reconciliation (L.O. 5)

The following information comes from the records of the Janesville Company:

From the Cash Receipts Journal — Page 22

Date	Debit Cash
Feb. 1	1,416
8	14,486
15	13,214
22	10,487
28	7,802
	47,405

From the Cash Payments Journal — Page 106

Date	Check Number	Credit Cash
Feb. 1	2076	1,218
3	2077	22
6	2078	6
7	2079	19,400
8	2080	2,620
12	2081	9,135
16	2082	14
17	2083	186
18	2084	5,662
		38,263

From the General Ledger

Cash						Account No. 111	
Date		Item	Post. Ref.	Debit	Credit	Balance Debit	Balance Credit
Jan.	31	Balance				10,570	
Feb.	28		CR22	47,405		57,975	
	28		CP106		38,263	19,712	

The bank statement for Janesville Company appears as follows:

FIRST NATIONAL BANK

Statement of Janesville Company
Janesville, OH

Checks/Debits			Deposits/Credits		Daily Balances	
Posting Date	Check No.	Amount	Posting Date	Amount	Date	Amount
02/02	2056	510.00	02/02	1,614.00	02/01	12,416.00
02/02	2075	32.00	02/09	14,486.00	02/02	13,488.00
02/03	2076	1,218.00	02/12	1,654.00CM	02/03	12,266.00
02/03	2072	4.00	02/16	13,214.00	02/05	12,244.00
02/05	2077	22.00	02/23	10,487.00	02/09	26,730.00
02/10	2079	19,400.00	02/28	101.00IN	02/10	6,065.00
02/10	2074	1,265.00			02/11	3,445.00
02/11	2080	2,620.00			02/12	5,099.00
02/17	2081	9,135.00			02/16	18,313.00
02/17	2082	14.00			02/17	9,164.00
02/18		40.00NSF			02/18	9,124.00
02/24	2084	5,662.00			02/23	19,611.00
02/28		17.00SC			02/24	13,949.00
					02/28	14,033.00

Code: CM—Credit Memo, DM—Debit Memo, IN—Interest, SC—Service Charge, NSF—Non-Sufficient Funds

The NSF check was received from T. Lambeth, a customer, for merchandise. The credit memorandum represents a $1,600 note collected by the bank plus interest. The February 2 deposit, recorded by Janesville as $1,416 in cash sales, was recorded correctly by the bank as $1,614. On February 1, there were only the following outstanding checks as reconciling items: No. 2056 at $510, No. 2072 at $4, No. 2073 at $35, No. 2074 at $1,265, and No. 2075 at $32.

Required

1. Prepare a bank reconciliation as of February 28, 19xx.
2. Prepare adjusting entries in general journal form.
3. What amount should appear on the balance sheet for cash as of February 28?

Financial Decision Case

Gabhart's
(L.O. 4)

Gabhart's is a retail department store with several departments. Its internal control procedures for cash sales and purchases are described below.

Cash sales Every cash sale is rung up by the sales clerk assigned to a particular department on the cash register for that department. The cash register produces a sales slip to be given to the customer with the merchandise. A carbon copy of the sales ticket is made on a continuous tape locked inside the machine. At the end of each day, a "total" key is pressed, and the machine prints the total sales for the day on the continuous tape. Then the sales clerk unlocks the machine, takes off the total sales figure, makes the entry in the accounting records for the day's cash sales, counts the cash in the drawer, retains the basic $50 change fund, and gives the cash received to the cashier. The sales clerk then files the cash register tape and is ready for the next day's business.

Purchases All goods are ordered by the purchasing agent upon the request of the various department heads. When the goods are received, the receiving clerk prepares a receiving report in triplicate. One copy is sent to the purchasing agent, one copy is forwarded to the department head, and one copy is kept by the receiving clerk. Invoices are forwarded immediately to the accounting department to ensure payment before the discount period elapses. After payment, the invoice is forwarded to the purchasing agent for comparison with the purchase order and the receiving report and is then returned to the accounting office for filing.

Required

For each of the above situations, identify at least one major internal control weakness and tell what you would suggest to improve the system.

Answers to Self-Test

1. d	3. c	5. b	7. a	9. c
2. b	4. d	6. c	8. b	10. a

CALDWELL NEEDLES ANDERSON

PART THREE MEASURING AND REPORTING ASSETS AND CURRENT LIABILITIES

In Parts One and Two, the basic accounting model was first presented and then extended to more complex applications. Part Three considers each of the major types of assets as well as the category of current liabilities and payroll accounting, with particular emphasis on the effect of their measurement on net income and their presentation in the financial statements. It also provides an overview of revenue and expense issues and discusses the effects of inflation on accounting.

Chapter 7 focuses on the major types of short-term liquid assets: cash and short-term investments, accounts receivable, and notes receivable.

Chapter 8 presents the accounting concepts and techniques associated with inventories and their importance to income measurement.

Chapter 9 deals with current liabilities and payroll accounting.

Chapter 10 discusses property, plant, equipment, natural resources, and intangible assets, as well as the concepts and techniques of depreciation, depletion, and amortization.

CHAPTER 7 SHORT-TERM LIQUID ASSETS

LEARNING OBJECTIVES

1. Describe accounting for cash and short-term investments.
2. Explain why estimated losses from uncollectible accounts are important to income determination and asset valuation.
3. Apply the percentage of net sales method and the accounts receivable aging method to accounting for uncollectible accounts.
4. Journalize entries involving the allowance method of accounting for uncollectible accounts.
5. Recognize types of receivables not classified as accounts receivable and specify their balance sheet presentation.
6. Define and describe a promissory note.
7. Make calculations involving promissory notes.
8. Journalize entries involving notes receivable.

In this chapter, you study the measurement and reporting issues associated with short-term liquid assets. **Short-term liquid assets** are assets that arise from cash transactions and the extension of credit. They include cash, short-term investments, accounts receivable, and notes receivable. They are useful because they are quickly available for paying current obligations. Of course, assets used in the functions of the business are less liquid. Among these productive assets are inventories; property, plant, and equipment; natural resources; and intangibles. After studying this chapter, you should be able to meet the learning objectives listed on the left.

Accounting for Cash and Short-Term Investments

Of all the short-term liquid assets, cash is the most liquid and the most readily available to pay debts. Cash is generally considered to consist of coin and currency on hand, checks and money orders received from customers, and deposits in bank checking accounts. The cash account may also include an amount that is not entirely free to be spent called a **compensating balance**. A compensating balance is a minimum amount that a bank requires a company to keep in its bank account as part of a credit-granting arrangement. This arrangement does, in fact, restrict cash and may reduce a company's liquidity. Therefore, the SEC requires companies to disclose in a note to the financial statements the amount of any compensating balance.

Sometimes during the year, a company may find that it has more cash on hand than it needs to pay current obligations. Because it is not wise to allow this cash to lie idle, especially in periods of high interest rates, the company may invest the excess cash in time deposits or certificates of deposit or in government securities or other marketable securities. Such investments are called **short-term investments** or **marketable securities** and are considered current assets because the intent is to hold the investments only until needed to pay current obligations.

OBJECTIVE 1
Describe accounting for cash and short-term investments

Though the term *marketable securities* is used widely, it is preferable to call them short-term investments because long-term investments may also contain securities that are just as marketable as the short-term investments. The difference is that management intends to hold the long-term investments for an indefinite period of time longer than one year.

Some companies are so successful that they accumulate large amounts of cash from earnings that they put into short-term investments. For example, at December 31, 1985, General Motors Corporation's balance sheet contained the following information (in millions):

Current Assets

Cash	$ 179.1
U.S. government and other marketable securities and time deposits—at cost, which approximates market of $5,534.6.	4,935.3
Total Cash and Marketable Securities	5,114.4

Short-term investments are at first recorded at cost. Suppose that on March 1, ST Company purchased U.S. Treasury bills, which are short-term debt of the U.S. government, for $97,000 and that the bills will mature in 120 days at $100,000. The following entry would be made by ST:

Mar. 1	Short-Term Investments	97,000	
	Cash		97,000
	Purchase of U.S. Treasury bills that mature in 120 days at $100,000		

Income on short-term investments is recorded as received. For example, dividends and interest on stocks and bonds held as short-term investments would be recorded as Dividend Income or Interest Income at the time it is received. In the case of the investment by ST Company, the interest is received when the bills are paid at maturity, as shown in the entry below:

June 30	Cash	100,000	
	Interest Income		3,000
	Short-Term Investments		97,000
	Receipt of cash on U.S. Treasury Bills and recognition of related income		

When short-term investments are sold, a gain or loss usually results. Suppose that ST Company sells 5,000 shares of an investment in Mobil Corporation on December 5. It bought the shares for $35 per share, including broker's commission. When it sells them at $25 per share net of (not including) broker's commissions, the following entry results:

Dec. 5	Cash	125,000	
	Loss on Sale of Investments	50,000	
	Short-Term Investments		175,000
	Sale of 5,000 shares of Mobil Corporation at $25 net of commissions		

In *Statement of Financial Accounting Standards No. 12,* the Financial Accounting Standards Board requires that investments in debt securities such as U.S. Treasury bills or corporate debt be listed at cost, unless there is reason to believe the value of the security is permanently impaired. However, the board requires that investments in equity securities such as capital stock be reported at the lower of historical cost or the market value determined at the balance sheet date.[1] For example, assume that at its year end of December 31, ST Company still owns 10,000 shares of Mobil Corporation that it purchased for $35 per share and that are now worth $25 per share. An adjusting entry is made to recognize the loss in value and to reduce the asset amount by means of a contra account, as follows:

Dec. 31	Loss on Decline in Short-Term Investments	100,000	
	Allowance to Reduce Short-Term Investments to Market		100,000
	To recognize decline in market value of short-term investments		

The loss is reported on the income statement, and although it is not usually shown as a separate item, the allowance account is reflected in the value assigned to short-term investments on the balance sheet, as follows:

Current Assets

Short-Term Investments (at lower of cost or market; cost equals $350,000)	$250,000

Subsequent increases in the market value of the investment in Mobil may be recorded, but only to the extent of bringing the short-term investment back up to cost. Increases in market value per share above cost are not recorded.

Note that accounting for investments is inconsistent with the concept of historical cost. Under historical cost the cost value would be presented on the balance sheet until the asset is sold. Accountants justify this inconsistency on the basis of the conservatism convention. That is, they recognize the potential loss immediately but put off recognition of any potential gain until it is actually realized.

1. *Statement of Financial Accounting Standards No. 12,* "Accounting for Certain Marketable Securities" (Stamford, Conn.: Financial Accounting Standards Board, 1975).

Accounting for Accounts Receivable

The other major types of short-term liquid assets are accounts receivable and notes receivable. Both result from credit sales to customers. Retail companies such as Sears, Roebuck and Company have made credit available to nearly every responsible person in the United States. Every field of retail trade has expanded by allowing customers the right to make payments a month or more after the date of sale. What is not so apparent is that credit at the wholesale and manufacturing levels has expanded even more than that at the retail level. The purpose of the rest of this chapter is to show the accounting for accounts and notes receivable, which play a key role in this credit expansion.

Accounts receivable are short-term liquid assets that arise from sales on credit to customers at either the wholesale or the retail level. This type of credit is often called **trade credit.**

Credit Policies and Uncollectible Accounts

Companies that make sales on credit naturally want to sell to customers who will pay. Therefore, most companies that sell on credit develop control procedures to increase the likelihood of selling only to customers who will pay when they are supposed to. As a result of these procedures, a company generally sets up a credit department. This department's responsibilities include the examination of each person or company that applies for credit and the approval or disapproval of the sale to that customer on credit. Typically, the credit department will ask for information on the customer's financial resources and debts. In addition, it may check personal references and established credit bureaus, which may have information about the customer. On the basis of this information, the credit department will decide whether to sell on credit to that customer. It may recommend the amount of payment, limit the amount of credit, or ask the customer to put up certain assets as security for the credit.

Regardless of how thorough and efficient its credit control system is, the company will always have some customers who will not pay. The accounts owed by such customers are called **uncollectible accounts**, or bad debts, and are a loss or an expense of selling on credit. Why does a company sell on credit if it expects that some of its accounts will not be paid? The answer is that the company expects to sell much more than it would if it did not sell on credit and, as a result, to make more profit.

Matching Losses on Uncollectible Accounts with Sales

In accounting for these uncollectible accounts, the basic rule of accounting is the matching rule. Expenses should be matched against the sales they help to produce. If bad debt losses are incurred in the process of increasing sales revenues, they should be charged against those sales revenues. A company does not know at the time of a credit sale that

OBJECTIVE 2
Explain why estimated losses from uncollectible accounts are important to income determination and asset valuation

the debt will not be collected. In fact, it may take a year or more to exhaust every possible means of collection. Even though the loss may not be specifically identified until a later accounting period, it is still an expense of the accounting period of the sale. Therefore, losses from the uncollectible accounts must be estimated for the accounting period, and this estimate becomes the expense for the fiscal year.

For example, let us assume that Cottage Sales Company made most of its sales on credit during its first year of operation. At the end of the year, accounts receivable amounted to $100,000. On this date, management reviewed the collectible status of the accounts receivable. Approximately $6,000 of the $100,000 of accounts reviewed were estimated to be uncollectible. Thus the uncollectible accounts expense for the first year of operation amounted to $6,000. The following adjusting entry would be made on December 31 of that year:

Dec. 31	Uncollectible Accounts Expense	6,000	
	Allowance for Uncollectible Accounts		6,000
	To record the estimated uncollectible accounts expense for the year 19xx		

The uncollectible accounts expense appears on the income statement as an operating expense. The **allowance for uncollectible accounts** appears in the balance sheet as a contra account and is deducted from the face value of accounts receivable.[2] It serves to reduce the accounts receivable to the amount that is expected to be realized, or collected in cash, as follows:

Current Assets		
Cash		$ 10,000
Short-Term Investments		15,000
Accounts Receivable	**$100,000**	
Less Allowance for Uncollectible Accounts	**6,000**	94,000
Inventory		56,000
Total Current Assets		$175,000

The allowance method of accounting for uncollectible accounts argues that in accordance with the matching rule, it is assumed that losses from an uncollectible account occur at the moment the sale is made to the customer. The Allowance for Uncollectible Accounts is used because the company does not know until after the sale that the customer will not pay. Since the amount of the loss must be estimated if it is to be matched

2. Note that although the purpose of the allowance for uncollectible accounts is to reduce the gross accounts receivable to the estimated amount collectible (estimated value), the purpose of another contra account, the Accumulated Depreciation account, is not to reduce the gross plant and equipment accounts to realizable value. The purpose of the Accumulated Depreciation account is to show how much of the cost of the plant and equipment has been allocated as an expense to previous accounting periods.

against the sales or revenue for the period, it is not possible to credit the account of any particular customer to reflect the overall estimate of the year's credit losses. Also, it is not possible to credit the Accounts Receivable controlling account in the general ledger because doing so would cause the controlling account to be out of balance with the many customers' accounts in the subsidiary ledger.

The Allowance for Uncollectible Accounts will often have other titles such as Allowance for Doubtful Accounts or Allowance for Bad Debts. Once in a while, the older phrase Reserve for Bad Debts will be seen, but in modern practice it should not be used. Bad Debts Expense is often used as another title for Uncollectible Accounts Expense.

Estimating Uncollectible Accounts Expense

Because it is impossible to know which accounts will be uncollectible at the time financial statements are prepared, it is necessary to give an estimate of the expense for the year that will cover the expected losses. Of course, estimates can vary widely. If one takes an optimistic view and projects a small loss from uncollectible accounts, the resulting net accounts receivable will be larger than if one takes a pessimistic view. Also, the net income will be larger under the optimistic view because the estimated expense will be smaller. The company's accountant makes an estimate based on past experience, modified by current economic conditions. For example, losses from uncollectible accounts are normally expected to be greater in periods of recession than in periods of economic growth. But the final decision as to how much is enough is made by management. This decision will depend on objective information such as the accountant's analyses and on certain qualitative factors such as how investors, bankers, creditors, and others may view the performance of the company. Regardless of the qualitative considerations, the estimated losses from uncollectible accounts should be realistic.

The accountant has two common methods available for estimating uncollectible accounts expense for an accounting period: the percentage of net sales method and the accounts receivable aging method.

OBJECTIVE 3
Apply the percentage of net sales method and the accounts receivable aging method to accounting for uncollectible accounts

Percentage of Net Sales Method. The **percentage of net sales method** asks the question, How much of this year's net sales will not be collected? The answer determines the amount of uncollectible accounts expense for the year.

For example, assume that the following balances represent the ending figures for Hassel Company for the year 19x9.:

Sales	
	$645,000

Sales Returns and Allowances	
$40,000	

Sales Discounts	
$5,000	

Allowance for Uncollectible Accounts	
	$3,600

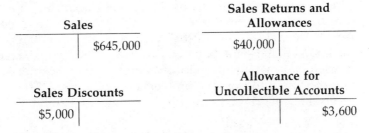

Assume that actual losses from uncollectible accounts for the past three years have been as follows:

Year	Net Sales	Losses from Uncollectible Accounts	Percentage
19x6	$ 520,000	$10,200	1.96%
19x7	595,000	13,900	2.34
19x8	585,000	9,900	1.69
Total	$1,700,000	$34,000	2.00%

Management believes that uncollectible accounts will continue to average about 2 percent of net sales. The uncollectible accounts expense for the year 19x9 is therefore estimated to be:

$$.02 \times (\$645{,}000 - \$40{,}000 - \$5{,}000) = .02 \times \$600{,}000 = \$12{,}000$$

net sales

OBJECTIVE 4 Journalize entries involving the allowance method of accounting for uncollectible accounts

The entry to record this estimate is:

Dec. 31	Uncollectible Accounts Expense	12,000	
	Allowance for Uncollectible Accounts		12,000
	To record uncollectible accounts expense at 2 percent of $600,000 net sales		

The Allowance for Uncollectible Accounts now has a balance of $15,600. This figure consists of the $12,000 estimated uncollectible accounts receivable from 19x9 sales and the $3,600 estimated uncollectible accounts receivable from previous years. They have not yet been matched with specific uncollectible accounts receivable resulting from sales in those years.

Accounts Receivable Aging Method. The **accounts receivable aging method** asks the question, How much of the year-end balance of accounts receivable will not be collected? The answer determines the amount that the allowance for uncollectible accounts is supposed to be at the end of the year. The difference between this amount and the actual balance of the Allowance account is the expense for the year. In theory, this method should produce the same result as the percentage of net sales method, but in practice it rarely does in any one year. The **aging of accounts receivable** is the process of listing each customer in accounts receivable according to the due date of the account. If a customer is past due on the account, there is a possibility that the account will not or cannot be paid. The further past due an account is, the greater the likelihood that the customer will not pay. The aging of accounts receivable is useful to management in evaluating its credit and collection policies and alerting it to possible problems of collection. The aging of accounts receivable for Myer Company is shown in Exhibit 7-1. Each account

Exhibit 7-1. Analysis of Accounts Receivable by Age

Myer Company
Analysis of Accounts Receivable by Age
December 31, 19xx

Customer	Total	Not Yet Due	1–30 Days Past Due	31–60 Days Past Due	61–90 Days Past Due	Over 90 Days Past Due
A. Arnold	$ 150		$ 150			
M. Benoit	400			$ 400		
J. Connolly	1,000	$ 900	100			
R. DiCarlo	250				$ 250	
Others	42,600	21,000	14,000	3,800	2,200	$1,600
Totals	$44,400	$21,900	$14,250	$4,200	$2,450	$1,600
Percentage	100.0%	49.3%	32.1%	9.5%	5.5%	3.6%

receivable is classified as being not yet due, or 1–30 days, 31–60 days, 61–90 days, or over 90 days past due. The percentage of total accounts receivable represented by each of these categories is calculated so that management may compare the analysis with previous periods.

The aging of accounts receivable method is useful to the accountant in determining the proper balance of the Allowance for Uncollectible Accounts. In Exhibit 7-2, estimates based on past experience show that only 1 percent of the accounts not yet due and 2 percent of the 1–30 days past due accounts will not be collected. Past experience also indicates that of the 31–60 days, 61–90 days, and over 90 days accounts, 10 percent, 30 percent, and 50 percent, respectively, will not be collected. In total, it is estimated that $2,459 of the $44,400 in accounts receivable will not be collected.

Let us assume that the current credit balance of the Allowance for Uncollectible Accounts for Myer Company is $800. Thus the estimated uncollectible accounts expense for the year is $1,659, which is calculated as follows:

Estimated Uncollectible Accounts	$2,459
Credit Balance—Allowance for Uncollectible Accounts	800[3]
Uncollectible Accounts Expense	$1,659

3. If the Allowance for Uncollectible Accounts had a debit balance, the amount of the debit balance would have to be added to the estimated uncollectible accounts to obtain the uncollectible accounts expense.

Exhibit 7-2. Calculation of Estimated Uncollectible Accounts

Myer Company
Estimated Uncollectible Accounts
December 31, 19xx

	Amount	Percentage Considered Uncollectible	Allowance for Uncollectible Accounts
Not yet due	$21,900	1	$ 219
1–30 days	14,250	2	285
31–60 days	4,200	10	420
61–90 days	2,450	30	735
Over 90 days	1,600	50	800
	$44,400		$2,459

The uncollectible accounts expense is recorded as follows:

Dec. 31	Uncollectible Accounts Expense	1,659	
	Allowance for Uncollectible Accounts		1,659
	To increase the allowance for uncollectible accounts to the level of expected losses		

Comparison of the Two Methods. Both methods try to determine the uncollectible accounts expense for the current accounting period in accordance with the matching rule, but they do so in different ways. The percentage of net sales method represents an income statement viewpoint. It is based on the proposition that of each dollar of sales a certain proportion will not be collected, and this proportion is the expense for the year. Because this method matches expenses against revenues, it is in accordance with the matching rule. However, this way of determining expense is independent of the current balance of the Allowance for Uncollectible Accounts. The estimated proportion of net sales not expected to be collected is added to the current balance of the Allowance account.

The aging of accounts receivable represents a balance sheet viewpoint and is a more direct valuation method. It is based on the proposition that of each dollar of accounts receivable outstanding, a certain proportion will not be collected, and this proportion should be the balance of the Allowance account at the end of the year. This method also agrees with the matching rule because the expense is the difference between what the account is and what it should be. This difference is assumed to be applicable to the current year.

Writing Off an Uncollectible Account

When it becomes clear that a specific account will not be collected, the amount should be written off to the Allowance for Uncollectible Accounts. Remember that it was already accounted for as an expense when the allowance was established. For example, assume that R. Deering, who owes the Myer Company $250, is declared bankrupt on January 15 by a federal court. The entry to *write off* this account is as follows:

Jan. 15	Allowance for Uncollectible Accounts	250	
	Accounts Receivable, R. Deering		250
	To write off receivable from R. Deering as uncollectible; Deering declared bankruptcy on January 15		

Note that the write-off does not affect the estimated net amount of accounts receivable because there is no expense involved and because the related allowance for uncollectible accounts has already been deducted from the receivables. The write-off simply reduces R. Deering's account to zero and reduces the Allowance for Uncollectible Accounts by a similar amount, as the following table shows:

	Balances Before Write-off	Balances After Write-off
Accounts Receivable	$44,400	$44,150
Less Allowance for Uncollectible Accounts	2,459	2,209
Estimated net value of Accounts Receivable	$41,941	$41,941

Why Accounts Written Off Will Differ from Estimates. The total of accounts receivable written off in any given year will rarely equal the estimated amount credited to the Allowance for Uncollectible Accounts. The Allowance account will show a credit balance when the accounts written off are less than the estimated uncollectible accounts. The Allowance account will show a debit balance when the accounts written off are greater than the estimated uncollectible accounts. The adjusting entry that is made to record the estimated uncollectible accounts expense for the current year will eliminate the debit balance at the end of the accounting period.

If the percentage of net sales method is used, the new balance of the Allowance account after the adjusting entry will equal the percentage of sales estimated to be uncollectible minus the debit balance. If the accounts receivable aging method is used, the amount of the adjustment must equal the estimated uncollectible accounts plus the debit balance in the Allowance for Uncollectible Accounts. Of course, if the estimates are consistently wrong, the balance of the Allowance account will become unusually large and will mean that management should reexamine the company's estimation rates.

Recovery of Accounts Receivable Written Off. Sometimes a customer whose account has been written off as uncollectible will later be able to pay the amount in full or in part. When this happens, it is necessary to make two journal entries: one to reverse the earlier write-off, which was incorrect in the first place; and another to show the collection of the account.

For example, assume that on September 1, R. Deering, after his bankruptcy on January 15, notified the company that he would be able to pay $100 of his account and sent a check for $50. The entries to record this transaction are as follows:

Sept. 1	Accounts Receivable, R. Deering	100	
	Allowance for Uncollectible Accounts		100
	To reinstate the portion of the account of R. Deering now considered collectible, which had been written off January 15		
1	Cash	50	
	Accounts Receivable, R. Deering		50
	To record collection from R. Deering		

The collectible portion of R. Deering's account must be restored to his account and credited to the Allowance for Uncollectible Accounts for two reasons. First, it was an error of judgment to write off the full $250 on January 15. Only $150 was actually uncollectible. Second, the Accounts Receivable subsidiary account for R. Deering should reflect his ability to pay part of the money he owed in spite of his bankruptcy. This action will give a clear picture of his credit record for future credit action.

Direct Charge-off Method

Some companies record uncollectible accounts by debiting expenses directly when bad debts are discovered instead of using the Allowance for Uncollectible Accounts. The **direct charge-off method** is not in accordance with good accounting theory because it makes no attempt to match revenues and expenses. Uncollectible accounts are charged to expenses in the accounting period in which they are discovered rather than in the period of the sale. On the balance sheet the accounts receivable are shown at gross value, not realizable value, because there is no Allowance for Uncollectible Accounts. Both the direct charge-off method and the allowance method of estimating uncollectible accounts expense are acceptable for use in computing taxable income under federal income tax regulations. Only the allowance method is used in this book because it is better from the standpoint of accounting theory.

Credit Balances in Accounts Receivable

Sometimes customers overpay their accounts because of mistakes or in anticipation of future purchases. When customer accounts show credit

OBJECTIVE 5 Recognize types of receivables not classified as accounts receivable and specify their balance sheet presentation

balances in the accounts receivable ledger, the balance of the Accounts Receivable controlling account should not appear on the balance sheet as the amount of the accounts receivable. The total of the customers' accounts with credit balances should be shown as a current liability because the company is liable to these customers for their overpayments.

Installment Accounts Receivable

Installment sales make up a significant portion of the accounts receivable of many retail companies. Department stores, appliance stores, and retail chains all sell goods that are paid for in a series of time payments. Companies such as J. C. Penney and Sears have millions of dollars in these **installment accounts receivable.** Although the payment period may be twenty-four months or more, installment accounts receivable are classified as current assets if such credit policies are customary in the industry. There are special accounting rules that apply to installment sales. Because these rules can be very complicated, the study of such practices is usually deferred until a more advanced accounting course.

Credit Card Sales

Many retailers allow customers to charge their purchases to a third-party company that the customer will pay later. These transactions are normally handled with credit cards. The five most widely used credit cards are American Express, Carte Blanche, Diners Club, MasterCard, and VISA. The customer establishes credit with the lender and receives a plastic card to use in making charge purchases. If the seller accepts the card, an invoice is made that is imprinted by the charge card and signed by the customer at the time of the sale. The seller then sends the invoice to the lender and receives cash. Because the seller does not have to establish the customer's credit, collect from the customer, or tie money up in accounts receivable, the seller receives an economic benefit that is provided by the lender. For this reason, the credit card company does not pay 100 percent of the total amount of the credit card sales invoices. The lender takes a discount of 2 to 6 percent on the credit card sales invoices.

One of two procedures is used in accounting for credit card sales, depending on whether the merchant must wait for collection from the credit card company or may deposit the sales invoices in a checking account immediately. The following example illustrates the procedure used in the first case. Assume that, at the end of the day, a restaurant has American Express invoices totaling $1,000. These sales are recorded as follows:

Accounts Receivable, American Express	1,000	
Sales		1,000
Sales made for which American Express cards were accepted		

The seller now mails the American Express invoices to American Express and later receives payment for them at 95 percent of their face value.

When cash is received, the entry is as follows:

Cash	950	
Credit Card Discount Expense	50	
Accounts Receivable, American Express		1,000
Receipt of payment from American Express for invoices at 95 percent of face value		

The second case is typical of sales made through bank credit cards such as VISA and MasterCard. For example, assume that the restaurant made sales of $1,000 on VISA credit cards and that VISA takes a 5 percent discount on the sales. Assume also that the sales invoices may be deposited in a special VISA bank account in the name of the company in much the same way that checks from cash sales may be deposited. These sales may be recorded as follows:

Cash	950	
Credit Card Discount Expense	50	
Sales		1,000
Sales for which VISA cards were accepted		

Other Accounts Receivable

The title Accounts Receivable on the balance sheet should be reserved for sales made to regular customers in the ordinary course of business. If loans or sales that do not fall in this category are made to employees, officers of a corporation, or owners, they should be shown separately on the balance sheet with an asset title such as Receivables from Employees and Officers.

Accounting for Notes Receivable

OBJECTIVE 6
Define and describe a promissory note

A **promissory note** is an unconditional promise to pay a definite sum of money on demand or at a future date. The person who signs the note and thereby promises to pay is called the *maker* of the note. The person to whom payment is to be made is called the *payee.* When the note is due in less than a year, the payee should record it as a note receivable in the current asset section of the balance sheet, and the maker should record it as a note payable in the current liability section of the balance sheet.

In this chapter, we are concerned primarily with notes received from customers. The nature of the business generally determined how frequently promissory notes are received from customers. Firms selling durable goods of high value, such as farm machinery and automobiles, will often take promissory notes in payment. One advantage of promissory notes in these situations is that the notes can be resold to banks as a financing method. Almost all companies will occasionally receive a note, and many companies obtain notes receivable in settlement of past-due accounts.

Computations Associated with Promissory Notes

OBJECTIVE 7
Make calculations involving promissory notes

In accounting for promissory notes, several terms are important. These terms are (1) maturity date, (2) duration of note, (3) interest and interest rate, (4) maturity value, (5) discount, and (6) proceeds from discounting.

Maturity Date. The **maturity date** is the date on which the note must be paid. It must either be stated on the promissory note or be determinable from the facts stated on the note. Among the most common statements of maturity date are the following:

1. A specific date, such as "November 14, 19xx"
2. A specific number of months after the date of the note, for example, "3 months after date"
3. A specific number of days after the date of the note, for example, "60 days after date"

There is no problem in determining the maturity date when it is stated. When the number of months from date of note is the maturity date, one simply uses the same day of the month as the note in the appropriate month in the future. For example, a note dated January 20 that is due two months from that date would be due on March 20.

When the computation of maturity date is based on a specific number of days, the maturity date must be determined on the basis of the passage of the exact number of days. In computing the maturity, it is important to exclude the date of the note and to include the maturity day. For example, a note dated May 20, and due in 90 days, would be due on August 18, computed as follows:

Days remaining in May (31 − 20)	11
Days in June	30
Days in July	31
Days in August	18
Total days	90

Duration of Note. Determining the **duration of note,** or its length of time in days, is the opposite problem from determining the maturity date. This calculation is important because interest must be calculated on the basis of the exact number of days. There is no problem when the maturity date is based on the number of days from date of note. However, if the maturity date is a specified date or a specified number of months from date, the exact number of days must be determined. Assume that the length of time of a note is from May 10 to August 10. The length of time is 92 days, determined as follows:

Days remaining in May (31 − 10)	21
Days in June	30
Days in July	31
Days in August	10
Total days	92

Interest and Interest Rate. The **interest** is the cost of borrowing money or the reward for loaning money, depending on whether one is the borrower or the lender. The amount of interest is based on three factors: the principal (the amount of money borrowed or loaned), the rate of interest, and the loan's length of time. The formula used in computing interest is as follows:

principal × rate of interest × time = interest

Interest rates are usually stated on an annual basis. For example, the interest on a $1,000, one-year, 8 percent note is computed as follows: $1,000 × 8/100 × 1 = $80.

If the term of the note were three months instead of a year, the interest charge would be $20, computed as follows: $1,000 × 8/100 × 3/12 = $20.

When the terms of a note are expressed in days, the exact number of days must be used in computing the interest. To keep the computation simple, let us compute interest on the basis of 360[4] days per year. Therefore, if the term of the above note were 45 days, the interest would be $10, computed as follows: $1,000 × 8/100 × 45/360 = $10.

Maturity Value. It is necessary to determine the **maturity value** of a note or the total proceeds of the note at maturity date. Maturity value is the face value of the note plus interest. The maturity value of a 90-day, 8 percent, $1,000 note is computed as follows:

maturity value = principal + interest
= $1,000 + ($1,000 × 8/100 × 90/360)
= $1,000 + $20
= $1,020

Occasionally, one will encounter a noninterest-bearing note, in which case the maturity value is the face value or principal amount.

Discount. To **discount** a note means to take out the interest in advance. The **discount** is the amount of interest deducted. It is very common for banks to use this method when loaning money on promissory notes. The amount of the discount is computed as follows:

discount = maturity value × rate × time

For example, assume that a noninterest-bearing $1,000 note due in 90 days is discounted at a 10 percent rate of interest:

discount = $1,000 × 10/100 × 90/360 = $25

Proceeds from Discounting. When someone borrows money on an interest-bearing note, the amount he or she receives or borrows is the face value or principal. When a note receivable is discounted, the amount the borrower receives is called the **proceeds from discounting** and must be computed as shown at the top of the next page:

4. Interest is computed in practice on the basis of 365 days in a year. In this book, use 360 days in a year to keep computations simple.

$$\textbf{proceeds} = \textbf{maturity value} - \textbf{discount}$$

Thus, in the preceding example, the proceeds would be computed as follows:

$$\begin{aligned} \text{proceeds} &= \$1{,}000 - (\$1{,}000 \times 10/100 \times 90/360) \\ &= \$1{,}000 - \$25 \\ &= \$975 \end{aligned}$$

This calculation is very simple when a noninterest-bearing note is involved, as illustrated here. However, the calculation is more complicated when an interest-bearing note is involved, as in the case when an interest-bearing note from a customer is discounted to the bank. In this situation, the maturity value must first be computed under the formula described for computing maturity value. Then the discount must be computed on the basis of the maturity value and, finally, the proceeds are determined by deducting the discount from the maturity value. For example, the proceeds of a $2,000, 8 percent, 90-day note, discounted on the date it is drawn at the bank at 10 percent, would be $1,989, determined as follows:

$$\begin{aligned} \textbf{maturity value} &= \textbf{principal} + \textbf{interest} \\ &= \$2{,}000 + (\$2{,}000 \times 8/100 \times 90/360) \\ &= \$2{,}000 + \$40 \\ &= \$2{,}040 \end{aligned}$$

$$\begin{aligned} \textbf{discount} &= \textbf{maturity value} \times \textbf{rate} \times \textbf{time} \\ &= \$2{,}040 \times 10/100 \times 90/360 \\ &= \$51 \end{aligned}$$

$$\begin{aligned} \textbf{proceeds} &= \textbf{maturity value} - \textbf{discount} \\ &= \$2{,}040 - \$51 \\ &= \$1{,}989 \end{aligned}$$

In this example, the note was discounted to the bank on the same day it was written. Usually some days will go by between the date the note is written and the date it is discounted. In such a case, the number of days used in computing the proceeds should be the days remaining until the maturity date of the note, because that is the length of time for which the bank is lending the money to the company holding the note. For example, assume the same facts as above except that the company holding the note waits 30 days to discount the note to the bank. In other words, at the date of discounting, there are 60 (90 − 30) days remaining until the maturity date. The proceeds are determined as follows:

$$\begin{aligned} \textbf{maturity value} &= \textbf{principal} + \textbf{interest} \\ &= \$2{,}040 \text{ (from above)} \end{aligned}$$

$$\begin{aligned} \textbf{discount} &= \textbf{maturity value} \times \textbf{rate} \times \textbf{time} \\ &= \$2{,}040 \times 10/100 \times 60/360 \\ &= \$34 \end{aligned}$$

$$\begin{aligned} \textbf{proceeds} &= \textbf{maturity value} - \textbf{discount} \\ &= \$2{,}040 - \$34 \\ &= \$2{,}006 \end{aligned}$$

The difference in discount of $17 ($51 − $34) between the two cases is equal to the discount on the 30 days lapsed between writing and discounting the note ($2,040 × 10/100 × 30/360 = $17).

Illustrative Accounting Entries

OBJECTIVE 8 Journalize entries involving notes receivable

The accounting entries for promissory notes receivable fall into five groups: (1) receipt of a note, (2) collection of a note, (3) recording a dishonored note, (4) discounting a note, and (5) recording adjusting entries.

Receipt of a Note. Assume that a 12 percent, 30-day note is received from a customer, J. Halsted, in settlement of an existing account receivable of $4,000. The entry for this transaction is as follows:

June 1	Notes Receivable	4,000	
	Accounts Receivable, J. Halsted		4,000
	Received 12 percent, 30-day note in payment of account		

Collection of a Note. When the note plus interest is collected 30 days later, the entry is as follows:

July 1	Cash	4,040	
	Notes Receivable		4,000
	Interest Income		40
	Collected 12 percent, 30-day note from J. Halsted		

Recording a Dishonored Note. When the maker of a note does not pay the note at maturity, the note is said to be dishonored. In the case of a **dishonored note,** an entry should be made by the holder or payee to transfer the amount due from the Notes Receivable account to an account receivable from the debtor. If it is assumed that J. Halsted did not pay his note on July 1 but dishonored it, the following entry would be made:

July 1	Accounts Receivable, J. Halsted	4,040	
	Notes Receivable		4,000
	Interest Income		40
	To record 12 percent, 30-day note dishonored by J. Halsted		

The interest earned is recorded because although J. Halsted did not pay the note, he is still obligated to pay both the principal amount and the interest.

Two things are accomplished by transferring dishonored notes receivable into an accounts receivable account. First, it leaves the Notes Receivable account with only notes that have not matured and are presumably negotiable and collectible. Second, it establishes a record in the borrower's account receivable that he or she has dishonored a note receivable. This information may be helpful in deciding whether to extend more credit to this customer in the future.

Discounting a Note. Many companies raise money for operations by selling notes receivable from customers to banks or finance companies for cash rather than holding them until maturity. This type of financing is usually called discounting because the bank deducts the interest from the maturity value of the note to determine the proceeds. The holder of the note (usually the payee) signs his or her name on the back of the note (as in endorsing a check) and delivers the note to the bank. The bank expects to collect the maturity value of the note (principal plus interest) on the maturity date. If the maker fails to pay, the endorser is liable to the bank for payment.

For example, assume that we take a \$1,000, 12 percent, 90-day note to the bank 60 days before maturity and that we discount it at 15 percent for cash. The cash to be received (proceeds from discounting) is calculated as the maturity value less the discount, recorded as follows:

Cash	1,004.25	
Notes Receivable		1,000.00
Interest Income		4.25
To record discounting of a 12 percent, 90-day note with 60 days left at 15 percent		
Maturity value:		
\$1,000 + (\$1,000 × 12/100 × 90/360)	= \$1,030.00	
Less discount:		
\$1,030 × 15/100 × 60/360	= 25.75	
Proceeds from discounted note receivable	\$1,004.25	

Before discussing the transaction, there are two things to note about the calculations. First, if the proceeds had been less than the note receivable, the difference would have been recorded as a debit to Interest Expense. For example, if the proceeds had been \$995.75 instead of \$1,004.25, Interest Expense would have been debited for \$4.25, and there would have been no entry to Interest Income. Second, neither the length of the discounting period nor the discount rate is the same as the term or the rate of interest of the note. This situation is typical.

Regarding the journal entry, notice that the account Notes Receivable is credited. Although this entry removes the note from the records, remember that if the maker cannot or will not pay the bank, the endorser is liable to the bank for the note. In accounting terminology, the endorser is said to be contingently liable to the bank. A **contingent liability** is a potential liability that can develop into a real liability if a possible subsequent event occurs. In this case, the subsequent event would be the nonpayment of the note by the maker.

Before the maturity date of the discounted note, the bank will notify the maker that it is holding the note and that payment should be made directly to the bank. If the maker pays the bank as agreed, then no entry is required in the records of the endorser. If the maker does not pay the note and interest on the due date, the note is said to be dishonored. To hold the endorser liable for the note, the bank must notify the endorser that the note is dishonored. The bank will normally notify the endorser by protesting the note. The bank does this by preparing and mailing a notice of protest to the endorser. The **notice of protest** is a sworn statement that the note was presented to the maker for payment and the maker refused to pay. The bank typically charges a **protest fee** for protesting the note, which must be paid when the endorser pays the bank the amount due on the dishonored note.

If the note discounted in the example above is dishonored by the maker on the maturity date, the following entry should be made by the endorser when paying the obligation:

Accounts Receivable, Name of Maker	1,040	
Cash		1,040
To record payment of principal and interest on discounted note (maturity value of $1,030), plus a protest fee of $10 to bank; the note was dishonored by the maker		

Additional interest accrues on the maturity value plus the protest fee until the note is paid or written off as uncollectible.

Recording Adjusting Entries. A promissory note received in one period may not be due until a following accounting period. Because the interest on the note accrues by a small amount each day of the duration of the note, it is necessary, according to the matching rule, to apportion the interest earned to the period in which it belongs. For example, assume that on August 31 a 60-day, 8 percent, $2,000 note was received and that the company prepares financial statements monthly. The following adjusting entry on September 30 is necessary to show how the interest earned for September has accrued:

Sept. 30	Accrued Interest Receivable	13.33	
	Interest Income		13.33
	To accrue 30 days' interest earned on note receivable $2,000 × 8/100 × 30/360 = $13.33		

The account Accrued Interest Receivable is a current asset on the balance sheet. Upon payment of the note plus interest on October 30, the following entry is made:[5]

Oct. 30	Cash	2,026.67	
	Note Receivable		2,000.00
	Accrued Interest Receivable		13.33
	Interest Income		13.34
	To record payment of note receivable plus interest		

As can be clearly seen from the above transactions, both September and October receive the benefit of one-half the interest earned.

5. Some firms may follow the practice of reversing the September 30 adjusting entry. Here we assume that a reversing entry is not made.

Chapter Review

Review of Learning Objectives

1. **Describe accounting for cash and short-term investments.**
Cash consists of coin and currency on hand, checks and money orders received from customers, deposits in bank accounts, certificates of deposit, and time deposits. Short-term investments, sometimes called marketable securities, are first recorded at cost. Afterwards, investments in debt securities are carried at cost unless there is a permanent drop in the market value. Investments in equity securities are reported at the lower of cost or market.

2. **Explain why estimated losses from uncollectible accounts are important to income determination and asset valuation.**
Because credit is offered to increase sales, it is reasonable that bad debts associated with the sales should be charged as expenses in the period in which the sale is made. However, because of the time lag between the sale and the time the account is judged to be uncollectible, the accountant must estimate the amount of bad debts in any given period.

3. **Apply the percentage of net sales method and the accounts receivable aging method to accounting for uncollectible accounts.**
Uncollectible accounts expense is estimated by either the percentage of net sales method or the accounts receivable aging method. When the first method is used, bad debts are judged to be a certain percentage of sales during the period. When the second method is used, certain percentages are applied to groups of the accounts receivable that have been arranged by due dates.

4. **Journalize entries involving the allowance method of accounting for uncollectible accounts.**
When the estimate of uncollectible accounts is made, and Allowance for Uncollectible Accounts is set up as a contra account to Accounts Receivable by a debit to expense and a credit to the Allowance account. When an individual account is determined to be uncollectible, it is removed from Accounts Receivable by debiting the Allowance account and crediting Accounts Receivable. If this account should later be collected, the earlier entry should be reversed and the collection recorded in the normal way.

5. **Recognize types of receivables not classified as accounts receivable and specify their balance sheet presentation.**
Accounts of customers with credit balances should not be classified as negative accounts receivable but as current liabilities on the balance sheet. Installment accounts receivable are classified as current assets if such credit policies are followed in the industry. Receivables from credit card companies should be classified as current assets. Receivables from employees, officers, stockholders, and others not made in the normal course of business should not be listed among accounts receivable. They may be either short- or long-term assets depending on when collection is expected to take place.

6. **Define and describe a promissory note.**
A promissory note is an unconditional promise to pay a definite sum of money on demand or at a future date. Companies selling durable goods of high value such as farm machinery and automobiles will often take promissory notes, which can be sold to banks as a financing method.

7. **Make calculations involving promissory notes.**
   In accounting for promissory notes, it is important to know how to calculate the following: maturity date, duration of note, interest, maturity value, discount, and proceeds from discounting. Discounting is the act of taking out the interest in advance when making a loan on a note.

8. **Journalize entries involving notes receivable.**
   The accounting entries for promissory notes receivable fall into five groups: receipt of a note, collection of a note, recording a dishonored note, discounting a note, and recording adjusting entries.

Review Problem
Entries for Uncollectible Accounts Expense and Notes Receivable Transactions

The Farm Implement Company sells merchandise on credit and also accepts notes for payment, which are discounted to the bank. During the past year ended June 30, the company had net credit sales of $1,200,000 and at the end of the year had total accounts receivable of $400,000 and a debit balance in the Allowance for Uncollectible Accounts of $2,100. In the past, approximately 1.5 percent of net sales have proved to be uncollectible. Also, an aging analysis of accounts receivable reveals that $17,000 in accounts receivable appears to be uncollectible.

The Farm Implement Company sold a tractor to R. C. Sims. Payment was received in the form of a $15,000, 9 percent, 90-day note dated March 16. On March 31, the note was discounted to the bank at 10 percent. On June 14, the bank notified the company that Sims had dishonored the note. The company paid the bank the maturity value of the note plus a fee of $15. On June 29, the company received payment in full from Sims plus additional interest from the date of the dishonored note.

Required

1. Prepare journal entries to record uncollectible accounts expense using (a) the percentage of net sales method and (b) the accounts receivable aging method.
2. Prepare journal entries relating to the note received from R. C. Sims.

Answer to Review Problem

1. Journal entries for uncollectible accounts prepared:
   a. Percentage of net sales method:

June 30	Uncollectible Accounts Expense	18,000	
	Allowance for Uncollectible Accounts		18,000
	To record estimated uncollectible accounts expense at 1.5 percent of $1,200,000		

   b. Accounts receivable aging method:

Date	Account	Debit	Credit
June 30	Uncollectible Accounts Expense	19,100	
	Allowance for Uncollectible Accounts		19,100
	To record estimated uncollectible accounts expense. The debit balance in the Allowance account must be added to the estimated uncollectible accounts		
	\$2,100 + \$17,000 = \$19,100		

2. Journal entries related to note prepared:

Date	Account	Debit	Credit
March 16	Notes Receivable	15,000.00	
	Sales		15,000.00
	Tractor sold to R. C. Sims; terms of note: 9%, 90 days		
31	Cash	15,017.97	
	Interest Income		17.97
	Notes Receivable		15,000.00
	To record note discounted at bank at 10 percent		
	Maturity value: \$15,000 + (\$15,000 × 9/100 × 90/360)	= \$15,337.50	
	Less discount (\$15,337.50 × 10/100 × 75/ 360)	= 319.53	
	Proceeds from discounted note receivable	\$15,017.97	
June 14	Accounts Receivable, R. C. Sims	15,352.50	
	Cash		15,352.50
	To record payment of principal and interest on discounted note (maturity value \$15,337.50), plus a \$15 fee to bank; the note was dishonored by Sims		
29	Cash	15,410.07	
	Accounts Receivable, R. C. Sims		15,410.07
	Received payment in full from R. C. Sims		
	\$15,352.50 + (\$15,352.50 × 9/100 × 15/360)		
	\$15,352.50 + \$57.57 = \$15,410.07		

Chapter Assignments

Questions

1. What items are included in the cash account? Is a compensating balance part of the cash account?
2. Why does a business need short-term liquid assets? Why is it acceptable to account for certain short-term investments by the lower-of-cost-or-market method?

3. Why does a company sell on credit if it expects that some of the accounts will not be paid? What role does a credit department play in selling on credit?
4. According to the accountant, at what point in the cycle of selling and collecting does the bad debt loss occur?
5. If management estimates that $5,000 of the year's sales will not be collected, what entry should be made at year end?
6. After adjusting and closing entries at the end of the year, suppose that the Accounts Receivable balance is $176,000, and the Allowance for Uncollectible Accounts balance is $14,500. (a) What is the collectible value of Accounts Receivable? (b) If the $450 account of a bankrupt customer is written off in the first month of the new year, what will be the resulting collectible value of Accounts Receivable?
7. What is the effect on net income of an optimistic versus a pessimistic view by management of estimated uncollectible accounts?
8. In what ways is the Allowance for Uncollectible Accounts similar to Accumulated Depreciation? In what ways is it different?
9. What procedure for estimating uncollectible accounts also gives management a view of the status of collections and the overall quality of accounts receivable?
10. What is the underlying reasoning behind the percentage of net sales and the accounts receivable aging methods of estimating uncollectible accounts?
11. Are the following terms different in any way: allowance for bad debts, allowance for doubtful accounts, allowance for uncollectible accounts?
12. Why should the entry for an account that has been written off as uncollectible be reinstated if the amount owed is subsequently collected?
13. What accounting rule is violated by the direct charge-off method of recognizing uncollectible accounts? Why?
14. Which of the lettered items below should be in Accounts Receivable? For those that do not belong in Accounts Receivable, tell where they do belong on the balance sheet: (a) installment accounts receivable from regular customers, due monthly for three years; (b) debit balances in customers' accounts; (c) receivables from employees; (d) credit balances in customers' accounts; (e) receivables from officers of the company; (f) accounts payable to a company that are less than accounts receivable from the same company.
15. What is a promissory note? Who is the maker? Who is the payee?
16. What are the due dates of the following notes: (a) a 3-month note dated August 16, (b) a 90-day note dated August 16, (c) a 60-day note dated March 25?
17. What is the difference between a sales discount and a discount on a note?
18. What is the difference between the interest on a note and the discount on a note?
19. A bank is offering Diane Wedge two alternatives for borrowing $2,000. The first alternative is a $2,000, 12 percent, 30-day note. The second alternative is a $2,000, 30-day, noninterest-bearing note discounted at 12 percent. (a) What entries are required by the bank to record the two loans? (b) What entries are needed by the bank to record the collection of the two loans? (c) Which alternative favors the bank, and why?

Classroom Exercises

Exercise 7-1. Accounting for Short-Term Investments
(L.O. 1)

During certain periods of its fiscal year, Harding Company invests its excess cash balances until they are needed at other times in the year. On January 16, the company invested $194,000 in 90-day U.S. Treasury bills that had a maturity value of $200,000. The bills matured on April 16 and the company received $200,000 in cash. On April 15, Harding purchased 5,000 shares of International Paper common stock at $35 per share and 10,000 shares of Commonwealth Edison common stock at $20 per share. On May 15, it received quarterly dividends of 92.25 cents per share from Commonwealth Edison and 60 cents per share from International Paper. On June 15, the company sold all the shares of International Paper for $38 per share. On June 30, the value of the Commonwealth Edison stock was $18 per share.

Prepare journal entries to record the transactions on January 16, April 16, April 15, May 15, June 15, and June 30. Also, show the balance sheet presentations of short-term investments on June 30.

Exercise 7-2. Adjusting Entries: Accounts Receivable Aging Method
(L.O. 3, 4)

The general ledger controlling account for accounts receivable of Parker Company shows a debit balance of $90,000 at the end of the year. An aging method analysis of the individual accounts indicates estimated uncollectible accounts to be $4,200.

Give the general journal entry to record the uncollectible accounts expense under each of the following assumptions: (1) The Allowance for Uncollectible Accounts has a credit balance of $300. (2) The Allowance for Uncollectible Accounts has a debit balance of $300.

Exercise 7-3. Adjusting Entry: Percentage of Net Sales Method
(L.O. 4)

At the end of the year, Janson Enterprises estimates the uncollectible accounts expense to be .5 percent of net sales of $9,200,000. The current credit balance of the Allowance for Uncollectible Accounts is $15,600. Give the general journal entry to record the uncollectible accounts expense.

Exercise 7-4. Aging Method and Net Sales Method Contrasted
(L.O. 3, 4)

At the beginning of 19xx, the balances for Accounts Receivable and the Allowance for Uncollectible Accounts were $810,000 and $56,700, respectively. During the current year, credit sales were $5,800,000 and collections on account were $5,700,000. In addition, $60,000 in uncollectible accounts were written off.

Make the year-end adjusting entry to record the Uncollectible Accounts expense and show the year-end balance sheet presentation of Accounts Receivable and the Allowance for Uncollectible Accounts under each of the following conditions:

a. Management estimates the percentage of uncollectible credit sales to be 1 percent.
b. Management estimates the percentage of end-of-year uncollectible accounts receivable to be 7 percent.

Exercise 7-5. Accounts Receivable Transactions
(L.O. 4)

Assuming that the allowance method is being used, prepare journal entries to record the transactions below and on the next page:

May 17, 19x8 Sold merchandise to Pam Earle for $1,200, terms n/10.
Sept. 20, 19x8 Received $400 from Pam Earle on account.

June 25, 19x9 Wrote off as uncollectible the balance of the Pam Earle account when she was declared bankrupt.

July 27, 19x9 Unexpectedly received a check for $200 from Pam Earle.

Exercise 7-6. Credit Card Sales Transactions (L.O. 5)

Prepare journal entries to record the following transactions for Diane's Specialty Shop:

Dec. 4 A tabulation of invoices at the end of the day showed $300 in American Express invoices and $400 in Diners Club invoices. American Express takes a discount of 4 percent, and Diners Club takes a 5 percent discount.

8 Received payment from American Express at 96 percent of face value and from Diners Club at 95 percent of face value.

9 A tabulation of invoices at the end of the day showed $200 in VISA invoices, which are deposited in a special bank account at full value less 5 percent discount.

Exercise 7-7. Interest Computations (L.O. 7)

Determine the interest on the following notes: (a) $10,360 at 12 percent for 60 days; (b) $6,000 at 9 percent for 90 days; (c) $10,000 at 6 percent for 30 days; (d) $12,000 at 15 percent for 120 days; (e) $4,500 at 12 percent for 30 days.

Exercise 7-8. Discounting Notes (L.O. 7)

In an effort to raise cash, Swann Company discounted two notes at the bank on September 15. The bank charged a discount rate of 12 percent applied to the maturity value.

Compute the proceeds from discounting of each of the following notes:

Date of Note	Amount	Interest Rate	Life of Note
a. Aug. 1	$ 4,500	9%	120 days
b. July 20	$22,000	10%	90 days

Exercise 7-9. Notes Receivable Transactions (L.O. 8)

Prepare general journal entries to record the following transactions:

Jan. 16 Sold merchandise to Western Corporation on account for $28,000, terms n/30.

Feb. 15 Accepted a $28,000, 12 percent, 60-day note from Western Corporation granting an extension on the previous sales.

Mar. 17 Discounted Western Corporation note at bank at 10 percent.

Apr. 16 Received notice that Western dishonored the note. Paid the bank the maturity value of the note plus a protest fee of $15.

May 15 Received payment in full from Western Corporation.

Exercise 7-10. Adjusting Entries: Interest Expense (L.O. 8)

Prepare journal entries to record the following:

Dec. 1 Received a 90-day, 12 percent note for $2,000 from a customer for a sale of merchandise.

31 Made end-of-year adjustment for accrued interest earned.

Mar. 1 Received payment in full for note and interest.

Interpreting Financial Information

Colgate-Palmolive Co.[6]
(L.O. 3)

Colgate-Palmolive is a major consumer goods company that sells over 3,000 products in 135 countries. From the company's annual report to the Securities and Exchange Commission, data pertaining to net sales and accounts related to accounts receivable for 1982, 1983, and 1984 were as follows (in 000's):

	1984	1983	1982
Net Sales	$4,910,000	$4,865,000	$4,888,000
Accounts Receivable	523,000	524,000	504,000
Allowance for Doubtful Accounts	18,600	21,200	24,500
Uncollectible Accounts Expense	15,000	16,700	15,800
Uncollectible Accounts Written Off	19,300	20,100	17,700
Recoveries of Accounts Previously Written Off	1,700	100	1,000

Required

1. Compute the ratios of Uncollectible Accounts Expense to Net Sales, Uncollectible Accounts Expense to Accounts Receivable, and Allowance for Doubtful Accounts to Accounts Receivable for 1982, 1983, and 1984. What appears to be management's attitude with respect to the collectibility of accounts receivable over the three year period?
2. Make the general journal entries related to the Allowance for Doubtful Accounts for 1984.

Problem Set A

Problem 7A-1. Percentage of Net Sales Method
(L.O. 3, 4)

On December 31 of last year, the balance sheet of Lee Company had accounts receivable of $314,000 and a credit balance in the Allowance for Uncollectible Accounts of $19,400. During the current year, the company's records included the following selected activities: sales on account, $1,215,000; sales returns and allowances, $75,000; collections from customers, $1,150,000; accounts written off as worthless, $16,000; written-off accounts unexpectedly collected, $2,000. In the past, the company had found that 1.5 percent of net sales would not be collected.

Required

1. Give the summary general journal entries to record each of the five items listed above.
2. Give the general journal entry to record the estimated uncollectible accounts expense for the year.
3. Open ledger accounts for the Accounts Receivable Controlling Account (112) and the Allowance for Uncollectible Accounts (113). Then enter the beginning balances in these accounts, and post the appropriate parts of the transactions in **1** and **2** to these accounts.

6. Figures for 1982, 1983, and 1984 reprinted by permission from the annual report of Colgate-Palmolive Company, 300 Park Avenue, New York, New York 10020.

Problem 7A-2. Accounts Receivable Aging Method (L.O. 3, 4)

Blocker Company uses the accounts receivable aging method to estimate uncollectible accounts. The Accounts Receivable controlling account and the Allowance for Uncollectible Accounts had balances of $86,000 and $6,000, respectively, at the beginning of the year. During the year, the company had sales on account of $473,000, sales returns and allowances of $4,200, worthless accounts written off of $7,075, and collections from customers of $450,730.

At the end of the year (December 31), a junior accountant for the company was preparing an aging analysis of accounts receivable. At the top of page 6 of his report, his totals appeared as follows:

Customer Account	Total	Not Yet Due	1–30 Days Past Due	31–60 Days Past Due	61–90 Days Past Due	Over 90 Days Past Due
Balance forward	$88,125	$48,650	$23,225	$8,930	$4,120	$3,200

He had the following accounts remaining to finish the analysis:

Account	Amount	Due Date
J. Baird	$ 870	Jan. 14 (next year)
A. Simons	590	Dec. 24
R. Mathern	1,955	Sept. 28
J. Carter	2,100	Aug. 16
B. Armstrong	375	Dec. 14
N. Li	2,685	Jan. 23 (next year)
T. Rodgers	295	Nov. 5
	$8,870	

The company has found from past experience that the following rates of estimated uncollectible accounts produce an adequate balance for the Allowance for Uncollectible Accounts:

Time Past Due	Percentage Considered Uncollectible
Not yet due	2
1–30 days	4
31–60 days	20
61–90 days	30
Over 90 days	50

Required

1. Complete the aging analysis of accounts receivable.
2. Using the beginning balance and the other data in the first paragraph, compute the end-of-year balance (before adjustments) for the Accounts Receivable Controlling account and the Allowance for Uncollectible Accounts.
3. Prepare an analysis computing the estimated uncollectible accounts.
4. Prepare a general journal entry to record the estimated uncollectible accounts expense for the year. (Round adjustment to the nearest dollar.)

Problem 7A-3. Notes Receivable Transactions (L.O. 8)

Kelly Manufacturing Company engaged in the following transactions involving promissory notes:

Jan. 14 Sold merchandise to John Moon Company for $14,200, terms n/30.
Feb. 13 Received $4,200 in cash from John Moon and received a 90-day, 8 percent promissory note for the balance of the account.
23 Discounted the note at the bank at 10 percent.
May 14 Because no notice that the note had been dishonored was received, it was assumed that John Moon paid the bank.
15 Received a 60-day, 12 percent note from Jean Fitt Company in payment of a past-due account, $6,000.
30 Discounted the note at the bank at 15 percent.
July 14 Received notice that Jean Fitt dishonored the note. Paid the bank the maturity value of the note plus a protest fee of $10.
20 Received a check from Jean Fitt for payment of the maturity value of the note, the $10 protest fee, and interest at 12 percent for the six days beyond maturity.
25 Sold merchandise to Jack Sales Company for $18,000, with payment of $3,000 cash down and the remainder on account.
31 Received a $15,000, 45-day, 10 percent promissory note from Jack Sales for the outstanding account.
Aug. 5 Discounted the note at the bank at 14 percent.
Sept. 14 Received notice that Jack Sales dishonored the note. Paid the bank the maturity value of the note plus a protest fee of $12.
25 Wrote off the Jack Sales Company account as uncollectible following news that the company had been declared bankrupt.

Required

Prepare general journal entries to record the above transactions.

Problem 7A-4. Notes Receivable Transactions (L.O. 8)

Joe's Auto Store engaged in the following transactions:

Jan. 2 Accepted a $10,800, 90-day, 14 percent note from Sylvia Swann as an extension on her past-due account.
5 Accepted a $1,800, 90-day, 12 percent note from Vaughn McDowell in payment of a past-due account receivable.
10 Accepted a $3,600, 90-day, 10 percent note from Roy Luther as an extension of a past-due account.
12 Discounted the Sylvia Swann note at the bank at 10 percent.
25 Discounted the Roy Luther note at the bank at 12 percent.
30 Accepted a $5,200, 90-day, 12 percent note from Mike Brown in lieu of immediate payment of a past-due account.
Apr. 2 Received notice that Sylvia Swann had dishonored her note. Paid the bank the maturity value plus a protest fee of $6.
5 Vaughn McDowell dishonored his note.
10 Received no notice of dishonor by Roy Luther and assumed he paid his obligation to the bank.
22 Received payment from Sylvia Swann for the total amount owed including maturity value, protest fee, and interest at 10 percent for the twenty days past maturity.
25 Wrote off the Vaughn McDowell account as uncollectible because he could not be located.

26 Delivered the Mike Brown note to bank for collection.
30 Received notice that Mike Brown paid his note plus interest in full to the bank. The bank credited the amount to Joe's account and charged a $5 collection fee.

Required

Prepare general journal entries to record the above transactions.

Problem 7A-5. Short-Term Financing by Discounting Customers' Notes
(L.O. 7, 8)

The Brewer Company is faced with a severe cash shortage because of slowing sales and past-due accounts. The financial vice president has studied the situation and has found a number of very large past-due accounts. He makes the following recommendations: (a) that the company seek promissory notes from past-due accounts to encourage the customers to pay on time and to earn interest on the money invested in these accounts, and (b) that the company generate cash by discounting the notes at the bank at the going rate of interest. During the first month of this program, the company was successful, as indicated by the following table:

Company	Amount of Note	Length of Note	Date of Note	Interest Rate	Discount Date	Discount Rate
J. T. Manufacturing Company	$130,000	60 days	Apr. 5	15%	Apr. 7	15%
Top-Notch Company	200,000	60 days	Apr. 10	12%	Apr. 13	15%
Williams Corporation	80,000	60 days	Apr. 15	14%	Apr. 20	15%

J. T. Manufacturing and Top-Notch Company paid their notes on the due dates. Williams Corporation dishonored its note on the due date.

Required

1. Prepare appropriate general journal entries for April.
2. What was the total cash generated during April by the vice president's plan?
3. Prepare appropriate general journal entries for June.
4. What is your evaluation of the plan? What offsetting factors occur in later months such as June?

Problem Set B

Problem 7B-1. Percentage of Net Sales Method
(L.O. 3, 4)

Kinder Company had an accounts receivable balance of $260,000 and a credit balance in the Allowance for Uncollectible Accounts of $12,600 at the beginning of 19xx. During the year, the company recorded the following transactions:

a. Sales on account, $973,000.
b. Sales returns and allowances, $47,800.
c. Collections from customers, $876,000.
d. Worthless accounts written off, $12,700.
e. Written-off accounts collected, $1,300.

The company's past history indicates that, in addition, 2.5 percent of net credit sales will not be collected.

Required

1. Record the summary general journal entries required for each of the five items listed on page 372.
2. Record the general journal entry for the estimated uncollectible accounts expense for the year.
3. Open ledger accounts for the Accounts Receivable Controlling Account (112) and the Allowance for Uncollectible Accounts (113). Then enter the beginning balances in these accounts, and post the appropriate parts of the transactions in **1** and **2** to the accounts.

Problem 7B-2. Accounts Receivable Aging Method
(L.O. 3, 4)

The Vassar Jewelry Store uses the accounts receivable aging method to estimate uncollectible accounts. The balances in its Accounts Receivable and Allowance for Uncollectible Accounts were $424,000 and $37,000, respectively, at the beginning of 19xx. During the year, the store had sales on account of $3,724,000, sales returns and allowances of $63,000, worthless accounts written off of $38,000, and collections from customers of $3,214,000.

As part of end-of-year (January 31) procedures, an aging analysis of accounts receivable is prepared. The analysis is partially complete. The totals of the analysis appear below.

Customer Account	Total	Not Yet Due	1–30 Days Past Due	31–60 Days Past Due	61–90 Days Past Due	Over 90 Days Past Due
Balance Forward	$777,800	$423,732	$159,912	$97,960	$56,992	$39,204

The following accounts remain to be classified in order to finish the analysis:

Account	Amount	Due Date
B. Hensel	$11,037	January 15
B. Rowsey	9,204	February 15 (next fiscal year)
S. Gilmore	8,664	December 20
J. Stiverson	780	October 1
R. Merritt	14,810	January 4
J. Osborn	6,316	November 15
M. Aures	4,389	March 1 (next fiscal year)
	$55,200	

From past experience, the company has found that the following rates for estimating uncollectible accounts produce an adequate balance for the Allowance for Uncollectible Accounts:

Time Past Due	Percentage Considered Uncollectible
Not yet due	2
1–30 days	5
31–60 days	15
61–90 days	25
Over 90 days	50

Required

1. Complete the aging analysis of accounts receivable.
2. Using the beginning balance and pertinent other data in the first paragraph, compute the end-of-year balance (before adjustments) for the Accounts Receivable Controlling Account and the Allowance for Uncollectible Accounts.
3. Prepare an analysis, computing the estimated uncollectible accounts.
4. Prepare a second journal entry to record the estimated uncollectible accounts expense for the year (round adjustment to the nearest dollar).

Problem 7B-3. Notes Receivable Transactions (L.O. 7, 8)

Tumey Manufacturing Company sells truck beds to various companies. To improve its liquidity, Tumey discounts any promissory notes it receives. The company engaged in the following transactions involving promissory notes:

Jan. 10	Sold beds to Edison Company for $20,000, terms n/10.
20	Accepted a 90-day, 13 percent promissory note in settlement of the account from Edision.
31	Discounted the note from Edison at the bank at 15 percent.
Apr. 20	Having received no notice that the note had been dishonored, Tumey assumed Edison paid the bank.
May 5	Sold beds to Shelton Company for $30,000, terms n/10.
15	Received $4,000 cash and a 60-day, 10 percent note for $26,000 in settlement of the Shelton account.
25	Discounted the note from Shelton to the bank at 15 percent.
July 14	Received notice that Shelton dishonored the note. Paid the bank the maturity value of the note plus a protest fee of $10.
Aug. 2	Wrote off the Shelton account as uncollectible after news that the company declared bankruptcy.
5	Received a 90-day, 11 percent note for $15,000 from Skycam Company in settlement of an account receivable.
15	Discounted the note from Skycam at the bank at 10 percent.
Nov. 30	Received notice that Skycam dishonored the note. Paid the bank the maturity value of the note plus a protest fee of $10.
Dec. 6	Received payment in full from Skycam, including 15 percent interest for the 6 days since the note was dishonored.

Required

Prepare general journal entries to record the above transactions.

Problem 7B-4. Notes Receivable Transactions (L.O. 7, 8)

The Ransack Company accepts notes as payment for sales to key customers. The transactions involving notes for August and October are presented below.

Aug. 6	Accepted a $6,000, 60-day, 10 percent note from Moser Company in payment for merchandise.

8 Accepted a $10,000, 60-day, 11 percent note from Kinney's Electronics in payment for merchandise.
13 Discounted the Moser Company note at the bank at 12 percent.
23 Discounted the Kinney's Electronics note at the bank at 13 percent.
28 Accepted a $12,000, 60-day, 9 percent note from Stockwell Company in payment for purchase of merchandise.
30 Accepted a $14,000, 60-day, 10 percent note from Tabor Company in payment for merchandise.
Oct. 5 Receiving no notice of dishonor by Moser Company, Ransack assumed Moser paid its obligation to the bank.
7 Received notice from the bank that Kinney's Electronics dishonored its note. Paid the bank the maturity value plus a protest fee of $12.
27 Delivered the Stockwell Company note to the bank for collection.
29 Tabor Company dishonored its note.
30 Received notice that Stockwell Company paid its note and interest. The bank charged a $12 collection fee.

Required

Prepare journal entries to record the above transactions.

Problem 7B-5. Short-Term Financing by Discounting Customers' Notes
(L.O. 7, 8)

The management of McDaniels Lawn Products sells its goods to distributors 120 days before the summer season. Mr. McDaniels has worked out a plan with his bank to finance receivables from the sales. The plan calls for the company to receive a 120-day, 9 percent note for each sale to a distributor. Each note will be discounted at the bank at the rate of 12 percent. This plan will provide McDaniels with adequate cash flow to operate his company.

During January, McDaniels made the following sales under the plan:

Company	Amount of Note	Date of Note	Discount Date*
Acme Hardware	$525,000	Jan. 7	Jan. 9
Marble Stores	750,000	12	15
Tom's Markets	250,000	19	24

*Assume 28 days in February

During May, all the distributors paid on their respective due dates except Marble Stores, which defaulted on its note. The note was paid in full 30 days late, including additional interest at 9 percent and a protest fee of $50.

Required

1. Prepare general journal entries to record McDaniels's January transactions (round calculations to nearest dollar).
2. What was the total cash generated in January from discounting the notes receivable?
3. Prepare general journal entries to record the May and June transactions on McDaniels Lawn Products records.
4. What is your evaluation of the plan? What risks is McDaniels's management taking?

Financial Decision Case

Elliot Electronics, Inc.
(L.O. 1, 2)

Two years ago Mark and Prudence Elliot began Elliot Electronics on a shoestring budget. Hard work and personal attention have brought success to their business, which sells television sets, video-tape machines, and other electronic entertainment devices. However, because of insufficient funds to finance credit sales, they have accepted only cash and bank credit cards. They are now considering a new policy of offering installment sales on terms of 25 percent down and 25 percent per month for three months, as well as continuing to accept cash and bank credit cards. They feel that this policy will boost sales greatly during the coming fall season. But to follow through on the new policy they will need a bank loan. To apply for the loan, they must make financial projections showing the effects of the new policy.

The Elliots project sales for the last third of the year as follows:

September	October	November	December
$30,000	$50,000	$80,000	$100,000

They also expect 20 percent of sales to be for cash, 30 percent to be by credit card on which a 5 percent fee is paid, and 50 percent to be on installment sales.

The Elliots have a financial agreement with their suppliers that requires them to buy and pay for their inventory in the month that they sell the items. This arrangement is called buying on consignment. Part of the Elliots' success has stemmed from their policy of selling at a discount price. They set the price at one-third above cost. (In other words, cost equals 75 percent of selling price.) This price is lower than that charged by most retail stores, and they intend to continue this policy. The Elliots feel that other cost associated with the new policy will increase cash outlays for operating expenses to $7,000 per month.

Required

1. Prepare a schedule that will show the impact of the new credit policy on cash receipts and payments for each of the four months. How much money in total will the Elliots need to borrow by December 31 to finance the new credit policy?
2. What will the level of accounts receivable be on December 31 if the Elliots' projections are met? What factors have they ignored? How would you change their projections to make them more realistic? What technique would you apply to accounts receivable at the end of each month to determine if the assumptions about collectibility are being met?

CHAPTER 8 INVENTORIES

LEARNING OBJECTIVES

1. Define nonmonetary assets, and state their relationship to the matching rule.
2. Define merchandise inventory, and show how inventory measurement affects income determination.
3. Calculate the pricing of inventory, using the cost basis according to the (a) specific identification method; (b) average-cost method; (c) first-in, first-out (FIFO) method; (d) last-in, first-out (LIFO) method.
4. Recognize the effects of each method on income determination in periods of changing prices.
5. Apply the perpetual inventory system to accounting for inventories and cost of goods sold.
6. Apply the lower-of-cost-or-market rule to inventory valuation.
7. Estimate the cost of ending inventory by using the (a) retail inventory method and (b) gross profit method.

This chapter begins by describing nonmonetary assets and their relationship to the matching rule. The rest of the chapter deals with inventory measurement, emphasizing its importance to income determination and explaining several different ways of determining, valuing, and estimating inventories. After studying this chapter, you should be able to meet the learning objectives listed at the left.

Nonmonetary Assets and the Matching Rule

On the one hand, **monetary assets** consist of cash and other assets representing the right to receive a specific amount of cash. **Nonmonetary assets**, on the other hand, are unexpired costs that will become expenses in future accounting periods. These assets are recorded at historical cost and are allocated to expense in accordance with the matching rule. It is not likely that the amount at which they are shown on the balance sheet would represent the amount of cash that could be gained from their sale because the allocation process is not an attempt to reflect the changing prices of the assets since their purchase.

Nonmonetary assets are of two kinds: short-term and long-term. **Short-term nonmonetary assets** come under the heading of current assets. Among these assets are prepaid rent, prepaid insurance, and other prepaid expenses. Inventories, too, are usually considered short-term nonmonetary assets.

Long-term nonmonetary assets or simply, **long-term assets**, must be allocated as expenses to two or more future years because they will have a positive effect on revenues during those years. In other words, they are unexpired costs that will expire over more than one future year. In most cases, long-term nonmonetary assets fall into the following three groups: (1) property, plant, and equipment; (2) natural resources; and (3) intangibles.

The most important accounting problem that arises in connection with all nonmonetary assets is the application of the matching rule. Nonmonetary assets are recorded at first as assets or unexpired costs. According to the matching rule, a portion of the cost must be transferred to an expense account in the accounting period that they benefit. We have seen, for example, that a three-year insurance policy is recorded as a debit to Prepaid Insurance and a credit to Cash or Accounts Payable. As time passes, it is necessary to use adjusting entries to charge the expired part of the policy to expense

OBJECTIVE 1
Define nonmonetary assets, and state their relationship to the matching rule

by debiting Insurance Expense and crediting Prepaid Insurance. To measure income properly, two important questions must be answered about each nonmonetary asset: (1) How much of the asset is used up or has expired during the current accounting period and should be transferred to expense? (2) How much of the asset is still unused or unexpired and should remain on the balance sheet as an asset?

Determining the amount of the expense will automatically establish the carrying value of the asset. In the case of insurance and other prepaid expenses, these calculations are fairly simple. However, the theoretical and practical problems associated with these measurements for inventories and long-term nonmonetary assets are among the most complex in accounting and have created much debate within and outside the accounting profession. For this reason, the rest of this chapter will deal with the application of the matching rule to inventories.

Inventories and Income Determination

OBJECTIVE 2
Define merchandise inventory, and show how inventory measurement affects income determination

The major source of revenue for retail or wholesale businesses is the sale of merchandise. In terms of dollars invested, the inventory of goods held for sale is one of the largest assets for a merchandising business. Because merchandise is continuously bought and sold, the cost of goods sold is the largest deduction from sales. In fact, it is often larger than all other expenses together.

Merchandise inventory consists of all goods that are owned and held for sale in the regular course of business, including incoming goods in transit if shipped FOB shipping point and outgoing goods if shipped FOB destination. Because it will normally be converted into cash within a year's time, merchandise inventory is considered a current asset. It is shown on the balance sheet just below Accounts Receivable because it is one step further removed from Cash.

In a manufacturing company, inventories are of three major kinds: raw materials to be used in making products, partly completed products (often called work in process), and finished goods ready for sale.

Objective of Inventory Measurement

The American Institute of Certified Public Accountants states, "A major objective of accounting for inventories is the proper determination of income through the process of matching appropriate costs against revenues."[1] Note that the objective is to determine the best measure of income, not the most realistic inventory value. As you will see, the two objectives are sometimes incompatible, in which case the objective of income determination takes precedence over a realistic inventory figure for the balance sheet.

1. American Institute of Certified Public Accountants, *Accounting Research Bulletins,* No. 43 (New York: AICPA, 1968), Ch. 4.

Review of Gross Margin and Cost of Goods Sold Computations

Because the computations of gross margin and cost of goods sold were presented earlier, a review might help to show how the cost assigned to inventory and these computations are related. The gross margin on sales earned during an accounting period is computed by deducting cost of goods sold from the net sales of the period.

Cost of goods sold is measured by deducting ending inventory from cost of goods available for sale. Because of these relationships, it may be shown that the higher the cost of ending inventory, the lower the cost of goods sold will be and the higher the resulting gross margin. Conversely, the lower the value assigned to ending inventory, the higher the cost of goods sold will be and the lower the gross margin. *In effect, the value assigned to the ending inventory determines what portion of the cost of goods originally available for sale will be deducted from net sales as cost of goods sold and what portion will be carried to the next period as beginning inventory.* Remember that the amount of goods available for sale includes the beginning inventory (unexpired costs passed from the last period to this period) plus net purchases during this period. The effects on income of errors in the cost of ending inventory are demonstrated in the next section.

Effects of Errors in Inventory Measurement

As seen above, the basic problem of separating goods available for sale into the two components, goods sold and goods not sold, is that of assigning a cost to the goods not sold or to the ending inventory. However, the determination of an ending inventory cost in effect decides the cost of goods sold. The reason is that whatever portion of the cost of goods available for sale is assigned to the ending inventory, the remainder is cost of goods sold.

For this reason, an error made in determining the inventory figure at the end of the period will cause an equal error in gross margin and net income in the income statement. The amount of assets and owner's equity in the balance sheet also will be misstated by the same amount. The consequences of overstatement and understatement of inventory are illustrated in the three simplified examples given below. In each case, beginning inventory, purchases, and cost of goods available for sale are correctly stated. In the first example, ending inventory has been stated correctly. In the second example, inventory is overstated by $6,000, and in the third example, inventory is understated by $6,000.

In these examples, the total cost of goods available for sale amounted to $70,000 in each case. The difference in net income resulted from how this $70,000 was divided between ending inventory and cost of goods sold.

Because the ending inventory in one period becomes the beginning inventory in the following period, it is important to recognize that an error in inventory valuation affects not only the current period but also the income statement for the following period. Using the same figures

Example 1. Ending Inventory Correctly Stated at $10,000

Cost of Goods Sold for the Year		Income Statement for the Year	
Beginning Inventory	$12,000	Net Sales	$100,000
Net Purchases	58,000	Cost of Goods Sold	60,000
Cost of Goods Available for Sale	$70,000	Gross Margin from Sales	$ 40,000
Ending Inventory	10,000	Expenses	30,000
Cost of Goods Sold	$60,000	Net Income	$ 10,000

Example 2. Ending Inventory Overstated by $6,000

Cost of Goods Sold for the Year		Income Statement for the Year	
Beginning Inventory	$12,000	Net Sales	$100,000
Net Purchases	58,000	Cost of Goods Sold	54,000
Cost of Goods Available for Sale	$70,000	Gross Margin from Sales	$ 46,000
Ending Inventory	16,000	Expenses	30,000
Cost of Goods Sold	$54,000	Net Income	$ 16,000

Example 3. Ending Inventory Understated by $6,000

Cost of Goods Sold for the Year		Income Statement for the Year	
Beginning Inventory	$12,000	Net Sales	$100,000
Net Purchases	58,000	Cost of Goods Sold	66,000
Cost of Goods Available for Sale	$70,000	Gross Margin from Sales	$ 34,000
Ending Inventory	4,000	Expenses	30,000
Cost of Goods Sold	$66,000	Net Income	$ 4,000

as examples 1 and 2 above, the income statements for two successive years in Exhibit 8-1 illustrate this carry-over effect.

Note that over a period of two years the errors will be offset or counterbalanced with regard to net income. In Exhibit 8-1, for example, the overstatement of ending inventory in 19x1 caused a $6,000 overstatement of beginning inventory in the following year, resulting in an understatement of income by the same amount. This offsetting effect is shown as follows:

	With Inventory Correctly Stated	With Inventory at Dec. 31, 19x1, Overstated	
		Reported Net Income Will Be	Reported Net Income Will Be Overstated (Understated)
Net Income for 19x1	$10,000	$16,000	$6,000
Net Income for 19x2	15,000	9,000	(6,000)
Total Net Income for Two Years	$25,000	$25,000	—

Because the total income for the two years is the same, there may be a tendency to think that one does not need to worry about inventory errors. This idea is not correct because it violates the matching rule, and many management decisions as well as creditor and investor decisions are made on an annual basis and depend on the accountant's determination of net income. The accountant has an obligation to make the net income figure as useful as possible.

The effects of errors in inventory on net income can be summarized as follows:

	Ending Inventory		Beginning Inventory	
	Understated	Overstated	Understated	Overstated
Net Income Overstated		×	×	
Net Income Understated	×			×

If we assume no income tax effects, a change or error in inventory of one amount results in a change or error in net income of the same amount. Thus the measurement of inventory is an important problem and is the subject of the remainder of this chapter.

Inventory Measurement

The cost assigned to ending inventory depends on two measurements: quantity and price. At least once each year, a business must take an actual physical count of all items of merchandise held for sale. This process is called taking a physical inventory, or simply taking inventory,

Exhibit 8-1. Effect of Error in Ending Inventory on Current and Succeeding Year

Effect of Error in Inventory
Income Statement
For the Year Ended December 31, 19x1

	Correct Statement of Ending Inventory		Overstatement of Ending Inventory	
Sales		$100,000		$100,000
Cost of Goods Sold				
Beginning Inventory, Dec. 31, 19x0	$12,000		$12,000	
Purchases	58,000		58,000	
Cost of Goods Available for Sale	$70,000		$70,000	
Less Ending Inventory, Dec. 31, 19x1	10,000		16,000	
Cost of Goods Sold		60,000		54,000
Gross Margin from Sales		$ 40,000		$ 46,000
Operating Expenses		30,000		30,000
Net Income		$ 10,000		$ 16,000

Effect on Succeeding Year
Income Statement
For the Year Ended December 31, 19x2

	Correct Statement of Beginning Inventory		Overstatement of Beginning Inventory	
Sales		$130,000		$130,000
Cost of Goods Sold				
Beginning Inventory, Dec. 31, 19x1	$10,000		$16,000	
Purchases	68,000		68,000	
Cost of Goods Available for Sale	$78,000		$84,000	
Less Ending Inventory, Dec. 31, 19x2	13,000		13,000	
Cost of Goods Sold		65,000		71,000
Gross Margin from Sales		$ 65,000		$ 59,000
Operating Expenses		50,000		50,000
Net Income		$ 15,000		$ 9,000

as described in Chapter 5. Although some companies take inventory at various times during the year, many companies take inventory only at the end of each year. Taking the inventory consists of (1) counting, weighing, or measuring the items on hand, (2) pricing each item, and (3) extending (multiplying) to determine the total.

Merchandise in Transit

Because merchandise inventory includes items owned by the company and held for sale, purchased merchandise in transit should be included in the inventory count if title to the goods has passed. As explained in Chapter 5, the terms of the shipping agreement must be examined to determine if title has passed. For example, outgoing goods shipped FOB destination would be included in merchandise inventory, whereas those shipped FOB shipping point would not. Conversely, incoming goods shipped FOB shipping point would be included in merchandise inventory, but those shipped FOB destination would not.

Merchandise on Hand Not Included in Inventory

At the time a physical inventory is taken, there may be merchandise on hand to which the company does not hold title. One category of such goods is an order for a customer on which the sale is completed and the goods in question now belong to the buyer and await delivery. This sale should be recorded and the goods segregated for delivery. A second category is goods held on consignment. A **consignment** is the placing of goods by the owner of the goods (known as the *consignor*) on the premises of another company (the *consignee*). Title to consigned goods remains with the consignor until the consignee sells the goods. Thus, if consigned goods are on hand, they should not be included in the physical inventory because they still belong to the consignor.

Pricing the Inventory at Cost

The pricing of inventory is one of the most interesting and most widely debated problems in accounting. As demonstrated above, the value placed on ending inventory may have a dramatic effect on net income for each of two consecutive years. Federal income taxes are based on income, so the valuation of inventory may have a considerable effect on the amount of income taxes to be paid. Federal income tax authorities have therefore been interested in the effects of various inventory valuation procedures and have specific regulations about the acceptability of different methods. So the accountant is sometimes faced with the problem of balancing the goals of proper income determination with those of minimizing income taxes payable.

There are a number of acceptable methods of valuing inventories in the accounts and on the financial statements. Most are based either on cost or on the lower of cost or market. Both methods are acceptable for income tax purposes. We will first explain variations of the cost basis of inventory valuation and then turn to the lower-of-cost-or-market method.

Cost Defined

According to the AICPA, "The primary basis of accounting for inventory is cost, which has been defined generally as the price paid or consideration given to acquire an asset. As applied to inventories, cost means in principle the sum of the applicable expenditures and charges directly or indirectly incurred in bringing an article to its existing condition and location."[2]

This definition of **inventory cost** has generally been interpreted in practice to include the following costs: (1) invoice price less cash discounts; (2) freight or transportation in, including insurance in transit; and (3) applicable taxes and tariffs.

Other costs, such as those for purchasing, receiving, and storage, should in principle also be included in inventory cost. In practice, however, it is so hard to allocate these costs to specific inventory items that they are in most cases considered an expense of the accounting period instead of an inventory cost.

Methods of Pricing Inventory at Cost

The prices of most kinds of merchandise vary during the year, and identical lots of merchandise may have been purchased at different prices. Also, when identical items are bought and sold, it is often impossible to tell which items have been sold and which are still in inventory. For this reason, it is necessary to make an assumption about the order in which items have been sold. Because the assumed order of sale may or may not be the same as the actual order of sale, the assumption is really an assumption about the *flow of costs* rather than the *flow of physical inventory*.

Thus the term **goods flow** refers to the actual physical movement of goods in the operations of the company, and the term **cost flow** refers to the association of costs with their *assumed* flow within the operations of the company. The assumed cost flow may or may not be the same as the actual goods flow. Though this statement may seem strange at first, there is nothing wrong with it. Several assumed cost flows are acceptable under generally accepted accounting principles. In fact, it is sometimes preferable to use an assumed cost flow that bears no relationship to goods flow because it gives a better estimate of income, which, as stated earlier, is the major goal of inventory valuation.

Accountants usually price inventory by using one of the following generally accepted methods, each based on a different assumption of cost flow: (1) specific identification method; (2) average-cost method; (3) first-in, first-out method (FIFO); and (4) last-in, first-out method (LIFO).

2. Ibid.

To illustrate the four methods, the following data for the month of June will be used:

Inventory Data, June 30

June 1		Inventory	50 units at $1.00	$ 50
6		Purchased	50 units at $1.10	55
13		Purchased	150 units at $1.20	180
20		Purchased	100 units at $1.30	130
25		Purchased	150 units at $1.40	210
Totals			500 units	$625
Sales			280 units	
On hand June 30			220 units	

Note that the total available for sale is 500 units, at a total cost of $625. Stated simply, the problem of inventory pricing is to divide the $625 between the 280 units sold and the 220 units on hand.

OBJECTIVE 3a
Calculate the pricing of inventory, using the cost basis according to the specific identification method

Specific Identification Method. If the units in the ending inventory can be identified as coming from specific purchases, the **specific identification method** may be used to price the inventories. For instance, assume that the June 30 inventory consisted of 50 units from the inventory on hand June 1, 100 units of the purchase of June 13, and 70 units of the purchase of June 25. The cost to be assigned to the inventory under the specific identification method would be $268, determined as follows:

Inventory, June 30—Specific Identification Method

50 units at $1.00	$ 50	Cost of Goods Available for Sale	$625
100 units at $1.20	120	→ **Less June 30 Inventory**	268
70 units at $1.40	98	Cost of Goods Sold	$357
220 units at a value of	**$268** ←		

The specific identification method might be used in the purchase and sale of high-priced articles such as automobiles, heavy equipment, and jewelry. However, although this method may appear to have a certain logic to it, it is not actually used much because it has two definite disadvantages. First, it is very difficult and impractical in most cases to keep track of the purchase and sale of individual items. Second, when a company deals in items of an identical nature, deciding which items are sold becomes arbitrary; thus the company can raise or lower income by choosing to sell the high- or low-cost items.

OBJECTIVE 3b
Calculate the pricing of inventory, using the cost basis according to the average-cost method

Average-Cost Method. Under the **average cost method**, it is assumed that the cost of inventory is the average cost of goods on hand at the beginning of the period plus all goods purchased during the period. Average cost is computed by dividing the total cost of goods available for sale by the total units available for sale. This gives a weighted-average unit cost that is applied to the units in the ending inventory. The ending inventory in the illustration when the average-cost method is used would be $1.25 per unit, or a total of $275, determined as follows:

Inventory, June 30—Average-Cost Method

June 1	Inventory	50 at $1.00	$ 50
6	Purchased	50 at $1.10	55
13	Purchased	150 at $1.20	180
20	Purchased	100 at $1.30	130
25	Purchased	150 at $1.40	210
Totals		500 units	$625

Average unit cost: $625 ÷ 500 = $1.25

→ **Ending inventory: 220 units @ $1.25 = $275**

Cost of Goods Available for Sale	$625
→ **Less June 30 Inventory**	**275**
Cost of Goods Sold	$350

The cost figure obtained for the ending inventory under the average-cost method is influenced by all the prices paid during the year and thus tends to level out the effects that cost increases and decreases during the year have on income. Some criticize the average-cost method because they feel that more recent costs should receive more attention and are more relevant for income measurement and decision making.

OBJECTIVE 3c
Calculate the pricing of inventory, using the cost basis according to the first-in, first-out (FIFO) method

First-In, First-Out (FIFO) Method. The **first-in, first-out (FIFO) method** is based on the assumption that the costs of the first items acquired should be assigned to the first items sold. The costs of the goods on hand at the end of a period are assumed to be from the most recent purchases and the costs assigned to goods that have been sold are assumed to be from the earliest purchases. The FIFO method of determining inventory cost may be adopted by any business, regardless of the actual physical flow of goods, because the assumption is made regarding the flow of costs and not the flow of goods.

For example, in our illustration, the June 30 inventory would be $301 when the FIFO method is used. It is computed as follows:

Inventory, June 30—First-In, First-Out Method

150 units at $1.40 from the purchase of June 25	$210
70 units at $1.30 from the purchase of June 20	91
→ **220 units at a value of**	**$301**

Cost of Goods Available for Sale	$625
→ **Less June 30 Inventory**	**301**
Cost of Goods Sold	$324

The effect of the FIFO method is to value the ending inventory at the most recent prices and include earlier prices in cost of goods sold. During periods of consistently rising prices, the FIFO method yields the highest possible amount of net income. One reason for this result is that businesses tend to increase selling prices as prices rise, regardless of the fact that inventories may have been purchased before the price rise. The reverse effect occurs in periods of price decreases. For these reasons a major criticism of FIFO is that it magnifies the effects of the business cycle on business income.

OBJECTIVE 3d
Calculate the pricing of inventory, using the cost basis according to the last-in, first-out (LIFO) method

Last-In, First-Out (LIFO) Method. The **last-in, first-out (LIFO) method** of costing inventories is based on the assumption that the costs of the last items purchased should be assigned to the first to be used or sold and that the cost of the ending inventory consists of the cost of merchandise purchased earliest.

Under this method, the June 30 inventory would be $249, computed as follows:

Inventory, June 30—Last-In, First-Out Method

50 units at $1.00 from June 1 inventory	$ 50
50 units at $1.10 from purchase of June 6	55
120 units at $1.20 from purchase of June 13	144
220 units at a value of	**$249**
Cost of Goods Available for Sale	$625
Less June 30 Inventory	249
Cost of Goods Sold	$376

The effect of LIFO is to value inventory at earliest prices and to include in cost of goods sold the cost of the most recent purchases of goods. This assumption, of course, does not agree with the actual physical movement of goods in most businesses.

However, there is a strong logical argument to support this method, based on the fact that a certain size inventory is necessary in a going concern. When inventory is sold, it must be replaced with more goods. The supporters of LIFO reason that the fairest determination of income occurs if the current costs of merchandise are matched against current sales prices, regardless of which physical units of merchandise are sold. When prices are moving either upward or downward, LIFO will mean that the cost of goods sold will show costs closer to the price level at the time the sales of goods are made. As a result, the LIFO method tends to show a smaller net income during inflationary times and a larger net income during deflationary times than other methods of inventory valuation. Thus the peaks and valleys of the business cycle tend to be smoothed out. The important factor here is that in inventory valuation the flow of costs and hence income determination is more important than the physical movement of goods and balance sheet valuation.

An argument may also be made against the LIFO method. Because the inventory valuation on the balance sheet reflects earlier prices, this value is often unrealistic with respect to the current value of the inventory. Thus such balance sheet measures as working capital and current ratio may be distorted and must be interpreted carefully.

Comparison of the Alternative Methods of Pricing Inventory

OBJECTIVE 4 Recognize the effects of each method on income determination in periods of changing prices

The specific identification, average-cost, FIFO, and LIFO methods of pricing inventory have now been illustrated. The specific identification method is based on actual costs, whereas the other three methods are based on assumptions regarding the flow of costs. Let us now compare the effects of the four methods on net income using the same data as before and assuming sales during June of $500.

	Specific Identification Method	Average-Cost Method	First-In, First-Out Method	Last-In, First-Out Method
Sales	$500	$500	$500	$500
Cost of Goods Sold				
Beginning Inventory	$ 50	$ 50	$ 50	$ 50
Purchases	575	575	575	575
Cost of Goods Available for Sale	$625	$625	$625	$625
Less Ending Inventory	268	275	301	249
Costs of Goods Sold	$357	$350	$324	$376
Gross Margin from Sales	**$143**	**$150**	**$176**	**$124**

Keeping in mind that in the illustration June was a period of rising prices, we can see that LIFO, which charges the most recent and in this case the highest prices to cost of goods sold, resulted in the lowest net income. Conversely, FIFO, which charges the earliest and in this case the lowest prices to cost of goods sold, produced the highest net income. The net income under the average-cost method is somewhere between those computed under LIFO and FIFO. Thus it is clear that this method has a less pronounced effect.

During a period of declining prices, the reverse effects would occur. The LIFO method would produce a higher net income than the FIFO method. It is apparent that the method of inventory valuation takes on the greatest importance during prolonged periods of price changes in one direction, either up or down.

Effect on the Financial Statements. Each of the four methods of inventory pricing presented above is acceptable for use in published financial statements. The FIFO, LIFO, and average-cost methods are widely used, as can be seen in Figure 8-1, which shows the inventory cost methods used by six hundred large companies. Each has its advantages and disadvantages, and none can be considered as best or perfect. The factors that should be considered in choosing an inventory method are the effects of each method on the balance sheet, the income statement, income taxes, and management decisions.

A basic problem in determining the best inventory measure for a particular company is that inventory appears on both the balance sheet and the income statement. As we have seen, the LIFO method is best suited for the income statement because it best matches revenues and cost of goods sold. But it is not the best measure of the current balance sheet value of inventory, particularly when there has been a prolonged period of price increases or decreases. The FIFO method, on the other hand, is best suited to the balance sheet because the ending inventory is closest to current values and thus gives a more realistic view of the current financial assets of a business. Readers of financial statements must be alert to inventory methods and be able to assess their effects.

Effect on Income Taxes. When prices are changing rapidly, management must base its sales policies on current replacement costs of the goods being sold. The LIFO method most nearly represents the measurement of net income based on these current costs. In addition, as seen in the illustration on page 308, in periods of rising prices LIFO shows a smaller profit. Thus, many businesses use LIFO to reduce the amount of income taxes to be paid.

Many accountants believe that the use of FIFO or average-cost methods in periods of rising prices causes businesses to report more than their true profit, resulting in the payment of excess income taxes. The profit is overstated because the company must now buy new inventory at higher prices, but some of the funds that should have been used for purchase of replacement inventory went to pay income taxes. During the rapid inflation of 1979 to 1982, billions of dollars reported as profits and paid in income taxes were believed to be the result of poor matching of current costs and revenues under the FIFO and average-cost methods. Consequently, many companies have since switched to the LIFO inventory method.

Figure 8-1. Inventory Cost Methods Used by 600 Large Companies

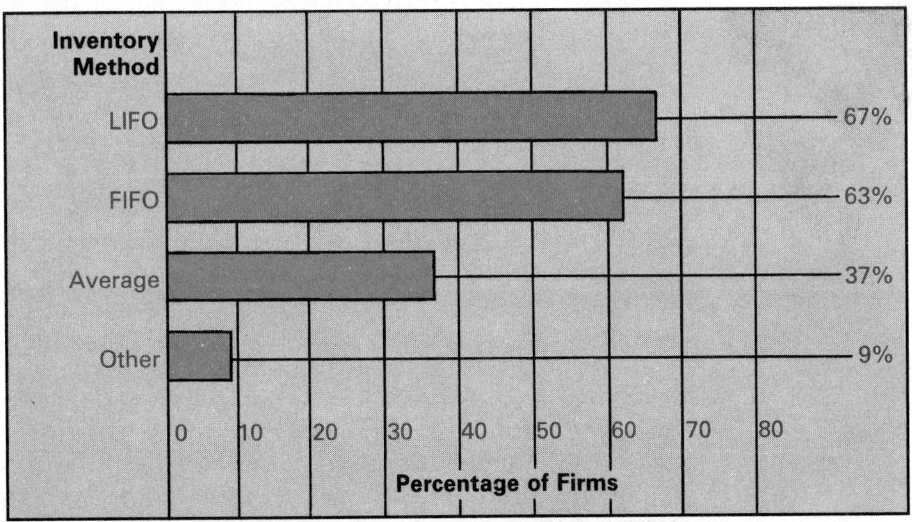

Total percentage exceeds 100 because some companies used different methods for different types of inventory.
Source: American Institute of Certified Public Accountants, *Accounting Trends and Techniques* (New York: AICPA, 1985).

Application of the Perpetual Inventory System

OBJECTIVE 5
Apply the perpetual inventory system to accounting for inventories and cost of goods sold

The system of inventories used so far in this book has been the **periodic inventory system**. Under this system no detailed record of inventory is kept during the year and a physical inventory must be taken at the end of the year to establish ending inventory. The cost of goods sold cannot be determined until the physical inventory is completed. Cost of goods sold is computed by adding the net cost of purchases to beginning inventory and subtracting the ending inventory.

Periodic inventory systems are used in many retail and wholesale businesses because they do not require a large amount of clerical work. The primary disadvantage of periodic inventory systems is the lack of detailed records as to what items of inventory are on hand at a point in time. Such detailed data would enable management to respond to customers' inquiries concerning product availability, order inventory more effectively to avoid being out of stock, and control the financial costs associated with the money invested in the inventory. The system that provides this type of data is the **perpetual inventory system**. Under this system, a continuous record of the inventory is maintained by keeping detailed records of the purchases and sales of inventory. As a result, the amount of inventory on hand and the cost of goods sold are known throughout the accounting period. In the past, the high clerical cost of maintaining this type of system meant that it was used primarily for goods of high value and low volume. However, with the advent of the computer and of electronic tags and markings, the perpetual inventory system has become easier and less expensive to operate and consequently has become much more prevalent. For example, the electronic markings of grocery items enable grocery stores to maintain perpetual inventory records; and the tags attached to products sold by clothing, department, and discount stores such as Sears and K mart enable them to have tight controls over inventory and ordering.

Handling the Perpetual Inventory System in the Accounting Records

The primary difference in accounting between the perpetual and the periodic inventory systems is that under the perpetual inventory system, the Merchandise Inventory account is continuously adjusted by entering purchases, sales, and other inventory transactions as they occur. Under the periodic inventory system, on the other hand, the Merchandise Inventory account stays at the beginning level until the physical inventory is recorded at the end of the accounting period. As a result, accounts you are familiar with under the periodic inventory system such as Purchases, Purchases Returns and Allowances, Purchases Discounts, and Freight In are not used. Also, as sales occur, the Cost of Goods Sold account is used to accumulate the cost of goods sold to customers. To illustrate these differences, the transactions of an office supply wholesaler are recorded under both the periodic and perpetual inventory systems as follows:

1. Received 100 cases of floppy disks for word processors at a cost of $12,000; terms 2/10, n/30, FOB destination. The net method of recording purchases is used.

Perpetual Inventory System			**Periodic Inventory System**		
Merchandise Inventory	11,760		Purchases	11,760	
Accounts Payable		11,760	Accounts Payable		11,760
Purchase of merchandise at net purchase price; (terms 2/10, n/30, FOB destination)			Purchase of merchandise at net purchase price; (terms 2/10, net/30, FOB destination)		

2. Sold 20 cases of floppy disks to a retailer at a total price of $3,000, terms n/10, FOB shipping point.

Perpetual Inventory System			**Periodic Inventory System**		
Accounts Receivable	3,000		Accounts Receivable	3,000	
Sales		3,000	Sales		3,000
Sales of 20 cases; terms n/10, FOB shipping point			Sales of 20 cases; terms n/10, FOB shipping point		
Cost of Goods Sold	2,352				
Merchandise Inventory		2,352			
To record cost of goods sold 20 cases × $117.60 = $2,352					

3. Arranged to return 10 cases of the floppy disks to supplier for full credit.

Perpetual Inventory System			**Periodic Inventory System**		
Accounts Payable	1,176		Accounts Payable	1,176	
Merchandise Inventory		1,176	Purchases Returns and Allowances		1,176
To record purchase return 10 cases × $117.60 = $1,176			To record purchase return		

4. Paid supplier in full within the discount period.

Perpetual Inventory System			**Periodic Inventory System**		
Accounts Payable	10,584		Accounts Payable	10,584	
Cash		10,584	Cash		10,584
Payment to supplier $11,760 − $1,176 = $10,584			Payment to supplier $11,760 − $1,176 = $10,584		

Note the differences in the first three transactions. In each case, under the perpetual inventory method, the Merchandise Inventory account is updated for the effect on the current status of the physical inventory; the Purchases and Purchases Returns and Allowances accounts are not used. Also, in transaction 2, the Cost of Goods Sold account is updated at the time of a sale.

At the end of the year, neither adjustments to Merchandise Inventory nor corresponding debits or credits to Income Summary are needed under the perpetual inventory system because the Merchandise Inventory account has been continually updated during the year and thus there is no need to establish the ending inventory in the records. The closing entry required is to close Cost of Goods Sold to Income Summary as an expense.

Maintaining the Detailed Perpetual Inventory Records

To keep track of the quantities and costs of the individual items stocked in merchandise inventory under the perpetual inventory system, it is necessary to maintain an individual record for each type of inventory. The Merchandise Inventory account is a controlling account for a subsidiary file of individual inventory records. This mechanism is very similar to that of the Accounts Receivable controlling account and its subsidiary ledger. In the inventory subsidiary file, each item has a card (or computer file in a computer system) on which purchases and sales are entered as they take place. A sample perpetual inventory card is shown in Exhibit 8-2 for another item held for sale by our office supply wholesaler. At any time, the card will show the number of pencil sharpeners on hand, and the total of all the cards is equal to the merchandise inventory.

As shown in Exhibit 8-2, on June 1 there is a balance of 60 pencil sharpeners that cost \$5 each. A sale on June 4 reduces the balance by 10 pencil sharpeners. On June 10, 100 pencil sharpeners are purchased at \$6 each. Now the inventory consists of 50 pencil sharpeners purchased at \$5 each and 100 pencil sharpeners purchased at \$6 each. The method of inventory valuation in Exhibit 8-2 is first-in, first-out, as can be determined by looking at the June 20 sale. The entire sale of 30 pencil sharpeners is taken from the 50 sharpeners still left from the beginning inventory. If the LIFO method were used, the sale would be deducted from the latest purchase of 100 pencil sharpeners at \$6 each. Under LIFO the resulting balance would be \$670 [(50 × \$5) + (70 × \$6)].

Exhibit 8-2. Perpetual Inventory Record Card, FIFO

Item: Pencil Sharpener, Model D-222

	Received			Sold			Balance		
Date	Units	Cost	Total	Units	Cost	Total	Units	Cost	Balance
June 1							60	5.00	300.00
4				10	5.00	50.00	50	5.00	250.00
10	100	6.00	600.00				50 100	5.00 6.00	850.00
20				30	5.00	150.00	20 100	5.00 6.00	700.00

Need for Physical Inventories Under the Perpetual Inventory System

The use of the perpetual inventory system does not eliminate the need for a physical inventory at the end of the accounting period. The perpetual inventory records show what should be on hand, not necessarily what is on hand. There may be losses due to spoilage, pilferage, theft, or other causes. If a loss has occurred, it is reflected in the accounts by a debit to Cost of Goods Sold and a credit to Merchandise Inventory. The individual inventory cards, which may also be the subsidiary ledger, must also be adjusted.

Valuing the Inventory at the Lower of Cost or Market (LCM)

OBJECTIVE 6
Apply the lower-of-cost-or-market rule to inventory valuation

Although cost is usually the most appropriate basis for valuation of inventory, there are times when inventory may properly be valued at less than its cost. If by reason of physical deterioration, obsolescence, or decline in price level the market value of the inventory falls below the cost, a loss has occurred. This loss may be recognized by writing the inventory down to market. The term **market** is used here to mean current replacement cost. For a merchandising company, market is the amount that the company would pay at the present time for the same goods, purchased from the usual suppliers and in the usual quantities. It may help in applying the **lower-of-cost-or-market (LCM) rule** by thinking of it as the "lower-of-cost-or-replacement-cost" rule.[3]

Methods of Applying LCM

There are three basic methods of valuing inventories at the lower of cost or market, as follows: (1) the item-by-item method, (2) the major category method, and (3) the total inventory method.

For example, a stereo shop could determine lower of cost or market for each kind of speaker, receiver, and turntable (item by item); for all speakers, all receivers, and all turntables (major categories); or for all speakers, receivers, and turntables together (total inventory).

Item-by-Item Method. When the **item-by-item method** is used, cost and market are compared for each item in the inventory. The individual items are then valued at their lower price.

3. In some cases, *market value* is determined by the *realizable value* of the inventory—the amount for which the goods can be sold rather than the amount for which the goods can be replaced. The circumstances in which realizable value determines market value are only occasionally encountered in practice and the valuation procedures are technical enough to be addressed in a more advanced accounting course.

Lower of Cost or Market with Item-by-Item Method

	Quantity	Per Unit Cost	Per Unit Market	Lower of Cost or Market
Category I				
Item a	200	$1.50	$1.70	$ 300
Item b	100	2.00	1.80	180
Item c	100	2.50	2.60	250
Category II				
Item d	300	5.00	4.50	1,350
Item e	200	4.00	4.10	800
Inventory at the lower of cost or market				**$2,880**

Major Category Method. Under the **major category method,** the total cost and total market for each category of items are compared. Each category is then valued at its lower amount.

Total Inventory Method. Under the **total inventory method,** the entire inventory is valued at both cost and market, and the lower price is used to value inventory. Since this method is not acceptable for federal income tax purposes, it is not illustrated here.

Lower of Cost or Market with Major Category Method

	Quantity	Per Unit Cost	Per Unit Market	Total Cost	Total Market	Lower of Cost or Market
Category I						
Item a	200	$1.50	$1.70	$ 300	$ 340	
Item b	100	2.00	1.80	200	180	
Item c	100	2.50	2.60	250	260	
Totals				$ 750	$ 780	$ 750
Category II						
Item d	300	5.00	4.50	$1,500	$1,350	
Item e	200	4.00	4.10	800	820	
Totals				$2,300	$2,170	2,170
Inventory at the lower of cost or market						**$2,920**

A Note on Inventory Valuation and Federal Income Taxes

The Internal Revenue Service has developed several rules for the valuation of inventories for federal income tax purposes. A company has a wide choice of methods, including cost or lower of cost or market and FIFO or LIFO. But once a method is chosen, it must be used consistently from one year to the next. The IRS must approve any changes in inventory valuation method for income tax purposes.[4] This requirement, of course, is also in agreement with the rule of consistency in accounting in that changes in inventory method would cause income to fluctuate too much and would make income statements hard to interpret from year to year. A company can change its inventory method if there is a good reason for doing so. The nature and effect of the change must be shown on its financial statements.

If a company uses the LIFO method in reporting income for tax purposes, the IRS requires that the LIFO method also be used in the accounting records. Also, the IRS will not allow the use of the lower-of-cost-or-market rule if the method of determining cost is the LIFO method. In this case, only the LIFO cost can be used. This rule does not preclude a company from using lower of LIFO cost or market for financial reporting purposes. As noted, another regulation bars the use of the total inventory method for determining lower of cost or market.

Valuing Inventory by Estimation

It is sometimes necessary or desirable to estimate the value of ending inventory. The methods most commonly used for this purpose are the retail method and the gross profit method.

Retail Method of Inventory Estimation

OBJECTIVE 7a Estimate the cost of ending inventory by using the retail inventory method

The **retail method**, as its name implies, is used in retail merchandising businesses. There are two principal reasons for the use of the retail method. First, management usually requires that financial statements be prepared at least once a month and, as it is time-consuming and expensive to take physical inventory each month, the retail method is used to estimate the value of inventory. Second, because items in a retail store normally have a price tag, it is common to take the physical inventory at retail from these price tags and reduce the total value to cost through use of the retail method.

When the retail method is used to estimate an end-of-period inventory, the records must show the amount of inventory at the beginning of the period at cost and at retail. The term *at retail* means the amount of the

4. A single exception to this rule is that taxpayers must notify the IRS of a change to LIFO from another method, but do not require advance IRS approval.

inventory at the marked selling prices of the inventory items. The records must also show the amount of goods purchased during the period both at cost and at retail. The net sales at retail are, of course, the balance of the Sales account less returns and allowances and discounts. A simple example of the retail method is shown below.

The Retail Method of Inventory Valuation

	Cost	Retail
Beginning Inventory	$ 40,000	$ 55,000
Net Purchases for the Period	107,000	145,000
Freight In	3,000	
Merchandise Available for Sale	$150,000	$200,000
Ratio of cost to retail price: $\frac{\$150,000}{\$200,000} = 75\%$		
Net Sales During the Period		160,000
Estimated Ending Inventory at Retail		$ 40,000
Ratio of cost to retail	75%	
Estimated Cost of Ending Inventory	$ 30,000	

Merchandise available for sale is determined both at cost and at retail by listing beginning inventory and net purchases for the period at cost and at the expected selling price of the goods, adding freight in to the cost column, and totaling. The ratio of these two amounts (cost to retail price) provides an estimate of the cost of each dollar of retail sales value. The estimated ending inventory at retail is then determined by deducting sales for the period from the retail price of the goods that were available for sale during the period. The inventory at retail is now converted to cost on the basis of the ratio of cost to retail.

The cost of ending inventory may also be estimated by applying the ratio of cost to retail to the total retail value of the physical count of the inventory. Applying the retail method in practice is often more difficult than this simple example because of certain complications such as changes in the retail price that take place during the year, different markups on different types of merchandise, and varying volumes of sales for different types of merchandise.

Gross Profit Method of Inventory Estimation

OBJECTIVE 7b
Estimate the cost of ending inventory by using the gross profit method

The **gross profit method** assumes that the ratio of gross margin for a business remains relatively stable from year to year. It is used in place of the retail method when records of the retail prices of beginning inventory and purchases are not kept. It is also useful in estimating the amount of inventory lost or destroyed by theft, fire, or other hazards. Insurance companies often use this method to verify loss claims.

The gross profit method is very simple to use. First, figure the cost of goods available for sale in the usual way (add purchases to beginning inventory). Second, estimate the cost of goods sold by deducting the estimated gross margin from sales. Third, deduct the estimated cost of goods sold from the goods available for sale. This method is shown below.

The Gross Profit Method of Inventory Valuation

1. Beginning Inventory at Cost		$ 50,000
Purchases at Cost		290,000
Cost of Goods Available for Sale		$340,000
2. Less Estimated Cost of Goods Sold		
Sales at Selling Price	$400,000	
Less Estimated Gross Margin of 30%	120,000	
Cost of Goods Sold		280,000
3. Estimated Cost of Ending Inventory		$ 60,000

Chapter Review

Review of Learning Objectives

1. **Define nonmonetary assets and state their relationship to the matching rule.** Nonmonetary assets are unexpired costs that will become expenses in future accounting periods. Typical nonmonetary assets are inventory; prepaid expenses; property, plant, and equipment; natural resources; and intangible assets. To apply the matching rule to nonmonetary assets, one must determine how much of the asset is used up or expired during the current accounting period and how much of the asset is still unused or unexpired. The former amount is an expense of the period; the latter is an asset.

2. **Define merchandise inventory and show how inventory measurement affects income determination.**
Merchandise inventory consists of all goods owned and held for sale in the regular course of business. The objective of accounting for inventories is the proper determination of income. If the value of ending inventory is understated or overstated, a corresponding error—dollar for dollar—will be made in net income. Furthermore, because the ending inventory of one period is the beginning inventory of the next, the misstatement affects two accounting periods, although the effects are opposite.

3. **Calculate the pricing of inventory, using the cost basis according to the (a) specific identification method; (b) average-cost method; (c) first-in, first-out (FIFO) method; (d) last-in, first-out (LIFO) method.**
The value assigned to the ending inventory is the result of two measurements: quantity and price. Quantity is determined by taking a physical inventory.

The pricing of inventory is usually based on the assumed cost flow of the goods as they are bought and sold. One of four assumptions is usually made regarding cost flow. These assumptions are represented by four inventory methods. Inventory pricing could be determined by the specific identification method, which associates the actual cost with each item of inventory but is rarely used. The average-cost method assumes that the cost of inventory is the average cost of goods available for sale during the period. The first-in, first-out (FIFO) method assumes that the costs of the first items acquired should be assigned to the first items sold. The last-in, first-out (LIFO) method assumes that the costs of the last items acquired should be assigned to the first items sold. The method chosen may or may not be equivalent to the actual flow of physical goods.

4. **Recognize the effects of each method on income determination in periods of changing prices.**

   During periods of rising prices, the LIFO method will show the lowest net income; FIFO, the highest; and average cost, in between. The opposite effects occur in periods of falling prices. No generalization can be made regarding the specific identification method.

5. **Apply the perpetual inventory system to accounting for inventories and cost of goods sold.**

   Under the periodic inventory system, the one used earlier in this book, inventory is determined by a physical count at the end of the accounting period. Under the perpetual inventory system, the inventory control account is constantly updated as sales and purchases are made during the accounting period. Also, as sales are made the Cost of Goods Sold account is used to accumulate the costs of those sales.

6. **Apply the lower-of-cost-or-market (LCM) rule to inventory valuation.**

   The lower-of-cost-or-market rule can be applied to the above methods of determining inventory at cost. This rule states that if the replacement cost (market) of the inventory is lower than what the inventory cost, the lower figure should be used. The Internal Revenue Service requires that if LIFO is used for tax purposes, it must also be used for book purposes, and that the lower-of-cost-or-market rule cannot be applied to the LIFO method.

7. **Estimate the cost of ending inventory by using the (a) retail inventory method and (b) the gross profit method.**

   Two methods of estimating the value of inventory are the retail inventory method and the gross profit method. Under the retail inventory method, inventory is determined at retail prices and is reduced to estimated cost by applying a ratio of cost to retail price. Under the gross profit method, cost of goods sold is estimated by reducing sales by estimated gross margin. The estimated cost of goods sold is then deducted from cost of goods available for sale to estimate the inventory.

Review Problem
Periodic and Perpetual Inventory Methods

The table on page 319 summarizes the beginning inventory, purchases, and sales of Psi Company's single product during January.

Required

1. Assuming that the company uses the periodic inventory method, compute the cost that should be assigned to ending inventory using (a) a FIFO basis and (b) a LIFO basis.

	Inventory			Purchases			
Date	**Units**	**Cost**	**Total**	**Units**	**Cost**	**Total**	**Sales Units**
Jan. 1	1,400	$19	$26,600				
4							300
8				600	$20	$12,000	
10							1,300
12				900	21	18,900	
15							150
18				500	22	11,000	
24				800	23	18,400	
31							1,350
Totals	1,400		$26,600	2,800		$60,300	3,100

2. Assuming that the company uses the perpetual inventory method, compute the cost that should be assigned to ending inventory using (a) a FIFO basis and (b) a LIFO basis. (Hint: It is helpful to use a form similar to the perpetual inventory card in Exhibit 8-2.)

Answer to Review Problem

	Units	Dollars
Beginning Inventory	1,400	$26,600
Purchases	2,800	60,300
Available for Sale	4,200	$86,900
Sales	3,100	
Ending Inventory	1,100	

1. Periodic inventory method
   a. FIFO basis
      Ending inventory consists of

Jan 24 purchases (800 × $23)	$18,400	
Jan. 18 purchases (300 × $22)	6,600	$25,000

   b. LIFO basis
      Ending inventory consists of

Beginning inventory (1,100 × $19)	$20,900

2. Perpetual inventory method
   a. FIFO basis

Date	Received			Sold			Balance		
	Units	Cost	Total	Units	Cost	Total	Units	Cost	Total
Jan. 1							1,400	$19	$26,600
4				300	$19	$ 5,700	1,100	19	20,900
8	600	$20	$12,000				1,100 600	19 20	32,900
10				1,100 200	19 20	24,900	400	20	8,000
12	900	21	18,900				400 900	20 21	26,900
15				150	20	3,000	250 900	20 21	23,900
18	500	22	11,000				250 900 500	20 21 22	34,900
24	800	23	18,400				250 900 500 800	20 21 22 23	53,300
31				250 900 200	20 21 22	28,300	300 800	22 23	25,000

b. LIFO basis

Date	Received			Sold			Balance		
	Units	Cost	Total	Units	Cost	Total	Units	Cost	Total
Jan. 1							1,400	$19	$26,600
4				300	$19	$ 5,700	1,100	19	20,900
8	600	$20	$12,000				1,100 600	19 20	32,900
10				600 700	20 19	25,300	400	19	7,600
12	900	21	18,900				400 900	19 21	26,500

	Received			Sold			Balance		
Date	Units	Cost	Total	Units	Cost	Total	Units	Cost	Total
15				150	21	3,150	400	19	
							750	21	23,350
18	500	22	11,000				400	19	
							750	21	
							500	22	34,350
24	800	23	18,400				400	19	
							750	21	
							500	22	
							800	23	52,750
31				800	23				
				500	22				
				50	21	30,450	400	19	
							700	21	22,300

Chapter Assignments

Questions

1. Why is inventory called a nonmonetary asset, and what measurements of nonmonetary assets must be taken to make a proper income determination? What is the relationship of nonmonetary assets to the matching rule?
2. What is merchandise inventory, and what is the primary objective of inventory measurement?
3. If the merchandise inventory is mistakenly overstated at the end of 19x8, what is the effect on (a) 19x8 net income, (b) 19x8 year-end balance sheet value, (c) 19x9 net income, (d) 19x9 year-end balance sheet value?
4. Fargo Sales Company is very busy at the end of its fiscal year on June 30. There is an order for 130 units of product in the warehouse. Although the shipping department tries, it cannot ship the product by June 30, and title has not yet passed. Should the 130 units be included in the year-end count of inventory?
5. What does the term *taking a physical inventory* mean?
6. What items are included in the cost of inventory?
7. In periods of steadily rising prices, which of the three inventory methods—average-cost, FIFO, or LIFO—will give the (a) highest inventory cost, (b) lowest inventory cost, (c) highest net income, and (d) lowest net income?
8. May a company change its inventory costing method from year to year? Explain.
9. Do FIFO and LIFO result in different quantities of ending inventory?
10. Under which method of cost flow are (a) the earliest costs assigned to inventory, (b) the latest costs assigned to inventory, (c) the average costs assigned to inventory?

11. What are the relative advantages and disadvantages of FIFO and LIFO from management's point of view?
12. Which of the following companies would find a perpetual inventory system practical: a drug store, a grocery store, a restaurant, an automobile dealer, a wholesale auto parts dealer? Why?
13. Which is more expensive to maintain: a perpetual inventory system or a periodic inventory system? Why?
14. What differences occur in recording sales, purchases, and closing entries under the perpetual and periodic inventory systems?
15. In the phrase "lower of cost or market," what is meant by "market"?
16. What methods can be used to determine lower of cost or market?
17. What effects do income taxes have on inventory valuation?
18. What are some reasons why management may want to use the gross profit method of determining inventory?
19. Does using the retail inventory method mean that inventories are measured at retail value on the balance sheet? Explain.
20. Which of the following inventory systems do not require a physical inventory: (a) perpetual, (b) periodic, (c) retail, (d) gross profit?

Classroom Exercises

Exercise 8-1. Effects of Inventory Errors (L.O. 2)

Condensed income statements for Jackson Company for two years are shown below.

	19x2	19x1
Sales	$44,000	$37,000
Cost of Goods Sold	26,000	19,000
Gross Margin on Sales	$18,000	$18,000
Operating Expenses	9,000	9,000
Net Income	$ 9,000	$ 9,000

After the end of 19x2, it was discovered that an error had been made in 19x1 that resulted in an understatement of the ending inventory of 19x1 by $4,000.

Compute the corrected net income for 19x1 and 19x2. What effect will the error have on net income and owner's equity for 19x3?

Exercise 8-2. Inventory Cost Methods (L.O. 3)

Jack's Farm Store had the following purchases and sales of fertilizer during the year:

Jan. 1	Beginning inventory	200 cases at $24 =	$ 4,800
Feb. 25	Purchased	100 cases at $26 =	2,600
June 15	Purchased	400 cases at $28 =	11,200
Aug. 15	Purchased	100 cases at $26 =	2,600
Oct. 15	Purchased	300 cases at $28 =	8,400
Dec. 15	Purchased	200 cases at $30 =	6,000
Totals		1,300 cases	$35,600
Total sales		1,000 cases	
Dec. 31 Ending inventory		300 cases	

Assume that all of the June 15 purchase and 200 cases each from the January 1 beginning inventory, the October 15 purchase, and the December 15 purchase were sold.

Determine the costs that should be assigned to cost of goods sold and ending inventory under each of the following assumptions: (1) Costs are assigned by the specific identification method. (2) Costs are assigned on an average-cost basis. (3) Costs are assigned on a FIFO basis. (4) Costs are assigned on a LIFO basis. What conclusions can you draw from your answers?

Exercise 8-3. Inventory Cost Methods (L.O. 3)

During its first year of operation, Reed Company purchased 5,500 units of a product at $20 per unit. During the second year, it purchased 6,000 units of the same product at $24 per unit. During the third year, it purchased 5,000 units at $30 per unit. Reed Company managed to have an ending inventory each year of 1,000 units. The company sells goods at a 100 percent markup over cost.

Prepare cost of goods sold statements that compare the value of ending inventory and the cost of goods sold for each of the three years using (1) the FIFO method and (2) the LIFO method. What conclusions can you draw from the resulting data about the relationships between changes in unit price and changes in the value of ending inventory?

Exercise 8-4. Perpetual and Periodic Inventory Methods (L.O. 5)

Record general journal entries using the net purchase method to record the following transactions under (1) the perpetual inventory system and (2) the periodic inventory system.

March 11	Received 5,000 cases of chloride tablets at a cost of $150 per case, terms 2/10, n/30, FOB destination.
March 15	Sold 100 cases of tablets for $250 per case, terms n/10, FOB shipping point.
March 17	Returned 30 cases that were damaged to suppliers for full credit.
March 20	Paid the supplier in full for the amount owed on the purchase of March 11.

Exercise 8-5. Lower-of-Cost-or-Market Method (L.O. 6)

Yaeger Company values its inventory, shown below, at the lower of cost or market. Compute Yaeger's inventory value using (1) the item-by-item method and (2) the major category method.

		Per Unit	
	Quantity	Cost	Market
Category 1			
Item aa	100	$1.00	$ .90
Item bb	120	2.00	2.20
Item cc	200	4.00	3.75
Category 2			
Item dd	600	6.00	6.50
Item ee	800	9.00	9.10

Exercise 8-6. Retail Method
(L.O. 7)

Jamie's Dress Shop had net retail sales of $220,000 during the current year. The following additional information was obtained from the accounting records:

	At Cost	At Retail
Beginning Inventory	$ 30,000	$ 45,000
Net Purchases	140,000	220,000
Freight In	7,550	

1. Estimate the company's ending inventory at cost using the retail method.
2. Assume that a physical inventory taken at year end revealed an inventory on hand of $38,000 at retail value. What is the estimated amount of inventory shrinkage (loss due to theft, damage, and so forth) at cost?
3. Prepare the journal entry to record the inventory shrinkage.

Exercise 8-7. Gross Profit Method
(L.O. 7)

Dale Nolan was at home watching television when he received a call from the fire department. His business was a total loss from fire. The insurance company asked him to prove his inventory loss. For the year, until the date of the fire, Dale's company had sales of $450,000 and purchases of $280,000. Freight in amounted to $13,700, and the beginning inventory was $45,000. It was Dale's custom to price goods in such a way as to have a gross margin of 40 percent on sales.

Compute Dale's estimated inventory loss.

Interpreting Accounting Information

Hershey Foods Corporation[5]
(L.O. 2, 4)

A portion of the income statement for 1983 and 1982 for Hershey Foods Corporation famous for its chocolate and confectionery products, appears as follows (in thousands):

	1983	1982
Net Sales	$1,706,105	$1,565,736
Cost of Goods Sold	1,168,109	1,084,748
Gross Margin	$ 537,996	$ 480,988
Selling, General, and Administrative Expense	332,831	301,586
Income from Operations	$ 205,165	$ 179,402
Interest Expense	15,814	7,859
Income before Income Taxes	$ 189,351	$ 171,543
Provision for Income Taxes	89,185	77,375
Net Income	$ 100,166	$ 94,168

In the summary of significant accounting policies, Hershey indicates that most of its inventories are maintained on a last-in, first-out (LIFO) basis. The company also reported that inventories on a LIFO cost basis were $178,585 in 1982 and $194,666 in 1983. In addition, it reports that if valued on a first-in, first-out basis inventories would have been $254,047 in 1982 and $259,542 in 1983.

5. Income statement figures for 1982 and 1983 reprinted by permission from the annual report of Hershey Foods Corporation, 14 East Chocolate Avenue, Hershey, PA 17033.

Required

1. Prepare a schedule comparing net income for 1983 on a LIFO basis with what it would have been on a FIFO basis. Use a corporate income tax rate of 47.1 percent.
2. Why do you suppose the management of Hershey chooses to use the LIFO inventory method? On what economic conditions, if any, do these reasons depend? Based on your calculations in **1** above, do you believe the economic conditions relevant to Hershey were advantageous for using LIFO in 1983?

Problem Set A

Problem 8A-1. Inventory Cost Methods
(L.O. 3)

The Magnet Door Company sold 2,000 doors during 19x8 at $150 per door. Its beginning inventory on January 1 was 125 doors at $50. Purchases during the year were as follows:

February	225 doors @ $52	August	300 doors @ $56
April	350 doors @ $55	October	200 doors @ $58
June	700 doors @ $60	November	250 doors @ $62

The company's selling and administrative costs for the year were $95,000, and the company uses the periodic inventory method.

Required

1. Prepare a schedule to compute the cost of goods available for sale.
2. Prepare an income statement under each of the following assumptions: (a) Costs are assigned to inventory on an average cost basis. (b) Costs are assigned to inventory on a FIFO basis. (c) Costs are assigned to inventory on a LIFO basis.

Problem 8A-2. Lower-of-Cost-or-Market Method
(L.O. 6)

The employees of Hobart's Shoes completed their physical inventory as shown below:

	Pairs of Shoes	Per Pair Cost	Per Pair Market
Men			
Black	300	$20	$25
Brown	325	21	21
Blue	100	25	23
Oxford	200	19	10
Women			
White	200	$25	$35
Red	150	23	20
Yellow	100	30	25
Blue	250	25	33
Brown	100	20	30
Black	150	20	25

Required

Determine the value of inventory at lower-of-cost-or-market using (1) the item-by-item method and (2) the major category method.

Problem 8A-3. Perpetual Inventory System (L.O. 5)

The beginning inventory, purchases, and sales of Product 65F for August and September are presented below:

Aug.	1	Beginning Inventory	60 units @ $50
	10	Purchases	100 units @ $52
	19	Sales	70 units
	27	Sales	20 units
Sept.	4	Purchases	120 units @ $53
	11	Sales	110 units
	15	Purchases	50 units @ $51
	23	Sales	80 units
	25	Purchases	100 units @ $54
	27	Sales	120 units

Required

1. Assume that the company maintains a perpetual inventory system on a FIFO basis and uses perpetual inventory cards similar to the one illustrated in Exhibit 8-2. Use the example in the text and record the transactions on such a card using two or more lines to show units on hand at each price or units sold when units costing different amounts are on hand or sold.
2. Assume that the company keeps its records on a LIFO basis and record the transactions on a second record card.
3. Prepare general journal entries to record the credit purchase on September 15 and the credit sale on September 23 for $8,000, assuming the LIFO basis of costing inventory. What is the amount and LIFO cost of the inventory at the end of September?
4. On September 30 the company counted a physical inventory of 26 units. Record any inventory loss necessary, assuming a LIFO basis.

Problem 8A-4. Periodic Inventory System (L.O. 3)

Assume the data presented in Problem 8A-3, except the company uses a periodic inventory system. The company closes its books at the end of each month.

Required

1. Compute the value of the ending inventory on August 31 and September 30 on a FIFO basis.
2. Compute the value of the ending inventory on August 31 and September 30 on a LIFO basis.
3. Prepare a general journal entry to record the sale on September 27 to Hastings Company on credit for $11,000.

Problem 8A-5. Retail Inventory Method (L.O. 7)

Sunray switched recently to the retail inventory method to estimate the cost of ending inventory. To test this method the company took a physical inventory one month after its implementation. Cost, retail, and the physical inventory data are presented on the following page:

	At Cost	At Retail
March 1 Beginning Inventory	$226,000	$302,800
Purchases	360,000	489,600
Purchases Returns and Allowances	(12,600)	(17,400)
Freight In	4,175	
Sales		530,000
Sales Returns and Allowances		(14,000)
March 31 Physical Inventory		247,400

Required

1. Prepare a schedule to estimate the dollar amount of Sunray's March 31 inventory using the retail method.
2. Use Sunray's cost ratio to reduce the retail value of the physical inventory to cost.
3. Calculate the estimated amount of inventory shortage at cost and at retail.

Problem 8A-6. Gross Profit Method (L.O. 7)

Kelly Oil Products warehouses its oil field products in a West Texas warehouse. The warehouse and most of its inventory were completely destroyed by a tornado on May 11. The company found some of its records, but it does not keep perpetual inventory records. The warehouse manager must estimate the amount of the loss for top management. He found the following information in the records:

Beginning inventory January 1	$620,000
Purchases January 2–May 11	300,000
Purchases Returns January 2–May 11	(15,000)
Freight in since January 2	2,000
Sales January 2–May 11	860,000
Sales Returns January 2–May 11	(20,000)

Inventory costing $180,000 was recovered and could be sold. The manager remembers the company's average gross margin on oil field products was 53 percent.

Required

Prepare a schedule showing an estimate of the inventory destroyed by the tornado.

Problem Set B

Problem 8B-1. Inventory Cost Methods (L.O. 3)

Clayton Company merchandises a single product called Mapco. The following data represent beginning inventory and purchases of product Mapco during the past year: January 1 inventory, 68,000 units at $12.00; February purchases, 80,000 units at $13.00; March purchases, 160,000 units at $12.40; May purchases, 120,000 units at $12.60; July purchases, 200,000 units at $12.80; September purchases, 160,000 units at $12.60; November purchases, 60,000 units at $13.20. Sales of product Mapco totaled 768,000 units at $20 per unit. Selling and administrative expenses totaled $4,736,000 for the year, and Clayton Company uses a periodic inventory method.

Required

1. Prepare a schedule to compute the cost of goods available for sale.
2. Prepare an income statement under each of the following assumptions: (a) Costs are assigned to inventory on an average-cost basis. (b) Costs are assigned to inventory on a FIFO basis. (c) Costs are assigned to inventory on a LIFO basis.

Problem 8B-2. Lower-of-Cost-or-Market Method (L.O. 6)

After taking the physical inventory, the accountant for Kerr Company prepared the inventory schedule shown below.

		Per Unit	
	Quantity	**Cost**	**Market**
Product line 1			
Item 11	170	$ 5	$ 5
Item 12	270	4	5
Item 13	210	8	7
Product line 2			
Item 21	110	15	17
Item 22	400	21	20
Item 23	70	18	20
Product line 3			
Item 31	370	26	20
Item 32	310	30	28
Item 33	120	34	39

Required

Determine the value of the inventory at lower of cost or market using (1) the item-by-item method and (2) the major category method.

Problem 8B-3. Perpetual Inventory System (L.O. 5)

The beginning inventory of Product E and data on purchases and sales for a two-month period are presented below.

Apr. 1	Inventory	50 units at $100
10	Purchase	100 units at $110
17	Sale	60 units
25	Sale	30 units
May 2	Purchase	100 units at $108
8	Sale	40 units
14	Purchase	50 units at $112
18	Sale	40 units
22	Purchase	50 units at $115
26	Sale	30 units
31	Sale	70 units

Required

1. Assume that the company maintains a perpetual inventory system on a FIFO basis and uses perpetual inventory cards similar to the one illustrated in Exhibit 8-2. Follow the example in the text and record the transactions on such a card using two or more lines to show units on hand at each price or units sold when units costing different amounts are on hand or sold.
2. Assume that the company keeps its records on a LIFO basis, and record the transactions on a second record card.
3. Assume that the May 31 sale was made to Hankins Corporation on credit for $14,000. Prepare a general journal entry to record the sale and cost of goods sold on a LIFO basis.
4. Assume the company takes a periodic inventory on May 31. The value of the inventory was $8,600. Record an inventory loss if necessary. Assume the FIFO basis of evaluating inventory.

Problem 8B-4. Periodic Inventory System
(L.O. 3)

Assume the same data as presented in Problem 8B-3, except that the company uses a periodic inventory system. The company closes its books at the end of each month.

Required

1. Compute the value of the ending inventory on April 30 and May 31 on a FIFO basis.
2. Compute the value of the ending inventory on April 30 and May 31 on a LIFO basis.
3. Prepare a general journal entry to record the sale on May 31 to Redfern Corporation on credit for $14,000.

Problem 8B-5. Retail Inventory Method
(L.O. 7)

Nolan Company operates a large discount store that uses the retail inventory method to estimate the cost of ending inventory. Management suspects that in recent weeks there have been unusually heavy losses from shoplifting or employee pilferage. To estimate the amount of the loss, the company has taken a physical inventory and will compare the results with the estimated cost of inventory. Data from the accounting records and from a year-end physical inventory are as follows:

	At Cost	At Retail
October 1 Beginning Inventory	$50,454	$ 71,600
Purchases	71,708	105,800
Purchases Returns and Allowances	2,043	3,200
Freight In	950	
Sales		109,183
Sales Returns and Allowances		933
October 31 Physical Inventory		61,750

Required

Prepare a schedule to do the following: (1) estimate the dollar amount of the store's year-end inventory using the retail method, (2) use the store's cost ratio to reduce the retail value of the physical inventory to cost, and (3) calculate the estimated amount of inventory shortage at cost and at retail.

Problem 8B-6. Gross Profit Method
(L.O. 7)

Burford Brothers is a large retail furniture company that operates in two adjacent warehouses. One warehouse serves as a showroom, and the other is used for storage of merchandise. On the night of April 22, a fire broke out in the storage warehouse and totally destroyed the merchandise stored there. Fortunately, the fire did not reach the showroom; so all the merchandise on display was saved. Although the company maintained a perpetual inventory system, its records were rather haphazard, and the last reliable physical inventory was taken on December 31. In addition, there was no control of the flow of the goods between the showroom and the warehouse. Thus it was impossible to tell what goods should be in either place. As a result, the insurance company required an independent estimate of the amount of loss. The insurance company examiners were satisfied with the following information:

1. Merchandise inventory on December 31	$ 719,125
2. Purchases, January 1 to April 22	1,193,068
3. Purchases returns, January 1 to April 22	5,353
4. Freight in, January 1 to April 22	26,550
5. Sales, January 1 to April 22	1,979,525
6. Sales returns, January 1 to April 22	14,900
7. Merchandise inventory in showroom on April 22	196,870
8. Average gross profit margin, 42 percent	

Required

Prepare a schedule showing the amount of inventory that should have been on hand on April 22, and estimate the amount of the loss.

Financial Decision Case

RTS Company
(L.O. 4)

Refrigerated Truck Sales Company (RTS Company) buys large refrigerated trucks from the manufacturer and sells them to companies and independent truckers who haul perishable goods such as frozen beef for long distances. RTS has been successful in this specialized niche of the industry because it provides a unique product and specialized service to these truckers. Because of the high cost of these trucks and the high cost of financing inventory, RTS tries to maintain as small an inventory as possible. In fact, at the beginning of March the company had no inventory or liabilities, as shown by the following balance sheet:

RTS Company
Balance Sheet
March 1, 19xx

Assets		Owner's Equity	
Cash	$500,000	Robert Trinker, Capital	$500,000
Total Assets	$500,000	Total Owner's Equity	$500,000

On March 5, RTS takes delivery of a truck at a price of $150,000. On March 15 after a rise in price, an identical truck is delivered to the company at a price of $160,000. On March 25, the company sells one of the trucks for $195,000. During March, expenses totaled $15,000. All transactions were paid in cash.

Required

1. Prepare income statements and balance sheets for RTS at March 31 using (a) the FIFO method of inventory valuation and (b) the LIFO method of inventory valuation. Explain the effects that each method has on the financial statements.
2. Assume that Robert Trinker, owner of RTS Company, follows the policy of withdrawing cash each period that is exactly equal to net income. What effect does this action have on each balance sheet prepared in **1**, and how do they compare with the balance sheet at the beginning of the month? Which inventory method, if either, do you feel is more realistic in representing RTS's income?
3. Assume that RTS receives notice of another price increase of $10,000 on refrigerated trucks, to take effect on April 1. How does this information relate to the withdrawal policy of the owner, and how will it affect next month's operations?

CHAPTER 9 CURRENT LIABILITIES AND PAYROLL ACCOUNTING

LEARNING OBJECTIVES

1. Define liability and explain how the problems of recognition, valuation, and classification apply to liabilities.
2. Identify, compute, and record definitely determinable and estimated current liabilities.
3. Define a contingent liability.
4. Identify and compute the liabilities associated with payroll accounting.
5. Record transactions associated with payroll accounting.

Liabilities are one of the three major parts of the balance sheet. The two major kinds of liabilities are current and long-term liabilities. This chapter deals with the nature and measurement of current liabilities. The subject of long-term liabilities is covered in Chapter 14. Because a number of current liabilities arise through the payroll process, the fundamentals of payroll accounting are also presented in this chapter. After studying this chapter, you should be able to meet the learning objectives listed on the left.

Nature and Measurement of Liabilities

Liabilities are the result of a company's past transactions and are legal obligations for the future payment of assets or the future performance of services. They are more than monetary obligations. For example, revenues received in advance are for goods or services that must be provided to customers. In most cases, the amount and due date are definite or subject to reasonable estimation. The problems of recognition, valuation, and classification apply equally to liabilities and assets.

Recognition of Liabilities

Timing is important in the recognition of liabilities. Very often failure to record a liability in an accounting period goes along with failure to record an expense. Thus it leads to an understatement of expense and an overstatement of income. Liabilities are recorded when an obligation occurs. This rule is harder to apply than it appears on the surface. When there is a transaction that obligates the company to make future payments, a liability arises and is recognized, as when goods are bought on credit. However, current liabilities often are not represented by a direct transaction. One of the major reasons for adjusting entries at the end of an accounting period is to recognize unrecorded liabilities. Among these accrued liabilities are salaries payable and interest payable. Other liabilities that can only be estimated, such as taxes payable, must also be recognized by adjusting entries.

OBJECTIVE 1
Define liability and explain how the problems of recognition, valuation, and classification apply to liabilities

On the other hand, a company may sometimes enter into an agreement for future transactions. For instance, a company may agree to pay an executive $50,000 a year for three years, or a public utility may agree to buy an unspecified quantity of coal at a certain price over the next five years. These contracts, though they are definite commitments, are not liabilities because they are for future—not past—transactions. As there is no current obligation, no liability is recognized.

Valuation of Liabilities

Liabilities are generally valued at the amount of money needed to pay the debt or at the fair market value of goods or services to be delivered. For most liabilities the amount is definitely known, but for some it must be estimated. For example, an automobile dealer who sells a car with a one-year warranty must provide parts and services during the year. The obligation is definite because the sale of the car has occurred, but the amount must be estimated.

Classification of Liabilities

Current liabilities are debts and obligations that are expected to be satisfied in one year or within the current operating cycle, whichever is longer. In most cases, they are paid out of current assets or by taking on another short-term liability. The classification of current liabilities directly matches the classification of current assets. Liabilities that will not be due during the next year or during the normal operating cycle are listed as **long-term liabilities**.

Common Categories of Current Liabilities

Current liabilities fall into two major groups: (1) definitely determinable liabilities and (2) estimated liabilities. Discussions on each follow.

Definitely Determinable Liabilities

OBJECTIVE 2
Identify, compute, and record definitely determinable and estimated current liabilities

Current liabilities that are set by contract or by statute and can be measured exactly are called **definitely determinable liabilities**. The accounting problems connected with these liabilities are to determine the existence and amount of the liability and to see that the liability is recorded properly. Definitely determinable liabilities include trade accounts payable, notes payable, dividends payable, sales and excise taxes payable, current portions of long-term debt, accrued liabilities, payroll liabilities, and deferred revenues.

Figure 9-1. Two Promissory Notes: One with Interest Stated Separately; One with Interest in Face Amount

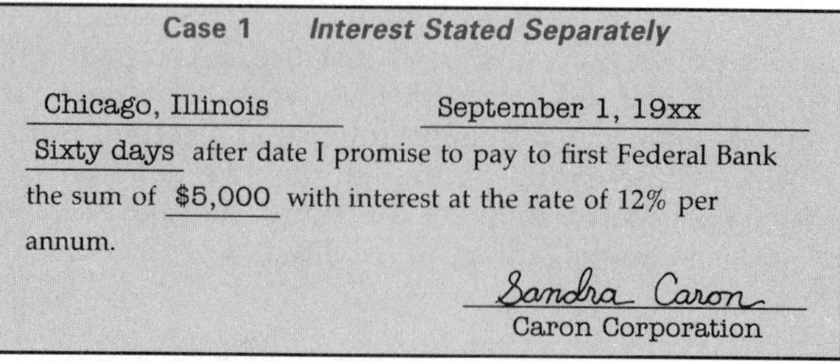

Case 1 ***Interest Stated Separately***

Chicago, Illinois September 1, 19xx

Sixty days after date I promise to pay to first Federal Bank the sum of $5,000 with interest at the rate of 12% per annum.

Sandra Caron
Caron Corporation

Case 2 ***Interest in Face Amount***

Chicago, Illinois September 1, 19xx

Sixty days after date I promise to pay to first Federal Bank the sum of $5,000 .

Sandra Caron
Caron Corporation

Trade Accounts Payable. Trade accounts payable are short-term obligations to suppliers for goods and services. The amount in the Trade Accounts Payable account is generally supported by an accounts payable subsidiary ledger. Under the voucher system, this account is called Vouchers Payable. Accounting for trade accounts payable has been treated at length earlier in the book.

Notes Payable. Short-term notes payable, which also arise out of the ordinary course of business, are obligations represented by promissory notes. The two major sources of notes payable are bank loans and payments to suppliers for goods and services. As with notes receivable, presented in Chapter 7, the interest on notes may be stated separately on the face of the note (Case 1 in Figure 9-1), or it may be deducted in advance by discounting (Case 2). The entries to record the note in each case are as follows:

Case 1—Interest stated separately

Aug. 31	Cash	5,000	
	Notes Payable		5,000
	To record 60-day, 12% promissory note with interest stated separately		

Case 2—Interest in face amount

Aug. 31	Cash	4,900	
	Discount on Notes Payable	100	
	Notes Payable		5,000
	To record 60-day, 12% promissory note with interest included in face amount		

$$\text{Discount} = \$5{,}000 \times \frac{60}{360} \times .12 = \$100$$

Note that in Case 1 the money borrowed equaled the face value of the note, whereas in Case 2 the money borrowed ($4,900) was less than the face value ($5,000) of the note. The amount of the discount equals the amount of the interest for sixty days. To show the correct amount of the liability on the balance sheet, the Discount on Notes Payable is deducted from the Notes Payable as a contra-liability account, as follows:

Current Liabilities		
Notes Payable	**$5,000**	
Less Discount on Notes Payable	**100**	**$4,900**

On October 30, when the note is paid, each alternative is recorded as follows:

Case 1—Interest stated separately

Oct. 30	Notes Payable	5,000	
	Interest Expense	100	
	Cash		5,100
	Payment of note with interest stated separately		

Case 2—Interest in face amount

Oct. 30	Notes Payable	5,000	
	Cash		5,000
	Payment of note with interest included in face value		
30	Interest Expense	100	
	Discount on Notes Payable		100
	To record interest expense on matured note		

Dividends Payable. Dividends are a distribution of earnings by a corporation. The payment of dividends is solely the decision of the corporation's board of directors. A liability does not exist until the board declares the dividends. There is usually a short time between the date of declaration and the date of payment of dividends. During that short time, the dividends declared are current liabilities of the corporation. Accounting for dividends is treated extensively in Chapters 12 and 13.

Sales and Excise Taxes Payable. Most states and many cities levy a sales tax on retail transactions. There are federal excise taxes on some products, such as automobile tires. The merchant who sells goods subject to these taxes must collect the taxes and remit, or pay, them periodically to the appropriate government agency. The amount of tax collected represents a current liability until it is remitted to the government. For example, assume that a merchant makes a $100 sale that is subject to a 5 percent sales tax and a 10 percent excise tax. Assuming that the sale took place on June 1, the correct entry to record the sale is as follows:

June 1	Cash	115	
	Sales		100
	Sales Tax Payable		5
	Excise Tax Payable		10
	To record sale of merchandise and collection of sales and excise taxes		

The sale is properly recorded at $100, and the tax collections are recorded as liabilities to be remitted at the proper time to the appropriate government agency.

Current Portions of Long-Term Debt. If a portion of long-term debt is due within the next year and is to be paid from current assets, then the current portion of long-term debt is properly classified as a current liability. For example, suppose that a $500,000 debt is to be paid in installments of $100,000 per year for the next five years. The $100,000 installment due in the current year should be classified as a current liability. The remaining $400,000 should be classified as a long-term liability.

Accrued Liabilities. A principal reason for adjusting entries at the end of an accounting period is to recognize and record liabilities that are not already recorded in the accounting records. This practice applies to any type of liability. For example, in previous chapters, adjustments relating to accrued salaries payable were made. As you will see, accrued liabilities can also apply to estimated liabilities. Here the focus is on interest payable, a definitely determinable liability. Interest accrues daily on interest-bearing notes. At the end of the accounting period, an adjusting entry should be made in accordance with the matching rule to record the interest obligation up to that point in time. Let us again use the example of the two notes presented earlier in this chapter. If we assume that the accounting period ends on September 30, or thirty days after the issuance of the sixty-day notes, the adjusting entries for each case would be as follows:

Case 1—Interest stated separately

Sept. 30	Interest Expense	50	
	Interest Payable		50
	To record interest expense for 30 days on note with interest stated separately		

Case 2—Interest in face amount

Sept. 30	Interest Expense	50	
	Discount on Notes Payable		50
	To record interest expense for 30 days on note with interest included in face amount		

In Case 2, current liabilities are increased by the credit to Discount on Notes Payable because this credit has the effect of increasing the net amount of Notes Payable from $4,900 on August 31 to $4,950 on September 30. On the latter date, the notes payable would appear on the balance sheet as follows:

Current Liabilities		
Notes Payable	$5,000	
Less Discount on Notes Payable	50	$4,950

Payroll Liabilities. A number of current liabilities are associated with payroll accounting. These liabilities are discussed in a major section at the end of this chapter.

Unearned or Deferred Revenues. **Unearned** or **deferred revenues** represent obligations for goods or services that the company must deliver in return for an advance payment from a customer. For example, most magazines accept payments for subscriptions in advance. The publisher then has a liability that expires when the magazine is delivered. Many businesses such as repair companies, construction companies, and special-order firms ask for a deposit or advance from a customer before they will begin work. These advances are also current liabilities until the goods or services are delivered.

Estimated Liabilities

Estimated liabilities are a company's definite obligations for which the exact amount cannot be known until a later date. Since there is no doubt as to the existence of the legal obligation, the primary accounting problem is to estimate and record the amount of the liability. Examples of estimated liabilities are income taxes, property taxes, product warranties, and vacation pay.

Income Tax. The income of a corporation is taxed by the federal government, most state governments, and some cities and towns. The amount of income tax liability depends on the results of operations. Often it is not certain until after the end of the year. However, because income taxes are an expense in the year in which income is earned, an adjusting entry is necessary to record the estimated tax liability. An example of this entry follows:

Dec. 31	Federal Income Tax Expense	53,000	
	Federal Income Tax Payable		53,000
	To record estimated federal income tax		

Remember that the income of sole proprietorships and partnerships is not subject to income taxes. Their owners must report their share of the firm's income on their individual tax returns.

Property Taxes Payable. Property taxes are taxes levied on real property such as land and buildings and on personal property such as inventory and equipment. Property taxes are a main source of revenue for local governments. Usually they are assessed annually against the property involved. Because the fiscal years of local governments and their assessment dates rarely correspond to those of the firm, it is necessary to estimate the amount of property taxes that applies to each month of the year. Assume, for instance, that a local government has a fiscal year of July 1 to June 30, that its assessment date is November 1 for the fiscal year beginning the previous July 1, and that its payment date is December 15. Assume also that on July 1, Janis Corporation estimates that its property tax assessment will be $24,000 for the coming year. The adjusting entry to be made on July 31, which would be repeated on August 31, September 30, and October 31, would be as follows:

July 31	Property Tax Expense	2,000	
	Estimated Property Tax Payable		2,000
	To record estimated property tax expense for the month $24,000 ÷ 12 months = $2,000		

On November 1, the firm receives a property tax bill for $24,720. The estimate made in July was too low. The monthly charge should have been $2,060 per month. Because the difference between the actual and the estimate is small, the company decides to absorb in November the amount undercharged in the previous four months. Therefore, the property tax expense for November is $2,300 [$2,060 + 4($60)] and is recorded as follows:

Nov. 30	Property Tax Expense	2,300	
	Estimated Property Tax Payable		2,300
	To record estimated property tax		

The Estimated Property Tax Payable account now has a balance of $10,300. The entry to record payment on December 15 would be as follows:

Dec. 15	Estimated Property Tax Payable	10,300	
	Prepaid Property Taxes	14,420	
	Cash		24,720
	To record payment of property taxes		

Beginning December 31 and each month afterward until June 30, property tax expense is recorded by a debit to Property Tax Expense and a credit to Prepaid Property Taxes in the amount of $2,060. The total of these seven entries will reduce the Prepaid Property Taxes account to zero on June 30.

Product Warranty Liability. When a firm places a warranty or guarantee on its product at the time of sale, a liability exists for the length of the warranty. The cost of the warranty is properly debited to an expense account in the period of sale because it is a feature of the product or service sold and thus was one of the reasons the customer made the purchase. On the basis of experience, it should be possible to estimate the amount the warranty will cost in the future. Some products or services will require little warranty service; others may require much. Thus there will be an average cost per product or service. For example, assume that a muffler company guarantees that it will replace any muffler free of charge if it fails any time as long as you own your car. The company charges a small service fee for replacing the muffler. This guarantee is an important selling feature for the firm's mufflers. In the past, 6 percent of the mufflers sold have been returned for replacement under the guarantee. The average cost of a muffler is $25. Assume that during July, 350 mufflers were sold. This accrued liability would be recorded as an adjustment at the end of July as follows:

July 31	Product Warranty Expense	525	
	Estimated Product Warranty Liability		525
	To record estimated product warranty expense, calculated as follows:		

Number of units sold	350
Rate of replacements under warranty	× .06
Estimated units to be replaced	21
Estimated cost per unit	× $25
Estimated liability for product warranty	$525

When a muffler is returned for replacement under the product warranty, the cost of the muffler is charged against the estimated product warranty liability account. For example, assume that a customer returns on December 5 with a defective muffler and pays a $10 service fee to have the muffler replaced. Assume that this particular muffler cost $20. The entry is as follows:

Dec. 5	Cash	10	
	Estimated Product Warranty Liability	20	
	Service Revenue		10
	Merchandise Inventory		20
	To record replacement of muffler under warranty		

Vacation Pay Liability. In most companies, employees earn the right to paid vacation days or weeks as they work during the year. For example, an employee may earn two weeks of paid vacation for each fifty weeks of work. Therefore, she or he is paid fifty-two weeks' salary for fifty weeks' work. Theoretically, the cost of the two weeks' vacation should be allocated as expense over the whole year. So vacation pay represents 4 percent (two weeks' vacation divided by fifty weeks) of a worker's pay. Every week worked earns the employee a small fraction (4 percent) of his or her vacation pay. Vacation pay liability can amount to a substantial amount of money. For example, Delta Airlines reported at its year end in 1985 a vacation pay liability of $82,844,000.

Suppose that a company with the above policy has a weekly payroll of $20,000. Since not all employees in every company will collect vacation pay because of turnover and rules regarding term of employment, it is assumed that 75 percent of employees will ultimately collect vacation pay. The computation of vacation pay expense is as follows: $20,000 × 4 percent × 75 percent = $600.

The entry to record vacation pay expense for the week ended April 20 is as follows:

Apr. 20	Vacation Pay Expense	600	
	Estimated Liability for Vacation Pay		600
	To record estimated vacation pay expense		

At the time that a person receives his or her vacation pay, an entry is made debiting Estimated Liability for Vacation Pay and crediting Cash or Wages Payable. For example, assume that an employee is paid $550 during a two-week vacation ending August 31; the entry is as follows:

Aug. 31	Estimated Liability for Vacation Pay	550	
	Cash (or Wages Payable)		550
	To record wages of employee on vacation		

Contingent Liabilities

OBJECTIVE 3
Define a contingent liability

A **contingent liability** is not an existing liability. Rather, it is a potential liability because it depends on a future event arising out of a past transaction. For instance, a construction company that built a bridge may have been sued by the state for using poor materials. The past transaction is the building of the bridge under contract. The future event whose outcome is not known is the suit against the company. Two conditions have been established by the FASB for determining when a loss contingency should be entered in the accounting records. They are that the liability must be probable and that it must be reasonably estimated.[1] Estimated liabilities such as the estimated income taxes liability, warranty liability, and vacation pay liability that were described earlier in this chapter meet these conditions. So they are accrued in the accounting records. Potential liabilities that do not meet both conditions are reported in the notes to the financial statements. Losses from such potential liabilities are recorded when the conditions set by the FASB are met. This example comes from a recent annual report of Exxon Corporation:

> The corporation, together with a number of other petroleum companies, is named as a respondent in an antitrust proceeding commenced by the Federal Trade

1. *Statement of Financial Accounting Standards No. 5,* "Accounting for Contingencies" (Stamford, Conn.: Financial Accounting Standards Board, 1975).

> Commission (FTC) in 1973 in which violati Commission Act are alleged. The FTC st may seek partial refining divestiture amo Several states have commenced separate law of federal and state monopoly and restraint o similar relief together with money damages.
>
> The allegations of unlawful practices in the the actions will be vigorously defended by t firmly believes the actions can be successfull ... broad relief sought, however, an adverse decision co ... significant effect upon the scope and nature of the corporation's operations. Final judicial determination is expected to take a number of years.

Contingent liabilities arise not only from lawsuits but also from income tax disputes, failure to follow government regulations, discounted notes receivable, and guarantees of the debt of other companies.

Introduction to Payroll Accounting

OBJECTIVE 4 Identify and compute the liabilities associated with payroll accounting

A major expense of most companies is the cost of labor and related payroll taxes. In some industries such as banking and airlines, payroll costs represent more than half of the operating costs. Payroll accounting is important because of the amounts of money involved and because the employer must conform to many complex laws governing taxes on payrolls. The employer has many reporting requirements and liabilities for the money withheld from employees' salaries and for payroll taxes.

Also, the payroll accounting system is subject to complaints and to possible fraud. Every employee must be paid on time and receive a detailed explanation of the amount of his or her pay. The payroll system calls for strong internal control and efficient processing and distribution of checks, as well as accurate reporting to the government agencies.

This section will focus on the liabilities, the records, and the control requirements of payroll accounting. The three general kinds of liabilities associated with payroll accounting are (1) liabilities for employee compensation, (2) liabilities for employee payroll withholdings, and (3) liabilities for employer payroll taxes.

It is important to distinguish between employees and independent contractors. Payroll accounting applies to employees of the company. Employees are paid a wage or salary by the company and are under its direct supervision and control. Independent contractors are not employees of the company, so they are not accounted for under the payroll system. They offer services to the firm for a fee but are not under its direct control or supervision. Some examples of independent contractors are certified public accountants, advertising agencies, and lawyers.

Liabilities for Employee Compensation

The employer is liable to employees for wages and salaries. The term **wages** refers to payment for the services of employees at an hourly rate or on a piecework basis. The term **salaries** refers to the compensation for employees who are paid at a monthly or yearly rate. Generally, these employees are administrators or managers.

Besides setting minimum wage levels, the federal Fair Labor Standards Act (also called the Wages and Hours Law) regulates overtime pay. Employers who take part in interstate commerce must pay overtime for hours worked beyond forty hours a week or more than eight hours a day. This overtime pay must be at least one and one-half times the regular rate. Work on Saturdays, Sundays, or holidays may also call for overtime pay under separate wage agreements. Overtime pay under union or other employment contracts may exceed these minimums.

For example, suppose that the employment contract of Robert Jones calls for a regular wage of $5 an hour, one and one-half times the regular rate for work over eight hours in any weekday, and twice the regular rate for work on Saturdays, Sundays, or holidays. He works the following days and hours during the week of January 18, 19xx:

Day	Total Hours Worked	Regular Time	Overtime
Monday	10	8	2
Tuesday	8	8	0
Wednesday	8	8	0
Thursday	9	8	1
Friday	10	8	2
Saturday	2	0	2
	47	40	7

Jones's wages would be figured as follows:

Regular time	40 hours × $5	$200.00
Overtime, weekdays	5 hours × $5 × 1.5	37.50
Overtime, weekend	2 hours × $5 × 2	20.00
Total wages		$257.50

Liabilities for Employee Payroll Withholdings

The amount paid to employees is generally less than the wages they have earned because the employer is required by law to withhold certain amounts from the employees' wages and send them directly to government agencies to pay taxes owed by the employees. In this group are FICA taxes, federal income taxes, and state income taxes. Also, certain withholdings are made for the employees' benefit and often at their request. In this group are pension payments, medical insurance premiums, life insurance premiums, union dues, and charitable contributions.

No matter what the reason is for the withholding from the employees' wages, the employer is liable for payment to the proper agency, fund, or organization.

FICA Tax. With the passage of the U.S. social security program in the 1930s, the federal government began to take more responsibility for the well-being of its citizens. The social security program offers retirement and disability benefits, survivor's benefits, and hospitalization and other medical benefits. One of the major extensions of the program provides hospitalization and medical insurance for persons over sixty-five.

The social security program is financed by taxes on employees, employers, and the self-employed. About 90 percent of the people working in the United States fall under the provisions of this program.

The Federal Insurance Contributions Act (FICA) set up the tax to pay for this program. The tax is paid by *both* employee and employer and is now based on the following schedule up to 1989.

	1987	**1988**	**1989**
FICA tax rate	7.15%	7.51%	7.51%
Maximum wage taxed under present law	$43,800.00	$45,600.00	$45,600.00
Present maximum tax	$ 3,131.70	$ 3,424.56	$ 3,424.56

Although this is the current schedule, it is subject to frequent amendments by Congress. In this text, we will use the figures given above.

The FICA tax applies to the pay of each employee up to a certain level. In 1987, it applies to the level of $43,800. There is no tax on individual earnings above this amount. So the largest possible FICA tax for each employee is $3,131.70 ($43,800 × .0715). The employee and the employer must each pay this amount. The employer deducts this tax from the employee's wages and sends the amount, along with other employees' withholdings of FICA taxes and the employer's FICA taxes to the government. Because of inflation and rising benefits under the social security system, these provisions are under constant study by Congress. They are subject to change and should be verified each year.

As an example of the FICA tax, suppose that Robert Jones will earn less than $43,800 this year and that the FICA withholding for taxes on his paycheck this week is $18.41 ($257.50 × .0715). The employer must pay an equal tax of $18.41 for a total of $36.82.

Federal Income Tax. The largest deduction from many employees' earnings is their estimated liability for federal income taxes. The system of tax collection for federal income taxes is to "pay as you go." The employer is required to withhold the amount of the taxes from employees' paychecks and turn it over to the Internal Revenue Service.

The amount to be withheld depends on the amount of each employee's earnings and on the number of the employee's exemptions. All employees are required by law to indicate their exemptions by filing a Form W-4 (Employee's Withholding Exemption Certificate). Each employee is entitled to one exemption for himself and one for each dependent. The Tax Reform Act of 1986 repealed additional exemptions for people who are blind or over 65. However, loss of these exemptions is recouped, in part, by an *additional standard deduction* for the elderly or blind. In our example, Robert Jones has four exemptions—one for himself, one for his wife, and one for each of two children.

The Internal Revenue Service provides employers with tables to aid them in computing the amount of withholdings. For example, Figure 9-2 is a withholding table for married employees who are paid weekly.[2] The withholding from Robert Jones's $257.50 weekly earnings is $15.00.

		Weekly Payroll Period—Employee Married										
And the wages are—		And the number of withholding allowances claimed is—										
At least	But less than	0	1	2	3	4	5	6	7	8	9	10 or more
		The amount of income tax to be withheld shall be—										
$200	$210	$20	$17	$14	$11	$ 8	$ 6	$ 3	$ 1	$ 0	$0	$0
210	220	21	18	15	12	9	7	4	2	0	0	0
220	230	22	19	17	14	11	8	6	3	1	0	0
230	240	24	21	18	15	12	9	7	4	2	0	0
240	250	26	22	19	16	14	11	8	6	3	1	0
250	260	27	24	21	18	15	12	9	7	4	2	0
260	270	29	25	22	19	16	13	11	8	5	3	1
270	280	30	27	24	21	18	15	12	9	7	4	2
280	290	32	29	25	22	19	16	13	10	8	5	3
290	300	34	30	27	24	21	18	15	12	9	7	4
300	310	35	32	28	25	22	19	16	13	10	8	5
310	320	37	33	30	27	23	20	18	15	12	9	6

Figure 9-2. Wage Bracket Table

State Income Tax. Most states have income taxes, and in most cases the procedures for withholding are similar to those for federal income taxes.

Other Withholdings. Some of the other withholdings, such as for a retirement or pension plan, are required of each employee. Others, such as withholdings for insurance premiums or savings plans, may be requested by the employee. The payroll system must allow for treating each employee separately with regard to withholdings and the records of these withholdings. The employer is liable to account for all withholdings and to make proper remittances.

2. This table is presented for illustrative purposes only. Actual withholding tables change periodically as changes occur in the tax rates or laws.

Computation of an Employee's Take-Home Pay: An Illustration

OBJECTIVE 5 Record transactions associated with payroll accounting

To continue with the example of Robert Jones, let us now compute his take-home pay. We know that his total earnings for the week of January 18 are $257.50, that his FICA tax rate at 7.15 percent is $18.41 (he has not earned over $43,800), and that his federal income tax withholding is $15.00. Assume also that his union dues are $2.00, his medical insurance premiums are $7.60, his life insurance premium is $6.00, he places $15.00 per week in savings bonds, and he contributes $1.00 per week to United Charities. His net (take-home) pay is computed as follows:

Gross earnings		$257.50
Deductions		
FICA tax	$18.41	
Federal income tax withheld	15.00	
Union dues	2.00	
Medical insurance	7.60	
Life insurance	6.00	
Savings bonds	15.00	
United Charities contribution	1.00	
Total withheld		(65.01)
Net (take-home) pay		$192.49

Employee Earnings Record. Each employer must keep a record of earnings and withholdings for each employee. Many companies today use computers to maintain these records, but small companies use manual records. The manual form of **employee earnings record** used for Robert Jones is shown in Exhibit 9-1. This form is designed to help the employer

Exhibit 9-1. Employee Earnings Record

Employee Earnings Record

Employee's Name Robert Jones	Social Security Number 444-66-9999	
Address 777 20th Street	Sex Male	Employee No. 705
Marshall, Michigan 52603	Single ____ Married X	Weekly Pay Rate $200
Date of Birth September 20, 1952	Exemptions (W-4) 4	Hourly Rate $5
Position Sales Assistant	Date of Employment July 15, 1978	Date Employment Ended ____

19xx		Earnings			Deductions							Payment		
Period Ended	Total Hours	Regular	Overtime	Gross	FICA Tax	Federal Income Tax	Union Dues	Medical Insurance	Life Insurance	Savings Bonds	Other: A—United Charities	Net Earnings	Check No.	Cumulative Gross Earnings
Jan. 4	40	200.00	0	200.00	14.30	8.00	2.00	7.60	6.00	15.00	A 1.00	146.10	717	200.00
11	44	200.00	30.00	230.00	16.45	12.00	2.00	7.60	6.00	15.00	A 1.00	169.95	822	430.00
18	47	200.00	57.50	257.50	18.41	15.00	2.00	7.60	6.00	15.00	A 1.00	192.49	926	687.50

Exhibit 9-2. Payroll Register

Payroll Register												Pay Period: Week ended January 18			
		Earnings			Deductions							Payment		Distribution	
Employee	Total Hours	Regular	Overtime	Gross	FICA Tax	Federal Income Tax	Union Dues	Medical Insurance	Life Insurance	Savings Bonds	Other: A—United Charities	Net Earnings	Check No.	Sales Salaries Expense	Office Salaries Expense
Linda Duval	40	160.00		160.00	11.44	11.00		5.80				131.76	923		160.00
John Franks	44	160.00	24.00	184.00	13.16	14.00	2.00	7.60			A 10.00	137.24	924	184.00	
Samuel Goetz	40	400.00		400.00	28.60	53.00		10.40	14.00		A 3.00	291.00	925	400.00	
Robert Jones	47	200.00	57.50	257.50	18.41	15.00	2.00	7.60	6.00	15.00	A 1.00	192.49	926	257.50	
Billie Matthews	40	160.00		160.00	11.44	14.00		5.80				128.76	927		160.00
Rosaire O'Brian	42	200.00	20.00	220.00	15.73	22.00	2.00	5.80				174.47	928	220.00	
James Van Dyke	40	200.00		200.00	14.30	20.00		5.80				159.90	929		200.00
		1,480.00	101.50	1,581.50	113.08	149.00	6.00	48.80	20.00	15.00	14.00	1,215.62		1,061.50	520.00

meet legal reporting requirements. Each deduction must be shown to have been paid to the proper agency and the employee must receive a report of the deductions made each year. Most columns are self-explanatory. Note, however, the column on the far right in Exhibit 9-1, where cumulative gross earnings (earnings to date) are recorded. This record helps the employer comply with the rule of applying FICA taxes only up to the maximum wage level. At the end of the year, the employer reports to the employee on Form W-2, the Wage and Tax Statement, the totals of earnings and deductions for the year so that the employee can complete his or her individual tax return. The employer sends a copy of the W-2 to the Internal Revenue Service. Thus the IRS can check on whether the employee has reported all income earned from that employer.

Payroll Register. The **payroll register** is a detailed listing of the firm's total payroll that is prepared each payday. A payroll register is presented in Exhibit 9-2. Note that the name, hours, earnings, deductions, and net pay of each employee are listed. Compare the January 18 entry in the employee earnings record (Exhibit 9-1) of Robert Jones with the entry for Robert Jones in the payroll register. Except for the first column, which lists the employee names, and the last column, which shows the wage or salary as either sales or office expense, the columns are the same. The columns help employers to record the payroll in the accounting records and to meet legal reporting requirements as noted above. The last two columns are needed to divide the expenses on the income statement into selling and administrative categories.

Recording the Payroll. The journal entry for recording the payroll is based on the total of the columns from the payroll register. The journal entry to record the payroll of January 18 is shown on page 347.

Note that each account debited or credited is a total from the payroll register. If the payroll register is considered a special-purpose journal like those in Appendix A, the column can be entered directly in the ledger accounts with the correct account numbers shown at the bottom of each column.

Jan. 18	Sales Salaries Expense	1,061.50	
	Office Salaries Expense	520.00	
	FICA Tax Payable		113.08
	Employees' Federal Income Tax Payable		149.00
	Union Dues Payable		6.00
	Medical Insurance Premiums Payable		48.80
	Life Insurance Premiums Payable		20.00
	Savings Bonds Payable		15.00
	United Charities Payable		14.00
	Salaries Payable		1,215.62
	To record weekly payroll		

Liabilities for Employer Payroll Taxes

The payroll taxes discussed so far were deducted from the employee's gross earnings, to be paid by the employer. There are three major taxes on salaries that the employer must also pay: the FICA tax, the federal unemployment insurance tax, and state unemployment compensation tax. These taxes are considered operating expenses.

FICA Tax. The employer must pay FICA tax equal to that paid by the employees. That is, from the payroll register in Exhibit 9-2, the employer would have to pay an FICA tax of $113.08, equal to that paid by the employees.

Federal Unemployment Insurance Tax. The Federal Unemployment Tax Act (FUTA) is another part of the U.S. social security system. It is intended to pay for operating programs to help unemployed workers. In this way, it is different from FICA taxes and state unemployment taxes. The dollars paid through FUTA provide for unemployment compensation. Unlike the FICA tax, which is levied on both employees and employers, the FUTA is assessed only against employers.

Although the amount of tax can vary, it amounted recently to 6.2 percent of the first $7,000 earned by each employee. The employer, however, is allowed a credit against this federal tax for unemployment taxes paid to the state. The maximum credit is 5.4 percent of the first $7,000 of each employee's earnings. Most states set their rate at this maximum. Therefore, the FUTA paid is 0.8 percent (6.2 percent − 5.4 percent) of the taxable wages.

State Unemployment Insurance Tax. All state unemployment plans provide for unemployment compensation to be paid to eligible unemployed workers. This compensation is paid out of the fund provided by the 5.4 percent of the first $7,000 earned by each employee. In some states, employers with favorable employment records may be entitled to pay less than the 5.4 percent.

Recording Payroll Taxes. According to Exhibit 9-2, the gross payroll for the week ended January 18 was $1,581.50. Because it was the first month of the year, all employees had accumulated less than the $43,800 and $7,000 maximum taxable salaries. Therefore, the FICA tax was $113.08 (equal to tax on employees); the FUTA was $12.65 (.008 × $1,581.50); and the state unemployment tax was $85.40 (.054 × $1,581.50). The entry to record this expense and related liability in the general journal is as follows:

Jan. 18	Payroll Tax Expense	211.13	
	FICA Tax Payable		113.08
	Federal Unemployment Tax Payable		12.65
	State Unemployment Tax Payable		85.40
	To record weekly payroll taxes expense		

Payment of Payroll and Payroll Taxes

After the weekly payroll is recorded, as illustrated earlier, a liability of $1,215.62 exists for salaries payable. How this liability will be paid depends on the system used by the company. Many companies use a special payroll account against which payroll checks are drawn. Under this system, a check must first be drawn on the regular checking account for net earnings and deposited in the special payroll account before the payroll checks are issued to the employees. If a voucher system is combined with a special payroll account, a voucher for the total salaries payable ($1,215.62) is prepared and recorded in the voucher register as a debit to Payroll Bank Account and a credit to Vouchers Payable.

The combined FICA taxes (both employees' and employer's share) and the federal income taxes must be paid to the Internal Revenue Service at least quarterly. Monthly payments are necessary if more than a certain amount of money is involved. The federal unemployment insurance taxes are paid yearly if the amount is less than $100. If it is more than $100, quarterly payments are necessary. The payment dates among the states vary. Other payroll deductions must be paid according to the particular contracts or agreements involved.

Chapter Review

Review of Learning Objectives

1. **Define liability and explain how the problems of recognition, valuation, and classification apply to liabilities.**
   Liabilities represent present legal obligations of the firm for future payment of assets or the future performance of services. They result from past transactions and should be recognized when there is a transaction that obligates the company to make future payments. Liabilities are valued at the amount of money necessary to satisfy the obligation of the fair market value of goods or services that must be delivered. Liabilities are classified as current or long-term.

2. **Identify, compute, and record definitely determinable and estimated current liabilities.**
   Two principal categories of current liabilities are definitely determinable liabilities and estimated liabilities. Although definitely determinable liabilities such as accounts payable, notes payable, dividends payable, accrued liabilities, and the current portion of long-term debt can be measured exactly, the accountant must still be careful not to overlook existing liabilities in these categories. Estimated liabilities such as liabilities for income taxes, property taxes, product warranties, and others definitely exist, but the amounts must be estimated and recorded properly.

3. **Define a contingent liability.**
   A contingent liability is a potential liability arising from a past transaction and dependent on a future event. Examples are lawsuits, income tax disputes, discounted notes receivable, guarantees of debt, and the potential cost of changes in government regulations.

4. **Identify and compute the liabilities associated with payroll accounting.**
   Labor costs are a large segment of the total cost of most businesses. In addition, three important categories of liabilities are associated with the payroll. The employer is liable for the compensation to the employee, for withholdings from the employee's gross pay, and for the employer portion of payroll taxes. The most common payroll withholdings are the FICA tax, federal and state income taxes, and employee-requested withholdings. The principal employer-paid taxes are FICA (an amount equal to that of the employee) and federal and state unemployment compensation taxes.

5. **Record transactions associated with payroll accounting.**
   The salary and deductions for each employee are recorded each pay period in the payroll register. From the payroll register the details of each employee's earnings are transferred to the employee's earnings record. The column totals of the payroll register are used to prepare a general journal entry that records the payroll and accompanying liabilities. One further general journal entry is needed to record the employer's share of the FICA taxes and the federal and state unemployment taxes.

Review Problem
Notes Payable Transactions and End-of-Period Entries

McLaughlin, Inc., whose fiscal year ends June 30, completed the following transactions involving notes payable:

May 11	Purchased a small crane by issuing a 60-day, 12 percent note for $54,000. The face of the note does not include interest.
16	Obtained a $40,000 loan from the bank to finance a temporary increase in receivables by signing a 90-day, 10 percent note. The face value includes interest.
June 30	Made end-of-year adjusting entry to accrue interest expense.
30	Made end-of-year closing entry pertaining to interest expense.
July 1	Made appropriate reversing entry.
10	Paid the note plus interest on the crane purchase.
Aug. 14	Paid off the note to the bank.

Required

1. Prepare general journal entries for the above transactions (page 36).
2. Open general ledger accounts for Notes Payable (212), Discount on Notes Payable (213), Interest Payable (214), and Interest Expense (721). Post the relevant portions of the entries to these general ledger accounts.

Answer to Review Problem

1. Journal entries prepared.

General Journal — **Page 36**

Date		Description	Post. Ref.	Debit	Credit
19xx					
May	11	Equipment		54,000	
		Notes Payable	212		54,000
		Purchase of crane with 60-day, 12 percent note			
	16	Cash		39,000	
		Discount on Notes Payable	213	1,000	
		Notes Payable	212		40,000
		Loan from bank obtained by signing 90-day, 10 percent note; discount $40,000 × .1 × 90/360 = $1,000			
June	30	Interest Expense	721	1,400	
		Discount on Notes Payable	213		500
		Interest Payable	214		900
		To accrue interest expense $1,000 × 45/90 = $500 $54,000 × .12 × 50/360 = $900			
	30	Income Summary		1,400	
		Interest Expense	721		1,400
		To close interest expense			
July	1	Discount on Notes Payable	213	500	
		Interest Payable	214	900	
		Interest Expense	721		1,400
		To reverse interest expense adjustment			
	10	Notes Payable	212	54,000	
		Interest Expense	721	1,080	
		Cash			55,080
		Payment of note on equipment $54,000 × .12 × 60/360 = $1,080			
Aug.	14	Notes Payable	212	40,000	
		Cash			40,000
		Payment of bank loan			
	14	Interest Expense	721	1,000	
		Discount on Notes Payable	213		1,000
		To record interest expense on notes payable			

2. Accounts opened and amounts posted.

Notes Payable — Account No. 212

Date		Item	Post. Ref.	Debit	Credit	Balance Debit	Balance Credit
May	11		J36		54,000		54,000
	16		J36		40,000		94,000
July	10		J36	54,000			40,000
Aug.	14		J36	40,000			—

Discount on Notes Payable — Account No. 213

Date		Item	Post. Ref.	Debit	Credit	Balance Debit	Balance Credit
May	16		J36	1,000		1,000	
June	30		J36		500	500	
July	1		J36	500		1,000	
Aug.	14		J36		1,000	—	

Interest Payable — Account No. 214

Date		Item	Post. Ref.	Debit	Credit	Balance Debit	Balance Credit
June	30		J36		900		900
July	1		J36	900			—

Interest Expense — Account No. 721

Date		Item	Post. Ref.	Debit	Credit	Balance Debit	Balance Credit
June	30		J36	1,400		1,400	
	30		J36		1,400	—	
July	1		J36		1,400		1,400
	10		J36	1,080			320
Aug.	14		J36	1,000		680	

Chapter Assignments

Questions

1. What are liabilities?
2. Why is the timing of liability recognition an important consideration in accounting?
3. At the end of the accounting period, Janson Company had a legal obligation to accept delivery and pay for a truckload of hospital supplies the following week. Is this legal obligation a liability?
4. Ned Johnson, a star college basketball player, received a contract from the Midwest Blazers to play professional basketball. The contract calls for a salary of $300,000 a year for four years, dependent on his making the team in each of those years. Should this contract be considered a liability and recorded on the books of the basketball team?
5. What is the rule for determining a current liability?
6. Where should the Discount on Notes Payable account appear on the balance sheet?
7. When can a portion of long-term debt be classified as a current liability?
8. Why are deferred revenues classified as liabilities?
9. What is definite about an estimated liability?
10. Why are income taxes payable considered to be estimated liabilities?
11. When does a company incur a liability for a product warranty?
12. What is a contingent liability, and how does it differ from an estimated liability?
13. What are some examples of contingent liabilities, and why is each a contingent liability?
14. Why is payroll accounting important?
15. How does an employee differ from an independent contractor?
16. What are three types of employer-related payroll liabilities?
17. Who pays the FICA tax?
18. What role does the W-4 form play in determining the withholding for estimated federal income taxes?
19. What withholdings might an employee voluntarily request?
20. Why is an employee earnings record necessary, and how does it relate to the W-2 form?
21. How can the payroll register be used as a special-purpose journal?

Classroom Exercises

Exercise 9-1. Excise and Sales Taxes (L.O. 2)

Lemke Speed Call billed its customers for the month of May for a total of $570,000, including 9 percent federal excise tax and 5 percent state sales tax.

1. Determine the proper amount of revenue to report for the month.
2. Prepare a general journal entry to record the revenue and related liabilities for the month.

Exercise 9-2. Interest Expense: Interest Not Included in Face of Note (L.O. 2)

On the last day of October, Sizemore Company borrows $40,000 from a bank on a note for sixty days at 12 percent interest.

Assume that interest is not included in the face amount. Prepare the following general journal entries: (1) October 31, recording of note; (2) November 30, accrual of interest expense; (3) November 30, closing entry; (4) December 1, reversing entry; (5) December 30, payment of note plus interest.

Exercise 9-3. Interest Expense: Interest Included in Face of Note (L.O. 2)

Assume the same facts as in Exercise 9-2, except that interest *is* included in the face amount of the note and the note is discounted at the bank on October 31. Prepare the following general journal entries: (1) October 31, recording of note; (2) November 30, accrual of interest expense; (3) November 30, closing entry; (4) December 1, reversing entry; (5) December 30, payment of note and recording of interest expense.

Exercise 9-4. Vacation Pay Liability (L.O. 4, 5)

Holiday Corporation currently allows each employee three weeks' paid vacation after working at the company for one year. On the basis of studies of employee turnover and previous experience, management estimates that 70 percent of the employees will qualify for vacation pay this year.

1. Assume that the August payroll for Holiday is $200,000. Figure the estimated employee benefit for the month.
2. Prepare a general journal entry to record the employee benefit for August.

Exercise 9-5. Payroll Transactions (L.O. 4, 5)

Jack Lime earns a salary of $60,000 during the year. FICA taxes are 7.15 percent up to $43,800. Federal unemployment insurance taxes are 6.2 percent of the first $7,000; however, a credit is allowed equal to the state unemployment insurance taxes of 5.4 percent on the $7,000. During the year, $15,000 was withheld for federal income taxes.

1. Prepare a general journal entry summarizing the payment of $60,000 to Lime during the year.
2. Prepare a general journal entry summarizing the employer payroll taxes on Lime's salary for the year.
3. Determine the total cost of employing Lime's for the year.

Exercise 9-6. Net Pay Calculation and Payroll Entries (L.O. 4, 5)

Sally Vett is an employee whose overtime pay is regulated by the Fair Labor Standards Act. Her hourly rate is $7.00, and during the week ended July 11, she worked forty-two hours. Sally claims two exemptions, including one for herself, on her W-4 form. So far this year she has earned $8,650. Each week $12 is deducted from her paycheck for medical insurance.

1. Compute the following items related to the pay for Sally Vett for the week of July 11: (a) gross pay, (b) FICA taxes (assume a rate of 7.15 percent), (c) federal income tax withholding (use Figure 11-2), and (d) net pay.
2. Prepare a general journal entry to record the wages expense and related liabilities for Sally Vett for the week ended July 11.

Exercise 9-7. Product Warranty Liability (L.O. 2)

Maze manufactures and sells electronic games. Each game costs $60 and sells for $100. In addition, each game carries a warranty that provides for free replacement if it fails for any reason during the two years following the sale. In the past, 6 percent of the games sold had to be replaced under the warranty. During October, Maze sold 48,000 games and 2,600 games were replaced under the warranty.

1. Prepare a general journal entry to record the estimated liability for product warranties during the month.
2. Prepare a general journal entry to record the games replaced under warranty during the month.

Exercise 9-8. Property Tax Liability
(L.O. 2)

A-1 Company accrues estimated liabilities for property taxes. The company's fiscal year ends December 31. The estimated property taxes for the year are $6,000. The bill for property taxes is usually received on March 1 and is due on May 1.

Prepare general journal entries for the following: January 31, accrual of property tax expense; February 28, accrual of property tax expense; March 31, accrual of property tax expense, assuming that the actual bill is $6,300; April 30, accrual of property tax expense; May 1, payment of property taxes; May 31, accrual of property tax expense.

Exercise 9-9. FICA and Unemployment Taxes
(L.O. 4)

Christo Company is subject to a 5.4 percent state unemployment insurance tax and an 0.8 percent federal unemployment insurance tax after credits. Currently, both federal and state unemployment taxes apply to the first $7,000 earned by each employee. FICA taxes in effect at this time are 7.15 percent for both employee and employer on the first $43,800 earned by each employee during this year.

During the current year, the cumulative earnings for each employee of the company are as follows:

Employee	Cumulative Earnings	Employee	Cumulative Earnings
Brown, E.	$28,620	Lavey, M.	$16,760
Caffey, B.	5,260	Lehman, L.	6,420
Evett, C.	32,820	Massie, M.	43,650
Harris, D.	30,130	Neal, M.	32,100
Hester, J.	52,250	Pruesch, R.	36,645
Jordan, M.	5,120	Widmer, J.	5,176

1. Prepare and complete a schedule with the following columns: Employee Name, Cumulative Earnings, Earnings Subject to FICA Taxes, Earnings Subject to Unemployment Taxes. Total the columns.
2. Compute the FICA taxes and the federal and state unemployment taxes.

Interpreting Accounting Information

Chrysler Corporation
(L.O. 1, 4, 5)

The automobile industry, especially Chrysler Corporation, has had difficult financial problems in recent years. Chrysler incurred operating losses of over $1 billion in both 1979 and 1980. It has received U.S. Government loan guarantees of $1 billion and more. Chrysler's short-term liquid assets (Cash, Marketable Securities, and Accounts Receivable) were $1,084.6 million in 1979 and $773.5 million in 1980. The company also reported short-term liabilities of $3,231.6 million in 1979 and $3,029.3 million in 1980. Sales totaled $12,001.9 million in 1979 and $9,225.3 million in 1980. In management's discussion and analysis of financial conditions and results of operations, it was noted that "Chrysler had to defer paying its major suppliers until it received the proceeds from the additional $400 million of federally guaranteed debt. Chrysler's liquidity and its long-term viability are predicated on a return to sustained profitable operations."

Epilogue: By 1983, Lee A. Iacocca, chief executive officer of Chrysler, could state in the 1983 annual report that "We repaid the $1.2 billion in loans guaranteed by the Federal Government. This action was taken seven years early." At the end of 1983, Chrysler had total short-term liquid assets of $2,753.8 million, consisting of Cash and Time Deposits of $111.6 million; Marketable Securities of $957.8 million; and Accounts Receivable (less allowance for uncollectible accounts of $25.5 million) of $1,684.4 million. Current liabilities were $3,453.9 million and sales for 1983 were $13,240.4 million.

Required

1. Compute Chrysler's ratio of short-term liquid assets to current liabilities for 1979 and 1980. Did Chrysler's short-term liquidity position improve or deteriorate from 1979 to 1980? What apparent effect did the 1980 federally guaranteed loan of $400 million have on the balance sheet and on the liquidity position?
2. Compute for 1983 the ratio you computed in question 1 for 1979 and 1980. Comment on Chrysler's situation in 1983 compared to 1979–1980.

Problem Set A

Problem 9A-1. Payroll Entries
(L.O. 4, 5)

The following payroll totals for the month of April were taken from the payroll register of Drollinger Corporation: sales salaries, $52,800; office salaries, $25,800; general salaries, $28,440; FICA taxes withheld, $7,653; income taxes withheld, $17,520; medical insurance deductions, $3,920; life insurance deductions, $1,880; salaries subject to unemployment taxes, $73,800.

Required

Prepare general journal entries to record the following: (1) accrual of the monthly payroll, (2) payment of the net payroll, (3) accrual of employer's payroll taxes (assuming an FICA tax equal to the amount for employees, a federal unemployment insurance tax of 0.8 percent, and a state unemployment tax of 5.4 percent), and (4) payment of all liabilities related to the payroll (assuming that all are settled at the same time).

Problem 9A-2. Product Warranty Liability
(L.O. 2)

Lighthouse Company is engaged in the retail sale of washing machines. Each machine has a twenty-four-month warranty on parts. If a repair under warranty is required, a charge for the labor is made. Management has found that 25 percent of the machines sold require some warranty work before the twenty-four months pass. Furthermore, the average cost of replacement parts has been $90 per repair. At the beginning of February, the account for the estimated liability for product warranties had a credit balance of $12,400. During February, 105 machines were returned under the warranty. The cost of the parts used in repairing the machines was $8,695, and $8,742 was collected as service revenue for the labor involved. Also, during the month, 430 new machines were sold.

Required

1. Prepare general journal entries to record each of the following: (a) the warranty work completed during the month, including related revenue; (b) the estimated liability for product warranties for machines sold during the month.
2. Compute the balance of the estimated product warranty liabilities at the end of the month.

Problem 9A-3. Notes Payable Transactions and End-of-Period Entries
(L.O. 2)

Healthcare Corporation, whose fiscal year ends June 30, completed the following transactions involving notes payable:

May 11	Signed a 90-day, 12 percent, $120,000 note payable to Citibank for a working capital loan. The face value included interest.
21	Obtained a 60-day extension on a $24,000 trade account payable owed to a supplier by signing a 60-day, $24,000 note. Interest is in addition to the face value at the rate of 14 percent.
June 30	Made end-of-year adjusting entry to accrue interest expense.
30	Made end-of-year closing entry pertaining to interest expense.
July 1	Made appropriate reversing entry.
20	paid off the note plus interest due the supplier.
Aug. 9	Paid amount due bank on 90-day note.

Required

1. Prepare general journal entries for the above transactions (page 28).
2. Open general ledger accounts for Notes Payable (212), Discount on Notes Payable (213), Interest Payable (214), and Interest Expense (721). Post the relevant portions of the entries to these general ledger accounts.

Problem 9A-4. Property Tax and Vacation Pay Liabilities
(L.O. 2, 4, 5)

Jaysee Corporation prepares monthly financial statements and ends its fiscal year on June 30. In July, your first month as accountant for the company, you find that the company has not previously accrued estimated liabilities. In the past, the company, which has a large property tax bill, has charged property taxes to the month in which the bill is paid. The tax bill for last year was $48,000, and it is estimated that the tax will increase by 10 percent in the coming year. The tax bill is usually received on September 1, to be paid November 1. You also discover that the company allows employees who have worked for the company for one year to take two weeks' paid vacation each year. The cost of these vacations had been charged to expense in the month of payment. Approximately 85 percent of the employees qualify for this benefit.

You suggest to management that proper accounting treatment for these expenses is to spread their cost over the entire year. Management agrees and asks you to make the proper adjustments.

Required

1. Figure the proper monthly charge to property taxes expense, and prepare general journal entries for the following:

July 31	Accrual of property tax expense
Aug. 31	Accrual of property tax expense
Sept. 30	Accrual of property tax expense (assume actual bill is $52,860).
Oct. 31	Accrual of property tax expense
Nov. 1	Payment of property tax
Nov. 30	Accrual of property tax expense

2. Assume that for July, the total payroll is $424,000, which includes $14,800 paid to employees who were on vacation. (a) Compute the vacation pay expense for July. (b) Prepare a general journal entry to record the accrual of vacation pay expense for July. (c) Prepare a general journal entry to record the wages of employees on vacation in July (ignore payroll deductions and taxes).

Problem 9A-5. Payroll Register and Related Entries
(L.O. 4, 5)

Cirulli Pasta has seven employees. The salaried employees are paid on the last biweekly payday of each month. Employees paid hourly receive a set rate for regular hours plus one and one-half times their hourly rate for overtime hours. They are paid every two weeks. The employees and company are subject to 7.15 percent FICA taxes on the first $43,800 earned by each employee. The unemployment insurance tax rates are 5.4 percent for the state and 0.8 percent for the federal government. The unemployment insurance tax applies to the first $7,000 earned by each employee and is levied only on the employer.

The company maintains a supplemental benefit plan that includes medical insurance, life insurance, and additional retirement funds for employees. Under the plan, each employee contributes 5 percent of his or her gross income as a payroll withholding, and the company matches this amount.

Data for the November 30 payroll, the last payday of November, follow:

Employee	Hours		Pay Rate	Cumulative Gross Pay Excluding Current Pay Period	Federal Income Tax to Be Withheld
	Regular	Overtime			
Battista, A.	80	5	$ 8.00	$ 4,867.00	$ 71.47
Cercone, M.	80	4	6.50	3,954.00	76.80
*Cirulli, C.	Salary		2,500.00	25,000.00	473.21
*Gallo, N.	80		5.00	8,250.00	32.25
*Mungioli, D.	Salary		2,000.00	20,000.00	294.40
Rizo, J.	80	20	10.00	12,000.00	103.65
Sposito, L.	Salary		1,500.00	15,000.00	210.00

*Denotes administrative; the rest are sales.

Required

1. Prepare a payroll register for the pay period ended November 30. The payroll register should have the following columns:

Employee	Deductions
Total Hours	FICA Tax
Earnings	Federal Income Tax
Regular	Supplemental Benefits Plan
Overtime	Net Pay
Gross	Distribution
Cumulative	Sales Expense
	Administrative Expense

2. Prepare a general journal entry to record the payroll and related liabilities for deductions for the period ended November 30.
3. Prepare general journal entries to record the expenses and related liabilities for the employer's payroll taxes and contribution to the supplemental benefit plan.

Problem Set B

Problem 9B-1. Payroll Entries
(L.O. 4, 5)

At the end of October, the payroll register for Goulding Corporation contained the following totals: sales salaries, $81,810; office salaries, $44,040; administrative salaries, $51,720; FICA taxes withheld, $11,808; federal income taxes withheld, $44,742; state income taxes withheld, $7,188; medical insurance deductions, $6,345; life insurance deductions, $5,586; union dues deductions, $648; salaries subject to unemployment taxes, $26,820.

Required

Prepare general journal entries to record the following: (1) accrual of the monthly payroll, (2) payment of the net payroll, (3) accrual of employer's payroll taxes (assuming an FICA tax equal to the amount for employees, a federal unemployment insurance tax of 0.8 percent, and a state unemployment tax of 5.4 percent), (4) payment of all liabilities related to the payroll (assuming that all are settled at the same time).

Problem 9B-2. Product Warranty Liability
(L.O. 2)

The Mixers Company manufactures and sells food processors. The company guarantees the processors for five years. If a processor fails, the customer is charged a percentage of the retail price for replacement. That percentage is based on the age of the processor. In the past, management found only 4 percent of the processors sold required replacement under the warranty. Of those replaced, an average of 25 percent of the cost is collected under the replacement pricing policy. The average food processor costs the company $110. At the beginning of September, the account for estimated liability for product warranties had a credit balance of $95,000. During September, 200 processors were returned under the warranty. The cost of replacement was $21,000, of which $4,830 was recovered under the replacement pricing policy. During the month, the company sold 2,000 food processors.

Required

1. Prepare general journal entries to record the food processors replaced under warranty and the estimated liability for product warranties for processors sold during the month.
2. Compute the balance of the estimated product warranty liabilities at the end of the month.

Problem 9B-3. Notes Payable Transactions and End-of-Month Period Entries
(L.O. 2)

Golini Paper Company, whose fiscal year ends December 31, completed the following transactions involving notes payable:

Nov. 25 Purchased a new loading cart by issuing a 60-day, 10 percent note for $15,000.
Dec. 16 Borrowed $20,000 from the bank to finance inventory by signing a 90-day, 12 percent note. The face value of the note includes interest.
31 Made end-of-the-year adjusting entry to accrue interest expense.

Dec. 31 Made end-of-the-year closing entry pertaining to interest expense.
Jan. 2 Made appropriate reversing entry.
24 Paid off the loading cart note to the bank.
Mar. 16 Paid off the inventory note to the bank.

Required

1. Prepare general journal entries for the above transactions (page 41).
2. Open general ledger accounts for: Notes Payable (212), Discount on Notes Payable (213), Interest Payable (214), and Interest Expense (721). Post the relevant portions of the entries to these general ledger accounts.

Problem 9B-4. Property Tax and Vacation Pay Liabilities (L.O. 2)

Dietch Corporation accrues estimated liabilities for property taxes and vacation pay. The company's fiscal year ends June 30. The property taxes for the previous year were $34,000 and are expected to increase 7 percent this year. Two-weeks' vacation pay is given to each employee after one year of service. Dietch management estimates that 80 percent of its employees will qualify for this benefit in the current year. In addition, the following facts are available:

—The property tax bill of $37,548 was received in September and paid on November 1.
—Total payroll for July was $89,600, including $8,052 that was paid to employees on paid vacations.

Required

1. Prepare the monthly journal entries to record accrued property taxes for July through November and actual property taxes paid. (Round to nearest dollar.)
2. a) Prepare a general journal entry to record the vacation accrual expense for July.
   b) Prepare a general journal entry to record the wages of employees on vacation in July (ignore payroll deductions and taxes).

Problem 9B-5. Payroll Register and Related Entries (L.O. 4, 5)

May Manufacturing employs seven people in the Drilling Division. All employees are paid an hourly wage except the foreman, who receives a monthly salary. Hourly employees are paid once a week and receive a set hourly rate for regular hours plus time-and-a-half for overtime. The employees and employer are subject to 7.15 percent FICA tax on the first $43,800 earned by each employee. The unemployment insurance tax rates are 5.4 percent for the state and 0.8 percent for the federal government. The unemployment insurance tax applies to the first $7,000 earned by each employee and is levied only on the employer. Each employee qualifies for the May Manufacturing Profit Sharing Plan. Under this plan each employee may contribute up to 10 percent of his or her gross income as a payroll withholding, and the company matches this amount.

The data for the last payday of October are on the following page.

Employee	Hours Regular	Hours Overtime	Pay Rate	Cumulative Earnings Prior to Current Pay Period	Percentage Contribution to Profit Sharing Plan	Federal Income Tax to be Withheld
Bridges, P.	40	4	$ 8.50	$14,350.00	2%	$ 40.50
Dixon, D.	40	2	9.00	11,275.00	5%	48.60
Gibson, M.	40	5	12.70	16,510.00	7%	35.60
Hendon, H.	Salary		4,000.00	40,000.00	9%	760.00
Jansen, G.	40	—	12.50	15,275.00	3%	60.50
Myers, R.	40	7	9.00	11,925.00	—	23.00
Webb, P.	40	3	7.50	10,218.00	—	20.75

Required

1. Prepare a payroll register for the period ended October 31. The payroll register should have the following columns:

Employee	Deductions
Total Hours	FICA Tax
Earnings	Federal Income Tax
Regular	Profit Sharing Plan
Overtime	Payment
Gross	Salaries Expense
Cumulative	

2. Prepare a general journal entry to record the payroll and related liabilities for deductions for the period ended October 31.
3. Prepare general journal entries to record the expenses and related liabilities to the employer's payroll taxes and contribution to the Profit Sharing Plan.

Financial Decision Case

Highland Television Repair
(L.O. 1, 2, 4)

Jerry Highland opened a small television repair shop on January 2, 19xx. He also sold a small line of television sets. Jerry's wife, Jane, was the sole salesperson for the television sets, and Jerry was the only person doing repairs. Jerry had worked for another television repair store for twenty years where he was the supervisor for six repairmen. The new business was such a success that he hired two assistants on March 1, 19xx. In October Jerry received a letter from the Internal Revenue Service informing him that he had failed to file any tax reports for his business since its inception and probably owed a considerable amount of taxes. Since Jerry has limited experience in maintaining business records, he has brought the letter and all his business records to you for help. The records include a checkbook, cancelled checks, deposit slips, invoices from his suppliers, notice of annual property taxes of $4,260 due to the city November 1, 19xx, and a promissory note to his father-in-law for $5,000. He wants you to determine what his business owes to the government and other parties.

You analyze all his records and determine the following:

Supplies Invoices	$ 2,650
Sales	70,650
Workers' Salaries	16,800
Repair Revenues	120,600

You learn that the shop workers are each paid $300 per week. Each is married and claims four income tax exemptions. The current FICA tax is 7 percent. The FUTA tax is 5.4 percent to the state and 0.8 percent to the federal government. Also, the state levies a sales tax of 5 percent on all retail sales of merchandise. Jerry has not filed a sales tax report to the state.

Required

1. Given these limited facts, determine Highland Television Repair's liabilities as of October 31, 19xx. (For employee income tax withholding, use Figure 9-2. Compute payroll-related liabilities on the two assistants only.)
2. What additional information would you want from Jerry to satisfy yourself that all liabilities have been identified?

CHAPTER 10 LONG-TERM ASSETS

LEARNING OBJECTIVES

1. Describe the nature, types, and problems of long-term assets.
2. Account for the cost of long-term assets.
3. Define depreciation, show how to record it, and state the factors that affect its computation.
4. Compute periodic depreciation under the (a) straight-line method, (b) production method, and (c) accelerated methods, including (1) sum-of-the-years'-digits method and (2) declining-balance method.
5. Apply depreciation methods to problems of partial years, revised rates, items of small unit value, groups of similar items, and accelerated cost recovery.
6. Apply the matching rule to the allocation of expired costs for capital expenditures and revenue expenditures.
7. Account for disposal of depreciable assets.
8. Identify natural resource accounting issues and compute depletion.
9. Apply the matching rule to intangible asset accounting problems.

In this chapter, you will study long-term assets. The focus will be on the major categories of long-term assets and accounting for their acquisition cost. You will also study the allocation of the costs of plant assets over their useful life through depreciation and the control of plant assets. The chapter concludes with an explanation of capital and revenue expenditures, disposal of plant assets, natural resources, and intangible assets. After studying this chapter, you should be able to meet the learning objectives listed on the left.

Long-Term Assets

Let us take a closer look at long-term nonmonetary assets, which were defined briefly in Chapter 8. **Long-term nonmonetary assets** (or simply **long-term assets**) are assets that (1) have a useful life of more than one year, (2) are acquired for use in the operation of the business, and (3) are not intended for resale to customers. For many years, it was common to refer to long-term assets as **fixed assets**, but use of this term is declining because the word *fixed* implies that they last forever.

Although there is no strict minimum length of time for an asset to be classified as long-term, the most common criterion is that the asset must be capable of repeated use for a period of at least a year. Included in this category is equipment that is used only in peak or emergency periods such as a generator.

Assets not used in the normal course of business should not be included in this category. Thus land held for speculative reasons or buildings that are no longer used in the ordinary business operations should not be included in the property, plant, and equipment category. Instead, they should be classified as long-term investments.

Finally, if an item is held for resale to customers, it should be classified as inventory—not plant and equipment—no matter how durable it is. For example, a printing press held for sale by a printing press manufacturer would be considered inventory, whereas the same printing press would be plant and equipment for a printing company that buys the press to use in its operations.

Life of Long-Term Assets

OBJECTIVE 1 Describe the nature, types, and problems of long-term assets

The primary accounting problem in dealing with short-term assets such as inventory and prepaid assets was to determine how much of the asset benefited the current period and how much should be carried forward as an asset to benefit future periods. Note that exactly the same problem applies to long-term assets since they are long-term unexpired costs.

It is helpful to think of a long-term asset as a bundle of services that are to be used in the operation of the business over a period of years. A delivery truck may provide 100,000 miles of service over its life. A piece of equipment may have the potential to produce 500,000 parts. A building may provide shelter for fifty years. As each of these assets is purchased, the company is paying in advance (prepaying) for 100,000 miles, 500,000 parts, or fifty years of service. In essence, each of these assets is a type of long-term prepaid expense. The accounting problem is to spread the cost of these services over the useful life of the asset. As the services benefit the company over the years, the cost becomes an expense rather than an asset.

Types of Long-Term Assets

Long-term assets are customarily divided into the following categories:

Asset	Expense
Tangible Assets	
Land	None
Plant, buildings, and equipment (plant assets)	Depreciation
Natural resources	Depletion
Intangible Assets	Amortization

Tangible assets have physical substance. Land is a tangible asset, and because it has an unlimited life it is the only asset not subject to depreciation or other expense. Plant, buildings, and equipment (referred to hereafter as plant assets) are subject to depreciation. **Depreciation** refers to periodic allocation of the cost of a tangible long-lived asset over its useful life. The term applies to manmade assets only. Note that accounting for depreciation is an allocation process, not a valuation process. This point is discussed in more detail later.

Natural resources differ from land in that they are purchased for the substances that can be taken from them and used up rather than for the value of their location. Among natural resources are the ore from mines, the oil and gas from oil and gas fields, and lumber from the forest. Natural resources are subject to depletion rather than to depreciation. The term **depletion** refers to the exhaustion of a natural resource through mining, cutting, pumping, or otherwise using up the resource, and to the way in which the cost is allocated.

Intangible assets are long-term assets that do not have physical substance and in most cases have to do with legal rights or advantages held. Among them are patents, copyrights, trademarks, franchises, organization costs, leaseholds, leasehold improvements, and goodwill. The allocation of intangible assets to the periods that they benefit is called **amortization.** Even though the current assets accounts receivable and prepaid expenses do not have physical substance, they are not intangible assets because they are not long-term.

The unexpired part of the cost of an asset is generally called its book value or *carrying value.* The latter term is used in this book when referring to long-term assets. The carrying value of plant assets, for instance, is cost less accumulated depreciation.

Problems of Accounting for Long-Term Assets

As with inventories and prepaid expenses, there are two important accounting problems connected with long-term assets. The first is determining how much of the total cost should be allocated to expense in the current accounting period. The second is figuring how much should remain on the balance sheet as an asset to benefit future periods. To solve these problems, four important questions (shown in Figure 10-1) must be answered:

1. How is the cost of the long-term assets determined?
2. How should the expired portion of the cost of the long-term assets be allocated against revenues over time?
3. How should later expenditures such as repairs, maintenance, and additions be treated?
4. How should disposal of long-term assets be recorded?

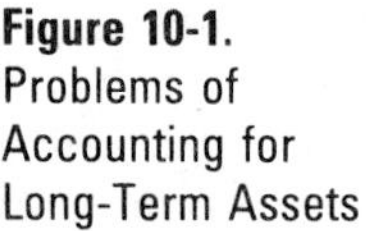

Figure 10-1. Problems of Accounting for Long-Term Assets

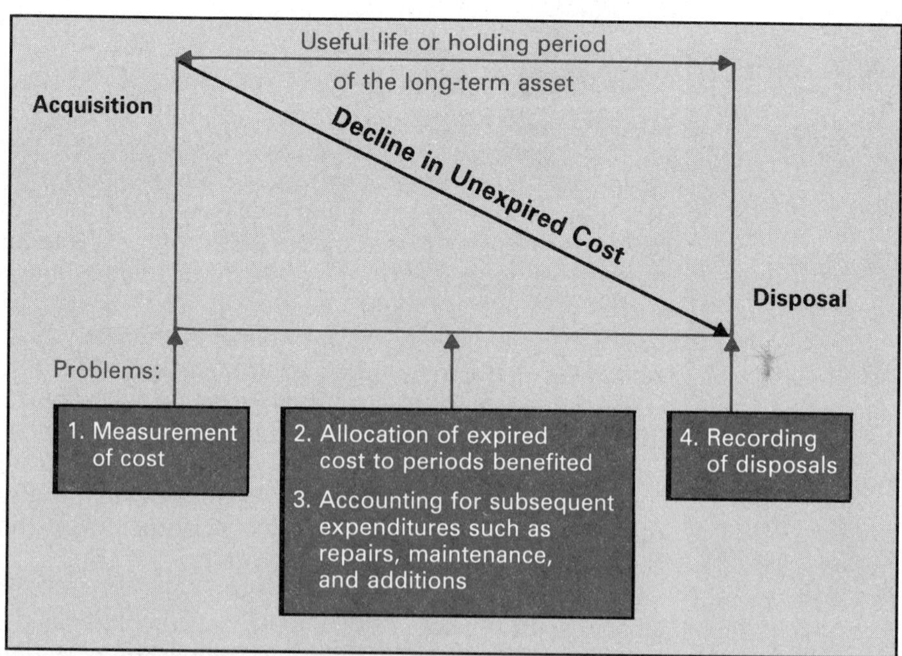

The remainder of this chapter deals with the answers to questions 1 and 2. The discussion of questions 3 and 4 and specific discussion of natural resources and intangibles will be postponed until later in the chapter.

Acquisition Cost of Property, Plant, and Equipment

OBJECTIVE 2
Account for the cost of long-term assets

The acquisition cost of property, plant, and equipment includes all expenditures reasonable and necessary to get them in place and ready for use. For example, the cost of installing and testing a machine is a legitimate cost of the machine. However, if the machine is damaged during installation, the cost of repairing the machine is an operating expense and is not a cost of the machine.

Cost is easiest to determine when a transaction is made for cash. In this case, the cost of the asset is equal to the cash paid for the asset plus expenditures for freight, insurance while in transit, installation, and other necessary related costs. If a debt is incurred in the purchase of the asset, the interest charges are not a cost of the asset but are a cost of borrowing the money to buy the asset. They are therefore an expense for the period. An exception to this principle is that interest costs during the construction of an asset are properly included as a cost of the asset.[1]

Expenditures such as freight, insurance while in transit, and installation are included in the cost of the asset because these expenditures are necessary for the asset to function. In accordance with the matching rule, therefore, they are allocated to the useful life of the asset rather than charged as an expense in the current period.

Some of the problems of determining the cost of a long-lived asset are demonstrated in the illustrations for land, buildings, equipment, land improvements, and group purchases presented in the next few sections.

Land

In buying land, there are often expenditures in addition to the price of the land that should be debited to the Land account. Some examples are commissions to real estate agents; lawyers' fees; accrued taxes paid by the purchaser; cost of draining, clearing, and grading; and assessments for local improvements such as streets and sewage systems.

Let us assume that a company buys land for a new retail operation. It pays a net purchase price of $170,000, pays brokerage fees of $6,000 and legal fees of $2,000, pays $10,000 to have an old building on the site torn down, receives $4,000 salvage from the old building, and pays $1,000 to have the site graded. The cost of the land will be $185,000, determined as shown on the next page.

1. "Capitalization of Interest Costs," *Statement of Financial Accounting Standards No. 34* (Stamford, Conn.: Financial Accounting Standards Board, 1979), par. 9–11.

Net purchase price		$170,000
Brokerage fees		6,000
Legal fees		2,000
Tearing down old building	$10,000	
Less salvage	4,000	6,000
Grading		1,000
		$185,000

Building

When an existing building is purchased, its cost includes the purchase price plus all repair and other expenses required to put it in usable condition. When a business constructs its own building, the cost includes all reasonable and necessary expenditures, such as those for materials, labor, part of the overhead and other indirect costs, the architects' fees, insurance during construction, interest on construction loans during the period of construction, the lawyers' fees, and building permits. If outside contractors are used in the construction, the net contract price plus other expenditures necessary to put the building in usable condition are included.

Equipment

The cost of equipment includes all expenditures connected with purchasing the equipment and preparing it for use. These expenditures include invoice price less cash discounts; freight or transportation, including insurance; excise taxes and tariffs; buying expenses; installation costs; and test runs to ready the equipment for operation.

Land Improvements

Improvements to real estate such as driveways, parking lots, and fences have a limited life and so are subject to depreciation. They should be recorded in an account called Land Improvements rather than in the Land account.

Group Purchases

Sometimes land and other assets will be purchased for a lump sum. Because land is a nondepreciable asset and has an unlimited life, separate ledger accounts must be kept for land and the other assets. For this reason, the lump-sum purchase price must be apportioned between the land and the other assets. For example, assume that a building and the land on which it is situated are purchased for a lump-sum payment of $85,000. The apportionment can be made by determining the price of each if purchased separately and applying the appropriate percentages to the lump-sum price. Assume that appraisals yield estimates of $10,000 for the land and $90,000 for the building if purchased separately. In that case, 10 percent, or $8,500, of the lum-sum price would be allocated to the land and 90 percent, or $76,500, would be allocated to the building, as shown on the next page.

	Appraisal	Percentage	Apportionment
Land	$ 10,000	10	$ 8,500
Building	90,000	90	76,500
Totals	$100,000	100	$85,000

Accounting for Depreciation

OBJECTIVE 3
Define depreciation, show how to record it, and state the factors that affect its computation

Depreciation accounting is described by the AICPA as follows:

> The cost of a productive facility is one of the costs of the services it renders during its useful economic life. Generally accepted accounting principles require that this cost be spread over the expected useful life of the facility in such a way as to allocate it as equitably as possible to the periods during which services are obtained from the use of the facility. This procedure is known as depreciation accounting, a system of accounting which aims to distribute the cost or other basic value of tangible capital assets, less salvage (if any), over the estimated useful life of the unit . . . in a systematic and rational manner. It is a process of allocation, not of valuation.[2]

This description contains several important points. First, all tangible assets except land—that is, plant and equipment assets—have a limited useful life. Because of the limited useful life, the cost of these assets must be distributed as expenses over the years that they benefit. The two major causes of the limited useful life of a depreciable asset are physical deterioration and obsolescence. The **physical deterioration** of tangible assets results from use and from exposure to the elements, such as wind and sun. Periodic repairs and a sound maintenance policy may keep buildings and equipment in good running order or "as good as new" and extract the maximum useful life from them, but every machine or building at some point must be discarded. The need for depreciation is not eliminated by repairs. The process of becoming out of date is called **obsolescence.** With fast-changing technology as well as fast-changing demands, machinery and even buildings often become obsolete before they wear out. Accountants do not distinguish between physical deterioration and obsolescence because they are interested in the length of the useful life of the asset regardless of what limits that useful life.

Second, the term *depreciation,* as used in accounting, does not refer to the physical deterioration of an asset or the decrease in market value of an asset over time. Depreciation means the allocation of the cost of a plant asset to the periods that benefit from the services of the asset. The term is used to describe the gradual conversion of the cost of the asset into an expense.

Third, depreciation is not a process of valuation. Accounting records are kept in accordance with the cost principle and thus are not meant to

2. *Financial Accounting Standards: Original Pronouncements as of July 1, 1977* (Stamford, Conn.: Financial Accounting Standards Board, 1977), ARB No. 43, Chap. 9, Sec. C, par. 5.

be indicators of changing price levels. It is possible that, through an advantageous buy and specific market conditions, the market value of a building may rise. Nevertheless, depreciation must continue to be recorded because it is the result of an allocation, not a valuation, process. Eventually the building will wear out or become obsolete regardless of interim fluctuations in market value.

Factors that Affect the Computation of Depreciation

The computation of depreciation for an accounting period is affected by (1) cost, (2) residual value, (3) depreciable cost, and (4) estimated useful life.

Cost. As explained above, cost is the net purchase price plus all reasonable and necessary expenditures to get the asset in place and ready for use.

Residual Value. The **residual value** of an asset is its estimated net scrap, salvage, or trade-in value as of the estimated date of disposal. Other terms often used are **salvage value** or **disposal value.**

Depreciable Cost. The **depreciable cost** of an asset is its cost less its residual value. For example, a truck that costs $12,000 and has a residual value of $3,000 would have a depreciable cost of $9,000.

Estimated Useful Life. The **estimated useful life** of an asset is the total number of service units expected from the asset. Service units may be measured in terms of years the asset is expected to be used, units expected to be produced, miles expected to be driven, or similar measures. In computing the estimated useful life of an asset, the accountant should consider all relevant information including (1) past experience with similar assets, (2) the asset's present condition, (3) the company's repair and maintenance policy, (4) current technological and industry trends, and (5) local conditions such as weather.

Methods of Computing Depreciation

OBJECTIVE 4
Compute periodic depreciation under each of four methods

Many methods are used to allocate the cost of a plant asset to accounting periods through depreciation. Each of them is proper for certain circumstances. The most common methods are (1) the straight-line method, (2) the production method, and (3) two accelerated methods known as the sum-of-the-years'-digits method and the declining-balance method.

Straight-Line Method

When the **straight-line method** is used to allocate depreciation, the depreciable cost of the asset is spread evenly over the life of the asset.

OBJECTIVE 4a
Compute periodic depreciation under the straight-line method

The straight-line method is based on the assumption that depreciation depends only on the passage of time. The depreciation expense for each period is computed by dividing the depreciable cost (cost of the depreciating asset less its residual value) by the number of accounting periods in the estimated useful life. The rate of depreciation is the same in each year. Suppose, for example, that a delivery truck costs $10,000 and has an estimated residual value of $1,000 at the end of its estimated useful life of five years. In this case, the annual depreciation would be 20 percent of depreciable cost or $1,800 under the straight-line method. This calculation is as follows:

$$\frac{\text{cost} - \text{residual value}}{\text{useful life}} = \frac{\$10{,}000 - \$1{,}000}{5} = \$1{,}800$$

The depreciation for the five years would be as follows:

Depreciation Schedule, Straight-Line Method

	Cost	Yearly Depreciation	Accumulated Depreciation	Carrying Value
Date of purchase	$10,000	—	—	$10,000
End of first year	10,000	$1,800	$1,800	8,200
End of second year	10,000	1,800	3,600	6,400
End of third year	10,000	1,800	5,400	4,600
End of fourth year	10,000	1,800	7,200	2,800
End of fifth year	10,000	1,800	9,000	1,000

There are three important points to note from the schedule for the straight-line depreciation method. First, the depreciation is the same each year. Second, the accumulated depreciation increases uniformly. Third, the carrying value decreases uniformly until it reaches the estimated residual value.

Production Method

OBJECTIVE 4b
Compute periodic depreciation under the production method

The **production method** of depreciation on assets is based on the assumption that depreciation is solely the result of use and that the passage of time plays no role in the depreciation process. If we assume that the delivery truck from the example above has an estimated useful life of 90,000 miles, the depreciation cost per mile would be determined as follows:

$$\frac{\text{cost} - \text{residual value}}{\text{estimated units of useful life}} = \frac{\$10{,}000 - \$1{,}000}{90{,}000 \text{ miles}} = \$.10 \text{ per mile}$$

If we assume that the mileage use of the truck was 20,000 miles for the first year, 30,000 miles for the second, 10,000 miles for the third, 20,000 miles for the fourth, and 10,000 miles for the fifth, the depreciation schedule for the delivery truck would appear as shown on the next page.

Depreciation Schedule, Production Method

	Cost	Miles	Yearly Deprecia-tion	Accumulated Deprecia-tion	Carrying Value
Date of purchase	$10,000	—	—	—	$10,000
End of first year	10,000	20,000	$2,000	$2,000	8,000
End of second year	10,000	30,000	3,000	5,000	5,000
End of third year	10,000	10,000	1,000	6,000	4,000
End of fourth year	10,000	20,000	2,000	8,000	2,000
End of fifth year	10,000	10,000	1,000	9,000	1,000

Note the direct relation between the amount of depreciation each year and the units of output or use. Also, the accumulated depreciation increases each year in direct relation to units of output or use. Finally, the carrying value decreases each year in direct relation to units of output or use until it reaches the actual residual value.

Under the production method, the unit of output or use that is used to measure estimated useful life for each asset should be appropriate for that asset. For example, the number of items produced may be appropriate for one machine, whereas the number of hours of use may be a better indicator of depreciation for another. This method should only be used when the output of an asset over its useful life can be estimated with reasonable accuracy.

Accelerated Methods

Accelerated methods result in relatively large amounts of depreciation in the early years and smaller amounts in later years. These methods, which are based on the passage of time, assume that many kinds of plant assets are most efficient when new, so they provide more and better service in the early years of useful life. It is consistent with the matching rule to allocate more depreciation to the early years than to later years if the benefits or services received in the early years are greater.

The accelerated methods also recognize that changing technologies make some equipment lose service value rapidly. Thus it is realistic to allocate more to depreciation in current years than in future years. New inventions and products result in obsolescence of equipment bought earlier, making it necessary to replace equipment sooner than if our technology changed more slowly.

Another argument in favor of accelerated methods is that repair expense is likely to be greater in future years than in current years. Thus, the total of repair and depreciation expense remains fairly constant over a period of years. This result naturally assumes that the services received from the asset are roughly equal from year to year.

Sum-of-the-Years'-Digits Method. Under the **sum-of-the-years'-digits method,** the years in the service life of an asset are added. Their sum becomes the denominator of a series of fractions, which are applied against the depreciable cost of the asset in allocating the total depreciation over the estimated useful life. The numerators of the fractions are the

OBJECTIVE 4c(1) Compute periodic depreciation under the sum-of-the-years'-digits method

individual years in the estimated useful life of the asset in their reverse order.

For the delivery truck used in the illustrations above, the estimated useful life is five years. The sum of the years' digits is as follows:[3]

$$1 + 2 + 3 + 4 + 5 = 15$$

The annual depreciation is then determined by multiplying each of the following fractions by the depreciable cost of $9,000 ($10,000 − $1,000): 5/15, 4/15, 3/15, 2/15, 1/15. The depreciation schedule for the sum-of-the-years'-digits method is as follows:

Depreciation Schedule, Sum-of-the-Years'-Digits Method

	Cost	Yearly Depreciation	Accumulated Depreciation	Carrying Value
Date of purchase	$10,000	—	—	$10,000
End of first year	10,000	(5/15 × $9,000) $3,000	$3,000	7,000
End of second year	10,000	(4/15 × $9,000) 2,400	5,400	4,600
End of third year	10,000	(3/15 × $9,000) 1,800	7,200	2,800
End of fourth year	10,000	(2/15 × $9,000) 1,200	8,400	1,600
End of fifth year	10,000	(1/15 × $9,000) 600	9,000	1,000

From the schedule, note that the depreciation is greatest in the first year and declines each year after that. Also, the accumulated depreciation increases by a smaller amount each year. Finally, the carrying value decreases each year by the amount of depreciation until it reaches the residual value.

OBJECTIVE 4c(2) Compute periodic depreciation under the declining-balance method

Declining-Balance Method. The **declining-balance method** is based on the same assumption as the sum-of-the-years'-digits method. Both methods result in higher depreciation charges during the early years of a plant asset's life. Though any fixed rate might be used under the method, the most common rate is a percentage equal to twice the straight-line percentage. When twice the straight-line rate is used, the method is usually called the **double-declining-balance method.**

In our earlier example, the delivery truck had an estimated useful life of five years. Consequently, under the straight-line method, the percentage depreciation for each year was 20 percent (100 percent ÷ 5 years).

3. The denominator used in the sum-of-the-years'-digits method can be computed quickly from the following formula:

$$S = \frac{N(N + 1)}{2}$$

where S equals the sum of the digits and N equals the number of years in the estimated useful life. For example, for an asset with an estimated useful life of ten years, the sum of the digits equals 55, calculated as follows:

$$S = \frac{10(10 + 1)}{2} = \frac{110}{2} = 55$$

Under the double-declining-balance method, the fixed-percentage rate is therefore 40 percent (2 × 20 percent). This fixed rate of 40 percent is applied to the *remaining carrying value* at the end of each year. Estimated residual value is *not* taken into account in figuring depreciation except in the last year, when depreciation is limited to the amount necessary to bring the carrying value down to the estimated residual value. The depreciation schedule for this method is shown below.

Depreciation Schedule, Double-Declining-Balance Method

	Cost		Yearly Depreciation	Accumulated Depreciation	Carrying Value
Date of purchase	$10,000		—	—	$10,000
End of first year	10,000	(40% × $10,000)	$4,000	$4,000	6,000
End of second year	10,000	(40% × $6,000)	2,400	6,400	3,600
End of third year	10,000	(40% × $3,600)	1,440	7,840	2,160
End of fourth year	10,000	(40% × $2,160)	864	8,704	1,296
End of fifth year	10,000		296*	9,000	1,000

*Depreciation limited to amount necessary to reduce carrying value to residual value.

Note that the fixed rate is always applied to the carrying value of the previous year. Next, the depreciation is greatest in the first year and declines each year after that. Finally, the depreciation in the last year is limited to the amount necessary to reduce carrying value to residual value.

Comparing the Four Methods

A visual comparison may help give you a better understanding of the four methods used to compute depreciation that are described above. Figure 10-2 compares periodic depreciation and carrying value under the four methods. In the graph that shows yearly depreciation, straight-line depreciation is uniform over the five-year period at $1,800. However, both accelerated depreciation methods (sum-of-the-years'-digits and declining-balance) begin at amounts greater than straight-line ($3,000 and $4,000, respectively), and decrease each year to amounts less than straight-line ($600 and $296, respectively). The production method does not produce a regular pattern of depreciation because of the random fluctuation of the depreciation base from year to year. These yearly depreciation patterns are reflected in the carrying value graph. For instance, the carrying value for the straight-line method is always greater than that for the accelerated methods. However, in the latter graph, each method starts in the same place (cost of $10,000 or 0) and ends at the same place (residual value of $1,000, or cost less residual value of $9,000). It is the patterns during the life of the asset that are different.

The depreciation methods used by six hundred large companies are illustrated in Figure 10-3 on page 374.

Figure 10-2. Graphical Comparison of the Four Methods of Determining Depreciation

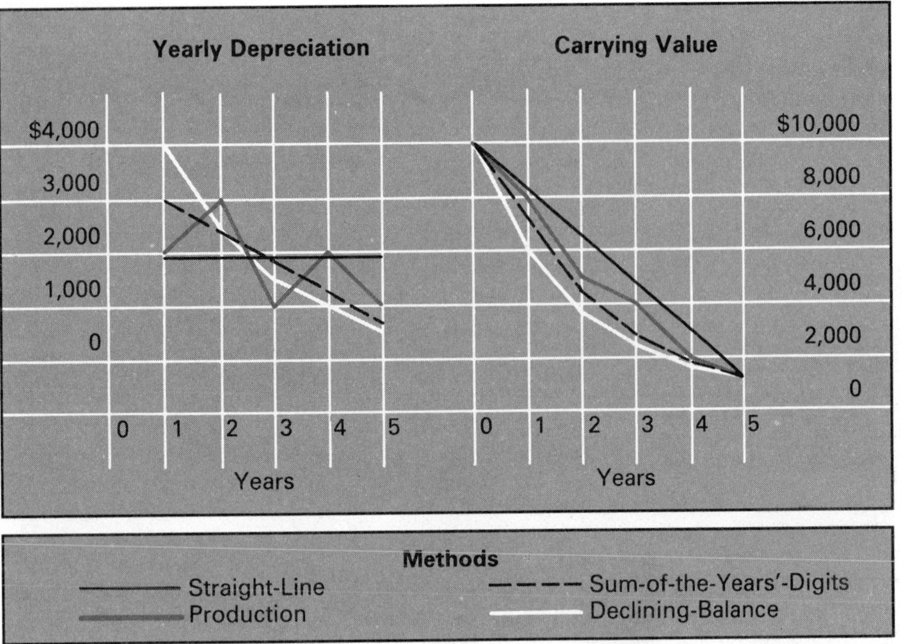

Special Problems of Depreciating Plant Assets

OBJECTIVE 5
Apply depreciation methods to problems of partial years, revised rates, items of small unit value, groups of similar items, and accelerated cost recovery

The illustrations used so far in this chapter have been simplified to explain the concepts and methods of depreciation. In real business practice, there is often a need to (1) calculate depreciation for partial years, (2) revise depreciation rates on the basis of new estimates of the useful life or residual value, (3) develop more practical ways of depreciating items of small unit value, (4) group items that are alike together in order to calculate depreciation, and (5) use the accelerated cost recovery method for tax purposes. The next sections discuss these five cases.

Depreciation for Partial Years

So far, the illustrations of the depreciation methods have assumed that the plant assets were purchased at the beginning or end of the accounting period. However, business people do not often buy assets exactly at the beginning or end of the accounting period. In most cases, they buy the assets when they are needed and sell or discard them when they are no longer useful or needed. The time of the year is normally not a factor in the decision. Consequently, it is often necessary to calculate depreciation for partial years.

For example, assume that a piece of equipment is purchased for $3,500 and that it has an estimated service life of six years, with an estimated residual value of $500 after that length of time. Assume also that it is purchased on September 5 and that the yearly accounting period ends

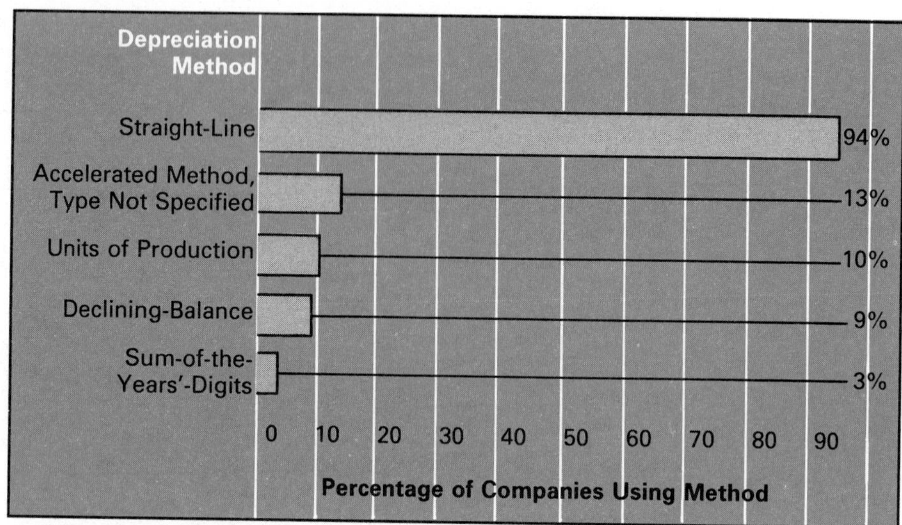

Figure 10-3. Depreciation Methods Used by 600 Large Companies

Total percentage exceeds 100 because some companies used different methods for different types of depreciable assets.
Source: American Institute of Certified Public Accountants, *Accounting Trends and Techniques* (New York, AICPA, 1985).

on December 31. Depreciation must be recorded for four months, or four-twelfths of the year. This factor is applied to the calculated depreciation for the entire year. The four months' depreciation under the straight-line method is calculated as follows:

$$\frac{\$3{,}500 - \$500}{6 \text{ years}} \times \tfrac{4}{12} = \$166.67$$

For other depreciation methods, most companies will compute the first year's depreciation and multiply by the partial year factor. For example, if the company used the double-declining-balance method on the above equipment, the depreciation would be computed as follows:

$$\$3{,}500 \times .33 \times \tfrac{4}{12} = \$385$$

Typically, the depreciation calculation is rounded off to the nearest whole month because a partial month's depreciation is not usually material and it makes the calculation easier. In this case, depreciation was recorded from the beginning of September even though the purchase was made on September 5. If the equipment had been purchased on September 16 or thereafter, depreciation would be charged beginning October 1, as if the equipment were purchased on that date. Some companies round off all partial years to the nearest one-half year for ease of calculation.

When a plant asset is disposed of, the depreciation on this asset must be brought up to the date of disposal. For example, if the asset is not disposed of at the beginning or end of the year, depreciation must be recorded for a partial year, reflecting the time to the date of disposal. The accounting treatment of disposals is covered later in this chapter.

Revision of Depreciation Rates

Because depreciation rates are based on an estimate of the useful life of an asset, the periodic depreciation charge is seldom precisely accurate.

Sometimes it is very inadequate or excessive. This situation may result from an underestimate or overestimate of the asset's useful life or perhaps from a wrong estimate of the residual value. What action should be taken when it is found, after using a piece of equipment for several years, that the equipment will not last as long as—or will last longer than—originally thought? Sometimes it is necessary to revise the estimate of the useful life, so that the periodic depreciation expense increases or decreases. In such a case, the method for correcting the depreciation program is to spread the undepreciated cost of the asset over the years of remaining useful life.

Under this method, the annual depreciation expense is increased or decreased so that the remaining depreciation of the asset will reduce its carrying value to residual value at the end of the remaining useful life. To illustrate, assume that a delivery truck was purchased for a price of $7,000, with a residual value of $1,000. At the time of the purchase, it was thought that the truck would last six years, and it was depreciated accordingly on the straight-line basis. However, after two years of intensive use, it is determined that the delivery truck will last only two more years and will continue to carry an estimated residual value of $1,000 at the end of the two years. In other words, at the end of the second year, the estimated useful life has been reduced from six years to four years. At that time, the asset account and its related accumulated depreciation account would appear as follows:

Delivery Truck

Debit		Credit
Cost	7,000	

Accumulated Depreciation, Delivery Truck

Debit	Credit	
	Depreciation, year 1	1,000
	Depreciation, year 2	1,000

The remaining depreciable cost is computed as follows:

cost	minus	depreciation already taken	minus	residual value	
$7,000	−	$2,000	−	$1,000	= $4,000

The new annual periodic depreciation charge is computed by dividing the remaining depreciable cost of $4,000 by the remaining useful life of two years. Therefore, the new periodic depreciation charge is $2,000. The annual adjusting entry for depreciation for the next two years would be as follows:

Dec. 31	Depreciation Expense, Delivery Truck	2,000	
	Accumulated Depreciation, Delivery Truck		2,000

This method of revising a depreciation program is used widely in industry and is acceptable for figuring taxable income. It is also supported by the Accounting Principles Board of the AICPA in Accounting Principles Board *Opinion No. 9* and *Opinion No. 20*.

Accounting for Assets of Low Unit Cost

Some classes of plant assets are made up of many individual items of low unit cost. In this category are included small tools such as hammers, wrenches, and drills, as well as dies, molds, patterns, and spare parts. Because of their large numbers, hard usage, breakage, and pilferage, assets such as these are relatively short-lived and require constant replacement. It is impractical to use the ordinary depreciation methods for such assets, and it is often costly to keep records of individual items.

There are two basic methods for accounting for plant assets of low unit cost. The first method is simply to charge the items as expenses when they are purchased. This method assumes that the annual loss on these items from use, depreciation, breakage, and other causes will approximately equal the amount of these items purchased during the year.

The second method used for plant assets of low unit cost is to account for them on an inventory basis. This method is best used when the amounts of items purchased vary greatly from year to year. The inventory basis of accounting for items of small unit value is very similar to the method of accounting for supplies, which you already know. Let us assume that a company account for spare parts on hand at the beginning of the accounting period is represented by a debit balance in the asset account Spare Parts. As spare parts are purchased during the accounting period, their cost is debited to this account. At the end of the period, a physical inventory of usable spare parts on hand in the factory is taken. This inventory amount is subtracted from the end-of-period balance in the Spare Parts account to determine the cost of spare parts lost, broken, and used during this period. This cost, assumed in this case to be $700, is then charged to an expense account as a work sheet adjustment with an adjusting entry as follows:

Dec. 31	Spare Parts Expense	700	
	Spare Parts		700
	To record cost of spare parts used or lost		

Group Depreciation

To say that the estimated useful life of an asset, such as a piece of equipment, is six years means that the average piece of equipment will last six years. In reality, some equipment may last only two or three years, and other equipment may last eight or nine years, or longer. For this reason and also for reasons of convenience, large companies will group items of similar plant assets such as trucks, power lines, office equipment, or transformers together for purposes of calculating depreciation. This method is called **group depreciation**. Group depreciation is used widely in all fields of industry and business. A recent survey of large businesses indicated that 65 percent used group depreciation for all or part of their plant assets.[4]

4. Edward P. McTague, "Accounting for Trade-Ins of Operational Assets," *The National Public Accountant* (January 1986), p. 39.

Cost Recovery for Federal Tax Purposes

In 1981, Congress dramatically changed the rules for tax depreciation by substituting for depreciation methods similar to those used for financial reporting a new method called **Accelerated Cost Recovery System (ACRS).** ACRS was a completely new and mandatory cost recovery system that for tax purposes discarded the concepts of estimated useful life and salvage value and instead required that a cost recovery allowance be computed (1) on the unadjusted cost of property being recovered (2) over a period of years prescribed by the law for all property of similar types. Recovery allowances could be calculated by the straight-line method or by prescribed percentages that approximated 150 percent declining-balance method with a half-year convention. ACRS recovery property is generally defined as tangible property subject to depreciation and placed in service after December 31, 1980 and before January 1, 1987.

In 1986, Congress passed the **Tax Reform Act of 1986,** arguably the most sweeping revision of Federal tax laws since the original enactment of the Internal Revenue Code in 1913. The new law retains the ACRS concepts of prescribed recovery periods for different classes of property, calculation of recovery allowances on the basis of the unadjusted cost of property, and elective use of the straight-line method or an accelerated method of cost recovery. The accelerated method prescribed in the new law for most property other than real estate is 200 percent declining balance with a half-year convention. Recovery of the cost of property placed in service after December 31, 1986 will be calculated as prescribed in the new law. Recovery of the cost of property placed in service before January 1, 1987 will continue to be calculated under ACRS. There is one exception. For property placed in service after July 31, 1986, and before January 1, 1987, the new law can be elected based on a property-by-property evaluation.

The intent of Congress, both in ACRS and in the Tax Reform Act of 1986, was to encourage businesses to invest in new plant and equipment by allowing them to write the assets off rapidly. Both ACRS and the new law accelerate the write-off of these investments in two ways. First, the recovery periods they prescribe are generally shorter than the estimated useful lives used for calculating book depreciation. Second, the accelerated methods allowed under ACRS and the new law provide for recovery of most of the cost of the investments early in the recovery period. Recovery will generally be more rapid under the Tax Reform Act of 1986 than under ACRS, because of the faster accelerated method allowed. In some cases, however, the new law provides longer recovery periods. For example, automobiles, light trucks, and light tools were classified as three-year property under ACRS. Under the new law, light tools continue to be three-year property, but automobiles and light trucks are five-year property. Table 10-1 shows the percentages of asset costs that can be written off under ACRS and the Tax Reform Act of 1986.

The use of ACRS may be demonstrated using the delivery truck from earlier in the chapter. It cost $10,000, had an estimated useful life of five years, and an estimated residual value of $1,000. Under ACRS, the delivery truck is a three-year property. The depreciation expense for Federal income tax purposes is determined for each year as follows:

Year	Computation	Depreciation Expense	Accumulated Depreciation	Carrying Value
				$10,000
1	(25% × $10,000)	$2,500	$ 2,500	7,500
2	(38% × $10,000)	3,800	6,300	3,700
3	(37% × $10,000)	3,700	10,000	-0-

Note that three years, rather than the estimated useful life of five years, is used to calculate depreciation. In addition, the estimated residual value is ignored, and the truck is depreciated to a carrying value of zero. No fractional year computations are made, regardless of when during the year the truck was put into service.

Under the Tax Reform Act of 1986, the truck is five-year property and is depreciated for tax purposes using the 200 percent declining balance method with a half-year convention. Depreciation expense for Federal tax purposes is calculated as follows:

Year	Computation	Depreciation Expense	Accumulated Depreciation	Carrying Value
				$10,000
1	($10,000 × 20%)	$2,000	$ 2,000	8,000
2	($10,000 × 32%)	3,200	5,200	4,800
3	($10,000 × 19.2%)	1,920	7,120	2,880
4	($10,000 × 11.52%)	1,152	8,272	1,728
5	($10,000 × 11.52%)	1,152	9,424	576
6	($10,000 × 5.76%)	576	10,000	-0-

Note that cost recovery under the new law is less rapid, despite the use of the 200 percent declining balance method, because the truck is now classified as five-year property.

Table 10-1. Old and New Depreciation Rates for Federal Income Tax Purposes

	ACRS Rates		Tax Reform Act of 1986 Rates*	
Year	3-Year Property	5-Year Property	3-Year Property	5-Year Property
1	25%	15%	33.33%	20%
2	38	22	44.45	32
3	37	21	14.81	19.2
4		21	7.41	11.52
5		21		11.52
6				5.76

* Because of the half year convention, an additional year is added on to each property year category (e.g. there are four depreciation percentages in the three year category).

Tax methods of depreciation are not usually acceptable for financial reporting under generally accepted accounting principles, because the recovery periods used are shorter than the depreciable assets' estimated useful lives. Accounting for the effects of differences between tax and book depreciation is discussed in Chapter 14.

Capital Expenditures and Revenue Expenditures

OBJECTIVE 6
Apply the matching rule to the allocation of expired costs for capital expenditures and revenue expenditures

The term **expenditure** refers to a payment or incurrence of an obligation to make a future payment for an asset, such as a truck, or a service rendered, such as a repair. When the payment or debt is for an asset or a service, it is correctly called an expenditure. A **capital expenditure** is an expenditure for the purchase or expansion of plant assets and is recorded in the asset accounts. An expenditure for repairs, maintenance, fuel, or other things needed to maintain and operate plant and equipment is called a **revenue expenditure** because it is an immediate charge as an expense against revenue. These are recorded by debits to expense accounts. Revenue expenditures are charged to expense because the benefits from the expenditures will be used up in the current period. For this reason, they will be deducted from the revenues of the current period in determining the net income. In summary, any expenditure that will benefit several accounting periods is considered a capital expenditure. Any expenditure that will benefit only the current accounting period is called a revenue expenditure.

It is important to note this careful distinction between capital and revenue expenditures. In accordance with the matching rule, expenditures of any type should be charged to the period that they benefit. For example, if a purchase of an automobile had been mistakenly charged as a revenue expenditure, the expense for the current period would be overstated on the income statement. As a result, current net income would be understated, and in future periods net income would be overstated. If, on the other hand, a revenue expenditure such as the painting of a building were charged to an asset account, the expense of the current period would be understated. Current net income would be overstated by the same amount, and net income of future periods would be understated.

For practical purposes many companies establish policies stating what constitutes a revenue or capital expenditure. For example, small expenditures for items that normally would be treated as capital expenditures may be treated as revenue expenditures because the amounts involved are not material in relation to net income. Thus a wastebasket, which might last for years, would be recorded as supplies expense rather than as a depreciable asset.

In addition to acquisition of plant assets, natural resources, and intangible assets, capital expenditures also include additions and betterments. **Additions** are enlargements to the physical layout of a plant asset. If a new wing is added to a building, the benefits from the expenditure will be received over several years, and the amount paid for it should be debited to the asset account. **Betterments** are improvements to plant assets that do not add to the physical layout of the asset. Installation of an air-conditioning system is an example of an expenditure for a betterment or improvement that will offer benefits over a period of years and so should be charged to the asset account.

Among the more usual kinds of revenue expenditures relating to plant equipment are the ordinary repairs, maintenance, lubrication, cleaning, and inspection necessary to keep an asset in good working condition.

Repairs fall into two categories: ordinary repairs and extraordinary repairs. **Ordinary repairs** are expenditures that are necessary to maintain an asset in good operating condition. Trucks must have tune-ups, tires and batteries must be replaced regularly, and other ordinary repairs must be made. Offices and halls must be painted regularly and have broken tiles or woodwork replaced. Ordinary repairs consist of any expenditures needed to maintain a plant asset in its normal state of operation. Such repairs are a current expense.

Extraordinary repairs are repairs of a more significant nature—they affect the estimated residual value or estimated useful life of an asset. For example, a boiler for heating a building may receive a complete overhaul, at a cost of several thousand dollars, which will extend the useful life of the boiler five years.

Typically, extraordinary repairs are recorded by debiting the Accumulated Depreciation account, under the assumption that some of the depreciation previously recorded has now been eliminated. The effect of this reduction in the Accumulated Depreciation account is to increase the book or carrying value of the asset by the cost of the extraordinary repair. Consequently, the new carrying value of the asset should be depreciated over the new estimated useful life. Let us assume that a machine costing $10,000 had no estimated residual value and an original estimated useful life of ten years. After eight years, the accumulated depreciation (straight-line method assumed) would be $8,000, and the carrying value would be $2,000 ($10,000 − $8,000). Assume that, at this point, the machine was given a major overhaul costing $1,500. This expenditure extends the useful life three years beyond the original ten years. The entry for extraordinary repair would be as follows:

Mar. 14	Accumulated Depreciation, Machinery	1,500	
	Cash		1,500
	To record extraordinary repair to machinery		

The annual periodic depreciation for each of the five years remaining in the machine's useful life would be calculated as follows:

Carrying value before extraordinary repairs	$2,000
Extraordinary repairs	1,500
Total	$3,500

$$\text{Annual periodic depreciation} = \frac{\$3{,}500}{5 \text{ years}} = \$700$$

If the machine remains in use for the five years expected after the major overhaul, the annual periodic depreciation charges of $700 will exactly write off the new carrying value, including the cost of extraordinary repairs.

Disposal of Depreciable Assets

OBJECTIVE 7
Account for disposal of depreciable assets

When items of plant assets are no longer useful in a business because they are worn out or obsolete, they may be discarded, sold, or traded in on the purchase of new plant and equipment. Regardless of the method of disposal, it is necessary to bring the depreciation up to the date of disposal and to remove both the cost and the accumulated depreciation of the asset from the accounts. This step is accomplished by debiting the Accumulated Depreciation account for the total depreciation to the date of disposal and crediting the asset account for the cost of the asset. A Gain or Loss on Disposal may result, depending on the facts of the situation.

If an asset lasts longer than its estimated life, as often occurs, and as a result is fully depreciated, it should not continue to be depreciated. In addition, the asset should not be written off until it is actually disposed of. The purpose of depreciation is to spread the depreciable cost of the asset over the future life of the asset. Thus the total accumulated depreciation should never exceed the total depreciable cost. If the asset is still used in the business, this fact should be supported by its cost and accumulated depreciation remaining in the ledger accounts. Proper records will thus be available for maintaining control over plant assets. If the asset is no longer used in the business, the cost and accumulated depreciation should be written off.

Assumptions for the Comprehensive Illustration

For accounting purposes, a plant asset may be disposed of in three ways: (1) discarded, (2) sold for cash, or (3) exchanged for another asset. To illustrate how each of these cases is recorded, assume the following facts. MGC Corporation purchased a machine on January 1, 19x0, for $6,500 and depreciated it on a straight-line basis over an estimated useful life of ten years. The residual value at the end of ten years was estimated to be $500. On January 1, 19x7, the balances of the relevant accounts in the plant ledger appeared as follows:

Machinery	
6,500	

Accumulated Depreciation, Machinery	
	4,200

On September 30, management disposed of the asset. The next few sections illustrate the accounting treatment to record depreciation for the partial year and the disposal under several assumptions.

Depreciation for Partial Year Prior to Disposal

When items of plant assets are discarded or disposed of in some other way, it is necessary to record depreciation expense for the partial year up to the date of disposal. This step is required because the asset was used until that date and under the matching rule the accounting period should receive the proper allocation of depreciation expense.

The depreciation expense for the partial year before disposal is calculated in exactly the same way as it is calculated for the partial year after purchase.

In this comprehensive illustration, MGC Corporation disposes of the machinery on September 30. The entry to record the depreciation for the first nine months of 19x7 is as follows:

Sept. 30	Depreciation Expense, Machinery	450	
	Accumulated Depreciation, Machinery		450
	To record depreciation for nine months prior to disposal of a machine:		

$$\frac{\$6{,}500 - \$500}{10} \times \frac{9}{12} = \$450$$

The relevant accounts in the plant ledger accounts appear as follows after the entry is posted:

Machinery	
6,500	

Accumulated Depreciation, Machinery	
	4,650

Recording Discarded Plant Assets

Even though it is depreciated over its estimated life, a plant asset rarely lasts exactly as long as its estimated life. If it lasts longer than its estimated life, it is not depreciated past the point that its carrying value equals its residual value. If the residual value is zero, the carrying value of a fully depreciated asset is zero until the asset is disposed of. If such an asset is discarded, no gain or loss results.

In the comprehensive illustration, however, the discarded equipment has a carrying value of $1,850 at the time of disposal. A loss equal to the carrying value should be recorded when the machine is discarded, as follows:

Sept. 30	Accumulated Depreciation, Machinery	4,650	
	Loss on Disposal of Machinery	1,850	
	Machinery		6,500
	Discarded machine no longer used in the business		

Recording Plant Assets Sold for Cash

The entries to record an asset sold for cash are similar to the one illustrated above except that the receipt of cash should also be recorded. The following entries show how to record the sale of a machine under three assumptions about the selling price. In the first case, the $1,850 of cash received is exactly equal to the carrying value of the machine ($1,850), so no gain or loss results:

Sept. 30	Cash	1,850	
	Accumulated Depreciation, Machinery	4,650	
	Machinery		6,500
	Sale of machine at carrying value; no gain or loss		

In the second case, the $1,000 cash received is less than the carrying value of $1,850, so a loss of $850 is recorded:

Sept. 30	Cash	1,000	
	Accumulated Depreciation, Machinery	4,650	
	Loss on Sale of Machinery	850	
	Machinery		6,500
	Sale of machine at less than carrying value; loss of $850 ($1,850 − $1,000) recorded		

In the third case, the $2,000 cash received exceeds the carrying value of $1,850, so a gain of $150 is recorded:

Sept. 30	Cash	2,000	
	Accumulated Depreciation, Machinery	4,650	
	Gain on Sale of Machinery		150
	Machinery		6,500
	Gain on sale of machine at more than carrying value, gain of $150 ($2,000 − $1,850) recorded		

Recording Exchanges of Plant Assets

Businesses also dispose of plant assets by trading them in on the purchase of other plant assets. Exchanges may involve similar assets, for example, an old machine traded in on a newer model, or dissimilar assets, for example, a machine being traded in on a truck. In either case, the purchase price is reduced by the amount of the trade-in allowance given for the asset traded in.

The basic accounting for exchanges of plant assets is similar to the accounting for sales of plant assets for cash. If the trade-in allowance received is greater than the book value of the asset surrendered, there has been a gain. If the allowance is less, there has been a loss. There are special rules for recognizing these gains and losses depending on the nature of the assets exchanged.

Exchange	Losses Recognized	Gains Recognized
For Financial Accounting Purposes		
Of Dissimilar Assets	Yes	Yes
Of Similar Assets	Yes	No
For Income Tax Purposes		
Of Dissimilar Assets	Yes	Yes
Of Similar Assets	No	No

Both gains and losses are recognized when a company exchanges dissimilar assets. For financial accounting purposes, gains on exchanges of similar assets are not recognized because the earning lives of the assets surrendered are not considered to be completed. When a company trades in an older machine on a newer machine of the same type, the economic substance of the transaction is the same as a major renovation and upgrading of the older machine. One can think of the trade-in as an extension of the life and usefulness of the original machine. Instead of recognizing a gain at the time of the exchange, the company records the new machine at the sum of the book value of the older machine plus any cash paid.[5]

Accounting for exchanges of similar assets is complicated by the fact that neither gains nor losses are recognized for income tax purposes. This is important because many companies choose to follow this practice in their accounting records. The reason usually given is for convenience.

As illustrated in Figure 10-4, a recent survey of large companies reveals that although 55 percent recognize both gains and losses, 32 percent report neither gains nor losses on trade-ins of individual assets. Only 13 percent recognize losses but not gains. Since all these options are used in practice, they are all illustrated in the following paragraphs.

Loss Recognized on the Exchange. To illustrate the recognition of a loss, let us assume that the firm in our comprehensive example exchanges the machine for a newer, more modern machine on the following terms:

Price of new machine	**$12,000**
Trade-in allowance for old machine	1,000
Cash payment required	$11,000

In this case the trade-in allowance ($1,000) is less than the carrying value ($1,850) of the old machine. Thus there is a loss on the exchange of $850 ($1,850 − $1,000). The following journal entry records this transaction under the assumption that the loss is to be recognized:

5. Accounting Principles Board, Opinion No. 29, "Accounting for Nonmonetary Transactions" (New York: American Institute of Certified Public Accountants, 1973); also see James B. Hobbs and D. R. Bainbridge, "Nonmonetary Exchange Transactions: Clarification of APB Opinion No. 29," *The Accounting Review* (January, 1982).

Figure 10-4. Recognition of Gains and Losses on Trade-ins of Individual Assets by 97 Large Companies

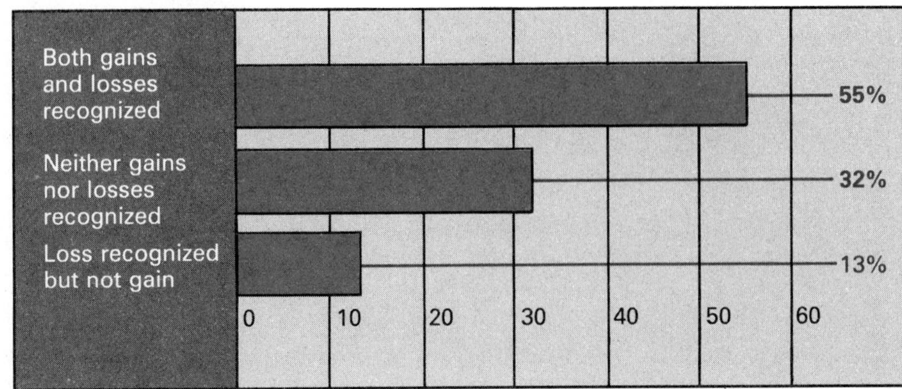

Source: Edward P. McTague, "Accounting for Trade-Ins of Operational Assets," *The National Public Accountant* (January, 1986), p. 39.

Sept. 30	**Machinery (new)**	**12,000**	
	Accumulated Depreciation, Machinery	4,650	
	Loss on Exchange of Machinery	850	
	Machinery (old)		6,500
	Cash		11,000
	Exchange of machine—cost of old machine and its accumulated depreciation removed from the records; new machine recorded at list price; loss recognized		

Loss Not Recognized on the Exchange. In the previous example in which a loss was recognized, the new asset was recorded at the purchase price of $12,000 and a loss of $850 was recorded. If the loss is not to be recognized, the cost basis of the new asset will reflect the effect of the unrecorded loss. The cost basis is computed by adding the cash payment to the carrying value of the old asset:

Carrying value of old machine	$ 1,850
Cash paid	11,000
Cost basis of new machine	**$12,850**

Note that no loss is recognized in the entry to record this transaction:

Sept. 30	**Machinery (new)**	**12,850**	
	Accumulated Depreciation, Machinery	4,650	
	Machinery (old)		6,500
	Cash		11,000
	Exchange of machines—cost of old machine and its accumulated depreciation removed from the records; new machine recorded at amount equal to carrying value of old machine plus cash paid; no loss recognized		

Depreciation of the new machine will be computed based on a cost of $12,850.

Gain Recognized on the Exchange. To illustrate the recognition of a gain, we will continue the same example, assuming the following terms of the exchange:

Price of new machine	**$12,000**
Trade-in allowance for old machine	3,000
Cash payment required	$ 9,000

Here the trade-in allowance ($3,000) exceeds the carrying value ($1,850) of the old machine by $1,150. Thus there is a gain on the exchange if we assume that the price of the new machine is not a figure that has been inflated for the purpose of allowing an excessive trade-in value. In other words, a gain exists if the trade-in allowance represents the fair market value of the old machine. Assuming this condition is true, the entry to record the transaction is as follows:

Sept. 30	**Machinery (new)**	**12,000**	
	Accumulated Depreciation, Machinery	4,650	
	Gain on Exchange of Machinery		1,150
	Machinery (old)		6,500
	Cash		9,000
	Exchange of machines—cost of old machine and its accumulated depreciation removed from the records; new machine recorded at sales price; gain recognized		

Gain Not Recognized on the Exchange. If the gain is not to be recognized in the accounting records, the cost basis of the new machine must indicate the effect of the unrecorded gain. This cost basis is computed by adding the cash payment to the carrying value of the old asset:

Carrying value of old machine	$ 1,850
Cash paid	9,000
Cost basis of new machine	**$10,850**

The entry to record the transaction is as follows:

Sept. 30	**Machinery (new)**	**10,850**	
	Accumulated Depreciation, Machinery	4,650	
	Machinery (old)		6,500
	Cash		9,000
	Exchange of machine—cost of old machine and its accumulated depreciation removed from the records; new machine recorded at amount equal to carrying value of old machine plus cash paid; no gain recognized		

The nonrecognition of the gain on the exchange is, in effect, a postponement of the gain. For example, in the illustration above, when the new machine is eventually discarded or sold, its cost basis will be $10,850 instead of its original price of $12,000. Since depreciation will be computed on the cost basis of $10,850, the "unrecognized" gain is reflected in less depreciation each year than if the gain had been recognized.

Accounting for Natural Resources

OBJECTIVE 8
Identify natural resource accounting issues and compute depletion

Natural resources are also known as **wasting assets.** Examples of natural resources are standing timber, oil and gas fields, and mineral deposits. The distinguishing characteristic of these wasting assets is that they are converted into inventory by cutting, pumping, or mining. For example, an oil field is a reservoir of unpumped oil, and a coal mine is a deposit of unmined coal.

Natural resources are shown on the balance sheet as long-term assets with descriptive titles such as Timber Lands, Oil and Gas Reserves, and Mineral Deposits. When the timber is cut, the oil is pumped, or the coal is mined, it becomes an inventory of the product to be sold.

Natural resources are recorded at acquisition cost, which may also include some costs of development. As the resource is converted through the process of cutting, pumping, or mining, the asset account must be proportionally reduced. The carrying value of oil reserves on the balance sheet, for example, is reduced by a small amount for each barrel of oil pumped. As a result, the original cost of the oil reserves is gradually reduced, and depletion is recognized by the amount of the decrease.

Depletion

The term depletion is used to describe not only the exhaustion of a natural resource but also the proportional allocation of the cost of a natural resource to the units removed. The costs are allocated in a way that is much like the production method used for depreciation. When a natural resource is purchased or developed, there must be an estimate of the total units that will be available, such as barrels of oil, tons of coal, or board-feet of lumber. The depletion cost per unit is determined by dividing the cost (less residual value, if any) of the natural resource by the estimated number of units available. The amount of the depletion cost for each accounting period is then computed by multiplying the depletion cost per unit by the number of units pumped, mined, or cut. For example, for a mine having an estimated 1,500,000 tons of coal, a cost of $1,800,000, and an estimated residual value of $300,000, the depletion charge per ton of coal is $1. Thus, if 115,000 tons of coal are mined and sold during the first year, the depletion charge for the year is $115,000. It is recorded as follows:

Dec. 31	Depletion Expense, Coal Mine	115,000	
	Accumulated Depletion, Coal Mine		115,000
	To record depletion of coal mine: 115,000 tons mined at $1 per ton		

On the balance sheet, the mine would be presented as follows:

Coal Mine	$1,800,000	
Less Accumulated Depletion	115,000	$1,685,000

A natural resource that is extracted in one year may not be sold until a later year. It is important to note that it is recorded as an *expense* in the year it is sold. The part not sold is considered inventory.

Depreciation of Closely Related Plant Assets

Natural resources often require special on-site buildings and equipment, such as conveyors, roads, tracks, and drilling and pumping devices, that are necessary to extract the resource. If the useful life of these assets is longer than the estimated time it will take to deplete the resource, a special problem arises. Because these long-term assets are often abandoned and have no useful purpose beyond the time when the resources are extracted, they should be depreciated on the same basis as the depletion is computed. For example, if machinery with a useful life of ten years is installed on an oil field that is expected to be depleted in eight years, the machinery should be depreciated over the eight-year period using the production method. In other words, each year's depreciation charge should be proportional to the depletion charge. If one-sixth of the oil field's total reserves is pumped in one year, then the depreciation should be one-sixth of the machinery's cost minus the scrap value. If the useful life of a long-term asset is less than the expected life of the depleting asset, the shorter life should be used to compute depreciation. In this case or when an asset is not to be abandoned when the reserves are fully depleted, other depreciation methods such as straight-line or accelerated methods are appropriate.

Accounting for Intangible Assets

OBJECTIVE 9 Apply the matching rule to intangible asset accounting problems

The purchase of an intangible asset is a special kind of capital expenditure. An intangible asset is long-term, but it has no physical substance. Its value comes from the long-term rights or advantages that it offers to the owner. Among the most common examples are patents, copyrights, leaseholds, leasehold improvements, trademarks and brand names, franchises, licenses, formulas, processes, and goodwill. Some current assets such as accounts receivable and certain prepaid expenses have no physical nature, but they are not called intangible assets because they are short-term. Intangible assets are both long-term and nonphysical.

Intangible assets are accounted for at acquisition cost, that is, the amount paid for them. Some intangible assets such as goodwill or trademarks may have been acquired at little or no cost. Even though they may have great value and are needed for profitable operations, they should not appear on the balance sheet unless they have been purchased from another party at a price established in the marketplace.

The accounting problems connected with intangible assets are the same as those connected with other long-lived assets. The Accounting Principles Board, in its *Opinion No. 17*, lists them as follows:

1. Determining an initial carrying amount
2. Accounting for that amount after acquisition under normal business conditions—that is, through periodic write-off or amortization—in a manner similar to depreciation
3. Accounting for that amount if the value declines substantially and permanently[6]

Besides these three problems, an intangible asset has no physical qualities and so in some cases may be impossible to identify. For these reasons, its value and its useful life may be quite hard to estimate.

The Accounting Principles Board has decided that a company should record as assets the costs of intangible assets acquired from others. However, the company should record as expenses the costs of developing intangible assets. Also, intangible assets that have a determinable life, such as patents, copyrights, and leaseholds, should be written off through periodic amortization over that useful life in much the same way as plant assets are depreciated. Even though some intangible assets, such as goodwill and trademarks, have no measurable limit on their lives, they should also be amortized over a reasonable length of time (but not more than forty years) because few things last forever.

To illustrate these procedures, assume that Soda Bottling Company purchases a patent on a unique bottle cap for $18,000. The entry to record the patent would be

Patent	18,000	
Cash		18,000
Purchase of bottle cap patent		

Note that if this company had developed the bottle cap internally instead of purchasing it from a third party the costs of developing the cap would have been expensed as incurred.

Assume now that Soda's management determines that, although the patent for the bottle cap will last for 17 years, the product using the cap will be sold only for the next six years. The entry to record the annual amortization would be

Amortization of Patent	3,000	
Patent		3,000
Annual amortization of patent: $18,000 ÷ 6 years = $3,000		

6. Adapted from Accounting Principles Board, *Opinion No. 17*, "Intangible Assets" (New York: American Institute of Certified Public Accountants, 1970), par. 2.

Table 10-2. Accounting for Intangible Assets

Type	Description	Special Accounting Problems
Patent	An exclusive right granted by the federal government for a period of 17 years to make a particular product or use a specific process.	The cost of successfully defending a patent in a patent infringement suit is added to the acquisition cost of the patent. Amortize over the useful life, which may be less than the legal life of 17 years.
Copyright	An exclusive right granted by the federal government to the possessor to publish and sell literary, musical, and other artistic materials for a period of the author's life plus 50 years. Includes computer programs.	Record at acquisition cost, and amortize over the useful life, which is often much shorter than the legal life. For example, the cost of paperback rights to a popular novel would typically be amortized over a useful life of two to four years.
Leasehold	A right to occupy land or buildings under a long-term rental contract. For example, Company A, which owns but does not want to use a prime retail location sells Company B the right to use it for ten years in return for one or more rental payments. Company B has purchased a leasehold.	Debit Leasehold for the amount of the payment, and amortize it over the remaining life of the lease. Payments to the lessor during the life of the lease should be debited to Lease Expense.
Leasehold Improvements	Improvements to leased property that become the property of the lessor (the person who owns the property) at the end of the lease.	Debit Leasehold Improvements for the cost of improvements, and amortize the cost of the improvements over the remaining life of the lease.
Trademark, Brand Name	A registered symbol or name giving the holder the right to use it to identify a product or service.	Debit the trademark or brand name for the acquisition cost, and amortize it over a reasonable life, not to exceed 40 years.
Franchise, License, Formula, Process	A right to an exclusive territory or to exclusive use of a formula, technique, or design.	Debit the franchise, license, formula, or process for the acquisition cost, and amortize it over a reasonable life, not to exceed 40 years.
Goodwill	The excess of the cost of a group of assets (usually a business) over the market value of the assets individually.	Debit Goodwill for the acquisition cost, and amortize it over a reasonable life, not to exceed 40 years.

Note that the Patent account is reduced directly by the amount of the amortization expense. This is in contrast to other long-term asset accounts in which depreciation or depletion is accumulated in a separate contra account.

If the patent becomes worthless before it is fully amortized, the remaining carrying value is written off as a loss. For instance, assume that after the first year Soda's chief competitor offers a bottle with a new type of cap that makes Soda's cap obsolete. The entry to record the loss would be

Loss on Patent	15,000	
Patent		15,000
To record loss resulting from patent's becoming worthless		

Accounting for the different types of intangible assets is outlined in Table 10-2.

Chapter Review

Review of Learning Objectives

1. **Describe the nature, types, and problems of long-term assets.**
   Long-term nonmonetary assets are unexpired costs that are used in the operation of the business, are not intended for resale, and have a useful life of more than one year. Long-term assets are either tangible or intangible. In the former category are land, plant assets, and natural resources. In the latter are trademarks, patents, franchises, goodwill, and other rights. The problems associated with accounting for long-term nonmonetary assets are the determination of cost, the allocation of expired cost, and the handling of repairs, maintenance, additions, and disposals.

2. **Account for the cost of long-term assets.**
   The acquisition cost of a long-term asset includes all expenditures reasonable and necessary to get it in place and ready for use.

3. **Define depreciation, show how to record it, and state the factors that affect its computation.**
   Depreciation is the periodic allocation of the cost of a plant asset over its estimated useful life. It is recorded by debiting Depreciation Expense and crediting a related contra-asset account called Accumulated Depreciation. Factors that affect its computation are its cost, residual value, depreciable cost, and estimated useful life.

4. **Compute periodic depreciation under the (a) straight-line method, (b) production method, and (c) accelerated methods, including (1) sum-of-the-years'-digits method and (2) declining-balance method.**
   Depreciation is commonly computed by the straight-line method, the production method, or one of the accelerated methods. The two most widely used

accelerated methods are the sum-of-the-years'-digits method and the declining-balance method. The straight-line method is related directly to the passage of time, whereas the production method is related directly to use. Accelerated methods, which result in relatively large amounts of depreciation in the early years and reduced amounts in later years, are based on the assumption that plant assets provide greater economic benefit in their early years than in later years.

5. **Apply depreciation methods to problems of partial years, revised rates, items of small unit value, groups of similar items, and accelerated cost recovery.**
In the application of depreciation methods, it may be necessary to calculate depreciation for partial years and to revise depreciation rates. In addition, it may be practical to apply these methods to groups of similar assets and to apply an inventory method to items of small unit value. For income tax purposes, rapid write-offs of depreciable assets are allowed through the accelerated cost recovery system.

6. **Apply the matching rule to the allocation of expired costs for capital expenditures and revenue expenditures.**
It is important to distinguish between capital expenditures, which are recorded as assets, and revenue expenditures, which are charged immediately against income. The error of classifying one as the other will have an important effect on net income. Expenditures for plant assets, additions, betterments, and intangible assets are capital expenditures. Extraordinary repairs are also treated as capital expenditures, whereas ordinary repairs are revenue expenditures.

7. **Account for disposal of depreciable assets.**
In the disposal of long-term assets, it is necessary to bring the depreciation up to the date of disposal and to remove the carrying value from the accounts by removing the cost from the asset account and the depreciation to date from the accumulated depreciation account. If a long-term asset is sold at a price different from carrying value, there is a gain or loss that should be recorded and reported in the income statement. In recording exchanges of similar plant assets, a gain or loss may also arise. According to the Accounting Principles Board, losses, but not gains, should be recognized at the time of the exchange. When a gain is not recognized, the new asset is recorded at the carrying value of the old asset plus any cash paid. For income tax purposes, neither gains nor losses are recognized.

8. **Identify natural resource accounting issues and compute depletion.**
Natural resources are wasting assets, which are converted to inventory by cutting, pumping, mining, or other forms of extraction. Natural resources are recorded at cost as long-term assets. They are allocated as expenses through depletion charges when the resources are depleted. The depletion charge is based on the ratio of the resource extracted to the total estimated resource. A major issue related to this subject is accounting for oil and gas reserves.

9. **Apply the matching rule to intangible asset accounting problems.**
Purchases of intangible assets should be treated as capital expenditures and recorded at acquisition cost, which in turn should be amortized over the useful life of the assets (but not more than forty years).

Review Problem
Depreciation Methods and Partial Years

Norton Construction Company purchased a cement mixer for $14,500. The mixer is expected to have a useful life of five years and a residual value of $1,000 at the end of that time. According to estimates by company engineers, the mixer has an estimated service life of 7,500 hours, of which 2,625 hours were used in 19x2. The company's year-end is December 31.

Required

1. Compute the depreciation expense for 19x2 assuming the cement mixer was purchased on January 1, 19x1, using the following methods: (a) Straight-line, (b) Production, (c) Sum-of-the-years'-digits, (d) Double-declining-balance (double straight-line rate).
2. Compute the depreciation expense for 19x2 assuming the cement mixer was purchased on July 1, 19x1, using the following methods; (a) Straight-line, (b) Production, (c) Sum-of-the-years'-digits, (d) Double-declining-balance (double straight-line rate).

Answer to Review Problem

1. Depreciation expense for 19x2 assuming purchase on January 1, 19x1:
   a. Straight-line method
      ($14,500 − $1,000) ÷ 5 = $2,700
   b. Production method
      $$(\$14{,}500 - \$1{,}000) \times \frac{2{,}625}{7{,}500} = \$4{,}725$$
   c. Sum-of-the-years'-digits
      $$(\$14{,}500 - \$1{,}000) \times \frac{4}{15} = \$3{,}600$$
   d. Double-declining-balance (double straight-line rate)
      First year: $14,500 × .4 = $5,800
      Second year: ($14,500 − $5,800) × .4 = $3,480
2. Depreciation expense for 19x2 assuming purchase on July 1, 19x1:
   a. Straight-line method

First year:	[($14,500 − $1,000) ÷ 5] × ½ =	$1,350
Second year:	[($14,500 − $1,000) ÷ 5] × ½ =	1,350
19x2 Total		$2,700

   b. Production method
      $$(\$14{,}500 - \$1{,}000) \times \frac{2{,}625}{7{,}500} = \$4{,}725$$
   c. Sum-of-the-years'-digits method

First year:	($14,500 − $1,000) × 5/15 × ½ =	$2,250
Second year:	($14,500 − $1,000) × 4/15 × ½ =	1,800
19x2 Total		$4,050

   d. Double-declining-balance method (double straight-line rate)

First year:	($14,500 × .4) × ½ =	$2,900
Second year:	[($14,500 − $5,800) × .4] × ½ =	1,740
19x2 Total		$4,640

Chapter Assignments

Questions

1. What are the characteristics of long-term nonmonetary assets?
2. Which of the following items would be classified as plant assets on the balance sheet: (a) a truck held for sale by a truck dealer, (b) an office building that was once the company headquarters but is now to be sold, (c) a typewriter used by a secretary of the company, (d) a machine that is used in the manufacturing operations but is now fully depreciated, (e) pollution-control equipment that does not reduce the cost or improve the efficiency of the factory, (f) a parking lot for company employees?
3. Why is it useful to think of plant assets as a bundle of services?
4. Why is land different from other long-term nonmonetary assets?
5. What in general is included in the cost of a long-term nonmonetary asset?
6. Which of the following expenditures incurred in connection with the purchase of a computer system would be charged to the asset account: (a) purchase price of the equipment, (b) interest on debt incurred to purchase the equipment, (c) freight charges, (d) installation charges, (e) cost of special communications outlets at the computer site, (f) cost of repairing door that was damaged during installation, (g) cost of adjustments to the system during first month of operation?
7. Hale's Grocery obtained bids on the construction of a dock for receiving goods at the back of its store. The lowest bid was $22,000. The company, however, decided to build the dock itself and was able to do it for $20,000, which it borrowed. The activity was recorded as a debit to Buildings for $22,000 and credits to Notes Payable for $20,000 and Gain on Construction for $2,000. Do you agree with the entry?
8. What do accountants mean by the term *depreciation,* and what is its relationship to depletion and amortization?
9. A firm buys a piece of technical equipment that is expected to last twelve years. Why might the equipment have to be depreciated over a shorter period of time?
10. A company purchased a building five years ago. The market value of the building is now greater than it was when the building was purchased. Should the company stop depreciating the building?
11. Evaluate the following statement: "A parking lot should not be depreciated because adequate repairs will make it last forever."
12. Is the purpose of depreciation to determine the value of equipment? Explain.
13. Contrast the assumptions underlying the straight-line depreciation method with the assumptions underlying the production depreciation method.
14. What is the principal argument supporting accelerated depreciation methods?
15. What does the balance of the Accumulated Depreciation account represent? Does it represent funds available to purchase new plant assets?
16. If a plant asset is sold during the year, why should depreciation be computed for the partial year prior to the date of the sale?
17. What basic procedure should be followed in revising a depreciation rate?
18. Explain why and how plant assets of small unit value can be accounted for on a basis similar to handling supplies inventory.
19. On what basis can depreciation be taken on a group of assets rather than on individual items?
20. What is the difference between depreciation for accounting purposes and accelerated cost recovery for income tax purposes?

21. What is the distinction between revenue expenditures and capital expenditures, and why is this distinction important?
22. What will be the effect on future years' income of charging an addition to a building as repair expense?
23. In what ways do an addition, a betterment, and an extraordinary repair differ?
24. How does an extraordinary repair differ from an ordinary repair? What is the accounting treatment for each?
25. If a plant asset is discarded before the end of its useful life, how is the amount of loss measured?
26. When similar assets are exchanged, at what amount is the new asset recorded for federal income tax purposes?
27. When an exchange of similar assets occurs in which there is an unrecorded loss for federal income tax purposes, is the taxpayer ever able to deduct or receive credit for the loss?
28. Old Stake Mining Company computes the depletion rate to be $2 per ton. During 19xx, the company mined 400,000 tons of ore and sold 370,000 tons. What is the total depletion for the year?
29. Under what circumstances can a mining company depreciate its plant assets over a period of time that is less than their useful lives?
30. Because accounts receivable have no physical substance, can they be classified as intangible assets?
31. Under what circumstances can a company have intangible assets that do not appear on the balance sheet?
32. When the Accounting Principles Board indicates that accounting for intangible assets involves the same problem as accounting for tangible assets, what problem is it referring to?

Classroom Exercises

Exercise 10-1. Determining Cost of Long-Term Assets (L.O. 2)

Isenhart Manufacturing purchased land next to its factory to be used as a parking lot. Expenditures incurred by the company were as follows: purchase price, $57,000; broker's fees, $4,000; title search and other fees, $350; demolition of a shack on the property, $1,000; grading, $750; parking lots, $10,000; lighting, $8,000; signs, $600.

Determine the amount that should be debited to the Land account.

Exercise 10-2. Group Purchase (L.O. 2)

James Trotter went into business by purchasing a car wash business for $200,000. The car wash assets included land, building, and equipment. If purchased separately, the land would have cost $75,000, the building $120,000, and the equipment $105,000. Determine the amount that should be recorded by Trotter in the new business's records for land, building, and equipment.

Exercise 10-3. Depreciation Methods (L.O. 4)

Cielo Oil purchased a drilling-equipment truck for $36,400. The company expected the truck to last five years or 200,000 miles, with an estimated residual value of $6,400 at the end of that time. During 19x2 the truck was driven 50,000 miles. The company's year-end is December 31.

Compute the depreciation for 19x2 under each of the following methods, assuming the truck was purchased on January 13, 19x1: (1) straight-line, (2) production, (3) sum-of-the-years'-digits, and (4) double-declining-balance at a rate double the straight-line rate.

Exercise 10-4. Depreciation Methods: Partial Years
(L.O. 5)

Using the same data as in Exercise 10-3, compute the depreciation for 19x2 under each of the following methods, assuming the truck was purchased on July 1, 19x1: (1) straight-line, (2) production, (3) sum-of-the-years'-digits, (4) double-declining-balance at a rate double the straight-line rate.

Exercise 10-5. Declining-Balance Method
(L.O. 4)

Obradovic Company purchased a word processor for $2,240. It has an estimated useful life of four years and an estimated residual value of $240.

Compute the depreciation charge for each of the four years using the double-declining-balance method at a rate double the straight-line rate.

Exercise 10-6. Straight-Line Method: Partial Years
(L.O. 4, 5)

Beltran Corporation purchased three machines during the year as follows:

February 10	Machine 1	$12,000
July 26	Machine 2	2,400
October 11	Machine 3	14,400

The machines are assumed to last six years and have no estimated residual value. The company's fiscal year corresponds to the calendar year.

Using the straight-line method, compute the depreciation charge for each machine for the year.

Exercise 10-7. Revision of Depreciation Rates
(L.O. 4, 5)

Lorain Hospital purchased a special x-ray machine for its operating room. The machine, which cost $147,360, was expected to last ten years, with an estimated residual value of $11,360. After two years of operation (and depreciation charges using the straight-line rate), it became evident that the x-ray machine would last a total of only seven years. At that time, the estimated residual value would remain the same.

Determine the new depreciation charge for the third year on the basis of the new estimated useful life.

Exercise 10-8. Accounting for Items of Small Unit Value
(L.O. 5)

Precision Air Conditioner Service Company maintains a large supply of small tools for servicing air conditioners. The company uses the inventory basis for accounting for the tools and assumes that depreciation expense is approximately equal to the cost of tools lost and discarded during the year. At the beginning of the year, the company had an inventory of small tools on hand in the amount of $6,150. During the year, small tools were purchased in the amount of $2,800. At the end of the year (December 31), a physical inventory revealed small tools in the amount of $5,575 on hand.

Prepare a general journal entry to record small tools expense for the year.

Exercise 10-9. Calculating Cost Recovery for Tax Purposes
(L.O. 5)

Quade Corporation purchased a truck for $25,000 and a heavy air compressor for $15,000. Management expects the truck to last six years and have a residual value of $2,000 and the air compressor to last for ten years with a residual value of $1,000. Under ACRS, the truck qualifies as 3-year property and the air compressor qualifies as 5-year property. Under the Tax Reform Act of 1986, both qualify as a 5-year property.

Compute the amount that may be deducted for depreciation on the company's tax return for each asset for the first two years of use, assuming (1) that both the truck and the compressor were placed in service in 1984, and (2) that both were placed in service in 1987.

Exercise 10-10. Extraordinary Repairs
(L.O. 6)

Huerta Manufacturing Company has an incinerator that originally cost $74,800 and now has accumulated depreciation of $58,300. The incinerator just completed its fifteenth year of service in an estimated useful life of twenty years. At the beginning of the sixteenth year, the company spent $19,300 repairing and modernizing the incinerator to comply with pollution control standards. Therefore, instead of five years, the incinerator is now expected to last ten more years. It will not, however, have more capacity than it did in the past or a residual value at the end of its useful life.

1. Prepare the entry to record the cost of the repairs.
2. Compute the book value of the incinerator after the entry.
3. Prepare the entry to record the depreciation (assuming straight-line method) for the current year.

Exercise 10-11. Disposal of Plant Assets
(L.O. 7)

A piece of equipment that cost $16,200 and on which $9,000 of accumulated depreciation had been recorded was disposed of on January 2, the first day of business of the current year.

Give general journal entries to record the disposal under each of the following assumptions: (1) It was discarded as having no value. (2) It was sold for $3,000 cash. (3) It was sold for $9,000 cash. (4) The equipment was traded in on similar equipment having a list price of $24,000. A $7,800 trade-in was allowed, and the balance was paid in cash. Gains and losses are to be recognized. (5) The equipment was traded in on similar equipment having a list price of $24,000. A $3,600 trade-in was allowed, and the balance was paid in cash. Gains and losses are to be recognized. (6) Same as (5) except that gains and losses are not to be recognized.

Exercise 10-12. Disposal of Plant Assets
(L.O. 7)

A commercial vacuum cleaner costing $2,450, with accumulated depreciation of $1,800, was traded in on a new model that had a list price of $3,050. A trade-in allowance of $500 was given.

1. Compute the carrying value of the old vacuum cleaner.
2. Determine the amount of cash required to purchase the new vacuum cleaner.
3. Compute the amount of loss on the exchange.
4. Determine the cost basis of the new vacuum cleaner assuming (a) the loss is recognized and (b) the loss is not recognized.
5. Compute the yearly depreciation on the new vacuum cleaner for both assumptions in **4**, assuming a useful life of five years, a residual value of $800, and straight-line depreciation.

Exercise 10-13. Natural Resource Depletion and Depreciation of Related Plant Assets
(L.O. 8)

Crescent Mining Corporation purchased land containing an estimated 12 million tons of ore for a cost of $4,400,000. The land without the ore is estimated to be worth $800,000. The company expects that all the usable ore can be mined in ten years. Buildings costing $400,000 with an estimated useful life of thirty years were erected on the site. Equipment costing $480,000 with an estimated useful life of ten years was installed. Because of the remote location, neither the buildings nor the equipment has an estimated residual value. During its first year of operation, the company mined 1 million tons of ore.

1. Compute the depletion charge per ton.
2. Compute the depletion that should be recorded for the year.

3. Determine the annual depreciation expense for the buildings, making it proportional to the depletion.
4. Determine the annual depreciation expense for the equipment, using the straight-line method and making the expense proportional to the depletion.

Exercise 10-14. Amortization of Copyrights and Trademarks
(L.O. 9)

1. McDowell Publishing Company purchased the copyright to a basic computer textbook for $10,000. The usual life of a textbook is about four years. However, the copyright will remain in effect for another 75 years.
   Calculate the annual amortization of the copyright.
2. Rice Company purchased a trademark from a well-known supermarket for $80,000. The management of the company argued that the trademark value would last forever and might even increase and so no amortization should be charged.
   Calculate the minimum amount of annual amortization that should be charged, according to guidelines of the appropriate Accounting Principles Board opinion.

Interpreting Accounting Information

Inland Steel
(L.O. 5)

Depreciation expense is a significant expense for companies in industries that have a high proportion of plant assets to other assets. Also, the amount of depreciation expense in a given year is affected by estimates of useful life and by choice of depreciation method. In 1982 Inland Steel, a major integrated steel producer, changed both the estimates of depreciable lives for major production assets and the method of depreciation from straight-line to a production method for other steel-making assets.

The company's 1982 annual report states, "Management review indicates that, on average, the major production assets continue in service significantly beyond their assigned depreciable lives. . . . Equipment lives which formerly ranged from 10 to 28 years have been increased to between 12 and 34 years." The report goes on to explain that the new production method of depreciation "recognizes that depreciation of production assets is substantially related to physical wear as well as the passage of time. This method, therefore, more appropriately allocates the cost of these facilities to the periods in which products are manufactured."

The report also summarized the effects of both actions on the year 1982 as follows:

Incremental Increase in Net Income	In Millions	Per Share
Lengthened lives	$15.7	$ .74
Production method		
Current year	10.5	.49
Prior years	4.0	.19
Total increase	$30.2	$1.42

During 1982, Inland Steel reported a net loss of $118,795,000 ($5.60 per share). Depreciation expense for 1982 was $125,296,000.

In explaining the changes, the comptroller of Inland Steel was quoted in an article in *Forbes* on November 22, 1982, as follows: "Why should we put ourselves at a disadvantage by depreciating more conservatively than other steel companies do?" But the article quotes a certified public accountant who argues that when a company slows its method of depreciation it "might be viewed by some people as reporting . . . lower quality earnings."

Required

1. Explain the accounting treatment when there is a change in the estimated lives of depreciable assets. What circumstances must exist for the production method to produce the effect it did in relation to the straight-line method? What would have been Inland's net income or loss if the changes had not been made? What may have motivated management to make the changes?
2. What does the controller of Inland Steel mean when he says that Inland has been "depreciating more conservatively than other steel companies"? Why might the changes at Inland indicate, as the accountant asserts, "lower quality earnings"? What risks might Inland face as a result of its decision to use the production method of depreciation?

Problem Set A

Problem 10A-1. Determining Cost of Assets (L.O. 2)

LAP Computers, Inc. constructed a new training center in 19x7. You were hired to manage the new center. A review of the accounting records lists the following expenditures debited to the Training Center account:

Attorney's Fee, land acquisition	$ 16,150
Contractor's Cost, building	460,000
Cost of Land	329,000
Architect's Fee, building design	50,200
Contractor's Cost, parking lot and sidewalk	70,700
Contractor's Cost, electrical	76,000
Landscaping	27,500
Costs of Surveying Land	4,600
Training Equipment, Tables, and Chairs	68,200
Contractor's Cost, installing training equipment	34,000
Cost of Grading the Land	7,000
Cost of Changes in Building to Soundproof Rooms	29,600
Total Account Balance	$1,172,950

During the Center's construction, someone from LAP Computer, Inc. worked full time on the project. He spent three months on the purchase and preparation of the site, seven months on the construction, one month on landscaping, and one month on equipment installation and training room furniture purchase and set-up. His salary of $36,000 was charged to administrative expense.

Required

1. Prepare a schedule with the following column (Account) headings: Land; Land Improvements; Building; and Equipment. Place each item from the list above in the appropriate column. Total the columns.

2. Prepare an entry to adjust the accounts associated with the training center, assuming the company's accounts have not been closed at the end of the year.

Problem 10A-2. Comparison of Depreciation Methods
(L.O. 4)

DAC Manufacturing Company purchased a robot for its manufacturing operations at a cost of $600,000. The robot has an estimated useful life of four years and an estimated residual value of $40,000. The robot is expected to last 20,000 hours. The robot was operated 6,000 hours in year 1, 9,000 hours in year 2, 4,000 hours in year 3, and 1,000 hours in year 4.

Required

1. Compute the annual depreciation for each year assuming the following depreciation methods: (1) straight-line, (2) production, (3) sum-of-the-years'-digits, and (4) double-declining-balance at double the straight-line rate.
2. What conclusions can you draw from the patterns of yearly depreciation and carrying value in **1**?

Problem 10A-3. Depreciation Methods and Partial Years
(L.O. 4, 5)

Debra Currie purchased a laundry company that caters to young college students. In addition to the washing machines and dryers, Debra installed a tanning machine, a video game machine, and a bar. Because each type of asset performs a different function, she has decided to use different depreciation methods. Data on each type of asset are summarized below:

Asset	Date Purchased	Cost	Installation Cost	Residual Value	Estimated Life	Depreciation Method
Washer/Dryer	3/15/x7	$ 1,500	$ 200	$ 260	4 years	Straight-line
Tanning Machine	4/1/x7	34,000	3,000	1,000	7,200 hours	Production
Video Game	6/31/x7	5,000	500	400	4 years	Sum-of-the-years'-digits
Bar	10/1/x7	3,400	600	600	10 years	Double declining balance

The tanning machine was operated 1,800 hours in 19x7; 2,700 hours in 19x8; and 2,100 hours in 19x9.

Required

Assuming the fiscal year ends December 31, compute the depreciation charges for 19x7, 19x8, and 19x9. Round your answers to the nearest dollar and present them by filling in a table with the headings shown below:

Asset	Computation	Depreciation		
		19x7	19x8	19x9

Problem 10A-4. Plant Asset Transactions, Revised Depreciation, and Spare Parts
(L.O. 2, 5)

Benox Auto Repair Company installed auto repair equipment on January 2, 19x7 that was purchased for $125,000. Delivery cost was $3,000, and installation cost was $2,000. Mr. Benox estimated the equipment would have a useful life of six years and a residual value of $10,000. On April 2, small tools for auto repairs were purchased for $1,300. Regular maintenance in 19x7 was $250, expended on November 1. At the end of the year, an inventory revealed $940 of small tools still on hand.

Regular maintenance for the equipment increased to $750 in 19x8. This expenditure was made on May 10. Mr. Benox determined that the machine would last only four years instead of the originally estimated six years. The new estimated residual value would be only $5,000. Also on June 10, 19x8, $420 of small tools were purchased, and the inventory of small tools showed $1,020 on hand at the end of the year.

Required

1. Prepare general journal entries for 19x7 to record the purchase of the equipment, costs associated with the purchase, maintenance costs, the transactions involving small tools, and year-end depreciation assuming the straight-line method of depreciation. Assume all purchases are made with cash.
2. Prepare general journal entries for 19x8 for maintenance, small tools, and depreciation expense using Mr. Benox's revised estimates.

Problem 10A-5. Capital and Revenue Expenditure Entries
(L.O. 6)

Joe Van Zee operates several low budget motels in the Midwest. The transactions below describe the capital and revenue expenditures for the first motel he purchased:

Dec. 21, 19x1	Purchased the motel at a cost of $825,000. The estimated life of the motel is 20 years, and the residual value is $100,000.
Dec. 31, 19x1	The motel was repainted and some minor roof problems were corrected at a cost of $50,000. These costs were necessary before the motel was opened to the public.
Jan. 12, 19x5	Made a small addition to the motel at a cost of $38,250. This cost did not impact on the life or residual value of the motel.
May 20, 19x5	Minor repairs were made to the doors of each room for $3,500.
Sept. 17, 19x5	Minor resurfacing was performed on the parking lot at a cost of $5,000.
Jan. 9, 19x8	Major repairs and renovation of $74,400 were completed. It was estimated that this work would extend the life of the motel by five years and increase the residual value by $10,000.

Required

1. Prepare general journal entries for each transaction.
2. Open ledger accounts for Motel (150) and Accumulated Depreciation, Motel (151), and post the relevant entries in **1** above through 19x9.
3. Compute depreciation expense for each year and partial year assuming the straight-line method is used and the company's fiscal year ends on December 31. Enter the amounts in the account for Accumulated Depreciation, Motel.
4. Prepare a general journal entry to record the sale of the motel on June 30, 19x9 for $770,000 in cash. Post the relevant portions of the entry to the two accounts opened in **2**.

Problem 10A-6. Recording Disposals (L.O. 7)

The Future Factory, Inc. purchased a computer that will assist it in designing factory layouts. The cost of the computer was $66,000. The expected useful life is five years. The company can probably sell the computer for $4,000 at the end of five years.

Required

Prepare journal entries to record the disposal of the computer at the end of the second year, assuming it was depreciated using the straight-line method and that

a. it is sold for $48,000.
b. it is sold for $35,000.
c. it is traded in on a similar computer costing $72,000, a trade-in allowance of $45,000 is given, the balance is paid in cash, and gains and losses are recognized.
d. same as **c**, except the trade-in allowance is $32,000.
e. same as **c**, except gains and losses are not recognized.
f. same as **d**, except gains and losses are not recognized.

Problem 10A-7. Leasehold, Leasehold Improvements, and Amortization of Patent (L.O. 9)

Part 1

Blair Guy purchased an eight-year sublease on a warehouse in Little Rock for $18,000. Blair will also pay rent of $300 a month. The warehouse needs the following improvements to meet Blair's needs:

Lighting Fixtures	$ 9,000	Heating System	$15,000
Replacement of a Wall	12,500	Break Room	6,100
Office Carpet	7,200	Loading Dock	4,200

The expected life of the loading dock and carpet is eight years. The other items are expected to last ten years. None of the improvements will have a residual value.

Required

Prepare general journal entries to record the following: (a) payment for the sublease; (b) first-year lease payment; (c) payments for the improvements; (d) amortization of leasehold for the year; (e) leasehold improvement amortization for the year.

Part 2

Dick Stenkowsky purchased a patent for $365,000 that applies to the manufacture of a unique tamper-proof lid for medicine bottles. Stenkowsky incurred legal costs of $135,000 in successfully defending the patent against use of the lid by a competitor. Stenkowsky estimated that the patent would be valuable for at least ten years. During the first two years of operation, Stenkowsky successfully marketed the lid. At the beginning of the third year, a study appeared in a consumers' magazine showing that the lid could, in fact, be removed by children. As a result, all orders for the lids were cancelled, and the patent was rendered worthless.

Required

Prepare journal entries to record the following: (a) purchase of the patent; (b) successful defense of the patent; (c) amortization expense for the first year; (d) write-off of the patent as worthless.

Problem Set B

Problem 10B-1. Determining Cost of Plant Assets
(L.O. 2, 4)

Rayco Corporation began operation on January 1 of the current year. At the end of the year, the company's auditor discovered that all expenditures involving long-term assets were debited to an account called Fixed Assets. An analysis of the account, which has a balance at the end of the year of $2,616,202, disclosed that it contained the following items:

Cost of land	$ 298,800
Surveying costs	3,300
Transfer and other fees	750
Broker's fees	21,144
Attorney's fees associated with land acquisition	7,048
Cost of removing unusable timber from land	50,400
Cost of grading land	4,200
Cost of digging building foundation	34,600
Architect's fee for building and land improvements (80 percent building)	64,800
Cost of building	655,000
Cost of sidewalks	11,400
Cost of parking lots	54,400
Cost of lighting for grounds	80,300
Cost of landscaping	11,800
Cost of machinery	1,034,000
Shipping cost on machinery	55,300
Cost of installing machinery	176,200
Cost of testing machinery	22,100
Cost of changes in building due to safety regulations required because of machinery	12,540
Cost of repairing building that was damaged in the installation of machinery	8,900
Cost of medical bill for injury received by employee while installing machinery	2,400
Cost of water damage to building during heavy rains prior to opening the plant for operation	6,820
Account balance	$2,616,202

The timber that was cleared from the land was sold to a firewood dealer for $4,000. This amount was credited to Miscellaneous Income. During the construction period, two supervisors devoted their full time to the construction project. These people earn $60,000 and $48,000, respectively. They spent two months on the purchase and preparation of the land, six months on the construction of the building (approximately one-sixth of which was devoted to improvements on the grounds), and two months on installation of machinery. The plant began operation on November 1, and the supervisors returned to their regular duties. Their salaries were debited to Factory Salary Expense.

Required

1. Prepare a schedule with the following column headings: Land, Land Improvements, Buildings, Machinery, and Losses. List the items appropriate to these

accounts and sort them out into their proper accounts. Negative amounts should be shown in parentheses. Total the columns.

2. Prepare an entry to adjust the accounts based on all the information given, assuming the company's accounts have not been closed at the end of the year.
3. Assume that the plant was in operation for two months during the year. Prepare an adjusting entry to record depreciation expense, assuming that the land improvements are depreciated over twenty years with no residual value, that the buildings are depreciated over thirty years with no estimated residual value, and that the machinery is depreciated over twelve years with the estimated residual value equal to 10 percent of cost. The company uses the straight-line method.

Problem 10B-2. Comparison of Depreciation Methods (L.O. 4)

Acaro Construction Company purchased a new crane for $334,500. The crane has an estimated residual value of $30,000 and an estimated useful life of six years. The crane is expected to last 10,000 hours. It was used 1,800 hours in year 1; 2,000 in year 2; 500 in year 3; 1,500 in year 4; 1,200 in year 5; and 1,000 in year 6.

Required

1. Compute the annual depreciation for each of the six years (round to nearest dollar where necessary) under each of the following methods: (1) straight-line, (2) production, (3) sum-of-the-years'-digits, (4) declining-balance at double the straight-line rate.
2. What conclusions can you draw from the patterns of yearly depreciation and carrying value in **1**?

Problem 10B-3. Depreciation Methods and Partial Years (L.O. 4, 5)

Amaro Corporation operates four types of equipment. Because of their varied functions, company accounting policy requires the application of four different depreciation methods to the equipment. Data on this equipment are summarized below.

Equipment	Date Purchased	Cost	Installation Cost	Estimated Residual Value	Estimated Life	Depreciation Method
1	1/12/x1	$57,500	$2,500	$ 5,000	8 years	Double-declining-balance
2	1/7/x1	76,675	2,750	7,500	6 years	Sum-of-the-years'-digits
3	7/9/x1	55,800	5,200	6,000	10 years	Straight-line
4	10/2/x1	96,900	2,700	11,200	20,000 hours	Production

Required

Assuming that the fiscal year ends December 31, compute the depreciation charges for 19x1, 19x2, and 19x3 by filling in a table with the headings shown below.

Equipment No.	Computations	Depreciation		
		19x1	19x2	19x3

Assume that production for Equipment 4 was 1,600 hours in 19x1; 3,500 hours in 19x2; and 2,700 hours in 19x3. Show your computations.

Problem 10B-4. Plant Asset Transactions, Revised Depreciation, and Spare Parts (L.O. 2, 5)

Dorothy Hammond entered the jewelry refinishing business in January 19x1. She was able to purchase refinishing equipment for $57,125. It cost her $5,200 to have the equipment moved to her building and $1,890 to have it installed. It cost another $1,065 to adjust the equipment. She estimated that the equipment would have a useful life of ten years and a residual value of $5,000. Small tools were purchased on May 14 at a cost of $490, and regular maintenance of the equipment purchased on September 16 came to $1,305. At the end of the year, an inventory revealed that $120 in small tools were still on hand.

During 19x2, small tools of $725 were purchased on April 18, and the physical inventory disclosed $230 on hand at the end of the year. Regular maintenance costs expended on October 4 increased to $2,070 during the year. Soon it became apparent that the equipment would last a total of only six years instead of the originally estimated ten years and the estimated residual value at the end of six years would be only $2,500.

Required

1. Prepare general journal entries for 19x1 to record the purchase of equipment, costs associated with the purchase, the transaction involving small tools, the upkeep costs, the year-end depreciation charge, and the small tools expense. The company uses the inventory method of recording small tools expense and the straight-line method for computing depreciation expense. Assume all purchases are made with cash.
2. Prepare general journal entries for 19x2 for small tools, maintenance, and depreciation expense. The depreciation expense should be based on the new estimates regarding the equipment.

Problem 10B-5. Comprehensive Capital and Revenue Expenditure Entries (L.O. 6)

Escobar's, Inc., operates a chain of self-service gasoline stations in several southern states. The transactions below describe the capital and revenue expenditures for one station.

Construction on the station was completed on July 1, 1970, at a cost of $310,000. It was estimated that the station would have a useful life of thirty-five years and a residual value of $30,000.

On September 15, 1974, scheduled painting and minor repairs affecting the appearance of the station were completed at a cost of $3,950.

On July 9, 1975, a new gasoline tank was added at a cost of $80,000. The tank did not add to the useful life of the station, but it did add $7,000 to its estimated residual value.

On October 22, 1979, the driveway of the station was resurfaced at a cost of $1,900.

The cost of major repairs and renovation, which were completed on July 3, 1980, was $55,000. It was estimated that this work would extend the life of the station by five years and would not increase the residual value.

A change in the routing of a major highway led to the sale of the station on January 2, 1983, for $200,000. The company received $20,000 in cash and a note for the balance of the $200,000.

Required

1. Prepare general journal entries for the following dates: (a) July 1, 1970; (b) September 15, 1974; (c) July 9, 1975; (d) October 22, 1979; and (e) July 3, 1980.
2. Open ledger accounts for Station (143) and for Accumulated Depreciation, Station (144), and post the relevant portions of the entries in **1**.
3. Compute depreciation expense for each year and partial year until the date of sale, assuming that the straight-line method is used and that the company's fiscal year ends on June 30. Enter the amounts in the account for Accumulated Depreciation, Station.
4. Prepare a general journal entry to record the sale of the station on January 2, 1983. Post the relevant portions of the entries to the two accounts opened in **2**.

Problem 10B-6. Recording Disposals (L.O. 7)

Holmes Construction Company purchased a cement mixer for $14,500. The mixer is expected to have a useful life of five years and a residual value of $1,000 at the end of that time.

Required

Prepare journal entries to record the disposal of the mixer at the end of the second year, assuming that the straight-line method is used and that (a) It is sold for $10,000 cash. (b) It is sold for $8,000 cash. (c) It is traded in on a similar mixer having a price of $16,500, a trade-in allowance of $10,000 is given, the balance is paid in cash, and gains or losses are recognized. (d) It is traded in on a similar mixer having a price of $16,500, a trade-in allowance of $8,000 is given, the balance is paid in cash, and gains and losses are recognized. (e) Same as **c** except gains or losses are not recognized. (f) Same as **d** except gains or losses are not recognized.

Problem 10B-7. Amortization of Exclusive License, Leasehold, and Leasehold Improvements (L.O. 9)

Part 1

On January 1, Castle Toys, Inc. (CTI) purchased the exclusive license to make dolls based on the characters in a new hit series on television called "High Flying." The exclusive license cost $1,500,000, and there was no termination date on the rights.

Immediately after signing the contract, the company sued a rival firm that claimed it had already received the exclusive license to the series characters. CTI successfully defended its rights at a cost of $250,000. During the first year and the next, CTI marketed toys based on the series. Because a successful television series lasts about five years, the company felt it could market the toys for three more years. However, before the third year of the series could get underway, a controversy arose between the two stars of the series and the producer. As a result, the stars refused to do the third year and the show was canceled, rendering exclusive rights worthless.

Required

Prepare journal entries to record the following: (a) purchase of the exclusive license; (b) successful defense of the license; (c) amortization expense, if any, for the first year; (d) news of the series cancellation.

Part 2

Judy Yu purchased a six-year sublease on a building from the estate of the former tenant, who had died suddenly. It was a good location for her business, and the annual rent of $2,400, which had been established ten years ago, was low for such a good location. The cost of the sublease was $6,300.

To use the building, Judy had to make certain alterations. First she moved some panels at a cost of $1,700 and installed others for $6,100. Then she added carpet, lighting fixtures, and a sign at costs of $2,900, $3,100, and $1,200, respectively. All items except the carpet would last for at least twelve years. The expected life of the carpet was six years. None of the improvements would have a residual value at the end of those times.

Required

Prepare general journal entries to record the following: (a) the payment for the sublease; (b) the payments for the alterations, panels, carpet, lighting fixtures, and sign; (c) the lease payment for the first year; (d) the expense, if any, associated with the sublease; (e) the expense, if any, associated with the alterations, panels, carpet, lighting fixtures, and sign.

Financial Decision Case

Primary Computer Company
(L.O. 4)

The Primary Computer Company manufactures computers for sale or rent. On January 2, 19x1, the company completed the manufacture of a computer for a total cost of $165,000. A customer leased the computer on the same day for a five-year period at a monthly rental of $4,000. Although the computer will last longer than five years, it is likely that it will be technologically obsolete by the end of the five-year period because of the rapid change in the manufacture of computers. However, it is possible that it will not be obsolete. Primary's management estimates that if the computer is obsolete, it can be sold for $15,000 at the end of the lease, and if it is not obsolete, it can be sold for $30,000 because it would probably last for another two years.

On the basis of its experience in leasing many computers, management estimates that the expenses associated with the lease of this computer will be as follows:

	Insurance and Property Taxes	Repairs and Maintenance
19x1	$6,000	$2,500
19x2	5,400	4,000
19x3	4,800	5,500
19x4	4,200	7,000
19x5	3,600	8,500

Required

1. What estimated useful life and estimated residual value do you recommend that Primary use for the computer? Explain.
2. Prepare two schedules that show for each year the lease revenue, expenses, and income before income taxes. Also, show on each schedule for each year the carrying value of the computer at the end of the year, and compute the ratio of income before income taxes to carrying value (return on assets). The first schedule should compute depreciation by using the straight-line method and the second schedule should use the sum-of-the-years'-digits method.
3. Compare the two schedules in **2,** and discuss the results. Which of the methods do you feel produces the most realistic pattern of income before taxes, and why?
4. If you were asked to determine the amount of cash generated each year from this lease (cash received minus cash disbursed), what effect, if any, would the method of depreciation have on your computations?

CALDWELL NEEDLES ANDERSON

PART FOUR ACCOUNTING FOR PARTNERSHIPS AND CORPORATIONS

In the earlier parts of this book, the sole proprietorship has been the major form of business organization discussed. In Part Four, introductory accounting concepts and practices of partnerships and corporations are presented.

Chapter 11 deals with the formation and liquidation of partnerships, as well as with how income and losses are distributed among partners.

Chapter 12 introduces accounting for the corporate form of business, including the issuance of capital stock and other transactions.

Chapter 13 focuses on accounting for retained earnings, a number of other transactions that affect the stockholders' equity of a corporation, and the parts that make up the corporate income statement.

Chapter 14 introduces the long-term liabilities of corporations, with special attention to accounting for bond liabilities.

CHAPTER 11 ACCOUNTING FOR PARTNERSHIPS

LEARNING OBJECTIVES

1. Identify the major characteristics of a partnership.
2. Identify the advantages and disadvantages of the partnership form of business.
3. Record partners' investments of cash and of other assets in forming a partnership.
4. Compute the income or losses that partners share, based on a stated ratio, the capital investment ratio, and salaries and interest to partners.
5. Record a person's admission to or withdrawal from a partnership.
6. Compute the distribution of assets to partners when they liquidate their partnership.

In the first half of this book, we used the sole proprietorship to illustrate the basic principles and practices of accounting. This chapter will focus on accounting for the partnership form of business organization. After studying this chapter, you should be able to meet the learning objectives listed on the left.

The Uniform Partnership Act, which has been adopted by most of the states, defines a **partnership** as "an association of two or more persons to carry on as co-owners of a business for profit." Generally, partnerships are formed when owners of small businesses wish to combine capital or managerial talents for some common business purpose.

Partnership Characteristics

Partnerships differ in many ways from other forms of business. The next few paragraphs describe some of the important characteristics of a partnership.

Voluntary Association

A partnership is a voluntary association of individuals rather than a legal entity in itself. Therefore, a partner is responsible under the law for his or her partner's business actions within the scope of the partnership. A partner also has unlimited liability for the debts of the partnership. Because of these potential liabilities, an individual must be allowed to choose the people who will join the partnership. A person should select as partners individuals who share his or her business objectives.

Partnership Agreement

A partnership is easy to form. Two or more competent people simply agree to be partners in some common business purpose. This agreement is known as the **partnership agreement** and does not have to be in writing. However, good business practice calls for a written document that clearly states the details of the partnership. The contract should include the name, location, and purpose of the business; the partners and their respective duties; the invest-

OBJECTIVE 1
Identify the major characteristics of a partnership

ments of each partner; the methods for distributing profits and losses; the admission or withdrawal of partners; the withdrawals of assets allowed each partner; and procedures for dissolving, or ending, the business.

Limited Life

Because a partnership is formed by a contract between partners, it has **limited life**: anything that ends the contract dissolves the partnership. A partnership is dissolved when (1) a partner withdraws, (2) a partner goes bankrupt, (3) a partner is incapacitated (as when a partner becomes ill), (4) a partner dies, (5) a new partner is admitted, (6) a partner retires, or (7) the partnership ends according to the partnership agreement (as when a major project is completed). However, the partnership agreement can be written to cover each of these situations. This would allow the partnership to legally continue. For example, if a partner dies, the partnership agreement may state that the remaining partner or partners purchase the deceased partner's capital at book value from the surviving beneficiaries.

Mutual Agency

Each partner is an agent of the partnership within the scope of the business. Because of this **mutual agency** feature, any partner can bind the partnership to a business agreement as long as he or she acts within the scope of normal operations of the business. For example, a partner in a used-car business can bind the partnership through the purchase or sale of used cars. However, this partner cannot bind the partnership to a contract for buying men's clothing or any other goods unrelated to the used-car business. Because of this mutual agency characteristic, it is very important for an individual to choose business partners who have integrity and business objectives similar to his or her own.

Unlimited Liability

Each partner is personally liable for all the debts of the partnership. If a partnership is in poor financial condition and cannot pay its debts, the creditors must first satisfy their claims from the assets of the partnership. When the assets of the business are not enough to pay all debts, the creditors may seek payment from the personal assets of each partner. If a partner's personal assets are used up before the debts are paid, the creditors may claim additional assets from the remaining partners who are able to pay the debts. Each partner could conceivably be required by law to pay all the debts of the partnership; therefore, all the partners have **unlimited liability** for their company's debt.

Co-ownership of Partnership Property

When individuals invest property in a partnership, they give up the right to their separate use of the property. The property becomes an asset of the partnership and is owned jointly by all the partners.

Participation in Partnership Income

Each partner has the right to share in the company's profits and the responsibility to share in its losses. The partnership agreement should state the method of distributing profits and losses to each partner. If the agreement describes how profits are to be shared but does not mention losses, the losses are distributed in the same way as profits. If the partners fail to describe the method of profit and loss distribution in the partnership agreement, the law states that profits and losses be shared equally.

Summary of the Advantages and Disadvantages of Partnerships

OBJECTIVE 2 Identify the advantages and disadvantages of the partnership form of business

Partnerships have both advantages and disadvantages. Several of the advantages are that the partnership is easy to form and to dissolve; it is able to pool capital resources and individual talents; it has no corporate tax burden (because the partnership is not a legal entity, it does not have to pay an income tax but must file an informational return); and it gives freedom and flexibility to its partners' actions. Several of the disadvantages of a partnership are that its life is limited; one partner can bind the partnership to a contract (mutual agency); the partners have unlimited personal liability; and it is hard in a partnership to raise large amounts of capital and to transfer ownership interest.

Accounting for Partners' Equity

Accounting for a partnership is very similar to accounting for a sole proprietorship. A major difference is that the owners' equity of a partnership is called **partners' equity**. In accounting for partners' equity, it is necessary to maintain separate capital and withdrawal accounts for each partner and to divide the profits and losses of the company among the partners. The differences in the capital accounts of a sole proprietorship and a partnership are illustrated below.

Sole Proprietorship

Blake, Capital	
	50,000

Blake, Withdrawals	
12,000	

Partnership

Desmond, Capital	
	30,000

Frank, Capital	
	40,000

Desmond, Withdrawals	
5,000	

Frank, Withdrawals	
6,000	

In the partners' equity section of the balance sheet, the balance of each partner's capital account is listed separately, as shown in the partial balance sheet on the next page.

Liabilities and Partners' Equity

Total Liabilities		$28,000
Partners' Equity		
Desmond, Capital	$25,000	
Frank, Capital	34,000	
Total Partners' Equity		59,000
Total Liabilities and Partners' Equity		$87,000

OBJECTIVE 3
Record partners' investments of cash and of other assets in forming a partnership

Each partner invests cash, other assets, or a combination of both in the partnership according to the agreement. When other assets are invested, the partners must agree on their value. The value of noncash assets should be their fair market value on the date they are transferred to the partnership. The assets invested by a partner are debited to the proper account, and the total amount is credited to the partner's capital account.

To illustrate the recording of partner's investments, we shall assume that Jerry Adcock and Rose Villa agree to combine their capital and equipment in a partnership for the purpose of operating a jewelry store. Adcock will invest $28,000 cash and $37,000 of furniture and displays, and Villa $40,000 cash and $20,000 of equipment, according to the partnership agreement. The general journal entries that record the initial investments of Adcock and Villa are as follows:

July 1	Cash	28,000	
	Furniture and Displays	37,000	
	Jerry Adcock, Capital		65,000
	To record the initial investment of Jerry Adcock in Adcock and Villa		
July 1	Cash	40,000	
	Equipment	20,000	
	Rose Villa, Capital		60,000
	To record the initial investment of Rose Villa in Adcock and Villa		

The values assigned to the assets in the above illustration would have had to be included in the partnership agreement. These values may differ from those carried on the partners' personal books. For example, the equipment that Rose Villa contributed may have had a value of only $12,000 on her books. However, after she purchased the equipment, its market value increased considerably. Regardless of book value, Villa's investment should be recognized at the fair market value of the equipment at the time of transfer, because that value represents the amount of money that Villa has put into the partnership.

Further investments are recorded in the same way. The partnership may also assume liabilities that are related to investments. For example, assume that after three months Rose Villa invests additional equipment with a fair market value of $45,000 in the partnership. Related to the equipment is a note payable for $37,000, which the partnership assumes.

The entry that records the transaction is as follows:

Oct. 1	Equipment	45,000	
	Notes Payable		37,000
	Rose Villa, Capital		8,000
	To record additional investment by Rose Villa in Adcock and Villa		

Distribution of Partnership Income and Losses

OBJECTIVE 4 Compute the income or losses that partners share, based on a stated ratio, the capital investment ratio, and salaries and interest to partners

A partnership's income and losses can be distributed according to any method that the partners specify in the partnership agreement. The agreement should be specific and clear to avoid disputes among the partners over later distributions of income and losses. However, if the partnership agreement does not mention the distribution of income and losses, the law requires that they be shared equally by all partners. Also, if the partnership agreement mentions only the distribution of income, the law requires that losses be distributed in the same ratio as income.

The income of a partnership normally has three components: (1) return to the partners for the use of their capital, (2) compensation for services that the partners have rendered, and (3) further economic income for the business risks the partners have taken. The breakdown of total income into its three components helps clarify how much each partner has contributed to the firm.

If all partners are spending the same amount of time, are contributing equal capital, and have similar managerial talents, then an equal sharing of income and losses would be fair. However, if one partner works full time in the firm whereas another partner devotes only one-fourth of his or her time, then the distribution of income or losses should reflect this difference. This arrangement would apply to any situation in which the partners contribute unequally to the business.

Several ways for partners to share income are (1) by stated ratio, (2) by capital investment ratio, and (3) by salaries to the partners and interest on partners' capital, with the remaining income shared according to a stated ratio.

Stated Ratio

One method of distributing income and losses is to give each partner a stated ratio of the total. If each partner is making an equal contribution to the firm, each may assume the same share of the income and losses. The equal contribution of the partners may take many forms. For example, each partner may have made an equal investment in the firm. On the other hand, one partner may be devoting more time and talent to the firm, whereas the second partner may make a larger capital investment.

Also, if the partners contribute unequally to the firm, unequal stated ratios can be appropriate, such as 60 percent, 30 percent, and 10 percent for a partnership of three persons.

To illustrate this method, we shall assume that Adcock and Villa had a net income last year of $30,000. The partnership agreement states that the percentages of income and losses distributed to Adcock and Villa will be 60 and 40, respectively. The computation of each partner's share of the income and the journal entry to show the distribution are as follows:

Adcock ($30,000 × 60%)	$18,000
Villa ($30,000 × 40%)	12,000
Net income	$30,000

June 30	Income Summary	30,000	
	Jerry Adcock, Capital		18,000
	Rose Villa, Capital		12,000
	To distribute the income for the year to the partners' capital accounts		

Capital Investment Ratio

If the invested capital produces the most income for the partnership business, then income and losses may be distributed according to capital investment. One way of distributing income and losses in this case is to use the ratio of capital balances of each partner at the beginning of the year. Another way is to use the average capital balance of each partner during the year.

To show how the first method works, we will assume the following balances for the capital accounts of Adcock and Villa for their first year of operation, which was July 1, 19x1, through June 30, 19x2. Income for the year was $140,000.

Jerry Adcock, Capital

Debit	Credit
	7/1 65,000

Jerry Adcock, Withdrawals

Debit	Credit
1/1 10,000	

Rose Villa, Capital

Debit	Credit
	7/1 60,000
	2/1 8,000

Rose Villa, Withdrawals

Debit	Credit
11/1 10,000	

Beginning capital balances for Adcock and Villa were as follows:

	Capital	Capital Ratio
Jerry Adcock	$ 65,000	65/125
Rose Villa	60,000	60/125
Total capital	$125,000	

The income that each partner will receive when distribution is based on beginning capital investment ratios is figured by multiplying the total income by each partner's capital ratio.

Jerry Adcock	$140,000 × 65/125 =	$72,800
Rose Villa	$140,000 × 60/125 =	67,200
		$140,000

The entry showing distribution of income is as follows:

June 30	Income Summary	140,000	
	Jerry Adcock, Capital		72,800
	Rose Villa, Capital		67,200
	To distribute the income for the year to the partners' capital accounts		

If Adcock and Villa use their beginning capital investments to determine the ratio for distributing income, they do not consider any withdrawals or further investments made during the year. However, such investments and withdrawals usually change the partners' capital ratio. Therefore, the partnership agreement should state which capital balances will determine the ratio for distributing income and losses.

If partners believe their capital balances will change very much during the year, they may select their average capital balances as a fairer means of distributing income and losses. To illustrate this method, we will assume that, during the first year, Jerry Adcock withdrew $10,000 on January 1, 19x2, and Rose Villa withdrew $10,000 on November 1, 19x1, and invested the additional $8,000 on February 1, 19x2. The income for the year's operation was $140,000. The calculations for the average capital balances and the distribution of income are as follows:

Average Capital Balances

Partner	Date	Capital Balance	×	Months Unchanged	=	Total				Average Capital
Adcock	7/x1–12/x1	$65,000	×	6	=	$390,000				
	1/x2–6/x2	55,000	×	6	=	330,000				
				12		$720,000	÷	12	=	$ 60,000
Villa	7/x1–10/x1	$60,000	×	4	=	$240,000				
	11/x1–1/x2	50,000	×	3	=	150,000				
	2/x2–6/x2	58,000	×	5	=	290,000				
				12		$680,000	÷	12	=	56,667
						Total average capital				$116,667

Average Capital Balance Ratios

$$\text{Adcock} = \frac{\text{Adcock's average capital balance}}{\text{total average capital}} = \frac{\$60{,}000}{\$116{,}667} = 51.4\%$$

$$\text{Villa} = \frac{\text{Villa's average capital balance}}{\text{total average capital}} = \frac{\$56{,}667}{\$116{,}667} = 48.6\%$$

Distribution of Income

Partner	Income × Ratio	=	Share of Income
Adcock	$140,000 × 51.4%	=	$ 71,960
Villa	$140,000 × 48.6%	=	68,040
	Total income		$140,000

Note that this calculation calls for determining (1) average capital balances, (2) average capital balance ratios, and (3) each partner's share of income or loss. To compute a partner's average capital balance, it is necessary to examine the changes that have taken place during the year in the partner's capital balance. These changes result from further investments and withdrawals. The partner's beginning capital is multiplied by the number of months the balance remains unchanged. After the balance changes, the new balance is multiplied by the number of months it remains unchanged. This process continues until the end of the year. The totals of these computations are added together, then divided by twelve, to determine the average capital balances. Once the average capital balances are determined, the method of figuring capital balance ratios for sharing income and losses is the same as that used for beginning capital balances.

The entry showing how the earnings for the year are distributed to the partners' capital accounts is as follows:

		Debit	Credit
June 30	Income Summary	140,000	
	Jerry Adcock, Capital		71,960
	Rose Villa, Capital		68,040
	To distribute the income for the year to the partners' capital accounts		

Salaries, Interest, and Stated Ratio

Partners generally do not contribute equally to a firm. To make up for these unequal contributions, some partnership agreements will allow for partners' salaries, interest on partners' capital balances, or a combination of both in the distribution of income. Salaries and interest of this kind are not deducted as expenses before the partnership income is determined. They represent a method of arriving at an equitable distribution of the income or loss.

To illustrate an allowance for partners' salaries, we shall assume that Adcock and Villa agree to the following salaries: $8,000 for Adcock and $7,000 for Villa. Any remaining income will be divided equally. Each salary is charged to the appropriate partner's withdrawal account when paid. If we assume the same $140,000 income for the first year, the calculations and journal entry for Adcock and Villa are as shown on the next page.

	Income of Partners		Income
	Adcock	Villa	Distributed
Total Income for Distribution			$140,000
Distribution of Salaries			
Adcock	$ 8,000		
Villa		$ 7,000	15,000
Remaining Income After Salaries			$125,000
Equal Distribution of Remaining Income			
Adcock	62,500		
Villa		62,500	125,000
Remaining Income			—
Income of Partners	$70,500	$69,500	$140,000

June 30	Income Summary	140,000	
	Jerry Adcock, Capital		70,500
	Rose Villa, Capital		69,500
	To distribute the income for the year to the partners' capital accounts		

Salaries allow for differences in the services that partners provide to the business. However, they do not consider differences in invested capital. To allow for capital differences, each partner may receive, in addition to salary, a stated interest on his or her invested capital. To illustrate, we will assume that Adcock and Villa agree to receive 10 percent interest on their beginning capital balances as well as annual salaries of $8,000 for Adcock and $7,000 for Villa. They will share any remaining income equally. The calculations for Adcock and Villa, if we assume income of $140,000, are at the top of the next page. The journal entry is

June 30	Income Summary	140,000	
	Jerry Adcock, Capital		70,750
	Rose Villa, Capital		69,250
	To distribute the income for the year to the partners' capital accounts		

If the partnership agreement allows for paying salaries or interest or both, these amounts must be allocated to the partners even if the profits are not enough to cover the salaries and interest. Such a situation would result in the partners' sharing a negative amount after salaries and interest are paid. If the company has a loss, these allocations must still occur. The negative amount after allocation of salaries and interest must be

	Income of Partners		Income Distributed
	Adcock	Villa	
Total Income for Distribution			$140,000
Distribution of Salaries			
Adcock	$ 8,000		
Villa		$ 7,000	15,000
Remaining Income After Salaries			$125,000
Distribution of Interest			
Adcock ($65,000 × 10%)	6,500		
Villa ($60,000 × 10%)		6,000	12,500
Remaining Income After Salaries and Interest			$112,500
Equal Distribution of Remaining Income			
Adcock	56,250		
Villa		56,250	112,500
Remaining Income			—
Income of Partners	$70,750	$69,250	$140,000

distributed according to the stated ratio in the partnership agreement. If the agreement does not mention a ratio, the negative amount is distributed equally. To illustrate this situation, we will assume that the partnership of Adcock and Villa agrees to the following conditions for the distribution of income and losses:

	Salaries	Interest	Beginning Capital Balance
Adcock	$70,000	10 percent of beginning	$65,000
Villa	60,000	capital balances	60,000

The income for the first year of operation was $140,000. The computation for the distribution of the income and loss is shown at the top of the next page. The journal entry is

June 30	Income Summary	140,000	
	Jerry Adcock, Capital		75,250
	Rose Villa, Capital		64,750
	To distribute the income for the year to the partners' capital accounts		

On the income statement for the partnership, the distribution of income or losses is shown below the net income figure. Exhibit 11-1 illustrates this point using the last example.

	Income of Partners		Income
	Adcock	Villa	Distributed
Total Income for Distribution			$140,000
Distribution of Salaries			
Adcock	$70,000		
Villa		$60,000	130,000
Remaining Income after Salaries			$ 10,000
Distribution of Interest			
Adcock ($65,000 × 10%)	6,500		
Villa ($60,000 × 10%)		6,000	12,500
Negative Amount After Distribution of Salaries and Interest			($2,500)
Adcock*	($1,250)		
Villa*		($1,250)	2,500
Remaining Income			—
Income of Partners	$75,250	$64,750	$140,000

* Notice that the negative amount was distributed equally because the agreement did not indicate how income and losses would be distributed after salaries and interest were paid.

Exhibit 11-1. Partial Income Statement for Adcock and Villa

Adcock and Villa
Partial Income Statement
For the Year Ended June 30, 19xx

Net Income		$140,000
Distribution to the partners		
Adcock		
Salary distribution	$70,000	
Interest on beginning capital balance	6,500	
Total	$76,500	
One-half of remaining negative amount	(1,250)	
Share of net income		$ 75,250
Villa		
Salary distribution	$60,000	
Interest on beginning capital balance	6,000	
Total	$66,000	
One-half of remaining negative amount	(1,250)	
Share of net income		64,750
Net Income Distributed		$140,000

Dissolution of a Partnership

OBJECTIVE 5
Record a person's admission to or withdrawal from a partnership

Dissolution of a partnership occurs when there is a change in the original association of the partners. When a partnership is dissolved, the partners lose their authority to continue the business as a going concern. This does not mean that the business operation is necessarily ended or interrupted. The remaining partners can act for the partnership in finishing the affairs of the business or in forming a new partnership. The dissolution of a partnership through admission of a new partner, withdrawal of a partner, or death of a partner will be discussed next.

Admission of a New Partner

Admission of a new partner will dissolve the old partnership because a new association has been formed. Dissolving the old partnership and creating a new one requires the consent of all the old partners. When a new partner is admitted, a new partnership agreement should describe the new arrangement in detail.

An individual may be admitted into a firm in one of two ways: (1) by purchasing an interest in the partnership from one or more of the original partners, or (2) by investing assets in the partnership.

Purchase Interest from Partner. When an individual is admitted to a firm by purchasing an interest from an old partner, each partner must agree to the change. The interest purchased must be transferred from the capital account of the selling partner to the capital account of the new partner.

For example, assume that Jerry Adcock of Adcock and Villa decides to sell his $70,000 interest in the business to Richard Davis for $100,000 on August 31, 19x3. Rose Villa agrees to the sale. The entry that records the sale on the partnership books would be:

Aug. 31	Jerry Adcock, Capital	70,000	
	Richard Davis, Capital		70,000
	To record the transfer of Jerry Adcock's equity to Richard Davis		

Note that the entry above records the book value of the equity and not the amount paid by Davis. The amount that Davis paid is a personal matter between him and Adcock. Because the amount paid did not affect the assets or liabilities of the firm, it should not be entered into the records.

For another example of a purchase, assume that Richard Davis purchases one-half of Jerry Adcock's $70,000 and one-half of Rose Villa's $80,000 interest in the partnership by paying a total of $100,000 to the two partners on August 31, 19x3. The entry that records this transaction on the partnership books would be:

Aug. 31	Jerry Adcock, Capital	35,000	
	Rose Villa, Capital	40,000	
	Richard Davis, Capital		75,000
	To record the transfer of one-half of Jerry Adcock's and Rose Villa's equity to Richard Davis		

Investment of Assets in Partnership. When a new partner is admitted by an investment in the partnership, both the assets and the owners' equity of the firm are increased. This is because, in contrast to the case of buying a partner out, the assets that the new partner invests become partnership assets, and this increase in assets creates a corresponding increase in owners' equity. For example, assume that Richard Davis wished to invest $75,000 for a one-third interest in the partnership of Adcock and Villa. The capital accounts of Adcock and Villa are $70,000 and $80,000, respectively. The assets of the firm are correctly valued. Thus the partners agree to admit Davis to a one-third interest in the firm for a $75,000 investment. Davis's $75,000 investment will equal a one-third interest in the firm after the investment is added to the previously existing capital, as shown below.

Adcock, Capital	$ 70,000
Villa, Capital	80,000
Davis's investment	75,000
Total capital after Davis's investment	$225,000

One-third interest $= \dfrac{\$225{,}000}{3} =$ $ 75,000

The entry to record this investment is:

Oct. 1	Cash	75,000	
	Richard Davis, Capital		75,000
	To record the admission of Richard Davis to a one-third interest in the company		

Bonus to Old Partners. Sometimes a partnership is so profitable or otherwise advantageous that a new investor will be willing to pay more than the actual dollar interest that he or she receives in the partnership. An individual may have to pay $100,000 for an $80,000 interest in a partnership. The $20,000 excess of the payment over the interest purchased is considered a **bonus** to the original partners. The bonus should be distributed to the original partners according to the partnership agreement. When the agreement does not cover the distribution of a bonus, it should be distributed to the original partners in accordance with the method of distributing income and losses.

As an illustration of the bonus method, assume that the Adcock and Villa Company has operated for several years and that the partners' capital balances and the new ratio for distribution of income and loss are as shown on the next page.

Partners	Capital Balances	Stated Ratio
Adcock	$160,000	55%
Villa	140,000	45%
	$300,000	100%

Richard Davis wishes to join the firm, and he offers to invest $100,000 for a one-fifth interest in the business and income. The original partners agree to the offer. The computation of the bonus to the original partners is as follows:

Partners' equity in the original partnership		$300,000
Cash investment by Richard Davis		100,000
Partners' equity in the new partnership		$400,000
Partners' equity assigned to Richard Davis ($400,000 × 1/5)		$ 80,000
Bonus to the original partners		
Investment by Richard Davis	$100,000	
Less equity assigned to Richard Davis	80,000	$ 20,000
Distribution of bonus to original partners		
Jerry Adcock ($20,000 × 55%)	$ 11,000	
Rose Villa ($20,000 × 45%)	9,000	$ 20,000

The journal entry that records the admission of Davis to the partnership is as follows:

Dec. 1	Cash	100,000	
	Jerry Adcock, Capital		11,000
	Rose Villa, Capital		9,000
	Richard Davis, Capital		80,000
	To record the sale of one-fifth interest in the firm to Richard Davis and the bonus he paid to the original partners		

Bonus to New Partner. There are several reasons why a partnership might seek a new partner. A firm in financial trouble might seek additional cash from a new partner. Or the original partners, wishing to expand the firm's markets, might require more capital than they themselves can provide. The partners might also know a person who would add a unique talent to the firm. Under these conditions, a new partner may be admitted to the partnership with the understanding that part of the original partners' capital will be transferred to the new partner's capital as a bonus.

For example, assume that Adcock and Villa have invited Richard Davis to join the firm. Davis is to invest $60,000 for a one-fourth interest in the company's capital and income. The capital balances of Adcock and Villa are $160,000 and $140,000, respectively. If Davis is to receive a one-fourth interest in the firm, the interest of the original partners represents a three-fourths interest in the business. The computation of the bonus to Davis follows.

Total equity in partnership		
Adcock, Capital		$160,000
Villa, Capital		140,000
Investment by Richard Davis		60,000
Partners' equity in the new partnership		$360,000
Partners' equity assigned to Richard Davis ($360,000 × 1/4)		$ 90,000
Bonus		
One-fourth interest, Richard Davis	$90,000	
Cash investment by Richard Davis	(60,000)	$ 30,000
Distribution from original partners		
Jerry Adcock ($30,000 × 55%)	$16,500	
Rose Villa ($30,000 × 45%)	13,500	$ 30,000

The journal entry that records the admission of Davis to the partnership is as follows:

Sept. 1	Cash	60,000	
	Jerry Adcock, Capital	16,500	
	Rose Villa, Capital	13,500	
	Richard Davis, Capital		90,000
	To record the investment of Richard Davis of cash and a bonus		

Withdrawal of a Partner

A partner has the right to withdraw from a partnership whenever he or she chooses. To avoid any disputes when a partner does decide to withdraw or retire from the firm, the partnership agreement should describe the appropriate actions to be taken. The agreement may specify (1) whether or not an audit will be performed by CPAs, (2) how the assets will be reappraised, (3) how a bonus is to be determined, and (4) by what method the withdrawing partner will be paid.

There are several ways in which a partner may withdraw from a partnership. A partner may (1) sell his or her interest to an outsider with the consent of the remaining partners, (2) sell his or her interest to another partner with the consent of the remaining partners, (3) withdraw assets that are equal to his or her capital balance, (4) withdraw assets that are greater than his or her capital balance (in this case the withdrawing partner will receive a bonus), or (5) withdraw assets that are less than his or her capital balance (in this case the remaining partners will receive a bonus). These alternatives are illustrated in Figure 11-1.

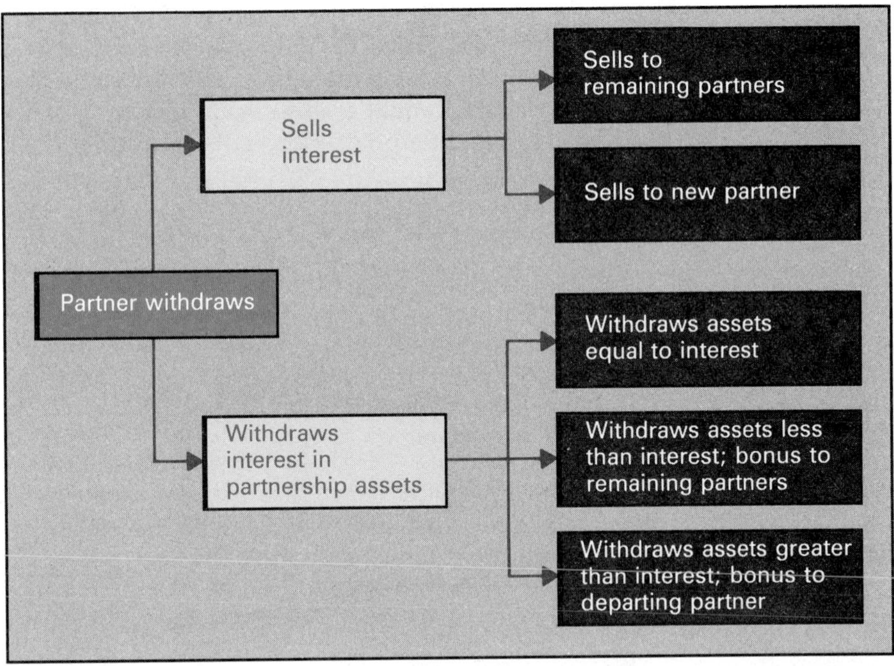

Figure 11-1. Alternative Ways for a Partner to Withdraw

Withdrawal by Selling Interest. When a partner sells his or her interest to an outsider or to another partner with the consent of the other partners, the transaction is personal and does not change the partnership assets or the owners' equity. For example, we will assume that the capital balances of Adcock, Villa, and Davis are $140,000, $100,000, and $60,000, respectively, for a total of $300,000.

Villa is withdrawing from the partnership and is reviewing two offers for her interest. The offers are to (1) sell her interest to Judy Jones for $120,000 or (2) sell her interest to Davis for $110,000. The remaining partners have agreed to either potential transaction. Because Jones and Davis will pay for Villa's interest from their personal assets, the partnership accounting records will show only the transfer of Villa's interest to Jones or Davis. The entries that record these possible transfers are as follows:

1. If Villa's interest is purchased by Jones:		
Rose Villa, Capital	100,000	
Judy Jones, Capital		100,000
To record sale of Villa's partnership interest to Jones		
2. If Villa's interest is purchased by Davis:		
Rose Villa, Capital	100,000	
Richard Davis, Capital		100,000
To record sale of Villa's partnership interest to Davis		

Withdrawal by Removing Assets. A partnership agreement may state that a withdrawing partner is allowed to remove assets from the firm equal to his or her capital balance. Assume that Richard Davis decides to withdraw from Adcock, Villa, Davis & Company. Davis's capital balance is $60,000. The partnership agreement states that he may withdraw cash from the firm equal to his capital balance. If there is not enough cash, he is to accept a promissory note from the new partnership for the balance. The remaining partners request that Davis take only $50,000 in cash because of a cash shortage at the time of his withdrawal. He agrees. The journal entry recording Davis's withdrawal follows:

Jan. 21	Richard Davis, Capital	60,000	
	Cash		50,000
	Notes Payable, Richard Davis		10,000
	To record the withdrawal of Richard Davis from the partnership		

When a withdrawing partner takes assets greater than his or her capital balance, the excess may be treated as a bonus to the withdrawing partner. The remaining partners absorb the bonus according to their stated ratios. On the other hand, the withdrawing partner may take out assets that represent less than his or her capital balance. A partner who withdraws under these conditions leaves a part of his or her capital in the business. The remaining partners will divide the remaining equity according to their stated ratios. This distribution is considered a bonus to the remaining partners. Alternative arrangements may exist through prior agreement in the partnership contract.

Death of a Partner

When a partner dies, the partnership is dissolved because the original association has changed. The partnership agreement should state the action to be taken on a partner's death. Normally the books are closed and financial statements prepared. These actions are necessary to determine the capital balance of each partner at the date of the death. The agreement may also indicate whether an audit should be conducted, assets appraised, and a bonus recorded as well as the procedures for settling with the heirs of the deceased partner. The conditions for such a settlement may be that the remaining partners purchase the deceased's equity, sell it to outsiders, or deliver certain business assets to the estate. If the firm intends to continue, a new partnership must be formed.

Liquidation of a Partnership

Liquidation of a partnership is the process of ending a business, which entails selling enough assets to pay the liabilities and distributing any remaining assets among the partners. Unlike the case of dissolution, if a partnership is liquidated, the business will not continue.

OBJECTIVE 6
Compute the distribution of assets to partners when they liquidate their partnership

The partnership agreement should indicate the procedures to be followed in the case of liquidation. Normally, the books should be adjusted and closed, with the income or loss being distributed to the partners. As the assets of the business are sold, any gain or loss should be distributed among the partners according to the established stated ratio. As cash becomes available, it must be applied first to outside creditors, then to partners' loans, and finally to the partners' capital balances.

The process of liquidation may have a variety of financial results. However, we will describe only the following three: (1) assets sold for a gain, (2) assets sold for a loss but absorbed by capital balances, and (3) assets sold for a loss when a partner's capital balance is insufficient to absorb the loss. For each alternative we will assume that the books have been closed for Adcock, Villa, Davis & Company and that the following balance sheet exists prior to liquidation:

Adcock, Villa, Davis & Company
Balance Sheet
February 2, 19xx

Assets		**Liabilities**	
Cash	$ 60,000	Accounts Payable	$120,000
Accounts Receivable	40,000	**Partners' Equity**	
Merchandise Inventory	100,000		
Plant Assets (net)	200,000	Adcock, Capital	85,000
Total Assets	$400,000	Villa, Capital	95,000
		Davis, Capital	100,000
		Total Liabilities and Partners' Equity	$400,000

The stated ratios of Adcock, Villa, and Davis will be 30, 30, and 40, respectively.

Gain on Sale of Assets

Let us assume that the following transactions occurred in the liquidation of Adcock, Villa, Davis & Company. The accounts receivable were collected for $35,000, and the inventory and plant assets were sold for $110,000 and $200,000, respectively. After the accounts payable were paid off, the partners shared the remaining cash. These transactions are summarized in the statement of liquidation in Exhibit 11-2. The journal entries that record the transactions are shown on the next two pages.

Exhibit 11-2. Statement of Liquidation Showing Gain on Sale of Assets

Adcock, Villa, Davis & Company
Statement of Liquidation
For the Period from February 2, 19xx through February 20, 19xx

Explanation	Cash	Other Assets	Accounts Payable	Adcock, Capital (30%)	Villa, Capital (30%)	Davis, Capital (40%)	Gain (or Loss) from Realization
Balance 2/2	$ 60,000	$340,000	$120,000	$ 85,000	$ 95,000	$100,000	
1. Collection of Accounts Receivable	35,000	(40,000)					($5,000)
	$ 95,000	$300,000	$120,000	$ 85,000	$ 95,000	$100,000	($ 5,000)
2. Sale of Inventory	110,000	(100,000)					10,000
	$205,000	$200,000	$120,000	$ 85,000	$ 95,000	$100,000	$ 5,000
3. Sale of Plant Assets	200,000	(200,000)					
	$405,000	—	$120,000	$ 85,000	$ 95,000	$100,000	$ 5,000
4. Payment of Liabilities	(120,000)		(120,000)				
	$285,000		—	$ 85,000	$ 95,000	$100,000	$ 5,000
5. Distribution of Gain or Loss from Realization				1,500	1,500	2,000	(5,000)
	$285,000			$ 86,500	$ 96,500	$102,000	—
6. Distribution to Partners	(285,000)			(86,500)	(96,500)	(102,000)	
	—			—	—	—	

	Journal Entries			Explanation on Statement of Liquidation
Feb. 13	Cash	35,000		1
	Gain or Loss from Realization	5,000		
	Accounts Receivable		40,000	
	To record collection of accounts receivable			
14	Cash	110,000		2
	Merchandise Inventory		100,000	
	Gain or Loss from Realization		10,000	
	To record the sale of inventory			

Date	Account	Debit	Credit	
Feb. 16	Cash	200,000		3
	Plant Assets		200,000	
	To record the sale of plant assets			
16	Accounts Payable	120,000		4
	Cash		120,000	
	To record the payment of accounts payable			
20	Gain or Loss from Realization	5,000		5
	Jerry Adcock, Capital		1,500	
	Rose Villa, Capital		1,500	
	Richard Davis, Capital		2,000	
	To record the distribution of the gain on assets ($10,000 gain minus $5,000 loss) to the partners			
20	Jerry Adcock, Capital	86,500		6
	Rose Villa, Capital	96,500		
	Richard Davis, Capital	102,000		
	Cash		285,000	
	To record the distribution of cash to the partners			

Note that cash distributed to the partners is the balance in their respective capital accounts. Cash is *not* distributed according to the partners' stated ratio.

Loss on Sale of Assets

We will discuss two cases involving losses on the sale of the company's assets. In the first case, the losses are small enough to be absorbed by the partners' capital balances. In the second case, one partner's share of the losses is too large for his or her capital balance to absorb.

When a firm's assets are sold at a loss, the partners share the loss on liquidation according to their stated ratio. For example, assume that during the liquidation of Adcock, Villa, Davis & Company, the total cash received from the collection of accounts receivable and the sale of inventory and plant assets was $140,000. The statement of liquidation appears in Exhibit 11-3, and the journal entries for the transaction are shown below and on the next page.

	Journal Entries			**Explanation on Statement of Liquidation** ↓
Feb. 15	Cash	140,000		1
	Gain or Loss from Realization	200,000		
	Accounts Receivable		40,000	
	Merchandise Inventory		100,000	
	Plant Assets		200,000	
	To record the collection of accounts receivable and the sale of the other assets			

Exhibit 11-3. Statement of Liquidation Showing Loss on Sale of Assets

Adcock, Villa, Davis & Company
Statement of Liquidation
For the Period from February 2, 19xx through February 20, 19xx

Explanation	Cash	Other Assets	Accounts Payable	Adcock, Capital (30%)	Villa, Capital (30%)	Davis, Capital (40%)	Gain (or Loss) from Realization
Balance 2/2	$ 60,000	$340,000	$120,000	$ 85,000	$ 95,000	$100,000	
1. Collection of Accounts Receivable and Sale of Inventory and Plant Assets	140,000	(340,000)					($200,000)
	$200,000	—	$120,000	$ 85,000	$ 95,000	$100,000	($200,000)
2. Payment of Liabilities	(120,000)		(120,000)				
	$ 80,000		—	$ 85,000	$ 95,000	$100,000	($200,000)
3. Distribution of Gain or Loss from Realization				(60,000)	(60,000)	(80,000)	200,000
	$ 80,000			$ 25,000	$ 35,000	$ 20,000	—
4. Distribution to Partners	(80,000)			(25,000)	(35,000)	(20,000)	
	—			—	—	—	

Feb. 16	Accounts Payable	120,000		2
	Cash		120,000	
	To record the payment of accounts payable			
20	Jerry Adcock, Capital	60,000		3
	Rose Villa, Capital	60,000		
	Richard Davis, Capital	80,000		
	Gain or Loss from Realization		200,000	
	To record the distribution of the loss on assets to the partners			
20	Jerry Adcock, Capital	25,000		4
	Rose Villa, Capital	35,000		
	Richard Davis, Capital	20,000		
	Cash		80,000	
	To record the distribution of cash to the partners			

In some liquidation cases, a partner's share of the losses is greater than his or her capital balance. In this situation, the partner must make up the deficit in his or her capital account from personal assets. For example, assume that after the sale of assets and the payment of liabilities the following conditions exist during the liquidation of Adcock, Villa, Davis & Company:

Assets		
Cash		$30,000
Partners' Equity		
Adcock, Capital	$25,000	
Villa, Capital	20,000	
Davis, Capital	(15,000)	$30,000

Richard Davis must pay $15,000 into the partnership from personal funds to cover his deficit. If we assume that he paid cash to the partnership, the following entry would record his cash contribution:

Feb. 20	Cash	15,000	
	Richard Davis, Capital		15,000
	To record the additional investment of Richard Davis to cover his liquidation losses		

After Davis's payment of $15,000, there is sufficient cash to pay Adcock and Villa their capital balances and thus to complete the liquidation. This transaction is recorded as follows:

Feb. 20	Jerry Adcock, Capital	25,000	
	Rose Villa, Capital	20,000	
	Cash		45,000
	To record the distribution of cash to the partners		

During liquidation, a partner might not have any additional cash to cover his or her obligations to the partnership. When this situation occurs, the remaining partners must share the loss according to their established stated ratio. This procedure is necessary because all partners have unlimited liability, which is characteristic of a partnership. Assume that Richard Davis cannot pay the $15,000 deficit in his capital account. Adcock and Villa must share the deficit according to the stated ratio. Their percentages are 30 and 30, respectively. Therefore, they will each pay 50 percent of the losses that Davis cannot pay. The new stated ratio for Adcock and Villa is computed as follows:

	Old Ratios	New Ratios
Adcock	30%	30/60 = 50%
Villa	30%	30/60 = 50%
	60%	100%

The journal entries that record these transactions are as follows:

Feb. 20	Jerry Adcock, Capital	7,500	
	Rose Villa, Capital	7,500	
	Richard Davis, Capital		15,000
	To record the transfer of Davis's deficit to Adcock and Villa		
20	Jerry Adcock, Capital	17,500	
	Rose Villa, Capital	12,500	
	Cash		30,000
	To record the cash distribution to the partners		

Richard Davis's inability to meet his obligations at the time of liquidation does not relieve him of his liabilities to Adcock and Villa. If he is able to pay his liabilities sometime in the future, Adcock and Villa may collect the amounts of Davis's deficit that they absorbed.

Chapter Review

Review of Learning Objectives

1. **Identify the major characteristics of a partnership.**
   A partnership has several major characteristics that distinguish it from other forms of business. A partnership is a voluntary association of two or more persons who combine their talents and resources to make a profit. This joint effort should be supported by a partnership agreement, specifying details of operation for the partnership. A partnership is easily dissolved by a partner's admission, withdrawal, or death, and therefore has a limited life. Each partner acts as an agent of the partnership within the scope of normal operations and is personally liable for the partnership's debts.

2. **Identify the advantages and disadvantages of the partnership form of business.**
   The advantages are ease of formation and dissolution, the opportunity to pool several individuals' talents and resources, the freedom of action each partner enjoys, and no tax burden. The disadvantages are the limited life of the partnership, the unlimited personal liability of the partners, the difficulty of transferring partners' interest and of raising large amounts of capital, and the risk inherent in each partner's being able to bind the partnership to a contract.

3. **Record partners' investments of cash and of other assets in forming a partnership.**
   Normally a partnership is formed when the partners contribute cash, other assets, or a combination of both to the business in accordance with the partnership agreement. The recording of initial investments entails a debit to the Cash or other asset account and a credit to the investing partner's capital account. The recorded amount of the other assets should be their fair value on the date of transfer to the partnership. In addition, a partnership may assume the investing partner's liabilities. When this occurs, the partner's capital account is credited with the difference between the assets invested and the liabilities assumed.

4. **Compute the income or losses that partners share, based on a stated ratio, the capital investment ratio, and salaries and interest to partners.**
   The partners should share income and losses in accordance with the partnership agreement. If the agreement says nothing about income and loss distributions, the partners will share them equally. Common methods used for distributing income and losses to partners include the use of stated ratios or capital investment ratios and the payment of salaries and interest on capital investments. Each method tries to measure each partners' contribution to the operations of the business. A stated ratio is usually based on the partners' relative contribution of effort to the partnership. If the capital investment ratio is used, the income (or losses) is divided strictly on the amount of capital provided to the partnership by each partner. The use of salaries and interest on capital investment takes into account both efforts (salary) and capital investment (interest) in dividing income (or losses) among the partners.

5. **Record a person's admission to or withdrawal from a partnership.**
   An individual is admitted to a partnership by purchasing a partner's interest or by contributing additional assets. When an interest is purchased, the old partner's capital is transferred to the new partner. When the new partner contributes assets to the partnership, it may be necessary to recognize a bonus to be shared or borne by the old partners.

   When a partner withdraws from a partnership, the partner either sells his or her interest in the business or withdraws company assets. When assets are withdrawn, the amount can be equal to, greater than, or less than the partner's capital interest. When assets that have a value greater than or less than the partner's interest are withdrawn, a bonus is recognized and distributed among the appropriate partners.

6. **Compute the distribution of assets to partners when they liquidate their partnership.**
   Liquidation of a partnership entails selling the assets necessary to pay the company's liabilities, then distributing any remaining assets to the partners. Any gain or loss on the sale of the assets is shared by the partners according to their stated ratio. When a partner has a deficit balance in a capital account, that partner must contribute personal assets equal to the deficit. When a partner does not have personal assets to cover a capital deficit, the deficit must be absorbed by the solvent partners according to their stated ratio.

Review Problem
Distribution of Income and Admission of Partner

Jack Holder and Dan Williams reached an agreement in 19x7 to pool their resources for the purpose of forming a partnership to manufacture and sell university T-shirts. In forming the partnership, Holder and Williams contributed $100,000 and $150,000, respectively. They drafted a partnership agreement stating that Holder was to receive an annual salary of $6,000 and Williams was to receive 3 percent interest annually on his original investment in the business. Income and losses after salary and interest were to be shared by Holder and Williams in a 2:3 ratio.

Required

1. Compute the income or loss that Holder and Williams share, and prepare the required journal entries, assuming the following income and loss before salary and interest: 19x7—$27,000 income; 19x8—$2,000 loss.

2. Assume that Jean Ratcliffe offers Holder and Williams $60,000 for a 15 percent interest in the partnership on January 1, 19x9. Holder and Williams agree to Ratcliffe's offer because they need her resources to expand the business. The capital balances of Holder and Williams are $113,600 and $161,400, respectively, on January 1, 19x9. Record the admission of Ratcliffe to the partnership, assuming that her investment is to represent a 15 percent interest in the total partners' capital and that a bonus is to be given to Holder and Williams in the ratio of 2:3.

Answer to Review Problem

1. Income distribution to partners computed:

	Income of Partner		Income
	Holder	Williams	Distributed
19x7			
Total Income for Distribution			$27,000
Distribution of Salary			
Holder	$ 6,000		(6,000)
Remaining Income After Salary			$21,000
Distribution of Interest			
Williams ($150,000 × 3%)		4,500	(4,500)
Remaining Income After Salary and Interest			$16,500
Distribution of Remaining Income			
Holder ($16,500 × 2/5)	6,600		
Williams ($16,500 × 3/5)		9,900	(16,500)
Remaining Income			—
Income of Partners	$12,600	$14,400	
19x8			
Total Income for Distribution			($2,000)
Distribution of Salary			
Holder	$ 6,000		6,000
Remaining Loss After Salary			($8,000)
Distribution of Interest			
Williams ($150,000 × 3%)		$ 4,500	4,500
Negative Amount After Distribution of Salary and Interest			($12,500)
Distribution of Remaining Loss in Profit/Loss Ratio			
Holder ($12,500 × 2/5)	(5,000)		
Williams ($12,500 × 3/5)		(7,500)	(12,500)
Remaining Income			—
Income of Partners	$ 1,000	($3,000)	

Journal entry—19x7

Income Summary	27,000	
Jack Holder, Capital		12,600
Dan Williams, Capital		14,400
To record the distribution (based on salary, interest, and stated ratio) of $27,000 profit for 19x7		

Journal entry—19x8

Dan Williams, Capital	3,000	
Income Summary		2,000
Jack Holder, Capital		1,000
To record the distribution (based on salary, interest, and stated ratio) of $2,000 loss for 19x8		

2. Admission of new partner recorded:

19x9			
Jan. 1	Cash	60,000	
	Jack Holder, Capital		3,900
	Dan Williams, Capital		5,850
	Jean Ratcliffe, Capital		50,250
	To record the $60,000 cash investment by Jean Ratcliffe for a 15 percent interest in the partnership, a bonus being allocated to original partners		

Computation

Ratcliffe, Capital = (original partners' capital + investment) × 15 percent
= ($113,600 + $161,400 + $60,000) × 15% = $50,250

Bonus = investment − Ratcliffe, Capital
= $60,000 − $50,250 = $9,750

Distribution of bonus:

Holder	= $9,750 × 2/5 =	$3,900
Williams	= $9,750 × 3/5 =	$5,850
Total bonus		$9,750

Chapter Assignments

Questions

1. Briefly define a partnership, and list several major characteristics of the partnership form of business.
2. What is the meaning of unlimited liability when applied to a partnership?
3. Abe and Bill are partners in a drilling operation. Abe purchased a drilling rig to be used in the partnership's operations. Is this purchase binding on Bill even though he was not involved in it?
4. The partnership agreement for Karla and Jean's partnership does not disclose how they will share income and losses. How would the income and losses be shared in this partnership?
5. What are several major advantages of a partnership? What are some possible disadvantages?
6. Edward contributes $10,000 in cash and a building with a book value of $40,000 and fair market value of $50,000 to the Edward and Francis partnership. What is the balance of Edward's capital account in the partnership if the building is recorded at its fair market value?
7. Gayle and Henry share income and losses in their partnership in a 3:2 ratio. The firm's net income for the current year is $80,000. How would the distribution of income be recorded in the journal?
8. Irene purchases Jane's interest in the Jane and Kane partnership for $62,000. Jane has a $57,000 capital interest in the partnership. How would this transaction be recorded in the partnership books?
9. Larry and Madison each own a $50,000 interest in a partnership. They agree to admit Nancy as a partner by selling her a one-third interest for $80,000. How large a bonus will be distributed to Larry and Madison?
10. Opel and Paul share income in their partnership in a 2:4 ratio. Opel and Paul receive salaries of $6,000 and $10,000, respectively. How would they share a net income before salaries of $22,000?
11. In the liquidation of a partnership, Robert's capital account showed a $5,000 deficit balance after all the creditors were paid. What obligation does Robert have to the partnership?
12. Describe how a dissolution of a partnership may differ from a liquidation of a partnership.
13. Tom Howard and Sharon Thomas are forming a partnership. What are some of the factors they should consider in deciding how income might be divided?

Classroom Exercises

Exercise 11-1. Partnership Formation (L.O. 3)

Charles Rossi and Phil Stem are electricians who wish to form a partnership and open a business. They have their attorney prepare their partnership agreement, which indicates that assets invested in the partnership will be recorded at their fair market value and liabilities will be assumed at book value. The assets contributed by each partner, the liabilities assumed, and their fair market and book values are shown at the top of the next page.

Prepare the journal entry necessary to record the original investments of Rossi and Stem in the partnership.

Assets	Charles Rossi	Phil Stem	Total
Cash	$40,000	$30,000	$70,000
Accounts Receivable	52,000	20,000	72,000
Allowance for Uncollectible Accounts	(4,000)	(3,000)	(7,000)
Supplies	1,000	500	1,500
Equipment	20,000	10,000	30,000
Liabilities			
Accounts Payable	(32,000)	(9,000)	(41,000)

Exercise 11-2. Distribution of Income and Losses (L.O. 4)

Jack O'Grady and Mary Foster agreed to form a partnership. O'Grady contributed $50,000 in cash, and Foster contributed assets with a fair market value of $100,000. The partnership in its initial year reported income of $30,000.

Determine how the partners would share the first year's income, and prepare the journal entry to distribute the income to the partners under each of the following conditions: (1) O'Grady and Foster failed to include stated ratios in the partnership agreement. (2) O'Grady and Foster agreed to share the income and losses in a 3:2 ratio. (3) O'Grady and Foster agreed to share the income and losses in the ratio of original investments. (4) O'Grady and Foster agreed to share the income and losses by allowing 10 percent interest on original investments and sharing any remainder equally.

Exercise 11-3. Distribution of Income: Salary and Interest (L.O. 4)

Assume that the partnership agreement of O'Grady and Foster in Exercise 11-2 states that O'Grady and Foster are to receive salaries of $5,000 and $6,000, respectively; that O'Grady is to receive 6 percent interest on his capital balance at the beginning of the year; and that the remainder of income and losses are to be shared equally.

Prepare the journal entries for distributing the income under the following conditions: (1) Income totaled $30,000 before deductions for salaries and interest. (2) Income totaled $12,000 before deductions for salaries and interest.

Exercise 11-4. Distribution of Income: Average Capital Balance (L.O. 4)

Barry and Joey operate a furniture rental business. Their capital balances on January 1, 19x7 are $40,000 and $60,000, respectively. Barry withdrew $8,000 cash from the business on April 1, 19x7. Joey withdrew $15,000 cash on October 1, 19x7. Barry and Joey distribute partnership income based on their average capital balances each year. Income for 19x7 was $50,000. Compute the income to be distributed to Barry and Joey using their average capital balances in 19x7.

Exercise 11-5. Admission of New Partner: Bonus to Old Partners (L.O. 5)

Larry, Steve, and Todd have equities in a partnership of $40,000, $40,000, and $60,000, respectively, and share income and losses in a ratio of 1:1:3. The partners have agreed to admit Devin to the partnership.

Prepare journal entries to record the admission of Devin to the partnership under the following assumptions: (1) Devin invests $60,000 for a one-fifth interest in the partnership, and a bonus is recorded for the original partners. (2) Devin invests $60,000 for a 40 percent interest in the partnership, and a bonus is recorded for Devin.

Exercise 11-6. Withdrawal of Partner
(L.O. 5)

Kenneth, Tobey, and Miles are partners who share income and losses in the ratio of 3:2:1. Miles's capital account has a $40,000 balance. Kenneth and Tobey have agreed to let Miles take $50,000 of the company's cash when he retires.

What journal entry must be made on the partnership's books when Miles retires, assuming that a bonus to Miles is recognized and absorbed by the remaining partners?

Exercise 11-7. Partnership Liquidation
(L.O. 6)

Assume the following assets, liabilities, and owners' equity of the Redd and McPhee partnership on December 31, 19xx:

Assets	=	Liabilities	+	Redd, Capital	+	McPhee, Capital
$40,000	=	$2,500	+	$22,500	+	$15,000

When the partners agree to liquidate the business, the assets are sold for $30,000 and the liabilities are paid. Redd and McPhee share income and losses in a ratio of 3:1.

1. What is the final cash distribution to the partners after liquidation?
2. Prepare journal entries for the sale of assets, payment of liabilities, distribution of loss from realization, and final distribution of cash to Redd and McPhee.

Exercise 11-8. Partnership Liquidation
(L.O. 6)

Lisa, Nicki, and Steve are partners in a tanning salon. The assets, liabilities, and capital balances as of July 19x7 are:

Assets	$120,000
Liabilities	40,000
Lisa, Capital	35,000
Nicki, Capital	10,000
Steve, Capital	35,000

Because competition is strong and business is declining, they have decided to sell the business. Lisa, Nicki, and Steve share profits and losses in a ratio of 3:1:1, respectively. The assets were sold for $60,000, and the liabilities were paid. Nicki has no other assets and will not be able to cover any deficits in her capital account. How will the ending cash balance be distributed to the partners?

Interpreting Accounting Information

Meriweather Clinic
(L.O. 2, 4)

The Meriweather Clinic is owned and operated by ten local doctors. The balance sheet for 19xx is shown on the next page.

Required

1. How should information on these lawsuits be disclosed in the December 31, 19xx, financial statements of the partnership?
2. Assume that the clinic settles out of court for a payment by the clinic of $70,000 from Cash and Short-Term Investments. What will be the effect of this payment on the clinic's December 31, 19xx, financial statements? Discuss the effect of the settlement on the doctors' personal financial returns.

Meriweather Clinic
Balance Sheet
December 31, 19xx

Assets			
Current Assets			
Cash		$ 58,000	
Short-Term Investments		12,000	
Accounts Receivable		20,000	
Unbilled Services		8,000	
Other		5,000	
Total Current Assets			$103,000
Property, Plant, and Equipment			
Buildings		$ 85,000	
Furniture and Equipment		35,000	
		$120,000	
Less Accumulated Depreciation		45,000	
Total Property, Plant, and Equipment			75,000
Total Assets			$178,000
Liabilities and Partners' Equity			
Current Liabilities			
Notes Payable	$15,700		
Current Portion of Long-Term Debt	20,000		
Accounts Payable	5,600		
Salaries Payable	4,500		
Other	2,000		
Total Current Liabilities		$ 47,800	
Long-Term Debt		75,000	
Total Liabilities			$122,800
Partners' Equity			55,200
Total Liabilities and Partners' Equity			$178,000

Recently, several patients have sued the clinic for malpractice for a total of $1,000,000. There is no mention of these suits in the partnership's financial statements.

Problem Set A

Problem 11A-1. Partnership Formation and Distribution of Income
(L.O. 3, 4)

James Butler and Julian Quinn agreed in January 19x6 to form a partnership to open a fitness center. James contributed $100,000 in cash to the business. Julian contributed the building and equipment with values of $100,000 and $50,000, respectively. The partnership had income of $28,000 in 19x6 and $35,000 in 19x7.

Required

1. Prepare the journal entry to record the investments of both partners.

2. Determine the share of income for each partner in 19x6 and 19x7 under each of the following conditions: (a) The partners agreed to share income equally. (b) The partners agreed to share income according to their original capital investment ratio. (c) The partners failed to include an income-sharing agreement in the partnership agreement. (d) The partners agreed to share income and losses by allowing interest of 10 percent on original investments and dividing the remainder equally. (e) The partners agreed to share income and losses by allowing salaries of $18,000 to Butler and $12,000 to Quinn, with the remainder to be shared equally. (f) The partners agreed to share income and losses by allowing interest of 10 percent on original investments, paying salaries of $18,000 to Butler and $12,000 to Quinn, and dividing the remainder equally.

Problem 11A-2. Distribution of Income: Salaries and Interest
(L.O. 4)

Pam and Tony are partners in a videotape rental business. They have agreed that Pam will operate the store and receive a salary of $36,000 per year. Tony will receive 8% interest on his original capital investment of $200,000. The remaining income or losses are to be shared by Pam and Tony in a 2:3 ratio.

Required

Determine each partner's share of income and losses under each of the following conditions, given the fact that income or loss is stated before distribution of salary and interest in each case:

1. The income was $72,000.
2. The income was $37,000.
3. The loss was $8,000.

Problem 11A-3. Admission of a Partner
(L.O. 5)

Sharon, Suzanne, and Genevieve are partners in a swimsuit store. Their capital balances as of March 31, 19x7, are as follows:

Sharon, Capital		Suzanne, Capital		Genevieve, Capital	
	45,000		15,000		30,000

Each partner has agreed to admit Kim to the partnership.

Required

Prepare the journal entries to record Kim's admission to the partnership under each of the following conditions: (a) Kim pays Sharon $12,500 for one-fifth of her interest. (b) Kim invests $20,000 cash in the partnership. (c) Kim invests $30,000 cash in the partnership for a 20 percent interest in the business. A bonus is to be recorded for the original partners on the basis of their capital balances on March 31, 19x7. (d) Kim invests $30,000 cash in the partnership for a 40 percent interest in the business. The original partners give Kim a bonus according to the ratio of their capital investment balances on March 31, 19x7.

Problem 11A-4. Partnership Liquidation
(L.O. 6)

Blazo, Levy, and Ray are partners in a retail lighting store and share income and losses in the ratio of 2:2:1, respectively. The partners have agreed to liquidate the partnership. The partnership balance sheet prior to liquidation is shown on the next page.

Blazo, Levy, and Ray Partnership
Balance Sheet
August 31, 19x7

Cash	$ 70,000	Accounts Payable	$ 90,000
Other Assets	220,000	Blazo, Capital	100,000
		Levy, Capital	60,000
		Ray, Capital	40,000
	$290,000		$290,000

The other assets were sold on September 1, 19x7, for $180,000. Accounts Payable were paid on September 4, 19x7. The remaining cash was distributed to the partners on September 11, 19x7.

Required

1. Prepare the following journal entries: (a) Sale of the other assets. (b) Payment of the accounts payable. (c) Distribution of the partners' gain or loss on liquidation. (d) Distribution to the partners of the remaining cash.
2. Prepare a statement of liquidation.

Problem 11A-5. Comprehensive Partnership Transactions
(L.O. 3, 4, 5, 6)

The following events pertain to a partnership formed by Tom Steele and Mark Drake to operate a floor cleaning company.

19x1

Feb. 14 The partnership was formed. Steele transferred to the partnership $40,000 cash, land worth $40,000, a building worth $240,000, and a mortgage on the building of $120,000. Drake transferred to the partnership $20,000 cash and equipment worth $80,000.

Dec. 31 During 19x1, the partnership made an income of only $42,000. The partnership agreement specified that income and losses were to be divided by allowing 8 percent interest on beginning capital investment, paying salaries of $20,000 to Steele and $30,000 to Drake, and dividing any remainder equally.

19x2

Jan. 1 To improve the prospects for the company, the partners decided to take in a new partner, Ellen Waters, who had experience in the floor cleaning business. Waters invested $78,000 for a 25 percent interest in the business. A bonus was transferred in equal amounts from the previous partners' capital accounts to Waters's capital account.

Dec. 31 During 19x2, the company earned an income of $43,600. The new partnership agreement specified that income and losses would be divided by allowing 8 percent interest on beginning capital balances after Waters's admission, paying salaries of $30,000 to Drake and $40,000 to Waters (no salary to Steele), and dividing the remainder equally.

19x3

Jan. 1 Because it appeared that the business could not support the three partners, the partners decided to liquidate the partnership. The asset and liability accounts of the partnership were as follows: Cash, $203,600; Accounts Receivable, $34,000; Land, $40,000; Building (net), $224,000; Equipment (net), $118,000; Accounts Payable, $44,000; Mortgage Payable, $112,000. The equipment was sold for $100,000, and the resulting loss was distributed equally to the partners' accounts. The accounts payable were paid. A statement of liquidation was prepared, and the remaining assets and liabilities were distributed. Steele agreed to accept cash plus the land and buildings at book value and the mortgage payable as payment for his share. Drake accepted cash and the accounts receivable for his share. Waters was paid in cash.

Required

Prepare general journal entries to record all the above facts. Support your computations with schedules, and prepare a statement of liquidation in connection with the January 1, 19x3, entries.

Problem Set B

Problem 11B-1. Partnership Formation and Distribution of Income
(L.O. 3, 4)

On January 1, 19x1, Mary Kellow and Roycee Wilson agreed to form a partnership to establish an educational consulting business. Kellow and Wilson invested cash of $60,000 and $40,000, respectively, in the partnership. The business had normal first-year problems, but during the second year the operation was very successful. For 19x1 they reported a $20,000 loss, and for 19x2 a $60,000 income.

Required

1. Prepare the journal entry to record both partners' investments.
2. Determine Kellow's and Wilson's share of the income or loss for each year, assuming each of the following methods of sharing income and losses: (a) The partners agreed to share income and losses equally. (b) The partners agreed to share income and losses in the ratio of 7:3 for Kellow and Wilson, respectively. (c) The partners agreed to share income according to their original capital investment ratio, but the agreement did not mention losses. (d) The partners agreed to share income and losses in the ratio of their capital investments at the beginning of the year. (e) The partners agreed to share income and losses by allowing interest of 10 percent on original investments and dividing the remainder equally. (f) The partners agreed to share income and losses by allowing interest of 10 percent on original investments, paying salaries of $15,000 to Kellow and $10,000 to Wilson, and dividing the remainder equally.

Problem 11B-2. Distribution of Income: Salaries and Interest
(L.O. 4)

Anthony, Patrick, and Neil are partners in the U-Rent Microcomputers Company. The partnership agreement states that Anthony is to receive 6 percent interest on his capital investment at the beginning of the year, Patrick is to receive a salary of $40,000 a year, and Neil will be paid interest of 5 percent on his average capital balance during the year. Anthony, Patrick, and Neil will share any income or loss after salaries and interest in a 5:3:2 ratio. Anthony's capital investment at the beginning of the year was $240,000, and Neil's average capital balance for the year was $280,000.

Required

Determine each partner's share of income and losses under each of the following assumptions:

1. The income was $468,400.
2. The income was $56,400.
3. The loss was $37,200.

Problem 11B-3. Admission of a Partner (L.O. 5)

Paonessa, Mallinder, and Clarke are partners in the Cookie Machine. The balances in the capital accounts of Paonessa, Mallinder, and Clarke as of November 30, 19xx, are $20,000, $30,000, and $50,000, respectively. The partners share income and losses in a ratio of 2:3:5.

Required

Prepare journal entries for each of the following conditions: (a) Roberts pays Clarke $50,000 for four-fifths of Clarke's interest. (b) Roberts is to be admitted to the partnership with a one-third interest for a $50,000 cash investment. (c) Roberts is to be admitted to the partnership with a one-third interest for an $80,000 investment. A bonus is to be distributed to the original partners when Roberts is admitted. (d) Roberts is to be admitted to the partnership with a one-third interest for a $41,000 cash investment. A bonus is to be given to Roberts upon admission.

Problem 11B-4. Partnership Liquidation (L.O. 6)

The balance sheet of the TOP Partnership as of July 31, 19xx, is shown below.

TOP Partnership
Balance Sheet
July 31, 19xx

Assets		**Liabilities**	
Cash	$ 3,000	Accounts Payable	$240,000
Accounts Receivable	60,000	**Partners' Equity**	
Inventory	132,000		
Equipment (net)	231,000	Tom, Capital	36,000
		Orville, Capital	90,000
		Pam, Capital	60,000
Total Assets	$426,000	Total Liabilities and Partners' Equity	$426,000

Tom, Orville, and Pam share income and losses in the ratio of 5:3:2. Because of a disagreement, the partners have agreed to liquidate the business.

Required

1. Prepare journal entries to liquidate the partnership and distribute any remaining cash. Assume that Tom cannot contribute any additional personal assets to the company during liquidation and the following transactions occurred during liquidation: (a) Accounts receivable were sold for 60 percent of their book value. (b) Inventory was sold for $138,000. (c) Equipment was sold for $150,000. (d) Accounts payable were paid in full. (e) Gain or loss from realization was distributed to the partners' capital accounts. (f) Tom's deficit was transferred to the remaining partners in their new profit and loss ratio. (g) The remaining cash was distributed to the partners.
2. Prepare a statement of liquidation.

Problem 11B-5. Comprehensive Partnership Transactions
(L.O. 3, 4, 5, 6)

Dave Sawyer and Joe Rappe formed a partnership on January 1, 19x1, to operate a computer software store. To begin the partnership, Dave transferred cash totaling $116,000 and office equipment valued at $84,000 to the partnership. Joe transferred cash of $56,000, land valued at $36,000, and a building valued at $300,000. In addition, the partnership assumed the mortgage of $232,000 on the building.

During the first year, the partnership reported a loss of $16,000 on December 31. In the partnership agreement, the owners had specified the distribution of income and losses by allowing interest of 10 percent on beginning capital, salaries of $20,000 to Dave and $48,000 to Joe, and the remaining amount to be divided in the ratio of 3:2.

On January 1, 19x2, the partners brought Jan Blocker, who was experienced in the software business, into the partnership. Jan invested $56,000 in the partnership for a 20 percent interest. The bonus to Jan was transferred from the original partners' accounts in the ratio of 3:2.

During 19x2, the partnership earned an income of $108,000. The new partnership agreement required that income and losses be divided by providing interest of 10 percent on beginning capital balances and salaries of $20,000, $48,000, and $60,000 for Dave, Joe, and Jan, respectively. Remaining amounts were to be divided equally.

Because of the lack of sufficient income, the partners decided to liquidate the partnership on January 1, 19x3. On that date, the assets and liabilities of the partnership were as follows: Cash, $244,000; Accounts Receivable, $152,000; Land, $36,000; Building (net), $280,000; Office Equipment (net), $108,000; Accounts Payable, $108,000; Mortgage Payable, $204,000.

The office equipment was sold for $72,000, and the accounts receivable were valued at $128,000. The resulting losses were distributed equally to the partners' capital accounts, and the accounts payable were paid. Dave agreed to accept the accounts receivable plus cash in payment for his partnership interest. Joe accepted the land, building, and mortgage payable at book value plus cash for his share in the liquidation. Jan was paid in cash.

Required

Prepare general journal entries to record all the above facts. Support your computations with schedules, and prepare a statement of liquidation in connection with the January 1, 19x3, entries.

Financial Decision Case

L & T Oyster Bar
(L.O. 4, 5)

The L & T Oyster Bar is owned by James Land and Larry Teague. The business has been very successful since its inception five years ago. James and Larry work ten to eleven hours a day at the business. They have decided to expand by opening up another bar in the north part of town. James has approached you about becoming a partner in their business. They are interested in you because of your past experience in operating a small oyster bar. In addition, they will need additional funds to expand their business.

Projected income after the expansion but before partner salaries for the next five years is

19x1	19x2	19x3	19x4	19x5
$100,000	$120,000	$130,000	$140,000	$150,000

Currently, James and Larry each draw $25,000 salary and share remaining profits equally. They are willing to give you an equal share of the business for $142,000. You will receive $25,000 salary and ⅓ of the remaining profits. You would work the same hours as James and Larry. Your expected salary for the next five years where you currently work is expected to be:

19x1	19x2	19x3	19x4	19x5
$34,000	$38,000	$42,000	$45,000	$50,000

Financial information for the L & T Oyster Bar is shown as follows:

Current assets	$ 45,000
Fixed assets	365,000
Current liabilities	50,000
Long-term liabilities	100,000
Land, capital	140,000
Teague, capital	120,000

Required

1. Compute your capital balance if you decide to join James and Larry in the partnership.
2. Analyze your expected income for the next five years. Should you invest in the L & T Oyster Bar?
3. Assume that you do not consider James and Larry's offer to be very attractive. Develop a counter offer that you would be willing to accept to join the partnership (be realistic in your proposed arrangement).

CHAPTER 12 CONTRIBUTED CAPITAL

LEARNING OBJECTIVES

1. Define a corporation, and state the advantages and disadvantages of the corporate form of business.
2. Account for organization costs.
3. Identify the components of stockholders' equity.
4. Account for cash dividends.
5. Calculate the division of dividends between common and preferred stockholders.
6. Account for the issuance of common and preferred stock for cash and other assets.
7. Account for stock subscriptions.
8. Account for the exercise of stock options.

There are fewer corporations than sole proprietorships and partnerships in the United States. However, the corporate form of business dominates the economy in total dollars of assets and output of goods and services. The major reason for this dominance is that it is easier for a corporation to amass a large amount of capital. The corporate form of business is also well suited to today's trends toward large organizations, international trade, and professional management.

This chapter begins by outlining some of the important characteristics of the corporate form of business. Then it explains accounting for organization costs and describes the components of stockholders' equity. The rest of the chapter focuses on accounting for the issuance of stock and other stock transactions. After studying this chapter, you should be able to meet the learning objectives listed on the left.

The Corporation

A **corporation** is defined as "a body of persons granted a charter legally recognizing them as a separate entity having its own rights, privileges, and liabilities distinct from those of its members."[1] In other words, the corporation is a legal entity separate from its owners. For this reason, corporate accounting is different in some ways from that for proprietorships and partnerships.

Formation of a Corporation

To form a corporation in most states an application is filed with the proper state official. The application contains the **articles of incorporation**. If approved by the state, these articles become, in effect, a contract between the state and the incorporators, called the company charter. After the charter is approved, the company is authorized to do business. The incorporators first hold a meeting to elect a board of directors and pass a set of bylaws to guide the operations of the corporation. The board of directors then

1. © 1973 Houghton Mifflin Company. Reprinted by permission from *The American Heritage Dictionary of the English Language*.

OBJECTIVE 1 Define a corporation, and state the advantages and disadvantages of the corporate form of business

holds a meeting to elect officers of the corporation. Finally, when beginning capital is raised through the issuance of shares of stock, the corporation is ready to begin operating.

Organization of a Corporation

The authority to manage the corporation is given by the stockholders to the board of directors and by the board of directors to the corporate officers (see Figure 12-1). That is, the stockholders elect the board of directors, which sets company policies and chooses the corporate officers. The officers in turn carry out the corporate policies by managing the business.

Stockholders. A unit of ownership in a corporation is called a **share of stock**. The articles of incorporation state the maximum or authorized number of shares of a stock that the corporation will be allowed to issue. The number of shares held by stockholders is the outstanding capital stock, and it may be less than the number of authorized shares. To invest in a corporation, a stockholder transfers cash or other resources to the corporation. In return, the stockholder receives shares of stock representing a proportionate share of ownership in the corporation. Afterward, the stockholder may transfer the shares at will. Corporations may have more than one kind of capital stock, but the first part of this chapter will refer only to common stock.

Individual stockholders do not normally take part in the day-to-day management of a corporation. However, a stockholder may serve as a member of the board if elected or as an officer of the company if appointed. But, in general, stockholders participate in management only through electing the board of directors and voting on particular issues at stockholders' meetings.

Stockholders will normally meet once a year to elect directors and carry on other business as provided for in the company's bylaws. Business transacted at these meetings may include the election of auditors, review of proposed mergers and acquisitions, changes in the charter, stock option plans, and issuance of additional stock and of long-term debt. Each stockholder has one vote for each share of voting stock held. Today, ownership of large corporations is spread over the entire country. As a result, only a few stockholders may be able to attend the annual stockholders' meeting. A stockholder who cannot attend the meeting may vote by proxy. The **proxy** is a legal document, signed by the

Figure 12-1. The Corporate Form of Business

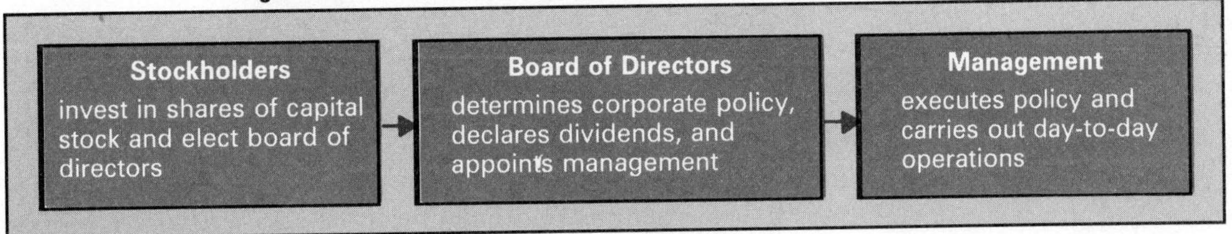
Stockholders
invest in shares of capital stock and elect board of directors
Board of Directors
determines corporate policy, declares dividends, and appoints management
Management
executes policy and carries out day-to-day operations

stockholder, giving another party the right to vote his or her shares. Normally, this right is given to the current management of the corporation.

Board of Directors. As noted, the stockholders elect the board of directors, which in turn decides on the major business policies of the corporation. Among the duties of the board are authorizing contracts, deciding on executive salaries, and arranging major loans with banks. The declaration of dividends is also an important function of the board of directors. Only the board has the authority to declare dividends. Dividends are distributions of resources, generally in the form of cash, to the stockholders. They are one way of rewarding stockholders for their investment in the corporation when it has been successful in earning a profit. (The other way is a rise in the market value of the stock.) There is usually a delay of two or three weeks between the time when the board declares a dividend and the date of the actual payment.

The make-up of the board of directors is different from company to company. In most cases, though, it contains several officers of the corporation and several outsiders. Today, it is common to form an **audit committee** with several outside directors to make sure that the board will be objective in judging management's performance. One of the audit committee's tasks is to hire the company's independent auditors and review their work.

Management. The board of directors appoints the managers of a corporation to carry out the company's policies and to run the day-to-day operations. The management consists of the operating officers, who are generally the president, vice presidents, controller, treasurer, and secretary. Besides being responsible for running the business, management has the duty to report the financial results of its administration to the board of directors and to the stockholders. Though management may and generally does report more often, it must report at least once a year. For large public corporations, these annual reports are available to the public. Parts of many of them have been used in this book.

Advantages of a Corporation

The corporate form of business organization has several advantages over the sole proprietorship and the partnership. Among these advantages are separate legal entity, limited liability, ease of capital generation, ease of transfer of ownership, lack of mutual agency, continuous existence, centralized authority and responsibility, and professional management.

Separate Legal Entity. A corporation is a separate legal entity that has most of the rights of a person except those of voting and marrying. As such, it may buy, sell, or own property, sue and be sued, enter into contracts with all parties, hire and fire employees, and be taxed.

Limited Liability. Because a corporation is a separate legal entity, it is responsible for its own actions and liabilities. For this reason, a corporation's creditors generally cannot look beyond the assets of the company to satisfy their claims. In other words, the creditors can satisfy their claims only against the assets of the corporation, not against the personal property of the owners of the company. Because owners of a corporation are not responsible for the debts of the company, their liability is limited to the amount of their investment. The personal property of sole proprietors and partners, however, may be available to creditors.

Ease of Capital Generation. It is fairly easy for a corporation to raise money because many people can take part in the ownership of the business by investing small amounts of money. As a result, a single corporation may be owned by many people.

Ease of Transfer of Ownership. The ownership of a corporation is represented by a transferable unit called a share of stock. The owner of the share of stock, or the stockholder, can buy and sell shares of stock without affecting the activities of the corporation or needing the approval of other owners.

Lack of Mutual Agency. There is no mutual agency with the corporate form of business. If a stockholder, acting as an owner, tries to enter into a contract for the corporation, the corporation will not be bound by the contract. But a partnership, where there is mutual agency, can be bound by a partner's actions.

Continuous Existence. Another advantage of the corporation being a legal entity separate from its owners is that an owner's death, incapacity, or withdrawal does not affect the life of the corporation. The life of a corporation is set by its charter and regulated by state laws.

Centralized Authority and Responsibility. The board of directors represents the stockholders and delegates the responsibility and authority for the day-to-day operation of the corporation to a single person, usually the president of the organization. This power is not divided among the many owners of the business. The president may delegate authority for certain segments of the business to others, but he or she is held accountable to the board of directors for the business. If the board is dissatisfied with the performance of the president, he or she can be replaced.

Professional Management. Large corporations are owned by many people who probably do not have the time or training to make timely operating decisions for the business. So, in most cases, management and ownership are separated in the manner described in the previous paragraph. This arrangement allows the corporation to hire the best talent available for managing the business.

Disadvantages of a Corporation

The corporate form of business has its disadvantages. Among the more important ones are government regulation, taxation, limited liability, and separate ownership and control.

Government Regulation. When corporations are created, they must meet the requirements of state laws. For this reason, they are said to be "creatures of the state" and are subject to greater control and regulation by the state than other forms of business. Corporations must file many reports with the states in which they are chartered. Also, corporations that are publicly held must file reports with the Securities and Exchange Commission and with the stock exchanges. Meeting these requirements becomes very costly.

Taxation. A major disadvantage of a corporation is **double taxation.** Because the corporation is a separate legal entity, its earnings are subject to federal and state income taxes. These taxes may approach 50 percent of the corporate earnings. If the corporation's after-tax earnings are then paid out to its stockholders as dividends, these earnings are again taxed as income to the stockholders who receive them. Taxation is different for the sole proprietorship and the partnership, whose earnings are taxed only as personal income to the owners.

Limited Liability. Earlier, limited liability was listed as an advantage of a corporation. This same feature, however, may limit the ability of a small corporation to borrow money. Credit of a small corporation is reduced because the stockholders have limited liability and the creditors will have claims only to the assets of the corporation. In such cases, the creditors will limit their loans to the level secured by the assets of the corporation or ask the stockholders to personally guarantee the loans.

Separation of Ownership and Control. Just as limited liability may be a drawback, so may the separation of ownership and control. Sometimes management makes decisions that are not good for the corporation as a whole. Poor communication can also make it hard for stockholders to exercise control over the corporation or even to recognize that management's decisions are harmful.

Organization Costs

OBJECTIVE 2
Account for organization costs

The costs of forming a corporation are called **organization costs.** These costs include such items as state incorporation fees, attorneys' fees for drawing up the articles of incorporation, and promoters' fees. Also included are the cost of printing stock certificates, accountants' fees for services rendered in registering the firm's initial stock, and other expenditures necessary for forming the corporation.

The benefits to be received from these costs should actually run through the entire life of the organization. For this reason, the costs should be capitalized as intangible assets and amortized over the years. However, the life of a corporation is normally unknown, so accountants amortize these costs over the early years of a corporation's life. Because federal income tax regulations allow organization costs to be amortized over five years or more, most companies amortize these costs over a five-year period, although the FASB will allow a period up to forty years. Organization costs normally appear as Other Assets or as Intangible Assets on the balance sheet.

To illustrate accounting practice for organization costs, we will assume that a corporation pays a lawyer $5,000 for services rendered in preparing the application for a charter with the state. The entry to record this cost would be as follows:

19x0			
July 1	Organization Costs	5,000	
	Cash		5,000
	To record $5,000 lawyer's fee for services rendered in corporate organization		

If the corporation amortizes the organization costs over a five-year period, the entry to record the amortization at the end of the fiscal year on June 30, 19x1, would be:

19x1			
June 30	Amortization Expense, Organization Costs	1,000	
	Organization Costs		1,000
	To record one year's amortization costs: $5,000 ÷ 5 years = $1,000		

The Components of Stockholders' Equity

OBJECTIVE 3 Identify the components of stockholders' equity

The major difference in accounting for corporations and accounting for sole proprietorships or partnerships involves the owners' equity. The assets and liabilities of a corporation are handled in the same way as they are for other forms of business. In a corporation's balance sheet, the owners' claims to the business are called **stockholders' equity**, as follows:

Stockholders' Equity

Contributed Capital		
Preferred Stock—$50 par value, 1,000 shares authorized and issued		$ 50,000
Common Stock—$5 par value, 30,000 shares authorized, 20,000 shares issued	$100,000	
Paid-in Capital in Excess of Par Value, Common	50,000	150,000
Total Contributed Capital		$200,000
Retained Earnings		60,000
Total Stockholders' Equity		$260,000

This equity section is different from the balance sheet presentation of a proprietorship and partnership in that it is divided into two parts: (1) contributed capital and (2) retained earnings. The **contributed capital** represents the investments made by the stockholders in the corporation. The retained earnings are the earnings of the business that are not distributed to the stockholders but are reinvested in the business.

The contributed capital part of stockholders' equity gives a great deal of information about the stock of a corporation. For example, the kinds of stock, their par value, and the number of shares authorized and issued are reported in this part of stockholders' equity. This information in the contributed capital part of stockholders' equity is the subject of the rest of this chapter. Retained earnings will be explained in Chapter 13.

Capital Stock

A unit of ownership in a corporation is called a share of stock. A **stock certificate** will be issued to the owner. It shows the number of shares of the corporation's stock owned by the stockholder. Stockholders can transfer their ownership at will, but they must sign their stock certificate and send it to the corporation's secretary. In large corporations listed on the organized stock exchanges, it is hard to maintain stockholders' records. Such companies may have millions of shares of stock, several thousand of which may change ownership every day. Therefore, these corporations often appoint independent registrars and transfer agents to aid in performing the secretary's duties. The registrars and the transfer agents are usually banks and trust companies. They are responsible for transferring the corporation's stock, maintaining stockholders' records, preparing a list of stockholders for stockholders' meetings, and paying the dividends. To help with the initial issue of capital stock, corporations often engage an underwriter. The underwriter is an intermediary, or contact, between the corporation and the investing public. For a fee—usually less than one percent of the selling price—the underwriter guarantees the sale of the stock. The corporation records the amount of the net proceeds of the offering—what the public paid less the underwriter's fee, legal and printing expenses, and any other direct costs of the offering—in its capital stock and additional paid-in capital accounts.

Authorization of Stock

When a corporation applies for a charter, the articles of incorporation indicate the maximum number of shares of stock a corporation will be allowed to issue. This number represents **authorized stock.** Most corporations get an authorization to issue more shares of stock than are necessary at the time of organization. This action enables the corporation to issue stock in the future to raise additional capital. For example, if a corporation is planning to expand later, a possible source of capital would be the unissued shares of stock that were authorized in its charter. If all authorized stock is issued immediately, the corporation must change its charter by applying to the state to increase the number of shares of authorized stock. The charter also shows the par value of the stock that has been authorized. The **par value** is the amount to be printed on each share of stock. It must be recorded in the capital stock accounts and constitutes the legal capital of a corporation. It usually bears little if any relationship to the market value or book value of the shares. When the corporation is formed, a memorandum entry may be made in the general journal giving the number and description of authorized shares.

Issued and Outstanding Stock

The **issued stock** of a corporation is the shares sold or otherwise transferred to the stockholders. For example, a corporation may have been authorized to issue 500,000 shares of stock but chose to issue only 300,000 shares when the company was organized. The 300,000 shares represent the issued stock. The holders of those shares own 100 percent of the corporation. The remaining 200,000 shares of stock are unissued shares. No rights or privileges are associated with them until they are issued. Shares of stock are said to be **outstanding stock** if they have been issued and are still in circulation. A share of stock would not be outstanding if it had been repurchased by the corporation or given back to the company by a shareholder. In such cases, a company can have more shares issued than are currently outstanding or held by the stockholders. Issued shares that are bought back and still held by the corporation are called *treasury stock* and are explained in Chapter 13.

Common Stock

A corporation may issue two basic types of stock: common stock and preferred stock. If only one kind of stock is issued, it is called **common stock**. The common stock is the **residual equity** of a company. This term means that all other creditor and preferred stockholder claims to the company's assets rank ahead of those of the common stockholders in case of liquidation. Because the common stock is generally the only stock carrying voting rights, it represents the means of controlling the corporation.

Dividends

OBJECTIVE 4
Account for cash dividends

A **dividend** is a distribution of assets of a corporation to its stockholders. Each stockholder receives assets, usually cash, in proportion to the number of shares of stock held. The board of directors has sole authority to declare dividends.

Dividends may be paid quarterly, semiannually, annually, or at other times decided on by the board. Most states do not allow the board to declare a dividend that exceeds retained earnings. Where such a dividend is declared, the corporation is essentially returning to the stockholders a part of their paid-in capital. This is called a **liquidating dividend** and is normally paid when a company is going out of business or is reducing its operations. However, having sufficient retained earnings does not in itself justify the distribution of a dividend. Cash or other readily distributable assets may not be available for distribution. In such a case the company might have to borrow money in order to pay a dividend. This is an action the board of directors may want to avoid.

There are three important dates associated with dividends. In order of occurrence, these are (1) the date of declaration, (2) the date of record, and (3) the date of payment. The date of declaration is the date the board of directors takes formal action declaring that a dividend will be paid. The date of record is the date on which ownership of the stock of a company, and therefore of the right to receive a dividend, is determined. Those individuals who own the stock on the date of record will be the ones to receive the dividend. After that date, the stock is said to be **ex-dividend** because if the shares of stock are sold from one person to another the right to the cash dividend remains with the first person and does not transfer with the shares to the second person. The date of payment is the date the dividend will be paid to the stockholders of record.

Cash Dividends. To illustrate the accounting for cash dividends, we will assume that the board of directors has decided that sufficient cash is available to pay a $56,000 cash dividend to the common stockholders. The dividend is declared on February 21, 19xx, to be paid March 31, 19xx, to stockholders of record on March 10, 19xx. The entries to record the declaration and payment of the cash dividend follow:

Date of declaration

Feb. 21	Dividends Declared	56,000	
	Dividends Payable		56,000
	To record the declaration of a cash dividend to common stockholders		

Date of record

Mar. 10	No entry is required because this date is used simply to determine the owners of the stock who will receive the dividends. After this date the shares are ex-dividend.

Date of payment

Mar. 31	Dividends Payable	56,000	
	Cash		56,000
	To record the payment of cash dividends		

Note that the liability for the dividend was recorded on the date of declaration because the legal obligation to pay the dividend was established on that date. No entry was required on the date of record, and the liability was liquidated, or settled, on the date of payment. At the end of the accounting period, the Dividends Declared account is a stockholders' equity account that is closed by debiting Retained Earnings and crediting Dividends Declared. Retained earnings are thereby reduced by the total dividends declared during the period.

Some companies do not pay dividends very often. For one reason, the company may not have any earnings. For another, the company may be growing and thus the assets generated by the earnings are kept in the company for business purposes such as expansion of the plant. Investors in such growth companies expect a return on their investment in the form of an increased market value of their stock.

Preferred Stock

The second kind of stock, called **preferred stock,** may be issued so that the company can obtain money from investors who have different investment goals. Preferred stock has preference over common stock in one or more areas. There may be several different classes of preferred stock, each with distinctive characteristics to attract different investors. Most preferred stock has one or more of the following characteristics: preference as to dividends, preference as to assets of the business in liquidation, convertibility or nonconvertibility, callable option, and no voting rights.

Preference as to Dividends. Preferred stocks ordinarily have a *preference* over common stock in the receipt of dividends, that is, the holders of preferred shares must receive a certain amount of dividends before the holders of common shares may receive dividends. The amount that preferred shareholders must be paid before common shareholders may be paid is usually stated in dollars per share or in a percentage of the face value of the preferred shares. For example, a corporation may issue a preferred stock and pay a dividend of $4 per share or it might issue a preferred stock of $50 par value and pay a yearly dividend of 8 percent of par value, which amounts to a $4 annual dividend.

OBJECTIVE 5
Calculate the division of dividends between common and preferred stockholders

Preferred shareholders have no guarantee of ever receiving dividends; the company must have earnings and the board of directors must declare dividends on preferred shares before any liability to pay them arises. The consequences of not declaring a dividend to preferred shareholders in the current year vary, however, according to the exact terms under which the shares were issued. If the company and shareholder agreed that the preferred shares were **noncumulative,** the board of directors' failure to declare a dividend for the current year has no effect on the company's obligation to pay preferred shareholders before common shareholders in future years. If the shares are **cumulative,** however, the fixed preference amount per preferred share accumulates from year to year, and the whole amount must be paid before any common dividends may be paid. Dividends guaranteed on cumulative preferred shares in previous years must be paid before common dividends declared in the current year.

Dividends that are not paid in the year they are due are called **dividends in arrears.** Assume that the preferred stock of a corporation is as follows: preferred stock, 5 percent cumulative, 10,000 shares, $100 par, $1,000,000. If in 19x1 no dividends were paid, at the end of that year there would be preferred dividends of $50,000 in arrears ($1,000,000 × 5% = $50,000). Thus if dividends are paid next year, the preferred stockholders' dividends in arrears plus the 19x2 preferred dividends must be paid before any dividends can be paid in 19x2 on common stock.

As an illustration, let us assume the following facts. On January 1, 19x1, a corporation issued 10,000 shares of $10 par, 6 percent cumulative preferred stock and 50,000 shares of common stock. The first year's operations resulted in income of only $4,000. The board of directors declared a $3,000 cash dividend to the preferred stockholders. The dividend picture at the end of 19x1 appears as follows:

19x1 dividends due preferred stockholders ($100,000 × 6%)	$6,000
19x1 dividends declared preferred stockholders	3,000
Preferred stock dividends in arrears	$3,000

Dividends in arrears are not recognized as liabilities of a corporation because there is no liability until the board declares a dividend. A corporation cannot be sure of making a profit. So, of course, it cannot promise dividends to stockholders. However, if a company has dividends in arrears, they should be reported either in the body of the financial statements or in a footnote. It is important to give this information to the users of these statements. The following footnote appeared in a steel company's annual report a few years ago:

> On January 1, 19xx, the company was in arrears by $37,851,000 ($1.25 per share) on dividends to its preferred stockholders. The company must pay all dividends in arrears to preferred stockholders before paying any dividends to common stockholders.

Let us suppose that in 19x2, the company in the example above earned income of $30,000 and wished to pay dividends to both the preferred and the common stockholders. But the preferred stock is cumulative. So the corporation must pay the $3,000 dividends in arrears on the preferred stock, plus the current year's dividends, before the common stockholders can receive a dividend. For example, assume that the corporation's board of directors declared a $12,000 dividend to be distributed to the preferred and common stockholders. The distribution of the dividend would be as follows:

19x2 declaration of dividends	$12,000	
Less 19x1 preferred stock dividends in arrears	3,000	
Available for 19x2 dividends		$ 9,000
Less 19x2 preferred stock dividend ($100,000 × 6%)		6,000
Remainder available to common stockholders		$ 3,000

The following entry is made when the dividend is declared:

Dec. 31	Dividends Declared	12,000	
	Dividends Payable		12,000

To record declaration of a
$9,000 cash dividend to
preferred stockholders and
a $3,000 cash dividend to
common stockholders

Preference as to Assets. Many preferred stocks have preference as to the assets of the corporation in the case of liquidation of the business. So when the business is ended, the preferred stockholders have a right to receive the par value of their stock or a larger stated liquidation value per share before the common stockholders receive any share of the company's assets. This preference may also include any dividends in arrears owed to the preferred stockholders.

Convertible Preferred Stock. A corporation may make its preferred stock more attractive to investors by adding a convertibility feature. Those who hold **convertible preferred stock** can exchange their shares of preferred stock, if they wish, for shares of the company's common stock at a ratio stated in the preferred stock contract. Convertibility is attractive to investors for two reasons. (1) Like all preferred stockholders, owners of convertible stock can be surer of regular dividends than can common stockholders. (2) If the market value of a company's common stock rises, the conversion feature will allow the preferred stockholders to share in this increase. The rise in value would come either through equal increases in the value of the preferred stock or through conversion to common stock.

For example, suppose that a company issues 1,000 shares of 8 percent, $100 par value convertible preferred stock for $100 per share. Each share of stock can be converted into five shares of the company's common stock at any time. The market value of the common stock is now $15 a share. In the past, the dividends on the common stock had been about $1 per share per year. The stockholder owning one share of preferred stock now holds an investment that is worth about $100 on the market, and the probability of dividends is higher than with common stock.

Assume that in the next several years the corporation's earnings increase, and the dividends being paid to common stockholders also increase, to $3 per share. In addition, the market value of a share of common stock increases from $15 to $30. The preferred stockholders can convert each of their preferred shares into five common shares and increase their dividends from $8 on each preferred share to the equivalent of $15 ($3 on each of five common shares). Furthermore, the market value of each share of preferred stock will be close to the $150 value of the five shares of common stock because the share may be converted into the five shares of common stock.

Callable Preferred Stock. Most preferred stocks are **callable preferred stocks.** That is, they may be redeemed or retired at the option of the issuing corporation at a certain price stated in the preferred stock contract. The stockholder must surrender a nonconvertible preferred stock to the corporation when requested to do so. If the preferred stock is convertible, the shareholder may either surrender the stock to the corporation or convert it into common stock when the corporation calls the stock. The call price, or redemption price, is usually higher than the par value of the stock. For example, a $100 par value preferred stock might be callable at $103 per share. When preferred stock is called and surrendered, the stockholder is entitled to (1) the par value of the stock, (2) the call premium, (3) the dividends in arrears, and (4) a prorated (by the proportion of the year to the call date) portion of the current period's dividend.

There are several reasons why a corporation may call its preferred stock. The first is that the company may wish to force conversion of the preferred stock to common because the cash dividend to be paid on the equivalent common stock is less than the dividend being paid on the preferred shares. Second, it may be possible to replace the outstanding preferred stock on the current market with a preferred stock at a lower dividend rate or with long-term debt which may have a lower after-tax cost. Third, the company may simply be profitable enough to retire the preferred stock.

Retained Earnings. Retained earnings, the other component of stockholders' equity, represents the claim of stockholders to the assets of the company resulting from profitable operations. Chapter 13 focuses on the retained earnings section of the balance sheet.

Accounting for Stock Issuance

OBJECTIVE 6
Account for the issuance of common and preferred stock for cash and other assets

A share of capital stock is either a par or a no-par stock. If the capital stock is par stock, the corporation charter states the par value, and this value must be printed on each share of stock. Par value may be 10¢, $1, $5, $100, or any other amount worked out by the organizers of the corporation. The par values of common stocks tend to be lower than those of preferred stocks.

Par value is the amount per share that is entered into the corporation's Capital Stock account and makes up the **legal capital** of the corporation. The legal capital is the minimum amount that can be reported as contributed capital. A corporation may not declare a dividend that would cause stockholders' equity to fall below the legal capital of the firm. Therefore, the par value is a minimum cushion of capital that protects creditors. Any amount received in excess of par value from the issuance of stock is recorded as Paid-in Capital in Excess of Par Value and represents a portion of the company's contributed capital.

No-par stock is capital stock that does not have a par value. There are several reasons for issuing stock without a par value. One is that some investors have confused par value with book or market value of stock and have thus made poor investment decisions. Another reason is that most states will not allow an original issuance of stock below par value and thereby limit a corporation's flexibility in obtaining capital.

No-par stock may be issued with or without a stated value. The board of directors of the corporation issuing the no-par stock may place a **stated value** on each share of stock. The stated value can be any value set by the board, but some states do indicate a minimum value per share. The stated value may be set before or after the shares are issued if the state law does not specify this point.

If a company issues a no-par stock without a stated value, then all proceeds of the stock's issuance are recorded in the Capital Stock account. This amount becomes the corporation's legal capital unless the amount is specified by state law. Because additional shares of the stock may be issued at different prices, the credit to the Capital Stock account will not be uniform per share. In this way it differs from par value stock or no-par stock with a stated value.

When no-par stock with a stated value is issued, the shares are recorded in the Capital Stock account at the stated value. Any amount received in excess of the stated value is recorded as Paid-in Capital in Excess of Stated Value. The excess of the stated value is a part of the corporation's contributed capital. However, the stated value is normally considered to be the legal capital of the corporation.

Issuance of Par Value Stock

When a par value stock is issued, the Capital Stock account is credited for the par value (legal capital) regardless of whether the proceeds are more or less than the par value. For example, assume that Bradley Corporation is authorized to issue 20,000 shares of $10 par value common stock and actually issues 10,000 shares at $10 per share. The entry to record the issuance of the stock at par value would be as shown below.

Jan 1.	Cash	100,000	
	Common Stock		100,000
	Issued 10,000 shares of $10 par value common stock for $10 per share		

Cash is debited for $100,000 (10,000 shares × $10), and Common Stock is credited for an equal amount because the stock was sold for par value (legal capital). If the stock had been issued for a price greater than par, the proceeds in excess of par would be credited to a capital account entitled Paid-in Capital in Excess of Par Value, Common. For example, assume that the 10,000 shares of Bradley common stock were sold for $12 per share. The entry to record the issuance of the stock at the price in excess of par value would be as follows:

Jan. 1	Cash	120,000	
	Common Stock		100,000
	Paid-in Capital in Excess of Par Value, Common		20,000
	Issued 10,000 shares of $10 par value common stock for $12 per share		

Cash is debited for the proceeds of $120,000 (10,000 shares × $12), and Common Stock is credited at total par value of $100,000 (10,000 shares × $10). Paid-in Capital in Excess of Par Value, Common, is credited for the difference of $20,000 (10,000 shares × $2). The premium paid for the stock is a part of the corporation's contributed capital and will be added to Common Stock in the stockholders' equity section of the balance sheet. The stockholders' equity section for Bradley Corporation immediately following the stock issue would appear as follows:

Contributed Capital	
Common Stock—$10 par value, 20,000 shares authorized, 10,000 shares issued and outstanding	$100,000
Paid-in Capital in Excess of Par Value, Common	20,000
Total Contributed Capital	$120,000
Retained Earnings	—
Total Stockholders' Equity	$120,000

If a corporation issues stock for less than par, an account entitled Discount on Capital Stock should be debited for the discount. The issuance of stock at a discount rarely occurs because it is illegal in many states and is thus not illustrated in this text.

Issuance of No-Par Stock

As mentioned earlier, stock may be issued without a par value. However, most states require that all or part of the proceeds from the issuance of no-par stock be designated as legal capital not subject to withdrawal, except in liquidation. The purpose is to protect the corporation's assets for the creditors.

Assume that the Bradley Corporation's capital stock is no-par common and that 10,000 shares are issued on January 1, 19xx, at $15 per share. The $150,000 (10,000 shares at $15) in proceeds would be recorded as shown in the following entry:

Jan 1.	Cash	150,000	
	Common Stock		150,000
	Issued 10,000 shares of no-par common stock at $15 per share		

Since the stock does not have a stated or par value, all proceeds of the issue are credited to Common Stock and are part of the company's legal capital.

Most states allow the board of directors to put a stated value on no-par stock, and this value represents the legal capital. Assume that Bradley's board puts a $10 stated value on its no-par stock. The entry to record the issue of 10,000 shares of no-par common stock with a $10 stated value for $15 per share would change from that in the last paragraph to the following:

Jan. 1	Cash	150,000	
	Common Stock		100,000
	Paid-in Capital in Excess of Stated Value, Common		50,000
	Issued 10,000 shares of no-par common stock of $10 stated value for $15 per share		

Note that the legal capital credited to Common Stock is the stated value as decided by the board of directors. Note also that the account Paid-in Capital in Excess of Stated Value, Common, is credited for $50,000. The $50,000 is the difference between the proceeds ($150,000) and the total stated value ($100,000). Paid-in Capital in Excess of Stated Value, Common, is presented on the balance sheet in the same way as Paid-in Capital in Excess of Par Value, Common, is presented for par value stock.

Issuance of Stock for Noncash Assets

In many stock transactions, stock is issued for assets or services other than cash. As a result, a problem arises as to what dollar amount should be recorded for the exchange. The generally preferred rule for such a transaction is to record the transaction at the fair market value of what is given up—in this case, the stock. If the fair market value of the stock cannot be determined, the fair market value of the assets or services may be used to record the transaction. Transactions of this kind usually include the use of stock to pay for land or buildings or for services of attorneys and promoters.

Where there is an exchange of stock for noncash assets, the board of directors has the right to determine the fair market value of the property. Thus, when the Bradley Corporation was formed, it issued 100 shares of its $10 par value common stock to its attorney for services rendered. At the time of the issuance, the market value of the stock could not be determined. However, for similar services the attorney would have billed the company for $1,500. The entry to record the noncash transaction follows:

Jan. 1	Organization Costs	1,500	
	Common Stock		1,000
	Paid-in Capital in Excess of Par Value, Common		500
	Issued 100 shares of $10 par value common stock for attorney's services		

Assume further that the Bradley Corporation exchanged 1,000 shares of its $10 par value common stock for a piece of land two years later. At the time of the exchange the stock was selling on the market for $16 per share and the value of the land could not be determined. The entry to record this exchange would be:

Jan. 1	Land	16,000	
	Common Stock		10,000
	Paid-in Capital in Excess of Par Value, Common		6,000
	Issued 1,000 shares of $10 par value common stock for a piece of land; market value of the stock $16 per share		

Stock Subscriptions

OBJECTIVE 7 Account for stock subscriptions

In some states, corporations may sell on a subscription basis. In a **stock subscription,** the investor agrees to pay for the stock on some future date or in installments at an agreed price. When a subscription is received, a contract exists and the corporation acquires an asset Subscriptions Receivable, which represents the amount owed on the stock, and a capital item Capital Stock Subscribed, which represents the par or stated value of the stock not yet fully paid for and issued. The Subscriptions Receivable account should be identified as either common or preferred stock. The Capital Stock Subscribed account should also be identified as either common or preferred stock. Whether or not the subscriber is entitled to dividends on the subscribed stock depends on the laws of the state in which the company is incorporated. In certain states, the stock is considered to be legally issued when a subscription contract is accepted, thereby making the subscriber a legal stockholder. However, in accounting for stock subscriptions, capital stock is not issued and recorded until the subscriptions receivable pertaining to the shares are collected in full and the stock certificate is delivered to the stockholder. Likewise, it may be assumed that dividends are not paid on common stock subscribed until it is fully paid for and the certificates issued.

To illustrate stock subscriptions, we will assume that on January 1, 19xx, the Bradley Corporation received subscriptions for 15,000 shares of $10 par value common stock at $15 per share. The entry to record the subscriptions would be as follows:

Jan. 1	Subscriptions Receivable, Common	225,000	
	Common Stock Subscribed		150,000
	Paid-in Capital in Excess of Par Value, Common		75,000
	Received subscriptions for 15,000 shares of $10 par value common stock at $15 per share		

If the full subscription price for 10,000 shares was collected on January 21, 19xx, the entry for the collection of the subscription would be:

Jan. 21	Cash	150,000	
	Subscriptions Receivable, Common		150,000
	Collected subscriptions in full for 10,000 shares of $10 par value common stock at $15 per share		

Because the 10,000 shares are fully paid for, it is appropriate to issue the common stock, as shown here:

Jan. 21	Common Stock Subscribed	100,000	
	Common Stock		100,000
	Issued 10,000 shares of $10 par value common stock		

Note that since the paid-in value in excess of par value was recorded in the January 1 entry, there is no need to record it again.

Assume that the financial statements are prepared on January 31, 19xx, before the remaining subscriptions are collected. The Subscriptions Receivable account of $75,000 ($225,000 – $150,000) would be classified as a current asset unless there was some reason why it would not be collected in the next year. The balance of $50,000 ($150,000 – $100,000) in the Common Stock Subscribed account represents the par value of the stock yet to be issued and is a temporary capital account. As such, it is properly shown as a part of stockholders' equity under Contributed Capital, as in the following illustration:

Contributed Capital		
Common Stock—$10 par value, 80,000 shares authorized		
Issued and outstanding, 10,000 shares	$100,000	
Subscribed but not issued, 5,000 shares	50,000	$150,000
Paid-in Capital in Excess of Par Value, Common		75,000
Total Contributed Capital		$225,000

Assume that one-half payment of $37,500 is received on February 5 for the remaining subscriptions receivable. The entry for the collection would be as follows:

Feb. 5	Cash	37,500	
	Subscriptions Receivable, Common		37,500
	Collected one-half payment for subscriptions to 5,000 common shares		

In this case, there is no entry to issue common stock because the subscription for the stock is not paid in full. If the subscriptions receivable are paid in full on February 20 the entries are as follows:

Feb. 20	Cash	37,500	
	Subscriptions Receivable, Common		37,500
	Collected subscriptions in full for 5,000 shares of $10 par value common stock for $15 per share		

Because the subscriptions are now paid in full, the common stock can be issued as follows:

Feb. 20	Common Stock Subscribed	50,000	
	Common Stock		50,000
	Issued 5,000 shares of $10 par value common stock		

Exercise of Stock Options

OBJECTIVE 8
Account for the exercise of stock options

Many companies encourage the ownership of the company's common stock through a **stock option plan.** A stock option plan is an agreement to issue stock to employees according to the terms of the plan. Under some plans, the option to purchase stock may apply to all employees equally, and the purchase of stock is made at a price that is approximately market value at the time of purchase. When this situation exists, the issue of stock is recorded in the same way any stock issue to an outsider is recorded. If, for example, we assume that on March 30, the employees of a company purchased 2,000 shares of $10 par value common stock, at the current market value of $25 per share, the entry would be shown as follows:

Mar. 30	Cash	50,000	
	Common Stock		20,000
	Paid-in Capital in Excess of Par Value, Common		30,000
	Issue of $10 par value common stock under employee stock option plan		

In other cases, the stock option plan may give the employee the right to purchase stock in the future at a fixed price. This type of plan, which usually applies to management personnel, serves to compensate and motivate the employee, because if the company's performance is such that the market value of the stock goes up, the employee can purchase the stock at the option price and sell it at the higher market price. The amount of compensation to the employee is measured by the difference between the option price and the market price on the date of granting the option, not on the date of issuing the stock. If no difference exists between the option price and the market price on the date of grant, no compensation exists. When the option is eventually exercised on the stock and is issued, the entry is similar to the previous entry. For example, assume that a company grants to key management personnel on July 1, 19x1, the option to purchase 50,000 shares of $10 par value common stock at the market value of $15 per share on that date. Assume that a company vice president exercises the option to purchase 2,000 shares on March 30, 19x2, when the market price is $25 per share. The entry to record the issue would be

Mar. 30	Cash	30,000	
	Common Stock		20,000
	Paid-in Capital in Excess of Par Value, Common		10,000
	Issue of $10 par value common stock under employee stock option plan		

Although the vice president has a gain of $20,000 ($50,000 market value minus $30,000 option price), no compensation expense is recorded. A compensation expense would have been recorded only if the option price were less than the $15 market price on July 1, 19x1, the date of grant. The handling of compensation when this situation exists is covered in more advanced courses.[1]

Chapter Review

Review of Learning Objectives

1. **Define a corporation, and state the advantages and disadvantages of the corporate form of business.**
Corporations, whose ownership is represented by shares of stocks, are separate entities for both legal and accounting purposes. The corporation is a separate legal entity having its own rights, privileges, and liabilities distinct from its owners. Like other forms of business entities, it has several advantages and disadvantages. The more common advantages are that (a) a corporation is a separate legal entity, (b) stockholders have limited liability, (c) it is easy to generate capital for a corporation, (d) stockholders can buy and sell shares of stock with ease, (e) there is a lack of mutual agency, (f) the corporation has a continuous existence, (g) authority and responsibility are centralized, and (h) it is run by a professional management team. Disadvantages of corporations include (a) a large amount of government regulation, (b) double taxation, (c) limited liability, and (d) the separation of ownership and control.

2. **Account for organization costs.**
The costs of organizing a corporation are recorded on a historical cost basis. As an intangible asset, organization costs are amortized over a reasonable period of time, usually five years.

3. **Identify the components of stockholders' equity.**
Stockholders' equity consists of contributed capital and retained earnings. Contributed capital may include more than one type of stock. Two of the most common types of stock are common stock and preferred stock. When only one type of security is issued, it is common stock. The holders of common stock have the right to elect the board of directors and vote on key issues of the corporation. In addition, common stockholders share in the earnings of the corporation, share in the assets of the corporation in case of liquidation, and maintain their percentage ownership.

1. Stock options are discussed here in the context of employee compensation. They can also be important features of complex corporate capitalization arrangements.

Preferred stock is issued to investors whose investment objectives differ from those of common stockholders. To attract these investors, corporations give them a preference to certain items. Preferred stockholders' rights normally include the privilege of receiving dividends ahead of common shareholders, the right to assets in liquidation ahead of common shareholders, and convertibility to common stock.

Retained earnings, the other component of stockholders' equity, represents the claim of stockholders to the assets of the company resulting from profitable operations.

4. **Account for cash dividends.**

   A liability for payment of cash dividends arises on the date of declaration by the board of directors. The date of record, on which no entry is required, establishes the shareholders who will receive the cash dividend on the date of payment.

5. **Calculate the division of dividends between common and preferred stockholders.**

   Most preferred stock is preferred as to dividends. This preference means that in allocating total dividends between common and preferred shareholders, the amount for the preferred stock is figured first. Then the remainder goes to common stock. If the preferred stock is cumulative and in arrears, the amount in arrears also has to be allocated to preferred before any allocation is made to common.

6. **Account for the issuance of common and preferred stock for cash and other assets.**

   A corporation's stock will normally be issued for cash and other assets or by subscription. The majority of states require that stock be issued at a minimum value called legal capital. Legal capital is represented by the par or stated value of the stock.

   When stock is issued for cash or other assets, the par or stated value of the stock is recorded as common or preferred stock. When the stock is sold at an amount greater than the par or stated value, the excess is recorded as Paid-in Capital in Excess of Par or Stated Value.

   Sometimes stock is issued for noncash assets. In these transactions, it is necessary to decide what value to use in recording the issuance of the stock. The general rule is to record the stock at the market value of the stock issued. If this value cannot be determined, then the fair market value of the asset received will be used to record the transaction.

7. **Account for stock subscriptions.**

   When stock is not fully paid for at the time of sale, it is not issued. However, the transaction is recorded by debiting Subscriptions Receivable (a current asset) and crediting Capital Stock Subscribed (a stockholders' equity account) for the par or stated value and crediting Paid-in Capital in Excess of Par or Stated Value for any difference. When the stock has been fully paid for and is issued, Capital Stock Subscribed is debited and Capital Stock is credited.

8. **Account for the exercise of stock options.**

   Stock option plans are established to allow a company's employees to own a part of the company. Usually the issue of stock to employees under stock option plans is recorded in a manner similar to the issue of stock to any outsider.

Review Problem
Stock Journal Entries, Stockholders' Equity, and Book Value Per Share

The Beta Corporation was organized in 19xx in the state of Arizona. The charter of the corporation authorized the issuance of 1,000,000 shares of $1 par value common stock and an additional 25,000 shares of 4 percent, $20 par value cumulative convertible preferred stock that is callable at $22 per share. Transactions that relate to the stock of the company for 19xx are shown below.

Feb. 12	Issued 100,000 shares of common stock for $125,000.
20	Issued 3,000 shares of common stock for accounting and legal services. The services were billed to the company at $3,600.
Mar. 15	Issued 120,000 shares of common stock to Edward Jackson in exchange for a building and land, which had an appraised value of $100,000 and $25,000, respectively.
Apr. 2	Accepted subscriptions on 200,000 shares of common stock for $1.30 per share.
July 1	Issued 25,000 shares of preferred stock for $500,000.
Sept. 30	Collected in full subscriptions related to 60 percent of the common stock subscribed and issued the appropriate stock to subscribers.
Dec. 31	The company reported earnings of $40,000 for 19xx, and the board declared dividends of $20,000, payable on January 15 to stockholders of record on January 8. Dividends include preferred stock cash dividend for one-half year.

Required

1. Prepare the journal entries necessary to record these stock-related transactions. Following the December 31 entry, show dividends payable for each class of stock.
2. Prepare the stockholders' equity section of the Beta Corporation balance sheet as of December 31.

Answer to Review Problem

1. Journal entries prepared:

Feb. 12	Cash	125,000	
	Common Stock		100,000
	Paid-in Capital in Excess of Par Value, Common		25,000
	To record the sale of 100,000 shares of $1 par value common stock for $1.25 per share		
20	Organization Costs	3,600	
	Common Stock		3,000
	Paid-in Capital in Excess of Par Value, Common		600
	To record issuance of 3,000 shares of $1 par value common stock for billed accounting and legal services of $3,600		

Date	Account / Explanation	Debit	Credit
Mar. 15	Building	100,000	
	Land	25,000	
	Common Stock		120,000
	Paid-in Capital in Excess of Par Value, Common		5,000
	To record issuance of 120,000 shares of $1 par value common stock for a building and tract of land appraised at $100,000 and $25,000		
Apr. 2	Subscriptions Receivable, Common Stock	260,000	
	Common Stock Subscribed		200,000
	Paid-in Capital in Excess of Par Value, Common		60,000
	To record subscription for 200,000 shares of $1 par value stock at $1.30 a share		
July 1	Cash	500,000	
	Preferred Stock		500,000
	To record sale of 25,000 shares of $20 par value preferred stock for $20 per share		
Sept. 30	Cash	156,000	
	Subscriptions Receivable, Common Stock		156,000
	To record collection in full of 60 percent subscriptions receivable: $260,000 × .60 = $156,000		
30	Common Stock Subscribed	120,000	
	Common Stock		120,000
	To record issuance of common stock		
Dec. 31	Income Summary	40,000	
	Retained Earnings		40,000
	To record the transfer of net income to retained earnings		
31	Dividends Declared	20,000	
	Dividends Payable		20,000
	To record the declaration of a $20,000 cash dividend to preferred and common stockholders		
	Preferred stock cash dividend $500,000 × .04 × ½ = $10,000		
	Total dividend $20,000		
	Less preferred stock cash dividend 10,000		
	Common stock cash dividend $10,000		
31	Retained Earnings	20,000	
	Dividends Declared		20,000
	To close Dividends Declared to Retained Earnings		

2. Stockholders' equity section of balance sheet prepared:

Beta Corporation
Stockholders' Equity
December 31, 19xx

Contributed Capital		
4% Cumulative Convertible Preferred Stock—$20 par value, 25,000 shares authorized, issued, and outstanding, callable at $22 per share		$ 500,000
Common Stock—$1 par value, 1,000,000 shares authorized, 343,000 shares issued and outstanding	$343,000	
Common Stock Subscribed	80,000	
Paid-in Capital in Excess of Par Value, Common	90,600	513,600
Total Contributed Capital		$1,013,600
Retained Earnings		20,000
Total Stockholders' Equity		$1,033,600

Chapter Assignments

Questions

1. What is a corporation, and how is it formed?
2. What is the role of the board of directors in a corporation, and how does it differ from the role of management?
3. What are the typical officers in the management of a corporation and their duties?
4. What are several advantages of the corporate form of business? Explain.
5. What are several disadvantages of the corporate form of business? Explain.
6. What are organization costs of a corporation?
7. What is the proper accounting treatment of organization costs?
8. What is the legal capital of a corporation, and what is its significance?
9. How is the value determined for recording stock issued for noncash assets?
10. Describe the accounting treatment of cash dividends.
11. What are stock subscriptions, and how are Subscriptions Receivable and Common Stock Subscribed classified on the balance sheet?
12. What does it mean for preferred stock to be cumulative, convertible, and/or callable?
13. What are dividends in arrears, and how should they be disclosed in the financial statements?
14. What is the proper classification of the following accounts on the balance sheet? (a) Organization Costs; (b) Common Stock; (c) Subscriptions Receivable, Preferred; (d) Preferred Stock Subscribed; (e) Paid-in Capital in Excess of Par Value, Common; (f) Paid-in Capital in Excess of Stated Value, Common; (g) Discount on Common Stock; (h) Retained Earnings.
15. What reasons can you think of for a company to have a stock option plan? Why would an employee want to participate in one?

Classroom Exercises

Exercise 12-1. Journal Entries and Stockholders' Equity
(L.O. 3, 6)

The Lopata Hospital Supply Corporation was organized in 19xx. The company was authorized to issue 100,000 shares of no-par common stock with a stated value at $5 per share, and 20,000 shares of $100 par value, 6 percent noncumulative preferred stock. On March 1 the company sold 50,000 shares of its common stock for $12 per share and 5,000 shares of its preferred stock for $100 per share.

1. Prepare the journal entries to record the sale of the stock.
2. Prepare the company's stockholders' equity section of the balance sheet immediately after the common and preferred stock were issued.

Exercise 12-2. Stockholders' Equity
(L.O. 3)

The accounts and balances shown below were taken from the records of Machado Corporation on December 31, 19xx.

Account Name	Balance Debit	Balance Credit
Common Stock—$10 par value, 60,000 shares authorized, 20,000 shares issued and outstanding		$200,000
Common Stock Subscribed		20,000
Preferred Stock—$100 par value, 9% cumulative, 10,000 shares authorized, 5,000 shares issued and outstanding		500,000
Paid-in Capital in Excess of Par Value, Common		170,000
Retained Earnings		12,000
Subscriptions Receivable, Common	$30,000	

Prepare a stockholders' equity section for Machado Corporation's balance sheet.

Exercise 12-3. Cash Dividends
(L.O. 4)

Patterson Corporation has authorized 200,000 shares of $10 par value common stock. There are 150,000 shares issued and 130,000 shares outstanding. On June 5, the board of directors declares a $.40 per share cash dividend to be paid on June 25 to shareholders of record on June 15. Prepare the journal entries necessary to record these events.

Exercise 12-4. Preferred Stock Dividends with Dividends in Arrears
(L.O. 5)

The Pokorny Corporation has 10,000 shares of its $100, 8 percent cumulative preferred stock outstanding and 50,000 shares of its $1 par value common stock outstanding. In its first four years of operation, the board of directors of Pokorny Corporation paid cash dividends as follows: 19x1, none; 19x2, $140,000; 19x3, $140,000; 19x4, $140,000.

Determine the total cash dividends and dividends per share paid to the preferred and common stockholders during each of the four years.

Exercise 12-5. Journal Entries: Stated Value Stock
(L.O. 6)

The Chen Corporation is authorized to issue 200,000 shares of no-par stock. The company recently sold 30,000 shares for $15 per share.

1. Prepare the journal entry to record the sale of the stock if there is no stated value.
2. Prepare the entry if a $5 stated value is authorized by the company's board of directors.

Exercise 12-6. Stock Journal Entries and Stockholders' Equity
(L.O. 6)

On July 1, 19xx, Dublin, a new corporation, issued 15,000 shares of its common stock for a corporate headquarters building. The building had a fair market value of $155,000 and a book value of $130,000. Because the corporation is new, it is not possible to establish a market value for the common stock.

Record the issuance of stock for the building, assuming the following conditions: (a) the par value of the stock is $9 per share, (b) the stock is no-par stock, and (c) the stock is no-par stock, but has a stated value of $2 per share.

Exercise 12-7. Preferred and Common Stock Dividends
(L.O. 5)

The Finnegan Corporation pays dividends at the end of each year. The dividends paid for 19x1, 19x2, and 19x3 were $50,000, $20,000, and $80,000, respectively.

Calculate the total amount of dividends paid each year to the common and preferred stockholders if each of the following capital structures is assumed: (1) 10,000 shares of $100 par, 6 percent noncumulative preferred stock and 30,000 shares of $10 par common stock. (2) 5,000 shares of $100 par, 6 percent cumulative preferred stock and 30,000 shares of $10 par common stock. There were no dividends in arrears at the beginning of 19x1.

Exercise 12-8. Organization Costs Journal Entries
(L.O. 2)

The Rosenthal Corporation was organized during 19x7. The company incurred the following costs in organizing the company: (1) Attorney's fees, market value of services $2,000, acceptance of 1,500 shares of $1 par common stock. (2) Paid the state $1,000 for incorporation fees. (3) Accountant accepted 1,000 shares of $1 par value common stock for services that would normally be billed at $1,250.

Prepare the journal entries necessary to record these transactions and to amortize organization costs for the first year, assuming that the company elects to write off organization costs over five years.

Exercise 12-9. Issuance of Stock for Noncash Assets
(L.O. 6)

The Flores Corporation issued 1,000 shares of its $10 par value common stock for some land. The land had a fair market value of $13,000.

Prepare the journal entries necessary to record the issuance of the stock for the land under each of the following conditions: (1) the stock was selling for $12 per share on the day of the transaction; and (2) management attempted to place a value on the common stock, but could not determine the value.

Exercise 12-10. Stock Subscriptions
(L.O. 7)

The Dunbar Corporation sold 10,000 shares of its $5 par value common stock by subscription for $9 per share on February 15, 19xx. Cash was received in installments from the purchasers: 50 percent on April 1 and 50 percent on June 1.

Prepare the entries necessary to record these transactions.

Exercise 12-11. Exercise of Stock Options (L.O. 8)

Record the following equity transaction of the Jefferson Company during 19xx:

May 5 Charles Jefferson exercised his option to purchase 5,000 shares of $5 par value common stock at an option price of $9. The market price per share on the option date was $9, and it was $23 on the exercise date.

Interpreting Accounting Information

United Airlines (L.O. 6)

United Airlines (UAL, Inc.) is one of the largest domestic airlines, with destinations in all fifty states plus the Orient. On February 18, 1986, the airline announced an issue of common stock in the *Wall Street Journal*, as follows:

4,400,000 Shares
UAL, Inc.
Common Stock
($5 par value)
Price $56¾ per share

On December 31, 1985 and 1984, a portion of the stockholders' equity section of balance sheet from UAL's 1985 Annual Report appeared as follows:

	1985	1984
	(in thousands)	
Common stock, $5 par value; authorized 50,000,000 shares; outstanding 34,484,544 shares in 1985 and 29,609,734 shares in 1984	172,423	148,049
Additional paid-in capital	555,427	421,100
Retained earnings	681,383	555,954

Required

1. Assuming all the shares are issued at the price indicated and that UAL receives the full proceeds, prepare the entry in UAL's accounting records to record the stock issue.
2. Prepare the portion of the stockholders' equity section of the balance sheet shown above after the issue of the common stock. Did UAL have to increase the authorized shares to undertake this stock issue?
3. How do you think the above results would differ if UAL's underwriter kept a fee of $.50 per share to assist it in issuing the stock so that UAL receives $56¼ per share?

Problem Set A

Problem 12A-1. Organization Costs, Stock and Dividend Journal Entries (L.O. 2, 4, 6)

Alpha Corporation began operations on September 1, 19xx. The corporation's charter authorized 300,000 shares of $4 par value common stock. Alpha Corporation engaged in the following transactions during the first quarter:

Sept. 1 Paid an attorney $7,000 to assist in organizing the corporation and obtaining the corporate charter from the state.
17 Issued 40,000 shares of common stock, $200,000.
Oct. 2 Issued 100,000 shares of common stock, $600,000.

Nov. 30 The board of directors declared a cash dividend of \$.20 per share to be paid on December 15 to stockholders of record on December 10.
30 Closed the Income Summary and Dividends Declared accounts for the first quarter. Revenue was \$170,000 and expenses \$120,000.

Required

1. Prepare general journal entries to record the first quarter transactions.
2. Prepare the stockholders' equity section of Alpha Corporation's November 30 balance sheet.
3. Assuming the payment to the attorney on September 1 was to be amortized over five years, what adjusting entry was made on November 30? Also, describe the resulting balance sheet presentation.

Problem 12A-2. Stock Journal Entries and Stockholders' Equity (L.O. 6, 7)

The corporate charter for Reville Corporation states the company is authorized to issue 500,000 shares of \$3 par value common stock. The company was involved with several stock transactions during March 19x8 as shown below: Assume no prior transactions.

March 3 Accepted subscriptions for 100,000 shares of its common stock at \$4 per share.
12 Issued 16,000 shares of stock for land and warehouse. The land and warehouse had a fair market value of \$25,000 and \$30,000, respectively.
22 Sold 50,000 shares of stock for \$250,000.
25 Collected full payment on 60,000 shares of the common stock subscribed on March 3 and issued the shares.

Required

1. Prepare the general journal entries to record the March transactions of Reville Corporation.
2. Prepare the stockholders' equity section of the Reville Corporation's balance sheet as of March 31.

Problem 12A-3. Preferred and Common Stock Dividends (L.O. 5)

The Schiff Corporation had both common stock and preferred stock outstanding from 19x4 through 19x6. Information about each stock for the three years is given below:

Type	Par Value	Shares Outstanding	Other
Preferred	\$100	20,000	5 percent cumulative
Common	10	600,000	

The company paid \$50,000, \$350,000, and \$500,000 dividends for 19x4 through 19x6, respectively.

Required

1. Determine the dividend per share paid to the common and preferred stockholders each year.
2. Repeat the computation, assuming the preferred stock was noncumulative.

Problem 12A-4. Comprehensive Stockholders' Equity Transactions
(L.O. 2, 3, 4, 6, 7)

The Redi-Made Plastics Corporation was chartered in the state of Kansas. The company was authorized to issue 15,000 shares of $100 par value 6 percent preferred stock and 150,000 shares of no-par common stock. The common stock has a $1 stated value. The stock-related transactions for March and April, 19xx are as follows:

March 3 Issued 10,000 shares of common stock for $50,000 worth of services rendered in organizing and chartering the corporation.
10 Received subscriptions for 50,000 shares of common stock at $6 a share.
15 Issued 15,000 shares of common stock for land, which has an asking price of $80,000. The common stock has a market value of $5 per share.
22 Issued 2,000 shares of preferred stock for $200,000.
30 Closed the Income Summary account. Net income for March was $17,000.
April 4 Issued 10,000 shares of common stock for $60,000.
10 Received payment in full for the stock subscriptions of March 10.
15 Declared a cash dividend for one month on the outstanding preferred stock and $.05 per share on common stock outstanding payable on April 30 to shareholders of record on April 25.
25 Record date for cash dividends.
30 Paid cash dividends.

Required

1. Prepare general journal entries for March and April.
2. Prepare the stockholders' equity section of the company's balance sheet as of April 30, 19xx.

Problem 12A-5. Comprehensive Stockholders' Equity Transactions
(L.O. 2, 3, 4, 6, 7, 8)

The Tulip Lighting Corporation was organized and authorized to issue 100,000 shares of 6 percent, $100 par value, noncumulative preferred stock and 3,000,000 shares of $5 par value common stock. The stock-related transactions for the first seven months of 19xx operations are as follows:

April 3 Issued 15,000 shares of common stock for legal and other organizational fees valued at $75,000.
29 Sold 200,000 shares of common stock for $7 a share.
May 5 Issued 40,000 shares of common stock for a building and land appraised at $150,000 and $80,000 respectively.
17 Received subscriptions for 300,000 shares of common stock at $8 a share.
June 17 Received full payment for 200,000 shares of common stock subscribed on May 17 and issued the stock.
30 Closed the Income Summary account for the first quarter of operations. Income was $200,000.
July 10 Issued 2,000 shares of common stock to employees under a stock option plan. The plan allows employees to purchase the stock at the current market price, which was $6.
17 Collected the full amount for the remaining 100,000 shares of common stock subscribed on May 17 and issued the stock.
Aug. 8 Issued 10,000 shares of common stock for $8 a share.
Sept. 11 Declared a cash dividend of $.10 per common share to be paid on September 25 to shareholders of record on September 18.

18 Cash dividend record date.
25 Paid the cash dividend to shareholders of record on September 18.
30 Closed the Income Summary account and Dividends Declared for the second quarter of operations. Income was $125,000.
Oct. 15 Issued 5,000 shares of preferred stock at par value.

Required

1. Prepare general journal entries to record the stock-related transactions of the Tulip Lighting Corporation.
2. Prepare the stockholders' equity section of Tulip Lighting Corporation's balance sheet as of October 31.

Problem Set B

Problem 12B-1. Organization Costs, Stock and Dividend Journal Entries, and Stockholders' Equity (L.O. 2, 4, 6)

On March 1, 19xx, Dublin Corporation began operations with a charter from the state that authorized 100,000 shares of $2 par value common stock and engaged in the following transactions:

Mar. 1 Issued 20,000 shares of common stock, $80,000.
2 Paid fees associated with obtaining the charter and organizing the corporation, $10,000.
Apr. 10 Issued 10,000 shares of stock, $50,000.
May 31 Closed the Income Summary account. Net income earned during the first quarter, $12,000.
31 The board of directors declared a $.10 per share cash dividend to be paid on June 15 to shareholders of record on June 10.

Required

1. Prepare general journal entries to record the above transactions.
2. Prepare the stockholders' equity section of Dublin Corporation's balance sheet on May 31, 19xx.

Problem 12B-2. Stock Journal Entries and Stockholders' Equity (L.O. 6, 7)

The Scalera Company, Inc., has been authorized by the State of Vermont to issue 1,000,000 shares of $1 par value common stock. The company began issuing its common stock in July of 19xx. During July the company had the following stock transactions:

July 10 Issued 29,000 shares of stock for a building and land with fair market value of $22,000 and $7,000, respectively.
15 Accepted subscriptions to 400,000 shares of its stock for $500,000.
20 Collected full payment on 200,000 shares of the common stock subscribed on July 15. Issued the appropriate shares.
23 Sold 15,000 shares of stock for $20,000 cash.
27 Collected full payment on 100,000 shares of the common stock subscribed on July 15 and issued the shares.

Required

1. Prepare the journal entries to record the stock transactions of Scalera Company, Inc., for the month of July.
2. Prepare the stockholders' equity section of Scalera's balance sheet as of July 31.

Problem 12B-3. Preferred and Common Stock Dividends
(L.O. 5)

The Chen Corporation had the following stock outstanding for 19x1 through 19x4:

Preferred stock—$50 par value, 4 percent cumulative, 10,000 shares authorized, issued, and outstanding
Common stock—$5 par value, 150,000 shares authorized, issued, and outstanding

The company paid $15,000, $15,000, $47,000, and $65,000 in dividends during 19x1, 19x2, 19x3, and 19x4, respectively.

Required

1. Determine the total amounts per share of dividends paid to common stockholders and preferred stockholders in 19x1, 19x2, 19x3, and 19x4.
2. Perform the same computations assuming that the preferred stock is noncumulative.

Problem 12B-4. Comprehensive Stockholders' Equity Transactions
(L.O. 2, 3, 4, 6, 7)

Andercald, Inc., was organized and authorized to issue 10,000 shares of $100 par value 9% preferred stock and 100,000 shares of no-par, $5 stated value common stock, on July 1, 19xx. Stock related transactions for Andercald are as follows:

July 1 Issued 10,000 shares of common stock at $9 per share.
1 Issued 500 shares of stock at $9 per share for services rendered in connection with the organization of the company.
2 Issued 1,000 shares of preferred stock at par value.
10 Received subscriptions for 10,000 shares of common stock at $10 per share.
10 Issued 5,000 shares of common stock for land on which the asking price was $60,000. Market value of stock was $10.
31 Closed the Income Summary account. Net income earned during July was $10,000.
Aug. 2 Received payment in full for the stock subscriptions of July 10.
10 Declared a cash dividend for one month on the outstanding preferred stock and $.02 per share on common stock outstanding payable on August 22 to shareholders of record on August 12.
12 Record date for cash dividends.
22 Paid cash dividends.

Required

1. Prepare general journal entries to record the above transactions.
2. Prepare the stockholders' equity section of the balance sheet as it would appear on July 31, 19xx.

Problem 12B-5. Comprehensive Stockholders' Equity Transactions
(L.O. 2, 3, 4, 6, 7, 8)

In January 19xx, the Flores Corporation was organized and authorized to issue 2,000,000 shares of no-par common stock and 50,000 shares of 5 percent, $50 par value, noncumulative preferred stock. The stock-related transactions of the first year's operations follow.

Jan. 19 Sold 15,000 shares of the common stock for $25,000. State law requires a minimum of $1 stated value per share.

Jan. 26 Accepted subscriptions for 20,000 shares of the common stock for $2 per share.
Feb. 7 Issued 30,000 shares of common stock for a building that had an appraised value of $45,000.
Mar. 22 Collected full payment for 12,000 shares of the common stock subscribed on January 26, 19xx, and issued the stock.
June 30 Closed the Income Summary account. Reported $80,000 income for the first six months of operations.
July 15 Issued 5,000 shares of common stock to employees under a stock option plan that allows any employee to buy shares at the current market price, which today is $3 per share.
Aug. 1 Collected the full amount on the remaining 8,000 shares of common stock subscribed and issued the stock.
Sept. 1 Declared a cash dividend of $.15 per common share to be paid on Sept. 25 to shareholders of record on Sept. 15.
15 Cash dividend record date.
25 Paid cash dividend to shareholders of record on Sept. 15.
Oct. 30 Issued 4,000 shares of common stock for a piece of land. The stock is selling for $3 per share, and the land has a fair market value of $12,500.
Nov. 10 Accepted subscriptions for 10,000 shares of the common stock for $2.50 per share.
Dec. 15 Issued 2,200 shares of preferred stock for $50 per share.
31 Closed the Income Summary account and Dividends Declared account. Reported $20,000 income for the last six months of operations.

Required

1. Prepare the journal entries to record all of the above transactions of Flores Corporation during 19xx.
2. Prepare the stockholders' equity section of Flores Corporation's balance sheet as of December 31, 19xx.

Financial Decision Case

Northeast Servotech Corporation
(L.O. 3)

The companies offering services to the computer technology industry are growing rapidly. Participating in this growth, Northeast Servotech Corporation has expanded rapidly in recent years. Because of its profitability, the company has been able to grow without obtaining external financing. This fact is reflected in its current balance sheet, which contains no long-term debt. The liability and stockholders' equity sections of the balance sheet are shown below.

Liabilities		
Current Liabilities		$ 500,000
Stockholders' Equity		
Common Stock, $10 par value, 100,000 shares issued and outstanding	$1,000,000	
Paid-in Capital in Excess of Par Value, Common	1,800,000	
Retained Earnings	1,700,000	
Total Stockholders' Equity		4,500,000
Total Liabilities and Stockholders' Equity		$5,000,000

The company is now faced with the possibility of doubling its size by purchasing the operations of a rival company for $4,000,000. If the purchase goes through, Northeast will become the top company in its specialized industry in the northeastern part of the country. The problem for management is how to finance the purchase. After much study and discussion with bankers and underwriters, management prepares three financing alternatives to present to the board of directors, which must authorize the purchase and the financing.

Alternative A: The company could issue $4,000,000 of long-term debt. Given the company's financial rating and the current market rates, it is believed that the company will have to pay an interest rate of 17 percent on the debt.

Alternative B: The company could issue 40,000 shares of 12 percent, $100 par value preferred stock.

Alternative C: The company could issue 100,000 additional shares of $10 par value common stock at $40.

Management explains to the board that the interest on the long-term debt is tax deductible and that the applicable income tax rate is 40 percent. The board members know that a dividend of $.80 per share of common stock was paid last year, up from $.60 and $.40 per share in the two years before that. The board has had a policy of regular increases in dividends of $.20 per share. The board feels that each of the three financing alternatives is feasible and now wishes to study the financial effects of each alternative.

Required

1. Prepare a schedule to show how the liability and stockholders' equity side of Northeast Servotech's balance sheet will look under each alternative, and figure the debt to equity ratio (total liabilities ÷ total stockholders' equity) for each.
2. Compute and compare the cash needed to pay the interest or dividend for each kind of financing net of income taxes in the first year. How may this requirement change in future years?
3. Evaluate the alternatives, giving the arguments for and against each.

CHAPTER 13 RETAINED EARNINGS AND CORPORATE INCOME STATEMENTS

LEARNING OBJECTIVES

1. Define retained earnings, and prepare a statement of retained earnings.
2. Account for stock dividends and stock splits.
3. Account for treasury stock transactions.
4. Prepare a statement of stockholders' equity.
5. Calculate book value per share, and distinguish it from market value.
6. Account for the appropriation of retained earnings.
7. Show the relationships among income taxes expense, deferred income taxes, and net of taxes.
8. Describe the disclosure on the income statement of discontinued operations, extraordinary items, and accounting changes.
9. Compute earnings per share.

This chapter continues the study of the stockholders' equity section of the balance sheet. It first covers the retained earnings of a corporation, the transactions that affect them, and the statement of retained earnings. The rest of the chapter examines the components of the corporate income statement. After studying this chapter, you should be able to meet the learning objectives listed on the left.

Retained Earnings Transactions

Stockholders' equity, as presented earlier, has two parts: contributed capital and retained earnings. The **retained earnings** of a company are the part of the stockholders' equity that represents claims to assets arising from the earnings of the business. Retained earnings equal the profits of a company since the date of its beginning less any losses, dividends to stockholders, or transfers to contributed capital. Exhibit 13-1 shows a statement of retained earnings of Caprock Corporation for 19xx. The beginning balance of retained earnings of $854,000 is increased by net income of $76,000 and decreased by cash dividends of $30,000, so that the ending balance is $900,000. This statement may disclose other transactions that are explained in the chapter.

A credit balance in the Retained Earnings account is important because it shows the combined claims against total assets that have come from operations but have not been satisfied by payment of dividends to the company's stockholders. It is important to note that retained earnings are not the assets themselves, but the existence of retained earnings means that assets generated by profitable operations have been kept in the company to help it grow or to meet other business needs. Note, however, that a credit balance in Retained Earnings does *not* mean that cash or any designated set of assets is directly associated with retained earnings. The fact that earnings have been retained means that assets as a whole have been increased.

Retained Earnings may carry a debit balance. Generally, this happens when a company's losses and distributions to stockholders are greater than its profits from operations. In such a case, the firm is said to have a **deficit** (debit balance) in retained earnings. This is shown in the stockholders' equity section of the balance sheet as a deduction from contributed capital.

Exhibit 13-1. A Statement of Retained Earnings

Caprock Corporation Statement of Retained Earnings For the Year Ended December 31, 19xx	
Retained Earnings, January 1	$854,000
Net Income, 19xx	76,000
Subtotal	$930,000
Less Cash Dividend, Common	30,000
Retained Earnings, December 31	$900,000

OBJECTIVE 1
Define retained earnings, and prepare a statement of retained earnings

Accountants have used various terms for the retained earnings of a business. One term is *surplus,* which implies that there are excess assets available for dividends. This is poor terminology as the existence of retained earnings carries no connotation of "excess" or "surplus." Because of possible misinterpretation, the American Institute of Certified Public Accountants recommends more fitting terms, such as *retained income, retained earnings, accumulated earnings,* or *earnings retained for use in the business.*[1]

Prior period adjustments are events or transactions that relate to earlier accounting periods but were not determinable in the earlier period. When they occur, they are shown on the statement of retained earnings as an adjustment in the account's beginning balance. The Financial Accounting Standards Board identifies only two kinds of prior period adjustments. The first is to correct an error in the financial statements of a prior year. The second is needed if a company realizes an income tax gain from carrying forward a preacquisition operating loss of a purchased subsidiary.[2] Prior period adjustments are rare in accounting.

Stock Dividends

OBJECTIVE 2
Account for stock dividends and stock splits

A **stock dividend** is a proportional distribution of shares of the company's stock to the corporation's stockholders. The distribution of stock does not change the assets and liabilities of the firm because there is not a distribution of assets as in a cash dividend. The board of directors may declare a stock dividend for several reasons:

1. It may wish to give stockholders some evidence of the success of the company without paying a cash dividend, which would affect the firm's working capital position.
2. The board's aim may be to reduce the market price of the stock by increasing the number of shares outstanding, though this goal is more often met by stock splits.

1. Committee on Accounting Terminology, *Accounting Terminology Bulletin No. 1,* "Review and Resume" (New York: American Institute of Certified Public Accountants, 1953), par. 69.
2. *Statement of Financial Accounting Standards No. 16,* "Prior Period Adjustments" (Stamford, Conn.: Financial Accounting Standards Board, June 1977), par. 11.

3. It may want to make a nontaxable distribution to stockholders. Stock dividends that meet certain conditions are not considered income, so a tax is not levied on this type of transaction.
4. It communicates that the permanent capital of the company has increased by transferring an amount from retained earnings to contributed capital.

The total stockholders' equity is not affected by a stock dividend. The effect of a stock dividend is to transfer a dollar amount from the Retained Earnings account to the contributed capital section on the date of declaration. The amount to be transferred is the fair market value (usually market price) of the additional shares to be issued. The laws of most states state the minimum to be transferred under a stock dividend. This minimum is normally the minimum legal capital (par or stated value). However, generally accepted accounting principles state that market value reflects the economic effect of small stock distributions (less than 20 or 25 percent of a company's outstanding common stock) better than the par or stated value does. For this reason, the market price should be used for proper accounting of small stock dividends.[3]

To illustrate the accounting for a stock dividend, we will assume that Caprock Corporation has the following stockholders' equity structure:

Contributed Capital	
Common Stock—$5 par value, 100,000 shares authorized, 30,000 issued and outstanding	$ 150,000
Paid-in Capital in Excess of Par Value, Common	30,000
Total Contributed Capital	$ 180,000
Retained Earnings	900,000
Total Stockholders' Equity	$1,080,000

Assume further that the board of directors declares a 10 percent stock dividend on February 24, distributable on March 31 to stockholders of record on March 15. The market price of the stock on February 24 was $20 per share. The entries to record the dividend declaration and distribution are as follows:

Date of declaration

Feb. 24	Retained Earnings	60,000	
	Common Stock Distributable		15,000
	Paid-in Capital in Excess of Par Value, Common		45,000
	To record the declaration of a 10% stock dividend on common stock, distributable on March 31, to stockholders of record on March 15: 30,000 shares × 10% = 3,000 shares 3,000 shares × $20/share = $60,000 3,000 shares × $5/share = $15,000		

3. *Accounting Research and Terminology Bulletin No. 43* (New York: American Institute of Certified Public Accountants, 1953), Chapter 7, Section B, par. 10.

Date of record

Mar. 15 No entry

Date of distribution

Date	Account	Debit	Credit
Mar. 31	Common Stock Distributable	15,000	
	Common Stock		15,000
	To record the distribution of stock dividend of 3,000 shares		

The effect of the above stock dividend is to transfer permanently the market value of the stock, $60,000, from Retained Earnings to Contributed Capital and to increase the number of shares outstanding by 3,000. Common Stock Distributable is credited for the par value of the stock to be distributed (3,000 × $5 = $15,000). In addition, when the market value is greater than the par value of the stock, Paid-in Capital in Excess of Par Value, Common must be credited for the amount that market value exceeds par value. In this case, total market value of the stock dividend ($60,000) exceeds the total par value ($15,000) by $45,000. No entry is required on the date of record. On the distribution date, the common stock is issued by debiting Common Stock Distributable and crediting Common Stock for the par value of the stock ($15,000).

Common Stock Distributable is not a liability, because there is no obligation to distribute cash or other assets. The obligation is to distribute additional shares of capital stock. If financial statements are prepared between the date of declaration and the distribution, Common Stock Distributable should be reported as part of Contributed Capital, as follows:

Contributed Capital	
Common Stock—$5 par value, 100,000 shares authorized, 30,000 issued and outstanding	$ 150,000
Common Stock Distributable, 3,000 shares	15,000
Paid-in Capital in Excess of Par Value, Common	75,000
Total Contributed Capital	$ 240,000
Retained Earnings	840,000
Total Stockholders' Equity	$1,080,000

Three points can be made from this example. First, the total stockholders' equity is unchanged before and after the stock dividend. Second, the assets of the corporation are not reduced as in the case of a cash dividend. Third, the proportionate ownership in the corporation of any individual stockholder is unchanged before and after the stock dividend. To illustrate these points, we will assume that a stockholder owns 1,000 shares before the stock dividend. After the 10 percent stock dividend is distributed, this stockholder would own 1,100 shares.

Stockholders' Equity	Before Dividend	After Dividend
Common Stock	$ 150,000	$ 165,000
Paid-in Capital in Excess of Par Value	30,000	75,000
Total Contributed Capital	$ 180,000	$ 240,000
Retained Earnings	900,000	840,000
Total Stockholders' Equity	$1,080,000	$1,080,000
Shares Outstanding	30,000	33,000
Book Value per Share	$36.00	$32.73

Stockholder's Investment		
Shares owned	**1,000**	**1,100**
Percentage of ownership	3⅓%	3⅓%
Book value of investment (3⅓% × $1,080,000)	$36,000	$36,000

Both before and after the stock dividend, the stockholders' equity totals $1,080,000 and the stockholder owns 3⅓ percent of the company. Book value of the investment stays at $36,000.

All stock dividends have an effect on the market price of a company's stock. But some stock dividends are so large that they have a material effect on the price per share of the stock. For example, a 50 percent stock dividend would cause the market price of the stock to drop about 33 percent. The AICPA has arbitrarily decided that large stock dividends, those greater than 20 to 25 percent, should be accounted for by transferring the par or stated value of the stock on the date of declaration from Retained Earnings to Contributed Capital.[4]

Stock Splits

A **stock split** occurs when a corporation increases the number of issued shares of stock and reduces the par or stated value proportionally. A company may plan a stock split when it wishes to lower the market value per share of its stock and increase the liquidity of the stock. This action may be necessary if the market value per share has become so high that it hinders the trading of the company's stock on the market. For example, suppose that the Caprock Corporation has 30,000 shares of $5.00 par value stock outstanding. The market value is $70.00 per share. The corporation plans a 2 for 1 split. This split will lower the par value to $2.50 and increase the number of shares outstanding to 60,000. If a stockholder previously owned 400 shares of the $5.00 par stock, he or she would own 800 shares of the $2.50 par stock after the split. When a stock split occurs, the market value tends to fall in proportion to the

4. Ibid., par. 13.

increase in outstanding shares of stock. For example, a 2 for 1 stock split would cause the price of the stock to drop by approximately 50 percent to about $35.00. The lower price plus the increase in shares tends to promote the buying and selling of shares.

A stock split does not, in itself, increase the number of shares authorized. Nor does it change the balances in the stockholders' equity section. It simply changes the par value and number of shares outstanding. Therefore, an entry is not necessary. However, it is appropriate to document the change by making a memorandum entry in the general journal, as follows:

July 15 The 30,000 shares of $5 par value common stock that are issued and outstanding were split 2 for 1, resulting in 60,000 shares of $2.50 par value common stock issued and outstanding.

The change for the Caprock Corporation is shown below.

Before Stock Split

Contributed Capital	
Common Stock—$5 par value, 100,000 shares authorized, 30,000 issued and outstanding	$ 150,000
Paid-in Capital in Excess of Par Value, Common	30,000
Total Contributed Capital	$ 180,000
Retained Earnings	900,000
Total Stockholders' Equity	$1,080,000

After Stock Split

Contributed Capital	
Common Stock—$2.50 par value, 100,000 shares authorized, 60,000 issued and outstanding	$ 150,000
Paid-in Capital in Excess of Par Value, Common	30,000
Total Contributed Capital	$ 180,000
Retained Earnings	900,000
Total Stockholders' Equity	$1,080,000

In cases where the number of split shares will exceed the number of authorized shares, the board of directors will have to authorize additional shares at the time of the stock split.

Treasury Stock Transactions

OBJECTIVE 3 Account for treasury stock transactions

Treasury stock is capital stock, either common or preferred, that has been issued and reacquired by the issuing company but has not been reissued or retired. The company normally gets the stock back by purchasing the shares on the market or through donations by stockholders. There are several reasons why a company purchases its own stock. (1) It may want to have stock available to distribute to employees through stock option plans. (2) It may be trying to maintain a favorable market for the company's stock. (3) It may want to increase the company's earnings per share. (4) It may want to have additional shares of the company's stock available for such activities as purchasing other companies. (5) It may be used as a strategy to prevent a hostile takeover of the company.

The effect of a treasury stock purchase is to reduce the assets and stockholders' equity of the company. It is not considered a purchase of assets, as purchase of the shares in another company would be. The treasury stock is capital stock that has been issued but is no longer outstanding. Treasury shares may be held for an indefinite period of time, reissued, or retired. Thus treasury stock is somewhat similar to unissued stock. That is, it has no rights until the stock is reissued. Treasury stock does not have voting rights, preemptive rights, rights to cash dividends, or rights to share in assets during liquidation of the company and it is not considered to be outstanding in the calculation of book value. However, there is one major difference between unissued shares and treasury shares. If a share of stock was originally issued at par value or greater and fully paid for, and then reacquired as treasury stock, it may be reissued at less than par value without a discount liability attaching to it.

Purchase of Treasury Stock. When treasury stock is purchased, it is normally recorded at cost. The transaction reduces both the assets and stockholders' equity of the firm. For example, assume that the Caprock Corporation purchases 1,000 shares of its common stock on the market at a price of $50 per share. The purchase would be recorded as follows:

Sept. 15	Treasury Stock, Common	50,000	
	Cash		50,000
	Acquired 1,000 shares of company's common stock for $50 per share		

Note that the treasury shares were recorded at cost. Any par value, stated value, or original issue price of the stock was ignored.

The stockholders' equity section of Caprock's balance sheet shows the cost of the treasury stock as a deduction from the total of Contributed Capital and Retained Earnings, as follows:

Contributed Capital	
Common Stock—$5 par value, 100,000 shares authorized, **30,000 shares issued, 29,000 shares outstanding**	$ 150,000
Paid-in Capital in Excess of Par Value, Common	30,000
Total Contributed Capital	$ 180,000
Retained Earnings	900,000
Total Contributed Capital and Retained Earnings	$1,080,000
Less Treasury Stock, Common (1,000 shares at Cost)	50,000
Total Stockholders' Equity	$1,030,000

Note that the number of shares issued has not changed although the number of outstanding shares has decreased as a result of the transaction.

Reissuance of Treasury Stock. The treasury shares may be reissued at cost, above cost, or below cost. For example, assume that the 1,000 treasury shares of the Caprock Corporation are sold for $50 per share. The entry to record this transaction is

Nov. 15	Cash	50,000	
	Treasury Stock, Common		50,000
	Reissued 1,000 shares of treasury stock for $50 per share		

When treasury shares are sold for an amount greater than their cost, the excess of the sales price over cost should be credited to Paid-in Capital, Treasury Stock. No gain should be recorded. For example, suppose that the 1,000 treasury shares of the Caprock Corporation are sold for $60 per share. The entry for the reissue would be

Nov. 15	Cash	60,000	
	Treasury Stock, Common		50,000
	Paid-in Capital, Treasury Stock		10,000
	To record the sale of 1,000 shares of treasury stock for $60 per share; cost was $50 per share		

If the treasury shares are reissued below their cost, the difference should be deducted from Paid-in Capital, Treasury Stock. When this account does not exist or is insufficient to cover the excess of cost over reissuance price, Retained Earnings should absorb the excess. No loss should be recorded. For example, suppose that on September 15 the Caprock Corporation bought 1,000 shares of its common stock on the market at a price of $50 per share. The company sold 400 shares of its stock on October 15 for $60 per share and the remaining 600 shares on December 15 for $42 per share. The entries to record these transactions are presented below.

Sept. 15	Treasury Stock, Common	50,000	
	Cash		50,000
	To record the purchase of 1,000 shares of treasury stock at $50 per share		
Oct. 15	Cash	24,000	
	Treasury Stock, Common		20,000
	Paid-in Capital, Treasury Stock		4,000
	To record the sale of 400 shares of treasury stock for $60 per share; cost was $50 per share		

Dec. 15	Cash	25,200	
	Paid-in Capital, Treasury Stock	4,000	
	Retained Earnings	800	
	Treasury Stock, Common		30,000
	To record sale of 600 shares of treasury stock for $42 per share; cost was $50 per share		

In the December 15 entry, Retained Earnings is debited for $800 because the 600 shares were sold for $4,800 less than cost. That amount is $800 greater than the $4,000 of paid-in capital generated by the sale of the 400 shares on October 15.

Retirement of Treasury Stock. If a company determines that it will not reissue stock it has purchased, it may, with the approval of its stockholders, decide to retire the stock. When shares of stock are retired, all items related to those shares should be removed from the related capital accounts. When stock that cost less than the original contributed capital is retired, the difference is recognized as Paid-in Capital, Retirement of Stock. However, if stock that cost more than was received when the shares were first issued is retired, the difference is a reduction in stockholders' equity and is debited to Retained Earnings. For instance, suppose that instead of reissuing the 1,000 shares of treasury stock purchased for $50,000, Caprock decides to retire the shares. Assuming the $5 par value common stock was originally issued at $6 per share, the entry to record the retirement is

Nov. 15	Common Stock	5,000	
	Paid in Capital in Excess of Par Value	1,000	
	Retained Earnings	44,000	
	Treasury Stock		50,000
	To record the retirement of 1,000 shares that cost $50 per share and were originally issued at $6 per share		

Statement of Stockholders' Equity

OBJECTIVE 4
Prepare a statement of stockholders' equity

The **statement of stockholders' equity** summarizes the changes in the components of the stockholders' equity section of the balance sheet. Companies are increasingly using this statement in place of the statement of retained earnings because it reveals much more about the year's stockholders' equity transactions. In Exhibit 13-2, for example, note that in the Tri-State Corporation's statement of stockholders' equity, the first line contains the beginning balances of each account in the stockholders' equity section. Each additional line in the statement discloses the effects of transactions that affect the accounts. It is possible to determine from this statement that during 19x2 Tri-State Corporation issued common stock, had a conversion of preferred stock into common stock, declared and issued a stock dividend on common stock, had a net purchase of

Exhibit 13-2. A Statement of Stockholders' Equity

Tri-State Corporation
Statement of Stockholders' Equity
For the Year Ended December 31, 19x2

	$100 Par Value Convertible, 8% Preferred Stock	$10 Par Value Common Stock	Paid-In Capital in Excess of Par Value	Retained Earnings	Treasury Stock	Total
Balance, December 31, 19x1	$400,000	$300,000	$300,000	$600,000	-0-	$1,600,000
Issuance of 5,000 Shares of Common Stock		50,000	200,000			250,000
Conversion of 1,000 Shares of Preferred Stock into 3,000 Shares of Common Stock	(100,000)	30,000	70,000			-0-
10 Percent Stock Dividend on Common Stock, 3,800 Shares		38,000	152,000	(190,000)		-0-
Purchase of 500 Shares of Treasury Stock					(24,000)	(24,000)
Net Income				270,000		270,000
Cash Dividends						
Preferred Stock				(33,000)		(33,000)
Common Stock				(38,600)		(38,600)
Balance, December 31, 19x2	$300,000	$418,000	$722,000	$608,400	($24,000)	$2,024,400

treasury shares, earned net income of $270,000, and paid cash dividends on both preferred and common stock. The ending balances of the accounts are presented at the bottom of the statement. Also, note that the Retained Earnings column has the same components as would the statement of retained earnings, if it were prepared separately.

Stock Values

The word *value* is associated with shares of stock in several ways. The terms *par value* and *stated value* have already been explained. They are each values per share that establish the legal capital of a company. Par value or stated value is arbitrarily set when the stock is authorized. Neither has any relationship to the book value or to the market value.

Book Value

OBJECTIVE 5
Calculate book value per share, and distinguish it from market value

The **book value** of a company's stock represents the total assets of the company less liabilities. Thus it is simply the owners' equity of the company or, to look at it another way, the company's net assets. The book value per share, therefore, represents the equity of the owner of one share of stock in the net assets of the corporation. This value, of course, does not necessarily equal the amount the shareholders would receive if the company were sold or liquidated. It is probably different, because most assets are recorded at historical cost, not at the current value at which they could be sold. To learn the book value per share when the company has only common stock outstanding, divide the total stockholders' equity by the total common shares outstanding. In computing shares outstanding, shares subscribed but not issued are included, but treasury stock (shares previously issued now held by the company) are not included. For example, on page 485, Caprock Corporation has total stockholders' equity of $1,030,000 and 29,000 shares outstanding after showing the purchase of treasury shares. The book value per share of Caprock's common stock is $35.52 ($1,030,000 ÷ 29,000 shares).

If a company has both preferred and common stock, the determination of book value per share is not so simple. The general rule is that the call value (or par value, if a call value is not specified) of the preferred stock plus any dividends in arrears is subtracted from total stockholders' equity to figure the equity pertaining to common stock. As an illustration, refer to the statement of stockholders' equity for Tri-State Corporation in Exhibit 13-2. Assuming there are no dividends in arrears and the preferred stock is callable at 105, the equity pertaining to common stock is figured as:

Total stockholders' equity	$2,024,400
Less equity allocated to preferred shareholders ($105 × 3,000 shares)	315,000
Equity pertaining to common shareholders	**$1,709,400**

There are 41,300 shares of common stock outstanding (41,800 shares issued less 500 shares of treasury stock). The book values per share would be as follows:

Preferred Stock: $315,000 ÷ 3,000 shares = $105 per share
Common Stock: $1,709,400 ÷ 41,300 shares = $41.39 per share

If we assume the same facts except that the preferred stock is cumulative and that one year of dividends is in arrears, the stockholders' equity would be allocated as follows:

Total Stockholders' Equity		$2,024,400
Less: Call value of outstanding preferred shares	$315,000	
Dividends in arrears (8% × $300,000)	24,000	
Equity allocated to preferred shareholders		**339,000**
Equity pertaining to common shareholders		**$1,685,400**

The book values per share under this assumption are:

Preferred Stock: $339,000 ÷ 3,000 shares = $113 per share
Common Stock: $1,685,400 ÷ 41,300 shares = $40.81 per share

Undeclared preferred dividends on cumulative preferred stock fall into arrears on the last day of the fiscal year (the date when the financial statements are prepared). Also, dividends in arrears do not apply to unissued preferred stock.

Market Value

The **market value** is the price that investors are willing to pay for a share of stock on the open market. While the book value is based on historical cost, the market value is usually determined by investors' expectations for the particular company and general economic conditions. That is, what people expect about the company's future profitability and dividends per share, how risky they view the company and its current financial condition, as well as the state of the money market, all will play a part in determining the market value of a corporation's stock. Although the book value per share often has little relationship to the market value per share, some investors use the relationship of the two measures as rough indicators of relative values of shares. For example, in July 1986 one major oil company, Texaco, had a market value per share of $31 compared with a book value per share of $55. At the same time, another large oil company, Exxon, had a market value per share of $61 and a book value per share of $40.

Appropriation of Retained Earnings

OBJECTIVE 6
Account for the appropriation of retained earnings

A corporation may wish to divide the Retained Earnings account into two parts: appropriated and unappropriated retained earnings. The reason for appropriating retained earnings is to separate a part of the Retained Earnings account on the balance sheet to give more information to the readers of the company's financial statements. When readers see **appropriated retained earnings** on the balance sheet, they know that some of the company's assets are to be used or set aside for purposes other than paying dividends.

Only the board of directors may appropriate retained earnings. The following are several reasons why it might do so:

1. A contractual agreement. For example, bond indentures may place a limitation on the dividends to be paid by the company.
2. State law. Many states will not allow dividends or the purchase of treasury stock to the extent of the impairment of the capital of a company.
3. Voluntary action by the board of directors. Many times a board will decide to retain assets in the business for future needs. For example, the company may be planning to build a new plant and may wish to show that dividends will be limited to save enough money for the

building. The company may also appropriate retained earnings to show the possible future loss of assets resulting from a lawsuit.

There are two ways of reporting retained earnings appropriations to readers of financial statements. First, the appropriation of retained earnings may be shown by a journal entry that transfers the appropriated amounts from Retained Earnings to another stockholders' equity account that is more descriptive, such as Retained Earnings Appropriated for Plant Expansion. Second, the report of appropriated retained earnings may be made by means of a note to the financial statements.

To illustrate the first case, assume the board of directors of Caprock Corporation recognizes the need to expand the company's plant capacity in the next two years. After studying several ideas, the board chooses to expand by retaining assets generated by earnings in the amount of $300,000. It acts on July 1, 19x2, to appropriate retained earnings in this amount. The entry to record the board's action is as follows:

July 1	Retained Earnings	300,000	
	Retained Earnings Appropriated for Plant Expansion		300,000
	To record the appropriation of retained earnings for plant expansion according to action of the board of directors on July 1, 19x2		

This transaction does not change the total retained earnings or stockholders' equity of the company. It simply divides retained earnings into two parts, appropriated and unappropriated. The appropriated part shows that assets in that amount are being used or will be used for the expansion. The unappropriated amount represents earnings kept in the business that could be used for dividends and other purposes. The division of retained earnings in Caprock's stockholders' equity section is:

Contributed Capital		
Common Stock—$5 par value, 100,000 shares authorized, 30,000 shares issued and outstanding		$ 150,000
Paid-in Capital in Excess of Par Value, Common		30,000
Total Contributed Capital		$ 180,000
Retained Earnings		
Appropriated for Plant Expansion	$300,000	
Unappropriated	600,000	
Total Retained Earnings		900,000
Total Stockholders' Equity		$1,080,000

The same facts about retained earnings appropriations could also be presented by reference to a note to the financial statements. For example:

Retained Earnings (Note 15)	$900,000

Note 15:
Because of plans for expanding the capacity of the clothing division, the board of directors has restricted retained earnings available for dividends by $300,000.

When the conditions for the appropriation are no longer present, the amount of the restriction should be transferred back to Unappropriated Retained Earnings. In fact, the only charge to an Appropriated Retained Earnings account is the one to transfer the balance back to Unappropriated Retained Earnings. For example, suppose that after two years Caprock finished the expansion of its plant at a cost of $325,000. The restriction of $300,000 on retained earnings is no longer needed. So the board acts on July 20, 19x4, to return the appropriated retained earnings to Unappropriated Retained Earnings. The entries to record the plant expansion and the transfer of retained earnings would be as follows:

July 20	Property, Plant, and Equipment	325,000	
	Cash		325,000
	To record the payment of $325,000 for plant expansion		
20	Retained Earnings Appropriated for Plant Expansion	300,000	
	Retained Earnings		300,000
	To eliminate appropriated retained earnings for plant expansion, according to the board of directors' action on July 20, 19x4		

Note that the appropriation of retained earnings does not restrict cash in any way. It simply explains to the readers of the financial statements that a certain amount of assets generated by earnings will remain in the business for the purpose stated. It is still management's job to make sure that there is enough cash or assets on hand to satisfy the restriction, and the removal of the restriction does not necessarily mean that the board of directors will now be able to declare a dividend.

Corporate Income Statements

This chapter and the one before it have shown how certain transactions are reflected in the stockholders' equity section of the corporate balance sheet, in the statement of stockholders' equity, and in the retained earnings statement. Chapter 27 deals with the statement of cash flows. The following sections will briefly describe some of the features of the corporate income statement.

The format of the income statement has not been specified by the accounting profession because flexibility has been considered more important than a standard income statement. Either the single-step or multistep form may be used (see Chapter 5). However, the accounting profession has taken the position that income for a period shall be an all-inclusive or **comprehensive income**.[5] This rule means that income or

5. *Statement of Financial Accounting Concepts No. 6,* "Elements of Financial Statements" (Stamford, Conn.: Financial Accounting Standards Board, 1985), pars. 70–77.

loss for a period should include all revenues, expenses, gains, and losses of the period, except for prior period adjustments. This approach to the measurement of income has resulted in several items being added to the income statement. These items include discontinued operations, extraordinary items, and accounting changes. In addition, earnings per share figures should be disclosed. Exhibit 13-3 illustrates the corporate income statement and the disclosures required. The following sections discuss these components of the corporate income statement, beginning with income taxes expense.

Exhibit 13-3. A Corporate Income Statement

Junction Corporation
Income Statement
For the Year Ended December 31, 19xx

Revenues			$925,000
Less Costs and Expenses			500,000
Income from Continuing Operations Before Taxes			$425,000
Income Taxes Expense			119,000
Income from Continuing Operations			$306,000
Discontinued Operations			
Income from Operations of Discontinued Segment (net of taxes, $35,000)		$90,000	
Loss on Disposal of Segment (net of taxes, $42,000)		(73,000)	17,000
Income Before Extraordinary Items and Cumulative Effect of Accounting Change			$323,000
Extraordinary Gain (net of taxes, $17,000)			43,000
Subtotal			$366,000
Cumulative Effect of a Change in Accounting Principle (net of taxes, $5,000)			(6,000)
Net Income			$360,000
Earnings per Common Share:			
Income from Continuing Operations	$3.06		
Discontinued Operations	.17		
Income Before Extraordinary Items	$3.23		
Extraordinary Gain (net of taxes)	.43		
Cumulative Effect of Accounting Change (net of taxes)	(.06)		
Net Income	$3.60		

Income Taxes Expense

OBJECTIVE 7
Show the relationships among income taxes expense, deferred income taxes, and net of taxes

Corporations determine their taxable income (the amount on which taxes will be paid) by subtracting allowable business deductions from includable gross income. The federal tax laws determine what business deductions are allowed and what must be included in gross income.[6]

The tax rates that apply to a corporation's taxable income are shown in Table 13-1. A corporation with a taxable income of $70,000 would have a federal income tax liability of $12,500. This amount is computed by adding $7,500 (the tax on the first $50,000 of taxable income) to $5,000 (25 percent times the $20,000 earned in excess of $50,000).

Income Taxes Expense is the expense recognized in the accounting records on an accrual basis to be applicable to income from continuing operations. This amount may or may not be equal to the amount of taxes actually paid by the corporation, an amount that is determined on the basis of the income tax code. For most small businesses it is convenient to keep their accounting records on the same basis as their tax records so that the income taxes expense on the income statement equals the income taxes liability to be paid to the Internal Revenue Service (IRS). This practice is usually acceptable when there is not a material difference between the income on an accounting basis and income on an income tax basis. However, the purpose of accounting is to determine net income in accordance with generally accepted accounting principles, whereas the purpose of the tax code is to determine taxable income and tax liability.

Management has an incentive to use methods for the purposes that will minimize the tax liability, but accountants, who are bound by accrual accounting and the materiality concept, cannot let the tax procedures dictate the method of preparing financial statements if the result is misleading. As a consequence, a material difference can occur between accounting and taxable incomes, especially in larger businesses. This difference in accounting and taxable incomes may result from a difference

Table 13-1. Tax Rate Schedule for Corporations

Taxable Income		Tax Liability	
Over	But Not Over		Of the Amount Over
—	$ 50,000	0 + 15%	—
$ 50,000	75,000	$ 7,500 + 25%	$ 50,000
75,000	100,000	13,750 + 34%	75,000
100,000	335,000	22,250 + 39%	100,000
335,000	—	113,900 + 34%	335,000

6. Rules for calculating and reporting taxable income in specialized industries such as banking, insurance, mutual funds, and cooperatives are highly technical and may vary significantly from those shown in this chapter.

in the timing of the recognition of revenues and expenses because of different methods used in determining the respective incomes. Some possible alternatives are shown below.

	Accounting Method	Tax Method
Revenue Recognition	Point of sale	Installment
Expense Recognition	Accrual or deferral	At time of expenditure
Inventories	Average-cost	FIFO
Depreciation	Straight-line	Accelerated cost recovery system (see Chapter 10)

Accounting for the difference between income taxes expense based on accounting income and the actual income taxes payable based on taxable income is accomplished by an accounting technique called **income tax allocation.** The amount by which income taxes expense differs from income taxes payable is reconciled in an account called **Deferred Income Taxes.** For example, if the Junction Corporation had income taxes expense of $119,000 shown on the income statement and actual income taxes payable to the IRS of $92,000, the entry to record the Income Taxes Expense applicable to income from continuing operations using the income tax allocation procedure would be as follows:

Dec. 31	Income Taxes Expense	119,000	
	Income Taxes Payable		92,000
	Deferred Income Taxes		27,000
	To record current and deferred income taxes		

Proponents of the income tax allocation procedure argue that this procedure is in accordance with the matching rule because the expense is directly related to the reported income for the period.

Presumably in a future year as the timing differences in accounting procedures change, the income taxes payable determined on IRS taxable income will exceed income taxes expense determined on GAAP accounting, and the deferred income taxes will become payable. When that situation occurs, the Deferred Income Taxes account will be debited because Income Taxes Payable will exceed Income Taxes Expense.

In any given year the amount of income taxes actually paid by a company may be determined by subtracting (or adding as the case may be) the Deferred Income Taxes for that year (as reported in the notes to the financial statements) from (or to) the Income Taxes Expense reported on the income statement.

Whether or not the Deferred Income Taxes credit balance is classified as a current or long-term liability depends on the classification of the asset or liability that gave rise to the timing difference.[7] For example, if the timing difference were due to different inventory methods, the

7. *Statement of Financial Accounting Standards No. 37,* "Balance Sheet Classifications of Deferred Income Taxes" (Stamford, Conn.: Financial Accounting Standards Board, 1980).

deferred tax liability would be classified as a current liability because inventory is classified as a current asset on the balance sheet. If the difference arose from different depreciation methods of plant assets, it would be a long-term liability because plant assets are long-term assets.

Some understanding of the importance of deferred income taxes to financial reporting may be gained from studying the financial statements of six hundred large companies surveyed in a recent year. Of those companies over 90 percent reported some sort of deferred taxes. Of that 90 percent, about 84 percent reported Deferred Income Taxes with a credit balance in the noncurrent long-term liability section.[8]

Net of Taxes

The phrase **net of taxes,** as used in Exhibit 13-3 and in the discussion below, means that the effect of applicable taxes (usually income taxes) has been considered when determining the overall effect of the item on the financial statements. The phrase is used on the corporate income statement when a company has items (such as those explained below) that must be disclosed in a separate section of the income statement. Each of these items should be reported at net of the income taxes applicable to that item to avoid distorting the net operating income figure. For example, assume that a corporation with $80,000 operating income before taxes has a total tax liability of $70,000 based on taxable income, including a capital gain of $100,000, on which a tax of $30,000 is due. Assume also that the gain is an extraordinary item (see Extraordinary Items, page 497) and must be disclosed as such. Thus,

Operating Income Before Taxes	$ 80,000
Income Taxes Expense **(actual taxes are $70,000, of which $30,000 is applicable to extraordinary gain)**	40,000
Income Before Extraordinary Item	$ 40,000
Extraordinary Gain (net of taxes) **($100,000 − $30,000)**	70,000
Net Income	$110,000

If all the taxes payable were deducted from operating income before taxes, both the income before extraordinary items and the extraordinary gain would be distorted. A company follows the same procedure in the case of an extraordinary loss. For example, assume the same facts as above except that total tax liability is only $10,000 because of a $100,000 extraordinary loss, which results in a $30,000 tax saving, as shown below.

Operating Income Before Taxes	$ 80,000
Income Taxes Expense **(actual taxes of $10,000 as a result of an extraordinary loss)**	40,000
Income Before Extraordinary Item	$ 40,000
Extraordinary Loss (net of taxes) **($100,000 − $30,000)**	(70,000)
Net Loss	$(30,000)

8. *Accounting Trends and Techniques* (New York: American Institute of Certified Public Accountants, 1985), p. 197.

If we apply these ideas to Junction Corporation in Exhibit 13-3, the total of the income tax items is $124,000. This amount is allocated among five statement components, as follows:

Income Taxes Expense on Income from Continuing Operations	$119,000
Income Tax on Income of Discontinued Segment	35,000
Income Tax Saving on Loss on Disposal of Segment	(42,000)
Income Tax on Extraordinary Gain	17,000
Income Tax Saving on Cumulative Effect of Change in Accounting Principle	(5,000)
Total Income Taxes Expense	$124,000

Discontinued Operations

OBJECTIVE 8 Describe the disclosure on the income statement of discontinued operations, extraordinary items, and accounting changes

Large companies in the United States usually have many segments. A segment of a business may be a separate major line of business or a separate class of customer. For example, a company that makes heavy drilling equipment may also have another line of business, such as mobile homes. These large companies may discontinue or otherwise dispose of certain segments of their business that are not profitable. **Discontinued operations** are segments that are no longer part of the ongoing operations of the business. Generally accepted accounting principles require that gains and losses from discontinued operations be reported separately in the income statement. The reasoning for the separate disclosure requirement is that the income statement will be more useful in evaluating the ongoing activities of the business if results from continuing operations are reported separately from discontinued operations. In a recent year, 74 (12 percent) of six hundred large companies reported losses from discontinued operations on the income statement.[9]

In Exhibit 13-3, the disclosure of discontinued operations has two parts. One part shows that the income during the year from operations of the segment of business that has been disposed of (or will be disposed of) to the decision date to discontinue was $90,000 (net of $35,000 taxes). The other part shows that the loss from disposal of the segment of business was $73,000 (net of $42,000 tax savings). The computation of the gains or losses will be covered in more advanced accounting courses. The disclosure has been described, however, to give a complete view of the content of the corporate income statement.

Extraordinary Items

The Accounting Principles Board, in its *Opinion No. 30,* defines **extraordinary items** as those "events or transactions that are distinguished by their unusual nature *and* by the infrequency of their occurrence."[10] As stated in the definition, the major criteria for these items are that they must be unusual and must not happen very often. Unusual and infrequent occurrences are explained in the opinion as follows:

9. Ibid., p. 239.
10. Accounting Principles Board, *Opinion No. 30,* "Reporting the Results of Operations" (New York: American Institute of Certified Public Accountants, 1973), par. 20.

Unusual Nature—the underlying event or transaction should possess a high degree of abnormality and be of a type clearly unrelated to, or only incidentally related to, the ordinary and typical activities of the entity, taking into account the environment in which the entity operates.

Infrequency of Occurrence—the underlying event or transaction should be of a type that would not reasonably be expected to recur in the foreseeable future, taking into account the environment in which the entity operates.[11]

If these items are both unusual and infrequent (and material in amount), they should be reported separately from continuing operations on the income statement. This disclosure will allow the reader of the statement to identify those gains or losses shown in the computation of income that would not be expected to happen again soon. Examples of items that usually are treated as extraordinary are (1) uninsured losses from floods, earthquakes, fires, and theft; (2) gains and losses resulting from the passing of a new law; (3) expropriation (taking) of property by a foreign government; and (4) gains or losses from early retirement of debt. These items should be reported in the income statement after discontinued operations. Also, the gain or loss should be shown net of applicable taxes. In a recent year, 74 (12 percent) of six hundred large companies reported extraordinary items on the income statement.[12] In Exhibit 13-3, the extraordinary gain was $43,000 after applicable taxes of $17,000.

Accounting Changes

Consistency, one of the basic conventions of accounting, means that, for accounting purposes, companies apply the same accounting principles from year to year. However, a company is allowed to make accounting changes if current procedures are incorrect or inappropriate. For example, a change from the FIFO to the LIFO inventory method may be made if there is adequate justification for the change. Adequate justification usually means that, if the change occurs, the financial statements will better show the financial activities of the company. A company's desire to lower the amount of income taxes to be paid is not seen as an adequate justification for an accounting change. If justification does exist and an accounting change is made during an accounting period, generally accepted accounting principles require disclosure of the change.

The cumulative effect of an accounting change is the effect that the new accounting principle would have had on net income of prior periods if it, instead of the old principle, had been applied in past years and is shown on the income statement immediately after extraordinary items.[13] For example, assume that for the prior five years the Junction Corporation has used the straight-line method in depreciating its machinery. The company changes to the sum-of-the-years'-digits method of depreciation this year. The following depreciation charges (net of taxes) were arrived at by the controller:

11. Ibid.
12. *Accounting Trends and Techniques* (New York: American Institute of Certified Public Accountants, 1985), p. 295.
13. Accounting Principles Board, *Opinion No. 20*, "Accounting Changes" (New York: American Institute of Certified Public Accountants, July 1971).

Cumulative, 5-year sum-of-the-years'-digits depreciation	$16,000
Less cumulative, 5-year straight-line depreciation	10,000
Cumulative effect of accounting change	$ 6,000

Relevant information about the accounting change is shown in the notes to the financial statements. The $6,000 difference (net of applicable income taxes) is the cumulative effect of the change in depreciation methods. The change results in an additional $6,000 depreciation expense for prior years being deducted in the current year in addition to the current year's depreciation costs included in the $500,000 costs and expenses section of the Income Statement. It must be shown in the current year's income statement as a reduction in income (see Exhibit 13-3). In a recent year, 83 (14 percent) of six hundred large companies reported changes in accounting procedures.[14] Further study of accounting changes is left up to more advanced accounting courses.

Earnings per Share

OBJECTIVE 9
Compute earnings per share

Readers of financial statements use earnings per share information to judge the performance of the company and to compare its performance with that of other companies. The Accounting Principles Board recognized the importance of this information in its *Opinion No. 15*. There it concluded that earnings per share of common stock should be presented on the face of the income statement.[15] As shown in Exhibit 13-3, the information is generally disclosed just below the net income figure. An earnings per share amount is always shown for (1) income from continuing operations, (2) income before extraordinary items and cumulative effect of accounting changes, (3) cumulative effect of accounting changes, and (4) net income. If the statement has a gain or loss from discontinued operations or a gain or loss on extraordinary items, earnings per share amounts may also be presented for these items.

A basic earnings per share amount is found when a company has only common stock and the same number of shares outstanding during the year. For example, it is assumed in Exhibit 13-3 that Junction Corporation, with a net income of $360,000, had 100,000 shares of common stock outstanding for the entire year. The earnings per share of common stock were computed as follows:

$$\text{earnings per share} = \frac{\text{net income}}{\text{shares outstanding}}$$

$$= \frac{\$360{,}000}{100{,}000 \text{ shares}}$$

$$= \$3.60 \text{ per share}$$

If, however, the number of shares outstanding changes during the year,

14. *Accounting Trends and Techniques* (New York: American Institute of Certified Public Accountants, 1985), p. 401.
15. Accounting Principles Board, *Opinion No. 15,* "Earnings per Share" (New York: American Institute of Certified Public Accountants, May 1969), par. 12.

it is necessary to figure a weighted-average number of shares outstanding for the year. Let us now suppose some different facts about Junction Corporation's outstanding shares. Let us assume that the common shares outstanding during various periods of the year were as follows: January–March, 100,000 shares; April–September, 120,000 shares; October–December, 130,000 shares. The weighted-average number of common shares outstanding and earnings per share would be found as shown:

100,000 shares × ¼ year	25,000
120,000 shares × ½ year	60,000
130,000 shares × ¼ year	32,500
Weighted-average shares outstanding	117,500

$$\text{Earnings per share} = \frac{\$360{,}000}{117{,}500 \text{ shares}}$$

$$= \$3.06 \text{ per share}$$

If a company has nonconvertible preferred stock outstanding, the dividend for this stock must be subtracted from net income before computing earnings per share for common stock. If we suppose that Junction Corporation has preferred stock on which the annual dividend is $23,500, earnings per share on common stock would be $2.86 [($360,000 − $23,500) ÷ 117,500 shares].

Companies with a capital structure in which there are no bonds, stocks, or stock options that could be converted into common stock are said to have a **simple capital structure**. The earnings per share for these companies are computed as shown above. Many companies, however, have a **complex capital structure**, which includes convertible stock and bonds. These convertible securities have the potential of diluting the earnings per share of common stock. Potential dilution means that a person's proportionate share of ownership in the company may be reduced by an increase in total shares outstanding through a conversion of stocks, bonds, or stock options. For example, suppose that a person owns 10,000 shares of a company, which equals 2 percent of the outstanding shares of 500,000. Now suppose that holders of convertible bonds convert the bonds into 100,000 shares of stock. The person's 10,000 shares would then be only 1.67 percent (10,000 ÷ 600,000) of the outstanding shares. In addition, the added shares outstanding would result in lower earnings per share and most likely a lower market price per share.

Since stock options and convertible preferred stocks or bonds have the potential to dilute earnings per share, they are referred to as **potentially dilutive securities**. A special subset of these convertible securities is called **common stock equivalents** because these securities are considered to be most like common stock. A convertible stock or bond is considered a common stock equivalent if the conversion feature is an important part of determining its original issue price. Special rules are applied by the accountant to determine if a convertible stock or bond is a common stock equivalent. A stock option, on the other hand, is by definition a common stock equivalent. The significance of common stock equivalents is that, when they exist, they are used in the earnings per share calculations explained in the next paragraph.

When a company has a complex capital structure, instead of presenting a single earnings per share figure, it must present two figures. The company must report a **primary earnings per share** and a **fully diluted earnings per share**. Primary earnings per share are calculated by including in the denominator the total of weighted-average common shares outstanding and common stock equivalents. On the other hand, fully diluted earnings per share are calculated by including in the denominator the total of all potentially dilutive securities, including common stock equivalents, and the weighted-average common shares of shares outstanding. The latter figure thus shows stockholders the maximum potential effect of dilution of their ownership in the company. An example of this disclosure is as follows:

	19x2	19x1
Net Income	$280,000	$200,000
Earnings per Share of Common Stock		
Primary	$2.25	$1.58
Fully Diluted	$2.00	$1.43

The computation of these figures is a complex process reserved for more advanced courses.

Chapter Review

Review of Learning Objectives

1. **Define retained earnings, and prepare a statement of retained earnings.**
Retained earnings are the part of stockholders' equity that comes from retaining assets earned in business operations. They are the claims of the stockholders against the assets of the company that arise from profitable operations. This account is different from contributed capital, which represents the claims against assets brought about by the initial and later investments by the stockholders. Both are claims against the general assets of the company, not against any specific assets that may have been set aside. It is important not to confuse the assets themselves with the claims against the assets. The statement of retained earnings will always show the beginning and ending balance of retained earnings, net income or loss, and cash dividends. It may also show prior period adjustments, stock dividends, and other transactions affecting retained earnings.

2. **Account for stock dividends and stock splits.**
A stock dividend is a distribution of shares by a corporation to its stockholders in proportion to the number of shares of stock held by each owner. A summary of the key dates and accounting treatment of stock dividends follows:

Key Date	Stock Dividend
Declaration date	Debit Retained Earnings for the market value of the stock to be distributed and credit Common Stock Distributable (par value) and Paid-in Capital in Excess of Par Value for the excess of market value over the stock's par value.
Record date	No entry.
Payment date	Debit Common Stock Distributable and credit Common Stock for the par value of the stock that was distributed.

A stock split is usually undertaken to reduce the market value and improve the liquidity of a company's stock. Since there is normally a decrease in the par value of the stock proportionate to the number of additional shares issued, there is no effect on the dollar amounts in the stockholders' equity accounts. The split should be recorded in the general journal by a memorandum entry only.

3. **Account for treasury stock transactions.**

The treasury stock of a company is stock that has been issued and reacquired but not reissued or retired. A company acquires its own stock for reasons such as creating stock option plans, maintaining a favorable market for the stock, increasing earnings per share, and purchasing other companies. Treasury stock is similar to unissued stock in that it does not have rights until it is reissued. However, treasury stock can be resold at less than par value without incurring a discount liability. The accounting treatment for treasury stock is summarized below.

Treasury Stock Transaction	Accounting Treatment
Purchase of treasury stock	Debit Treasury Stock and credit Cash for the cost of the shares.
Reissuance of treasury stock at cost	Debit Cash and credit Treasury Stock for the cost of the shares.
Reissuance of treasury stock at an amount greater than the cost of the shares	Debit Cash for the reissue price of the shares and credit Treasury Stock for the cost of the shares and Paid-in Capital, Treasury Stock for the excess.
Reissuance of treasury stock at an amount less than the cost of the shares	Debit Cash for the reissue price; debit Paid-in Capital, Treasury Stock for the difference between reissue price and the cost of the shares; and credit Treasury Stock for the cost of the shares. If Paid-in Capital, Treasury Stock does not exist or is not large enough to cover the difference, Retained Earnings should absorb the difference.

4. **Prepare a statement of stockholders' equity.**
   The statement of stockholders' equity shows the changes during the year in each component of the stockholders' equity section of the balance sheet.

5. **Calculate book value per share, and distinguish it from market value.**
   Book value per share is the owners' equity per share. It is calculated by dividing stockholders' equity by the number of common shares outstanding plus shares subscribed. When preferred stock exists, the call or par value plus any dividends in arrears are deducted first from total stockholders' equity before dividing by common shares outstanding plus shares subscribed. Market value per share is the price investors are willing to pay based on their expectations about the future earning ability of the company.

6. **Account for the appropriation of retained earnings.**
   For reasons such as plant expansion, a company may need to retain a portion of its assets in the business rather than distribute them to the stockholders as dividends. Management may communicate the plans to stockholders and other users of the company's financial statements by appropriation of retained earnings. In this way a portion of Retained Earnings is transferred to an account such as Retained Earnings Appropriated for Plant Expansion. A more common way to disclose the appropriation is through a note to the financial statements. When the reason for the appropriation no longer exists, the appropriated amount can be returned to the Retained Earnings account or the note removed from the financial statements.

7. **Show the relationships among income taxes expense, deferred income taxes, and net of taxes.**
   Income taxes expense are the taxes applicable to income from operations on an accrual basis. Income tax allocation is necessary when differences between accrual-based accounting income and taxable income cause a material difference in income taxes expense as shown on the income statement and the actual income tax liability. The difference between the accrued income taxes and the actual income taxes is debited or credited to an account called Deferred Income Taxes.

   Net of taxes is a phrase used to indicate that the effect of taxes has been considered when showing an item on the income statement.

8. **Describe the disclosure on the income statement of discontinued operations, extraordinary items, and accounting changes.**
   There are several accounting items that must be disclosed separately from continuing operations and net of income taxes on the income statement because of their unusual nature. These items include a gain or loss on discontinued operations, extraordinary items, and the cumulative effect of accounting changes.

9. **Compute earnings per share.**
   Stockholders and other users of financial statements use earnings per share data to evaluate the performance of a company, estimate future earnings, and evaluate their investment opportunities. Therefore, earnings per share data are presented on the face of the income statement. The amounts are computed by dividing the income applicable to common stock by the common shares outstanding for the year. If the number of shares outstanding has varied during the year, then the weighted-average shares outstanding should be used in the computation. When the company has a complex capital structure, a dual presentation of primary and fully diluted earnings per share data must be disclosed on the face of the income statement.

Review Problem
Statement of Stockholders' Equity and Corporate Income Statement

Two important corporate financial statements are presented in this chapter: the statement of stockholders' equity and the income statement. Review Exhibit 13-2 for the format and components of the statement of stockholders' equity. Note that the changes in each component of stockholders' equity are disclosed. Also note that retained earnings are affected by net income and cash and stock dividends.

Review the corporate income statement in Exhibit 13-3 carefully and identify the major components, which are indicated by bold color. They are income taxes expense, discontinued operations, extraordinary gain, cumulative effect of a change in accounting principle, and earnings per common share. Be sure that you can describe the nature and content of each of these components.

Chapter Assignments

Questions

1. What are retained earnings, and how do they relate to the assets of a corporation?
2. When does a company have a deficit in retained earnings?
3. What items are identified by generally accepted accounting principles as prior period adjustments?
4. Describe the significance of the following dates as they relate to dividends: (a) date of declaration, (b) date of record, and (c) date of payment.
5. How does the accounting treatment of stock dividends differ from that of cash dividends?
6. What is the difference between a stock dividend and a stock split? What is the effect of each on the capital structure of a corporation?
7. What is the purpose of appropriating retained earnings?
8. Define treasury stock. Why would a company purchase its own stock?
9. What are prior period adjustments and on what statements do they appear?
10. Would you expect a corporation's book value per share to equal its market value per share? Why or why not?
11. "Accounting income should be geared to the concept of taxable income because the public understands the concept of taxable income." Comment on this statement and tell why income tax allocation is necessary.
12. Santa Fe Southern Pacific Railroad had about $1.8 billion of deferred income taxes in 1982, equal to about 31 percent of total liabilities. By 1984, deferred income taxes had reached almost $2.3 billion, or about 38 percent of total liabilities. Given management's desire to put off the payment of taxes as long as possible, the long-term growth of the economy and inflation, and the definition of a liability (probable future sacrifices of future benefits arising from present obligations), can you give an argument for not accounting for deferred income taxes?
13. Explain the two major criteria for extraordinary items. How should extraordinary items be disclosed in financial statements?
14. How are earnings per share disclosed in financial statements?
15. When an accounting change occurs, what financial statement disclosures are necessary?

16. When does a company have a simple capital structure? a complex capital structure?
17. What is the difference between primary and fully diluted earnings per share?
18. Why should the gain or loss on discontinued operations be disclosed separately on the income statement?

Classroom Exercises

Exercise 13-1. Statement of Retained Earnings (L.O. 1)

The Maggio Corporation had a Retained Earnings balance on January 1, 19x2, of $130,000. During 19x2, the company reported a profit of $56,000 after taxes. In addition, the company located a $22,000 (net of taxes) error that resulted in an overstatement of prior years' income and meets the criteria of a prior period adjustment. During 19x2, the company declared cash dividends totaling $8,000.

Prepare the company's statement of retained earnings for the year ended December 31, 19x2.

Exercise 13-2. Journal Entries: Stock Dividends (L.O. 2)

The Broadnax Company has 20,000 shares of its $1 par value common stock outstanding.

Record the following transactions as they relate to the company's common stock:

July 17 Declared a 10 percent stock dividend on common stock to be distributed on August 10. Market value of the stock was $5 per share on this date.
31 Record date.
Aug. 10 Distributed the stock dividend declared on July 17.
Sept. 1 Declared a 50¢ per share cash dividend on common stock to be paid on Sept. 16 to stockholders of record on Sept. 10.

Exercise 13-3. Stock Split (L.O. 2)

The Mansfield Company currently has 100,000 shares of $1 par value common stock outstanding. The board of directors declared a 2 for 1 stock split on May 15, when the market value of the common stock was $2.50 per share. The Retained Earnings balance on May 15 was $700,000. Paid-in Capital in Excess of Par Value, Common Stock, on this date was $20,000.

Prepare the stockholders' equity section of the company's balance sheet before and after the stock split. What journal entry, if any, would be necessary to record the stock split?

Exercise 13-4. Treasury Stock Transactions (L.O. 3)

Prepare the journal entries necessary to record the following stock transactions of the Epps Company during 19xx:

May 5 Purchased 200 shares of its own $1 par value common stock for $5.00, the current market price.
17 Sold 75 shares of treasury stock purchased on May 5 for $5.50 per share.
21 Sold 50 shares of treasury stock purchased on May 5 for $5.00 per share.
28 Sold the remaining 75 shares of treasury stock purchased on May 5 for $4.75 per share.

Exercise 13-5. Book Value for Preferred and Common Stock (L.O. 5)

The stockholders' equity section of the Feldman Corporation's balance sheet is shown below.

Stockholders' Equity

Contributed Capital		
Preferred Stock—$100 per share, 6% cumulative, 10,000 shares authorized, 100 shares issued and outstanding*		$ 10,000
Common Stock—$5 par value, 100,000 shares authorized, 10,000 shares issued, 9,000 outstanding	$50,000	
Paid-in Capital in Excess of Par Value, Common	8,000	58,000
Total Contributed Capital		$ 68,000
Retained Earnings		45,000
Total Contributed Capital and Retained Earnings		$113,000
Less Treasury Stock, Common (1,000 shares at cost)		15,000
Total Stockholders' Equity		$ 98,000

* The preferred stock is callable at $104 per share, and one year's dividends are in arrears.

Determine the book value per share for both the preferred and the common stock.

Exercise 13-6. Appropriation of Retained Earnings (L.O. 6)

The board of directors of the Maldonado Company has approved a major plant expansion during the coming year. The expansion should cost approximately $550,000. The board has taken action to appropriate retained earnings of the company in the amount of $550,000 on July 17, 19x1. On August 20, 19x2, the expansion was completed at a total cost of $525,000 and paid for with cash. Also, on that date, the appropriation of retained earnings was removed.

1. Prepare the necessary journal entries for July 17, 19x1, and August 20, 19x2.
2. If the company had unappropriated retained earnings of $976,000 immediately before the August 20, 19x2, entries, what were the total retained earnings immediately before and after August 20, 19x2?

Exercise 13-7. Use of Corporate Income Tax Rate Schedule (L.O. 7)

Using the corporate tax rate schedule on page 494, compute the income tax liability for the following situations:

Situation	Taxable Income
A	$ 60,000
B	90,000
C	280,000

Exercise 13-8. Income Tax Allocation (L.O. 7)

The Dudec Corporation reported the following accounting income before income taxes, income taxes expense, and net income for 19x2 and 19x3:

	19x2	19x3
Accounting income before taxes	$140,000	$140,000
Income taxes expense	44,150	44,150
Net income	$ 95,850	$ 95,850

Also on the balance sheet, deferred income taxes liability increased by $19,200 in 19x2 and decreased by $9,400 in 19x3.

1. How much did Dudec Corporation actually pay in income taxes in 19x2 and 19x3?
2. Prepare journal entries to record income taxes expense in 19x2 and 19x3.

Exercise 13-9. Corporate Income Statement (L.O. 8)

Assume that the Ryback Furniture Company's chief financial officer gave you the following information: Net Sales, $1,500,000; Cost of Goods Sold, $700,000; Extraordinary Gain (applicable income tax on gain of $3,500), $16,000; Loss from Discontinued Operations (applicable income tax benefit of $30,000), $82,000; Loss on Disposal of Discontinued Operations (applicable income tax benefit of $13,000), $48,000; Selling Expenses, $50,000; Administrative Expenses, $40,000; Income Taxes Expense on Continuing Operations, $300,000.

From this information, prepare the company's income statement for the year ended June 30, 19xx. (Ignore earnings per share information.)

Exercise 13-10. Earnings per Share (L.O. 9)

During 19x1, the Potts Corporation reported a net income of $1,265,000. On January 1, Potts had 500,000 shares of common stock outstanding. The company issued an additional 300,000 shares of common stock on October 1. In 19x1, the company had a simple capital structure.

During 19x2, there were no transactions involving common stock, and the company reported net income of $1,840,000.

1. Determine the weighted-average number of common shares outstanding each year.
2. Compute earnings per share for each year.

Exercise 13-11. Statement of Stockholders' Equity (L.O. 4)

The stockholders' equity section of Groveport Corporation's balance sheet on December 31, 19x2, appears as follows:

Contributed Capital	
Common stock—$1 par value, 500,000 shares authorized, 400,000 shares issued and outstanding	$ 400,000
Paid-in Capital in Excess of Par Value, Common	500,000
Total Contributed Capital	$ 900,000
Retained Earnings	1,700,000
Total Stockholders' Equity	$2,600,000

Prepare a statement of stockholders' equity at December 31, 19x3, assuming the following transactions occurred during 19x3:

a. Issued 5,000 shares of $100 par value, 9 percent cumulative preferred stock at par.
b. Issued 40,000 shares of common stock in connection with the conversion of bonds having a carrying value of $300,000.
c. Declared and issued a 2 percent stock dividend. The market value on the date of declaration is $7 per share.
d. Purchased 10,000 shares of common stock for the treasury at a cost of $8 per share.
e. Earned a net income of $300,000.
f. Paid the full year's dividend on preferred stock and a 20¢ per share on common stock outstanding at the end of the year.

Interpreting Accounting Information

13-1.
Lockheed Corporation
(L.O. 8)

Presented below are several excerpts from an article that appeared in the February 2, 1982, *Wall Street Journal* entitled "Lockheed Had Loss in 4th Quarter, Year; $396 Million TriStar Write-Off Is Cited":

As expected, Lockheed Corp. took a $396 million write-off to cover expenses of its production phase-out of L-1011 TriStar commercial jets, resulting in a net loss of . . . $289 million for the year.

Roy A. Anderson, Lockheed Chairman, said he believed the company had "recognized all costs, including those yet to be incurred, that are associated with the phase-out of the TriStar program." He said he thinks the company now is in a sound position to embark on a program of future growth and earnings improvement.

Included in the $396 million total write-off are remaining deferred production start-up costs, adjustments for redundant inventories and provisions for losses and other costs expected to be incurred while TriStar production is completed. In addition to the write-off, discontinued operations include a $70 million after-tax loss associated with 1981 L-1011 operations. The comparable 1980 L-1011 loss was $108 million.

The $289 million 1981 net loss consists of the TriStar losses, reduced by the previously reported [extraordinary after-tax] gain of $23 million from the exchange of debentures. . . .

For the year, Lockheed had earnings from continuing operations of $154 million, a 14% gain from $135 million in 1980. In 1981 the company had a $466 million loss from discontinued operations, resulting in a net loss of $289 million. A year earlier, the concern had a $108 million loss from discontinued operations, resulting in a net profit of $28 million.[16]

Required

1. Interpret the financial information from the *Wall Street Journal* by preparing a partial income statement for Lockheed for 1981, beginning with "income from continuing operations." Be prepared to explain the nature of each item on the income statement.
2. How do you explain the fact that on the New York Stock Exchange, Lockheed common stock closed at $50 per share, up 75¢ on the day after the quoted announcement of a net loss of $289 million and up from $41 per share two months earlier?

16. Reprinted by permission of *The Wall Street Journal*,

13-2.
NBI, Inc.
(L.O. 7)

NBI, Inc., is one of a number of high-technology companies that have experienced explosive growth during the last five years. NBI, known affectionately as "Nothing But Initials," was begun in the mid-1970s to design, develop, manufacture, and market a variety of information-processing and word-processing applications for the office. The tables below present information from the income taxes note to the financial statements in the company's adapted annual report.

The provision for income taxes was different than the amount computed by applying the federal statutory rate to pre-tax income for financial reporting purposes. The reasons for this difference are as follows (amounts are in thousands):

	1986	1985	1984
Federal tax computed at statutory rate	**$10,562**	$ 2,615	$9,022
Increase (reduction) resulting from:			
State taxes, net of federal tax benefit	**461**	200	795
Losses of foreign subsidiaries not recognized for tax purposes	**542**	557	—
Investment tax credit	**(425)**	(1,015)	(589)
Dividends excluded from taxation	**(298)**	(283)	—
Earnings of DISC	**(356)**	(51)	(307)
Research and experimentation tax credit	**(891)**	(888)	(706)
Other	**(410)**	(40)	412
Income taxes as shown on income statement	**$ 9,185**	$ 1,095	$8,627

The principal components of deferred income tax expense are as follows (amounts are in thousands):

	1986	1985	1984
Tax depreciation in excess of book depreciation	**$ 668**	$ (161)	$ (163)
Equipment sales treated as leases for tax purposes	**872**	167	1,723
Equipment leases treated as sales for tax purposes	**41**	61	134
Net distribution from DISC	**154**	(373)	177
Equipment sales reported on installment method for tax purposes	**840**	1,487	—
Investment adjustments deferred for tax purposes	**(304)**	—	—
Other	**(21)**	31	61
Deferred income taxes expense	**$2,250**	$1,212	$1,932

The initials DISC in the tables are those of a foreign division of the company that is not subject to federal income taxes.

Required

1. How much in income taxes was paid in 1985 and 1986? Prepare journal entries to record the overall income tax liability for 1985 and 1986, using income tax allocation procedures.
2. What does the investment tax credit tell you about NBI's investment in plant assets in 1986 compared to 1985? What does the tax depreciation component of the deferred income tax expense tell you about the depreciation methods used for accounting purposes as compared to those used for tax purposes?
3. On the balance sheet date in 1986, NBI classifies deferred income taxes as a long-term liability. If NBI keeps growing as it has and given the definition of a liability, do you see any possible problem with calling deferred income taxes a liability?

Problem Set A

Problem 13A-1. Treasury Stock Transactions
(L.O. 3)

The Brendan Corporation was involved in the following treasury stock transactions during 19x7: (a) purchased 30,000 shares of its $1 par value common stock at $2.50 per share; (b) purchased 5,000 shares of its common stock at $2.80 per share; (c) sold 19,000 shares purchased in **a** for $55,100; (d) sold the other 11,000 shares purchased in **a** for $23,000; (e) sold 3,000 of the remaining shares of treasury stock for $1.60 per share; (f) retired all the remaining shares of treasury stock. All shares were originally issued at $1.50 per share.

Required

Record the treasury stock transactions in general journal form.

Problem 13A-2. Treasury Stock and Retained Earnings Transactions
(L.O. 3, 6)

The following transactions occurred in 19x7 for the Follett Corporation:

Feb. 5	The board of directors voted to appropriate $125,000 of retained earnings in anticipation of the construction of a new warehousing facility.
Mar. 21	Purchased 10,000 shares of the company's $2 par value common stock at $6 per share.
May 16	Sold 4,000 shares of the treasury stock purchased on March 21 for $7 per share.
Aug. 3	Completed the new warehouse at a cost of $140,000 and removed the appropriation of retained earnings in connection with the warehouse expansion.
Oct. 15	Sold 5,000 shares of the treasury stock purchased on March 21 for $3.50 per share.
Nov. 15	Decided to retire, effective immediately, the remaining shares held in the treasury. The shares were originally issued at $3 per share.

Required

Record the transactions for Follett Corporation in general journal form.

Problem 13A-3. Dividend Transactions, Retained Earnings, and Stockholders' Equity
(L.O. 1, 2, 6)

The stockholders' equity section of the Morgan Blind and Awning Company as of January 1, 19x7 is as follows:

Contributed Capital	
Common Stock—$1 par value, 3,000,000 shares authorized, 400,000 issued and outstanding	$400,000
Paid-in Capital in Excess of Par Value, Common	100,000
Total Contributed Capital	$500,000
Retained Earnings	450,000
Total Stockholders' Equity	$950,000

The company was involved in the following stockholders' equity transactions during 19x7:

Mar. 5	Declared a $.20 per share cash dividend to be paid on April 6 to stockholders of record on March 20.
20	Date of record.
Apr. 6	Paid the cash dividend.
June 17	Declared a 10 percent stock dividend to be distributed to stockholders of record on August 5. The market value of the stock was $7 per share.
Aug. 5	Date of record.
17	Distributed the stock dividend.
Oct. 2	Split its stock 3 for 1.
Dec. 9	Appropriated retained earnings for pending lawsuit in the amount of $65,000.
27	Declared a cash dividend of $.05 per share payable January 27, 19x8 to stockholders of record on January 14, 19x8.
31	Closed the Income Summary with a credit balance of $200,000 to Retained Earnings.
31	Closed Dividends Declared to Retained Earnings.

Required

1. Record the 19x7 transactions in general journal form.
2. Prepare a statement of retained earnings.
3. Prepare the stockholders' equity section of the company's balance sheet as of December 31, 19x7.

Problem 13A-4. Corporate Income Statement
(L.O. 8, 9)

Income statement information for the Harine Corporation during 19x1 is as follows: (a) administrative expenses, $90,000; (b) cost of goods sold, $400,000; (c) cumulative effect of accounting change in inventory methods (net of taxes $34,000) that decreased income, $60,000; (d) extraordinary loss from storm (net of tax $12,000), $20,000; (e) income taxes expense, continuing operations, $120,000; (f) sales, $930,000; (g) selling expenses, $200,000.

Required

Prepare Harine Corporation's income statement for 19x1, including earnings per share information assuming a weighted average of 200,000 shares of common stock outstanding for 19x1.

Problem 13A-5. Comprehensive Stockholders' Equity Transactions
(L.O. 1, 2, 3, 5)

The stockholders' equity on June 30, 19x5 of the Troge Company is as follows:

Contributed Capital	
Common Stock—no-par value, $2 stated value, 400,000 shares authorized, 150,000 shares issued and outstanding	$ 300,000
Paid-in Capital in Excess of Stated Value, Common	460,000
Total Contributed Capital	$ 760,000
Retained Earnings	240,000
Total Stockholders' Equity	$1,000,000

Stockholders' equity transactions for the next fiscal year are presented below:

a. The board of directors declared a 2 for 1 stock split.
b. The board of directors obtained authorization to issue 100,000 shares of $100 par value 4 percent noncumulative preferred stock that is callable at 105.
c. Issued 10,000 shares of common stock for a building appraised at $20,000.
d. Purchased 6,000 shares of the company's common stock for $15,000.
e. Issued 20,000 shares of the preferred stock for $100 per share.
f. Sold 4,000 shares of the treasury stock for $9,000.
g. Declared cash dividends of $4 per share on the preferred stock and $.10 per share on the common stock.
h. Paid the preferred and common stock cash dividends.
i. Declared a 5 percent stock dividend on the common stock. The market value was $9 per share. The stock dividend was distributable after the end of the fiscal year.
j. Net income for the year was $170,000.
k. Closed Dividends Declared to Retained Earnings.

Required

1. Make the general journal entries to record the transactions.
2. Prepare the company's Retained Earnings statement at June 30, 19x6.
3. Prepare the Stockholders' Equity section of the company's balance sheet at June 30, 19x6.
4. Compute the book values per share of preferred and common stock on June 30, 19x5 and 19x6.

Problem Set B

Problem 13B-1. Treasury Stock Transactions
(L.O. 3)

The following treasury stock transactions occurred during 19xx for the Huang Company: (a) Purchased 25,000 shares of its $1 par value common stock on the market for $20 per share. (b) Sold 7,000 shares of the treasury stock for $21 per share. (c) Sold 6,000 shares of the treasury stock for $19 per share. (d) Sold 10,000 shares of the treasury stock remaining for $17 per share. (e) Purchased an additional 3,000 shares for $18 per share. (f) Retired all the remaining shares of treasury stock. All shares were originally issued at $4 per share.

Required

Record these transactions in general journal form.

Problem 13B-2. Treasury Stock and Retained Earnings Transactions (L.O. 3, 6)

A review of the stockholders' equity records of Logan Cotton Mills disclosed the following transactions during 19xx:

Jan. 30	Purchased 20,000 shares of the company's $5 par value common stock for $10. The stock was originally issued for $9.
Mar. 5	The board of directors voted to appropriate $265,000 of retained earnings because of a contractual agreement to purchase cotton delinting equipment.
Apr. 16	Sold 1,000 shares of the company's stock purchased on January 30 for $12 per share.
Aug. 17	Sold 1,000 shares of the company's stock purchased on January 30 for $9 per share.
Sept. 10	Purchased the cotton delinting equipment at a total cost of $285,000, including installation, and removed the appropriation of retained earnings in connection with the purchase contract.
Nov. 5	Sold 2,000 shares of the company's stock purchased on January 30 for $9 per share.
Dec. 31	Decided to retire, effective immediately, the remaining shares held in the treasury.

Required

Record the transactions of Logan Cotton Mills in general journal form.

Problem 13B-3. Dividend Transactions, Retained Earnings, and Stockholders' Equity (L.O. 1, 2, 6)

The balance sheet of the Hurwitz Clothing Company disclosed the following stockholders' equity as of September 30, 19x1:

Contributed Capital	
Common Stock—$2 par value, 1,000,000 shares authorized, 250,000 shares issued and outstanding	$500,000
Paid-in Capital in Excess of Par Value, Common	60,000
Total Contributed Capital	$560,000
Retained Earnings	400,000
Total Stockholders' Equity	$960,000

The following stockholders' equity transactions were completed during the year in the order presented:

19x1	
Dec. 17	Declared a 10 percent stock dividend to stockholders of record on January 1. The market value per share on the date of declaration was $4.
19x2	
Jan. 20	Distributed the stock dividend.
Apr. 14	Declared a 25¢ per share cash dividend. Cash dividend payable May 15 to stockholders of record on May 1.
May 15	Paid the cash dividend.
June 17	Split its stock 2 for 1.
Sept. 14	Appropriated retained earnings for plant expansion in the amount of $95,000.

15 Declared a cash dividend of 10¢ per share payable October 10 to stockholders of record October 1
30 Closed Income Summary ($50,000 credit balance) to Retained Earnings.
30 Closed Dividends Declared to Retained Earnings.

Required

1. Record the above transactions in general journal form.
2. Prepare a statement of retained earnings.
3. Prepare the stockholders' equity section of the company's balance sheet as of September 30, 19x2.

Problem 13B-4. Corporate Income Statement (L.O. 8, 9)

Information concerning operations of the DeSoto Shoe Company during 19xx is as follows: (a) Administrative Expenses, $100,000; (b) Cost of Goods Sold, $350,000; (c) Cumulative effect of an accounting change that increased income, change in depreciation methods (net of taxes $20,000), $42,000; (d) Extraordinary Item, Loss from Earthquake (net of taxes $46,000), ($60,000); (e) Sales (net), $800,000; (f) Selling Expenses, $80,000; (g) Income Taxes Expense applicable to continuing operations, $135,000.

Required

Prepare the company's income statement for the year ended December 31, 19xx, including earnings per share information. Assume a weighted average of 100,000 common stock shares outstanding during the year.

Problem 13B-5. Stockholders' Equity and Comprehensive Stockholders' Equity Transactions (L.O. 1, 2, 3, 5)

On December 31, 19x1, the stockholders' equity section of the Kotsouris Company appeared as shown below.

Contributed Capital	
Common Stock—$4 par value, 100,000 shares authorized, 40,000 shares issued and outstanding	$ 160,000
Paid-in Capital in Excess of Par Value, Common	580,000
Total Contributed Capital	$ 740,000
Retained Earnings	316,000
Total Stockholders' Equity	$1,056,000

Selected transactions involving stockholders' equity are as follows: (a) During January, the board of directors obtained authorization for 20,000 shares of $20 par value noncumulative preferred stock that carried an indicated dividend rate of $2 per share and was callable at $21 per share. The company sold 12,000 shares at $20 per share and issued another 2,000 in exchange for a building valued at $40,000. (b) During March, the board of directors also declared a 2 for 1 stock split on the common stock. (c) In April, after the stock split, the company purchased 3,000 shares of common stock for the treasury at an average price of $6 per share; 1,000 of these shares were subsequently sold at an average price of $8 per share. (d) During July, declared and paid a cash dividend of $2 per share on preferred stock and 20¢ per share on common stock. (e) The board of directors declared a 15 percent stock dividend in November when the common stock was selling for $10. The stock dividend had not been distributed by the end of the year. (f) Net loss for 19xx was $115,000. (g) Closed Dividends Declared to Retained Earnings.

Required

1. Prepare journal entries to record the above transactions.
2. Prepare the company's statement of retained earnings for the year ended December 31, 19x2.
3. Prepare the stockholders' equity section of the company's balance sheet as of December 31, 19x2.
4. Compute book value per share for preferred and common stock on December 31, 19x1 and 19x2.

Financial Decision Case

Metzger Steel Corporation
(L.O. 2, 3)

Metzger Steel Corporation (MSC) is a small specialty steel manufacturer located in northern Alabama that has been owned by the Metzger family for several generations. Arnold Metzger III is a major shareholder in MSC by virtue of having inherited 200,000 shares of common stock in the company. Previously, Arnold has not shown much interest in the business because of his enthusiasm for archaeology, which takes him to far parts of the world. However, when he received minutes of the last board of directors meeting, he questioned a number of transactions involving the stockholders' equity of MSC. He asks you, as a person with a knowledge of accounting, to help him interpret the effect of these transactions on his interest in MSC.

First, you note that at the beginning of 19xx the stockholders' equity of MSC appeared as follows:

Metzger Steel Corporation
Stockholders' Equity
January 1, 19xx

Contributed Capital	
Common Stock—$10 par value, 5,000,000 shares authorized, 1,000,000 shares issued and outstanding	$10,000,000
Paid-in Capital in Excess of Par Value, Common	25,000,000
Total Contributed Capital	$35,000,000
Retained Earnings	25,000,000
Total Stockholders' Equity	$60,000,000

Then, you read the relevant parts of the minutes of the December 15 meeting of the board of directors of MSC as they appear below:

Item A: A report by the president of the following transactions involving the company's stock during the last quarter:

October 15 Sold 500,000 shares of authorized common stock through the investment banking firm of A. B. Abbott at a net price of $50 per share.

November 1 Purchased 100,000 shares for the corporate treasury from Sharon Metzger at a price of $55 per share.

Item B: The board declared a two-for-one stock split (accomplished by halving the par value and doubling each stockholder's shares), followed by a 10 percent stock dividend. The board then declared the annual cash dividend of $2.00 per share on the resulting shares. All these transactions are applicable to stockholders of record on December 20 and are payable on January 10. The market value of Metzger stock on the board meeting date after the stock split was estimated to be $30.

Item C: The chief financial officer stated that he expected the company to report a net income for the year of $4,000,000.

Required

1. Prepare a stockholders' equity section of MSC's balance sheet as of December 31, 19xx, that reflects the status of the above transactions. (Hint: use T accounts to analyze the transactions. Also, use a T account to keep track of the shares of common stock outstanding.)
2. Compute the book value per share and percent ownership of the company at the beginning and at the end of the year for Arnold's holdings. Explain the differences. Would you say that Arnold's position has improved or not during the year?

CHAPTER 14 LONG-TERM LIABILITIES

LEARNING OBJECTIVES

1. Identify and contrast the major characteristics of bonds.
2. Record the issuance of bonds at face value, between interest dates, and at a discount or premium.
3. Amortize bond discount and premium by using the effective interest method, and make year-end adjustments.
4. Account for the retirement of bonds and the conversion of bonds into stock.
5. Compute sinking fund requirements, and prepare accounting entries associated with sinking fund bonds payable.
6. Explain the basic features of mortgages payable, long-term leases, and pensions as long-term liabilities.

This chapter introduces long-term liabilities. It describes the nature of bonds and the accounting treatment for bonds payable and other long-term liabilities such as mortgages, long-term leases, and pension liabilities. After studying this chapter, you should be able to meet the learning objectives listed on the left.

A corporation has many sources of funds from which to finance operations and expansion. As you learned earlier, corporations acquire cash and other assets by having profitable operations, getting short-term credit, and issuing stock. Another source of funds for a business is long-term debt in the form of bonds or notes. When a company issues bonds or notes, it promises to pay the creditor periodic interest plus the principal of the debt on a certain date in the future. Notes and bonds are long-term if they are due more than one year from the balance sheet date. In practice, long-term notes can range from two to ten years to maturity and long-term bonds and mortgages from ten to fifty years to maturity.

Nature of Bonds

A **bond** is a security representing money borrowed by a corporation from the public. (Other kinds of bonds are those issued by the United States government, state and local governments, and foreign companies and countries to raise money.) Bonds must be repaid at a certain time and require periodic payments of interest. Interest is usually paid semiannually, or twice a year. These bonds must not be confused with stocks. Because stocks are shares of ownership, stockholders are owners. Bondholders, however, are creditors. Bonds are promises to repay the amount borrowed, called the principal, and a certain rate of interest at specified future dates.

The holder of a bond receives a **bond certificate** as evidence of the company's debt to the bondholder. In most cases, the face value (denomination) of the bond is $1,000 or some multiple of $1,000. A **bond issue** is the total number of bonds that are issued at the same time. For example, a $1,000,000 bond issue may consist of a thousand $1,000 bonds. The issue may be bought and held by many investors. So the corporation usually enters into a supplementary agreement, called a **bond indenture**. The bond indenture defines the rights, privileges, and limitations of bondholders. The bond indenture will generally describe such things

OBJECTIVE 1
Identify and contrast the major characteristics of bonds

as the maturity date of the bonds, interest payment dates, interest rate, and characteristics of the bonds such as callable features. Repayment plans and restrictions are also usually covered.

The prices of bonds are stated in terms of a percentage of face value. If a bond issue is quoted at 103½, this means that a $1,000 bond would cost $1,035 ($1,000 × 103½%). When a bond sells at exactly 100, it is said to sell at face or par value. When it sells at above 100, it is said to sell at a premium and when below face value, at a discount. A $1,000 bond quoted at 87.62 would be selling at a discount and would cost the buyer $876.20.

A bond indenture can be written to fit the needs of an individual company and its financing needs. As a result, the bonds being issued by corporations in today's financial markets have many different features. Several of the more important features are described below.

Secured or Unsecured Bonds

Bonds may be either secured or unsecured. If issued on the general credit of the company, they are **unsecured bonds** (also called **debenture bonds**). **Secured bonds** give the bondholders a pledge of certain assets of the company as a guarantee of repayment. The security identified by a secured bond may be any specific asset of the company or a general category such as property, plant, and equipment.

Term or Serial Bonds

When all the bonds of an issue mature at the same time, they are called **term bonds.** For example, a company may issue $1,000,000 worth of bonds, all due twenty years from the date of issue. If the maturity dates of a bond issue are spread over several maturity dates, the bonds are **serial bonds.** A company may issue serial bonds to make it easier to get together cash for retiring the bonds. An example of serial bonds would be a $1,000,000 issue that called for retiring $200,000 of the principal every five years. This arrangement means that after the first $200,000 payment is made, only $800,000 of the bonds would remain outstanding for the next five years. In other words, $1,000,000 is outstanding for the first five years, and $800,000 is outstanding for the second five years.

Registered or Coupon Bonds

Most bonds that are issued today are **registered bonds.** On registered bonds the name and address of the owner must be recorded with the issuing company. In this way the company keeps a register of the owners and pays interest by check to the bondholders of record on the interest payment date. **Coupon bonds** are generally not registered with the corporation but have interest coupons attached to them. Each coupon states the amount of interest due and the payment date. The coupons are removed from the bond on the interest payment dates and presented at a bank for collection. In this way the interest is paid to the holder of the coupon.

Accounting for Bonds Payable[1]

OBJECTIVE 2 Record the issuance of bonds at face value, between interest dates, and at a discount or premium

When the board of directors decides to issue bonds, it generally presents the proposal to the stockholders. If the stockholders agree to the issue, the company then prints the certificates and draws up a deed of trust. The bonds are then authorized for issuance. It is not necessary to make a journal entry for the authorization, but most companies prepare a memorandum in the Bonds Payable account describing the issue. This note gives the amount of bonds authorized, interest rate, interest payment dates, and life of the bonds.

Once the bonds are issued, the corporation must pay interest to the bondholders during the life of the bonds (in most cases semiannually) and the principal of the bonds at maturity.

Balance Sheet Disclosure of Bonds

Bonds payable and either unamortized discount or premium (which will be explained later) are generally shown on a company's balance sheet as long-term liabilities. However, as explained in Chapter 7, if the maturity date of the bond issue is one year or less and the bonds will be retired by the use of current assets, bonds payable should be listed as current liabilities. If the issue is to be paid with segregated assets or replaced by another bond issue, then they should still be shown as long-term liabilities.

Important provisions of the bond indenture are reported in the notes to the financial statements, often with a list of all bond issues, the kind of bonds, interest rate, any security connected with the bonds, interest payment dates, maturity date, and effective interest rate.

Bonds Issued at Face Value

As an example, suppose that the Vason Corporation has authorized the issuance of $100,000 of 9 percent, five-year bonds on January 1, 19x0. Interest is to be paid on January 1 and July 1 of each year. Assume that the bonds are sold on January 1, 19x0, for their face value. The entry to record the issuance is as follows:

Jan. 1	Cash	100,000	
	Bonds Payable		100,000
	Sold $100,000 of 9%, 5-year bonds at face value		

As stated above, interest is paid on July 1 and January 1 of each year. Thus the corporation would owe the bondholders $4,500 interest on July 1, 19x0. The interest computation is shown on the next page:

1. At the time this chapter is being written, the market interest rates on corporate bonds are quite volatile. Only the bold and reckless predict which way they will go. Therefore, the examples and problems in this chapter use a variety of interest rates that are convenient for demonstrating the concepts.

$$\begin{aligned} \text{interest} &= \text{principal} \times \text{rate} \times \text{time} \\ &= \$100{,}000 \times .09 \times \tfrac{1}{2}\ \text{year} \\ &= \$4{,}500 \end{aligned}$$

The interest paid to the bondholders on each semiannual interest payment date would be recorded as follows:

July 1	Bond Interest Expense	4,500	
	Cash (or Interest Payable)		4,500
	Paid (or accrued) semiannual interest to bondholders of 9%, 5-year bonds		

Sales of Bonds Between Interest Dates

Bonds may be issued on their interest date as in the example above, but many times they are sold between interest dates. The generally accepted method of handling bonds issued in this manner is to collect from the investor the interest that has accrued since the last interest payment date. Then when the next interest period arrives, the corporation pays the investor the interest for the entire period. Thus the interest collected when bonds are sold is returned to the investor on the next interest payment date.

There are two reasons for following this procedure. First, there is a practical reason. If a company were issuing bonds on several different days and did not collect the accrued interest, records would have to be maintained for each bondholder and date of purchase. In such a case, the interest due each bondholder would have to be computed on the basis of different time periods. It becomes clear that large bookkeeping costs would be incurred under this system. On the other hand, if accrued interest is collected when the bonds are sold, then on the interest payment date the corporation can pay the interest due for the entire period, eliminating the extra computations and costs.

The second reason for collecting accrued interest in advance is that when this amount is netted against the full interest paid on the interest payment date, the resulting interest expense is the amount for the time the money has been borrowed.

For example, assume that the Vason Corporation sold $100,000 of 9 percent, five-year bonds for face value on April 1, 19x0, rather than on January 1, 19x0, the issue date. The entries to record the sale of the bonds and payment of interest on July 1, 19x0, follow:

Apr. 1	Cash	102,250	
	Bond Interest Expense		2,250
	Bonds Payable		100,000
	Sold 9%, 5-year bonds at face value plus 3 months' accrued interest		
	$\$100{,}000 \times .09 \times \frac{3}{12} = \$2{,}250$		

As shown on page 520, Cash is debited for the amount received, \$102,250 (face value of \$100,000 plus three months' accrued interest of \$2,250). Bond Interest Expense is credited for the \$2,250 of accrued interest, and Bonds Payable is credited for the face value of \$100,000. When the first semiannual interest date arrives, the following entry is made:

July 1	Bond Interest Expense	4,500	
	Cash (or Interest Payable)		4,500
	Paid (or accrued) semiannual interest $100,000 × .09 × ½ = $4,500		

Note that here the full half-year interest is both debited to Bond Interest Expense and credited to Cash because the corporation only pays bond interest every six months and in full six-month amounts. Also note that the actual interest expense for the three months that the bonds were outstanding is \$2,250. This amount is the net balance of the \$4,500 debit to Bond Interest Expense on July 1 less the \$2,250 credit to Bond Interest Expense on April 1. We can see these steps clearly in the posted entries in the ledger account for Bond Interest Expense:

Bond Interest Expense — **Account No. 723**

Date		Item	Post. Ref.	Debit	Credit	Balance Debit	Balance Credit
19x0							
Apr.	1				2,250		2,250
July	1			4,500		2,250	

The Effect of the Market Rate of Interest on Bond Prices

The face value of a bond and its face interest rate are fixed. One hundred thousand dollars in bonds at 9 percent will pay \$9,000 a year or \$4,500 every six months until maturity. However, bonds are bought and sold by investors in the market every day, and interest rates in the market change from day to day. The corporation has no control over the market rate of interest. Vason Corporation can receive face value or \$100,000 for the bonds only if the current market or effective rate of interest is 9 percent for bonds with the same conditions and quality. If the current market rate of interest on this kind of bond issue has gone up to 10 percent, Vason could receive less than \$100,000 from the bond investor. In other words, given a market rate of interest of 10 percent, the wise investor will not pay \$100,000 for a yearly interest payment of \$9,000.

On the other hand, if the market rate goes down to 8 percent, Vason Corporation will be able to issue the bonds for more than $100,000 because similar bonds will yield only 8 percent.

When issuing bonds, most companies try to set the face interest rate as close as possible to the market interest rate. However, a company must decide in advance what the face interest rate will be to allow time to file with regulatory bodies, publicize the issue, and print the certificates. So there is often a difference in the market or effective rate of interest and the face rate of interest on the issue date. The result is that the issue price of the bond does not equal the principal or face value of the bond. If the issue price is less than the face value, the bonds are said to be issued at a **discount**. The discount equals the excess of face value over issue price. If the issue price is more than the face value, the bonds are said to be issued at a **premium**. The premium is equal to the excess of the issue price over the face value.

Using Present Value to Value a Bond[2]

Present value is relevant here because the value of bonds is based on the present value of two components of cash flow: (1) a series of fixed interest payments and (2) a single payment at maturity. To determine the present value of a bond, use Tables D-3 and D-4 in Appendix D. The amount of interest that a bond pays is fixed over its life. During its life, however, the market rate of interest varies from day to day. Thus the amount that investors are willing to pay for the bond changes as well.

Assume, for example, that a particular bond has a face value of $10,000 and pays a fixed amount of interest of $450 (9 percent annual rate) every six months. The bond is due in five years. If the market rate of interest today is 14 percent, how much is the present value of the bond?

Because the compounding period is more than once a year, it is necessary to convert the annual rate to a semiannual rate of 7 percent (14% ÷ two six-month periods per year) and to use ten periods (five years × two six-month periods per year). Using this information, we compute the present value of the bond:

Present value of 10 periodic payments (from Table D-4): $450 × 7.024	=	$3,160.80
Present value of a single payment (from Table D-3): $10,000 × 0.508	=	5,080.00
Present value of $10,000 bond	=	$8,240.80

The market rate of interest has increased so much since the bond was issued (from 9 percent to 14 percent) that the value of the bond is only $8,240.80 today. This amount is all that investors would be willing to pay at this time for an income from this bond of $450 every six months and return of the $10,000 principal in five years.

2. A knowledge of present value concepts, as presented in Appendix C, is helpful in understanding this section.

Bonds Issued at a Discount

As a case of issuing bonds at a discount, suppose that the Vason Corporation issues its $100,000 of five-year, 9 percent bonds at 96.149 when the market rate of interest is 10 percent. The entry to record the issuance of the bonds at a discount is:

Jan. 1	Cash		96,149	
	Unamortized Bond Discount		3,851	
	Bonds Payable			100,000
	Sold $100,000 of 9%, 5-year bonds			
	Face Amount of Bonds	$100,000		
	Less Purchase Price of Bonds ($100,000 × .96149)	96,149		
	Unamortized Bond Discount	$ 3,851		

As shown above, Cash is debited for the amount received ($96,149), Bonds Payable is credited for the face amount ($100,000) of the bond liability, and the difference ($3,851) is debited to Unamortized Bond Discount. If a balance sheet is prepared right after this issuance of bonds at a discount, the liability for bonds payable is as follows:

Long-Term Liabilities		
9% Bonds Payable, due 1/1/x5	$100,000	
Less Unamortized Bond Discount	3,851	$96,149

As can be seen, the Unamortized Bond Discount is deducted from the face amount of the bonds to arrive at the carrying value or present value of the bonds. The bond discount is described as unamortized because it will be amortized (written off) over the life of the bonds. For this reason, the carrying value of the bonds will gradually increase. By the time the maturity date of the bonds arrives, the carrying value of the bonds will equal their face value.

Calculation of Total Interest Cost

When bonds are issued at a discount, the effective interest rate paid by the company is greater than the face interest rate on the bonds. The reason is that the interest cost to the company is the stated interest payments *plus* the amount of the bond discount. That is, the company did not receive the full face value of the bonds upon issue, but it must pay back the full face amount at maturity. The difference between the issue price and the face value must be added to the interest payments to arrive at the actual interest expense. The full cost to the Vason Corporation of issuing the bonds at a discount is as follows:

Cash to be paid to bondholders	
Face value at maturity	$100,000
Interest payments ($100,000 × .09 × 5 years)	45,000
Total cash to bondholders	$145,000
Cash received from bondholders	96,149
Total interest cost	$ 48,851

Or alternatively

Interest payments ($100,000 × .09 × 5 years)	$ 45,000
Unamortized Bond Discount	3,851
Total interest cost	$ 48,851

The total interest cost of $48,851 is made up of $45,000 in interest payments and the $3,851 of bond discount. So the bond discount increases the interest paid on the bonds from the stated to the effective interest rate.

The discount must be spread or allocated over the remaining life of the bonds as an increase in the interest expense each period. This process of allocation is called amortization of the bond discount. Thus, interest expense for each period will exceed the actual payment of interest by the amount of bond discount amortized during the period.

It is interesting to note that some companies and governmental units have begun to issue bonds that do not have periodic interest payments. These bonds, called **zero coupon bonds**, are simply a promise to pay a fixed amount at the maturity date. These bonds are issued at a large discount, and the only interest earned by the buyer or interest paid by the issuer is the discount. For example, a $100,000, five-year bond issued at a time when the market rate is 14 percent, compounded semiannually, would sell for only $50,800. This amount is the present value of a single payment (from Table D-3, 7 percent for ten periods equals 0.508). The discount of $49,200 ($100,000 − $50,800) is the total interest cost and is amortized over the life of the bond, as shown in the following sections.

Amortizing the Bond Discount

There are two ways of amortizing the discount: the straight-line method and the effective interest method.

OBJECTIVE 3 Amortize bond discount and premium by using the effective interest method, and make year-end adjustments

Straight-Line Method. The **straight-line method** is the easier of the two and makes the amortization of the discount equal for each interest period. In this case, suppose that the interest payment dates for the Vason bond issue are January 1 and July 1. The bond discount is amortized and the interest cost is figured in four steps, as follows:

1. Total interest payments = interest payments per year × life of bonds
$$= 2 \times 5$$
$$= 10$$

2. Amortization of bond discount per interest payment
$$= \frac{\text{bond discount}}{\text{total interest payments}} = \frac{\$3,851}{10} = \$385$$

3. Regular cash interest payment
   = face value × face interest rate × time
   = $100,000 × .09 × ½
   = $4,500
4. Total interest cost per interest date
   = interest payment + amortization of bond discount
   = $4,500 + $385 = $4,885

On July 1, 19x0, the semiannual interest date, the entry would be as follows:

July 1	Bond Interest Expense	4,885	
	Unamortized Bond Discount		385
	Cash (or Interest Payable)		4,500
	Paid (or accrued) semiannual interest to bondholders and amortized discount on 9%, 5-year bonds		

Note that the bond interest expense is $4,885, but the amount received by the bondholder is the $4,500 face interest payment. The difference of $385 is the credit to Unamortized Bond Discount. This will lower the debit balance of the Unamortized Bond Discount and so will raise the carrying value of the bonds payable by $385 each interest period. When the bond issue matures, there will be no balance in the Unamortized Bond Discount account, and the carrying value of the bonds payable will be $100,000. This is exactly equal to the amount due to bondholder.

Even though the straight-line method has long been used, it has a certain weakness. Because the carrying value goes up each period and the bond interest expense stays the same, the straight-line method leads to a decreasing rate of interest over time. Also, using the straight-line method to amortize a premium leads to a rising rate of interest over time. For this reason, the APB has ruled that the straight-line method can be used only where it does not lead to a material difference from the effective interest method.[3] As will be seen, the effective interest rate method presupposes a constant rate of interest over the life of the bond. This rate will be constant if the total interest expense changes a little each interest period in response to the changing carrying value of the bond.

Effective Interest Method. We will describe how to compute the interest and amortization of bond discount for each interest period under the **effective interest method**. One must apply a constant interest rate to the carrying value of the bonds at the beginning of the interest period. This rate would be the market rate (effective rate) at the time the bonds were issued. The amount to be amortized becomes the difference between the interest computed by using the constant rate (effective rate) and the actual interest paid to the bondholders.

3. Accounting Principles Board, *Opinion No. 21,* "Interest on Receivables and Payables" (New York: American Institute of Certified Public Accountants, 1971), par. 15.

As an example of this method, let us use the same facts as in the earlier case ($100,000 bond issue at 9 percent, five-year maturity, interest paid twice a year). The market or effective rate of interest at the time is 10 percent. The bonds were sold for $96,149, which means a discount of $3,851. The amounts of interest and amortization of the bond discount are shown in Table 14-1.

The following points should help to explain how the amounts in the table are computed:

Column A: The carrying value of the bonds is the face value of the bonds less unamortized bond discount ($100,000 − $3,851 = $96,149).

Column B: The interest expense to be recorded is the effective interest. It is found by multiplying the carrying value of the bonds by the effective interest rate for one-half year ($96,149 × .10 × ½ = $4,807).

Column C: The interest paid in the period is the face value of the bonds multiplied by the interest rate for the bonds multiplied by the interest time period ($100,000 × .09 × ½ = $4,500).

Column D: The discount amortized is the difference between the effective interest expense to be recorded and the interest to be paid on the interest payment date ($4,807 − $4,500) = $307).

Table 14-1. Interest and Amortization of Bond Discount: Effective Interest Method

	A	B	C	D	E	F
Semi-annual Interest Period	Carrying Value at Beginning of Period	Semiannual Interest Expense at 10% to Be Recorded* (5% × A)	Semiannual Interest to Be Paid to Bondholders (4½% × $100,000)	Amortization of Discount (B − C)	Unamortized Bond Discount at End of Period	Carrying Value at End of Period (A + D)
0					$3,851	$ 96,149
1	$96,149	$4,807	$4,500	$307	3,544	96,456
2	96,456	4,823	4,500	323	3,221	96,779
3	96,779	4,839	4,500	339	2,882	97,118
4	97,118	4,856	4,500	356	2,526	97,474
5	97,474	4,874	4,500	374	2,152	97,848
6	97,848	4,892	4,500	392	1,760	98,240
7	98,240	4,912	4,500	412	1,348	98,652
8	98,652	4,933	4,500	433	915	99,085
9	99,085	4,954	4,500	454	461	99,539
10	99,539	4,961**	4,500	461	—	100,000

*Rounded to nearest dollar.
**Error due to rounding.

Column E: The unamortized bond discount is the balance of the bond discount at the beginning of the period less the current period amortization of the discount ($3,851 − $307 = **$3,544**). The unamortized discount decreases each interest payment period because it is amortized as a portion of interest expense.

Column F: The carrying value of the bonds at the end of the period is the carrying value at the beginning of the period plus the amortization during the period ($96,149 + $307 = **$96,456**). Notice that the sum of the carrying value and unamortized discount (column E + column F) always equals the face value of the bonds ($96,456 + $3,544 = $100,000).

The entry to record the interest expense is exactly like the one shown when the straight-line method is applied. However, the amounts debited and credited to the various accounts are different. The entry for July 1, 19x0, using the effective interest method, would be

July 1	Bond Interest Expense	4,807	
	Unamortized Bond Discount		307
	Cash (or Interest Payable)		4,500
	Paid (or accrued) semiannual interest to bondholders and amortized discount on 9%, 5-year bonds		

Note also that an interest and amortization table does not have to be prepared to determine the amortization of discount for any one interest payment period. It is necessary only to multiply the carrying value by the effective interest rate and subtract the interest payment from the result. For example, the amount of discount to be amortized in the seventh interest payment period equals $412 [($98,240 × .05) − $4,500].

Bonds Issued at a Premium

When bonds have a face interest rate that is above the market rate for similar investments, they will be issued at a price above the face value, or at a premium. For example, assume that the Vason Corporation issued $100,000 of bonds for $104,100 when the market rate of interest is 8 percent. This means that they will be purchased by investors at 104.1 percent of their face value. The entry to record their issuance would be as follows:

Jan. 1	Cash	104,100	
	Unamortized Bond Premium		4,100
	Bonds Payable		100,000
	Sold $100,000 of 9%, 5-year bonds at 104.1		

Right after this entry is made, bonds payable would be presented on the balance sheet as shown on the next page.

Long-Term Liabilities		
9% Bonds Payable, due 1/1/x5	$100,000	
Unamortized Bond Premium	4,100	$104,100

The carrying value of bonds payable is $104,100, which is equal to the face value of the bonds plus the unamortized bond premium. The cash received from the issuance of the bonds is also $104,100. This means that the purchasers were willing to pay a premium of $4,100 to get these bonds because the face interest on them was greater than the market rate. The $4,100 premium represents an amount that will not be paid back to the bondholders at maturity. For this reason, it is amortized over the life of the bonds as a decrease in Bond Interest Expense. Note in the calculation in Table 14-2 the difference from the amortization of bond discount, which raised interest expense. The bond premium, on the other hand, serves to lower total interest costs below the amount paid to bondholders.

Cash to be paid to bondholders:	
Face value at maturity	$100,000
Interest payments ($100,000 × .09 × 5)	45,000
Total cash paid to bondholders	$145,000
Cash received from bondholders	104,100
Total interest costs	$ 40,900

Table 14-2. Interest and Amortization of Bond Premium: Effective Interest Method

	A	B	C	D	E	F
Semi-annual Interest Period	Carrying Value at Beginning of Period	Semiannual Interest Expense at 8% to Be Recorded* (4% × A)	Semiannual Interest to Be Paid to Bondholders (4½% × $100,000)	Amortization of Premium (C − B)	Unamortized Bond Premium at End of Period	Carrying Value at End of Period (A − D)
0					$4,100	$104,100
1	$104,100	$4,164	$4,500	$336	3,764	103,764
2	103,764	4,151	4,500	349	3,415	103,415
3	103,415	4,137	4,500	363	3,052	103,052
4	103,052	4,122	4,500	378	2,674	102,674
5	102,674	4,107	4,500	393	2,281	102,281
6	102,281	4,091	4,500	409	1,872	101,872
7	101,872	4,075	4,500	425	1,447	101,447
8	101,447	4,058	4,500	442	1,005	101,005
9	101,005	4,040	4,500	460	545	100,545
10	100,545	3,955**	4,500	545	—	100,000

*Rounded to nearest dollar.
**Error due to rounding.

Amortizing Bond Premium

When bonds are issued at a premium, the amount of the premium must be spread over the life of the bonds to lower the interest expense. As noted earlier in describing bond discounts, the effective interest method is the more acceptable way of amortizing bond premium. Using the same facts as above, the amortization of the bond premium under the effective interest method is shown in Table 14-2. This table is much like Table 14-1. The difference is that interest expense for the period is the amount of interest paid less the amount of the premium amortized for the period. The first interest payment is recorded as follows:

		Debit	Credit
July 1	Bond Interest Expense	4,164	
	Unamortized Bond Premium	336	
	Cash (or Interest Payable)		4,500
	Paid (or accrued) semiannual interest to bondholders and amortized premium on 9%, 5-year bonds		

Note that the interest expense to be recorded each period decreases. It goes down because the carrying value to which the effective interest rate is applied becomes less in each period. Also note that the Unamortized Bond Premium drops to zero and the carrying value decreases to the face value over the life of the bond.

To find the amount of premium amortization in any one interest payment period, we subtract the effective interest expense (the carrying value times the effective interest rate) from the interest payment. In semiannual interest period 5, for example, the amortization of premium equals \$393 [(\$102,674 × .04) − \$4,500].

Bond Issue Costs

Of course, there are costs connected with the issuance of bonds. Most bonds are sold through underwriters. The underwriters receive a fee for taking care of the details of marketing the issue or for taking a chance on getting the selling price. Since bond issue costs benefit the whole life of the bond issue, it makes sense to spread these costs over that period. It is generally accepted practice to establish a separate account for bond issue costs and amortize them over the life of the bonds. However, issue costs decrease the amount of money received by the company for the bond issue. Thus they have the effect of raising the discount or lowering the premium on the issue. As a result, bond issue costs may be spread over the life of the bonds through the amortization of discount or premium. Because this method simplifies the record keeping, it is assumed in the text and problems of this book that all bond issues at either a discount or premium are priced at the net of bond issue costs.

Year-End Accrual for Bond Interest Expense

It is not often that bond interest payment dates will correspond to a company's fiscal year. An adjustment therefore must be made at the end of the accounting period to accrue the interest expense on the bonds from the last payment date to the end of the fiscal year. Further, if there is any discount or premium on the bonds it must also be amortized for the fractional period. Remember that in the earlier example, Vason Corporation issued $100,000 in bonds on January 1 at 104.1. The company's fiscal year ends September 30, 19x0. In the period since the interest payment and amortization of premium on July 1, three months' interest has accrued, and the following adjusting entry must be made:

Sept. 30	Bond Interest Expense	2,075.50	
	Unamortized Bond Premium	174.50	
	Interest Payable		2,250.00
	Accrued interest on 9% bonds payable for three months and amortized one-half of the premium for second interest payment period		

This entry covers one-half of the second interest period. The Unamortized Bond Premium is debited for $174.50, which is one-half of $349—the amortization of premium for the second period from Table 14-2. Accrued Interest Payable is credited for $2,250, for three months' interest ($100,000 × .09 × ¼) on the face value of the bonds. The net debit figure of $2,075.50 ($2,250 − $174.50) is the Bond Interest Expense for the three-month period.

When the January 1, 19x1, payment date arrives, the entry to pay the bondholders and amortize the premium is as follows:[4]

Jan. 1	Bond Interest Expense	2,075.50	
	Interest Payable	2,250.00	
	Unamortized Bond Premium	174.50	
	Cash		4,500.00
	Paid semiannual interest including that previously accrued and amortized the premium for the period since the end of the fiscal year		

As shown above, one-half ($2,250) of the amount paid ($4,500) was accrued on September 30. The Unamortized Bond Premium is debited for the remaining amount from Table 14-2 to be amortized for the period ($349.00 − $174.50 = $174.50). The resulting Bond Interest Expense is the amount that applies to the three-month period from September 30 to January 1.

Bond discounts are recorded at year end in the same way as bond premiums. The difference is that the amortization of bond discounts will increase interest expense instead of decreasing it as a premium does.

4. This entry assumes that a reversing entry of the accrual was not made on October 1. Some firms may prefer to use reversing entries.

Retirement of Bonds

OBJECTIVE 4
Account for the retirement of bonds and the conversion of bonds into stock

Most bond issues provide for a call feature. This feature gives the corporation a chance to buy back and retire the bonds at a given price, usually above face value, before maturity. Such bonds are known as **callable bonds.** They give the corporation flexibility in financing its operations. If bond interest rates drop, the company can call its bonds and reissue debt at a lower interest rate. The bond indenture will state the time period and the prices at which the bonds can be redeemed.

As an illustration of this feature, assume that Vason Corporation may call or retire the $100,000 bond issue (the one issued at a premium) at 105 and that it decides to do so on July 1, 19x3. To avoid complexity, this illustration assumes retirement on an interest payment date. Because the bonds were issued on January 1, 19x0, the retirement takes place on the seventh interest payment date. Assume that the entry for the interest payment (which must be made) and the amortization of premium have been made. Then the entry to retire the bonds is as follows:

19x3			
July 1	Bonds Payable	100,000	
	Unamortized Bond Premium	1,447	
	Loss on Retirement of Bonds	3,553	
	Cash		105,000
	Retired 9% bonds at 105		

In this entry, the cash paid is the face value times the call price ($100,000 × 1.05 = $105,000). The Unamortized Bond Premium can be found in column E of Table 14-2. The loss on retirement of bonds occurs because the call price of the bonds is greater than the carrying value ($105,000 − $101,447 = $3,553). The loss is presented as an extraordinary item on the income statement, as explained in Chapter 13.

Sometimes a rise in the market interest rate will cause the market value of the bonds to fall considerably below the face amount of the bond. If it has the cash to do so, the company may find it advantageous to purchase the bonds on the open market and retire them, rather than to wait and pay them off at face value. When this occurs, it is called **early extinguishment of debt,** and an extraordinary gain is recognized for the difference between the purchase price of the bonds and the face value of the bonds retired. For example, assume that due to a rise in interest rates, Vason Corporation was able to purchase the $100,000 bond issue on the open market at 85, making it unnecessary to call the bonds at the higher price of 105. Then the entry would be as follows:

19x3			
July 1	Bonds Payable	100,000	
	Unamortized Bond Premium	1,447	
	Cash		85,000
	Gain on Early Extinguishment of Debt		16,447
	Purchased and retired 9% bonds at 85		

Conversion of Bonds into Stock

Bonds that may be exchanged for other securities of the corporation (in most cases common stock) are called **convertible bonds**. These bonds may be exchanged if the bondholder wishes. The conversion feature may be added to make the bonds more attractive to some investors. The convertible bond gives the investor a chance of making more money because if the market price of the common stock rises, the value of the bond rises. However, if the price of the common stock does not rise, the investor still holds the bond and receives the periodic interest payment as well as the principal at the maturity date.

When bonds are converted into common stock, the basic accounting rule is that the common stock is recorded at the carrying value of the bonds. The bond liability and associated unamortized discount or premium are written off the books. For this reason, no gain or loss is recorded on the transaction. For example, suppose that the bonds in the earlier case are not called on July 1, 19x3. Instead, Vason Corporation's stockholders decide to convert all the bonds to $8 par value common stock under a convertible provision of 40 shares of common stock for each $1,000 bond. The entry would be

19x3			
July 1	Bonds Payable	100,000	
	Unamortized Bond Premium	1,447	
	Common Stock		32,000
	Paid-in Capital in Excess of Par Value, Common		69,447
	Converted 9% bonds payable into common stock at a rate of 40 shares for each $1,000 bond		

The Unamortized Bond Premium is found in the semiannual interest period of Table 14-2. At a rate of 40 shares for each $1,000 bond, 4,000 shares will be issued at a total par value of $32,000 (4,000 × $8). The Common Stock account is credited for the amount of the par value of the stock issued. Another account, called Paid-in Capital in Excess of Par Value, Common, is credited for the difference between the carrying value of the bonds and the par value of the stocks issued ($101,447 − $32,000 = $69,447). No gain or loss is recorded on this transaction.

Bond Sinking Fund

Many bond issues require that funds be set aside over the life of the issue. This is done to satisfy investors that money will be available to pay the bondholders at maturity. This segregation of assets is called a **bond sinking fund**. The bond indenture will usually state that the

Table 14-3. Growth of Annual Investments in Sinking Fund

	A	B	C	D
End of Year	Fund Balance at Beginning of Year	Deposit	Interest at 8% (8% × A)	Fund Balance at End of Year (A + B + C)
1	$ —	$17,044.49	$ —	$ 17,044.49
2	17,045.65	17,044.49	1,363.56	35,452.54
3	35,452.54	17,044.49	2,836.20	55,333.23
4	55,333.23	17,044.49	4,426.66	76,804.38
5	76,804.38	17,044.49	6,144.35	99,993.22*

*Off 6.78 due to rounding.

corporation will make periodic deposits over the life of the bonds. The trustee has control of the fund, and is charged with investing the deposits in income-producing securities. It is intended that the deposits plus the earnings on the investment be large enough to pay the bonds at maturity. Because the assets in the sinking fund cannot be used by the corporation for current operations, the sinking fund is classified as a long-term investment on the balance sheet.

OBJECTIVE 5
Compute sinking fund requirements, and prepare accounting entries associated with sinking fund bonds payable

When a corporation establishes a sinking fund, it must determine how much cash will be set aside each period to pay the bonds. The amount will depend on the estimated rate of return the investments can earn. Let us illustrate the accounting for a bond sinking fund. Assume that the Vason Corporation agrees with a trustee to set aside enough cash at the end of each year of its bond issue to accumulate the $100,000 maturity value. The trustee will be able to earn an 8 percent return on the investment of the cash deposited by the company. To pay the bonds in five years, the company must deposit $17,045.65 at the end of each year.[5] The investments will grow to a point where the sinking fund is equal to the principal at the maturity date, as shown in Table 14-3.

The entry to record the creation of the sinking fund and the annual deposit would be as follows:

Dec. 31	Bond Sinking Fund	17,044.49	
	Cash		17,044.49
	Paid the annual deposit to the bond sinking fund		

Every year the sinking fund trustee invests these funds to get the best return possible. The trustee collects interest and dividends and reports

5. This annual payment may be computed by using Table D-2 in Appendix D. Divide the principal by the future value of an annuity for five periods at 8 percent compound interest to find the amount of the annuity ($100,000 ÷ 5.867 = $17,045.65).

them to the corporation. As an illustration, assume that the cash set aside by the Vason Corporation earned the necessary $1,363.56 the second year. The earnings would be recorded as shown in the following entry:

Dec. 31	Bond Sinking Fund	1,363.65	
	Income from Bond Sinking Fund		1,363.65
	To record income from investment in the bond sinking fund		

The earnings of the sinking fund would appear on the income statement as Other Revenue.

If investments in the sinking fund are sold and result in a gain or loss, the transaction should be recognized by increasing or decreasing the bond sinking fund. For example, if the sale of an investment results in a $1,000 loss, the entry will be:

May 21	Loss on Sale of Sinking Fund Investment	1,000	
	Bond Sinking Fund		1,000
	To record loss on investment in bond sinking fund		

When the bonds mature, the trustee must sell the investments to obtain the cash to pay the bondholders. The amount earned in the fund over the years will rise and fall. Thus the actual cash realized is not likely to equal exactly the amount necessary to pay the bondholders. When excess cash is available, it should be transferred to Cash. If there is less cash than necessary to retire the bonds, the corporation must provide additional cash. For example, assume that at the bond maturity date the sinking fund had a carrying value of $100,100 and realized a total of $99,600 when liquidated. The entry to pay the bonds follows:

Dec. 31	Bonds Payable	100,000	
	Loss on Sale of Sinking Fund Assets	500	
	Sinking Fund		100,100
	Cash		400
	To record liquidation of sinking fund and payment of bonds at maturity		

The loss would be shown in the income statement as part of Other Income and Expense.

Other Long-Term Liabilities

A company may have other long-term liabilities besides bonds—the most common are mortgages payable, long-term leases, and pensions.

Mortgages Payable

OBJECTIVE 6
Explain the basic features of mortgages payable, long-term leases, and pensions as long-term liabilities

A **mortgage** is a type of long-term debt secured by real property. It is usually paid in equal monthly installments. Each monthly payment is partly interest on the debt and partly a reduction in the debt. To illustrate this point, Table 14-4 shows the first three monthly payments on a $50,000, 15 percent mortgage. The mortgage was obtained on June 1 and the monthly payments are $900. According to the table, the entry to record the July 1 payment would be as shown below.

July 1	Mortgage Payable	275	
	Mortgage Interest Expense	625	
	Cash		900
	Made monthly mortgage payment		

Note from the entry and from Table 14-4 that the July 1 payment represents interest expense of $625 ($50,000 × .15 × 1/12) and a reduction in the debt of $275 ($900 − $625). So the unpaid balance is reduced by the $275 to $49,725 in July. Therefore the interest expense for August is slightly less than it was for July.

Table 14-4. Monthly Payment Schedule on $50,000, 15 Percent Mortgage

	A	B	C	D	E
Payment Date	Unpaid Balance at Beginning of Period	Monthly Payment	Interest for 1 Month at 1¼% on Unpaid Balance* (1¼% × A)	Reduction in Debt (B − C)	Unpaid Balance at End of Period (A − D)
June 1					$50,000
July 1	$50,000	$900	$625	$275	49,725
Aug. 1	49,725	900	622	278	49,447
Sept. 1	49,447	900	618	282	49,165

*Rounded to nearest dollar.

Long-Term Leases

There are different ways in which a company may get new operating assets. One way is to borrow the money and buy the asset. Another is to rent the equipment on a short-term lease. A third way is to obtain the equipment on a long-term lease. The first two methods cause no unusual accounting problems. In the first case, the asset and liability are recorded at the amount paid, and the asset is subject to periodic depreciation. In the second case, the lease is short-term or cancelable, and the risks of ownership lie with the lessor. This type of lease is called an **operating lease.** It is proper accounting to treat operating lease payments as an expense and to debit the amount of each monthly payment to Rent Expense.

The third case, a long-term lease, is one of the fastest-growing ways of financing operating equipment in the U.S. economy. It has several advantages. For instance, it requires no immediate cash payment. The rental payment is deducted in full for tax purposes. And it costs less than a short-term lease. Acquiring the use of a plant asset under a long-term lease does cause several accounting problems, however. Often, such leases may not be canceled. Also, their length may be about the same as the useful life of the asset. Finally, they provide for the lessee to buy the asset at a nominal price at the end of the lease. The lease is much like an installment purchase because the risks of ownership lie with the lessee. The lessee company's available assets have increased and its legal obligations (liabilities) have increased because it must make a number of payments over the life of the asset. So this "off-the-balance-sheet financing" leads to a balance sheet that omits a material asset and a material liability.

Noting this problem, the Financial Accounting Standards Board has described such a long-term lease as a **capital lease.** This term reflects the terms of the lease, which make the transaction more like a purchase/sale on installment. The FASB has ruled that in the case of a capital lease, the lessee must record an asset and a long-term liability equal to the value of the total lease payments during the lease term. In doing so, the lessee must use the present value at the beginning of the lease.[6] In much the same way as the mortgage payments above, each lease payment becomes partly interest expense and partly a repayment of debt. Further, depreciation expense is figured on the asset and entered on the records.

Suppose, for example, that Isaacs Company enters into a long-term lease for a machine used in its manufacturing operations. The lease terms call for an annual payment of $4,000 for six years, which approximates the useful life of the machine. (See Table 14-5.) At the end of the lease period, the title to the machine passes to Isaacs. This lease is clearly a capital lease and should be recorded according to FASB *Statement No. 13*.

A lease is a periodic payment for the right to use an asset or assets. Present value techniques, explained in Appendix C, can be used to value the asset and the corresponding liability associated with a capital lease. The present value of the lease payments may be computed as follows, if Isaacs' usual interest cost is 16 percent:

periodic payment	×	factor (Table D-4) (16%, 6 years)	=	present value
$4,000	×	3.685	=	$14,740

6. *Statement of Financial Accounting Standards No. 13*, "Accounting for Leases" (Stamford, Conn.: Financial Accounting Standards Board, 1976), par. 10.

The entry to record the lease contract is

Leased Asset, Equipment	14,740	
Lease Obligations		14,740

Leased Asset, Equipment is classified as a long-term asset and Lease Obligations is classified as a long-term liability. Each year, Isaacs must record depreciation on the leased asset. If we assume a six-year life and no salvage value, the entry will be

Depreciation Expense	2,456.67	
Accumulated Depreciation, Leased Equipment		2,456.67

The amount of the interest expense for each year would be computed by multiplying the interest rate (16 percent) by the amount of the remaining lease obligation. Table 14-5 shows these calculations. Using the data in Table 14-5, the first lease payment is recorded as follows:

Interest Expense (col. B)	2,358.40	
Lease Obligations (col. C)	1,641.60	
Cash		4,000.00

Table 14-5. Payment Schedule on 16 Percent Capital Lease

	A	B	C	D
Year	Lease Payment	Interest (16%) on Unpaid Obligation (D × 16%)	Reduction of Lease Obligation (A − B)	Balance of Lease Obligation
Beginning				$14,740.00
1	$ 4,000	$2,358.40	$ 1,641.60	13,098.40
2	4,000	2,095.74	1,904.26	11,194.14
3	4,000	1,791.06	2,208.94	8,985.20
4	4,000	1,437.63	2,562.37	6,422.83
5	4,000	1,027.65	2,972.35	3,450.48
6	4,000	549.52*	3,450.48	—
	$24,000	$9,260.00	$14,740.00	

*The last year's interest equals the lease payment minus the remaining balance of the lease obligation ($549.52 = $4,000 − $3,450.48) and does not exactly equal $552.08 ($3,450.48 × .16) because of cumulative rounding errors.

Pensions

Most employees who work for medium and large companies are covered by some sort of pension plan. A **pension plan** is a contract between the company and its employees wherein the company agrees to pay benefits after retirement. Most companies contribute the full cost of the pension, but sometimes the employees also pay a part of their salary or wages toward their pension. The contributions from both parties are generally paid into a **pension fund**, and the benefits are paid out of this fund to retirees. In most cases, pension benefits consist of monthly payments to employees after retirement and other payments on death or disability.

There are two kinds of pension plans. Under *defined contribution plans*, the employer is required to contribute an annual amount determined in the current year on the basis of agreements between the company and its employees or resolution of the board of directors. Retirement payments will depend on the amount of pension payments the accumulated contributions can support. Under *defined benefit plans*, the employer's required annual contribution is the amount required to fund pension liabilities that arise as a result of employment in the current year but whose amount will not be finally determined until the retirement and death of the persons currently employed. Here the amount of the contribution required in the current year depends on a fixed amount of future benefits but uncertain current contributions, whereas under a defined contribution plan, the uncertain future amount of pension liabilities depends on the cumulative amounts of fixed current contributions.

Accounting for annual pension expense under defined contribution plans is simple. After determining what contribution is required, Pension Expense is debited and a liability (or Cash) is credited.

Accounting for annual expense under defined benefit plans is one of the most complex topics in accounting, thus the intricacies are reserved for more advanced courses. However, in concept, the procedure is simple. Just as one contributes to a sinking fund to retire future bond liabilities, so one must contribute to a fund to pay future defined pension liabilities. There is a wide range of pension plans and methods to accrue pension expenses whose amounts will not be known for many years.[7] Most of these complications have to do with computing the pension costs that should be recognized in the current year. The amount of expense that employers must recognize in the current year is determined on the basis of actuarial calculations. Such calculations are extremely sensitive to the actuary's assumptions.

Once the amount of these costs is determined, the entry is the same as under the defined contribution plans: Pension Expense is debited and a current liability (or Cash) is credited. A pension liability exists at the year end if the full contribution has not been paid. This liability can be short-term, long-term, or a combination of both depending on the terms of the pension plan.

7. *Statement of Financial Accounting Standards No. 87*, "Employers' Accounting for Pensions" (Stamford, Conn.: Financial Accounting Standards Board, 1985).

In calculating the amount of the pension expense under a defined benefits plan, compound interest tables are used to find the present value of the future payments (defined benefits) for employees covered by the pension plan. The choice of the interest rate on which to compute the present value has major impact on the pension expense. In general, given a specified level of future pension benefits, the choice of a lower interest rate will cause a larger expense than the choice of a higher interest rate. For example, Goodyear Tire & Rubber Company reported pension expense in 1983 of $108,200,000. Borg-Warner reported a pension expense of $52,400,000 in 1983. It appears that Goodyear's pension obligation was about twice as large as Borg-Warner's. However, in the notes to the financial statements Goodyear reports that it used a rate of 8.5 percent to find the present value. Borg-Warner used a rate of 11 percent—a much less conservative rate than Goodyear's. Had Borg-Warner used a rate of 8.5 percent, the present value of its pension obligations would have been larger and the amount of the expense would have been much closer to Goodyear's. A difference of 2.5 percent in pension fund earnings over a long period of time can mean a difference of millions of dollars in the current year's expense. Only time will tell which company made a wise estimate of the pension expense.

Chapter Review

Review of Learning Objectives

1. **Identify and contrast the major characteristics of bonds.**
   When bonds are issued, the corporation enters into a contract with the bondholders, called a bond indenture. The bond indenture identifies the major conditions of the bonds. A corporation may issue several types of bonds, each having different characteristics. For example, a bond issue may require security or be unsecured. It may be payable at a single time (term) or at several times (serial). Also, it may be registered in the name of the holder, or the holder may be unidentified and have to return coupons to receive interest payable.

2. **Record the issuance of bonds at face value, between interest dates, and at a discount or premium.**
   When bonds are issued, the bondholders will pay an amount equal to, greater than, or less than the face value of the bond. A bondholder will pay face value for the bonds when the interest rate on the bonds approximates the market rate for similar investments. The issuing corporation records the issuance of bonds as a long-term liability called Bonds Payable equal to the face value of the bonds.

   If the bonds are sold on dates between the interest payment dates, the issuing corporation collects from the investor the interest that has accrued since the last interest payment date. When the next interest payment date arrives, the corporation pays the bondholder interest for the entire interest period.

Bonds are issued at a rate less than the face value of the bonds when the bond interest rate is below the market rate for similar investments. The difference between face value and issue price is called a discount and is debited to Unamortized Bond Discount.

If the interest rate on bonds is greater than the return on similar investments, investors will be willing to pay more than face value for the bonds. The difference between the issue price and face value is called a premium and is credited to Unamortized Bond Premium.

3. **Amortize bond discount and premium by using the effective interest method, and make year-end adjustments.**

When bonds are sold at a premium or discount, the result is an adjustment of the interest rate on the bonds from the face rate to an effective rate that is close to the market rate when the bonds were issued. Therefore, bond premiums or discounts have the effect of increasing or decreasing the interest paid on the bonds over their life. Under these conditions, it is necessary to amortize the premium or discount over the life of the bonds in a way that will adjust the interest expense from the stated interest to the effective interest. The effective interest method is the accepted method for amortizing bond discount or premium.

The effective interest method results in a constant rate of interest on the carrying value of the bonds. To find interest and the amortization of premiums or discounts we apply the effective interest rate to the carrying value (face value plus premium or minus discount) of the bonds at the beginning of the interest period. The amount of premium or discount to be amortized is the difference between the interest figured by using the effective rate and that obtained by using the stated rate.

When the end of a corporation's fiscal year does not agree with interest payment dates, the corporation must accrue bond interest expense from the last interest payment date to the end of the company's fiscal year. This accrual results in the inclusion of the interest expense in the year incurred.

4. **Account for the retirement of bonds and the conversion of bonds into stock.**

Callable bonds may be retired before maturity at the option of the issuing corporation. The call price is usually an amount greater than the face value of the bonds. Thus the corporation must usually recognize a loss on the retirement of the bonds. An extraordinary gain may be recognized on early extinguishment of debt, which results when a company purchases its bonds on the open market. This retirement method can be advantageous due to a rise in the market interest rate that causes the market value of the bonds to fall.

Convertible bonds allow the bondholder to convert bonds to stock of the issuing corporation. In this case, the common stocks being issued are recorded at the carrying value of the bonds being converted. No gain or loss is recognized.

5. **Compute sinking fund requirements, and prepare accounting entries associated with sinking fund bonds payable.**

Some bond issues require the issuing corporation to segregate assets of the company over the life of the bonds so cash will be available to pay the bonds at maturity. The segregated assets are called a bond sinking fund. The corporation deposits cash in the fund over the life of the bonds. The deposits plus earnings on the deposits are planned so they will be sufficient to pay the face value of the bonds at maturity.

6. **Explain the basic features of mortgages payable, long-term leases, and pensions as long-term liabilities.**
A mortgage is a type of long-term debt secured by real property. It is usually paid in equal monthly installments. Each payment is partly interest expense and partly debt repayment. If a long-term lease is a capital lease, the risks of ownership lie with the lessee. For a capital lease, an asset and a long-term liability should be recorded. The liability should be equal to the present value at the beginning of the lease of the total lease payment during the lease term. Like a mortgage payment, each lease payment is partly interest and partly reduction of debt. The recorded asset is subject to depreciation. A company is also required to record pension expense in the current period. The annual expense should be equal to the amortization of the present value of future benefits that are estimated to be paid to employees under a pension plan.

Review Problem
Interest and Amortization of Bond Discount and Bond Retirement

The Merrill Manufacturing Company is currently expanding its metal window division in Utah. The company does not have enough capital for the expansion. Thus management has sought and received approval from the board of directors to issue bonds for this activity. The company plans to issue $5,000,000 of 8 percent, five-year bonds in 19x1. Interest is paid on December 31 and June 30 of each year. The bonds are callable at 104. The bonds are sold on January 1, 19x1, at 96. The bonds have to be sold at a discount because the market rate for similar investments is 9 percent. The company plans to amortize the bond discount by using the effective interest method. On July 1, 19x3, one-half of the bonds were called and retired.

Required

1. Prepare an interest and amortization schedule for the first five interest payment dates.
2. Prepare the journal entries to record the sale of the bonds, the first two interest payments and the bond retirement.

Answer to Review Problem

1. Schedule for first five periods prepared. (See interest and amortization schedule at the top of page 542.)

Interest and Amortization of Bond Discount*

Semiannual Interest Payment	Carrying Value at Beginning of Period	Semi-annual Interest Expense (9% × ½)	Semi-annual Interest Paid per Period (8% × ½)	Amortization of Discount	Unamortized Bond Discount at End of Period	Carrying Value at End of Period
Jan. 1, 19x1					$200,000	
June 30, 19x1	$4,800,000	$216,000	$200,000	$16,000	184,000	$4,816,000
Dec. 31, 19x1	4,816,000	216,720	200,000	16,720	167,280	4,832,720
June 30, 19x2	4,832,720	217,472	200,000	17,472	149,808	4,850,192
Dec. 31, 19x2	4,850,192	218,259	200,000	18,259	131,549	4,868,451
June 30, 19x3	4,868,451	219,080	200,000	19,080	112,469	4,887,531

*Rounded to nearest dollar.

2. Journal entries prepared.

Date	Account	Debit	Credit
19x1			
Jan. 1	Cash	4,800,000	
	Unamortized Bond Discount	200,000	
	Bond Payable		5,000,000
	Sold $5,000,000 of 8% bonds at 96		
June 30	Bond Interest Expense	216,000	
	Unamortized Bond Discount		16,000
	Cash		200,000
	Paid semiannual interest payment		
Dec. 31	Bond Interest Expense	216,720	
	Unamortized Bond Discount		16,720
	Cash		200,000
	Paid semiannual interest payment		
19x3			
July 1	Bonds Payable	2,500,000	
	Loss on Retirement of Bonds Payable	156,235	
	Unamortized Bond Discount		56,235
	Cash		2,600,000
	Called $2,500,000 of 8% bonds and retired them at 104		

Chapter Assignments

Questions

1. What is the difference between a bond certificate, a bond issue, and a bond indenture? What are some examples of items found in a bond indenture?
2. What is the essential difference between the bonds in the case of (a) secured versus debenture bonds, (b) term versus serial bonds, and (c) registered versus coupon bonds?
3. Napier Corporation sold $500,000 of 5 percent bonds on the interest payment date. What would the proceeds from the sale be if the bonds were issued at 95, at 100, at 102?
4. If you were buying a bond on which the face interest rate was less than the market interest rate, would you expect to pay more or less than par value for the bonds? Why?
5. Why does the amortization of a bond discount increase interest expense to an amount above the amount of interest paid? Why does a premium have the opposite effect?
6. When bonds are issued between interest dates, why is it necessary for the issuer to collect an amount equal to accrued interest from the buyer?
7. When the effective interest rate method of amortizing bond discount or premium is used, why does the amount of interest expense change from period to period?
8. Why would a company want to exercise the callable provision of a bond when it can wait longer to pay off the debt?
9. What are the advantages of convertible bonds or convertible preferred stock to the company and to the investor?
10. The long-term investment section of the DeLoach Corporation balance sheet contains an account called Bond Sinking Fund. What is the purpose of this account?
11. What are the two components of a uniform monthly mortgage payment?
12. Under what conditions is a long-term lease called a capital lease? Why would such a lease result in recording both an asset and a liability? What items would appear on the income statement as a result of such a lease?
13. What is a pension plan? What assumptions have to be made to account for the expenses associated with the plan?
14. What is the difference between a defined contribution plan and a defined benefit plan? In general, how is expense determined under each?

Classroom Exercises[8]

Exercise 14-1. Bond Issue Entries (L.O. 2)

Raritan is authorized to issue $800,000 in bonds on June 1. The bonds carry a face interest rate of 9 percent, which is to be paid on June 1 and December 1.

Prepare journal entries for the issue of the bonds by Raritan under the assumptions that (a) the bonds are issued on September 1 at 100 and (b) the bonds are issued on June 1 at 105.

Exercise 14-2. Sale of Bonds and Interest Payments (L.O. 2, 3)

The Chippewa Drapery Company sold $600,000 of its 9½ percent, twenty-year bonds on April 1, 19xx, at 106. The semiannual interest payment dates are April 1 and October 1. The effective interest rate is approximately 8.9 percent. The company's fiscal year ends September 30.

Prepare journal entries to record the sale of these bonds on April 1, the accrual of interest and amortization of premium on September 30, and the first interest payment on October 1. Use the effective interest method to amortize the premium.

Exercise 14-3. Journal Entries for Interest and Amortization of Discount (L.O. 2, 3)

On March 1, 19x1, the Occidental Corporation issued $600,000 of five-year, 10 percent bonds. The semiannual interest payment dates are March 1 and September 1. Because the market rate for similar investments was 11 percent, the bonds had to be issued at a discount. The discount on the issuance of the bonds was $24,335.

Prepare the journal entries to record the bond issue on March 1, 19x1, and the payments of interest and amortization of the discount on September 1, 19x1, and March 1, 19x2. Use the effective interest method. (Ignore year-end accruals.)

Exercise 14-4. Journal Entries for Interest Payments (L.O. 3)

The long-term debt section of the Genesis Corporation's balance sheet at the end of its fiscal year, December 31, 1983, is shown below:

Long-Term Liabilities		
Bonds Payable—8%, interest payable 1/1 and 7/1, due 12/31/98	$500,000	
Unamortized Bond Discount	(40,000)	$460,000

Prepare the journal entries relevant to the interest payments on July 1, 1984, December 31, 1984, and January 1, 1985. Assume an effective interest rate of 10 percent.

Exercise 14-5. Bond Retirement Journal Entry (L.O. 4)

The Del Ray Corporation has outstanding $700,000 of 8 percent bonds callable at 104. On September 1, immediately after recording the payment of the semiannual interest, the unamortized bond discount equaled $21,000. On that date, $400,000 of the bonds were called and retired.

Prepare the entry to record the retirement of the bonds on September 1.

8. Bond interest rates are most often quoted in eighths of a percent. Some exercises and problems in this chapter quote the rates in tenths of a percent to ease the burden of computation.

Exercise 14-6. Bond Conversion Journal Entry (L.O. 4)

The Dyson Corporation has $500,000 of 6 percent convertible bonds outstanding. There is $20,000 of unamortized discount remaining on these bonds after the July 1, 19x8 semiannual interest payment. The bonds are convertible at the rate of 40 shares of $5 par value common stock for each $1,000 bond. On July 1, 19x8 bondholders presented $300,000 of the bonds for conversion.

Prepare the journal entry to record the conversion of the bonds.

Exercise 14-7. Mortgage Payable (L.O. 6)

Herrman Corporation purchased a building by signing a long-term $150,000 mortgage with monthly payments of $2,000. The mortgage carries an interest rate of 12 percent.

1. For the first three months, prepare a monthly payment schedule showing the monthly payment, the interest for the month, the reduction in debt, and the unpaid balance. (Round to the nearest dollar.)
2. Prepare a journal entry to record the purchase and the first two monthly payments.

Exercise 14-8. Valuing Bonds Using Present Value (L.O. 2)

Ravenswood, Inc., is considering two bond issues. (a) One is a $200,000 bond issue that pays semiannual interest of $16,000 and is due in twenty years. (b) The other is a $200,000 bond issue that pays semiannual interest of $15,000 and is due in fifteen years. Assume that the market rate of interest for each bond is 12 percent.

Calculate the amount that Ravenswood, Inc., will receive if both bond issues occur. (Calculate the present value of each bond issue and sum.)

Exercise 14-9. Zero Coupon Bonds (L.O. 2)

The Commonwealth of Virginia is considering issuing zero coupon bonds, which have no periodic interest payments. It needs to raise $50,000,000 for highway repairs. The current market rate of interest for the bonds is 10 percent. What face value of bonds must be issued to raise the needed funds, assuming the bonds will be due in thirty years and compounded annually? How would your answer change if the bonds were due in fifty years? How would both answers change if the market rate of interest were 8 percent instead of 10 percent?

Exercise 14-10. Time Value of Money and Early Extinguishment of Debt (L.O. 2, 4)

Mercurio, Inc., has a $300,000, 8 percent bond issue that was issued a number of years ago at face value. There are now ten years left on the bond issue, and the market rate of interest is 16 percent. Interest is paid semiannually.

1. Figure the current market value of the bond issue, using present value tables.
2. Record the retirement of the bonds, assuming the company purchased the bonds on the open market at the calculated value.

Exercise 14-11. Recording Lease Obligations (L.O. 6)

Chemco Corporation has leased a piece of equipment that has a useful life of twelve years. The terms of the lease are $17,400 per year for twelve years. Chemco is able to borrow money currently for a long-term interest rate of 15 percent.

1. Calculate the present value of the lease.
2. Prepare the journal entry to record the lease agreement.
3. Prepare the entry to record depreciation of the equipment for the first year.
4. Prepare the entries to record the lease payment for the first two years.

Interpreting Accounting Information

Franklin Savings Association[9]
(L.O. 2, 3)

A notice appeared in the November 16, 1984, *Wall Street Journal* stating that Franklin Savings Association of Kansas was issuing $2.9 billion in zero coupon bonds. Zero coupon means that "The Bonds do not pay interest periodically. The only scheduled payment to the holder of a Bond will be the amount at maturity." The details of two components of the issue are as follows:

$800,000,000 Bonds due December 12, 2014, at 3.254%
$500,000,000 Bonds due December 12, 2024, at 1.380%

plus accrued amortization, if any, of original issue discount from December 12, 1984, to date of delivery

Required

1. Assuming all the bonds are issued on December 12, 1984, make the general journal entry to record each component shown above.
2. Determine the approximate effective interest rate on each of the two components of the bond issue. Assume that interest is compounded annually. (Hint: Use Table B-3.)
3. Prepare general entries to record Bond Interest Expense for each of the first two years (December 12, 1985 and 1986) on the component of the bond due in 2014 (ignore effects of fiscal year-ends). What advantages or disadvantages are there to Franklin in issuing zero coupon bonds?

Problem Set A

Problem 14A-1. Bond Transactions
(L.O. 2, 3)

Levitan Corporation has $20,000,000 of 10½ percent, twenty-year bonds dated June 1, with interest payment dates of May 30 and November 30. The company's fiscal year ends December 31. It uses the effective interest method to amortize premium or discount.

Required

1. Prepare general journal entries for August 1, November 30, and December 31. Assume the bonds are issued at face value plus accrued interest on August 1.
2. Prepare general journal entries for June 1, November 30, and December 31. Assume the bonds were issued at 103 on June 1, to yield an effective interest rate of 10.1 percent.
3. Prepare general journal entries for June 1, November 30, and December 31. Assume the bonds were issued at 97 on June 1, to yield an effective interest rate of 10.9 percent.

Problem 14A-2. Bonds Issued at Discount and Premium
(L.O. 2, 3)

Padorr Corporation found it necessary to raise capital by issuing bonds twice during 19x1. The following transactions describe these financing activities:

19x1

Jan. 1 Issued $2,000,000 of its own 9⅕ percent, 10-year bonds dated January 1, 19x1, with interest payable on June 30 and December 31. The bonds were sold at 98.1, resulting in an effective interest rate of 9.5 percent.

Apr. 1 Issued $2,000,000 of its own 9⅘ percent, 10-year bonds dated April 1, 19x1, with interest payable on March 31 and September 30. The bonds were sold at 102, resulting in an effective interest rate of 9.5 percent.

9. Figures from the *Wall Street Journal* notice reprinted by permission from Franklin Savings Association, One Franklin Plaza, Ottawa, Kansas 66067.

June 30 Paid semiannual interest on the January 1 issue and amortized the discount, using the effective interest rate method.
Sept. 30 Paid semiannual interest on the April 1 issue and amortized the premium, using the effective interest rate method.
Dec. 31 Paid semiannual interest on the January 1 issue and amortized the discount, using the effective interest rate method.
31 Made an adjusting entry to accrue interest on the April 1 issue and amortize one-half the premium applicable to the second interest period.

19x2
Mar. 31 Paid semiannual interest on the April 1 issue and amortized the premium applicable to the second half of the second interest period.

Required

Prepare general journal entries to record the bond transactions.

Problem 14A-3. Bond and Mortgage Transactions Contrasted
(L.O. 2, 3, 6)

Tolbert Manufacturing Company is expanding its operations by building and equipping a new plant. It is financing the building and land by issuing a $10,000,000, thirty-year mortgage, which carries an interest rate of 12 percent and requires monthly payments of $118,000. The company is financing the equipment and working capital for the new plant by issuing $10,000,000, twenty-year bonds, which carry a face interest rate of 11 percent, payable semiannually on March 31 and September 30. Selected transactions during 19x1 and 19x2 related to these two financing issues are as follows:

19x1
Jan. 1 Signed mortgage in exchange for land and building. Land represents 10 percent of total price.
Feb. 1 Made first mortgage payment.
Mar. 1 Made second mortgage payment.
31 Issued bonds for cash at 96, a price that results in an effective interest rate of 11.5 percent.
Apr. 1 Made third mortgage payment.
May 1 Made fourth mortgage payment.
June 1 Made fifth mortgage payment.
30 Made year-end adjusting entry to accrue interest on bonds and amortize the discount, using the effective interest method.
July 1 Made sixth mortgage payment.
Aug. 1 Made seventh mortgage payment.
Sept. 1 Made eight mortgage payment.
30 Made first interest payment on bonds and amortized the discount for the time period since the end of the fiscal year.

19x2
Mar. 31 Made second interest payment on bonds and amortized the discount for the time period since the last interest payment.

Required

1. Prepare a monthly payment schedule for the mortgage for ten months with the following headings (round amounts to the nearest dollar): Payment Date Unpaid Balance at Beginning of Period, Monthly Payment, Interest for One Month at 1% on Unpaid Balance, Reduction in Debt, and Unpaid Balance at End of Period.

2. Prepare the journal entries for the selected transactions. (Ignore the mortgage payments between October 1, 19x1, and March 1, 19x2.)

Problem 14A-4. Bond Interest and Amortization Table and Bond Retirements
(L.O. 3, 4)

Ayala Corporation is authorized to issue $20,000,000 of six-year unsecured bonds. The bonds carry a face interest rate of 9 percent, payable semiannually on June 30 and December 31. Each $2,000 bond is convertible into forty shares of $20 par value common stock. The bonds are callable at 105 any time after June 30, 19x4.

All bonds are issued on July 1, 19x1, at 95.568, a price yielding effective interest of 10 percent.

On July 1, 19x4, one-half of the outstanding bonds were called by the company and retired.

Required

1. Prepare a table similar to Table 14-1, showing the interest and amortization of bond discount for twelve interest payment periods. Use the effective interest method (round results to the nearest dollar).
2. Prepare general journal entries for the bond issue, interest payments and amortization of bond discounts, and bond retirement on the following dates: July 1, 19x1; December 31, 19x1; June 30, 19x4; July 1, 19x4; and December 31, 19x4.

Problem 14A-5. Comprehensive Bond Transactions
(L.O. 2, 3, 4)

The Bosmed Corporation, a company with a June 30 fiscal year, engaged in the following long-term bond transactions over a three year period:

19x5

Nov. 1 Issued $10,000,000 of 12 percent debenture bonds at face value plus accrued interest. Interest is payable on January 31 and July 31, and the bonds are callable at 104.

19x6

Jan. 31 Made the semiannual interest payment on the 12 percent bonds.

June 30 Made the year-end accrual of interest payment on the 12 percent bonds.

July 31 Issued $20,000,000 of 10 percent convertible bonds at 105. Interest is payable on June 30 and December 31, and each $1,000 in bonds is convertible into 30 shares of $10 par value common stock. The market rate of interest is 9 percent.

31 Made the semiannual interest payment on the 12 percent bonds.

Dec. 31 Made the semiannual interest payment on the 10 percent bonds and amortized the bond premium.

19x7

Jan. 31 Made the semiannual interest payment on the 12 percent bonds.

Feb. 28 Called and retired all the 12 percent bonds, including accruing the interest to the date of the conversion.

June 30 Made the semiannual interest payment on the 10 percent bonds and amortized the bond premium.

July 1 Accepted for conversion into common stock all the 10 percent bonds.

Required

Prepare general journal entries to record the bond transactions making all necessary accruals and using the effective interest rate method.

Problem Set B

Problem 14B-1. Bond Transactions (L.O. 2, 3)

Papyrus Corporation has $10,000,000 of 9½ percent, twenty-five-year bonds dated March 1, with interest payable on March 1 and September 1. The company's fiscal year ends on November 30, and it uses the effective interest method to amortize premium or discount.

Required

1. Prepare general journal entries for June 1, September 1, and November 30. Assume that the bonds were issued on June 1 at face value plus accrued interest.
2. Prepare general journal entries for March 1, September 1, and November 30. Assume that the bonds were issued at 102.5 on March 1, to yield an effective interest rate of 9.2 percent.
3. Prepare general journal entries for March 1, September 1, and November 30. Assume that the bonds were issued at 97.5 on March 1, to yield an effective interest rate of 9.8 percent.

Problem 14B-2. Bonds Issued at Discount and Premium (L.O. 2, 3)

Munoz Corporation sold bonds twice during 19x2. A summary of the transactions involving these bonds is presented below.

19x2

Jan. 1 Issued $2,000,000 of its own 9⁹⁄₁₀ percent, ten-year bonds dated January 1, 19x2, with interest payable on December 31 and June 30. The bonds were sold at 102.6, resulting in an effective interest rate of 9.4 percent.

Mar. 1 Issued $1,000,000 of its own 9⅕ percent, ten-year bonds dated March 1, 19x2, with interest payable March 1 and September 1. The bonds were sold at 98.2, resulting in an effective interest rate of 9.5 percent.

June 30 Paid the semiannual interest on the January 1 issue and amortized the premium, using the effective interest rate method.

Sept. 1 Paid the semiannual interest on the March 1 issue and amortized the discount, using the effective interest rate method.

Dec. 31 Paid the semiannual interest on the January 1 issue and amortized the premium, using the effective interest rate method.

31 Made an end-of-year adjusting entry to accrue the interest on the March 1 issue and amortize two-thirds of the discount applicable to the second interest period.

19x3

Mar. 1 Paid the semiannual interest on the March 1 issue and amortized the remainder of the discount applicable to the second interest period.

Required

Prepare the general journal entries to record the bond transactions.

Problem 14B-3. Bond and Mortgage Transactions Contrasted (L.O. 2, 3, 6)

Kessler Grocery Stores, Inc., is expanding its operations by buying a chain of four outlets in another city. To finance this purchase of land and buildings, Kessler is getting a $2,000,000 mortgage that carries an interest rate of 12 percent and requires monthly payments of $27,000. To finance the rest of the purchase, Kessler is issuing $2,000,000 of 12½ percent unsecured bonds due in twenty years, with interest payable December 31 and June 30. Selected transactions relating to these two financing activities are listed on the next page.

Jan. 1 Issued the bonds for cash at 104 to yield an effective rate of 12 percent.
Feb. 1 Issued the mortgage in exchange for land and buildings. The land represents 15 percent of the purchase price.
Mar. 1 Made the first mortgage payment.
31 Made the year-end adjusting entry to accrue interest on the bonds and amortize the premium, using the effective interest method.
Apr. 1 Made the second mortgage payment.
May 1 Made the third mortgage payment.
June 1 Made the fourth mortgage payment.
30 Made the first semiannual interest payment on the bonds and amortized the premium for the time period since the end of the fiscal year.
July 1 Made the fifth mortgage payment.
Dec. 1 Made the tenth mortgage payment.
31 Made the second semiannual interest payment on the bonds and amortized the premium for the time period since the last payment.

Required

1. Prepare a payment schedule for the mortgage for ten months with these headings (round amounts to nearest dollar): Payment Date, Unpaid Balance at Beginning of Period, Monthly Payment, Interest for One Month at 1% on Unpaid Balance, Reduction in Debt, and Unpaid Balance at End of Period.
2. Prepare the journal entry for the selected transactions. (Ignore the mortgage payments of August 1 through November 1.)

Problem 14B-4. Bond Interest and Amortization Table and Bond Retirements
(L.O. 3, 4)

Okawa Corporation is authorized to issue $6,000,000 of unsecured bonds, due March 31, 19x6. The bonds carry a face interest rate of 11$\frac{3}{5}$ percent, payable semiannually on March 31 and September 30. The bonds are callable at 104 any time after March 31, 19x4.

All the bonds are issued on April 1, 19x1, at 102.261, a price that yields effective interest of 11 percent.

On April 1, 19x4, Okawa Corporation calls one-half of the outstanding bonds and retires them.

Required

1. Prepare a table similar to Table 14-2 to show the interest and amortization of the bond premium for ten interest payment periods, using the effective interest method (round results to nearest dollar).
2. Prepare general journal entries for the bond issue, interest payments and amortization of bond premium, and bond retirement on: April 1, 19x1; September 30, 19x1; March 31, 19x4; April 1, 19x4; and September 30, 19x4.

Problem 14B-5. Comprehensive Bond Transactions
(L.O. 2, 3, 4)

Over a period of three years, UAX Corporation, a company with a December 31 year end, engaged in the following transactions involving two bond issues:

19x1
July 1 Issued $20,000,000 of 12 percent convertible bonds at 96. The bonds are convertible into $20 par value common stock at the rate of twenty shares of stock for each $1,000 bond. Interest is payable on June 30 and December 31, and the market rate of interest is 13 percent.
Dec. 31 Made semiannual interest payment and amortized bond discount.
19x2
June 1 Issued $10,000,000 of 9 percent bonds at face value plus accrued interest.

Interest is payable on February 28 and August 31. The bonds are callable at 105, and the market rate of interest is 9 percent.

30 Made semiannual interest payment on 12 percent bonds and amortized the bond discount.

Aug. 31 Made semiannual interest payment on 9 percent bonds.

Dec. 31 Made semiannual interest payment on 12 percent bonds, amortized discount, and accrued interest on 9 percent bonds.

19x3

Feb. 28 Made semiannual interest payment on 9 percent bonds.

June 30 Made semiannual interest payment on 12 percent bonds.

July 1 Accepted for conversion into common stock all 12 percent bonds.

July 31 Called and retired all 9 percent bonds including accrued interest.

Required

Prepare general journal entries to record the bond transactions making all necessary accruals and using the effective interest rate method.

Financial Decision Case

Gianni Chemical Corporation (L.O. 2, 6)

The Gianni Chemical Corporation plans to build a new plant that will produce liquid fertilizer to sell to agricultural markets. The plant is expected to cost $200,000,000 and will be located in the southwestern part of the United States. The company's chief financial officer, Julio Bassi, has spent the last several weeks studying different means of financing the plant's construction. In talking with bankers and other financiers, he has decided that there are two basic choices. The plant can be financed through the issuance of long-term bonds or through a long-term lease. The two options can be summarized as follows:

a. Issuance of $200,000,000 of 25-year, 16 percent bonds that are secured by the new plant. Interest on the bonds is payable semiannually.
b. Signing of a 25-year lease calling for semiannual lease payments of $16,350,000.

Now that Bassi knows what the two basic choices are, he wants to look at the accounting effects of each choice on the financial statements. He estimates that the useful life of the plant is 25 years, at which time it is expected to have an estimated residual value of $20,000,000.

Required

1. Prepare the entries to record issuance of the bonds in exchange for the fertilizer plant. Assume that the transaction occurs on the first day of the fiscal year, which is July 1. Also prepare entries to pay the interest expense and interest payable and to record depreciation on the plant during the first year. Assume that the straight-line method is used. Describe the effects that these transactions will have on the balance sheet and income statement.
2. Prepare the entries required to treat the long-term lease as a capital lease. Assume that the plant is occupied on the first day of the fiscal year, July 1, and that an interest rate of 16 percent applies. Also prepare entries to record the lease payments and to record depreciation during the first year. Describe the effects that these transactions will have on the balance sheet and income statement. (A knowledge of present value, which is dealt with in Chapter 7 and Table D-4 in Appendix D, is necessary to do part 2.)
3. What factors would you consider important to deciding which alternative to choose? Contrast the annual cash requirement of each alternative.

CALDWELL NEEDLES ANDERSON

PART FIVE BASIC CONCEPTS OF MANAGEMENT ACCOUNTING

The first four parts of this book dealt primarily with financial accounting and the measurement and reporting problems pertaining to general-purpose financial statements used by people outside the business entity, such as bankers and stockholders. The basic concepts and practices of internal or management accounting are explored in the final four parts of this text.

Part Five introduces the student to the basic concepts, terminology, and practices underlying management accounting. Specific types of information are needed by management to support day-to-day and long-term decisions. The management accountant provides these data.

Chapter 15 describes the field of management accounting, compares management accounting with financial accounting, and focuses on analysis of nonfinancial data which is common in the work environment of the management accountant.

Chapter 16 discusses the basic terminology used in accounting for internal operations. Reporting of manufacturing costs is also highlighted and illustrated.

Chapters 17 and 18 center on two approaches to product costing. After defining the concept of absorption costing and describing the development and use of predetermined overhead rates, Chapter 17 focuses on product costing within the job order cost accounting system. Chapter 18 analyzes product costing in a process cost accounting environment.

CHAPTER 15 INTRODUCTION TO MANAGEMENT ACCOUNTING

LEARNING OBJECTIVES

1. Describe the field of management accounting.
2. Distinguish between management accounting and financial accounting.
3. Compare the information needs of a manager of: (a) a manufacturing company; (b) a bank; and (c) a department store.
4. Identify the important questions a manager must consider before preparing a managerial report.
5. Prepare analyses of nonfinancial data.
6. State the differences between accounting for a manufacturing and a merchandising company.

This chapter begins your study of management accounting. In the first fourteen chapters, financial accounting issues and practices were emphasized. There are fundamental differences between the two disciplines, and those differences will be outlined. Management accounting will be defined and the practices and procedures associated with it will be introduced. This chapter includes a discussion of the information needs of managers and the important questions that must be answered before a report or analysis can be prepared. Since much of a management accountant's work deals with nonfinancial data, several cases will be used to illustrate these important types of reports.

The chapter concludes by comparing accounting for manufacturing and merchandising companies and by looking at the requirements for becoming a Certified Management Accountant (CMA). After studying this chapter, you should be able to meet the learning objectives listed on the left.

Financial Accounting Versus Management Accounting: Making the Transition

Management accounting, which is an extension of financial accounting, applies primarily to a company's internal operations and the decisions managers must make to carry out a company's mission. Different rules are applicable to accounting information created and prepared for management's use than to information reported to the general public. It is important that you understand the significance of these rules.

To help you make the transition from financial accounting to management accounting, think for a moment about your own life. You exist in an environment and a society composed of hundreds of rules and regulations. Some are social conduct rules, and others are legal, moral, ethical, and religious rules. Collectively, they determine your environment. Now, reflect on your home life as you were growing up. Remember all of those special rules laid down as law by your parents? Keep your room clean. Do your chores and your homework before going out. Dinner is served at 6:30 P.M., no later! Be on your best behavior when your grandparents arrive. When you entered your home, did you leave your external rules at the doorstep and assume an entirely new set when you went inside? Of course not. You simply added a new set of rules to those standards and created your own environment within your home.

When looking at the world of accounting, consider financial accounting as comprising all rules governing the accounting for and reporting of financial information that must be disclosed to people outside the company. Special rules apply to the gathering of this information, putting it into a workable accounting system, and combining it into a meaningful set of financial statements at year end. All this is done primarily for people outside the company, such as stockholders, bankers, creditors, and brokers.

The rules applicable to management accounting are similar to those special rules in the home described earlier. Management accounting exists primarily for the benefit of people inside the company. Usually there is a lot more information available to managers than to people outside the company. And what you can do with that information to make it more meaningful to those managers is limited only by your imagination, not a set of rigid rules. Your overall guideline or limit is that the report or analysis must be meaningful and answer the question or issue under review.

There are many accounting procedures and policies from financial accounting that carry over into management accounting, so you should not put what you have learned thus far on the shelf. Many of these areas, such as depreciation techniques, cash collection and disbursement procedures, inventory valuation methods, and the recognition of what is an asset or a liability, will be needed in your study of management accounting. A new set of rules for generating information for internal managers will be described in the remaining chapters of this book.

One important, additional point needs mentioning. A knowledge of management accounting is just as important to your career as a knowledge of financial accounting. If you plan to become a CPA, you will need your management accounting background when auditing a manufacturing company or service organization. If you become an accountant for a company or government organization, management accounting principles will be part of your daily life. And if you are destined for a position in marketing, finance, or management, you will have to deal with management accountants to obtain information to run your department or business. In other words, no matter what you do in the business world, you must rely on management accounting in one way or another.

Management Accounting

OBJECTIVE 1
Describe the field of management accounting

The field of management accounting consists of specific types of information gathering and reporting functions and related accounting techniques and procedures. When collectively applied to a company's financial and production data, management accounting procedures will satisfy management's information needs.

All business managers require accurate, timely information for pricing, planning, and decision-making purposes. Managers of production, merchandising, government, and service-oriented enterprises all depend on management accounting information. Management accounting is often associated with large multidivisional corporations with many segments engaged in manufacturing and assembly. These large corporations need more complex accounting and reporting systems than do small, one-owner businesses, such as a neighborhood grocery store or a shoe store. Even though large corporations need large *amounts* of information, small- and medium-size businesses need certain *types* of financial information just as much as large corporations. The types of data needed to ensure efficient operating conditions do not depend entirely on an organization's size.

The National Association of Accountants, in *Statement No. 1A* of its series of *Statements on Management Accounting,* defined **management accounting** as:

> . . . the process of identification, measurement, accumulation, analysis, preparation, and communication of financial information used by management to plan, evaluate, and control within the organization and to assure appropriate use and accountability for its resources.[1]

Three types of financial information are needed to effectively manage a company: (1) manufacturing and service-oriented companies need product costing information; (2) all companies need data to plan and control operations; and (3) managers need special reports and analyses to support their decisions. Product costing is the first type of information. It uses cost accounting techniques to gather production information, assign specific costs to product batches, and calculate product unit costs. Product costing techniques are discussed in Chapters 17 and 18.

Data for planning and control are organized in ways that help management plan production and its related costs. As production goes on and expected costs are incurred, formal control procedures are used to compare planned and actual costs so the effectiveness of operations and management can be measured. Chapters 19–23 focus on these planning and control functions of management accounting.

Special reports and analyses help management in decision making. All management decisions should be supported by analyses of alternate courses of action. The accountant is expected to supply information for these decisions. Several approaches used by accountants are discussed in Chapters 24, 25, and 26.

Comparing Management Accounting with Financial Accounting

Students often have problems coping with management accounting concepts and procedures because they have been trained in the procedures

1. National Association of Accountants, *Statement No. 1A* (New York, 1982).

OBJECTIVE 2
Distinguish between management accounting and financial accounting

and rules governing financial accounting. Management accounting has rules, too, but it is much more open and places fewer restrictions on the accountant's day-to-day efforts. Fewer restrictions mean somewhat less defined methods for doing things. Therefore, in this section you will take a closer look at the differences between management accounting and financial accounting. The comparison focuses primarily on (1) primary users of information; (2) types of accounting systems; (3) restrictive guidelines; (4) units of measurement; (5) focal point for analysis; (6) frequency of reporting; and (7) degree of reliability in the information generated. These areas of comparison are summarized in Table 15-1.

Primary Users of Information

The users of traditional financial statements are external to the company preparing the report. Internal management is responsible for preparing a company's annual financial statements, but this information is disclosed primarily for external users.

Table 15-1. Comparison of Financial and Management Accounting

Areas of Comparison	Financial Accounting	Management Accounting
1. Primary users of information	Persons and organizations outside the business entity	Various levels of internal management
2. Types of accounting systems	Double-entry systems	Not restricted to double-entry system; any useful system
3. Restrictive guidelines	Adherence to generally accepted accounting principles	No guides or restrictions: only criterion is usefulness
4. Units of measurement	Historical dollar	Any useful monetary or physical measurement, such as—labor hour or machine hour; if dollars are used, may be historical or future dollars
5. Focal point for analysis	Business entity as a whole	Various segments of the business entity
6. Frequency of reporting	Periodically on regular basis	Whenever needed; may not be on a regular basis
7. Degree of reliability	Demands objectivity; historical in nature	Heavily subjective for planning purposes, but objective data are used when relevant; futuristic in nature

In comparison, internal reports and analyses prepared by the management accountant are used by every member of management. The content of the reports varies, depending on the level of management being served, the department or segment being analyzed, and the purpose underlying each report. Emphasis is placed on supplying relevant information to people responsible for particular activities. Examples of different types and uses of internally generated information include: unit cost analyses for product costing purposes, budgets for planning future operations, control reports by responsibility unit for measuring performance, relevant cost reports for short-run decision making, and capital budgeting analyses for corporate long-run planning.

Types of Accounting Systems

Financial statements prepared for external use are made up of dollar totals, which reflect the balances of all accounts included in a company's general ledger. Before financial data are entered into the general ledger, the amounts must be coded, adjusted, and translated into a form suitable for a double-entry accounting system. Special journals, ledgers, and other analyses used to process financial accounting information are based on the double-entry system.

The analyses and flow of accounting data inside a company need not depend on the double-entry format. Data may be gathered for small segments or large divisions and may be expressed in units of measurement other than historical dollars. The information need not flow into and through general ledger accounts as in financial accounting. Special reports may be prepared for a particular manager's use with the process ending there. Under these conditions the information storage and retrieval system must have greater capabilities than those required for financial accounting. The major criterion in designing internal accounting systems is that the generated reports and analyses must be *useful* for meeting the information needs of management.

Restrictive Guidelines

Financial accounting is concerned with analyzing, classifying, recording, and reporting a company's financial activities. Since financial statements are prepared primarily for people external to the company, accountants must adhere to generally accepted accounting standards and principles that govern the recording, measuring, and reporting of financial information. Although necessary for protective and credibility purposes, generally accepted accounting principles confine accountants to a finite number of accounting practices. Examples of such restrictions include principles that involve matching revenues with expenses, stating inventories at lower of cost or market, reporting fixed assets at acquisition costs, realizing revenue in appropriate periods, and reporting on a consistent basis.

Management accounting has only one restrictive guideline: the accounting practice or technique used must produce *useful* information. Before tackling a problem, the management accountant must decide what information will be useful to the recipient of the report. He or she must then choose the appropriate concepts, procedures, and techniques to solve the problem. To illustrate, suppose management at Erin Company is deciding whether to purchase a piece of equipment. Return on investment information is relevant to the decision. Before return on investment can be computed, however, the financial effect of the new machine on company operations must be determined. This analysis requires estimates of increases in product sales, changes in variable and fixed manufacturing and selling costs, and changes in administrative costs. Once these amounts have been estimated, the management accountant must select an appropriate method for determining the machine's return on investment. Several approaches are available, and the method selected should be the most accurate one for the circumstances. Since the information is only for internal use, there is no need to stay within the restrictive guidelines for recording and reporting information to people outside the company.

Units of Measurement

The fourth area of comparison between financial and management accounting is the units of measurement used as a basis for reports and analyses. Financial accounting serves a stewardship or accountability function by providing financial information on a company's past events. All information is presented in dollar amounts. The common unit of measurement associated with financial accounting is the historical dollar. Transactions that are summarized in the financial statements have already occurred and the financial effects are objectively measurable.

Management accountants are not restricted to using the historical dollar and can employ any measurement unit *useful* in a situation. Historical dollars may be used in the short run for cost control analyses and for measuring trends for routine planning tasks. However, most management decisions are based on analyses using expected future dollars. Most decisions require forecasts and projections of operating data and must be based on estimates of future dollar flows. In addition to monetary units, the management accountant uses such measures as labor hours, machine hours, and product or service units as bases for analysis. The common denominator underlying all measurement, reporting, and analysis activities in management accounting is usefulness to a situation.

Focal Point for Analysis

Typically, financial accounting records and reports information on assets, equities, and net income of a *company as a whole*. Financial statements summarize transactions of an organization. Management accounting, on the other hand, usually involves analyses of *various segments* of a business, such as cost centers, profit centers, divisions, or departments, or some specific aspect of its operations. Reports can range from analyzing revenues and expenses of an entire division to investigating materials used by one department.

Frequency of Reporting

Financial statements developed for external use are usually prepared on a regular basis: monthly, quarterly, and/or annually. Periodic reporting at regular intervals is a basic concept of financial accounting. Management accounting reports may be prepared monthly, quarterly, and/or annually on a regular basis, or they may be requested daily or on an irregular basis. The key issues are that each report generated must be useful to its recipient and be prepared whenever needed.

Degree of Reliability

Financial information included in financial statements prepared for external use is past data, summarized as of a particular date for the user. This information results from transactions that already have happened. For this reason the information is determined *objectively* and is verifiable. Management accounting is concerned primarily with planning and control of internal operations. Planning and managerial decision making are activities that are more future related. Past expense and revenue transactions, although useful for establishing trends, are not usually relevant to planning activities and must be replaced by *subjective* estimates of future events.

These seven areas of comparison should help you make the transition from financial accounting to management accounting. A management accountant is typically involved with analyses dealing with units of output, machine hours, or direct labor hours in addition to reports centering on dollar amounts. Budgeted data are important to the management accountant, and the analysis of management's plans is a continual concern. In many cases reports generated by the management accountant have a direct bearing on the company's profitability and are considered confidential to management. Leaks of such information could give the competition an unfair advantage in the marketplace. So, whereas financial accounting's main emphasis is on full and accurate accounting for and disclosure of a company's operating results, management accounting's thrust is on helping management accomplish its objectives.

Information Needs of Management

OBJECTIVE 3
Compare the information needs of a manager of: (a) a manufacturing company; (b) a bank; and (c) a department store

When talking about accounting for management, one includes the information needs of management in all types of businesses. Although it is customary to discuss manufacturing operations when addressing the topic of management accounting, you must remember that any manager in any business, from a conglomerate to a family grocery store, relies daily on management accounting information. Service organizations, such as banks, hotels, public accounting firms, insurance companies, and attorneys' offices, need internal accounting information to determine the costs of providing their services and the prices to charge. Retail organizations, such as Sears Roebuck & Co. and Neiman-Marcus, use management accounting reports to manage operations and maximize profits. Nonprofit and government units and agencies use internal accounting information to develop budgets and performance reports during normal operations.

Understanding the importance and significance of management accounting reports and analyses is critical to your study of business. Management accounting principles and procedures are not just for accountants. Management personnel, financial analysts, real estate brokers, insurance agents, bankers, marketing research people, economists, hotel managers, and sales people are just a few of the managers making decisions from information supplied by the management accountant. Every person employed in a management-related job must help develop and rely on management accounting information.

To illustrate how widely management accounting information is used, we will now examine three types of business enterprises: a manufacturing company, a bank, and a department store. The reports and analyses needed by each management team will be identified. After a brief discussion of each type of business, information needs will be charted and compared.

The Manufacturing Company

One of the most important aspects of management accounting for a manufacturing company is to provide product costing information. This should be understandable, since a manufacturer's primary purpose is to take raw materials, such as wood, steel, and rubber, and transform them into finished products, such as furniture, automobiles, and tires. Product costing information is used to identify weak production areas, control costs, support pricing decisions, and set inventory values. Budgets are also an integral part of the flow of management information. Such documents are used as both planning and control tools. Managers in a manufacturing company also require continuous information about production planning and scheduling, product-line management and development, cash management, capital expenditure decision analysis, and selling and distribution expense analysis. Information is also needed for reporting purposes and for computing state and federal taxes.

Information used to make operating decisions is extremely important to manufacturing managers. Special orders may be received, and the manager must be able to respond prudently. When several products are involved, constant monitoring of the sales mix is important. Having to decide whether it is more economical to make a part or purchase it from an outside vendor is common in the manufacturing environment. Often, two or more products emerge from a common raw material such as gasoline and motor oil from crude oil. Such a situation often requires information to support a decision either to (1) sell the product when it can be first identified or (2) process it further to make a more salable and profitable product. These are but a few of the information needs of managers in a manufacturing company.

The Bank

If a manufacturing company is in business to make a product, what is the primary purpose of a bank? No, not to make money!! At least not to physically make the green stuff. The United States Mint prints and distributes this country's money. Of course, the bank is in business to make a profit, but so is the manufacturer. The bank provides its customers with various services for a fee. Loans are available, and interest is assessed as payment for the service. Checking accounts usually have either a monthly fee or a minimum balance requirement, so the bank can lend the money and earn interest income. A small charge is assessed for certified checks, and fees are charged for safe deposit boxes. Although the list of services is larger for larger banks, the idea of providing financial services for a fee describes the banking business.

Bank managers require many types of internally generated reports. The key to managing a bank's resources rests with its accounting information system. Balancing and monitoring cash reserves is critical. Managers are responsible for customers' savings accounts and federal deposit reserves required by the Federal Reserve Board and other government agencies. Federal auditors and independent auditors are required to make surprise visits to check on how banks manage their funds.

In addition to using the cash balancing and monitoring system, bank managers use budgets and service-line analysis reports extensively. Cash management for internal use is also important. Bank managers make capital expenditure decisions in much the same way as managers in manufacturing. Although normal operating decisions differ in many ways, the bank manager must continually analyze the services provided and the optimal service mix of the bank, just as the manufacturing manager must analyze the products manufactured and the optimal product mix to be produced. Loan activities require an effective system for credit verification with related reporting. Monitoring of loan payments and delinquent loans is very important.

Recently, banks have started adopting product costing procedures. Since a bank's products are its services, it needs information to determine if its services operate efficiently and are cost effective. Therefore, information on cost per loan, cost per savings transaction, and cost per checking account maintenance has become increasingly important to bank managers.

The Department Store

Instead of being a normal customer, imagine yourself as a store manager. You have just stepped inside the local J.C. Penney department store. What is the most important thing you should be concerned about here? Product costing information? Cost of maintaining a checking account? Traffic in the parking lot? No, none of these things. But there are three correct answers: customers, personnel, and merchandise. The most important asset of a department store is its merchandise. And it is the manager who is responsible for the following: (1) ordering proper items in economical quantities; (2) safely storing merchandise once it is received;

(3) displaying items so customers will be attracted to them; (4) marketing merchandise through the local media; (5) and distributing items to customers.

But to manage these areas of responsibility, a manager needs a complete accounting information system made up of reports, requisitions, controls, and analyses. Marketing surveys and other types of marketing research often support merchandise purchases made by a company's buyer. Also, knowing the most economical quantity to order helps keep costs down. And inventory records are critical once the merchandise has been received. These documents supply the manager with information on merchandise quality, deterioration, obsolescence, losses caused by theft, quantity on hand, reorder point, and current demand data.

As you can see, a store manager needs internal accounting information to control merchandise. But store managers are involved in other areas as well, including: (1) budgeting; (2) cash management; (3) product sales-line analyses; (4) capital expenditure analyses; (5) product selling cost analyses; (6) report preparation for all levels of management and taxing authorities; and (7) operating decisions concerning sales mix, special orders, and personnel placement. All these reports and analyses involve management accounting assistance.

Comparison of Information Needs of Managers

In Table 15-2 the information needs of the managers in a manufacturing company, a bank, and a department store are compared. Each manager has his or her special needs, depending on the type of business activity involved. A banker, for example, has different concerns and interests than a department store manager. Yet, despite the differences, managers have many similar needs. Budgets are found in any successful business. Cash management is always important. Special operating decisions and capital expenditure decisions are always required. Preparing reports and reporting information on taxes is part of any profitable enterprise. In short, many types of management accounting information are important to all managers.

How to Prepare a Management Accounting Report or Analysis

OBJECTIVE 4
Identify the important questions a manager must consider before preparing a managerial report

Are you ready to begin your study of management accounting? You have already seen how important this discipline is to your future, whether you become a management accountant or another type of business manager. Regardless of your future business position, you will be required to prepare reports and analyses. Such preparation does not depend on formats memorized while you were a student in an accounting class. Of course, you may want to refer to your old textbook for help and assistance, but report formats and structures are decided by the person developing the report and time constraints of the project.

Table 15-2. Comparison of Information Needs of Management

Reports and Analyses	Manufacturing Company	Bank	Department Store
Product/service costing			
For cost control	X	X	X
For pricing decisions	X	X	
For inventory valuation	X		
Budget preparation	X	X	X
Cash management system			
Normal operating funds	X	X	X
Funds held/managed for others		X	
Production planning	X		
Product-line management	X		
Service-line management		X	
Merchandise-line management			X
Capital expenditure analysis	X	X	X
Distribution/selling			
Expense analysis	X		X
Special reporting activities	X	X	X
Inventory control systems			
Raw materials	X		
Work in process	X		
Finished goods	X		
Merchandise			X
Funds on deposit		X	
Operating decisions			
Special orders	X		X
Sales mix	X		X
Service mix		X	
Make or buy	X		
Sell or process further	X		
Preparation of tax reports	X	X	X

In each of the following chapters, you will find report formats that help convey each chapter's contents. Most are formats that have been used in business, and they provide useful information.

As a manager, however, you should think of a report in the same way that an athlete thinks of an athletic record. Every record will someday be broken and a new record set. Every report can be improved on, and a manager should strive to create new and more informative ones. When a specific information need arises, your textbook will probably be unavailable as a reference. What you will need instead are a few simple guidelines for preparing new reports or improving old ones.

Report preparation depends on the four W's: **Why? What? Who?** and **When?**

Why? The question, "Why are you going to prepare this report?" is answered by the purpose of the report. The purpose establishes the report's characteristics and is instrumental in answering the other three questions. Therefore, the manager should write down the purpose of a report before creating it. Many reports prepared by circumventing this step are unfocused and do not fulfill the intended need.

What? Once the purpose of a report is stated, its maker must decide what information the report should contain to satisfy that purpose. In addition, the presentation method should be established. The information should be relevant to the decision and easy to read and understand. Cluttered reports do not communicate information. A report should address the purpose directly.

Who? The "who" question can take several forms: For whom are you preparing the report? To whom should the report be distributed? Who will read it? All three answers will dictate the report's format. If the report is prepared for only one manager, it may be less structured than one being distributed to a dozen managers or sent to stockholders. Widely distributed reports normally contain concise, summarized information, whereas reports prepared for a company's president are more detailed.

When? When is the report due? Timing is the key to effective reporting. A report is useful only when its information is timely. Preparation time is often limited by a report's urgency. Quick reports often lack accuracy. This tradeoff between accuracy and urgency is a normal constraint, and it is one the report maker must become accustomed to and master.

Illustrative Cases: Analysis of Nonfinancial Data

OBJECTIVE 5
Prepare analyses of nonfinancial data

In making the transition from financial accounting to management accounting, you must become accustomed to dealing with units of measurement other than a typical historical dollar. Most people connect accounting with the analysis of money. However, this chapter will begin your study of management accounting with a different perspective. Although management accountants do prepare analyses expressed in dollars, they also confront problems requiring solutions formulated around such items as labor hours, machine hours, units of output, number of employees, and number of requests for a service.

The purpose of this section is to illustrate three decision support situations, all requiring nonfinancial data. Since the information needs of a manufacturing company, a bank, and a department store have already been compared, the nonfinancial cases will also center on these types of businesses.

Case One: Granville Manufacturing Company, Hough, Mississippi. The Granville Manufacturing Company produces a special product called

"Form-fit Ski Boots." Shoe moldings are cast in the Molding Department. This department employs seven people, three direct labor employees who run the molding machines and four helpers. Data on hours worked in February are summarized below.

Granville Manufacturing Company
Summary of Labor Hours—Molding Department
For February 19x8

	Hours Worked							
	Week 1		Week 2		Week 3		Week 4	
Employee	Direct Labor	Helper Labor	Direct Labor	Helper Labor	Direct Labor	Helper Labor	Direct Labor	Helper Labor
T. Brown	44		40		46		37	
L. Erickson	48		36		40		44	
K. Golden		40		36		36		40
C. Hune	40		40		44		48	
P. Hugstad		42		44		44		40
R. Miyaki		32		48		32		48
L. Mulhulland		48		48		46		48

Management has determined that twelve pairs of boots should be produced for each hour of direct labor worked. Actual production for February is shown below.

Week 1	1,428 pairs
Week 2	1,227 pairs
Week 3	1,348 pairs
Week 4	1,302 pairs

Required

Analyze production activity for February. Should management be concerned about productivity in the Molding Department? What information supports your answer?

Solution to Case One

The schedule in Exhibit 15-1 analyzes labor hours worked by the Molding Department and production output in relation to target units of output. As you can see, the department is consistently under the set target. Causing even more concern, the percentage under target increases by almost 2 percent each week. This is a bad sign, and the productivity of machine operators should be investigated. Remember, this does not say the employees are at fault. The cause could be bad materials or inefficient machines. The analysis simply says that something is wrong, and it must be analyzed and corrected.

Exhibit 15-1. Analysis of Nonfinancial Data—Manufacturing Company

Granville Manufacturing Company
Analysis of Labor Hours—Molding Department
For February 19x8

Summary of Labor Hours Worked:

	Hours Worked									
	Week 1		Week 2		Week 3		Week 4		Totals	
Employee	Direct Labor	Helper Labor	Direct Labor	Helper Labor	Direct Labor	Helper Labor	Direct Labor	Helper Labor	Direct Labor	Helper Labor
T. Brown	44		40		46		37		167	
L. Erickson	48		36		40		44		168	
K. Golden		40		36		36		40		152
C. Hune	40		40		44		48		172	
P. Hugstad		42		44		44		40		170
R. Miyaki		32		48		32		48		160
L. Mulhulland		48		48		46		48		190
	132	162	116	176	130	158	129	176	507	672

Analysis of production:

	Week 1	Week 2	Week 3	Week 4	Totals
Units* that should have been produced (12 × direct labor hours)	1,584	1,392	1,560	1,548	6,084
Units produced	1,428	1,227	1,348	1,302	5,305
Units under target	156	165	212	246	779
Percent under target	9.85%	11.85%	13.59%	15.89%	12.80%

* Unit equals one pair of boots.

Case Two: Winter Springs National Bank. Candice Hall supervises tellers at Winter Springs National Bank. The bank has six drive-up windows, each requiring a full-time teller. Historically, each teller has serviced an average of thirty customers per hour. However, on November 1 management imposed a new check-scanning procedure, which has decreased the number of customers serviced per hour.

Data on the number of customers serviced for the three-month period ending December 31, 19x9, are shown in Part A of Exhibit 15-2. Each teller works an average of 170 hours per month. Based on a history of rush and slack periods, window #1 has traditionally been the busiest. Each window thereafter receives progressively less business. The average of 30 customers per hour is an average of all six windows.

Ms. Hall is preparing a report for management on the effects of the new procedure. To assist her, you have been asked to calculate a new average for customers serviced per hour for both November and December.

Solution to Case Two

Part B of Exhibit 15-2 shows an analysis of the number of customers serviced over the three months by each teller window. Using the 170-hour monthly average per teller, you can compute the number of customers serviced per hour by dividing the number of customers serviced by 170. By averaging the customer service rates for six tellers, you get 28.45 and 28.57 for November and December respectively. As you can see, the service rate has decreased. But December's average is higher than November's, so the tellers are becoming more accustomed to the new procedure.

Exhibit 15-2. Analysis of Nonfinancial Data—Bank

Winter Springs National Bank
Summary of Number of Customers Serviced
For the Quarter Ended December 31, 19x9

Part A

	Number of Customers Serviced			
Window	**October**	**November**	**December**	**Quarter Totals**
#1	5,428	5,186	5,162	15,776
#2	5,220	4,980	4,920	15,120
#3	5,280	4,820	4,960	15,060
#4	5,120	4,840	4,880	14,840
#5	5,100	4,700	4,840	14,640
#6	4,452	4,494	4,380	13,326
Totals	30,600	29,020	29,142	88,762

Part B

	Number of Customers Serviced Per Hour			
Window	**October**	**November**	**December**	**Quarter Totals**
#1	31.93	30.51	30.36	30.93
#2	30.71	29.29	28.94	29.65
#3	31.06	28.35	29.18	29.53
#4	30.12	28.47	28.71	29.10
#5	30.00	27.65	28.47	28.71
#6	26.19	26.44	25.76	26.13
Totals	180.01	170.71	171.42	174.05
Average per hour per window	30.00*	28.45	28.57	29.01*

* difference due to rounding.

Case Three: Halfacre Dry Goods Store. Halfacre Dry Goods Store, a high-volume establishment, features home delivery to entice customers. Located in Newport Beach, California, the company uses four delivery trucks to handle its home-delivery business. Recently, demand for home delivery has increased significantly. The controller, Mr. Marion, had developed two alternatives for solving the store's delivery-demand problem. The first alternative was to purchase a fifth truck and hire a fifth driver. The second alternative was to hire a person to schedule deliveries more efficiently, thereby saving time and increasing the number of deliveries per truck. Before committing to the truck-purchase alternative, Mr. Marion decided to try the scheduling idea.

Delivery data for the most recent four-week period are shown in Exhibit 15-3. The scheduler began her duties at the beginning of week three. She immediately broke down the territory into four delivery regions. Actual deliveries were scheduled by location within each region to cut down mileage and backtracking. Mr. Marion's goal was to increase deliveries by 10 percent. Did the scheduler work out, or should Mr. Marion purchase a fifth truck?

Solution to Case Three

Total deliveries per week were

First week	1,750
Second week	1,730
Third week	1,920
Fourth week	2,080

To achieve Mr. Marion's goal, there must be at least 1,925 weekly deliveries (1,750 × 110%). From the information given, the scheduler seems to be meeting the target set by Mr. Marion.

Exhibit 15-3. Analysis of Nonfinancial Data—Department Store

Halfacre Dry Goods Store
Analysis of Deliveries
For the Four Weeks Ending January 28, 19x8

Weekly Average, Previous Year	Truck	Number of Deliveries: First Week	Second Week	Third Week	Fourth Week	Total Deliveries
400	#1	360	380	440	460	1,640
450	#2	480	460	500	540	1,980
400	#3	390	410	420	480	1,700
500	#4	520	480	560	600	2,160
1,750		1,750	1,730	1,920	2,080	7,480

Merchandising Versus Manufacturing Operations

OBJECTIVE 6
State the differences between accounting for a manufacturing and a merchandising company

Much of this text has been about the merchandising organization. Thus, it is important here to explain the differences in accounting for manufacturing firms and merchandising firms. Many types of businesses gather information on costs, but doing so is especially important in manufacturing. Figures 15-1 and 15-2 show how the computation of cost of goods sold differs between manufacturing and merchandising companies.

A merchandising company normally buys a product ready for resale when it is received. Nothing needs to be done to the product to make it salable except possibly to prepare a special package or display. As shown in Figure 15-1, total beginning merchandise inventory plus purchases is the basis for computing both the cost of goods sold and ending merchandise inventory balances. Costs assigned to unsold items make up the ending inventory balance. The difference between the cost of

Figure 15-1. Cost of Goods Sold: A Merchandising Company

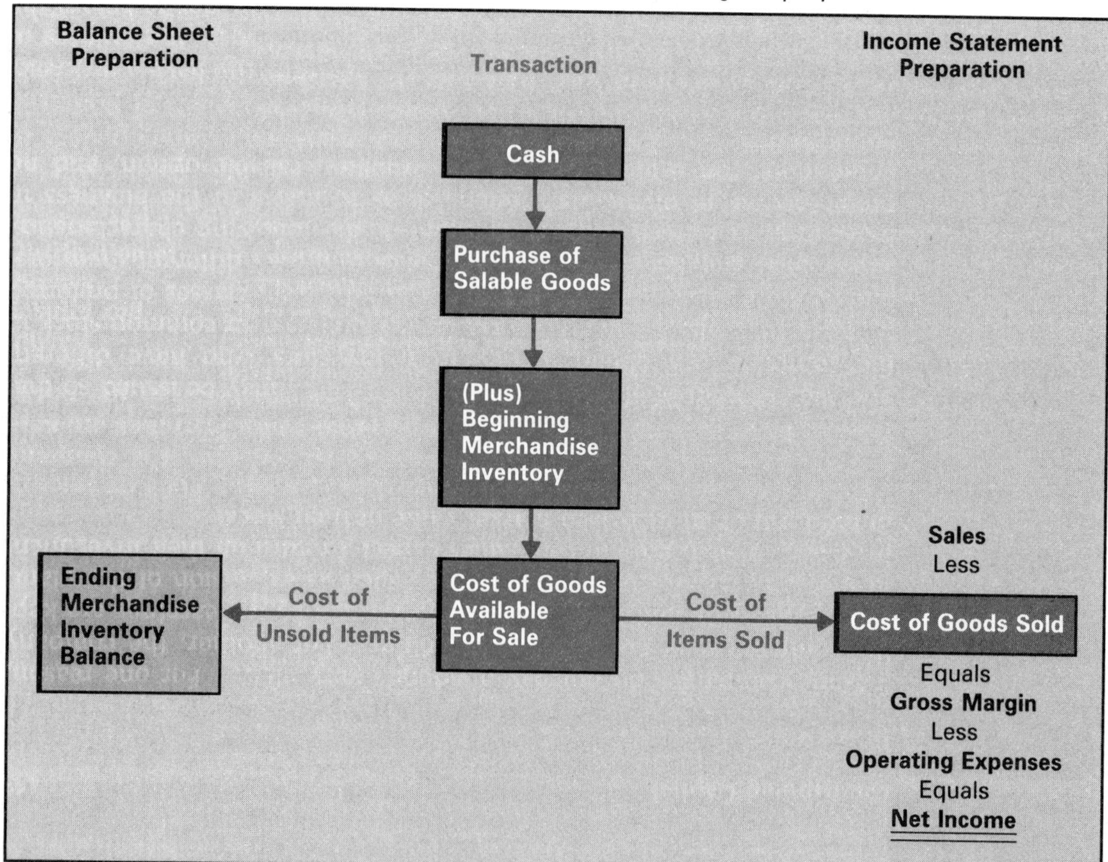

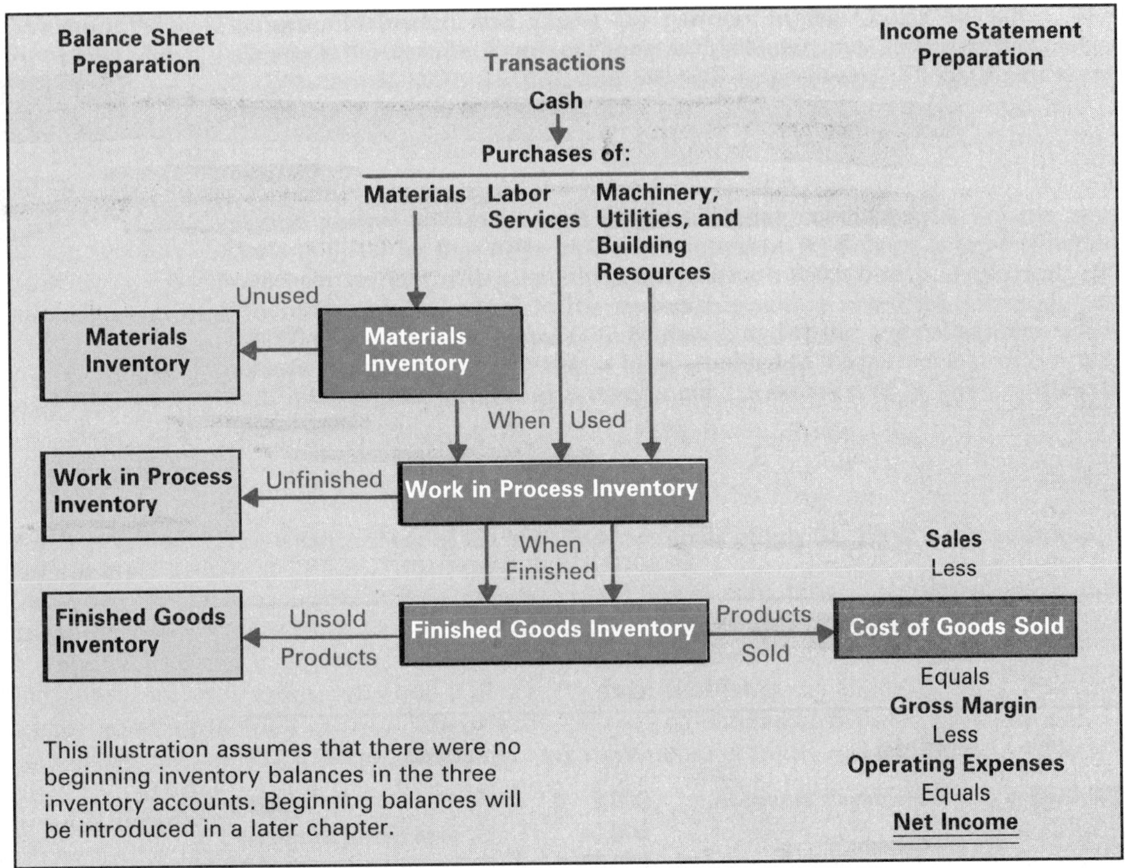

Figure 15-2. Cost of Goods Sold: A Manufacturing Company

goods available for sale and the ending inventory amount is the cost of goods sold during the period. The following example shows this computation:

Beginning merchandise inventory	$ 2,000
Plus total purchases of salable goods	8,000
Cost of goods available for sale	10,000
Less ending merchandise inventory	(2,700)
Cost of goods sold	$ 7,300

This example and Figure 15-1 show how easy it is to compute the cost of goods sold for a merchandising company. The only expenditure occurs when salable goods are purchased. Any items unsold at year end make up the ending inventory balance. The remainder of the purchase costs (plus any balance in beginning merchandise inventory) are reported as Cost of Goods Sold.

Computing the cost of goods sold for a manufacturing company is more complex. As shown in Figure 15-2, instead of one inventory account, a manufacturer maintains three inventory accounts: Materials Inventory, Work in Process Inventory, and Finished Goods Inventory.

Purchased materials unused during the production process make up the year-end Materials Inventory balance. The cost of materials used plus the costs of labor services and factory overhead are transferred to the Work in Process Inventory account when the materials, labor services, and overhead items are used in the production process. (Factory overhead includes such items as utility costs, depreciation of factory machinery and building, and supplies.)

The three types of costs discussed above are often called simply materials, labor, and overhead (abbreviated M, L, and OH). These costs are accumulated in the Work in Process Inventory account during an accounting period. When a batch or order is completed, all manufacturing costs assigned to the completed units are moved to the Finished Goods Inventory account. Costs remaining in the Work in Process Inventory account belong to partly completed units. These costs make up the ending balance in the Work in Process Inventory account.

The Finished Goods Inventory account is set up in much the same way as the Merchandise Inventory account in Figure 15-1. Costs of completed goods are entered into the Finished Goods Inventory account. Then, as shown in Figure 15-2, costs attached to unsold items at year end make up the ending balance in the Finished Goods Inventory account. All costs related to units sold are transferred to the Cost of Goods Sold account and reported on the income statement. To make this flow of costs clearer, the next chapter will discuss the three manufacturing cost elements: direct materials, direct labor, and factory (manufacturing) overhead. The three manufacturing inventory accounts will also be discussed. They will then be integrated into the computation of cost of goods sold.

The Certified Management Accountant

In 1972 the National Association of Accountants (NAA) created the Institute of Certified Management Accountants (ICMA), a separate wing of NAA. This wing is responsible for establishing and maintaining a program leading to the Certified Management Accountant designation.[2] The program was developed to recognize professional competence in the field of management accounting. This program parallels the CPA certificate program at the American Institute of Certified Public Accountants, which recognizes professional competence in the public accounting field.

Management accounting has come a long way since its inception as a recognized accounting discipline. Because of this, management accounting can no longer be considered a minor part of the accounting profession.

2. Certificate in Management Accounting Established by NAA," *Management Accounting* (March 1972), p. 13.

The management accountant has a right to be recognized, and the CMA program has been designed for this purpose.

The CMA Examination. To become a CMA, one must exhibit proficiency in the following areas on the CMA exam: (1) economics and business finance; (2) organization and behavior, including ethical considerations; (3) public reporting standards, auditing and taxes; (4) internal reporting and analysis, and (5) decision analysis, including modeling and information systems.

Admission to the CMA Program. Admission to the CMA program requires an applicant to satisfy one of the following conditions:

1. Hold a baccalaureate degree in any major from an accredited college or university
2. Achieve a score satisfactory to the Credentials Committee of the ICMA on either the Graduate Record Examination (GRE) or the Graduate Management Admissions Test (GMAT)
3. Be a Certified Public Accountant or hold a comparable professional qualification outside the United States approved by the Credentials Committee.[3]

Chapter Review

Review of Learning Objectives

1. **Describe the field of management accounting.**
   Management accounting is the process of identifying, measuring, accumulating, analyzing, preparing, and communicating information used by management. This information is used to plan, evaluate, and control the organization and to ensure that its resources are appropriately used and accounted for. The field of management accounting is made up of appropriate accounting techniques and procedures for information gathering and reporting. When applied to a company's financial and production data, management accounting procedures will satisfy management's information needs. The information needed includes: (a) product costing information; (b) data for planning and control of operations; and (c) special reports and analyses to support management decisions.

2. **Distinguish between management accounting and financial accounting.**
   Management accounting and financial accounting can be contrasted by using seven areas of comparison. People and organizations outside the business unit are the primary users of financial accounting information, whereas various levels of internal management use management accounting information. There is no restriction on the types of accounting systems one can use in management accounting, but financial accounting centers on the double-entry system. Restrictive guidelines for financial accounting are composed of all generally

3. More information about the CMA program and the examination can be obtained by writing to the Institute of Certified Management Accountants, 10 Paragon Drive, P.O. Box 405, Montvale, New Jersey 07645-0405.

accepted accounting standards, whereas management accounting's only restriction is that the information be useful to the recipient. Although the historical dollar is the main unit of measurement in financial accounting, any useful unit of measurement may be used. The business unit as a whole is the focal point of any analysis in financial accounting, but a management accounting analysis may focus on a division, a department, or even a machine. *Frequency of reporting* is on a regular, periodic basis in financial accounting, in management accounting, on an as-needed basis. Financial accounting deals with things that have happened, so its degree of reliability demands objectivity, whereas management accounting often focuses on the future and can become heavily subjective.

3. **Compare the information needs of a manager of: (a) a manufacturing company; (b) a bank; and (c) a department store.**

   The information needs of a manager of a manufacturing company, a bank, or a department store vary, depending on the type of business activity involved. The manufacturer needs product costing information and is involved with various types of inventory. The banker requires special analyses for fund management and control. A department store manager needs merchandise control information. But despite these differences, each of these managers requires many types of similar information, such as budgets, tax reports, operating decision analyses, cash management, and capital expenditure data.

4. **Identify the important questions a manager must consider before preparing a managerial report.**

   Report preparation depends on the four "W" questions: Why? What? Who? and When? The why question is answered by the purpose of the report. Once that has been stated, the report maker must determine what information the report should contain to satisfy that purpose. The who question can take several forms: For whom are you preparing the report? To whom should the report be distributed? Who will read it? Finally, there is the question of when. When is the report due?

5. **Prepare analyses of nonfinancial data.**

   Most people connect the discipline of accounting with the analysis of money. Management accountants do prepare analyses expressed in dollars, but they also confront problems requiring solutions formulated around labor hours, machine hours, units of output, number of employees, and number of requests for service.

6. **State the differences between accounting for a manufacturing and a merchandising company.**

   Accounting methods used by a manufacturing company differ in important ways from those used by a merchandising company. Management accountants at a manufacturing company must maintain an internal accounting system for classifying and assigning production and production-related costs to the products manufactured. A manufacturing accounting system uses three inventory accounts: Materials Inventory, Work in Process Inventory, and Finished Goods Inventory. Manufacturing costs must flow through all three inventory accounts. This flow results in a more complex internal accounting system.

   Merchandise accounting concentrates on the business that purchases a product ready for resale when it is received. Only one account, Merchandise Inventory, is used to record and account for items in inventory. Because the items in merchandise inventory are purchased in salable condition, the cost flow from time of purchase to time of sale involves a maximum of four of the following accounts, depending upon whether the periodic or perpetual system is used: Cash or Accounts Payable, Purchases or Merchandise Inventory, Freight In, and Cost of Goods Sold.

Review Problem

Nonfinancial Data

Ken Becker Surfaces, Inc., is a house painting company located in Rock Island, Illinois. The company employs twelve painters. Mr. Becker manages the operation and does all of the estimating and billing work. Two painters specialize in interior painting, three painters are exterior trim specialists, and the remaining seven are semi-skilled, all-purpose painters. Mr. Becker prepared the following projection of work hours for the month of June:

	Projected Hours to be Worked				
	Week #1	Week #2	Week #3	Week #4	Totals
Mason Apartments:					
Interior	60	60	48	32	200
Exterior trim	100	60	48	24	232
General painting	180	160	120	60	520
Gantry Building:					
Interior	20	20	32	48	120
Exterior trim	20	60	72	96	248
General painting	100	120	160	220	600
Totals	480	480	480	480	1,920

On July 2, Mr. Becker assembled the following actual hour data:

	Actual Hours Worked				
	Week #1	Week #2	Week #3	Week #4	Totals
Mason Apartments:					
Interior	72	76	68	52	268
Exterior trim	88	56	44	20	208
General painting	220	180	144	76	620
Gantry Building:					
Interior	24	32	48	64	168
Exterior trim	16	52	64	88	220
General painting	116	136	184	260	696
Totals	536	532	552	560	2,180

Mr. Becker is concerned about the excess labor hours worked during June. The July forecast needs to be developed but he needs further analysis of June's data before proceeding.

Required:

1. Prepare an analysis that shows the number of hours over or under projected hours for each job's assignments for June.
2. From your analysis in part **1**, what trouble areas would you point out to Mr. Becker? Suggest some solutions.

Answer to Review Problem

1.

	Hours Worked (Over) or Under Projected Hours				
	Week #1	Week #2	Week #3	Week #4	Totals
Mason Apartments:					
Interior	(12)	(16)	(20)	(20)	(68)
Exterior trim	12	4	4	4	24
General painting	(40)	(20)	(24)	(16)	(100)
Gantry Building:					
Interior	(4)	(12)	(16)	(16)	(48)
Exterior trim	4	8	8	8	28
General painting	(16)	(16)	(24)	(40)	(96)
Totals	(56)	(52)	(72)	(80)	(260)

2. Both the interior and semi-skilled painters are taking more time to complete the jobs than was anticipated by Mr. Becker. Either his estimates were wrong, the quality of the painting materials was poor, or some of the painters need to be reprimanded or dismissed.

Chapter Assignments

Questions

1. Describe the field of management accounting, including the three areas in which management needs information.
2. Identify how the primary users of information, types of accounting systems, and restrictive guidelines differ between management accounting and financial accounting.
3. Compare management accounting and financial accounting. Include units of measurement, focal point of analysis, frequency of reporting, and degree of reliability in your comparison.
4. Does the size of a business dictate the type or amount of financial information needed by management? Explain your answer.
5. What types of information are important to a manager in a manufacturing company?
6. How do the information needs of a bank manager differ from those of a manager in a department store? What needs are similar?
7. Why should a person specializing in marketing, finance, or management be familiar with management accounting?
8. What are the four "W" questions related to report preparation? Explain the importance of each question.
9. An analysis of nonfinancial data is important to the management accountant. Why?
10. What is the difference between a merchandising company and a manufacturing company? Include a description of inventory cost flows for each type of company in your answer.
11. List the five parts of the CMA examination.

Classroom Exercises

Exercise 15-1. Definitions of Management Accounting
(L.O. 1)

There are many definitions and descriptions of management accounting. The National Association of Accountants, in *Statement No. 1A* in its series *Statements on Management Accounting*, defined management accounting as

> . . . the process of identification, measurement, accumulation, analysis, preparation, and communication of financial information used by management to plan, evaluate, and control within the organization and to assure appropriate use and accountability for its resources. Management accounting also comprises the preparation of financial reports for nonmanagement groups such as shareholders, creditors, regulatory agencies, and tax authorities:[4]

In *The Modern Accountant's Handbook*, management (managerial) accounting is described as

> "Managerial accounting, although generally anchored to the financial accounting framework, involves a broader information-processing system. It deals in many units of measure and produces a variety of reports designed for specific purposes. Its scope encompasses the past, the present, and the future. Its purposes include short- and long-range planning, cost determination, control of activities, assessment of objectives and program performance, and provision of basic information for decision making.[5]

4. National Association of Accountants, *Statement No. 1A* (New York, 1982).
5. Edwards and Black, *The Modern Accountant's Handbook* (Homewood, IL: Dow Jones-Irwin, 1976), p. 830.

1. Compare these two statements on management accounting.
2. "It is impossible to distinguish the point at which financial accounting ends and management accounting begins." Explain this statement.

Exercise 15-2. Types of Accounting Systems (L.O. 2)

Many management accounting analyses are not limited by the double-entry accounting system. Two such analyses are shown below.

a. Budgeted materials purchases for March

Aluminum ingots	$ 80,000
Copper ingots	140,000
Silver ingots	500,000
Total estimated materials costs	$720,000

b. Determining an appropriate selling price for a new product

Estimated manufacturing costs per unit	$51.00
Operating expenses (40% of manufacturing costs)	20.40
Profit factor (25% of manufacturing & operating costs)	17.85
Projected selling price	$89.25

1. Do the above analyses require a journal entry to become effective?
2. When will the above information enter the general ledger?

Exercise 15-3. Management Information Needs (L.O. 3)

The following statement was overheard by Linda Hutcheson, the newly appointed senior budget analyst for the LaRue Corporation. The statement was made by the vice president of sales in a conversation with the controller.

Budgets are made up of guesswork and do not apply to sales people. Budgets tend to restrict our movement and thereby inhibit sales efforts and hold down sales. Budgets should be applicable only to production people who need to keep their costs down and concentrate on efficient operating plans and procedures.

Do you agree with the vice president? Defend your answer, basing your arguments on the information needs of managers.

Exercise 15-4. Management Structure and Information Needs (L.O. 4)

The F. D. Fowler Corporation employs executives in the following positions:

Production manager	Division 1
Management accountant	Division 2
Sales manager	Division 1
Sales manager	Division 2
Vice president	Engineering
Chief engineer	Division 2
Corporate controller	
Chairman of the board	

Vice president	Sales
Production manager	Division 2
Management accountant	Division 1
Corporate secretary/treasurer	
Chief engineer	Division 1
Production vice president	
President	
Corporate legal counsel	

1. Prepare a diagram or chart, showing the organizational hierarchy of this management team. **Hint:** Start at the top with the chairman of the board and work down. Show positions with seemingly similar power and stature on the same horizontal level.
2. What types of information would the corporate controller request from the management accountant of Division 2 before designing a reporting system for the sales area?

Exercise 15-5. Nonfinancial Data Analysis (L.O. 5)

Sachdev Landscapes, Inc., specializes in lawn installations requiring Kentucky bluegrass sod. The sod comes in 1-yard squares. The company uses the guideline of 250 square yards per person per hour to evaluate the performance of its sod layers.

During the first week of March, the following actual data were collected:

Employee	Hours Worked	Square Yards of Sod Planted
R. Elam	38	9,120
G. W. Krull	45	11,250
J. B. Boatsman	40	9,800
E. E. Milam	42	8,820
H. P. Schaefer	44	11,440
F. L. Neumann	45	11,250

Evaluate the performance of the six employees.

Exercise 15-6. Manufacturer Versus Merchandiser (L.O. 6)

Tahoe Corporation has two divisions, the Incline Division and the Keys Division, that operate as autonomous units. Incline manufactures powerboats. Keys, as a marine supplies merchandiser, is responsible for sales and service of Incline's products.

1. Explain the flow of operating costs through the records of each division, and describe each type of cost.
2. What will be the differences in each division's financial statements?

Exercise 15-7. Balance Sheet Interpretation (L.O. 6)

Gist Corporation is located in Houston, Texas. The corporation's balance sheet on July 31 is shown on the next page.

Gist Corporation
Balance Sheet
As of July 31, 19x8

Assets

Current Assets			
Cash		$ 16,400	
Accounts Receivable		290,000	
Materials Inventory		18,700	
Work in Process Inventory		50,600	
Finished Goods Inventory		40,400	
Prepaid Factory Insurance		23,100	
Small Tools		24,000	
Total Current Assets			$ 463,200
Machinery and Equipment			
Factory Machinery	$720,000		
Less Accumulated Depreciation	132,000	$588,000	
Office Equipment	$ 94,000		
Less Accumulated Depreciation	47,000	47,000	
Total Machinery and Equipment			635,000
Total Assets			$1,098,200

Liabilities and Stockholders' Equity

Liabilities			
Current Liabilities			
Accounts Payable		$ 22,500	
Income Taxes Withheld		30,000	
FICA Taxes Payable		12,000	
United States Government Bonds Payable		2,000	
Union Dues Payable		3,500	
Federal Income Taxes Payable		32,600	
Total Liabilities			$ 102,600
Stockholders' Equity			
Common Stock		$750,000	
Retained Earnings, July 1, 19x8	$205,600		
Net Income, July 19x8	40,000		
Retained Earnings, July 31, 19x8		245,600	
Total Stockholders' Equity			995,600
Total Liabilities and Stockholders' Equity			$1,098,200

1. Is Gist Corporation a merchandising firm or a manufacturing company?
2. Identify at least five reasons for your answer to **1** above.

Interpreting Accounting Information

Financial Statement Users: Otto Enterprises (L.O. 2)

Otto Enterprises is a corporation. It produces and distributes household cleaning products nationally. Common and preferred stocks of the company are traded on a regional stock exchange. There are four divisions in the firm, and each is headed by a vice president. The following condensed financial statements appeared in Otto's annual report for 19x7:

Otto Enterprises
Balance Sheet
December 31, 19x7

Assets		Liabilities and Stockholders' Equity		
Current Assets		Liabilities		
Cash	$ 20,000	Current Liabilities		
Receivables (net)	10,000	Accounts Payable	$20,000	
Inventories	30,000	Accrued Liabilities	5,000	
Prepaid Expenses	5,000	Total Current Liabilities		$25,000
Total Current Assets	$ 65,000	Bonds Payable		40,000
		Total Liabilities		$ 65,000
Buildings and Equipment (net)	75,000	Stockholders' Equity		
		Preferred Stock	$20,000	
Total Assets	$140,000	Common Stock	40,000	
		Retained Earnings	15,000	
		Total Stockholder's Equity		75,000
		Total Liabilities and Stockholders' Equity		$140,000

Otto Enterprises
Income Statement
For the Year 19x7

Net Sales	$200,000
Cost of Goods Sold	95,000
Gross Margin on Sales	$105,000
Selling & Administrative Expenses	80,000
Operating Income	$ 25,000
Interest Expenses	5,000
Income Before Taxes	$ 20,000
Income Taxes	5,000
Net Income ($.30 per share)	$ 15,000

Required

Discuss the usefulness of the annual report in decisions and evaluations normally made by the following people:

a. Holders of Otto common stock
b. Holders of Otto preferred stock
c. Potential stockholders in Otto securities
d. Company president and board of directors
e. Company bondholders
f. Vice presidents of each division
g. Plant superintendents
h. District sales managers
i. Cost center supervisors in each plant
j. Salaried employees who are nonsupervisory

Problem Set A

Problem 15A-1. Approach to Report Preparation (L.O. 3, 4)

Lanzilloti Industries, Inc., is deciding whether to expand its "Jeans by Louis" line of men's clothing. Sales in units of this product were 22,500, 28,900, and 36,200 in 19x6, 19x7, and 19x8 respectively. The product has been very profitable, averaging 35 percent profit (above cost) over the three-year period. Lanzilloti has ten sales representatives covering seven states in the Northeast. Present production capacity is about 40,000 jeans per year. There is adequate plant space for additional equipment, and the labor needed can be easily hired and trained.

The company's management is made up of four vice presidents: vice president of marketing, vice president of production, vice president of finance, and vice president of data processing. Each of these people is directly responsible to the president, Louis Lanzilloti.

Required

1. What types of information will Mr. Lanzilloti need before he can decide whether to expand the "Jeans by Louis" product line?
2. Assume one of the reports needed to support Mr. Lanzilloti's decision is an analysis of sales over the past three years. This analysis should be broken down by sales representatives. Answer the four "W" questions as they pertain to this report.
3. Design a format for the report in **2** above.

Problem 15A-2. Nonfinancial Data Analysis: Manufacturing (L.O. 5)

St. Patrick Surfboards, Inc., manufactures state-of-the-art surfboards and related equipment. Charles Reilly is manager of the New England branch. The production process is made up of the following departments and tasks: (1) Molding Department, where the board's base is molded; (2) Sanding Department, where the base is sanded after being taken out of the mold; (3) Fiber-Ap Department, where a fiber glass coating is applied; and (4) Finishing Department, where a finishing coat of fiber glass is applied and the board is inspected. After the molding process all functions are performed by hand.

Mr. Reilly is concerned about the labor hours being worked by his employees. The New England branch utilizes a two-shift labor force. The actual hours worked for the past four weeks are summarized on the next page.

Actual Hours Worked—First Shift

Department	Week #1	Week #2	Week #3	Week #4	Totals
Molding	420	432	476	494	1,822
Sanding	60	81	70	91	302
Fiber-Ap	504	540	588	572	2,204
Finishing	768	891	952	832	3,443

Actual Hours Worked—Second Shift

Department	Week #1	Week #2	Week #3	Week #4	Totals
Molding	360	357	437	462	1,616
Sanding	60	84	69	99	312
Fiber-Ap	440	462	529	506	1,937
Finishing	670	714	782	726	2,892

Expected labor hours per product for each operation are: Molding, 3.4 hours; Sanding, .5 hours; Fiber-Ap, 4.0 hours; and Finishing, 6.5 hours. Actual units completed were as follows:

Week	First Shift	Second Shift
1	120	100
2	135	105
3	140	115
4	130	110

Required

1. Prepare an analysis to determine the average actual labor hours worked per board for each phase of the production process and for each shift.
2. Using the information from **1** above and the expected labor hours per board for each department, prepare an analysis, showing the differences in each phase of each shift. Identify reasons for the differences.

Problem 15A-3. Nonfinancial Data Analysis: Bank (L.O. 5)

Torrington State Bank was formed in 1869. It has had a record of slow, steady growth since inception. Management has always kept the processing of information as current as technology allows. Belinda Kessing, manager of the SUNY branch, is upgrading the check-sorting equipment in her office. There are eight check-sorting machines in operation. Information on the number of checks sorted by machine for the past eight weeks is summarized on the next page.

Machine	Weeks One	Two	Three	Four	Five	Six	Seven	Eight
AA	89,260	89,439	89,394	90,288	90,739	90,658	90,676	90,630
AB	91,420	91,237	91,602	91,969	91,950	92,502	92,446	92,816
AC	94,830	95,020	94,972	95,922	96,401	96,315	96,334	96,286
AD	91,970	91,786	92,153	92,522	92,503	93,058	93,002	93,375
AE	87,270	87,445	87,401	88,275	88,716	88,636	88,654	88,610
BA	92,450	92,265	92,634	93,005	92,986	93,544	93,488	93,862
BB	91,910	92,094	92,048	92,968	93,433	93,349	93,368	93,321
BC	90,040	89,860	90,219	90,580	90,562	91,105	91,051	91,415
BD	87,110	87,190	87,210	130,815	132,320	133,560	134,290	135,770
BE	94,330	94,519	94,471	95,416	95,893	95,807	95,826	95,778

The SUNY branch has increased its checking business significantly over the past two years. Ms. Kessing has decided to purchase either additional check-sorting machines or attachments for the existing machines to increase productivity. Five weeks ago the Green Company convinced her to experiment with one such attachment, and it was placed on Machine BD. Ms. Kessing is impressed with the attachment but has yet to decide between the two alternate courses of action.

Required: (show computations to support your answers)

1. If the Green Company attachment costs about the same as a new check-sorting machine, which alternative should Ms. Kessing choose?
2. Would you change your recommendation if two attachments could be purchased for the price of one check-sorting machine?
3. If three attachments could be purchased for the price of one check-sorting machine, what action would you recommend?

Problem 15A-4. Manufacturing Company Balance Sheet
(L.O. 6)

The analysis at the top of the following page represents the balance sheet accounts at Cassagio Manufacturing Company after closing entries were made. Net income for the year is still identified for the purposes of report preparation.

Required

Using the information in the analysis and proper form, prepare a balance sheet for the Cassagio Manufacturing Company as of December 31, 19x9.

Hint: Production Supplies and Tools are a current asset. Patents are classified as "Other Assets."

Ledger Accounts	Debit	Credit
Cash	$ 16,000	
Accounts Receivable	30,000	
Materials Inventory, 12/31/x9	42,000	
Work in Process Inventory, 12/31/x9	17,400	
Finished Goods Inventory, 12/31/x9	52,700	
Production Supplies and Tools	8,600	
Land	200,000	
Factory Building	400,000	
Factory Equipment	250,000	
Sales Warehouse	148,000	
Accumulated Depreciation, Building		$ 110,000
Accumulated Depreciation, Equipment		72,000
Accumulated Depreciation, Warehouse		35,000
Patents	27,300	
Accounts Payable		19,800
Accrued Property Taxes		12,000
Income Taxes Payable		50,000
Mortgage Payable, due in one year		20,000
Mortgage Payable		380,000
Common Stock		260,000
Retained Earnings, 1/1/x9		100,000
Net Income for 19x9		133,200
	$1,192,000	$1,192,000

Problem Set B

Problem 15B-1. Approach to Report Preparation
(L.O. 3, 4)

Debbie Most recently purchased Lawn & Garden Supplies, Inc., a wholesale distributor of lawn- and garden-care equipment and supplies. The company, headquartered in Baltimore, Maryland, has four distribution centers: Boston, Massachusetts; Rye, New York; Reston, Virginia; and Lawrenceville, New Jersey. These distribution centers service fourteen eastern states. Company profits were $125,400, $237,980, and $467,200 for 19x7, 19x8, and 19x9 respectively.

Shortly after purchasing the company, Ms. Most appointed people to fill the following positions: vice president, marketing; vice president, distribution; corporate controller; and vice president, research and development. Ms. Most has called a meeting of her management group. She would like to create a deluxe retail lawn and garden center that would include a large, fully landscaped plant and tree nursery. The purposes of the retail center would be (1) to test equipment and supplies before selecting them for sales and distribution and (2) to showcase the effects of using the company's products. The retail center must also make a profit on sales.

Required

1. What types of information will Ms. Most need before deciding whether to create the retail lawn and garden center?
2. Assume one of the reports needed to support Ms. Most's decision analyzes locations for the new retail center. The report came from the vice president of research and development. Respond to the four "W" questions as they pertain to this report.
3. Design a format for the report in **2** above.

Problem 15B-2. Nonfinancial Data Analysis: Manufacturing
(L.O. 5)

Flagstaff Enterprises makes sports shoes for every major sports activity. The "Awesome Shoe" is one of the company's leading products. This shoe is lightweight, long wearing, and inexpensive. Production of the Awesome Shoe is composed of five operations and tasks: (1) Cutting/Lining Department, where cloth tops are cut and lined; (2) Molding Department, where the shoe's rubber base is formed; (3) Bonding Department, where the cloth top is bonded to the rubber base; (4) Soling Department, where the sole is attached to the rubber base; and (5) Finishing Department, where the shoe is trimmed, stitched, and laced.

Recently, manufacturing costs have been increasing for the Awesome Shoe. Controller Ron Pitt has been investigating the production process to determine the problems. Everything points to the labor hours required to make the shoe. Actual labor hours worked in a recent week are shown below.

Actual Hours Worked

Operation	Monday	Tuesday	Wednesday	Thursday	Friday	Total
Cutting/lining	300	310	305	300	246	1,461
Molding	144	186	183	200	246	959
Bonding	456	434	488	450	492	2,320
Soling	408	434	366	400	492	2,100
Finishing	600	620	549	625	615	3,009

The company has estimated that the following labor hours for each department should be needed to complete a pair of Awesome Shoes: Cutting/lining, .2 hour; Molding, .1 hour; Bonding, .4 hour; Soling, .3 hour; and Finishing, .5 hour. During the week under review, the number of actual pairs of Awesome Shoes produced were: 1,200 pairs on Monday; 1,240 pairs on Tuesday; 1,220 pairs on Wednesday; 1,250 pairs on Thursday; and 1,230 pairs on Friday.

Required

1. Prepare an analysis to determine the average actual labor hours worked per day per pair of shoes for each operation in the production process.
2. Comparing the average actual labor hours worked from **1** above and the expected labor hours per pair of shoes per department, prepare an analysis, showing differences in each operation for each day. Identify reasons for those differences.

Problem 15B-3. Nonfinancial Data Analysis: Airport (L.O. 5)

The Medford County Airport at Long Plains, Nebraska, has experienced increased air traffic over the past year. How passenger traffic flow is handled is important to airport management. Because of the requirement that all passengers must be checked for possible weapons, passenger flow has slowed significantly. Medford County Airport uses eight metal-detector devices to screen passengers. The airport is open from 6:00 a.m. to 10:00 p.m. daily, and present machinery allows a maximum of 45,000 passengers to be checked each day.

Four of the metal-detector machines have been selected for special analysis to determine if additional equipment is needed or if a passenger traffic director could solve the problem. The passenger traffic director would be responsible for guiding people to different machines and instructing them on the detection process. Management hopes this procedure will quicken passenger traffic flow. Makers of the machinery have stated that each machine can handle an average of 400 passengers per hour. Data on passenger traffic through the four machines for the past ten days is shown below.

Passengers Checked by Metal Detector Machines

Dates	Machine I	Machine II	Machine III	Machine IV	Totals
March 6	5,620	5,490	5,436	5,268	21,814
March 7	5,524	5,534	5,442	5,290	21,790
March 8	5,490	5,548	5,489	5,348	21,875
March 9	5,436	5,592	5,536	5,410	21,974
March 10	5,404	5,631	5,568	5,456	22,059
March 11	5,386	5,667	5,594	5,496	22,143
March 12	5,364	5,690	5,638	5,542	22,234
March 13	5,678	6,248	6,180	6,090	24,196
March 14	5,720	6,272	6,232	6,212	24,436
March 15	5,736	6,324	6,372	6,278	24,710

In the past passenger traffic flow has favored Machine I because of its location. Overflow traffic goes to Machines II, III, and IV in that order.

The passenger traffic director began her duties on March 13. If this choice of alternatives results in at least a ten percent increase in passengers handled, management will employ a second traffic director for the remaining four machines. It will then scrap the idea of purchasing additional metal detectors.

Required (Show computations to support your answers)

1. Did the passenger traffic director pass the minimum test set up by management, or should airport officials purchase additional metal-detector machines?
2. Is there anything unusual in the analysis that management should have looked into regarding the rate of passenger traffic flow?

Problem 15B-4. Manufacturing Company Balance Sheet (L.O. 6)

Espey Industries, Inc., manufactures racing hubs for sports car enthusiasts. Information on balances in balance sheet accounts at year-end are shown on the following page. Closing entries have been made, but net income has been separated so year-end financial statements can be prepared.

Ledger Accounts	Debit	Credit
Cash	$ 24,000	
Accounts Receivable	47,000	
Materials Inventory, 12/31/x8	51,000	
Work in Process Inventory, 12/31/x8	37,900	
Finished Goods Inventory, 12/31/x8	64,800	
Production Supplies	5,700	
Small Tools	9,330	
Land	160,000	
Factory Building	575,000	
Factory Equipment	310,000	
Accumulated Depreciation, Building		$ 219,000
Accumulated Depreciation, Factory Equipment		117,000
Patents	33,500	
Accounts Payable		36,900
Accrued Insurance		6,700
Income Taxes Payable		61,500
Mortgage Payable, due in one year		18,000
Mortgage Payable		325,000
Common Stock		200,000
Retained Earnings, 1/1/x8		196,000
Net Income for 19x8		138,130
	$1,318,230	$1,318,230

Required

Using the information above and the proper form, prepare a balance sheet for Espey Industries, Inc., as of December 31, 19x8.
Hint: Production Supplies and Small Tools are current assets. Patents are classified as "Other Assets."

Management Decision Case

McCartney Manufacturing Company: Nonfinancial Data Analysis
(L.O. 4, 5)

Being a subcontractor in the jet aircraft industry, McCartney Manufacturing Company specializes in the production of housings for landing gear on jet airplanes. The company, located in Selden, New York, employs approximately 150 people. Two shifts, a day shift and a night shift, work forty-hour weeks normally. Production begins on machine #1, where the housing material is cut from huge sheets of metal into pieces weighing 1,800 pounds each. Machine #2 bends the pieces into cylinder-shaped products and trims off the rough edges. On machine #3 the seam of the cylinder is welded, and the entire piece is pushed into a large die to mold the housing into its final shape.

Scrap is a costly problem for the company. Management has asked the controller, Chuck Heck, to prepare an analysis of scrap for the past four-week period.

The analysis performed by Mr. Heck produced the information on the production of units summarized in the following tables:

Units of Production—Day Shift

Machine	Week #1	Week #2	Week #3	Week #4	Totals
1A*	1,020	1,008	996	990	4,014
1B*	1,024	1,020	1,026	1,032	4,102
2	2,020	2,006	2,018	2,012	8,056
3	1,998	2,004	2,014	2,012	8,028

Units of Production—Night Shift

Machine	Week #1	Week #2	Week #3	Week #4	Totals
1A*	1,010	1,014	1,018	1,024	4,066
1B*	1,026	1,012	996	990	4,024
2	1,996	1,992	1,990	1,984	7,962
3	1,988	1,986	1,986	1,980	7,940

* It takes output of two Machine #1's to supply inputs for a single Machine #2.

Note that the total number of units being worked on decreases as production moves from Machine #1 to Machine #2 and from Machine #2 to Machine #3. Assume that this decrease represents units that are scrapped because of poor workmanship or faulty equipment.

Actual scrap generation is summarized in the following tables below and at the top of the following page:

Pounds of Scrap Generation—Day Shift

Machine	Week #1	Week #2	Week #3	Week #4	Totals
1A	36,720	54,288	71,856	82,440	245,304
1B	36,864	36,720	36,936	37,152	147,672
2	43,200	39,600	7,200	18,000	108,000
3	39,600	3,600	7,200	0	50,400

Pounds of Scrap Generation—Night Shift					
Machine	Week #1	Week #2	Week #3	Week #4	Totals
1A	36,360	36,504	36,648	36,864	146,376
1B	36,936	58,032	75,456	78,840	249,264
2	72,000	61,200	43,200	54,000	230,400
3	14,400	10,800	7,200	7,200	39,600

Company officials expect the following production quotas and amounts of scrap:

Machine #1: Cuts 25 pieces per hour; scrap from trimmings and spoilage equals 2 percent of output weight.

Machine #2: Bends 50 pieces per hour; spoilage occurs at a rate of one per two hundred pieces attempted.

Machine #3: Welds and forms 50 pieces per hour; one out of every 400 pieces is found to be defective at the end of the process. These pieces cannot be reworked and are scrapped.

Required

1. Using actual production data, prepare an analysis of pounds of scrap generation expected for an average day shift and night shift.
2. Using the data computed in **1** above and the actual information on scrap generation, analyze the differences between actual and expected scrap poundage.
3. What areas of the production process should Mr. Heck investigate further? Why?
4. Do you suspect machine failure or human inefficiency to be the root of the problem? Defend your answer.

CHAPTER 16 PRODUCTION COSTS: TERMS, CLASSIFICATIONS, AND REPORTING

LEARNING OBJECTIVES

1. State the differences between the three manufacturing cost elements: (a) direct materials costs; (b) direct labor costs; and (c) factory overhead costs.
2. Identify the source documents used to collect information on manufacturing cost accumulation.
3. Compute a product's unit cost.
4. Distinguish between product costs and period costs.
5. Describe the nature, contents, and flow of costs through the Materials, Work in Process, and Finished Goods inventory accounts.
6. Prepare a statement of cost of goods manufactured.
7. Prepare an income statement for a manufacturing company.
8. Apply cost classification concepts to a service-oriented business.

Management accounting includes three interrelated functions that comprise a company's internal accounting system: (1) determining product or service costs for inventory valuation and cost control purposes; (2) providing information for the planning and control phases of internal operations; and (3) aiding top management in decision-making activities. All three functions require cost information from past, current, or future operations.

In this chapter we will acquaint you with the various kinds of manufacturing costs and their classification and reporting possibilities. Emphasis is placed on the manufacturing environment, primarily because these cost classifications and reporting techniques are used extensively by companies involved in manufacturing. As stated earlier, however, management accounting is also important to companies in service-related industries. Thus, following the discussion of accounting for manufacturing costs, this chapter concludes by briefly covering some of these concepts and their application to a service business.

Your study of management accounting continues with an analysis of the three manufacturing cost elements: direct materials costs, direct labor costs, and factory overhead costs. Computing a product's unit cost sums up that discussion and leads into an analysis of the three manufacturing inventory accounts: Materials Inventory, Work in Process Inventory, and Finished Goods Inventory. Studying manufacturing cost flow within the accounting system is an appropriate way to introduce reporting in a manufacturing setting. The statement of cost of goods manufactured is a prerequisite to preparing an income statement for a production-oriented company. After studying this chapter, you should be able to meet the learning objectives listed on the left. A work sheet analysis based on perpetual and periodic inventories is covered in a special analysis in The Windham Company Practice Case.

Manufacturing Cost Elements

Manufacturing costs can be classified in many ways. Some costs can be traced directly to one product or batch of products. Other costs cannot be traced directly to products. In gathering information for business decisions, a particular cost may be important to one

OBJECTIVE 1
State the differences between the three manufacturing cost elements: (a) direct materials costs; (b) direct labor costs; and (c) factory overhead costs

type of decision analysis and ignored in another. When changing from an external financial reporting approach to an internal or management accounting approach, some costs take on different characteristics. In fact, manufacturing costs can be reclassified in different ways, depending on the goal of the cost analysis.

The most common classification scheme, as mentioned before, is to group manufacturing costs into one of three classes: (1) direct materials costs; (2) direct labor costs; and (3) indirect manufacturing costs. This last class of costs is often referred to as factory overhead. **Direct costs** can be traced to specific products. **Indirect costs** must be assigned to products by some general plan for allocation.

Direct Materials Costs

All manufactured products are made from basic direct materials. The basic material may be iron ore for steel, sheet steel for automobiles, or flour for bread. These examples show the link between a basic raw material and a final product.

The way a company buys, stores, and uses materials is important. Timely purchasing is important because if the company runs out of materials, the manufacturing process will be forced to shut down. Shutting down production results in no products, unhappy customers, and loss of sales and profits. Buying too many direct materials, on the other hand, can lead to high storage costs.

Proper storage of materials will avoid waste and spoilage. Large enough storage space and orderly storage procedures are essential. Materials must be handled and stored properly to guarantee their satisfactory use in production. Proper records make it possible to find goods easily. Such records also reduce problems caused by lost or misplaced items.

Direct materials are materials that become part of the finished product and can be conveniently and economically traced to specific product units. The costs of these materials are direct costs. In some cases, even though a material becomes part of a finished product, the expense of actually tracing the cost of a specific material is too great. Examples include nails in furniture, bolts in automobiles, and rivets in airplanes. These minor materials and other production supplies that cannot be conveniently or economically traced to specific products are accounted for as **indirect materials.** Indirect materials costs are part of factory overhead costs, which are discussed later in this chapter.

OBJECTIVE 2
Identify the source documents used to collect information on manufacturing cost accumulation

Direct Materials Purchases. Direct materials are a sizable expenditure each year, so special care must be taken in purchasing them. A company must be careful to buy proper amounts and to ensure it receives quality goods. An efficient purchasing system uses several important documents to account for direct materials purchases. These documents were described in Chapter 6. The **purchase requisition** (or **purchase request**), which starts in the production department, is used to begin the materials purchasing process. The requisition describes the items to be purchased and the quantities needed. It must be approved by a qualified manager or supervisor.

From the information on the purchase requisition, the purchasing department prepares a formal **purchase order.** Some copies of the purchase order are sent to the vendor or supplier; the remaining copies are kept for internal use. When the ordered goods are received, a **receiving report** is prepared. It is matched against the descriptions and quantities listed on the purchase order. Usually, the materials are inspected as soon as they arrive for inferior quality or damage. The purchasing process is complete when the company gets an invoice from the vendor and approves it for payment.

Direct Materials Usage. Controlling direct materials costs does not end with the receipt and inspection of purchased goods. The materials must be stored in a safe place. They must be counted at regular intervals. And they should be issued into production only with the approval of a production supervisor. It is important to keep the materials storage areas clean and orderly and to lock up valuable items. Regular physical counts are necessary to see how many units are on hand and to test the inventory accounting system. Materials should be issued to production only when an approved **materials requisition** form is presented to the storeroom clerk. The materials requisition form, shown in Figure 16-1, is essential for controlling direct materials. Besides providing the supervisor's approval signature, the materials requisition describes the types and quantities of goods needed and received.

Direct Labor Costs

Labor services are, in essence, purchased from employees working in the factory. In addition, other types of labor are purchased from people and organizations outside the company. However, the labor cost usually associated with manufacturing is that of factory personnel. These personnel include machine operators; maintenance workers; managers and supervisors; support personnel; and people who handle, inspect, and store materials. Because these people are all connected in some way with the production process, their wages and salaries must be accounted for as production costs and, finally, as costs of products. However, it is difficult to trace many of these costs directly to individual products.

To help overcome this problem, the wages of machine operators and other workers involved in actually shaping the product are classified as direct labor costs. **Direct labor** costs include all labor costs for specific work performed on products that can be conveniently and economically traced to end products. Labor costs for production-related activities that cannot be connected with or conveniently or economically traced to end products are called **indirect labor** costs. These costs include the wages and salaries of such workers as machine helpers, supervisors, and other support personnel. Like indirect materials costs, indirect labor costs are accounted for as factory overhead costs.

Figure 16-1.
The Materials Requisition Form

Benton Publishing Company
Boston, Massachusetts

Materials Requisition

No. 49621

Charge to Job No. 14-629

Requested by Jim Roberts

Date 4/27/x9

Department Binding

Part Number	Description	Quantity Requested	Quantity Issued	Unit Cost	Total Cost
16T	Glue	140 gallons	60 gallons	$12.40	$744.00

Issued by L. Sanchez

Approved by A. Schroeder

Received by J. Roberts

Date Received 5/1/x9

Labor Documentation. Labor time-records are important to both the employee and the company. The employee wants to be paid at the correct rate for all hours worked. The company does not want to underpay or overpay its employees. In addition, company management wants a record kept of hours worked on products or batches of products made during the period. For these reasons accounting for wages and salaries requires careful attention.

The basic time-record is called an employee **timecard.** On each employee's timecard either the supervisor or a time clock records the employee's daily starting and finishing times. Normally, a company uses another set of labor cards to help verify the time recorded on the timecards and to keep track of labor costs per job or batch of goods produced. These documents, called **job cards,** record the time spent by an employee on a certain job. Each eight-hour period recorded on a timecard may be supported by several job cards. Special job cards also record machine downtime, which may stem from machine repair or product design changes. Job cards verify the time worked by each employee and help control labor time per job.

Gross Versus Net Payroll. Accounting for direct and indirect labor costs often causes misunderstanding. People sometimes confuse gross payroll with net payroll. For internal accounting purposes, gross wages and salaries are used. **Net payroll** is the amount paid to the employee after all payroll deductions have been subtracted from gross wages. Payroll deductions, such as those for federal income taxes and social security taxes, are paid by the employee. The employer just withholds them and pays them to the government and other organizations for the employee. **Gross payroll** is a measure of the total wages and salaries earned by employees, including payroll deductions. It is used to compute total manufacturing costs. The following example shows the difference between gross and net payroll:

Gross wages earned		
40 hours at $10/hour		$400.00
Less deductions		
Federal income taxes withheld	$82.50	
FICA taxes withheld	26.00	
U.S. government savings bond	37.50	
Union dues	12.50	
Insurance premiums	21.00	
Total deductions		179.50
Net wages paid (amount of check)		$220.50

The employee receives net wages of only $220.50, even though the company pays $400.00 in wages and deductions. The amounts withheld from the employee's gross wages are paid by the company to the taxing agencies, savings plan, union, and insurance companies. Gross payroll in this case is $400.00, and it is the gross payroll that must be accounted for as a cost of production and assigned to products or jobs. Net payroll is primarily important to the employee.

Labor-related Costs. Other labor-related manufacturing costs fall into two categories: employee benefits and employer payroll taxes. Employee benefits are considered part of an employee's compensation package. They may include paid vacations, holiday and sick pay, and an employee pension plan. Other benefits might be life and medical insurance, performance bonuses, profit sharing, and recreation facilities. Most of these costs vary in direct proportion to labor costs.

Besides the payroll taxes paid by the employee, there are payroll-related taxes paid by the employer. For every dollar of social security (FICA) tax withheld from the paycheck, the employer usually pays an equal amount. The company must also pay state and federal unemployment compensation taxes. Agreements between management and labor as well as government regulations are sources of some labor-related costs. Company management may spend other money on a voluntary basis for the benefit of its employees.

Most labor-related costs are incurred in direct proportion to wages and salaries earned by the employees. As much as possible, labor-related costs dependent on direct labor costs and conveniently traceable to them should be accounted for as part of direct labor. All other labor-related costs should be classified as factory overhead. However, because of the size and complexity of payroll systems, most labor-related costs are not traced to individual employees. Such costs are normally calculated from wages and salaries by means of a predetermined rate based on past experience. For instance, a company may incur twelve cents of labor-related costs for every dollar of wages and salaries earned by employees. In this case labor-related costs average 12 percent of labor costs. Therefore, if direct labor totaled $6,000 for a period of time, total direct labor cost would be $6,720 ($6,000 plus 12 percent, or $720, in labor-related costs). Total indirect labor cost would be computed in the same manner, as shown in the next section.

Factory Overhead

The third manufacturing cost element is a catchall for manufacturing costs that cannot be classified as direct materials or direct labor costs. **Factory overhead** costs are a varied collection of production-related costs that cannot be practically or conveniently traced to end products. This collection of costs is also called manufacturing overhead, factory burden, and indirect manufacturing costs. Examples of the major classifications of factory overhead costs are listed below.

Indirect materials and supplies: nails, rivets, lubricants, and small tools

Indirect labor costs: lift-truck driver's wages, maintenance and inspection labor, engineering labor, machine helpers, and supervisors

Other indirect factory costs: building maintenance, machinery and tool maintenance, property taxes, property insurance, pension costs, depreciation on plant and equipment, rent expense, and utilities expense

Although this list is incomplete, it includes many common overhead costs and shows how varied they are.

Overhead Cost Behavior. Cost behavior is an important concept in management accounting. Manufacturing costs tend either to rise and fall with the volume of production or to stay the same within certain ranges of output. **Variable manufacturing costs** increase or decrease in direct proportion to the number of units produced. Examples include: direct materials costs; direct labor costs; indirect materials and supply costs; most indirect labor costs; and small-tool costs.

Production costs that stay fairly constant during the accounting period are called **fixed manufacturing costs.** Even with changes in productive output, these costs tend to stay the same. Examples of fixed manufacturing costs are fire insurance premiums, factory rent, supervisors' salaries, and depreciation on machinery. Some costs are called semivariable because part of the cost is fixed and part varies with usage. Telephone charges (basic charge plus long-distance charges) and utility bills are generally semivariable.

Cost behavior will be explored further in Chapter 19. In accounting for factory overhead costs, cost behavior analysis helps assign these indirect costs to units of output.

Overhead Cost Allocation. A cost is classified as a factory overhead cost when it cannot be directly traced to an end product. Yet a product's total cost obviously includes factory overhead costs. Somehow factory overhead costs must be identified with and assigned to specific products or jobs. Because direct materials and direct labor costs are traceable to products, assigning their costs to units of output is relatively easy. Factory overhead costs, however, must be assigned to products by some cost allocation method. Cost allocation methods are explained in Chapters 17 and 19.

Unit Cost Determination

OBJECTIVE 3
Compute a product's unit cost

Direct materials, direct labor, and factory overhead costs constitute total manufacturing costs for a period of time or a batch of products. Product unit cost for each job completed is computed by dividing the total cost of materials, labor, and factory overhead for that job by the total units produced. For example, assume that Roland Products, Inc., produced 3,000 units of output for Job 12K. Costs for Job 12K included the following: direct materials, $3,000; direct labor, $5,400; and factory overhead, $2,700. The company's unit cost for Job 12K would be computed as follows:

Direct materials ($3,000/3,000 units)	$1.00
Direct labor ($5,400/3,000 units)	1.80
Factory overhead ($2,700/3,000 units)	.90
Total unit cost ($11,100/3,000 units)	$3.70

The unit cost described above was computed when the job ended and when all information was known. What about situations needing this information a month before the job is started? Unit cost figures must then be estimated. Assume that accounting personnel developed these estimates for another product: $2.50 per unit for direct materials, $4.50 per unit for direct labor, and 50 percent of direct labor cost for factory overhead. The unit cost would then be as follows:

Direct materials	$2.50
Direct labor	4.50
Factory overhead (50% of $4.50)	2.25
Total unit cost	$9.25

This $9.25 unit cost is based on estimates. Still, it is useful for job costing and as a starting point for product pricing.

Product and Period Costs

OBJECTIVE 4
Distinguish between product costs and period costs

Product costs and *period costs* are two terms commonly used in analyzing costs. **Product costs** consist of the three manufacturing cost elements: direct materials, direct labor, and factory overhead. They are incurred in making products and are inventoriable. That is, product costs are associated with the materials, work in process, and finished goods inventories. They provide values for the ending balances of these inventories on year-end financial statements. Product costs are also considered unexpired costs because, as inventory balances, they are company assets. Assets, as shown in earlier chapters, are economic resources expected to benefit future operations.

Period costs (expenses) are costs that cannot be inventoried. Examples include selling and administrative expenses, since selling and administrative resources are used up in the same period in which they originate. Period costs are linked to services consumed during the current period and would never be used to determine a product's unit cost or to establish ending inventory balances.

Periodic Versus Perpetual Inventory Methods in Manufacturing Accounting

Cost flow in accounting for manufacturing costs depends on how a company chooses to handle its inventories. In Chapter 8, we discussed the periodic and perpetual inventory methods. Because these methods are related to management accounting systems, we also include a brief discussion here. A company using the periodic inventory method records materials purchases in a separate purchases account and assigns manufacturing costs to individual labor accounts and various factory overhead cost accounts in the general ledger. Beginning inventory balances in the general ledger remain unchanged during the period. No costs flow through the Materials, Work in Process, and Finished Goods Inventory accounts during the accounting period. Year-end inventory values are found by counting the items on hand and placing a cost on these goods. Inventory accounts are then adjusted to reflect the cost of the ending inventories.

If a company uses the perpetual inventory method, manufacturing costs flow through inventory accounts as goods and services are bought and used in the production process. Inventory account balances are updated perpetually. In this way it is possible to know these account balances at any point in time. Materials purchased are debited to the Materials Inventory account. The cost of materials used, direct labor, and factory overhead items are entered into the Work in Process Inventory account. The cost of completed units is debited directly to the Finished Goods Inventory account.

The perpetual inventory method is in common use. Greater accuracy and better inventory control are the major benefits of this approach.

However, a perpetual inventory system is expensive to install and maintain. For this reason, many medium-size and small manufacturing companies use a periodic inventory approach.

Manufacturing Inventory Accounts

Most manufacturing companies use the perpetual inventory approach. In the remaining sections of this book, you are to assume that a company uses the perpetual inventory method unless otherwise indicated. Accounting for inventories is the more difficult part of manufacturing accounting when compared with merchandising accounting. Instead of dealing with one account—Merchandise Inventory—*three* accounts must be used: Materials Inventory, Work in Process Inventory, and Finished Goods Inventory.

Materials Inventory

OBJECTIVE 5
Describe the nature, contents, and flow of costs through the Materials, Work in Process, and Finished Goods inventory accounts

The **Materials Inventory** account, also called the Stores and Materials Inventory Control account, is made up of the balances of materials and supplies on hand. This account is maintained in much the same way as the Merchandise Inventory account. The main difference is in the way that the costs of items in inventory are assigned. For the merchandising company, goods taken out of inventory are items that have been sold. When a sale is made, an entry is needed to debit Cost of Goods Sold and to credit Merchandise Inventory for the cost of the item. Materials, on the other hand, are usually not purchased for resale but for use in manufacturing a product. Therefore, an item taken out of Materials Inventory and requisitioned into production is transferred to the Work in Process Inventory account (not Cost of Goods Sold). Figure 16-2 compares the accounting treatment of merchandise inventory with that of materials inventory.

Work in Process Inventory

All manufacturing costs incurred and assigned to products being produced are classified as **Work in Process Inventory** costs. This inventory account has no counterpart in merchandise accounting. A thorough understanding of the concept of Work in Process Inventory is vital in manufacturing accounting. Figure 16-3 shows the various costs that become part of Work in Process Inventory and the way costs are transferred out of the account.

The requisitioning of materials into production, shown initially in Figure 16-2, begins the production process. These materials must be cut, molded, assembled, or in some other way changed into a finished product. To make this change, people, machines, and other factory resources (buildings, electricity, supplies, and so on) must be used. All of these costs are manufacturing cost elements, and all of them enter into accounting for Work in Process Inventory.

Direct labor dollars earned by factory employees are also product costs. Since these people work on specific products, their labor costs are assigned to those products by including the labor dollars earned as part of the Work in Process Inventory account. (Specific product costing is the topic

Figure 16-2. Materials Inventory Versus Merchandise Inventory Accounting (Perpetual)

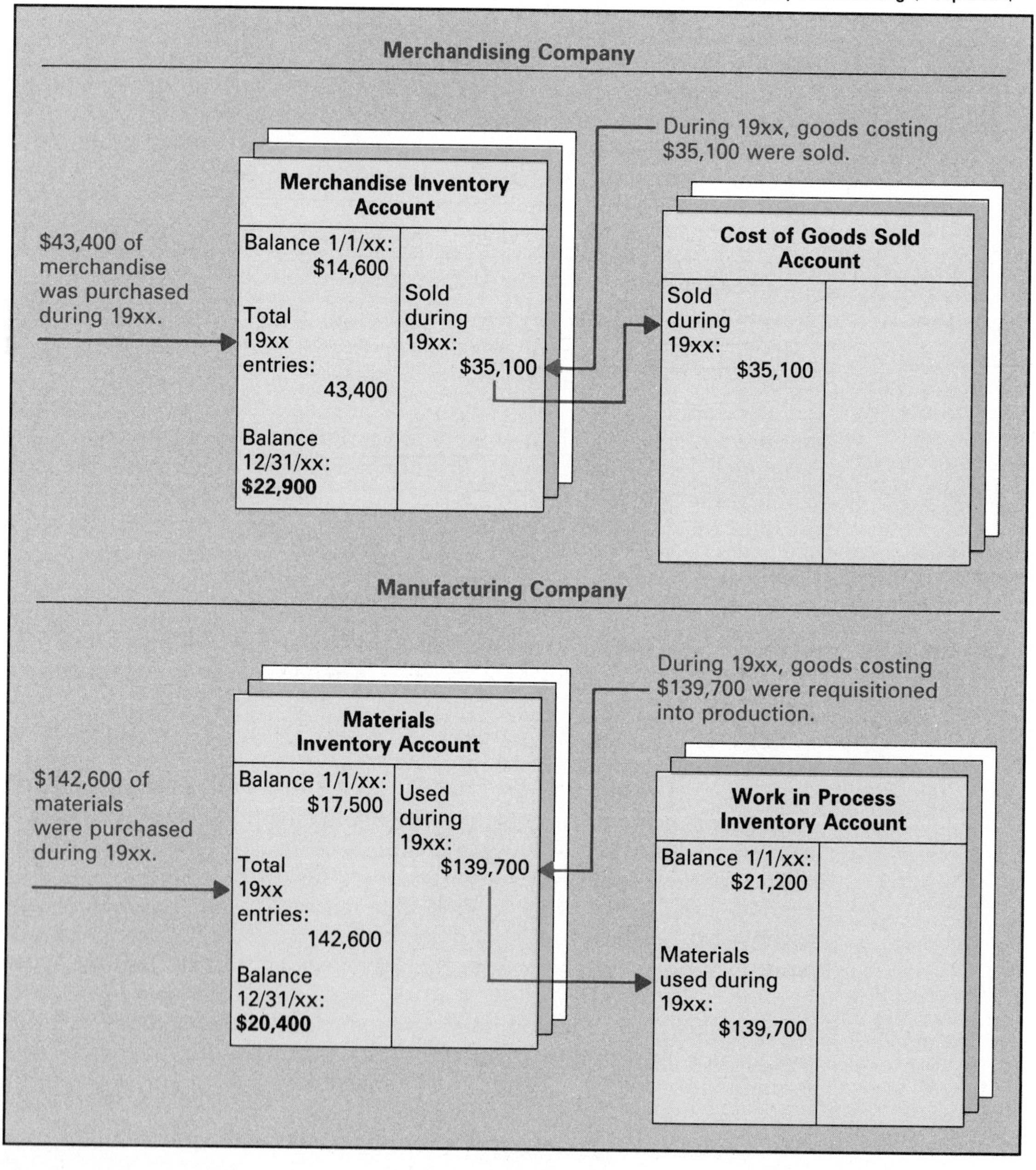

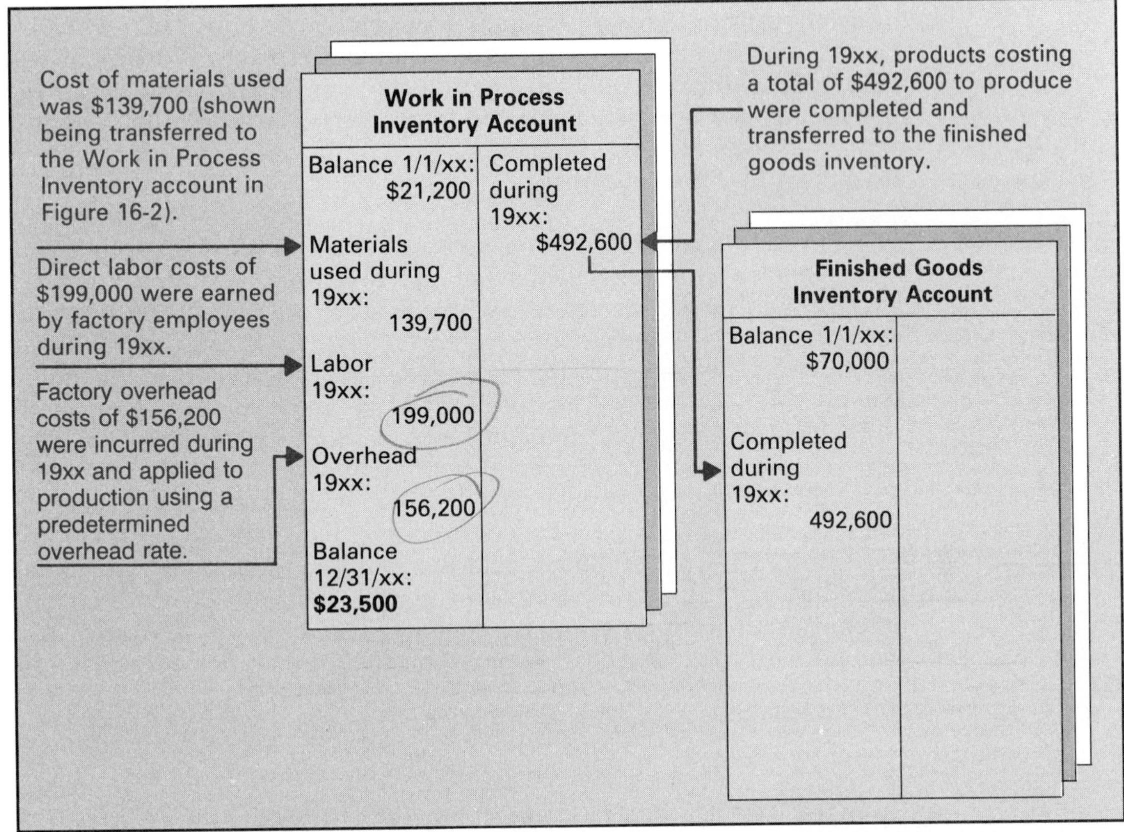

Figure 16-3. The Work in Process Inventory Account (Perpetual)

of the next two chapters. At this point you should assume that all direct labor costs will be included in the Work in Process Inventory account.)

Overhead costs are product costs and must be assigned to specific products. Thus they, too, are included in the Work in Process Inventory account. As discussed earlier, there are too many overhead costs to account for on an individual basis. To reduce the amount of work needed to assign these costs to products, they are accumulated and accounted for under one account title: Factory Overhead Control. These costs are then assigned to products by using an overhead rate. Using this rate, called a predetermined overhead rate, costs are transferred from the Factory Overhead account to the Work in Process Inventory account. In the example in Figure 16-3, factory overhead costs of $156,200 were charged to the Work in Process Inventory account. The predetermined overhead rate will be discussed in Chapter 17.

As products are completed, they are put into the finished goods storage area. These products now have materials, direct labor, and factory overhead costs assigned to them. When products are completed, their costs no longer belong to work (products) in process. Therefore, when the completed products are sent to the storage area, their costs are transferred from the Work in Process Inventory account to the Finished Goods Inventory account. The balance remaining in the Work in Process Inventory account ($23,500 in Figure 16-3) represents costs assigned to products partly completed and still in process at the end of the period.

Finished Goods Inventory

The **Finished Goods Inventory** account, like Materials Inventory, has some characteristics of the Merchandise Inventory account. You have already seen how costs are moved from the Work in Process Inventory account to the Finished Goods Inventory account. At this point Finished Goods Inventory takes on the characteristics of Merchandise Inventory. If you compare the Merchandise Inventory account analysis in Figure 16-2 with the accounting for Finished Goods Inventory in Figure 16-4, you will see that the credit side of both accounts is handled in the same way. Both examples show that when goods or products are sold, the costs of those goods are moved from the Finished Goods Inventory account to the Cost of Goods Sold account. However, the accounting procedures affecting the debit side of the Finished Goods Inventory account differ from those for the Merchandise Inventory account. In a manufacturing firm salable products are produced rather than purchased.

Figure 16-4. Accounting for Finished Goods Inventory (Perpetual)

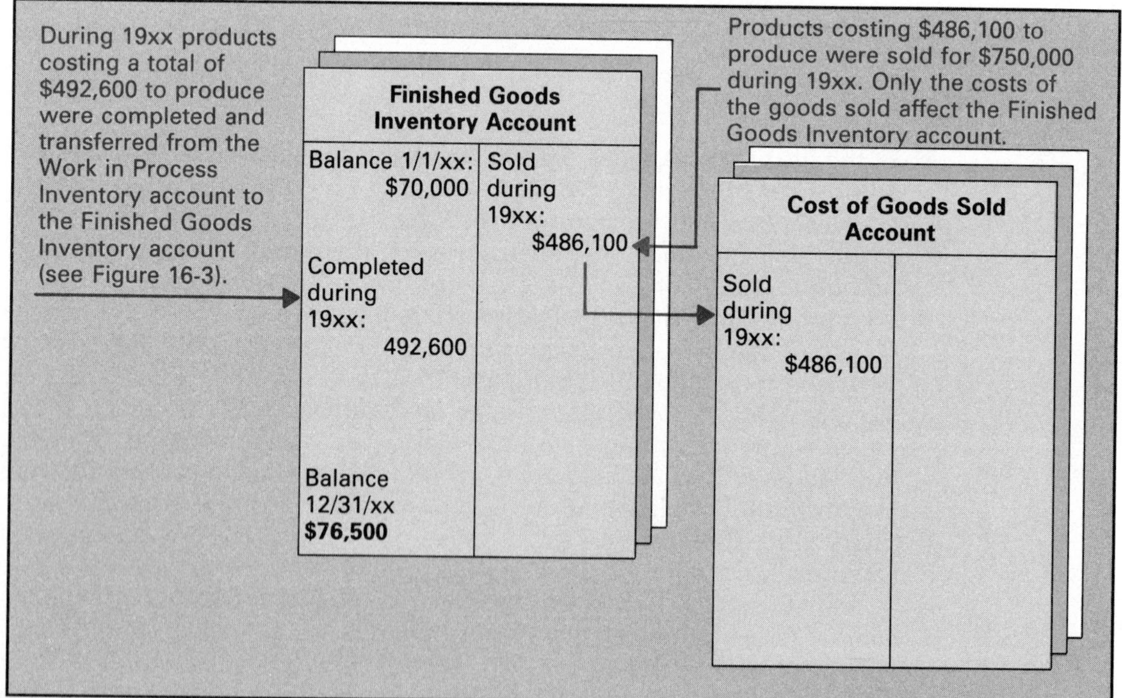

All costs debited to Finished Goods Inventory represent transfers from the Work in Process Inventory account. At the end of an accounting period, the balance in the Finished Goods Inventory account is made up of the costs of products completed but unsold as of that date.

Manufacturing Cost Flow

Product costing, inventory valuation, and financial reporting depend on a defined, structured flow of manufacturing costs. This **manufacturing cost flow** was outlined in the discussion of the three manufacturing inventory accounts. Figure 16-5 sums up the entire cost-flow process as it relates to accounts in the general ledger. At this point do not worry about the actual journal entries needed to make this cost flow operational. These entries will be illustrated in Chapter 17.

Here we will concentrate on the general pattern of manufacturing cost flow, as shown in Figure 16-6. The cost flow begins with costs being incurred. Manufacturing costs start in many ways. They may be cash payments, incurred liabilities, fixed asset depreciation, or expired prepaid expenses. Once these costs have been incurred, they are recorded as either direct materials, direct labor, or factory overhead costs. As the resources are used up, the company transfers its costs to the Work in Process Inventory account. When production is completed, costs assigned to finished units are transferred to the Finished Goods Inventory account. In much the same way, costs attached to units sold are transferred to the Cost of Goods Sold account. Before going on, compare the cost flow as it moves through the general ledger accounts in Figure 16-5 with the general pattern shown in Figure 16-6. Both figures show the same type of cost flow.

The Manufacturing Statement

Financial statements of manufacturing companies differ little from those of merchandising companies. Depending on the industry, the account titles found on the balance sheet (statement of financial position) are the same in most corporations. (Examples include Cash, Accounts Receivable, Buildings, Machinery, Accounts Payable, and Capital Stock.) Even the income statements for a merchandiser and a manufacturer are similar. However, a closer look shows that the heading Cost of Goods Manufactured is used in place of the Purchases account. Also, the Merchandise Inventory account is replaced by Finished Goods Inventory. Note these differences on the income statement of the Windham Company (Exhibit 16-1).

The key to preparing an income statement for a manufacturing company is to determine the cost of goods manufactured. This dollar amount is

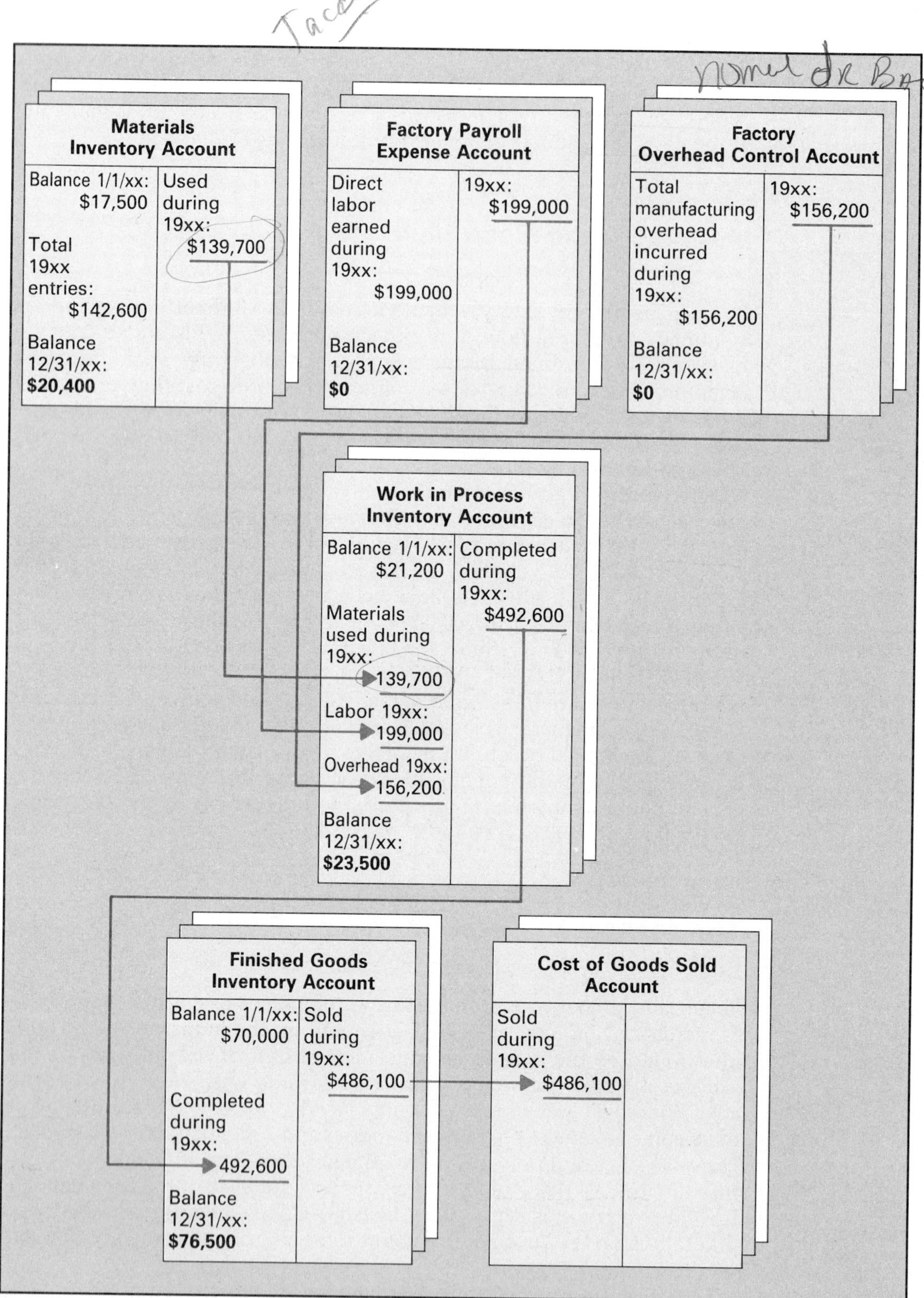

Figure 16-5. Manufacturing Cost Flow: An Example

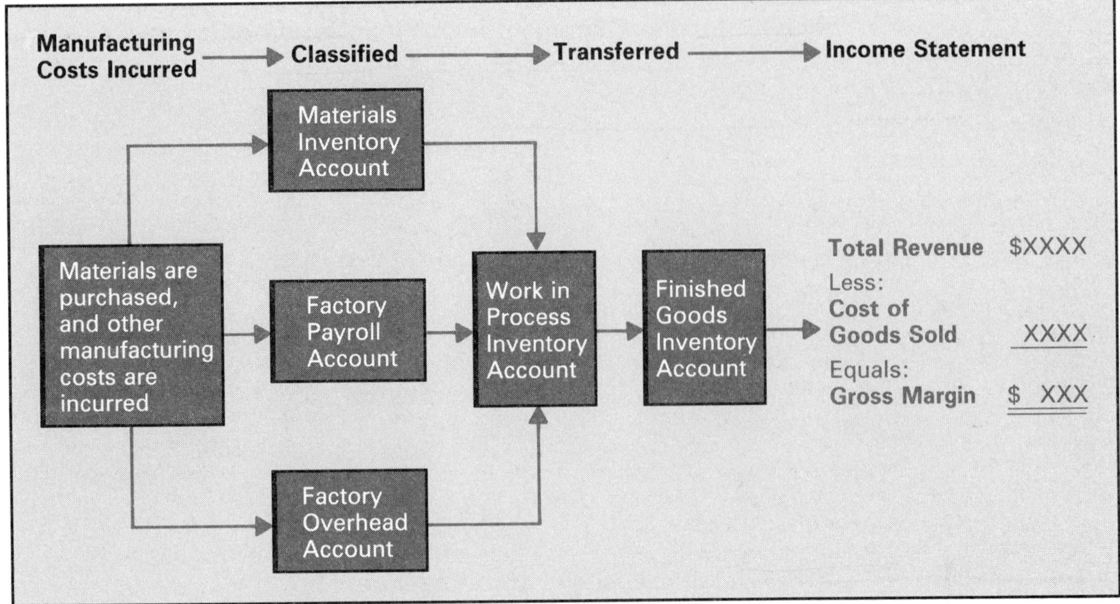

Figure 16-6. Manufacturing Cost Flow: Basic Concepts

the end result of a special manufacturing statement, the statement of cost of goods manufactured, which is prepared to support the figure on the income statement.

Statement of Cost of Goods Manufactured

OBJECTIVE 6
Prepare a statement of cost of goods manufactured

The flow of manufacturing costs, shown in Figures 16-2 through 16-6, provides the basis for accounting for manufacturing costs. In this process all manufacturing costs incurred are considered product costs. They are used to compute ending inventory balances and cost of goods sold. The costs flowing from one account to another during the year have been combined into one number in the illustrations to help show the basic idea. In fact, hundreds of transactions occur during a year, and each transaction affects part of the cost flow process. At the end of the year, the flow of all manufacturing costs incurred during the year is summarized in the **statement of cost of goods manufactured**. This statement gives the dollar amount of costs for products completed and moved to Finished Goods Inventory during the year. The amount for cost of goods manufactured should be the same as the amount transferred from the Work in Process Inventory account to the Finished Goods Inventory account during the year.

The statement of cost of goods manufactured is shown in Exhibit 16-2. Even though this statement is rather complex, it can be pieced together in three steps. The *first step* is to compute the cost of materials used. Add the materials purchases for the period to the beginning balance in the Materials Inventory account. This subtotal represents the cost of

Exhibit 16-1. Income Statement for a Manufacturing Company

Windham Company
Income Statement
For the Year Ended December 31, 19xx

Net Sales			$750,000
Cost of Goods Sold			
Finished Goods Inventory, Jan. 1, 19xx		**$ 70,000**	
Cost of Goods Manufactured (Exhibit 16-2)		**492,600**	
Total Cost of Finished Goods Available for Sale		**$562,600**	
Less Finished Goods Inventory, Dec. 31, 19xx		**76,500**	
Cost of Goods Sold			**486,100**
Gross Margin from Sales			$263,900
Operating Expenses			
Selling Expenses			
Salaries and Commissions	$46,500		
Advertising	19,500		
Other Selling Expenses	7,400		
Total Selling Expenses		$ 73,400	
General and Administrative Expenses			
Administrative Salaries	$65,000		
Franchise and Property Taxes	72,000		
Other G & A Expenses	11,300		
Total General and Administrative Expenses		148,300	
Total Operating Expenses			221,700
Income from Operations			$ 42,200
Less Interest Expense			4,600
Net Income Before Taxes			$37,600
Income Taxes Expense			11,548
Net Income			$ 26,052

materials available for use during the year. Then subtract the balance of the ending Materials Inventory from the cost of materials available for use. The difference is the cost of materials used during the accounting period.

Computation of Cost of Materials Used

Beginning Balance: Materials Inventory	$ 17,500
Plus Materials Purchases (net)	142,600
Cost of Materials Available for Use	$160,100
Less Ending Balance: Materials Inventory	20,400
Cost of Materials Used	$139,700

Exhibit 16-2. Statement of Cost of Goods Manufactured

Windham Company
Statement of Cost of Goods Manufactured
For the Year Ended December 31, 19xx

	Materials Used		
	Materials Inventory, Jan. 1, 19xx	$ 17,500	
	Materials Purchases (net)	142,600	
Step One	Cost of Materials Available for Use	$160,100	
	Less Materials Inventory, December 31, 19xx	20,400	
	Cost of Materials Used		$139,700
	Direct Labor		199,000
	Factory Overhead Costs		
	Indirect Labor	$ 46,400	
	Power	25,200	
Step Two	Depreciation Expense, Machinery and Equipment	14,800	
	Depreciation Expense, Factory Building	16,200	
	Small Tools Expense	2,700	
	Factory Insurance Expense	1,600	
	Supervision Expense	37,900	
	Other Factory Costs	11,400	
	Total Factory Overhead Costs		156,200
	Total Manufacturing Costs		$494,900
	Add Work in Process Inventory, January 1, 19xx		21,200
Step Three	Total Cost of Work in Process During the Year		$516,100
	Less Work in Process Inventory, December 31, 19xx		23,500
	Cost of Goods Manufactured		$492,600

Before going to the next step, trace these numbers back to the Materials Inventory account in Figure 16-2 to see how that account is related to the statement of cost of goods manufactured.

Calculating total manufacturing costs for the year is the *second step*. As shown in Figure 16-3, the costs of materials used and direct labor are added to total factory overhead costs incurred during the year. This step is shown below as well as in Exhibit 16-2.

Computation of Total Manufacturing Costs

Cost of Materials Used	$139,700
Plus Direct Labor Costs	199,000
Plus Total Factory Overhead Costs	156,200
Total Manufacturing Costs	$494,900

The *third step* shown in Exhibit 16-2 changes total manufacturing costs into total cost of goods manufactured for the year. Add the beginning Work in Process Inventory balance to total manufacturing costs for the period to arrive at the total cost of work in process during the year. From this amount subtract the ending Work in Process Inventory balance for the year to get the cost of goods manufactured.

Computation of Cost of Goods Manufactured

Total Manufacturing Costs	$494,900
Plus Beginning Balance: Work in Process Inventory	21,200
Total Cost of Work in Process During the Year	$516,100
Less Ending Balance: Work in Process Inventory	23,500
Cost of Goods Manufactured	$492,600

The term *total manufacturing costs* must not be confused with the cost of goods manufactured. **Total manufacturing costs** are the total costs for materials used, direct labor, and factory overhead incurred and charged to production during an accounting period. **Cost of goods manufactured** consists of the total manufacturing costs attached to units of a product *completed* during an accounting period. To understand the difference between these two dollar amounts, review the computation just shown. Total manufacturing costs of $494,900 incurred during the current year are added to the beginning balance in Work in Process Inventory. Costs of $21,200 in the beginning balance, by definition, are costs from an earlier period. The costs of two accounting periods are now being mixed to arrive at the total cost of work in process during the year, or $516,100. The costs of ending products still in process ($23,500) are then subtracted from the total cost of work in process during the year. The remainder, $492,600, is the cost of goods manufactured (completed) during the year. It is assumed that the items in beginning inventory were completed first. Costs attached to the ending Work in Process Inventory are part of the current period's total manufacturing costs. But they will not become part of the cost of goods manufactured until the next accounting period when the products are completed.

Cost of Goods Sold and the Income Statement

OBJECTIVE 7
Prepare an income statement for a manufacturing company

Exhibits 16-1 and 16-2 demonstrate the relationship between the statement of cost of goods manufactured and the income statement. The total amount of cost of goods manufactured during the period is carried over to the income statement. There it is used to compute cost of goods sold. The cost of goods manufactured is added to the beginning balance of Finished Goods Inventory to get the total cost of finished goods available for sale during the period. The cost of goods sold is then computed by subtracting the ending balance in Finished Goods Inventory (cost of goods completed but unsold) from the total cost of finished goods available for sale. Cost of goods sold is considered an expense for the period in which the related products were sold.

Computation of Cost of Goods Sold

Beginning Balance: Finished Goods Inventory	$ 70,000
Plus Cost of Goods Manufactured	492,600
Total Cost of Finished Goods Available for Sale	$562,600
Less Ending Balance: Finished Goods Inventory	76,500
Cost of Goods Sold	$486,100

Note that the above computation is similar to the computation of cost of goods sold in the income statement in Exhibit 16-1. The other parts of the income statement in Exhibit 16-1 should be familiar from earlier discussions in this text.

Product Costs in a Service-oriented Business

OBJECTIVE 8
Apply cost classification concepts to a service-oriented business

Costs are classified as product or period costs for many reasons, including: (1) to determine the unit manufacturing costs so inventories can be valued and selling prices created and verified; (2) to report production costs on the income statement; and (3) to analyze costs for control purposes. When someone shifts from a manufacturing environment to a service-oriented environment, the only major difference is that he or she is no longer dealing with a physical product that can be assembled, stored, and valued. Services are rendered and cannot be stored up or placed in a vault.

So how does this affect the types of cost classifications? Only one cost classification is affected, *the materials costs*. No longer is something being made from a type of material. Rendering a loan service, representing someone in a court of law, selling an insurance policy, or computing a person's taxes are typical services performed by professionals. If you were asked to compute the unit cost of one of these services, what types of costs would you be dealing with?

The most important cost would be the professional labor involved, and the same definition is applicable; that is, the direct labor cost must be traceable to the service rendered. In addition to the labor cost, any type of business, whether it is manufacturing, service, or not-for-profit oriented, will incur various overhead costs. In a service business those overhead costs associated with and incurred for the purpose of offering a service are classified as service overhead (like factory) and, along with professional labor costs, are considered service costs (like product costs) rather than period costs.

As an example, assume the Loan Department at the Orange Bank of Commerce wants to determine the total costs incurred in processing a typical loan application. Their policy for the past five years has been to charge a $150 fee for processing a home-loan application. Ms. Kim Lazar, chief loan officer, thinks the fee is far too low, considering the way operating costs have soared in the past five years. You have been asked to compute the cost of processing a typical home-loan application.

The following information concerning the processing of a loan application has been given to you:

Direct Professional Labor:	
Loan Processor's Monthly Salary:	
4 people @ $3,000 each	$12,000
Indirect Monthly Loan Department Related Overhead Costs:	
Chief Loan Officer's Salary	$ 4,500
Telephone Expense	750
Depreciation, Building	2,800
Depreciation, Equipment	1,750
Depreciation, Automobiles	1,200
Legal Advice	2,460
Legal Forms/Supplies	320
Customer Relations	640
Credit Check Function	1,980
Advertising	440
Internal Audit Function	2,400
Utilities Expense	1,690
Clerical Personnel	3,880
Miscellaneous	290
Total Overhead Costs	$25,100

In addition, you discover that all appraisal and title search activities are performed by people outside the bank, and their fees are treated as separate loan costs. One hundred home-loan applications are usually processed each month.

The Loan Department performs several functions in addition to home-loan application tasks. Roughly one-half of the department is involved in loan collection activities. After determining how many of the processed loans were not home loans, you conclude that only 25 percent of the overhead costs of the Loan Department were applicable to the processing of home-loan applications. A computation for the cost of processing one home-loan application is given below.

Direct Professional Labor Cost:	
$12,000 ÷ 100	$120.00
Service Overhead Cost:	
$25,100 × 25% ÷ 100	62.75
Total Processing Cost Per Loan	$182.75

Finally, you conclude that the loan officer was correct; the present fee does not cover the current costs of processing a typical home-loan application. However, doubling the loan fee seems inappropriate. To allow for a profit margin, the loan fee could be raised to $225 or $250.

Chapter Review

Review of Learning Objectives

1. **State the differences between the three manufacturing cost elements: (a) direct materials costs; (b) direct labor costs; and (c) factory overhead costs.**
   Direct materials are materials and parts that become part of the finished product and can be conveniently and economically traced to specific product units. Direct labor costs include all labor costs for specific work performed on products that can be conveniently and economically traced to end products. All other production-related costs are classified and accounted for as factory overhead costs. These costs cannot be practically or conveniently traced to end products, so they must be assigned to the products by some cost allocation method. The classifying of manufacturing costs into the three elements described above is important for product costing, inventory valuation, and product pricing.

2. **Identify the source documents used to collect information on manufacturing cost accumulation.**
   Purchase requisitions list the items or materials needed by the production departments. The purchasing department then uses the purchase order to order the items. When the items or materials come in from vendors, the receiving report is used to identify the items and to match them against purchase orders to ensure the correct items were received. The materials requisition is used to request items and to prove that items or materials were issued into the production process. Timecards record each employee's daily starting and finishing times. Job cards record time spent by each employee on each job. Job cards are matched against timecards to verify the time worked by each employee and to control labor time per job.

3. **Compute a product's unit cost.**
   The unit cost of a product is made up of the costs of materials, labor, and factory overhead. These three cost components are accumulated for a batch of products as they are produced. When the batch has been completed, the number of units produced is divided into the total costs incurred to determine product unit cost.

4. **Distinguish between product costs and period costs.**
   Product costs consist of the three manufacturing cost elements: direct materials, direct labor, and factory overhead. Such costs are incurred in making products and can be inventoried. Period costs are costs that cannot be inventoried and are linked to services consumed during the period, such as selling and administrative expenses.

5. **Describe the nature, contents, and flow of costs through the Materials, Work in Process, and Finished Goods inventory accounts.**
   The flow of costs through inventory accounts begins when costs are incurred for materials, direct labor, and factory overhead. Materials costs flow first into the Materials Inventory account. This account is used to record the costs of materials when they are received and again when they are issued for use in a company's production process. All manufacturing-related costs—materials, direct labor, and factory overhead—are recorded in the Work in Process Inventory account as they enter the production process. When products are completed, their costs are transferred from the Work in Process Inventory

account to the Finished Goods Inventory account. Costs remain in the Finished Goods Inventory account until the products are sold. At that time their costs are transferred to the Cost of Goods Sold account.

6. **Prepare a statement of cost of goods manufactured.**
Preparing a statement of cost of goods manufactured involves three steps. The first is to compute the cost of materials used. Total materials purchases are added to the beginning balance of Materials Inventory to arrive at the cost of materials available for use. From this amount the ending Materials Inventory balance is subtracted to get the cost of materials used. The second step is to compute the total manufacturing costs for the period. Costs of direct labor and factory overhead are added to the cost of materials used to arrive at this amount. The third step is to compute the cost of goods manufactured. Total manufacturing costs and the beginning balance in the Work in Process Inventory account are added. Their sum is called total cost of work in process during the year. By subtracting the ending Work in Process Inventory balance from total cost of work in process, you get the cost of goods manufactured.

7. **Prepare an income statement for a manufacturing company.**
The major change to make in preparing an income statement for a manufacturing company is the requirement that the cost of goods manufactured be determined before the cost of goods sold is computed. Cost of goods manufactured is added to the beginning balance of Finished Goods Inventory to arrive at the total cost of finished goods available for sale. When the ending balance of Finished Goods Inventory (cost of unsold goods) is subtracted from the total cost of goods available for sale, the difference represents the costs attached to the goods sold.

8. **Apply cost classification concepts to a service-oriented business.**
Most types of costs incurred by a manufacturer and called product costs are also incurred by a service-oriented company. The only major difference is that you are no longer dealing with a physical product that can be assembled, stored, and valued. Services are rendered and cannot be stored up or placed into a vault. Only the materials cost classification is affected when applying the various cost classifications to service companies. To determine the cost of performing a particular service, professional labor and service-related overhead costs are included in the analysis.

Review Problem
Cost of Goods Manufactured—Three Fundamental Steps

The management of the Augusta Company requires the controller to prepare a statement of cost of goods manufactured in addition to the year-end balance sheet and income statement. During 19x8, $405,625 of materials were purchased. Operating data and inventory account balances for 19x8 follow:

Account	Balance
Direct Labor (31,420 hours at $8.50 per hour)	$267,070
Plant Supervision	52,500
Indirect Labor (62,280 hours at $5.25 per hour)	326,970
Factory Insurance	8,100

Account	Balance
Utilities	$29,220
Depreciation, Factory Building	46,200
Depreciation, Equipment	42,800
Manufacturing Supplies	9,460
Repairs and Maintenance	14,980
Selling and Administrative Expenses	96,480
Materials Inventory, Jan. 1, 19x8	94,210
Work in Process Inventory, Jan. 1, 19x8	101,640
Finished Goods Inventory, Jan. 1, 19x8	148,290
Materials Inventory, Dec. 31, 19x8	96,174
Work in Process Inventory, Dec. 31, 19x8	100,400
Finished Goods Inventory, Dec. 31, 19x8	141,100

Required

To review the three basic steps for computing cost of goods manufactured, do the following:

1. Prepare a schedule showing the calculation of the cost of materials used during the year.
2. Given the cost of materials used, develop an analysis to find total manufacturing costs for the year.
3. Given total manufacturing costs for the year, prepare an analysis to find the cost of goods manufactured during the year.

Answer to Review Problem

1. Computation of cost of materials used:

Beginning Balance: Materials Inventory	$ 94,210
Plus Materials Purchases	405,625
Cost of Materials Available for Use	$ 499,835
Less Ending Balance: Materials Inventory	96,174
Cost of Materials Used	$ 403,661

2. Computation of total manufacturing costs:

Cost of Materials Used		$ 403,661
Plus Direct Labor		267,070
Plus Factory Overhead Cost:		
Plant Supervision	$ 52,500	
Indirect Labor	326,970	
Factory Insurance	8,100	
Utilities	29,220	
Depreciation, Factory Building	46,200	
Depreciation, Equipment	42,800	
Manufacturing Supplies	9,460	
Repairs and Maintenance	14,980	
Total Factory Overhead Costs		530,230
Total Manufacturing Costs		$1,200,961

3. Computation of cost of goods manufactured:

Total Manufacturing Costs	$1,200,961
Plus Beginning Balance: Work in Process Inventory	101,640
Total Cost of Work in Process During the Year	$1,302,601
Less Ending Balance: Work in Process Inventory	100,400
Cost of Goods Manufactured	$1,202,201

Chapter Assignments

Questions

1. What are the three kinds of costs included in a product's cost?
2. What is the difference between a period cost and a product cost?
3. Define a direct cost. How is it different from an indirect cost?
4. Define direct materials.
5. Describe the following: purchase requisition (request), purchase order, and receiving report.
6. How is direct labor different from indirect labor?
7. What are the two kinds of labor-related costs? Discuss each one.
8. What characteristics identify a cost as being part of factory overhead?
9. What is meant by cost behavior?
10. How does the periodic inventory method differ from the perpetual inventory method?
11. Identify and describe the three inventory accounts used by a manufacturing company.
12. What is meant by manufacturing cost flow?
13. Describe how to compute the cost of materials used.
14. How do total manufacturing costs differ from the cost of goods manufactured?
15. How is the cost of goods manufactured used in computing the cost of goods sold?
16. "The concept of product costs is not applicable to service-oriented companies." Is this statement correct? Defend your answer.
17. Since service-oriented companies do not maintain Work in Process and Finished Goods inventories, what use do they have for unit cost information?
18. Identify two types of service companies, state their primary services, and discuss a method that could control the costs of these services.

Classroom Exercises

Exercise 16-1. Manufacturing Cost Flow
(L.O. 1, 2, 5)

Using the ideas illustrated in Figures 16-5 and 16-6 and discussed in this chapter, describe in detail the flow of materials costs through the recording process of a cost accounting system. Include in your answer all general ledger accounts affected and all recording documents used. Prepare your answer in proper order.

Exercise 16-2. Documentation
(L.O. 2)

Rolla Company manufactures a complete line of music boxes. Seventy percent of its products are standard items produced in long production runs. The remaining thirty percent are special orders, involving specific requests for tunes.

These special-order boxes cost from three to six times more than the standard product because additional materials and labor are used.

Shawna Lynne, controller, recently received a complaint memorandum from Mr. Heinrichshaus, production supervisor, about the new network of source documents added to the cost accounting system. These new documents include a materials purchase requisition, a purchase order form, a materials receiving report, and a materials use requisition. Mr. Heinrichshaus claims these forms create extra "busy work" and interrupt the normal flow of production.

Prepare a written response from Ms. Lynne, fully explaining the purpose of each document.

Exercise 16-3. Unit Cost Determination
(L.O. 3)

The Reis Winery is one of the finest and oldest established wineries in the country. One of its most famous products is an exquisite red table wine called Leon Millot. This wine is made from Leon Millot grapes grown in Missouri's Ozark region. Recently, management has become concerned about the increasing cost of making Leon Millot and needs to find out if the current $9 per bottle selling price is adequate. The following information is given to you for analysis:

Batch size:	10,550 bottles
Costs:	
Materials:	
Leon Millot Grapes	$16,880
Chancellor Grapes	4,220
Bottles	5,275
Labor:	
Pickers/Loaders	2,110
Crusher	422
Processors	9,495
Bottler	633
Storage & Racking	11,605
Production overhead:	
Depreciation, Equipment	2,743
Depreciation, Building	5,275
Utilities	1,055
Indirect Labor	6,330
Supervision	9,495
Supplies	3,165
Storage Fixtures	2,532
Chemicals	2,110
Repairs	1,477
Miscellaneous	633
Total production costs	$85,455

1. Compute the unit cost per bottle for materials, labor, and production overhead.
2. What would you advise company management regarding the price per bottle of Leon Millot wine? Defend your answer.

Exercise 16-4. Cost Classification (L.O. 4)

The following is a list of typical costs incurred by a garment maker: (a) gasoline and oil for salesperson's automobile; (b) telephone charges; (c) dyes for yardage; (d) seamstresses' regular hourly labor; (e) thread; (f) president's subscription to *The Wall Street Journal;* (g) sales commissions; (h) business forms used in the office; (i) buttons and zippers; (j) depreciation of sewing machines; (k) property taxes on the factory; (l) advertising; (m) brand labels; (n) administrative salaries; (o) interest on business loans; (p) starch and fabric conditioners; (q) patterns; (r) hourly workers' vacation pay; (s) roof repair to office; (t) packaging.

1. At the time these costs are incurred, which ones will be classified as period costs? Which ones will be treated as product costs?
2. Of the costs identified as product costs, which are direct costs? Which are indirect costs?

Exercise 16-5. Concept of Three Types of Inventories (L.O. 5)

"For manufacturing companies the concept of inventories must be expanded to include three types: Materials Inventory, Work in Process Inventory, and Finished Goods Inventory."

Briefly explain how the three inventory accounts function and how they relate to each other.

Exercise 16-6. Periodic Versus Perpetual Inventory Methods (L.O. 1)

1. In as much detail as possible, discuss the differences between the periodic and the perpetual inventory methods. Be sure to describe the kinds of businesses that might use each method.
2. Would the periodic or perpetual inventory method be more suitable for each business listed below? Be able to defend your answers.

a. Home appliance retailer
b. Grocery store
c. Computer hardware company
d. Retailer of fine jewelry
e. Sporting goods store
f. Grain elevator
g. Discount department store
h. Auto parts store
i. Pool supplies store
j. Paper manufacturer
k. Fertilizer manufacturer
l. Tire manufacturer
m. Cosmetics outlet for exclusive distributorship
n. Car dealer
o. Office supplies store

Exercise 16-7. Cost of Materials Used (L.O. 6)

Data for the cost of materials for the month that ended July 31, 19xx, are as follows: Materials Inventory on July 1, 19xx, was $34,200, and Materials Inventory on July 31, 19xx, totaled $41,910. During July the company purchased $120,600 in materials on account from Angels Company and $42,200 in materials for cash from Mets Company. In addition, $60,000 was paid on the Angels account balance.

Compute the cost of materials used during July 19xx.

Exercise 16-8. Computing Total Manufacturing Costs (L.O. 6)

The partial trial balance of Waring Millinery, Inc., is shown on the next page. Inventory accounts still reflect balances at the beginning of the period. Period end balances are $57,000, $85,800, and $36,200 for Materials Inventory, Work in Process Inventory, and Finished Goods Inventory, respectively.

	Debit	Credit
Accounts Receivable	$157,420	
Materials Inventory	68,400	
Work in Process Inventory	74,400	
Finished Goods Inventory	41,400	
Accounts Payable		$ 89,250
Sales		911,940
Purchases	301,600	
Direct Labor	191,200	
Operating Supplies Expense, Factory	21,700	
Depreciation Expense, Machinery	54,100	
Fire Loss	82,000	
Insurance Expense, Factory	9,700	
Indirect Labor Expense	56,900	
Supervisory Salaries, Factory	32,700	
President's Salary	39,900	
Property Tax Expense, Factory	9,400	
Other Indirect Manufacturing Expenses	26,500	

From the above information, prepare a schedule (in good form) for computing total manufacturing costs for the period ending May 31, 19xx.

Exercise 16-9. Statement of Cost of Goods Manufactured
(L.O. 6)

Information on the manufacturing costs incurred by the Ferrigno Company for the month ended August 31, 19xx, is as follows:

Purchases of materials during August were $49,000.
Direct labor was 10,400 hours at $5.75 per hour.
These factory overhead costs were incurred: Utilities, $2,870; Supervision, $18,600; Indirect Supplies, $6,000; Depreciation, $5,200; Insurance, $830; and Miscellaneous, $700.
Inventories on August 1 were as follows: Materials, $58,600; Work in Process, $53,250; Finished Goods, $40,500.
Inventories on August 31 were as follows: Materials, $60,100; Work in Process, $47,400; Finished Goods, $42,450.

From the information given, prepare a statement of cost of goods manufactured.

Exercise 16-10. Computing Cost of Goods Sold
(L.O. 6, 7)

Rosati Distilleries, Inc., produces a deluxe line of wines and beverages. During 19xx, the company operated at record levels with sales totaling $965,000. The accounting department has already determined that total manufacturing costs for the period were $455,500. Operating expenses for the year were $199,740. Inventory balances were as follows:

	Jan. 1, 19xx	Dec. 31, 19xx
Materials Inventory	$35,490	$28,810
Work in Process Inventory	67,400	51,980
Finished Goods Inventory	94,820	79,320

Assuming a 34 percent tax rate, prepare an income statement for the year ended December 31, 19xx.

Exercise 16-11. Cost Accounting for a Service-Oriented Business
(L.O. 8)

Preparing appraisals of both residential and commercial real estate is the main function of Abbey Appraisers, Inc. Most of its procedures are similar in time and nature for each class of property appraised. Dana Abbey, president of the company, is concerned about increased costs and the apparent need to increase appraisal fees. For the current year the company charges $450 for a residential appraisal and $900 for a commerical appraisal.

The following information pertains to the month of August 19x9, which has just ended:

Professional Labor	
Appraisers	
Two @ 160 hours @ $24 per hour	$7,680
Apprentices	
Three @ 180 hours @ $10 per hour	5,400
Appraisal Overhead	
Clerical Staff	1,551
Forms and Supplies	282
Utilities	423
Depreciation, Automobile	752
Depreciation, Building	329
Depreciation, Office Equipment	470
Automobile Expenses	282
Supervision	1,880
Library Maintenance & Update	564
Telephone Expense	376
Valuation Service	1,128
Equipment Repairs	517
Liability Insurance	1,316
Outside Consultants	658
Miscellaneous	235

During August, 34 residential and 30 commercial appraisals were completed. Expected hours are as follows:

	Residential	Commercial
Appraisers	3.5 hours	7.0 hours
Apprentices	5.0 hours	10.0 hours

Overhead is normally apportioned to residential and commercial jobs on a one-third, to two-thirds basis, respectively.

1. Determine if Abbey Appraisers, Inc., made a profit during August.
2. Should the appraisal fees be increased? If so, by how much?

Interpreting Accounting Information

Gregor Manufacturing Company
(L.O. 6, 7)

Gregor Manufacturing Company manufactures sheet-metal products for heating and air conditioning installations. For the past several years its income has declined, and this past year, 19x9, was particularly bad. The company's statements of cost of goods manufactured and its income statements for 19x8 and 19x9 are shown on the next two pages. You have been asked to comment on the company's profit situation and to give reasons for its deterioration.

Required

1. In preparing your comments, compute the following ratios for each year:
   a. Ratios of cost of materials used to total manufacturing costs, direct labor to total manufacturing costs, and total factory overhead costs to total manufacturing costs.
   b. Ratios of gross margin from sales to sales, operating expenses to sales, and net income to sales.
2. From your evaluation of ratios computed in **1**, state the probable causes of the decline in net income.
3. What other factors or ratios do you believe should be considered?

Gregor Manufacturing Company
Statements of Cost of Goods Manufactured
For the Years Ended December 31, 19x9 and 19x8

	19x9		19x8	
Materials Used				
Materials Inventory, January 1	$ 89,660		$ 92,460	
Materials Purchases	789,640		760,040	
Cost of Materials Available for Use	$879,300		$852,500	
Less Materials Inventory, December 31	94,930		89,660	
Cost of Materials Used		$ 784,370		$ 762,840
Direct Labor		871,410		879,720
Factory Overhead Costs				
Indirect Labor	$ 82,660		$ 71,980	
Power Expense	34,990		32,550	
Insurance Expense	22,430		18,530	
Supervision	125,330		120,050	
Depreciation Expense	75,730		72,720	
Other Factory Expenses	41,740		36,280	
Total Factory Overhead Costs		382,880		352,110
Total Manufacturing Costs		$2,038,660		$1,994,670
Add Work in Process Inventory, January 1		148,875		152,275
Total Cost of Work in Process During the Year		$2,187,535		$2,146,945
Less Work in Process Inventory, December 31		146,750		148,875
Cost of Goods Manufactured		$2,040,785		$1,998,070

Gregor Manufacturing Company
Income Statements
For the Years Ended December 31, 19x9 and 19x8

	19x9		19x8	
Net Sales		$3,442,960		$3,496,220
Cost of Goods Sold				
Finished Goods Inventory, January 1	$ 192,640		$ 184,820	
Cost of Goods Manufactured	2,040,785		1,998,070	
Total Cost of Finished Goods Available for Sale	$2,233,425		$2,182,890	
Less Finished Goods Inventory, December 31	186,630		192,640	
Cost of Goods Sold		2,046,795		1,990,250
Gross Margin from Sales		$1,396,165		$1,505,970
Operating Expenses				
Sales Salaries and Commissions Expense	$ 494,840		$ 429,480	
Advertising Expense	216,110		194,290	
Other Selling Expenses	82,680		72,930	
Administrative Expenses	342,600		295,530	
Total Operating Expenses		1,136,230		992,230
Income from Operations		$ 259,935		$ 513,740
Other Revenues and Expenses				
Interest Expense		54,160		56,815
Net Income Before Taxes		$ 205,775		$ 456,925
Income Taxes Expense (34 percent)		69,964		155,355
Net Income		$ 135,811		$ 301,570

Problem Set A

Problem 16A-1. Unit Cost Computation (L.O. 3)

ERV Industries, Inc., manufactures videodiscs for several leading recording studios in the United States and Europe. Department 1401 is responsible for the electronic circuitry in each disc. Some parts are purchased from outside vendors; others are produced internally. Department 1211 applies the plastic-like surface to the discs and packages them for shipment.

A recent order for 2,000 discs from the SAM Company was produced during July. Parts other than the direct materials used in the production and assembly processes were purchased for this job from UMSL Corporation. Those parts cost $3,960. Also, department 1401 incurred the following costs for this job: direct materials used, $1,300; direct labor, $1,680; and factory overhead, $1,460. Costs incurred by Department 1211 included: $1,120 in direct materials used; $420 in direct labor; and $600 in factory overhead. All 2,000 units were completed and shipped during the month.

Required

1. Compute the unit cost for each of the two departments.
2. Compute the total unit cost for the SAM Company order.
3. The selling price for this order was $5.30 per unit. Was the selling price adequate? List the assumptions and/or computations on which you based your answer. What suggestions would you make to ERV Industries' management concerning the pricing of future orders?

Problem 16A-2. Factory Overhead: Cost Flow (L.O. 1, 2)

A working knowledge of the make-up of the cost category called factory overhead is essential to understanding the elements, purpose, and operation of a cost accounting system.

Required

1. Identify the characteristics of factory overhead.
2. Are factory overhead costs always indirect costs? Why?
3. List three examples of a factory overhead cost.
4. Diagram the flow of factory overhead costs in a manufacturing environment. List the documents used to record these costs, and link the documents to specific parts of the cost flow diagram.
5. Merlot Industries in Grapevine, California, produces oak wine barrels. The oak wood is purchased in large slabs and milled to size. Metal barrel-rings are purchased from an outside vendor. The following factory overhead costs were incurred in June: indirect mill labor, $21,420; indirect assembly labor, $18,210; administrative salaries, $8,100; depreciation expense for equipment, $2,800; factory rent, $3,400; utilities expense, $1,800; and small tools expense, $1,410. Identify each of the above costs as either a variable cost or a fixed cost. Give reasons for your answers.

Problem 16A-3. Cost of Goods Manufactured: Three Fundamental Steps (L.O. 6)

England Company manufactures a line of aquatic equipment, including a new gill-like device that produces oxygen from water and replaces large, cumbersome pressurized air tanks. Management requires a quarterly statement of cost of goods manufactured as well as an income statement. As the company's accountant, you have determined the following account balances for the quarter ended October 31, 19xx:

Purchases of Materials During Quarter	$360,000
Small Tools Expense	8,240
Factory Insurance Expense	2,690
Factory Utilities Expense	7,410
Depreciation Expense, Building	16,240
Depreciation Expense, Equipment	12,990
Selling Expenses	32,600
Plant Supervisor's Salary	16,250
Direct Labor	214,700
Indirect Labor	81,400
Repairs and Maintenance, Factory	21,200
Miscellaneous Factory Overhead	14,120
Indirect Materials and Supplies, Factory	39,400
Materials Inventory, August 1, 19xx	51,600

Materials Inventory, October 31, 19xx	56,240
Work in Process Inventory, August 1, 19xx	34,020
Work in Process Inventory, October 31, 19xx	41,900
Finished Goods Inventory, August 1, 19xx	39,200
Finished Goods Inventory, October 31, 19xx	40,200

Required

Highlight the three basic steps used in preparing the statement of cost of goods manufactured by doing the following:

1. Prepare an analysis in which you calculate the cost of materials used during the quarter.
2. Using the figure calculated in **1**, prepare a schedule, showing the total manufacturing costs for the quarter.
3. From the amount computed in **2**, prepare a final schedule in which you can derive the cost of goods manufactured for the quarter.

Problem 16A-4. Statement of Cost of Goods Manufactured (L.O. 6)

Wasa Manufacturing Company produces replicas of Viking ships. These models are sold at Scandinavian gift shops throughout the world. Financial records of the company provide the following information: inventory balances on May 1, 19x7: Materials, $110,400; Work in Process, $96,250; and Finished Goods, $42,810. April 30, 19x8, inventory balances were: Materials, $116,250; Work in Process, $87,900; and Finished Goods, $51,620.

During the 19x7–x8 fiscal year, $494,630 in materials were purchased, and payroll records indicate that direct labor costs totaled $315,970. Overhead costs for the period included: indirect materials and supplies, $27,640; indirect labor, $92,710; depreciation expense, building, $19,900; depreciation expense, equipment, $14,240; heating expense, $9,810; electricity, $8,770; repairs and maintenance expense, $5,110; liability and fire insurance expense, $2,980; property taxes, building, $3,830; design and rework expense, $16,770; and supervision expense, $95,290. Other costs for the period included shipping costs, $41,720, and administrative salaries, $102,750.

Required

Using the information provided above, prepare a statement of cost of goods manufactured for the fiscal year ended April 30, 19x8.

Problem 16A-5. Statement Preparation: Manufacturing Company (L.O. 6, 7)

The Peach River Company produces lighting fixtures. All parts are purchased, and the primary function of the company is to assemble the fixtures. Information for the quarter ended December 31, 19x7, is as follows:

	October 1	December 31
Inventories:		
Materials		
Fixtures	$ 46,810	$ 52,020
Shades	16,660	15,940
Electrical parts	29,890	30,470
Wire	11,250	10,840
Work in Process	87,910	90,130
Finished Goods	106,520	101,260

During the three-month period, the company purchased $72,480 in fixtures; $21,660 in shades; $32,780 in electrical parts; and $9,460 in wire. Direct labor for the period was 16,000 hours at an average wage rate of $7.50 per hour. Factory overhead costs for the period were: indirect labor, $38,870; assembly supplies, $3,930; factory rent, $3,000; insurance expense, $940; repairs and maintenance, $3,880; and depreciation of equipment, $2,600. Total sales for the three months were $601,770, and general, selling, and administrative expenses totaled $196,820. Assume an income tax rate of 34 percent.

Required

1. Compute the cost of each of the four materials used during the quarter.
2. Using good form, prepare a statement of cost of goods manufactured for the quarter ended December 31, 19x7.
3. Using your answer in **2**, prepare an income statement for the same period.

Problem Set B

Problem 16B-1. Unit Cost Computation (L.O. 3)

Hugo Industries has recently finished production on Job HA-32. The corporation's cost accountant is ready to calculate the unit cost for this order. Relevant information for the month ended March 31, 19xx, follows. The number of units produced was 38,480. Cost information for Department F-14 included 3,210 liters at $3.00 per liter for direct materials used, 168 hours at $8.50 per hour for direct labor incurred, and $2,514 in factory overhead. Cost data for Department G-12 included 900 liters at $5.57 per liter for direct materials used, 400 hours at $7.80 per hour for direct labor incurred, and $6,570 in factory overhead. Cost data for Department H-15 included 2,005 liters at $5.00 per liter for direct materials used, 420 hours at $8.00 per hour for direct labor incurred, and $4,711 in factory overhead. Each unit produced was processed through three departments, F-14, G-12, and H-15, in that order. There was no ending Work in Process Inventory as of March 31, 19xx.

Required

1. Compute the unit cost for each of the three departments. Carry to one tenth of a cent.
2. Compute the total unit cost.
3. Order HA-32 was specially made for the Jessie Company. The selling price was $53,325. Determine whether the selling price was appropriate. List the assumptions or computations on which you base your answer. What advice, if any, would you offer to the management of Hugo Industries on the pricing of future orders?

Problem 16B-2. Direct Materials: Cost Flow (L.O. 1, 2)

A solid working knowledge of direct materials cost is important for understanding the elements, purpose, and operation of a cost accounting system.

Required

1. Name the characteristics of direct materials and indirect materials.
2. Give at least two examples for each of the two cost categories listed in **1**.
3. Prepare a diagram, showing the flow of all materials costs for a manufacturing concern. Show which documents are used to record materials costs, and relate these documents to specific parts in the cost flow diagram.

4. If a direct materials invoice for $600 is dated September 2, with terms 2/10 and n/30, how much should be paid if the invoice is paid on September 8? On September 29?

Problem 16B-3. Cost of Goods Manufactured: Three Fundamental Steps (L.O. 6)

McGillicuddy Metallurgists, Inc., is a large manufacturing firm that prepares financial statements on a quarterly basis. Assume you are working in the firm's accounting department. Preparing a statement of the cost of goods manufactured is one of your regular, quarterly duties. Account balances are as follows for the quarter ended March 31, 19xx:

Office Supplies Expense	$ 2,870
Depreciation Expense, Plant and Equipment	15,230
President's Salary	26,000
Property Taxes, Office	950
Equipment Repairs Expense, Factory	2,290
Plant Supervisors' Salaries	19,750
Insurance Expense, Plant and Equipment	2,040
Direct Labor	148,310
Utilities Expense, Plant	4,420
Indirect Labor	16,000
Manufacturing Supplies Expense	4,760
Small Tools Expense	900
Materials Inventory, Jan. 1, 19xx	597,950
Materials Inventory, Mar. 31, 19xx	615,030
Work in Process Inventory, Jan. 1, 19xx	729,840
Work in Process Inventory, Mar. 31, 19xx	715,560
Finished Goods Inventory, Jan. 1, 19xx	575,010
Finished Goods Inventory, Mar. 31, 19xx	602,840
Purchases of Materials During the Quarter	1,425,330

Required

Highlight the three basic steps in preparing the statement of cost of goods manufactured by doing the following:

1. Prepare an analysis in which you calculate the cost of materials used during the quarter.
2. Using the figure calculated in **1**, prepare a schedule, showing the total manufacturing costs for the quarter.
3. From the figure derived in **2**, prepare a final schedule, showing cost of goods manufactured for the quarter.

Problem 16B-4. Statement of Cost of Goods Manufactured (L.O. 6)

Winemakers Andor and Tizson operate a large vineyard in California that produces a full and varied line of wines. The company, whose fiscal year begins on November 1, has just completed a record-breaking year, which ended October 31, 19x7. Production figures for this period are as follows:

Account	Nov. 1, 19x6	Oct. 31, 19x7
Materials Inventory	$ 3,956,200	$ 4,203,800
Work in Process Inventory	7,371,000	6,764,500
Finished Goods Inventory	10,596,400	10,883,200

Materials purchased during the year amounted to $3,750,000. Direct labor hours totaled 242,500, at an average labor rate of $5.20 per hour. The following factory overhead costs were incurred during the year: depreciation expense, plant and equipment, $885,600; operating supplies expense, $507,300; property tax expense, plant and equipment, $214,200; material handlers' labor expense, $1,013,700; small tools expense, $72,400; utilities expense, $1,936,500; and employee benefits expense, $746,100.

Required

Using proper form, prepare a statement of cost of goods manufactured from the information provided.

Problem 16B-5. Statement Preparation: Manufacturing Company (L.O. 6, 7)

The Spencer Pharmaceuticals Corporation manufactures various drugs, which are marketed internationally. Inventory information for April 19x8 was as follows:

	April 1	April 30
Materials:		
Natural Minerals	$ 88,700	$ 70,600
Basic Organic Compounds	124,300	111,400
Catalysts	40,500	28,900
Suspension Agents	32,900	42,200
Total Materials	$286,400	$253,100
Work in Process	$108,800	$ 97,200
Finished Goods	$211,700	$214,100

Purchases of materials for April were: natural minerals, $24,610; basic organic compounds, $50,980; catalysts, $42,670; and suspension agents, $24,340. Direct labor costs were computed on the basis of 30,000 hours at $6 per hour. Actual factory overhead costs incurred in April were: operating supplies, $5,700; janitorial and material-handling labor, $29,100; employee benefits, $110,800; heat, light, and power, $54,000; depreciation, factory, $14,400; property taxes, $8,000; and expired portions of insurance premiums, $12,000. Net sales for April were $1,188,400. General and administrative expenses were $162,000. Income is taxed at a rate of 34 percent.

Required

1. Compute the cost of each of the four materials used during April.
2. Using good form, prepare a statement of cost of goods manufactured for the month ended April 30.
3. Using your answer in **2**, prepare an income statement for the same period.

Management Decision Case

St. James Municipal Hospital (L.O. 1, 2, 3, 8)

Hospitals are run in a competitive environment, and they rely heavily on cost data to keep their pricing structures in line with those of competitors. St. James Municipal Hospital is such a case. Located in a large city, the hospital offers three broad types of service. *General services* (dietary, housekeeping, maintenance, patient-care coordination, and general and administrative services) are the first type of service. *Ancillary services* (anesthesiology, blood bank, central and sterile supply, electrodiagnosis, laboratory, operating and recovery room, pharmacy, radiology, and respiratory therapy) are the second type. *Nursing care services* (acute or intensive care units, intermediate care units, neonatal (newborn) nursery, and nursing administration) are the third type.

The hospital's controller is Donnie Kristof. She is reviewing the billing procedure for patients using the thirty intensive care units (ICUs) in the facility. Each unit contains a regular hospital bed and a great deal of special equipment. Special suction equipment, oxygen flow meters at bedside, endotracheal tubes to assist breathing, a portable respirator, back-up suction machinery, and multiple IVs (intravenous feeding lines) with automatic drip counters are among the equipment in each unit. An H.P. Swan Ganz machine has a cardiac catheter tube that, when inserted into the heart, constantly monitors the pressure inside the heart chambers. One of the most important pieces of equipment at each bedside in the ICU is the cardiac monitor that displays the patient's heartbeat. A set of central monitors at the nurses' station helps nurses watch for instances of tachycardia (excessively rapid heartbeat), arrhythmia (irregular heartbeat), or bradycardia (abnormally slow heartbeat). An alarm system attached to the monitor warns the nurses when the patient's heartbeat is over or under acceptable limits. To equip an ICU today costs about $85,000 per room. Use of the equipment is billed to the patient at a rate of $150 per day. This charge includes a 25 percent markup to cover hospital overhead and profit.

Other ICU patient costs include the following:

Doctors' Care	2 hours per day @ $160 per hour (actual)
Special Nursing Care	8 hours per day @ $35 per hour (actual)
Regular Nursing Care	24 hours per day @ $18 per hour (average)
Medicines	$37 per day (average)
Medical Supplies	$34 per day (average)
Room Rental	$50 per day (average)
Food and Service	$40 per day (average)

For billing purposes, as with equipment charges, the hospital adds 25 percent to all costs to cover its operating costs and profit.

Required

1. From the costs listed, identify the direct costs used in determining the "cost per patient day" for an ICU.
2. Compute the cost per patient day.
3. Compute the billing per patient day, using the hospital's markup rate, which covers operating expenses and profit.
4. Many hospitals use separate markup rates for each cost when preparing billing statements. Industry averages revealed the following markup rates:

Doctors' Care	30%	Medical Supplies	50%
Special Nursing Care	40%	Room Rental	20%
Regular Nursing Care	50%	Food and Service	25%
Medicines	50%	Equipment	30%

   Using these rates, recompute the billing per patient day for an ICU.
5. Using the information in **3** and **4**, which billing procedure would you recommend to the hospital's director? Why?

CHAPTER 17 PRODUCT COSTING: THE JOB ORDER SYSTEM

LEARNING OBJECTIVES

1. Identify the differences between job order costing and process costing.
2. Describe the concept of absorption costing.
3. Compute a predetermined overhead rate, and use this rate to apply overhead costs to production.
4. Dispose of underapplied or overapplied overhead.
5. Explain the relationship between product costing and inventory valuation.
6. Describe cost flow in a job order cost accounting system.
7. Journalize transactions in a job order cost accounting system.
8. Compute product unit cost for a specific job order.

Determining a product's unit cost is one of the basic functions of a cost accounting system. Business success depends on product costing information in several ways. First, unit costs are an important element in determining an adequate, fair, and competitive selling price. Second, product costing information often forms the basis for forecasting and controlling operations and costs. Finally, product unit costs are needed to arrive at ending inventory balances.

One important reason for having a cost accounting system is to figure out the cost of manufacturing an individual product or batch of products. Such cost accounting systems vary from one company to another. But each system is designed to give information that company management thinks is important. In this chapter the basic information on manufacturing accounting, discussed in Chapter 16, is applied to a traditional product costing system: the job order costing system. A **job order** is a customer order for a specific number of specially designed, made-to-order products. Thus, you will learn to compute product costs in job order situations. Then you will link these costs to units completed and transferred to Finished Goods Inventory.

However, before discussing a specific product cost accounting system, more background information is needed. In the first part of this chapter, the two most common product costing systems—job order costing and process costing—are compared. Next, the concept of absorption costing is explained. Then, predetermined overhead rates and their application to specific jobs or products are discussed. The primary emphasis is then placed on describing and illustrating the job order cost accounting system. After studying this chapter, you should be able to meet the learning objectives listed on the left. A work sheet analysis based on perpetual inventories is covered in a special analysis in The Windham Company Practice Case.

Job Order Versus Process Costing

Job order costing and process costing are the two traditional, basic approaches to product cost accounting systems. Actual cost accounting systems may differ widely. However, all are based on one

OBJECTIVE 1
Identify the differences between job order costing and process costing

of these product costing concepts. The systems are then adjusted to fit a particular industry, company, or operating department. The objective of the two systems is the same. Both are meant to provide product unit cost information for product pricing, cost control, inventory valuation, and income statement preparation. End-of-period values for the Cost of Goods Sold, the Work in Process Inventory, and the Finished Goods Inventory accounts are computed by using product unit cost data.

Characteristics of Job Order Costing

A **job order cost accounting system** is a product costing system used in making one-of-a-kind or special-order products. In such a system direct materials, direct labor, and factory overhead costs are assigned to specific job orders or batches of products. In computing unit costs, the total manufacturing costs for each job order are divided by the number of good units produced for that order. Industries that use a job order cost accounting system include those that make ships, airplanes, large machines, and other types of special orders.

The primary characteristics of a job order cost system are as follows: (1) It collects all manufacturing costs and assigns them to specific jobs or batches of product. (2) It measures costs for each completed job rather than for set time periods. (3) It uses just one Work in Process Inventory account in the general ledger. This account is supported by a subsidiary ledger of job order cost sheets for each job still in process at period end.

Characteristics of Process Costing

A **process cost accounting system** is a product costing system used by companies that make many similar products or that have a continuous production flow. In either case, it is more economical to account for product-related costs for a period of time (a week or a month) than to try to assign them to specific products or job orders. Unit costs are computed by dividing total manufacturing costs assigned to a department or work center during a week or month by the number of good units produced during that time period. If a product is routed through four departments, four unit cost amounts are added together to find the product's total unit cost. Companies producing paint, oil and gas, automobiles, bricks, or soft drinks use some type of process costing system.

The main characteristics of a process cost accounting system are as follows: (1) Manufacturing costs are grouped by department or work center, with little concern for specific job orders. (2) The system emphasizes a weekly or monthly time period rather than the time it takes to complete a specific order. (3) The system uses several Work in Process Inventory accounts—one for each department or work center in the manufacturing process. Process costing will be discussed in detail in Chapter 18.

The Concept of Absorption Costing

OBJECTIVE 2
Describe the concept of absorption costing

Product costing is possible only when the accounting system can define the types of manufacturing costs to be included in the analysis. For instance, should all factory overhead costs be considered costs of making the product, or only the variable factory overhead costs? Usually, it is assumed that product costing is governed by the concept of absorption costing. **Absorption costing** is an approach to product costing that assigns *all* types of manufacturing costs to individual products. The costs of direct materials, direct labor, variable factory overhead, and fixed factory overhead are all assigned to products. The product costing systems discussed in both this chapter and Chapter 18 apply the absorption costing concept.

Direct materials and direct labor costs are not difficult to handle in product costing because they can be conveniently and economically traced to products. Factory overhead costs, on the other hand, are not so easy to trace directly to products. For example, for a company making lawn and garden equipment, how much machine depreciation should be assigned to a single lawnmower? How about the costs of electrical power and indirect labor? One solution would be to wait until the end of the accounting period. All variable and fixed factory overhead costs incurred could then be added up. This amount could next be divided by the number of units produced during the period. This procedure would be an acceptable method of computing unit cost if the following two conditions exist: (1) All products are alike and require the same manufacturing operations. (2) Computation of product unit costs can wait until the end of the period. Such a situation is seldom found in industry. A company usually makes many different products, and it needs product costing information to set prices for goods before they are produced. Therefore, under absorption costing a predetermined overhead rate must be used to allocate factory overhead costs to products.

Predetermined Overhead Rates

OBJECTIVE 3
Compute a predetermined overhead rate, and use this rate to apply overhead costs to production

Factory overhead costs are a problem for the management accountant. Actual overhead costs fluctuate from month to month because of the timing of fixed overhead costs. Therefore, some method must be used to allocate overhead costs to products. How can these costs be estimated and assigned to certain products or jobs before the end of the accounting period? The most common way is to use a **predetermined overhead rate** for each department or other operating unit. This rate can be defined as an overhead cost factor used to assign factory overhead costs to specific products or jobs. It is based on *estimated* overhead costs and production levels for the period. The rate is computed by following the three steps explained on the following page.

1. **Estimate factory overhead costs.** Using cost behavior analysis, estimate all factory overhead costs. Do so for each production department in the coming accounting period. (Cost behavior analysis is useful in this procedure and will be discussed in Chapter 19.) Add the totals for all the production departments. For example, suppose the total costs of rent, utilities, insurance, and so on for the coming year are expected to be $450,000.
2. **Select a basis for allocating costs, and estimate its amount.** A way must be found to connect overhead costs to the products produced by using some measure of production activity. Common measures of production activity are labor hours, dollars of direct labor cost, machine hours, or units of output. The basis chosen should link the overhead cost to the product produced in a meaningful way. For instance, if an operation is more labor-hour than machine-hour intensive (as in the typical assembly line), then labor hours would be a good basis to use in overhead allocation. In the example suppose that overhead per hour of direct labor is the most useful measure. Management believes that 25,000 hours of direct labor will be used during the year.
3. **Divide the total overhead costs estimated for the period by the total estimated basis (hours, dollars, or units).** The result is the predetermined overhead rate. The computation for this example is as follows:

$$\begin{aligned}\begin{array}{c}\text{predetermined overhead rate}\\ \text{per direct labor hour}\end{array} &= \frac{\text{total estimated overhead costs}}{\text{total estimated direct labor hours}}\\ &= \frac{\$450{,}000}{25{,}000\text{ hours}}\\ &= \$18\text{ of overhead per direct labor hour}\end{aligned}$$

Overhead costs are then applied to each product, using this rate. Now, assume it takes one-half hour of direct labor to produce one unit. The overhead rate is $18 per direct labor hour. That unit is therefore assigned a factory overhead cost of $9. This amount is then added to the direct materials and direct labor costs already assigned to the product. The sum is the total unit cost.

Importance of Good Estimates

The whole process of overhead cost allocation depends on two factors for its success. One is a careful estimate of the total amount of overhead. The other is a good forecast of production activity, which will be used as the allocation basis.

Estimating total overhead costs is critical. If this estimate is wrong, the overhead rate will be wrong. The result will be that either too much or too little overhead cost will be assigned to the products produced. Therefore, in developing this estimate, the management accountant must be careful to include all factory overhead items and make accurate forecasts of their costs.

Overhead costs are generally estimated in the normal budgeting process. Expected overhead costs are gathered from all departments involved either directly or indirectly in the production process. The accounting department receives and totals each department's schedules of estimated costs. Costs of supporting service departments, such as maintenance and electrical departments, have only an indirect connection with products. Therefore, these costs must be distributed among the production departments. They can then be included as part of total factory overhead when computing the predetermined overhead rate of the period.

Forecasting production activity is also critical to the success of overhead cost allocation. First, a decision must be made as to which activity base is most appropriate—labor hours, labor dollars, machine hours, or units of output. The basis chosen should be one that relates to the overhead cost in a causal or beneficial way. For example, a greater number of machine hours would cause higher electricity costs and depreciation charges. Therefore, departments that are equipment intensive, such as those in which one person runs twenty-five or thirty machines by remote control, would use machine hours as the allocation basis. The object is to pick the one activity base that varies most with total overhead costs. Selecting an inappropriate activity base will mean that overhead costs assigned to individual jobs or products will not be closely related to actual overhead costs.

Exhibit 17-1 sums up the whole process of overhead cost allocation. In the first phase the predetermined overhead rate is computed. This is done by estimating total overhead costs and total production activity. In the second phase the predetermined overhead rate is used to compute the amount of overhead costs to be applied to products or jobs during the period.

Exhibit 17-1. Overhead Cost Allocation

Phase I: Computing the Predetermined Overhead Rate

Develop Overhead Cost Estimates
Estimate overhead costs for each production department.

Develop Allocation (Activity) Basis Estimates
1. Select an allocation basis for each production department that has a causal or beneficial relationship to the costs being assigned to the end product or job.
2. Carefully estimate the activity level of each department for the coming period.

$$\frac{\text{total estimated overhead costs}}{\text{total estimated activity basis}} = \text{predetermined overhead rate}$$

Phase II: Using the Rate to Assign Overhead Costs

predetermined overhead rate × amount of activity per job order = overhead cost assigned to that particular job order or batch of products

Underapplied or Overapplied Overhead

OBJECTIVE 4
Dispose of underapplied or overapplied overhead

Much time and effort can go into estimating and allocating factory overhead costs. Still, actual overhead costs and actual production activities seldom agree with these estimates. Changes in anticipated costs or increases/decreases in the activity base cause differences (or variances) to occur. Differences in either area cause factory overhead to be **underapplied** or **overapplied.** That is, the amount of overhead costs assigned to products is less or more than the actual amount of overhead costs incurred. These actual overhead costs must be accounted for by making a quarterly or annual adjustment. Monthly differences between actual overhead incurred and overhead costs applied are normally not adjusted. In many cases monthly differences tend to offset one another, leaving only a small adjustment to be made at year-end.

An example will illustrate the accounting problems of using predetermined overhead rates. Assume that the accounting records of the West Company show the overhead transactions below. Also assume that all overhead costs are debited to one general ledger controlling account—the Factory Overhead Control account—instead of to individual overhead accounts.

May	25	Paid utility bill for three months, $1,420.
	27	Recorded usage of indirect materials and supplies, $940.
June	21	Paid indirect labor wages, $2,190.
Aug.	12	Paid property taxes on factory building, $620.
Sept.	9	Recorded expiration of prepaid insurance premium, $560.
Nov.	27	Recorded depreciation of machinery and equipment for the year, $1,210.

These transactions resulted in the following entries:

Date		Account	Debit	Credit
May	25	Factory Overhead Control*	1,420	
		Cash		1,420
		To record payment of 3-month utility bill		
May	27	Factory Overhead Control*	940	
		Materials (or Supplies) Inventory		940
		To record usage of indirect materials and supplies		
June	21	Factory Overhead Control*	2,190	
		Factory Payroll		2,190
		To distribute indirect labor from factory payroll		
Aug.	12	Factory Overhead Control*	620	
		Cash		620
		To record payment of property taxes on factory building		
Sept.	9	Factory Overhead Control*	560	
		Prepaid Insurance		560
		To record expiration of insurance premiums		

Nov. 27	Factory Overhead Control*	1,210	
	Accumulated Depreciation, Machinery and Equipment		1,210
	To record depreciation for the year		

*When the Factory Overhead Control account is used, all types of factory overhead costs are debited when incurred to the Factory Overhead Control account. A subsidiary ledger containing each individual overhead account is maintained. This procedure is illustrated later in the chapter.

The previous entries record actual overhead expenses. However, they do not help in assigning these costs to products. Nor do they help in transferring costs to the Work in Process Inventory account. Such a transfer must occur before product unit costs can be computed.

Here, the predetermined overhead rate is useful. Assume that the predetermined overhead rate for the period was $2.50 per direct labor hour. The following list of jobs completed during the period shows the number of direct labor hours for each job. It also shows the overhead cost applied to each one.

Job	Direct Labor Hours	×	Rate	=	Overhead Applied
16-2	520		$2.50		$1,300
19-4	718		2.50		1,795
17-3	622		2.50		1,555
18-6	416		2.50		1,040
21-5	384		2.50		960
	2,660				$6,650

A journal entry like the one below was used to record the application of predetermined overhead costs to each job worked on during the period. This entry charges Work in Process Inventory with a prorated share of estimated overhead costs and records the amount applied to Job 16-2. Normally, this entry is made when payroll is recorded, since overhead costs can be applied only after the number of labor hours is known. But in this example weekly and monthly labor data are unavailable. Thus, estimated overhead is applied to the completed job.

June 1	Work in Process Inventory	1,300	
	Factory Overhead Applied		1,300
	To record application of overhead costs to Job 16-2		

Similar entries would be prepared for each job worked on during the period.

After posting all actual overhead transactions discussed earlier, overhead costs applied and actual overhead costs can be compared. The resulting general ledger account entries and balances are shown at the top of the next page.

Factory Overhead Control (Incurred)

5/25	1,420	
5/27	940	
6/21	2,190	
8/12	620	
9/9	560	
11/27	1,210	
Bal.	**6,940**	

Factory Overhead Applied

	Job 16-2	1,300
	Job 19-4	1,795
	Job 17-3	1,555
	Job 18-6	1,040
	Job 21-5	960
	Bal.	**6,650**

At year end these records of the West Company show that overhead has been *under*applied by $290 ($6,940 – $6,650). More actual overhead costs were incurred than were applied to products. The predetermined overhead rate was a little low. That is, it did not apply all overhead costs incurred to products produced. The $290 must now be added to the production costs of the period.

Two courses of action are available. First, if the $290 difference is considered small, or if most of the items worked on during the year have been sold, the entire amount can be charged to Cost of Goods Sold. This approach is the most common one because it is easy to apply. The adjusting entry would be as follows:

Factory Overhead Applied	6,650	
Cost of Goods Sold	290	
Factory Overhead Control		6,940
To close out overhead accounts and to charge underapplied overhead to the Cost of Goods Sold account		

Another method is used if the amount of the adjustment is large or if many of the products worked on during the year are unsold at year end. When this approach is used, underapplied or overapplied overhead is divided at year end among the Work in Process Inventory, Finished Goods Inventory, and Cost of Goods Sold accounts. For example, assume that at year end the products the West Company worked on during the year were located as follows: 30 percent in Work in Process Inventory, 20 percent in Finished Goods Inventory, and 50 percent sold. In such a case the following entry would be made:

Factory Overhead Applied	6,650	
Cost of Goods Sold (50% of $290)	145	
Work in Process Inventory (30% of $290)	87	
Finished Goods Inventory (20% of $290)	58	
Factory Overhead Control		6,940
To close out overhead accounts and to account for underapplied factory overhead		

The breakdown of the $290 into the three accounts could be based on the number of units worked on during the period, the direct labor hours incurred and attached to units in the three accounts, or the dollar balances in the three accounts. The Review Problem at the end of this chapter provides more guidance in accounting procedures for underapplied or overapplied overhead.

Product Costing and Inventory Valuation

OBJECTIVE 5
Explain the relationship between product costing and inventory valuation

One of the main goals of a cost accounting system is to supply management with information about production costs. This information is useful in many ways. It assists those making internal decisions. It helps the accountant control costs. And through inventory valuation it forms the link between financial accounting and management accounting.

All manufacturing costs incurred during a period must be accounted for in the year-end financial statements. However, not all of these costs will appear on the income statement. Only those costs assigned to units sold will be reported on the income statement. Costs assigned to units sold have "expired." They were used up in producing revenue. Costs assigned to unsold units (ending inventory) are "unexpired," or unused, costs. They are classified as assets and included in either the Work in Process Inventory or the Finished Goods Inventory on the balance sheet. Product unit cost information is needed to compute end-of-period balances in the Work in Process Inventory and the Finished Goods Inventory as well as to compute the cost of goods sold.

The Job Order Cost Accounting System

OBJECTIVE 6
Describe cost flow in a job order cost accounting system

As shown, a job order cost system is designed to gather manufacturing costs for a specific order or batch of products and to aid in determining product unit costs. Price-setting decisions, production scheduling, and other management tasks depend on information from a company's cost accounting system. For these reasons it is necessary to maintain a system that gives timely, correct data about product costs. In Chapter 16 the three main cost elements—materials, labor, and factory overhead—were discussed. Here, these costs are accounted for in a job order cost system.

Incurrence of Materials, Labor, and Factory Overhead Costs

A basic part of a job order cost system is the set of procedures and journal entries used when the company incurs materials, labor, and factory overhead costs. To help control these costs, businesses use various documents for each transaction. The effective use of these procedures and documents promotes accounting accuracy. Such use also makes for a smooth, efficient flow of cost information through the accounting record system. Note that all inventory balances in a job order cost system are kept on a perpetual basis.

Materials. Careful use of materials improves a company's overall efficiency. It conserves production resources and can bring about large cost savings. At the same time, good records ensure accountability and cut down waste. Controlling the physical materials and keeping good records enhances profits.

To help record and control materials costs, accountants rely heavily on a connected series of cost documents. These documents include the purchase request, purchase order, receiving report, inventory records, and materials requisition. Each of these documents was discussed in Chapter 16 and is an important link in accounting for materials costs. Direct materials costs are traced to specific jobs or products. Costs of indirect materials and supplies are charged to factory overhead.

Labor. Labor is one production resource that cannot be stored and used later. So it is important to link labor costs to each job or product. Labor timecards and job cards are used to record labor costs as they are incurred. Indirect labor costs are routed through the Factory Overhead Control account.

Factory Overhead. All indirect manufacturing costs are classified as factory overhead. Unlike materials and direct labor, overhead costs do not call for special documents. Vendors' bills support most payments. Factory depreciation expenses and prepaid expenses are charged to the Factory Overhead Control account through journal entries. Overhead costs may be accounted for in separate accounts, but that is not done in a job order cost system. As shown earlier, factory overhead costs are all debited to a Factory Overhead Control account.

A control account, you will recall, sums up several similar account balances to reduce accounting detail. A separate subsidiary account is also kept for each type of factory overhead cost. These separate accounts make up a subsidiary ledger to the Factory Overhead Control account.

Factory overhead costs, by nature, cannot be traced directly to jobs or products. For this reason an estimate of factory overhead costs is applied to products by means of the predetermined overhead rate. This process was discussed earlier, and it will be illustrated later in this chapter (see Exhibit 17-2) on pages 640–641.

The Work in Process Inventory Account

Job order costing focuses on the flow of costs through the Work in Process Inventory account. All manufacturing costs incurred and charged to production are routed through the Work in Process Inventory. Figure 17-1 shows cost flow in a job order cost system. Materials costs are debited to Work in Process Inventory. But indirect materials and supplies are debited to the Factory Overhead Control account. All labor costs traceable to specific jobs are debited to Work in Process Inventory. But

Figure 17-1.
Job Order
Cost Flow

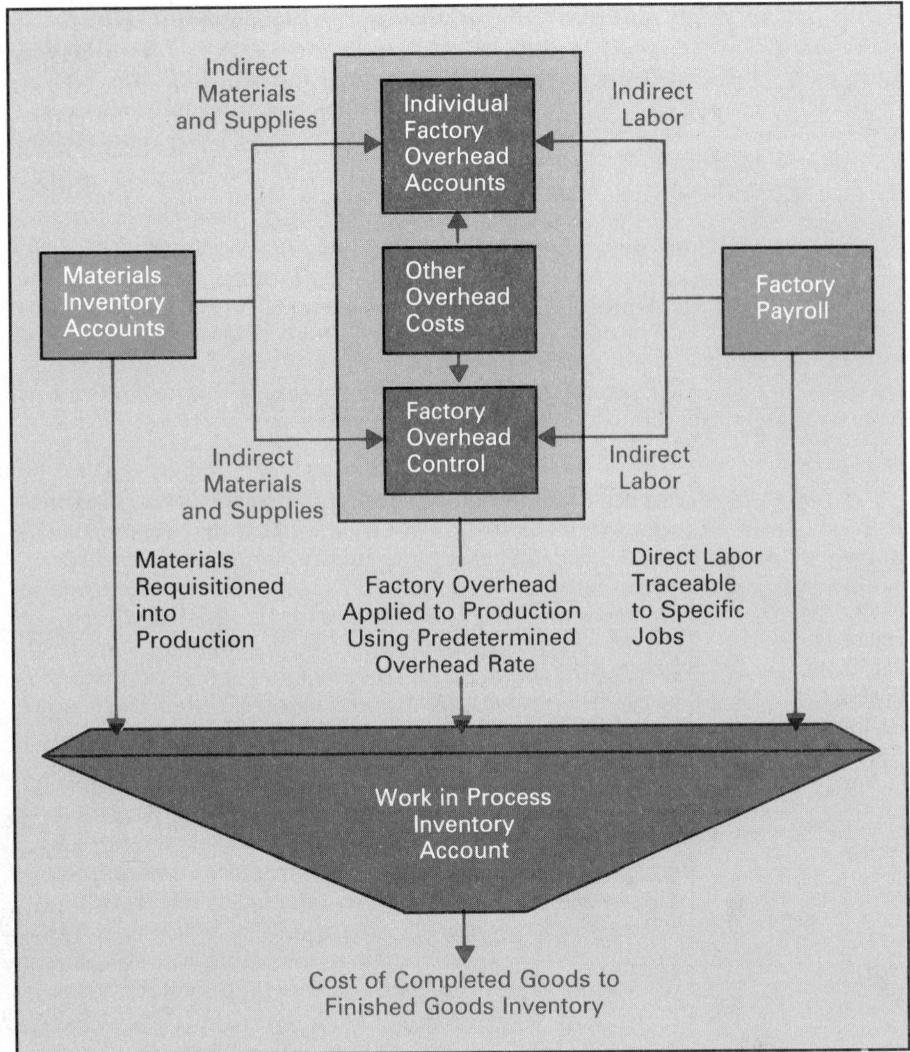

indirect labor costs are charged against the Factory Overhead Control account balance. By using a predetermined overhead rate, overhead costs are applied to specific jobs by debiting Work in Process Inventory and crediting Factory Overhead Applied.

Attaching costs of direct materials, direct labor, and factory overhead to specific jobs and products is not an automatic process. Even though all manufacturing costs are debited to Work in Process Inventory, a separate accounting procedure is necessary for linking those costs to specific jobs. For this purpose a subsidiary ledger made up of **job order cost cards** is used. There is one job order cost card for each job being worked on, and all costs for that job are recorded on it. As costs are debited to Work in Process Inventory, the costs must also be reclassified by job and added to their job order cost cards.

A typical job order cost card is shown in Figure 17-2. Each card has space for materials, direct labor, and factory overhead costs. There is also space to write the job order number, product specifications, name of customer, date of order, projected completion date, and summary cost data. As each department incurs materials and labor costs, the job order cost cards are updated. Factory overhead, as applied, is also posted to the job order cost cards. Job order cost cards for incomplete jobs make up the subsidiary ledger for the Work in Process Inventory Control account. To ensure that the ending balance in the Work in Process Inventory Control account is right, compare it with the total costs shown on the job order cost cards.

Accounting for Finished Goods

Once a job has been completed, all costs assigned to that job order are moved to Finished Goods Inventory. This is done in the accounting records by debiting the Finished Goods Inventory account and crediting

Figure 17-2. Job Order Cost Card

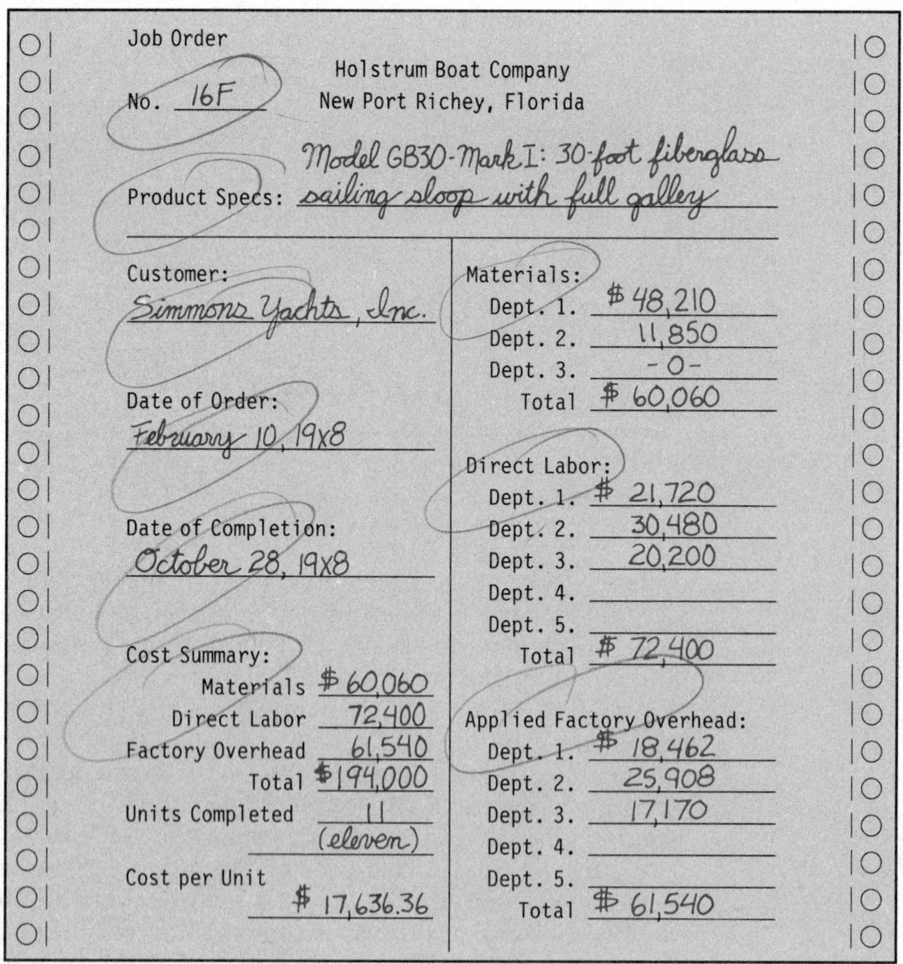

Job Order
No. 16F

Holstrum Boat Company
New Port Richey, Florida

Product Specs: Model GB30-Mark I: 30-foot fiberglass sailing sloop with full galley

Customer: Simmons Yachts, Inc.

Date of Order: February 10, 19x8

Date of Completion: October 28, 19x8

Cost Summary:

Materials	$60,060
Direct Labor	72,400
Factory Overhead	61,540
Total	$194,000
Units Completed	11 (eleven)
Cost per Unit	$17,636.36

Materials:

Dept. 1.	$48,210
Dept. 2.	11,850
Dept. 3.	-0-
Total	$60,060

Direct Labor:

Dept. 1.	$21,720
Dept. 2.	30,480
Dept. 3.	20,200
Dept. 4.	
Dept. 5.	
Total	$72,400

Applied Factory Overhead:

Dept. 1.	$18,462
Dept. 2.	25,908
Dept. 3.	17,170
Dept. 4.	
Dept. 5.	
Total	$61,540

the Work in Process Inventory account. When this entry is made, the job order cost card should be removed from the subsidiary ledger file. It is then used to help update the finished goods inventory records.

When goods are shipped, the order for them is recorded as a sale. Accounts Receivable is debited and Sales is credited for the entire selling price. But the cost of the goods shipped must also be accounted for. The proper procedure is to debit Cost of Goods Sold and to credit Finished Goods Inventory for the *cost* of the goods shipped.

To learn the mechanics of operating the system just described, you really need to go through an analysis of transactions and related journal entries. While studying the journal entry analysis that follows, review the preceding paragraphs. Try to keep in mind the cost flow concept shown in Figure 17-1.

Journal Entry Analysis

OBJECTIVE 7
Journalize transactions in a job order cost accounting system

Because a job order cost system emphasizes cost flow, you must understand journal entries that record various costs as they are incurred. You also must know the entries that transfer costs from one account to another. In fact, these entries along with job order cost cards and other subsidiary ledgers for materials and finished goods inventories are a major part of the job order cost system. As each area in the analysis of the Holstrum Boat Company is covered, the related transaction will be described first. The journal entry needed to record the transaction will follow. Each section will end with a discussion of the unique features of the transaction or the accounts being used. Exhibit 17-2 shows the entire job order cost flow through the general ledger, including supporting subsidiary ledgers. As each entry is discussed, trace its number and related debits or credits as shown in Exhibit 17-2.

Materials Purchased. In recording direct materials purchases, note the differences between journal entries used in the perpetual inventory approach and those used for periodic inventories. For example, Holstrum Boat Company purchased the following materials: Material 5X for $28,600 and Material 14Q for $17,000. Materials purchases were recorded at cost in the Materials Inventory Control account.

		Debit	Credit
Entry 1:	Materials Inventory Control	45,600	
	Accounts Payable (or Cash)		45,600
	To record purchase of $28,600 of Material 5X and $17,000 of Material 14Q		

This procedure differs in several ways from the recording of purchases discussed before in this text. First, the debit is to an inventory account instead of a purchases account because the inventory system is perpetual. All costs of materials flow through the inventory account. Second, there is a difference in the entry above because of the use of a **control** or **controlling account**. The term *control* means the account is an accumulation of several account balances. Some companies have hundreds of

Exhibit 17-2. The Job Order Cost System—Holstrum Boat Company

Materials Inventory Control

Beg. Bal.	61,500	Requisitions:	
(1) Purchases	45,600	Materials	94,000 (3)
(2) Purchases	4,100	Supplies	4,800 (3)
End. Bal. 12,400			

Work in Process Inventory Control

Beg. Bal.	20,000		
(3) Materials Used	94,000	Completed	194,000 (10)
(6) Direct Labor	82,000	Adjustment	135 (13)
(9) Overhead	69,700		
End. Bal. 71,565			

Factory Payroll

(4) Wages Earned	120,000	Direct Labor	82,000 (6)
		Indirect Labor	38,000 (6)

Factory Overhead Control

(3) Supplies Used	4,800	To Close	69,200 (13)
(6) Indirect Labor	38,000		
(7) Other	14,400		
(8) Adjustments	12,000		

Factory Overhead Applied

(13) To Close	69,700	Applied	69,700 (9)

Subsidiary Ledgers

Materials Ledger

Material 5X

Beg. Bal.	41,500	Used	62,000
Purchases	28,600		
End. Bal. 8,100			

Material 14Q

Beg. Bal.	18,500	Used	32,000
Purchases	17,000		
End. Bal. 3,500			

Supplies Inventory

Beg. Bal.	1,500	Used	4,800
Purchases	4,100		
End. Bal. 800			

Job Order Cost Cards

Job 16F

Beginning Balance	20,000
Materials	51,900
Direct Labor	66,000
Factory Overhead	56,100
Completed Cost	194,000

Job 23H

Materials	42,100
Direct Labor	16,000
Factory Overhead	13,600
Year-End Adjustment	(135)
Ending Balance	71,565

Exhibit 17-2. *(continued)*

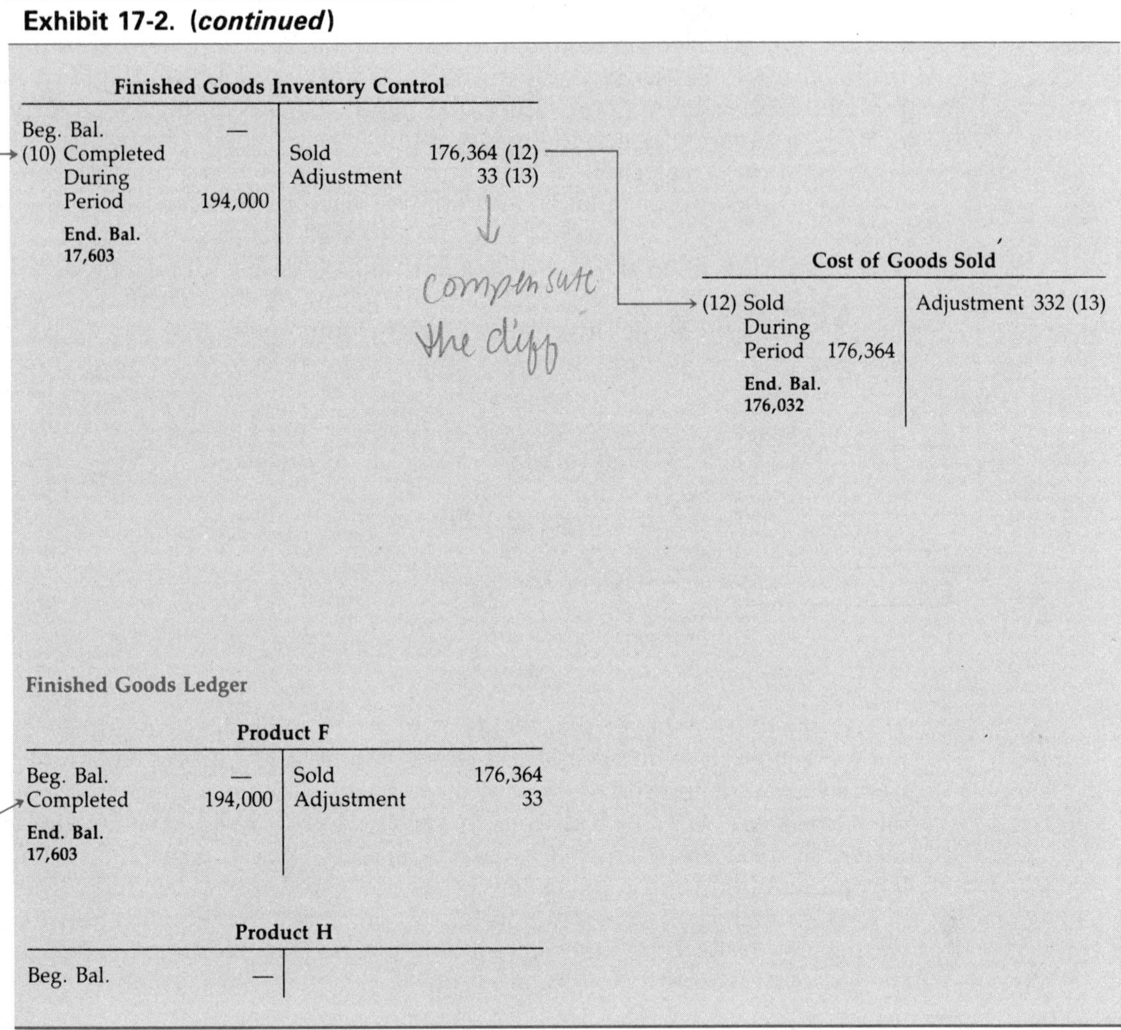

items in inventory. To keep a separate account for each item in the general ledger would make the ledger crowded and hard to work with. A control account is used for each area in which several similar items are being accounted for and only one cumulative total appears in the general ledger. Each control account is supported by a subsidiary ledger that holds all individual account balances. When entry 1 is posted to the general ledger, the accounts in the materials ledger are also updated (see Exhibit 17-2).

Purchase of Supplies. The following transaction and entry are for the purchase of supplies for production. The company purchased $4,100 in operating supplies for the manufacturing process.

		Debit	Credit
Entry 2:	Materials Inventory Control	4,100	
	Accounts Payable (or Cash)		4,100
	To record the purchase of operating supplies		

The procedures used to account for the purchase of supplies are much like those used to record direct materials purchases. Supplies Inventory in the example is assumed to be one subsidiary account, and is part of the total Materials Inventory Control account. If the supplies inventory is large, a separate general ledger account may be used. Regardless of which method is selected, the accountant should be able to give reasons to support the approach taken and follow this approach consistently.

Requisitioning of Materials and Supplies. When a properly prepared materials requisition form is received, the following direct materials and supplies are issued from inventory to production: Material 5X for $62,000, Material 14Q for $32,000, and operating supplies for $4,800.

		Debit	Credit
Entry 3:	Work in Process Inventory Control	94,000	
	Factory Overhead Control	4,800	
	Materials Inventory Control		98,800
	To record issuance of $62,000 of Material 5X, $32,000 of Material 14Q, and $4,800 of operating supplies into production		

The entry above shows that $94,000 of direct materials and $4,800 of indirect materials were issued. The debit to the Work in Process Inventory Control account records the cost of direct materials issued to production. Such costs are directly traceable to specific job orders. As the direct materials costs are charged to work in process, amounts for individual jobs are entered on the job order cost cards. As shown in Exhibit 17-2, $51,900 in materials were used on Job 16F, and materials costing $42,100 were used on Job 23H. Indirect materials costs (supplies) are debited to the Factory Overhead Control account.

Labor Costs. Recording labor costs for a manufacturing company takes three journal entries. Chapter 9 illustrated and discussed journal entries to record payroll for a merchandising company. Recording payroll for a manufacturing company is more complex, but the same basic payroll documents and transactions are used. In accounting for factory labor costs, however, some new account titles are needed. Costs are assigned to specific products and jobs.

The first labor cost entry records the total payroll liability of the company. Although only $107,640 in net earnings are to be paid to employees, the gross direct and indirect labor costs will be used for product and job costing. In the transaction described in entry 4, payroll liability for the period was recorded as follows: gross direct labor wages, $82,000; gross indirect labor wages, $38,000; gross administrative salaries, $36,000; FICA (social security) taxes withheld, $9,360; federal income taxes withheld, $39,000. Entry 4 is shown at the top of the following page.

		Debit	Credit
Entry 4:	Factory Payroll	120,000	
	Administrative Salaries Expense	36,000	
	FICA Tax Payable		9,360
	Employees' Federal Income Tax Payable		39,000
	Wages and Salaries Payable		107,640
	To record payroll liability for the period		

A follow-up entry is now needed to account properly for labor costs. The next entry, entry 5, will record the payment of the payroll liability established in entry 4. In this transaction, payroll checks for the period were prepared and given to the employees.

		Debit	Credit
Entry 5:	Wages and Salaries Payable	107,640	
	Cash		107,640
	To record payment of payroll		

The total payroll dollars for factory personnel first debited to the Factory Payroll account must now be moved to the production accounts. Gross direct labor costs are debited to Work in Process Inventory Control, and total indirect wages (including factory supervisors' salaries) are debited to Factory Overhead Control. Factory Payroll is credited to show that the total amount has been distributed to the production accounts.

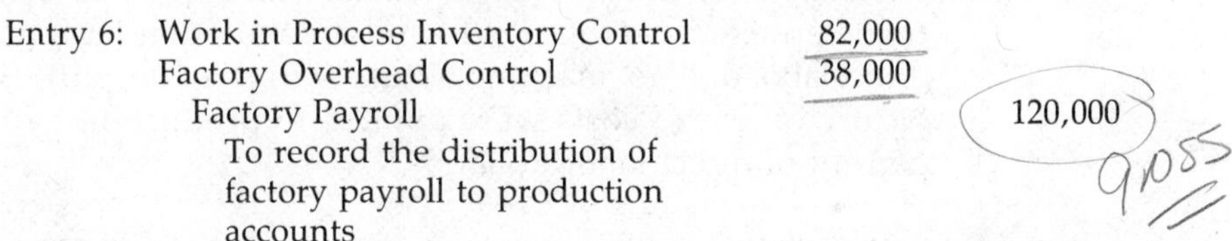

		Debit	Credit
Entry 6:	Work in Process Inventory Control	82,000	
	Factory Overhead Control	38,000	
	Factory Payroll		120,000
	To record the distribution of factory payroll to production accounts		

In addition, direct labor costs are recorded by job on job order cost cards. The distribution of $66,000 to Job 16F and $16,000 to Job 23H is shown in Exhibit 17-2.

Other Factory Overhead Costs. As factory overhead costs other than indirect materials and labor charges are incurred, the sum of these costs is charged (debited) to the Factory Overhead Control account. Each cost is identified in the explanation of the journal entry. In the example, factory overhead costs were paid as follows: electricity, $3,100; maintenance and repair, $8,400; insurance, $1,300; and property taxes, $1,600.

		Debit	Credit
Entry 7:	Factory Overhead Control	14,400	
	Cash		14,400
	To record incurrence of the following overhead costs: electricity, $3,100; maintenance and repair, $8,400; insurance expense, $1,300; and property taxes, $1,600		

From the information in the journal entry explanation, individual subsidiary ledger accounts are updated. Because of the amount of information already included in Exhibit 17-2, the subsidiary ledger for the Factory Overhead Control account is not shown. However, the subsidiary ledger would include an account for each type of factory overhead cost. The costs would be accounted for in much the same way as those described for the materials ledger and the job order cost cards.

The next transaction is an adjusting entry needed to record depreciation on factory equipment for the period.

Entry 8:	Factory Overhead Control	12,000	
	Accumulated Depreciation, Equipment		12,000
	To record depreciation on factory equipment for the period		

This entry is out of order, since adjusting entries are usually prepared after all transactions for the period have been recorded. But it is introduced at this point because depreciation of factory equipment is a part of total factory overhead costs. The actual depreciation expense account will be part of the overhead subsidiary ledger.

Factory Overhead Applied. Factory overhead is applied by using a predetermined overhead rate and an allocation base (direct labor hours, direct labor dollars, machine hours, or units of output). In this transaction factory overhead costs were applied to production by using a rate of 85 percent of direct labor dollars.

Entry 9:	Work in Process Inventory Control	69,700	
	Factory Overhead Applied		69,700
	To apply factory overhead costs to production		

The amount of overhead charged to production is found by multiplying the overhead rate by the units of the applicable overhead allocation base. In the example 85 percent was multiplied by the direct labor dollars ($82,000), which came to $69,700 ($82,000 × .85). This amount was debited to the Work in Process Inventory Control account. Because the overhead application is related to direct labor dollars, the job order cost cards may be updated by the same procedure. Job 16F is assigned $56,100 in overhead costs ($66,000 × .85). Job 23H receives a charge of $13,600 ($16,000 × .85). These amounts have been posted to the job order cost cards in Exhibit 17-2.

Accounting for Completed Units. As various job orders are completed, their costs are moved to the Finished Goods Inventory Control account. In this case, goods costing $194,000 for Job 16F were completed and transferred to Finished Goods Inventory (see the job order cost card, Exhibit 17-2).

Entry 10:	Finished Goods Inventory Control	194,000	
	Work in Process Inventory Control		194,000
	To record transfer of completed goods for Job 16F from Work in Process Inventory to Finished Goods Inventory		

When a job is completed, its job order cost card is pulled from the Work in Process subsidiary ledger. The card is then used to help update the Finished Goods ledger. Specifically, costs recorded on the job order cost card are used to compute unit costs and to determine the amount of the transfer entry (see Exhibit 17-2).

Accounting for Units Sold. The final phase of manufacturing cost flow is to transfer costs from the Finished Goods Inventory Control account to the Cost of Goods Sold account. At this point ten sailing sloops from Job 16F were shipped to the customer. The selling price for the goods shipped was $260,000. The cost to manufacture these products totaled $176,364.

Entry 11:	Accounts Receivable	260,000	
	Sales		260,000
	To record sale of portion of Job 16F		

Entry 12:	Cost of Goods Sold	176,364	
	Finished Goods Inventory Control		176,364
	To record the transfer of the cost of shipped goods for Job 16F from Finished Goods Inventory to Cost of Goods Sold		

Both the entry to record the sale and the entry to establish the cost of the goods sold are shown here. Entry 12 is made at the same time the sale is recorded. When the costs of the products sold are transferred out of the Finished Goods Inventory Control account, the Finished Goods ledger (subsidiary ledger) should also be updated, as shown in Exhibit 17-2.

Underapplied or Overapplied Overhead Disposition. At the end of an accounting period, the Factory Overhead Control account and the Factory Overhead Applied account are totaled. Then an entry to close these accounts and dispose of any underapplied or overapplied overhead is made.

		Debit	Credit
Entry 13:	Factory Overhead Applied	69,700	
	Work in Process Inventory Control		135
	Finished Goods Inventory Control		33
	Cost of Goods Sold		332
	Factory Overhead Control		69,200
	To close out factory overhead account balances and to dispose of the overapplied balance		

In this transaction factory overhead was overapplied by $500. So, as the Factory Overhead Control and Factory Overhead Applied accounts were closed, the $500 difference was distributed among Work in Process Inventory Control, Finished Goods Inventory Control, and Cost of Goods Sold. These changes were made based on each account's balance before the adjustment. The following analysis shows how these figures were computed.

The following T accounts summarize the overhead account balances before entry 13. Numbers in parentheses refer to earlier journal entries.

Factory Overhead Control

Debit		Credit
(3)	4,800	
(6)	38,000	
(7)	14,400	
(8)	12,000	
	69,200	

Factory Overhead Applied

Debit	Credit	
	(9)	69,700
		69,700

Overhead has been overapplied by $500 ($69,700 − $69,200). This amount can be either credited to the Cost of Goods Sold account or distributed among the Work in Process Inventory Control, Finished Goods Inventory Control, and Cost of Goods Sold accounts. Since it is assumed the amount is significant, it is distributed among the three accounts on the basis of their ending balances (see Exhibit 17-2). The following table shows how the distribution amounts were computed:

Account	Ending Balance	Percentage of Each to Total	×	Amount to Be Allocated	=	Allocation of Overapplied Overhead
Work in Process Inventory Control	$ 71,700	27.0		$500		$135
Finished Goods Inventory Control	17,636	6.6		500		33
Cost of Goods Sold	176,364	66.4		500		332
Totals	$265,700	100.0				$500

After entry 13 has been posted to the general ledger, the accounts affected will look like those in Exhibit 17-2. In addition, all subsidiary ledgers affected by the overhead adjustment must be updated. In the example the entire $135 adjustment to Work in Process was credited to Job 23H. Because Job 16F had been completed, its share of the adjustment was assigned to the Finished Goods Inventory Control and the Cost of Goods Sold accounts.

Computing Product Unit Costs

OBJECTIVE 8
Compute product unit cost for a specific job order

The process of computing product **unit cost** is fairly simple in a job order costing system. All costs of materials, direct labor, and factory overhead for each job are recorded on a job order cost card as the job progresses to completion. When the job is finished, all costs on the job order cost card are totaled. The unit cost is then computed by dividing total manufacturing costs for the job by the number of good units produced. Job 16F was completed in the journal entry analysis just finished. The cost data for this job are shown on the job order cost card in Figure 17-2. Eleven sailing sloops were produced at a total cost of $194,000, which worked out to a cost of $17,636.36 per sloop before adjustments. Note in Exhibit 17-2 that only ten of the sloops were actually shipped during the year. One still remains in Finished Goods Inventory Control.

Fully and Partly Completed Products

In a job order costing system, as shown, manufacturing costs are accumulated, classified, and reclassified several times. As products near completion, all manufacturing costs for their production are linked to them. These costs then follow the products first to Finished Goods Inventory Control and then to Cost of Goods Sold. Exhibit 17-2 illustrates the accounting procedures and cost flows of units worked on during the period. Dollar amounts in that exhibit came from posting the journal entries just discussed.

At period end some costs remain in the Work in Process Inventory Control and the Finished Goods Inventory Control accounts. The ending balance of $71,565 in Work in Process Inventory Control is from costs attached to partly completed units in Job 23H. These costs are traceable to the specific job order cost cards for partly completed jobs in the subsidiary ledger. Finished Goods Inventory Control also has an ending balance. Of all units completed during the period, one sloop from Job 16F, costing $17,603 (after the adjustment), has not been sold or shipped. Its cost now appears as the ending balance in Finished Goods Inventory Control.

Chapter Review

Review of Learning Objectives

1. **Identify the differences between job order costing and process costing.**
Both job order costing and process costing are basic, traditional approaches to product cost accounting. However, they have different characteristics. A job order costing system is used for unique or special-order products. In such a system, materials, direct labor, and factory overhead costs are assigned to specific job orders or batches of products. In determining unit costs, the total manufacturing cost assigned to each job order is divided by the number of good units produced for that order. A process costing system is used by companies that produce many similar products or have a continuous production flow. These companies find it more economical to account for product-related costs for a period of time (a week or month) than to assign them to specific products or job orders. Unit costs in a process costing system are found by dividing total manufacturing costs for a department or work center during a time period by the number of good units produced.

2. **Describe the concept of absorption costing.**
Absorption costing is an approach to product costing that assigns a representative portion of *all* manufacturing costs to individual products. The costs of direct materials, direct labor, variable factory overhead, and fixed factory overhead are all assigned to products.

3. **Compute a predetermined overhead rate, and use this rate to apply overhead costs to production.**
A predetermined overhead rate is computed by dividing total estimated overhead costs for a period by the total activity basis expected for that period. Factory overhead costs are applied to a job order by multiplying the predetermined overhead rate by the amount of the activity base (such as labor hours) used for the job order.

4. **Dispose of underapplied or overapplied overhead.**
If there is any difference between the balances in the Factory Overhead Control and Factory Overhead Applied accounts at year end, there are two ways to dispose of the difference. If the difference is small, it should be assigned to the Cost of Goods Sold account. Often, however, the amount of the adjustment is large or the costs of the products worked on during the period are spread among the Work in Process Inventory, Finished Goods Inventory, and Cost of Goods Sold accounts. In such cases the difference should be assigned proportionately to these three accounts.

5. **Explain the relationship between product costing and inventory valuation.**
Product costing techniques are necessary to attach costs to job orders or units of product worked on during a given time period. At period end when financial statements are prepared, these product costs are used in costing the Work in Process and Finished Goods Inventories.

6. **Describe cost flow in a job order cost accounting system.**
A job order cost accounting system generally follows the concept of absorption costing. It also uses the perpetual approach to inventory maintenance and valuation. Within these limits, materials and supplies costs are first debited to the Materials Inventory Control account. Labor costs are debited to the

Factory Payroll account. And the various factory overhead costs are debited to the Factory Overhead Control account. As the products are being manufactured, costs of direct materials and direct labor are transferred to the Work in Process Inventory Control account. Factory overhead costs are applied and charged to the Work in Process Inventory Control account by using a predetermined overhead rate. These overhead cost charges are credited to the Factory Overhead Applied account. When products or jobs are completed, the costs assigned to them are transferred to the Finished Goods Inventory Control account. These same costs are transferred to the Cost of Goods Sold account when the products are sold and shipped.

7. **Journalize transactions in a job order cost accounting system.**
Mastery of a job order costing system requires that the user be able to prepare journal entries for each of the following transactions: (a) purchase of materials; (b) purchase of operating supplies; (c) requisition of materials and supplies into production; (d) recording of payroll liability; (e) payment of payroll to employees; (f) distribution of factory payroll to production accounts; (g) cash payment of overhead costs; (h) recording of noncash overhead costs, such as depreciation of factory and equipment; (i) application of factory overhead costs to production; (j) transfer of costs of completed jobs from the Work in Process Inventory Control account to the Finished Goods Inventory Control account; (k) sale of products and transfer of related costs from the Finished Goods Inventory Control account to the Cost of Goods Sold account; and (l) disposition of underapplied or overapplied factory overhead.

8. **Compute product unit cost for a specific job order.**
Product costs in a job order costing system are computed by first totaling all manufacturing costs accumulated on a particular job order cost card. This amount is then divided by the number of good units produced for that job to find the unit cost for the order. Unit cost information is entered onto the job order cost card and used for inventory valuation purposes.

Review Problem
Journal Entry Analysis: Job Order Costing System

The Astro Manufacturing Company produces "uniframe" desk and chair assemblies and study carrels for libraries. The firm uses a job order cost system and a current factory overhead application rate of 220 percent of direct labor dollars. The following transactions and events occurred during September 19xx:

Sept.	4	Direct materials costing $9,540 and purchased on account were received.
	7	The production department requisitioned $2,700 of materials and $650 of operating supplies.
	14	Gross factory payroll of $16,000 was paid to factory personnel. Of this amount $11,500 represents direct labor, and the remaining amount is indirect labor. (Prepare only the entry to distribute factory payroll to production accounts.)
	14	Factory overhead costs were applied to production.
	16	Supplies costing $3,500 and direct materials costing $17,000 were received. Both were ordered on 9/11/xx and purchased on account.
	20	$9,000 of direct materials and $1,750 of supplies were requisitioned into production.

26 The following overhead costs were paid: heat, light, and power, $1,400; repairs by outside firm, $1,600; property taxes, $2,700.
28 Gross factory payroll of $15,600 was earned by factory personnel. Of this amount indirect wages and supervisors' salaries totaled $6,400. Prepare only the entry to distribute factory payroll to production accounts.
28 Factory overhead costs were applied to production.
29 Completed units costing $67,500 were transferred to Finished Goods Inventory.
30 Depreciation of plant and equipment for September was $24,000. During the same period $1,200 in prepaid fire insurance expired.
30 Library carrel units costing $32,750 were shipped to a customer for a total selling price of $53,710.

Required

1. Record journal entries for all the above transactions and events.
2. Assume that: (a) the beginning balance in Materials Inventory Control was $4,700; (b) the beginning balance in Work in Process Inventory Control was $6,200; and (c) the beginning balance in Finished Goods Inventory Control was $9,000. Compute the ending balances in these inventory accounts.
3. Determine the amount of underapplied or overapplied overhead.
4. If 131 carrels were included in the order sold and shipped on September 30, compute the cost and selling price per carrel shipped.

Answer to Review Problem

1. Journal entries:

Sept. 4	Materials Inventory Control	9,540	
	Accounts Payable		9,540
	To record purchase of direct materials on account		
7	Work in Process Inventory Control	2,700	
	Factory Overhead Control	650	
	Materials Inventory Control		3,350
	To record requisition of direct materials and supplies into production		
14	Work in Process Inventory Control	11,500	
	Factory Overhead Control	4,500	
	Factory Payroll		16,000
	To distribute payroll to production accounts		
14	Work in Process Inventory Control	25,300	
	Factory Overhead Applied		25,300
	To apply factory overhead costs to production ($11,500 × 220%)		

Date	Account	Debit	Credit
Sept. 16	Materials Inventory Control	20,500	
	Accounts Payable		20,500
	To record purchase of $3,500 of operating supplies and $17,000 of direct materials		
20	Work in Process Inventory Control	9,000	
	Factory Overhead Control	1,750	
	Materials Inventory Control		10,750
	To record requisition of direct materials and supplies into production		
26	Factory Overhead Control	5,700	
	Cash		5,700
	To record payment of the following overhead costs: heat, light, and power, $1,400; outside repairs, $1,600; and property taxes, $2,700		
28	Work in Process Inventory Control	9,200	
	Factory Overhead Control	6,400	
	Factory Payroll		15,600
	To distribute payroll to production accounts		
28	Work in Process Inventory Control	20,240	
	Factory Overhead Applied		20,240
	To apply factory overhead costs to production ($9,200 × 220%)		
29	Finished Goods Inventory Control	67,500	
	Work in Process Inventory Control		67,500
	To transfer costs of completed goods to Finished Goods Inventory		
30	Factory Overhead Control	25,200	
	Accumulated Depreciation, Plant and Equipment		24,000
	Prepaid Insurance		1,200
	To charge Factory Overhead Control for expired asset costs		
30	Accounts Receivable	53,710	
	Sales		53,710
	To record sales for September		
30	Cost of Goods Sold	32,750	
	Finished Goods Inventory Control		32,750
	To record transfer of costs from Finished Goods Inventory to Cost of Goods Sold		

2. Ending balances of inventory accounts:

Materials Inventory Control

Beg. Bal	4,700	9/7	3,350
9/4	9,540	9/20	10,750
9/16	20,500		
	34,740		**14,100**
End. Bal.	**20,640**		

Work in Process Inventory Control

Beg. Bal.	6,200	9/29	67,500
9/7	2,700		
9/14	11,500		
9/14	25,300		
9/20	9,000		
9/28	9,200		
9/28	20,240		
	84,140		**67,500**
End. Bal.	**16,640**		

Finished Goods Inventory Control

Beg. Bal.	9,000	9/30	32,750
9/29	67,500		
	76,500		**32,750**
End. Bal.	**43,750**		

3. Underapplied or overapplied overhead:

Factory Overhead Control

9/7	650		
9/14	4,500		
9/20	1,750		
9/26	5,700		
9/28	6,400		
9/30	25,200		
End. Bal.	**44,200**		

Factory Overhead Applied

		9/14	25,300
		9/28	20,240
		End. Bal.	**45,540**

Factory overhead is overapplied by $1,340 ($45,540 − $44,200).

4. Cost and selling price per unit:

Cost per unit: $32,750 ÷ 131 = $250 per unit
Selling price per unit: $53,710 ÷ 131 = $410 per unit

Chapter Assignments

Questions

1. What is the common goal of a job order cost accounting system and a process cost accounting system?
2. Explain the concept of absorption costing.
3. What is the connection between manufacturing cost flow and the perpetual inventory method?
4. Describe the steps used to arrive at a predetermined overhead rate based on direct labor hours.

5. What are the factors for success in applying overhead to products and job orders?
6. What is meant by underapplied or overapplied overhead?
7. Describe two ways to adjust for underapplied or overapplied overhead.
8. "Some costs of direct materials, direct labor, and factory overhead used during a period will be reported in the company's income statement. Others will be reported in the company's balance sheet." Discuss the accuracy of this statement.
9. What are the differences between a job order cost system and a process cost system? (Focus on the characteristics of each system.)
10. In what way is timely purchasing a do-or-die function?
11. How does materials usage influence the efficiency of operations?
12. "Purchased labor resource services cannot be stored." Discuss this statement.
13. Discuss the role of the Work in Process Inventory account in a job order cost system.
14. What is the purpose of a job order cost card? Identify the types of information recorded on such a card.
15. Define the terms *control account* and *subsidiary ledger*. How are they related?
16. Cost and management accounting are often overshadowed by financial accounting, since it is better publicized. Describe the importance of a product costing system to (a) the preparation of financial statements and (b) profitability.

Classroom Exercises

Exercise 17-1. Cost System: Industry Linkage (L.O. 1)

Which of the following types of manufactured products would normally be produced using a job order costing system? Which would be produced using a process costing system? (a) paint; (b) automobiles; (c) 747 jet aircraft; (d) bricks; (e) large milling machines; (f) liquid detergent; (g) aluminum compressed-gas cylinders of standard size and capacity; (h) aluminum compressed-gas cylinders with a special fiber-glass overwrap for a Mount Everest expedition; (i) nails from wire; (j) television sets; (k) printed wedding invitations; (l) a limited edition of lithographs; (m) pet flea collars; (n) high-speed lathes with special-order threaded drills; (o) breakfast cereal; and (p) an original evening gown.

Exercise 17-2. Concept of Absorption Costing (L.O. 2)

Using the absorption costing concept, determine a product's unit cost from the following costs incurred during March: (a) $3,500 in Liability Insurance, Factory; (b) $2,900 in Rent Expense, Sales Office; (c) $4,100 in Depreciation Expense, Factory Equipment; (d) $20,650 in Materials Used; (e) $3,480 in Indirect Labor, Factory; (f) $1,080 in Factory Supplies; (g) $1,510 in Heat, Light, and Power, Factory; (h) $2,600 in Fire Insurance, Factory; (i) $4,250 in Depreciation Expense, Sales Equipment; (j) $3,850 in Rent Expense, Factory; (k) $28,420 in Direct Labor; (l) $3,100 in Manager's Salary, Factory; (m) $5,800 in President's Salary; (n) $8,250 in Sales Commissions; (o) $2,975 in Advertising Expenses. The Inspection Department reported that 150,800 good units were produced during March.

Exercise 17-3. Overhead Application Rate (L.O. 3)

Gustafson Compumatics specializes in the analysis and reporting of complex inventory costing projects. Materials costs are minimal, consisting entirely of operating supplies, such as data processing cards, inventory sheets, and other recording tools. Labor is the highest single expense item, and it totaled $645,250 for 72,400 hours of work in 19x7. Factory overhead costs for 19x7 were $825,450, and this amount was applied to specific jobs on the basis of labor hours worked.

In 19x8 the company anticipates a 30 percent increase in overhead costs. Labor costs will increase by as much as $130,000, and the number of hours worked during 19x8 is expected to increase 20 percent.

1. Determine the total amount of factory overhead anticipated by the company in 19x8.
2. Compute the predetermined overhead rate for 19x8. (Round your answer to the nearest penny.)
3. During April 19x8 the following jobs were completed and the related hours worked: Job 16A4, 2,490 hours; Job 21C2, 5,220 hours; and Job 17H3, 4,270 hours. Prepare the journal entry required to apply overhead costs to operations for April.

Exercise 17-4. Predetermined Overhead Rate Computation (L.O. 3)

The overhead costs used by Gerald Industries, Inc., to compute its predetermined overhead rate for 19x8 were as follows:

Indirect Materials and Supplies	$ 66,200
Repairs and Maintenance	28,900
Outside Service Contracts	27,300
Indirect Labor	79,100
Factory Supervision	52,900
Depreciation, Machinery	85,000
Factory Insurance	38,200
Property Taxes	7,500
Heat, Light, and Power	11,700
Miscellaneous Factory Overhead	6,045
	$402,845

A total of 45,600 direct labor hours were used as the 19x8 allocation base.

In 19x9 all overhead costs except depreciation, property taxes, and miscellaneous factory overhead are expected to increase by 10 percent. Depreciation should increase by 15 percent, and a 20 percent increase in property taxes and miscellaneous factory overhead is expected. Plant capacity in terms of direct labor hours used will increase by 3,850 hours in 19x9.

1. Compute the 19x8 predetermined overhead rate.
2. Compute the predetermined overhead rate for 19x9.

Exercise 17-5. Disposition of Overapplied Overhead (Extension of Exercise 17-3) (L.O. 4)

By the end of 19x8, Gustafson Compumatics had compiled a total of 81,340 hours worked. The overhead incurred during the year was $999,850.

1. Using the predetermined overhead rate computed in Exercise 17-3, determine the total amount of overhead applied to operations during 19x8.
2. Compute the amount of overapplied overhead for the year.
3. Prepare the journal entry to close out the overhead accounts and to dispose of the overapplied overhead amount for 19x8. Assume that the amount is insignificant.

Exercise 17-6. Disposition of Underapplied Overhead (L.O. 4)

The Hendel Manufacturing Company ended the year with a total of $26,200 in underapplied overhead. Because management thinks this amount is significant, this unfavorable difference should be distributed among the three appropriate accounts in proportion to their ending balances. The ending account balances are Materials Inventory Control, $214,740; Work in Process Inventory Control,

$312,500; Finished Goods Inventory Control, $250,000; Cost of Goods Sold, $687,500; Factory Overhead Control, $215,400; and Factory Overhead Applied, $189,200.

Using good form, close out the factory overhead accounts, and dispose of the underapplied overhead. Show your work in journal entry form. Separately, give supporting computations.

Exercise 17-7. Job Order Cost Flow (L.O. 6)

The three manufacturing cost elements—direct materials, direct labor, and factory overhead—flow through a job order cost system in a structured, orderly fashion. Specific general ledger accounts, subsidiary ledgers, and source documents are used to verify and record cost information. In paragraph and diagram form, describe cost flow in a job order cost accounting system.

Exercise 17-8. Work in Process Inventory Account: Journal Entry Analysis (L.O. 7)

On July 1 there was a $29,073 beginning balance in the Work in Process Inventory account of the Glaser Specialty Company. Production activity for July was as follows: (a) Materials costing $138,820, along with $17,402 of operating supplies, were requisitioned for production. (b) Total factory payroll for July was $184,239, of which $43,989 were payments for indirect labor. (Assume that payroll has been recorded but not distributed to production accounts.) (c) Factory overhead was applied at a rate of 80 percent of direct labor costs.

1. Prepare journal entries to record the materials, labor, and overhead costs for July.
2. Compute the ending balance in the Work in Process Inventory Control account. Assume a transfer of $381,480 to the Finished Goods Inventory Control account occurred during the period.

Exercise 17-9. Unit Cost Computation (L.O. 8)

Webster Corporation manufactures a line of women's apparel known the world over as Robertson Fashions. During February the corporation worked on three special orders, A-16, A-20, and B-14. Cost and production data for each order are as follows:

	Job A-16	Job A-20	Job B-14
Direct materials:			
Fabric Q	$ 6,840	$10,980	$14,660
Fabric Z	10,400	8,200	12,440
Fabric YB	4,260	5,920	8,900
Direct labor:			
Seamstress labor	12,900	18,400	26,200
Layout labor	7,450	9,425	12,210
Packaging labor	2,950	3,875	5,090
Factory overhead:			
90% of direct labor dollars	?	?	?
Number of units produced	600	675	1,582

1. Compute the total cost associated with each job, and indicate subtotals for each cost category in your analysis.
2. Compute each job's unit cost. (Round to the nearest penny.)

Interpreting Accounting Information

Internal Management Information: Dean Company and Witter Corporation
(L.O. 3, 5)

Both Dean Company and Witter Corporation use predetermined overhead rates for product costing, inventory pricing, and sales quotations. The two businesses are about the same size, and they compete in the corrugated-box industry. Dean Company's management believes that since the predetermined overhead rate is an estimated measure, the controller's department should spend little effort developing the rate. The company computes the rate once a year based on a trend analysis of last year's costs. It does not monitor the accuracy of the rate.

Witter Corporation takes a more sophisticated approach. One person in the controller's office is assigned the responsibility of developing predetermined overhead rates on a monthly basis. All cost inputs are checked out carefully to ensure the estimates are realistic. Accuracy checks are a routine procedure during each month's closing analysis. Foreseeing normal business changes is part of the overhead rate analyst's regular performance evaluation by her supervisor.

1. Describe the advantages and disadvantages of each company's approach to overhead rate determination.
2. Which company has taken the most cost-effective approach in developing predetermined overhead rates? Defend your answer.
3. Is an accurate overhead rate most important for product costing, inventory valuation, or sales quotations? Why?

Problem Set A

Problem 17A-1. Application of Factory Overhead
(L.O. 3, 4)

Hosseini Laser Products, Inc., uses a predetermined overhead rate in its production, assembly, and testing departments. One rate is used for the entire company, and it is applied based on direct labor hours. The current year's rate was determined by analyzing data from the previous two years and projecting the current year's information, adjusted to reflect expected changes. Mr. Roubi is about to compute the rate for 19x8, and the following data were compiled to assist him in this project:

	19x6	19x7
Direct labor hours	32,500	36,250
Factory overhead costs:		
Indirect materials	$ 32,500	$ 42,250
Indirect labor	26,200	31,440
Factory supervision costs	46,800	51,480
Factory utilities	7,400	8,880
Labor-related costs	18,100	19,910
Depreciation, factory	9,700	10,670
Depreciation, machinery	15,700	18,840
Factory property taxes	2,200	2,640
Factory insurance	1,900	2,280
Miscellaneous factory expenses	3,400	3,740
Total overhead	$163,900	$192,130

In 19x8 the percentage increase of each factory overhead cost item is expected to be the same as its 19x6–19x7 increase. Direct labor hours are anticipated to be 39,650 hours during 19x8.

Required

1. Compute the overhead rate for 19x8. (Round answer to three decimal places.)
2. During 19x8 Hosseini Laser Products, Inc., produced the following jobs with related direct labor hours:

Job	Actual Direct Labor Hours
B142	7,240
B164	4,960
B175	7,800
B201	10,280
B218	11,310
B304	1,460

Determine the amount of factory overhead applied to each job in 19x8. What was the total overhead applied during the year?
3. Prepare the journal entry needed to close the overhead accounts and to dispose of the under or overapplied overhead. Actual factory overhead for 19x8 was $247,840. Assume the difference between actual and applied overhead costs is considered insignificant.

Problem 17A-2. Job Order Cost Flow
(L.O. 6, 8)

Alice James is chief financial officer for Meridian Industries, makers of special-order printers for home personal computers. Her records for February 19x8 reveal the following information:

Beginning Inventory balances:	
Materials Inventory Control	$42,450
Work in Process Inventory Control	26,900
Finished Goods Inventory Control	31,200
Materials purchased and received:	
February 6	$ 6,200
February 12	7,110
February 24	5,890
Direct labor costs:	
February 14	$14,750
February 28	15,230
Materials requisitioned into production:	
February 4	$ 8,080
February 13	4,940
February 25	9,600

Job order cost cards for jobs in process on February 28:

Job No.	Materials	Direct Labor	Factory Overhead
H310	$2,220	$1,860	$2,232
H414	3,080	2,410	2,892
H730	2,180	1,940	2,328
H916	4,290	2,870	3,444

The predetermined overhead for the month was 120 percent of direct labor dollars. Sales for February totaled $153,360, which represents an 80 percent markup over cost of production.

Required

1. Using T accounts, reconstruct the transactions for February.
2. Compute the cost of units completed during the month.
3. What was the total cost of units sold during February?
4. Determine the ending inventory balances.
5. During the first week of March, Jobs H310 and H414 were completed. No additional materials costs were incurred, but Job H310 needed $920 more in direct labor and Job H414 required additional direct labor of $1,240. Job H310 was composed of 40 units, and Job H414 contained 55 units. Compute each job's unit cost.

Problem 17A-3. Job Order Costing: Unknown Quantity Analysis
(L.O. 6)

Baggett Enterprises makes an assortment of computer support equipment. Mr. Ruggle, the new controller for the organization, can find only partial information from the past two months, which is shown below. The current year's predetermined overhead rate is 80 percent of direct labor dollars.

	May	June
Materials Inventory Control, Beginning	$46,240	(e)
Work in Process Inventory Control, Beginning	66,480	(f)
Finished Goods Inventory Control, Beginning	54,260	(g)
Materials Purchased	(a)	$96,120
Materials Requisitioned	82,220	(h)
Direct Labor Costs	(b)	71,250
Factory Overhead Applied	52,400	(i)
Cost of Units Completed	(c)	221,400
Cost of Units Sold	209,050	(j)
Materials Inventory Control, Ending	48,810	51,950
Work in Process Inventory Control, Ending	(d)	(k)
Finished Goods Inventory Control, Ending	56,940	61,180

Required

Using the information given, compute the unknown values. Show all your work.

Problem 17A-4. Job Order Costing: Journal Entry Analysis and T Accounts
(L.O. 7)

Vagge, the finest name in parking attendant apparel, has been in business for more than thirty years. These colorful and stylish uniforms are special ordered by exclusive hotels and country clubs around the world. During April 19x9 Vagge Industries, Inc., encountered the transactions described below. Factory overhead was applied at a rate of 90 percent of direct labor cost.

April 1 Materials costing $39,400 were purchased on account.
3 Materials costing $16,850 were requisitioned into production.
4 Operating supplies costing $12,830 were purchased for cash.
8 The company issued checks for the following factory overhead costs: utilities, $1,310; factory insurance, $1,825; repairs charges, $2,640.

10 The cutting department manager requisitioned $18,510 in materials and $6,480 in operating supplies into production.
15 Payroll was distributed to the employees. Gross wages and salaries were: direct labor, $72,900; indirect labor, $41,610; factory supervision, $22,900; and sales commissions, $32,980.
15 Overhead was applied to production.
22 Overhead expenses were paid: utilities, $1,270; factory maintenance, $1,380; and factory rent, $4,250.
23 The receiving department recorded purchases and receipts of $21,940 in materials and $8,260 in operating supplies.
27 Production requisitions for $18,870 in materials and $6,640 in operating supplies were recorded.
30 The following gross wages and salaries were paid to employees: direct labor, $74,220; indirect labor, $39,290; factory supervision, $24,520; and sales commissions, $36,200.
30 Factory overhead was applied to production.
30 Units completed during the month were transferred to Finished Goods Inventory Control; total cost was $298,400.
30 Sales on account of $398,240 were shipped to customers. Their cost was $264,200.
30 Adjusting entries for the following were recorded:

Depreciation, factory equipment	$1,680
Factory property taxes	1,130

Required

1. Record the journal entries for all April transactions and events. For the payroll entries, concern yourself only with the distribution of factory payroll to the production accounts.
2. Post the entries prepared in part **1** to T accounts, and determine the partial accounts balances.
3. Compute the amount of underapplied or overapplied overhead for April.

Problem 17A-5. Job Order Costing: Comprehensive Journal Entry Analysis (L.O. 7)

Merriman Information Systems Company is a division of Hilbrich International, Inc. The company designs unique management information systems and produces specialty computer equipment for such industries as heavy road-construction machinery and underwater search equipment. A job order cost accounting system is used, and the current year's predetermined overhead rate is 80 percent of direct labor dollars.

The Materials Inventory Control account had a balance of $286,750 at the beginning of business on March 1, 19x8. Materials Inventory Subsidiary records revealed the following breakdown: sheet metal, $64,820; casings, $46,110; computer components, $164,880; and supplies inventory, $10,940. There were three jobs in process on March 1, 19x8, and job order cost cards showed the following amounts: Job P-284, $96,250; Job E-302, $61,810; and Job G-325, $22,250. The Work in Process Inventory Control account balance at March 1 was $180,310. All Finished Goods Inventory items had been sold and shipped in February, and no balance existed in the account at the beginning of March. In addition, the Factory Payroll, Factory Overhead Control, and Factory Overhead Applied accounts had no balances carried forward from February because these accounts are closed at the end of each month.

The following transactions were incurred during March:

March 1 Received recent purchases along with invoices: sheet metal, $26,440, and casings, $14,980.
2 Requisitioned $2,710 in operating supplies into production.
4 Paid factory overhead costs: electricity, $1,240; water, $290; heat, $1,450; and repairs and maintenance, $620.
5 Received new purchases along with invoices: computer components $42,810; casings, $12,550; and operating supplies, $3,070.
7 Requisitioned materials into production:
Job E-302: sheet metal, $6,480, and computer components, $12,270.
Job G-325: casings, $4,760, and computer components, $16,960.
Job G-410: sheet metal, $12,420; casings, $5,130; and computer components $3,230.
9 Requisitioned operating supplies costing $1,840 into production.
14 Recorded and distributed semimonthly payroll liability to the production accounts: total direct labor, $57,020 (Job P-284, $13,940; Job E-302, $16,720; Job G-325, $20,110; and Job G-410, $6,250); indirect labor wages, $36,190; administrative salaries, $54,200; FICA taxes withheld, $10,320; and federal income taxes withheld, $26,534.
14 Applied factory overhead costs to production.
16 Received purchases of materials along with invoices: sheet metal, $14,520; casings, $13,960; computer components, $26,280; and operating supplies, $3,110.
18 Requisitioned materials into production:
Job E-302: computer components, $12,890.
Job G-325: casings, $14,780, and computer components, $20,520.
Job G-410: sheet metal, $11,460; casings, $11,220; and computer components, $14,610.
Job Y-160: sheet metal, $7,810; casings, $8,730; and computer components, $3,230.
20 Requisitioned operating supplies into production, $4,620.
23 Paid factory overhead expenses: property taxes, $2,470; unemployment compensation taxes, factory, $460; repairs, $1,680; contractual, indirect labor, $2,170; and rent, $1,110.
28 Recorded semimonthly payroll liability and distributed it to the production accounts: total direct labor, $63,080 (Job P-284, $6,210; Job E-302, $9,760; Job G-325, $22,560; Job G-410, $18,940; and Job Y-160, $5,610); indirect labor, $38,770; administrative salaries, $56,540; FICA taxes withheld, $11,090; and federal income taxes withheld, $28,510.
28 Applied factory overhead costs to production.
29 Completed and transferred Jobs P-284 and E-302 to Finished Goods Inventory control.
30 Recorded depreciation on equipment, $1,090.
31 Sold and shipped Job P-284 to customer; selling price, $267,940.
31 Closed out Factory Overhead Control and Factory Overhead Applied accounts and distributed the difference to the Cost of Goods Sold account.

Required

1. Prepare journal entries for all of the preceding transactions and events.
2. Prepare T accounts for all of the general ledger and subsidiary ledger accounts relevant to the job order costing system. Enter the beginning balances when applicable, and post the journal entries prepared in part **1** to these accounts.

3. Check the accuracy of ending inventory control account balances by reconciling them with the totals of their respective subsidiary ledger accounts.

Problem Set B

Problem 17B-1. Application of Factory Overhead
(L.O. 3, 4)

Crowley Cosmetics Company applies factory overhead costs on the basis of direct labor dollars. The current, predetermined overhead rate is computed by using data from the two prior years, in this case 19x7 and 19x8, adjusted to reflect expectations for the current year, 19x9. Using the information below, the controller prepared the overhead rate analysis for 19x9.

	19x7	19x8
Direct labor dollars	$57,500	$69,000
Factory overhead costs:		
Indirect labor	$23,100	$30,030
Employee fringe benefits	19,000	21,850
Manufacturing supervision	14,800	16,280
Utilities	9,350	13,090
Factory insurance	10,000	13,500
Janitorial services	9,000	11,250
Depreciation, factory and machinery	7,750	9,300
Miscellaneous manufacturing expenses	4,750	5,225
Total overhead	$97,750	$120,525

For the year 19x9 each item of factory overhead costs is expected to increase by the same percentage as it did from 19x7 to 19x8. Direct labor expense is expected to total $82,800 for the year 19x9.

Required

1. Compute the overhead rate for 19x9. Round answer to nearest whole percent.
2. The company actually surpassed its sales and operating expectations. Jobs completed during 19x9 and the related direct labor dollars were as follows: Job 2214, $14,000; Job 2215, $16,000; Job 2216, $11,000; Job 2217, $18,000; Job 2218, $22,000; and Job 2219, $9,000. The total was $90,000. Determine the amount of factory overhead to be applied to each job and to total production during 19x9.
3. Prepare the journal entry needed to close the overhead accounts and to dispose of the underapplied or overapplied overhead. Assume that $160,245 in factory overhead was incurred in 19x9. Also assume that the difference between actual and applied overhead costs is considered insignificant.

Problem 17B-2. Job Order Cost Flow
(L.O. 6, 8)

September 1 inventory balances of Granger House, manufacturers of high-quality children's clothing, were as follows:

Materials Inventory Control	$41,360
Work in Process Inventory Control	25,112
Finished Goods Inventory Control	27,120

Additional information on operating events in September is summarized at the top of the following page.

Job order cost cards for jobs in process as of September 30, 19x7, revealed the following:

Job No.	Materials	Direct Labor	Factory Overhead
24A	$1,496	$1,390	$1,529
24B	1,392	1,480	1,628
24C	1,784	1,960	2,156
24D	1,408	1,760	1,936

Materials purchased and received in September:

September 4	$23,120
September 16	18,600
September 22	21,920

Direct labor costs for September:

September 15 payroll	$33,680
September 29 payroll	35,960

Predetermined overhead rate: 110 percent of direct labor dollars

Materials requisitioned into production during September:

September 6	$27,240
September 23	28,960

Finished goods with a 75 percent markup over cost were sold during September for $350,000.

Required

1. Using T accounts, reconstruct the transactions for September.
2. Compute the cost of units completed during the period.
3. What was the total cost of units sold during September?
4. Determine the ending inventory balances.
5. During the first week of October, Jobs 24A and 24C were completed. No additional materials costs were incurred, but Job 24A required $960 more in direct labor, and Job 24C needed additional direct labor of $1,610. Job 24A was composed of 1,200 pairs of trousers, and Job 24C's customer ordered 950 shirts. Compute each job's unit cost.

Problem 17B-3. Job Order Costing: Unknown Quantity Analysis (L.O. 6)

Partial operating data for the Duckworth Picture Company for March and April are given below. Management has decided on an overhead rate of 140 percent of direct labor dollars for the current year.

	March	April
Beginning Materials Inventory Control	(a)	(e)
Beginning Work in Process Inventory Control	$ 99,505	(f)
Beginning Finished Goods Inventory Control	89,764	$ 77,660
Materials Requisitioned	58,025	(g)
Materials Purchased	57,090	60,116
Direct Labor Costs	48,760	54,540
Factory Overhead Applied	(b)	(h)
Cost of Units Completed	(c)	229,861

Cost of Goods Sold	165,805	(i)
Ending Materials Inventory Control	43,014	38,628
Ending Work in Process Inventory Control	(d)	(j)
Ending Finished Goods Inventory Control	77,660	40,515

Required

Using the data provided, compute the amount of each lettered unknown. Show your computations.

Problem 17B-4. Job Order Costing: Journal Entry Analysis and T Accounts (L.O. 7)

Schoenthal Manufacturing, Inc., produces electric golf carts. These carts are special-order items, so a job order cost accounting system is needed. Factory overhead is applied at the rate of 80 percent of direct labor cost. Below is a listing of events and transactions for January.

Jan. 1 Materials costing $196,400 were purchased on account.
2 $38,500 in operating supplies were purchased on account.
4 Production personnel requisitioned materials costing $184,200 and operating supplies costing $32,100 into production.
10 The following overhead costs were paid: utilities, $4,400; factory rent, $3,500; and maintenance charges, $2,800.
15 Payroll was distributed to employees. Gross wages and salaries were as follows: direct labor, $138,000; indirect labor, $52,620; sales commissions, $32,400; and administrative salaries, $38,000.
15 Overhead was applied to production.
19 Operating supplies costing $37,550 and materials listed at $210,450 were purchased on account.
21 Materials costing $202,750 and operating supplies costing $39,400 were requisitioned into production.
26 Production completed during the month was transferred to Finished Goods Inventory Control. Total costs assigned to these jobs were $473,590.
31 The following gross wages and salaries were paid to employees: direct labor, $152,000; indirect labor, $56,240; sales commissions, $31,200; and administrative salaries, $38,000.
31 Overhead was applied to production.
31 Products costing $404,520 were shipped to customers during the month. Total selling price of these goods was $536,800, and the sales should be recorded at month end.
31 The following overhead costs (adjusting entries) should be recorded: prepaid insurance expired, $4,900; property taxes (payable at year end), $4,200; and depreciation, machinery, $53,500.

Required

1. Record the journal entries for all January transactions and events. For the payroll entries concern yourself only with the distribution of factory payroll to the production accounts.
2. Post the entries prepared in part **1** to T accounts, and determine the partial account balances.
3. Compute the amount of underapplied or overapplied factory overhead on January 31.

Problem 17B-5. Job Order Costing: Comprehensive Journal Entry Analysis (L.O. 7)

The Benz Manufacturing Company maintains a job order cost accounting system. The company uses an overhead application rate of 130 percent of direct labor costs.

Accounting records on August 1 showed that the Materials Inventory Control account balance was $93,390 and the materials subsidiary ledger balances were $41,800 for mixing fluid, $38,610 for MX powder, and $12,980 for supplies inventory. The Work in Process Inventory Control account balance was $85,060, and the subsidiary ledger job order cost card balances were $61,910 for Job 16-A; $19,730 for Job 18-A; and $3,420 for Job 20-A. The Finished Goods Inventory Control account balance was $67,850, and the finished goods subsidiary ledger balances were: none for Product 16; $29,240 for Product 18; and $38,610 for Product 20.

The Factory Payroll, Factory Overhead Control, and Factory Overhead Applied accounts have no balances carried forward from July because these accounts are closed at the end of each month. The following transactions and events occurred during August.

Aug. 1 Operating supplies totaling $8,740 were requisitioned into production.
4 $55,650 in mixing fluid and $36,720 in MX powder were received and purchased on account.
6 The following factory overhead costs were paid in cash: factory rent, $2,850; heat, light, and power, $1,290; repairs and maintenance, $5,240; and outside contractual services, $6,525.
9 The following semimonthly payroll liability was recorded: gross direct labor wages, $40,250 (Job 16-A, $26,640; Job 18-A, $7,800; and Job 20-A, $5,810); gross indirect labor wages, $19,420; gross administrative salaries, $9,250; FICA taxes withheld, $4,535; federal income taxes withheld, $16,320.
9 Factory payroll was distributed to the production accounts.
9 Factory overhead costs were applied to production.
12 $14,120 in operating supplies were purchased and received on account.
13 $35,280 in mixing fluid and $19,960 in MX powder were requisitioned into production for Job 18-A.
14 Payroll checks for the liability recorded on August 9 were prepared and distributed to the employees.
15 Property taxes of $4,100 were paid and chargeable to factory overhead.
18 Job 16-A was completed and transferred to Finished Goods Inventory.
20 $21,890 in mixing fluid and $16,770 in MX powder were requisitioned into production for Job 20-A.
23 The following semimonthly payroll liability was recorded: gross direct wages, $31,220 (Job 18-A, $19,410; Job 20-A, $11,810); gross indirect labor wages, $18,140; gross administrative salaries, $8,250; FICA taxes payable, $3,460; and federal income taxes withheld, $14,980.
23 Factory payroll was distributed to production accounts.
23 Factory overhead costs were applied to production.
26 A major portion of Job 16-A was sold and shipped to a customer. Four thousand liters were shipped at a cost of $23 per liter. This shipment sold for $139,840.
28 Payroll checks for the liability recorded on August 23 were prepared and distributed to the employees.
30 Depreciation on machinery of $14,940 for the month was recorded.
30 The Factory Overhead Control and the Factory Overhead Applied accounts were closed out, and the difference was distributed to the Cost of Goods Sold account.

Required

1. Prepare journal entries for all of the preceding transactions and events.
2. Prepare T accounts for all general ledger and subsidiary ledger accounts relevant to the job order costing system. Enter the beginning balances when applicable, and post the journal entries prepared in part **1** to these accounts.
3. Check the accuracy of ending inventory control account balances by comparing them with the totals on the subsidiary ledger accounts.

Management Decision Case

Fornstrom Manufacturing Company
(L.O. 5, 6, 8)

Fornstrom Manufacturing Company is a small family-owned business that makes specialty plastic products. Since it was started three years ago, the company has grown quickly and now employs ten production people. Because of its size, the company uses a job order cost accounting system designed around a periodic inventory method. Work sheets and special analyses are used to account for manufacturing costs and inventory valuations.

Two months ago the company's accountant quit. You have now been called in to assist management. The following information has been given to you:

Beginning inventory balances (1/1/x7):	
Materials	$20,420
Work in Process (Job K-2)	69,100
Finished Goods (Job K-1)	81,700

Materials requisitioned into production during 19x7:	
Job K-2	$19,000
Job K-4	38,800
Job K-6	58,000

Direct labor for the year:	
Job K-2	$37,300
Job K-4	46,480
Job K-6	75,600

The company purchased materials only once during the year, and all jobs use the same material. Purchases totaled $96,500. For the current year the company has been using an overhead application rate of 125 percent of direct labor dollars. So far in 19x7, two jobs, K-2 and K-4, have been completed. Jobs K-1 and K-2 have been shipped to customers. Job K-1 was made up of 3,000 units. Job K-2 contained 5,500 units. Job K-4 has 4,800 units.

Required

1. Reconstruct the job order cost sheets for each job worked on during the period. What were the unit costs for jobs K-1, K-2, and K-4? Round answer to nearest cent.
2. From the information given and using T account analysis, compute the current balances in the three inventory accounts and the cost of goods sold.
3. The president has asked you to analyze the current job order cost accounting system. Should the system be changed? How? Why? Prepare an outline of your response to the president.

CHAPTER 18 PRODUCT COSTING: THE PROCESS COST SYSTEM

LEARNING OBJECTIVES

1. Explain the role of the Work in Process Inventory account(s) in a process cost accounting system.
2. Describe product flow and cost flow through a process cost accounting system.
3. Compute equivalent production for situations with and without units in the beginning Work in Process Inventory.
4. Compute product unit cost for a specific time period (unit cost analysis schedule).
5. Prepare a cost summary schedule that assigns costs to units completed and transferred out of the department during the period, and find the ending Work in Process Inventory balance.
6. Make the journal entry(ies) needed to transfer costs of completed units out of the Work in Process Inventory account.

A major goal in using any cost accounting system is to find product unit costs and to set ending values for Materials, Work in Process, and Finished Goods inventories. Continuous product flows (liquids) and long production runs of identical or standard products generally require a process cost accounting system. With this system, manufacturing costs are not traced to specific products or job orders. Instead, they are averaged over the units produced in each period of time.

Process costing depends on three schedules: (1) the schedule of equivalent production; (2) the unit cost analysis schedule; and (3) the cost summary schedule. From the information in these three schedules, it is possible to tell what costs to attach to units completed and transferred out of the department. Then, a journal entry is used to transfer these costs out of the Work in Process Inventory account. Those costs remaining in the Work in Process Inventory account belong to units still in process at period end.

This chapter will analyze the process cost accounting system and explain how to calculate product unit costs. It will also explain how to compute and verify the period-end balance for the Work in Process Inventory account and the costs assigned to units completed. These units will have been transferred either to the next department or to the Finished Goods Inventory account. After studying this chapter, you should be able to meet the learning objectives listed on the left.

In Chapter 17 we compared the characteristics of job order costing and process costing. You will remember that a process cost accounting system is used by companies in such environments as the paint, oil, fastener (screws and bolts), gas, and beverage industries. These companies produce large amounts of similar products or have a continuous production flow. A process costing system has the following characteristics: (1) cost data are collected by department or work center, with little concern for specific job orders; (2) a weekly or monthly time period is emphasized rather than the time it takes to complete a specific order; and (3) the accounting system uses several Work in Process Inventory accounts—one for each department or work center in the manufacturing process.

Cost Flow Through Work in Process Inventory Accounts

Accounting for the costs of materials, direct labor, and factory overhead does not differ much between job order costing and process costing. Under both systems costs must be recorded and eventually charged to production. Materials and supplies must be purchased and requisitioned into production. Direct labor wages must be paid to the employees and charged to production accounts. And costs of various types of factory overhead are assigned to production. Journal entries such as those described in Chapter 17 record these transactions and events. So as you can see, the flow of costs *into* the Work in Process Inventory account is very similar in the two product costing systems.

The major difference between job order cost accounting and process cost accounting is the way costs are assigned to products. In a job order cost system, costs are traced to specific jobs and products. In a process cost system, however, an averaging technique is used. For computing unit cost in the process cost system, all products worked on during a specific time period (a week or a month) are used as the output base. Total costs of materials, direct labor, and factory overhead accumulated in the Work in Process Inventory account (or accounts) are divided by the equivalent units worked on during the period. This procedure may seem clear enough, but technical aspects make it more difficult than it first appears. These aspects are discussed below.

Work in Process Inventory Accounts

OBJECTIVE 1
Explain the role of the Work in Process Inventory account(s) in a process cost accounting system

The Work in Process Inventory account is the focal point of process costing. Unlike the job order approach, a process cost system is not limited to one Work in Process Inventory account. In fact, process costing uses as many Work in Process Inventory accounts as there are departments or steps in the production process. The process shown in Figure 18-1 has two departments. Finished units of Department 1 become the direct materials input of Department 2. As shown in this figure, the three cost elements flow into the Work in Process Inventory account of Department 1. The total unit cost of each completed product from Department 1 moves to Department 2 along with the completed unit. In Department 2 the products from Department 1 are processed further. No more materials are needed in Department 2, but as shown in Figure 18-1, more labor is used and factory overhead is assigned, usually on the basis of labor cost or hours.

When the completed products are finished, they are transferred from Work in Process Inventory (Department 2) to Finished Goods Inventory. At that point each unit's cost amount is made up of five cost inputs. Three are from Department 1 and two from Department 2. A detailed breakdown, using *hypothetical* dollar amounts, is shown on the next page.

Figure 18-1. Cost Elements and Process Cost Accounts

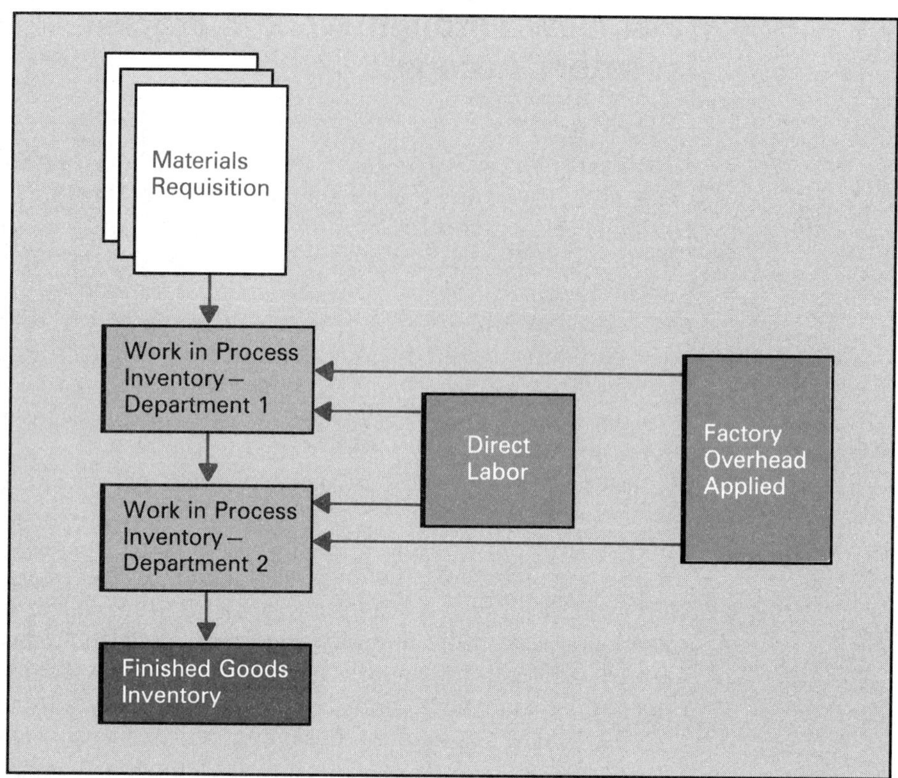

Total Unit Cost

Department 1		
Materials	$1.40	
Direct Labor	1.10	
Factory Overhead	.55	
Total, Department 1		$3.05
Department 2		
Direct Labor	$1.90	
Factory Overhead	2.09	
Total, Department 2		3.99
Total Unit Cost (to Finished Goods Inventory)		$7.04

Production Flow Combinations

There are hundreds of ways that product flows can combine with department or production processes. Two basic structures are illustrated in Figure 18-2. Example 1 shows a *series* of three processes or departments. The completed product of one department becomes the direct materials input of the next department. (Figure 18-1 also showed a series of departments.) The number of departments in a series can range from

Figure 18-2. Cost Flow for Process Costing

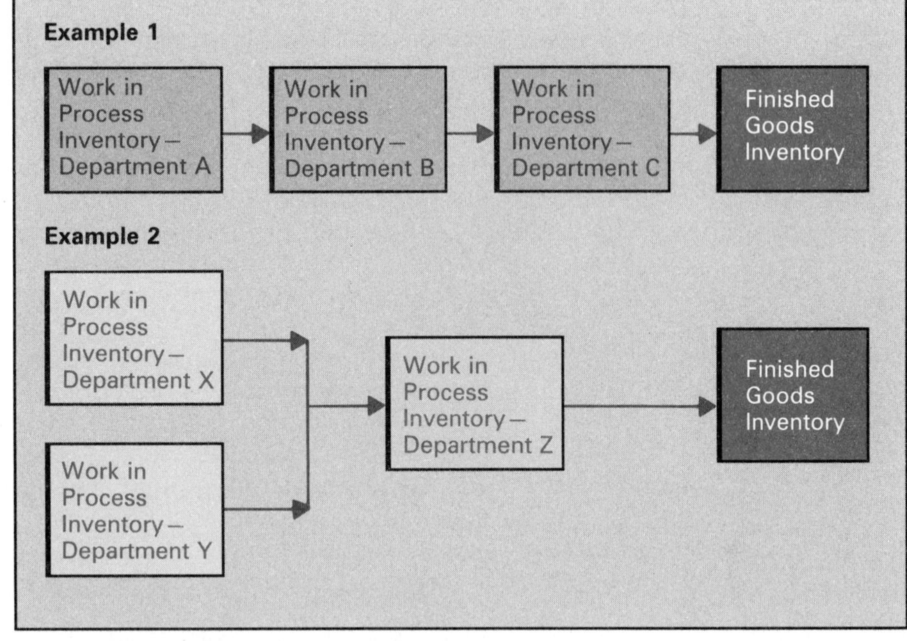

two to more than a dozen. The important point to remember is that product unit cost is the sum of the cost elements used in all departments.

OBJECTIVE 2 Describe product flow and cost flow through a process cost accounting system

Example 2 in Figure 18-2 shows a different type of production flow. Again, there are three departments. In this example, however, the product does not flow through all departments in a simple 1-2-3 order. Here, two separate products are developed, one in Department X and another in Department Y. Both products then go to Department Z, where they are joined with a third direct material input. The unit cost transferred to Finished Goods Inventory when the products are completed includes cost elements from Departments X, Y, and Z. The possible combinations of departments or processes are limitless.

Note: The three-schedule cost analysis shown in this chapter must be prepared for *each* department for *each* time period. Thus, a company with three production departments and two monthly time periods must prepare six *sets* of the three-schedule analysis.

The Concept of Equivalent Production

A key component of a process cost accounting system is the computation of equivalent units of production for each accounting period. This computation is needed to arrive at product unit costs.

Remember that in process costing, an averaging approach is used. All manufacturing costs incurred by a department or production process are divided by the units produced during the period. No attempt is made to associate costs with particular job orders. There are, however, several important questions: How many units were produced? Do you count only those units completed during the period? What about partly completed units in the beginning Work in Process Inventory? Do you count units even if only part of the work needed to complete them was done during this period? What about products in ending Work in Process Inventory? Is it proper to focus only on those units started and completed during the period?

OBJECTIVE 3
Compute equivalent production for situations with and without units in the beginning Work in Process Inventory

The answers to all these questions are linked to the concept of equivalent production. **Equivalent production** (also called **equivalent units**) is a measure of units produced in a period of time. This measure is expressed in terms of fully completed or equivalent whole units produced. Partly completed units are restated in terms of equivalent whole units. The number of equivalent units produced must be found. It is equal to the sum of (1) total units started and completed during the period and (2) an amount for partly completed products. This amount is a restatement of these units in terms of equivalent whole units. A *percentage of completion* factor is used to calculate the number of equivalent whole units. Figure 18-3 illustrates the equivalent unit computation. Three automobiles were started and completed during February. In addition, one-half (.5) of Car A is completed in February, and three-quarters (.75) of Car E is completed. To find the total equivalent units for the month, the units started and completed (3.0) and the units partly completed (.5 and .75) are added together. Therefore, equivalent production for February for direct labor and factory overhead is 4.25 units.

Once you know the number of equivalent units produced, you can compute unit costs for materials and conversion costs for each department in the production process. **Conversion costs** are the combined total of direct labor and factory overhead costs incurred by a production department. The equations for computing unit cost amounts appear below. (Note the role of equivalent units.)

$$\text{Unit cost for materials} = \frac{\text{total materials costs}}{\text{equivalent units—materials}}$$

$$\text{Unit cost for conversion costs} = \frac{\text{total labor and factory overhead costs}}{\text{equivalent units—conversion costs}}$$

Computing equivalent units of production for materials usually differs from computing equivalent units of production for conversion costs. As shown in Figure 18-3, materials are usually all added in at the beginning of a process. Therefore, materials for Car A were added in January and do not influence equivalent units for materials in February. However, materials for Car E were *all* added to production in February. By adding 3.0 (units started and completed—Cars B, C, and D) and 1.0 (unit started but not completed—Car E) you get the equivalent units of production for materials for February (4.0 units).

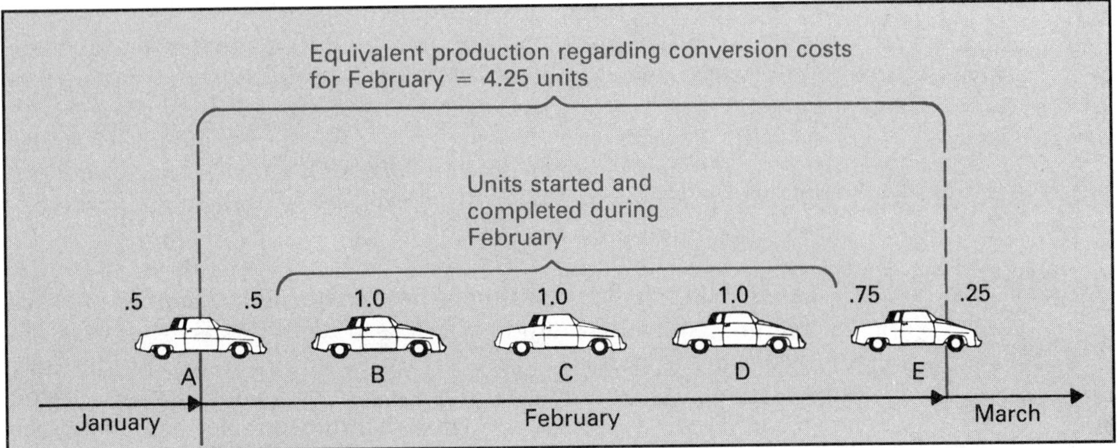

Figure 18-3. Equivalent Unit Computation

Facts: Conversion costs (those for direct labor and factory overhead) are incurred uniformly as each car moves through production. Equivalent production for February is 4.25 units as to conversion costs. But materials costs are all added to production at the beginning of the process. Since four cars entered production in February (cars B, C, D, and E), equivalent production for the month is 4.0 units as to materials costs.

FIFO Costing Approach

Figure 18-3 illustrates the *FIFO product flow* normally associated with process cost accounting. Industries that produce liquid products or engage in long production runs of identical products use the process costing method. With such a production flow, the first unit to enter the production process during a period is the first to be completed (automobile A in Figure 18-3). Therefore, the FIFO product flow is part of the process cost accounting system.

FIFO cost flow is an assumption underlying the FIFO method of determining product unit cost. This method assigns costs to products based on FIFO product flow and the work performed in a given time period. It is one of two methods used for product costing in a process cost accounting system. The second method is known as the average costing approach. Although a bit more accurate, the FIFO approach is a more complex method and will be left for a more advanced course in cost accounting. The FIFO approach is mentioned only to make you aware of an alternative method to the one disclosed in the following sections.

The Average Costing Approach

Cost flow and accountability need not follow the same assumptions as those supporting the flow of products. Such is the case with the average costing approach to process cost accounting. As stated earlier, products flow in a first-in, first-out (FIFO) manner in a process costing environment.

It is assumed that beginning inventory items are completed as new ones are brought into the production process. But following the average costing approach, you do not account for costs in the same manner as actual product flow. *The average process costing method is based on the assumption that the items in beginning Work in Process Inventory were started and completed during the current period.* Although a bit less accurate than the FIFO costing approach, this method is easier to understand and work with. It is illustrated below.

No Beginning Work in Process Inventory. To begin this detailed analysis for calculating equivalent production, assume there are no units in beginning Work in Process Inventory. Thus, you need to consider only (1) units started and completed during the period and (2) units started but not completed. By definition, units started but not completed are the balance in the ending Work in Process Inventory. Equivalent production is figured in parts as follows:

Part 1: Units started and completed = (number of units) × 100 percent

Part 2: Equivalent units in ending work in process inventory = (number of units) × (percentage of completion)

The *sum* of these two amounts is the equivalent whole units completed during the period. The percentage of completion figures are supplied by engineers or supervisors in the production departments.

Earlier an important point about computing unit cost was noted. Direct labor and factory overhead costs are usually lumped together and called conversion costs. The reason is that both costs are usually incurred uniformly throughout the production process. Combining them is convenient. Materials costs are generally not incurred uniformly throughout the process. They are normally incurred either at the beginning of the process (materials input) or at the end of it (packing materials). Because of this difference, the equivalent unit amount for materials will not be the same as that for conversion costs. Separate computations are necessary.

For example, assume that the records of Danelid Clothing, Inc., for January 19xx show the following information: (a) 47,500 units were started during the period; (b) 6,200 units were partly complete at period end; (c) units in ending Work in Process Inventory were 60 percent complete; (d) materials were added at the *beginning* of the process; (e) conversion costs were incurred *uniformly* throughout the process; and (f) no units were lost or spoiled during the month.

In the **schedule of equivalent production,** equivalent production is computed for the period for both materials and conversion costs. This schedule is shown for Danelid Clothing in Exhibit 18-1. Because there were no units in beginning Work in Process Inventory, dashes are entered in that row. As you can see, 41,300 units were started and completed during the period (47,500 units started less 6,200 units not completed). All 41,300 received 100 percent of the materials, labor, and overhead effort needed to complete them. Therefore, 41,300 equivalent units are recorded in both the Materials Costs and Conversion Costs columns.

Exhibit 18-1. Equivalent Units: No Beginning Inventory

Danelid Clothing, Inc.
Schedule of Equivalent Production
For the Month Ended January 31, 19xx

Units—Stage of Completion	Units to Be Accounted For	Equivalent Units: Materials Costs	Equivalent Units: Conversion Costs
Beginning inventory—units completed in this period	—	—	—
Units started and completed in this period (47,500–6,200)	41,300	41,300	41,300
Ending inventory—units started but not completed in this period	6,200		
(Materials—100% complete)		6,200	
(Conversion costs—60% complete)			3,720
Totals	47,500	47,500	45,020

Accounting for equivalent units in ending inventory is a bit more complicated. These 6,200 units received all materials inputs because materials were added to each product as it entered the production process. Therefore, in the materials column 6,200 equivalent units are entered. However, as you know, conversion costs are added uniformly as the products move through the process. The 6,200 units in ending inventory are only 60 percent complete. So the number of equivalent whole units can be calculated by multiplying the number of actual units by the percentage completed. In Exhibit 18-1 the amount of equivalent units for conversion costs of ending inventory is 6,200 units × 60% completion = 3,720 equivalent units. As a result of these computations for January, there are 47,500 equivalent units for materials costs and 45,020 equivalent units for conversion costs.

With Beginning Work in Process Inventory. A situation with no beginning Work in Process Inventory is almost never found in industry. By definition, process costing techniques are used in industries in which production flows continuously or in which there are long runs of identical products. In these cases, there is always something in process at month end. So there are always units in beginning Work in Process Inventory in the next period. Now, turn to the situation on the next page, which expands on the example used above.

During February 19xx, unit production information for Danelid Clothing, Inc., was as follows: (a) 6,200 units in beginning work in process inventory; (b) beginning inventory items were 60 percent completed; (c) 57,500 units were started during the period; (d) 5,000 units were in ending Work in Process Inventory; and (e) ending inventory was 45 percent completed as to conversion costs (all materials have been added).

The presence of beginning inventories makes it a little more difficult to compute equivalent units. Exhibit 18-2 illustrates the computation of equivalent units using the *average costing approach* when beginning inventory items must be accounted for. Remember, in average costing you treat all units in beginning Work in Process Inventory as if they were started and completed in the current period. With the inclusion of beginning inventories, equivalent production is calculated in three parts as follows:

Part 1: Equivalent units in beginning inventory = number of units × 100 percent

Part 2: Units started and completed = number of units × 100 percent

Part 3: Equivalent units in ending inventory:

Materials costs = number of units × percentage of completion
Conversion costs = number of units × percentage of completion

Exhibit 18-2. Equivalent Units: With Beginning Inventory

Danelid Clothing, Inc.
Schedule of Equivalent Production
For the Month Ended February 29, 19xx

Units—Stage of Completion	Units to Be Accounted For	Equivalent Units: Materials Costs	Equivalent Units: Conversion Costs
Beginning inventory—units completed in this period	6,200	6,200	6,200
Units started and completed in this period	52,500	52,500	52,500
Ending inventory—units started but not completed in this period	5,000		
(Materials—100% complete)		5,000	
(Conversion costs—45% complete)			2,250
Totals	63,700	63,700	60,950

February operations of Danelid Clothing, Inc., involve both beginning and ending balances in Work in Process Inventory. As shown in Exhibit 18-2, the 6,200 units in beginning inventory are extended at their full amount to the materials costs and conversion costs columns of the schedule. This treatment is the same as that given to the 52,500 units started and completed during February (57,500 units started minus 5,000 unfinished units). Units started and completed receive the full amount of materials costs and conversion costs. Ending inventory is 100 percent complete as to materials (5,000 units). It is 45 percent complete as to conversion costs (5,000 × 45% = 2,250). The end result is that February produced 63,700 equivalent units that had materials costs and 60,950 equivalent units that had conversion costs. (Note that these illustrations cover only two of the hundreds of possible process costing situations that could arise with varying percentages of completion.)

Cost Analysis Schedules

OBJECTIVE 4
Compute product unit cost for a specific time period (unit cost analysis schedule)

So far, accounting for *units* of productive output has been emphasized. In the schedule of equivalent production, the total units to be accounted for were determined. Then, equivalent units for materials costs and conversion costs were computed. Once the unit information is sorted out and equivalent unit figures have been computed, the dollar information can be considered. Now, manufacturing costs, cost per equivalent unit, and inventory costing are brought into the analysis.

Unit Cost Analysis Schedule

The **unit cost analysis schedule** is the second of the three schedules used in process costing. It does two things: (1) It adds all costs charged to the Work in Process Inventory account of each department or production process. (2) It computes cost per equivalent unit for materials and conversion costs. A unit cost analysis schedule is shown in Exhibit 18-3.

Unit costs are arrived at in two steps. The first step in the schedule is to summarize all costs for the period. These costs are made up of costs of materials and conversion costs incurred in the current period plus the costs included in the beginning Work in Process Inventory. (The Total Costs to Be Accounted For later serves as a figure for checking the third schedule—the cost summary schedule.)

The second step in the unit cost analysis is to divide the costs by the number of equivalent units. Total costs for materials are divided by the equivalent units for materials. In the same way, total conversion costs are divided by the equivalent units for conversion costs. When you use the average cost flow assumption, units and costs in beginning inventory are included in figuring the period's costs per equivalent unit.

Exhibit 18-3. Unit Cost Determination: No Beginning Inventories

Danelid Clothing, Inc.
Unit Cost Analysis Schedule
For the Month Ended January 31, 19xx

	Total Costs				Equivalent Unit Costs		
	Costs from Beginning Inventory	Costs from Current Period	Total Costs to Be Accounted For	÷	Equivalent Units	=	Cost per Equivalent Unit
Materials	—	$154,375	$154,375		47,500		$3.25
Conversion costs	—	258,865	258,865		45,020		5.75
Totals	—	$413,240	$413,240				$9.00

Exhibit 18-4. Ending Inventory Computation: No Beginning Inventories

Danelid Clothing, Inc.
Cost Summary Schedule
For the Month Ended January 31, 19xx

	Cost of Goods Transferred to Finished Goods Inventory	Cost of Ending Work in Process Inventory
Beginning inventory		
None	—	
Units started and completed*		
41,300 units × $9.00 per unit	$371,700	
Ending inventory*		
Materials: 6,200 units × $3.25		$ 20,150
Conversion costs: 3,720 units × $5.75		21,390
Totals	$371,700	$ 41,540
Check of computations:		
Costs to Finished Goods Inventory		$371,700
Cost of ending Work in Process Inventory		41,540
Total costs accounted for (unit cost analysis schedule)		$413,240

*Note: Unit figures come from the schedule of equivalent production for January (Exhibit 18-1).

Cost Summary Schedule

OBJECTIVE 5
Prepare a cost summary schedule that assigns costs to units completed and transferred out of the department during the period, and find the ending Work in Process Inventory balance

The final phase of the process costing analysis is to distribute the total costs accumulated during the period among all the units of output. Some costs may stay in ending Work in Process Inventory. Others must go with the units completed and transferred out of the department. Costs are assigned by means of the **cost summary schedule.** Information in this schedule comes from both the schedule of equivalent production and the unit cost analysis schedule.

It is fairly easy to compute the total costs to be transferred out of the department. Suppose that 16,500 units were completed during the period and moved to Finished Goods Inventory. Cost per equivalent unit was found to be \$3.30. Therefore, \$54,450 (16,500 × \$3.30) is transferred out of Work in Process Inventory by making a journal entry. All costs remaining in Work in Process Inventory after costs of completed units have been transferred out represent the cost of ending units in process.

To complete the analysis, add together the total cost of units transferred and the costs belonging to ending Work in Process Inventory. Then, compare the total with the total costs to be accounted for in the unit cost analysis schedule. If the two totals are not equal, there has been an arithmetic error (normally due to rounding).

Illustrative Analysis

To fully explain the form and use of the cost schedules, the Danelid Clothing, Inc., example will be expanded. Besides the equivalent unit information discussed earlier, the company has the following cost data:

January, 19xx	
Beginning Work in Process Inventory	—
Cost of materials used	\$154,375
Conversion costs for the month	258,865
February, 19xx	
Cost of materials used	\$190,060
Conversion costs for the month	319,930

From these data the equivalent unit costs, total costs transferred to Finished Goods Inventory, and the ending balance in Work in Process Inventory for January and February 19xx will be computed.

January. The unit cost analysis schedule for January is shown in Exhibit 18-3. Total costs to be accounted for are \$413,240. Of this amount, costs for materials are \$154,375, and conversion costs are \$258,865. When these costs are divided by the equivalent unit amounts (computed in Exhibit 18-1), you get costs per equivalent unit of \$3.25 for materials (\$154,375 ÷ 47,500) and \$5.75 for conversion costs (\$258,865 ÷ 45,020). Total unit cost for the period is \$9.00. The per unit cost amounts are used in the cost summary schedule shown in Exhibit 18-4 to compute costs transferred to Finished Goods Inventory and the cost assigned to ending Work in Process Inventory.

In Danelid's cost summary schedule for January, shown in Exhibit 18-4, no units were in process at the beginning of January, so no costs are entered for beginning inventory. (Even though there was no beginning inventory for January, the headings are included so the form can be used for any process costing situation.) Units transferred to Finished Goods Inventory in January are made up entirely of units started and completed, since there were no units in beginning inventory. These 41,300 units cost $9.00 each to produce (total cost per equivalent unit). So $371,700 must be transferred to Finished Goods Inventory.

During January $413,240 was debited to Work in Process Inventory. Of that amount, $371,700 was transferred to Finished Goods Inventory. The difference of $41,540 remaining in the account is the ending Work in Process Inventory balance. This amount is verified in Exhibit 18-4. Using the ending inventory amounts from the schedule of equivalent production in Exhibit 18-1 and the costs per equivalent unit from the cost analysis schedule in Exhibit 18-3, you can make the following computations:

Materials costs: 6,200 equivalent units × $3.25 per unit	$20,150
Conversion costs: 3,720 equivalent units × $5.75 per unit	21,390
Ending Work in Process Inventory balance	$41,540

The check of computations at the bottom of Exhibit 18-4 ensures that all the arithmetic is right. Total costs computed in Exhibit 18-3 have been accounted for.

February. The cost analysis for February is a bit more difficult because units and costs in beginning Work in Process Inventory must be considered. February operating results are analyzed in Exhibits 18-5 and 18-6. Total costs to be accounted for in February are $551,530. Included in this

Exhibit 18-5. Unit Cost Determination: With Beginning Inventories

Danelid Clothing, Inc.
Unit Cost Analysis Schedule
For the Month Ended February 29, 19xx

	Total Costs				Equivalent Unit Costs		
	Costs from Beginning Inventory	Costs from Current Period	Total Costs to Be Accounted For	÷	Equivalent Units	=	Cost per Equivalent Unit
Materials	$20,150	$190,060	$210,210		63,700		$3.30
Conversion costs	21,390	319,930	341,320		60,950		5.60
Totals	$41,540	$509,990	$551,530				$8.90

amount is the beginning inventory balance of $41,540 (see Exhibit 18-4) plus current costs from February of $190,060 and $319,930 for materials and conversion costs, respectively. These costs are then added to the materials and conversion costs carried over from January in the Work in Process Inventory account. The total costs to be accounted for are then divided by the equivalent unit figures computed in Exhibit 18-2. February's $8.90 cost per equivalent unit includes $3.30 per unit for materials and $5.60 per unit for conversion costs.

The February cost analysis is finished by preparing the cost summary schedule (Exhibit 18-6). Costs transferred to Finished Goods Inventory total $522,430. This amount includes costs of $55,180 for the 6,200 units in beginning inventory and the costs of $467,250 for the 52,500 units started and completed during February.

The ending Work in Process Inventory balance of $29,100 is made up of $16,500 in materials costs and $12,600 in conversion costs. At the bottom of the cost summary schedule, a check ensures that no arithmetic errors were made.

Exhibit 18-6. Ending Inventory Computation: With Beginning Inventories

Danelid Clothing, Inc.
Cost Summary Schedule
For the Month Ended February 29, 19xx

	Cost of Goods Transferred to Finished Goods Inventory	Cost of Ending Work in Process Inventory
Beginning inventory*		
6,200 units × $8.90 per unit	$ 55,180	
Units started and completed*		
52,500 units × $8.90 per unit	467,250	
Ending inventory*		
Materials: 5,000 units × $3.30		$ 16,500
Conversion costs:		
2,250 units × $5.60		12,600
Totals	$522,430	$ 29,100
Check of computations:		
Costs to Finished Goods Inventory		$522,430
Costs of ending Work in Process Inventory		29,100
Total costs to be accounted for (unit cost analysis schedule)		$551,530

*Note: Unit figures come from schedule of equivalent production (Exhibit 18-2).

Journal Entry Analysis

OBJECTIVE 6
Make the journal entry(ies) needed to transfer costs of completed units out of the Work in Process Inventory account

Although schedules for (1) equivalent production, (2) unit cost analysis, and (3) cost summary have been emphasized, none of these schedules offers a direct way to transfer costs in the accounting records. All three schedules deal mostly with the Work in Process Inventory account. The goal of doing a process costing analysis is to compute dollar totals for goods completed and transferred to Finished Goods Inventory and for partly completed products staying in the Work in Process Inventory account. However, the three schedules alone do not cause costs to flow through accounts in the general ledger. They only give the information needed for journal entries. It is the journal entries that actually move costs from one account to another.

The final step in a process costing analysis, then, is a journal entry to transfer costs of completed products out of Work in Process Inventory. Remember that all entries analyzed in Chapter 17 are also necessary in a process costing system. Only one entry is highlighted here, however, because it is directly involved with the transfer of costs of completed goods. To transfer the costs of units completed, you debit Finished Goods Inventory (or the Work in Process Inventory of a subsequent department) and credit Work in Process Inventory. The amount of the cost transfer was calculated in the cost summary schedule.

In the example of Danelid Clothing, Inc., the following entries would be made at the end of each time period:

Jan. 31	Finished Goods Inventory	371,700	
	Work in Process Inventory		371,700
	To transfer cost of units completed in January to Finished Goods Inventory		
Feb. 29	Finished Goods Inventory	522,430	
	Work in Process Inventory		522,430
	To transfer cost of units completed in February to Finished Goods Inventory		

Once the entries are posted, the Work in Process Inventory account would appear as follows on February 29, 19xx:

Work in Process Inventory

Balance	—	Transferred to Finished	
Jan. materials	154,375	Goods in Jan.	371,700
Jan. conversion costs	258,865		
Balance 1/31/xx	**41,540**		
Feb. materials	190,060	Transferred to Finished	
Feb. conversion costs	319,930	Goods in Feb.	522,430
Balance 2/29/xx	**29,100***		

*This amount is confirmed by the cost summary schedule in Exhibit 18-6.

In the analysis of Danelid Clothing, Inc., it is assumed that the company had only *one* production department, and the example centered on two consecutive monthly accounting periods. Because only one production department was used, only one Work in Process Inventory account was needed. The following example deals with *two* production departments in a series. The product passes from the first to the second department and then to Finished Goods Inventory. This production flow is similar to that illustrated in Figure 18-1. When the production process requires two departments, the accounting system must maintain two Work in Process Inventory accounts, one for each department. This situation calls for more work, but the computations are the same. The key point is to treat *each* department and related Work in Process Inventory account in a separate analysis. The three schedules must be prepared for *each* department. Departments should be analyzed in the same order in which they appear in the series.

Illustrative Problem: Two Production Departments

Zarycki Manufacturing Company produces a liquid chemical for converting salt water into fresh water. The production process involves the Mixing Department and the Cooling Department. Every unit produced must be processed by both departments. Cooling is the final operation.

In the Mixing Department a basic chemical powder, Material BP, is added to salt water, heated to 88° Celsius, and mixed for two hours. Assume that no evaporation occurs and that Material BP is added at the beginning of the process. Conversion costs are incurred uniformly throughout the process. Operating data for the Mixing Department for April 19xx are as follows:

Beginning Work in Process Inventory	
Units (30% complete)	1,450 liters
Costs: Materials	$ 13,050
Conversion costs	1,760
Ending Work in Process Inventory	
All units 60% complete	
April operations	
Units started	55,600 liters
Costs: Materials used	$488,990
Conversion costs	278,990
Units completed and transferred to the Cooling Department	54,800 liters

Required

1. Using good form, prepare: (a) a schedule of equivalent production; (b) a unit cost analysis schedule; and (c) a cost summary schedule.
2. From information in the cost summary schedule, prepare the proper journal entry for transferring costs of completed units for April out of the Mixing Department.

Solution

1. Before doing the three schedules and preparing the journal entry, you should make a special analysis of the units (liters) worked on during April. To complete the schedule of equivalent production, you must first find the number of units started and completed and the number of units in ending Work in Process Inventory. These amounts were not given above, but they could have been easily computed.

Units started and completed:		
	Units completed and transferred (given)	54,800 liters
Less:	Units in beginning inventory (given)	1,450 liters
Equals:	Units started and completed	53,350 liters

Units in ending inventory:		
	Units started during April (given)	55,600 liters
Less:	Units started and completed (above)	53,350 liters
Equals:	Units in ending inventory	2,250 liters

Once you know the number of units started and completed and the number of units in ending Work in Process Inventory, you can prepare the three schedules in the cost analysis (shown on the next page).

2. The costs of completed units for April are now ready to be transferred from the Mixing Department to the Cooling Department. The required journal entry would be as follows:

Work in Process—Cooling Department	756,240	
Work in Process—Mixing Department		756,240
To transfer cost of units completed in April from Mixing Department to Cooling Department		

Note that the $756,240 is being transferred from one Work in Process Inventory account to another. The $756,240 attached to the units transferred into the Cooling Department during April would be accounted for in the same way as materials used in the Mixing Department. All other procedures and schedules illustrated in the Mixing Department example would be used again for the Cooling Department. See the special problem at the end of this chapter for the accounting treatment of the Cooling Department.

Zarycki Manufacturing Company
Mixing Department
Process Cost Analysis
For the Month Ended April 30, 19xx

1a. Schedule of Equivalent Production

Units—Stage of Completion	Units to Be Accounted For	Equivalent Units: Materials Costs	Equivalent Units: Conversion Costs
Beginning inventory	1,450	1,450	1,450
Units started and completed in this period	53,350	53,350	53,350
Ending inventory—units started but not completed in this period	2,250		
(Materials—100% complete)		2,250	
(Conversion costs—60% complete)			1,350 (60% of 2,250)
Totals	57,050	57,050	56,150

1b. Unit Cost Analysis Schedule

	Total Costs: Costs from Beginning Inventory	Total Costs: Costs from Current Period	Total Costs: Total Costs to Be Accounted For	÷	Equivalent Unit Costs: Equivalent Units	=	Equivalent Unit Costs: Cost per Equivalent Unit
Materials	$13,050	$488,990	$502,040		57,050		$ 8.80
Conversion costs	1,760	278,990	280,750		56,150		5.00
Totals	$14,810	$767,980	$782,790				$13.80

1c. Cost Summary Schedule

	Cost of Goods Transferred to Cooling Department	Cost of Ending Work in Process Inventory
Beginning inventory		
1,450 units × $13.80 per unit	$ 20,010	
Units started and completed		
53,350 units × $13.80 per unit	736,230	
Ending inventory		
Materials: 2,250 units × $8.80		$19,800
Conversion costs:		
1,350 units × $5.00		6,750
Totals	$756,240	$26,550
Check on computations:		
Costs to Cooling Department	$756,240	
Cost of ending Work in Process Inventory	26,550	
Total costs accounted for (unit cost analysis schedule)	$782,790	

Chapter Review

Review of Learning Objectives

1. **Explain the role of the Work in Process Inventory account(s) in a process cost accounting system.**
   The Work in Process Inventory account is the heart of the process cost accounting system. Each production department or operating unit has its own Work in Process Inventory account. All costs charged to that department flow into this inventory account. Special analysis, using three schedules, is needed at period end to determine the costs flowing out of the account. All special analyses in process cost accounting are related to costs in the Work in Process Inventory account.

2. **Describe product flow and cost flow through a process cost accounting system.**
   Products in a process costing environment are liquids or long production runs of identical products. Therefore, products flow in a FIFO fashion (first in, first out). Once a product is started into production, it flows on to completion. Manufacturing costs are handled differently. Current costs of materials, direct labor, and factory overhead are added to costs in beginning inventory when computing unit costs. The unit costs are then assigned either to completed units or to units in ending Work in Process Inventory.

3. **Compute equivalent production for situations with and without units in the beginning Work in Process Inventory.**
   The number of equivalent units is found with the aid of a schedule of equivalent production. Units worked on during the period are classified as being: (a) in beginning inventory (started last period and completed this period); (b) started and completed this period; *or* (c) started this period and still in process at period end. A percentage of completion data is used to compute equivalent units separately for materials and conversion costs.

4. **Compute product unit cost for a specific time period (unit cost analysis schedule).**
   Unit costs are found with the aid of a unit cost analysis schedule. Materials costs for units in beginning inventory and costs for the current period are added together. The same is done for conversion costs. Next, the total cost of materials is divided by the equivalent unit amount for materials. The same procedure is followed for conversion costs. Then, unit cost for materials and unit cost for conversion costs are added to reach total unit cost.

5. **Prepare a cost summary schedule that assigns costs to units completed and transferred out of the department during the period, and find the ending Work in Process Inventory balance.**
   The first part of the cost summary schedule helps you to compute costs assigned to units completed and transferred out during the period. This part is done in two steps: (a) Units in beginning inventory are assigned a full share of production costs. (b) Units started and completed during the current period are also assigned a full share of production costs. The total of these two calculations represents costs attached to units completed and transferred out during the period. The second part of the cost summary schedule assigns costs to units still in process at period end. Unit costs for materials and conversion costs are multiplied by their respective equivalent units. The total

of these two dollar amounts represents the ending Work in Process Inventory balance for the period.

6. **Make the journal entry(ies) needed to transfer costs of completed units out of the Work in Process Inventory account.**
   The first part of the cost summary schedule is completed (the part that assigns costs to units completed and transferred out during the period). Then, a journal entry should be prepared to transfer these costs out of the Work in Process Inventory account. A credit is made to the inventory account for the whole amount. The debit can be either to Finished Goods Inventory or to another Work in Process Inventory account, depending on the network of production departments in the process.

Special Review Problem: Costs Transferred In

This problem reviews the three-schedule analysis used in process costing. It also introduces two new situations common in process costing.

1. **Transferred-in costs.** Accounting for the second in a series of Work in Process Inventory accounts is much like accounting for the first department's costs. The only difference is that instead of accounting for current materials costs, you are dealing with *costs transferred in* during the period. All procedures used to account for costs transferred in are exactly the same as those used for materials costs and units. *When accounting for costs and units transferred in, treat them as you would materials added at the beginning of the process.*
2. **Rounding of numerical answers.** Unlike the problems discussed so far in this chapter, most real-world unit costs do not work out to even-numbered dollars and cents. The concept of rounding helps deal with this problem. Remember these three simple rules: (a) Round off all unit cost computations to three decimal places. (b) Round off cost summary data to the nearest dollar. (c) On the cost summary schedule, any difference caused by rounding should be added to or subtracted from the amount being transferred out of the department before the journal entry is prepared.

The purpose of this review problem is to illustrate the accounting approach for the second in a series of production departments and to show how to use cost rounding. We will go on with the example of the Zarycki Manufacturing Company's Cooling Department. Operating data for the Cooling Department for April 19xx are shown below. No new materials are added in this department. Only conversion costs are added in the cooling process.

Beginning Work in Process Inventory		
Units (40% complete)		2,100 liters
Costs: Transferred-in	$ 29,200	
Conversion costs	2,654	
Ending Work in Process Inventory		
All units 60% complete		
April operations		
Units transferred-in		54,800 liters
Costs: Transferred-in	$756,240	
Conversion costs	172,130	
Units completed and transferred to Finished Goods Inventory		54,450 liters

Required

1. Using good form, prepare: (a) a schedule of equivalent production; (b) a unit cost analysis schedule; and (c) a cost summary schedule.
2. From the cost summary schedule, prepare the journal entry to transfer costs of completed units for April to Finished Goods Inventory.

Answer to Special Review Problem

1. Before doing the three-schedule analysis, you should first analyze the unit information, just as before.

Units started and completed:		
	Units completed and transferred (given)	54,450 liters
Less:	Units in beginning inventory (given)	2,100 liters
Equals:	Units started and completed	52,350 liters
Units in ending Work in Process Inventory:		
	Units transferred in during April (given)	54,800 liters
Less:	Units started and completed (above)	52,350 liters
Equals:	Units in ending inventory	2,450 liters

With this unit information you can then prepare the three schedules below and on the following page.

Zarycki Manufacturing Company
Cooling Department
Process Cost Analysis
For the Month Ended April 30, 19xx

1a. Schedule of Equivalent Production

Units—Stage of Completion	Units to Be Accounted For	Equivalent Units: Transferred In	Equivalent Units: Conversion Costs
Beginning inventory—units completed in this period	2,100	2,100	2,100
Units started and completed in this period	52,350	52,350	52,350
Ending inventory—units started but not completed in this period	2,450		
(Transferred-in costs—100% complete)		2,450	
(Conversion costs—60% complete)			1,470
Totals	56,900	56,900	55,920

1b. Unit Cost Analysis Schedule

	Total Costs				Equivalent Unit Costs		
	Costs from Beginning Inventory	Costs from Current Period	Total Costs to Be Accounted For	÷	Equivalent Units	=	Cost per Equivalent Unit
Transferred-in costs	$29,200	$756,240	$785,440		56,900		$13.804*
Conversion costs	2,654	172,130	174,784		55,920		3.126*
Totals	$31,854	$928,370	$960,224				$16.930

1c. Cost Summary Schedule

	Cost of Goods Transferred to Finished Goods Inventory	Cost of Ending Work in Process Inventory
Beginning inventory		
2,100 units × $16.930 per unit	$ 35,553	
Units started and completed		
52,350 units × $16.930 per unit	886,286†	
Ending inventory		
Transferred-in costs: 2,450 units × $13.804		$33,820†
Conversion costs: 1,470 units × $3.126		4,595†
Totals	$921,839	$38,415
Check on computations:		
Costs to Finished Goods Inventory	$921,839	
Costs in ending Work in Process Inventory	38,415	
Error caused by rounding—subtract from costs transferred to Finished Goods Inventory	(30)	
Total costs to be accounted for (unit cost analysis schedule)	$960,224	

*Answer is rounded to three decimal places. †Answer is affected by using rounded unit cost amounts.

2. The costs of completed units for April are now ready to be transferred from the Cooling Department to Finished Goods Inventory. The proper journal entry is:

Finished Goods Inventory ($921,839 − $30)	921,809	
Work in Process—Cooling Department		921,809
To record the transfer of cost of completed units in April from the Cooling Department to Finished Goods Inventory		

Chapter Assignments

Questions

1. What types of production are suited to a process cost accounting system?
2. "For job order costing, *one* Work in Process Inventory account is used. However, in process costing there are often *several* Work in Process Inventory accounts in use." Explain.
3. Define *equivalent units.*
4. Why do actual unit data need to be changed to equivalent unit data for product costing purposes in a process costing system?
5. Define *conversion costs.* Why is this concept used in process costing computations?
6. What are the three schedules used in process costing analysis?
7. Why is it easier to compute equivalent units without units, rather than with them, in beginning inventory?
8. What are the purposes of the unit cost analysis schedule?
9. What two important dollar amounts come from the cost summary schedule? How do they relate to the year-end financial statements?
10. Describe how to check the accuracy of results in a cost summary schedule.
11. What is the significance of the journal entry used to transfer costs of completed products out of the Work in Process Inventory account?
12. What is a transferred-in cost? Where does it come from? Why is it handled like materials added at the beginning of the process?

Classroom Exercises

Exercise 18-1. Work in Process Inventory Accounts: Total Unit Costs
(L.O. 4)

Scientists at Brooks Laboratories, Inc., have just perfected a liquid substance called D.K. Rid, which dissolves tooth decay without the dentist needing to use the infamous drill. The substance, which is generated from a complex process using five departments, is very costly. Cost and equivalent unit data for the latest week are as follows (units are in ounces):

	Materials Costs		Conversion Costs	
Dept.	Dollars	Equivalent Units	Dollars	Equivalent Units
A	$25,000	4,000	$34,113	4,110
B	23,423	3,970	26,130	4,020
C	48,204	4,120	20,972	4,280
D	—	—	22,086	4,090
E	—	—	15,171	3,890

From the data above, compute (a) the unit cost for each department and (b) the total unit cost of producing an ounce of D.K. Rid.

Exercise 18-2. Process Cost Flow Diagram
(L.O. 2)

Benz Paint Company uses a process costing system to analyze the costs incurred in making paint. Production of Quality Brand starts in the Blending Department, where materials SM and HA are added to a water base. The solution is heated to 70° Celsius and then transferred to the Mixing Department, where it is mixed for one hour. Then, the paint goes to the Settling/Canning Department, where it is cooled and put into 4-liter cans. Direct labor and factory overhead charges are incurred uniformly throughout each part of the process.

In diagram form, show product flow for Quality Brand paint.

Exercise 18-3. Equivalent Units: No Beginning Inventories
(L.O. 3)

Slumpstone bricks are produced by the Strefeler Stone Company. Although it has only been operating for twelve months, the company already enjoys a good reputation for quality bricks. During its first year materials for 460,500 bricks were put into production, and 456,900 bricks were completed and transferred to Finished Goods Inventory. The remaining bricks were still in process at year end, 65 percent completed. In their process costing system, all materials are added at the beginning of the process. Conversion costs are incurred uniformly throughout the production process.

From the information provided, prepare a schedule of equivalent production for the year. Use the average costing approach.

Exercise 18-4. Equivalent Units: Beginning Inventories
(L.O. 3)

Harwood Enterprises makes Sweetwater Shampoo for professional hair stylists. On January 1, 19x7, 18,400 liters of shampoo were in process, 70 percent complete as to conversion costs and 100 percent complete as to materials. During the year, 212,500 liters of materials were put into production. Data for Work in Process Inventory on December 31, 19x7, were as follows: shampoo, 7,500 liters; stage of completion, 60 percent of conversion costs and 100 percent of materials content.

From this information, prepare a schedule of equivalent production for the year. Use the average costing approach.

Exercise 18-5. Equivalent Units: Beginning Inventories
(L.O. 3)

The Lucas Company, a major producer of liquid vitamins, uses a process cost accounting system. During January, 65,000 gallons of Material CIA and 20,000 gallons of Material CMA were put into production. Beginning Work in Process Inventory was 27,500 gallons of product, 80 percent complete as to labor and overhead. Ending Work in Process Inventory was made up of 18,000 gallons, 25 percent complete as to conversion costs. All materials were added at the beginning of the process.

From the above information, prepare a schedule of equivalent production for January, 19xx. Use the average costing approach.

Exercise 18-6. Unit Cost Determination
(L.O. 4)

Guide Kitchenwares, Inc., manufactures heavy-duty cookware. Production has just been completed for July. Beginning Work in Process Inventory was (a) materials, $20,200 and (b) conversion costs, $26,800. Costs of materials used in July were $128,057. Conversion costs for the month were $152,858. During July, 45,190 units were started and completed. A schedule of equivalent production for July has already been prepared. It shows 54,910 equivalent units as to conversion costs and 55,450 equivalent units as to materials.

With this information, prepare a unit cost analysis schedule for July, 19xx. Use the average costing approach.

Exercise 18-7. Cost Summary Schedule (L.O. 5)

The Bjorn Danish Bakery, which produces its world famous "Kringle" coffee bread, uses a process cost system for internal record-keeping purposes. Production for August was as follows: (a) Beginning inventory of 14,900 units; costs attached from the preceding period were materials at $7,400 and conversion costs at $6,700. (b) Units started and completed totaled 124,100 Kringles during the month. (c) Ending Work in Process Inventory was: materials, 9,000 units, 100 percent complete as to materials and 80 percent complete as to conversion costs. (d) Unit costs per equivalent unit have been computed for August: Materials, 50¢; Conversion Costs, 65¢.

Using the information given, compute the cost of goods transferred to Finished Goods Inventory, the cost of ending Work in Process Inventory, and the total costs to be accounted for. Use the average costing approach.

Exercise 18-8. Cost Transfer: Journal Entry Required (L.O. 3, 6)

The following cost summary schedule was prepared for the La Cava Paste Company for the year ended July 31, 19xx.

1. From the information given, prepare the journal entry for July 31, 19xx.
2. Draw up the company's schedule of equivalent production. Assume that materials are added at the beginning of the process.

La Cava Paste Company
Cost Summary Schedule
For the Year Ended July 31, 19xx

	Cost of Goods Transferred to Finished Goods Inventory	Cost of Ending Work in Process Inventory
Beginning inventory		
9,140 units × $2.60	$ 23,764	
Units started and completed		
74,960 units × $2.60	194,896	
Ending inventory		
Materials: 8,400 units × $1.40		$11,760
Conversion costs: 4,200 units × $1.20		5,040
Totals	$218,660	$16,800

Interpreting Accounting Information

Internal Management Information: Tennant Tire Corporation (L.O. 4)

Tennant Tire Corporation makes several lines of automobile and truck tires. The company operates in a competitive marketplace, so it relies heavily on cost data from its process cost accounting system. It uses this information to set prices for its most competitive tires. The company's "Blue Radial" line has lost some of its market share during each of the past four years. Management believes price breaks allowed by the three competitors are the major reason for the decline in sales.

The company controller, Linda Sugarman, has been asked to review the product costing information that supports price decisions on the Blue Radial line. In preparing her report, she collected the following accurate data related to 19x8, the last full year of operations.

	Units	Dollars
Equivalent units: Materials costs	88,540	
Conversion costs	86,590	
Manufacturing costs: Materials		$1,981,050.00
Direct labor		770,410.00
Factory overhead applied		1,540,820.00
Unit cost data: Materials		23.50
Conversion costs		27.00
Work in Process Inventory:		
Beginning (30% complete)	4,240	
Ending (50% complete)	6,900	

There were 80,400 units started and completed during 19x8. The costs attached to the year's beginning Work in Process Inventory were materials costs, $99,640, and conversion costs, $26,700.

Sugarman found that little spoilage had occurred. The proper cost allowance for spoilage was included in the predetermined overhead rate of $2.00 per direct labor dollar. Examination of direct labor cost, however, revealed that $173,180 was charged twice to the production account, the second time in error.

So far in 19x9 Blue Radial has been selling for $91 per tire. This price was based on the 19x8 unit cost data plus 50 percent to cover operating costs and 20 percent of the sum of these two cost factors for profit. During 19x9 the three competitors' prices have been about $85 per tire.

In the company's process costing system, all materials are added at the beginning of the process, and conversion costs are incurred uniformly throughout.

Required

1. Point out how such a cost-charging error could affect the company.
2. Prepare a revised unit cost analysis schedule for 19x8. Use the average costing approach.
3. What should have been the minimum selling price per tire in 19x9?
4. Suggest to the controller ways of preventing such errors in the future.

Problem Set A

Problem 18A-1. Process Costing: No Beginning Inventories
(L.O. 3, 4, 5, 6)

Winter Industries specializes in making "Slik," a high-moisture, low-alkaline wax used to protect and preserve skis. Production of a new, improved brand of Slik began January 1, 19xx. For this new product, Materials A14 and C9 are introduced at the beginning of the production process along with a wax-based product. During January, 260 pounds of A14, 820 pounds of C9, and 5,600 pounds of wax base were used at a cost of $10,400, $8,460, and $11,200, respectively. Direct labor of $12,976 and factory overhead costs of $25,952 were incurred uniformly throughout the month. By January 31, 19xx, 6,200 pounds of Slik had been completed and transferred to Finished Goods Inventory. Much of the already finished product had been shipped to customers. Since no spoilage occurred, the pounds not yet finished stayed in production, on the average 60 percent completed.

Required

1. Using proper form, prepare: (a) a schedule of equivalent production; (b) a unit cost analysis schedule; and (c) a cost summary schedule for Winter Industries for January.
2. From the cost summary schedule, prepare the journal entry to transfer costs of completed units for January to Finished Goods Inventory.

Problem 18A-2. Process Costing: With Beginning Inventories
(L.O. 3, 4, 5, 6)

Many of the products made by Baucom Plastics Company are standard replacement parts for telephones and involve long production runs. One of these parts, a wire clip, is produced continuously. During April materials for 50,500 units of wire clips were put into production (1 unit contains 1,000 clips). Total cost of materials used during April was $2,273,000. Direct labor costs for the month totaled $1,135,000. Factory overhead is applied to production using a rate of 150% of direct labor costs. Beginning Work in Process Inventory contained 3,200 units, 100 percent complete as to materials and 50 percent complete as to conversion costs. Costs attached to the units in beginning inventory totaled $232,000, including $143,500 in materials costs. There were 2,500 units in ending Work in Process Inventory; all materials have been added, and the units are 80 percent complete as to conversion costs.

Required

1. Using good form, and assuming an average costing approach and no loss due to spoilage, prepare: (a) a schedule of equivalent production; (b) a unit cost analysis schedule; and (c) a cost summary schedule.
2. From the cost summary schedule, prepare a journal entry to transfer costs of units completed in April to Finished Goods Inventory.

Problem 18A-3. Process Costing: With Beginning Inventories
(L.O. 3, 4, 5, 6)

Lasciandro Liquid Extracts Company produces a line of fruit extracts for use in producing such homemade products as wines (grapes), jams and jellies, pies, and meat sauces. Fruits are introduced into the production process in pounds, and the product unit emerges in quarts. (Note: 1 pound of input equals 1 quart of output.) On June 1, 19x9, there were 6,250 units in process; all materials had been added, and the units were 90 percent completed as to conversion costs. There were $12,810 in materials costs and $7,319 in conversion costs attached to the beginning Work in Process Inventory. During June, 50,300 pounds of fruit were added: apples, 20,500 pounds, costing $36,900; grapes, 18,600 pounds, costing $40,920; and bananas, 11,200 pounds, costing $28,125. Direct labor for the month of June totaled $12,662, and overhead costs were applied at the rate of 400 percent of direct labor dollars. On June 30, 7,400 units of work remained in process; all materials had been added, and 70 percent of conversion costs had been incurred.

Required

1. Using good form and an average costing approach, prepare the following schedules for June: (a) a schedule of equivalent production; (b) a unit cost analysis schedule; and (c) a cost summary schedule.
2. From the cost summary schedule, prepare a journal entry to transfer the costs of completed units to Finished Goods Inventory.

Problem 18A-4. Process Costing: One Process/ Two Time Periods (L.O. 3, 4, 5, 6)

Cassagio Laboratories produces liquid detergents that leave no soap film. All elements are biodegradable. The production process has been automated so the product can now be produced in one operation instead of separately going through heating, mixing, and cooling. All materials are added at the beginning of the process, and conversion costs are incurred uniformly throughout the process. Operating data for July and August are shown below.

	July	August
Beginning Work in Process Inventory		
Units (pounds)	4,650	?
Costs: Materials costs	$ 4,750	?
Conversion costs	1,580	?
Production during the period		
Units started (pounds)	63,000	65,600
Current period costs:		
Materials costs	$64,253	$68,346.00
Conversion costs	54,367	54,867.50
Ending Work in Process Inventory		
Units (pounds)	6,100	7,200

Beginning Work in Process Inventory was 40 percent complete as to conversion costs, and point of completion information for ending work in process inventories was: July, 70 percent; August, 60 percent. Assume that loss from spoilage and evaporation was negligible.

Required

1. Using good form and an average costing approach, prepare the following schedules for July: (a) a schedule of equivalent production; (b) a unit cost analysis schedule; and (c) a cost summary schedule.
2. From the cost summary schedule, prepare a journal entry to transfer costs of completed units in July to Finished Goods Inventory.
3. Repeat **1** and **2** for August.

Problem 18A-5. Process Costing: With Beginning Inventories/ Two Departments (L.O. 3, 4, 5, 6)

David Ganz Enterprises produces dozens of products linked to the housing construction industry. Its most successful product is called "Sta-Soft" plaster, a mixture that is easy to apply and is used to finish off wall surfaces after dry-wall sheets have been positioned. Its unique quality is that the substance never hardens until it comes into contact with the dry wall. Sta-Soft is produced using three processes: blending, conditioning, and canning. All materials are introduced at the beginning of the blending operation, except for the can, which is added at the end in the final canning operation. Direct labor and factory overhead costs are applied to the products uniformly throughout each process. Production and cost information for September 19x8 are summarized below.

Blending Department. Beginning Work in Process Inventory contained 11,460 pounds of Sta-Soft, 60 percent complete as to conversion costs. There were $38,900 assigned to these units, $28,600 of which were for materials costs. During September, 121,140 pounds of materials were put into production, costing $302,900. Direct labor for the month was $88,210, and an equal amount of factory overhead costs were charged to the work in process. Ending Work in Process Inventory was made up of 16,240 pounds, 50 percent complete as to conversion costs.

Conditioning Department. During September, 116,360 pounds of Sta-Soft were received from the Blending Department. Beginning Work in Process Inventory consisted of 5,250 pounds, costing $30,250 ($21,000 were transferred-in costs). Direct labor costs incurred during September totaled $115,625, and factory overhead costs applied were $138,751. Ending Work in Process Inventory contained 4,450 pounds, 60 percent complete as to conversion costs.

Assume there was no measurable loss due to spoilage or waste in the month.

Required

1. Using proper form and an average costing approach, prepare the following schedules for the Blending Department for September: (a) a schedule of equivalent production; (b) a unit cost analysis schedule; and (c) a cost summary schedule.
2. From the cost summary schedule, prepare the journal entry needed to transfer costs of completed units for September from the Blending Department to the Conditioning Department.
3. Prepare the same schedules for the Conditioning Department that were requested in **1.**
4. Prepare the journal entry needed to transfer costs of completed units from the Conditioning Department to the Canning Department.

Problem Set B

Problem 18B-1. Process Costing: No Beginning Inventories
(L.O. 3, 4, 5, 6)

The Solinko Chewing Gum Company, which produces several flavors of bubble gum, began production of a new kumquat-flavored gum on June 1, 19xx. Two basic materials, gum base and kumquat-flavored sweetener, are blended at the beginning of the process. Direct labor and factory overhead costs are incurred uniformly throughout the blending process. During June, 270,000 kilograms of gum base and 540,000 kilograms of kumquat-flavored sweetener were used at costs of $324,000 and $162,000, respectively. Direct labor charges were $720,620, and factory overhead costs applied during June were $368,020. The ending Work in Process Inventory was 43,200 kilograms. All materials have been added to these units, and 25 percent of the conversion costs have been assigned.

Required

1. Using proper form, prepare: (a) a schedule of equivalent production; (b) a unit cost analysis schedule; and (c) a cost summary schedule for the Blending Department for June.
2. From the cost summary schedule, prepare the journal entry to transfer costs of completed units for June from the Blending Department to the Forming and Packing Department.

Problem 18B-2. Process Costing: With Beginning Inventories
(L.O. 3, 4, 5, 6)

O'Hara Food Products, Inc., makes high-vitamin, calorie-packed wafers used by professional sports teams to supply quick energy to players. Production of these thin white wafers is through a continuous product flow process. The company, which uses a process costing system based on the average costing approach, recently purchased several automated machines so the wafers could be produced in a single department. The materials are all added at the beginning of the process. The cost for the machine operator's labor and production-related overhead are incurred uniformly throughout the process.

In February a total of 115,600 liters of materials were put into production; cost of the materials was $294,780. Two liters of materials are used to produce one unit of output (one unit = 144 wafers). Labor costs for February were $60,530. Factory overhead was $181,590. Beginning Work in Process Inventory on February 1 was 28,000 units. The units were 100 percent complete as to materials and 40 percent as to conversion costs. The total cost of beginning inventory was $126,420, with $64,220 assigned to the cost of materials. The ending Work in Process Inventory of 24,000 units is fully complete as to materials, but only 30 percent complete as to conversion costs.

Required

1. Using good form and assuming no loss due to spoilage, prepare: (a) a schedule of equivalent production; (b) a unit cost analysis schedule, rounding off unit cost computations to *four* decimal places; and (c) a cost summary schedule.
2. From the cost summary schedule, prepare a journal entry to transfer costs of completed units in February to Finished Goods Inventory.

Problem 18B-3. Process Costing: With Beginning Inventories
(L.O. 3, 4, 5, 6)

Ezckannagha Bottling Company makes and sells several types of soft drinks. Materials (sugar syrup and artificial flavoring) are added at the beginning of production in the Mixing Department. Direct labor and factory overhead costs are applied to products throughout the process. The following information is for the Citrus Punch product for August. Beginning Work in Process Inventory (60 percent complete) was 4,800 liters. Ending inventory (50 percent complete) was 7,200 liters. Production data showed 180,000 liters started. A total of 177,600 liters was completed and transferred to the Bottling Department. Beginning inventory data showed $1,200 for materials and $1,152 for conversion costs. Current period costs were $45,000 for materials and $71,328 for conversion costs.

Required

1. Using good form and an average costing approach, prepare the following schedules for the Mixing Department for August: (a) a schedule of equivalent production; (b) a unit cost analysis schedule; and (c) a cost summary schedule.
2. From the cost summary schedule, prepare a journal entry to transfer the cost of completed units to the Bottling Department.

Problem 18B-4. Process Costing: One Process/ Two Time Periods
(L.O. 3, 4, 5, 6)

The Kockentiedt Natural Products Company, which owns thousands of beehives, produces organic honey for sale to health food stores. No materials other than the honey from the hives are used. The production operation is a simple one in which the impure honey is added at the beginning of the process. A series of filterings follows, leading to a pure finished product. Production data for April and May are shown below.

	April	May
Beginning Work in Process Inventory		
Units (liters)	14,200	?
Costs: Materials	$ 17,600	?
Conversion costs	23,860	
Production during the period		
Units started (liters)	388,000	410,000
Current period costs:		
Materials	$ 481,128	$ 491,008
Conversion costs	1,046,748	1,137,304
Ending Work in Process Inventory		
Units (liters)	24,800	33,800

For the incomplete inventory figures, assume that all materials have already been added. Beginning inventory for April was 60 percent complete as to conversion costs, and ending inventory was 20 percent complete. Ending inventory for May was 30 percent complete as to conversion costs. Costs of labor and factory overhead are incurred uniformly throughout the filtering process. Assume there was no loss from spoilage or evaporation.

Required

1. Using good form and an average costing approach, prepare the following schedules for April: (a) a schedule of equivalent production; (b) a unit cost analysis schedule; and (c) a cost summary schedule.
2. From the cost summary schedule, prepare a journal entry to transfer costs of completed units in April to Finished Goods Inventory.
3. Repeat **1** and **2** for May.

Problem 18B-5. Process Costing: With Beginning Inventories/ Two Departments
(L.O. 3, 4, 5, 6)

Canned fruits and vegetables are the main products of Culley/Grove Foods, Inc. When canned peaches are being prepared, all basic materials go in at the beginning of the Mixing Department's process. When mixed, the solution goes to the Cooking Department. There, it is heated to 100° Celsius and left to simmer for twenty minutes. When cooled, the mixture goes to the Canning Department for final processing. Throughout these operations direct labor and factory overhead costs are incurred uniformly. No materials are added in the Cooking Department.

Cost data and other information for January are shown below.

Production Cost Data	**Materials**	**Conversion Costs**
Mixing Department		
Beginning inventory	$ 28,800	$ 4,800
Current Period Costs	432,000	182,400
	Transferred-in Costs	**Conversion Costs**
Cooking Department		
Beginning Inventory	$ 63,000	$ 13,320
Current Period Costs	?	671,040
Work in Process Inventories		
Beginning Inventories:		
Mixing Department (40% complete)		12,000 liters
Cooking Department (20% complete)		18,000 liters
Ending Inventories:		
Mixing Department (70% complete)		16,000 liters
Cooking Department (80% complete)		20,000 liters

Unit Production Data	**Mixing Department**	**Cooking Department**
Units started during January	180,000 liters	176,000 liters
Units transferred out during January	176,000 liters	174,000 liters

Assume that no spoilage or evaporation loss occurred during January. (Before completing this problem, refer to the Special Problem on pages 685–687.)

Required

1. Using proper form and an average costing approach, prepare the following schedules for the Mixing Department for January: (a) a schedule of equivalent production; (b) a unit cost analysis schedule; and (c) a cost summary schedule.
2. From the cost summary schedule, prepare the journal entry to transfer costs of completed units for January from the Mixing to the Cooking Department.
3. Prepare the same schedules requested in **1** for the Cooking Department.
4. Prepare the journal entry to transfer costs of completed units in January from the Cooking Department to the Canning Department.

Management Decision Case

CT&H Cola, Inc.
(L.O. 3, 4)

For the past four years, three companies have dominated the soft drink industry, controlling 85 percent of market share. CT&H Cola, Inc., ranks second nationally in soft drink sales with gross revenues last year of $27,450,000. Management wants to introduce a new low-calorie drink called Slimit Cola.

Soft drinks at CT&H are completely processed in a single department. All materials are added at the beginning of the process. Fluids are bottled at the end of the process into bottles costing one cent each. Direct labor and factory overhead costs are applied uniformly throughout the process.

Corporate controller Robert Buttery believes that costs for the new cola will be similar to those for the company's Cola Plus drink. Last year the following data related to Cola Plus:

	Units	**Costs**
Work in Process Inventory		
January 1, 19x8[1]	12,840	
Materials Costs		$ 10,280
Conversion Costs		3,876
December 31, 19x8[2]	17,800	
Materials Costs		14,240
Conversion Costs		7,476
Units Started During the Year	918,760	
Costs for 19x8		
Liquid Materials Added		735,000
Direct Labor		344,925
Factory Overhead Applied		206,955
Bottles		219,312

[1] 50% complete [2] 70% complete Note: Each unit is a 24-bottle case

Variable operating and selling costs are $1.10 per unit. Fixed operating and selling costs are assigned to products at the rate of $.50 per unit. The two major competitors have already introduced a diet cola into the marketplace. Company A's product sells for $4.00 per unit; Company B's, for $3.95.

All costs in 19x9 are expected to increase by 10 percent over 19x8 costs. The company tries to earn a profit of at least 12 percent over cost.

Required

1. What factors should be considered in setting a selling price for Slimit Cola?
2. Using the average costing approach, compute (a) the total production cost per unit and (b) the total cost per unit of Cola Plus for 19x8.
3. What is the expected total cost per unit of Slimit Cola for 19x9?
4. Recommend a unit price range for selling Slimit Cola and give your reason(s).

CALDWELL NEEDLES ANDERSON

PART SIX MANAGEMENT PLANNING AND CONTROL

Part Five introduced you to the field of management accounting, focusing on the development of useful cost information for product costing and management reporting purposes. Emphasis was placed on the first of three aspects of management accounting: management's need for product or service costing information.

In Part Six we analyze the second aspect of the field of management accounting, management's need for data used for operations planning and control. Special concepts and techniques are used for cost planning and control. When integrated with an existing accounting system, these concepts and techniques are used to develop reports that facilitate budgetary control activities.

Chapter 19 introduces cost planning and control, specifically focusing on cost behavior patterns, cost-volume-profit relationships, and cost allocation problems and techniques.

Chapter 20 explains the responsibility accounting system and introduces the principles of performance evaluation. The evaluations of managers of a cost/expense center, a profit center, and an investment center are illustrated.

Chapter 21 uses the cost planning tools described in Chapters 19 and 20 to implement the planning function of the budgetary control process. Emphasis is placed on budgeting principles and preparation, including the preparation of a cash budget.

Chapters 22 and 23 conclude your study of the budgetary control process. In Chapter 22, the standard costing system is introduced, and materials and labor variances are analyzed. Chapter 23 continues your study of standard costing by analyzing the overhead variances and accounting for their disposition. Evaluating employee performance using variances is discussed.

CHAPTER 19 COST-VOLUME-PROFIT ANALYSIS AND COST ALLOCATION

LEARNING OBJECTIVES

1. Define and classify variable costs, semivariable costs, and fixed costs.
2. Compute the break-even point in units of output and in sales dollars.
3. Use contribution margin analysis to estimate levels of sales that will produce planned profits.
4. State the role of cost objectives in the cost allocation process.
5. Assign costs of supporting service functions to production departments.
6. Allocate common costs to joint products.

Cost planning and control are vital to the ongoing life of a company. Good cost planning results in efficient production, and cost control contributes to profits. Knowledge of cost behavior patterns, cost-volume-profit relationships, and cost allocation procedures help a company achieve good cost planning and control. Cost allocation techniques are used not only to assign costs after they have been incurred, but also to plan future activities. After studying this chapter, you should be able to meet the learning objectives listed on the left.

Cost Behavior

Before estimating a future cost or preparing a budget, a manager must know the basic behavior patterns of costs. We can define **cost behavior** as the way costs respond to changes in activity or volume. To understand cost behavior, we need to look at the basic characteristics and the accounting classifications of costs. This knowledge is useful for predicting future costs and analyzing past cost performance.

Variable and Fixed Costs

Almost any cost can be classified as either a variable cost or a fixed cost. Some cost totals increase or decrease along with increases or decreases in productive output. Other costs remain constant. (Although we focus on cost behavior as it relates to production, you should realize that some costs are *not* measured in terms of production. Sales commissions, for example, depend on the number of units sold, or total sales revenue, not on production measures.)

Total costs that change in direct proportion to changes in productive output (or any other volume measure) are called **variable costs**. To see how variable costs work, consider the example of an automaker. Each new car has four tires, and each tire costs $38. Thus, the total cost of tires (four tires per automobile) is $152 for one automobile, $304 for two, $456 for three, $608 for four, $760 for five, $1,520 for ten, and $15,200 for one hundred. In the production of automobiles, the total cost of tires is a variable cost. On a per unit basis, however,

OBJECTIVE 1
Define and classify variable costs, semivariable costs, and fixed costs

a variable cost remains constant. In this case the cost of tires per automobile is $152 ($38 × 4) whether one car or one hundred cars are produced.

In discussing variable costs, we assume that there is a linear relationship between cost and volume. Figure 19-1 shows this relationship. In this example, each unit of output requires $2.50 of labor cost. Total labor costs grow in direct proportion to the increase in units of output.

But not all variable costs behave this way. Electricity rates per kilowatt hour, for instance, go down as the use of electricity goes up. Although variable in some ways, this cost pattern is more like that of semivariable costs, which are discussed in the next section of this chapter. For now, we will assume that variable costs have a linear relationship to volume, as shown in Figure 19-1.

Fixed costs behave in an entirely different manner. Total **fixed costs** remain constant within a relevant range of volume or activity. A **relevant range** of activity is the range in which actual operations are likely to occur. Supervisory salaries are a good example of a fixed cost. Assume that a local manufacturing company needs one supervisor for an eight-hour work shift. Production can range from 0 to 500,000 units per month per shift. The supervisor's salary is $2,000 per month, and the relevant range is 0 to 500,000 units. The cost behavior analysis is as follows:

Units of Output	Total Supervisory Salaries per Month
100,000	$2,000
200,000	2,000
300,000	2,000
400,000	2,000
500,000	2,000
600,000	4,000

Figure 19-1.
A Common Cost Behavior Pattern: Variable Cost

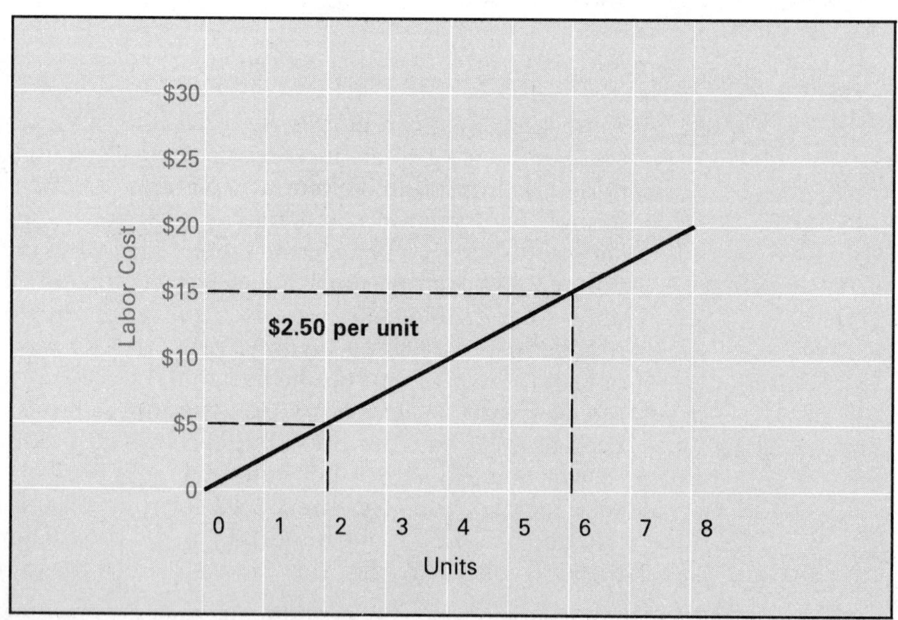

As noted, a maximum of 500,000 units can be produced per shift. So any output over 500,000 units calls for another work shift and another supervisor.

On a per unit basis, fixed costs go down as volume goes up. In our example, supervisory costs per unit would change as follows:

Volume of Activity	Cost per Unit
100,000 units	\$2,000/100,000 = \$.02
200,000 units	\$2,000/200,000 = \$.01
300,000 units	\$2,000/300,000 = \$.0067
400,000 units	\$2,000/400,000 = \$.005
500,000 units	\$2,000/500,000 = \$.004
600,000 units	**\$4,000**/600,000 = **\$.0067**

The per unit cost increased at the 600,000 unit level because volume was not within the relevant range and another supervisor was hired.

Total fixed costs stay the same for all levels of activity within the relevant range. A graphic view of this fixed overhead cost is shown in Figure 19-2. Fixed overhead costs of \$2,000 are needed for the first 500,000 units of production. Fixed costs hold steady at \$2,000 for any level of output within the relevant range. But output over 500,000 units calls for another supervisor, and the cost level jumps to \$4,000.

Semivariable and Mixed Costs

Some costs cannot be classified as either variable or fixed. A **semivariable cost** has both variable cost and fixed cost components. Part of the cost is fixed, and part changes with the volume of output. Telephone expense is an example. Monthly telephone charges are made up of a service

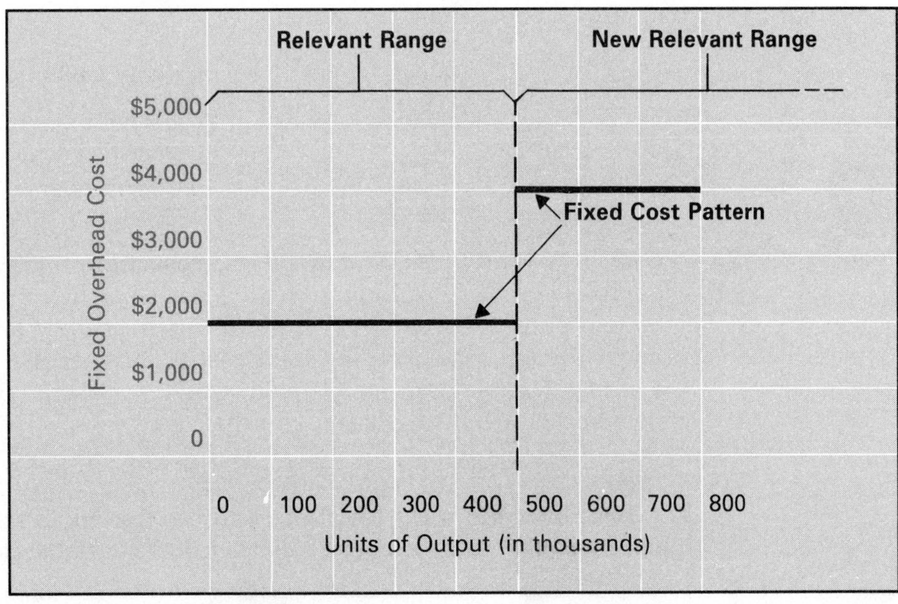

Figure 19-2. A Common Cost Behavior Pattern: Fixed Cost

charge plus extra charges for extra telephones and long-distance calls. The service charge and the cost of extra telephones are fixed costs. But the long-distance charges are variable because they depend on monthly use.

Mixed costs are also made up of variable and fixed costs. **Mixed costs** result when more than one kind of cost is charged to the same general ledger account. The Repairs and Maintenance account is a good example of an account balance made up of mixed costs. Labor charges to this account may vary in proportion to the amount of repairs done. However, only one repair and maintenance worker may be employed on a full-time basis (a fixed cost), and extra help is hired only when needed (a variable cost). Depreciation costs for repair and maintenance machinery are also fixed costs, but costs of repair supplies depend on use. *For purposes of cost planning and control, semivariable and mixed costs must be divided into their respective variable and fixed cost parts.* They can then be grouped with other variable and fixed costs for analysis.

When dealing with semivariable or mixed costs, several methods are available to differentiate variable costs from fixed costs. The *high-low approach* is one such method. Assume the following monthly totals appeared in the Repairs and Maintenance account for the first six months of the year:

Month	Total Costs	Volume in Labor Hours
January	$1,864	1,200
February	2,008	1,400
March	2,152	1,600
April	1,936	1,300
May	1,720	1,000
June	1,792	1,100

The high-low method identifies high-cost and low-cost items, along with their respective volume levels. The amount of the changes between the high and the low items are noted.

	Cost	Activity Level
High	$2,152	1,600 labor hours
Low	1,720	1,000 labor hours
Difference	$ 432	600 labor hours

As activity went up 600 labor hours, costs rose $432. Therefore, the variable rate is $432/600 hours, or $.72 per labor hour.

To compute the fixed cost, multiply each activity level by $.72, and subtract the amount from the total cost. Thus, at the 1,600 labor hour level, total variable costs equal 1,600 × $.72 = $1,152. Total costs minus variable costs equal fixed costs. In this case:

$$\$2,152 - \$1,152 = \$1,000 \text{ (fixed costs)}$$

The same procedure can be applied to each month's figures in order to break down the entire account balance into its variable cost and fixed cost components.

Operating Capacity: Definition and Cost Influence

Operating capacity plays an important part in our study of cost behavior and in budgetary control. Operating capacity is the upper limit on production output and related costs, so it is essential information when predictions are being made. Because variable costs increase or decrease in direct proportion to expected volume or output, it is important to know what is meant by the term *operating capacity*. **Theoretical, or ideal, capacity** is the maximum productive output a department or company could reach for a given period if all machinery and equipment were operated at optimum speed without interruptions. Theoretical capacity is useful in thinking about maximum production levels. However, it has little value for day-to-day operations. No company operates at ideal capacity. **Practical capacity** is theoretical capacity reduced by normal and expected work stoppages. Production may be interrupted by machine downtime for retooling, repair and maintenance, or employee work breaks. These normal interruptions and the resulting lower output should be considered when measuring capacity.

A company seldom operates at either ideal or practical capacity. **Excess capacity**, which is extra machinery and equipment kept on hand on a standby basis, is part of practical and ideal capacity. Such extra equipment may be used when regular equipment is being repaired. Or during a slow season, a company may use only part of its equipment. Or it may work just one or two shifts instead of around the clock. Because of these circumstances normal capacity, rather than ideal or practical capacity, is often used for planning. **Normal capacity** is the average annual level of operating capacity needed to meet expected sales demands. This demand figure is adjusted for seasonal changes and for business and economic cycles. Therefore, normal capacity is a realistic measure of what *is likely* to be produced, rather than what *can* be produced, by an operating unit.

Cost-Volume-Profit Relationships

Cost behavior patterns underlie the relationship between costs, volume of output, and profit. These relationships are studied through **cost-volume-profit analysis (or C-V-P analysis)**. They are useful for predicting future operating results. A company may use C-V-P analysis as a planning tool when the sales volume is known and management needs to find out how much profit will result. Another way of planning is to begin with a target profit. Then, through C-V-P analysis a company can decide the level of sales needed to reach that profit.

For cost control purposes, C-V-P analysis is a way of measuring how well departments in the company are doing. At the end of a period, the company analyzes sales volume and related actual costs to find actual profit. It measures performance by comparing actual costs with expected costs. These expected costs are computed by applying C-V-P analysis to actual sales volume. The result is a performance report on which management can base the control of operations. This process is explained further in Chapter 21.

C-V-P Analysis: Break-even Point and Profit Planning

Cost-volume-profit analysis is based on the relationships between operating costs, sales volume, sales revenue, and target net income. Before starting C-V-P analysis, we must first classify costs as either variable costs (VC) or fixed costs (FC). Sales (S) are computed by multiplying units sold by the selling price per unit. Target net income (NI) is decided by management. The usual formula for C-V-P analysis is

$$\text{Sales revenue} = \text{variable costs} + \text{fixed costs} + \text{net income}$$

Or, more simply,

$$S = VC + FC + NI$$

If we move the variable costs (VC) and fixed costs (FC) to the left side of the equal sign and change the positive signs to negative, this same equation begins to look like the income statement:

$$S - VC - FC = NI$$

OBJECTIVE 2
Compute the break-even point in units of output and in sales dollars

Break-even Point. The **break-even point** is the point at which total revenue equals total costs incurred. Thus, it is the point at which a company begins to earn a profit. When planning new ventures or product lines, you can quickly measure the likelihood of success by finding the project's break-even point. If, for instance, break-even is 50,000 units and the total market is only 25,000, the idea should be promptly abandoned. When finding a company's or a product's break-even point, only sales (S), variable cost (VC), and fixed cost (FC) are used. There is no net income (NI) when a company breaks even. The goal is to find the level of activity at which sales revenue equals the sum of all variable and fixed costs. Break-even data can be stated in break-even sales units or break-even sales dollars. The general equations for finding the break-even point are

$$S = VC + FC \quad \text{or} \quad S - VC - FC = 0$$

An example will show how the equation can be used to find break-even units and dollars. Reed Products, Inc., makes wooden stands for portable television sets. Variable costs are \$25 per unit, and fixed costs average \$20,000 per year. Each wooden stand sells for \$45. Given this information, we can figure the break-even point for this product in sales units and dollars.

Break-even point in sales units (represented by x)

$$\begin{aligned} S &= VC + FC \\ \$45x &= \$25x + \$20,000 \\ \$20x &= \$20,000 \\ x &= 1,000 \text{ units} \end{aligned}$$

Break-even point in sales dollars

$$\$45/\text{unit} \times 1{,}000 \text{ units} = \$45{,}000$$

We can also make a rough estimate of the break-even point by using a graph. This method is less exact, but it does yield meaningful data. Figure 19-3 shows a break-even analysis for Reed Products. This standard break-even chart has five parts: (1) a horizontal axis in volume or units; (2) a vertical axis in dollars; (3) a horizontal line for the upper limit of fixed costs ($20,000); (4) a total cost line beginning at the point where the fixed cost line crosses the vertical axis and sloping upward to the right (the slope of the line depends on the variable costs per unit); and (5) a total revenue line beginning at the origin of the vertical and horizontal axes and sloping upward to the right (the slope depends on the selling price per unit). At the point where the total revenue line crosses the total cost line, revenues equal total costs. The break-even point, stated in either units or dollars of sales, can be found by extending lines from this point to the axes. As shown in Figure 19-3, Reed Products will break even when 1,000 television stands have been made and sold for $45,000 in sales.

Figure 19-3. Graphic Break-even Analysis: Reed Products, Inc.

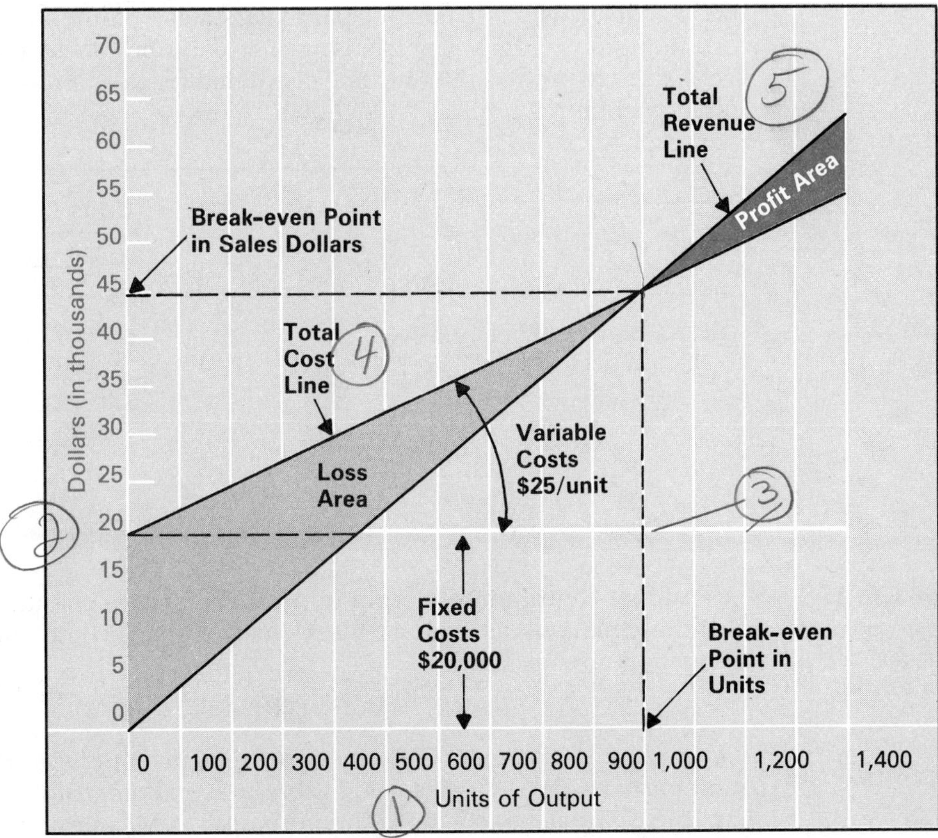

Profit Planning. The break-even process can be easily extended to include profit planning. Assume that Reed Products' president, Elaine Shirl, has set $10,000 in profit as the goal for the year. If all the previous data stay the same, how many television stands must Reed Products make and sell to reach the target profit? The answer is figured below (x = number of units).

$$\begin{aligned} S &= VC + FC + NI \\ \$45x &= \$25x + \$20{,}000 + \$10{,}000 \\ \$20x &= \$30{,}000 \\ x &= 1{,}500 \text{ units} \end{aligned}$$

To check the accuracy of this answer, put all known data into the equation for an income statement

$$\begin{aligned} S - VC - FC &= NI \\ (1{,}500 \text{ units} \times \$45) - (1{,}500 \times \$25) - (\$20{,}000) &= \$10{,}000 \\ \$67{,}500 - \$37{,}500 - \$20{,}000 &= \$10{,}000 \end{aligned}$$

Contribution Margin Concept

Our analysis of cost-volume-profit relationships is not complete until we add a new concept. **Contribution margin** is the excess of revenues over *all* variable costs related to a particular sales volume. A product line's contribution margin represents its net contribution to paying off fixed costs and to profits. Net income computed for Reed Products, Inc., using the contribution approach, is shown below.

	Units Produced and Sold	
	1,000	**1,500**
Sales revenue ($45 per unit)	$45,000	$67,500
Less variable costs ($25 per unit)	25,000	37,500
Contribution margin	$20,000	$30,000
Less fixed costs	20,000	20,000
Net income	—	$10,000

OBJECTIVE 3
Use contribution margin analysis to estimate levels of sales that will produce planned profits

Adding contribution margin into C-V-P analysis changes the make-up of the equations as well as the format of the income statement. The equation now becomes

$$[S - VC = CM] - FC = NI$$

Contribution margin (CM) is what remains after variable costs are subtracted from total sales. So the break-even point (BE) can be expressed as the point at which contribution margin (CM) minus total fixed costs

(FC) equals zero. That is, break-even occurs when CM − FC = 0. In terms of units of product, the break-even point equation is changed as follows:

$$(\text{CM/unit} \times \text{BE units}) - \text{FC} = 0$$

At this point we need to develop an equation that isolates the expression *BE units*. The equation can be rearranged as follows:

1. Move FC to the right side of the equation

$$\text{CM/unit} \times \text{BE units} = \text{FC}$$

2. Divide both sides of the equation by CM/unit

$$\frac{\text{CM/unit} \times \text{BE units}}{\text{CM/unit}} = \frac{\text{FC}}{\text{CM/unit}}$$

3. After canceling terms, the end result is

$$\text{BE units} = \frac{\text{FC}}{\text{CM/unit}}$$

For profit planning the equation is adjusted to include target net income as follows:

$$\text{Target unit sales} = \frac{\text{FC} + \text{NI}}{\text{CM/unit}}$$

To illustrate the use of these equations, we will put in the data given earlier for Reed Products.

$$\text{BE units} = \frac{\text{FC}}{\text{CM/unit}} = \frac{\$20{,}000}{\$45 - \$25} = \frac{\$20{,}000}{\$20} = 1{,}000 \text{ units}$$

$$\text{Target unit sales} = \frac{\text{FC} + \text{NI}}{\text{CM/unit}} = \frac{\$20{,}000 + \$10{,}000}{\$20} = \frac{\$30{,}000}{\$20} = 1{,}500 \text{ units}$$

Once mastered, use of the contribution margin simplifies the finding of the break-even point and planning for profits.

Assumptions Underlying C-V-P Analysis

Cost-volume-profit figures are useful only when certain assumptions hold true and certain conditions exist. If one or more of these assumptions and conditions are absent, the results of the analysis may be misleading. These assumptions and conditions are as follows:

1. Behavior of variable and fixed costs can be measured accurately.
2. Costs and revenues have a close linear approximation. For example, if costs rise, revenues will rise proportionately.
3. Efficiency and productivity will hold steady within the relevant range of activity.
4. Cost and price variables will also hold steady during the period being planned.

5. The product sales mix will not change during the planning period.
6. Production and sales volume will be about equal.

Illustrative Problem: Profit Planning—Contribution Margin Approach

Producing college textbooks is made up of many complex steps. All of them add to the cost of published materials. Good paper and binding materials add much to the cost as well as to the useful life of a book. Nathan Publishing Company is taking a careful look at a new manuscript on management information systems. Early estimates are that variable costs per book will be $6.80 and total fixed costs will be $60,000. The company plans to market the book wholesale at $12.80 per copy.

Required

1. Using the contribution margin approach, compute the number of copies the book must sell for the company to earn a profit of $30,000.
2. Using the same approach and assuming that fixed costs are cut to $50,000, determine the number of copies that must be sold to earn a target profit of $61,000.
3. Given the original information and assuming that 21,000 copies of the book can be sold, find the selling price the company must set to earn a profit of $80,700.
4. The company's marketing director says the most optimistic sales estimate for the book would be 36,000 copies. Assume that the highest possible price the company can charge is $13.20 and that variable costs per unit cannot be reduced below $6.80. How much more can be spent on fixed advertising costs if the new target profit is $40,000?

Solution

1. Target units computed

Unit sales = (FC + NI) ÷ CM per unit
= ($60,000 + $30,000) ÷ ($12.80 − $6.80)
= $90,000 ÷ $6
= 15,000 copies

2. Units required for higher profit and lower costs computed

Unit sales = (FC + NI) ÷ CM per unit
= ($50,000 + $61,000) ÷ ($12.80 − $6.80)
= $111,000 ÷ $6
= 18,500 copies

3. Selling price determined

Unit sales = (FC + NI) ÷ CM per unit
21,000 = ($60,000 + $80,700) ÷ ($x$ − $6.80)

Multiplying both sides of the equation by $(x - \$6.80)$, we get

$$\begin{aligned} 21{,}000(x - \$6.80) &= \$140{,}700 \\ 21{,}000x - \$142{,}800 &= \$140{,}700 \\ 21{,}000x &= \$283{,}500 \\ x &= \$13.50 \end{aligned}$$

4. Increased amount for advertising determined

$$\begin{aligned} \text{Unit sales} &= (\text{FC} + \text{NI}) \div \text{CM per unit} \\ 36{,}000 &= (x + \$40{,}000) \div (\$13.20 - \$6.80) \\ 36{,}000 &= (x + \$40{,}000) \div \$6.40 \end{aligned}$$

Multiplying both sides of the equation by \$6.40, we get

$$\begin{aligned} \$6.40(36{,}000) &= x + \$40{,}000 \\ \$230{,}400 &= x + \$40{,}000 \\ x &= \$230{,}400 - \$40{,}000 \\ x &= \$190{,}400 \end{aligned}$$

Total fixed costs allowed	\$190,400
Less original fixed cost estimate	60,000
Additional dollars available for advertising	\$130,400

Cost Allocation

Cost allocation, or assignment, is important to every part of management accounting, including the determination of unit costs for products and services. Some operating costs (direct costs) can be easily traced and assigned to products or services. But other costs (indirect costs) must be assigned by using some form of allocation method. The need for cost allocation goes beyond just identifying product or service costs. Every report a company's accountants prepare requires some form of cost allocation. Depreciation expense on a building, for example, is often allocated to the departments housed in that building. Depreciation expense is originally established by allocating an investment's total cost to various time periods. Even the president's salary is allocated to the various divisions of a company.

In accounting for operating costs, each cost must be assigned to products, services, departments, or jobs before accounting reports can be prepared. Without proper cost allocation techniques, management accountants cannot do their work. Management accountants have three major tasks in preparing internal accounting documents: (1) They must find product or service unit costs. (2) They must work out cost budgets and cost controls for management. (3) They must prepare reports to aid and support management decisions. Each task requires proper cost allocation procedures.

Several terms are unique to the concept of cost allocation and should be discussed further. For instance, the terms *cost allocation* and *cost assignment* are often used interchangeably, although *cost allocation* is the more popular of the two. For our purposes **cost allocation** is the process of assigning a specific cost to a specific cost objective.[1] Understanding such terms as *cost center, cost objective, direct cost,* and *indirect cost* is also vital to the study of cost allocation.

A **cost center** is any organizational segment or area of activity for which there is a reason to accumulate costs. Examples of cost centers include the company as a whole, corporate divisions, specific operating plants, departments, and even specific machines or work areas. Once a cost center has been selected, methods can be worked out to assign costs accurately to that cost center. No accounting report about a cost center can be prepared until all the proper cost allocation procedures have been carried out.

OBJECTIVE 4
State the role of cost objectives in the cost allocation process

A **cost objective** is the destination of an assigned cost.[2] If the purpose of a certain cost analysis is to evaluate the operating performance of a division or department, the cost objective would be that department or division (cost center). But if product costing is the reason for accumulating costs, a specific product, order, or an entire contract could be the cost objective. The important point is that cost classification and cost allocation results differ, depending on the cost objective being analyzed.

Now, we can expand the definitions of direct and indirect costs used earlier in relation to product costing. A **direct cost** is any cost that can be conveniently and economically traced to a *specific cost objective.* Direct materials costs and direct labor costs are normally thought of as direct costs. However, costs considered to be direct will vary with individual cost objectives. In general the number of costs classified as direct increases with the size of the cost objective. If the cost objective is a large division of a company, then electricity, maintenance, and special tooling costs of the division may be classified as direct costs. An **indirect cost** is any cost that cannot be conveniently or economically traced and assigned to a specific cost objective. In an actual situation any production cost not classified as a direct cost is an indirect cost.

Allocation of Manufacturing Costs

All manufacturing costs can be traced or assigned to a company's divisions, departments, or units of productive output. Direct costs, such as the cost of direct materials, can be assigned to specific products, departments,

1. Cost Accounting Standard 402, promulgated by the Cost Accounting Standards Board in 1972, defined the term *allocate* as follows: "To assign an item of cost, or group of items of cost, to one or more cost objectives. This term includes both direct assignment of cost and the reassignment of a share from an indirect cost pool."
2. Cost Accounting Standard 402, promulgated by the Cost Accounting Standards Board in 1972, defined the term *cost objective* as follows: "A function, organizational subdivision, contract or other work unit for which cost data are desired and for which provision is made to accumulate and measure the cost of processes, products, jobs, capitalized projects, etc."

or jobs. Many manufacturing costs, however, are indirect costs incurred for the benefit of more than one product or department. These costs should be allocated to the departments and products that benefit from the costs. For example, electricity cost is incurred for the benefit of all departments or divisions of a company. This cost must be allocated to all work done during a week or a month. Assigning all of it to one department would not give a true picture of events. This benefit theory and the methods used to distribute costs are basic to cost allocation.

The cost allocation process is shown in Figure 19-4. All three cost elements are included: materials, labor, and factory overhead. The costs of lumber and the cabinet maker's wages are direct costs of the product. Examples of factory overhead costs include depreciation of the table saw, clean-up and janitorial services, and nails. All factory overhead costs are indirect costs of the product and must be assigned by means of an allocation method. In this example, the cost objective is the product. Various cost classifications and cost allocation methods are used depending upon the specific cost objective being analyzed.

To summarize, allocation of production costs calls for assigning direct and indirect manufacturing costs to specific cost objectives. A cost may be a direct cost to a large cost objective (a large division) but an indirect cost to a smaller cost objective (a product). In each case all manufacturing costs are assigned to the specific cost objectives being analyzed as either direct or indirect costs.

The Role of Cost Assignment in Corporate Reporting

Accounting reports are prepared for all levels of management, from the president down to the department manager or supervisor. The president is responsible for all costs of the company. A department manager, on the other hand, is only responsible for costs connected to that one department. Reports must be prepared for all cost centers, including the

Figure 19-4. Cabinet Making: Assigning Manufacturing Costs to the Product

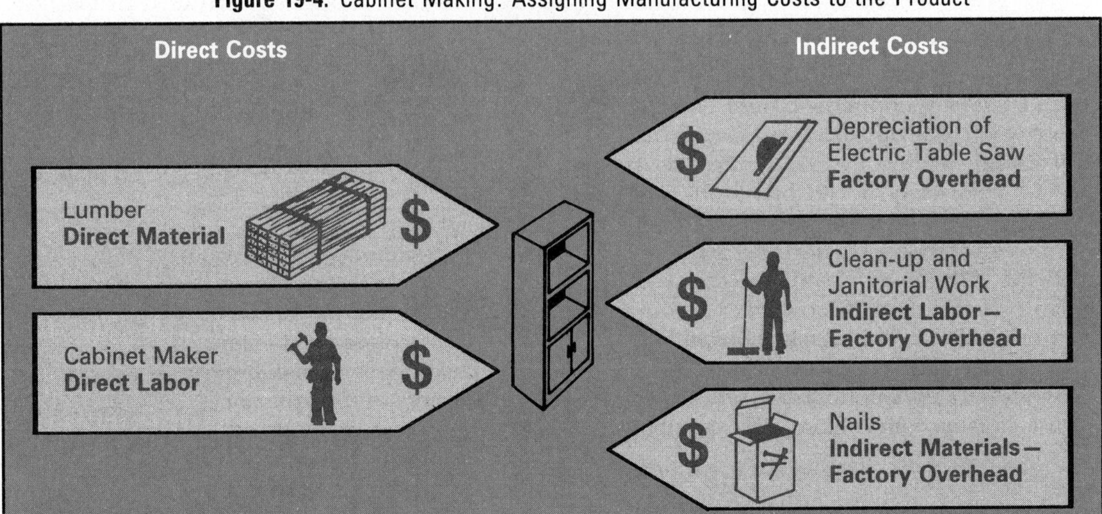

company as a whole, each division, and all departments in each division. The same costs shown in departmental reports will appear again in divisional and corporate reports, but perhaps in summary form.

As focus shifts from one cost center or cost objective to another, so does the ease with which costs can be traced. Here is where cost allocation comes into the picture. The different types of accounting reports can be prepared only with the aid of cost allocation techniques. As costs are reclassified and assigned to smaller cost centers or cost objectives, they become more difficult to trace. More costs are accounted for as indirect when emphasis shifts from divisional to departmental reporting. When the size of the cost objective is reduced to focus on a single product, only direct materials and direct labor costs can be directly traced. All other costs are classified as indirect and must be parceled out to the different products. This distribution calls for special procedures.

Table 19-1 shows how three manufacturing costs are traced differently as cost objectives change. Direct materials costs can be traced directly to any level of cost objective shown. They are a direct cost at the divisional, departmental, and product levels. All 40,000 pounds of sugar were issued to Division A. So they can be traced directly to that division. Only half (20,000 pounds) of the division's sugar was used by Department XZ. So only that amount can be traced directly to that department. At the product level every unit of Product AB requires one-half pound of sugar. The cost of that one-half pound is a direct cost that can be traced to the product. Depreciation of Factory Building G, which is used entirely by Division A, can be traced directly to Division A. For any smaller cost objectives, though, it becomes an indirect cost. Building depreciation expense must be shared by the various cost centers in the building. Such costs must be allocated to departmental or product cost objectives, using an allocation base, such as space occupied or direct labor hours. Depreciation costs of Machine 201 can be traced directly to either Division A or Department XZ. When Product AB is the cost objective, however, depreciation of machinery is considered an indirect manufacturing cost. It is accounted for as a factory overhead cost. Factory overhead costs are accumulated and then allocated to the products produced in Department XZ, as we saw in previous chapters. The principles of classifying and tracing costs discussed here play a part in the preparation of all internal accounting reports.

Assigning Costs of Supporting Service Functions

OBJECTIVE 5 Assign costs of supporting service functions to production departments

Every company and manufacturing process depends on the aid of many supporting service functions or departments. A **supporting service function** is not directly involved in production, but it is an operating unit or department needed for the overall operation of the company. Examples include a repair and maintenance department, a production scheduling department, a central power department, an inspection department, and materials storage and handling.

Labor costs and various indirect operating costs are accumulated for each service function. The costs of these supporting departments are

Table 19-1. Cost Classification and Traceability

Costs	Cost Objectives		
	Division A	**Department XZ**	**Product AB**
Direct Materials	*Direct costs:* 40,000 pounds of sugar issued from inventory specifically for Division A.	*Direct cost:* 20,000 of the 40,000 pounds of sugar issued from inventory were used by Department XZ (can be directly traced).	*Direct cost:* Every unit of Product AB requires one-half pound of sugar.
Depreciation of Factory Building G	*Direct cost:* Factory Building G is used entirely by Division A. Therefore, all depreciation expenses from usage of Factory Building G can be directly traced to Division A.	*Indirect cost:* Department XZ is one of four departments in Factory Building G. Depreciation of Factory Building G is allocated to the four departments according to square footage used by each department.	*Indirect cost:* Depreciation of Factory Building G is an indirect product cost. It is allocated to individual products as part of factory overhead charges applied to products using direct labor hours as a base.
Depreciation of Machine 201	*Direct cost:* Machine 201 is located in Department XZ and is used exclusively by Division A (can be directly traced).	*Direct cost:* Machine 201 is used only by Department XZ. Therefore, its depreciation charges can be directly traced to Department XZ.	*Indirect cost:* Depreciation of Machine 201 cannot be directly traced to individual products it produces. Such depreciation charges are accounted for as part of factory overhead costs.

incurred for the purpose of producing a product. So the costs incurred by supporting service functions are product costs. They should be treated as indirect manufacturing costs and assigned to products through the Factory Overhead account. This type of cost allocation is done in two steps. First, the costs of the supporting service function are allocated to the departments or cost centers that benefited from the services. After this step the assigned costs are included in the production department's Factory Overhead account and allocated to the end product.

Allocating factory overhead costs to products was discussed in Chapter 17. Here, we will concentrate on assigning supporting service department costs to production departments. A service function must benefit other departments to justify its existence. It is on this concept of benefit that supporting service department costs are assigned to production departments. Benefit must be measured on some basis that shows how the service performed relates to the department receiving the service.

Table 19-2 gives examples of bases used to allocate costs of supporting service functions. Each should be used when there is a benefit relationship between the service function and the production departments. Each service request may represent an equal amount of benefit or service to the receiving department. In that case the number of service requests can be the basis. Or total benefit may be measured by the number of labor hours needed to complete the service. Then labor hours can be the basis. Similar relationships justify the use of kilowatt hours or the number of materials requisitions as the allocation basis. The following problem will help you understand the process of assigning supporting service department costs.

Illustrative Problem: Assigning Service Department Costs

Saleh Metal Products Company has six production departments. The company also has three supporting service departments. One is the Repairs and Maintenance (R & M) Department. Costs of the R & M Department are assigned to the six production departments on the basis of the number of service requests each department makes.

The production departments made the following number of service requests during February: 16 requests by the Cutting Department, 21 by the Extruding Department, 8 by the Shaping Department, 31 by the Threading Department, 24 by the Polishing Department, and 25 by the Finishing Department.

Table 19-2. Cost Allocation Bases for Assigning Costs of Supporting Service Functions

Possible Allocation Basis	When to Use It
1. Number of service requests	Used when each service takes the same amount of time or when a record of service requests is maintained and no other basis is available
2. Labor hours	Used when service labor hours are recorded for each service performed; a very good basis when the different services take different amounts of time
3. Kilowatt hours used	Used to distribute the costs of a central power department maintained by the company
4. Number of materials requisitions	Used to allocate costs of a materials storage area

Costs incurred and charged against the R & M Department during February are shown below.

Supplies and Parts	
Small Tools	$ 1,850
Lubricants and Supplies	940
Replacement Parts	2,100
Labor	
Repair and Maintenance	3,910
Supervision	1,600
Depreciation	
Equipment	1,290
Machinery	1,620
Other Operating Costs	2,440
Total Costs for February	$15,750

Required

1. Using the number of service requests, prepare a schedule allocating the R & M Department's operating costs for February to the six production departments.
2. Name and discuss another possible allocation basis for assigning the R & M Department's costs to the six production departments.

Solution

1. The goal of this part of the problem is to see what portion of February R & M costs should be assigned to each production department. The specific dollar amounts are found by using a ratio of the benefits each production department received to total benefits rendered by the R & M Department. Using the number of service requests as the cost allocation basis, we can approach this problem in two ways:
   a. Find the average cost per request, and multiply this amount by each department's number of service requests

$$\frac{\text{Total cost}}{\text{Total service requests}} = \frac{\$15{,}750}{125} = \$126 \text{ per request}$$

R & M Department cost allocation for February

To Cutting Department (16 × $126)	$ 2,016
To Extruding Department (21 × $126)	2,646
To Shaping Department (8 × $126)	1,008
To Threading Department (31 × $126)	3,906
To Polishing Department (24 × $126)	3,024
To Finishing Department (25 × $126)	3,150
Total Costs Allocated	$15,750

b. The other approach is to take the ratio of each department's requests to the total number of requests and multiply by the total costs to be allocated. R & M Department cost allocation for February:

To Cutting Department (16/125) ($15,750)	$ 2,016
To Extruding Department (21/125) ($15,750)	2,646
To Shaping Department (8/125) ($15,750)	1,008
To Threading Department (31/125) ($15,750)	3,906
To Polishing Department (24/125) ($15,750)	3,024
To Finishing Department (25/125) ($15,750)	3,150
Total Costs Allocated	$15,750

The allocations are the same by method **b** as by method **a**, as they should be.

2. Labor hours used would be another possible allocation basis. Time records can be kept for each service call. Then costs can be allocated by finding the average R & M Department cost per labor hour. This cost is then multiplied by the number of service labor hours used by each production department.

Allocation of Joint Production Costs

OBJECTIVE 6
Allocate common costs to joint products

Joint, or common, costs present a special need for cost allocation. A **joint cost** (or common cost) is one that relates to two or more products produced from a common input or raw material and that can be assigned only by means of arbitrary cost allocation after the products become identifiable. Joint products cannot be identified as separate products during most of the production process. Only at a particular point in the manufacturing process, called the **split-off point**, do separate products evolve from a common processing unit. Joint products are often found in such industries as petroleum refining, wood processing, and meat packing. In all these industries more than one end product arises from a single kind of input.

In the beef processing industry, the final cuts of meat (steaks, roasts, hamburger) do not appear until the end of the process. However, the cost of the steer, transportation costs, storage and hanging costs, and labor costs were incurred to get the side of beef ready for final butchering. How do we assign these joint costs to specific cuts of beef? This type of cost allocation is the objective of accounting for joint costs.

Figure 19-5 shows a joint production situation and the accounting problem of allocating joint costs. The joint costs of $420,000 can be assigned to Product AA and Product BB in several ways. We outline the two most commonly used methods in the following paragraphs.

Physical Volume Method

One way to allocate joint production costs to specific products is called the **physical volume method**. This approach uses a measure of physical

Figure 19-5. Joint Product Cost Allocation

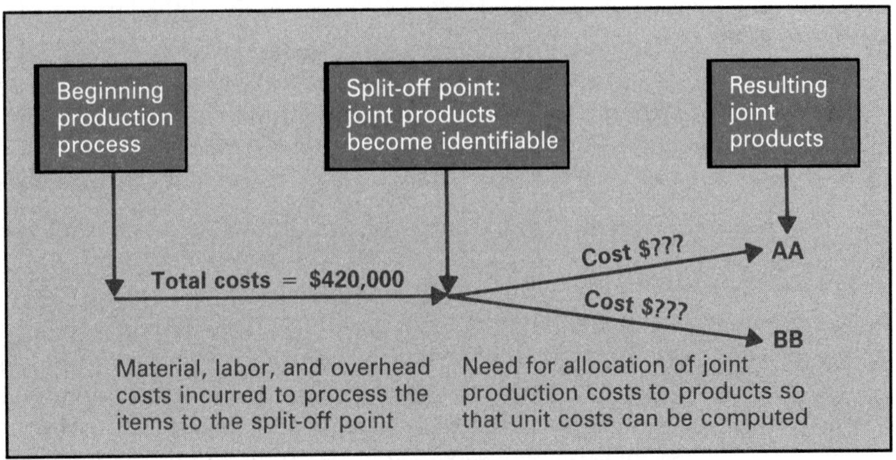

volume (units, pounds, liters, or grams) as the basis for joint cost allocation. An example will show how the physical volume method applies to the problem in Figure 19-5.

Assume that the Phillips Company makes two grades of paint from the same mixture of substances. During August, 75,000 liters of various ingredients were put into the production process. The final output for the month was 25,000 liters of Product AA and 50,000 liters of Product BB. Total joint production costs for August were $420,000. They were made up of $190,000 for direct materials, $145,000 for direct labor, and $85,000 for factory overhead. The joint products cannot be identified until the end of the production process. Product AA sells for $9 per liter; Product BB for $6 per liter.

Now, let us use the physical volume method of assigning joint costs. We take total liters as the allocation basis. Then, we apply a ratio of the physical volume of each product to total physical volume.

	Total Liters	Allocation Ratio	Joint Cost Allocation	
Product AA	25,000	$\frac{25,000}{75,000}$ or ⅓	$140,000	($420,000 × ⅓)
Product BB	50,000	$\frac{50,000}{75,000}$ or ⅔	280,000	($420,000 × ⅔)
Totals	75,000		$420,000	

Product AA generates $225,000 in revenues (25,000 liters at $9 per liter). Thus, the gross margin for this product line will be $85,000. We compute this by subtracting $140,000 of assigned joint costs from the total revenues of $225,000. Product BB sells for a total of $300,000 (50,000 liters at $6 per liter) and will show only $20,000 in gross margin ($300,000 minus $280,000 of assigned joint costs).

The physical volume method is easy to use. However, it often seriously distorts net income. This distortion results because the physical volume of joint products may not be proportionate to each product's ability to generate revenue. In our example, Product BB's net income suffered because its high-volume content attracted two-thirds of the production costs even though its selling price was much less than Product AA.

Relative Sales Value Method

A different way to allocate joint production costs depends on the relative sales value of the products. The **relative sales value method** allocates joint production costs to products in proportion to each product's ability to generate revenue. Extending the Phillips Company data, we can make the following analysis. (Costs are assigned to joint products on the basis of their relative sales value when they first become identifiable as specific products—that is, at the split-off point.)

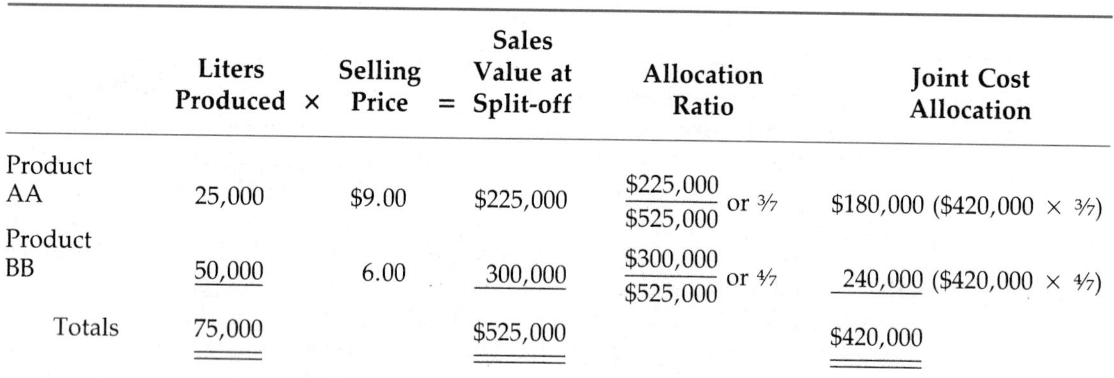

	Liters Produced ×	Selling Price =	Sales Value at Split-off	Allocation Ratio	Joint Cost Allocation
Product AA	25,000	$9.00	$225,000	$225,000 / $525,000 or 3/7	$180,000 ($420,000 × 3/7)
Product BB	50,000	6.00	300,000	$300,000 / $525,000 or 4/7	240,000 ($420,000 × 4/7)
Totals	75,000		$525,000		$420,000

Product AA has a relative sales value of $225,000 at split-off, and Product BB's relative sales value totals $300,000. The resulting cost allocation ratios are 3/7 and 4/7, respectively, for Products AA and BB. Applying these ratios to the total joint cost of $420,000, we assign $180,000 to Product AA and $240,000 to Product BB.

	Product AA		Product BB	
	Physical Volume Method	Relative Sales Value Method	Physical Volume Method	Relative Sales Value Method
Sales	$225,000	$225,000	$300,000	$300,000
Cost of goods sold	140,000	180,000	280,000	240,000
Gross margin	$ 85,000	$ 45,000	$ 20,000	$ 60,000
Gross margin as percent of sales	37.8%	20%	6.7%	20%

If we compare the two joint cost allocation methods, we see a wide difference in gross margin for the two product lines.

The major advantage of the relative sales value method is that it allocates joint costs according to a product's ability to absorb the cost. For this reason equal gross margin percentages will always result when products are valued at the split-off point. Our example shows that under the relative sales value method, gross margin as a percentage of sales is 20 percent for both Product AA and Product BB.

As mentioned earlier, these approaches to assigning joint production costs are arbitrary. The reason for using arbitrary approaches is that it is difficult to determine just how the end products (cost objectives) specifically benefited from the incurred cost. These approaches—whether the physical volume method or the relative sales value method—should be used only when it is impossible to tell how the cost benefited the cost objective. Most cost assignment methods used for determining product unit costs are based on a beneficial relationship.

Chapter Review

Review of Learning Objectives

1. **Define and classify variable costs, semivariable costs, and fixed costs.**
   Variable costs are total costs that change in direct proportion to changes in productive output. Direct materials and direct labor are examples of variable costs. Semivariable costs act like both variable and fixed costs. That is, part of the cost is fixed and part changes with the volume of output. Examples are power costs and telephone charges. Total fixed costs remain constant within a relevant range of volume or activity. Examples of fixed costs include supervisors' salaries and depreciation charges.

2. **Compute the break-even point in units of output and in sales dollars.**
   The break-even point is the point at which total revenue equals total costs incurred. In formula form break-even occurs when S = VC + FC (sales equals variable costs plus fixed costs). In terms of contribution margin, the formula is

$$\text{BE units} = \frac{\text{FC}}{\text{CM/unit}}$$

   Once the number of break-even units is known, it can be multiplied by the product's selling price to get the break-even point in dollars of sales.

3. **Use contribution margin analysis to estimate levels of sales that will produce planned profits.**
   The addition of projected net income (NI) to the break-even equation makes it possible to plan levels of operation that yield target profits. The formula in terms of contribution margin is

$$\text{Target unit sales} = \frac{\text{FC} + \text{NI}}{\text{CM/unit}}$$

4. **State the role of cost objectives in the cost allocation process.**
   A cost objective is the destination of an assigned cost. The cost objective varies according to the focus of a particular report. It may range from an

entire company or a division down to one particular product. Cost allocation is the process of assigning a specific cost to a specific cost objective. Cost objectives provide a target for the allocation process.

5. **Assign costs of supporting service functions to production departments.** Costs incurred by supporting service departments must be accounted for as indirect manufacturing costs. They are allocated to production departments on a benefit basis—a beneficial relationship of cost to cost objective. Several allocation bases exist. Each is suitable for a certain relationship between the service used and the production department receiving the service.

6. **Allocate common costs to joint products.** Joint products evolve from a common processing unit. They cannot be identified as specific products until the split-off point in the process. All manufacturing costs incurred prior to the split-off point are shared by all the joint products. At the split-off point, costs are assigned to individual products by either the physical volume method or the relative sales value method.

Review Problem
Break-even/Profit Planning Analysis

TK Organs, Inc., is a major producer of large pipe organs. Model ERV is a two-manual organ with a large potential market. Data from 19x7 operations for Model ERV are summarized below.

Variable Costs per Unit	
Direct Materials	$ 3,700
Direct Labor	5,200
Factory Overhead	2,600
Selling Expenses	2,500
Total Fixed Costs	
Factory Overhead	$390,000
Advertising	110,000
Administrative Expenses	136,000
Selling Price per Unit	29,900

Management is pondering alternate courses of action for 19x8. Each alternative should be treated as an independent action and not tied to the other alternatives.

Required

1. Compute the 19x7 break-even point in units.
2. Calculate the amount of net income generated if 45 ERV models were sold in 19x7.
3. For 19x8:
   a. Calculate the number of units that must be sold to generate a $190,800 profit. Assume that costs and selling price remain constant.
   b. Calculate the net income if the company increases the number of units sold by 20 percent and cuts the selling price by $900 per unit.
   c. Determine the number of units that must be sold to break even if advertising is increased by $47,700.

d. If variable costs are cut by 10 percent, find the number of units that must be sold to generate a profit of $315,500.

Answer to Review Problem

1. Break-even point in units for 19x7 computed

Variable costs per unit	$ 14,000
Contribution margin per unit:	
$29,900 − $14,000	15,900
Total fixed costs	$636,000

$$\text{Break-even point} = \frac{\text{FC}}{\text{CM/unit}} = \frac{\$636{,}000}{\$15{,}900} = \underline{\underline{40}} \text{ units}$$

2. Net income for 45 units calculated

Units sold	45
Units required to break even	40
Units over break-even	5

19x7 net income = $15,900 per unit × 5 = $79,500

Contribution margin equals sales minus all variable costs. CM/unit equals the amount of sales dollars remaining, after variable costs have been subtracted, to cover fixed costs and provide a profit for the company. If all fixed costs have been absorbed by the time break-even is reached, the whole contribution margin of each unit sold in excess of break-even represents profit.

3. a. Number of units required to generate a given profit calculated

$$\text{Unit sales} = \frac{\text{FC} + \text{NI}}{\text{CM/unit}}$$

$$= \frac{\$636{,}000 + \$190{,}800}{\$15{,}900} = \frac{\$826{,}800}{\$15{,}900} = 52 \text{ units}$$

3. b. Net income under specified conditions calculated

Units to be sold = 45 × 120% = 54 units
New selling price = $29,000
Contribution margin = $29,000 − $14,000 = $15,000

$$\text{BE units} = \frac{\$636{,}000}{\$15{,}000} = 42.4 \text{ units}$$

Units to be sold in excess of break-even

54 − 42.4 = 11.6 units

Projected net income

11.6 units × $15,000/unit = $174,000

3. c. Number of break-even units under specified conditions determined

$$\text{BE units} = \frac{\$636{,}000 + \$47{,}700}{\$15{,}900}$$

$$= \frac{\$683{,}700}{\$15{,}900} = \underline{\underline{43 \text{ units}}}$$

3. d. Number of units required to generate a given profit determined

Variable costs per unit = \$14,000 × .9 = \$12,600
Contribution margin per unit = \$29,900 − \$12,600 = \$17,300

$$\text{Unit sales} = \frac{\$636{,}000 + \$315{,}500}{\$17{,}300} = \frac{\$951{,}500}{\$17{,}300} = \underline{\underline{55 \text{ units}}}$$

Chapter Assignments

Questions

1. What makes variable costs different from other costs?
2. "Fixed costs remain constant in total but decrease per unit as output increases." Explain this statement.
3. What is meant by relevant range of activity?
4. Why is a telephone charge considered a semivariable cost?
5. What is the difference between practical capacity and ideal capacity?
6. Why does a company seldom operate at either ideal or practical capacity?
7. What is normal capacity? Why is this expression of capacity more relevant and useful than either ideal or practical capacity?
8. What is the relationship between cost-volume-profit analysis and the concept of cost behavior?
9. Define what the break-even point is. State why information on break-even is useful to management.
10. Define contribution margin. How is this concept useful?
11. State the equation that determines target unit sales, using the elements of fixed costs, net income, and contribution margin.
12. What conditions must be met for cost-volume-profit computations to be accurate?
13. What is a cost objective, and what is its role in management accounting?
14. "As the size of the cost center or cost objective decreases, the ability to trace cost and revenue becomes more limited." Explain this statement.
15. What is a supporting service department? Give examples.
16. What is a joint manufacturing cost?
17. Describe the physical volume method of allocating joint costs to products. List the advantages and disadvantages of the physical volume method.
18. Should joint costs be allocated to a product on the basis of the product's ability to generate revenue? Explain your answer.

Classroom Exercises

Exercise 19-1. Identification of Variable and Fixed Costs (L.O. 1)

From the following list of costs of productive output, indicate which are usually considered variable costs and which are fixed costs: (a) packing materials for stereo components; (b) real estate taxes; (c) gasoline for a delivery truck; (d) property insurance; (e) depreciation expense of buildings (straight-line method); (f) supplies; (g) indirect materials used; (h) bottles used in the sale of liquids; (i) license fees for company cars; (j) wiring used in radios; (k) machine helper's wages; (l) wood used in bookcases; (m) city operating license; (n) employer's share of social security payments; (o) machine operators' wages; and (p) cost of required outside inspection on each unit produced. Could any of these costs be considered a semivariable cost? Explain.

Exercise 19-2. Semivariable Costs/High-Low Method (L.O. 1)

McMahan Electronics Company manufactures major appliances. It just had its most successful year because of increased interest in its refrigerator line. While preparing the budget for next year, Mr. James, the company's controller, came across the following data related to utility costs:

Month	Power Costs	Volume in Machine Hours
July	$58,000	6,000
August	52,000	5,000
September	50,000	4,500
October	48,000	4,000
November	42,000	3,500
December	40,000	3,000

Using the high-low method, determine: (1) the variable power cost per machine hour; (2) the monthly fixed power cost; and (3) the total variable power and fixed power costs for the six-month period.

Exercise 19-3. Break-even Analysis (L.O. 2)

Ustinowich Manufacturing Company makes head covers for golf clubs. The company expects to make a profit next year. It anticipates fixed manufacturing costs to be $106,500 and fixed general and administrative expenses to be $102,030. Variable manufacturing and selling costs per set of head covers will be $3.65 and $1.75, respectively. Each set will sell for $11.40.

1. Compute the break-even point in sales units.
2. Compute the break-even point in sales dollars.
3. If the selling price were increased to $12.00 per unit and fixed general and administrative expenses were cut by $33,465, what would the new break-even point be in units?
4. Prepare a graph to illustrate the break-even point in **2**.

Exercise 19-4. Profit Planning (L.O. 2, 3)

Short-term automobile rentals are the specialty of Coffey Auto Loans, Inc. Average variable operating expenses have been $6.25 per day per automobile. The company owns thirty cars. Fixed operating costs for the next year are expected to be $75,050. Average daily rental revenue per automobile is expected to be $17.75. Management would like to earn $25,000 during the year.

1. Calculate the number of total daily rentals the company must have during the year to earn the target profit.
2. On the basis of your answer to **1**, determine the average number of days each automobile must be rented.
3. Find the total rental revenue for the year that is needed to earn the $25,000 profit.
4. What would the total rental revenue be if fixed operating costs could be lowered by $2,525 and target earnings increased to $35,000?

Exercise 19-5. Contribution Margin/Profit Planning
(L.O. 3)

Thom Systems, Ltd., makes undersea missiles for nuclear submarines. Management has just been offered a government contract that may result in a profit for the company. The contract purchase price is $30,000 per unit, but the number of units to be purchased has not been decided. The company's fixed costs are budgeted at $3,970,000. Variable costs are $18,500 per unit.

1. Compute the number of units at the stated contract price the company should agree to make in order to earn a target income of $5,000,000.
2. Using a lighter material, the variable unit cost can be reduced by $2,000, but that will cause total fixed overhead to increase by $7,500. How many units must now be produced to make $5,000,000 in profit?
3. Using the factors in **2**, how many additional units need to be produced to increase profit by $1,350,000?

Exercise 19-6. Cost Allocation Basis
(L.O. 4)

A plan for cost assignment is vital to corporate reporting, product costing, and inventory valuation. Examples of costs and related cost objectives are listed below.

Cost	Cost Objectives
Materials-handling costs	Product
Plant depreciation costs	Division
Repair and Maintenance Department costs	One of five production departments served
Corporate president's salary	Division

1. Which costs would be direct costs of the related cost objective? Which would be indirect costs?
2. For each indirect cost choose a cost allocation basis that provides a logical relationship between the cost and the cost objective. Defend your answers.

Exercise 19-7. Cost Allocation— Direct Versus Indirect
(L.O. 4)

Classifying a cost as direct or indirect depends on the cost objective. Depreciation of a factory building is a direct cost when the plant is the cost objective, but when the cost objective is a product, the depreciation cost becomes indirect.

For the costs listed at the top of the following page, indicate for each cost objective whether it would be an indirect cost (I) or a direct cost (D). Be able to defend your answers.

	Cost Objective		
	Division	Department	Product
Direct labor			
Departmental supplies			
Division head's salary			
President's salary			
Department manager's salary			
Direct materials			
Fire insurance on specific machine			
Property taxes, division plant			
Department repairs and maintenance			

Exercise 19-8. Service Department Cost Allocation (L.O. 5)

Delta Fundraising, Inc., has six departments that must share the services of a single central computer. Management has decided that the best basis for cost allocation is the minutes of computer time used by each department. Usage per department for the first week in June was as follows: 3,096 minutes for Department A; 4,128 minutes for Department B; 4,560 minutes for Department C; 2,064 minutes for Department D; 1,032 minutes for Department E; and 5,160 minutes for Department F. The total for all departments was 20,040 minutes. The total cost of operating the computer during the month was $14,028.

Determine the computer expense to be assigned to each department for the one-week period.

Exercise 19-9. Joint Cost Allocation— Relative Sales Value Method (L.O. 6)

In the processing of pulp for making paper, two distinct grades of wood pulp come out of a common crushing and mixing process. Ward Paper Products, Inc., produced 44,000 liters of pulp during January. Direct materials inputs cost the company $86,000. Labor and overhead costs for the month were $56,000 and $36,000, respectively. Output for the month was as follows:

Product	Quantity	Market Value at Split-off
Grade A pulp	28,000 liters	$14.00 per liter
Grade B pulp	16,000 liters	$10.50 per liter

Using the relative sales value method, allocate common production costs to Grade A pulp and Grade B pulp.

Exercise 19-10. Joint Cost Allocation— Physical Volume Method (L.O. 6)

Kennedy Company of Massachusetts produces molasses and refined sugar, joint products that emerge from juice extracted from sugar beets. The company will use the physical volume method to assign common, or joint, costs to the two products. The allocation base is liters. During February, Kennedy Company put 320,000 liters of sugar beet juice into production. The final products from this input were 48,000 liters of molasses and 272,000 liters of refined sugar. These joint product costs were incurred during February: $3,640 for materials;

$9,240 for direct labor; and $11,520 for factory overhead. Thus, total joint costs amounted to $24,400.

Assuming no loss through evaporation, assign a portion of joint production costs to each product.

Interpreting Accounting Information

Rio Pinar Golf and Tennis Club
(L.O. 1)

Officials of the Rio Pinar Golf and Tennis Club are putting together a budget for the year ending December 31, 19x9. Several problems have caused the budget to be delayed by more than four weeks. Mr. Ray Landry, club treasurer, indicated that the delay was caused by three expense items. These items were difficult to account for because they were called "semivariable or mixed costs," and he did not know how to break them down into their variable and fixed components for the budget. An accountant friend and golfing partner helped him identify the problem and told him to use the high-low method to divide the costs into their variable and fixed parts.

The three cost categories are: (a) Water Expense; (b) Electricity Expense; and (c) Repairs and Maintenance Expense. Information pertaining to last year's spending patterns and the measurement activity connected with each cost are as follows:

	Water Expense		Electricity Expense		Repairs and Maintenance	
Month	**Amount**	**Gallons Used**	**Amount**	**Kilowatt Hours**	**Amount**	**Labor Hours**
Jan.	$ 21,990	125,000	$ 7,500	210,000	$ 7,578	220
Feb.	19,740	110,000	8,255	240,200	7,852	230
Mar.	18,690	103,000	8,165	236,600	7,304	210
Apr.	21,240	120,000	8,960	268,400	7,030	200
May	22,740	130,000	7,520	210,800	7,852	230
June	26,115	152,500	7,025	191,000	8,126	240
July	28,740	170,000	6,970	188,800	8,400	250
Aug.	30,840	184,000	6,990	189,600	8,674	260
Sept.	28,740	170,000	7,055	192,200	8,948	270
Oct.	26,790	157,000	7,135	195,400	8,674	260
Nov.	22,740	130,000	8,560	252,400	8,126	240
Dec.	20,040	112,000	8,415	246,600	7,852	230
Totals	$288,405	1,663,500	$92,550	2,622,000	$96,416	2,840

Required

1. Using the high-low method, compute the variable cost rates used last year for each expense. What was the monthly fixed cost for water, electricity, and repairs and maintenance?
2. Compute the total variable cost and total fixed cost for each expense category for last year.

3. Mr. Landry believes that for the coming year the variable water rate will go up by $.05, the electricity rate will increase by $.005, and the repairs rate will rise by $1.20. Usage of all items and their fixed cost amounts will remain constant. Compute the projected total cost for each category.

Problem Set A

Problem 19A-1. Break-even Analysis (L.O. 2)

Borman & Fess, a law firm in downtown San Francisco, is thinking of developing a legal clinic for middle- and low-income residents. Paraprofessional help will be employed, and a $16 per hour billing rate will be used. These paraprofessional employees will be law students who will work for $8 per hour. Other variable costs are anticipated to be $4.40 per hour, and annual fixed costs are expected to total $18,000.

Required

1. Compute the break-even point in billable hours.
2. Compute the break-even point in total billings.
3. Find the new break-even point in total billings if fixed costs go up by $2,340.
4. Using the original figures, compute the break-even point in total billings if the billing rate is decreased by $1 per hour, variable costs are decreased by $.40 per hour, and fixed costs are decreased by $3,600.

Problem 19A-2. Profit Planning—Contribution Margin Approach (L.O. 2, 3)

Peat Financial Corporation is a subsidiary of Marwick Enterprises. Processing loan applications is the major task of the corporation. Last year, Mr. Bob Singleton, manager of the Loan Department, established the policy of charging a fee for every loan processed, amounting to $150 per application. Next year's costs are projected to be as follows: (a) variable costs: loan consultant wages, $12.50 per hour (usually takes 6 hours to process a loan application); (b) supplies, $1.20 per application; and (c) other variable costs, $.30 per application. Fixed costs include: depreciation of equipment, $7,500; building rental, $13,000; promotional costs, $11,500; and other fixed costs, $15,040.

Required

1. Using the contribution margin approach, compute the number of loan applications the company must process to (a) break even and (b) earn a profit of $14,700.
2. Continuing the same approach, compute the number of applications that must be processed to earn a target profit of $20,000 if promotional costs increase by $5,725.
3. Assuming the original information and the processing of 1,000 applications, compute the new loan application fee the company must use if the target profit is $41,460.
4. Mr. Singleton believes that processing 1,500 loan applications is the maximum his staff can handle. How much more can be spent on promotional costs if the highest fee tolerable to the customer is $200, if variable costs cannot be reduced, and if the target net income for such an application load is $50,000?

Problem 19A-3. Allocation Process—Cost–Base Relationship (L.O. 4)

Five types of costs incurred by a typical manufacturing company are shown below. Each cost must be allocated to a cost objective.

Type of Cost	Cost Objective
1. Cost Accounting Department	Production departments
2. Engineering (service) Department	Products
3. Materials handling function	Products
4. Cafeteria (service) function	Production departments
5. Production Scheduling Department	Production departments

A number of allocation bases can be used to assign these costs to their respective cost objectives. They include: (a) machine hours; (b) direct labor hours; (c) direct labor dollars; (d) engineering labor hours; (e) number of employees; (f) total labor hours; (g) units handled; (h) percentage of service costs; (i) number of service requests; and (j) direct charges.

Required

1. For each of the five types of costs, select the allocation base(s) that best expresses the beneficial relationship between the cost and the cost objective. State the reasons for your answers.
2. Some companies group all the costs listed above into one factory overhead cost "pool" and allocate them to products, using just one allocation base, such as direct labor hours. What are the advantages and disadvantages of this approach?

Problem 19A-4. Service Department Expense Allocation (L.O. 5)

Tenants at the Two Flights Up Office Complex on Park Avenue enjoy the benefits of the pooled concept for supporting services. All operating costs are incurred centrally and allocated to the seven tenant businesses on the basis of usage. Word processing is one of these centralized services. For August the following costs were related to the word processing function: (a) operator labor, five people at $1,200 monthly salary each; (b) supplies, $820; (c) equipment depreciation, $1,250; (d) space rental, $2,000; (e) utilities expense, $550; and (f) overhead charge, $1,380. Thus, total allocable costs for August amounted to $12,000.

Usage of the word processing pool is recorded by hours of usage, which is also the basis for allocating the cost each month. During August tenant usage was as follows: (a) Hanna Catering Service, 64 hours; (b) Wooten Realtors, Inc., 142 hours; (c) High & Wide, Attorneys at Law, 211 hours; (d) Wilson Inventory Service, 85 hours; (e) Evers & Nagel, CPAs, 180 hours; (f) Boxwell Sporting Goods, 63 hours; and (g) Byrd Hair Styling Supplies Company, 55 hours.

Required

1. Assign the costs of the word processing function for August to each of the seven tenant businesses on the basis of hours used.
2. Explain other bases of allocation that could have been used to assign costs. Discuss the advantages and disadvantages of each allocation base.

Problem 19A-5. Joint Cost Allocation (L.O. 6)

The processing of crude oil is necessary before its joint products, gasoline, motor oil, and kerosene, can be produced. Paton Petroleum Products, Inc., a Chicago-based company, specializes in quality products. During April the company used 1,500,000 gallons of crude oil at $.20 per gallon, paid $225,000 in direct labor wages, and applied $180,000 of factory overhead to the crude oil processing department. Production during the period yielded 850,000 gallons of gasoline, 150,000 gallons of motor oil, and 400,000 gallons of kerosene. Evaporation caused the loss of 100,000 gallons. This amount of evaporation is normal, and its cost should be included in the costing of good units produced. Selling prices of the joint products are: $.60 per gallon of gasoline, $.85 per quart of motor oil, and $.18 per gallon of kerosene. Assume that there were no beginning or ending Work in Process inventories and that everything produced was sold during the period. (Note: four quarts equal one gallon.)

Required

1. Using the physical volume method, allocate joint costs to the three joint products.
2. Using the relative sales value method, allocate joint costs to each of the three products.
3. Prepare a schedule that compares the gross margin at split-off point that results from the two methods of allocation for the three products. Compute gross margin both in total dollars and as a percentage of sales.
4. Gasoline could be processed further beyond the split-off point and become a top premium product. If the company incurred $153,500 in additional processing costs for gasoline in April, the selling price could be increased to $.80 per gallon. Under these circumstances, and assuming that joint cost is allocated using the relative sales value method, how much additional profit would be earned from the sale of gasoline? Should the company process the gasoline beyond split-off?

Problem Set B

Problem 19B-1. Break-even Analysis (L.O. 2)

At the beginning of each year, the accounting department at Woolley Lighting, Ltd., must find the point at which projected sales revenue will equal total budgeted variable and fixed costs. The company makes custom-made, durable, low-voltage yard lighting systems. Each system sells for an average of $738. Variable costs per unit are $410. Total fixed costs for the year are estimated to be $328,000.

Required

1. Compute the break-even point in sales units.
2. Compute the break-even point in sales dollars.
3. Find the new break-even point in sales units if fixed costs go up by $9,840.
4. Using the original figures, compute the break-even point in sales units if the selling price decreases to $730 per unit, fixed costs go up by $33,580, and variable costs decrease by $38 per unit.

Problem 19B-2. Profit Planning—Contribution Margin Approach (L.O. 2, 3)

Raoul Dean is president of the Baylor Plastics Division of Waco Industries. Management is considering a new product line that features a large bird posed in a running posture. Called "Chargin' Cardinal," this product is expected to have worldwide market appeal and become the mascot of many high school and university athletic teams. Expected variable unit costs are as follows: (a) direct materials, $8.90; (b) direct labor, $5.48; (c) production supplies, $.42; (d) selling costs, $3.80; and (e) other, $2.90. The following are annual fixed costs: depreciation, building and equipment, $26,000; advertising, $65,000; and other, $11,510. The company plans to sell the product for $55.00.

Required

1. Using the contribution margin approach, compute the number of products the company must sell to (a) break even and (b) earn a profit of $70,350.
2. Continuing with the same approach, compute the number of products that must be sold to earn a target profit of $140,230 if advertising costs rise by $40,000.
3. Assuming the original information and sales of 10,000 units, compute the new selling price the company must use to make $131,490 profit.
4. According to the vice president of marketing, Joyce Dean, the most optimistic annual sales estimate for the product would be 25,000 items. How much more can be spent on fixed advertising costs if the highest possible selling price the company can charge is $46.50, if variable costs cannot be reduced, and if target net income for 25,000 unit sales is $251,000?

Problem 19B-3. Allocation Process: Cost–Base Relationship (L.O. 4)

Below are five types of costs for a typical manufacturing company. Each cost is allocated to a cost objective.

Type of Cost	Cost Objective
1. Cost of corporate computer center	Production departments
2. Depreciation of division factory buildings	Production departments
3. Tool and die making cost (service department)	Production departments
4. Material storage cost	Products
5. Repairs and Maintenance Department costs	Production departments

A number of allocation bases could be used to assign the costs listed above to their respective cost objectives. They include: (a) direct labor dollars; (b) direct labor hours; (c) machine hours; (d) facility or service usage hours; (e) direct materials costs; (f) square footage; and (g) number of service requests.

Required

1. For each of the five types of costs, select the allocation base that best expresses the beneficial relationship between the cost and the cost objective. State reasons for your answers.
2. What would be wrong with including all these costs in one overhead cost pool and allocating them to production departments on the basis of direct labor dollars? What would be the advantage of such an approach?

Problem 19B-4. Service Department Expense Allocation
(L.O. 5)

Goldenrod Community Hospital has one respirator that must be shared by the hospital's six departments. To judge efficiency and to aid in future budgeting, each department's operating income or loss is figured separately each month. Before these calculations can be made, expenses that are considered "common" expenses must be allocated to each department. Depreciation and maintenance expenses connected directly to the respirator are allocated to departments according to hours of usage.

The costs for upkeep of the respirator for July are as follows: (a) depreciation was $1,100 on the respirator and $240 on supplemental machinery; (b) labor costs were $6,000 for the operators and $1,800 for maintenance; and (c) materials costs were $3,200 for oxygen, $480 for small replacement parts, $960 for supplies, and $620 for other operating costs. Thus, total costs for October were $14,400.

Respirator usage by department for July was as follows: 173.0 hours for the Oncology Department, 32.6 hours for the Orthopedics Department, 88.2 hours for the Nephrology Department, 73.8 hours for the Geriatrics Department, 37.4 hours for the Pediatrics Department, and 75.0 hours for the Maternity Department.

Required

1. Assign respirator costs for July to each of the six departments according to hourly usage.
2. Explain other bases of allocation that could be used to assign costs. Discuss the advantages and disadvantages of each allocation basis.

Problem 19B-5. Joint Cost Allocation
(L.O. 6)

Three distinct grades of chocolate sauce are made by the Thatcher Toppings Company. The initial ingredients for all three grades of chocolate sauce are first blended together. After this blending other ingredients are added to produce the three grades. The Extra-Rich blend sells for $4.20 per liter. The Quality blend sells for $3.60 per liter. And the Regular blend sells for $3.00 per liter. In July, 372,000 liters of ingredients were put into production, with output as follows: 81,840 liters of Extra-Rich blend, 148,800 liters of Quality blend, and 141,360 liters of Regular blend. Joint costs for the period are made up of $301,200 for direct materials, $246,000 for direct labor, and $196,800 for factory overhead. Assume there were no beginning or ending inventories and no loss of input during production.

Required

1. Using the physical volume method, allocate joint costs to the three chocolate sauce blends.
2. Using the relative sales value method, allocate joint costs to the three blends.
3. Prepare a schedule that compares the gross profit at split-off point that results from the two allocation methods for the three products. Compute gross margin both in total dollars and as a percentage of sales.
4. Additional processing costs could be incurred after split-off for a special ingredient for the Extra-Rich blend that would push up its selling price. If the company incurred $81,840 for this ingredient in this period, it is thought that the selling price could be increased to $6.00 per liter. Following these assumptions and assuming that joint costs are allocated using the relative sales value method, how much profit would be earned from Extra-Rich sales? Should the company add the extra ingredient?

Management Decision Case

Fullerton State Bank
(L.O. 5, 7)

California Bancorp is the parent corporation for two statewide banks, Fullerton State Bank and Long Beach State Bank. The Fullerton State Bank is the responsibility of its president, Mr. John Lawrence. Four senior vice presidents report to him and coordinate the activities of Marketing, Operations, Commercial Loans, and Investments. In addition, the Internal Audit Division reports directly to the Board of Directors. Within Operations there are five departments, as follows:

Departments	Functions
Controller's Department:	General ledger maintenance Assistant controller Special cost and revenue analyses
Data Processing Department:	Programming Systems design Data entry Computer operators Systems maintenance
Customer Service Department:	Tellers New account representatives Customer concerns
Bookkeeping Department:	Customer statement preparation Telephone and wire dollar transfers Service and vault charges
Proof Department:	Proving of bulk deposits Internal check clearing-house

The Customer Service Department is considered the primary department of this division, with the remaining four being support service departments.

According to the controller's department, fixed costs of the division are shared by all five departments and should therefore be grouped together in a fixed overhead cost pool and allocated based on total salary dollars. During 19xx the entire division expects to pay $1,200,000 in salaries. Projected costs to be charged to the fixed overhead cost pool include:

Depreciation, Furniture and Fixtures	$25,800
Telephone Charges	640/month plus $100/month for long-distance calls
Property Taxes	19,240
Electricity Expense	820/month plus $.001 per kilowatt hour of usage[1]
Rent, Buildings	36,000
Insurance Expense	11,960
Gas Heating Expense	1,040/month plus $.005 per cubic foot of gas consumption[2]
Equipment Leasing Expense	165,000

[1] 46,400,000 kilowatt hours are expected to be used.
[2] 1,640,000 cubic feet of gas are expected to be consumed.

Required

1. Compute the fixed overhead cost rate for the Operations Division for 19xx.
2. During 19xx the departments incurred the following salary costs:

Controller's	$236,480
Data Processing	372,920
Customer Service	279,400
Bookkeeping	166,400
Proof	144,800

   Determine the fixed overhead costs that were allocated to each department during the year.
3. Ms. Shu-Jen Chen, manager of the Data Processing Department, received a performance report for the year ended December 31, 19xx, as shown below. How good was Ms. Chen's performance? Critique the performance report as part of your answer.

The Fullerton State Bank
Operations Division
Data Processing Department
Performance Report
For the Year Ended December 31, 19xx

Amount Budgeted	Cost/Expense Item	Actual Amount	Over (Under) Budget
$ 96,000	Salaries, programmers	$ 95,060	$ (940)
96,000	Salaries, system designers	85,080	(10,920)
120,000	Salaries, computer operators	127,820	7,820
64,000	Salary, manager	64,960	960
25,620	Salaries, bank administration	37,520	11,900
165,000	Equipment leasing	172,880	7,880
30,000	Computer supplies	28,420	(1,580)
80,000	Software purchases	73,480	(6,520)
6,000	Data storage diskettes	6,560	560
4,920	Depreciation, furniture and fixtures	4,920	0
90,240	Fixed divisional overhead	111,876	21,636
27,000	Back-up data file maintenance	25,540	(1,460)
10,000	Bank-wide overhead	10,500	500
4,000	Miscellaneous expenses	3,280	(720)
$818,780	Totals	$847,896	$29,116

CHAPTER 20 RESPONSIBILITY ACCOUNTING AND PERFORMANCE EVALUATION

LEARNING OBJECTIVES

1. Define responsibility accounting and describe a responsibility accounting system.
2. Identify the cost and revenue classifications that are controllable by a particular manager.
3. Distinguish between a cost/expense center, a profit center, and an investment center.
4. Identify and describe the behavioral principles of performance evaluation.
5. State the operational principles of performance evaluation and explain how they are interrelated.
6. Prepare a performance evaluation report for (a) a cost/expense center; (b) a profit center; and (c) an investment center.

Whenever the term *management* is used, one can assume that an organization is being discussed. An organization consists of many people doing different types of jobs. One does not use the term *management* to describe the leadership of a husband and wife-operated grocery store down the street even though the owners are also the managers. Whether a company needs levels of managers depends on its size. The bigger the organization, the more managers it needs to keep everything running smoothly. As a company grows, its functional operations and the responsibilities associated with those functions tend to become decentralized. **Decentralization** means that control of the company's operations is spread among several people. Decentralization requires a special approach to managing an enterprise.

In this chapter you will learn how accounting assists management in controlling the operations of a decentralized company. One approach to this task is to use a process called responsibility accounting. Responsibility accounting is the foundation on which plans and budgets are developed in a decentralized organization. A responsibility accounting system is also important in controlling actual operations.

After defining responsibility accounting and illustrating such a system, this chapter will focus on the costs and revenues a manager can control or take responsibility for. The chapter will then emphasize the responsibilities of various centers in a decentralized company, that is, cost/expense centers, profit centers, and investment centers. The chapter concludes by looking at the performance evaluation process of a decentralized company. Particular attention is directed toward the behavioral and operational principles of performance evaluation.

After studying this chapter, you should be able to meet the learning objectives listed on the left.

Responsibility Accounting

Responsibility accounting is an information reporting system that (1) classifies financial data according to areas of responsibility in an organization and (2) reports the activities of managers by including only revenue and cost categories that are controllable by a particular

OBJECTIVE 1 Define responsibility accounting and describe a responsibility accounting system

manager. Also called **activity accounting** and **profitability accounting**, a responsibility accounting system personalizes accounting reports. Such a system emphasizes **responsibility centers**, which includes: (1) cost/expense centers; (2) revenue/profit centers; and (3) investment centers. By concentrating on these responsibility centers, a responsibility accounting system classifies and reports cost and revenue information according to responsibility areas assigned to managers or management positions.

Even though a company uses a responsibility accounting system, it still needs to collect normal cost and revenue data. To do so, a company must use normal recording methods and make normal debit and credit entries. A general ledger, special journals, and a defined chart of accounts are also used. Responsibility accounting focuses on the *reporting*—not the *recording*—of operating cost and revenue data. Once the financial data from daily operations have been recorded in the accounting system, specific costs and revenues can be reclassified and reported for specific areas of managerial responsibility.

Reporting operating costs requires special report formats and reporting techniques. The goal of the statement of cost of goods manufactured is to translate manufacturing cost data into information useful for purposes of inventory valuation, profit measurement, and external reporting. As discussed in Chapter 16, all costs of materials, direct labor, and factory overhead are used to compute the cost of goods manufactured. However, management needs more than the data included in the statement of cost of goods manufactured. Management also needs information on many day-to-day activities. Budget preparation, revenue and cost analyses, cost control procedures, and managerial performance evaluation all call for a special system for classifying and reporting information. A responsibility accounting system and its network of reports satisfies this need.

Organizational Structure and Reporting

A responsibility accounting system is made up of several responsibility centers. There is a responsibility center for each area or level of managerial responsibility, and a report is generated for each center. The report for a responsibility center includes only those cost and revenue items the manager of that center can control. If a manager cannot influence a cost or revenue item, it is either not included in the manager's report or it is segregated. Such segregation prevents the item from influencing the manager's performance evaluation. Cost and revenue controllability is discussed later in this chapter.

A look at a corporate organization chart and a series of related managerial reports will show how a responsibility accounting system works. Figure 20-1 shows a typical management hierarchy with its three vice presidents reporting to the corporate president. The sales and finance areas have been condensed, however, to emphasize the manufacturing area. The production managers of divisions A and B report to the vice president of manufacturing. In Division B the managers of the Stamping Department, Painting Department, and Assembly Department report to the division's production manager.

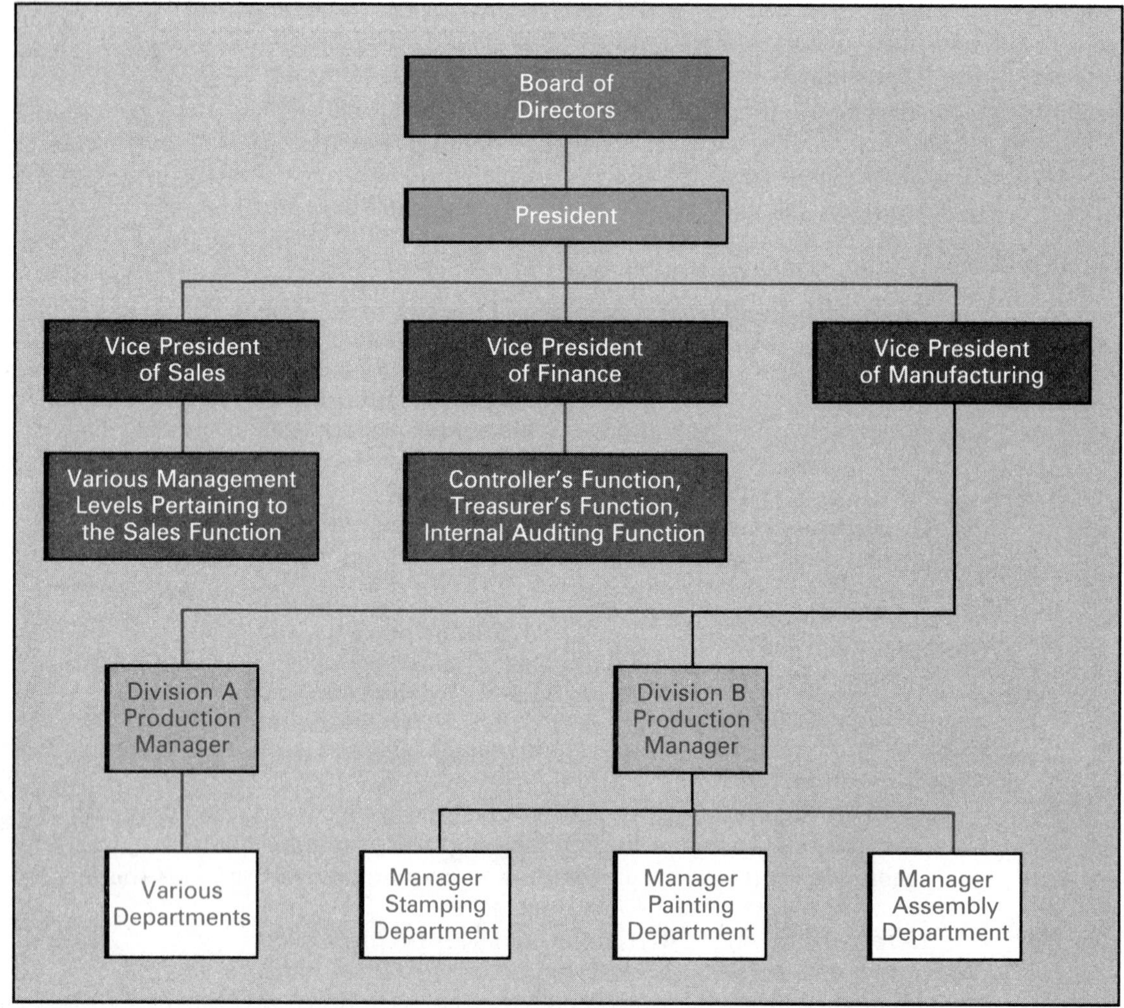

Figure 20-1. Organization Chart Emphasizing the Manufacturing Area

In a responsibility accounting system, operating reports for each level of management are tailored to individual needs. Because a responsibility accounting system provides a report for every manager, and because lower-level managers report to higher-level managers, the same costs and revenues may appear in several reports. However, when lower-level operating data are included in reports to higher-level managers, the data are summarized.

Exhibit 20-1 illustrates how the responsibility reporting network is tied together. At the department level the report lists cost items under the manager's control and compares expected (or budgeted) costs with actual costs. This comparison is a measure of operating performance. The manager who receives the report on the Stamping Department should be

Exhibit 20-1. Reporting Within a Responsibility Accounting System

Manufacturing: Vice President — **Monthly Report: November**

Amount Budgeted	Controllable Cost	Actual Amount	Over (Under) Budget
$ 281,400	Central production scheduling	$ 298,100	$16,700
179,600	Office expenses	192,800	13,200
19,800	Operating expenses	26,200	6,400
	Divisions		
339,500	A	348,900	9,400
426,200	B	399,400	(26,800)
$1,246,500	Totals	$1,265,400	$18,900

Division B: Production Manager — **Monthly Report: November**

Amount Budgeted	Controllable Cost	Actual Amount	Over (Under) Budget
	Division expenses		
$101,800	Salaries	$ 96,600	$ (5,200)
39,600	Utilities	39,900	300
25,600	Insurance	21,650	(3,950)
	Departments		
46,600	Stamping	48,450	1,850
69,900	Painting	64,700	(5,200)
142,700	Assembly	128,100	(14,600)
$426,200	Totals	$399,400	$(26,800)

Stamping Department: Manager — **Monthly Report: November**

Amount Budgeted	Controllable Cost	Actual Amount	Over (Under) Budget
$22,500	Direct materials	$23,900	$1,400
14,900	Factory labor	15,200	300
2,600	Small tools	1,400	(1,200)
5,100	Maintenance salaries	6,000	900
1,000	Supplies	1,200	200
500	Other costs	750	250
$46,600	Totals	$48,450	$1,850

particularly concerned with direct materials costs and maintenance salaries, for they are significantly over budget. Also, the underutilization of small tools may signal problems with that department's productivity.

The production manager of Division B is responsible for the three operating departments plus controllable divisionwide costs. The production manager's report includes a summary of results from the Stamping Department as well as from all other areas of responsibility. At the division level the report does not present detailed data on each department. Only department totals appear. As shown in Exhibit 20-1, the data are even more condensed in the vice president's report. Only corporate and summarized divisional data on costs controllable by the vice president are included. Note that the $1,200 for supplies, shown in the Stamping Department report, is part of the vice president's report. The cost is included in the $399,400. But like all costs reported at higher levels, specific identity has been lost.

Cost and Revenue Controllability

OBJECTIVE 2
Identify the cost and revenue classifications that are controllable by a particular manager

Management wants to incur the lowest possible costs while still producing a quality product or providing a useful service. Profit-oriented businesses want to maximize their profits. Not-for-profit organizations, such as government units or charitable associations, seek to accomplish a mission while operating within their appropriations or budgets. To achieve these goals, management must know the origin of a cost or revenue item and be able to identify the person who controlls it.

A manager's **controllable** costs and revenues are those that result from his or her actions, influence, and decisions. If a manager can regulate or influence a cost or revenue item, the item is controllable at that level of operation. Or if managers have the authority to acquire or supervise the use of a resource or service, they control its cost.

Determining controllability is the key to a successful responsibility accounting system. In theory it means that every dollar of a company's incurred costs or earned revenue is traceable to and controllable by at least one manager. However, identifying controllable costs at lower management levels is often difficult. These managers seldom have full authority to acquire or supervise the use of resources and services. For example, if resources are shared with another department, a manager has only partial control and influence over such costs. For this reason managers should help identify the costs for which they will be held accountable in their performance reviews. If cost and revenue items can be controlled by the person responsible for the area in which they originate, then an efficient, meaningful reporting system can be designed for measuring operating performance and pinpointing trouble spots.

The activity of a responsibility center dictates the extent of the manager's responsibility. If a responsibility center only involves costs or expenditures, it is called a cost/expense center. On the other hand, if a manager is responsible for both revenues and costs, the department is called a profit center. And finally, if a manager is involved in decisions to invest in plant, equipment, and other capital resources and is also responsible for revenues and costs, the unit is called an investment center.

Cost/Expense Center

OBJECTIVE 3 Distinguish between a cost/expense center, a profit center, and an investment center

Any organizational unit, such as a department or division, whose manager is responsible only for costs incurred by that unit is known as a **cost center or expense center.** The manager of a cost or expense center has no direct influence over revenue generation or decisions to invest in capital equipment. Instead, he or she is charged with the responsibility of producing a quality product or service at a reasonable but minimal cost.

The two terms *cost center* and *expense center* are both used in this discussion because both are used in business. *Cost center* is the term used more often. However, it has two distinct meanings. When discussing the accumulation of cost data, the term often refers to the smallest segment for which costs are accumulated and analyzed. Thus, if a machine were being analyzed and costs were collected for that analysis, the machine would be a cost center. When the term *cost center* is used in connection with responsibility centers and responsibility accounting, it means an organizational unit with a manager who is accountable for the unit's actions. To avoid confusion, expense center could be used to describe this type of responsibility center. But because that term is less widely used than *cost center,* this text will refer to such organizational units as cost/expense centers.

What makes a cost controllable? Earlier a cost was said to be controllable if the manager could influence its incurrence and amount. A manager cannot pick and choose the costs he or she can control. Those costs must be operating costs incurred by the cost/expense center. Such costs must also be variable depending on the center's activity. Fixed costs for supervising a cost/expense center should also be included in costs controllable by the manager. All other fixed costs, such as depreciation, insurance premiums, and property taxes, as well as the operating overhead allocated to the center cannot be controlled by the manager of a cost/expense center.

Cost/expense centers are unique in that their inputs (costs) are measurable in dollars, but their outputs (products or services) are not. Such organizational units must therefore add value to a product or service or support the business in another way. Cost/expense centers are not directly connected with the sale of a product or service. Consider the Teller Department and the Data Processing Department of your local bank. Their roles in the continued successful operations of the bank are obvious. Tellers are critical to good customer relations and the orderly receipt and withdrawal of funds by customers. The Data Processing Department is responsible for accurately recording all funds received and expended by the bank. Yet, neither department generates revenue. Hence, both departments are considered cost/expense centers in the bank's responsibility accounting system. And respective managers are responsible for only the costs incurred to operate each department.

Profit Center

When the manager of an organizational unit is responsible for revenues, costs, and resulting profits, the responsibility center is known as a **profit center**. The term *revenue center* is sometimes used in practice. Nevertheless, a pure revenue center is one in which the department or business segment's manager is only responsible for revenue generation. The costs incurred to generate that revenue are not used to measure the manager's performance. Such a situation is quite uncommon. *Profit center* is the more common term used to describe a business unit in which the manager is responsible for generating revenues and incurring costs in such a way as to maximize profits.

Managers of profit centers are accountable for both the amount of revenues their departments generate and the costs incurred to reach that revenue level. A profit center is operated much like a separate minibusiness, since it shows a profit or loss for its actions during a particular period. Profit centers are useful in decentralized companies. From a control standpoint, it is much easier to monitor operations if the enterprise is broken up into minibusinesses (profit centers). Large, decentralized companies are difficult to manage because of the size and diversity of the products sold or services rendered. By operating within a responsibility accounting system, a company can place managers in charge of dozens of small profit centers. Each manager is then responsible for the expected profit from his or her operating unit.

Controllable costs for a profit center are determined much as they are for a cost/expense center. A cost is controllable only if the manager can decide if it should be incurred. Revenues of a profit center can also be controlled or influenced by the center's manager. Such revenues are used to determine a center's net income.

Large retail establishments provide a clear picture of how profit centers are used. Department stores usually have several departments, such as children's clothing, cosmetics, women's clothing, menswear, and jewelry. Each department sells directly to the public, with each manager being responsible for generating a profit from sales in his or her department.

Must an organizational unit be directly involved with selling a company's product or service to be a profit center? No. An artificial selling price can be created for a department's output even if the product or service is not in a finished or saleable condition when leaving the department. This process is known as transfer pricing, and it is discussed in detail in Chapter 24. For purposes of this discussion, however, the analyses will be limited to those business units involved in direct selling activities.

Investment Center

In an investment center the concept of a responsibility center is carried one step further. The manager must be responsible for the revenues, costs and related profits of the department or business unit for it to qualify as an investment center. In addition, the manager must be evaluated on the effective use of assets employed to generate those profits. In other words, an **investment center** is a profit center whose manager can make significant decisions about the assets used by the center. On the surface there is little difference between a profit center and an investment center. But a closer look shows a very basic difference—top management turns over the control of the center's assets to its manager. In a profit center, top management determines the quantity and quality of assets employed by a department. If such assets are old or nonproductive, the manager can request improved equipment but cannot decide whether to replace or repair it.

Since the manager of an investment center has control over assets, he or she must be evaluated based on the effective use of those assets. Not only is the amount of profit earned important, but so is the center's **return on investment.** *Return on investment* is computed as follows:

$$\text{Return on investment} = \frac{\text{Net income}}{\text{Dollar value of the assets employed in generating that income}}$$

The numerator, net income, can either be before or after taxes. In the examples here, before-tax net income is used to make the analysis simpler. But remember that after-tax net income is commonly used in practice. The denominator is usually the average cost of assets employed to generate a center's profit. Although much has been written and debated about the methods of assigning value to the assets employed, the most common approach is to use the historical cost of the assets and not reduce their value to book value. Such an approach tends to keep the denominator constant, and the results from year to year are more comparable. If book values are used, the denominator is decreased over the life of an asset. Thus, one would expect the return on investment to increase.

To evaluate the performance of an investment center's manager, one must know the quantity and value of the assets under his or her control. One must also know the controllable costs and revenues for the period. Controllable costs and revenues are identified in the same manner as was discussed for a profit center. Because an investment center is similar to an autonomous business enterprise, more costs are usually controllable by the manager. Such costs as insurance premiums, depreciation of the center's assets, and property taxes traced to the center are controllable by the manager. The value of the assets employed must be computed by someone familiar with the investment center. The manager should be able to verify this amount, since he or she will be accountable for it at the end of the accounting period.

Later in this chapter, we will analyze three departments of Petosa Retail Centers, Inc. The focus will be on evaluating the performance of each of the three managers. However, determining the type of responsibility center being evaluated has a direct bearing on deciding which cost and/or revenue items should be used in the evaluation process. In the Petosa case, the Maintenance Contract Department is accounted for as a cost/expense center; the Home Furnishings Department is treated as a profit center; and the Custom Draperies and Blinds Department is an investment center. But before the case can be discussed, you must study the process of performance evaluation.

Performance Evaluation

Performance evaluation is the application of financial measurement techniques so actual results can be compared with expectations and performance judged. This definition seems straightforward enough. An individual's performance is measured by comparing actual and budgeted results of operations. But the process is not so easy. Successful performance evaluation is the result of several factors, some involving company policies, others, human factors.

Performance evaluation is an important part of a company's budgetary control program. An effective budgetary control program includes policies and procedures for: (1) preparing operational plans; (2) establishing responsibility for performance; (3) communicating operational plans to key personnel; (4) evaluating areas of responsibility; and (5) learning the causes of any variations between budgeted and actual results and making the needed corrections.

Operating policies alone will not provide a company with an effective performance evaluation system. The human aspect is critical to its success. People do the planning and perform the actions needed to generate a profit. They are also the evaluators and the evaluated.

Behavioral Principles of Performance Evaluation

OBJECTIVE 4
Identify and describe the behavioral principles of performance evaluation

Some basic guidelines regarding people must be part of any effective cost and revenue control system. Behavioral considerations should include those listed below.

1. Managers should have input into the standards and goals set for their areas of responsibility.
2. Top management's support of the evaluation process should be evident.
3. Only *controllable* cost and revenue items with *significant* variances should be the focus of performance reports.
4. Opportunity for manager response should be part of the evaluation process.

All considerations assume that an effective reward system (compensation) for attaining set goals was previously established.

1. **Managers should have input into the standards and goals set for their areas of responsibility.** The manager responsible for an operating area must have direct input into the goal-setting process of his or her area. Having a desire to perform is a key factor in meeting goals and attaining targets. When a manager believes that an operating target is unrealistic, or that plans were developed without the participation of personnel from the department, the desire to reach those goals may not materialize. To prevent this negative reaction, top management should encourage participative goal setting. When departmental managers are involved in setting the targets against which they are to be evaluated, their incentive to perform is increased. They perceive such goals as attainable and not a set of unrealistic targets set arbitrarily by top management.

2. **Top management's support of the evaluation process should be evident.** Top management must show its support by clearly communicating goals and plans, including each person's exact responsibilities, to all people involved. Failure to communicate plans to managers is a common cause of inefficient operating performance. Such communication accomplishes two important aspects of the budgetary control process. First, communication spells out in detail management's expectations of each manager. After discussing the plans with a superior, a manager knows the targets he or she should aim for and is more motivated to attain those targets. Second, the developing of an evaluation system and the communicating of that system to managers says that top management is deeply involved in the performance evaluation process and will support quests to meet set targets. Without the continued support of top management, a performance evaluation system fails to accomplish its objectives.
3. **Only controllable cost and revenue items with significant variances should be the focus of performance reports.** As previously discussed, performance reports should contain only those cost and revenue categories that a manager can influence or control. Holding someone responsible for costs outside of his or her control causes negative feelings and decreases the effectiveness of the control process and the evaluation system. In addition, when there are many cost and revenue categories within a manager's domain, it is more effective to limit the items reported on the performance report to those with significant variations from budget. This process focuses attention on those areas needing immediate action, so the manager will not waste time evaluating insignificant differences.
4. **Opportunity for manager response should be a part of the evaluation process.** Managers should have a chance to provide top management with feedback on their performance. Top management should praise good performance and not take it for granted. Silence does not imply good performance; it means bad management. If performance is poor or substandard, the responsible person should have a chance to defend his or her actions. There may be a good reason for a variance. Perhaps the cause was beyond the person's control. The key is to make the manager feel that he or she is an important part of the management team and not just someone on whom blame is placed when top management performs poorly.

Operational Principles of Performance Evaluation

OBJECTIVE 5
State the operational principles of performance evaluation and explain how they are interrelated

Making a performance evaluation system operable requires that a set of operational principles be followed. Note that they are linked closely with the behavioral principles already discussed. The operational principles of performance evaluation are listed below.

1. Provide accurate and suitable measures of performance.
2. Communicate expectations to appropriate managers and segment leaders to be evaluated.
3. Identify the responsibilities of each manager.

4. Compare actual performance with a suitable base.
5. Prepare performance reports that highlight areas of concern.
6. Analyze important cause and effect relationships.

1. **Provide accurate and suitable measures of performance.** Expectations of a manager's performance must be realistic to accomplish budgetary control. Accurate and suitable measures of performance should include predetermined budgets and standards, performances of other people in comparable jobs, and past performances in the same job classification. A manager will be able to do an effective job if these performance measures are provided and if they represent attainable goals. Nonfinancial measures, such as labor hours or units of output, can be used to measure performance and may be as useful as dollar measures.
2. **Communicate expectations to appropriate managers and segment leaders to be evaluated.** When developing its performance evaluation process, a company should ensure that its system of communicating expectations to managers at all levels is well-defined. The communications system should be two-way. It should go down through the organizational hierarchy and up from the lowest level of management to the chairman of the board. Each side must listen to the concerns and solutions of the other. Feedback is vital to the success of a performance evaluation system.
3. **Identify the responsibilities of each manager.** Before expecting a person to do something, one should inform him or her of what is expected. Identifying the specific responsibilities of each manager is part of the performance evaluation process. This step is usually accomplished when the company's responsibility accounting system is devised. One way to ensure the failure of a performance evaluation process is to have managers held accountable for actions they thought were another's responsibility.
4. **Compare actual performance with a suitable base.** When evaluating performance, one must compare what actually happened with a measure of what was anticipated or expected. This measure may be a budget prepared before the current period began, the average performance on a particular task over the past three or four years, a standard cost (discussed in Chapters 22 and 23), or simply a rough estimate of expectations. The point is that without some anticipated base, one has nothing to evaluate actual results against. And without that measurement ability, performance cannot be evaluated.
5. **Prepare performance reports that highlight areas of concern.** The preparation of performance reports is an important step in the performance evaluation process. Information contained in these reports should specify a manager's responsibilities. These responsibilities may be limited to cost and revenue items that depart enough from anticipated targets to warrant analysis. If a manager's area of responsibility involves only fifteen or twenty cost and revenue items, then all controllable costs and revenues may be included. But if there are

more than twenty, only those needing analysis for being far over or under target should be included. Remember, only controllable cost and revenue items belong in a manager's performance report.

6. **Analyze important cause-and-effect relationships.** Isolating a variation between a budgeted amount and an actual cost is just the beginning of the performance evaluation process. Some people believe that once this variation has been determined, someone is guilty and should be reprimanded. But a performance report is more than a set of numbers compared with one another. One cost or revenue variation from budget may help cause a second reaction (domino effect). A performance report should reveal cause-and-effect factors and significant relationships. If, for instance, a furniture manufacturer purchases poor-quality lumber, labor costs might soar because the wood is difficult to work with. Such qualitative information can often explain differences between budgeted and actual dollars. Much of this information must come from the manager being evaluated.

Implementing a Performance Reporting System

You have now learned about the elements needed to develop a performance reporting system.

1. A performance reporting system is based on the concept of responsibility accounting. As mentioned earlier, responsibility accounting is an information reporting system that classifies financial data according to specific areas of responsibility. By creating a detailed organization chart of the company, all managerial positions that will become part of the performance reporting system can be identified and areas of responsibility determined.
2. Adequate performance measures must be determined.
3. Specific duties and operating expectations must be identified and communicated to each manager.
4. A communications system must be established, and it must involve managers in determining their targets and goals for the period.
5. A reporting format must be devised, and it must contain only those cost and revenue items under a manager's control.
6. Once the budgeted and actual amounts have been measured and compared, the manager is expected to explain the significant differences on his or her report.
7. A manager and his or her superior must work out methods to correct problems.
8. A strong system of rewards and feedback is necessary for the performance evaluation process to succeed.

With these performance evaluation elements in mind, let us analyze the performance reporting techniques of Petosa Retail Centers, Inc.

Illustrative Case: Petosa Retail Centers, Inc.

Discussing performance evaluation in terms of behavioral principles and operational principles helps describe the process. But there is a large difference between discussing the concept and actually doing an evaluation. The Petosa Retail Centers, Inc., case analysis, discussed below, illustrates the process of performance evaluation in a decentralized company. Emphasis is placed on determining the costs and revenues a manager can control and on structuring and designing performance reports. The case analysis compares performance evaluation and reporting for a cost/expense center, a profit center, and an investment center.

Petosa Retail Centers, Inc., competes directly with Sears Roebuck and J.C. Penney for customers who want a store with a full line of household goods and services. Petosa's stores, which are in all major metropolitan areas, are located near Sears' and Penney's stores. Store layouts closely resemble those of competitors. Because of its large size, the company operates as a decentralized organization. In all 117 stores, the departments are large and are supervised by highly trained managers.

The analysis below concentrates on three supervisors and their performance reports. Bill Drown manages a service-oriented cost/expense center, Julia Mulligan supervises a profit center within a service business, and Nickolas Chrysochos supervises a production and service department that is treated as an investment center.

Maintenance Contract Department

OBJECTIVE 6a Prepare a performance evaluation report for a cost/ expense center

Organization. Bill Drown manages the Maintenance Contract Department at Petosa's Nashville, Tennessee, store. The company's Appliance and Gardening Departments sell maintenance contracts to customers who buy appliances and lawn and gardening equipment. These contracts guarantee that for a set annual contract price, all labor and parts needed to keep the item in operating order will be supplied by the Maintenance Contract Department of a Petosa store. The maintenance contracts are sold by the appliance and gardening equipment sales people and not by people working for Bill Drown. Hence, the Maintenance Contract Department and Mr. Drown do not have revenue responsibility.

Mr. Drown is responsible for thirty maintenance and repair people and a fleet of eighteen vans stocked with a full line of parts. Half the vans are involved in appliance repair activities; the other nine are used for lawn and garden equipment repairs. Twelve employees are support personnel involved in scheduling, purchasing, and stocking activities as well as in assisting the eighteen full-time maintenance repair people who operate the vans. The department is housed in its own building, which has room for parts storage and two bays for repairing the vans.

Operating Results for March. The costs identified with the Maintenance Contract Department for March 1988 are shown on the next page. The format is the original one received by Mr. Drown. As you can see, the report lists all costs assigned to the Contract Maintenance Department

Petosa Retail Centers, Inc.
Maintenance Contract Department
Operating Report
For March 1988

Supervisor: B. Drown	**Budgeted**	**Actual**
Labor:		
Appliance repair	$ 5,400	$ 5,940
Lawn and garden equipment repair	5,400	5,310
Support	6,000	6,240
Supervision	2,600	2,600
Labor-related benefits	3,600	3,920
Repair parts, appliances	12,500	10,800
Repair parts, lawn and garden equipment	16,400	17,250
Fuel, vans	2,250	2,520
Oil, tires, and repairs, vans	2,880	2,430
Depreciation, vans	2,400	3,000
Maintenance and upkeep, building	2,500	2,350
Property taxes, building	600	750
Depreciation, building	2,200	2,650
Insurance, building	450	510
Utilities, building	300	280
Local store overhead	2,100	4,070
Corporate general and administrative costs	6,290	8,880
Total costs	$73,870	$79,500

Performance: Operating costs were $5,630 over budget.

for both budgeted and actual data. At the bottom of the report, performance is said to be $5,630 over budget. The report, however, provides little additional information. Although the columns are totaled, there is no information on the over- or under-budget spending in individual cost categories. Also, included in the listing of costs are several which Mr. Drown cannot control.

Petosa's national headquarters has recently installed a responsibility accounting system for all 117 stores. Mr. Drown was asked to help prepare a format for the responsibility accounting report for his department. Of the costs included in his regular monthly performance report, Mr. Drown identified the following as being out of his control:

1. Fixed/allocated costs
   a. Depreciation, vans
   b. Property taxes, building
   c. Depreciation, building
   d. Insurance, building
2. Local store overhead
3. Corporate general and administrative costs

Using this information, the controller of the Nashville store put together a new report format.

The revised performance report for the Maintenance Contract Department for March is shown in Exhibit 20-2. Costs not controllable by Mr. Drown are summarized at the bottom. Those costs that Mr. Drown can

Exhibit 20-2. Performance Reporting: Cost/Expense Center

Petosa Retail Centers, Inc.—Nashville, Tennessee
Maintenance Contract Department
Performance Report
For the Month Ended March 31, 1988

Supervisor: Bill Drown	Budgeted	Actual	Difference Over (Under) Budget
Costs Controllable by Supervisor			
Labor costs			
Maintenance repair personnel			
Appliance repair	$ 5,400	$ 5,940	$ 540
Lawn and garden equipment repair	5,400	5,310	(90)
Support personnel	6,000	6,240	240
Supervision	2,600	2,600	0
Labor-related benefits costs	3,600	3,920	320
Repair parts			
Appliances	12,500	10,800	(1,700)
Lawn and garden equipment	16,400	17,250	850
Van costs			
Fuel	2,250	2,520	270
Oil, tires, and repairs	2,880	2,430	(450)
Building costs			
Maintenance and upkeep	2,500	2,350	(150)
Utilities	300	280	(20)
Total controllable costs	$59,830	$59,640	$ (190)
Costs Uncontrollable by Supervisor			
Fixed/allocated costs			
Depreciation, vans	$ 2,400	$ 3,000	$ 600
Property taxes, buiding	600	750	150
Depreciation, building	2,200	2,650	450
Insurance, building	450	510	60
Local store overhead	2,100	4,070	1,970
Corporate general and administrative costs	6,290	8,880	2,590
Total uncontrollable costs	$14,040	$19,860	$5,820
Total costs	$73,870	$79,500	$5,630

influence are reported first. He can control and has responsibility for labor and labor-related costs, repair parts, van costs, and building costs.

Mr. Drown's performance during March was much better than that stated on the old performance report. Overall, his controllable costs were $190 under budget. Areas he needs to work on are labor costs, appliance repair ($540 over budget); repair parts, lawn and garden equipment ($850 over budget); and repair parts, appliances ($1,700 under budget). There may be a connection between the low cost of parts and the high cost of labor in the appliance repair area. Repair personnel people may be using a lot of time trying to fix existing parts rather than replacing them when making repairs. Such action could also lead to lower-quality repair service. Mr. Drown should take action in this area. Other than those areas mentioned, he seems to be doing a good job. Although the new report format still shows the department as $5,630 over budget, Mr. Drown is only accountable for the controllable costs of his unit.

Home Furnishings Department.

OBJECTIVE 6b Prepare a performance evaluation report for a profit center

Organization. Julia Mulligan is the supervisor of the Home Furnishings Department in Petosa's Irving, Texas, store. This location is convenient for customers living in both Dallas and Fort Worth, making the Irving store one of the largest Petosa stores in the country. Home furnishings include furniture, beddings, glassware, rugs, and carpeting. This department occupies 20 percent of the store's floor space allotted to sales. Storage space for inventory takes up almost 40 percent of the store's warehouse space.

Since Ms. Mulligan is responsible for both the purchase and sale of all goods listed as home furnishings, her department is considered a profit center. She employs thirty sales people, four buyers, and twelve support people who work as sales-floor stockers, warehouse personnel, and delivery people. These three areas—sales, buying, and support—are operated as minidepartments, and each has a manager who reports to Ms. Mulligan.

Operating Results for March. The original performance report received by Ms. Mulligan for the Home Furnishings Department for March is shown on page 752. The report is divided into revenue and costs sections, and department income is shown. Budgeted and actual information is reported for each category. Ms. Mulligan's performance was judged to be $6,602 under the net income budgeted for the department.

As with the Nashville, Tennessee, store, the Irving, Texas, store is shifting to the new responsibility accounting reporting system. With the cooperation of her store's controller, Ms. Mulligan identified the following items as being out of her control:

1. Depreciation, sales floor
2. Depreciation, warehouse
3. Local store overhead
4. Corporate general and administrative costs

Petosa Retail Centers, Inc.
Home Furnishings Department
Operating Report
For March 1988

Supervisor: J. Mulligan	Budgeted	Actual
Revenue		
Furniture sales	$187,500	$191,900
Carpeting sales	126,250	129,600
Other sales	98,500	106,200
Total revenue	$412,250	$427,700
Costs		
Cost of goods sold, furniture	$112,500	$111,302
Cost of goods sold, carpet	75,750	84,240
Cost of goods sold, other	68,950	63,720
Selling, commissions	16,490	17,108
Selling, supervision	1,200	1,250
Buying, salaries	5,600	5,000
Buying, supervision	1,200	1,200
Support, wages	8,400	8,160
Support, supervision	1,000	1,100
Department supervision	3,250	3,250
Employee benefits	7,428	7,610
Utilities, sales floor	4,200	4,450
Depreciation, sales floor	8,600	14,250
Utilities, warehouse	2,800	3,100
Depreciation, warehouse	4,700	5,900
Delivery costs	3,300	3,550
Local store overhead	13,450	15,120
Corporate general and administrative costs	26,980	37,540
Total costs	$365,798	$387,850
Department income	$ 46,452	$ 39,850

Performance: Department income was $6,602 under budget.

With this input from Ms. Mulligan, the controller recast the performance report as shown in Exhibit 20-3.

As reflected in the new report, Ms. Mulligan produced department income in March that was $12,478 over budget. All cost categories were well within normal range. Selling commissions were $618 over budget, but that should be expected since sales were $15,450 over budget. Buying salaries were low, and the difference was probably caused by being one buyer short during the month.

What has not been shown in Exhibit 20-3, however, is the performance

Exhibit 20-3. Performance Reporting—Profit Center

Petosa Retail Centers, Inc.—Irving, Texas
Home Furnishings Department
Performance Report
For the Month Ended March 31, 1988

Supervisor: Julia Mulligan	Budgeted	Actual	Difference Over (Under) Budget
Costs Controllable by Supervisor			
Revenue from sales			
Furniture	$187,500	$191,900	$ 4,400
Carpet	126,250	129,600	3,350
Other	98,500	106,200	7,700
Total revenue	$412,250	$427,700	$15,450
Cost of goods sold			
Furniture	$112,500	$111,302	$ (1,198)
Carpet	75,750	84,240	8,490
Other	68,950	63,720	(5,230)
Total cost of goods sold	$257,200	$259,262	$ 2,062
Gross margin from sales	$155,050	$168,438	$13,388
Operating costs			
Selling			
Commissions	$ 16,490	$ 17,108	$ 618
Supervision	1,200	1,250	50
Buying			
Salaries	5,600	5,000	(600)
Supervision	1,200	1,200	0
Support			
Wages	8,400	8,160	(240)
Supervision	1,000	1,100	100
Department supervision	3,250	3,250	0
Employee benefits	7,428	7,610	182
Space costs			
Utilities, sales floor	4,200	4,450	250
Utilities, warehouse	2,800	3,100	300
Delivery costs	3,300	3,550	250
Total controllable costs	$ 54,868	$ 55,778	$ 910
Controllable department income	$100,182	$112,660	$12,478
Costs Uncontrollable by Supervisor			
Depreciation, sales floor	$ 8,600	$ 14,250	$ 5,650
Depreciation, warehouse	4,700	5,900	1,200
Local store overhead	13,450	15,120	1,670
Corporate general and administrative costs	26,980	37,540	10,560
Total uncontrollable costs	$ 53,730	$ 72,810	$19,080
Net department income	$ 46,452	$ 39,850	$ (6,602)

of the three minidepartment managers. For this purpose the sales, cost of goods sold, and gross margin from sales data are summarized below.

	Budgeted	Actual	Difference Over (Under) Budget
Gross Margin from Sales			
Furniture sales	$ 75,000	$ 80,598	$ 5,598
Carpeting sales	50,500	45,360	(5,140)
Other sales	29,550	42,480	12,930
Totals	$155,050	$168,438	$13,388

This analysis is revealing. Even though the department's overall gross margin was $13,388, the carpeting minidepartment had a gross margin of $5,140 *under* budget for March. Looking further into the data, carpet sales were $3,350 over budget, but the cost of carpet sold was $8,490 *over* budget. Ms. Mulligan should request information from her carpeting manager about this situation. Either someone has been buying carpet at increased prices and/or of increased quality, or sales prices are too low. Of course, these reasons may be connected. In any event, Ms. Mulligan has a serious problem to deal with, even though overall department income is very favorable.

Custom Draperies and Blinds Department.

OBJECTIVE 6c Prepare a performance evaluation report for an investment center

Organization. Nickolas Chrysochos supervises the Custom Draperies and Blinds Department at the Petosa store in Seattle, Washington. He has three full-time sales people working for him, and they are responsible for soliciting orders for custom-made draperies and window blinds. A major portion of this department's work involves making custom draperies for homes on special order. The sales people visit customers' homes and take all measurements for each order.

In addition to the sales staff, Mr. Chrysochos employs six drapery makers, five blinds makers, and four indirect labor personnel. The department uses a job order costing system for cost accumulation purposes. Seventy percent of the department's work is custom-made goods, and 30 percent of sales are ready-made draperies and blinds. Three sales clerks handle sales of ready-made goods.

The company considers the Custom Draperies and Blinds Department to be an investment center, since Mr. Chrysochos is responsible for buying such capital assets as machinery and equipment, which are used to make the custom draperies and blinds. He is also responsible for three automobiles used for sales, 2,000 square feet of sales floor in the main building, and the drapery production shop located in its own building adjacent to the store.

Petosa Retail Centers, Inc.
Custom Draperies and Blinds Department
Operating Report
For March 1988

Supervisor: N. Chrysochos **Investment base: $1,559,600**	**Budgeted**	**Actual**
Revenue		
Custom drapery sales	$ 75,450	$ 79,410
Custom blinds sales	59,250	62,190
Ready-made sales	57,730	56,280
Total revenue	$192,430	$197,880
Costs		
Cost of goods sold		
Custom draperies, materials	$ 30,180	$ 33,480
Custom draperies, labor	15,090	19,100
Custom draperies, factory overhead	7,545	8,020
Custom blinds, materials	29,625	30,040
Custom blinds, labor	11,850	12,130
Custom blinds, factory overhead	5,925	6,125
Ready-made draperies and blinds	40,411	38,290
Selling commissions, custom-made	8,082	8,496
Selling commissions, ready-made	1,732	1,688
Automobile expenses, selling	4,620	3,750
Automobile depreciation, selling	8,160	8,430
Department supervision	2,700	2,700
Employee benefits	7,891	8,823
Utilities, sales floor	1,200	1,320
Depreciation, sales floor	1,610	1,750
Local store overhead	2,350	2,290
Corporate general and administrative costs	1,780	3,650
Total costs	$180,751	$190,082
Department income	$ 11,679	$ 7,798
Department rate of return	.75%	.50%

Performance: Department income was $3,881 under budget.
Department return on investment for March was .5% (6% annualized), which is .25% under the anticipated monthly return of .75%.

Operating Results for March. Mr. Chrysochos' performance report for March, which follows the original format, is summarized above. Because the Custom Draperies and Blinds Department is an investment center, performance is judged by both the department's income and its return on investment. As shown, Mr. Chrysochos' overall performance was well below expectations. Department income was $3,881 *below* expectations for March. This situation meant that on the $1,559,600 investment base for the department, only a .5 percent return was realized. Target monthly return on investment was .75 percent.

As with the other stores, the Seattle, Washington, store changed to a responsibility accounting reporting system in March. After reviewing the cost and revenue categories with Mr. Chrysochos, the store's controller identified the following items as being out of the control of the department's supervisor:

1. Local store overhead
2. Corporate general and administrative costs

Using this information, the controller revised Mr. Chrysochos' performance report. It is shown in Exhibit 20-4.

Unlike the reports for Mr. Drown and Ms. Mulligan, the new reporting format for the Custom Draperies and Blinds Department does not turn an unfavorable situation into a favorable one. Mr. Chrysochos has problems generating a favorable gross margin from sales. There are also two or three operating cost categories that he should be concerned about. A further look at gross margin revealed the following:

	Budgeted	Actual	Difference Over (Under) Budget
Gross Margin from Sales			
Custom draperies	$22,635	$18,810	$(3,825)
Custom blinds	11,850	13,895	2,045
Ready-mades	17,319	17,990	671
Totals	$51,804	$50,695	$(1,109)

There is a definite problem in the production of custom draperies. Mr. Chrysochos should analyze all aspects of that area. Are cloth and other materials prices too high? Is there too much labor employed for the volume of business? Do the sales people need to revise retail price figures used to develop customer quotes? There may be several possible causes for the poor performance. Other areas of concern include sales commissions for custom-made products and employee benefits. The high cost of benefits may be related to excess labor in the custom draperies area.

As shown, regardless of the result for each manager, the new reporting format has helped determine ways to improve performance. Responsibility accounting provides the tools necessary to establish a performance reporting system that highlights cost and revenue areas under the control of a manager.

Exhibit 20-4. Performance Reporting: Investment Center

Petosa Retail Centers, Inc.—Seattle, Washington
Custom Draperies and Blinds Department
Performance Report
For the Month Ended March 31, 1988

Supervisor: Nickolas Chrysochos Investment base: $1,559,600	Budgeted	Actual	Difference Over (Under) Budget
Costs Controllable by Supervisor			
Revenue from sales			
Custom draperies	$ 75,450	$ 79,410	$3,960
Custom blinds	59,250	62,190	2,940
Ready-mades	57,730	56,280	(1,450)
Totals	$192,430	$197,880	$5,450
Cost of goods sold			
Custom draperies			
Materials	$ 30,180	$ 33,480	$3,300
Labor	15,090	19,100	4,010
Factory overhead	7,545	8,020	475
Subtotals	$ 52,815	$ 60,600	$7,785
Custom blinds			
Materials	$ 29,625	$ 30,040	$ 415
Labor	11,850	12,130	280
Factory overhead	5,925	6,125	200
Subtotals	$ 47,400	$ 48,295	$ 895
Ready-made draperies and blinds	$ 40,411	$ 38,290	($2,121)
Total cost of goods sold	$140,626	$147,185	$6,559
Gross margin from sales	$ 51,804	$ 50,695	($1,109)
Operating costs			
Sales commissions, custom-mades	$ 8,082	$ 8,496	$ 414
Sales commissions, ready-mades	1,732	1,688	(44)
Auto expenses	4,620	3,750	(870)
Auto depreciation	8,160	8,430	270
Department supervision	2,700	2,700	0
Employee benefits	7,891	8,823	932
Sales space costs			
Utilities, sales floor	1,200	1,320	120
Depreciation, sales floor	1,610	1,750	140
Total controllable costs	$ 35,995	$ 36,957	$ 962
Controllable departmental income	$ 15,809	$ 13,738	($2,071)
Controllable department rate of return	1.01%	0.88%	−0.13%
Costs Uncontrollable by Supervisor			
Local store overhead	$ 2,350	$ 2,290	($60)
Corporate general and administrative costs	1,780	3,650	1,870
Total uncontrollable costs	$ 4,130	$ 5,940	$1,810
Net departmental income	$ 11,679	$ 7,798	($3,881)

Chapter Review

Review of Learning Objectives

1. **Define responsibility accounting and describe a responsibility accounting system.**

   Responsibility accounting is an information reporting system that (1) classifies financial data according to areas of responsibility in an organization and (2) reports the activities of managers by including only revenue and cost categories a manager can control. A responsibility accounting system personalizes accounting reports. It is composed of a series of reports, one for each person in a company's organization chart.

2. **Identify the cost and revenue classifications that are controllable by a particular manager.**

   A manager's controllable costs and revenues are those that can be influenced by his or her actions and decisions. If a manager can regulate or influence a cost or revenue item, it is controllable at that level of operation. If a manager has the authority to acquire or supervise the use of a resource or service, he or she controls its cost.

3. **Distinguish between a cost/expense center, a profit center, and an investment center.**

   Any organizational unit, such as a department or division, whose manager is responsible only for costs incurred by that unit is known as a cost/expense center. Cost/expense centers have no direct connection with the sale of a product or service. When a unit manager is responsible for revenues, costs, and resulting profits, the responsibility center is known as a profit center. To qualify as an investment center, the organization must evaluate its managers on how effectively assets are used to generate profits.

4. **Identify and describe the behavioral principles of performance evaluation.**

   Behavioral principles of performance evaluation state that: (1) managers should have input into the standards and goals set for their areas of responsibility; (2) top management's support of the evaluation process should be evident; (3) only controllable cost and revenue items with significant variances should be the focus of performance reports; and (4) managers should be given opportunities to respond to evaluations.

5. **State the operational principles of performance evaluation and explain how they are interrelated.**

   Operational principles of performance evaluation stipulate that management: (1) provide accurate and suitable measures of performance; (2) communicate expectations with appropriate managers and segment leaders to be evaluated; (3) identify the responsibilities of each manager; (4) compare actual performance with a suitable base; (5) prepare performance reports that highlight areas of concern; and (6) analyze important cause-and-effect relationships. These principles are all based on concern for the manager and his or her areas of responsibility.

6. **Prepare a performance evaluation report for: (a) a cost/expense center; (b) a profit center; and (c) an investment center.**

   The key to preparing performance evaluation reports is to divide the report between those items a manager can and cannot control. A performance report for a cost/expense center contains only cost items, whereas a report for a profit and investment center contains both revenue and cost items. In addition, the report for an investment center provides information on the center's investment base and the rate of return on invested dollars.

Review Problem
Allocation and Responsibility of Overhead

Idaho Instruments Company is a high-tech firm engaged in the assembly of laser welders. The company is very employee oriented and has a complete workout room and indoor running track that can be used by any employee at any time, day or night. Included in the company's health facility is a special cafeteria serving only low cholesterol, low sodium foods. In 19x8, the cafeteria operated at a net loss of $178,950. Company policy is to allocate this cost to all responsibility centers since every employee has the opportunity to eat at the cafeteria. Management is considering three allocation bases, number of employees, meals purchased by employees, and total labor hours, from which to select the allocation base. Below are the data supporting each of the bases under consideration:

Responsibility Center	Number of employees	Meals purchased by employees	Total labor hours
Materials handling	9	655	50,400
Inventory storage	18	3,275	16,800
Electrical	63	10,480	100,800
Assembly	135	18,340	285,600
Engineering	54	9,170	134,400
Inspection	27	5,240	58,800
Accounting/Finance	9	2,620	33,600
Marketing/Sales	81	9,825	117,600
Purchasing/Shipping	18	1,965	8,400
Research/Design	36	3,930	33,600
Totals	450	65,500	840,000

Required:

1. Allocate the net loss of the cafeteria to the ten responsibility centers, using as a basis: (a) number of employees; (b) meals purchased by employees; and (c) total labor hours.
2. For purposes of traceability, which of the three allocation bases best associates the cafeteria's cost with the cost objective (responsibility centers)? Why?
3. For purposes of performance evaluation, which of the cafeteria loss distributions computed in part 1 above leads to the most effective control of costs? Defend your answer.

Answer to Review Problem

1. Amount to be allocated: $178,950

1a. Using number of employees basis:

Responsibility Center	Number of Employees	Percent Number of Employees	Amount Allocated to Each Department
Materials handling	9	2.0	$ 3,579.00
Inventory storage	18	4.0	7,158.00
Electrical	63	14.0	25,053.00
Assembly	135	30.0	53,685.00
Engineering	54	12.0	21,474.00
Inspection	27	6.0	10,737.00
Accounting/Finance	9	2.0	3,579.00
Marketing/Sales	81	18.0	32,211.00
Purchasing/Shipping	18	4.0	7,158.00
Research/Design	36	8.0	14,316.00
Totals	450	100.0	$178,950.00

1b. Using meals purchased by employees basis:

Responsibility Center	Meals Purchased by Employees	Percent Meals Purchased by Employees	Amount Allocated to Each Department
Materials handling	655	1.0	$ 1,789.50
Inventory storage	3,275	5.0	8,947.50
Electrical	10,480	16.0	28,632.00
Assembly	18,340	28.0	50,106.00
Engineering	9,170	14.0	25,053.00
Inspection	5,240	8.0	14,316.00
Accounting/Finance	2,620	4.0	7,158.00
Marketing/Sales	9,825	15.0	26,842.50
Purchasing/Shipping	1,965	3.0	5,368.50
Research/Design	3,930	6.0	10,737.00
Totals	65,500	100.0	$178,950.00

1c. Using total labor hours as basis:

Responsibility Center	Total Labor Hours	Percent Total Labor Hours	Amount Allocated to Each Department
Materials handling	50,400	6.0	$ 10,737.00
Inventory storage	16,800	2.0	3,579.00
Electrical	100,800	12.0	21,474.00
Assembly	285,600	34.0	60,843.00
Engineering	134,400	16.0	28,632.00
Inspection	58,800	7.0	12,526.50
Accounting/Finance	33,600	4.0	7,158.00
Marketing/Sales	117,600	14.0	25,053.00
Purchasing/Shipping	8,400	1.0	1,789.50
Research/Design	33,600	4.0	7,158.00
Totals	840,000	100.0	$178,950.00

2. For purposes of traceability

Of the three allocation bases, meals purchased by employees has to be the only basis with a direct connection between the loss and the cost objective. The loss is directly connected with the number of meals served. Therefore, number of meals served is the best allocation base to satisfy the test of traceability.

3. For purposes of performance evaluation

For the purpose of performance evaluation, none of the three bases are applicable. Only CONTROLLABLE costs should be included in a manager's performance evalution. None of the managers in the above departments have any control over cafeteria costs.

Chapter Assignments

Questions

1. Define responsibility accounting.
2. Describe a responsibility accounting system.
3. What is a responsibility center?
4. How does a company's organizational structure affect its responsibility accounting system?
5. "In a responsibility accounting system, operating reports for each level of management are tailored to individual needs." Discuss this statement.
6. What role does controllability play in a responsibility accounting system?
7. Describe a cost/expense center. Give two examples.
8. What is a profit center?
9. How does a profit center differ from a revenue center?
10. "A profit center is operated much like a separate minibusiness." Explain.
11. Describe an investment center.
12. Compare a cost/expense center, a profit center, and an investment center.
13. Describe how return on investment is computed.
14. What role does return on investment play in the evaluation of an investment center?
15. Define performance evaluation.
16. Identify the four behavioral principles of performance evaluation.
17. What is meant by participative goal setting?
18. State the six operational principles of performance evaluation.
19. Explain the importance of a good communications system in performance evaluation.
20. Explain how a responsibility accounting system is linked to effective performance evaluation of managers.

Classroom Exercises

Exercise 20-1. Responsibility Accounting/ Organization Chart (L.O. 1)

Pima Tennis and Golf Resort is in Apache, Arizona, at the foothills of the Painted Desert. Management has just hired your accounting firm to create and install a responsibility accounting system for reporting and performance evaluation purposes. Pima has two 18-hole golf courses, 24 lighted tennis courts, and a 450-room lodge.

The following managerial positions are to be included in your analysis.

Manager, golf course maintenance
Manager, customer relations
Manager, collections, payables, and billings
Manager, building maintenance
Vice president, accounting and finance
Manager, resort reservations
Manager, resort grounds maintenance
Vice president, resort occupancy
President and chairman of the board
Manager, tennis court maintenance
Manager, room cleaning/customer services
Manager, tennis and golf activities
Vice president, building and grounds
Manager, cash management
Manager, discount convention sales
Manager, budgeting and reporting

Use these managerial positions to prepare an organization chart for use in developing a responsibility accounting system.

Exercise 20-2. Controllable Versus Uncontrollable Costs (L.O. 2, 3)

For each of the following costs, state whether it is controllable or uncontrollable for a supervisor of (1) a profit center and (2) an investment center:

Cost of goods purchased, Shoe Department
Electricity costs, allocated using an overhead application rate
Depreciation, store equipment
Insurance expense, fire insurance on equipment
Buyer's salary, Home Appliance Department
Advertising expense, Video & Sounds Department
President's salary, manufacturing company
Auto and truck repair costs, Electrical Department
Contribution to local university, Garden Tools Department
Building repair costs, Reupholstering Department

Exercise 20-3. Responsibility Accounting/ Organizational Structure (L.O. 1, 2)

The following job titles are used by the Gregor Shewman Company:

Sales manager
Vice president, manufacturing
President
Cashier
Controller
Production supervisor
Vice president, sales
Purchasing agent
Internal auditor
Supervisor, repairs and maintenance
Warehouse manager
Marketing manager
Engineering research manager
Personnel manager
Treasurer
Vice president, administration

1. Design an organization chart using these job titles.
2. For each job title, list some possible costs for which the person holding each position would be responsible.

Exercise 20-4. Cost/Expense Center: Performance Report (L.O. 2, 6)

The Pima Tennis and Golf Resort, described in Exercise 20-1, has now been divided into responsibility centers. Mr. Ralph Beach is manager of golf course maintenance, which has been designated as a cost/expense center. During February the following costs, shown with their respective budgeted amounts, were incurred:

	Budgeted	Actual
Maintenance labor	$ 5,700	$ 6,200
Depreciation, equipment	3,000	3,300
Fuel and equipment repairs	2,450	2,200
Supervisors' salaries	2,500	2,500
Maintenance supplies	1,350	1,110
Sod and grass seed	3,100	3,340
Employee benefits	900	1,040
Resort overhead	5,000	5,790
Upkeep of storage sheds	400	240
Vandalism insurance	750	790
Depreciation, resort buildings	4,200	4,600
Small tools	400	260
Fertilizer and insect control powders	5,000	4,670
New trees and shrubberies	2,000	2,940
Water expense	2,600	2,180
Sprinkler system, parts and repairs	1,800	1,260
Totals	$41,150	$42,420

Prepare a performance report for Mr. Beach for February. Use a responsibility accounting format.

Exercise 20-5. Identification of Controllable Costs (L.O. 2)

Anderman Corporation produces computer equipment. Production has a three-tier management structure as follows:

Vice president, production
← Plant superintendent
← Production supervisors

Various production costs are accounted for each period. Examples include

Repair and maintenance costs	Superintendent's salary
Material handling costs	Materials usage costs
Direct labor	Storage, finished goods inventory
Supervisors' salaries	Property taxes, plant
Plant maintenance of grounds	Depreciation, plant
Depreciation, equipment	

1. Identify each cost item as a variable or fixed cost.
2. Identify the manager responsible for each cost.

Exercise 20-6. Performance Report: Profit Center (L.O. 2, 6)

Thomas Dry Goods, Ltd., is a worldwide merchandising concern with headquarters in London, England. Thomas's store in Tempe, Arizona, is installing a responsibility accounting reporting system. A summary of the Cosmetics Department's revenues and expenses for April are shown below.

	Budgeted	Actual
Sales, women's cosmetics	$54,600	$56,100
Sales, men's cosmetics	28,700	31,200
Total sales	$83,300	$87,300
Cost of goods sold, women's cosmetics	$38,000	$41,600
Cost of goods sold, men's cosmetics	15,700	17,740
Selling commissions	5,200	5,325
Buyer's salary	2,000	2,100
Supervisor's salary	2,400	2,400
Advertising expense	8,100	8,650
Depreciation, building	1,400	1,600
Depreciation, furniture and fixtures	800	950
Fire insurance expense	250	250
Travel expenses of buyer	1,640	2,110
Local store overhead charges	4,200	5,400
Total costs	$79,690	$88,125
Net income (loss) before taxes	$ 3,610	$ (825)

Assuming the Cosmetics Department is a profit center, prepare a performance report, in income statement format, for the department manager, Ms. Rosalind.

Exercise 20-7. Evaluating Performance: Investment Center (L.O. 6)

Operating results of the Boating Accessories Department of Robles Industries for January 19x9, is shown on the following page.

Analyze this performance report. State your opinion of Ms. Selbor's performance. Was her performance report structured properly? As part of your analysis, prepare a gross margin report for the three sales categories.

Exercise 20-8. Behavioral Considerations (L.O. 4)

An effective budget converts the objectives and goals of management into data. A budget often serves as a blueprint of management's operating plans.

A budget is frequently the basis of control. Management's performance can be evaluated by comparing actual results with budgeted results.

Thus, creating the budget is essential to the success of an organization. Implementing the budget and getting to the ultimate goal, requires extensive use of human resources. How the people involved perceive their roles is important if the budget is to be used effectively as a management tool for planning, communicating, and controlling.

Discuss the behavioral implications of budgetary planning and control when a company's management employs

1. An imposed budgetary approach
2. A participative budgetary approach

(ICMA adapted)

Robles Industries
Performance Report
Boating Accessories Department
For the Month Ended January 31, 19x9

Supervisor: Aide Selbor Investment Base: $883,500	Budgeted	Actual	Difference Over (Under) Budget
Controllable by Supervisor			
Sales			
Boat motors	$ 52,400	$ 56,340	$3,940
Water-sports equipment	36,500	31,890	(4,610)
Boat-repair parts	18,200	16,430	(1,770)
Total sales	$107,100	$104,660	($2,440)
Cost of goods sold			
Boat motors	$ 36,680	$ 34,640	($2,040)
Water-sports equipment	21,900	19,220	(2,680)
Boat-repair parts	14,560	15,690	1,130
Total cost of goods sold	$ 73,140	$ 69,550	($3,590)
Gross margin from sales	$ 33,960	$ 35,110	$1,150
Less operating costs			
Heating and electricity	$ 1,460	$ 1,660	$ 200
Depreciation, building	1,980	2,240	260
Fire insurance, building	450	450	0
Employee fringe benefits	2,130	2,350	220
Supervisors' costs	4,600	4,850	250
Storewide overhead costs	2,880	3,260	380
Department overhead costs	1,920	1,430	(490)
Other operating costs	870	240	(630)
Total operating costs	$ 16,290	$ 16,480	$ 190
Controllable department income	$ 17,670	$ 18,630	$ 960
Controllable department return on investment	2.00%	2.11%	0.11%
Uncontrollable by Supervisor			
Depreciation, equipment	$ 3,800	$ 3,800	$ 0
Selling commissions	8,787	8,079	(708)
Repair labor	5,060	5,510	450
Total uncontrollable operating costs	$ 17,647	$ 17,389	($ 258)
Net department income before taxes	$ 23	$ 1,241	$1,218

Interpreting Accounting Information

Internal Management Information: California Produce Company (L.O. 2, 6)

The Packing and Storage Department at California Produce Company is run by Elaine Waring. A responsibility accounting system was recently installed. A performance report is prepared monthly for each of the company's cost centers.

Ms. Waring's performance report for May is shown below. Top management notices that the $2,935 is 8.04 percent over budget, far above the 4 percent tolerance agreed on. Amounts allocated to the Packing and Storage Department were figured by means of appropriate allocation bases.

California Produce Company
Performance Report
Packing and Storage Department
For the Month Ended May 31, 19xx

Amount Budgeted	Cost Item	Actual Amount	Over (Under) Budget
$ 3,500	Packing materials	$ 3,600	$ 100
1,800	Packing supplies	1,700	(100)
8,240	Wages, packing	8,110	(130)
5,680	Wages, storage	5,820	140
4,500	Salaries, packing and storage	4,500	0
1,600	Salaries, vice president's staff	3,100	1,500
1,840	Depreciation, packing machinery	1,820	(20)
3,200	Depreciation, storage warehouse	3,200	0
1,250	Depreciation, companywide office building	2,500	1,250
870	Electric power, packing and storage	910	40
490	Electric power, main office	580	90
575	Heating, packing and storage	600	25
380	Heating, main office	420	40
780	Equipment rental, packing	750	(30)
410	Equipment rental, main office	450	40
290	Insurance expense, packing and storage	290	0
160	Insurance expense, total company	180	20
460	Equipment maintenance expense, packing and storage	440	(20)
220	Lift truck expense, packing and storage	200	(20)
250	Miscellaneous expense	260	10
$36,495	Totals	$39,430	$2,935

Required

1. Using the concept of controllable costs, identify the costs that should not be in Ms. Waring's performance report.
2. Recast the performance report, using only those costs controllable by the department's supervisor.
3. How should Ms. Waring respond to top management?

Problem Set A

Problem 20A-1. Allocation and Responsibility of Overhead
(L.O. 2, 6)

Eagle Manufacturing Company operates as a decentralized enterprise. There are seven responsibility centers in the factory area: molding, finishing, storage, receiving, shipping, scheduling, and inspection. During February the Factory Overhead account was charged with $382,400 in indirect management related expenses. Management wants these costs allocated to responsibility centers. It is considering three allocation bases: square footage, total costs incurred, and labor hours. The following information was provided to support the allocation analysis:

Department	Square Footage	Total Costs Incurred	Labor Hours
Molding	3,500	$ 435,060	640
Finishing	2,625	217,530	1,920
Storage	4,375	72,510	320
Receiving	1,750	145,020	1,280
Shipping	875	217,530	640
Scheduling	1,750	72,510	320
Inspection	2,625	290,040	1,280
	17,500	$1,450,200	6,400

Required

1. Allocate the balance in the Factory Overhead account to the seven departments, using as a basis: (a) square footage; (b) total costs incurred; and (c) labor hours.
2. For purposes of performance evaluation, which of the factory overhead distributions computed in **1** above leads to the most effective control of costs? Defend your answer.

Problem 20A-2. Cost/Expense Centers: Performance Evaluation
(L.O. 2, 6)

Burrows Brothers Specialty Company makes two types of road construction barricades. Department A produces brightly colored, cone-shaped support structures to identify detour areas. Department B specializes in colored crossbars, which are mounted onto vehicles to divert traffic from heavy construction areas. Frank Burrows manages Department A; Ron Burrows, Department B. Operating data for April are shown at the top of the next page. Each department is considered a cost/expense center because sales of each item are the Marketing Department's responsibility.

Required

1. Prepare a performance report for each of the two departments. Assume the company employs a responsibility accounting system.
2. Evaluate the performance of the two managers, using data provided in **1** above.

	Department A		Department B	
	Budgeted	Actual	Budgeted	Actual
Direct materials	$ 14,200	$ 16,100	$ 15,000	$ 14,100
Direct labor	34,100	35,400	41,000	40,200
Factory overhead				
Indirect labor	21,000	22,050	24,600	24,250
Supplies	3,400	3,520	6,400	6,650
Depreciation, building	2,100	2,350	2,700	2,800
Depreciation, equipment	3,600	3,900	3,700	4,200
Property taxes, factory	750	810	850	930
Electricity	1,340	1,360	1,410	1,400
Repairs, machinery	1,600	1,450	1,800	1,900
Insurance, building	900	1,020	950	1,100
Advertising expense	1,500	2,100	2,000	2,200
Packaging costs	6,400	6,600	7,100	6,940
Departmental supervision	5,900	6,100	5,900	6,240
General and administrative overhead	8,200	12,500	9,100	13,200
Interest expense				
Corporate loans	960	1,210	1,080	1,340
Total costs	$105,950	$116,470	$123,590	$127,450
Units of output	17,588	18,620	25,820	25,260

Problem 20A-3. Profit Centers: Performance Evaluation (L.O. 2, 6)

Label & Mori, a national men's clothing chain, has two stores in Honolulu, Hawaii. Wayne is the manager of the Manoa store; Joe, the Aloha store. The general ledger for the Hawaii branch revealed the following data for April 1–June 30, 19x6:

	Budgeted		Actual	
	Debit	Credit	Debit	Credit
Shoe sales				
Manoa store		$124,500		$122,100
Aloha store		110,900		114,750
Clothing sales				
Manoa store		296,000		286,900
Aloha store		245,000		256,200
Cost of goods sold, shoes				
Manoa store	$ 56,000		$ 55,940	
Aloha store	49,900		51,230	
Cost of goods sold, clothing				
Manoa store	262,800		259,790	
Aloha store	234,750		239,160	
Salaries and selling commissions	74,584		75,897	
Depreciation, store fixtures				
Manoa store	15,200		15,400	
Aloha store	12,400		12,400	
Depreciation, buildings				
Manoa store	8,100		8,300	
Aloha store	6,700		6,900	
Utilities expense	9,340		9,540	
Advertising expense	13,000		15,790	
Miscellaneous selling expenses	4,660		4,679	
Insurance expense	2,400		2,600	
Corporate administrative salaries	12,500		14,600	
Interest expense, corporate loans	5,200		5,600	
Totals	$767,534	$776,400	$777,826	$779,950

Wayne and Joe are responsible for store revenues and specific store expenditures. They do not make decisions about store buildings or fixtures. Corporate expenses are allocated to the stores by the company's home office.

Salaries of $14,500 and $13,500 were budgeted for the Manoa and Aloha stores, respectively. Actual costs for salaries were $16,200 in Manoa and $12,900 in Aloha. Selling commissions were 6 percent of total sales dollars in both stores for budgeted and actual sales as follows:

	Budgeted	**Actual**
Manoa Store	$25,230	$24,540
Aloha Store	$21,354	$22,257

Utilities expense

	Budgeted	**Actual**
Manoa Store	$5,240	$5,600
Aloha Store	$4,100	$3,940

Advertising expense

	Budgeted	**Actual**
Manoa Store	$7,400	$9,640
Aloha Store	$5,600	$6,150

Miscellaneous selling expenses

	Budgeted	**Actual**
Manoa Store	$2,520	$2,454
Aloha Store	$2,140	$2,225

All insurance expense is assigned to the Manoa and Aloha Stores on a 70 percent/30 percent basis, respectively.

All salaries and expenses for corporate administration are assigned to the Manoa and Aloha Stores on a 60 percent/40 percent basis, respectively.

Required

1. Prepare a performance report for the quarter ended June 30, 19x6, using a responsibility accounting format for the Manoa Store.
2. Prepare a performance report for the quarter ended June 30, 19x6, using a responsibility accounting format for the Aloha Store.
3. Compare the performances of Wayne and Joe. As part of your report, prepare a gross margin analysis for each product line.

Problem 20A-4. Performance Evaluation: Centralized Versus Decentralized Organization in an Investment Center (L.O. 2, 4, 5, 6)

Ferris Leather Processors, Inc., has twelve processing plants throughout the country. Its home office is Kansas City, Missouri. Organizationally, the corporation is operated in a centralized manner with each plant targeting operations to the goals and budgets set by the home office. The targeted rate of return on investment is 12 percent before taxes for each plant.

Two plants being investigated for low operating results are in Michigan. One is in Big Rapids, the other, just outside of Mackinaw City. The plant in Big Rapids specializes in leather accessories. It is managed by Dick Hanna. Leather clothing is the specialty of the Mackinaw City plant, which is managed by Dean Scheerens.

Leather goods are purchased centrally in raw finished form and shipped to each plant in bulk shipping cases. Each plant then cleans, shapes, and packages the goods for shipment to customers. Sales are made by sales people connected with each plant, but advertising decisions and expenditures are made by the home office. All decisions on purchasing equipment and building space as well as truck fleet rental are made in Kansas City. Operating losses of other plants and general and administrative corporate expenses are allocated to each plant.

The performance report for the year ending May 31, 19x9, is shown on the facing page.

Required

1. Identify the problems inherent in the organizational structure used by Ferris Leather Processors, Inc. Also identify the behavorial and operational performance evaluation principles not being followed by Ferris.
2. Recast the information given into a performance evaluation summary. Assume that Ferris's organizational structure is decentralized and that it uses a responsibility accounting reporting format. Also assume that everything except buyer's expenses and other corporate allocations is under the control of each manager.
3. Compute the rates of return for each plant, using the data generated in **2** above.

Ferris Leather Processors, Inc.
Performance Report
For the Year Ended May 31, 19x9

	Leather Accessories Plant		Leather Clothing Plant	
	Budgeted	**Actual**	**Budgeted**	**Actual**
Sales				
Accessories	$1,400,000	$1,610,700	$ 0	$ 0
Clothing	0	0	2,750,000	3,242,000
Miscellaneous	250,000	239,400	350,000	410,290
Total sales	$1,650,000	$1,850,100	$3,100,000	$3,652,290
Cost of goods sold				
Accessories	$ 490,000	$ 669,400	$ 0	$ 0
Clothing	0	0	1,237,500	1,652,900
Miscellaneous	95,000	105,760	140,000	163,400
Cleaning and shaping labor	184,500	192,400	265,000	291,700
Outside contractual services	62,000	67,200	115,000	122,800
Corporate buyer's expenses	116,600	146,250	235,000	292,100
Special packaging costs	186,200	190,700	290,000	301,040
Depreciation expense, equipment	32,700	35,100	52,500	52,500
Depreciation expense, building	26,900	27,900	44,800	51,640
Utilities expense	12,870	14,230	22,600	23,770
Telephone expense	3,200	3,470	5,400	5,880
Delivery trucks, fuel	4,250	4,510	7,500	7,390
Delivery trucks, repairs	3,900	4,110	5,800	5,410
Truck rental expense	10,400	10,400	20,800	20,800
Property taxes	17,500	19,100	31,200	33,810
Fire and liability insurance	2,400	2,600	3,900	3,950
Sales commissions	66,000	74,000	124,000	146,090
Other selling expenses	22,200	23,840	41,300	40,240
Advertising expense	49,300	67,400	84,200	102,720
Loss, Portland, Oregon, plant	16,100	17,900	16,100	17,900
Plantwide overhead	14,900	13,600	26,700	25,160
Corporate expense, general and administrative	42,500	51,400	81,600	97,270
Total expenses	$1,459,420	$1,741,270	$2,850,900	$3,458,470
Plant net income before taxes	$ 190,580	$ 108,830	$ 249,100	$ 193,820
Investment base	$1,588,160	$1,588,160	$2,075,830	$2,075,830
Plant return on investment	12.00%	6.85%	12.00%	9.34%

Problem 20A-5. Performance Evaluation (L.O. 2, 3, 6)

George Johnson was hired on July 1, 19x9, as assistant general manager of the Botel Division of Staple, Inc. Besides becoming acquainted with the division and the general manager's duties, Mr. Johnson was given specific responsibility for developing the 19x0 and 19x1 budgets. When he was hired, it was understood that he would be elevated to general manager of the division on January 1, 19x1, when the current general manager retired. This was done. As general manager in 19x1, he was obviously responsible for the 19x2 budget.

Staple, Inc., is a multiproduct company that is highly decentralized. Each division is quite autonomous. The corporate staff approves operating budgets prepared by the divisions but seldom makes major changes in them. The corporate staff actively participates in decisions requiring capital investment for expansion or replacement and makes final decisions. Divisional management is responsible for implementing the capital investment program. The major method used by Staple, Inc., to measure divisional performance is contribution return on a division's net investments. The budgets below were approved by the corporation. (Revision of the 19x2 budget is considered unnecessary even though 19x1 actual departed from the 19x1 budgeted.)

Comparative profit report ($000 omitted)

	Actual			Budget	
Botel Division	**19x9**	**19x0**	**19x1**	**19x1**	**19x2**
Sales	$1,000	$1,500	$1,800	$2,000	$2,400
Less					
Divisional variable costs					
Materials and labor	$ 250	$ 375	$ 450	$ 500	$ 600
Repairs	50	75	50	100	120
Supplies	20	30	36	40	48
Less					
Division-managed costs					
Employee training	30	35	25	40	45
Maintenance	50	55	40	60	70
Less					
Division-committed costs					
Depreciation	120	160	160	200	200
Rent	80	100	110	140	140
Total	$ 600	$ 830	$ 871	$1,080	$1,223
Divisional net contribution	$ 400	$ 670	$ 929	$ 920	$1,177
Divisional investment					
Accounts receivable	$ 100	$ 150	$ 180	$ 200	$ 240
Inventory	200	300	270	400	480
Fixed assets	1,590	2,565	2,800	3,380	4,000
Less					
Accounts and wages payable	(150)	(225)	(350)	(300)	(360)
Net investment	$1,740	$2,790	$2,900	$3,680	$4,360
Contribution return on net investment	23%	24%	32%	25%	27%

Required

1. Identify Mr. Johnson's responsibilities under the management and measurement program described above.
2. Evaluate the performance of Mr. Johnson in 19x1.
3. Recommend to the president any changes in the responsibilities assigned to managers or in the measurement methods used to evaluate division managers.

(ICMA adapted)

Problem Set B

Problem 20B-1. Allocation and Responsibility of Overhead (L.O. 2, 6)

A division of Hal Reneau Enterprises makes special-order horse saddles for customers in the Southeast. Seven responsibility centers are used to manage the production operation: cutting, trimming, inspection, packing, storage/shipping, central receiving, and scheduling. Management has asked you to make a comparative analysis of the allocation methods that assign corporate overhead costs to these centers. The following data were developed for your use:

Department	Total Costs Incurred	Labor Hours	Labor Dollars
Cutting	$ 428,120	1,200	$ 16,800
Trimming	535,150	1,800	22,400
Inspection	214,060	2,400	11,200
Packing	107,030	1,800	16,800
Storage/Shipping	428,120	1,800	11,200
Central Receiving	321,090	1,800	22,400
Scheduling	107,030	1,200	11,200
	$2,140,600	12,000	$112,000

During July, $165,940 in corporate overhead were assigned to the Saddle Production Division for distribution to the responsibility centers.

Required

1. Allocate the balance of corporate overhead charges to the seven departments, using as a basis: (a) total costs incurred, (b) labor hours, and (c) labor dollars.
2. For purposes of performance evaluation, which of the overhead distributions computed in **1** above most effectively controls costs? Defend your answer.

Problem 20B-2. Cost/Expense Center: Performance Evaluation (L.O. 2, 6)

The City of Dalescotts has hired you as a consultant. Your job is to evaluate the performance of the city's Street Maintenance Department. Ms. Linda Mitchusson is the department's supervisor. To assist you in your analysis, similar costs for the Street Maintenance Department of the City of Fordrock have been assembled. These data for May are shown at the top of the following page.

	City of Dalescotts Street Maintenance Department		City of Fordrock Street Maintenance Department	
	Budgeted	**Actual**	**Budgeted**	**Actual**
Materials				
Concrete	$ 60,400	$ 58,100	$ 29,500	$ 34,600
Bedrock	52,900	48,990	22,000	24,280
Asphalt	294,800	281,420	146,100	159,200
Labor				
Heavy construction	116,740	118,410	62,400	64,100
Light construction	72,220	73,930	41,000	41,940
Overhead				
Helper labor	105,200	110,560	62,900	64,110
Equipment repairs	9,400	9,820	6,150	6,020
Vehicle repairs	4,210	4,470	2,050	2,000
Fuel expense	6,240	6,810	3,940	4,090
Depreciation, equipment	10,100	10,800	6,200	6,200
Depreciation, vehicles	17,000	19,450	11,000	13,200
Liability insurance	2,040	2,240	1,400	1,600
Operating supplies	3,210	3,620	1,800	1,890
Electricity expense	1,740	2,110	910	940
Construction-site housing	6,940	6,910	3,900	4,140
Supervision	9,280	9,280	6,100	6,310
City overhead charges	12,980	13,800	8,200	8,860
Mayor's election activities	4,200	4,400	2,600	3,600
City council charges	7,900	8,800	4,200	5,190
Total costs	$797,500	$793,920	$422,350	$452,270
Number of road repair requests honored	35	31	22	28

1. Prepare a performance report for each of the two departments. Assume the two cities employ responsibility accounting systems.
2. Evaluate the performance of Ms. Mitchusson, using data provided in **1** above.

Problem 20B-3. Profit Centers: Performance Evaluation

Jim Peters and Larry Scott manage the E & W and PW branches of Recruiters Appliances, Inc. All goods sold by these stores fall into two groups, white goods and brown goods. White goods include refrigerators, freezers, washing machines, and clothes dryers. Brown goods include televisions, radios, and stereos. The general ledger for Recruiters Appliances, Inc., for February revealed the following information:

	Budgeted		Actual	
	Debit	Credit	Debit	Credit
Sales, white goods				
E & W store		$125,400		$136,550
PW store		152,100		146,640
Sales, brown goods				
E & W store		86,200		97,240
PW store		120,700		116,120
Cost of goods sold, white goods				
E & W store	$ 68,970		$ 74,560	
PW store	83,655		81,650	
Cost of goods sold, brown goods				
E & W store	51,720		56,940	
PW store	72,420		70,880	
Salaries and selling commissions	56,552		58,595	
Utilities expense	3,630		3,860	
Advertising expense	14,000		16,060	
Insurance expense	2,400		2,600	
Depreciation expense, fixtures				
E & W store	5,900		6,100	
PW store	8,200		9,980	
Rent expense	7,700		8,000	
Miscellaneous selling expenses	3,870		3,970	
Corporate administrative salaries	8,400		8,600	
Interest expense, corporate loans	2,500		2,900	
Totals	$389,917	$484,400	$404,695	$496,550

Mr. Peters and Mr. Scott are responsible for store profits based on each store's sales and expenditures, which are made and approved by each manager. None of the managers make decisions concerning fixture purchases, but all are responsible for store rent. Corporate expenses are allocated to each store from the corporation's home office.

Salaries of $8,200 and $9,600 were budgeted for the E & W and PW stores, respectively. Actual salaries were $8,450 for E & W and $10,410 for PW. Selling commissions were as follows:

	Budgeted	Actual
E & W Store	$16,928	$18,710
PW Store	$21,824	$21,025

Utilities expense was:

	Budgeted	Actual
E & W Store	$1,640	$1,750
PW Store	$1,990	$2,110

Advertising expense was:

	Budgeted	Actual
E & W Store	$6,200	$6,450
PW Store	$7,800	$9,610

Insurance expense was assigned to E & W and PW stores on a 35 percent/65 percent basis, respectively.

Rent expense was:

	Budgeted	Actual
E & W Store	$3,200	$3,200
PW Store	$4,500	$4,800

Miscellaneous selling expenses were:

	Budgeted	Actual
E & W Store	$1,690	$1,870
PW Store	$2,180	$2,100

Corporate administrative salaries and interest expense were assigned to E & W and PW stores on a 40 percent/60 percent basis, respectively.

Required

1. Prepare a monthly performance report, based on a responsibility accounting format, for the E & W store.
2. Prepare a monthly performance report, based on a responsibility accounting format, for the PW store.
3. For your report, compare the performances of Mr. Peters and Mr. Scott. Include a gross margin analysis of white goods and brown goods.

Problem 20B-4. Investment Center Performance Evaluation: Centralized Versus Decentralized Organization (L.O. 2, 4, 5, 6)

Fritzemeyer Motors, Inc., is a retail automobile sales company with eight divisions in the Midwest. The company specializes in automobiles manufactured in Sweden and England. Organizationally, the company is operated in a centralized fashion. Each division patterns its budgets to the goals and targets set by the home office in Iowa City, Iowa. Top management has said that it expects a 14 percent rate of return on investment for the current quarter.

Two of the eight divisions have not been operating at the expected level. The troubled operations are in Akron, Ohio, and Peoria, Illinois. Akron is managed by Dick Metcalf; Peoria, by Mike Lane.

All automobiles are purchased by the home office and shipped to the divisions. Each division then cleans and otherwise prepares them for sale. Sales commissions are earned by local sales people, but advertising and promotion costs are controlled by the home office. All decisions concerning the purchase of equipment and buildings are made by central management. Operating losses of other divisions as well as corporate general and administrative expenses are allocated to the divisions.

The performance report for the two divisions for the quarter ended September 30, 19x8, is shown on the following page.

Fritzemeyer Motors, Inc.
Performance Report
For the Quarter Ended September 30, 19x8

	Akron Ohio, Division		Peoria, Illinois, Division	
	Budgeted	Actual	Budgeted	Actual
Sales				
Swedish-made autos	$ 836,000	$ 914,440	$ 704,000	$ 802,390
English-made autos	736,000	702,960	552,000	562,610
Parts and repairs	125,500	136,130	98,600	101,840
Total sales	$1,697,500	$1,753,530	$1,354,600	$1,466,840
Cost of goods sold				
Swedish-made autos	$ 601,600	$ 690,440	$ 472,400	$ 561,230
English-made autos	504,800	491,960	353,600	363,740
Parts	37,650	47,560	29,580	34,660
Repair labor	43,925	49,880	34,510	37,230
Sales commissions, autos	141,480	145,566	113,040	129,675
Corporate buyer's expense	21,250	26,900	15,460	22,310
Utilities expense	4,250	4,320	3,980	3,920
Demonstration auto expense	2,750	3,810	3,250	3,140
Depreciation, demonstration autos	2,100	2,260	2,800	2,990
Depreciation, equipment	3,600	3,600	3,250	3,350
Depreciation, building	2,750	2,950	2,600	2,600
Telephone charges	1,440	1,520	1,350	1,390
Advertising expense	11,780	14,790	21,400	23,110
Promotion costs	8,550	9,920	10,640	9,750
Other selling expenses	2,340	2,440	2,280	2,280
Property taxes	920	970	880	910
Insurance, fire and liability	790	790	640	730
Divisional overhead	4,250	4,530	5,350	5,260
Loss, Lincoln, Nebraska, division	2,600	3,100	2,600	3,100
Corporate general and administrative expenses	7,250	7,750	6,150	6,320
Total expenses	$1,406,075	$1,515,056	$1,085,760	$1,217,695
Divisional net income before taxes	$ 291,425	$ 238,474	$ 268,840	$ 249,145
Investment base	$2,081,600	$2,081,600	$1,920,280	$1,920,280
Divisional return on investment	14.00%	11.46%	14.00%	12.97%

Required

1. What problems are inherent in the organizational structure used by Fritzemeyer Motors, Inc.? In your discussion include the behavioral and operational performance evaluation principles not being followed.

2. Recast the information given into a performance evaluation summary based on a decentralized organizational structure. Use a responsibility accounting reporting format. Assume that control is shifted to each manager for everything except buyer's expenses and other corporate allocations.
3. Compute the rates of return for each division, using the data generated in **2.**

Problem 20B-5. Responsibility Accounting and Budgets
(L.O. 2, 3, 4, 5)

Argon County Hospital is located in the county seat. Argon county is a well-known summer resort area. The county's population doubles during the vacation months of May through August, and hospital activity more than doubles. Although Argon is a relatively small hospital, its pleasant surroundings have attracted a well-trained and competent medical staff.

An administrator was hired a year ago to improve the hospital's business activities. Among the new ideas introduced was responsibility accounting. This program was announced in a memo accompanying quarterly cost reports supplied to department heads. Previously, cost data were presented to department heads infrequently. Excerpts from the announcement and the report received by the laundry supervisor are presented below:

Argon County Hospital
Performance Report: Laundry Department
For the Months July–September, 19x3

	Budget	Actual	(Over) Under Budget	Percent (Over) Under Budget
Patient days	9,500	11,900	(2,400)	(25)
Pounds processed, laundry	125,000	156,000	(31,000)	(25)
Costs				
Laundry labor	$ 9,000	$12,500	($3,500)	(39)
Supplies	1,100	1,875	(775)	(70)
Water, water heating and softening	1,700	2,500	(800)	(47)
Maintenance	1,400	2,200	(800)	(57)
Supervisor's salary	3,150	3,750	(600)	(19)
Allocated administrative costs	4,000	5,000	(1,000)	(25)
Equipment depreciation	1,200	1,250	(50)	(4)
	$21,550	$29,075	($7,525)	(35)

Administrator's comments:
Costs are significantly above budget for the quarter. Particular attention should be paid to labor, supplies, and maintenance. The hospital has adopted a responsibility accounting system. From now on you will receive quarterly reports, which will compare the costs of operating your department with budgeted costs. The reports will highlight differences (variations) so you can zero in on departures from budgeted costs. (This is called management by exception.) Responsibility accounting means you are accountable for keeping the costs in your department within budget. Variations from the budget will help you identify out-of-line costs. The size of the variation will indicate which costs are most important. Your first report accompanies this announcement.

The annual budget for 19x3 was constructed by the new administrator. Quarterly budgets were computed as one-fourth of the annual budget. The administrator compiled the budget by analyzing costs from the prior three years. The analysis showed that all costs increased each year and that the increases were more rapid between the second and third years. The administrator considered establishing a budget according to an average of the prior three years' costs, hoping that installation of the system would reduce costs to this level. However, because of rapidly increasing prices, 19x2 costs, less 3 percent, were finally chosen for the 19x3 budget. The activity level measured by patient days and pounds of laundry processed was set at 19x2 volume, which was approximately equal to the volume in each of the past three years.

Required

1. Comment on the method used to construct the budget.
2. What information should be communicated by variations from budget?
3. Does the report effectively communicate the level of efficiency of this department? Give reasons for your answer.

(ICMA adapted)

Management Decision Case

Kelly Petroleum Company
(L.O. 1, 4, 5, 6)

Kelly Petroleum Company has a large oil and natural gas project in Oklahoma. The project has been organized into two production centers (Petroleum Production and Natural Gas Production) and one service center (Maintenance).

Don Pepper, maintenance center manager, has organized his maintenance workers into work crews that serve the two production centers. The crews perform preventive maintenance and repair equipment both in the field and in the central maintenance shop.

Pepper is responsible for scheduling all maintenance work in the field and at the central shop. Preventive maintenance is performed according to a set schedule established by Pepper and approved by production center managers. Breakdowns are given immediate priority in scheduling, so downtime is minimized. Thus, preventive maintenance must occasionally be postponed, but every attempt is made to reschedule it within three weeks.

Preventive maintenance is the responsibility of Pepper. However, if a significant problem is discovered during the work, a production center supervisor authorizes and supervises the repair after checking with Pepper.

When a breakdown in the field occurs, the production centers contact Pepper to initiate the repairs. The work is supervised by a production center supervisor. Machinery and equipment must sometimes be replaced while they are being repaired in the central shop. This procedure is followed only when the time to make a repair would significantly interrupt operations. Equipment replacement is recommended by the maintenance work crew supervisor and approved by a production center supervisor.

Routine preventive maintenance and breakdowns of automotive and mobile equipment used in the field are completed in the central shop. All repairs and maintenance activities in the central shop are under the direction of Pepper.

Maintenance Center Accounting Activities

Pepper has records identifying the work crews assigned to each job in the field, the number of hours spent on the job, and the parts and supplies used.

In addition, records for the central shop (jobs, labor hours, and parts and supplies) have been maintained. However, this detailed maintenance information is not incorporated into Kelly's accounting system.

Pepper develops the annual budget for the maintenance center by: (1) planning the preventive maintenance needed during the year; (2) estimating the number and seriousness of breakdowns; and (3) estimating shop activities. He then estimates the labor, parts, and supply costs and develops budget amounts by line item. Because the timing of the breakdowns is impossible to plan, Pepper divides the annual budget by 12 to derive monthly budgets.

All costs incurred by work crews in the field and in the central shop are accumulated monthly. They are then allocated to the two production cost centers based on the field hours worked in each production center. This method of cost allocation has been used because of Pepper's recommendation that it was easy to implement and understand. Furthermore, he believed that a better allocation system was impossible to incorporate into monthly reports because of the wide range of salaries paid to maintenance workers and the fast turnover of materials and parts.

The November cost report for the Maintenance Center, provided by the Accounting Department, is shown below.

Oklahoma Project
Maintenance Center Cost Report
For the Month of November 1989
(in thousands of dollars)

	Budget	Actual	Petroleum Production	Natural Gas Production
Shop hours	2,000	1,800	—	—
Field hours	8,000	10,000	6,000	4,000
Labor, electrical	$ 25.0	$ 24.0	$ 14.4	$ 9.6
Labor, mechanical	30.0	35.0	21.0	14.0
Labor, instrumentation	18.0	22.5	13.5	9.0
Labor, automotive	3.5	2.8	1.7	1.1
Labor, heavy equipment	9.6	12.3	7.4	4.9
Labor, equipment operation	28.8	35.4	21.2	14.2
Labor, general	15.4	15.9	9.5	6.4
Parts	60.0	86.2	51.7	34.5
Supplies	15.3	12.2	7.3	4.9
Lubricants and fuels	3.4	3.0	1.8	1.2
Tools	2.5	3.2	1.9	1.3
Accounting and data processing	1.5	1.5	.9	.6
Total	$213.0	$254.0	$152.3	$101.7

Production Center Manager's Concerns

Both production center managers have been upset with the cost allocation method. Furthermore, they believe the report is virtually useless as a cost control device. Actual costs always seem to deviate from the monthly budget, and the proportion charged to each production center varies significantly from month to month. Maintenance costs have increased substantially since 1987, and production managers believe they have no way of judging whether such an increase is reasonable.

The two production managers, Pepper, and representatives of corporate accounting met to discuss these concerns. They concluded that a responsibility accounting system should be developed to replace the current system. In their opinion a responsibility accounting system would alleviate the production managers' concerns and accurately reflect activity in the Maintenance Center.

Required

1. Explain the purposes of a responsibility accounting system. Also, discuss how such a system could resolve the concern of production center managers.
2. Describe behavioral advantages generally attributed to responsibility accounting systems that management should expect if the system is effectively introduced into the maintenance center.
3. Describe a report format for the maintenance center based on an effective responsibility accounting system. Explain which, if any, of the maintenance center's costs should be charged to the two production centers.

(ICMA adapted)

CHAPTER 21 THE BUDGETING PROCESS

LEARNING OBJECTIVES

1. Describe the structure and contents of a budget.
2. Identify the five groups of budgeting principles, and explain the principles in each group.
3. Define the concept of budgetary control.
4. Identify the components of a master budget, and describe how they relate to each other.
5. Prepare a period budget.
6. State the purpose and make-up of a cash budget.
7. Prepare a cash budget.

The budgetary control process includes cost planning and cost control. In this chapter the focus is on cost planning. We outline the principles of budgeting, which deal with long-term and short-term goals, human responsibilities, housekeeping, and follow-up. Using these principles along with a number of cost accounting tools explained earlier in the book, we describe the preparation of period budgets, the master budget, and the cash budget. After studying this chapter, you should be able to meet the learning objectives listed on the left.

What Is a Budget and What Does It Look Like?

To someone who has never worked with a budget, such a document may be thought of as a cure-all for the financial problems of an enterprise. Why? Because the word *budget* has been heard in this context by almost everyone. Do you recall any discussion on television or in the newspapers regarding our federal budget? We have all heard about deficit spending by the U.S. government over the past four or five decades. And the cure for this deficit spending is to "balance the budget." This statement is misleading because the spending processes cannot be used to balance the budget. What politicians and news commentators are really saying is: to reduce or reverse the current deficit, one must ensure that the intake is greater than the payout. But there is only one way to balance a budget, and that is by preparing the document so the revenue side equals the expenditure side. That is all there is to it.

A budget is a financial document created before anticipated transactions occur and is often called a financial plan of action. The key to understanding the term *budget* is to realize that it is nothing more than a piece of paper on which financial data are printed. These data have been projected for a series of events that have yet to occur. It is a printed crystal ball of a set of financial transactions.

The federal budget contains all anticipated revenues and expenditures of the government for a time period. In order to balance this budget, one must ensure that the numbers on one side add up to the numbers on the other side. A budget is composed of anticipated dollar amounts, and the document itself cannot help balance anything. The people making taxing and appropriation decisions are the only ones who can make a balanced budget become a reality.

OBJECTIVE 1
Describe the structure and contents of a budget

Now that you have a feel for how a budget operates as a financial document, what does a budget look like? Well, a budget can take on an infinite number of shapes and forms. The structure depends on what is being budgeted, the size of the organization preparing the budget, the degree to which the budgeting process is integrated into the financial structure of the enterprise, and the amount of training the preparer has in his or her background. Unlike the formal income statement or the balance sheet, a budget does not have a standard form to be memorized by the student of budgeting. A budget can be as simple as the projected sales and costs of a corner soft drink stand or as complicated as the financial projections of General Motors Corporation for the upcoming year.

A budget should contain enough information presented in an orderly manner so that its purpose is communicated to the reader. Too much information tends to cloud the meaning and accuracy of the data. Too little information may result in overspending because the reader did not understand the spending limits suggested by the document. A budget need not contain both revenue and expense components nor does it have to be balanced. A Materials Purchases Budget, for example, contains only projected expenditures for materials for the period being analyzed. A budget can also be made up *entirely* of nondollar data, such as hours, units of product, or number of services.

When preparing a budget, make sure you include a clearly stated title or heading and the time period under consideration. Clearly label the budget's components and list the unit and financial data in an orderly manner. The actual format of the budget is developed by the budget preparer. Of course, a company may have developed its own budget format for recurring budget instruments used on a regular basis. But if a new service or product needs budget information to support its value to the company, the document need not follow other budget structures and formats. The only underlying concept that must be followed is that the information contained in the budget should be accurate as possible and meaningful to the recipient.

Exhibit 21-1 contains two examples of simple budgets prepared for diverse purposes. They are presented for illustrative purposes only and should not be considered as official guidelines for budget preparation when doing the chapter assignments. You should use your imagination and create your own budget formats. Example 1 is the revenues and expenditures budget of the Boosters Club for the homecoming football game of the State University Knights. Example 2 contains projections of hotel occupancy for the Down Home Resort. Note that in Example 2, the budget contains no dollar information and is not balanced.

Exhibit 21-1. Examples of Budgets

Example 1.

State University Knights
Boosters Club
Revenue and Expenditure Budget
Homecoming Activities—19x9

Budgeted revenues		
Football concession sales	$22,500	
Homecoming dance tickets 1,200 @ $20	24,000	
Parking fees	425	
Total budgeted revenues		$46,925
Budgeted expenditures		
Dance music group	$ 8,500	
Hall rental	2,000	
Refreshments	3,600	
Printing costs	1,450	
Concession purchases	12,200	
Clean-up costs	4,720	
Miscellaneous	800	
Total budgeted expenditures		33,270
Excess of revenues over expenditures		$13,655

Example 2.

Down Home Resort
Room Occupancy Budget
For the Year Ending December 31, 19x7

	Projected Occupancy							
	Singles (50)		Doubles (80)		Minisuites (10)		Luxury Suites (6)	
Month	Rooms	%	Rooms	%	Rooms	%	Rooms	%
Jan.	20	40.0	30	37.5	2	20.0	1	16.7
Feb.	24	48.0	36	45.0	3	30.0	1	16.7
Mar.	28	56.0	42	52.5	4	40.0	2	33.3
Apr.	32	64.0	50	62.5	5	50.0	2	33.3
May	44	88.0	60	75.0	6	60.0	2	33.3
June	46	92.0	74	92.5	7	70.0	3	50.0
July	50	100.0	78	97.5	9	90.0	4	66.7
Aug.	50	100.0	80	100.0	10	100.0	5	83.3
Sept.	48	96.0	78	97.5	10	100.0	6	100.0
Oct.	34	68.0	60	75.0	8	80.0	5	83.3
Nov.	30	60.0	46	57.5	2	20.0	3	50.0
Dec.	34	68.0	50	62.5	4	40.0	4	66.7

Basic Principles of Budgeting

The preparation of an organization's budget is the single most important aspect of its success. First, it forces management to look ahead and try to see the future of the organization in terms of both long-term and short-term goals and events. Second, it requires that the whole management team, from the lowest-level supervisor to the chairman of the board of directors, work together to make and carry out the yearly plans. Finally, by comparing the budget with actual results, it is possible to review performance at all levels of management. The principles of effective budgeting are summarized in Table 21-1. Each group of principles will be explained further to show how closely connected the principles are to the whole budgeting process.

Table 21-1. Principles of Effective Budgeting

Group A: Long-Range Goals Principles

1. Develop long-range goals for the enterprise.
2. Convert the long-range goals into statements about long-range plans for product lines or services offered and associated profit plans in broad quantitative terms.

Group B: Short-Range Goals and Strategies Principles

3. Restate the long-range plan in terms of short-range plans for product lines or services available and a detailed profit plan.
4. Prepare a set of budget development plans and a specific timetable for the whole period.

Group C: Human Responsibilities and Interaction Principles

5. Identify the budget director and staff.
6. Identify all participants in budget development.
7. Practice participative budgeting.
8. Obtain the full support of top management, and communicate this support to budget participants.
9. Practice full communications during the entire budgeting process.

Group D: Budget Housekeeping Principles

10. Practice realism in the preparation of all budgets.
11. Require that all budget preparation deadlines be met.
12. Use flexible application procedures.

Group E: Follow-up Principles

13. Maintain a continual budgeting process, and monitor the budget throughout the period.
14. Develop a system of periodic performance reports linked to assigned responsibilities.
15. Review problem areas to be studied before further planning takes place.

Long-Range Goals Principles

Annual operating plans cannot be made unless those responsible for preparing the budget know the direction in which top management expects the organization to go. Long-range goals must be set by top management. Statements about the expected quality of products or services and about growth rates and percentage-of-market targets are among the long-range goals. Economic and industry forecasts, employee-management relationships, and the structure and role of top management in leading the organization also bear on these goals.

OBJECTIVE 2
Identify the five groups of budgeting principles, and explain the principles in each group

It is necessary to name those responsible for achieving the long-term goals and to set actual targets and expected timetables. For example, Kinlin Corporation has as one of its long-term goals the control of 15 percent of its product's market. At present the company holds only 4 percent of the market. The company's long-term goals may state that the vice president of marketing is to develop plans and strategies so the company controls 10 percent of the market in five years and increases its share to 15 percent by the end of ten years.

Once all the organization's goals have been developed, they should be brought together into a total long-range plan. This plan should state a broad range of targets and goals and direct management in trying to reach them. Specific statements about long-term goals, then, are the basis for preparing the annual budget.

Short-Range Goals and Strategies Principles

Using long-range goals, management must prepare yearly operating plans and targets. The short-range plan or budget involves every part of the enterprise and is much more detailed than long-range goals. The first order of business each year is to restate long-range goals in terms of what should be accomplished during the year. Statements must be made about sales targets by product or service line, profit expectations by division or product line, personnel needs and expected changes, and plans for introducing new products or services. Budget statements must also cover materials and supplies needed; forecasts of such overhead costs as electric power and expected costs of property taxes and insurance; and all capital expenditures, such as new buildings, machinery, and equipment. These short-range targets and goals are woven together to form the organization's operating budget for the year.

An important part of the process described above is the approach to collecting and processing the information that goes into the annual budget. Once the short-range goals are set by management, the controller or budget director takes charge of preparing the budget. He or she designs a complete set of budget development plans and a timetable with deadlines for all levels and parts of the year's operating plan. Specific people must be named to carry out each part of the budget's development and their responsibilities, targets, and deadlines clearly described. The last step in the budget's development is to clearly communicate the plan to the participants. It may seem all too obvious that everyone should be fully aware of the need for and importance of budget development. But do not forget that each of the participants in the budgeting process has another job in the organization. The production supervisor, for instance, is most interested in what is happening on the production floor. Thinking about the next year's activities does not help to meet the current month's production targets. The same can be said for the district sales managers, financial and cost accounting people, and the rest of the staff. It is the budget director's responsibility to organize the budget information, and a key part of that process is making sure each participant knows what he or she is expected to do and when information is due.

Human Responsibilities and Interaction Principles

Budgeting success or failure is largely determined by how well the human aspects of the process are handled. From top management down to the lowest-level supervisor in the organization, *all* appropriate people must take part actively and honestly if the process is to be successful. To get this kind of cooperation, each person must feel that he or she is an important link in the organizational chain.

Choosing a budget director (and staff if necessary) is important to an effective budgeting system. This person must be able to communicate well with people both above and below in the organization's hierarchy. Top management gives the budget targets and organizational goals to the budget director. This person in turn assigns those targets and goals to managers at various levels. The managers then try to put into operation the goals and targets assigned to them. Problem areas found by managers are communicated to the budget director who, after careful analysis, must pass the information on to top management. The targets and goals are then reassessed, restructured, and passed back to the budget director, and the process begins over again. Since the budget director acts as an information-gathering center and clearing house for the budgeting process, its success depends on this person.

All participants in the budget development process should be identified and told early of their responsibilities in the program. The identification process begins with high-level managers. These people must then identify lower-level managers under their supervision who will actually prepare the data. At the lower levels the organization's main activities take place, whether they are production, sales, health care, or education. From these managers the information must flow through all supervisory levels up to top management. Each one of these people plays a part in developing the budget and putting it to work. It is the budget director's job to coordinate all the budgeting activities of the managers.

Participative budgeting means that all levels of supervisory and data input personnel take part in the budgeting process in a meaningful, active way. If every manager has significant input into the goals and expectations of his or her unit, personal motivation will be woven into the budgeting process. This sort of interaction and cooperation is what participative budgeting is all about.

Top management's role is also very important to the budgeting process. If top management simply dictates and sends down targets and goals for others to carry out, participative budgeting is not being practiced. Such dictated targets are often hard to attain and do not motivate lower-level managers to try to reach them. Similarly, if top management simply lets the budget director handle everything, other managers are likely to think that budgeting is a low priority and may not take it seriously. To have an effective budgeting program, top management must communicate its support and enthusiasm to all levels of management and allow the managers to take part in a meaningful way. If this happens, the principle of practicing full communication has also been followed.

Budget Housekeeping Principles

In terms of housekeeping the budget process depends heavily on three things. First, a realistic approach must be taken by the participants. Second, all deadlines must be met. Third, the organization must use flexible application procedures.

Realism is a two-way street. Top management must first suggest realistic targets and goals. Then, each manager must provide realistic information and not place departmental goals ahead of the goals of the whole organization. Inflated expenditure plans or deflated sales targets in one or two cases may make life easier for a manager's unit. However, they can cause the entire budget to be inaccurate and hard to use as a guide and control mechanism for the organization as a whole.

The reason for having and meeting budget development deadlines is clear. Budget preparation depends on the timely cooperation of many people. If one or two people ignore a deadline for submitting information to their supervisor or the budget director, the budget will not be ready on time. Top management should communicate the importance of the budget development timetable to all participants and should review timely budget data submission as part of each manager's performance evaluation.

Budgets are important guides to the actions of management. However, they should always be treated as guides and not as absolute truths. Remember that budgets are prepared almost a year in advance of the actual operating cycle. During that time unexpected changes may take place. A manager cannot simply ignore these changes just because they were not a part of the original budget. Instead, a means of dealing with revenue and expenditure changes should be worked out as part of budget implementation. A procedure for notifying the budget director of a change and receiving approval for it takes care of the matter and does not upset the performance of the manager's operating unit.

Follow-up Principles

Budget follow-up and data feedback are really part of the control aspect of budgetary control and will be explained further in Chapters 22 and 23. The follow-up principles play an important role in budgeting. Since we are dealing with projections and estimates as the budget is being developed, it is important that the budget be checked continuously and corrected whenever necessary. If a budget is found to be in error, it makes more sense to correct the error than to work with a less accurate guide.

Organizational or departmental expectations can also be unrealistic. Such problems are found when performance reports are used to compare actual results with budgeted or planned operating results. These reports are the backbone of the responsibility accounting system presented in Chapter 20. The budgeting cycle is complete when problems are identified in the performance evaluation of the last budgeting cycle and are analyzed and restructured to become targets or goals of the next budgeting cycle.

The Need for Budgetary Control and Planning

OBJECTIVE 3
Define the concept of budgetary control

Planning and controlling costs and operations are keys to good management. The process of (1) developing plans for a company's expected operations and (2) controlling operations to help carry out those plans is known as **budgetary control**. In Chapter 19 you studied cost behavior patterns and cost-volume-profit analysis, which are two tools used in developing a company's annual budget and profit goals. Profit planning is important to all successful, profit-oriented companies as part of their budgeting program. In this chapter we will deal mainly with the planning element.

A successful business does not reap the benefits of effective budgetary control by operating in a haphazard way from day to day. The company must first set quantitative goals, define the roles of individuals, and set intermediate operating targets. Companies begin by making both long-term and short-term operating plans.

First, they must prepare and maintain a long-term plan covering a five- or ten-year period. Such plans are general. They usually describe product line changes, expansion of plant and facilities, machinery replacement, and changes in marketing strategies. Long-term plans are important because they provide broad goals to work toward through yearly operations.

Yearly operating plans do not automatically grow out of long-term plans. Even though long-term plans provide broad goals, they do not contain specific instructions on how to get the expected results through annual production and sales efforts. Given the five- or ten-year plan, management must translate long-term objectives into more specific goals for each year. Once the goals have been defined for the next accounting period, various levels of managers must work out details of the operations needed to meet them. This task centers on a one-year time period and stated targets.

Short-term or one-year plans are generally formulated in a set of period budgets (also known as detailed operating budgets). A **period budget** is a forecast of a year's operating results for a segment or function of a company. It is a quantitative expression of planned activities. Period budgets are prepared by the whole management team. They require timely information and careful coordination. This process converts unit sales and production forecasts into revenue and cost estimates for each of the many operating segments of the company. Everyone involved in budgeting should make these forecasts as accurate and realistic as possible.

Period budget preparation relies heavily on several management accounting tools already discussed. Knowledge of cost behavior patterns and use of cost-volume-profit analysis help management project departmental or product-line revenues and costs. Profit planning is possible only after all cost behavior patterns have been identified. Responsibility accounting, with its network of managerial responsibilities and information flows, provides a blueprint for the structure of the budget-data gathering process. These tools, together with the concepts of cost allocation and cost accumulation, provide the foundation for preparing an organization's budget.

The Master Budget

OBJECTIVE 4
Identify the components of a master budget, and describe how they relate to each other

A **master budget** is a combined set of departmental or functional period budgets that have been consolidated into forecasted financial statements for the whole company. Each of the separate budgets gives the projected costs and revenues for that part of the company. When combined, these budgets show all anticipated transactions of the company for a future accounting period. With this information the anticipated results of the company's operations can be put together with the beginning general ledger balances to prepare forecasted statements of the company's net income and financial position for the time period.

Three steps lead to the completed master budget: (1) The period budgets are prepared. (2) The forecasted income statement is prepared. (3) The forecasted balance sheet is prepared. After describing each of these components, we will explain how budgets are prepared.

Detailed Period Budgets

Period budgets are generally prepared for each departmental or functional cost and revenue producing segment of the company. These budgets consist of the following: (1) sales budget (in units); (2) production budget (in units); (3) selling expense budget; (4) revenue budget; (5) materials usage budget; (6) materials purchase budget; (7) labor hour requirement budget; (8) labor dollar budget; (9) factory overhead budget; (10) general and administrative (G & A) expense budget; and (11) capital expenditures budget. Although these budgets are referred to by functional area, data are usually developed and transmitted to the budget director in departmental form and consolidated into the functional format described.

Sales Budget. The unit sales forecast is the starting point of the budgeting process and probably the most critical. The sales target is developed by top management with input from marketing and production. Since the entire cost portion of the budget is developed from this forecast, you can see how important it is to the master budget.

Production Budget. Once the sales target in units has been established, the units needed from production can be computed. Management must first determine if the Finished Goods Inventory level should remain the same or be increased or decreased. The unit sales forecast along with the desired changes in Finished Goods Inventory are then used to determine the unit production schedule.

Selling Expense Budget. Selling expenses, such as sales commissions and automobile expenses, may be variable. Other selling-related costs, such as advertising expenses and supervisory salaries, may be fixed. The selling expense budget is the responsibility of the sales department and can be prepared as soon as the sales budget has been completed.

Revenue Budget. The revenue budget is the result of decisions to establish the unit sales forecast and the unit selling prices. Forecasted unit sales are multiplied by selling prices to yield the expected revenue for the budget period.

Materials Usage and Purchase Budgets. The materials usage and purchase budgets can be prepared separately or as part of the same document. Materials usage is determined by the production budget and the anticipated changes in Materials Inventory levels. This information will generate the units of materials to be purchased. Multiplying the number of units to be purchased by the estimated purchase price for those materials will yield the materials purchase budget.

Labor Hour Requirement and Labor Dollar Budgets. As with the previous two budgets, the forecasted labor hours and labor dollars can be structured into two separate budgets or done in one comprehensive schedule. Labor hours can be determined as soon as the unit production budget has been set. Labor hours needed per unit are multiplied by the anticipated units of production to compute labor hour requirements for the budget period. These labor hours, when multiplied by the various hourly labor rates, yield the labor dollar budget.

Factory Overhead Budget. The budget for factory overhead has two purposes: (1) to integrate overhead cost budgets developed by production and service department managers and (2) to compute factory overhead rates for the forthcoming accounting period after accumulating that information.

General and Administrative Expense Budget. In preparing a master budget, general and administrative expenses must be projected to provide information for the cash budgeting process. The G & A expense budget also serves as a means of controlling these costs. Most elements of this budget are fixed costs.

*Capital Expenditure Budget.* Determining capital facility needs and obtaining investment resources for such expenditures are complex areas of management accounting. Deciding what to buy or build and establishing the criteria for decisions regarding return on investment are topics covered in Chapter 26 and explored fully in an advanced management accounting course. For our purposes information regarding capital facility investment decisions influences the cash budget, the interest expense and depreciation expense on the forecasted income statement, and the plant and equipment account balances on the forecasted balance sheet. Therefore, these decisions must be anticipated and integrated into the master budget.

Relationships Between the Period Budgets

Period budgets are closely related to each other. Following the sales unit forecast, the production budget can be prepared. The selling expense budget also depends on the sales forecast. Direct materials usage and resulting purchase requirements are related to the production forecast. The production budget also leads to labor and factory overhead budgets. In most cases plans for general and administrative expenses and capital expenditures are made by top management. However, much of this information may be gathered at the departmental level and included in these period budgets. The key point to remember is that the whole budgeting process begins with the sales unit forecast. Figure 21-1 shows how these period budgets set the stage for determining the effects of planned operations on the company's financial position.

Forecasted Income Statement

Once the period budgets have been prepared, the controller or the budget director can begin to put all the information together. He or she prepares a cost of goods sold forecast from data in the direct materials, direct labor, and factory overhead budgets. Revenue information is figured from the unit sales budget. Using the expected revenue and cost of goods sold data and adding information from the selling expense and general and administrative expense budgets, the controller can prepare the forecasted income statement. This step is also shown in Figure 21-1.

Financial Position Forecast

The last step in the master budget process is to prepare a financial position forecast or projected balance sheet for the company, assuming that planned activities actually take place. As Figure 21-1 shows, all budget data are used in this process. The controller prepares a cash flow forecast, or cash budget, from all planned transactions requiring cash inflow or expenditure. A more detailed explanation of cash budgeting follows later in this chapter. In preparing the forecasted statement of financial position, the budget director must know the projected cash balance and must have determined the net income and amount of capital expenditures.

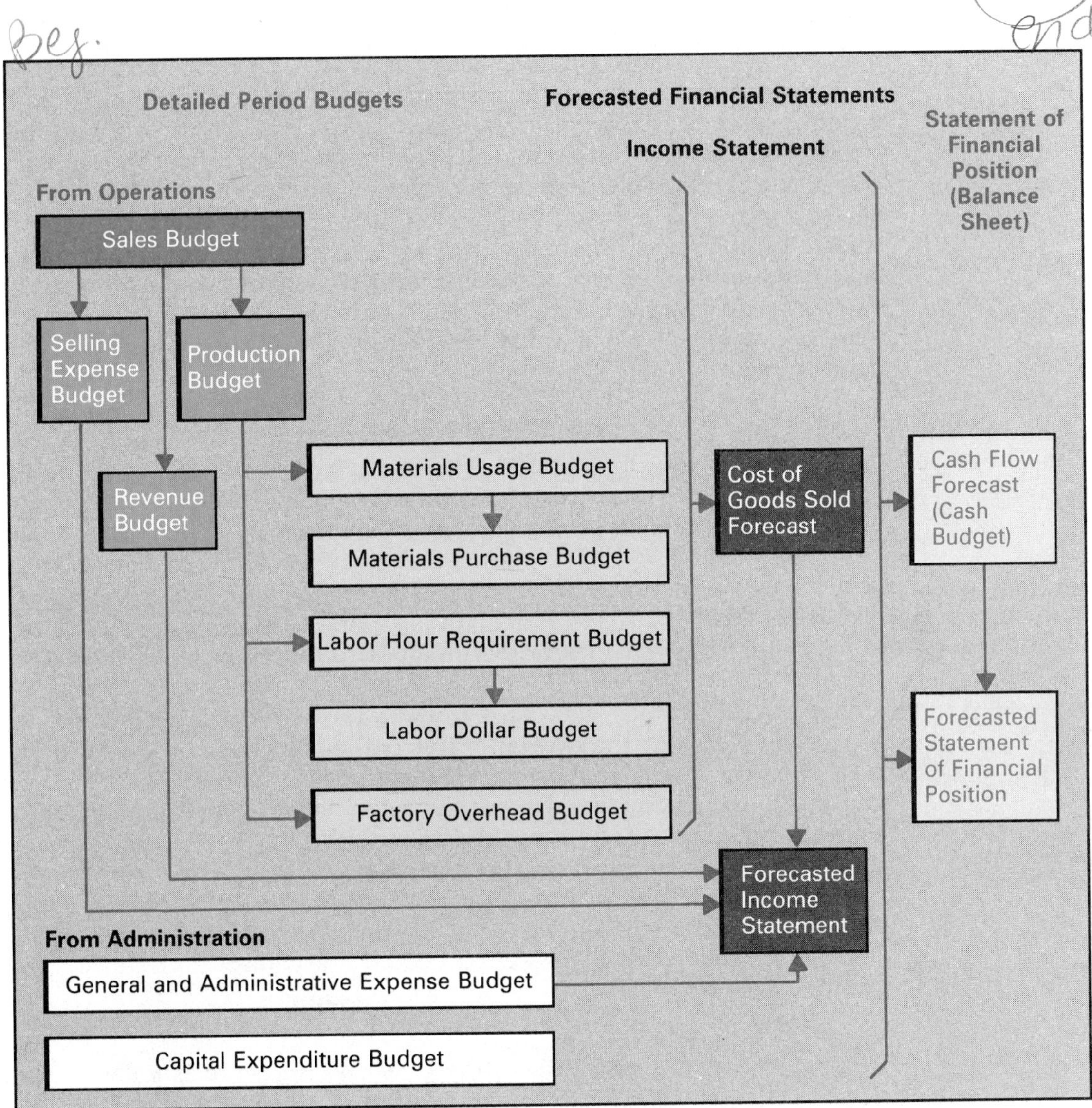

Figure 21-1. Preparation of Master Budget

All of the expected transactions shown in the period budgets must be classified and posted to general ledger accounts. The projected financial statements are the end product of the budgeting process. At this point management must decide whether to accept the proposed master budget as well as the planned operating results or ask the budget director to change the plans and do parts of the budget over.

Budget Implementation

Budget implementation is the responsibility of the budget director. Two important things determine the success of this process. The first is proper communication of budget expectations and production and profit targets to key people in the company. All people involved in the operations of the business must know what is expected of them and receive directions on how to reach their goals. Second, and equally important, is support and encouragement by top management. No matter how sophisticated the budgeting process is, it will succeed only if middle- and lower-level managers can see that top management is truly interested in the final outcome and willing to reward people for meeting budget goals.

Illustrative Problem: Budget Preparation

OBJECTIVE 5
Prepare a period budget

Period budget preparation and the make-up of the master budget vary from one company to another. Therefore, it is impossible to cover all procedures found in actual practice. Our problem will show only one approach to preparing period budgets. However, by applying the tools of cost behavior, C-V-P analysis, and responsibility accounting to a particular case, one can prepare any kind of budget. There is also no standard format to use for budget preparation. Your only guidelines are that the budget is clear and understandable and communicates information to the reader.

Downes Steelworks, Inc., manufactures cans from 4- by 8-foot sheets of steel of different thicknesses. The number of cans produced from each sheet of steel depends on the height and diameter of the cans. During 19xx the company expects the following sales and unit changes in inventory:

Can Size	Unit Sales	Unit Change in Finished Goods Inventory
6″ × 3″	1,250,000	150,000 (increase)
8″ × 4″	710,000	8,000 (decrease)

Direct materials requirements for these two products are as follows:

Can Size	Sheet Steel Type	Average Usable Cans per Sheet	Average Usable Lids per Sheet
6″ × 3″	No. 16	90	500
8″ × 4″	No. 22	45	270

Usage is the same over a twelve-month period. On the first day of each operating quarter, 25 percent of the year's direct materials requirements will be purchased, starting January 1. Assume no changes in the balances of the Materials Inventory and Work in Process Inventory accounts.

Required

Prepare a direct materials usage budget and a direct materials purchases budget for 19xx. Expected prices for the year are \$11.00 per sheet for No. 16 and \$13.40 per sheet for No. 22.

Solution

Before preparing the required budgets, you must first compute the total number of cans (including lids for tops and bottoms) to be produced per sheet of steel. The following relationships were supplied by the Engineering Department.

6″ × 3″ can: 450 cans (plus 900 lids) require 6.8 sheets of steel, so you can manufacture 66.176 cans and lids per sheet of steel

8″ × 4″ can: 135 cans (plus 270 lids) require 4 sheets of steel, so you can manufacture 33.75 cans and lids per sheet of steel

Downes Steelworks, Inc.
Materials Usage Budget
For the Year Ended December 31, 19xx

	Number of Cans
6″ × 3″ Can	
Expected Sales	1,250,000
Plus Increase in Inventory	150,000
Total To Be Produced	1,400,000

No. 16 Sheets To Be Used

$$\frac{\text{Units to be produced}}{\text{Cans per sheet}} = \frac{1{,}400{,}000 \text{ cans}}{66.176 \text{ cans/sheet}} = 21{,}155.71 \text{ or } 21{,}156 \text{ sheets}$$

8″ × 4″ Can	
Expected Sales	710,000
Less Decrease in Inventory	8,000
Total To Be Produced	702,000

No. 22 Sheets To Be Used

$$\frac{\text{Units to be produced}}{\text{Cans per sheet}} = \frac{702{,}000 \text{ cans}}{33.75 \text{ cans/sheet}} = 20{,}800 \text{ sheets}$$

Downes Steelworks, Inc.
Materials Purchases Budget
For the Year Ended December 31, 19xx

Sheet Steel Type	Unit Cost/Sheet	Sheets to Be Purchased Quarterly*	Total Quarterly Purchase Cost	Annual Cost
No. 16	$11.00	5,289	$58,179	$232,716
No. 22	13.40	5,200	69,680	278,720
Total Purchases Budget				$511,436

*Purchases of one-fourth of annual usage on January 1, April 1, July 1, and October 1.

Cash Budgeting

Cash flow is one of the most important aspects of the operating cycle of a business. Within the master budget preparation cycle, the cash budget is developed after all period budgets are final and the forecasted income statement is complete. A **cash flow forecast**, or **cash budget**, is a projection of cash receipts and cash payments for a future period of time. It sums up the cash results of planned transactions in all phases of a master budget. Generally, it shows the company's projected ending cash balance and the cash position for each month of the year. This permits periods of high and low cash availability to be anticipated. Large cash balances mean funds of the company may not have been used to earn the best possible rate of return. Low cash reserves may mean that the company will be unable to make current payments on amounts it owes. To prevent either of these problems, careful cash planning is necessary.

The cash budget has two main parts—forecasted cash receipts and forecasted cash disbursements. Sales budgets, cash or credit sales data, and accounts receivable collection data are used to figure expected cash receipts for the period. Other sources of cash, such as the sale of stock, the sale of assets, or loans, also enter into cash receipts planning.

Expected cash disbursements are taken from period budgets. The person preparing the cash budget must know how direct materials, labor, and other goods and services will be purchased. That is, are they to be paid for with cash immediately or purchased on account with the cash payment delayed for a period of time? When dealing with accounts payable, it is important to know the company's payment policies. Besides its use in regular operating expenses, cash is also used for buying equipment and paying off loans and other long-term liabilities. All of this information must be available before an accurate cash budget can be prepared.

Cash Budgeting: Purposes and Nature

OBJECTIVE 6
State the purpose and make-up of a cash budget

The cash budget serves two purposes. First, it shows the ending cash balance, which is needed to complete the projected balance sheet (see Figure 21-1). Second, it highlights periods of excess cash reserves or cash shortages. The first purpose focuses on the role of the cash budget in the master budget preparation cycle. The second purpose reflects its use as a tool of cash management, which is important to any business. Without cash a business cannot function. By comparing projected cash receipts and cash payments, the budget director can advise financial executives of the months the company will need extra short-term financing because of cash shortages. Similarly, the budget director can point out times when excess cash will be available for short-term investments.

A cash budget combines information from several period budgets. All elements of cash flow, both cash inflows (cash receipts) and cash outflows (cash disbursements or payments) are brought together to show expected cash flows of the company. The cash budget of Neehon Shohkoo, Inc., is shown in Exhibit 21-2. To highlight the first quarter of the year, detailed cash inflows and outflows are shown for January, February, and March. The remaining nine months are lumped together in this annual cash forecast.

Now, let's explore the relationship of the cash budget shown in Exhibit 21-2 to the parts of the master budget shown in Figure 21-1. Somewhere in all business transactions, cash must come into the picture. Since the master budget is a summary of all expected transactions for a future time period, it must also be the key to all expected cash transactions. To prepare the cash budget, then, one must analyze the master budget in terms of cash inflows and outflows. Table 21-2 focuses on the relationships between the master budget and the cash budget and explains how the cash budget for Neehon Shohkoo, Inc., shown in Exhibit 21-2, is created. For the next year the company expects only cash receipts from sales. Note that 60 percent of all sales are for cash. Thirty-eight percent are credit sales collected in the following month. All of the necessary cash inflow information comes from the sales and sales revenue budgets.

Exhibit 21-2. Typical Cash Budget

Neehon Shohkoo, Inc.
Cash Budget
For the Year Ending December 31, 19xx

	January	February	March	April–December	Totals
Cash receipts					
Sales—previous month (38%*)	$ 10,773	$ 7,182	$ 10,773	$ 14,364	$ 43,092
Sales—current month (60%*)	11,340	17,010	22,680	368,928	419,958
Total receipts	$ 22,113	$24,192	$ 33,453	$383,292	$463,050
Cash disbursements					
Direct materials	$ 7,146	$ 7,146	$ 7,622	$ 72,434	$ 94,348
Operating supplies	237	—	—	710	947
Direct labor	3,700	3,850	4,220	34,940	46,710
Factory overhead	3,440	3,480	3,750	32,580	43,250
Selling expenses	8,585	10,000	11,420	109,870	139,875
General and administrative expenses	4,500	4,500	4,500	40,500	54,000
Capital expenditures	4,200	—	7,920	14,780	26,900
Income taxes	—	—	22,640	**	22,640
Interest expense	6,000	—	—	8,920	14,920
Total disbursements	$ 37,808	$28,976	$ 62,072	$314,734	$443,590
Cash increase (decrease)	$(15,695)	$(4,784)	$(28,619)	$ 68,558	$ 19,460
Beginning cash balance	36,275	20,580	15,796	(12,823)	36,275
Ending cash balance	$ 20,580	$15,796	$(12,823)	$ 55,735	$ 55,735

*2% of sales result in bad debt expense.
**No payments. Estimated loss for the year.

Table 21-2. Master Budget and Cash Budget Interrelationships

Elements of the Cash Budget	Sources of the Information
Cash Receipts	
Cash sales	Sales budget (cash sales)
Cash collections of previous sales	Sales budget (credit sales) plus collection record—percent collected in first month, second month, etc.
Proceeds from sale of assets	Forecasted income statement
Loan proceeds	Previous month's information on cash budget
Cash Disbursements	
Direct materials	Materials purchase budget
Operating supplies	Factory overhead budget and materials purchase budget
Direct labor	Labor dollar budget
Factory overhead	Factory overhead budget
Selling expenses	Selling expense budget
General and administrative expenses	General and administrative expense budget
Capital expenditures	Capital expenditure budget
Income taxes	Estimated from previous year's income statement and current year's projections
Interest expense	Forecasted income statement
Loan payments	Loan record

Note: Other sources of cash receipts and possible cash disbursements exist. The above analysis covers only the most common types of cash inflows and outflows.

Information supporting cash disbursement forecasts comes from several sources. Cash used to purchase direct materials and operating supplies is determined by changing the materials purchase budget into a cash flow analysis. Materials are generally purchased on account. Every company should have a policy about payment on account as part of its cash management. If the company's policy is to pay everything within the discount period, cash flow would occur in 10 or 20 days if the terms of the purchase are 2/10, n/30 or 3/20, n/60. If, however, the company wants to hold its cash for the maximum time, cash payments would not be made for 30 or 60 days. In most cases direct labor cash flow, for obvious reasons, is delayed very little. Information from the labor dollar budget is used to support the cash payments for both direct and indirect labor services. Cash payments for all factory overhead other than operating supplies and indirect labor are figured by using the factory overhead budget.

Cash requirements for selling expenses, general and administrative expenses, and capital expenditures are determined from their respective budgets. Again, the timing of the cash exchange is important. Selling expenses, such as gasoline purchases and sales brochures, may be made on credit, and the actual payment may be postponed for thirty days or more. The same may be true for large capital expenditures. When preparing a cash budget, one must concentrate on the time of actual cash flow, not the time of the original sale or purchase transaction.

The final two cash disbursements shown in Exhibit 21-2 are for income taxes and interest expense. Corporations usually make quarterly tax payments, which are applied against an estimate of the current year's tax liability. Any excess owed at year end is due on the fifteenth day of the third month following the close of the company's fiscal year. Interest expense payments may be made monthly, quarterly, semiannually, or annually, depending on the terms of the loan agreement. This information can be found in the organization's loan record.

Once the cash receipts and cash disbursements have been established, the cash increase or decrease for the period is computed. The resulting increase or decrease is added to the period's beginning cash balance to arrive at the projected cash balance at period end. In the case of Neehon Shohkoo, the first three months will put a heavy drain on cash reserves, but positive cash flow will return during the last nine months of the year. The company seems to have a favorable cash position for the year except at the end of March. Depending on cash payment patterns, the company may need to take out a small loan to cover the cash shortage and protect itself in case a large unexpected payment becomes due. On the other hand, a $55,735 balance in cash at year end may be too much extra cash. So management may want to plan on investing this money in short-term securities.

Illustrative Problem

OBJECTIVE 7
Prepare a cash budget

Worrell Information Processing Company provides word processing services to its clients. Worrell uses state-of-the-art computerized information processing equipment. It employs five keyboard operators who each average 120 hours of work a month. The following information was developed by the budget officer:

	Actual—19x8		Forecast—19x9		
	November	December	January	February	March
Client billings (sales)	$25,000	$35,000	$25,000	$20,000	$40,000
Selling expenses	4,500	5,000	4,000	4,000	5,000
General and administrative expenses	7,500	8,000	8,000	7,000	7,500
Operating supplies purchased	2,500	3,500	2,500	2,500	4,000
Factory overhead	3,200	3,500	3,000	2,500	3,500

The company has a bank loan of $12,000 at a 12 percent annual interest rate. Interest is paid monthly, and $2,000 of the principal is due on February 28, 19x9. No capital expenditures are anticipated for the first quarter of the coming year. Income taxes for calendar year 19x8 of $4,550 are due and payable on March 15, 19x9. The company's five employees earn $7.50 an hour, and all costs of payroll-related labor benefits are included in factory overhead.

For the revenue and cost items included in the chart just given, assume the following conditions:

Client Billings:	60% are cash sales collected during the current period 30% are collected in the month following the sale 10% are collected in the second month following the sale
Operating Supplies:	Paid in the month purchased
Selling Expenses, General and Administrative Expenses & Factory Overhead:	Paid in the month following the cost's incurrence

The beginning cash balance on January 1, 19x9, is expected to be $13,840.

Required

Prepare a monthly cash budget for the Worrell Information Processing Company for the three-month period ending March 31, 19x9.

Solution

The three-month cash budget for the Worrell Information Processing Company is shown in Exhibit 21-3. Details supporting the individual computations are shown below.

	January	**February**	**March**
Cash from client billings			
Current month = 60%	$15,000	$12,000	$24,000
Previous month = 30%	10,500	7,500	6,000
Month before last = 10%	2,500	3,500	2,500
Totals	$28,000	$23,000	$32,500
Operating supplies			
All paid in the month purchased	$ 2,500	$ 2,500	$ 4,000
Direct labor			
5 employees × 120 hours/month × $7.50/hour	$ 4,500	$ 4,500	$ 4,500
Factory overhead			
Paid in the following month	$ 3,500	$ 3,000	$ 2,500
Selling expenses			
Paid in the following month	$ 5,000	$ 4,000	$ 4,000
General and administrative expenses			
Paid in the following month	$ 8,000	$ 8,000	$ 7,000

Interest expense			
January and February = 1% of $12,000	$ 120	$ 120	
March = 1% of $10,000			$ 100
Loan payment	—	$ 2,000	—
Income tax payment	—	—	$ 4,550

The ending cash balances of $18,220, $17,100, and $22,950 for January, February, and March 19x9, respectively, appear to be comfortable but not too large for the company.

Exhibit 21-3. Example of a Period Budget

Worrell Information Processing Company
Monthly Cash Budget
For the Three-Month Period Ending March 31, 19x9

	January	February	March	Totals
Cash receipts				
Client billings	$28,000	$23,000	$32,500	$83,500
Cash disbursements				
Operating supplies	$ 2,500	$ 2,500	$ 4,000	$ 9,000
Direct labor	4,500	4,500	4,500	13,500
Factory overhead	3,500	3,000	2,500	9,000
Selling expenses	5,000	4,000	4,000	13,000
General and administrative expenses	8,000	8,000	7,000	23,000
Interest expense	120	120	100	340
Loan payment	—	2,000	—	2,000
Income tax payment	—	—	4,550	4,550
Total disbursements	$23,620	$24,120	$26,650	$74,390
Cash increase (decrease)	$ 4,380	$(1,120)	$ 5,850	$ 9,110
Beginning cash balance	13,840	18,220	17,100	13,840
Ending cash balance	$18,220	$17,100	$22,950	$22,950

Chapter Review

Review of Learning Objectives

1. **Describe the structure and contents of a budget.**
There is no standard form or structure for a budget. A budget's structure depends on what is being budgeted, the size of the organization preparing the budget, the degree to which the budgeting process is integrated into the financial structure of the enterprise, and the amount of training the budget preparer has in his or her background. A budget should contain enough information presented in an orderly manner to communicate its purpose to

the budget's reader or user. Too much information tends to obscure the meaning and accuracy of the data. Too little information can result in overspending because the reader did not understand the spending limits suggested by the document.

2. **Identify the five groups of budgeting principles, and explain the principles in each group.**

   The five groups of budgeting principles are: (1) long-range goals principles; (2) short-range goals and strategies principles; (3) human responsibilities and interaction principles; (4) budget housekeeping principles; and (5) follow-up principles. Every organization needs to set long-range goals and convert them into plans for product line or service offerings. Short-range goals and strategies must be restated in terms of the annual product line or service offerings and associated profit plans. The budget development plans and timetable must also be set up. The human side includes identifying a budget director, staff, and participants. These people must be informed of their duties and responsibilities. It is essential to practice participative budgeting, obtain the full support of top management, and ensure full and open communication among all participants. Being realistic, requiring that all deadlines be met, and using flexible application procedures are the housekeeping principles of budgeting. Finally, budget follow-up includes maintaining a continual budgeting process and using a system of periodic reports to measure performance of the operating segments. Problems are identified for analysis and inclusion into the next period's planning activities.

3. **Define the concept of budgetary control.**

   The budgetary control process consists of the cost planning function and the cost control function. Cost planning and control are key functions leading to effective management. Budgetary control is the total process of (1) developing plans for a company's expected operations and (2) controlling operations to help carry out those plans.

4. **Identify the components of a master budget, and describe how they relate to each other.**

   A master budget is a combined set of departmental or functional period budgets that have been consolidated into forecasted financial statements for the whole company. First, the detailed operating or period budgets are prepared. These are the sales budget, production budget, selling expense budget, revenue budget, materials usage budget, materials purchases budget, labor hour requirements budget, direct labor dollars budget, factory overhead budget, general and administrative expense budget, and capital expenditures budget. The selling expense budget, revenue budget, and the production budget are computed from the sales budget data. Materials usage, labor hour and dollars, and factory overhead budgets arise from the production budget. Materials purchases can be pinned down only after materials use is known. General and administrative expenses and proposed capital expenditures are determined by top management. Once these budgets have been prepared, a forecasted income statement, a forecasted cash flow statement (cash budget), and a forecasted balance sheet can be prepared, assuming that all planned activities actually occur.

5. **Prepare a period budget.**

   A period budget, also known as an operating budget, is the forecast of a year's operating results for a segment of a company. It is a quantitative expression of planned activities. For examples of period budgets, see the illustrative problems on pages 799 and 803. The period budgeting process converts unit sales and production forecasts into revenue and cost estimates for each of the many operating segments of the company.

6. **State the purpose and make-up of a cash budget.**
The cash budget's purposes are (1) to disclose the firm's projected ending cash balance and (2) to show the cash position for each month so that periods of excess cash or cash shortages can be planned for. Cash management is critical to the success of an organization, and the cash budget is a major tool used in that process. The cash budget begins with the projection of all expected sources of cash (cash receipts). Next, all expected cash disbursements or payments are found by analyzing all other period budgets within the master budget. The difference between these two totals is the cash increase or decrease anticipated for the period. This total combined with the period's beginning cash balance yields the ending cash balance.

7. **Prepare a cash budget.**
A cash budget or cash flow forecast is a projection of the cash receipts and payments for a future period of time. It summarizes the cash results of planned transactions in all parts of a master budget. For an example, see Exhibit 21-2.

Additional Illustrative Problem

Hank Fishkind is president of Fishkind Economic Forecasting Services, Inc. Last year's forecasted income statement for the company is shown below.

Fishkind Economic Forecasting Services, Inc.
Forecasted Income Statement
For the Year Ending December 31, 19x7

Revenues		
Consulting fees	$246,500	
Special forecasts	137,800	
Total revenues		$384,300
Operating expenses		
Economic information service costs	$111,400	
Outside economists' fees	62,100	
Travel costs	12,800	
Salaries: staff	60,000	
executives	80,000	
Rent, building	6,400	
Depreciation, equipment	3,900	
Utilities	1,800	
Supplies	2,100	
Brochure printing	3,500	
Computer services	6,700	
Miscellaneous	900	
Total operating expenses		351,600
Income before taxes		$ 32,700
Federal income taxes (30%)		9,810
Net income after taxes		$ 22,890

During 19x8 the following changes are anticipated:

a. Consulting fees and special forecasts revenues are expected to increase by 20 percent.
b. Economic information service costs are scheduled for a 30 percent increase in January 19x8.
c. Outside economists' fees and travel costs will rise 10 percent.
d. All salaries will be increased by 20 percent.
e. Rent, depreciation, and utility expenses are expected to stay the same throughout next year.
f. Supplies costs will decrease by 10 percent.
g. Brochure printing costs will rise by 40 percent.
h. Computer services costs will double because of expanded services.
i. Miscellaneous expenses should total $1,000 in 19x8.

Required

Prepare the forecasted income statement for 19x8.

Solution

Fishkind Economic Forecasting Services, Inc.
Forecasted Income Statement
For the Year Ending December 31, 19x8

Revenues		
Consulting fees ($246,500 × 1.2)	$295,800	
Special forecasts ($137,800 × 1.2)	165,360	
Total revenues		$461,160
Operating expenses		
Economic information service costs ($111,400 × 1.3)	$144,820	
Outside economists' fees costs ($62,100 × 1.1)	68,310	
Travel costs ($12,800 × 1.1)	14,080	
Salaries: staff ($60,000 × 1.2)	72,000	
executives ($80,000 × 1.2)	96,000	
Rent, building	6,400	
Depreciation, equipment	3,900	
Utilities	1,800	
Supplies ($2,100 × .9)	1,890	
Brochure printing ($3,500 × 1.4)	4,900	
Computer services ($6,700 × 2)	13,400	
Miscellaneous	1,000	
Total operating expenses		428,500
Income before taxes		$ 32,660
Federal income taxes (30%)		9,798
Net income after taxes		$ 22,862

Chapter Assignments

Questions

1. "The structure of a budget varies with the task and its circumstances." Is this statement true? Defend your answer.
2. Describe the concept of budgetary control. Why is it important?
3. Distinguish between long-term plans and yearly operating plans.
4. What is a period budget?
5. How does responsibility accounting help in period budget preparation?
6. What is a master budget? What is its purpose?
7. Why is the preparation of a forecasted cash flow statement or cash budget so important to a company?
8. Name the three main phases of the budget preparation cycle.
9. Identify and discuss the interrelationship of detailed operating budgets.
10. What are the long-range goals principles of budgeting?
11. One of the budgeting principles we listed was "Restate the long-range plan in terms of short-range plans for product lines or services available and a detailed profit plan." What is the purpose of this principle?
12. Why is it necessary to identify all participants in budget development?
13. Describe participative budgeting.
14. State the budget housekeeping principles.
15. Why use a continuous budgeting process?
16. What is the connection between periodic performance reports and responsibility accounting?
17. In the budget preparation cycle, what steps must precede preparation of the cash budget?
18. How are the areas of sales and purchases on account handled when drawing up the cash budget?

Classroom Exercises

Exercise 21-1. Budgeting Principles
(L.O. 2)

Long-range goals principles and short-range goals and strategies principles are critical to a successful budgeting system. Assume that you work in the accounting department of a small wholesale warehousing business. The president has just returned from an industry association meeting where he attended a seminar on the values of a budgeting system. He wants to develop a budgeting system and has asked you to direct it.

State the points that you should communicate to the president about the initial development steps of the process. Concentrate on the two sets of principles mentioned above.

Exercise 21-2. Budgetary Control
(L.O. 3)

You are a new employee of Sacks Laboratories, Inc., and have been assigned to the controller's department. This department employs 25 paraprofessionals (nondegreed people) who fill clerical and other repetitive skills positions. All are in need of supplemental knowledge in the budgetary control area.

The controller has asked you to team up with another accountant to prepare and present a four-hour seminar on budgetary control to these paraprofessional employees. Your particular assignment is to concentrate on the planning phase of budgetary control. Prepare an outline of the topics and ideas you would cover in this seminar.

Exercise 21-3. Master Budget Components (L.O. 4)

Snorek Prototype Research, Inc., is in its sixth year of operation. Known for "accomplishing the impossible," the corporation has grown from a moonlighting operation in an engineer's garage to a company employing 120 professionals and 15 staff employees. High-tech prototype design is Snorek's main product.

Two years ago the financial vice president hired a controller who was instructed to install a complete budgeting system. To date the budgeting system consists of the following:

Sales Revenue Forecast
Cash Budget
Capital Expenditure Budget

The financial vice president has called you (the company's independent CPA) for advice and ideas regarding a complete budgeting system.

Prepare a response to your client, indicating what will be needed to put together an annual master budget.

Exercise 21-4. Production Budget Preparation (L.O. 5)

The Holstrum Specialty Door Company's forecast of unit sales for 19x6 is as follows: (a) January, 40,000; (b) February, 50,000; (c) March, 60,000; (d) April, 70,000; (e) May, 60,000; (f) June, 50,000; (g) July, 40,000; (h) August, 50,000; (i) September, 60,000; (j) October, 70,000; (k) November, 80,000; and (l) December, 60,000.

The forecast of unit sales for January 19x7 is 50,000. Beginning Finished Goods Inventory on January 1, 19x6, contained 15,000 doors. Company policy states that minimum Finished Goods Inventory is 15,000 units and that the maximum is one-half of the following month's sales. Maximum productive capacity is 65,000 units per month.

Using the information given above, prepare a monthly production budget, stating the number of units to be produced. Note that the company wants a fairly constant productive output so a constant work force can be maintained. How many units will be in Finished Goods Inventory on December 31, 19x6?

Exercise 21-5. Direct Materials Purchases Budget (Linked to Exercise 21-4) (L.O. 5)

Refer to the data for the Holstrum Specialty Door Company in Exercise 21-4. Prepare a direct materials purchases budget for January, February, and March 19x6, assuming the following breakdown of parts needed:

Hinges	4 sets/door	$8.00/set
Door Panels	4 panels/door	$17.00/panel
Other Hardware	1 lock/door	$11.00/lock
	1 handle/door	$2.50/handle
	2 sets roller tracks/door	$22.00/set of two roller tracks
	8 rollers/door	$1.00/roller

All direct materials are purchased in the month before their use in production.

Exercise 21-6. Factory Labor Budget (L.O. 5)

Sterling Metals Company manufactures three products in a single plant with four departments: Cutting, Grinding, Polishing, and Packing. The company has estimated costs for products T, M, and B and is currently analyzing direct labor hour requirements for the budget year 19xx. The routing sequence and departmental data are presented below.

Unit of Product	Estimated Hours per Unit: Cut	Grind	Polish	Pack	Total Estimated Direct Labor Hours/Unit
T	.6	1.0	.4	.2	2.2
M	1.0	—	2.8	.6	4.4
B	1.6	3.0	—	.4	5.0
Hourly labor rate	$8	$6	$5	$4	
Annual DLH capacity	900,000	1,200,000	1,248,000	360,000	

The annual direct labor hour capacity for each department is based on a normal two-shift operation. Hours of labor exceeding capacity are provided by overtime labor at 150 percent of normal hourly rates. Budgeted unit production in 19xx for the products is 210,000 of T, 360,000 of M, and 300,000 of B.

Prepare a monthly direct labor hour requirements schedule for 19xx and the related direct labor cost budget. Assume that direct labor hour capacity is the same each month. Production should be close to constant each month.

Exercise 21-7. Cash Budget Preparation—Revenues
(L.O. 6, 7)

Storevik Car Care, Inc., is an automobile maintenance and repair organization with outlets throughout the midwestern United States. Ms. Shanley, budget director for the home office, is assembling next quarter's operating cash budget. Sales are projected as follows:

	On Account	Cash
October	$742,000	$265,800
November	680,000	250,000
December	810,500	279,400

Past collection results for sales on account indicate the following pattern:

Month of sale	40%
1st month following sale	30%
2nd month following sale	28%
Uncollectible	2%

Sales on account during August and September were $846,000 and $595,000, respectively.

Required

1. What is the purpose of preparing a cash budget?
2. Compute the amount of cash to be collected from sales during each month of the last quarter.

Exercise 21-8. Cash Budget Preparation— Expenditures (L.O. 7)

Cabernet Corporation relies heavily on its cash budget to predict periods of high or low cash. The company considers proper cash management to be its primary short-range strategy for achieving higher profits. All materials and supplies are purchased on account with terms of either 2/10, n/30 or 2/30, n/60. Discounts are taken whenever possible, but payment is not made until the final day of the discount period. Purchases for the next quarter are expected to be as follows:

Date	Terms	Gross Amount	Date	Terms	Gross Amount
July 10	2/10, n/30	$ 6,400	Aug. 31	2/10, n/30	$ 6,800
July 16	2/30, n/60	8,200	Sept. 4	2/10, n/30	9,400
July 24	2/30, n/60	7,400	Sept. 9	2/10, n/30	8,100
Aug. 6	2/10, n/30	6,200	Sept. 18	2/10, n/30	7,500
Aug. 12	2/30, n/60	10,400	Sept. 20	2/10, n/30	10,400
Aug. 18	2/30, n/60	10,500	Sept. 24	2/30, n/60	9,400
Aug. 30	2/10, n/30	11,600	Sept. 29	2/10, n/30	4,900

Three purchases in June affected July cash flow: June 6, 2/30, n/60, $14,200; June 21, 2/30, n/60, $10,400; and June 24, 2/10, n/30, $6,400.

From the information given, compute total cash outflow for July, August, and September resulting from the purchases identified above.

Interpreting Accounting Information

Internal Management Information: Hedlund Corporation (L.O. 1, 2, 4)

Hedlund Corporation is a manufacturing company with annual sales of $25,000,000. The controller, Mr. Milton, appointed Ms. Maybelle as budget director. She created this budget formulation policy based on a calendar-year accounting period:

May 19x7 — Meeting of corporate officers and budget director to discuss corporate plans for 19x8.

June 19x7 — Meeting(s) of division managers, department heads, and budget director to communicate 19x8 corporate objectives. At this time relevant background data are distributed to all managers and a time schedule is established for development of 19x8 budget data.

July 19x7 — Managers and department heads continue to develop budget data. Complete 19x8 monthly sales forecasts by product line and receive final sales estimates from sales vice president.

Aug. 19x7 — Complete 19x8 monthly production activity and anticipated inventory level plans. Division managers and department heads should communicate preliminary budget figures to budget director for coordination and distribution to other operating areas.

Sept. 19x7 — Development of preliminary 19x8 master budget. Revised budget data from all functional areas to be received. Budget director will coordinate staff activities, integrating manpower requirements, direct materials and supplies requirements, unit cost estimates, cash requirements, and profit estimates into 19x8 master budget.

Oct. 19x7 — Meeting with corporate officers to discuss preliminary 19x8 master budget. Any corrections, additions, or deletions are to be communicated to budget director by corporate officers; all authorized changes are to be incorporated into the 19x8 master budget.

Nov. 19x7 Submit final draft of 19x8 master budget to corporate officers for approval. Publish approved budget and distribute to all corporate officers, division managers, and department heads.

Required

1. Comment on the proposed budget formulation policy.
2. What changes in the policy would you recommend?

Problem Set A

Problem 21A-1. Divisional Budget Preparation (L.O. 5)

Lester Twichell is budget director for Villa Park Spectaculars, Inc., a division of Diversified, Ltd., a multinational company based in California. Villa Park Spectaculars organizes and coordinates art shows and auctions throughout the world. Budgeted and actual costs and expenses for 19x7 are compared in the schedule below.

	19x7 Amounts	
Expense Item	**Budget**	**Actual**
Salary Expense, Staging	$ 130,000	$ 146,400
Salary Expense, Executive	390,000	423,600
Travel Costs	220,000	236,010
Auctioneer Services	170,000	124,910
Space Rental Costs	135,500	133,290
Printing Costs	76,000	81,250
Advertising Expense	94,500	101,640
Insurance, Merchandise	32,400	28,650
Insurance, Liability	22,000	23,550
Home Office Costs	104,600	99,940
Shipping costs	22,500	26,280
Miscellaneous	12,500	11,914
Total Expenses	$1,410,000	$1,437,434
Net Receipts	$2,750,000	$2,984,600

For 19x8 the following fixed costs have been budgeted: executive salaries, $400,000; advertising expense, $95,000; merchandise insurance, $20,000; liability insurance, $34,000; for a total of $549,000. Additional information follows:

a. Net receipts are expected to be $2,900,000 in 19x8.
b. Staging salaries will increase 50% over 19x7 actual figures.
c. Travel costs are expected to be 11% of net receipts.
d. Auctioneer services will be billed at 9.5% of net receipts.
e. Space rental costs will go up 20% from 19x7 budgeted amounts.
f. Printing costs are expected to be $85,000 in 19x8.

g. Home office costs are budgeted for $125,000 in 19x8.
h. Shipping costs are expected to rise 20% over 19x7 budgeted amounts.
i. Miscellaneous expenses for 19x8 will be budgeted at $4,000.

Required

1. Prepare the division's budget for 19x8. Assume that only services are being sold and there is no cost of sales. (Net receipts equal gross margin.) Use a 30 percent federal income tax rate.
2. Should the budget director be worried about the trend of the company's operations? Be specific.

Problem 21A-2. Factory Overhead Expense Budget (L.O. 5)

Stalcup Manufacturing Company has a home office and three operating divisions. The home office houses top management personnel, including all accounting functions. The factory overhead costs incurred during 19x7 are summarized below.

Expense Categories	East Division	West Division	Central Division	Total	Expected Increase in 19x8
Indirect Labor	$ 34,500	$ 38,600	$ 40,200	$113,300	10%
Indirect Materials	14,800	15,200	16,000	46,000	20%
Supplies	13,900	13,900	14,000	41,800	10%
Utilities	16,200	17,400	17,100	50,700	10%
Computer Services	30,400	36,900	38,600	105,900	—
Insurance	13,400	13,500	13,600	40,500	10%
Repairs and Maintenance	15,600	16,000	15,400	47,000	20%
Miscellaneous	11,100	11,200	11,300	33,600	10%
Totals	$149,900	$162,700	$166,200	$478,800	

Expected percentage increases for 19x8 are shown for all categories except computer services. These services will increase by different amounts for each division: East Division, 25%; West Division, 30%; and Central Division, 40%. In 19x7 the home office was charged $52,500 for computer service costs. This amount is expected to rise by 25 percent in 19x8. During 19x8 the company will rent a new software package at an annual cost of $70,000.

Required

1. Find the total expected cost of computer services for 19x8 for the three divisions and the home office.
2. Assume the rental charge for the new software package is allocated to computer service users on the basis of their costs for normal computer use as a percentage of total computer service charges. Compute the allocation of the rental charges to the three divisions and the central office. (Use the 19x8 amounts computed in **1** above, and round to one percentage decimal place.)
3. Prepare the divisional factory overhead expense budget for Stalcup Manufacturing Company for 19x8.

Problem 21A-3. Master Budget
(L.O. 4, 5)

Abramson Video Company, Inc., produces and markets two popular video games, "Grant Avenues" and "Thornton Adventures." The company's closing balance sheet account balances for 19x7 are as follows: (a) Cash, $17,450; (b) Accounts Receivable, $21,900; (c) Materials Inventory, $18,510; (d) Work in Process Inventory, $28,680; (e) Finished Goods Inventory, $31,940; (f) Prepaid Expenses, $3,420; (g) Plant and Equipment, $262,800; (h) Accumulated Depreciation, Plant and Equipment, $52,560; (i) Other Assets, $9,480; (j) Accounts Payable, $76,640; (k) Mortgage Payable, $88,000; (l) Common Stock, $100,000; (m) Retained Earnings, $76,980.

Period budgets for the first quarter of 19x8 revealed the following: (a) materials purchases, $48,100; (b) materials usage, $50,240; (c) labor expense, $72,880; (d) factory overhead expense, $41,910; (e) selling expenses, $45,820; (f) general and administrative expenses, $60,230; (g) capital expenditures, $0; (h) ending cash balances by month: January—$34,610, February—$60,190, and March—$96,240; (i) Cost of Goods Manufactured, $163,990; and (j) Cost of Goods Sold, $165,440. Sales per month are projected to be $165,210 for January, $114,890 for February, and $132,860 for March. The accounts receivable balance will probably double during the quarter, and accounts payable will decrease by 25 percent. Mortgage payments for the quarter will total $6,000, of which $2,000 is interest expense. Prepaid expenses are expected to go up by $20,000, and other assets are projected to increase 50 percent over the budget period. Depreciation for plant and equipment (already included in the factory overhead budget) averages 10 percent per year. Federal income taxes are 30 percent of profits and are payable in April.

Required

1. Prepare a forecasted income statement for the quarter ending March 31, 19x8.
2. Prepare a forecasted statement of financial position as of March 31, 19x8.

Problem 21A-4. Basic Cash Budget
(L.O. 7)

David Schuelke is president of United Nurseries of Idaho, Inc. This corporation has four locations in the State of Idaho and has been in business for six years. Each retail outlet offers over 200 varieties of plants and trees to its customers. Milly Cooper, the controller, has been asked to prepare a cash budget for the president for the Southern Division for the first quarter of 19x8. Projected data supporting the budget are summarized below. Collection history for the accounts receivable shows that 30 percent of all credit sales are collected in the month of sale, 60 percent in the month following the sale, and 8 percent in the second month following the sale. Two percent of credit sales are uncollectible. Purchases are all paid for in the month following the purchase. The cash balance as of December 31, 19x7, was $4,875.

Sales (60 percent on credit):

November, 19x7	$80,000
December, 19x7	90,000
January, 19x8	40,000
February, 19x8	70,000
March, 19x8	30,000

Purchases:

December, 19x7	28,400
January, 19x8	49,350
February, 19x8	21,720
March, 19x8	32,400

Salaries and wages were $14,600 in January; $18,600 in February; and $12,600 in March. Monthly costs were: (a) utilities, $1,110; (b) collection fees, $1,350; (c) rent, $2,850; (d) equipment depreciation, $3,720; (e) supplies, $3,240; (f) small tools, $570; and (g) miscellaneous, $850.

Required

1. Prepare a cash budget by month for the Southern Division for the first quarter of 19x8.
2. Should United Nurseries of Idaho, Inc., anticipate taking out a loan during the quarter? How much should be borrowed? When? (Note: Management maintains a $3,000 minimum cash balance at each of its four locations.)

Problem 21A-5. Cash Budget Preparation: Comprehensive (L.O. 7)

Olson's Wellness Centers, Inc., operates three fully equipped personal health facilities in Minneapolis, Minnesota. In addition to the health facilities, the corporation maintains a complete medical center specializing in preventive medicine. Emphasis is placed on regular workouts and medical examinations. Care is taken to keep everything in good running order so members' personal fitness programs are not interrupted.

Budgeted Cash Receipts: First Quarter, 19x8

Membership dues
- Memberships: December 19x7, 970; Jan., 980; Feb., 1,010; and Mar., 1,025.
- Dues: $80 per month, payable on the 10th day (80 percent collected on time; 20 percent collected one month late).
- Special aerobics classes: Jan., $2,480; Feb., $3,210; and Mar., $4,680.
- Suntan sessions: Jan., $1,240; Feb., $1,620; and Mar., $2,050.
- High-protein food sales: Jan., $3,890; Feb., $4,130; and Mar., $5,280.
- Medical examinations: Jan., $34,610; Feb., $39,840; and Mar., $43,610.

Budgeted Cash Disbursements: First Quarter, 19x8

Salaries/Wages
- Corporate officers: $20,000/month
- Medical doctors: 2 @ $6,000/month
- Nurses: 3 @ $2,500/month
- Clerical staff: 2 @ $1,200/month
- Aerobics instructors: 3 @ $900/month
- Clinic staff: 6 @ $1,400/month
- Maintenance staff: 3 @ $1,000/month
- Health food servers: 3 @ $800/month

Purchases
Muscle-tone machines: Jan., $16,400; Feb., $12,800; and Mar., $0
Pool supplies: $420 per month
Health food: Jan., $2,290; Feb., $2,460; and Mar., $2,720
Medical supplies: Jan., $9,400; Feb., $10,250; and Mar., $11,640
Medical clothing: Jan., $6,410; Feb., $2,900; and Mar., $2,450
Medical equipment: Jan., $10,200; Feb., $2,400; and Mar., $4,900
Advertising: Jan., $1,250; Feb., $2,190; and Mar., $3,450
Utilities expense: Jan., $6,450; Feb., $6,890; and Mar., $7,090
Insurance, fire: Jan., $2,470
liability: Mar., $4,980
Property taxes: $4,760 due in Jan.
Federal income taxes: 19x7 taxes of $22,000 due in Mar., 19x8
Miscellaneous: Jan., $1,625; Feb., $1,800; and Mar., $2,150

The beginning cash balance for 19x8 is anticipated to be $20,840.

Required

Prepare a cash budget for Olson's Wellness Centers, Inc., for the first quarter of 19x8. Use the following column headings:

Item January February March Total

Problem Set B

Problem 21B-1. Budget Preparation (L.O. 5)

The main product of Revell Enterprises, Inc., is a multipurpose hammer that carries a lifetime guarantee. The steps in the manufacturing process have been combined by using modern, automated equipment. A list of cost and production information for the Revell hammer follows:

Direct materials
Anodized steel: 2 kilograms per hammer at $.60 per kilogram
Leather strapping for handle: ½ square meter per hammer at $4.80 per square meter
(Packing materials are returned to the manufacturer and, thus, are not included as part of Cost of Goods Sold.)
Direct labor
Forging operation: $10.50 per direct labor hour, 12 minutes per hammer
Leather-wrapping operation: $10.00 per direct labor hour; 24 minutes per hammer
Factory overhead
Forging operation: rate equals 70% of department's direct labor dollars
Leather-wrapping operation: rate equals 50% of department's direct labor dollars

For the three months ended December 31, 19xx, management expects to produce 48,000 hammers in October, 42,000 hammers in November, and 40,000 hammers in December.

Required

1. For the three-month period ending December 31, 19xx, prepare monthly production cost information for manufacturing the Revell hammer. In your budget analysis, show a detailed breakdown of all costs involved and the computation methods used.
2. Prepare a quarterly production cost budget for the hammer. Show monthly cost data and combined totals for the quarter for each cost category.

Problem 21B-2. General and Administrative Expense Budget (L.O. 5)

Rogne Metal Products, Inc., has four divisions and a centralized management structure. The home office is located in Spencer, Iowa. General and administrative expenses of the corporation for 19x8 and expected percentage increases for 19x9 are presented below.

Expense Categories	19x8 Expenses	Expected Increase in 19x9
Administrative Salaries	$125,000	20%
Facility Depreciation	37,000	10%
Operating Supplies	24,500	20%
Insurance and Taxes	6,000	10%
Computer Services	200,000	40%
Clerical Salaries	55,000	15%
Miscellaneous	12,500	10%
Total	$460,000	

To determine divisional profitability, all general and administrative expenses except for computer services are allocated to divisions on a total labor dollar basis. Computer service costs are charged directly to divisions on the basis of percent of total usage charges. Computer charges and direct labor costs in 19x8 were as follows:

	Computer Charges	Direct Labor
Division A	$ 50,000	$150,000
Division B	44,000	100,000
Division C	36,000	125,000
Division D	30,000	125,000
Home Office	40,000	
Total	$200,000	

Required

1. Prepare the general and administrative expense budget for Rogne Metal Products, Inc., for 19x9.
2. Prepare a schedule of budgeted cost charges for computer service for each division and the home office. Assume that percentage of usage time and cost distribution in 19x9 will be the same as in 19x8.

3. Determine the amount of general and administrative expense to be allocated to each division in 19x9. Assume the same direct labor cost distribution percentages in 19x8. Do not include costs budgeted in **2**.

Problem 21B-3. Master Budget (L.O. 4, 5)

The Bank of Seminole County has asked the president of Naruse Laser Products, Inc., for a forecasted income statement and balance sheet for the quarter ended June 30, 19x9. These documents will be used to support the company's request for a loan. A quarterly master budget is prepared on a routine basis by the company, so the president indicated that the requested documents would be forwarded to the bank in the near future.

To date (April 2) the following period budgets have been developed: Sales: April, \$210,400; May, \$154,220; and June, \$155,980. Materials purchases for the period, \$86,840; anticipated materials usage, \$92,710; labor expenses, \$81,460; projected factory overhead, \$69,940; selling expenses for the quarter, \$72,840; general and administrative expenses, \$90,900; capital expenditures, \$125,000 (to be spent on June 29); Cost of Goods Manufactured, \$256,820; and Cost of Goods Sold, \$262,910.

Balance sheet account balances at March 31, 19x9, were: Cash, \$28,770; Accounts Receivable, \$33,910; Materials Inventory, \$41,620; Work in Process Inventory, \$46,220; Finished Goods Inventory, \$51,940; Prepaid Expenses, \$9,200; Plant, Furniture, and Fixtures, \$498,600; Accumulated Depreciation, Plant, Furniture, and Fixtures, \$99,720; Patents, \$89,680; Accounts Payable, \$49,610; Notes Payable, \$105,500; Common Stock, \$250,000; and Retained Earnings, \$295,110.

Monthly cash balances for the quarter are projected to be: April 30, \$20,490; May 31, \$5,610; and June 30, (\$13,958). During the quarter accounts receivable are supposed to increase by 60 percent, patents will go up by \$7,500, prepaid expenses will remain constant, accounts payable will go down by 20 percent, and the company will make a \$5,000 payment on the note payable (\$4,100 is principal reduction). The federal income tax rate is 30 percent, and the second quarter's tax is paid in July. Depreciation for the quarter will be \$6,420, which is already included in the factory overhead budget.

Required

1. Prepare a forecasted income statement for the quarter ended June 30, 19x9.
2. Prepare a forecasted statement of financial position as of June 30, 19x9.

Problem 21B-4. Basic Cash Budget (L.O. 7)

Produce World, Inc., is the creation of John Versackas, an immigrant from Lithuania. Mr. Versackas's dream was to develop the biggest produce store with the widest selection of fresh fruits and vegetables in the Northern Illinois area. In three short years he accomplished his objective. Eighty percent of his business is conducted on credit with area retail enterprises, and 20 percent of the produce sold is to walk-in customers at his retail outlet on a cash only basis. Collection experience shows that 20 percent of all credit sales are collected during the month of sale, 50 percent are received in the month following the sale, and 29 percent are collected in the second month after the sale. One percent of credit sales are uncollectible.

Mr. Versackas has asked you to prepare a cash budget for his business for the quarter ending September 30, 19x9. Operating data for the period is as follows: Total sales in May were $125,000; in June, $140,000. Anticipated sales include July, $115,000; August, $157,500; and September, $215,800. Purchases for the quarter are expected to be $67,400 in July; $92,850 in August; and $101,450 in September. All purchases are for cash. Other projected costs for the quarter include: (a) salaries and wages of $39,740 in July, $42,400 in August, and $51,600 in September; (b) monthly costs of $3,080 for heat, light, and power; (c) $950 for bank collection fees; (d) $4,850 for rent; (e) $5,240 for supplies; (f) $2,410 for depreciation of equipment; (g) $1,570 for equipment repairs; and (h) $1,150 for miscellaneous expenses. The corporation's cash balance at June 30, 19x9, was $8,490.

Required

1. Prepare a cash budget by month for the quarter ending September 30, 19x9.
2. Should Produce World, Inc., anticipate taking out a bank loan during the quarter? How much should be borrowed? When? (Note: Management maintains a $5,000 minimum monthly cash balance.)

Problem 21B-5. Cash Budget Preparation: Comprehensive (L.O. 7)

Texas Mountain Ski Resort, Inc., located in the Texas panhandle, has been in business for twenty-two years. Although the skiing season is difficult to predict, the company operates under the assumption that all of its revenues will be generated during the first three months of the calendar year. Routine maintenance and repair work is done during the remaining nine-month period. The following projections for 19x9 were developed by Lou Vlasho, company budget director:

Cash Receipts

Lift tickets: January, 14,800 people at $21; February, 12,400 people at $22; and March, 14,800 people at $23

Food sales: January, $72,000; February, $66,000; and March, $72,000

Skiing lessons: January, $258,000; February, $234,000; and March, $258,000

Equipment sales and rental: January, $992,000; February, $896,000; and March, $992,000

Liquor sales: January, $114,000; February, $102,000; and March, $114,000

Cash Disbursements

Salaries:

- Ski area:
  - Lift operators: 10 people at $2,000 per month for January, February, and March (first quarter)
  - Instruction and equipment rental: 22 people at $2,200 per month for first quarter
- Maintenance: $33,000 per month for first quarter and $94,000 for the rest of the year
- Customer service: shuttle-bus drivers: 5 people at $1,200 per month for first quarter

Medical: six people at $4,400 per month for first quarter
Food service: sixteen people at $1,000 per month for first quarter

Purchases:

- Food: $20,000 per month for the first quarter
- Ski equipment: purchases of $440,000 in both January and February plus a $600,000 purchase in December 19x9
- Liquors: $40,000 in each month of the first quarter
- Tickets and supplies: $50,000 in January, $40,000 in February, and $80,000 in December 19x9
- Advertising: $30,000 in January, $20,000 in February, and $80,000 from April through the end of the year
- Fire and liability insurance: January and June premium payments of $7,000
- Medical facility costs: $5,000 per month during first quarter
- Utilities: $3,000 per month for the first quarter and $1,000 per month for the rest of the year
- Lift maintenance: $15,000 per month for the first quarter and $10,000 per month for the rest of the year
- Property taxes: $280,000 due in June
- Federal income taxes: 19x8 taxes of $564,000 due in March

The beginning cash balance for 19x9 is anticipated to be $10,000.

Required

Prepare a cash budget for Texas Mountain Ski Resort, Inc., for 19x9, using the following column headings:

Item	January	February	March	April–December	Total

Management Decision Case

P.C. Enterprises
(L.O. 1, 2, 5)

During the past ten years, P.C. Enterprises has practiced participative budgeting all the way from the maintenance personnel to the president's staff. Gradually, however, the objectives of honesty and decisions made in the best interest of the company have given way at the divisional level to division-benefiting decisions and budgets biased in favor of divisional interests. Mr. Vrana, corporate controller, has asked Ms. Somer, budget director, to carefully analyze this year's divisional budgets before incorporating them into the company's master budget.

The Western Division was first of six divisions to submit its 19x7 budget request to the corporate office. Its summary income statement and accompanying notes are presented on the next page.

Required

1. Recast the Western Division's Forecasted Income Statement into the following format (round percentages to two decimal places):

	Budget—12/31/x6		Budget—12/31/x7	
Account	**Amount**	**Percent of Sales**	**Amount**	**Percent of Sales**

2. Actual results for 19x6 revealed the following information about revenues and cost of goods sold:

	Amount	Percent of Sales
Sales: Radios	$ 760,000	43.30
Appliances	560,000	31.91
Telephones	370,000	21.08
Miscellaneous	65,000	3.70
Total revenues	$1,755,000	100.00*
Less Cost of Goods Sold	763,425	43.50
Gross margin	$ 991,575	56.50

On the basis of this information and your analysis in **1**, what should the budget director say to officials of the Western Division? Mention specific areas of the budget that need to be revised.

*Error due to rounding.

P.C. Enterprises
Western Division
Forecasted Income Statement
For the Years Ending December 31, 19x6 and 19x7

	Budget 12/31/x6	Budget 12/31/x7	Increase (Decrease)
Revenues			
Sales: radios	$ 840,000	$ 900,000	$ 60,000
appliances	690,000	750,000	60,000
telephones	265,000	300,000	35,000
miscellaneous	82,400	100,000	17,600
Total revenues	$1,877,400	$2,050,000	$172,600
Less cost of goods sold	750,960	717,500[1]	(33,460)
Gross margin	$1,126,440	$1,332,500	$206,060
Operating Expenses			
Wages: warehouse	$ 84,500	$ 92,250	$ 7,750
purchasing	67,800	74,000	6,200
delivery/shipping	59,400	64,780	5,380
maintenance	32,650	35,670	3,020
Salaries: supervisory	60,000	92,250	32,250
executive	120,000	164,000	44,000
Purchases, supplies	17,400	20,500	3,100
Merchandise moving equipment:			
maintenance	72,400	82,000	9,600
depreciation	62,000	71,750[2]	9,750
Building rent	96,000	102,500	6,500
Sales commissions	187,740	205,000	17,260
Insurance: fire	12,670	20,500	7,830
liability	18,200	20,500	2,300
Utilities	14,100	15,375	1,275
Taxes: property	16,600	18,450	1,850
payroll	26,520	41,000	14,480
Miscellaneous	4,610	10,250	5,640
Total operating expenses	$ 952,590	$1,130,775	$178,185
Net income before taxes	$ 173,850	$ 201,725	$ 27,875

1. Less expensive merchandise will be purchased in 19x7 to boost profits.
2. Depreciation is increased because of the need to buy additional equipment to handle increased sales.

CHAPTER 22 INTRODUCTION TO STANDARD COST ACCOUNTING

LEARNING OBJECTIVES

1. Describe the nature and purpose of standard costs.
2. Describe and differentiate among the three types of standard costs: ideal standards, basic standards, and currently attainable standards.
3. Identify the six elements of a standard unit cost and describe the factors to consider in developing each element.
4. Compute a standard unit cost.
5. Compute and evaluate direct materials and direct labor variances.
6. Prepare journal entries to record transactions involving direct materials and direct labor variances in a standard cost system.

Standard cost accounting is a tool used by management for cost planning and cost control. When a company uses standard costs, all costs affecting the three inventory accounts and the Cost of Goods Sold account are stated in terms of standard or predetermined costs rather than actual costs incurred. A standard cost system is used with a job order or process costing system and is not a full cost accounting system by itself. Together with cost behavior relationships and cost-volume-profit analyses, the incorporation of standard costs into a cost accounting system provides the foundation for the budgetary control process. Standard costs are useful for: (1) evaluating the performance of workers and management; (2) preparing budgets and forecasts; and (3) deciding on appropriate selling prices.

Because standard cost accounting is so important and represents such a major change in costing concepts, this topic will be covered in two chapters. In this chapter we will look at the nature and purpose of standard costs, their make-up, their development, and their use in product costing. We will also introduce variance analysis for direct materials and direct labor and their journal entry recording. In Chapter 23 we will (1) continue to focus on variance analysis, this time in the overhead cost area and (2) analyze variances as a basis for performance evaluation.

After studying this chapter you should be able to meet the learning objectives listed on the left.

Nature and Purpose of Standard Costs

Standard costs are realistically predetermined costs for direct materials, direct labor, and factory overhead. They are usually expressed as cost per unit of finished product. Predetermined overhead costs, which we discussed in Chapter 17, are different from standard costs. The concept of standard costing focuses on total unit cost, which includes all three manufacturing cost elements. It goes beyond factory overhead cost. In addition, a more detailed analysis is used when computing standard costs.

Predetermined overhead costing and standard costing do, however, share two important elements: both forecast dollar amounts to

OBJECTIVE 1 Describe the nature and purpose of standard costs

be used in product costing, and both depend on expected costs of budgeted items. But this is where the similarity ends. Standard costs depend on more than the simple projections of past costs that are used to develop predetermined overhead rates. They are based on engineering estimates, forecasted demand, worker input, time-and-motion studies, and direct materials types and quality. However, we should not play down the role of the predetermined overhead rate. It provides some of the same data as the standard overhead rate. And standard costing is both sophisticated and expensive. If a company cannot afford to add standard costing to its cost system, it should still continue to use predetermined overhead rates.

Standard costing is a total cost concept. It is made up of costs for direct materials, direct labor, and factory overhead. In a fully integrated standard cost system, all actual manufacturing cost data are replaced by standard (or predetermined) cost data. Accounts such as Direct Materials Inventory, Work in Process Inventory, Finished Goods Inventory, and Cost of Goods Sold are all stated in terms of standard costs. All debit and credit entries made to these accounts are in terms of standard costs, not actual costs. All inventory balances are figured by using standard unit costs. Separate records of actual costs are kept to compare standard costs (what should have been spent) with actual costs. The two are usually compared at the end of each accounting period, whether weekly, monthly, or quarterly. If large differences (variances) exist, the management accountant looks for the cause of the differences. This process, known as variance analysis, is one of the most effective cost control tools. We discuss it later in this chapter and in Chapter 23.

Standard costs are introduced into a cost accounting system for several reasons. These costs are useful for preparing operating budgets. They make it easier to pinpoint production costs that need to be controlled. They help in setting realistic prices. And they basically simplify cost accounting procedures for inventories and product costing. Although expensive to set up and maintain, a standard cost accounting system can save a company a lot of money by reducing waste and inefficiency.

Budgetary Control and Standard Costs

Budgetary control involves the successful planning of a company's operating activities and the control of operations to help attain those plans. In management accounting terms, the objectives of budgetary control are:

1. To help establish procedures for preparing a company's planned costs and revenues
2. To help coordinate and communicate these plans to levels of management
3. To formulate a basis for effective cost control.

Standard costs play a major role in budgetary control. Standard materials, labor, and factory overhead costs are useful in projecting anticipated costs. For example, assume that Arnold Company estimates that it will manufacture 35,000 type-A products during the coming year. Each product requires 2½ hours of labor (labor time standard) at a cost of $7.50 per hour (standard labor rate per hour). Planned labor costs for the year on this product would be

$$35{,}000 \text{ products} \times 2.5 \text{ hours} \times \$7.50 = \$656{,}250$$

This example involves estimates of the number of products, standard labor hours per product, and standard labor cost per hour. Such forecasted information facilitates planning by coordinating plans throughout the enterprise and by communicating information to managers responsible for production volume and factory labor. The estimate of 35,000 products provides the production superintendent with an output goal for the year. Production personnel know that these 35,000 units should be produced by using an average of 2½ labor hours on each unit with an average labor rate of $7.50 per hour.

Assume that at year end the Arnold Company had incurred actual labor costs of $662,350 to manufacture this product. In standard costing terms a variance had been incurred:

$$\text{Actual cost} - \text{standard cost} = \text{variance}$$

or

$$\$662{,}350 - \$656{,}250 = \$6{,}100(\text{U})$$

A variance is the difference between actual results and related standard or budgeted results. In the example, actual costs exceeded standard costs, which resulted in an unfavorable variance. An unfavorable variance is designated by the symbol "U." If actual costs are less than standard costs, the variance is favorable and is noted by the symbol "F."

Variance analysis is used in the cost control phase of the budgetary control process. With the aid of standard costs, you can compute and analyze variances. Once the causes of a variance have been determined, corrective measures are implemented to prevent nonstandard performance in future periods.

What caused the Arnold Company to incur $6,100 more in labor costs than anticipated? From the information given no single reason or cause can be isolated. The following list of possible causes indicates the types of factors that should be investigated to obtain an appropriate explanation:

1. The company produced more than 35,000 products during the year.
2. More than 2½ labor hours were used per product.
3. The average labor rate exceeded the standard labor rate of $7.50.
4. The variance resulted from a combination of factors included in items 1, 2, and 3.

Standard cost variances measure the degree of nonstandard performance. Additional information must be obtained to identify the causes related to such performance. The Arnold Company example introduced you to cost control through the analysis of variances. This concept will be expanded on later in this chapter and in Chapter 23.

Behaviorial Effects of Standard Costs

A standard cost should be viewed as a target cost by managers in each area of the company's operations. The operating objective is to achieve the standard performance target in terms of materials usage and costs, labor time and costs, and overhead costs to produce a given volume of products or to provide a defined amount of service. Standard costs are carefully determined, but they are seldom precise, since estimates are used in the computations. Meeting the standard performance target should be considered a reasonable measure of operating performance when evaluating managers. When actual costs are compared with related standards, variances should be expected. Significant or large variances pinpoint operating efficiencies or inefficiencies. Remember, variances can be positive as well as negative.

If standard costs are to be accepted as targets or performance goals, the standards must be attainable and managers and employees must consider them reasonable. Standards that are unattainable will soon be recognized, and they will cease to inspire managers to operate efficiently. Therefore, a successful standard cost system must include motivational considerations. All managers and employees should be advised of their specific areas of responsibility and should take part in developing related standards and budget targets. Basing standard costs on both motivational factors and efficient operating considerations will assist management in reaching overall corporate objectives.

Types of Standard Costs

OBJECTIVE 2
Describe and differentiate among the three types of standard costs: ideal standards, basic standards, and currently attainable standards

Standard costs can be characterized as ideal standards, basic standards, or currently attainable standards. Each type of standard cost is useful, but ideal standards and basic standards require certain adjustments before they can be used to evaluate performance or assess the value of inventory.

Ideal Standards

Ideal standards, also called theoretical, or perfection, standards, are based on a maximum efficiency level with no breaks or work stoppages. These standards allow for minimum materials, labor time, and other cost constraints in producing a product or creating a service. Performance equivalent to the attainment of ideal standards is rarely accomplished because people and machines have periods of downtime. Standards based on this maximum efficiency approach are effective only when operating personnel are aware of this factor and are rewarded for performing at a percentage, say 85 or 90 percent, of standard.

For example, assume that Machine 1 can produce a maximum of 300 units per hour, which is the ideal standard. Mr. M. Jackson, operator of the machine, is told by the supervisor that the target is to produce an average of 270 units per hour, even though the ideal standard is 300 units per hour. By adjusting ideal production standards downward, realistic operating goals can be communicated to employees to promote employee motivation. Ideal standards are based on theoretical capacity and result in minimum unit costs.

Illustration A in Figure 22-1 depicts an ideal standard cost for direct labor. The standard is set at such a high level that it can never be attained. To be useful, the standards must be adjusted. The cost standard must be increased to a reasonable level. Once the standard is adjusted, actual performance can be compared with the adjusted standard data for evaluation purposes. In the figure the actual labor cost varied above and below the adjusted standard amount, causing both unfavorable and favorable variances.

The concept of an ideal standard does provide a picture of a worker's or machine's maximum efficiency. However, ideal standards are difficult to understand and employ; and therefore, are seldom used in practice.

Basic Standards

Basic standards are projections that are seldom revised or updated to reflect current operating costs and price level changes. They remain the same after being computed for the first time. Basic standards are used primarily to measure trends in operating performance. Although useful, basic standards must be adjusted before they can be used to evaluate performance.

Figure 22-1. Graphic Illustration of Ideal and Basic Standards

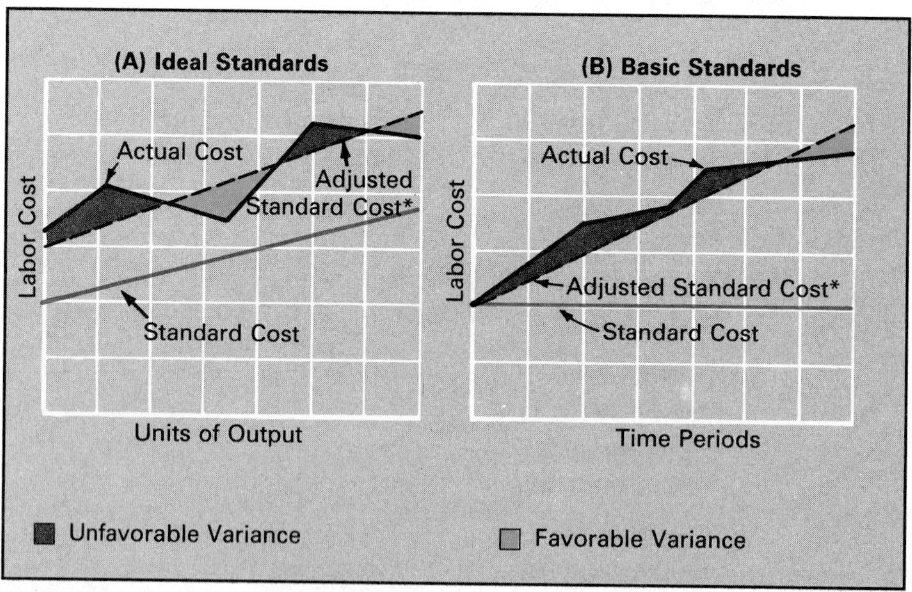

*Adjusted standard cost = standard cost × 1.5

*Adjusted standard increase above basic standard because of inflation and other factors

Basic standards are illustrated in Part B of Figure 22-1. The standard cost does not change over time. To be useful the basic standard must be adjusted to reflect price level changes and improvements in operator and machine efficiency. Once the basic standard has been adjusted, actual cost can be plotted and compared with the expected cost. In Figure 22-1(B), actual cost is above adjusted standard cost for the first few time periods. Then, actual unit costs level off, and the adjusted standard is greater than the actual. The result is a favorable variance.

Like ideal standards, basic standards require adjustment before becoming useful targets. Because of this factor basic standards tend to be confusing and lack motivational properties. They also have limited use in practice.

Currently Attainable Standards

Currently attainable standards are standard costs that are updated periodically to reflect changes in operating conditions and current price levels for direct materials, direct labor, and factory overhead costs. Unlike ideal standards, currently attainable standards measure reasonable performance under average operating conditions. Normal efficiency is assumed. Under these conditions direct labor standards include allowances for recurring machine downtime and work stoppages by employees. Direct materials standards are based on current market prices and include allowances for normal scrap and spoilage loss.

Currently attainable standards are acceptable for purposes of product costing, performance evaluation, planning, and employee motivation. Unless otherwise indicated, the remaining illustrations and problems in this text assume the use of currently attainable standards. Currently attainable standards yield inventory valuations that closely approximate actual unit costs and are acceptable for external financial reporting purposes.

Development of Standard Costs

OBJECTIVE 3
Identify the six elements of a standard unit cost, and describe the factors to consider in developing each element

A standard unit cost has six parts: (1) direct materials price standard; (2) direct materials quantity standard; (3) direct labor time standard; (4) direct labor rate standard; (5) standard variable factory overhead rate; and (6) standard fixed factory overhead rate. To develop a standard unit cost, we must identify and analyze each of these items.

Standard Direct Materials Cost. The **standard direct materials cost** is found by multiplying the standard price for direct materials by the standard quantity for direct materials. If the price standard for a certain item is \$2.75 and a job calls for eight of these items, the standard direct materials cost for that job is \$22.00 (8 × \$2.75).

The **direct materials price standard** is a careful estimate of the cost of a certain type of direct material in the next accounting period. Possible price changes, changes in quantities available, and new supplier sources must be considered when determining this standard. Any of these could influence the price standard. A company's purchasing agent is responsible for developing price standards for all direct materials. The purchasing agent also follows through with actual purchases at the projected standard prices.

The standard use of direct materials is one of the most difficult standards to forecast. The **direct materials quantity standard** is an estimate of expected quantity use. It is influenced by product engineering specifications, quality of direct materials, age and productivity of machinery, and the quality and experience of the work force. Production managers are usually responsible for establishing and policing direct materials quantity standards. However, other people, such as engineers, the purchasing agent, and machine operators, can provide input into the development of these standards.

Standard Direct Labor Cost. The **standard direct labor cost** for a product, task, or job order is figured by multiplying the standard hours of direct labor by the standard wage for direct labor. Assume that a product takes 1.5 standard direct labor hours to produce and that the standard labor rate is $8.40 per hour. Even if the person actually making the product is paid only $7.90 per hour, $12.60 ($8.40 × 1.5) of standard direct labor cost would be charged to the Work in Process Inventory account.

Current time-and-motion studies of workers and machines as well as past employee and machine performance are the basic inputs for a **direct labor time standard.** Such standards express the time it takes for each department, machine, or process to complete production on one unit or batch of output. In many cases standard time per unit will be a small fraction of an hour. Meeting time standards is the department manager's or supervisor's responsibility. These standards should be revised whenever a machine is replaced or the quality of workers changes.

Labor rates are either set by labor contracts or defined by the company, so standard labor rates are fairly easy to develop. **Direct labor rate standards** are the hourly labor costs that are expected to prevail during the next accounting period for each function or job classification. Although rate ranges are established for each type of worker and rates vary within these ranges, an average standard rate is developed for each task. Problems in controlling costs arise when a highly paid worker performs a lower-level task. For instance, a machine operator making $9.25 per hour may actually perform the work of a set-up person earning $4.50 per hour. Here, the actual cost for the work will be at variance with the standard direct labor rate.

Standard Factory Overhead Cost. Basically, a **standard factory overhead cost** is an estimate of variable and fixed overhead in the next accounting period. The variable overhead cost and the fixed overhead cost depend on standard rates computed in much the same way as the predetermined overhead rate discussed in Chapter 17. There are only two differences. First, the standard overhead rate is made up of two parts, the rate for variable costs and the rate for fixed costs. Second, more time and effort are put into calculating standard overhead rates.

The reason for computing the variable rate and the fixed rate separately is that different application bases are generally appropriate. The **standard variable overhead rate** is usually computed on the basis of *expected* direct labor hours. (Other bases may be used if direct labor hours are not a good barometer of variable costs.) The formula is as follows:

$$\text{Standard variable overhead rate} = \frac{\text{total budgeted variable overhead costs}}{\text{expected number of standard direct labor hours}}$$

The **standard fixed overhead rate**, on the other hand, is most often computed on the basis of **normal operating capacity**. This basis is expressed in the same terms as those used to compute the variable overhead rate.

$$\text{Standard fixed overhead rate} = \frac{\text{total budgeted fixed overhead costs}}{\text{normal capacity in terms of standard direct labor hours}}$$

By using normal capacity as the denominator, all fixed overhead costs should be applied to units produced by the time normal capacity is reached.

If actual output exceeds expectations and the standard hours allowed for good units produced is more than normal capacity, a favorable situation exists because more fixed overhead has been applied than was actually incurred. But if actual output does not meet expectations and is less than normal capacity, all expected fixed overhead costs have not been applied to production units—an unfavorable condition. The difference (variance) between factory overhead incurred and factory overhead applied will be discussed in greater detail in Chapter 23.

Updating and Maintaining Standards

Currently attainable standards will not remain currently attainable unless they are periodically reviewed and updated. Changing prices, new personnel, new machinery, changing quality of direct materials, and new labor contracts all tend to make currently attainable standards obsolete. Obsolete standards lead to unrealistic budgets, poor cost control, and unreasonable unit costs for inventory valuation.

To prevent standards from becoming obsolete, a company should install a program designed to update standards and maintain them at currently attainable levels. If labor rates are increased, labor rate standards should be adjusted immediately. If a new, more efficient piece of machinery is purchased to replace a relatively inefficient machine, labor time standards and material quantity standards should be updated. In addition to these obvious adjustments, a system for revising standard costs should require that every standard be analyzed for adequacy at least once a year. With this type of annual review system, a company will have standards that approximate currently attainable levels.

Using Standards for Product Costing

Using standard costs does away with the need to compute unit costs from actual cost data for every week or month or for each batch. Once standards are developed for direct materials, direct labor, and factory overhead, a total standard unit cost can be computed anytime.

Standard cost elements can be used to find the following: (1) cost of purchased direct materials entered into Materials Inventory; (2) cost of goods requisitioned out of Materials Inventory and into Work in Process Inventory; (3) cost of direct labor charged to Work in Process Inventory; (4) cost of factory overhead applied to Work in Process Inventory; (5) cost of goods completed and transferred to Finished Goods Inventory; and (6) cost of units sold and charged to the Cost of Goods Sold account. In other words, all transactions (entries) affecting the three inventory accounts and Cost of Goods Sold will be expressed in terms of standard costs, no matter what the actual costs incurred. An illustrative problem will show how this concept works.

Illustrative Problem: Use of Standard Costs

OBJECTIVE 4
Compute a standard unit cost

McCall Industries, Inc., uses standard costs in its St. Louis, Missouri, division. Recently, the company changed the standards for its line of automatic pencils to agree with current costs for the year 19xx. New standards include the following: Direct materials price standards are $7.20 per square foot for casing material and $1.50 for each movement mechanism. Direct materials quantity standards are .125 square foot of casing material per pencil and one movement mechanism per pencil. Direct labor time standards are .01 hour per pencil for the Stamping Department and .05 hour per pencil for the Assembly Department. Direct labor rate standards are $6.00 per hour for the Stamping Department and $7.20 per hour for the Assembly Department. Standard factory overhead rates are $18.00 per direct labor hour for the standard variable overhead rate and $12.00 per direct labor hour for the standard fixed overhead rate.

Required

Compute the standard manufacturing cost of one automatic pencil.

Solution

Standard cost of one pencil is computed as follows:

Direct materials costs	
Casing ($7.20/sq ft × .125 sq ft)	$ .90
One movement mechanism	1.50
Direct labor costs	
Stamping Department (.01 hr/pencil × $6.00/hr)	.06
Assembly Department (.05 hr/pencil × $7.20/hr)	.36
Factory overhead	
Variable overhead (.06 hr/pencil × $18.00/hr)	1.08
Fixed overhead (.06 hr/pencil × $12.00/hr)	.72
Total standard cost per pencil	$4.62

Journal Entry Analysis

Recording standard costs is much like recording actual cost data. The only major difference is that any amount for direct materials, direct labor, or factory overhead entered into the Work in Process Inventory account is stated at standard cost. This means that the Work in Process Inventory account is stated entirely at standard cost. Any transfer of units to Finished Goods Inventory or to the Cost of Goods Sold account will automatically be at standard unit cost. When actual costs for direct materials, direct labor, and factory overhead are different from standard costs, the difference is recorded in a variance account. (We will discuss such accounts in a later section.) In the following analysis, we assume that all costs incurred are at standard cost. Again, we use McCall Industries as an example.

Transaction: Purchased 400 square feet of casing material at standard cost.

		Debit	Credit
Entry:	Materials Inventory	2,880	
	Accounts Payable		2,880
	To record purchase of 400 sq ft of casing material at $7.20/sq ft		

(It does not matter if the actual purchase price is higher or lower than the standard price. The same $2,880 standard cost is still entered into the Materials Inventory account. See also the journal entry for purchases on page 836.)

Transaction: Requisitioned 60 square feet of casing material and 240 movement mechanisms into production.

		Debit	Credit
Entry:	Work in Process Inventory	792	
	Materials Inventory		792
	To record requisition of 60 sq ft of casing material (at $7.20/sq ft) and 240 movement mechanisms (at $1.50 each) into production		

Transaction: At period end 300 pencils were completed and transferred to Finished Goods Inventory.

		Debit	Credit
Entry:	Finished Goods Inventory	1,386	
	Work in Process Inventory		1,386
	To record the transfer of 300 completed units to Finished Goods Inventory (300 pencils × $4.62/pencil)		

The above analysis shows only a few examples of the journal entries used in recording standard cost information. The examples given later in this chapter and in Chapter 23 are more realistic because they are joined with the analysis of variances. Our purpose here is just to show that when a standard cost accounting system is used, standard costs, rather than actual costs, flow through the production and inventory accounts.

Benefits and Drawbacks of a Standard Costing System

The principal advantages of a standard costing system for planning, control, and product costing are as follows:

1. The setting of standards requires a thorough analysis of all cost functions and often discloses inefficiencies.
2. Standard cost information is more useful than historical cost data for product costing and pricing.
3. Standard costs are the basis of an effective budgetary control system.
4. The speed with which regular operating data is recorded is increased.
5. Clearly defined lines of cost responsibility and authority are established by a standard costing system.
6. The setting of standards forces management to plan efficient operations.
7. Performance evaluation is enhanced through variance analysis.

There are also certain limitations regarding standard costing systems. The use of standard costing is not practical for every company because a standard cost system is expensive to develop. In addition, maintenance and updating requirements are costly. Before deciding to install a standard cost system, management should conduct some type of cost-benefit analysis. If the potential benefits exceed the costs, then standard costing should be introduced into the cost accounting system.

Variance Analysis: Direct Materials and Direct Labor

Variance analysis is a cost control tool provided by standard cost accounting systems. Standard costs provide the foundation for effective budgetary control. The development and use of standard costs facilitate the planning phase of budgetary control. However, budgetary control is successful only if management's effectiveness and operating efficiency can be analyzed. Such analyses involve cost control and are achieved by measuring and evaluating performance. **Variance analysis** is the process of computing the amount of and isolating the causes of differences between actual costs and standard costs.

As stated, a major objective of variance analysis is to measure management's effectiveness and operating efficiency. Comparisons of actual operating results with budgeted or planned operating activities are the foundation for performance evaluation. If actual operating costs deviate from anticipated costs, a cost variance is incurred. A variance indicates that management has failed to accomplish a stated objective. Variance analysis helps determine the reasons for unsatisfactory or superior operating results.

Variance analysis involves two phases: (a) computing individual variances and (b) determining the cause(s) of each variance. The remaining sections of this chapter concentrate on computing materials and labor variances. Overhead variance computations, analysis of causes, reporting of variances to managers, and accounting for the disposition of variances, which are covered in Chapter 23, conclude the study of standard cost variance analysis.

OBJECTIVE 5
Compute and evaluate direct materials and direct labor variances

Direct Materials Variances. To identify direct materials variances, we compare standard amounts for price and quantity with actual prices and quantities of materials used. Let us assume, for example, that Pearce Company makes leather chairs. Each chair should use 4 yards of leather (standard quantity), and the standard price of leather is $6.00 per yard. During August, 760 yards of leather, costing $5.90 per yard, were purchased and used to produce 180 chairs. The total direct materials cost variance is computed below.

Actual cost	
Actual quantity × actual price =	
760 yd at $5.90/yd =	$4,484
Standard cost	
Standard quantity × standard price =	
(180 chairs × 4 yd/chair) at $6.00/yd =	
720 yd at $6.00/yd =	$4,320
Total direct materials cost variance	$ 164(U)

Remember, the "U" following the dollar amount indicates an unfavorable situation. (A favorable situation would be indicated by an "F.") The special problem facing Pearce Company is that part of this variance is caused by price differences and part is caused by direct materials usage. To find the area or people responsible for these variances, the total direct materials cost variance must be broken down into two parts: the direct materials price variance and the direct materials quantity variance.

The **direct materials price variance** is the difference between the actual price and the standard price, multiplied by the actual quantity purchased. For the Pearce Company it would be computed as follows:

Actual price	$5.90
Less standard price	6.00
Difference	$ .10(F)

Price variance = (actual price − standard price) × actual quantity
= $.10(F) × 760 yards
= $76(F)

The **direct materials quantity variance** is the difference between the actual quantity used and the standard quantity that should have been used, multiplied by the standard price.

Actual quantity	760 yd
Less standard quantity (180 × 4 yd/chair)	720 yd
Difference	40 yd(U)

Quantity variance = (actual quantity − standard quantity) × standard price
= 40 yd(U) × $6/yd
$240(U)

As a check of these answers, the sum of the price variance and the quantity variance should equal the total direct materials cost variance.

Price variance	$ 76(F)
Quantity variance	240(U)
Total direct materials cost variance	$164(U)

Sometimes it is easier to see cost relationships when shown in a diagram. Figure 22-2 illustrates the cost variance analysis described above. Materials are purchased at actual cost but entered into the Materials Inventory account at standard price. Therefore, the materials price variance of $76(F) is determined before costs are entered into Materials Inventory. The materials quantity variance results from using too much or too little materials in making the product. Spoilage and waste occur, of which some may be unavoidable and, thus, anticipated when computing the standard quantity amount. A materials quantity variance occurs when the standard quantity is not used. If more quantity is used, as in the Pearce Company example, an unfavorable materials quantity variance results; here, $240(U). As shown, standard quantity times standard price is the amount entered into the Work in Process Inventory account.

Normally, the purchasing agent is responsible for price variances, and the production department supervisors are accountable for quantity variances. In cases such as this one, however, the less expensive materials may have been of such poor quality that higher scrap rates resulted. Each situation must be evaluated according to specific circumstances and not in terms of general guidelines.

Direct Labor Variances. The approach to finding variances in direct labor costs parallels the approach to finding direct materials variances. Total direct labor variance is the difference between the actual labor cost and standard labor cost for the good units produced. Expanding the Pearce Company example, we find that each chair requires 2.4 standard labor hours, and the standard labor rate is $8.50 per hour. During August, 450 direct labor hours were used to make 180 chairs at an average

Figure 22-2.
Materials Variance Analysis

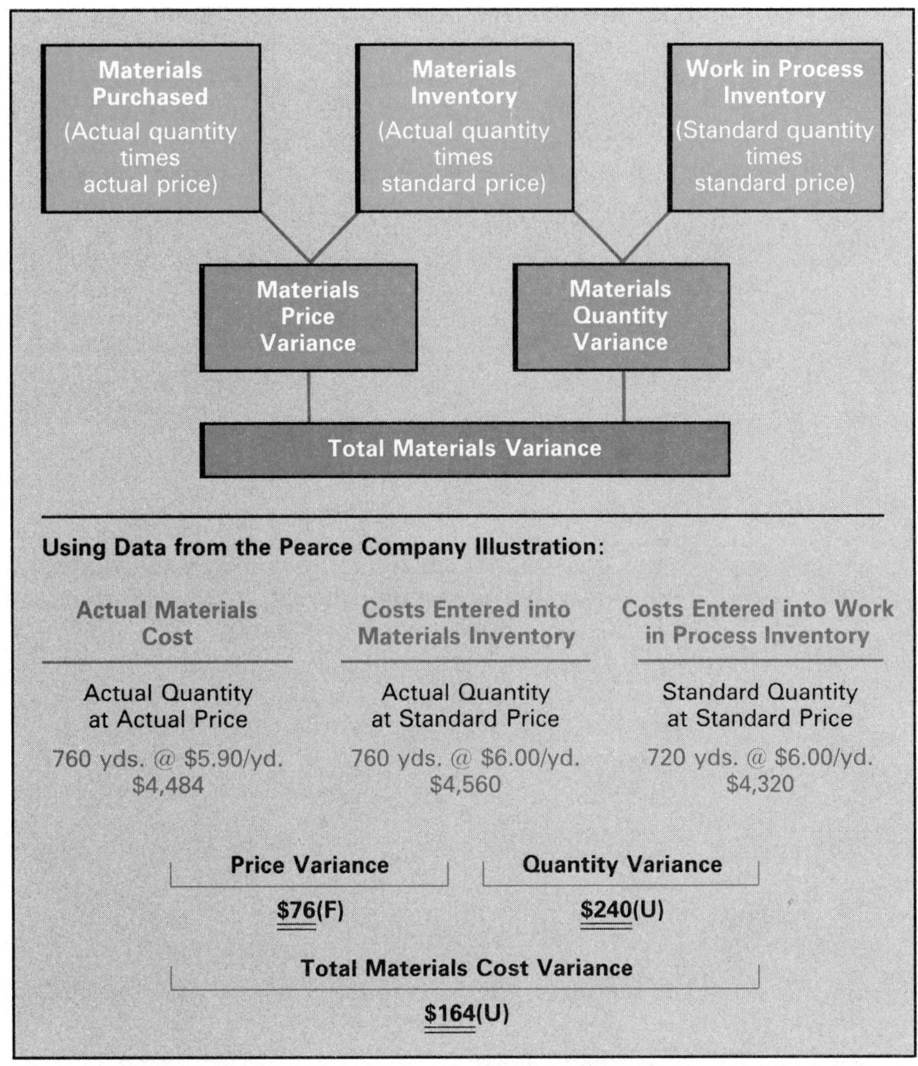

pay rate of $9.20 per hour. The total direct labor cost variance is computed as shown below.

Actual cost	
Actual hours × actual rate = 450 hr × $9.20/hr =	$4,140
Standard cost	
Standard hours allowed × standard rate =	
(180 chairs × 2.4 hr/chair) × $8.50/hr =	
432 hr × $8.50/hr =	3,672
Total direct labor cost variance	$ 468(U)

Both the actual hours per chair and the actual labor rate varied from standard. For effective cost control, management must know how much of the total cost arose from varying labor rates and how much from varying labor hour usage. This information is found by computing the labor rate variance and the labor efficiency variance separately.

The **direct labor rate variance** is the difference between the actual labor rate and the standard labor rate, multiplied by the actual hours worked.

Actual rate	$9.20
Less standard rate	8.50
Difference	$ .70(U)

Rate variance = (actual rate − standard rate) × actual hours
= .70(U) × 450 hours
= $315(U)

The **direct labor efficiency variance** is the difference between actual hours worked and standard hours allowed for the good units produced, multiplied by the standard labor rate.

Actual Hours Worked	450 hr
Less Standard Hours Allowed (180 chairs × 2.4 hr/chair)	432 hr
Difference	18 hr(U)

Efficiency variance = (actual hours − standard hours allowed) × standard rate
= 18 hr(U) × $8.50/hr
= $153(U)

The following check shows that the variances were computed correctly.

Rate variance	$315(U)
Efficiency variance	153(U)
Total direct labor cost variance	$468(U)

Labor rate variances are generally the responsibility of the Personnel Department. A rate variance often happens when a person is hired at an incorrect rate or performs the duties of a higher- or lower-paid employee. Labor efficiency variances can be traced to departmental supervisors. As with direct materials variances, an unfavorable labor efficiency variance can occur if an inexperienced, lower-paid person is assigned to a task requiring greater skill. Management should judge each situation only after looking at all circumstances.

The analysis shown in Figure 22-2 can be easily adjusted to fit the computations for labor variances. Figure 22-3 contains a summary of the direct labor variance analysis. Unlike materials variances, the labor rate and efficiency variances are usually computed and recorded at the same

Figure 22-3. Direct Labor Variance Analysis

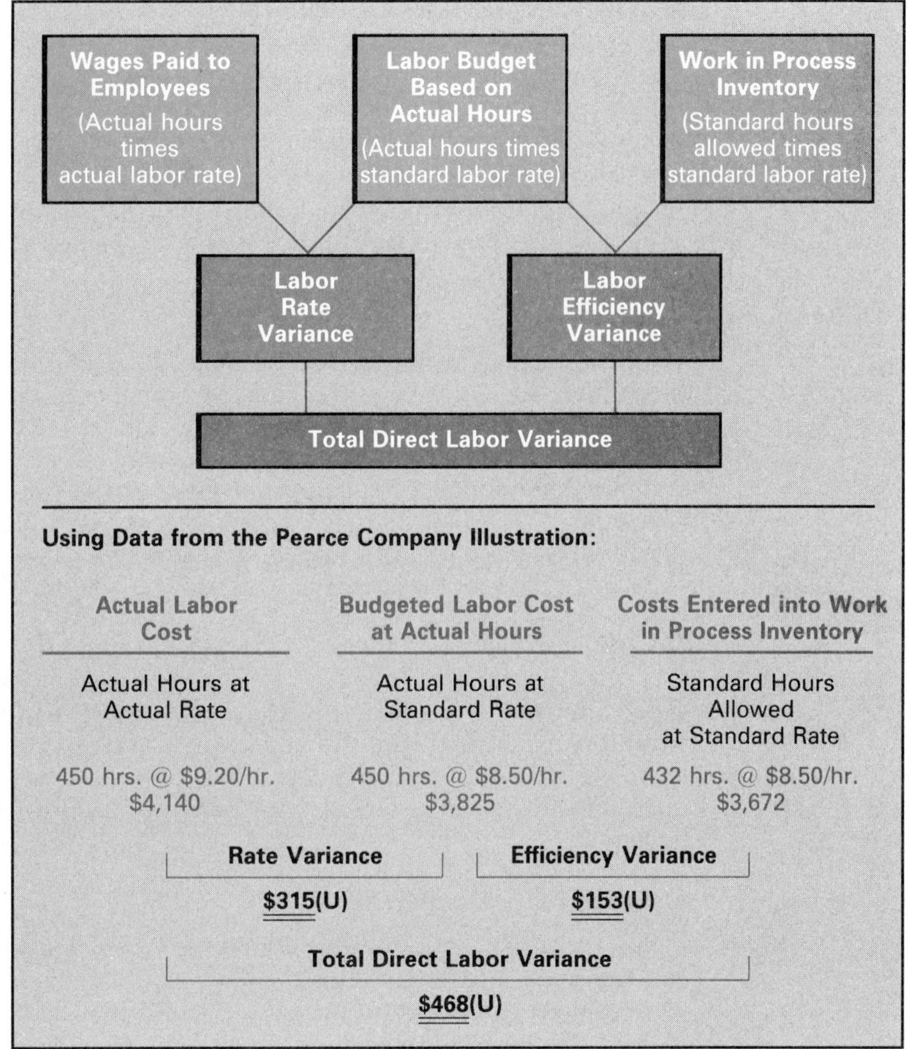

time. The reason for this approach is that labor is not stored in an inventory account before use, as are materials. The labor rate variance is the difference between wages paid to employees (actual direct labor expense) and the labor budget based on actual hours (direct labor expense if standard direct labor rates were paid). The difference between the labor budget based on actual hours and the labor cost entered into the Work in Process Inventory is the labor efficiency variance. Efficiency relates to the time taken to complete a task. Here, efficiency is measured as the difference between actual hours worked and standard hours allowed for the good units produced during the period. This difference is multiplied by the standard labor rate to compute the variance. Data from the Pearce Company were inserted into the lower portion of Figure 22-3 to illustrate this approach to labor variance analysis.

Variances in the Accounting Records

OBJECTIVE 6
Prepare journal entries to record transactions involving direct materials and direct labor variances in a standard cost system

When variances from standard costs develop, special journal entries are needed. The few simple rules below will make this recording process easier to remember.

1. *All* inventory balances are recorded at standard cost, as stated earlier.
2. Separate accounts are created for each type of variance.
3. *Unfavorable* variances are *debited* to their accounts, and *favorable* variances are *credited*.

With these rules in mind, we will now record the direct materials and direct labor transactions of the Pearce Company described earlier.

Note that it is possible to operate a standard cost system without putting variances into the records with journal entries. Variances can be computed on work sheets, and actual costs can be run through accounts. This approach is less costly to operate. However, it loses the advantage of consistent pricing of products and inventories. It also makes it harder to record product cost flow.

Journal Entries for Direct Materials Transactions

There are two key points in this transaction: (1) The increase in Materials Inventory is recorded at the actual quantity purchased but priced at standard cost. (2) Accounts Payable is stated at the actual cost (actual quantity purchased × actual price paid per unit) to record the proper liability.

a. Direct Materials Purchase:

Materials Inventory (760 yds @ $6)	4,560	
Direct Materials Price Variance		76
Accounts Payable (actual cost)		4,484
To record purchase of direct materials and resulting variance		

b. Direct Materials Requisition:

Work in Process Inventory (720 yds @ $6)	4,320	
Direct Materials Quantity Variance	240	
Materials Inventory (760 yds @ $6)		4,560
To record usage of direct materials and resulting variance		

Note the important aspects of this entry: (1) Everything in the Work in Process Inventory is recorded at standard cost, which here means standard quantity × standard price. (2) Actual quantity at standard price must come out of Materials Inventory because that is how it was first recorded. Remember that quantities purchased may actually be used in smaller amounts. In our example, the entire amount of the purchase was used during the period.

Journal Entry for Direct Labor Transactions

Work in Process Inventory (432 hr @ \$8.50/hr)	3,672	
Direct Labor Rate Variance	315	
Direct Labor Efficiency Variance	153	
Factory Payroll (450 hr @ \$9.20/hr)		4,140
To charge labor cost to Work in Process and to identify the resulting variances		

When recording labor costs, the same rules hold true as for recording the requisition of materials: (1) Work in Process Inventory is charged with standard labor cost (standard hours allowed × standard labor rate). (2) Factory Payroll must be credited for the actual labor cost of the workers (actual hours worked × actual labor rate earned). The variances, if computed properly, will balance out the difference between these two amounts.

Graphical Approach to Variances

Variance analysis using formulas and symbols is not always understood by the beginning student. Often, a graphical approach provides a clearer picture of what a variance involves and the components necessary for its determination. As an example, the labor efficiency variance is derived from labor hour input-output comparisons, whereas labor rate comparisons lead to labor rate variances. A graphic illustration of these variances is shown in Figure 22-4. The vertical axis represents direct labor pay

Figure 22-4. Labor Variances—Graphic Illustration

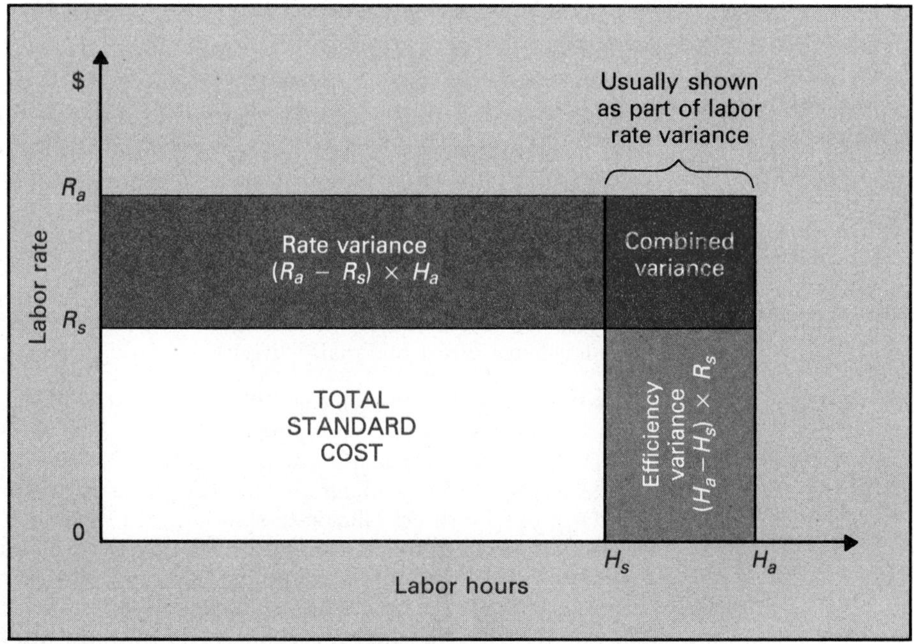

rates; the horizontal axis, direct labor hours. Total standard labor cost is shown by the large unshaded box and is computed by multiplying the standard direct labor rate (R_s) by the standard hours allowed (H_s). Actual labor cost is actual direct labor rate (R_a) multiplied by actual hours worked (H_a), and includes the shaded and unshaded parts of the diagram. As depicted in Figure 22-4

$$\text{Rate variance} = (R_a - R_s) \times H_a$$
$$\text{Efficiency variance} = (H_a - H_s) \times R_s$$

Since actual labor costs exceed standard labor costs, the diagram illustrates the unfavorable labor rate and efficiency variances. If H_s were greater than H_a or R_s greater than R_a, favorable variances would result. The combined variance is really caused because both actual hours and actual rate exceeded standard. Since actual hours are used in computing the labor rate variance, this variance includes the combined variance shown in the illustration.

Chapter Review

Review of Learning Objectives

1. **Describe the nature and purpose of standard costs.**
   Standard costs are realistically predetermined costs for direct materials, direct labor, and factory overhead. They are usually expressed as cost per unit of finished product. They are introduced into a cost accounting system to help in the budgetary control process. Standard costs are used to evaluate performance and prepare operating budgets. They are also used to identify areas of the production process requiring cost control measures, to set realistic prices, and to simplify cost accounting procedures for inventories and product costing.

2. **Describe and differentiate among the three types of standard costs: ideal standards, basic standards, and currently attainable standards.**
   Ideal standards are perfection cost standards that allow for minimum direct materials, direct labor, and other cost constraints in manufacturing a product. Performance equivalent to ideal standard level is rarely accomplished. Basic standards are seldom revised or updated to reflect current operating costs and price level changes. They are left unchanged and are used primarily to measure trends in operating performance. Currently attainable standards are updated periodically to reflect changes in operating conditions and current price levels for direct materials, direct labor, and factory overhead costs.

3. **Identify the six elements of a standard unit cost, and describe the factors to consider in developing each element.**
   The six elements of a standard unit cost are: (1) the direct materials price standard; (2) the direct materials quantity standard; (3) the direct labor time standard; (4) the direct labor rate standard; (5) the standard variable factory overhead rate; and (6) the standard fixed factory overhead rate. The direct materials price standard is found by carefully considering expected price increases, changes in quantities available, and possible new supplier sources. The direct materials quantity standard is an expression of forecasted, or

expected, quantity usage. It is affected by product engineering specifications, quality of direct materials used, age and productivity of the machines being used, and the quality and experience of the machine operators and set-up people. The direct labor time standard is based on current time-and-motion studies of workers and machines and past employee and machine performance. Labor union contracts and company personnel policies lead to direct labor rate standards. Standard variable and fixed factory overhead rates are found by taking total budgeted or forecasted variable and fixed factory overhead costs and dividing by an appropriate application base, such as standard direct labor hours or normal capacity.

4. **Compute a standard unit cost.**
   A product's total standard unit cost is computed by adding together the following costs: (1) direct materials cost (equals direct materials price standard × direct materials quantity standard); (2) direct labor cost (equals direct labor time standard × direct labor rate standard); and (3) factory overhead cost (equals standard variable and standard fixed factory overhead rates × standard direct labor hours per unit).

5. **Compute and evaluate direct materials and direct labor variances.**
   Cost variances, or differences between actual and standard costs, can be computed for direct materials and direct labor. The direct materials price and quantity variances help explain differences between actual and standard direct materials costs. Direct labor cost differences are analyzed by means of the direct labor rate variance and the direct labor efficiency variance. Each variance results from specific causes, and these causes help pinpoint reasons for the differences between actual and standard costs.

6. **Prepare journal entries to record transactions involving direct materials and direct labor variances in a standard cost system.**
   Journal entries are used to integrate standard cost variance information into the accounting records. Unfavorable variances create debit balances, and favorable variances are credited. General ledger accounts are maintained for direct materials price variance, direct materials quantity variance, direct labor rate variance, and direct labor efficiency variance. The key point to remember in preparing journal entries to record transactions in a standard costing system is that all entries affecting Materials Inventory, Work in Process Inventory, Finished Goods Inventory, and Cost of Goods Sold accounts *must* be recorded at standard cost.

Review Problem: Standard Process Costing System

The journal entry analysis described in this chapter centers on the use of standard costs in a job order costing system. Standard costs, however, are also applicable to a *process costing system*. Assume the following circumstances:

Bates, Inc., uses a standard process costing system in its East Texas plant, which manufactures a special chemical product. The standard cost per unit of finished product is

Direct materials (4 gal @ $2.50/gal)	$10.00
Direct labor (6 hours @ $4/hour)	24.00
Factory overhead (6 hours @ $5/hour)	30.00
Unit standard cost (4 gal container)	$64.00

All direct materials are introduced at the start of the process, and conversion costs are applied uniformly throughout the process. Assume an *average* cost flow approach. Also assume that any loss of materials is caused by normal evaporation or spoilage. During April 19x3 the Processing Department transferred 3,000 units to Finished Goods Inventory. Work in Process inventories at the beginning and end of April were 2,000 and 6,000 gallons, respectively. All partially processed units are considered 50 percent complete for conversion cost purposes. Actual production costs in beginning Work in Process Inventory and from usage in April were: (a) direct materials, 18,100 gallons, costing $2.25 per gallon and (b) conversion costs of $192,500.

Required

1. Using the *average* process costing approach, prepare the following schedules for the month of April:
   a. A schedule of equivalent production
   b. A unit cost analysis schedule
   c. A cost summary schedule
2. Prepare the journal entry to transfer costs of goods completed from Work in Process Inventory to Finished Goods Inventory.
3. Compute the materials price variance and the materials quantity variance for the period.

Answer to Review Problem

1a and 1b. The primary purpose of the Schedule of Equivalent Production is to provide data for computing unit cost in the Unit Cost Analysis Schedule. Since only standard costs are used in entries to the Work in Process Inventory account, unit cost will always be at standard. Therefore, it is unnecessary to complete parts 1a and 1b of this problem.

1c. Before completing the Cost Summary Schedule, you should study the following analysis of units:

Units in beginning inventory (2,000 gal ÷ 4)	500
Units started	4,000*
Units to be accounted for	4,500
Units completed and transferred	3,000
Units in ending inventory (6,000 gal ÷ 4)	1,500
Units to be accounted for	4,500
Units started and completed: 4,000 − 1,500 =	2,500

*This amount is computed after you determine the number of units to be accounted for.

1c. (continued)

Bates, Inc.
Cost Summary Schedule
For the Month Ended April 30, 19x3

	Cost of Goods Transferred to Finished Goods Inventory	Cost of Ending Work in Process Inventory
Beginning inventory		
500 units × $64/unit	$ 32,000	
Units started and completed		
2,500 units × $64/unit	160,000	
Ending inventory		
Materials		
1,500 units × $10/unit		$ 15,000
Conversion costs		
750 units × $54/unit		40,500
	$192,000	$ 55,500
Computation check		
Cost to Finished Goods Inventory		$192,000
Cost to Ending Work in Process Inventory		55,500
Total Standard Costs to be Accounted For		$247,500

2. The journal entry for April would be

Finished Goods Inventory	192,000	
Work in Process Inventory		192,000
To transfer costs of units completed in April from Work in Process Inventory to Finished Goods Inventory		

3. The materials price variance and the materials quantity variance for the period are computed as follows:

Actual cost of materials	
18,100 gal @ $2.25/gal =	$40,725
Standard cost of materials	
4,500 units × 4 gal × $2.50/gal =	45,000
Total materials cost variance	$ 4,275(F)

Materials price variance	
($2.25 − $2.50) × 18,100 gal =	
$.25(F) × 18,100 gal =	$ 4,525(F)
Materials quantity variance	
(18,100 − (4,500 × 4)) × $2.50/gal =	
100(U) × $2.50/gal =	250(U)
Total materials cost variance	$ 4,275(F)

Chapter Assignments

Questions

1. Define the following terms and concepts:
   a. Standard costs
   b. Budgetary control
   c. Ideal standards
   d. Basic standards
   e. Currently attainable standards
   f. Direct materials price variance
   g. Direct materials quantity variance
   h. Direct labor rate variance
   i. Direct labor efficiency variance
2. Describe how standard costs are useful in the budgetary control process.
3. Identify and differentiate between the three types of standard costs.
4. What characteristics do predetermined overhead costing and standard costing share? How do these costing approaches differ?
5. "Standard costing is a total cost concept in that standard unit costs are determined for direct materials, direct labor, and factory overhead." Explain this statement.
6. Identify and describe the six standard cost elements used to compute total standard unit cost.
7. What factors could influence a direct materials price standard?
8. "Standard labor cost is a function of efficiency and unionization." Is this a true statement? Defend your answer.
9. What general ledger accounts are affected by installing a standard cost system?
10. Why is it important to update standard costs?
11. "In a standard costing system, all inventories are valued at standard cost." Is this statement true? For reporting purposes, when must standard costs be replaced by actual costs?
12. State and discuss three advantages of using a standard costing system.
13. What is the principal disadvantage of a standard costing system?
14. What motivational considerations are important when developing standard costs?
15. Compare and contrast the usefulness of ideal standards, basic standards, and currently attainable standards.
16. What is a variance?
17. What is the formula for computing a direct materials quantity variance?
18. How would you interpret an unfavorable direct materials price variance?

Classroom Exercises

Exercise 22-1
Purpose of Standard Costs
(L.O.1)

Mr. Ron Bawmann is a senior accountant for a large public accounting firm Rock & Island, CPAs. One of his duties is to counsel and advise clients regarding needed improvements or additions to their accounting systems. His newest client, Augustana Industries of Rock Island, Illinois, manufactures rubber gaskets for automobile engines. These products are homogeneous and are produced in long production runs. The company, which uses a process cost accounting system, has been experiencing both labor and materials inefficiencies. Total cost increases have far exceeded the labor rate and materials price increases.

Augustana's president, an engineer, has asked Mr. Bawmann for advice. The president would like to know more about a standard cost accounting system and how it could possibly help control costs in her company.

Prepare a reply to the president.

Exercise 22-2 Types of Standard Costs (L.O. 2)

Accountants Torrington, Connor, and Leene are involved in a heavy discussion concerning the development of materials cost standards for their company's rock-music disc products.

Torrington: I think we should use maximum production data and minimum cost information to compute these standards. Our organization is operated at a very efficient level. Our standards should reflect this high level of productivity.

Connor: Listen, hip means being realistic. We must take a close look at what our productivity levels are and try to anticipate changes in our purchase prices when computing these standards.

Leene: You both are missing the boat. We already have a set of standards that have been used since my daddy worked for this company. They were useful then, and they are still useful now. They have been tested over the years, and the company has remained profitable during the entire period.

1. Identify the types of standards each accountant is advocating.
2. Discuss the advantages and disadvantages of each type of standard. Include behavioral considerations in your responses.

Exercise 22-3. Keeping Standards Current (L.O. 3)

Peters Paper Company recently installed a complete standard process cost accounting system. Mr. N. A. Always, controller of the Irvine Division, is concerned about keeping cost standards on a current basis. He is thinking about establishing a standard maintenance system and has asked Ms. U. R. Next, assistant controller, to take charge of the project and to outline the system.

List the suggested policies, procedures, and people that Ms. Next should include in her analysis.

Exercise 22-4. Standard Unit Cost Computation (L.O. 4)

Accountants and engineers of the Boyce Saw Company developed the following direct materials cost and usage standards and direct labor time and rate standards for producing a small chain saw, one of the company's main products. Direct materials required are: a saw motor casing at \$4.75, an operating chain at \$3.50, a 3-horsepower motor at \$19.90, and a chain housing at \$6.25. Direct labor consists of .5 hour for a materials inspector at \$7.50 per hour, .5 hour for an assembler at \$9.00 per hour, and .25 hour for a product tester at \$8.00 per hour. Factory overhead charges are figured at a variable rate of \$10.00 per direct labor hour and at a fixed rate of \$7.40 per direct labor hour.

Compute the total standard manufacturing cost of one chain saw.

Exercise 22-5. Standard Unit Cost Computation (L.O. 4)

Hedlund Aerodynamics, Inc., makes electronically equipped weather-detecting balloons for university meteorological departments. Recent effects of nationwide inflation have caused the company's management to recompute its standard costs.

New direct materials price standards are \$620.00 per set for electronic components and \$4.00 per square meter for heavy-duty canvas. Direct materials quantity standards include one set of electronic components per balloon and 95 square meters of heavy-duty canvas per balloon. Direct labor time standards are 14.5 hours per balloon for the Electronics Department and 12.0 hours per balloon for the Assembly Department. Direct labor rate standards are $9.00 an hour for the Electronics Department and $8.50 an hour for the Assembly Department. Standard factory overhead rates are $12.00 per direct labor hour for the standard variable overhead rate and $9.00 per direct labor hour for the standard fixed overhead rate.

Using the production standards provided, compute the standard manufacturing cost of one weather balloon.

Exercise 22-6. Direct Materials Price and Quantity Variances (L.O. 5)

The Marcos Elevator Company manufactures small hydroelectric elevators with a maximum capacity of ten passengers each. One of the direct materials used by the Production Department is heavy-duty carpet for the elevator floors. The direct materials quantity standard used for the month ended April 30, 19xx, was 8 square yards per elevator. During April the purchasing agent was able to purchase this carpet for $8 per square yard. Standard price for the period was $10. Eighty-two elevators were completed and sold during April, and the Production Department used 9.6 square yards of carpet per elevator.

Calculate the direct materials price variance and quantity variance for April 19xx.

Exercise 22-7. Direct Labor Rate and Efficiency Variances (L.O. 5)

Winter Park Foundry, Inc., produces castings used by other companies in the production of machinery. For the past two years the largest-selling product has been a casting for an eight-cylinder engine block. Standard direct labor hours per engine block are 1.8 hours. The labor contract requires that all direct labor employees be paid $9.50 an hour. During June, 16,500 engine blocks were produced. Actual direct labor hours and cost for June were 30,000 hours and $288,000, respectively.

1. Compute the direct labor rate variance for June for the engine block product line.
2. Using the same data, compute the direct labor efficiency variance for June for the engine block product line. (Check your answer. Assume that total direct labor variance is $5,850(U).)

Exercise 22-8. Journal Entries—Standard Costing (L.O. 6)

Isolated transactions of the Cent Franc Corporation for August 19x8 are listed below. The company uses a standard job order costing system.

August 6:	Purchased Direct Materials:	
	Actual Cost	$13,450
	Standard Cost	14,500
August 9:	Requisitioned a total of $7,500 in direct materials from inventory into production. An analysis of standard quantities required indicates that $400 worth of excess materials, which were spoiled, were included in the requisition.	
August 12:	Paid factory wages and salaries and credited Factory Payroll account for $17,650. An analysis of factory wages disclosed that unfavorable labor variances of $400 were incurred, including a labor rate variance of $750(U).	

Prepare journal entries to record the above transactions.

Exercise 22-9. Standard Cost Journal Entries (L.O. 6)

Bush-Hunt Battery Company produces batteries for automobiles, motorcycles, and mopeds. Transactions for direct materials and direct labor for March were as follows:

1. Purchased 1,000 type A battery casings for $6.50 each on account; standard cost, $7.00 per casing.
2. Purchased 5,000 type 4C lead battery plates for $2.40 each on account; standard cost, $2.25 per plate.
3. Requisitioned 32 type A battery casings and 128 type 4C lead plates into production. Order No. 647 called for 30 batteries, each using a standard quantity of four plates per casing.
4. Direct labor costs for Order No. 647 were as follows:

Department H	
Actual labor	26 hours @ $5/hour
Standard labor	24 hours @ $5/hour
Department J	
Actual labor	10 hours @ $6.50/hour
Standard labor	12 hours @ $7.00/hour

Prepare journal entries for the four transactions above.

Interpreting Accounting Information

Direct Materials Variances: Portsmouth Industries (L.O. 1, 3)

Portsmouth Industries produces a diverse line of paper products and uses a standard cost system for all inventories. Material 42H is a chemical dye used in several departments and in many products. The company has recently experienced a trend of unfavorable quantity variances for material 42H. The production vice president received a summary report of September's operations, which disclosed the following results:

Material 42H issued to production	438,000 lbs
Standard allowance for good production	412,000 lbs
Over standard	26,000 lbs
Current price (September 30, 19x5)	× $5.50
Unfavorable variance	$143,000

On inquiring, the vice president discovered that the purchase price of 42H has increased 8 percent since the beginning of the year. The standard allowances were derived by a clerical assistant who worked all day searching through completed production reports. The vice president could not readily determine the products or the departments that accounted for this quantity variance.

Required

Assume you are the production vice president. Write a memorandum to the company's controller that summarizes weaknesses in the standard cost system and that recommends appropriate changes.

Problem Set A

Problem 22A-1. Standard Cost Per Unit (L.O. 4)

Three production departments are used by the Columbia Products Company to produce "Bold," a leading men's after-shave lotion. The product requires processing in the Blending, Cooling, and Bottling departments, in that order. The following data were used to establish standard materials, labor, and overhead costs for each 4-ounce unit of Bold:

Direct Materials	Purchase Quantities and Prices	Normal Evaporation Loss
Sweet water	10,000 gallons @ $40.00/100 gallons	20%
Herbs and spices	1,500 pounds @ $180.00/100 pounds	
Bottles	1,000 bottles @ $.80/bottle	

Note: Average batch size is 1,000 gallons before evaporation, and 500 pounds of herbs and spices are added to each 1,000-gallon batch.

Labor	Blending	Cooling	Bottling
Standard time per batch in each department	7 hours	2 hours	12 hours
Number of direct labor workers required per batch	2	1	4
Standard wage rate per hour	$4.40	$4.25	$4.30

Factory Overhead (plantwide rates):

Standard variable overhead rate	$3.46/direct labor dollar
Standard fixed overhead rate	$5.94/direct labor dollar

Required

Compute the standard production cost of

a. One batch of Bold
b. One 4-ounce bottle of Bold
(Note: 1 gallon = 128 ounces.)

Problem 22A-2. Development of Standards: Direct Materials (L.O. 3, 4)

Lou & Costello, Ltd., assemble clock movements for grandfather clocks. Each movement has four components to assemble: the clock facing, the clock hands, the time movement, and the spring assembly. For the current year, 19x7, the company used the following standard costs: facing, $14.60; hands, $16.90, time movement $46.10; and spring assembly, $22.50.

Prices and sources of materials are expected to change in 19x8. Seventy percent of the facings will be supplied by Company A at $16.50 each, and the remaining thirty percent will be purchased from Company B at $17.90 each. The hands are produced for Lou & Costello by Abbott Hardware, Inc., and will cost $19.75 per set in 19x8. Time movements will be purchased from three Swiss sources: Company Q, 20 percent of total need at $48.50 per movement; Company R, 30 percent at $49.50; and Company S, 50 percent at $51.90. Spring assemblies will be purchased from a French company and are expected to increase in cost by 30 percent.

Required

1. Determine the total standard materials cost per unit for 19x8.
2. If the company could guarantee the purchase of 2,500 sets of hands from Abbott Hardware, Inc., the unit cost would be reduced by 10 percent. Find the resulting standard materials unit cost.
3. Substandard spring assemblies can be purchased at $25.50, but 15 percent of them will be unusable and nonreturnable. Compute the standard direct materials unit cost if the company follows this procedure, assuming the original facts of the case for the remaining data. The cost of the defective materials will be spread over good units produced.

Problem 22A-3. Developing and Using Standard Costs
(L.O. 3, 4, 6)

Prefabricated, factory-built houses are the specialty of Young Homes, Inc., of Buffalo, New York. Although many models are produced and it is possible to "special order" a home, 60 percent of the company's business comes from the sale of the El Dorado home. The El Dorado is a three-bedroom, 2,200 square foot home, and the front entrance section is its real selling feature. Six basic materials are used to manufacture this section, and their 19x7 standard costs are as follows: (a) wood framing materials, $120; (b) the deluxe front door, $180; (c) door hardware, $60; (d) exterior siding, $210; (e) electrical materials, $80; (f) and interior finishing materials, $140. The three types of labor used for this section and their respective 19x7 standard costs are: (a) carpenter, 10 hours at $12.00 per hour; (b) door specialist, 4 hours at $15.00 per hour; and (c) electrician, 3 hours at $16.00 per hour. The company used 50 percent of direct labor dollars as an overhead rate for 19x7.

During 19x8 the following changes are anticipated:

Wood framing materials	increase by 20 percent
Deluxe front door	will need two suppliers; Supplier A, 40 percent of need @ $190 per door; Supplier B, 60 percent of need @ $200 per door
Door hardware	increase by 10 percent
Exterior siding	decrease by $10 per section
Electrical materials	increase by 20 percent
Interior finishing materials	remain the same
Carpenter wages	increase by $1 per hour
Door specialist wages	remain the same
Electrician wages	increase by 10 percent
Factory overhead rate	decrease to 40 percent of direct labor cost

Required

1. Compute the total standard direct materials cost per front entrance section for 19x8.
2. Using your answer from **1** and other information from the problem, compute the 19x8 standard manufacturing cost for the El Dorado's front entrance section.

3. From the information above, prepare journal entries for the following 19x8 transactions:

Jan. 6	Purchased 120 front doors from Supplier A for $22,800.
Jan. 14	Requisitioned 60 sets of hardware into production to complete a job calling for 56 section units.
Jan. 30	Transferred the 56 completed sections to Finished Goods Inventory.

Problem 22A-4. Materials and Labor Variances (L.O. 5, 6)

Reggie Trophies Company produces a variety of athletic awards, most in the form of trophies or mounted replicas of athletes in action. Mr. Jackson, president of the company, is developing a standard cost accounting system. Trophies differ in size, and Reggie has six standard sizes. The deluxe trophy stands three feet above the base. Materials standards include one pound of metal and 3 ounces of plastic supported by a 6-ounce wooden base. Standard prices for 19x9 were: $2.25 per pound of metal; $.20 per ounce of plastic; and $.50 per ounce of wood.

Direct labor is used in both the Molding and Trimming/Finishing departments. Deluxe trophies require labor standards of .2 hours of direct labor in the Molding Department and .4 hours in the Trimming/Finishing Department. Standard labor rates for deluxe trophies include $8.50 per hour in Molding and $8.00 per hour in Trimming/Finishing.

During January 19x9, 14,400 deluxe trophies were made. The actual production data were as follows:

Materials:	
Metal	15,840 pounds @ $2.20/pound
Plastic	46,080 ounces @ $.25/ounce
Wood	86,400 ounces @ $.60/ounce
Labor:	
Molding	3,600 hours @ $8.60/hour
Trimming/Finishing	5,040 hours @ $8.10/hour

Required

1. Compute the direct materials price and quantity variances for metal, plastic, and wood bases.
2. Compute the direct labor rate and efficiency variances for the Molding and the Trimming/Finishing departments.
3. Prepare journal entries to record the transactions involving materials and labor for the period.

Problem 22A-5. Standard Process Costing (L.O. 4, 5, 6)

"Beauty Gloss" is the primary paint product of Mary Jo Key Paints, Inc. The company produces its paint products in two departments, Mixing and Canning, and employs a standard process costing system. Three direct materials, water, Material M, and Material J, are added on a per batch basis at the beginning of the mixing process. Only gallon-size cans are added in the Canning Department at the end of the process. Labor costs are incurred uniformly throughout both departments.

Standard Cost Data per 25-gallon Batch		Mixing Department	Canning Department
Direct materials:	Water	20 gal @ $.02/gal	
	Material M	4 gal @ $4.85/gal	
	Material J	1 gal @ $13.20/gal	
	Gallon cans		25 cans @ $.80/can
Direct labor		6 hours @ $8.50/hr	4 hours @ $6.50/hr
Factory overhead		$12/direct labor hr	$16/direct labor hr
Beginning inventories		Four batches, 40% complete	Six batches, 20% complete
Ending inventories		Two batches, 80% complete	Four batches, 60% complete
Batches started during August:		120 batches	?

Assume that nothing was lost because of spoilage or evaporation.

Actual costs incurred for August:	
Water: 2,400 gal @ $.022 per gal	$ 52.80
Material M: 480 gal @ $4.90	2,352.00
Material J: 120 gal @ $13.40	1,608.00
Gallon cans: 3,100 @ $.85	2,635.00
Direct labor, Mixing 730 hrs @ $8.50/hr	6,205.00
Direct labor, Canning 500 hrs @ $6.60/hr	3,300.00
Factory overhead, Mixing	8,850.00
Factory overhead, Canning	7,690.00
Total	$32,692.80

Required

1. Compute the number of batches started and completed in each department in August.
2. Compute the standard cost per batch of paint.
3. Using the *average* costing approach and process costing schedules when necessary, compute the costs attached to completed units and ending Work in Process Inventory in each department for August.
4. Prepare the appropriate journal entries to transfer the cost of completed work out of each department's Work in Process Inventory account.
5. Compute the materials price and quantity variances for Materials M and J for August.

Problem Set B

Problem 22B-1. Standard Cost Formulation (L.O. 3, 4)

Gorge Company has developed material, labor, and overhead standards for its principal product, "Quanto." Each unit of Quanto requires inputs of materials A and B plus work in the cutting and polishing operations. Standards per unit of Quanto were developed as follows:

Materials	Pounds	Price/lb	Labor	Hours	Rate
A	5	$4	Cut	3	$5
B	8	$2	Polish	2	$6

The standard overhead rate, including both variable and fixed costs, was established at $11.50 per direct labor hour.

Required

a. Prepare a summary of standard costs for one unit of Quanto.
b. If 8,000 good units of Quanto are produced during a period, what is the standard quantity allowed for material usage? What are the standard hours allowed for labor time?
c. Assume that 10,000 units of Quanto are produced during a period when the actual overhead incurred is $600,000. Determine the amount of under- or over-applied factory overhead.

Problem 22B-2. Development of Standards: Direct Labor
(L.O. 3, 4)

A planned change in the employee labor rate structure has caused the Red Sox Salt Company to develop a new standard direct labor cost for its product. Standard direct labor costs per 1,000 pounds of a new and healthy form of salt in 19x7 were: (a) 1.5 hours in the Sodium Preparation Department at $10.40 per hour; (b) 1.8 hours in the Chloride Mixing Department at $11.00 per hour; and (c) 1.4 hours in the Cleaning and Packaging Department at $7.50 per hour. Labor rates are expected to increase in 19x8 by 10 percent in the Sodium Preparation Department, decrease by 10 percent in the Chloride Mixing Department, and decrease by 12 percent in the Cleaning and Packaging Department. New machinery in the Chloride Mixing Department will lower the direct labor time standard by 20 percent per 1,000 pounds of salt. All other time standards are expected to remain the same.

Required

1. Compute the standard direct labor cost per 1,000 pounds of salt in 19x8.
2. Management has a plan to improve productive output by 20 percent in the Sodium Preparation Department. If such results are achieved in 19x8, determine (a) the effect on the direct labor time standard and (b) the resulting total standard direct labor cost per 1,000 pounds of salt.
3. Unskilled labor can be hired to staff all departments in 19x8, with the result that all labor rates paid in 19x7 would be cut by 60 percent in the new year. Such a change in labor skill would cause the direct labor time standards to increase by 50 percent over their anticipated 19x8 levels using skilled labor. Compute the standard direct labor cost per 1,000 pounds of salt if this change occurs.

Problem 22B-3. Developing and Using Standard Costs
(L.O. 3, 4, 6)

The Otani Supply Company makes swimming-pool equipment and accessories. To make swimming-pool umbrellas, waterproof canvas is first sent to the Cutting Department. In the Assembly Department the canvas is stretched over the umbrella's ribs on the center pole and opening mechanism. Then, the umbrella is mounted on a heavy base before being packed for shipment.

The company uses a standard cost accounting system. Direct labor standards for each pool umbrella for 19x9 are: (a) direct labor of .2 hour charged to the Cutting Department at $8.00 per hour and (b) .8 hour charged to the Assembly Department at $9.50 per hour. Variable factory overhead is 150 percent, and fixed overhead is 130 percent of total direct labor dollars.

During 19x8 the company used the following direct materials standards: Waterproof canvas was $2.60 per square yard for 4 square yards per umbrella.

The standard for a unit consisting of pole, ribs, and opening mechanism was $10.50 per unit. The base was $6.40 per unit.

Quantity standards are expected to remain the same during 19x9. However, the following price changes are likely: The cost of waterproof canvas will increase by 20 percent. The pole, ribs, and opening mechanism will be purchased from three vendors. Vendor A will provide 10 percent of the total supply at $10.60 per unit. Vendor B will provide 60 percent at $10.80. Vendor C will supply 30 percent at $11.00. The cost of each base will increase 20 percent.

Required

1. Compute the total standard direct materials cost per umbrella for 19x9.
2. Using your answer from **1** and information from the problem, compute the 19x9 standard manufacturing cost of one pool umbrella.
3. Using your answers from **1** and **2**, prepare journal entries for the following 19x9 transactions:

Jan. 20	Purchased 5,500 square yards of waterproof canvas at $3.20 per square yard on account.
Feb. 1	Requisitioned 625 pole, rib, and opening mechanism assemblies into production to complete a job calling for 600 umbrellas.
Mar. 15	Transferred 300 completed pool umbrellas to Finished Goods Inventory.

Problem 22B-4. Materials and Labor Variances (L.O. 5, 6)

The Connecticut Fruit Packaging Company makes plastic berry baskets for food wholesalers. Each basket is made of .8 grams of liquid plastic and .6 grams of an additive, which provides the color and hardening agents. The standard prices are $.006 per gram of liquid plastic and $.008 per gram of additive.

Labor is of three kinds: molding, trimming, and packing. The labor time standard per 1,000-box batch and the rate standards are as follows: molding, .6 hour per batch at an hourly rate of $10; trimming, .5 hour per batch at an hourly rate of $8; and packing, .4 hour at $5 per hour.

During 19xx the company produced 450,000 berry baskets. Actual materials used were 367,000 grams of liquid plastic at a cost of $1,835 and 267,000 grams of additive, at a cost of $2,403. Direct labor included 275 hours for molding, costing $2,695; 230 hours for trimming, costing $1,863; and 175 hours for packing, costing $910.

Required

1. Compute the direct materials price and quantity variances for both the liquid plastic and the additive. Show a check of your answers.
2. Compute the direct labor rate and efficiency variances for the molding, trimming, and packing processes. Show a check of your answers.
3. Prepare journal entries to record the transactions involving materials and labor for the period.

Problem 22B-5. Standard Process Costing (L.O. 3, 4, 5)

Ruf-Jaw Cosmetics, Inc., produces "Realwite," a brand of toothpaste sold primarily to smokers. One producing department is used, and costs are accumulated through a standard process costing system. All direct materials are added at the beginning of the process except for packaging tubes, which are force filled at the end of the process. Labor and overhead costs are applied uniformly throughout the process. Cost reports for July 19x8 reveal the following data:

Work in Process Inventory, July 1, 19x8:
400 lbs, 40% completed
Standard costs attached:

Materials	$220.00
Conversion costs	140.80

July 19x8 standard cost data:
Direct materials added:
Paste: 4,500 lbs at standard cost of $.50/lb
Grit: 500 lbs at standard cost of $1.00/lb
Tubes: 2-oz tubes used at standard cost of $.25/tube
Direct labor:
One standard direct labor hour allowed for each 5 lbs processed
Standard labor rate = $2.10/standard direct labor hour
Manufacturing overhead:
Standard variable overhead rate = $1.40/DLH
Standard fixed overhead rate = $.90/DLH
Work in Process Inventory, July 31, 19x8:
900 lbs, 60% completed

During the month no spoilage occurred. The company uses the *average* process costing method.

Required

1. Compute the number of tubes started and completed during July.
2. Compute the standard cost per tube of toothpaste.
3. Using process costing schedules when necessary, compute the costs attached to completed units and ending Work in Process Inventory at July 31, 19x8.
4. Prepare the appropriate journal entry to transfer the cost of completed units to Finished Goods Inventory.
(Note: 16 ounces = 1 pound)
5. Actual cost data for direct materials for July are summarized below:
Paste: 4,600 lbs at $.52/lb
Grit: 480 lbs at $.96/lb
Tubes: No quantity variance existed but the tubes used cost $.28 each

Compute the materials price and quantity variances for the month.

Management Decision Case

Standard Costing and Employee Behavior: Mighty Mac Company
(L.O. 1, 2, 3)

Mighty Mac Company is expanding its Punch Press Department and wants to purchase three new punch presses from Equipment Manufacturers, Inc. Engineers at Equipment Manufacturers made mechanical studies, indicating that for Mighty Mac's intended use, the output rate for one press should be 1,000 pieces per hour. Mighty Mac has similar presses in operation. Production from these presses now averages 600 pieces per hour.

A study of the Mighty Mac experience shows that the average is derived from the following individual outputs:

Worker	Daily Output
A. Curley	750
B. Holdmeyer	750
C. Orme	600
D. Peach	500
E. Priest	550
F. Quade	450
Total	3,600
Average	600

Mighty Mac's management plans to institute a standard cost accounting system soon. Company engineers support a standard based on 1,000 pieces per hour. The Accounting Department wants 750 pieces per hour. The department supervisor suggests 600 pieces per hour.

Required

a. What argument is each proponent likely to offer to support his or her case?
b. Which alternative best reconciles the need for both cost control and better motivation to improve performance? Why?

(ICMA adapted)

CHAPTER 23 VARIANCE ANALYSIS AND PERFORMANCE REPORTING

LEARNING OBJECTIVES

1. Review the principles of performance evaluation.
2. Prepare a flexible budget.
3. Compute overhead variances, using both the two-way and three-way analyses.
4. Prepare journal entries involving overhead variances.
5. Dispose of variance balances at period end.
6. Describe the concept of management by exception.
7. Evaluate employee performance, using variances.

Standard cost accounting is an important tool for measuring operating performance. Variance analysis helps identify areas with operating problems as well as efficient departments or work areas. Cost variances are usually associated with performance evaluation in the manufacturing environment. But as the review problem demonstrates, standard costing and variance analysis are equally important when promoting profitability and operating efficiency in service-oriented businesses as well as in selling and distributing products in a manufacturing company. Materials variances are unique to manufacturing activities, whereas labor variances and overhead variances may be computed for service enterprises as well as for manufacturing companies.

In this chapter the principles of performance evaluation will be revisited. Then, a study of the flexible budget will lead into a discussion of the two-way and the three-way approaches to overhead variance analysis. Once variances have been computed, the chapter will explain how they are entered into the accounting records through journal entries and how their balances are disposed of before final financial statements for the period are prepared. The chapter concludes with a discussion of the concept of management by exception and a look at performance reporting based on variance analysis. After studying this chapter, you should be able to meet the learning objectives listed on the left.

Principles of Performance Evaluation Revisited

The principles of performance evaluation were identified and discussed in Chapter 20. However, before continuing to discuss standard costing and related variance analyses, it is important to review the performance evaluation principles so they can be applied once variances have been determined. After all, variances are computed to assist management in attaining optimal operating results. The actual variance numbers are useless until they are integrated into a performance report and evaluated. Determining the causes of variances is critical to moving toward optimal productivity and profitability.

OBJECTIVE 1
Review the principles of performance evaluation

Management's policies are intended to satisfy the overall objective of the enterprise—maximizing profitability for the profit-oriented company and successfully completing the mission of the not-for-profit organization. These company policies are important, but alone they will not effectively control operations. Performance must be accurately measured, comparatively analyzed and evaluated, and properly reported. Throughout the performance evaluation process, one must consider the behavior of the people involved, which is vital to successful performance. The human aspect is the most important part of trying to meet corporate goals. People do the planning, people perform the operations of the enterprise, people evaluate, and people are evaluated. The following performance evaluation principles were discussed in Chapter 20:

Behavioral Principles

1. **Managers should have input into the standards and goals set for their areas of responsibility.**
2. **Management's support for the evaluation process should be evident.**
3. **Only controllable cost and revenue items with significant variances should be the focus of performance reports.**
4. **Opportunity for a manager to respond should be a part of the evaluation process.**

Operational Principles

1. **Provide accurate and suitable measures of performance,** including (1) predetermined standards or budgets; (2) others' performance in comparable jobs; and (3) past performance. Nonfinancial measures, such as labor hours or units of output, may be used to measure performance and may be as useful as dollar measures.
2. **Communicate expectations to appropriate managers and segment leaders who will be evaluated.** Expectations should be clearly stated and contain relevant input from the manager being evaluated.
3. **Identify the responsibilities of each manager.** A manager assumes the obligation of being held accountable for a defined number of areas when he or she accepts a position.
4. **Compare actual performance to a suitable base.** Evaluating performance requires comparison because performance must be compared with some anticipated target or standard. Suitable measures of performance were mentioned above.
5. **Prepare performance reports that highlight areas of concern.** The information contained in a performance report should be specific about the manager's responsibilities, controllable by the manager, and represent a significant enough departure from the anticipated target to warrant analysis.
6. **Analyze important cause-and-effect relationships.** A performance report is more than a set of numbers to be compared against one another. One variation may help cause another (domino effect). A performance report should reveal cause-and-effect factors and significant relationships. Nonquantitative information is often used to explain differences. Much of this information should come from the manager being evaluated.

In Chapter 20 performance evaluation and analysis was based on comparisons of actual data with budgeted data. Such comparisons make the analysis of current productivity against past or budgeted output possible. Still, pinpointing responsibility is often difficult. Standard costing helps solve this problem by enabling management to create a performance reporting system oriented toward specific managers and their areas of responsibility. This type of system is also based on cause-and-effect relationships, which help managers explain reasons for the variances.

The discussion of standard costing will now continue by analyzing overhead costs and computing related variances. The chapter concludes by looking at performance analysis based on standard cost accounting and the materials, labor, and overhead variances generated by the system.

Cost Control Through Variance Analysis

The performance evaluation, which is an important part of cost control, should emphasize the comparison of what happened (actual results) against what was expected to happen (budgeted). Therefore, this discussion will continue to focus on the differences between (1) actual costs and budgeted costs and (2) actual costs and standard costs.

Cost variances are usually associated with performance evaluation in the manufacturing environment. But as the illustrative problem and several problems in the assignment materials show, standard costs for evaluating service-oriented enterprises and such functions as selling in a manufacturing company are equally important to profitability and operating efficiency.

Flexible Budgets

OBJECTIVE 2
Prepare a flexible budget

Budgets were emphasized in Chapter 21, which focused on the planning process. Why, then, you might ask, should the concept of flexible budgets be introduced as part of cost control rather than as a planning tool? This has been done because a flexible budget (also called a variable budget) is primarily a cost control tool to help evaluate performance. A **flexible budget** is a summary of expected costs for a range of activity levels; it is geared to changes in the level of productive output. The budgets discussed as part of the planning function are called static, or fixed, budgets because they describe just one level of expected sales and production activity. The master budget, including all of the period budgets, is usually prepared for an expected or normal level of sales and productive output.

For budgeting or planning purposes, a set of static budgets based on a single level of output is good enough for management's needs. These budgets show management the desired picture of operating results. They also provide a target for managers to use in developing monthly and weekly operating plans. However, these budgets often prove inadequate for judging operating results. Exhibit 23-1 presents data for Arizona Industries, Inc. Actual costs exceed budgeted costs by $14,300, or 7.2 percent. Such an overrun is thought to be significant by most managers. But was there really a cost overrun? As explained in the notes to Exhibit 23-1, the budgeted amounts are based on expected output of 17,500 units, but actual output was 19,100 units.

Before analyzing the performance of the Tucson Division, you must change the budgeted data to reflect an output of 19,100 units. In this example, the static budget for 17,500 units is of no use in judging performance. This is because you should expect more costs to be incurred in producing 19,100 units than in producing 17,500. The role of a flexible budget is to provide forecasted data that can be adjusted automatically for changes in the level of output. Exhibit 23-2 presents a flexible budget for Arizona Industries, Inc., with budgeted data for 15,000, 17,500, and 20,000 units of output. The important part of this illustration is the flexible budget formula shown at the bottom. This budget formula is an

Exhibit 23-1. Performance Analysis: Comparison of Actual and Budgeted Data

Arizona Industries, Inc.
Performance Report—Tucson Division
For the Year Ended December 31, 19xx

Cost Item	Budget*	Actual†	Difference Under (Over) Budget
Direct materials	$ 42,000	$ 46,000	$ (4,000)
Direct labor	68,250	75,000	(6,750)
Factory overhead			
Variable			
Indirect materials	10,500	11,500	(1,000)
Indirect labor	14,000	15,250	(1,250)
Utilities	7,000	7,600	(600)
Other	8,750	9,750	(1,000)
Fixed			
Supervisory salaries	19,000	18,500	500
Depreciation	15,000	15,000	—
Utilities	4,500	4,500	—
Other	10,900	11,100	(200)
Totals	$199,900	$214,200	$(14,300)

* Budget based on expected productive output of 17,500 units.
† Actual cost of producing 19,100 units.

equation that can be used to determine the correct budgeted cost for any activity level. It consists of a per unit amount for variable costs and a total amount for fixed costs. In Exhibit 23-2, the $8.60 variable cost per unit is computed in the upper right column, and the $49,400 is found in the fixed-cost section of the analysis. Using this formula, you can draw up a budget for the Tucson Division at any level of output.

In Exhibit 23-1, budgeted data should have been adjusted for expected costs at the 19,100-unit level before such data could be compared with actual dollar amounts. Exhibit 23-3 shows a performance report using flexible budget data. Unit variable cost amounts have been multiplied by 19,100 units to arrive at total budgeted figures. Fixed overhead information has been carried over from the flexible budget developed in Exhibit 23-2. As the new performance report shows, costs exceeded

Exhibit 23-2. Flexible Budget Preparation

Arizona Industries, Inc.
Flexible Budget Analysis—Tucson Division
For the Year Ended December 31, 19xx

Cost Item	Unit Levels of Activity			Variable Cost per Unit*
	15,000	17,500	20,000	
Direct materials	$ 36,000	$ 42,000	$ 48,000	$2.40
Direct labor	58,500	68,250	78,000	3.90
Variable factory overhead				
Indirect materials	9,000	10,500	12,000	.60
Indirect labor	12,000	14,000	16,000	.80
Utilities	6,000	7,000	8,000	.40
Other	7,500	8,750	10,000	.50
Total variable costs	$129,000	$150,500	$172,000	$8.60
Fixed factory overhead				
Supervisory salaries	$ 19,000	$ 19,000	$ 19,000	
Depreciation	15,000	15,000	15,000	
Utilities	4,500	4,500	4,500	
Other	10,900	10,900	10,900	
Total fixed costs	$ 49,400	$ 49,400	$ 49,400	
Total costs	$178,400	$199,900	$221,400	

Flexible budget formula:
(Variable cost per unit × number of units produced) + budgeted fixed costs
= ($8.60 × units produced) + $49,400

Note: Activity expressed in units was used as the basis for this analysis. When units are used, direct material and direct labor costs are included in the analysis. Flexible budgets are commonly restricted to overhead costs. In such a situation direct labor hours are used in place of units produced.

* Computed by dividing the dollar amount in any column by the respective activity level.

Exhibit 23-3. Performance Analysis Using Flexible Budget Data

Arizona Industries, Inc.
Performance Report—Tucson Division
For the Year Ended December 31, 19xx

Cost Item (Variable Unit Cost)	Budget Based on 19,100 Units Produced	Actual Costs at 19,100-Unit Level	Differences Under (Over) Budget
Direct materials ($2.40)	$ 45,840	$ 46,000	$(160)
Direct labor ($3.90)	74,490	75,000	(510)
Factory overhead			
Variable			
Indirect materials ($.60)	11,460	11,500	(40)
Indirect labor ($.80)	15,280	15,250	30
Utilities ($.40)	7,640	7,600	40
Other ($.50)	9,550	9,750	(200)
Fixed			
Supervisory salaries	19,000	18,500	500
Depreciation	15,000	15,000	—
Utilities	4,500	4,500	—
Other	10,900	11,100	(200)
Totals	$213,660	$214,200	$(540)

budgeted amounts during the year by only $540, or two-tenths of one percent. Using the flexible budget concept, you can see that the performance of the Tucson Division is almost on target. Performance has now been measured and analyzed accurately.

Overhead Variance Analysis

Controlling overhead costs is more difficult than controlling direct materials and direct labor costs because responsibility for overhead costs is difficult to pin down. In addition, the analysis of factory (or service) overhead variances is more complex than analysis of materials and labor variance. These two factors explain reasons for many students' problems in coping with and adjusting to overhead variance analysis.

In this chapter the computing of overhead variances is viewed first from a conceptual level. Then, the difference between overhead costs incurred and overhead costs applied, which is the total overhead variance, is broken down into a two-way variance analysis. To further help explain the overhead variances, the third and final step is to expand the two-way approach into a three-way variance analysis. The goal, remember, is to explain to management through variance analysis reasons the company's cost targets were not met.

Conceptual View. The analysis of overhead variances is based on several ideas and concepts already discussed in this book. Figure 23-1 shows the underlying concepts of overhead variance analysis and their relationships to one another. The concept of operating capacity was discussed in Chapter 19. Although theoretical and practical capacity levels can be defined and computed, they are idealistic and nonrepresentative of the expected operating level of the enterprise. **Normal capacity,** which is the average annual level of operating capacity needed to meet expected sales demands, was selected as the most appropriate operating level on which to gauge expectations. Of course, this expectation level will also be the basis for comparing actual operating results and for analyzing performance.

Normal capacity plays a unique role in overhead variance analysis. As you should recall, when the standard overhead rates were computed in Chapter 22, the standard fixed overhead rate was computed by dividing the total budgeted fixed overhead costs by normal capacity in terms of standard direct labor hours. When analyzing variances of fixed overhead costs, you must again use the concept of normal capacity to help explain the variance.

Figure 23-1. Conceptual Foundation: Overhead Variance Analysis

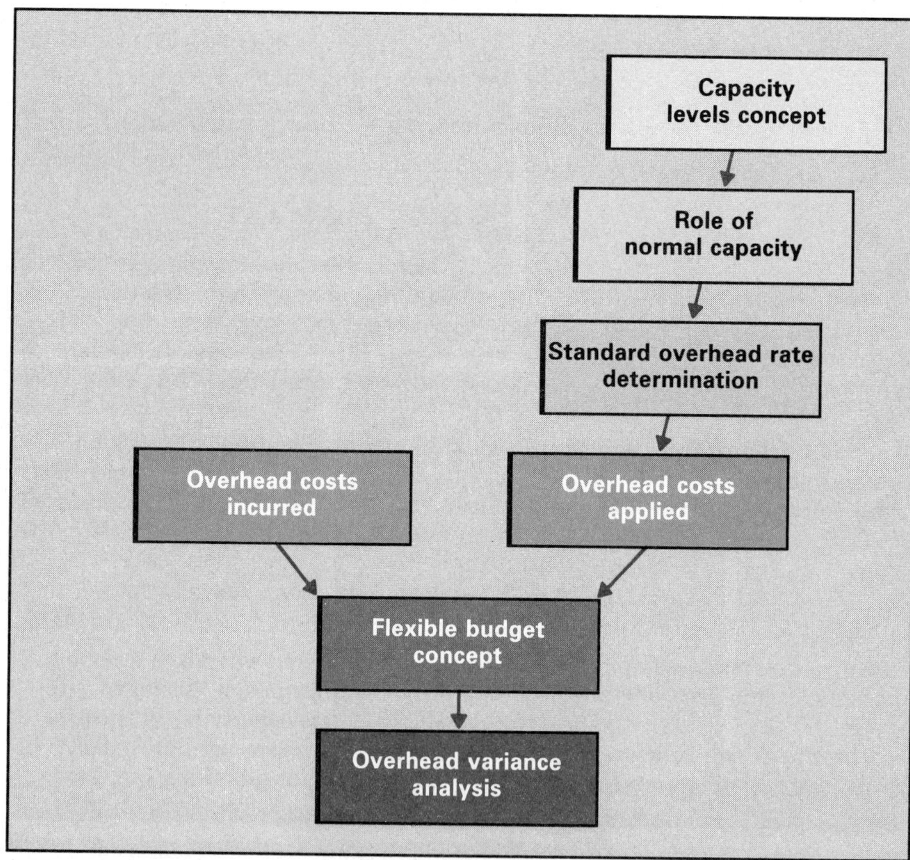

Once variable and fixed standard overhead rates have been computed, overhead can be applied to units produced much as it was applied to Work in Process Inventory in Chapter 17. The over- or underapplied overhead, the difference between actual overhead costs incurred and overhead costs applied to units produced, now becomes the **total overhead variance.**

The next step, as shown in Figure 23-1, is to incorporate the flexible budget concept into the analysis. As explained earlier, performance cannot be properly analyzed unless actual costs incurred are compared with budgeted or standard costs that should have been incurred at the actual level of output. The tool available for this adjustment process is the **flexible budget** and the **flexible budget formula.** This formula is a key ingredient when computing overhead variances, as you will see later in this chapter.

In summary, the analysis of overhead variances depends on several fundamental concepts that should be familiar to you from previous discussions. If you have forgotten some of this information, you should review these topics before going on to the analysis of overhead variances.

OBJECTIVE 3a
Compute overhead variances, using the two-way analysis

Two-Way Variance Analysis. Analyses of factory overhead variances vary in sophistication. One approach is to compute the total overhead variance, then divide this amount into two parts: (1) the controllable overhead variance and (2) the overhead volume variance. The controllable overhead variance is easily linked to areas of responsibility, so the term *controllable* is important. If you return to the Pearce Company example begun in Chapter 22, you will see that additional data is needed to continue the variance analysis into the overhead cost accounts. The flexible budget of overhead costs for the period revealed the following formula:

$5.75/direct labor hour + $1,300 in monthly fixed overhead costs

Normal capacity was set at 400 direct labor hours per month. The company incurred $4,100 in actual overhead costs during August.

Before finding the overhead variances, you must calculate the total standard overhead rate. The total standard overhead rate has two parts. One part is the variable rate of $5.75 per direct labor hour. The other is the standard fixed overhead rate, which is found by dividing budgeted fixed overhead ($1,300) by normal capacity. This works out to $3.25 per direct labor hour ($1,300/400 hours). Therefore, the total standard overhead rate used to apply overhead was $9.00 per direct labor hour ($5.75 + $3.25). The total fixed overhead costs divided by normal capacity provides a rate that assigns all fixed overhead costs to products (or services) if total expected output is achieved. As you will recall from Chapter 22, the standard hours per chair are 2.4 direct labor hours. If 400 direct labor hours are normal for a month, then the output of chairs should be around 167 (400 hours/2.4 hours per chair). Given this information, you can now calculate the total overhead variance for the Pearce Company as follows:

Actual overhead costs incurred		$4,100
Standard overhead costs applied to good units produced:		
$9.00/direct labor hour × (180 chairs × 2.4 hour/chair)		3,888
Total overhead variance		$ 212(U)

The **controllable overhead variance** is the difference between the actual overhead incurred and the factory overhead budgeted for the level of production reached. Thus, the controllable variance for the Pearce Company for August would be as follows:

Actual overhead costs incurred		$4,100
Less budgeted factory overhead (flexible budget) for 180 chairs:		
Variable overhead cost:		
(180 chairs × 2.4 hour/chair) × $5.75/direct labor hour	$2,484	
Budgeted fixed overhead cost	1,300	
Total budgeted factory overhead		3,784
Controllable overhead variance		$ 316(U)

The **overhead volume variance** is the difference between the factory overhead budgeted for the level of production achieved and the overhead applied to production, using the standard overhead rate. Continuing with the Pearce Company example, you have

Budgeted factory overhead (see above)	$3,784
Less factory overhead applied:	
(180 chairs × 2.4 hour/chair) × $9.00/direct labor hour	3,888
Overhead volume variance	$ 104(F)

By checking the computations, you will find that the two variances do equal the total overhead variance.

Controllable overhead variance	$316(U)
Overhead volume variance	104(F)
Total overhead variance	$212(U)

In this example, the company spent more than it should have, so the controllable variance is unfavorable.

Use of existing facilities and capacity is measured by the overhead volume variance. A volume variance will occur only if more or less capacity than normal is actually used. In the example, 400 direct labor hours is the measure of normal use of facilities. In producing 180 chairs, the company should have used 432 standard direct labor hours (standard hours allowed). Fixed overhead costs are applied on the basis of standard hours allowed. In the example, overhead would be applied on the basis of 432 hours, but the fixed overhead rate was computed by using 400 hours (normal capacity). Thus, more fixed costs would be applied to products than were budgeted. Because the products can absorb no more than actual costs incurred, this level of production would tend to lower unit cost. When more than expected capacity is used, the result is a favorable overhead volume variance. When less than normal capacity is used, less than all fixed overhead costs will be applied to units produced. It is then necessary to add the amount of underapplied fixed overhead to the cost of the good units produced, thereby increasing their unit cost. This condition is unfavorable.

Figure 23-2 sums up the discussion of overhead variance analysis. All procedures shown are exactly the same as those explained above. To figure the controllable variance, subtract the budgeted overhead amount (using a flexible budget) for the level of output achieved from actual overhead costs incurred. A positive answer means an unfavorable variance, because actual costs were greater than those budgeted. The controllable variance is favorable if the difference is negative. Subtracting total overhead applied from overhead budgeted at the level of output achieved produces the volume variance. As before, a positive answer means an unfavorable variance, and a negative answer means a favorable variance. The data from the Pearce Company example are shown in the lower part of Figure 23-2. Carefully check the solution in the figure with that given earlier.

OBJECTIVE 3b
Compute overhead variances, using the three-way analysis

Three-Way Variance Analysis. As the title indicates, the three-way approach to overhead variance analysis divides the total overhead variance into three parts instead of the two parts just studied. Remember, the purpose of variance analysis is to break down variations from budgeted information so one can determine reasons for changes from planned operations. The three-way approach to overhead variance analysis breaks the controllable overhead variance into two parts and identifies an *overhead spending variance* and an *overhead efficiency variance.* The overhead volume variance is the third overhead variance, and it is computed as in the two-way variance analysis.

The **overhead spending variance** is the difference between the actual overhead costs incurred and the amount that should have been spent, based on actual hours worked or other productive input measures. Therefore, actual overhead costs incurred are compared with the costs of a flexible budget based on actual hours worked. When the Pearce Company example is expanded, the spending variance is computed as follows:

Actual overhead costs incurred		**$4,100.00**
Less budgeted factory overhead (flexible budget) for 450 hours worked:		
Variable overhead cost:		
450 hours × $5.75 per direct labor hour	**$2,587.50**	
Budgeted fixed overhead cost	**1,300.00**	
Total budgeted factory overhead		**3,887.50**
Overhead Spending Variance		**$ 212.50(U)**

Figure 23-2. Two-way Overhead Variance Analysis

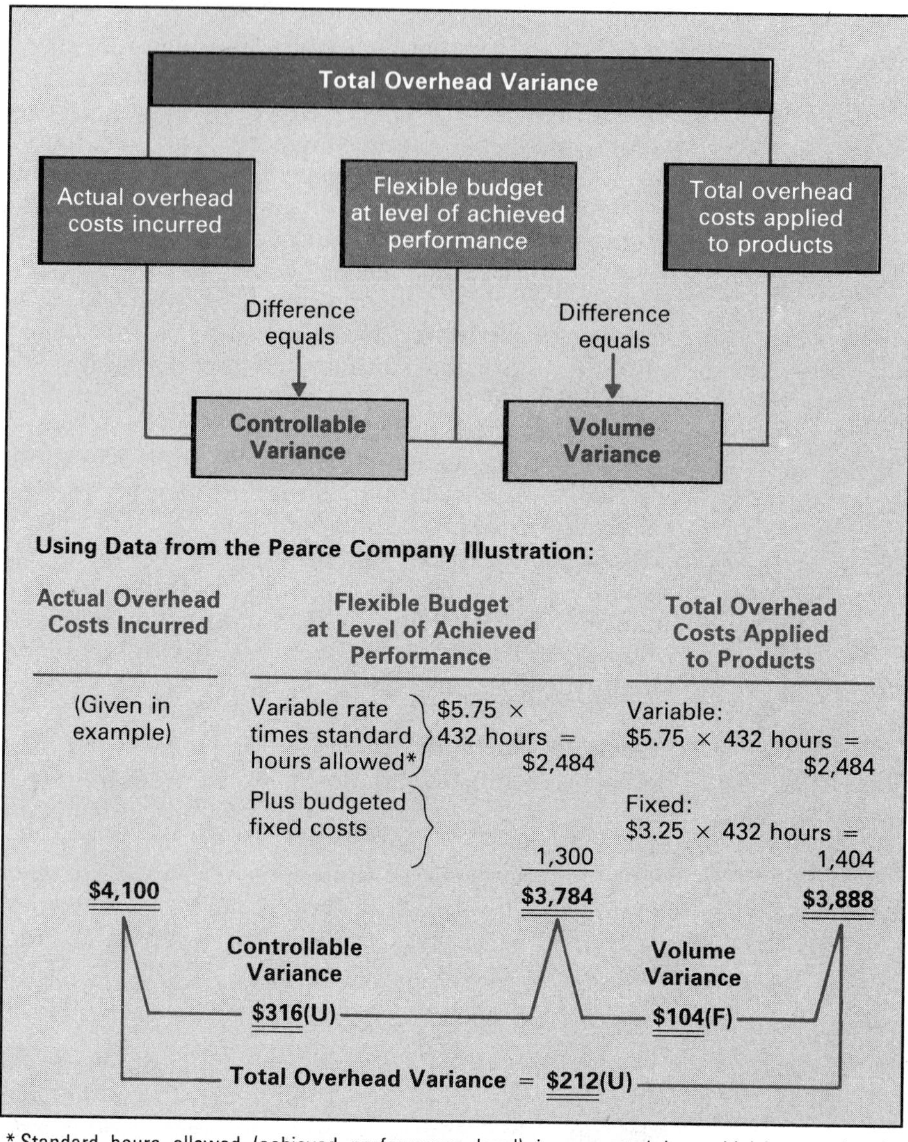

* Standard hours allowed (achieved performance level) is computed by multiplying good units produced by required standard time per unit. Here, the computation is as follows:

180 chairs produced × 2.4 hours per chair = 432 standard hours allowed

Note that the total overhead spending variance can be broken down into its variable and fixed components. In the example, actual overhead incurred was given in total and details were not provided. If the actual variable and fixed cost components were given, however, you could easily generate a variable overhead spending variance and a fixed overhead spending variance. This further breakdown would provide additional information to the supervisor. If most of the spending variance involved fixed costs, much of the variance would be difficult for the manager to control. If, on the other hand, most of the spending variance were caused by noncompliance with variable cost targets, those responsible should be held accountable for the differences.

The **overhead efficiency variance** is linked directly with the labor efficiency variance. An efficiency variance arises when actual hours worked differ from standard hours allowed for good units produced. The overhead efficiency variance is the difference between actual direct labor hours worked and standard labor hours allowed, multiplied by the standard variable overhead rate. Computing the overhead efficiency variance involves comparing two flexible budgets, one based on actual hours worked and the other based on standard hours allowed for good units produced. The overhead efficiency variance is computed as follows:

Budgeted factory overhead (flexible budget) for actual hours worked:		
Variable overhead cost:		
450 hours × $5.75 per direct labor hour	**$2,587.50**	
Budgeted fixed overhead cost	**1,300.00**	
Total budgeted overhead for actual hours worked		**$3,887.50**
Budgeted factory overhead (flexible budget) for standard hours allowed:		
Variable overhead cost:		
(180 chairs × 2.4 hours per chair) × $5.75 per direct labor hour	**$2,484.00**	
Budgeted fixed overhead cost	**1,300.00**	
Total budgeted overhead for standard hours allowed		**3,784.00**
Overhead efficiency variance		**$ 103.50(U)**

Note that by design the overhead efficiency variance is the difference between variable costs only. When two flexible budgets are compared, the fixed cost component is identical for each budget. The difference must come from the variable costs.

The overhead efficiency variance identifies the portion of the total overhead variance that occurs automatically when a labor efficiency variance develops. If the labor efficiency variance is unfavorable, the overhead efficiency variance will also be unfavorable. The person responsible for the labor efficiency variance is also responsible for the overhead efficiency variance.

As stated earlier, the **overhead volume variance** is computed as in the two-way approach. If you need to review its computation, refer to page 862 and Figure 23-3, which illustrates three-way overhead variance analysis.

In the upper portion of Figure 23-3, the total overhead variance is broken down into the three variances: (1) spending variance; (2) efficiency variance; and (3) volume variance. In addition, the cost totals compared to arrive at each variance are identified. Note that the only difference between Figure 23-2 and Figure 23-3 is the introduction of the *flexible budget for effort expended.* Using this flexible budget, one can break down

Figure 23-3. Three-Way Overhead Variance Analysis

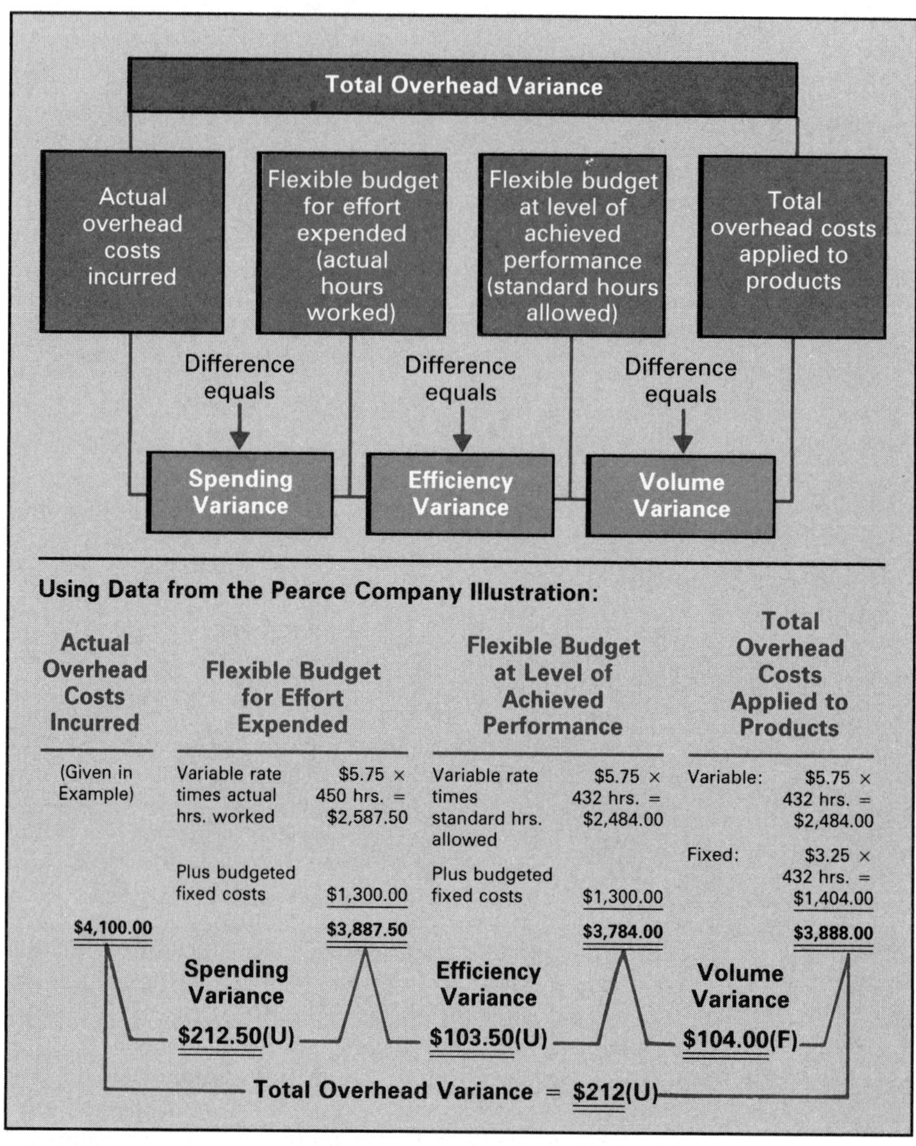

the controllable overhead variance into overhead spending variance and overhead efficiency variance.

In the bottom portion of Figure 23-3, the actual computation of the three variances is summarized. To check your answers to the three variances, the following calculation should be done:

Overhead spending variance	$212.50(U)
Overhead efficiency variance	103.50(U)
Overhead volume variance	104.00(F)
Total overhead variance	$212.00(U)

Illustrative Problem: Variance Analysis

Broadt Manufacturing Company has a standard cost system and keeps all cost standards up-to-date. The company's main product is heating pipe, which is made in a single department. The standard variable costs for one unit of finished pipe are:

Direct materials (two sq meters @ $1.50)	$ 3.00
Direct labor (1.5 hours @ $7.00)	10.50
Variable overhead (1.5 hours @ $4.00)	6.00
Standard variable cost/unit	$19.50

Normal capacity is 18,000 direct labor hours, and budgeted fixed overhead costs for the year were $36,000. During the year, 12,200 units were produced and sold. Related transactions and actual cost data for the year were as follows: Direct materials consisted of 24,500 square meters purchased and used; unit purchase costs were $1.40 per square meter. Direct labor consisted of 18,200 direct labor hours worked at an average labor rate of $7.20 per hour. Factory overhead incurred consisted of variable overhead costs of $73,500 and fixed overhead costs of $36,000.

Required

Using the data above, compute the following:

1. Standard hours allowed
2. Standard fixed overhead rate
3. Direct materials price variance
4. Direct materials quantity variance
5. Direct labor rate variance
6. Direct labor efficiency variance
7. Overhead spending variance
8. Overhead efficiency variance
9. Controllable overhead variance
10. Overhead volume variance

Solution

1. Standard hours allowed = good units produced × standard direct labor hours per unit

$$12{,}200 \text{ units} \times 1.5 \text{ hours/unit} = \underline{\underline{18{,}300 \text{ hrs}}}$$

2. Standard fixed overhead rate $= \dfrac{\text{budgeted fixed overhead costs}}{\text{normal capacity}}$

$$= \frac{\$36{,}000}{18{,}000 \text{ hours}}$$

$$= \underline{\underline{\$2.00}}\text{/direct labor hour}$$

Solution (continued):

3. Direct materials price variance

Price difference:		
	Actual price paid	$1.40/sq meter
	Less standard price	1.50/sq meter
	Difference	$ .10(F)

Direct materials price variance = (actual price − standard price) × actual quantity
= .10(F) × 24,500 sq meters
= $2,450(F)

4. Direct materials quantity variance

Quantity difference:		
	Actual quantity used	24,500 sq meters
	Less standard quantity (12,200 units × 2 sq meters)	24,400 sq meters
	Difference	100(U)

Direct materials quantity variance = (actual quantity − standard quantity) × standard price
= 100(U) × $1.50/sq meter
= $150(U)

5. Direct labor rate variance

Rate difference:		
	Actual labor rate	$7.20/hour
	Less standard labor rate	7.00/hour
	Difference	$ .20(U)

Direct labor rate variance = (actual rate − standard rate) × actual hours
= .20(U) × 18,200 hours
= $3,640(U)

6. Direct labor efficiency variance

Difference in hours:		
	Actual hours worked	18,200 hours
	Less standard hours allowed	18,300 hours
	Difference	100(F)

Direct labor efficiency variance = (actual hours − standard hours allowed) × standard rate
= 100 hours(F) × $7.00/hour
= $700(F)

7. Overhead spending variance

Overhead costs incurred:		
Variable	$73,500	
Fixed	36,000	$109,500
Less flexible budget for effort expended:		
Actual hours worked × variable overhead rate:		
18,200 labor hours × $4/hour	$72,800	
Plus budgeted fixed costs	36,000	108,800
Overhead spending variance		$ 700(U)

8. Overhead efficiency variance

Flexible budget for effort expended (see computation in 7 above)		$108,800
Less flexible budget at level of achieved performance		
Standard hours allowed × variable overhead rate:		
18,300 labor hours × $4/hour	$73,200	
Plus budgeted fixed costs	36,000	109,200
Overhead efficiency variance		$ 400(F)

9. Controllable overhead variance

Actual overhead costs incurred		$109,500
Less budgeted factory overhead for 18,300 hours:		
Variable overhead cost:		
18,300 hours at $4.00/hour	$73,200	
Budgeted fixed factory overhead	36,000	
Total budgeted factory overhead		109,200
Controllable overhead variance		$ 300(U)

10. Overhead volume variance

Total budgeted factory overhead (see computation in 9 above)		$109,200
Less factory overhead applied:		
Variable: 18,300 hours at $4/hour	$73,200	
Fixed: 18,300 hours at $2/hour	36,600	
Total factory overhead applied		109,800
Overhead volume variance		$ 600(F)

Recording Overhead Variances

OBJECTIVE 4
Prepare journal entries involving overhead variances

In Chapter 22 variances associated with materials and labor costs were recorded. As you will recall, there are a few simple rules to follow when recording transactions involving variances: (1) record all inventory balances at standard cost; (2) create separate accounts for each type of variance; (3) *debit unfavorable* variances to their accounts, and (4) *credit favorable* variances.

Recording overhead variances differs in timing and technique from recording variances related to direct materials and direct labor. First, for a manufacturing company, factory overhead (the total of variable and fixed amounts) is charged to Work in Process Inventory at standard cost (direct labor hours allowed × standard variable and fixed overhead rates). The entry is identical to the one used in Chapter 17 to apply factory overhead to production except that here standard overhead rates are used. This same entry is used for both the two-way and three-way approaches to overhead variance analysis. Second, the overhead variances are identified and recorded when the Factory Overhead Applied and Factory Overhead Control accounts are closed out at period end. These entries are illustrated below, using information from the Pearce Company example.

Journal Entry to Apply Factory Overhead to Production

Work in Process Inventory		
(432 standard hours allowed at $9/hour)	3,888	
Factory Overhead Applied		3,888
To apply factory overhead costs to Work in Process Inventory at standard cost		

Following this entry, there is a $4,100 debit balance in the Factory Overhead Control account and a $3,888 credit balance in the Factory Overhead Applied account.

Two-way Analysis: Journal Entry to Record Variances

Factory Overhead Applied	3,888	
Controllable Overhead Variance	316	
Overhead Volume Variance		104
Factory Overhead Control		4,100
To close out Factory Overhead Control and Applied accounts and record the resulting variances		

Three-way Analysis: Journal Entry to Record Variances

Factory Overhead Applied	3,888.00	
Overhead Spending Variance	212.50	
Overhead Efficiency Variance	103.50	
Overhead Volume Variance		104.00
Factory Overhead Control		4,100.00
To close out Factory Overhead Control and Applied accounts and record the resulting variances		

Once transactions involving direct materials, direct labor, factory overhead, and related variances have been recorded for the Pearce Company, the recording cycle must be completed. This is done by preparing entries to transfer completed units to finished goods inventory and units sold to cost of goods sold and by disposing of balances in the variance accounts at period end.

Journal Entry for Transfer of Completed Units to Finished Goods Inventory

There is now $11,880 in standard costs recorded in the Work in Process Inventory account. Assuming that these 180 chairs have been completed, the following entry would be made:

Finished Goods Inventory		
(180 chairs at $66/chair)	11,880	
Work in Process Inventory		11,880
To record transfer of completed units to finished goods inventory		

The standard unit price of $66 was computed from information in Chapter 22 and this chapter as follows:

Direct materials:	
4 yards @ $6/yard	$24.00
Direct labor	
2.4 hours @ $8.50/hour	20.40
Factory overhead	
2.4 hours @ $9/hour	21.60
Total standard unit cost	$66.00

Because all costs went into the Work in Process Inventory account at standard cost, standard cost is also used when costs are transferred out of the account.

Journal Entry to Transfer Cost of Units Sold to Cost of Goods Sold Account

Assume that the 180 chairs completed were sold on account for $169 per chair and shipped to a customer.

Accounts Receivable (180 chairs at $169/chair)	30,420	
Sales		30,420
To record sale of 180 chairs		
Cost of Goods Sold	11,880	
Finished Goods Inventory		11,880
To record transfer of standard cost of units sold to Cost of Goods Sold account		

Journal Entry to Dispose of End-of-Period Variance Account Balances

OBJECTIVE 5 Dispose of variance balances at period end

The balances in the variance accounts at the end of the period are disposed of much as over- or underapplied overhead was earlier. Here, it is assumed that all units worked on were completed and sold. Therefore, a period-end journal entry is made to close all variances to Cost of Goods Sold. Remember, the balances of the variances related to direct materials and direct labor are brought forward from Chapter 22.

Cost of Goods Sold	844.00	
Direct Materials Price Variance	76.00	
Overhead Volume Variance	104.00	
Direct Materials Quantity Variance		240.00
Direct Labor Rate Variance		315.00
Direct Labor Efficiency Variance		153.00
Overhead Spending Variance*		212.50
Overhead Efficiency Variance*		103.50
To close all variance account balances to Cost of Goods Sold		

If balances still exist at period end in Materials Inventory, Work in Process Inventory, and Finished Goods Inventory and the variance amounts are significant, then the net amount of the variances ($844 here) should be divided among the inventory accounts and Cost of Goods Sold in proportion to their balances.

Note that part of the price variance will be allocated to the Materials Inventory. No other variance is connected with items in materials inventory. If the variances are significant, then items in materials inventory and products in work in process inventory, finished goods inventory, and cost of goods sold are either materially understated or overstated. Remember that for reporting purposes, inventory can only be stated at standard cost if its value corresponds to currently attainable prices. The existence of significant variances indicates that inventories are not stated at currently attainable prices and standard costs are not set at currently attainable cost levels. Therefore, by allocating variances back to all items in inventory and cost of goods sold, you are really restating the variances at actual costs. They can then be used to prepare financial statements.

Performance Reporting and Cost Controllability

The budgetary control process requires that management formulate a basis for effective cost control. Standard cost variance analysis is a useful tool in achieving this objective. Once variances have been computed,

* This entry assumes the use of the three-way analysis of overhead variances. If the two-way analysis were used, the overhead spending variance and the overhead efficiency variance would be combined into the controllable overhead variance, and it would be credited for $316.

managers responsible for the variances should be asked to give reasons for incurring them. In addition, management accounting personnel should try to determine other causes for each variance. This review process makes managers conscious of their cost responsibilities, permits timely standard cost revisions, and leads to effective cost control through a continuous evaluation process of past and future costs.

Responsibility for Variances

Responsibility for efficient or inefficient operating results passes from the company president down the corporate hierarchy to managers in charge of divisions and smaller segments of the company. Specific titles of individuals responsible for each type of standard cost variance differ between companies. The analysis shown in Table 23-1 indicates the managers generally held accountable for cost variances. When reviewing Table 23-1, remember that each company takes a unique approach to how it establishes a responsibility accounting system. Thus, the titles and variance responsibilities shown may differ from the ones encountered in business. It is important to understand, however, that each variance can be traced to someone in the company who should answer for the difference between budgeted and actual results.

Table 23-1. Responsibility for Standard Cost Variances

Variance	Personnel Responsible
Materials price variance	Purchasing agent or purchasing department manager
Materials quantity variance	Plant superintendent, departmental supervisors, machine operators, quality control department, and material handlers
Labor rate variance	Employment department manager, departmental supervisors, and plant superintendent
Labor efficiency variance	Plant superintendent, departmental supervisors, production scheduling department, quality control department, material handlers, and machine operators
Overhead spending variance	*Variable portion*—responsibility of individual supervisors, expected to keep actual expenses within budget *Fixed portion*—responsibility of top management
Overhead efficiency variance	Same personnel responsible for labor efficiency variance
Overhead volume variance	Top management and production schedulers

Source: Henry R. Anderson and Mitchell H. Raiborn, *Basic Cost Accounting Concepts* (Boston: Houghton Mifflin, 1977), p. 380. Reprinted by permission.

Causes of Variances

Operating performance can be evaluated by comparing actual results with either budgeted data or standard cost data. Budgeted data tend to be less precise than standard cost data, but both provide cost goals. In this section we will focus on performance evaluation based on standard costs. The first step is to find out if a variance exists. Determining variances helps locate areas of operating efficiency or inefficiency so corrective steps can be taken. But the key to effectively controlling operations involves more than finding the variance amount. *Finding the reason(s) for the variance is essential.* Once the reason(s) is known, steps can be taken to correct the trouble spot.

There are many possible causes for each standard cost variance. The list in Table 23-2 is not all-inclusive, but it does indicate reasons commonly used to explain why variances arise. Standard cost variances are reported to managers so they can identify causes of specific variances. Based on a functioning responsibility accounting system, the accounts associated with those variances are controllable by the managers. When reviewing the list, remember that some causes can result from events in the company not under the control of the manager being reviewed. Also remember that there are degrees of legitimacy, and only the supervisor's experience can help sort out sound reasons for inefficient operations.

Management by Exception: Using Standard Costs

OBJECTIVE 6 Describe the concept of management by exception

To facilitate performance evaluation, management needs a system for analyzing operations so areas functioning above or below expectations can be identified. Many companies are so large that it is virtually impossible to review all operating areas. Locating and analyzing only the areas of unusually good or bad performance is called **management by exception.** Variance analysis is the primary accounting tool that management uses in exception reporting. Techniques are developed to isolate variances (differences) between standard and actual costs for direct materials, direct labor, and factory overhead. A variance must exceed, either favorably or unfavorably, a minimum amount or percentage difference before being considered an exception. The variance is then subjected to careful analysis to determine its cause. For example, assume management decides that performance within plus or minus 4 percent of budget or target is acceptable. When reviewing performance reports, a manager only analyzes cost areas in which differences exceed these limits. In Figure 23-4 only direct materials C and E are outside the 4 percent limit, and their purchasing practices will be analyzed. The standard or target unit costs mark the spots where the vertical bars should end. Actual unit costs are shown in parentheses under the letters identifying the materials.

Management by exception is a useful tool for controlling operations. Once the system is implemented, efforts are automatically directed toward major trouble spots. Management is freed from many details, enabling them to concentrate on more creative facets of the business.

Table 23-2. Possible Causes of Standard Cost Variances

Materials price variance
Recent purchase price changes not incorporated into the standard cost
Quantity purchase discount changes caused by changes in ordering policies
Substitute raw materials different from original material specifications
Freight cost changes

Materials quantity variance
Poor material handling
Inferior workmanship by machine operator
Faulty equipment
Less expensive grade of raw material, causing excessive scrap
Inferior quality control inspection

Labor rate variance
Recent pay rate changes within industry
Employee hired at incorrect skill and experience level
Labor strike, causing utilization of unskilled help
Labor layoff, causing skilled labor to be retained to prevent resignations and job switching
Employee sickness and vacation time

Labor efficiency variance
Machine breakdown
Inferior raw materials
Poor supervision
Lack of timely material handling
Poor employee performance
Erratic production scheduling
Inferior engineering specifications
New, inexperienced employee

Overhead spending variance
Unexpected price changes
Excessive indirect labor usage
Excessive indirect material usage
Changes in employee overtime
Machine and personnel failures
Depreciation rate changes

Overhead efficiency variance
See labor efficiency variance

Overhead volume variance
Failure to utilize normal capacity
Lack of sales orders
Too much idle capacity
Inefficient or efficient utilization of existing capacity

Source: Henry R. Anderson and Mitchell H. Raiborn, *Basic Cost Accounting Concepts* (Boston: Houghton Mifflin, 1977), p. 381. Reprinted by permission.

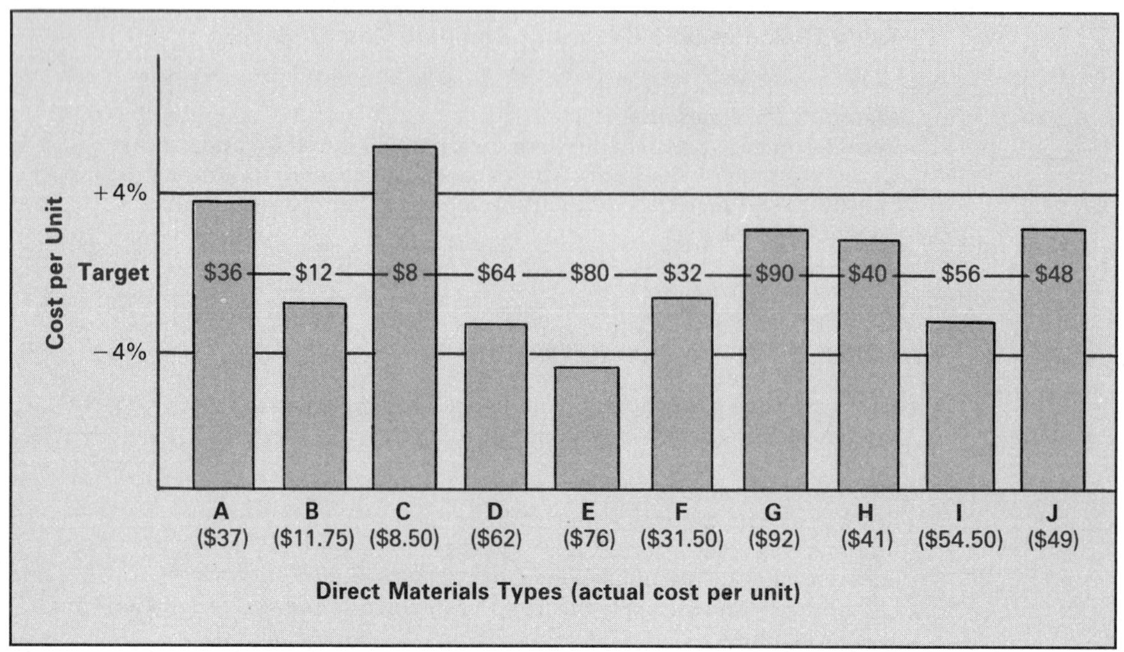

Figure 23-4. The Management by Exception Technique

Performance Reports Using Standard Costs

OBJECTIVE 7
Evaluate employee performance, using variances

As discussed in Chapter 20, performance reports should be tailored to areas of responsibility. The report should be accurate and clearly stated, and it should only contain cost or revenue items the manager receiving the report can control. In Exhibit 23-4 a performance report uses variance data from the Pearce Company example pertinent to the production department supervisor. The production supervisor is responsible for: (a) direct materials used and related direct materials quantity variance); (b) direct labor hours used and related direct labor and overhead efficiency variances; and (c) the cost areas used to compute the overhead spending variance. Dollar figures in Exhibit 23-4 are limited to these costs. It is important to leave enough space on the performance report for the manager to write in reasons for the variances.

The report shown in Exhibit 23-4 is simpler than most. Normally, such a report shows several items of direct materials, two or more direct labor classifications, and many items of overhead costs. In addition, companies do not all use the same format. In fact, as seen in Chapter 20, these differences can be significant. But the ingredients most important to any performance report are present in Exhibit 23-4. They are: (1) appropriate title and identity of area or person being evaluated; (2) pertinent data supporting the computations; (3) a detailed breakdown of the cost and/ or revenue items being analyzed, including the variance amounts; and (4) a specified place where the manager can respond about the variances. These elements should be included in all performance reports.

Exhibit 23-4. Performance Report Using Variance Analysis

Pearce Company
Production Department Performance Report—Cost Variance Analysis
For the Month Ended August 31, 19xx

400 hours: normal capacity (direct labor hours)
432 hours: capacity performance level achieved (standard hours allowed)
180 chairs: good units produced

Cost Analysis

	Cost		Variance	
	Budgeted	**Actual**	**Amount**	**Type**
Direct materials used (leather)	$ 4,320	$ 4,560	$240.00(U)	Quantity variance
Direct labor usage	3,672	3,825	153.00(U)	Efficiency variance
Factory overhead	3,784	4,100	212.50(U)	Spending variance
			103.50(U)	Efficiency variance
Totals	$11,776	$12,485	$709.00(U)	

Reasons for Variances
Direct materials quantity variance: (1) inferior quality-control inspection and (2) cheaper grade of direct materials caused excessive scrap
Direct labor efficiency variance: (1) inferior direct materials and (2) new, inexperienced employee
Overhead spending variance: (1) excessive indirect material usage; (2) changes in employee overtime; and (3) unexpected price changes
Overhead efficiency variance: reasons the same as those for direct labor efficiency variance

Chapter Review

Review of Learning Objectives

1. **Review the principles of performance evaluation.**
Performance evaluation principles consist of both behavioral principles and operational principles. The behavioral principles are: (1) managers should have input into the standards set for their area of responsibility; (2) management support of the evaluation process should be evident; (3) only controllable cost and revenue items with significant variances should be included in the performance reports; and (4) opportunity for manager response should be part of the evaluation. Operational principles include: (1) providing accurate and suitable measures of performance; (2) communicating with appropriate managers and segment leaders to be evaluated; (3) identifying the responsibilities of each manager; (4) comparing actual performance with a suitable base; (5) preparing performance reports that highlight areas of concern; and (6) analyzing important cause-and-effect relationships.

2. **Prepare a flexible budget.**
   A flexible budget summarizes anticipated costs prepared for various activity levels. It is geared toward changes in the level of productive output. Variable and fixed costs are given for several levels of capacity or output, with each column showing the total expected cost for an output level. Once prepared, the flexible budget is used to determine the flexible budget formula. This formula, which can be applied to any level of productive output, is a key tool in evaluating performance of individuals and departments.

3. **Compute overhead variances, using both the two-way and three-way analyses.**
   Cost variances for overhead costs can be computed using either the two-way or the three-way approach. Using two-way analysis, one can develop a controllable variance and a volume variance. The three-way approach to overhead variances refines the total overhead variances into a spending variance, an efficiency variance, and a volume variance. Comparing the two approaches, one finds that the three-way approach breaks the controllable variance of the two-way approach into a spending variance and an efficiency variance. The volume variance remains the same for both methods. Each variance results from specific causes, and these causes help pinpoint reasons for the differences between actual and standard costs.

4. **Prepare journal entries involving overhead variances.**
   The journal entries required to record overhead variances differ little from the set of entries illustrated for the job order costing system in Chapter 17. Actual overhead costs are still recorded in the overhead control account, and overhead costs applied using standard overhead rates are credited to the overhead applied account. The difference between the actual and applied overhead accounts represents the total overhead variance. When these two accounts are closed at period end, variances from standard cost can be assigned accounts in the general ledger and debited (unfavorable) or credited (favorable) to them. Only standard costs are charged to materials, work in process, and finished goods inventories. All differences between standard and actual costs are entered into the variance accounts.

5. **Dispose of variance balances at period end.**
   At the close of an accounting period, balances in variance accounts are disposed of. This disposal is accomplished by either (1) closing them to cost of goods sold if the balances are small or if most or all of the goods produced during the period were sold or (2) dividing the net variance balance among work in process inventory, finished goods inventory, and cost of goods sold in proportion to their balances. The price variance, if significant, should be allocated separately because a portion should be assigned to materials inventory to convert that account balance into actual costs. Inventory balances can be stated at standard cost on period-end financial statements only when variance amounts are insignificant.

6. **Describe the concept of management by exception.**
   Management by exception is a performance evaluation technique used to highlight significant variances from budgeted or planned operations and to analyze their causes. Variances within specific limits set by management are not analyzed. This technique is especially useful for companies trying to control a large number of cost centers or cost categories.

7. **Evaluate employee performance, using variances.**
   Introducing variances from standard costs into the performance report lends a degree of accuracy to the evaluation process. Variances tend to pinpoint

efficient and inefficient operating areas more than comparisons between budgeted and actual data. The key factors in preparing a performance report based on standard costs and related variances are: (a) to establish a responsibility accounting system and identify those responsible for each variance; (b) to determine the causes for each variance; (c) to establish a system of management by exception; and (d) to develop a reporting format suited to the task. Following these basic rules will provide the supervisor with an effective tool for cost control and evaluation.

Review Problem: Standard Costing in a Service Industry: Annuity Life Insurance Company

The Annuity Life Insurance Company (ALIC) markets several types of life insurance policies, but its permanent, twenty-year life annuity policy (P20A) is the company's most desired product. The P20A policy sells in $10,000 increments and features variable percentages of whole-life insurance and single-payment annuity, depending on the potential policyholder's needs and age. There is an entire department devoted to developing and marketing the P20A policy. ALIC has determined that both the policy developer and policy salesperson contribute to creating each policy. Therefore, ALIC categorizes these people as direct labor for variance analysis, cost control, and performance evaluation purposes. For unit costing purposes, each $10,000 increment is considered one unit. Thus, a $90,000 policy comprises 9 units.

Standard unit cost information for the period is as follows:

Direct labor	
Policy developer:	
3 hours at $12/hour	$ 36.00
Policy salesperson:	
8.5 hours at $14.20/hour	120.70
Operating overhead	
Variable overhead:	
11.5 hours at $26/hour	299.00
Fixed overhead:	
11.5 hours at $18/hour	207.00
Standard unit cost	$662.70

Actual costs incurred during January for the 265 units sold were as follows:

Direct labor	
Policy developers:	
848 hours at $12.50/hour	$10,600.00
Policy salespeople:	
2,252.5 hours at $14/hour	31,535.00
Operating overhead:	
Variable operating overhead	78,440.00
Fixed operating overhead	53,400.00

Normal monthly capacity was 260 units, and the budgeted fixed operating overhead for the month was $53,820.

Required

1. Compute the standard hours allowed in January for policy developers and for policy salespeople.
2. What were the total actual costs incurred for January? What should have been the total standard costs for that period?
3. Compute the labor rate and efficiency variances for policy developers and for policy salespeople.
4. Compute the overhead variances for January, using both the two-way variance approach and the three-way variance approach.
5. Identify possible causes for each variance, and develop possible solutions.

Answer to Review Problem

1. Standard hours allowed = good units produced × standard hours per unit

Policy developers

Standard hours allowed	=	265 × 3.00
	=	795 hours

Policy salespeople

Standard hours allowed	=	265 × 8.50
	=	2,252.5 hours

2. Actual costs

Direct labor:		
Policy developers		$ 10,600.00
Policy salespeople		31,535.00
Total direct labor cost		$ 42,135.00
Operating overhead:		
Variable operating overhead		$ 78,440.00
Fixed operating overhead		53,400.00
Total operating overhead		$131,840.00
Total actual costs		$173,975.00
Standard costs that should have been incurred for 265 units		
Direct labor:		
Policy developers	(795 × $12.00)	$ 9,540.00
Policy salespeople	(2,252.5 × $14.20)	31,985.50
Total direct labor cost		$ 41,525.50
Operating overhead:		
Variable operating overhead	(265 × $299.00)	$ 79,235.00
Fixed operating overhead	(265 × $207.00)	54,855.00
Total operating overhead		$134,090.00
Total standard costs		$175,615.50
Total variance from standard cost: ($173,975.00 − $175,615.50)		$ 1,640.50(F)

3. Labor variances

Labor rate variances	=	(actual rate − standard rate)	× actual hours
Policy developers	=	($12.50 − $12.00)	× 848 hours
	=	$424.00(U)	
Policy salespeople	=	($14.00 − $14.20)	× 2,252.5 hours
	=	$450.50(F)	
Efficiency variances	=	(actual hours − standard hours)	× standard rate
Policy developers	=	(848.0 − 795.0)	× $12.00
	=	$636.00(U)	
Policy salespeople	=	(2,252.5 − 2,252.5)	× $14.20
	=	$0.00	

Check:	
Total actual labor cost	$ 42,135.00
Total standard labor cost	41,525.50
Total labor variance	$ 609.50(U)
Rate variances:	
Developers	$ 424.00(U)
Salespeople	450.50(F)
Efficiency variances:	
Developers	636.00(U)
Salespeople	0.00
Total labor variance	$ 609.50(U)

4(a). Overhead variances using the two-variance approach

Total overhead variance:	
Actual overhead costs incurred	$131,840.00
Standard overhead costs applied to good units produced:	
units produced × std hours/unit × total rate/hour	
265 × 11.50 × $44.00	134,090.00
Total overhead variance	$ 2,250.00(F)
Controllable overhead variance:	
Actual overhead costs incurred	$131,840.00
Less budgeted factory overhead (flexible budget) for 265 units:	
Variable overhead cost:	
units × hours/unit × rate/hour	
265 × 11.50 × $26.00	$ 79,235.00
Plus budgeted fixed overhead cost	53,820.00
Total budgeted factory overhead	$133,055.00
Controllable overhead variance	$ 1,215.00(F)

Overhead volume variance:	
Budgeted factory overhead (from previous page)	$133,055.00
Less factory overhead applied:	
units produced × std hours/unit × total rate/hour	
265 × 11.50 × $44.00	134,090.00
Overhead volume variance	$ 1,035.00(F)

Check of computations:	
Controllable overhead variance	$ 1,215.00(F)
Overhead volume variance	1,035.00(F)
Total overhead variance	$ 2,250.00(F)

4(b). Overhead variances using the three-variance approach

Spending variance:	
Actual variable overhead cost	$ 78,440.00
Budgeted variable overhead (3,100.5 actual hours worked):	
3,100.5 × $26.00/hour	80,613.00
Variable spending variance	$ 2,173.00(F)
Actual fixed overhead cost	$ 53,400.00
Budgeted fixed overhead cost	53,820.00
Fixed spending variance	$ 420.00(F)
Spending variance	$ 2,593.00(F)

Efficiency overhead variance:	
Budgeted factory overhead (flexible budget for actual hours worked)	
Variable overhead cost:	
hours worked × rate paid	
3,100.5 × $26.00	$ 80,613.00
Budgeted fixed overhead cost	53,820.00
Total budgeted overhead for actual hours worked	$134,433.00
Budgeted factory overhead (flexible budget for standard hours allowed):	
Variable overhead cost:	
units × hour/unit × rate/hour	
265 × 11.50 × $26.00	$ 79,235.00
Budgeted fixed overhead cost	53,820.00
Total budgeted overhead for standard hours allowed	$133,055.00
Overhead efficiency variance	$ 1,378.00(U)

Overhead volume variance:	
Budgeted factory overhead (from above)	$133,055.00
Less factory overhead applied:	
units produced × std hours/unit × total rate/hour	
265 × 11.50 × $44.00	134,090.00
Overhead volume variance	$ 1,035.00(F)

Check of computations:	
Spending variance	$ 2,593.00(F)
Efficiency variance	1,378.00(U)
Overhead volume variance	1,035.00(F)
Total overhead variance	$ 2,250.00(F)

5. Although the total rate variance was favorable, a closer look shows that it is made up of a $424 unfavorable variance for policy developers and a $450 favorable variance for policy salespeople. There are several possible reasons for the unfavorable variance of $424. For instance, the industry's pay rate may have increased, forcing ALIC to increase the rate paid to policy developers. Or perhaps, needing more developers, ALIC hired those of greater skill and, thus, at a greater pay rate. A possible cause of the favorable labor rate variance could be a high turnover rate with new people being hired at a lower rate. An approach to the variance would be to determine if the actual rates were caused by a one-time situation, making them temporary, or by permanent changes in the labor market. If the change is permanent, the standard should be changed.

   The unfavorable labor efficiency variance was caused entirely by policy developers, who took more time to complete 265 units than the standard allowed. This situation may have been caused by a high number of new, inexperienced employees. Also, the developers completed 5 more units than normal capacity. This may have resulted in longer than normal work days and a decrease in efficiency because of fatigue.

   The total overhead variance was favorable. The three-way breakdown of the total variance showed favorable spending and volume variances and an unfavorable efficiency variance. This means that either someone did a good job controlling overhead costs and should be commended or the standards were set too low and should be adjusted. The overhead costs may have been less than expected because of an unexpected price change, a decrease in the amount of indirect labor used, such as less clerical staff; or a decrease in the utilities consumed. The cause of the favorable fixed overhead spending variance may have resulted from a lowering of the rent or a decrease in depreciation charges because some office equipment was sold.

   The volume variance was actually favorable because five more units were sold than expected. This should again result in a reward for the person responsible and possibly an adjustment of normal capacity if it was set too low. Finally, the overhead efficiency variance was unfavorable for the same reason the labor efficiency variance was unfavorable.

Chapter Assignments

Questions

1. Define the following:
   a. Flexible budget
   b. Total overhead variance
   c. Controllable overhead variance
   d. Overhead spending variance
   e. Overhead efficiency variance
   f. Overhead volume variance

g. Variance disposition
h. Management by exception

2. "Performance is evaluated or measured by comparing what happened with what should have happened." What is meant by this statement? Relate your comments to the budgetary control process.
3. What is the purpose of a flexible budget?
4. What are the two parts of a flexible budget formula? How are they related?
5. Distinguish between the controllable overhead variance and the overhead volume variance.
6. How can a variance help management achieve effective control of operations?
7. If standard hours allowed are more than normal hours, will the period's overhead volume variance be favorable or unfavorable? Explain your answer.
8. Can an unfavorable direct materials quantity variance be caused, at least in part, by a favorable direct materials price variance? Explain.
9. "Variance analysis is an integral part of standard cost accounting." Explain this statement.
10. The two phases of standard cost variance analysis are (1) the initial computing of variances and (2) the identification of underlying causes. Discuss the relationship between these two phases.
11. What three rules underlie the recording of standard cost variances?
12. What circumstances cause a material quantity variance to be favorable?
13. Identify some possible causes of an unfavorable labor rate variance.
14. If the labor efficiency variance in the Pumping Department is unfavorable, would you also expect an unfavorable overhead efficiency variance in the department? Support your answer.
15. Discuss the relevance and importance of normal capacity and flexible budgets when determining overhead variances.
16. Identify and discuss the operating principles of performance evaluation.
17. Compare the two-way and three-way approaches to overhead variance analysis. Which is the better approach? Why?
18. How do you determine if an overhead efficiency variance is favorable or unfavorable?
19. Identify the supervisor(s) normally responsible for the material quantity variance.
20. Who is responsible for the overhead volume variance? How are these people held accountable for this variance?

Classroom Exercises

Exercise 23-1. Performance Evaluation Principles (L.O. 1)

Jill Langhorn was recently promoted to supervisor of the Water Conservation Department in the Mississippi Valley Bureau of Resources. Part of her duties as supervisor include managing a work force of fifty-two people. There are three assistant supervisors answering directly to Ms. Langhorn: Phil Hueidon, Brent Bergermust, and Barbara Terswal. All three people have been with the department longer than Ms. Langhorn. All three have good records with the Bureau, and each one is sensitive to his or her role in the department. Ms. Langhorn has never evaluated anyone before and has come to you, her immediate supervisor, for suggestions about preparing performance evaluations on these assistant supervisors.

Prepare a written response to Ms. Langhorn. Include an analysis of the principles of performance evaluation.

Exercise 23-2. Flexible Budget Preparation (L.O. 2)

Fixed overhead costs for the Karolinski Kostume Company for 19xx are expected to be: (a) depreciation, $84,000; (b) supervisor's salaries, $76,000; (c) property taxes and insurance, $24,000; and (d) other fixed overhead, $12,000. Total fixed overhead is therefore expected to be $196,000. Variable costs per unit are expected to be: (a) direct materials, $5.00; (b) direct labor, $7.50; (c) operating supplies, $1.50; (d) indirect labor, $2.00; and (e) other variable overhead costs, $1.00.

Prepare a flexible budget for the following levels of production: 16,000 units, 18,000 units, and 20,000 units. What is the flexible budget formula for 19xx?

Exercise 23-3. Factory Overhead Variances: Two-way Approach (L.O. 3a)

The Lowry Company produces handmade lobster pots, which are sold to distributors throughout New England. The company incurred $22,200 of actual overhead costs in May. Budgeted standard overhead costs were $8 of variable overhead costs per direct labor hour plus $2,500 in fixed overhead costs for May. Normal capacity was set at 2,000 direct labor hours per month. In May the company produced 800 lobster pots. The time standard is 3 direct labor hours per lobster pot.

Compute the controllable overhead variance, the overhead volume variance, and the total overhead variance for May.

Exercise 23-4. Overhead Variance Analysis: Three-way Approach (L.O. 3b)

Budgeted fixed factory overhead for the Cahill Manufacturing Company is $29,565 per month. Variable overhead costs are budgeted at $2.60 per direct labor hour. Normal capacity for a given month is established at 8,100 direct labor hours. Actual operating data for November 19x9 were as follows:

Variable overhead costs	$21,240
Fixed overhead costs	29,840
Actual direct labor hours	8,310 hours
Standard hours allowed	8,120 hours

Compute the following amounts and label all answers carefully:

a. Total overhead applied
b. Over- or underapplied overhead
c. Overhead spending variance
d. Overhead efficiency variance
e. Overhead volume variance
f. Total overhead variance

Exercise 23-5. Overhead Variance Analysis: Three-way Approach (L.O. 3b)

Chisarizk Industries uses a standard cost accounting system, which utilizes flexible budget procedures for planning and control purposes. The monthly flexible budget for overhead costs is $200,000 of fixed costs plus $4.80 per machine hour. Normal capacity of 100,000 machine hours is used to compute the standard fixed overhead rate.

During December 19x9 plant workers recorded 105,000 actual machine hours. The standard machine hours allowed for good production during December were only 98,500. Actual costs incurred during December were $541,000 of variable overhead and $204,500 of fixed overhead.

1. Compute the under- or overapplied overhead during December.
2. Prepare an analysis of the overhead spending variance, overhead efficiency variance, and overhead volume variance. Show all computations.

Exercise 23-6. Journal Entries and Overhead Variances
(L.O. 3, 4)

John Espey is president of Cecil Appliance Repair Company, which employs more than seventy repair people when the normal operating schedule is met. During January 19x8, 11,200 standard hours allowed were produced by working 10,800 actual hours. The company's flexible budget for overhead costs is $3.40 per direct labor hour plus $22,300 in budgeted fixed costs. Actual costs for January were $36,800 of variable overhead and $23,050 of fixed overhead. Normal capacity is 11,150 direct labor hours per month.

1. Compute the overhead spending variance, the overhead efficiency variance, and the overhead volume variance for January.
2. Assuming actual overhead costs have been recorded, apply overhead to repair jobs worked on during the period.
3. Close the overhead applied and control accounts, and record overhead variances for the month.

Exercise 23-7. Disposing of Overhead Variance Account Balances
(L.O. 5)

Long Island Company's controller, Myrna Fischman, is about to close the year's financial records. The following data related to overhead still appear in the accounting records:

Overhead spending variance	$ 1,660(U)
Overhead efficiency variance	2,720(F)
Overhead volume variance	200(F)
Work in process inventory	50,000
Finished goods inventory	75,000
Cost of goods sold	375,000

1. Prepare the journal entry to dispose of the variance balances. Assume that the total overhead variance is closed to Cost of Goods Sold.
2. Assuming the variance balances are significant, close the variance accounts for work in process inventory, finished goods inventory, and cost of goods sold.

Exercise 23-8. Management by Exception
(L.O. 6)

Falcetta-Frank Instruments, Inc., produces scientific apparatus for food inspection. During the past five years, the corporation has grown from having sales of $3,500,000 to having sales exceeding $25,000,000. Over 500 types of materials are used in the production process, and labor skills of more than 80 specialists are utilized. The controller has been asked by the vice president of finance to develop an improved method of controlling costs. A standard cost accounting system was introduced two years ago, but the numerous variances identified by the system are not systematically analyzed for cause. Rapid growth, which has caused many of the variances, is also the reason the controller's department had no time to concentrate on the variances.

1. Describe the concept of management by exception.
2. Discuss how management by exception might be employed by the controller of Falcetta-Frank Instruments, Inc.

Exercise 23-9. Evaluating Performance Through Variances
(L.O. 3, 7)

Evaluating the operating performance of the Morris Health Club is the responsibility of its controller, Charles Cheetham. The following information was available for March 19x8:

	Budget	Actual
Variable costs		
Operating labor	$ 5,760	$ 7,350
Utility costs	1,440	1,680
Repairs and maintenance	2,880	3,570
Fixed costs		
Depreciation, equipment	1,300	1,340
Rent expense	1,640	1,640
Other fixed costs	852	930
Totals	$13,872	$16,510

Normal operating hours call for six operators, working 160 hours each per month. During March seven operators worked an average of 150 hours each.

With this limited information, compute as many variances as possible for labor and overhead, and prepare a performance report for the month.

Interpreting Accounting Information

Internal Management Information: Nassau Realtors
(L.O. 2, 7)

Ms. Paluska, the managing partner of Nassau Realtors, Inc., received the performance report shown on page 888. The report showed the company had experienced its biggest year in home resales since it began operating fifteen years ago. The report indicates that although fees were over budget by $244,800, all cost categories were also over budget, cutting the increase in net income to only $18,470.

During 19x7 company sales personnel marketed 186 homes, averaging $155,000 per unit. Budgeted data were based on 150 homes sold at an average market value of $165,000. Selling fees for all realty work are 6 percent of the selling price. Data supporting the budget figures were as follows:

Commissions: Salespersons: 25 percent of total fees
Listing agents: 20 percent of total fees
Listing companies: 25 percent of total fees
(Thirty-five percent of homes sold by Nassau were listed by another company.)
Other variable expenses: Automobile expenses, $180 per sale
Advertising expenses, $420 per sale
Home repairs expenses, $230 per sale
Word processing expenses, $115 per sale
General overhead: 25 percent of total fees

Required

1. Recast the performance report, using a flexible budget based on the number of units sold.
2. Interpret the revised performance report for Ms. Paluska.

Nassau Realtors, Inc.
Performance Report
For the Year Ended December 31, 19x7

	Budget for the Year	Actual Fees and Costs	Variance Under (Over) Budget
Total Selling Fees	$1,485,000	$1,729,800	$(244,800)
Expenses			
Commissions			
Salespersons	$ 371,250	$ 432,450	$ (61,200)
Listing agents	297,000	345,960	(48,960)
Listing companies	129,938	151,358	(21,420)
Other variable expenses			
Automobile expenses	27,000	28,630	(1,630)
Advertising	63,000	72,940	(9,940)
Home repair expenses	34,500	43,110	(8,610)
Word processing expenses	17,250	19,880	(2,630)
General overhead expenses	371,250	443,190	(71,940)
Total expenses	$1,311,188	$1,537,518	$(226,330)
Net Income Before Taxes	$ 173,812	$ 192,282	$ (18,470)

Problem Set A

Problem 23A-1. Performance Analysis/ Management by Exception (L.O. 6, 7)

Management at Alpha Motor Assembly, Inc., just introduced a management by exception component into its standard costing system. For the first few months, the purchase and use of materials will be emphasized. Variances are considered significant, and they need special analysis for cause if they fall outside the following tolerances:

Price variance: + or − 5% of the item's total purchase price
Quantity variance: + or − 3% of the item's cost charged to Work in Process Inventory

During February the data shown on the top of the next page were generated:

Required

1. Prepare and complete a six-column analysis of these materials. Use the following column headings: Price Variance, Total Purchase Price, Percent of Variance, Quantity Variance, Cost of Materials Charged to Work in Process Inventory, and Percent of Variance.
2. Identify the variances to be analyzed for cause. Use the tolerances prescribed by management.
3. List three possible causes for each significant variance. Try identifying causes different from those in the book.

Type of Material	Quantities (Units)			Prices	
		Used			
	Purchased	Actual	Standard	Actual	Standard
Motor A	14,200	13,700	13,500	$112	$110
Motor B	7,410	6,300	6,250	181	185
Motor C	4,820	4,605	4,600	212	200
Casing I	8,900	6,924	6,900	46	45
Casing II	20,000	17,992	17,450	38	44
Electrical components	26,400	24,492	24,350	22	20
Wood base R	15,400	13,020	12,840	82	88
Wood base Q	8,200	7,210	7,200	89	92
Metal base	4,800	4,460	4,310	125	120
Hardware components	25,600	24,380	24,350	26	29

Problem 23A-2. Variance Review: Missing Information (L.O. 3)

Over- or underapplied overhead is the reason for analyzing overhead variances. These variances are interrelated. Howard Felt Corporation and Temple Company have standard costing systems. Each one uses the three-way approach to overhead variance analysis.

Required

For each company fill in the unknown amounts below by analyzing the data for each organization. Capacities are expressed in direct labor hours. Hint: Use the structure of Figure 23-3 as a guide to your analysis.

	Howard Felt Corporation	Temple Company
Actual direct labor hours	17,100	______
Standard hours allowed	17,500	8,800
Normal capacity in direct labor hours	______	9,000
Total overhead rate per direct labor hour	______	______
Standard variable overhead rate	$ 2.50	$ 1.80
Actual variable and fixed overhead	______	$43,850
Total overhead costs applied	______	$44,000
Budgeted fixed overhead	$76,500	______
Total overhead variance	______	______
Overhead spending variance	$ 700(F)	______
Overhead efficiency variance	______	$ 360(F)
Overhead volume variance	$ 2,250(F)	______

Problem 23A-3. Labor and Overhead Variance Analysis
(L.O. 3, 7)

Allied Discount Auto Repairs, Inc., is a high-volume business employing 125 mechanics in four locations. In order to charge discount rates, Allied is departmentalized. Standard costing is used for cost control purposes. The Overhaul/8 Department specializes in eight-cylinder engine overhauls. The following standards, which are in effect for the current period, cover the overhaul of an eight-cylinder engine:

Direct labor	
Senior mechanic:	
6.5 hours @ $14.20/hour	$ 92.30
Junior mechanic:	
12.4 hours @ $10.50/hour	130.20
Shop overhead	
Variable overhead:	
18.9 hours @ $19/hour	359.10
Fixed overhead:	
18.9 hours @ $8/hour	151.20
Standard cost per overhaul	$732.80

During September, the Overhaul/8 Department incurred the following costs:

Direct labor	
Senior mechanics:	
1,057 hours @ $14/hour	$14,798
Junior mechanics:	
1,963 hours @ $11/hour	21,593
Shop overhead	
Variable shop overhead	54,100
Fixed shop overhead	22,200

Normal capacity for the Overhaul/8 Department per month is 140 jobs. During September, 151 complete overhauls were achieved. Budgeted fixed-shop overhead is $21,168 per month.

Required

1. Compute the standard hours allowed for September for senior mechanics and junior mechanics.
2. What was the total actual labor cost and overhead cost for September? What was the total standard cost (labor and overhead) charged to the Overhaul/8 Department for the month?
3. Compute the direct labor rate and efficiency variances for senior mechanics and junior mechanics.
4. Compute the shop overhead variances for September, using the two-variance approach and the three-variance approach.
5. Identify possible causes for each variance, and develop possible solutions to the causes.

Problem 23A-4. Direct Materials, Direct Labor, and Factory Overhead Variances
(L.O. 3)

During 19x8 Navas Laboratories, Inc., researched and perfected a cure for the common cold. Called "Cold-Gone," the series of five tablets sells for $9.50 per package. Standard costs for this product were developed in late 19x8 for use in 19x9. The costs per package were as follows: (a) chemical ingredients, 5 ounces at $.20/ounce; (b) materials for a safety package, $.80; (c) direct labor, .2 hours at $10/hour; (d) standard variable factory overhead, $2.00/direct labor hour; and (e) standard fixed factory overhead, $3.00/direct labor hour.

The first quarter of 19x9, the normal season for colds, saw demand for the new product rise above the wildest expectations of management. During these three months the company produced and sold five million packages of Cold-Gone. Production for the first week in April revealed the following: (a) 40,000 packages were produced; (b) 205,000 ounces of chemicals were used, costing $36,900; (c) materials for 40,400 packages were used, costing $34,340; (d) 8,140 direct labor hours cost $79,772; (e) total variable factory overhead cost, $15,650; and (f) total fixed factory overhead cost, $25,400. Budgeted fixed factory overhead for the period was $23,400.

Required

Compute (1) all direct materials price variances; (2) all direct materials quantity variances; (3) direct labor rate variance; (4) direct labor efficiency variance; (5) controllable overhead variance; and (6) overhead volume variance.

Problem 23A-5. Comprehensive: Standard Cost Journal Entry Analysis
(L.O. 3, 4, 5)

Westchester Lamp Company manufactures several lines of home and business lights and lighting systems. Mahogany table lamps are one of the company's most popular product lines. Since this wood is difficult to work with, special woodcarvers are employed. Deborah Goorbin, controller, has developed the following cost, quantity, and time standards for one table lamp for the current year:

Direct materials: wood, 10″ × 8″ × 18″ block of mahogany, $16.00; electrical fixture and cord, $6.50; and shade and mounting, $8.20

Direct labor: woodcarvers, 6 hours @ $12.50/hour, and assemblers and packers, 1.2 hours @ $8.00/hour

Factory overhead: variable rate, $2.60/direct labor hour, and fixed rate, $3.10/direct labor hour.

Mahogany table lamps sell for $350 each.

Selected transactions for August 19x8 are described as follows:

August 3 Purchased 700 blocks of mahogany for $11,060 on account.

4 Requisitioned 60 blocks of wood into production for Order #16, calling for 50 lamps.

5 Purchased 500 electrical fixture kits for $3,300 and 600 lamp shades and mountings for $4,950 on account.

7 Requisitioned 54 electrical fixture kits and 50 lamp shades and mountings into production for the same order of 50 lamps.

14 Semimonthly payroll was paid, and it included the following wages for Order #16: woodcarvers, 310 hours, $3,720, and assemblers and packers, 66 hours, $561. These labor efforts completed Order #16.

14 Factory overhead was applied to Order #16 units worked on during the payroll period.

16 Requisitioned 74 blocks of wood into production for Order #26, totaling 70 lamps.
19 Requisitioned 78 electrical fixture kits and 75 lamp shades and mountings into production for Order #26.
30 Labor for the previous half month was paid. Labor costs associated with Order #26 included: woodcarvers, 430 hours, $5,246, and assemblers and packers, 90 hours, $765.
30 Factory overhead was applied to work performed on Order #26 during the past two weeks.
30 Orders #16 and #26 were completed and transferred to Finished Goods Inventory.
31 Orders #16 and #26 were shipped to customers at the contracted price.

Beginning inventory information included: Materials Inventory Control, $31,410; Work in Process Inventory Control, $0; and Finished Goods Inventory Control, $14,600.

During August actual factory overhead for these two orders was $2,100, variable, and $2,850, fixed. All actual overhead costs were recorded in the Factory Overhead Control account. Budgeted fixed factory overhead was $2,697 for August.

Required

1. Compute the standard cost for one mahogany table lamp.
2. Prepare the entries necessary to record the above transactions, and show calculations for each variance. For the direct labor entries, record only the distribution of direct labor to Work in Process Inventory Control.*
3. Analyze the factory overhead accounts, and compute the controllable and volume variances.
4. Prepare the entry to dispose of the overhead accounts and record the overhead variances.
5. Close all variance account balances to the Cost of Goods Sold account.

Problem Set B

Problem 23B-1. Performance Analysis/ Management by Exception
(L.O. 6, 7)

Top management at the Jagat Jain Hotel in Niagara, New York, is interested in the effectiveness of the new management by exception program in their standard costing system. Past experience indicates that analyzing all variances is too cumbersome. In the new program the only labor variances considered significant enough to need special analysis for cause are those falling outside the tolerances given below.

Rate variance: + or − 8% of the total standard labor cost for that category
Efficiency variance: + or − 10% of the total standard labor cost for that category

During March the following data were generated:

* Round answers to nearest dollar.

Labor Category	Labor Hours		Labor Rates	
	Actual	Standard	Actual	Standard
Bellmen	1,040	960	$ 5.80	$ 6.00
Cashiers	710	640	11.20	11.00
Registration clerks	1,570	1,440	9.40	9.00
Maids	5,240	4,800	4.80	4.50
Room service	1,390	1,280	5.00	5.50
Maintenance	1,080	960	6.40	7.00
Catering	3,390	3,200	7.70	7.50
Conference sales staff	910	800	11.20	10.00
Parking attendants	1,880	1,600	4.20	4.00

Required

1. Prepare and complete a five-column analysis, using the following column headings: Standard Labor Cost, Rate Variance, Percent of Variance, Efficiency Variance, and Percent of Variance.
2. Identify the variances to be analyzed for cause. Use the tolerances prescribed by management.
3. List three possible causes for each significant variance. Try identifying some causes different from those in the book.

Problem 23B-2. Variance Review: Missing Information
(L.O. 3)

Overhead variances are interrelated. The Meltzer Company and the Taylor Corporation both use standard costing systems. These systems depend on a standard overhead rate when overhead costs are applied to units produced.

Required

Fill in the unknown amounts below by analyzing the data given for each company. Capacities are expressed in direct labor hours. Hint: Use Figure 23-3 as guide.

	Meltzer Company	Taylor Corporation
Actual direct labor hours	7,500	4,200
Standard hours allowed	______	4,100
Normal capacity in direct labor hours	______	______
Total overhead rate per direct labor hour	$ 3.20	______
Standard variable overhead rate	$ 1.00	$ 4.00
Actual variable and fixed overhead	$26,200	______
Total overhead costs applied	$25,600	______
Budgeted fixed overhead	______	$24,000
Total overhead variance	______	$ 600(F)
Overhead spending variance	______	______
Overhead efficiency variance	______	$ 400(U)
Overhead volume variance	$ 440(F)	______
Controllable overhead variance	______	$ 8,200(U)

Problem 23B-3. Labor and Overhead Variance Analysis
(L.O. 3, 7)

Massasoit Secretarial Service operates a legal transcript department for their clients. Two people, a legal paraprofessional and a typist are assigned to each case. Based on past history a price is quoted for each job. This price is calculated on the basis of expected hours of work. A standard cost system is employed for cost control purposes. The following standards are in effect for July for each case:

Labor	
Legal paraprofessional:	
25 hours at $14/hour	$ 350.00
Typist:	
40 hours at $9.50/hour	380.00
Overhead	
Variable overhead:	
65 hours at $8/hour	520.00
Fixed overhead:	
65 hours at $5.40/hour	351.00
Standard cost/case	$ 1,601.00

During October the Transcript Department incurred the following costs:

Labor	
Legal paraprofessional:	
890 hours at $15/hour	$13,350.00
Typist:	
1,360 hours at $9/hour	12,240.00
Overhead	
Variable overhead	18,550.00
Fixed overhead	11,990.00

During July work on 35 full (equivalent) cases was completed and billed. Normal capacity is thought to be 32 cases per month. Budgeted fixed overhead is $11,232.

Required

1. Compute the standard hours allowed for July for legal paraprofessionals and typists.
2. What were the total actual labor cost and actual overhead cost for July? How much labor cost should have been incurred? How much overhead cost was applied to the case accounts during July?
3. Compute the labor rate and efficiency variances for legal paraprofessionals and for typists.
4. Compute the overhead variances for July, using the two-variance approach and the three-variance approach.
5. Identify possible causes for each variance, and develop possible solutions.

Problem 23B-4. Direct Materials, Direct Labor, and Factory Overhead Variances
(L.O. 3)

Monroe Shoe Company has a Sandal Division that produces a line of all-vinyl thongs. Each pair of thongs calls for .2 meter of vinyl material that costs $2.00 per meter. Standard direct labor hours and cost per pair of thongs are .2 hour and $1.25 (.2 hour × $6.25 per hour), respectively. The division's current standard variable overhead rate is $1.20 per direct labor hour, and the standard fixed overhead rate is $.70 per direct labor hour.

In August the Sandal Division manufactured and sold 50,000 pairs of thongs. During the month 9,980 meters of vinyl material were used, at a total cost of

$20,958. The total actual overhead costs for August were $19,250. The total number of direct labor hours worked were 10,120, and August's factory payroll for direct labor was $60,720. Normal monthly capacity for the year was set at 48,000 pairs of thongs.

Required

Compute: (1) direct materials price variance; (2) direct materials quantity variance; (3) direct labor rate variance; (4) direct labor efficiency variance; (5) controllable overhead variance; and (6) overhead volume variance. Show checks of your computations.

Problem 23B-5. Comprehensive: Standard Cost Journal Entry Analysis
(L.O. 3, 4, 5)

Plucinski Bottle Company makes wine bottles for many of the major wineries in California's Napa and Sonoma valleys as well as for wineries in the grape growing regions around Cupertino and Santa Cruz, California. Ken Fredonia, as controller of the company, installed these cost, quantity, and time standards for 19x8:

Direct materials: 2 five-gallon pails of a special silicon dioxide and phosphorus pentoxide-based compound per one gross (144) of bottles; cost, $8 per pail
Direct labor: Forming Department—.2 hour per gross at $8.80 per direct labor hour; Finishing/Polishing Department—.1 hour per gross at $7.40 per direct labor hour
Factory overhead: variable—$2.20 per direct labor hour; fixed—$1.80 per direct labor hour

The direct materials are added at the beginning of the forming process. Much of the machinery is automated, and the compound is heated, mixed, and poured into molds in a short time. Once cooled, the new bottles move via conveyor belt to the Finishing/Polishing Department. Again, the process is highly automated. Machines scrape off excess material on the bottles and then polish all outside and inside surfaces. After polishing, the bottles are fed into large cartons for shipping to customers.

During March 19x8 the following selected transactions occurred:

March 2 Purchased 12,000 pails of compound at $7.80 per pail on account.
3 Requisitioned 2,612 pails of compound into production for an order calling for 1,300 gross of wine bottles.
6 Requisitioned 5,880 pails of compound into production for an order of 2,900 gross of wine bottles.
12 Transferred 3,400 gross of bottles to finished goods inventory.
15 Requisitioned 4,630 pails of compound into production for an order calling for 2,300 gross of wine bottles.
16 For the two-week period ending March 14, actual labor costs included 860 direct labor hours in the Forming Department at $8.50 per hour and 410 direct labor hours in the Finishing/Polishing Department at $7.50 per hour. During the pay period, 4,200 gross of good bottles were produced.
16 Factory overhead was applied to units worked on during the previous two weeks.
18 Purchased 9,000 pails of compound at $8.10 per pail on account.
20 Requisitioned 6,960 pails of compound into production for an order of 3,500 gross of wine bottles.
28 Transferred 6,000 gross of bottles to finished goods inventory.

30 For the two-week period ending March 28, actual labor costs included 1,040 direct labor hours in the Forming Department at $9.00 per hour and 550 direct labor hours in the Finishing/Polishing Department at $7.50 per hour. During the pay period 5,300 gross of *good* bottles were produced.

30 Factory overhead was applied to units worked on during the two-week period.

31 During March, 9,800 gross of wine bottles were sold on account and shipped to customers. Selling price for these bottles was $36 per gross.

Actual factory overhead for February was $6,350 in variable and $5,300 in fixed overhead. These amounts were recorded in the Factory Overhead Control account. Budgeted fixed factory overhead was $5,000 for March. Beginning inventory information included: Materials Inventory, $21,360; Work in Process Inventory, $10,064; and Finished Goods Inventory, $17,760.

Required

1. Compute the standard cost per gross of wine bottles.
2. Prepare the entries necessary to record the above transactions, showing calculations for each variance. For the direct labor entries, record only the distribution of direct labor to Work in Process Inventory Control.
3. Analyze the factory overhead accounts, and compute the controllable and volume variances.
4. Prepare the entry to dispose of the overhead accounts, and record the overhead variances.
5. Close all variance account balances to the Cost of Goods Sold account.

Management Decision Case

Taube Aquatic Corporation
(L.O. 3, 6)

Taube Aquatic Corporation produces water-sports gear, including safety cushions, water skis, towing lines, goggles, and snorkeling equipment. Much of the operation involves assembling parts purchased from outside vendors. However, all rubber parts are produced by the company in the Shaping Department. Face masks and goggles are assembled in the Face Wear Department, using purchased clear-plastic lenses and fastener devices. Rubber mask casings and head straps are transferred in from the Shaping Department. Anthony Zazzara is in charge of the Shaping Department, and Jo Ann Wolfe supervises the Face Wear Department.

At the end of April 19x8, the Accounting Department developed the performance reports for the two departments shown on the next page. When asked to comment on his performance, Zazzara stated, "Compared with the Face Wear Department, my performance is very good. Most of the $1,670(U) net variance arose because of two new, inexperienced workers, who increased the average labor hours for the department. Since overhead is applied based on direct labor hours, an unfavorable controllable variance was expected."

Ms. Wolfe was quite upset at Mr. Zazzara's comments. She said, "First of all, one of the variances is in error. The standard for direct labor usage should be $9,020, since 1,100 standard hours allowed were earned at an $8.20 standard labor rate. Also, the additional 100 standard hours allowed would cause the controllable variance to decrease by $420 because of the standard variable overhead rate of $4.20 per direct labor hour." She continued, "Now let's focus on the large unfavorable quantity and efficiency variances. All my production problems can be traced to the poor quality of mask casings coming from the Shaping Department. Poor workmanship meant dozens of spoiled mask assemblies, and my people had to work overtime to meet customer orders for the period. Had we had decent mask casings, we would have had an overall favorable performance for the period. Either the quality of the mask casings improves or I will ask to have them purchased from an outside vendor in the future."

Required

1. Recompute the variances and the performance report for the Face Wear Department. Assume Ms. Wolfe is correct.
2. Which supervisor's performance should be further analyzed? Why?
3. If you were vice president of production, what steps would you take to correct the situation? Develop a plan.

Taube Aquatic Corporation
Shaping Department
Performance Report—Cost Variance Analysis
For the Month Ended April 30, 19x8

Supervisor: Anthony Zazzara

	Costs		Variance	
	Standard	**Actual**	**Amount**	**Type**
Direct materials used	$17,800	$18,000	$ 200(U)	Quantity variance
Direct labor usage	9,640	10,120	860(F)	Rate variance
			1,340(U)	Efficiency variance
Factory overhead	6,400	7,390	990(U)	Controllable variance
Totals	$33,840	$35,510	$1,670(U)	

Taube Aquatic Corporation
Face Wear Department
Performance Report—Cost Variance Analysis
For the Month Ended April 30, 19x8

Supervisor: Jo Ann Wolfe

	Costs		Variance	
	Standard	**Actual**	**Amount**	**Type**
Direct materials used	$12,600	$16,450	$3,850(U)	Quantity variance
Direct labor usage	8,200	11,580	20(F)	Rate variance
			3,400(U)	Efficiency variance
Factory overhead	5,460	7,220	1,760(U)	Controllable variance
Totals	$26,260	$35,250	$8,990(U)	

CALDWELL NEEDLES ANDERSON

PART SEVEN ACCOUNTING FOR MANAGEMENT DECISION MAKING

The third aspect of management accounting, providing information to support management decision making, is the focal point of Part Seven of this text. Our basic philosophy is that pricing decisions, transfer pricing policies, short-run decision analyses, and capital expenditure decision analyses are fundamental applications of management accounting concepts and techniques. Pricing decisions are based on cost analyses as well as on external market factors. Short-run decisions require a thorough knowledge of cost and revenue activities. Capital expenditure decisions are made following extensive analyses of future cost and revenue projections.

Chapter 24 exposes the difficulties of setting an accurate price for a good or a service. External as well as internal factors are used in the price setting process. Transfer pricing can be either cost- or market-based. Transfer prices are created prices that do cause internal employee problems when used to evaluate performance.

Chapter 25 introduces the concepts of relevant decision information, variable costing, contribution margin reporting, and incremental decision analysis. Examples of short-run decisions include make or buy, special order, scarce resource/sales mix, elimination of unprofitable segments, and sell or process further considerations.

Chapter 26 first looks at the steps in the capital expenditure decision process. Then the techniques of accounting rate of return, payback period, and net present value are discussed. The concept of the time value of money and income tax influences on the capital expenditure decision analysis conclude the chapter.

CHAPTER 24 PRICING DECISIONS, INCLUDING TRANSFER PRICING

LEARNING OBJECTIVES

1. Describe traditional economic pricing concepts.
2. Identify external and internal factors on which prices are based.
3. State the objectives managers use to establish prices of goods and services.
4. Create prices by applying the methods and tools of price determination.
5. Define and discuss transfer pricing.
6. Distinguish between a cost-based transfer price and a market-based transfer price.
7. Develop a transfer price.
8. Measure a manager's performance by using transfer prices.

Deciding on an appropriate price is among a manager's most difficult day-to-day decisions. Such decisions affect the long-term life of any profit-oriented enterprise. To stay in business, a company's selling price must (1) be equal to or lower than the competition's price; (2) be acceptable to the customer; and (3) recover all costs incurred in bringing the product or service to a marketable condition. If a manager deviates from these three pricing rules, there must be a specific short-run objective. Breaking these pricing rules for a long period will force a company into bankruptcy.

Transfer pricing involves the setting of artificial prices on goods moving from one profit center to another within a company. Because such prices are used only for internal decisions and performance evaluation, they are unknown to the outside world. A set of rules different from those used to set external prices govern the development of transfer prices. Transfer prices force segments to compete for a company's resources and influence managers' behavior. Although not as critical to a company's future as external prices, transfer prices can influence operating efficiency and profitability. On completion of this chapter, you should be able to meet the learning objectives listed on the left.

The Pricing Decision

The process of establishing a correct price is more of an art than a science. True, there are many mechanical approaches to price setting, and each produces a price. But who knows if that price is the most correct? Six pricing methods may well produce six prices. The art of price setting stems from the ability to read the marketplace and anticipate customer reaction to a product and its price. Pricing methods do not provide a manager with the ability to react to the market. Much of market savvy is developed through years of experience in dealing with customers and products in an industry. Intuition also plays a major role in price setting.

So why study pricing methods then? The methods discussed in the following pages illustrate the process of developing a specific price under defined circumstances or objectives. Some of the methods provide the manager with the minimum price he or she can charge and still make a profit. Other prices are based on the competition and market conditions. The concept of setting prices according to "whatever the market will bear" will produce still another figure.

In making a final pricing decision, the manager must consider all these projected prices. The more data the manager has, the more he or she will be able to make a well-informed decision. But remember, pricing methods and approaches yield only decision data. The manager must still select the appropriate price and be evaluated on the consequences.

The Art of Setting a Price

Maison & Jardin is a gourmet restaurant in Altamonte Springs, Florida. Besides excellent food, the establishment boasts of fine wines. Among its selections of California red wine is a 1982 Cabernet Sauvignon from Shafer Vineyards in Napa Valley, California. The restaurant's normal charge for a bottle of this wine is $18.50. However, for one or more reasons, this wine is being featured as the "special selection of the month." Perhaps there is an oversupply of the wine, the wine has matured and must be sold, or the vineyard is running a special promotion.

Listed below are prices the restaurant is now charging for this wine.

	Price per Bottle
Purchased by the glass, $5.25 (4 glasses per bottle)	$21.00
Purchased by the bottle with your meal	16.75
Purchased by the bottle to take home	11.95
Purchased by the case to take home ($119.50 ÷ 12)	9.96

What is the correct price for a bottle of this wine?

The listed prices are all appropriate based on differing circumstances. The $18.50 price is based on the cost of the bottle, reputation of the vineyard, prices of wines of comparable quality, vintage (1982), mixture of varietal grapes, and alcohol level.

Once a bottle of quality red wine has been opened, the wine begins to oxidize. It then spoils in two or three hours. Therefore, when wine is sold by the glass, the restaurant risks losing part of the bottle to spoilage. Thus, $5.25 per glass seems appropriate under the circumstances.

To promote a specific product, many businesses run special sales. A restaurant is no different. This month Maison & Jardin's management decided to reduce the bottle's price by $1.75 to lure customers into trying this product with their meal.

Although the take-home feature is unusual, the pricing is appropriate. Part of the cost for a bottle of wine served with a meal is for the cost of serving it. The wine steward must fetch the bottle, bring a cooling device for white wine to the table, uncork the bottle, decant a bottle of older wine, present the wine for customer approval, and continue pouring the wine during the meal. In the example, the restaurant reduced the price of a take-home bottle by $4.80. This means the cost of serving a bottle of wine and the restaurant's profit margin on this labor is somewhere around $5.00 per bottle. And that price has been included in the price shown on the wine list.

Finally, consider the case price. On a per bottle basis, the case price is $1.99 less than purchasing it by the bottle to take home. This reduction is known as quantity discounting, a concept widely followed in the free enterprise system. As with the take-home bottle price, reduced handling costs support the use of quantity discount pricing.

Pricing is a fascinating topic to study and learn. It is the key to a successful business. Any entrepreneur is a student of pricing during his or her entire career. The ability to set the one perfect price will never be mastered, for changes in circumstances will always justify a different price. Please keep this truth in mind as you begin this study of pricing decisions.

Traditional Economic Pricing Concepts

OBJECTIVE 1
Describe traditional economic pricing concepts

The traditional approach to pricing is based on microeconomic theory. Pricing has a major role in the concepts underlying the theory of the firm. At the base of this concept, the firm is in business to maximize profits. Although each product has its own set of revenues and costs, microeconomic theory states that profit will be maximized when the difference between total revenues and total costs is the greatest. Recall the discussion of break-even analysis in Chapter 19. Figure 19-3 (page 707) illustrated a typical break-even chart. To the left of the break-even point of 1,000 units, the company will lose money, since total costs exceed total revenues. To the right of the break-even point, profit will be realized, since total revenues are greater than total costs. But where is the point at which profits are maximized, and what is the role of pricing in this discussion?

Total Revenue and Total Cost Curves. By looking at Figure 19-3, you see that the outlook for profits is a bit misleading. The profit area seems to increase significantly as more and more products are sold. Therefore, it seems that if the company could produce an infinite number of products, maximum profit would be realized. But this situation is untrue, and microeconomic theory tells you why.

Figure 24-1A shows the economist's view of the break-even chart. On it there are two break-even points, between which is a large space labeled *profit*. Notice that the total revenue line is curved rather than straight. The theory is that as one markets a product, price reductions will be necessary to sell additional units. Competition and other factors will cause such decreases. Total revenue will continue to increase, but the rate of increase will diminish as more units are sold. Therefore, the total revenue line curves toward the right.

Costs react in an opposite fashion. Over the assumed relevant range in Chapter 19, variable and fixed costs were fairly predictable, with fixed costs remaining constant and variable costs being the same per unit. The result was a straight line for total costs. Following microeconomic theory costs per unit will increase over time, since fixed costs will change. As one moves into different relevant ranges, such fixed costs as supervision and depreciation increase. In addition, as the company pushes for more and more products from limited facilities, repair and maintenance costs

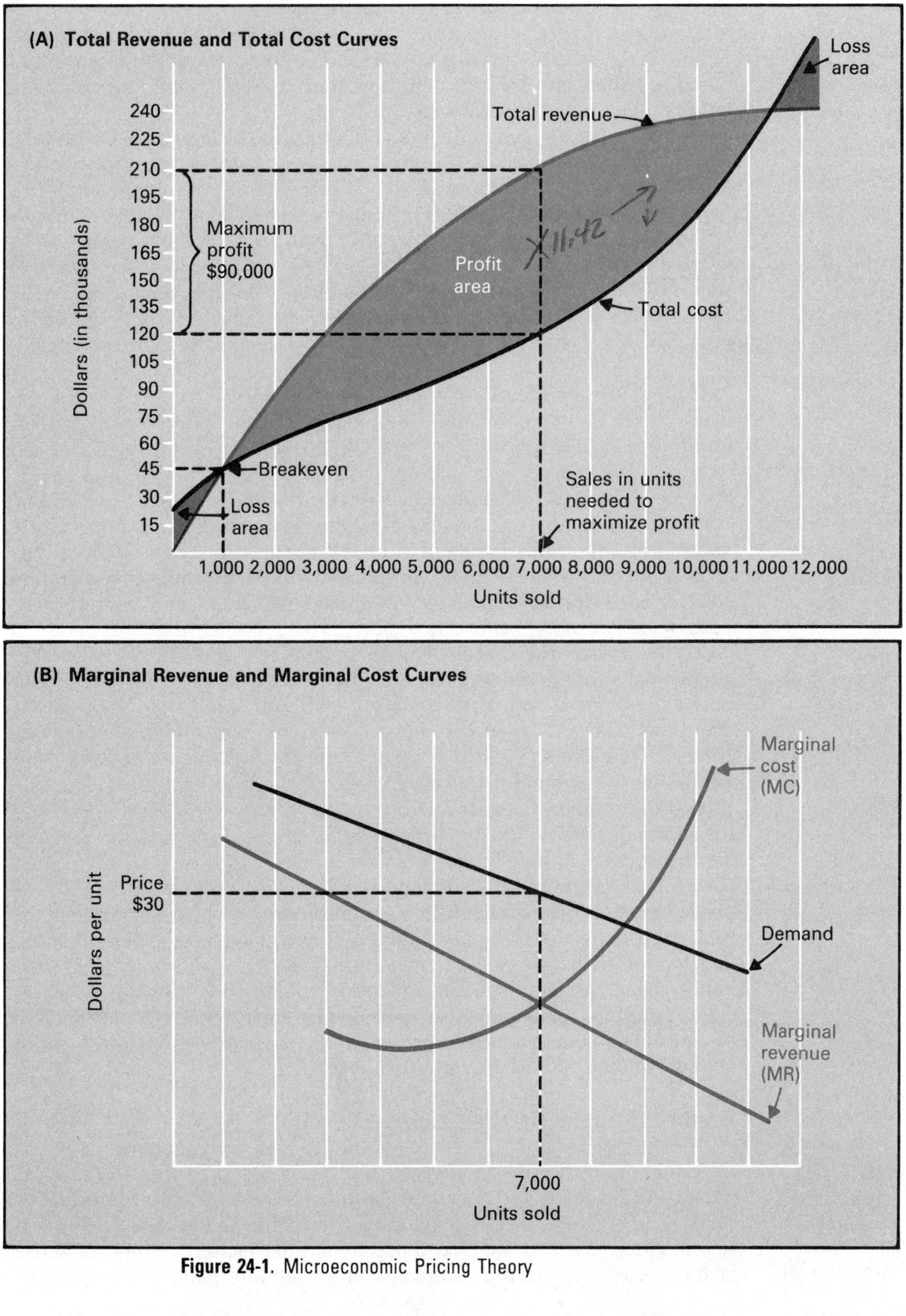

(A) Total Revenue and Total Cost Curves

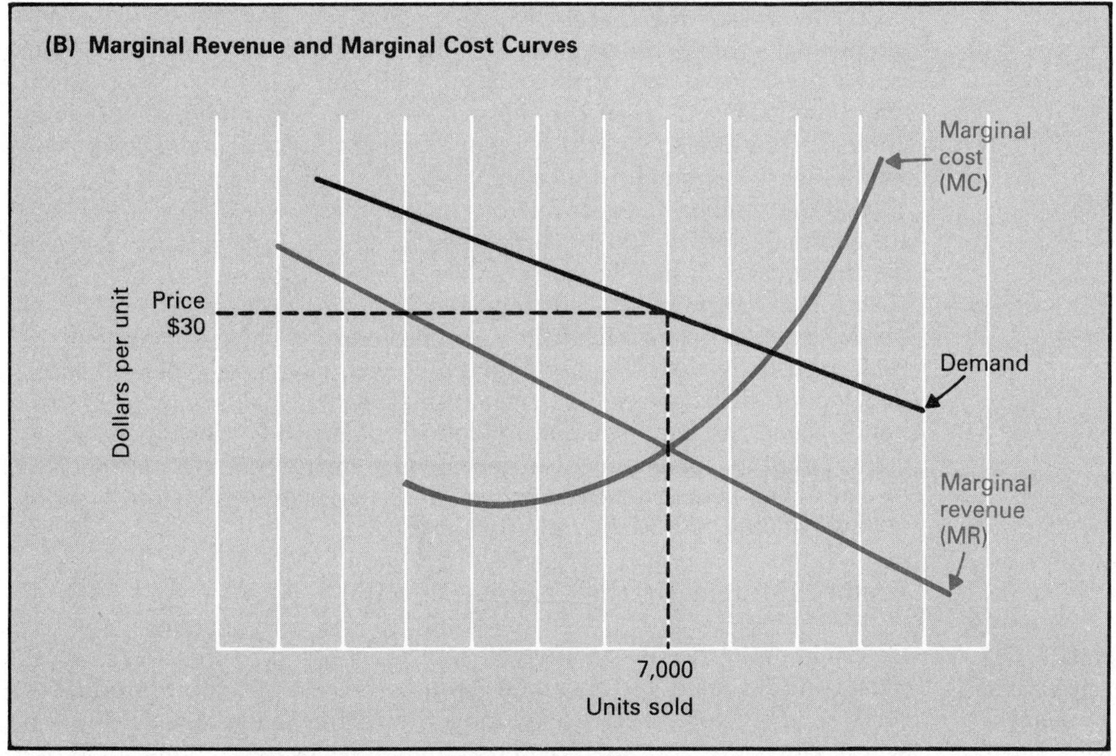

Figure 24-1. Microeconomic Pricing Theory

increase. And as the push from management increases, total costs rise at an accelerating rate per unit. The result is that the total cost line in Figure 24-1A begins curving upward. The total revenue line and total cost lines then cross again. Beyond that crossing point the company suffers a loss on additional sales.

Profits are maximized at the point at which the difference between total revenue and total cost is the greatest. In Figure 24-1A, this point is assumed to be 7,000 units of sales. At that sales level, total revenue will be $210,000; total cost, $120,000; and profit, $90,000. In theory if one additional unit is sold, profit per unit will drop, because total cost is rising at a faster rate than total revenues. As you can see, if the company sells 11,000 units, total profits will be almost entirely eaten up by the rising costs. Therefore, in the example, 7,000 sales units is the optimum operating level, and the price charged at that level is the correct price.

Marginal Revenue and Marginal Cost Curves. Economists use the concepts of marginal revenue and marginal cost to help pinpoint an optimum price for a good or service. **Marginal revenue** is the change in total revenue caused by a one-unit change in output. **Marginal cost** is the change in total cost caused by a one-unit change in output. Graphic curves for marginal revenue and marginal cost are derived by measuring and plotting the rate of change in total revenue and total cost at various activity levels. Were you to compute marginal revenue and marginal cost for each unit sold in the example and plot them onto a graph, the lines would resemble those in Figure 24-1B. Notice that the marginal cost line crosses the marginal revenue line at 7,000 units. After that point total profits will decrease as additional units are sold. Marginal cost will exceed marginal revenue for each unit sold over 7,000. Profit will be maximized when the marginal revenue and marginal cost lines intersect. By projecting this point onto the product's demand curve, you can locate the optimal price, which is $30 per unit.

If all information used in microeconomic theory were certain, picking the optimal price would be fairly easy. But most information used in the previous analysis relied on projected amounts for unit sales, product costs, and revenues. Just computing total demand for a product or service from such data is difficult. And projecting repair and maintenance costs is usually done by using unsupported estimates. Nevertheless, developing such an analysis usually makes the analyst aware of cost patterns and the unanticipated influences of demand. For this reason it is important for management to consider the microeconomic approach to pricing when setting product prices. But information from this type of analysis should not be the only data relied on.

Factors Influencing the Pricing Decision

OBJECTIVE 2
Identify external and internal factors on which prices are based

Determining a price is an involved and difficult procedure. A manager must consider many factors when creating the best price for a product or service. Therefore, before exploring the methods used to compute a selling price, we will analyze those influential factors. Some of those factors are external to the company; others are internal.

External Factors. Each product or service has a targeted market that determines demand. Strong consideration should be given to this market before choosing a final price. External factors to be considered in setting a price are summarized in Table 24-1. Those factors include the following considerations:

1. What is total demand for the item?
2. Are there one or several competing products in the marketplace?
3. What prices are being charged by others already selling the item?
4. Do customers want the least expensive product or are they more interested in quality than in price?
5. Is the product so unique or new that the company is the only source in the marketplace?

All these questions should be answered by the person developing the price. If competition is keen and the quality is similar, market price will set the ceiling for any new entry into the market. If, however, a product is unique or new, a more flexible pricing environment exists. Customers' needs and desires are important for any new product. If quality is of primary importance, as is the case for top-of-the-line automobiles, then emphasis should be placed on using quality inputs. The price will be adjusted upward accordingly.

In summary: it is important to know the marketplace, including customers' needs and the competition, before determining a final price.

Table 24-1. Factors to Consider When Setting a Price

External Factors:

Total demand for product or service
Number of competing products or services
Quality of competing products or services
Current prices of competing products or services
Customers' preferences for quality versus price
Sole source versus heavy competition
Seasonal demand or continual demand
Life of product or service

Internal Factors:

Cost of product or service
  Variable costs
  Full absorption costs
  Total costs
Price geared toward return on investment
Loss leader or main product
Quality of materials and labor inputs
Labor intensive or automated process
Markup percentage updated
Usage of scarce resources

Internal Factors. Several internal factors also influence the price of a good or service, and these are also summarized in Table 24-1. Basic among these factors is an item's cost. What cost basis should be considered when determining price—variable costs, full absorption costs, or total costs? Should the price be based on a desired rate of return on assets? Is the product a loss leader, created to lure customers into considering additional, more expensive products? Where should one draw the line on the quality of materials and supplies? Is the product labor intensive or can it be produced by using automated equipment? If markup percentages are used to establish prices, were they updated to reflect current operating conditions? Are the company's scarce resources being overtaxed by introducing an additional product or service, and does the price reflect this use of scarce resources?

As with external factors each of these questions should be answered before a manager establishes a price for a product or service. Underlying every pricing decision is the fact that all costs incurred must be recovered in the long run or the company will no longer be in business.

Pricing Policy Objectives

OBJECTIVE 3
State the objectives managers use to establish prices of goods and services

The long-run objectives of a company should include a pricing policy. Such policies differentiate one company from another. For example, consider the pricing policies of Mercedes and Ford or Neiman-Marcus and K-Mart. All four companies are successful, but their pricing policies are quite different. Of primary importance in setting company objectives is identifying the market being served and meeting the needs of that market. Possible pricing policy objectives include

1. Identifying and adhering to short-run and long-run pricing strategies
2. Maximizing profits
3. Maintaining or gaining market share
4. Setting socially responsible prices
5. Maintaining stated rate of return on investment
6. Ensuring prices support trend of total sales increases

Pricing strategies depend on many factors and conditions. Companies producing standard items for a competitive marketplace will have different pricing strategies from firms making custom-designed items. In a competitive market pricing can be reduced to gain market share by displacing sales of competing companies. Continuous upgrading of a product or service can help in this area. The company making custom-designed items can be more conservative in its pricing strategy.

Maximizing profits has always been considered the underlying objective of any pricing policy. Although still a dominant factor in price setting, profit maximization has been tempered in recent years by other more socially acceptable goals. Maintaining or gaining market share is closely related to pricing strategies. However, market share is important only if sales are profitable. To increase market share by reducing prices below cost can be disastrous unless this move is accompanied by other compensating objectives and goals.

Prices have a social effect, and companies are concerned about their public image. Recall the discussion about Mercedes, Ford, Neiman-

Marcus, and K-Mart. Does each one have an individual image in your mind? And are prices not a part of that image? Other social concerns, such as legal constraints and ethical considerations, also affect many companies' pricing policies.

Other pricing policy objectives include maintaining a minimum return on investment and concentrating on continuous sales growth. Return on investment involves markup percentages designed to provide a buffer between costs and prices. Such an objective is linked closely with the profit maximization objective. Maintaining a continuous sales growth is important for several reasons. First, it provides management with a strong measure of performance for shareholders. Second, sales growth can be used to measure whether market share is increasing. Finally, such a policy provides managers with yearly incentives and targets.

Pricing Methods

OBJECTIVE 4 Create prices by applying the methods and tools of price determination

There are as many pricing methods in business as there are people developing prices. And although managers may use one or two traditional approaches, at some point they must deviate from those approaches and use their experience.

Several pricing methods are available that can be adopted by the pricing manager. A good starting point is for a manager to develop a price based on the cost of producing a good or service. Here, four methods based on cost will be discussed: (1) variable cost pricing; (2) gross margin pricing; (3) profit margin pricing; and (4) return on assets pricing. Remember that in a competitive environment, market prices and conditions also influence price. However, when prices do not cover a company's costs, the company will fail in the long run.

To illustrate the four methods of cost-base pricing, our example will use data on the Ron Jones Company. The Ron Jones Company assembles parts purchased from outside vendors into an Electric Car-Wax Buffer. Total costs and unit costs incurred in the previous accounting period to produce 14,750 wax buffers were as follows:

	Total Costs	Unit Costs
Variable production costs		
Materials and parts	$ 88,500	$ 6.00
Direct labor	66,375	4.50
Variable factory overhead	44,250	3.00
Total variable production costs	$199,125	$13.50
Fixed factory overhead	$154,875	$10.50
Selling, general, & administrative expenses		
Selling expenses	$ 73,750	$ 5.00
General expenses	36,875	2.50
Administrative expenses	22,125	1.50
Total selling, general, & administrative, expenses	$132,750	$ 9.00
Total costs and expenses	$486,750	$33.00

No changes in unit costs are expected this period. Desired profit for the period is $110,625. The company uses assets totaling $921,875 in producing the wax buffers. A 12 percent return on these assets is expected.

Variable Cost Pricing. One approach to cost-based pricing is to establish selling prices at a certain percentage above each item's variable production costs. This approach is called **variable cost pricing.** Basing a pricing decision on variable costs traceable to a product is useful if: (1) the amount of assets attributable to each product in a company's line of products is similar and (2) if the ratio of variable production costs to remaining operating costs is similar for each type of product. As in all cost-based methods for determining price, the method must attach a fair share of total costs to each product. In the case of variable cost pricing, the following formulas are used:

$$\text{Markup percentage} = \frac{\text{desired profit} + \text{total fixed production costs} + \text{total selling, general, \& administrative expenses}}{\text{total variable production costs}}$$

$$\text{Variable cost-based price} = \text{variable production costs per unit} + (\text{markup percentage} \times \text{variable production costs per unit})$$

In the markup percentage formula, the numerator is composed of all costs, expenses, and targeted profit that must be recovered by the selling price over and above variable production costs. By adding together desired profit; total fixed production costs; and total selling, general, and administrative costs in the numerator, the resulting markup factor forces these items to be considered in any decision on selling price. The denominator is the total variable production costs, since this is the amount on which the markup factor is being based.

Once the markup percentage is computed, an item's selling price can be determined. The second formula above illustrates this process. After calculating a product's variable production costs, one multiplies the markup percentage by the variable production costs per unit. The markup is then added to a unit's variable production costs to arrive at the selling price.

To examine this process, data from the Ron Jones Company will be used. The formulas and computations are shown below.

$$\text{Markup percentage} = \frac{\$110{,}625 + \$154{,}875 + \$132{,}750}{\$199{,}125}$$

$$= \frac{\$398{,}250}{\$199{,}125}$$

$$= 200.00\%$$

$$\text{Variable cost-based price} = \$13.50 + (\$13.50 \times 200\%)$$

$$= \$40.50$$

The numerator in the markup percentage formula contains the desired profit ($110,625); total fixed production costs ($154,875); and total selling, general, and administrative expenses ($132,750). This total amount ($398,250) is divided by total variable production costs ($199,125). The resulting markup percentage is 200 percent. To compute the variable cost-based price, one adds the markup of $27.00 ($13.50 × 200%) to the variable cost base of $13.50 per unit. The product should sell for $40.50 if all costs and expenses are to be covered and the desired profit realized.

Gross Margin Pricing. A second approach to determining a selling price based on costs is known as **gross margin pricing.** Gross margin is the difference between sales and total production costs of those sales. The markup percentage under the gross margin method is designed to include everything not included in gross margin in the computation of the selling price. The gross margin markup percentage is composed of selling, general, and administrative expenses and desired profit. Because an accounting system often provides management with unit production cost data, both variable and fixed, this method of determining selling price can be easily applied. The formulas used are shown below.

$$\text{Markup percentage} = \frac{\text{desired profit} + \text{total selling, general, and administrative expenses}}{\text{total production costs}}$$

$$\text{Gross margin-based price} = \text{total production costs per unit} + (\text{markup percentage} \times \text{total production costs per unit})$$

The numerator in the markup percentage formula contains desired profit plus total selling, general, and administrative expenses. As you can see, this numerator is divided by total production costs to arrive at the markup factor.

For the Ron Jones Company, the markup percentage and selling price are computed as shown below.

$$\text{Markup percentage} = \frac{\$110{,}625 + \$132{,}750}{\$199{,}125 + \$154{,}875} = \frac{\$243{,}375}{\$354{,}000} = 68.75\%$$

$$\text{Gross margin-based price} = \$13.50 + \$10.50 + (\$24.00 \times 68.75\%) = \$40.50$$

The numerator in the markup percentage formula is the sum of the desired profit ($110,625) and total selling, general, and administrative expenses ($132,750). The denominator contains all production costs, variable costs of $199,125, and fixed production costs of $154,875. Gross margin markup is 68.75 percent of total production costs, or $16.50 ($24 × 68.75%). Adding $16.50 to the total production cost base yields a selling price of $40.50.

As you can see, the same selling price was computed by using both the variable cost and gross margin approaches. Since the same base data were used in the computations, the answers should be the same. The only item that changed in the two methods was the base (variable production costs versus total production costs). The markup percentage compensated for this change, and the same selling price resulted. The remaining cost-based methods will also result in the same selling price, although the return on assets approach could have different results.

Profit Margin Pricing. When using the profit margin approach, the markup percentage includes only the desired profit factor. For this method to be effective, all costs and expenses must be broken down into unit cost data. Since selling, general, and administrative costs tend to be more difficult to allocate to products or services than variable and fixed production costs, only arbitrary assignments can be used. However, arbitrary allocations can be misleading and may result in poor price setting. As long as market and competition factors are accounted for before establishing a final price, profit margin pricing can be used as a starting point in any price-setting decision analysis.

In the markup percentage computation below, all costs have shifted from the numerator to the denominator.

$$\text{Markup percentage} = \frac{\text{desired profit}}{\text{total costs and expenses}}$$

$$\text{Profit margin-base price} = \text{total costs and expenses per unit} + (\text{markup percentage} \times \text{total costs and expenses per unit})$$

As shown, only desired profit remains in the numerator. The denominator contains all production and operating costs related to the product or service being priced. In the profit margin pricing formula, total costs and expenses per unit are multiplied by the markup percentage to obtain the appropriate profit margin. The selling price is computed by adding profit margin to total unit costs.

Refer again to data on the Ron Jones Company. Notice that the following analysis computes the markup percentage and unit selling price by using the profit margin pricing approach:

$$\begin{aligned}
\text{Markup percentage} &= \frac{\$110{,}625}{\$199{,}125 + \$154{,}875 + \$132{,}750} \\
&= \frac{\$110{,}625}{\$486{,}750} \\
&= \underline{\underline{22.73\%}} \\
\text{Profit margin-based price} &= \$13.50 + \$10.50 + \$9.00 \\
&\quad + (\$33.00 \times 22.73\%) \\
&= \underline{\underline{\$40.50}}
\end{aligned}$$

Only the $110,625 in desired profit margin remains in the numerator, whereas the denominator increased to $486,750. The denominator represents total costs and expenses to be incurred. Markup percentage for this situation is 22.73 percent. The selling price is again \$40.50. However, in this computation the markup percentage of 22.73 percent is applied to the total cost of \$33.00 to obtain the profit margin of \$7.50 per unit (\$33.00 + \$7.50 = \$40.50).

Return on Assets Pricing. Return on assets pricing changes the objective of the price determination process. Earning a profit margin on total costs is replaced by earning a profit equal to a specified rate of return on assets employed in the operation. Since a business's primary objective should be earning a minimum desired rate of return, the return on assets pricing approach has a great appeal and support.

Assuming a company has a stated minimum desired rate of return, you can use the following formula to calculate return on assets-based price.

Return on assets-based price = total costs and expenses per unit + (desired rate of return × total costs of assets employed ÷ anticipated units to be produced)

The return on assets-based price is computed by first dividing the cost of assets employed by projected units to be produced. This number is then multiplied by the rate of return to obtain desired earnings per unit. Desired earnings per unit plus total costs and expenses per unit yields unit selling price.

For the Ron Jones Company, one can compute the selling price per unit needed to earn a 12 percent return on the \$921,875 asset base when estimated production is 14,750 units as shown below.

Return on assets-based price = \$13.50 + \$10.50 + \$9.00 + [12% × (\$921,875 ÷ 14,750)]
= \$40.50

The desired profit amount has been replaced by an overall company rate of return on assets. By dividing cost of assets employed by projected units of output and multiplying the result by the minimum desired rate of return, one obtains a unit profit factor of \$7.50 [12% × (\$921,875 ÷ 14,750)]. By adding this profit factor to total unit costs and expenses, one obtains a selling price of \$40.50.

Summary of the Cost-based Pricing Methods. The four cost-based pricing methods are summarized in Figure 24-2. All four methods—variable cost pricing, gross margin pricing, profit margin pricing, and return on assets pricing—will yield the same selling price if applied to the same data. Therefore, companies select their methods based on their degree of trust in a cost base. The cost base from which they can choose are: (1) variable costs per unit; (2) total product costs per unit; or (3) total costs and expenses per unit. Often total product costs per unit are readily available, which makes gross margin pricing a good benchmark on which to compute selling prices. Return on assets pricing is also a good pricing

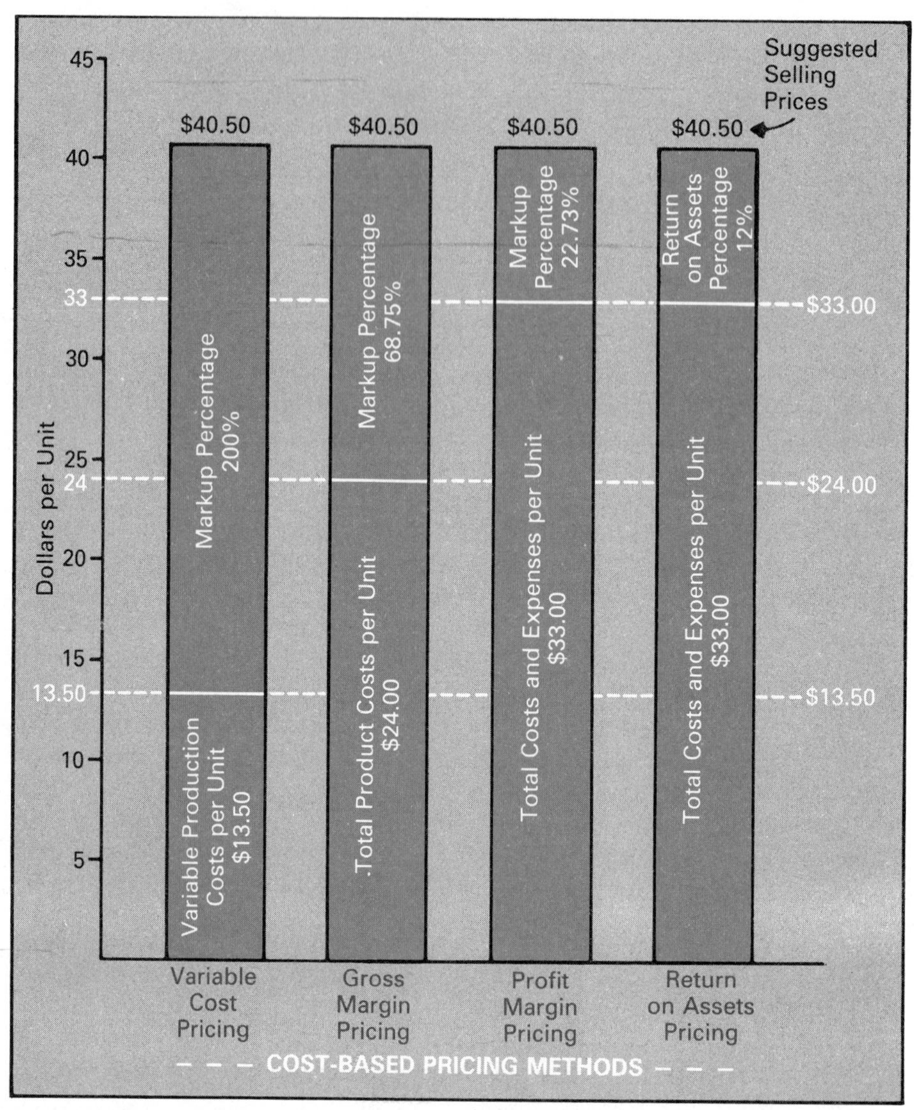

Figure 24-2. Cost-based Pricing Methods: Ron Jones Company

method if the cost of the assets used on a product can be identified and a cost amount determined. If not, the method yields inaccurate results.

Pricing of Services. Service-oriented businesses take a different approach to pricing of their products. Although a service has no physical existence, it must still be priced and billed to the customer. Most service organizations use a form of **time and materials pricing** to arrive at the price of a service. Service companies, such as appliance repair shops, home-addition specialists, pool cleaners, and automobile repair businesses, arrive at prices by using two computations, one for labor and one for materials and parts. As with the cost-based approaches, a markup percentage is used to add the cost of overhead to the direct costs of labor, materials, and parts. If materials and parts are not a component of the service being performed, then only direct labor costs are used as a basis for developing price. For professionals, such as attorneys, accountants, and consultants, a factor representing all overhead costs is applied to the base labor costs to establish a price for the services.

Ben's Auto Pampering just completed working on Mr. Crenshaw's 1983 Jaguar XJ6. Parts used to repair the vehicle cost $340. The company's 40 percent markup rate on parts covers parts-related overhead costs. Labor involved nine hours of time from a Jaguar specialist whose wages are $15 per hour. The current overhead markup rate on labor is 80 percent. To see how much Mr. Crenshaw will be billed for these auto repairs, review the following computation:

Repair parts used	$340	
Overhead charges		
$340 × 40%	136	
Totals parts charges		$476
Labor charges		
9 hours @ $15/hour	$135	
Overhead charges		
$135 × 80%	108	
Total labor charges		243
TOTAL BILLING		$719

Final Notes on Pricing Methods. As emphasized earlier, pricing is an art, not a science. Although one can use several methods to mechanically compute the price of something, many factors external to the good or service influence price. Once the cost of a good or service is determined, the decision maker must account for such factors as competitors' prices, customers' expectations, and the cost of substitute goods and services. Pricing is a risky part of operating a business, and care must be taken to establish that all-important selling price.

Special-order pricing takes a different approach to price determination. This topic, along with other short-run operating decisions, is covered in Chapter 25.

Transfer Pricing

OBJECTIVE 5
Define and discuss transfer pricing

In Chapter 20 the concept of responsibility centers was introduced. As you learned, cost/expense centers and profit centers are important to a decentralized organization because they help alleviate some of the difficulty of controlling diverse operations. Responsibility for a company's functions are placed with managers, and their performance is measured by comparing actual results with budgeted or projected results.

Profit measurement and return on investment are important gauges of performance in decentralized divisions. But at cost centers where only costs are involved, many people have difficulty measuring performance. This problem becomes more complicated when divisions within a company exchange goods or services and assume the role of customer or supplier to another division. As a result, transfer prices are used. A **transfer price** is the price at which goods are exchanged among a company's divisions. Such prices allow intracompany transactions to be measured and accounted for. These prices also affect the revenues and costs of the divisions involved. Furthermore, since a transfer price contains an estimated amount of profit, a manager's ability to meet a targeted profit can be measured. Although often called fictitious or created prices, company transfer prices as well as related policies are closely connected with performance evaluation.

Transfer Pricing Characteristics

The subject of transfer pricing is complex. Some people believe totally in the benefits of using transfer prices. Others believe they should never be used because they are not real prices. To illustrate how transfer prices are used and to help explain the difficult operational and behavioral aspects of such prices, we will analyze two situations requiring such prices. Figure 24-3 shows a pictorial view of how products flow at the Creative Pulp Company. This company is composed of three divisions: the Pulp Division, the Cardboard Division, and the Box Division. Example I shows the Pulp Division transferring wood pulp to the Cardboard Division for use in making cardboard. The Cardboard Division also has the option of purchasing the pulp from an outside supplier. The cost of making the pulp, including materials, labor, variable overhead, and fixed overhead, is $12.90 per pound. By adding a 10 percent factor to cover miscellaneous and divisional overhead expenses as well as a small profit, the proposed transfer price amounts to $14.19 per pound. The outside supplier will sell the pulp to the company for $14.10 per pound. What should the manager of the Cardboard Division do?

Clearly, pressure is on the manager of the Pulp Division to lower the transfer price to an amount equal to or less than $14.10, the market price. If this action is taken, however, the $.09 per pound reduction will directly affect profits of the Pulp Division. In turn, that situation will affect the manager's performance. On the other hand, if the manager of the Cardboard Division agrees or is forced to pay the $14.19 price to benefit overall company operating results, that person's profit and performance will be negatively affected. Thus, the question arises: is either amount a fair price? Such a problem would not occur if costs were simply accumulated as the product travels through the production process. The Pulp Division could be treated as a cost center and the manager's performance evaluated on the basis of only budgeted and actual costs. But then the Pulp Division's return on investment could not be measured. These are the conflicting objectives of performance evaluation in a decentralized organization.

A second common situation is shown in Example II of Figure 24-3. Instead of an outside supplier's influencing an internal transfer price, the Cardboard Division has an outside customer. The manager of the Cardboard Division must decide whether to sell cardboard to the outside customer for $28.10 per pound or supply the Box Division at $27.90 per pound. (The $27.90 covers all costs plus a profit margin.)

Figure 24-3. Intracompany Transfer Pricing Examples—Creative Pulp Company

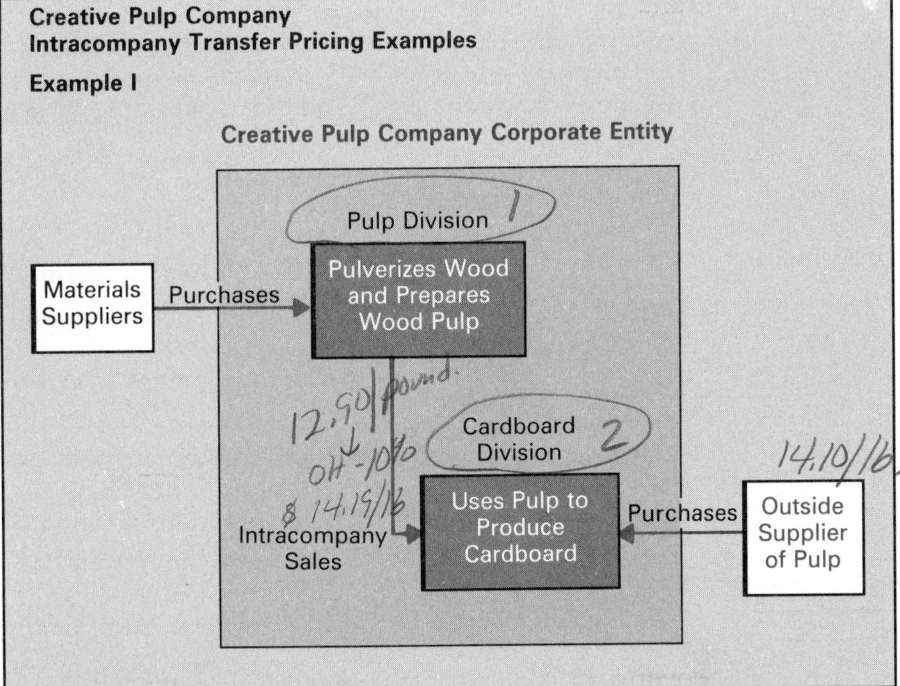

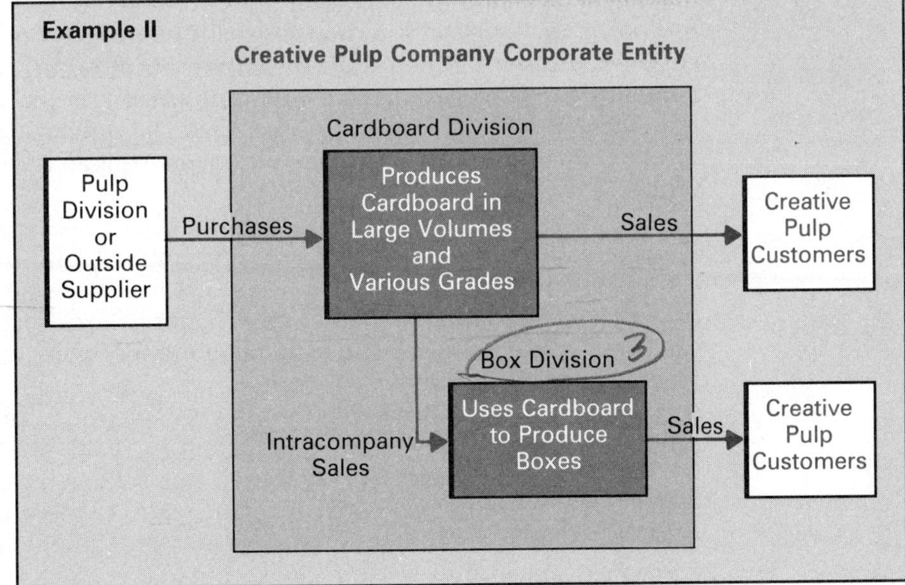

Several possible problems must be considered here. Is the outside customer going to make boxes that compete with the company's Box Division? Should the Box Division pay a market value transfer price so the Cardboard Division's manager can be evaluated properly? What about the Box Division? Should that manager suffer because all profits were siphoned off by managers of the Pulp and Cardboard divisions?

These are but a few of the problems involved in using transfer prices. So, perhaps you can now better understand why there are both proponents and opponents of this concept. From the example, it is easy to understand why transfer prices often cause internal bickering between managers. But measuring a manager's performance is still a major objective of decentralized companies. And the use of transfer prices is one important approach to that objective.

Transfer Pricing Methods

OBJECTIVE 6
Distinguish between a cost-based transfer price and a market-based transfer price

There are two primary approaches to developing a transfer price.

1. The price may be based on the cost of the item until its transfer to the next department or process.
2. A market value may be used if the item has an existing external market when transferred.

Both of these pricing situations were present in the Creative Pulp Company example described earlier. There, the Pulp Division would be inclined to use the cost method, since no apparent outside market exists for the pulp product. The only user of pulp is the Cardboard Division. However, the Box Division will probably have to pay a market-related price for the cardboard, since the Cardboard Division can either sell its product outside or transfer it to the Box Division.

In a situation in which no external markets are involved, division managers in a decentralized company may agree on a *cost-plus transfer price* or a *negotiated transfer price*. A **cost-plus transfer price** is the sum of costs incurred by the producing division plus an agreed on profit percentage. The weakness of cost-plus pricing is that cost recovery is guaranteed to the selling division. And guaranteed cost recovery fails to detect inefficient operating conditions as well as excessive cost incurrence.

A **negotiated transfer price**, on the other hand, is bargained for by the managers of the buying and selling divisions. From the cost-plus side, a transfer price may be based on an agreement to use a standard cost plus a profit percentage. This approach emphasizes cost control through the use of standard costs while still allowing the selling division to return a profit even though it is a cost center. A negotiated transfer price may also be based on a market price that was reduced in the bargaining process.

Market transfer prices are discussed but seldom used without being subjected to negotiations between managers. Using market prices may cause the selling division to ignore negotiation attempts from the buying division manager and sell directly to outside customers. If this causes an internal shortage of materials and forces the buying division to purchase materials from the outside, overall company profits may be lowered even when the selling division makes a profit. Such use of market prices works against a company's overall operating objectives. Therefore, when market prices are used to develop transfer prices, they are normally used only as a basis for negotiation.

Developing a Transfer Price

OBJECTIVE 7
Develop a transfer price

Many of the normal pricing considerations introduced earlier in this chapter are also present in the development of a transfer price. The first step is to compute the unit cost of the item being transferred. Next, management must determine the appropriate profit markup. If the semifinished product (1) has an existing external market for the selling division to consider or (2) can be purchased in similar condition by the buying division from an outside source, then the market price must be included in the analysis used to develop a transfer price. The final step is to have the managers negotiate a compromise between the two prices.

Now, look again at the Creative Pulp Company example. The division manager's computations supporting the $14.19 cost-plus transfer price are shown in Exhibit 24-1.

Exhibit 24-1. Transfer Price Computation

Creative Pulp Company
Pulp Division—Transfer Price Computation

Cost Category	Budgeted Costs	Cost per Unit
Materials		
Wood	$1,584,000	$ 3.30
Scrap wood	336,000	0.70
Labor		
Shaving/cleaning	768,000	1.60
Pulverizing	1,152,000	2.40
Blending	912,000	1.90
Overhead		
Variable	936,000	1.95
Fixed	504,000	1.05
Subtotals	$6,192,000	$12.90
Costs allocated from corporate office	144,000	
Target profit, 10% of division's costs	619,200	1.29
Total costs and profit	$6,955,200	
Cost-plus transfer price		$14.19

This one-year budget is based on the expectation that the Cardboard Division will require 480,000 pounds of pulp. Unit costs are stated in the right column. Notice that allocated corporate overhead is not included in the computation of the transfer price. Only costs related to the Pulp Division are included. The profit markup percentage of 10 percent adds $1.29 to the final transfer price of $14.19.

At this point management could dictate that the $14.19 price be used. On the other hand, the manager of the Cardboard Division could bring the outside purchase price of $14.10 per pound to the attention of management. Usually, such situations end up being negotiated to determine the final transfer price. Each side has a position and strong arguments to support a price. And each manager's performance will be compromised by adopting the other's price.

In the example, both managers brought their concerns to the attention of top management. A unique settlement was reached. Since internal profits must be erased before financial statements are prepared, management allowed the Pulp Division to use the $14.19 price and the Cardboard Division the $14.10 price for purposes of performance evaluation. Obviously, the company did not want the Cardboard Division buying pulp from another company. At the same time, the Pulp Division had the right to a 10 percent profit. Such approaches are often used to maintain harmony within a corporation. In this case it allowed top management to measure the managers' performance while avoiding behavioral issues. After the period was over, all fictitious profits were canceled by using adjusting entries before preparing end-of-year financial statements. The final product, in this case the boxes, had a profit factor that took into account all operations of the business.

Measuring Performance by Using Transfer Prices

OBJECTIVE 8 Measure a manager's performance by using transfer prices

When transfer prices are used, performance reports on managers of cost centers will contain revenue and income figures used in the evaluation. The Pulp Division performance report in Exhibit 24-2 is a good example.

The Pulp Division supplied 500 more pounds of pulp than anticipated for the month. Sales were priced at $14.19 per pound. The variable costs per unit shown earlier were used to extend budgeted and actual amounts for materials, labor, and variable overhead. The result was that the manager of the Pulp Division earned a March profit of $43,350, which was $1,170 over budget. The transfer price made it possible for the division to be evaluated as if it were a profit center, even though the division does not sell to outside customers. Were the Pulp Division still accounted for as a cost center, the manager would have to explain costs' being $5,925 over budget instead of divisional income's being over target.

(*Note:* Management may want the budget column restated at 42,500 pounds for evaluation purposes.)

Exhibit 24-2. Performance Report Using Transfer Prices

Creative Pulp Company
Pulp Division—Performance Report
For March 19x0

	Budget (42,000 pounds)	Actual (42,500 pounds)	Difference Over/(Under) Budget
Costs Controllable by Supervisor			
Sales to Cardboard Division	$595,980	$603,075	$7,095
Cost of goods sold			
Materials:			
Wood	$138,600	$140,250	$1,650
Scrap wood	29,400	29,750	350
Labor:			
Shaving/cleaning	67,200	68,000	800
Pulverizing	100,800	102,000	1,200
Blending	79,800	80,750	950
Overhead:			
Variable	81,900	82,875	975
Fixed	44,100	44,100	0
Total cost of goods sold	$541,800	$547,725	$5,925
Gross margin from sales	$ 54,180	$ 55,350	$1,170
Costs Uncontrollable by Supervisor			
Cost allocated from corporate office	$ 12,000	$ 12,000	$ 0
Division's income	$ 42,180	$ 43,350	$1,170

Final Note on Transfer Prices

Problems in transfer price policy arise when buying divisions elect to purchase from outside suppliers. A selling division with adequate capacity to fulfill the buying division's demands should sell to that division at any price that recovers incremental costs. Incremental costs of intracompany sales include all variable costs of production and distribution plus any fixed costs directly traceable to intracompany sales. If a buying division can acquire products from outside suppliers at an annual cost that is less than the supplying division's incremental costs, then purchases should be made from the outside supplier. This is because overall company profits will be enhanced. A thorough analysis of the supplying division's operations should also be conducted.

Chapter Review

Review of Learning Objectives

1. **Describe traditional economic pricing concepts.**
The traditional approach to pricing is based on microeconomic theory. Microeconomic theory states that profits will be maximized at the point at which the difference between total revenue and total cost is greatest. Total revenue then tapers off, since as a product is marketed, price reductions are necessary to sell more units. Total cost increases when large quantities are produced because fixed costs change. To locate the point of maximum profit, marginal revenue and marginal cost must be computed and plotted. Profit is maximized at the point at which the marginal revenue and marginal cost curves intersect.

2. **Identify external and internal factors on which prices are based.**
Many factors influence the process of determining a selling price. Factors external to a company include: (a) total demand for the product or service; (b) number of competing products or services; (c) competitor's quality and price; (d) customer preference; (e) seasonal demand; and (f) life of product. Internal factors are: (a) costs of producing the product or service; (b) purpose and quality of product; (c) type of process used—labor intensive versus automated; (d) markup percentage procedure; and (e) amount of scarce resources used.

3. **State the objectives managers use to establish prices of goods and services.**
The long-run objectives of a company should include statements on pricing policy. Possible pricing policy objectives include: (a) adhering to short- and long-run pricing strategies; (b) maximizing profits; (c) maintaining or gaining market share; (d) ensuring prices are socially responsible; (e) maintaining a stated rate of return on investments; and (f) ensuring prices support a trend of total sales increases.

4. **Create prices by applying the methods and tools of price determination.**
Several pricing methods can be adopted by the pricing manager. However, experience in pricing a product often leads to adjustments in the formula used. Pricing methods include: (a) variable cost pricing; (b) gross margin pricing; (c) profit margin pricing; and (d) return on assets pricing. Time and materials pricing is often used by service-oriented businesses.

5. **Define and discuss transfer pricing.**
A transfer price is the price at which goods are exchanged between a company's divisions. Since a transfer price contains an amount of estimated profit, a manager's ability to meet a profit target can be measured, even for a typical cost center. Although often called fictitious or created prices, company transfer prices and related policies are closely connected with performance evaluation.

6. **Distinguish between a cost-based transfer price and a market-based transfer price.**
There are two primary approaches to developing transfer prices: (a) the price may be based on the cost of the item up to the point at which it is transferred to the next department or process or (2) a market value may be used if an item has an existing external market when transferred. A cost-plus transfer price is the sum of costs incurred by the producing division plus an agreed on profit percentage. A market-based transfer price is geared to external

market prices. In most cases a negotiated transfer price is used, that is, one that was bargained for between the managers of the selling and buying divisions.

7. **Develop a transfer price.**
Many of the normal pricing considerations are also present in the development of a transfer price. The first step is to compute the unit cost of the item being transferred. Next, management must determine the appropriate profit markup. Then, those involved in the intracompany transfer must discuss any relevant market prices before negotiating a final transfer price.

8. **Measure a manager's performance by using transfer prices.**
When transfer prices are used, performance reports on managers of cost centers must contain revenue and income figures used in the evaluation process. Actual performance reports on cost centers will look just like those used for profit centers. Evaluation procedures will also be similar in that the manager of the cost center will have to explain any differences between budgeted and actual revenues and income.

Review Problem
Cost-based Pricing

The Bengtson Toy Company makes a complete line of toy vehicles including three types of trucks, a pickup, a dumpster, and a flatbed. These toy trucks are produced in assembly line fashion beginning with the Stamping operation and continuing through the Welding, Painting, and Detailing Departments. Projected costs of each toy truck and allocation percentages for fixed and common costs are shown below.

Cost Categories		Total Projected Costs	Toy Pickup Truck	Toy Dumpster Truck	Toy Flatbed Truck
Materials:	Metal	$137,000	$62,500	$29,000	$45,500
	Axles	5,250	2,500	1,000	1,750
	Wheels	9,250	3,750	2,000	3,500
	Paint	70,500	30,000	16,000	24,500
Labor:	Stamping	53,750	22,500	12,000	19,250
	Welding	94,000	42,500	20,000	31,500
	Painting	107,500	45,000	24,000	38,500
	Detailing	44,250	17,500	11,000	15,750
Indirect labor		173,000	77,500	36,000	59,500
Operating supplies		30,000	12,500	7,000	10,500
Variable production costs		90,500	40,000	19,000	31,500
Fixed production costs		120,000	45%	25%	30%
Distribution costs		105,000	40%	20%	40%
Variable marketing costs		123,000	55,000	26,000	42,000
Fixed marketing costs		85,400	40%	25%	35%
General and administrative costs		47,600	40%	25%	35%

Bengtson's policy is to earn a minimum of 30 percent over total cost on each type of toy produced. Expected sales for 19x9 are: Pickup, 50,000 units; Dumpster, 20,000 units; and Flatbed, 35,000 units. Assume no change in inventory levels.

Required:

1. Compute the selling price for each toy truck using the gross margin pricing method.
2. Check your answers in **1** by computing the selling prices using the profit margin pricing method.
3. If the competition's selling price for a similar pickup truck is around $14.00, would this influence Bengtson's pricing decision? Give reasons defending your answer.

Answer to Review Problem

Before the various selling prices are computed, the cost analysis must be completed and restructured in order to supply the information needed for the pricing computations.

Cost Categories		Total Projected Costs	Toy Pickup Truck	Toy Dumpster Truck	Toy Flatbed Truck
Materials:	Metal	$ 137,000	$ 62,500	$ 29,000	$ 45,500
	Axles	5,250	2,500	1,000	1,750
	Wheels	9,250	3,750	2,000	3,500
	Paint	70,500	30,000	16,000	24,500
Labor:	Stamping	53,750	22,500	12,000	19,250
	Welding	94,000	42,500	20,000	31,500
	Painting	107,500	45,000	24,000	38,500
	Detailing	44,250	17,500	11,000	15,750
Indirect labor		173,000	77,500	36,000	59,500
Operating supplies		30,000	12,500	7,000	10,500
Variable production costs		90,500	40,000	19,000	31,500
Fixed production costs		120,000	54,000	30,000	36,000
Total production costs		$ 935,000	$410,250	$207,000	$317,750
Distribution costs		$ 105,000	$ 42,000	$ 21,000	$ 42,000
Variable marketing costs		123,000	55,000	26,000	42,000
Fixed marketing costs		85,400	34,160	21,350	29,890
General and administrative costs		47,600	19,040	11,900	16,660
Total selling, general and administrative costs		$ 361,000	$150,200	$ 80,250	$130,550
Total Costs		$1,296,000	$560,450	$287,250	$448,300
Desired Profit		$ 388,800	$168,135	$ 86,175	$134,490

1. Pricing using the gross margin approach.
Markup percentage formula:

$$\text{Markup percentage} = \frac{\text{Desired profit} + \text{Total selling, general, and administrative costs}}{\text{Total production costs}}$$

Gross margin pricing formula:
Gross margin-based price = Total production costs per unit + (markup percentage × total production costs)

Pickup truck:

$$\text{Markup percentage} = \frac{\$168{,}135 + \$150{,}200}{\$410{,}250} = \underline{\underline{77.60\%}}$$

Gross margin-based price = (\$410,250/50,000) + (\$410,250/50,000) × 77.6% = $\underline{\underline{\$14.57}}$

Dumpster truck:

$$\text{Markup percentage} = \frac{\$86{,}175 + \$80{,}250}{\$207{,}000} = \underline{\underline{80.40\%}}$$

Gross margin-based price = (\$207,000/20,000) + (\$207,000/20,000) × 80.4% = $\underline{\underline{\$18.67}}$

Flatbed truck:

$$\text{Markup percentage} = \frac{\$134{,}490 + \$130{,}550}{\$317{,}750} = \underline{\underline{83.41\%}}$$

Gross margin-based price = (\$317,750/35,000) + (\$317,750/35,000) × 83.41% = $\underline{\underline{\$16.65}}$

2. Pricing using the profit margin approach.
Markup percentage formula:

$$\text{Markup percentage} = \frac{\text{Desired profit}}{\text{Total costs and expenses}}$$

Profit margin pricing formula:
Profit margin-based price = Total costs expenses per unit + (markup percentage × total costs and expenses)

Pickup truck:

$$\text{Markup percentage} = \frac{\$168{,}135}{\$560{,}450} = \underline{\underline{30.00\%}}$$

Profit margin-based price = (\$560,450/50,000) + (\$560,450/50,000) × 30% = $\underline{\underline{\$14.57}}$

Dumpster truck:

$$\text{Markup percentage} = \frac{\$86{,}175}{\$287{,}250} = \underline{\underline{30.00\%}}$$

Profit margin-based price = (\$287,250/20,000) + (\$287,250/20,000) × 30% = $\underline{\underline{\$18.67}}$

Flatbed truck:

$$\text{Markup percentage} = \frac{\$134{,}490}{\$448{,}300} = \underline{\underline{30.00\%}}$$

Profit margin-based price = (\$448,300/35,000) + (\$448,300/35,000) × 30% = $\underline{\underline{\$16.65}}$

3. Competition's influence on price.
   If the competition's toy pickup truck was similar in quality as well as design and looks, then Bengtson's management would have to consider the $14.00 price range. At $14.57, they have a 30 percent profit factor built in to their price. Break even is at $11.21 ($14.57/1.3). Therefore, they have the ability to reduce the price below the competition and still make a significant profit.

Chapter Assignments

Questions

1. List some considerations a decision maker must allow for when setting the price of a product or service.
2. Discuss the concept of making pricing decisions based on whatever the market will bear.
3. In the traditional economic pricing concept, what role does total revenue play in maximizing profit?
4. Why is profit maximized where marginal revenue equals marginal cost?
5. Identify five pricing policy objectives. Discuss each one briefly.
6. Do prices have a social effect? How or in what way?
7. List some external factors to consider when establishing an item's price.
8. List the internal factors one should use to gauge pricing decisions.
9. Describe the variable cost pricing method. Under what conditions will it yield useful data?
10. What is the gross profit pricing method? How is the markup percentage calculated under this method?
11. Differentiate the profit margin pricing method from the return on assets pricing method.
12. In the pricing of services, what is meant by time and materials pricing?
13. What is a transfer price?
14. Why are transfer prices associated with decentralized corporations?
15. Why is a transfer price often referred to as a fictitious or created price?
16. Describe the cost-plus approach to setting transfer prices.
17. How are market prices used to develop a transfer price? Under what circumstances are market prices relevant to a transfer pricing decision?
18. "Most transfer prices are negotiated prices." Explain this statement.

Classroom Exercises

Exercise 24-1. Traditional Economic Pricing Theory (L.O. 1)

McCome & Fritz are product designers. The firm has just completed a contract to develop a portable telephone. The telephone must be recharged only once a week and can be used up to one mile from the receiver. Initial fixed costs for this product are $4,000. The designers estimate the product will break even at the $5,000/100-unit mark. Total revenues will again equal total cost at the $25,000/900-unit point. Marginal cost is expected to equal marginal revenue when 550 units are sold.

1. Sketch total revenue and total cost curves for this product. Mark the vertical axis at each $5,000 increment; the horizontal axis at each 100-unit increment.
2. From your total revenue and total cost curves in **1** above, estimate the unit selling price at which profits will be maximized.

Exercise 24-2. External and Internal Pricing Factors
(L.O. 2)

Stanley Panin's Tire Outlet features more than a dozen brands of tires in many sizes. Two of the brands are Yerelle and Pokohama, both imported into the United States. The tire size, 205/70—VR15, is available in both brands. The following information was obtained:

	Yerelle	Pokohama
Selling prices		
Single tire, installed	$145	$124
Set of four tires, installed	520	460
Cost per tire	100	70

As shown, selling prices include installation costs. Each Yerelle tire costs $20 to mount and balance; each Pokohama tire, $15 to mount and balance.

1. Compute each brand's unit selling price for both a single tire and a set of four.
2. Was cost the major consideration in supporting these prices?
3. What other factors could have influenced these prices?

Exercise 24-3. Pricing Policy Objectives
(L.O. 3)

Lynda Lane, Ltd. is an international clothing company specializing in retailing medium-priced goods. Retail outlets are located throughout the United States, France, Germany, and Great Britain. Management is interested in creating an image of giving the customer the most quality for the dollar. Selling prices are developed to draw customers away from competitor's stores. First-of-the-month sales are a regular practice of all stores, and customers are accustomed to this practice. Company buyers are carefully trained to seek out quality goods at inexpensive prices. Sales are targeted to increase a minimum of 5 percent per year. All sales should yield a 15 percent return on assets. Sales personnel are expected to wear Lane's clothing while working, and all personnel can purchase clothing at 10 percent above cost. Cleanliness and an orderly appearance are required at all stores. Competitors' prices are checked daily.

Identify the pricing policy objectives of Lynda Lane, Ltd.

Exercise 24-4. Price Determination
(L.O. 4)

Sopkiewicz Industries has just patented a new product called "Toms," an automobile wax for lasting protection against the elements. Annual information developed by the company's controller for use in price determination meetings is shown below.

Variable production costs	$1,530,000
Fixed factory overhead	540,000
Selling expenses	360,000
General and administrative expenses	202,500
Desired profit	337,500

2632500
2970,000
$5.85

Annual demand for the product is expected to be 450,000 cans.

1. Compute the projected unit cost for one can of Toms.
2. Prepare formulas for computing the markup percentage and selling price for one can. Using the gross margin pricing method compute these amounts.
3. To check your answer to **2** above, compute the selling price of one can of Toms using the profit margin pricing method.

Exercise 24-5. Pricing a Service (L.O. 4)

Utah has just passed a law making it mandatory to have every head of cattle inspected at least once a year for a series of communicable diseases. Halbert Jensen Enterprises is considering entering this inspection business. After extensive studies Mr. Jensen has developed the following annual projections:

Direct service labor	$425,000
Variable service overhead costs	350,000
Fixed service overhead costs	237,500
Marketing expenses	162,500
General & administrative expenses	137,500
Minimum desired profit	125,000
Cost of assets employed	781,250

Mr. Jensen believes his company would inspect 125,000 head of cattle per year. On average the company now earns a 16 percent return on assets.

1. Compute the projected cost of inspecting each head of cattle.
2. Determine the price to charge for inspecting each head of cattle. Use the gross margin pricing method.
3. Using the return on assets method, compute the unit price to charge for this inspection service.

Exercise 24-6. Transfer Price Comparison (L.O. 5, 6)

David Koeppen and Gordon Pirrong are developing a transfer price for the first section of an automatic pool-cleaning device. The housing is made in Department AA. It is then passed onto Department DG, wherein final assembly occurs. Unit costs for the housing are as follows:

Cost Categories	Unit Costs
Materials	$2.10
Direct labor	1.65
Variable factory overhead	1.15
Fixed factory overhead	0.80
Profit markup, 20% of cost	?

An outside supplier can supply the housing for $6.80 per unit.

1. Develop a cost-plus transfer price for the housing.
2. What should the transfer price be? Support your answer.

Exercise 24-7. Developing a Cost-Plus Transfer Price (L.O. 7)

Management at Kaldenberg Industries has just decided to use a set of transfer prices for intracompany transfers between departments. Management's objective is to include return on assets in the performance evaluation of managers at its cost centers. Data from the Molding Department for the past six months are

Account	Total Costs	Expected Increases/Decreases
Raw plastic, ADG	$238,600	+10%
Raw plastic, XJS	398,700	−10%
Direct labor, Melting	145,300	—
Direct labor, Blending	167,200	—
Direct labor, Shaping	195,100	+ 5%
Variable factory overhead	92,300	+20%
Fixed factory overhead	125,900	—

During the six-month period, 52,500 plastic units were produced. The same number of units are expected to be completed during the next six-month period. The company uses a 15 percent profit markup percentage.

1. Compute estimated total costs for the Molding Department for the next six months.
2. Develop a cost-plus transfer price for the plastic unit.

Exercise 24-8. Transfer Prices and Performance Evaluation (L.O. 8)

The Jensen Fireplace Accessories Company uses transfer prices when evaluating division managers. Data from the Forging Department for April 19x9 are as follows:

	Budget	Actual
Steel ingots	$80,360	$ 80,780
Iron ingots	45,920	46,160
Brass ingots	183,680	184,640
Direct labor	235,340	236,570
Variable factory overhead	74,620	75,010
Fixed factory overhead	34,440	34,440
Corporate selling expenses	17,410	18,700
Corporate administrative expenses	18,200	19,100

A special alloy is prepared from iron, steel, and brass before beginning the forging operation.

The division's transfer price is $13.11 per unit. During April the budget called for 57,400 units, and 57,700 units were actually produced and transferred.

Prepare a performance report for the Forging Division.

Interpreting Accounting Information

Transfer Price Determination: Orlando Industries, Inc. (L.O. 6, 7)

Two major operating divisions, the Cabinet Division and the Electronics Division, make up Orlando Industries, Inc. The company's major products are deluxe console television sets. The TV cabinets are manufactured by the Cabinet Division, while the Electronics Division produces all electronic components and assembles the sets. The company uses a decentralized organizational structure.

The Cabinet Division not only supplies cabinets to the Electronics Division, but it also sells cabinets to other TV manufacturers. Based on a normal sales order of 40 cabinets, the following unit cost breakdown for a deluxe television cabinet was developed:

Materials	$ 22.00
Direct labor	25.00
Variable factory overhead	14.00
Fixed factory overhead	16.00
Variable selling expenses	9.00
Fixed selling expenses	6.00
Fixed general & administrative expenses	8.00
Total unit cost	$100.00

The Cabinet Division's normal profit margin is 20 percent, and the regular selling price of a deluxe cabinet is $120. Divisional management recently decided that $120 will also be the transfer price used for all intracompany transactions.

Management at the Electronics Division is unhappy with that decision. They claim the Cabinet Division will show superior performance at the expense of the Electronics Division. Competition recently forced the company to lower prices. Because of a newly established transfer price for the cabinet, Electronics' portion of the profit margin on deluxe television sets was lowered to 18 percent. To counteract the new intracompany transfer price, management at the Electronics Division announced that effective immediately, all cabinets will be purchased from an outside supplier. They will be purchased in lots of 200 cabinets at a unit price of $110 per cabinet.

The corporate president, J. J. Johnson, has called a meeting of both divisions in order to negotiate a fair intracompany transfer price. The following prices were listed as possible alternatives:

Current market price	$120 per cabinet
Current outside purchase price (This price is based on a large-quantity purchase discount. It will cause increased storage costs for the Electronics Division.)	$110 per cabinet
Total unit *manufacturing* costs plus a normal 20 percent profit margin $77.00 + $15.40	$92.40 per cabinet
Total unit costs, excluding variable selling expenses, plus a normal 20 percent profit margin $91.00 + $18.20	$109.20 per cabinet

Required

1. What price should be established for intracompany transactions? Defend your answer by showing the shortcomings of each alternative.
2. Were there an outside market for all units produced by the Cabinet Division at the $120 price would you change your answer to **1** above? Why?

Problem Set A

Problem 24A-1. Cost-based Pricing (L.O. 2, 4)

Bodrero Coffee Company produces special types of blended coffee. Its products are used in exclusive restaurants throughout the world. Quality is the primary objective of the company. A team of quality consultants is employed to continuously assess the quality of the purchased coffee beans, and the blending procedures and ingredients used. The company's controller is in the process of determining prices for the coming year. Three blends are currently produced; Regular Blend, Mint Blend and Choco Blend. Expected profit on each blend is 20 percent above costs. Expected production for 19x8 is: 120,000 pounds of Regular Blend, 50,000 pounds of Mint Blend, and 30,000 pounds of Choco Blend.

Required

1. Compute the selling price for each blend, using the gross margin pricing method.
2. Check your answers in **1** above by computing selling prices. Use the profit margin pricing method.
3. If the competition's selling price for the Choco Blend averaged $24.50 per pound, should this influence the controller's pricing decision? Explain.

Total anticipated costs and percentages of total costs per blend are shown below for 19x8.

Cost Categories	Percentage of Total Costs: Regular Blend	Mint Blend	Choco Blend	Total Projected Costs
Coffee beans	60%	25%	15%	$770,000
Chocolate	0%	10%	90%	45,000
Mint leaf	10%	80%	10%	32,000
Labor				
Cleaning	60%	25%	15%	148,000
Blending	40%	30%	30%	372,000
Roasting	60%	25%	15%	298,000
Indirect labor	60%	25%	15%	110,000
Supplies	30%	40%	30%	36,500
Other variable factory overhead	60%	25%	15%	280,000
Fixed factory overhead	60%	25%	15%	166,000
Variable selling expenses	40%	30%	30%	96,500
Fixed selling expenses	40%	30%	30%	42,000
General & administrative expenses	34%	33%	33%	146,000

Problem 24A-2. Pricing Decision
(L.O. 2, 4)

Curtis Hawkins & Company is an assembly jobber specializing in home appliances. One division, Hart Operations, focuses most efforts on assembling a standard single-slice toaster. Projected costs on this product for 19x9 are as follows:

Cost Description	Budgeted Costs
Toaster casings	$1,344,000
Electrical components	1,860,000
Direct labor, electrical	2,520,000
Direct labor, assembly	1,128,000
Variable indirect assembly costs	780,000
Fixed indirect assembly costs	1,740,000
Variable selling expenses	1,032,000
Fixed selling expenses	504,000
General operating expenses	840,000
Administrative expenses	816,000

Estimated annual demand for the single-slice toaster is 1,200,000 per year. The above budgeted amounts were geared to this demand. The company wants to make a $1,260,000 profit.

Competitors have just published their wholesale prices for the coming year. They range from $10.80 to $11.32 per toaster. The Curtis Hawkins toaster is known for its high quality, and it competes with products at the top end of the price range. Even with its high quality, however, every $.10 increase above the top competitor's price causes a drop in demand of 120,000 units below the original estimate. Assume all price changes are in $.10 increments.

Required

1. Compute the anticipated selling price. Use the gross margin pricing method.
2. Based on competitors' prices, what should the Curtis Hawkins Toaster sell for in 19x9? Defend your answer.
3. Would your pricing structure in **2** above change if the company had only limited competition at their quality level? If so, in what direction? Why?

Problem 24A-3. Time and Materials Pricing (L.O. 4)

Thomason Construction Company specializes in additions to custom homes. Last week a potential customer called for a quote on a two-room addition to the family home. After visiting the site and taking all relevant measurements, Annette Thomason returned to the office to work on drawings for the addition. As part of the process of preparing a bid, a total breakdown of cost is required.

The company follows the time and materials pricing system and uses data from the previous six months to compute markup percentages for overhead. Separate rates are used for materials and supplies and for labor. During the past six months, $28,500 of materials and supplies-related overhead was incurred and $142,500 of materials and supplies were billed. Labor cost for the six-month period was $341,600. Labor-related overhead was $136,640. Add 20 percent to each markup percentage to cover desired profit. According to Ms. Thomason's design, the materials, supplies, and labor shown below are needed to complete the job:

Quantity		Unit Price
Materials		
150	2″ × 4″ × 8′ cedar	$ 1.10
50	2″ × 6″ × 8′ cedar	2.05
14	2″ × 8″ × 8′ cedar	4.50
25	4′ × 8′ sheets, ½″ plywood	10.40
6	Framed windows	80.00
3	Framed doors	110.00
30	4′ × 8′ sheets, siding	14.00
Supplies		65.00

Hours		Hourly Rate
Labor		
120	Laborers/helpers	$ 9.50
80	Semiskilled carpenters	11.00
60	Carpenters	14.50

Required

1. Compute markup percentages for overhead and profit for both materials and supplies and for labor.

2. Prepare a complete billing for this job. Include itemized amounts for each type of materials, supplies, and labor. Follow the time and material pricing approach and show total price for the job.

Problem 24A-4. Developing Transfer Prices (L.O. 5, 7)

Seven years ago Ed Browning formed The Browning Corporation and began producing sound equipment for home use. Because of the highly technical and competitive nature of the industry, Browning established the Research and Development Division. That division is responsible for continually evaluating and updating critical electronic parts used in the corporation's products. The R & D staff has been very successful, contributing to the corporation's ranking as America's leader in the industry.

Two years ago, R & D took on the added responsibility of producing all microchip circuit boards for Browning's sound equipment. One of Browning's specialties is a sound dissemination board (SDB) used in videocassette recorders (VCRs). The SDB greatly enhances the sound quality of Browning's VCRs.

Demand for the SDB has increased significantly in the past year. As a result, R & D has increased its production and assembly labor force. Three outside customers want to purchase the SDB for their sound products. To date, R & D has been producing SDBs for internal use only.

The controller of the R & D Division wants to create a transfer price for the SDBs applicable to all intracompany transfers. The following data show projections for the next six months:

Costs

Materials:	
boards	$ 253,050
chips	1,229,100
wire posts	325,350
wire	144,600
electronic glue	433,800
Labor:	
Board preparation	759,150
Assembly	1,988,250
Testing	650,700
Supplies	90,375
Indirect labor	524,175
Other variable overhead costs	180,750
Fixed overhead, SDBs	397,650
Other fixed overhead, corporate	506,100
Variable selling expenses, SDBs	1,012,200
Fixed selling expenses, corporate	578,400
General corporate operating expenses	795,300
Corporate administrative expenses	614,550

A profit factor of at least 20 percent must be added to total unit cost for internal transfer purposes. Outside customers are willing to pay $36 for each SDB. Estimated demand over the next six months is 235,000 SDBs for internal use and 126,500 SDBs for external customers.

Required

1. Compute the cost of producing and distributing one SDB.
2. What transfer price should R & D use? What factors influenced your decision?

Problem 24A-5. Transfer Prices and Performance Evaluation (L.O. 8)

"That Culpepper Division is robbing us blind!" This statement by the director of the White Division was heard during the board of directors meeting at Arkansas Company. The company produces umbrellas in a two-step process. The Culpepper Division prepares the fabric tops and transfers them to the White Division. The White Division produces the ribs and handles, secures the tops, and packs all finished umbrellas for shipment.

Because of the director's concern, the company controller gathered the following data on the past year:

	Culpepper Division	White Division	Company Totals
Sales			
Regular	$880,000	$2,720,000	$3,600,000
Deluxe	720,000	2,300,000	3,020,000
Materials			
Cloth	360,000	0	360,000
Aluminum	0	660,000	660,000
Closing mechanisms	0	1,560,000	1,560,000
Labor	480,000	540,000	1,020,000
Variable factory overhead	90,000	240,000	330,000
Fixed divisional overhead	150,000	210,000	360,000
Selling expenses	60,000	180,000	240,000
General operating expenses	72,000	192,000	264,000
Company administrative expenses	84,000	108,000	192,000

During the year, 400,000 regular umbrellas and 200,000 deluxe umbrellas were completed and transferred or shipped by the two divisions. Transfer prices used by the Culpepper Division were:

Regular	$ 2.20
Deluxe	3.60

The regular umbrella wholesales for $6.80; the deluxe model, for $11.50. Selling, general operating, and company administrative costs are allocated to divisions by a preconceived formula.

Management has indicated the transfer price should include a 20 percent profit factor on total division costs.

Required

1. Prepare a performance report on the Culpepper Division.
2. Prepare a performance report on the White Division.
3. Compute each division's rate of return on controllable and on total division costs.
4. Do you agree with the director's statement?
5. What procedures would you recommend to the board of directors?

Problem Set B

Problem 24B-1. Cost-based Pricing (L.O. 2, 4)

Jackson Publishing Company specializes in health awareness books. Because the field of health awareness is very competitive, Anne Jackson, the company's president, maintains a strict policy about selecting books to publish. Jackson wants to publish only books whose projected earnings are 20 percent above total projected costs. Three titles were accepted for publication during 19x0. The authors were Krotec, Vawter, and Boyll. Projected costs for each book and allocation percentages for fixed and common costs are shown below.

Cost Categories	Total Projected Costs	Krotec Book	Vawter Book	Boyll Book
Labor				
Editing	$184,000	$55,200	$ 92,000	$36,800
Proofing	86,500	25,950	43,250	17,300
Development	94,400	28,320	47,200	18,880
Design	122,600	36,780	61,300	24,520
Royalty costs	120,000	36,000	60,000	24,000
Printing costs	248,600	74,580	124,300	49,720
Supplies	34,200	10,260	17,100	6,840
Variable production costs	142,000	42,600	71,000	28,400
Fixed production costs	168,000	35%	40%	25%
Distribution costs	194,000	30%	50%	20%
Variable marketing costs	124,600	37,380	62,300	24,920
Fixed marketing costs	69,400	35%	40%	25%
General & administrative costs	52,400	35%	40%	25%

Expected sales for 19x0 are as follows: Krotec, 25,000 copies; Vawter, 30,000 copies; and Boyll, 40,000 copies.

Required

1. Compute the selling price for each book. Use the gross margin pricing method.
2. Check your answers in **1** above by computing selling prices under the profit margin pricing method.
3. If the competition's average selling price for a book on the same subject as Boyll's is $16, should this influence Jackson's pricing decision? State your reasons.

(Hint: In **1** and **2**, treat royalty costs as production costs.)

Problem 24B-2. Pricing Decision (L.O. 2, 4)

Jain & Gawel, Ltd., design and assemble handguns for police departments across the country. Only four other companies compete in this specialty market. The most popular police handgun is the Jain & Gawel .357-caliber magnum, model 87, made of stainless steel. Jain & Gawel estimates there will be 47,000 requests for this model in 19x8.

Estimated costs related to this product for 19x8 are shown below.

Description	Budgeted Costs
Gun casing	$ 573,400
Ammunition chamber	404,200
Trigger mechanism	1,151,500
Direct labor, assembly	991,700
Direct labor, finishing & testing	606,300
Variable indirect assembly costs	789,600
Fixed indirect assembly costs	338,400
Variable selling expenses	188,000
Fixed selling expenses	305,500
General operating expenses	183,300
Administrative expenses	126,900

The above budget is based on the demand previously stated. The company wants to earn a $846,000 profit in 19x8.

Last week the four competitors released their wholesale prices for the next year.

Gunsmith A	$128.40
Gunsmith B	122.90
Gunsmith C	119.80
Gunsmith D	126.50

Jain & Gawel handguns are known for their high quality. They compete with handguns at the top of the price range. Despite the high quality, however, every $5.00 price increase above the top competitor's price causes an 11,000-unit drop in demand from what was originally estimated. (Assume all price changes are in $5.00 increments.)

Required

1. Compute the anticipated selling price. Use the gross margin pricing method.
2. Based on competitors' prices, what should the Jain & Gawel handgun sell for in 19x8? Defend your answer.
3. Would your pricing structure in **2** above change if the company had only limited competition at this quality level? If so, in what direction? Why?

Problem 24B-3. Time and Materials Pricing (L.O. 4)

Cluff-Mack Maintenance, Inc., repairs heavy construction equipment and vehicles. Recently, the Ashton Construction Company had one of their giant "Earthmovers" overhauled and its tires replaced. Repair work for this size of vehicle usually takes from one week to ten days. Extensive effort must be used to lift the vehicle enough to gain access to the engine. Parts are normally so large, a crane must be used to put them into place.

Cluff-Mack uses the time and materials pricing method for billing. A markup percentage is applied to the cost of parts and materials to cover materials-related overhead. A similar approach is used for labor-related overhead costs.

During the previous year the company incurred $779,040 in materials-related overhead costs and paid $486,900 for materials and parts. During that same time period, direct labor employees earned $347,200, and labor-related overhead of $520,800 was incurred. A factor of 20 percent is added to markup percentages to cover desired profit.

A summary of the materials and parts used and the labor needed to repair the giant Earthmover are shown below.

Quantity		Unit Price	Hours		Hourly Rate
Materials and parts			Labor		
24	Spark plugs	$ 2.40	42	Mechanic	$18.20
20	Oil, quarts	3.90	54	Assistant Mechanic	10.00
12	Hoses	11.60			
1	Water pump	964.00			
30	Coolant, quarts	6.50			
18	Clamps	5.90			
1	Distributor cap	128.40			
1	Carburetor	214.10			
4	Tires	1,020.00			

Required

1. Compute the markup percentages for overhead and profit for (1) materials and parts and (2) labor.
2. Prepare a complete billing for this job. Include itemized amounts for each type of material, part, and labor. Follow the time and materials pricing approach and show the total price for the job.

Problem 24B-4. Developing Transfer Prices (L.O. 5, 7)

Beta Company has two divisions, Alpha and Psi. For several years Alpha Division has manufactured a special glass container, which it sells to the Psi Division at the prevailing market price of $20. Alpha produces the glass containers only for Psi and does not sell the product to outside customers. Annual production and sales volume is 20,000 containers. A unit cost analysis for Alpha showed:

Cost Categories	Costs per Container
Direct materials	$ 2.00
Direct labor, ½ hour	5.00
Variable factory overhead	4.00
Traceable fixed costs $40,000 ÷ 20,000	2.00
General & administrative overhead, $6 per hour	3.00
Variable shipping costs	1.00
Unit cost	$17.00

General and administrative overhead represents such allocated joint fixed costs of production as building depreciation, property taxes, fire insurance, and salaries of production executives. A normal profit allowance of 20 percent is used in determining transfer prices.

Required

1. What would be the appropriate transfer price for Alpha Division to use in billing its transactions with Psi Division?
2. If Alpha Division decided to sell some containers to outside customers, would your answer to **1** above change? Defend your answer.

Problem 24B-5. Transfer Prices and Performance Evaluation
(L.O. 8)

Edmonds Brick Company has two divisions involved in producing and selling bricks. The Mining Division produces clay, which is sold in 100-pound bags to the Production Division. All output of the Mining Division is shipped to the Production Division. These transfers are priced at the average unit cost of production and distribution. The Production Division sells each brick for $1. Each brick requires 1 pound of clay as raw material. Operating results for 19x7 for the two divisions are summarized below.

	Mining Division	Production Division
Total production costs	$ 700,000	$4,500,000
Selling, general, & administrative expenses	300,000	1,500,000
Total costs and expenses	$1,000,000	$6,000,000

In 19x7 the Mining Division produced and shipped 10 million pounds of clay, which were billed to the Production Division at $.10 per pound. The Production Division manufactured and sold 10 million bricks in 19x7. Other mines sell comparable clay material for $.30 per pound.

Required

1. Assume intracompany transfers are priced at average cost. Prepare an income statement for each division.
2. Assume intracompany transfers are billed at market price. Prepare an income statement for each division.

Management Decision Case

Heitz Company
(L.O. 4)

The Heitz Company manufactures office equipment for retail stores. Tom Grant, Vice President of Marketing, has proposed that Heitz introduce two new products, an electric stapler and an electric pencil sharpener.

Grant has requested that the Profit Planning Department develop preliminary selling prices for the two new products for his review. Profit Planning is to follow the company's standard policy for developing potential selling prices. It is to use all data available on each product. Data accumulated by Profit Planning on the two new products are reproduced below.

	Electric Stapler	Electric Pencil Sharpener
Estimated annual demand in units	12,000	10,000
Estimated unit manufacturing costs	$10.00	$12.00
Estimated unit selling & administrative expenses	$4.00	Not available
Assets employed in manufacturing	$180,000	Not available

Heitz plans to use an average of $2,400,000 in assets to support operations in the current year. The condensed pro forma operating income statement presented below represents Heitz's planned costs and return on assets for the entire company for all products.

Heitz Company
Pro Forma Operating Income Statement
For the Year Ended May 31, 19x5
($000 omitted)

Revenue	$4,800
Cost of goods sold, manufacturing costs	2,880
Gross profit	$1,920
Selling & administrative expenses	1,440
Operating profit	$ 480

Required

1. Calculate a potential selling price for the:
   (1) electric stapler using return-on-assets pricing.
   (2) electric pencil sharpener using gross margin pricing.
2. Could a selling price for the electric pencil sharpener be calculated using return-on-assets pricing? Explain your answer.
3. Which of the two pricing methods—return-on-asset pricing or gross margin pricing—is more appropriate for decision analysis? Explain your answer.
4. Discuss the additional steps Tom Grant is likely to take after he receives the potential selling prices for the two new products (as calculated in Requirement 1) to set an actual selling price for each of the two products.

(ICMA adapted)

CHAPTER 25 SHORT-RUN DECISION ANALYSIS

LEARNING OBJECTIVES

1. Define and identify information relevant to decision making.
2. Describe the steps in the management decision cycle.
3. Calculate unit costs, using variable costing procedures.
4. Prepare an income statement, using the contribution margin reporting format.
5. Develop decision data, using the technique of incremental analysis.
6. Evaluate alternatives involving: (a) make-or-buy decisions; (b) special-order decisions; (c) scarce-resource/sales-mix decisions; (d) decisions to eliminate unprofitable segments; and (e) sell or process-further decisions.

One of this book's main tenets is that the management accountant supplies management with three basic types of information: (1) product costing data for pricing and inventory valuation; (2) cost analyses for operational planning and control; and (3) special analyses to support management decision making. Product costing techniques and planning and control procedures were studied in earlier chapters. Decision making is the focus of Chapters 24, 25, and 26. After studying this chapter, you should be able to meet the learning objectives listed on the left.

Top management often depends on the management accountant for information to support its decision-making activities. Such information reveals important data about each alternate decision. To evaluate decision alternatives, the accountant uses special decision models, analyses, and reporting techniques. Decisions concerning long-term capital expenditures are the most complex, and they will be studied in depth in the next chapter. This chapter emphasizes day-to-day operating decisions and information needed for implementation. After discussing the role of strategic planning, defining the term *relevant information*, and exploring management's decision cycle, this chapter discusses decision models. These models include variable costing procedures, contribution margin reporting, and the technique of incremental analysis. The remainder of the chapter focuses on specific types of decisions: (1) make-or-buy; (2) special-order; (3) scarce-resource/sales-mix; (4) unprofitable segment elimination; and (5) sell or process-further.

Strategic Plans of Management

Strategic planning establishes an organization's basic objectives. This planning activity is critical to having a successful business. Without strategic plans, management is without guidance or direction for its actions. Picture an airplane that has just taken off without a destination. The pilot is without direction and does not know where to go. Such is also true for a company without a strategic plan.

Management develops its strategic plan by creating company objectives, an organizational structure, and policies concerning growth and product or service lines. Identifying defined markets to which its products or services should be targeted is also a strategic matter, as are any other factors affecting the organization's structure.

Strategic planning is important to the topics covered in this chapter because it provides the framework for applying short-run period planning. All management decisions should be consistent with a company's strategic plans. For example, assume that management at Datalife Corporation, a supplier of quality computer equipment for the past twelve years, established a new objective: to enter the telecommunications field. Before this change in its strategic plan, management had no guidelines when deciding about: (1) purchasing a company specializing in telecommunications materials or (2) converting an existing product line from a low-profit computer memory chip to a special, potentially high-profit telecommunications memory chip. Without the new strategic plan, both decisions would have been negative because Datalife was not in the telecommunications business. With the change in its strategic plan, management will now consider these and other matters involving the telecommunications industry. As you study decision analyses in this chapter and in Chapter 26, remember that before any positive decision is made, it should be consistent with the organization's strategic plan.

Relevant Information for Management

OBJECTIVE 1
Define and identify information relevant to decision making

The management decision process calls for comparing two or more possible solutions to a problem and deciding which one is the best. Supplying relevant information to management for each alternative is the responsibility of the management accountant. Members of top management should evaluate the possible solutions to a particular problem. To do so, they should not have to wade through pages and pages of data to find out how each alternative will affect the operations of the business. Many of the facts may be the same for each alternative. For instance, total sales may not be affected by a proposal to reduce labor costs by installing automatic machinery. If there are three possible courses of action (three machines to choose from) and total sales are the same in each case, the sales data would not influence the decision. In addition, the accountant often uses past data in preparing cost estimates of decision alternatives. However, it is the cost estimates that are relevant to the decision, not the historical data. **Relevant decision information** is future cost, revenue, or resource usage data, and it will be different for the various alternatives being evaluated. A decision must be made on the basis of the alternatives available. Information that is alike for those alternatives or costs or transactions that have already happened, will not be helpful in picking out the best alternative. Relevant information is limited to future data that differ among the possible alternatives.

Management Decision Cycle

OBJECTIVE 2
Describe the steps in the management decision cycle

The decision-making process is an unstructured area of responsibility. Many decisions are unique and do not lend themselves to strict rules, steps, or timetables. However, certain events accompany each kind of management decision analysis. Figure 25-1 shows the events that make up the management decision cycle. Following the discovery of a problem or resource need, the accountant should seek out all possible courses of action that are open to management and will solve the problem or meet the need. After identifying the alternatives, the accountant prepares a complete analysis for each action, showing its total cost, cost savings, or financial effects on business operations. Each type of decision calls for different information. When all the information has been gathered and organized in a meaningful way, management can decide on the best course of action. After the decision has been carried out, the accountant should prepare a post-decision audit analysis to provide feedback to management on the results of the decision. If further action is needed, the decision cycle begins all over again. If not, this particular decision process has been completed.

Accounting Tools and Reports for Decision Analysis

The accountant usually plays the role of data supplier in the management decision process. Certain accounting tools and reports are used for this purpose. Management expects decision information to be accurate, timely, refined, and presented in a readable way. For this reason the accountant must be concerned not only with the information itself but with the reporting format as well.

Variable costing, which is the basis for contribution margin reporting practices, and incremental analysis are the two most common decision support tools used by the accountant. Each technique helps identify information relevant to a decision. Each technique also provides the accountant with a special decision-reporting format.

Decision Models in Management Accounting

When numerous alternatives are to be evaluated, the decision-making process becomes complex. In addition, many decisions are nonrecurring and cannot be resolved by relying on past experience. To facilitate a complex analysis, this chapter provides a guide to developing a decision model. A **decision model** is a symbolic or numerical representation of the variables and parameters affecting a decision. **Variables** are factors controlled by management. **Parameters** are uncontrollable factors and

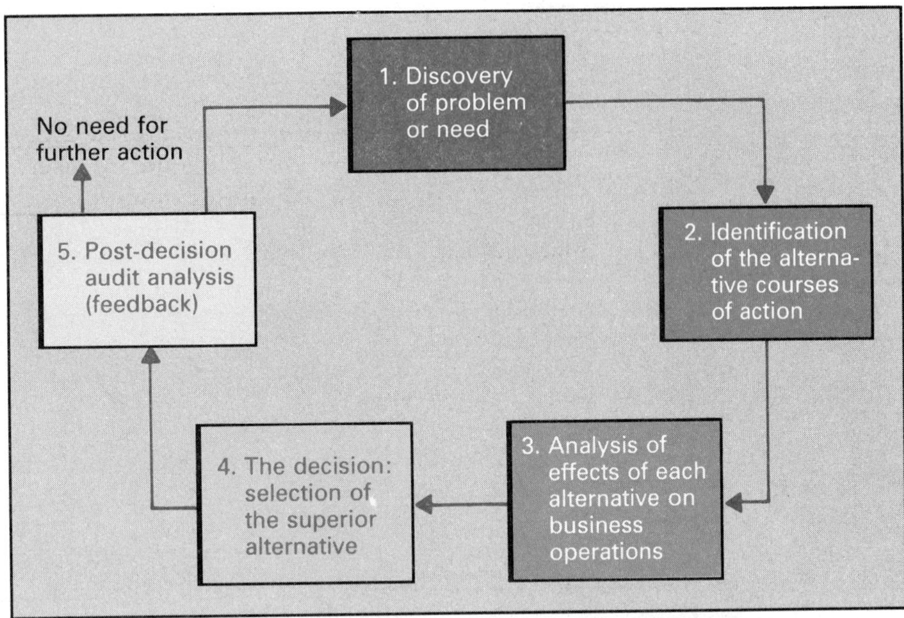

Figure 25-1. The Management Decision Cycle

operating constraints and limitations. As an example, suppose you need to develop a decision model to evaluate new product lines. Your analysis would involve such parameters as customer demand, market growth, competitors' actions, and production capacity limitations. Variables in this decision model would include product selling prices, production costs, and manufacturing methods. The key to developing such a model is to identify relevant variables and parameters and put the information together in an informative manner.

Steps in the model-building process are outlined in Figure 25-2. Parameters affecting the decision are first defined, then possible alternatives are identified. In steps 3 and 4, appropriate cost and revenue information is developed and analyzed. After the irrelevant information has been eliminated, the relative benefits of each alternative are summarized and presented to management. Output of the decision model is a comparative analysis, using the measurement criterion selected for the particular decision problem. This analysis is a formal report to management, and it should include

1. A brief description of the project or problem situation
2. A comparative financial analysis of each alternative
3. A summary of the relative advantages of each alternative

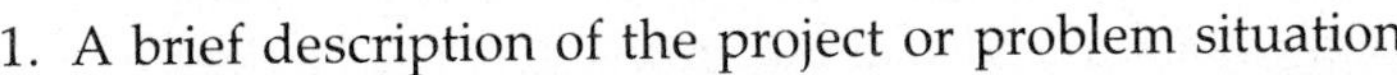

Variable Costing

Variable costing (also called direct costing) is an approach to product costing. However, variable costing is also the basis for developing an

Figure 25-2. Steps in Developing a Decision Model

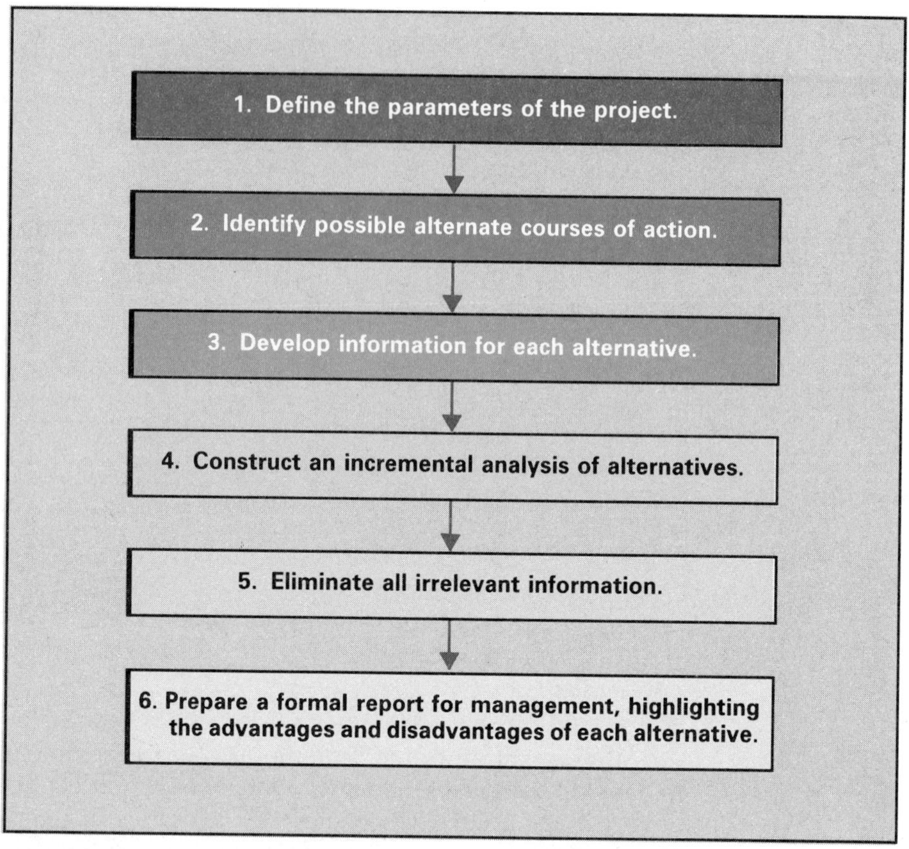
1. Define the parameters of the project.
2. Identify possible alternate courses of action.
3. Develop information for each alternative.
4. Construct an incremental analysis of alternatives.
5. Eliminate all irrelevant information.
6. Prepare a formal report for management, highlighting the advantages and disadvantages of each alternative.

income statement using the contribution margin format. This income statement design is useful in decision-making activities. Unlike absorption costing, which assigns all manufacturing costs to products, **variable costing** uses only the variable manufacturing costs for product costing and inventory valuation. Direct materials costs, direct labor costs, and variable factory overhead costs are the only cost elements used to figure product costs. Fixed factory overhead costs are considered costs of the current accounting period.

Support for variable costing stems from the fact that a company has fixed operating costs whether it operates or not. For this reason those who favor variable costing argue that such costs do not have a direct relationship to the product and should not be used to find the product's unit cost. Fixed manufacturing costs are linked more closely with time than with productive output. Opponents of variable costing say that without fixed manufacturing costs, production would stop. Therefore, such costs are an integral part of a product's cost.

Whatever side you are on, two points are certain. The first is that variable costing is *very* useful for internal management decision purposes. The second is that neither the Internal Revenue Service nor the public accounting profession accepts variable costing for external reporting purposes. They reject it because fixed costs are not included in inventory and cost of goods sold. Therefore, this approach cannot be used for computing federal income taxes or for reporting the results of operations and financial position to stockholders and others outside the company.

OBJECTIVE 3 Calculate unit costs, using variable costing procedures

Product Costing. For purposes of product costing, variable costing treats fixed manufacturing costs differently from production costs that vary with output. A point often overlooked is that fixed manufacturing costs are also left out of all inventories. For this reason the value of inventories arrived at by means of variable costing is lower than the value of those computed by means of absorption costing.

An example will help explain the differences between these two product costing approaches. McClure Industries, Inc., produces grills for outdoor cooking. During 19xx the company put a new, disposable grill into production. A summary of 19xx cost and production data for the grill follows: direct materials costs, $59,136; direct labor, $76,384; variable factory overhead, $44,352; and fixed factory overhead, $36,960. There were 24,640 units completed and 22,000 units sold during 19xx. There were no beginning or ending work in process inventories.

Using this data, we can find the unit cost as well as the ending inventory and cost of goods sold amounts for 19xx under a variable costing approach and under an absorption costing approach. This information is summarized in Exhibit 25-1. Unit production cost under variable costing is $7.30 per grill, whereas unit cost is $8.80 working with absorption costing. Ending finished goods inventory balances are not the same because of the $1.50 difference in unit cost. Because fewer costs remain in inventory at year end with variable costing amounts, it is logical that greater costs will appear on the income statement. As shown in Exhibit 25-1, $197,560 of current manufacturing costs are considered costs of the period, to be subtracted from revenue in the variable costing income statement. Only $193,600 is shown as Cost of Goods Sold when absorption costing is used. The difference of $3,960 (2,640 units in inventory × $1.50 fixed costs per unit) is shown as part of inventory under absorption costing.

Contribution Margin Reporting Format

OBJECTIVE 4 Prepare an income statement, using the contribution reporting format

Performance Analysis: The Income Statement. The use of variable costing leads to differences in financial reporting as well as in product costing. Putting together the concepts of contribution margin and variable costing results in an entirely new form of income statement. This new form emphasizes cost variability and segment or product line contributions to income. Costs are no longer classified as either manufacturing or nonmanufacturing costs. Instead, attention is focused on separating variable costs from fixed costs.

Adding to the McClure Industries example will help explain this point. Assume the following additional information for 19xx: selling price per grill is $24.50. Variable selling costs per grill are $4.80. Fixed selling expenses are $48,210, and fixed administrative expenses are $82,430. Net

Exhibit 25-1. Variable Costing Versus Absorption Costing

McClure Industries, Inc.
Unit Cost and Ending Inventory Values
For the Year Ended December 31, 19xx

	Variable Costing	Absorption Costing
Contribution Margin		
Unit Cost		
Direct materials ($59,136 ÷ 24,640 units)	$ 2.40	$ 2.40
Direct labor ($76,384 ÷ 24,640 units)	3.10	3.10
Variable factory overhead ($44,352 ÷ 24,640 units)	1.80	1.80
Fixed factory overhead ($36,960 ÷ 24,640 units)	—	1.50
Total unit cost	$ 7.30	$ 8.80
Ending Finished Goods Inventory		
2,640 units at $7.30	$ 19,272	
2,640 units at $8.80		$ 23,232
Cost of Goods Sold for 19xx		
22,000 units at $7.30	$160,600	
22,000 units at $8.80		$193,600
Plus fixed factory overhead	36,960	
Costs appearing on 19xx income statement	$197,560	$193,600
Total costs to be accounted for	$216,832	$216,832

income under both variable costing and absorption costing procedures is compared in Exhibit 25-2. The contribution margin format is presented first. Note that the term *gross margin* is replaced by the term *contribution margin* and that only variable costs (including variable selling costs) are subtracted from sales to get the contribution margin. Contribution margin is the amount that each segment or product line is contributing to the fixed costs and profits of the company. Net income calculated by using the conventional statement is shown in the lower part of Exhibit 25-2. Note that net income is different under the two methods. This difference, $3,960, is the same amount noted earlier. It is the part of fixed manufacturing overhead cost that is inventoried when absorption costing is used.

Contribution Reporting and Decisions. Variable costing and the contribution approach to income reporting are used a great deal in decision analysis. Their most common use is in deciding whether to continue a segment, division, or product line. Other uses are in the evaluation of new product lines and in sales-mix studies. Decisions about the contribution of sales territories also use the contribution approach to income reporting. These uses will be explained later when specific kinds of decisions are looked at.

Exhibit 25-2. The Income Statement: Contribution Versus Conventional Formats

McClure Industries, Inc.
Disposable Grill Division
Income Statement
For the Year Ended December 31, 19xx

Contribution Format

Sales		$539,000
Variable Cost of Goods Sold		
Variable Cost of Goods Available for Sale	$179,872	
Less Ending Inventory	19,272*	
Variable Cost of Goods Sold	$160,600*	
Plus Variable Selling Costs (22,000 units at $4.80)	105,600	266,200
Contribution Margin		$272,800
Less Fixed Costs		
Fixed Manufacturing Costs	$ 36,960	
Fixed Selling Expenses	48,210	
Fixed Administrative Expenses	82,430	167,600
Net Income Before Taxes		$105,200

Conventional Format

Sales		$539,000
Cost of Goods Sold		
Cost of Goods Manufactured	$216,832*	
Less Ending Inventory	23,232*	193,600*
Gross Margin from Sales		$345,400
Selling Expenses		
Variable	$105,600	
Fixed	48,210	
Administrative Expenses	82,430	236,240
Net Income (before taxes)		$109,160

* Detailed computations are found in Exhibit 25-1.

Incremental Analysis

OBJECTIVE 5 Develop decision data, using the technique of incremental analysis

Incremental analysis, an approach often used in decision reporting, compares different alternatives by looking only at information differences. Only relevant information, decision data that differ between alternatives, are of concern. For decision purposes, only future data are included. By focusing on the differences between alternatives, incremental analysis helps highlight important points. It makes the evaluation easier for the decision maker. And it reduces the time needed to choose the best course of action.

For example, assume that the Eubanks Company is trying to decide which one of two machines, C or W, to buy. Management has been able to collect the following annual operating estimates on the two machines:

	Machine C	Machine W
Increase in revenue	$16,200	$19,800
Increase in annual operating costs		
Direct materials	2,800	2,800
Direct labor	4,200	6,100
Variable factory overhead	2,100	3,050
Fixed factory overhead (depreciation included)	5,000	5,000

The best method of comparing these two decision alternatives is to prepare an analysis that will show increases or decreases in revenues and costs relevant to the decision. This analysis is shown below.

Eubanks Company
Incremental Decision Analysis

	Machine C	Machine W	Difference in Favor of Machine W
Increase in revenues	$16,200	$19,800	$3,600
Increase in operating costs			
Direct materials	$ 2,800	$ 2,800	—
Direct labor	4,200	6,100	1,900
Variable factory overhead	2,100	3,050	950
Fixed factory overhead	5,000	5,000	—
Total operating costs	$14,100	$16,950	$2,850
Resulting increase in net income	$ 2,100	$ 2,850	$ 750

If you assume that the purchase price and useful life of the two machines are the same, the analysis shows that Machine W will generate $750 more in net income than Machine C. Thus, the decision would be to purchase Machine W. Direct materials costs and fixed factory overhead costs need not be included in the analysis, since they are similar for each alternative. These irrelevant costs are shown here only for purposes of explanation.

Special Reports

Qualitative as well as quantitative data are useful in decision making. When only quantitative data are being considered, most problems of choosing between alternatives can be solved by using either contribution reporting or incremental analysis. However, in some decisions there are many alternatives, each of which is the best one in certain circumstances. One may be more profitable, but another may further diversify a company's product line. A third alternative may help prevent a huge layoff of personnel in some part of the country, thus bolstering the company's goodwill there. Even though many equally good qualitative decision alternatives may be available, management must choose only one course of action. In cases such as those described above, the accountant must use imagination and prepare the special decision report that is best under the circumstances.

For most special decision reports, there is no one correct, set structure. These reports are created by skilled, experienced accountants to fit individual situations. Students of management accounting often have difficulty with decision analysis problems because there are infinite ways to develop these analyses. Students are used to referring back to the text for examples of problem-solving techniques and simply inserting new numbers into a format to solve exercises and problems. Because this is a principles-level book, examples in the text may be used to solve most of the problems. But remember that as the accountant progresses in the field of management accounting, each adventure requires that he or she create a reporting format appropriate to the circumstances. Such challenges contribute to the dynamic nature of this discipline.

Operating Decisions of Management

Management depends on the accountant to supply relevant information for many kinds of decisions. Therefore, this chapter will now turn to data relevant to: (1) the make-or-buy decision; (2) the special-order decision; (3) the scarce-resource/sales-mix decision; (4) the decision to eliminate an unprofitable segment and (5) the sell or process-further decision.

Make-or-Buy Decisions

One common group of decision analyses centers on the many parts used in product assembly operations. Management is continually faced with the decision as to whether to make or buy some or all parts. The goal

OBJECTIVE 6a
Evaluate alternatives involving make-or-buy decisions

of the **make-or-buy decision** is to identify those cost and revenue elements relevant to this kind of decision. Below is the information to be considered.

To Make	To Buy
Need for expensive machinery	Purchase price of item
Other variable costs of making the item	Rent or net cash flow to be generated from vacated space in factory
Repair and maintenance expenses	Salvage value of machinery

To illustrate a make-or-buy decision, the case of the Klock Electronics Company is presented. The firm has been purchasing a small transistor casing from an outside supplier for the past five years at a cost of $1.25 per casing. However, the supplier has just informed Klock Electronics that the price will be raised by 20 percent, effective immediately. The company has idle machinery that could be used to produce the casings. Also, management has found that the costs of producing the casings would be $84 per 100 casings for direct materials, six minutes of labor per casing at $4 per direct labor hour, and variable factory overhead at $2 per direct labor hour. Fixed factory overhead would include $4,000 of depreciation per year and $6,000 of other fixed costs. Annual production and usage would be 20,000 casings. The space and machinery to be used would not be usable if the part were purchased. Should Klock Electronics Company make or buy the casings?

From the information given, the company should make the casings. An incremental cost analysis of the two decision alternatives is presented

Exhibit 25-3. Incremental Analysis: Make-or-Buy Decision

Klock Electronics Company
Incremental Decision Analysis
Current Year—Annual Usage

	Make	Buy	Difference in Favor of Make
Raw materials			
(20,000 ÷ 100 × $84)	$16,800	—	$(16,800)
Direct labor			
(20,000 ÷ 10 × $4)	8,000	—	(8,000)
Variable factory overhead			
(20,000 ÷ 10 × $2)	4,000	—	(4,000)
Fixed factory overhead			
Depreciation*	**4,000**	**4,000**	—
Other*	**6,000**	**6,000**	—
To purchase completed casings			
20,000 × $1.50	—	30,000	30,000
Totals	$28,800	$30,000	$ 1,200

* Irrelevant because these amounts are the same for both decision alternatives. Amounts have not been included in totals.

in Exhibit 25-3. All costs connected with the decision are shown in the analysis. Because the machinery has already been purchased and neither the machinery nor the required factory space has any other use, the fixed factory overhead costs are the same for both alternatives. For this reason they are not relevant to the decision. The costs of making the needed casings (leaving out the fixed overhead costs) are $28,800. The cost of buying 20,000 casings will be $30,000 at the increased purchase price. It is clear, then, that $1,200 will be saved if the casings are made within the company.

Using incremental analysis is a good approach to the make-or-buy decision. This approach allows the analyst to use all decision data available and quickly identify anything irrelevant to the final decision.

Special-Order Decisions

OBJECTIVE 6b Evaluate alternatives involving special-order decisions

Management is often faced with **special-order decisions**, that is, whether to accept special product orders. These orders are normally for large numbers of similar products to be sold at prices below those listed in advertisements. Because management did not expect such orders, the orders were not included in any annual cost or sales estimates. Generally, these orders are one-time events and should not be included in estimates of subsequent years' operations. (Because standard products are sold to the public at stated prices, legal advice on federal price discrimination laws should be obtained before accepting special orders.)

To illustrate special-order analysis, consider Landry Sporting Goods, Inc., which manufactures a complete line of sporting equipment. Kelliher Enterprises operates a large chain of discount stores and has approached the Landry company with a special order. The order calls for 30,000 deluxe baseballs to be shipped with bulk packaging of 500 baseballs per box. Kelliher is willing to pay $2.45 per baseball.

The following data were developed by the Landry accounting department: annual expected production, 400,000 baseballs; current year's production, 410,000 baseballs; maximum production capacity, 450,000 baseballs. Additional data are presented below.

Unit cost data	
Direct materials	$ .60
Direct labor	.90
Factory overhead	
Variable	.50
Fixed ($100,000 ÷ 400,000)	.25
Packaging per unit	.30
Advertising ($60,000 ÷ 400,000)	.15
Other fixed selling and administrative costs ($120,000 ÷ 400,000)	.30
Total	$ 3.00
Unit selling price	$ 4.00
Total estimated bulk packaging costs (30,000 baseballs: 500 per box)	$2,500

Should Landry Sporting Goods, Inc., accept the Kelliher offer?

A profitability analysis reveals that the special order from Kelliher Enterprises should be accepted. Exhibit 25-4 contains a comparative analysis based on the contribution reporting format. Net income before taxes is computed for the Baseball Division for operations both with and without the Kelliher order.

The only costs affected by the order are for direct materials, direct labor, variable factory overhead, and packaging. Materials, labor, and overhead costs are shown for sales of 410,000 and 440,000 baseballs, respectively. Sales data were computed, using these same unit amounts. Packaging costs will increase, but only by the amount of the added bulk packaging costs. All other costs will remain the same. The net result of accepting the special order is an $11,000 increase in contribution margin (and net income before taxes). This amount can be verified by the following computations:

$$
\begin{aligned}
\text{Net gain} &= [(\text{unit selling price} - \text{unit variable mfg. costs}) \times \text{units}] - \text{bulk pack costs} \\
&= [(\$2.45 - \$2.00)\ 30{,}000] - \$2{,}500 \\
&= \$13{,}500 - \$2{,}500 = \underline{\underline{\$11{,}000}}
\end{aligned}
$$

For special-order analysis both the comparative contribution reporting approach and incremental analysis can be used. In the above case contribution reporting was chosen because of the misleading fixed cost

Exhibit 25-4. Contribution Reporting: Special Product Order

Landry Sporting Goods, Inc.
Comparative Decision Analysis
Special Product Order—Baseball Division

	Without Kelliher Order	With Kelliher Order
Sales	$1,640,000	$1,713,500
Less variable costs		
Direct materials	$ 246,000	$ 264,000
Direct labor	369,000	396,000
Variable factory overhead	205,000	220,000
Packaging costs	123,000	125,500
Total variable costs	$ 943,000	$1,005,500
Contribution margin	$ 697,000	$ 708,000
Less fixed costs		
Factory overhead	$ 100,000	$ 100,000
Advertising	60,000	60,000
Selling and administrative	120,000	120,000
Total fixed costs	$ 280,000	$ 280,000
Net income before taxes	$ 417,000	$ 428,000

data in the problem. Contribution reporting highlights the effect of variable cost changes on contribution margin and net income.

Scarce-Resource/Sales-Mix Analysis

OBJECTIVE 6c
Evaluate alternatives involving scarce-resource/sales-mix decisions

Profit can be maximized only when the profitability of all product lines is known. Optimal use of scarce resources, such as labor hours or machine hours, is part of this maximizing process. The question is: which product or products contribute most to company profitability in relation to the amount of capital assets or other scarce resources needed to produce the item(s)? To answer this question, the management accountant must first measure the contribution margin of each product. Next, he or she must determine a set of ratios of contribution margin to the required capital equipment or other scarce resource. This analysis identifies products or services yielding the most contribution margin per unit of scarce resource. Once this step has been completed, management should request a marketing study to establish the upper limits of demand for the most profitable products or services. If profitability per product or service can be computed and market demand exists, then management should shift its emphasis to the most profitable products or services.

Many decisions can be related to the approach described here. **Sales-mix analysis** means determining the most profitable combination of product sales when a company produces more than one product or offers more than one service. The contribution margin approach to decision analysis, as described above, can also be used for several other types of decisions. Closely connected with sales-mix analysis is the product line profitability study designed to discover if any products are losing money for the company. Although the contribution margin approach is used, the objective is different. There is no longer interest in maximizing profits based on the use of scarce resources. Instead, interest centers on eliminating the unprofitable product line(s) or service(s). Identifying unprofitable corporate divisions or segments is another type of decision analysis relying on the contribution margin approach. Decisions to eliminate unprofitable products or services and unprofitable corporate segments are based on similar analyses of contribution margin. These types of decisions are discussed in the next section of this chapter.

An example of sales-mix analysis will aid understanding. The management of Christenson Enterprises is analyzing its sales mix. The company manufactures three products—C, A, and L—using the same production equipment for all three. Total productive capacity is being used. Below are the product line statistics.

	Product C	Product A	Product L
Current production and sales (units)	20,000	30,000	18,000
Machine hours per product	2	1	2.5
Selling price per unit	$24.00	$18.00	$32.00
Unit variable manufacturing costs	$12.50	$10.00	$18.75
Unit variable selling costs	$ 6.50	$ 5.00	$ 6.25

Should the company try selling more of one product and less of another?

Exhibit 25-5. Contribution Reporting: Sales-Mix Analysis

Christenson Enterprises
Sales-mix Analysis
Contribution Reporting Format

	Product C	Product A	Product L
Sales price	$24.00	$18.00	$32.00
Variable costs			
Manufacturing	$12.50	$10.00	$18.75
Selling	6.50	5.00	6.25
Total	$19.00	$15.00	$25.00
Contribution margin (A)	$ 5.00	$ 3.00	$ 7.00
Machine hours required per unit (B)	2	1	2.5
Contribution margin per machine hour (A ÷ B)	$ 2.50	$ 3.00	$ 2.80

Because total productive capacity is being used, the only way to expand production of one product is to reduce production of another product. The sales-mix analysis of Christenson Enterprises is shown in Exhibit 25-5. Although contribution reporting is used here, contribution margin per product is not the important figure when deciding about shifts in sales mix. In the analysis Product L has the highest contribution margin. However, all products use the same machinery and all machine hours are filled. Therefore, machine hours become the scarce resource.

The analysis in Exhibit 25-5 goes one step beyond the computation of contribution margin per unit. Such a sales-mix decision should use two decision variables: (1) contribution margin per unit and (2) machine hours required per unit. For instance, Product C requires two machine hours to generate $5 of contribution margin. But Product A would generate $6 of contribution margin using the same two machine hours. For this reason, contribution margin is calculated per machine hour. Based on this information, management can readily see that it should produce and sell as much of Product A as possible. Next, it should push Product L. If any productive capacity remains, it should produce Product C.

Decisions to Eliminate Unprofitable Segments

OBJECTIVE 6d Evaluate alternatives involving decisions to eliminate unprofitable segments

Whether to eliminate an unprofitable product, service, division, or other corporate segment is another type of operating decision management may face. The analysis prepared for this type of decision is an extension of the normal performance evaluation of the segment. As an overview the analysis of unprofitable segments compares: (1) operating results of the corporation with the segment in question included against (2) operating results for the same period that do not include data from that segment. The key to this analysis is to be able to isolate the segment, product, or service in question. Variable costs associated with a product or segment are easy to identify and account for. But each product or segment also has fixed costs associated with it. The fixed costs are commonly referred to as **traceable fixed costs**.

To analyze the financial consequences of eliminating a segment, one must concentrate on the incremental profit effect of the decision. The decision analysis consists of comparing contribution margin income statements for the company. One statement includes the segment under review, and the second excludes this information. The basic decision is a problem of choosing to keep the product, service, or segment or to eliminate it.

Assume management at Hugh Corporation wants to determine if Division B should be eliminated. Exhibit 25-6 provides basic cost and

Exhibit 25-6. Divisional Profit Summary and Decision Analysis

Hugh Corporation
Divisional Profit Summary and Decision Analysis

A. Income Statements

	Divisions D and E	Division B	Total Company
Sales	$135,000	$15,000	$150,000
Less variable costs	52,500	7,500	60,000
Contribution margin	$ 82,500	$ 7,500	$ 90,000
Less traceable fixed costs	55,500	16,500	72,000
Divisional income	$ 27,000	($ 9,000)	$ 18,000
Less unallocated fixed costs			12,000
Income before taxes			$ 6,000

B. Incremental Decision Analysis

	Company Profitability if It Elects To: Keep Division B	Company Profitability if It Elects To: Eliminate Division B	Benefit or (Cost) To Eliminate Division B	
Sales	$150,000	$135,000	($15,000)	sales decrease
Less variable costs	60,000	52,500	7,500	cost reduction
Contribution margin	$ 90,000	$ 82,500	($ 7,500)	CM decrease
Less total fixed costs	84,000	67,500	16,500	cost reduction
Income before taxes	$ 6,000	$ 15,000	$ 9,000	profit increase

revenue data and illustrates a format for evaluating alternate decisions. This analysis requires that an income statement be prepared for each alternative and that profits be compared. All traceable fixed costs of Division B are assumed to be avoidable. **Avoidable costs** are costs that will be eliminated if a particular product, service or corporate segment is discontinued. As the analysis in Exhibit 25-6 shows, the profits of Hugh Corporation will increase by $9,000 if Division B is eliminated.

Another way of looking at this decision is to concentrate on the third column in part B of Exhibit 25-6. Revenue and cost factors that are different under each alternative can be analyzed to explain the profit difference of $9,000. The incremental factors are analyzed in Exhibit 25-7. If all fixed costs traceable to Division B are avoidable, then the operating loss of $9,000 is also avoidable if the division is eliminated. The primary concept is to isolate avoidable costs, which may not always correspond with traceable costs. Avoidable costs are incremental costs, since these amounts are incurred only if the division exists.

In trying to understand the significance of determining an accurate amount of avoidable costs, assume you discover that executives and supervisors in Division B will be reassigned to other divisions if Division B is eliminated. Included in the $16,500 of traceable fixed costs for Division B are salaries of $12,000 for these people. This assumption now changes the profit effect of eliminating Division B, as shown below.

Advantage of eliminating Division B	
Reduction of variable expenses	$ 7,500
Reduction of fixed expenses ($16,500 − $12,000)	4,500
Total benefits	$12,000
Disadvantage of eliminating Division B	
Reduction in sales	$15,000
Decrease in profit as a result of eliminating Division B (2 − 1)	$ 3,000

By following these revised assumptions, you compute that avoidable fixed costs for Division B are $4,500 (traceable fixed costs of $16,500 less the $12,000 cost of people to be reassigned to other divisions). Generally, it is unprofitable to eliminate any segment for which contribution margin exceeds avoidable fixed costs. This rule is actually a condensed version of the incremental profit analysis.

If you apply this rule to the Hugh Corporation example, the analysis would be as follows:

Division B

Contribution margin	$7,500
Less avoidable fixed costs	4,500
Profit contribution	$3,000

In such an analysis corporate profits would actually decrease by $3,000 if Division B were eliminated. This conclusion is valid even though operating reports for Division B disclose a loss of $9,000.

Exhibit 25-7. Incremental Revenue and Cost Analysis

Hugh Corporation
Incremental Revenue and Cost Analysis

Advantage of Eliminating Division B	Amount
Increase in sales	None
Decrease in costs ($7,500 + $16,500)	$24,000
Total advantage	$24,000

Disadvantage of Eliminating Division B	Amount
Decrease in sales	$15,000
Increase in costs	None
Total disadvantage	$15,000
Incremental profit from eliminating Division B advantage less disadvantage	$ 9,000

As shown in Exhibit 25-6, the decision analysis used to decide about eliminating an unprofitable segment (product line, service, or division) requires two decision analysis tools: (1) contribution margin reporting and (2) incremental analysis. Contribution margin reporting helped identify traceable and avoidable fixed costs relevant to the decision, whereas incremental analysis assisted in comparing the operating results with and without the segment.

Sell or Process-Further Decisions

OBJECTIVE 6e Evaluate alternatives involving sell or process-further decisions

The sell or process-further decision was briefly mentioned when analyzing the allocation of joint or common processing costs in Chapter 19. The choice between selling a product at the split-off point or processing it further is a short-run operating decision about joint products. The decision to process a joint product beyond split-off requires an analysis of incremental revenues and costs of the two alternate courses of action. Additional processing adds value to a product and increases its selling price above the amount it may have been sold for at split-off. The decision to process further depends on whether the increase in total revenue exceeds additional costs for processing beyond split-off. *Joint costs incurred before split-off do not affect the decision.* These costs are incurred regardless of the point at which the products are sold. Thus, they are irrelevant to the decision. Only future costs differing between alternatives are relevant to the decision.

Maximizing company profits is the objective of sell or process-further decisions. For example, assume that Buttery Gardening Supplies, Inc., produces various products to enhance plant growth. In one process three products emerge from the joint initial phase. They are called "Gro-Pow," "Gro-Pow II," and "Gro-Supreme." For each 20,000-pound batch of materials converted into products, $120,000 in joint production costs are incurred. At split-off 50 percent of the output becomes Gro-Pow, 30 percent becomes Gro-Pow II, and 20 percent becomes Gro-Supreme. Each product is processed beyond split-off, and the following additional variable costs are incurred:

Product	Pounds	Additional Processing Costs
Gro-Pow	10,000	$24,000
Gro-Pow II	6,000	38,000
Gro-Supreme	4,000	33,500
Totals	20,000	$95,500

Christine & Hill, landscapers, has offered to purchase all joint products at split-off for the following prices per pound: Gro-Pow, $8; Gro-Pow II, $24; and Gro-Supreme, $40. To help the landscapers decide whether to sell at split-off or process the products further, Buttery management requested an incremental analysis. This analysis is to compare increases in revenue and increases in processing costs for each alternative.

Exhibit 25-8 reveals the selling prices of the three products at split-off and if processed further. The exhibit also contains the incremental analysis. As illustrated, products Gro-Pow and Gro-Supreme should be processed further, since each will cause a significant increase in overall company profit. If Gro-Pow II can be sold to Christine & Hill, the company will avoid a $2,000 loss from further processing. Note that the $120,000 joint processing costs are irrevelant to the decision, since they will be incurred with either alternative.

Measuring incremental costs for additional processing beyond split-off can create problems. Additional costs of materials, labor, and variable overhead are incremental, since these costs are caused by additional processing. However, supervisors' salaries, property taxes, insurance, and other fixed costs incurred regardless of the production decision are not incremental costs. Incremental processing costs should include only production costs if a product is processed beyond split-off. Fixed overhead costs common to other production activity must be excluded from a sell or process-further incremental analysis.

Exhibit 25-8. Incremental Analysis—Sell or Process-Further Decision

Buttery Gardening Supplies, Inc.
Incremental Analysis—Sell or Process-Further Decision

Unit selling price data

Product	If Sold at Split-off	If Sold After Additional Processing
Gro-Pow	$ 8.00	$12.00
Gro-Pow II	24.00	30.00
Gro-Supreme	40.00	50.00

given

Incremental analysis per 20,000 pound batch

Product	(1) Pounds	(2) Total Revenue if Sold at Split-off	(3) Total Revenue if Sold After Processing Further	(4) Incremental Revenue (3) − (2)	(5) Incremental Costs	(6) Effect on Overall Profit (4) − (5)
Gro-Pow	10,000	$ 80,000	$120,000	$40,000	$24,000	$16,000
Gro-Pow II	6,000	144,000	180,000	36,000	38,000	(2,000)
Gro-Supreme	4,000	160,000	200,000	40,000	33,500	6,500

given given

Chapter Review

Review of Learning Objectives

1. **Define and identify information relevant to decision making.**
Any future cost, revenue, or resource usage data utilized in decision analyses that will be different for alternative courses of action are considered relevant decision information. Recognition of relevant data comes from developing a comparative analysis of the decision alternatives.

2. **Describe the steps in the management decision cycle.**
The decision cycle begins with discovery of a problem or resource need. Then, various alternative courses of action to solve the problem or meet the need are identified. Next, a complete analysis to determine the effects of each alternative on business operations is prepared. With this supporting data the decision maker chooses the best alternative. After the decision has been carried out, the accountant should do a post-audit to see if the decision was correct or if other needs have arisen.

3. **Calculate unit costs, using variable costing procedures.**
Variable costing uses only variable *manufacturing* costs for product costing and inventory valuation. Direct materials costs, direct labor costs, and variable factory overhead costs are the only elements used to compute product costs. Fixed factory overhead costs are considered costs of the current period and are not included in inventories.

4. **Prepare an income statement, using the contribution margin reporting format.**
Unlike the conventional form of income reporting that depends on the absorption costing concept, the contribution form is based on variable costing procedures. Variable costs of goods sold and variable selling expenses are subtracted from sales to arrive at contribution margin. All fixed costs, including those from manufacturing, selling, and administration, are subtracted from contribution margin to determine net income (before taxes).

5. **Develop decision data, using the technique of incremental analysis.**
Incremental analysis is a form of decision reporting in which various decision alternatives are identified and differences in information about them are examined. When all revenue and cost data are examined in this way, data relevant to the decision are highlighted, since they are the ones where differences exist. Revenue and cost items that are the same under the various alternatives are irrelevant to the decision.

6. **Evaluate alternatives involving: (a) make-or-buy decisions; (b) special-order decisions; (c) scarce-resource/sales-mix decisions; (d) decisions to eliminate unprofitable segments; and (e) sell or process-further decisions.**
Make-or-buy decision analysis helps management decide whether to buy a part used in product assembly or to make the part inside the company. This analysis centers on an incremental view of the costs of each alternative. Special-order decisions concern unused capacity and finding the lowest acceptable selling price of a product. Generally, fixed costs are irrelevant to the decision, since these costs were covered by regular operations. Contribution margin is a key decision yardstick. Sales-mix analysis is used to find the most profitable combination of product sales when a company makes more than one product using a common scarce resource. A similar approach may be used for decisions about profitable sales territories, service lines, or corporate segments. Comparative analyses using the contribution reporting format are important in all of these studies. The decision to eliminate unprofitable products, services, or company segments requires an incremental analysis. This analysis should compare operating results that include the questionable segment against operating results without the segment's traceable and avoidable revenues and costs. Both income statements are prepared by following the contribution margin reporting format. Sell or process-further decisions are also based on comparisons of incremental revenues and costs of the two alternatives. Joint processing costs are irrelevant to the decision, since they are identical for either alternative.

Review Problem: Short-run Operating Decision Analysis

In 1981 Frank Calacchi formed National Services, Inc., a company specializing in repair and maintenance services dealing with the home and its surroundings. To date National has six offices in major cities across the country. Fourteen services, ranging from plumbing repair to appliance repair to lawn care, are offered to the home owner. During the past two years the company's profitability has decreased, and Mr. Calacchi wants to determine which service lines are not meeting the company's profit targets. Once the unprofitable service lines are identified, he will either eliminate them or set higher prices. If higher prices are set, all variable and fixed operating, selling, and general administration costs will be covered by the price structure. The following data from the most recent year-end closing was available for the analysis. Four service lines are under serious review.

National Services, Inc.
Service Profit and Loss Summary
For the Year Ended December 31, 19x8

	Auto Repair Service	Boat Repair Service	Tile Floor Repair Service	Tree Trimming Service	Total Company Impact
Sales	$297,500	$114,300	$126,400	$97,600	$635,800
Less variable costs					
Direct labor	$119,000	$ 40,005	$ 44,240	$34,160	$237,405
Operating supplies	14,875	5,715	6,320	4,880	31,790
Small tools	11,900	4,572	5,056	7,808	29,336
Replacement parts	59,500	22,860	25,280	0	107,640
Truck expenses	0	11,430	12,640	14,640	38,710
Selling expenses	44,625	17,145	18,960	9,760	90,490
Other variable costs	5,950	2,286	2,528	1,952	12,716
Total	$255,850	$104,013	$115,024	$73,200	$548,087
Contribution margin	$ 41,650	$ 10,287	$ 11,376	$24,400	$ 87,713
Less traceable fixed costs	74,200	29,600	34,700	28,400	166,900
Service margin	($32,550)	($ 19,313)	($ 23,324)	($ 4,000)	($ 79,187)
Less nontraceable joint fixed costs					32,100
Net income before taxes					($111,287)
Avoidable fixed costs included in traceable fixed costs above	$ 35,800	$ 16,300	$ 24,100	$ 5,200	$ 81,400

Required

1. Analyze the performance of the four services being reviewed.
2. Should Mr. Calacchi eliminate any of the service lines? Why?
3. Identify some possible causes for poor performance by the services.
4. What factors would lead you to raise the fee for a service rather than eliminate the service?

Answer to Review Problem

1. When analyzing the performance of four service lines for possible elimination, you should concentrate on the revenues and costs to be eliminated if the service is eliminated. You should start your analysis with contribution margin because all sales and variable costs will be eliminated. By subtracting the avoidable fixed costs from contribution margin, you will find the profit or loss that will be eliminated if the service is eliminated.

	Auto Repair Service	Boat Repair Service	Tile Floor Repair Service	Tree Trimming Service	Total Company Impact
Contribution margin	$41,650	$10,287	$11,376	$24,400	$87,713
Less avoidable fixed costs	35,800	16,300	24,100	5,200	81,400
Profit (loss) lost if service is eliminated	$ 5,850	($ 6,013)	($12,724)	$19,200	$ 6,313

2. From the analysis in part 1, you can see that the company will improve by $18,737 ($6,013 + $12,724) if the Boat Repair Service and the Tile Floor Service are eliminated.
3. There are several possible causes for poor performance by the four services. Among them are the following:
   a. Low service fee being charged
   b. Inadequate advertising of the service
   c. High direct labor costs
   d. Other variable costs too high
   e. Poor management of fixed cost levels
   f. Excessive management costs
4. In order to judge the adequacy of the service fees being charged, you should first look at the contribution margin percentages. This additional bit of information will help support pricing decisions for the four services.

	Auto Repair Service	Boat Repair Service	Tile Floor Repair Service	Tree Trimming Service
Sales	$297,500	$114,300	126,400	$97,600
Contribution margin	$ 41,650	$ 10,287	$ 11,376	$24,400
Contribution margin percentage	14.00%	9.00%	9.00%	25.00%

As you can see, only 9 percent of the selling price is available for fixed costs and profit from the Boat Repair and Tile Floor Repair services. This is a thin margin with which to work. An increase in fees seems appropriate. Even fees for the Auto Repair Service may need to be increased.

Also, remember there were large amounts of unavoidable and nontraceable fixed costs reported. These costs may need to be analyzed, too. Although they may be avoidable, these costs must be covered by fees if the company is to remain profitable.

Chapter Assignments

Questions

1. Define strategic planning.
2. "Strategic planning provides the basic framework for applying short-run period planning." Do you agree? Why?
3. What is meant by the term *relevant decision information*? What are the two important characteristics of such information?
4. Describe and discuss the five steps of the management decision cycle.
5. Describe the concept of variable costing. How does variable costing differ from absorption costing?
6. Is variable costing widely used for financial reporting purposes? Defend your answer.
7. What is the connection between variable costing and the contribution margin approach to reporting?
8. Are variable costs always relevant? Defend your response.
9. Identify and discuss the steps required to build a decision model.
10. What are the objectives of incremental analysis? What types of decision analyses depend on the incremental approach?
11. Illustrate and discuss some qualitative inputs into decision analysis.
12. How does one determine which data are relevant to a make-or-buy decision?
13. Under what circumstances should profit contribution per machine hour be considered in a make-or-buy decision?
14. When pricing a special order, what justifies excluding fixed overhead costs from the analysis? Under what circumstances are fixed costs relevant to the pricing decision?
15. What questions must be answered in trying to make the most of product line profitability? Give examples of approaches to the solution of this question.
16. For sales-mix decisions, what criteria can be used to select products that will maximize net income?
17. Why is the term *avoidable cost* used in relation to alternatives to eliminating a segment.
18. Distinguish between the terms *avoidable cost* and *traceable cost.*
19. Why are joint processing costs irrelevant to the decision to sell a product at split-off or process it further?
20. Is incremental analysis important to the sell or process-further decision? Why?

Classroom Exercises

Exercise 25-1. Relevant Data and Incremental Analysis
(L.O. 1, 5)

Mr. Richard, business manager for Bebee Industries, must select a new typewriter for his secretary. Rental of Model A, which is like the typewriter now being used, is $400 per year. Model B, a deluxe typewriter, rents for $600 per year, but it will require a new desk for the secretary. The annual desk rental charge is $200. The secretary's salary of $500 per month will not change. If Model B is rented, $80 in training costs will be incurred. Model B has greater capacity and is expected to save $550 per year in part-time secretarial wages. Upkeep and operating costs will not differ between the two models.

1. Identify the relevant data in this problem.
2. Prepare an incremental analysis to aid the business manager's decision.

Exercise 25-2. Relevant Costs and Revenues (L.O. 1)

Old Dominion Enterprises manufactures various household metal products, such as window frames, light fixtures, and doorknobs. In 19x8 the company produced 20,000 square doorknobs but sold only 2,000 units at $10.00 each. The remaining units cannot be sold through normal channels. For inventory purposes costs on December 31, 19x8, included the following data on unsold units:

Direct materials	$2.00
Direct labor	3.00
Variable overhead	.50
Fixed overhead	1.50
Cost per knob	$7.00

The 18,000 square knobs can be sold to a scrap dealer in another state for $3.50 each. A business license for this state will cost Old Dominion $400. Shipping expenses will average $.05 per knob.

1. Identify the relevant costs and revenues for the scrap-sale alternative.
2. Assume the square knobs can be reprocessed to produce round knobs, which normally have the same $7.00 unit cost components and sell for $8.00 each. Rework costs will be $4.50 per unit. Determine the most profitable alternative, reprocessing or selling scrap.

Exercise 25-3. Variable Costing: Unit Cost Computation (L.O. 3)

Suny Corporation produces a full line of energy-tracking devices. These devices can detect and track all forms of thermochemical energy-emitting space vehicles. The following cost data are provided: direct materials cost $985,000 for four units. Direct labor for assembly is 1,590 hours per unit at $11.50 per hour. Variable factory overhead is $28.00 per direct labor hour. Fixed factory overhead is $1,792,000 per month (based on an average production of 28 units per month). Packaging materials come to $27,200 for four units, and packaging labor is 20 hours per unit at $8.50 per hour. Advertising and marketing cost $196,750 per month, and other fixed selling and administrative costs are $287,680 per month.

1. From the cost data above, find the unit production cost, using both variable costing and absorption costing methods.
2. Assume the current month's ending inventory is fifteen units. Compute the inventory valuation under both variable and absorption costing methods.

Exercise 25-4. Income Statement: Contribution Reporting Format (L.O. 4)

The income statement in the conventional reporting format for Brosi Products, Inc., for the year ended December 31, 19xx, appeared as shown.

Fixed manufacturing costs of $27,600 and $850 are included in Cost of Goods Available for Sale and Ending Inventory, respectively. Total fixed manufacturing costs for 19xx were $26,540. There were no beginning or ending work in process inventories. All administrative expenses are considered to be fixed.

Using this information, prepare an income statement for Brosi Products, Inc., for the year ended December 31, 19xx, using the contribution reporting format.

Brosi Products, Inc.
Income Statement
For the Year Ended December 31, 19xx

Sales		$396,400
Cost of goods sold		
Cost of goods available for sale	$225,290	
Less ending inventory	12,540	212,750
Gross margin from sales		$183,650
Less operating expenses		
Selling expenses		
Variable	$ 99,820	
Fixed	26,980	
Administrative expenses	37,410	164,210
Net income before taxes		$ 19,440

Exercise 25-5. Make-or-Buy Decision (L.O. 6a)

One part for a radio assembly being produced by Mount Vernon Audio Systems, Inc., is being purchased for $155 per 100 parts. Management is studying the possibility of manufacturing these parts. Cost and production data are as follows: annual production (usage) is 60,000 units. Fixed costs (all of which remain unchanged whether the part is made or purchased) are $28,500. Variable costs are $.65 per unit for direct materials, $.45 per unit for direct labor, and $.40 per unit for manufacturing overhead.

Using incremental decision analysis, decide whether the company should make the part or continue to purchase it from an outside vendor.

Exercise 25-6. Special-Order Decision (L.O. 6b)

Alvin, Kabot, & Hunter, Ltd., produces antique-looking lamp shades. Management has just received a request for a special-design order and must decide whether to accept it. The special order calls for 8,000 shades to be shipped in a total of 200 bulk pack cartons. Shipping costs of $60 per carton will replace normal packing and shipping costs. The purchasing company is offering to pay $24 per shade plus packing and shipping expenses.

The following information has been provided by the accounting department: Annual expected production is 250,000 shades, and the current year's production (before special order) is 260,000 shades. Maximum production capacity is 280,000 shades. Unit cost data include $6.20 for direct materials, $8.00 for direct labor, variable factory overhead of $5.80, and fixed factory overhead of $3.50 ($875,000/250,000). Normal packaging and shipping costs per unit come to $2.50, and advertising is $.36 per unit ($90,000/250,000). Other fixed administrative costs are $.88 per unit ($220,000/250,000). Thus, total normal cost per unit is $27.24. Per unit selling price is set at $38.00. Total estimated bulk packaging costs ($60 per carton × 200 cartons) are $12,000.

Determine whether this special order should be accepted.

Exercise 25-7. Scarce-Resource Usage (L.O. 6c)

Massasoit, Inc., manufactures two products, which require both machine processing and labor operations. Although there is unlimited demand for both products, Massasoit could devote all of its capacities to a single product. Unit prices, cost data, and processing requirements are shown below:

	Product A	Product M
Unit selling price	$40	$110
Unit variable costs	$20	$ 45
Machine hours per unit	.4	1.4
Labor hours per unit	2	6

In 19x9 the company will be limited to 160,000 machine hours and 120,000 labor hours.

1. Compute the quantities of each product to be produced in 19x9.
2. Prepare an income statement for the product volume computed in 1.

Exercise 25-8. Elimination of Unprofitable Segment (L.O. 6d)

Stockholm Glass, Inc., has three divisions, Atta, Nio, and Tio. The divisional income summaries for 19x8 revealed the following:

	Atta Division	Nio Division	Tio Division	Total Company
Sales	$390,000	$433,000	$837,000	$1,660,000
Variable costs	247,000	335,000	472,000	1,054,000
Contribution margin	$143,000	$ 98,000	$365,000	$ 606,000
Less traceable fixed costs	166,000	114,000	175,000	455,000
Divisional income	($ 23,000)	($ 16,000)	$190,000	$ 151,000
Less unallocated fixed costs				82,000
Net income before taxes				$ 69,000

A detailed analysis of the traceable fixed costs revealed the following:

	Atta Division	Nio Division	Tio Division
Avoidable fixed costs	$154,000	$ 96,000	$139,000
Unavoidable fixed costs	12,000	18,000	36,000
Total	$166,000	$114,000	$175,000

Based on the 19x8 income summaries, determine whether it would be profitable for the company to eliminate one or more of its segments. Identify which division(s) should be eliminated, and compute how much the resulting increase in total net income would be before taxes.

Exercise 25-9. Sell or Process-Further Decision (L.O. 6e)

Ron Owens Marketeers, Inc., has developed a promotional program for a large shopping center in Hopewell, New Jersey. After investing $360,000 into the promotion campaign, the firm is ready to present its client with: (1) a TV advertising program, (2) a series of brochures for mass mailing, and (3) a special rotating "BIG SALE" schedule for ten of the twenty-eight tenants in the shopping center. Revenue from the original contract with the shopping center is shown below. Also shown is an offer for an add-on contract, which extends the original contract terms.

	Contract Terms	
	Original Contract Terms	**Extended Contract Including Add-on Terms**
TV advertising program	$420,000	$480,000
Brochure package	110,000	130,000
Rotating "BIG SALE" schedule	70,000	90,000
Totals	$600,000	$700,000

Mr. Owens estimates that the following additional costs will be incurred by extending the contract:

	T.V. Program	Brochures	BIG SALE Schedule
Direct labor	$30,000	$ 9,000	$7,000
Variable overhead costs	22,000	14,000	6,000
Fixed overhead costs*	12,000	4,000	2,000

* 20% are unavoidable fixed costs applied to this contract.

1. Compute the costs that will be incurred for each part of the add-on portion of the contract.
2. Should Ron Owens Marketeers, Inc., accept the add-on contract or ask for a final settlement check on the original contract only? Defend your answer.
3. If management of the shopping center indicated the terms of the add-on contract were negotiable, how should the Owens group respond?

Interpreting Accounting Information

Internal Management Information: Falcetta Can Opener Company, Special-Order Decision
(L.O. 6b)

Falcetta Can Opener Company is a subsidiary of Frank Appliances, Inc. The can opener produced by Falcetta is in strong demand. Sales during the present year, 19x9, are expected to hit the 1,000,000 mark. Full plant capacity is 1,150,000 units, but the 1,000,000-unit mark was considered normal capacity for the current year. The following unit price and cost breakdown is applicable in 19x9:

	Per Unit
Sales price	$45.00
Less manufacturing costs	
Materials	$ 9.00
Direct labor	7.00
Overhead: variable	4.00
fixed	6.00
Total manufacturing costs	$26.00
Gross margin	$19.00
Less selling and administrative expenses:	
Selling: variable	$ 2.50
fixed	2.00
Administrative, fixed	3.00
Packaging, variable*	1.50
Total selling and administrative expenses	$ 9.00
Net profit before taxes	$10.00

* Three types of packaging are available:

Deluxe	$1.50/unit
Plain	$1.00/unit
Bulk pack	$ .50/unit

During November the company received three special-order requests from large chain-store companies. These orders are not part of the budgeted 1,000,000-unit sales for 19x9, but company officials think that sufficient capacity exists for one order to be accepted.

Orders received and their terms follow:

Order 1: 75,000 can openers @ $40.00/unit, deluxe packaging

Order 2: 90,000 can openers @ $36.00/unit, plain packaging

Order 3: 125,000 can openers @ $31.50/unit, bulk packaging

Since these orders were made directly to company officials, no variable selling costs will be incurred.

1. Analyze the profitability of each of the three special orders.
2. Which special order should be accepted?

Problem Set A

Problem 25A-1. Variable Costing: Contribution Approach to Income Statement (L.O. 3, 4)

Interior designers often use the deluxe carpet products of McCoy Mills, Inc. The Thomas Blend is the company's top-of-the-line product. In March 19x8 McCoy produced 137,500 square yards and sold 124,900 square yards of Thomas Blend. Factory operating data for the year included: (a) direct materials used, $1,203,125; (b) direct labor, .75 direct labor hours per square yard at $12 per hour; (c) variable factory overhead, $240,625; and (d) fixed factory overhead, $343,750. Other expenses included: variable selling expenses, $149,880; fixed selling expenses, $155,000; and fixed general and administrative expenses, $242,500. Total sales revenue equaled $3,747,000. All production occurred in March, and there was no work in process at month end. Goods are usually shipped when completed, but at the end of March, 12,600 square yards still awaited shipment.

Required

1. Compute the unit cost and ending finished goods inventory value, using (a) variable costing procedures and (b) absorption costing procedures.
2. Prepare the year-end income statement for McCoy Mills, Inc., using (a) the contribution format based on variable costing data and (b) the conventional format based on absorption costing data.

Problem 25A-2. Make-or-Buy Decision (L.O. 6a)

The Dimon Furniture Company of Utica, New York, is famous for its lines of dining-room furniture. One full department is engaged in the production of the "Annette" line, an elegant but affordable dining-room set. To date the company has been manufacturing all pieces of the set, including the six chairs that go with each set.

Management has just received word that a company in Greenville, South Carolina, is willing to produce the chairs for Dimon Furniture Company at a total purchase price of $6,240,000 for the annual demand. Company records show that the following costs have been incurred producing the chairs: (a) wood materials, $1,250 for 100 chairs; (b) cloth materials, $650 for 100 chairs; (c) direct labor, 1.2 hours per chair at $12.00 per hour; (d) variable factory overhead, $6.00 per direct labor hour; and (e) fixed factory overhead: depreciation, $455,000; other, $309,400. Fixed factory overhead would continue whether or not the chairs are produced. Assume that idle facilities cannot be used for any other purpose and that annual usage is 156,000 chairs.

Required

1. Prepare an incremental decision analysis to determine whether the chairs should be made by the company or purchased from the outside supplier in Greenville.
2. Compute the unit cost to make one chair and to buy one chair.

Problem 25A-3. Special-Order Decision (L.O. 6b)

On March 16 the Jean Harry Boat Division of Anderson Industries received a special-order request for 320, 10-foot aluminum row-type fishing boats. Operating on a fiscal year ending May 31, the division already had orders that would allow them to produce at budget levels for the period. However, extra capacity existed to produce the 320 additional boats.

Terms of the special order called for a selling price of $225 per boat, with the customer paying all shipping costs. No sales personnel were involved in soliciting this order.

The 10-foot fishing boat has the following cost estimates associated with it: (a) direct materials, aluminum, two 4′ × 8′ sheets at $45 per sheet; (b) direct labor, 8 hours at $12 per hour; (c) variable factory overhead, $3.50 per direct labor hour; (d) fixed factory overhead, $5.50 per direct labor hour; (e) variable selling expenses, $36.50 per boat; and (f) variable shipping expenses, $27.25 per boat.

Required

1. Prepare an analysis for management of the Jean Harry Division to use in deciding whether to accept or reject the special order. What decision should be made?
2. What would be the lowest possible price the Jean Harry Division could charge per boat for this special order and still make a $3,000 profit on it?

Problem 25A-4. Scarce-Resource/ Sales-Mix Analysis (L.O. 6c)

The vice president of finance for Arizona Machine Tool, Inc., is evaluating the profitability of the company's four product lines. During the current year the company will operate at full machine-hour capacity. The production data shown below have been compiled:

Product	Current Year's Production (Units)	Total Machine Hours Used
24F	60,000	150,000
37N	100,000	200,000
29T	40,000	40,000
40U	180,000	90,000

Sales and operating cost data are as follows:

	Product 24F	Product 37N	Product 29T	Product 40U
Selling price per unit	$40.00	$50.00	$60.00	$70.00
Unit variable manufacturing cost	16.00	34.00	42.00	58.00
Unit fixed manufacturing cost	8.00	6.00	5.00	4.00
Unit variable selling cost	4.00	4.00	9.00	6.50
Unit fixed administrative cost	6.00	4.00	6.00	3.50

Required

1. Compute the machine hours needed to produce one unit of each product type.
2. Determine the contribution margin of each product type.
3. Which product line(s) should be pushed by the company's sales force? Why?

Problem 25A-5. Analysis to Eliminate an Unprofitable Product (L.O. 6d)

Seven years ago Norton & Wilson Publishing Company produced its first book. Since that time the company has added four more books to its product list. Management is considering proposals for three more new books, but editorial capacity limits the company to producing seven books. Before deciding which of the proposed books to publish, management wants you to evaluate the performance of its present book list. Revenue and cost data for the recent year are shown below. Each book is identified by the author or authors.

Norton & Wilson Publishing Company
Product Profit and Loss Summary
For the Year Ended December 31, 19x6

	Marc & Bjorn	Polk & Lorenz	Wojeck & Williams	Harrison	Bornren	Company Totals
Sales	$813,800	$782,000	$634,200	$944,100	$707,000	$3,881,100
Less variable costs						
Materials and binding	$325,520	$312,800	$190,260	$283,230	$212,100	$1,323,910
Editorial services	81,380	78,200	63,420	47,205	70,700	340,905
Author royalties	130,208	125,120	101,472	151,056	113,120	620,976
Sales commissions	162,760	156,400	95,130	141,615	141,400	697,305
Other selling costs	40,682	54,740	31,708	28,334	70,700	226,164
Total	$740,550	$727,260	$481,990	$651,440	$608,020	$3,209,260
Contribution margin	$ 73,250	$ 54,740	$152,210	$292,660	$ 98,980	$ 671,840
Less traceable fixed costs	87,250	91,240	79,610	100,460	72,680	431,240
Product margin	($ 14,000)	($ 36,500)	$ 72,600	$192,200	$ 26,300	$ 240,600
Less nontraceable joint fixed costs						82,400
Net income before taxes						$ 158,200
Avoidable fixed costs included in traceable fixed costs above	$ 31,200	$ 35,100	$ 29,400	$ 39,100	$ 28,800	$ 163,600

Projected data for the proposed new books are: Book A, sales, $450,000, contribution margin, $45,000; Book B, sales, $725,000, contribution margin, $25,200; and Book C, sales, $913,200, contribution margin, $115,500.

Required

1. Analyze the performance of the five books being published.
2. Should the company eliminate any of its present products? If so, which one(s)?
3. List possible causes for the poor performance of the books you selected to eliminate.
4. Identify the new books you would use to replace those eliminated. Justify your answer.

Problem Set B

Problem 25B-1. Variable Costing: Contribution Approach to Income Statement
(L.O. 3, 4)

Roofing tile is the major product of the Maine/Orono Corporation. The company had a particularly good year in 19x9. It produced 82,650 cases (units) of tile and sold 78,400 cases. Direct materials used cost $363,660; direct labor was $239,685; variable factory overhead was $247,950; fixed factory overhead was $165,300; variable selling expenses were $117,600; fixed selling expenses were $134,325; and fixed administrative expenses were $99,750. Selling price was $20 per case. There were no partially completed jobs in process at the beginning or the end of the year. Finished goods inventory had been used up at the end of the previous year, 19x8.

Required

1. Compute the unit cost and ending finished goods inventory value, using (a) variable costing procedures and (b) absorption costing procedures.
2. Prepare the year-end income statement for the Maine/Orono Corporation, using (a) the contribution format based on variable costing data and (b) the conventional format based on absorption costing data.

Problem 25B-2. Make-or-Buy Decision
(L.O. 6a)

The Goldey Beacom Refrigerator Company purchases and installs defrost clocks in its products. The clocks cost $232 per case, and each case contains 24 clocks. The supplier recently gave notice that effective in thirty days, the price will rise by 50 percent. The company has idle equipment that could be used to produce similar defrost clocks with only a few changes in the equipment.

The following cost estimates have been prepared under the assumption that the company could make the product itself. Direct materials would cost $172.80 per 24 clocks. Direct labor required would be 6 minutes per clock at a labor rate of $18.00 per hour. Variable factory overhead would be $4.30 per clock. Fixed factory overhead, which would be incurred under either decision alternative, would be $96,400 a year for depreciation and $239,200 a year for other expenses. Production and usage are estimated to be 96,000 clocks a year. (Assume the idle equipment could not be used for any other purpose.)

Required

1. Prepare an incremental decision analysis to decide whether the defrost clocks should be made within the company or purchased from the outside supplier at the higher rate.
2. Compute the unit cost to make one clock and to buy one clock.

Problem 25B-3. Special-Order Decision
(L.O. 6b)

Hughson Resorts, Ltd., has approached NYC Technical Printers, Inc., with a special order to produce 300,000 two-page brochures. Most of the work done by NYC Technical consists of recurring short-run orders. Hughson Resorts is offering a one-time order, but NYC Technical does have the capacity to handle the order over a two-month period.

Hughson's management has stated that the company would be unwilling to pay more than $38 per thousand brochures. The following cost data were assembled by NYC Technical's controller for this decision analysis: direct materials (paper) would be $22.50 per thousand brochures. Direct labor costs would be $4.80 per thousand brochures. Direct materials (ink) would be $2.40 per thousand brochures. Variable production overhead would be $4.20 per thousand brochures. Machine maintenance (fixed cost) is $1.00 per direct labor dollar. Other fixed production overhead amounts to $2.40 per direct labor dollar. Variable packing costs would be $4.30 per thousand brochures. Also, the share of general and administrative expenses (fixed costs) to be allocated would be $5.25 per direct labor dollar.

Required

1. Prepare an analysis for NYC Technical's management to use in deciding whether to accept or reject the offer by Hughson Resorts, Ltd. What decision should be made?
2. What is the lowest possible price NYC Technical can charge per thousand and still make a $6,000 profit on the order?

Problem 25B-4. Scarce-Resource/ Sales-Mix Analysis (L.O. 6c)

Management at Coppin Chemical Company is evaluating its product mix in an attempt to maximize profits. For the past two years, Coppin has produced five products, and all have a large market in which to expand market share. Marjorie Lyles, Coppin's controller, has gathered data from current operations and wants you to analyze it for her. Sales and operating data are as follows:

	Product AE42	Product BF53	Product CG64	Product DH75	Product EI86
Variable production costs	$ 51,000	$ 81,000	$101,920	$ 97,440	$156,800
Variable selling costs	10,200	5,400	12,480	20,160	26,880
Fixed production costs	20,400	21,600	29,120	18,480	22,400
Fixed administrative costs	3,400	5,400	6,240	10,080	8,960
Total sales	$102,000	$126,000	$166,400	$151,200	$224,000
Units produced and sold	85,000	45,000	26,000	14,000	32,000
Machine hours used*	17,000	18,000	20,800	16,800	22,400

* Coppin's scarce resource, machine hours, is operating at full capacity.

Required

1. Compute the machine hours needed to produce one unit of each product.
2. Determine the contribution margin per machine hour for each product.
3. Which product line(s) should be targeted for market share expansion? Why?

Problem 25B-5. Analysis to Eliminate an Unprofitable Segment (L.O. 6d)

Bednarz Sporting Goods, Inc., is a nationwide distributor of sporting equipment. The home office is located in Winter Springs, Florida, and four branch distributorships are in Phenix City, Alabama; Rockford, Illinois; Temecula, California; and Helena, Montana. Operating results for 19x8 are on the next page. All amounts in the summary are in thousands of dollars.

Bednarz Sporting Goods, Inc.
Segment Profit and Loss Summary
For the Year Ended December 31, 19x8

	Phenix Branch	Rockford Branch	Temecula Branch	Helena Branch	Total Company
Sales	$6,008	$6,712	$6,473	$8,059	$27,252
Less variable costs					
Purchases	$3,471	$4,119	$3,970	$5,246	$16,806
Wages and salaries	694	702	687	841	2,924
Sales commissions	535	610	519	881	2,545
Selling expenses	96	102	79	127	404
Total	$4,796	$5,533	$5,255	$7,095	$22,679
Contribution margin	$1,212	$1,179	$1,218	$ 964	$ 4,573
Less traceable fixed costs	972	1,099	808	1,059	3,938
Branch margin	$ 240	$ 80	$ 410	($ 95)	$ 635
Less nontraceable joint costs					325
Net income before taxes					$ 310

The corporate president, Mr. Shapiro, is upset with overall corporate operating results and particularly with results of the Helena branch. He has requested the controller to work up a complete profitability analysis of the four branch operations and to study the possibility of closing the Helena branch. The controller needed the following information before the analysis could be completed:

1. Shipping costs were 20 percent of the cost of goods purchased by the Helena branch.
2. Of the uncontrollable fixed costs traceable to the branch operations, the following were avoidable:

Phenix	$782,000
Rockford	$989,000
Temecula	$648,000
Helena	$849,000

3. An analysis of sales revealed

	Average Growth, Last Five Years	Growth, 19x8	Future Average Growth Rate
Phenix	8%	7%	5%
Rockford	7%	5%	6%
Temecula	10%	13%	8%
Helena	22%	20%	10%

Required

1. Analyze the performance of each branch president. (*Hint:* Convert the segment profit and loss summary to a common-size statement)
2. Should the corporation eliminate the Helena branch?
3. Are there other branches Mr. Shapiro should be concerned about? Why?
4. List possible causes for the corporation's poor performance.

Management Decision Case

Metzger Company: Sell or Process-Further Decision
(L.O. 6e)

Management at Metzger Company is considering a proposal to install a third production department within its factory building. With the company's present production setup, raw material is processed through Department I to produce materials A and B in equal proportions. Material A is then processed through Department II to yield product C. Material B is sold as-is at $20.25 per pound. Product C has a selling price of $100.00 per pound. Current per-pound standard costs used by Metzger Company follow:

	Department I (Materials A & B)	Department II (Product C)	(Material B)
Prior department's cost	$ —	$53.03	$13.47
Direct materials	20.00	—	—
Direct labor	7.00	12.00	—
Variable overhead	3.00	5.00	—
Fixed overhead			
Traceable	2.25	2.25	—
Allocated (⅔, ⅓)	1.00	1.00	—
	$33.25	$73.28	$13.47

These standard costs were developed by using an estimated production volume of 200,000 pounds of raw material as the standard volume. The company assigns Department I costs to materials A and B in proportion to their net sales values at the point of separation. These values are computed by deducting subsequent standard production costs from sales prices. The $300,000 in common fixed overhead costs are allocated to the two producing departments on the basis of the space used by the departments.

The proposed Department III would be used to process Material B into Product D. It is expected that any quantity of Product D can be sold for $30 per pound. Standard costs per pound under this proposal were developed by using 200,000 pounds of raw material as the standard volume. Those costs are as follows:

	Department I (Materials A & B)	Department II (Product C)	Department III (Product D)
Prior department's costs	$ —	$52.80	$13.20
Direct materials	20.00	—	—
Direct labor	7.00	12.00	5.50
Variable overhead	3.00	5.00	2.00
Fixed overhead			
Traceable	2.25	2.25	1.75
Allocated (½, ¼, ¼)	.75	.75	.75
	$33.00	$72.80	$23.20

Required

1. If (a) sales and production levels are expected to remain constant in the foreseeable future, and (b) there are no foreseeable alternate uses for the factory space, should Metzger Company install Department III and produce Product D? Show calculations to support your answer.
2. Instead of constant sales and production levels, suppose that under the present production setup, $1,000,000 in additions to the factory building must be made every ten years to accommodate growth. Also suppose that proper maintenance gives these factory additions an infinite life and that all such maintenance costs are included in the standard costs set forth in the text. How would the analysis you performed in **1** be changed if installation of Department III shortened the interval at which the $1,000,000 in factory additions are made from ten years to six years? Be as specific as possible in your answer.

(ICMA adapted)

CHAPTER 26 CAPITAL EXPENDITURE DECISIONS

LEARNING OBJECTIVES

1. Define and discuss the capital expenditure decision process.
2. Identify and describe steps in the capital expenditure decision cycle.
3. Describe the purpose of the minimum desired rate of return, and explain the methods used to arrive at this rate.
4. Identify information relevant to the capital expenditure decision process.
5. Evaluate capital expenditure proposals, using: (a) the accounting rate-of-return method and (b) the payback period method.
6. Apply the concept of time value of money.
7. Evaluate capital expenditure proposals, using the discounted cash flow—present-value method.
8. Analyze capital expenditure decision alternatives that incorporate the effects of income taxes.
9. Rank proposals competing for limited capital expenditure funds.

Capital expenditure decisions involve time periods that can span several years and capital asset purchases representing significant dollar amounts. The success or failure of capital expenditure decisions often makes the difference between operating at a profit or a loss. These long-term decisions require projections of revenues and expenses for many years. Whenever one deals with long-range predictions, much uncertainty is incorporated into the decision process. Therefore, the management accountant must consider all likely outcomes of proposed projects and use realistic rate-of-return forecasts when preparing decision support information for management. After studying this chapter, you should be able to meet the learning objectives listed on the left.

In this chapter you will first look at the capital expenditure decision process, the steps in the decision cycle, and the meaning and computation of the minimum desired rate of return. After a lengthy review of information relevant to this decision process, the text analyzes three primary evaluation methods, including: (1) accounting rate of return; (2) payback period; and (3) discounted cash flow—present value. In relation to the discounted cash-flow approach, the concept of time value of money is discussed. The capital expenditure evaluation methods are first analyzed by using before-tax amounts. They are then reanalyzed, using after-tax amounts. These analyses are done so you can see how income taxes affect these decisions. The chapter concludes with an approach to ranking various proposals competing for limited capital expenditure funds.

The Capital Expenditure Decision Process

Among the most important types of decisions facing management are those about when and how much to spend on capital facilities for the company. These are called **capital expenditure decisions.** Under this heading are decisions about installing new equipment, replacing old equipment, expanding the production area by adding to a building, buying or building a new factory, or acquiring another company. All of these major spending decisions call for careful analysis by the accountant and generally involve comparative analysis of two or more alternatives.

Capital Budgeting: A Cooperative Venture

OBJECTIVE 1 Define and discuss the capital expenditure decision process

The capital expenditure decision-making process, often referred to as **capital budgeting,** consists of identifying the need for a facility, analyzing courses of action to meet that need, preparing reports for management, choosing the best alternative, and rationing capital expenditure funds among competing resource needs. This process calls for input from people in every part of the business organization. Finance people are expected to supply a target cost of capital or desired rate of return for the decision analysis and an estimate of how much money can be spent on any one project. Without this kind of information, a decision cannot be reached. Marketing people identify areas of the business that need plant and facility expansion through their predictions of future sales trends. Management people at all levels help identify facility needs and often prepare preliminary cost estimates of the desired facility. These same people help carry out capital expenditure decisions by trying to keep actual results within cost and revenue estimates.

The accountant gathers and organizes the decision information into a workable, readable form. Generally, he or she applies one or more evaluation methods to the information gathered for each alternative. The most common capital expenditure proposal evaluation methods are: (1) the accounting rate-of-return method; (2) the payback period method; and (3) the discounted cash-flow, or present-value, method. Once these methods have been applied, management can make a choice based on the criteria used for the decision.

The Capital Expenditure Decision Cycle[1]

OBJECTIVE 2 Identify and describe steps in the capital expenditure decision cycle

Capital expenditure decision analysis involves the evaluation of alternate proposals for large capital expenditures, including considerations for financing the projects. Referred to earlier as capital budgeting, capital expenditure decision analyses affect both short-term and long-term planning activities of management. Figure 26-1 illustrates the time span of the capital expenditure planning process. Most companies have developed a long-term plan, either a five- or ten-year projection of operations. Large capital expenditures should be an integral part of a long-term plan. Anticipated additions or changes to a product line, replacements of equipment, and acquisitions of other companies are examples of items to be included in long-term capital expenditure plans. In addition, capital expenditure needs may arise from changes in current operations and may not be part of the company's long-term plan.

In Chapter 21 the master budget was discussed. Do you remember that one of the period budgets in the master budget is a capital expenditure budget? How does that capital expenditure budget fit into the planning process, capital budgeting, and the capital expenditure decision process?

1. The comments in this section are summarized from Henry R. Anderson and Rickard P. Schwartz, "The Capital Facility Decision," *Management Accounting* (National Association of Accountants, February, 1971).

Figure 26-1. Time Span of Capital Expenditure Planning Process

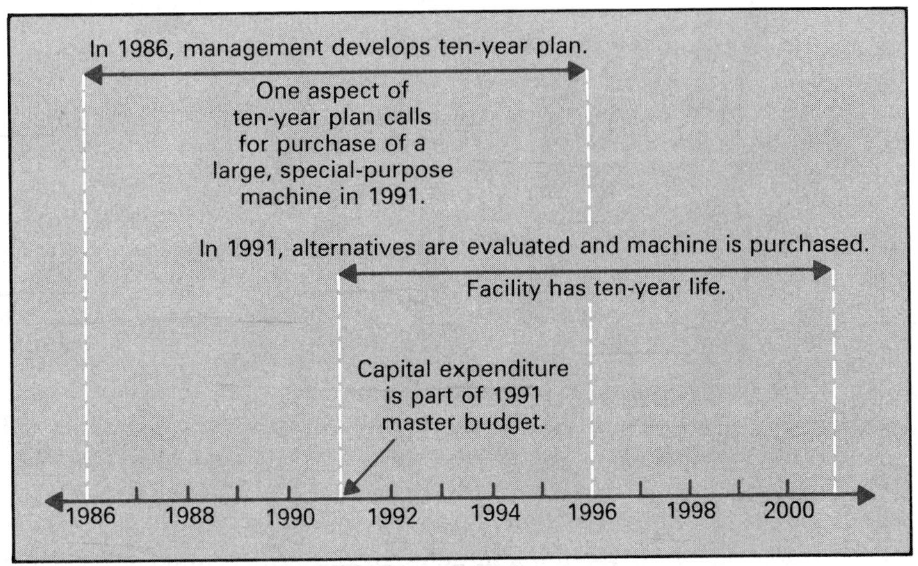
In 1986, management develops ten-year plan.
One aspect of ten-year plan calls for purchase of a large, special-purpose machine in 1991.
In 1991, alternatives are evaluated and machine is purchased.
Facility has ten-year life.
Capital expenditure is part of 1991 master budget.
1986
1988
1990
1992
1994
1996
1998
2000

To understand this fit, compare it with your current personal situation. You want to become a college graduate. That is your long-term plan. To succeed at this plan, you must take a specific number of courses over a defined time period, usually four years. Each of your semester schedules can be compared with the capital expenditure budget in a company's master budget. Long-term plans, such as your goal of a college degree, are not very specific. They are expressed in broad, goal-oriented terms.

As time passes, each annual budget must help accomplish long-term plans. Look again at Figure 26-1. In 1991 the company plans to purchase a large, special-purpose machine. When the ten-year plan was developed, only a broad statement about a plan to purchase the machine was included. There was nothing in the ten-year plan concerning the cost of the machine or the anticipated operating details and costs. The annual master budget for 1991 contains this detailed information. And it is in 1991 that the capital expenditure decision analysis will occur. So, even though capital expenditure decisions that will affect the company for many years are discussed and estimates of future revenues and expenditures are made, the analysis is for the current period. This point is often confusing and needs to be emphasized here so the remainder of the chapter can be studied in the proper perspective. When you have finished Chapter 26, you will have also completed the master budget structured in Chapter 21.

Evaluating capital expenditure proposals, deciding on proposals to be authorized, and implementing capital expenditures are long, involved procedures. Figure 26-2 depicts the capital expenditure, or capital facility, decision cycle. The management accountant's primary responsibilities in the decision process center on three functions: (1) final evaluation of proposals; (2) methods of evaluation; and (3) post-completion audit. The first two functions use proposal evaluation methods described later in this chapter. But the management accountant also has related responsibilities in other areas of the decision process. Figure 26-2 places the various phases of capital expenditure planning in perspective. The following paragraphs discuss each phase of that process.

Environmental Factors. The capital expenditure, or capital facility, decision cycle occurs within a defined time period and under constraints imposed by economic policies, conditions, and objectives originating at corporate, industry, and/or national levels. Coordinating short- and long-term capital investment plans within this dynamic environment is management's responsibility, and it is vital to profitable operations.

Detection of Capital Facility Needs. Identifying the need for a new capital facility is the starting point of the decision process. Ideas for capital investment opportunities may originate from past sales experience, changes in sources and quality of raw materials, managerial suggestions, production bottlenecks caused by obsolete equipment, new production or distribution methods, or personnel complaints. Capital facility needs are also identified.

1. Proposals to add new products to the product line
2. Proposals to expand capacity in existing product lines
3. Proposals to reduce costs in production of existing products without altering operation levels

Request for Capital Expenditure. A formal request for a capital expenditure is prepared by the appropriate manager to facilitate control over capital expenditures. The proposed request should include a complete description of the facility under review, reasons a new facility is needed, alternate means of satisfying the need, estimated costs and related cost savings for each alternative, and engineering specifications.

Preliminary Analysis of Requests. In a large company with a highly developed capital expenditure decision process, information contained in requests for a capital expenditure is often verified before initial screening of proposals. The management accountant plays a major role in this activity by helping to identify undesirable or nonqualifying proposals, computational errors, and deficiencies in request information.

Initial Screening. Initial screening processes are used by companies with several branch plants and a highly developed program for capital expenditures. The objective of initial screening is to ensure that the only proposals going forward for further review are those that meet company's objectives and the minimum desired rate of return established by management.

Acceptance-Rejection Standards. When there are many requests for capital expenditures and limited funds for capital investment, one must establish some acceptance-rejection standard. Such a standard may be expressed as a minimum desired rate of return or as a minimum cash-flow payback period. As shown in Figure 26-2, acceptance-rejection

Figure 26-2. The Capital Facility Decision Cycle

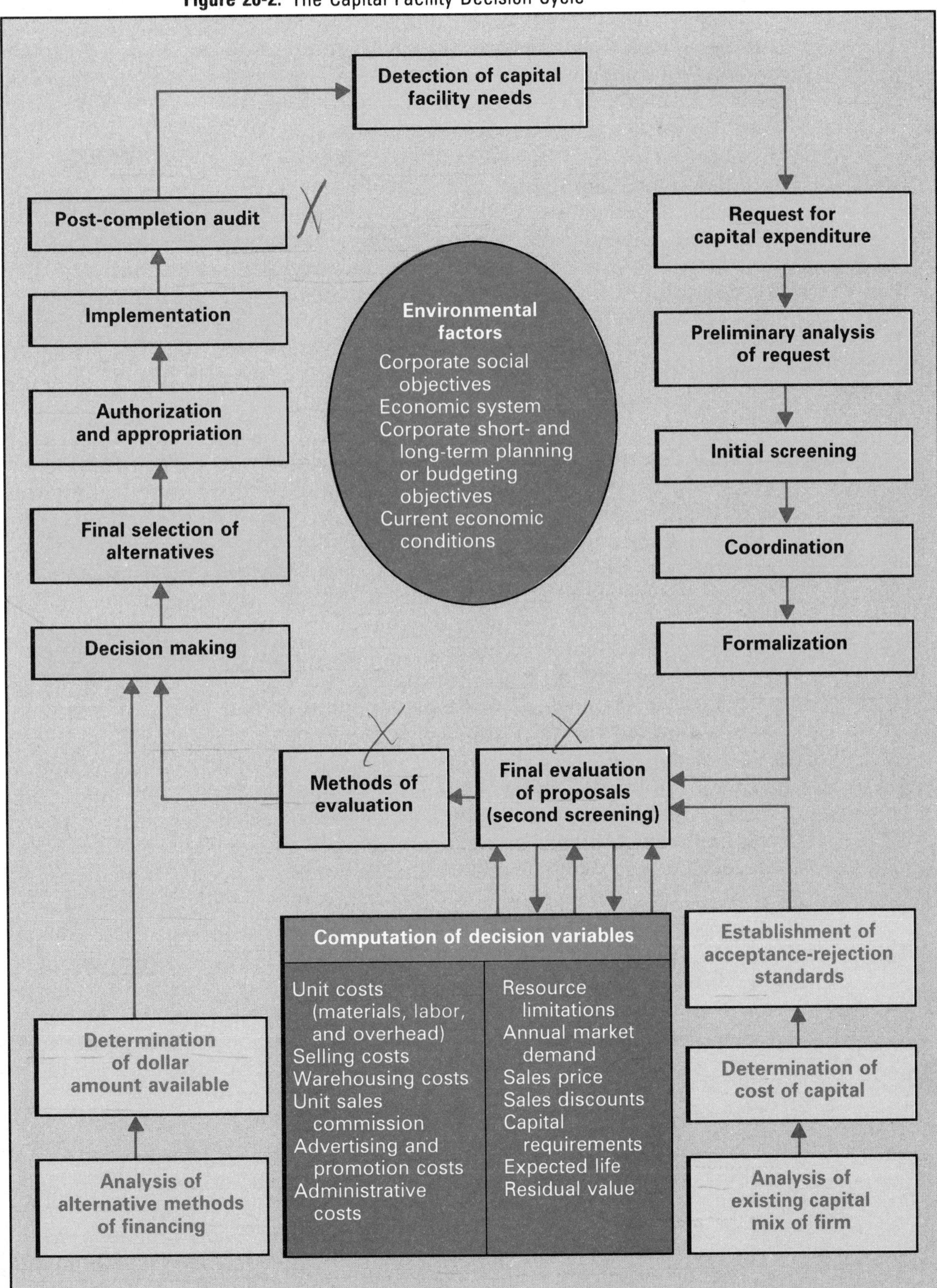

Source: Henry R. Anderson and Rickard P. Schwartz, "The Capital Facility Decision," *Management Accounting* (National Association of Accountants, February 1971), p. 30.

standards are used in the screening processes to identify projects expected to yield inadequate or marginal returns. This step also identifies proposed projects with high demand and return expectations. Cost of capital information is often used to establish minimum desired rates of return on investment. Developing these rates will be discussed in detail later in this chapter.

Coordination and Formalization. Before the final screening of proposed projects, alternate proposals must be coordinated and formalized for the decision maker. Coordination involves relating proposed projects to company objectives. Formalization is concerned with structuring the expenditure request to highlight its advantages and to summarize cost-benefit information for top management. Department or division managers often compete for limited capital expenditure funds. The more convincing a capital expenditure request is, the more likely it is to receive final authorization.

Final Evaluation of Proposals. Final evaluation of proposals involves verifying decision variables and applying capital expenditure proposal evaluation methods. The management accountant is primarily responsible for these procedures. The circular-flow diagram shown in Figure 26-2 lists several variables that may be relevant to a capital expenditure request. Generally, the variables in capital facility decisions are: (1) project life; (2) estimated cash flow; and (3) investment cost. Each variable in a proposal should be checked for accuracy.

Methods of Evaluation. Techniques used for proposal evaluation include the accounting rate-of-return method; the payback period method; and the present-value, or discounted cash-flow, method. Using management's minimum acceptance-rejection standard as a cutoff point, the management accountant evaluates all proposals, using one or more evaluation methods. The approach selected should be used consistently to facilitate project comparison.

Final Selection of Alternatives. After passing through the final screening process, acceptable capital expenditure requests are given to management for final review. Before deciding which requests to implement, management must consider the funds available for capital expenditures. Requests that have made it through screening and evaluation are ranked in order of profitability or payback potential. The final capital expenditure budget is then prepared by allocating funds to the selected proposals.

Authorization, Appropriation, and Implementation. Positive action by the board of directors on the proposed capital expenditure budget represents formal authorization. Such authorization includes the appropriation of the funds to acquire, construct, and/or install capital facilities. The implementation period begins with authorization and ends when the facility is operational.

Post-completion Audit. The decision process does not end when the facility is operational. The accountant should perform a post-completion audit for each project to evaluate the accuracy of forecasted results. Any weakness found in the decision process should be corrected to avoid the same problem in future decisions.

The post-completion audit is a difficult decision step. To isolate how a decision affects a company's overall operating results requires extensive analysis. Only when an entire new plant is constructed can one isolate and identify relevant information and measure a facility's performance. The main problems in the post-completion audit are: (1) that long-term projects must be evaluated by concentrating on cash flows over the project's life; (2) that a particular decision may influence the operations of existing facilities; and (3) that profitability resulting from a decision may be difficult to isolate and identify.

In summary, the capital expenditure, or capital facility, decision cycle is vital to managing a company. By making correct decisions about capital expenditures, management provides for the continued existence of the company. A series of incorrect decisions on capital expenditures could cause a company to fail. This topic by itself could fill several books. You will study various parts of the capital expenditure decision cycle in several other business courses. Each exposure will help you to fully appreciate the importance of the decision process. In the remaining parts of this chapter, you will look at aspects of a decision that are the responsibility of the management accountant, including the development of a minimum desired rate of return on investment, proposal evaluation methods, and ranking of acceptable proposals. The topic of post-completion audit is a major responsibility of the management accountant. But as stated earlier, such a process is difficult, and its analysis will be left for a more advanced course in operational auditing.

Desired Rate of Return on Investment

Choosing the best capital expenditure alternative is not always the approach taken in the decision-making process. Most companies have a set minimum rate of return, below which the expenditure request is automatically refused. If none of the capital expenditure requests is expected to meet the minimum desired rate of return, all requests will be turned down.

OBJECTIVE 3
Describe the purpose of the minimum desired rate of return, and explain the methods used to arrive at this rate

Why do companies use such a cutoff point? The idea is that if an expenditure request falls below the minimum rate of return, the funds can be used more profitably in another part of the company. Supporting poor-return proposals will lower the company's profitability later.

Deciding on a company's minimum desired rate of return is not simple. Each measure that can be used to set a cutoff point has certain advantages. The most common measures used are: (1) cost of capital; (2) corporate return on investment; (3) industry's average return on investment; and (4) bank interest rate. How to find the cost of capital will be described in some detail. Then, the use of other measures will be briefly explained.

Cost of Capital Measures. Of all the measures for desired rates of return listed above, cost of capital measures are the most widely used and discussed. The goal is to find the cost of financing the company's activities. However, to finance its activities, a company borrows funds and issues preferred and common stock. At the same time the company tries to operate at a profit. Each of these financing alternatives has a different cost rate. Furthermore, each company uses a different mix of these sources to finance current and future operations.

To set a desired cutoff rate of return, management can use cost of debt, cost of preferred stock, cost of equity capital, or cost of retained earnings. In many cases a company will average these cost results to establish an **average cost of capital** measure. Sophisticated methods are used to compute these financial return measures.[2] But the purpose here is simply to identify measures used. Thus, only a brief description of each type of cost of financing is presented.

Cost of debt is the ratio of loan charges to net proceeds of the loan. The effects of income taxes and the present value of interest charges must be taken into account, but the rate is essentially the ratio of costs to loan proceeds. **Cost of preferred stock** is the stated dividend rate of the individual stock issue. Tax effects are unimportant in this case because dividends, unlike interest charges, are a nondeductible expense. **Cost of equity capital** is the rate of return to the investor and is what makes stock valuable in the market. It is not just the dividend rate to the stockholder, because the dividend rate can be raised or lowered almost at will by management. This concept is very complex, but it has sound authoritative financial support.[3] **Cost of retained earnings** is the opportunity cost, or the dividends given up by the stockholder. Such a cost is linked closely with the cost of equity capital just described. The point is that a firm's cost of capital is hard to compute because it is a weighted average of the cost of various financing methods. However, this figure is the best estimate of a minimum desired rate of return.

Weighted average cost of capital is computed by first finding the cost rate for each source or class of capital-raising instrument. The second part of the computation is to figure the percentage of each source of capital to the total debt and equity financing of the company. Weighted average cost of capital is the sum of the products of each financing source's percentage multiplied by its cost rate. For example, assume the Leventhal Company's financing structure is as follows:

Cost Rate	Source of Capital	Amount	Capital Mix (Percentage of Each to Total)
10%	Debt financing	$150,000	30
8%	Preferred stock	50,000	10
12%	Common stock	200,000	40
14%	Retained earnings	100,000	20
	Totals	$500,000	100

2. See James C. Van Horne, "Cost of Capital of the Firm," *Financial Management and Policy*, 6th ed. (Englewood Cliffs, N.J.: Prentice-Hall, Inc., 1983), Chapter 8, pp. 213–227.
3. Ibid.

Weighted average cost of capital of 11.4 percent would be computed in the following way:

Source of Capital	Cost Rate	×	Ratio of Capital Mix	=	Portion of Weighted Average Cost of Capital
Debt financing	.10		.30		.030
Preferred stock	.08		.10		.008
Common stock	.12		.40		.048
Retained earnings	.14		.20		.028
Weighted average cost of capital					.114

Other Cutoff Measures. If cost of capital information is unavailable, management can use one of three less accurate but still useful amounts as the minimum desired rate of return. The first is average total corporate return on investment. The reasoning used to support such a measure is that any capital investment that produced a return lower than an amount earned historically by the company would negatively affect future operations. A second method is to use an industry's averages of the cost of capital. Most sizable industry associations supply such information. As a last resort a company might use the current bank lending rate. But because most companies are both debt and equity financed, this rate seldom reflects an accurate rate of return.

Capital Expenditure Evaluation Methods

Although many methods are used to evaluate capital expenditure proposals, the most common are: (1) the accounting rate-of-return method; (2) the payback period method; and (3) the net present-value approach, which is the most common discounted cash-flow method. These three methods are discussed in detail below. However, before discussing evaluation methods, we will first discuss types of information relevant to capital expenditure decision evaluations.

Information Relevant to Capital Expenditure Decision Evaluations

OBJECTIVE 4
Identify information relevant to the capital expenditure decision process

When evaluating capital expenditure alternatives, one must identify the types and compute the amounts of information relevant to capital expenditure proposals.

Cost Savings Versus Net Cash Flow. When evaluating a capital expenditure alternative, you must be interested in how the item will perform and how it will benefit the company. The accounting rate-of-return, payback period, and net present-value methods help in determining how a capital expenditure will increase an organization's profitability or liquidity.

However, each evaluation method uses different information as a basis for analysis. Net income is used in computing the accounting rate of return. This amount is calculated in the normal fashion, and increases in net income resulting from the capital expenditure must be determined for each alternative.

Net cash inflow, the balance of increases in cash receipts over increases in cash payments resulting from the capital expenditure, is used in evaluating capital projects when either the payback period or net present-value method is employed. In some cases equipment replacement decisions may involve several alternatives that do not increase current revenue. In these cases cost savings resulting from each alternative may be used in evaluating the proposals. Both net cash flow and cost savings can be used as a basis for the evaluation, and neither should be confused with the other. As long as decision alternatives are measured and evaluated consistently, the analysis will be beneficial to management in making its decisions.

Book Value of Assets. **Book value** is the undepreciated portion of the original cost of a fixed asset. When evaluating a decision to replace an asset, the book value of the old asset is irrelevant, since it is a past, or historical, cost and will not be altered by the decision. Net proceeds from its sale or disposal are relevant because these proceeds affect cash flows. Also, such proceeds may be different for each alternative being considered to replace the asset. Gains or losses incurred in an exchange or sale of an old asset are relevant because of their tax consequences. The tax implications of capital expenditure decision evaluations are explained later in the chapter.

Disposal or Salvage Values. As explained above, sales proceeds from the disposal of an old asset represent current cash inflows and are relevant to evaluating capital expenditure decisions. Projected disposal or salvage values of alternative new replacement equipment are also relevant to the decision analysis. These values represent future cash inflows. And because the values usually differ between decision alternatives, they fit the definition of relevant decision information discussed in Chapter 25. Remember, these salvage values will be received at the end of the asset's estimated life.

Depreciation Expense. All methods of evaluating capital expenditure proposals—except for the accounting rate-of-return method—use cash-flow information. Since depreciation is a **noncash expense**, it is irrelevant to decision analyses based on cash flow. However, because depreciation expense reduces net income and income tax expense, this cash savings is relevant to the evaluation process. The effect of tax savings on capital expenditure decisions is discussed later in this chapter.

Even Versus Uneven Cash Flows. As discussed above, future net cash inflows or cost savings are relevant to evaluations of capital expenditure proposals when the payback period or net present-value method is used.

Projections of these cash flows may be the same for each year of the asset's life or vary from year to year. Unequal, or uneven, cash flows are common and must be analyzed yearly in the evaluation process. Equal, or even, cash flows require less detailed analysis. Evaluations for projects with even and uneven cash flows are illustrated and explained later in this chapter.

Accounting Rate-of-Return Method

OBJECTIVE 5a Evaluate capital expenditure proposals, using the accounting rate-of-return method

Among the methods used to measure estimated performance of a capital investment, the **accounting rate-of-return method** is a crude but easy approach. With this method one measures expected performance by using two variables: (1) estimated annual after-tax net income from the project and (2) average investment cost. The basic equation is as follows:

$$\text{Accounting rate of return} = \frac{\text{project's average annual after-tax net income}}{\text{average investment cost}}$$

To compute average annual after-tax net income, one uses the revenue and expense data prepared for evaluating the project. Average investment in the proposed capital facility is figured as follows:[4]

$$\text{Average investment} = \frac{\text{total investment} + \text{salvage value}}{2}$$

For example, assume the Cox-Erickson Company is interested in purchasing a new bottling machine. Only projects that promise to yield more than a 16 percent return are acceptable to management. Estimates for the proposal include revenue increases of \$17,900 a year and operating cost increases of \$8,500 a year (including depreciation). The cost of the machine is \$51,000. Its salvage value is \$3,000. The company's income tax rate is 34 percent. Should the company invest in the machine? To answer the question, compute the accounting rate of return as follows:

$$\text{Accounting rate of return} = \frac{(\$17{,}900 - \$8{,}500) \times .66}{(\$51{,}000 + \$3{,}000) \div 2}$$

$$= \frac{\$6{,}204}{\$27{,}000} = \underline{\underline{22.98\%}}$$

The projected rate of return is higher than the 16 percent minimum desired rate, so management should think seriously about making the investment.

4. The procedure of adding salvage value to the numerator may seem illogical. However, a fixed asset is never depreciated below its salvage value. Average investment is computed by determining the midpoint of the depreciable portion of the asset and adding back the salvage value. Another way of stating the above formula is

$$\text{Average investment} = \frac{\text{total investment} - \text{salvage value}}{2} + \text{salvage value}$$

Such a statement reduces to the formula used above.

Because this method is easy to understand and apply, it is widely used. However, it is important to know the disadvantages of the accounting rate-of-return method. First, the use of averages tends to equalize all information, leading to errors in annual income and investment data. Second, the method is unreliable if estimated annual net income differs from year to year. Finally, the time value of money is not considered in the computations. Thus, future and present dollars are treated as equal.

Cash Flow and the Payback Period Method

OBJECTIVE 5b
Evaluate capital expenditure proposals, using the payback period method

Instead of measuring the rate of return on investments, many managers would rather estimate the cash flow to be generated by a capital investment. In such cases the goal is to determine the minimum length of time it will take to get back the initial investment. If two investment alternatives are being studied, the choice will be the investment that pays back its initial amount in the shortest time. This period of time is known as the payback period, and the capital investment evaluation approach is called the **payback period method.**

You compute the payback period as follows:

$$\text{Payback period} = \frac{\text{cost of investment}}{\text{annual net cash inflow}}$$

To apply the payback period method to the proposed capital investment of the Cox-Erickson Company discussed earlier, you need further information. You need to determine the net cash flow. To do so, you find and eliminate the effects of all noncash revenue and expense items included in the analysis of net income. In this case it is assumed that the only noncash expense or revenue amount is machine depreciation. To calculate this amount, you must know the asset's life and the depreciation method. Suppose the Cox-Erickson Company uses the straight-line depreciation approach, and the new bottling machine will have a ten-year estimated service life. Using this information and the facts given earlier, the payback period is computed as shown.

$$\begin{aligned}
\text{Annual depreciation} &= \frac{\text{cost} - \text{salvage value}}{10\text{ (years)}} \\
&= \frac{\$51{,}000 - \$3{,}000}{10} \\
&= \underline{\underline{\$4{,}800}} \text{ per year}
\end{aligned}$$

$$\begin{aligned}
\text{Payback period} &= \frac{\text{cost of machine}}{\text{cash revenue} - \text{cash expenses} - \text{taxes}} \\
&= \frac{\$51{,}000}{\$17{,}900 - (\$8{,}500 - \$4{,}800) - \$3{,}196} \\
&= \frac{\$51{,}000}{\$11{,}004} \\
&= \underline{\underline{4.6347}} \text{ years}
\end{aligned}$$

If the company's desired payback period is five years or less, the capital investment proposal would be approved.

Payback has the advantage of being easy to compute and understand, and for this reason it is widely used. However, the disadvantages of this approach far outweigh the advantages. First, the method does not measure profitability. Second, the present value of cash flows from different periods is not recognized. Finally, emphasis is on the time it takes to get out of the investment rather than on the long-run return on the investment.

Time Value of Money

OBJECTIVE 6
Apply the concept of time value of money

Today there are many opportunities to do something with investment capital besides buying fixed assets. Consequently, management expects an asset to yield a reasonable return during its useful life. Capital expenditure decision analysis calls for evaluating estimates for several future time periods. It is unrealistic for cash flows from different periods to have the same values when measured in current dollars. For this reason treating all future income flows alike ignores the time value of money. Both the accounting rate-of-return and payback period evaluation methods have this disadvantage.

The time value of money implies that cash flows of equal dollar amounts separated by an interval of time have different values. The values differ because of the effect of compound interest. For example, assume that Greg Sundevil was awarded a $20,000 settlement in a lawsuit over automobile damages from an accident. The terms of the settlement dictate that the first payment of $10,000 is to be paid today, December 31, 1988. The second $10,000 installment is due on December 31, 1992. What is the value today (its present value) of the total settlement? Assume that Mr. Sundevil could earn 10 percent interest on his current funds. To compute the present value of the settlement, you must go to Table D-3 in Appendix D. There, you will find the multiplier for 4 years at 10 percent, which is 0.683. The settlement's present value is computed below.

Present value of first payment on Dec. 31, 1988	$10,000
Present value of second payment to be received on Dec. 31, 1992: ($10,000 × .683)	6,830
Present value of the total settlement	$16,830

If Mr. Sundevil had the choice of (1) accepting the $20,000 settlement as offered or (2) receiving $16,830 today as total compensation for the lawsuit, he would be indifferent.

As seen, the $10,000 to be received in four years is not worth $10,000 today. If funds can be invested to earn 10 percent interest, then each $1 to be received in four years is worth only $.683 today. To prove the indifference statement above, look at the value of the total settlement to

Mr. Sundevil on December 31, 1992, for each choice. In this analysis Table D-1 in Appendix D is used because this example deals with future values based on compounding of interest.

(1) Accepting the $20,000 settlement as offered	
December 31, 1988 payment after earning four years of interest income @ 10% annual rate ($10,000 × 1.464)	$14,640.00
December 31, 1992 payment	10,000.00
Total amount at December 31, 1992	$24,640.00

(2) Receiving $16,830 on 12/31/88 as total compensation for the lawsuit December 31, 1988 payment after earning four years of interest income @ 10% annual rate ($16,830 × 1.464)	$24,639.12*

* difference due to rounding

The analysis above was based on single payments received either today or on a future date. Now, assume that Debbie Aztec was just told that she won the lottery. Her winnings are $1,000,000, to be paid in $50,000 amounts over the next 20 years. If she could choose to receive the value of the winnings today and earn 9 percent interest on her savings, how much should she settle for? Since a *series* of payments is being dealt with, you must use Table D-4 in Appendix D to locate the applicable multiplier of 9.129, which represents the discounting of 20 future payments back to the present assuming a 9 percent rate-of-return factor.

Present value of 20 annual future payments of $50,000 commencing one year from now if one assumes a 9% interest factor is used ($50,000 × 9.129)	$456,450

In other words, Ms. Aztec would be indifferent if given the choice of (1) receiving $1,000,000 in 20 future annual installments of $50,000 each or (2) receiving $456,450 today. To prove this point, determine the future value of the two alternatives by using data from Table D-2 in Appendix D. Such data are used because this example deals with a series of future payments and the compounding of interest on those payments.

(1) Receiving $1,000,000 in 20 future annual installments of $50,000 each ($50,000 × 51.16)	$2,558,000.00
(2) Receiving $456,450 today, using Table D-1 because you are dealing with a single payment ($456,450 × 5.604)	$2,557,945.80*

* difference due to rounding

When dealing with the time value of money, one uses compounding to find the future value of an amount now held. To find the present value of an amount to be received, one uses discounting.

When determining future values, you should refer to tables D-1 and D-2 in Appendix D. To determine present values of future amounts of money, use tables D-3 and D-4 in Appendix D. Also, remember that tables D-1 and D-3 deal with a single payment or amount, whereas tables D-2 and D-4 are used for a *series* of *equal* annual amounts. There are additional exercises in Appendix C if you need more practice with the time value of money.

Discounted Cash Flow: Present-value Method[5]

OBJECTIVE 7 Evaluate capital expenditure proposals, using the discounted cash flow—present-value method

The concept of **discounted cash flow** helps overcome the disadvantages of the accounting rate-of-return and payback period methods in evaluating capital investment alternatives. By using the present-value tables in Appendix D, it is possible to discount future cash flows back to the present. This approach to capital investment analysis is called the **present-value method.** Multipliers used to find the present value of a future cash flow are in the present-value tables. Which multipliers to use is computed by connecting the minimum desired rate of return and the life of the asset or length of time for which the amount is being discounted. Each element of cash inflow and cash outflow to be realized over the life of the asset is discounted back to the present. If the present value of all expected future net cash inflows is greater than the amount of the current investment, the expenditure meets the minimum desired rate of return, and the project should be carried out.

The present-value method is used in different ways, depending on whether annual cash flows are equal or unequal. If all annual cash flows (inflows less outflows) are equal, the discount factor to be used will come from Table D-4 in Appendix D. This table gives multipliers for the present value of $1 received *each period* for a given number of time periods. One computation will cover the cash flows of all time periods involved. If, however, expected cash inflows and outflows differ from one year to the next, each year's amount must be discounted back to the present. Discount factors used in this kind of analysis are found in Table D-3 in Appendix D. Multipliers in Table D-3 are used to find the present value of $1 to be received (or paid out) at the end of a given number of time periods.

An example will help to show the difference in the present-value analysis of expenditures with equal and unequal cash flows. Suppose the Bibb Metal Products Company is deciding which of two stamping machines to buy. The Blue Machine has equal expected annual net cash inflows, and the Black Machine has unequal annual amounts. Information on the two machines follows:

5. This section is based on the concept of present value. Appendixes C and D explain this concept and provide tables of multipliers for computations.

	Blue Machine	Black Machine
Purchase price: January 1, 19x4	$16,500	$16,500
Salvage	0	0
Expected life	5 years	5 years
Estimated net cash inflows:		
19x4	$5,000	$6,000
19x5	$5,000	$5,500
19x6	$5,000	$5,000
19x7	$5,000	$4,500
19x8	$5,000	$4,000

The company's minimum desired rate of return is 16 percent. Which—if either—of the two alternatives should be chosen?

The evaluation process is shown in Exhibit 26-1. An analysis involving equal annual cash flows is easier to prepare. Present value of net cash inflows for the five-year period for the Blue Machine is found by multiplying $5,000 by 3.274. The multiplier, 3.274, is found in Table D-4 in Appendix D by using the 16 percent minimum desired rate of return and a five-year life for the Blue Machine. Present value of the total cash inflows from the Blue Machine is $16,370. Comparing this figure with the $16,500 purchase price results in a *negative* net present value of $130.

Analysis of the Black Machine alternative gives a different result. As shown in Exhibit 26-1, unequal net cash inflows cause more work.

Exhibit 26-1. Present-value Analysis: Equal Versus Unequal Cash Flows

Bibb Metal Products Company
Capital Expenditure Analysis
19x3

Blue Machine		
Present value of cash inflows	$5,000 × 3.274 =	$16,370.00
Less purchase price of machine		16,500.00
Negative net present value		($ 130.00)
Black Machine		
Present value of cash inflows		
19x4	($6,000 × .862)	$ 5,172.00
19x5	($5,500 × .743)	4,086.50
19x6	($5,000 × .641)	3,205.00
19x7	($4,500 × .552)	2,484.00
19x8	($4,000 × .476)	1,904.00
Total		$16,851.50
Less purchase price of machine		(16,500.00)
Positive net present value		$ 351.50

Multipliers for this part of the analysis are found by using the same 16 percent rate. But five multipliers, one for each year of the life of the asset, must be used. Table D-3 in Appendix D applies here, since each annual amount must be individually discounted back to the present. For the Black Machine, the $16,851.50 present value of net cash inflows is more than the $16,500.00 purchase price of the machine. Thus, there is a positive net present value of $351.50.

A positive net present-value figure means the return on the asset exceeds the 16 percent minimum desired rate of return. A negative figure means the rate of return is below the minimum cutoff point. In the Bibb Metal Products case, the right decision would be to purchase the Black Machine.

Incorporating time value of money into the evaluation of capital expenditure proposals is the major advantage of the present-value method. This method also deals mainly with total cash flows from the investment over its useful life, so it brings total profitability into the analysis as well. The major disadvantage of the present-value method is that many managers do not trust or understand the procedure. They prefer the payback period method or the accounting rate-of-return method because the computations are easier.

Income Taxes and Business Decisions

Tax Effects on Capital Expenditure Decisions

OBJECTIVE 8
Analyze capital expenditure decision alternatives that incorporate the effects of income taxes

Income taxes are an important cost of doing business, and they often have an important impact on business decisions. The aim of capital budgeting evaluation techniques, such as payback period and net present value, is to measure and compare the relative benefits of proposed capital expenditures. These measurements focus on cash receipts and payments for a given project. For profit-oriented companies income taxes are important in capital budgeting analyses because they affect the amount and timing of cash flows. For this reason capital expenditure evaluation analysis must take tax effects into account.

Corporate income tax rates range from 15 percent on low income to 34 percent on income of more than $335,000.

Taxable Income	Tax Rate
$0 to $50,000	15%
$50,000 to $75,000	$ 7,500 + 25% of amount over $50,000
$75,000 to $100,000	$ 13,750 + 34% of amount over $75,000
$100,000 to $335,000	$ 22,250 + 39% of amount over $100,000
over $335,000	$110,000 + 34% of amount over $335,000

Because of different tax rates and changes from year to year, this text will show the effects of income taxes on cash flow by simply using a corporate tax rate of 34 percent on taxable income.

Now, suppose a project makes the contribution to annual net income as shown below.

Cash revenues	$400,000
Cash expenses	(200,000)
Depreciation	(100,000)
Income before taxes	$100,000
Income taxes at 34%	(34,000)
Income after taxes	$ 66,000

Annual cash flow for this project can be determined by two different procedures:

1. Cash flow—receipts and disbursements

Revenues (cash inflow)	$400,000
Cash expenses (outflow)	(200,000)
Income taxes (outflow)	(34,000)
Net cash inflow	$166,000

2. Cash flow—income adjustment procedure

Income after taxes	$ 66,000
Add: noncash expenses (depreciation)	100,000
Less: noncash revenues	—
Net cash inflow	$166,000

In both computations the net cash inflow is $166,000, and the total effect of income taxes is to lower the net cash flow by $34,000.

Revenues and gains from the sale of equipment increase taxable income and tax payments. When dealing with cash inflows, you must distinguish between a gain on the sale of an asset and the proceeds received from the sale. *Gains* are the amount received over and above the book value of the asset, whereas *proceeds* include the whole sales price and represent the cash inflow. Gains are not cash-flow items, but they do raise tax payments. If equipment with a book value of $80,000 is sold for $180,000 in cash, the gain is $100,000. By assuming that this gain is taxable at the same rate of 34 percent,[6] you would analyze the cash flow as follows:

Proceeds from sale		$180,000
Gain on sale	$100,000	
Capital gains tax rate	× .34	
Cash outflow (tax increase)		(34,000)
Net cash inflow		$146,000

As cash flows from the receipt of revenues and proceeds from the sale of assets are reduced because of income taxes, so, too, are the amounts

6. Capital gains will be taxable at the same rates as ordinary income from 1988 on.

of potential expenses (cash outflows). Cash expenses lower net income and result in cash outflows only to the extent that they exceed related tax reductions. This generalization is true for both cash operating expenses and losses on the sale of fixed assets. The following examples show the cash-flow effects of increases in cash and noncash expenses and losses on the sale of equipment:

Cash expenses		
Increase in cash operating expenses	$100,000	
Less: tax reduction at 34%	(34,000)	
Net increase in cash outflow	$ 66,000	
Noncash expenses		
Annual depreciation expense	$200,000	
Corporate tax rate	× .34	
Tax reduction = cash savings	$ 68,000	
Loss on the sale of an asset		
Proceeds from sale		$150,000
Loss on sale	$100,000	
Corporate tax rate	× .34	
Reduction of taxes and cash outflow		34,000
Total cash inflow resulting from sale		$184,000

Depreciation expense is not a cash-flow item, but it does provide a cash benefit equal to the amount of the reduction in taxes. Losses on the sale of fixed assets are also not cash-flow items, but they provide a cash benefit by reducing the amount of taxes to be paid in cash. For illustrations of the above ideas, see the review problem for this chapter (page 996).

Minimizing Taxes Through Planning

When operating a business, there are many ways to plan so tax liability is as low as possible. One of the most important is the timing of business transactions. For example, a corporation that is nearing $50,000 in taxable income for the year may want to put off an income-producing transaction until just after year end to avoid the higher tax rate. Or it may speed up making certain expenditures for the same reason.

Another important way to reduce tax liability through operating decisions is by the timing of transactions involving depreciable business assets and land. For example, if possible, no such asset should be sold at a gain less than six months from date of purchase.

It is always good management to try taking advantage of provisions of the tax law that allow preferential treatment. For example, the tax law has often been used to encourage investment in areas thought to be important for national goals. Because these goals change over the years, the tax law has been used to promote everything from emergency war equipment to pollution-control devices. Special credits are also allowed for certain spending that lowers unemployment or encourages the hiring of such underemployed groups as the handicapped.

Ranking Capital Expenditure Proposals

OBJECTIVE 9 Rank proposals competing for limited capital expenditure funds

Generally, a company's requests for capital funds exceed the amount of dollars available for capital expenditures. Even after proposals have been evaluated and selected under minimum desired acceptance-rejection standards, there are normally too many to fund adequately. At that point the proposals must be ranked according to their rates of return or profitability. A second selection process is then imposed.

Assume that five acceptable proposals are competing for the same limited capital expenditure funds. Boston Enterprises has $4,500,000 to spend this year in capital improvements. It currently uses an 18 percent minimum desired rate of return. Below are the proposals under review.

Project	Rate of Return	Capital Expenditure
A	32%	$1,460,000
B	30%	1,890,000
C	28%	460,000
D	24%	840,000
E	22%	580,000
Total		$5,230,000

How would you go about selecting the capital expenditure proposals to be implemented for the year? Projects A, B, and C are obvious contenders, and their combined dollar needs total $3,810,000. There are $690,000 in capital funds remaining. Project D should be examined to see if it can be implemented for $150,000 less. If not, then Project E should be selected. The selection of projects A, B, C, and E means there will be $110,000 in uncommitted capital expenditure funds for the year.

Chapter Review

Review of Learning Objectives

1. **Define and discuss the capital expenditure decision process.**
Capital expenditure decisions are concerned with when and how much to spend on a company's capital facilities. The capital expenditure decision-making process, often referred to as capital budgeting, consists of: (a) identifying the need for a facility; (b) analyzing courses of action to meet the need; (c) preparing reports for management; (d) choosing the best alternative; and (e) rationing capital expenditure funds among competing resource needs.

2. **Identify and describe steps in the capital expenditure decision cycle.**
The capital expenditure decision cycle begins with detecting a facility's need. A proposal or request is then prepared and analyzed before being subjected

to one or two screening processes, depending on the size of the business involved. Using various evaluation methods and a minimum desired rate of return, the proposal is determined to be either acceptable or unacceptable. If acceptable, the proposal is ranked with all other acceptable proposals. Total dollars available for capital investment are used to determine which of the ranked proposals to authorize and implement. The final step is a post-completion audit to determine the accuracy of the forecasted data used in the decision cycle and to find out if some of the projections need corrective action.

3. **Describe the purpose of the minimum desired rate of return, and explain the methods used to arrive at this rate.**

   The minimum desired rate of return acts as a screening mechanism. It eliminates capital expenditure requests with anticipated low returns from further consideration. By using such an approach to decision making, many unprofitable requests are turned away or discouraged without a great deal of wasted executive time. The most common measures used to compute minimum desired rates of return include: (a) cost of capital; (b) corporate return on investment; (c) industry average return on investment; and (d) federal and bank interest rates. The weighted average cost of capital and average return on investment are the most widely used measures.

4. **Identify information relevant to the capital expenditure decision process.**

   The definition of relevant information—that it be future data differing between two or more alternatives to a decision—is also applicable in the capital expenditure decision process. In addition, determining cost savings or net cash inflow from a project is important. Book values and depreciation expense of assets awaiting replacement are irrelevant. Net proceeds from the sale of an old asset and estimated salvage value of a new facility are relevant, for they represent future cash flows. Gains and losses on the sale of old assets and depreciation expense on replacement equipment are relevant to future cash flows only as they affect cash payments for income taxes. Even versus uneven cash flows materially affect the decision analysis process.

5. **Evaluate capital expenditure proposals, using (a) the accounting rate-of-return method and (b) the payback period method.**

   When using the accounting rate-of-return method to evaluate two or more capital expenditure proposals, the alternative that yields the highest ratio of net income after taxes to average cost of investment is chosen. When using the payback period method to evaluate a capital expenditure proposal, emphasis is placed on the shortest time period needed to recoup the original amount of the investment in cash.

6. **Apply the concept of time value of money.**

   Time value of money implies that cash flows of equal dollar amounts at different times have different values because of the effect of compound interest. Of the evaluation methods discussed in this chapter, only the net present-value method is based on the concept of time value of money.

7. **Evaluate capital expenditure proposals, using the discounted cash flow—present-value method.**

   The discounted cash flow—present-value method of evaluating capital expenditures depends very much on the time value of money. Present values of future cash flows are studied to see if they are more than the current cost of the capital expenditure being evaluated.

8. **Analyze capital expenditure decision alternatives that incorporate the effects of income taxes.**
   Income taxes affect the results of all capital expenditure analyses. Care must be taken to look at both sides of income tax effects. Revenues and gains on the sale of assets increase taxes. Increased expenditures, noncash expenditures, and losses from the sale of assets decrease taxes. Tax-related inflows result from capital losses, increased expenses, and noncash expenditures, whereas tax-related cash outflows arise when a company has capital gains from the sale of fixed assets or from increased sales revenue.
9. **Rank proposals competing for limited capital expenditure funds.**
   When ranking capital expenditure proposals, acceptable projects are listed in their order of estimated rate of return. They are then authorized in their order of ranking until all capital expenditure funds appropriated for the year have been taken. If funds remain because the selection process was halted by a project too large to be funded, a smaller proposal, lower in priority, may be authorized.

Review Problem: Tax Effects on a Capital Expenditure Decision

The Rudolph Construction Company specializes in developing large shopping centers. The company is considering the purchase of a new earth-moving machine and has gathered the following information:

Purchase price	$600,000
Salvage value	$100,000
Useful life	4 years
Effective tax rate[7]	34%
Depreciation method	Straight-line
Desired before-tax payback period	3 years
Desired after-tax payback period	4 years
Minimum before-tax rate of return	15%
Minimum after-tax rate of return	9%

The before-tax cash flow estimates are as follows:

Year	Revenues	Expenses	Net Cash Flow
1	$ 500,000	$260,000	$240,000
2	450,000	240,000	210,000
3	400,000	220,000	180,000
4	350,000	200,000	150,000
Totals	$1,700,000	$920,000	$780,000

Required

1. Using before-tax information, analyze the Rudolph Construction Company's investment in the new earth-moving machine. In your analysis use: (a) the accounting rate-of-return method; (b) the payback period method; and (c) the present-value method.
2. Repeat **1** above, using after-tax information.

7. All company operations combined result in a 34% tax rate. Because of this, do not use specific tax rates in the tax schedule.

Answer to Review Problem

1. Before-tax calculations

The increase in net income is as follows:

Year	Before-tax Net Cash Flow	Depreciation	Income Before Taxes
1	$240,000	$125,000	$115,000
2	210,000	125,000	85,000
3	180,000	125,000	55,000
4	150,000	125,000	25,000
Totals	$780,000	$500,000	$280,000

1a. (Before-tax) Accounting rate-of-return method

$$\text{Accounting rate of return} = \frac{\text{average annual net income}}{\text{average investment cost}}$$

$$= \frac{\$280{,}000 \div 4}{(\$600{,}000 + \$100{,}000) \div 2} = \frac{\$70{,}000}{\$350{,}000} = 20\%$$

1b. (Before-tax) Payback period method

Total cash investment		$600,000
Less cash-flow recovery		
Year 1	$240,000	
Year 2	210,000	
Year 3 (5/6 of $180,000)	150,000	(600,000)
Unrecovered investment		—

Payback period $2\frac{5}{6}$ years, 2.833 years, or 2 years, 10 months

1c. (Before-tax) Present-value method (multipliers are from Table D-3)

Year	Net Cash Flow	Present-value Multiplier	Present Value
1	$240,000	.870	$208,800
2	210,000	.756	158,760
3	180,000	.658	118,440
4	150,000	.572	85,800
4	100,000 (salvage)	.572	57,200
Total present value			$629,000
Less cost of original investment			(600,000)
Positive net present value			$ 29,000

2. After-tax calculations

The increase in net income after taxes is as shown on the following page:

Year	Before-tax Net Cash Flow	Depreciation	Income Before Taxes	Taxes (34%)	Income After Taxes
1	$240,000	$125,000	$115,000	$39,100	$ 75,900
2	210,000	125,000	85,000	28,900	56,100
3	180,000	125,000	55,000	18,700	36,300
4	150,000	125,000	25,000	8,500	16,500
Totals	$780,000	$500,000	$280,000	$95,200	$184,800

The after-tax cash flow is as follows:

Year	Net Cash Flow Before Taxes	Taxes	Net Cash Flow After Taxes
1	$240,000	$39,100	$200,900
2	210,000	28,900	181,100
3	180,000	18,700	161,300
4	150,000	8,500	141,500
Totals	$780,000	$95,200	$684,800

2a. (After-tax) Accounting rate-of-return method

$$\text{Accounting rate of return} = \frac{\text{average annual after-tax net income}}{\text{average investment cost}}$$

$$= \frac{\$184{,}800 \div 4}{(\$600{,}000 + \$100{,}000) \div 2} = \frac{\$46{,}200}{\$350{,}000} = \underline{\underline{13.2\%}}$$

2b. (After-tax) Payback period method:

Total cash investment		$600,000
Less cash-flow recovery		
Year 1	$200,900	
Year 2	181,100	
Year 3	161,300	
Year 4 (.401 × $141,500)	56,700	(600,000)
Unrecovered investment		—

Payback period 3.401 years

2c. (After-tax) Present-value method (multipliers are from Table D-3):

Year	Net Cash Inflow After Taxes	Present-value Multiplier	Present Value
1	$200,900	.917	$184,225
2	181,100	.842	152,486
3	161,300	.772	124,524
4	141,500	.708	100,182
4	100,000 (salvage)	.708	70,800
Total present value			$632,217
Less cost of original investment			(600,000)
Positive net present value			$ 32,217

Rudolph Construction Company: Summary of Decision Analysis

	Before-tax		After-tax	
	Desired	**Predicted**	**Desired**	**Predicted**
Accounting rate of return	15%	20%	9%	13.2%
Payback period	3 years	2.833 years	4 years	3.401 years
Present value	—	$29,000	—	$32,217

Based on the calculations in **1** and **2** above, the Rudolph Company's proposed investment in the earth-moving machine meets all company criteria for such investments. Given these results, the company should invest in the machine.

Chapter Assignments

Questions

1. What is a capital expenditure? Give examples of types of capital expenditures.
2. Define capital budgeting.
3. Discuss the interrelationship of the following steps in the capital expenditure decision cycle:
   a. Determination of dollar amount available
   b. Final selection of alternatives
   c. Final evaluation of proposals
4. What are some difficulties encountered in trying to implement the post-completion audit step in the capital expenditure decision cycle?
5. Describe some approaches companies use in arriving at a minimum desired rate of return to use as its acceptance-rejection standard in capital expenditure decision making.
6. What is the importance of equal versus unequal cash flows in capital expenditure decisions? Are they relevant to the accounting rate-of-return method? the payback period method? the net present-value method?
7. What is a crude but easy method for evaluating capital expenditures? List the advantages and disadvantages of this method.
8. What is the formula used for determining payback period? Is this decision measuring technique accurate? Defend your answer.
9. Distinguish between cost savings and net cash flow.
10. "To treat all future income flows alike ignores the time value of money." Discuss this statement.
11. Explain the relationship of compound interest to determination of present value.
12. What is the objective of using the concept of discounted cash flows?
13. "In using discounted cash-flow methods, the book value of an asset is irrelevant, whereas current and future salvage values are relevant." Is this statement valid? Defend your answer.
14. In evaluating equipment replacement decisions with net present-value measures, what justifies ignoring depreciation of the old equipment?
15. What is the role of cost of capital when using the net present-value method to evaluate capital expenditure proposals?
16. Why is it important to consider income taxes when evaluating a capital expenditure proposal?

17. Aljeannie Company has: (a) net cash inflow from operations for 19x9 of $63,000; (b) noncash expenditures of $12,000; and (c) an asset sale that netted $54,000 in proceeds and involved a $20,000 capital gain. Using the 34 percent tax rate for normal income and capital gains, compute the company's tax liability.
18. When selecting capital expenditure proposals for implementation, final ranking of proposals may not follow the order in which they were presented. Why?

Classroom Exercises

Exercise 26-1. Capital Expenditure Decision Cycle (L.O. 2)

Newell Anthony was just promoted to supervisor of building maintenance for the Bob Carr Theatre complex in Grove City, Pennsylvania. The complex comprises seventeen buildings. Omni Entertainment, Inc., Mr. Anthony's employer, uses an integral system for evaluating capital expenditure requests from its twenty-two supervisors. Mr. Anthony has approached you, the corporate controller, for advice on preparing his first proposal. He would also like to become familiar with the entire decision cycle.

1. What advice would you give Mr. Anthony before he prepares his first capital expenditure request proposal?
2. Explain the capital expenditure decision cycle for Mr. Anthony.

Exercise 26-2. Minimum Desired Rate of Return (L.O. 3)

The controller of Jessie Corporation wants to establish a minimum desired rate of return and would like to use a weighted average cost of capital. Current data about the corporation's financing structure are as follows: debt financing, 50 percent; preferred stock, 20 percent; common stock, 20 percent; and retained earnings, 10 percent. After-tax cost of debt is 8 percent. Dividend rates on the preferred and common stock issues are 6 and 10 percent, respectively. Cost of retained earnings is 12 percent.

Compute the weighted average cost of capital.

Exercise 26-3. Using the Present-value Tables (L.O. 6)

For each of the following situations, identify the correct multiplier to use from the tables in Appendix D. Also, compute the appropriate present value.

a. Annual net cash inflow of $20,000 for five years, discounted at 16%
b. An amount of $35,000 to be received at the end of ten years, discounted at 12%
c. The amount of $22,000 to be received at the end of two years, and $16,000 to be received at the end of years four, five, and six, discounted at 10%
d. Annual net cash inflow of $32,500 for twelve years, discounted at 14%
e. The following five years of cash inflows, discounted at 10%

Year 1	$35,000
Year 2	30,000
Year 3	40,000
Year 4	50,000
Year 5	60,000

f. The amount of $70,000 to be received at the beginning of year seven, discounted at 14%

Exercise 26-4. Present-value Computations (L.O. 6)

Three machines are being considered in a replacement decision. All have about the same purchase price and an estimated ten-year life. The company uses a 12 percent minimum desired rate of return as its acceptance-rejection standard. Below are the estimated net cash inflows for each machine.

Year	Machine A	Machine B	Machine C
One	$22,000	$10,000	$17,500
Two	23,000	12,000	17,500
Three	24,000	14,000	17,500
Four	23,000	19,000	17,500
Five	22,000	20,000	17,500
Six	21,000	22,000	17,500
Seven	16,000	23,000	17,500
Eight	14,000	24,000	17,500
Nine	8,000	25,000	17,500
Ten	4,000	20,000	17,500
Salvage Value	1,000	20,000	10,000

1. Compute the net present value for each machine.
2. Which machine should the company purchase?

Exercise 26-5. Analysis of Relevant Information (L.O. 4)

Harold Randolph & Co., a scrap-metal company, supplies area steel companies with recycled materials. The company collects scrap metal, sorts and cleans the material, and compresses it into one-ton blocks for easy handling. Increased demand for recycled metals has caused Mr. Randolph to consider purchasing an additional metal-compressing machine. He has narrowed the choice to the two models shown below. The company's management accountant has gathered the information related to each model.

	Model One	Model Two
Purchase price	$50,000	$ 60,000
Salvage value	6,000	10,000
Annual depreciation*	4,400	5,000
Resulting increases in		
Annual sales	86,000	100,000
Annual operating costs:		
Materials	30,000	35,000
Direct labor	20,000	20,000
Operating supplies	1,800	2,000
Indirect labor	12,000	18,000
Insurance and taxes	800	1,000
Plant rental	4,000	4,000
Electricity	500	560
Other overhead	2,500	2,840

* computed using the straight-line method

1. Identify the costs and revenues relevant to the decision.
2. Prepare an incremental cash-flow analysis for year one.

Exercise 26-6. Capital Expenditure Decision: Accounting Rate-of-Return Method (L.O. 5a)

Castleberry Corporation manufactures metal hard hats for on-site construction workers. Recently, management tried to raise productivity to meet the growing demand from the real estate industry. The company is now thinking about a new stamping machine. Management has decided that only projects yielding a 16 percent return before taxes will be accepted. The following projections for the proposal are given: the new machine will cost $255,000. Revenue will increase $85,600 per year. The salvage value of the new machine will be $35,000. Operating cost increases (including depreciation) will be $64,600 per year.

Using the accounting rate-of-return method, decide whether the company should invest in the machine. (Show all computations to support your decision, and ignore income tax effects.)

Exercise 26-7. Capital Expenditure Decision: Payback Period Method (L.O. 5b)

Shively Sounds, Inc., a manufacturer of stereo speakers, wants to add a new injection molding machine. This machine can produce speaker parts the company now buys from outsiders. The machine has an estimated life of fourteen years and will cost $164,000. Gross cash revenue from the machine will be about $267,500 per year, and related cash expenses should total $186,000. Taxes on income are estimated to be $36,000 a year. The payback period as set by management should be four years or less.

On the basis of the data given, use the payback period method to determine whether the company should invest in this new machine. Show computations to support your answer.

Exercise 26-8. Capital Expenditure Decision: Present-value Method (L.O. 7)

Esther Falkowitz and Associates wants to buy an automatic extruding machine. This piece of equipment would have a useful life of six years, would cost $75,000, and would increase annual after-tax net cash inflows by $19,260. Assume there is no salvage value at the end of six years. The company's minimum desired rate of return is 14 percent.

Using the present-value method, prepare an analysis to determine whether the company should purchase the machine.

Exercise 26-9. Ranking Capital Expenditure Proposals (L.O. 9)

Managers of the Santa Ana Furniture Company have all capital expenditure proposals for the year, and they are ready to make their final selections. The following proposals and related rate-of-return amounts were received during the period:

Project	Amount of Investment	Rate of Return
AB	$ 450,000	19%
CD	500,000	34%
EF	654,000	12%
GH	800,000	28%
IJ	320,000	22%
KL	240,000	18%

Project	Amount of Investment	Rate of Return
MN	180,000	16%
OP	400,000	26%
QR	560,000	14%
ST	1,200,000	23%
UV	1,600,000	20%

Assume the company's minimum desired rate of return is 15 percent and \$5,000,000 are available for capital expenditures during the year.

1. List the acceptable capital expenditure proposals in order of profitability.
2. Which proposals will be selected for this year?

Interpreting Accounting Information

Internal Management Information: Rancho California Federal Bank
(L.O. 7)

Automatic round-the-clock tellers are the newest thing in the banking industry. Several companies have developed these computerized money machines and are bombarding bank managers with sales people and advertising brochures. Rancho California Federal Bank plans to install such a device and has decided on the S-JC machine. Ms. Chen, the controller, has prepared the decision analysis shown below. She has recommended purchase of the machine based on the positive net present value shown in the analysis.

Rancho California Federal Bank
Capital Expenditure Decision Analysis
Before-tax Net Present-value Approach
March 2, 19x6

Year	Net Cash Inflow	Present-value Multipliers	Present Value
1	\$ 65,000	.909	\$ 59,085
2	85,000	.826	70,210
3	95,000	.751	71,345
4	110,000	.683	75,130
5	75,000	.621	46,575
5 (salvage)	40,000	.621	24,840
Total present value			\$347,185
Initial investment		\$440,000	
Less proceeds from the sale of teller machines		110,000	
Net capital investment			330,000
Positive net present value			\$ 17,185

The S-JC machine has an estimated life of five years and an expected salvage value of $40,000. Its purchase price would be $440,000. Two existing teller machines, each having a book value of $35,000, would be sold for a total of $110,000 to a neighboring bank in Temecula. Annual operating cash inflow is expected to increase in the following manner:

Year 1	$ 65,000
Year 2	85,000
Year 3	95,000
Year 4	110,000
Year 5	75,000

The bank uses straight-line depreciation. The before-tax minimum desired rate of return is 16 percent, and a 10 percent rate is used for interpreting after-tax data. Assume a 34 percent tax rate for normal operations and capital gains items.

Required

1. Analyze the work of Ms. Chen. What changes need to be made in her capital expenditure decision analysis?
2. What would you recommend to bank management about the S-JC machine purchase?

Problem Set A

Problem 26A-1. Accounting Rate-of-Return and Payback Period Methods
(L.O. 5a, 5b)

St. Cloud Corporation wants to buy a new rubber-stamping machine. The machine will provide the company with a new product line, pressed-rubber food trays for kitchens. Two machines are being considered, and the data applicable to each machine are shown below.

	Lawrence Machine	Lange Machine
Estimated annual increase in revenue	$570,000	$600,000
Purchase price	300,000	340,000
Salvage value	30,000	34,000
Traceable annual costs		
Materials	216,420	165,200
Direct labor	130,500	184,600
Factory supervision	26,000	26,000
Indirect labor	62,480	82,750
Electrical power	7,200	7,200
Other factory overhead	42,800	33,550
Useful life in years	10	12

Depreciation is computed using the straight-line method net of salvage value. Assume a 34 percent income tax rate. The company's minimum desired after-tax rate of return is 16 percent, and the maximum allowable payback period is 5 years.

Required

1. From the information given, compute how the company's net income after taxes will change by each alternative.
2. For each machine compute the projected accounting rate of return.
3. Compute the payback period for each machine.
4. From the information generated in **2** and **3** above, decide which machine should be purchased? Why?

Problem 26A-2. Minimum Desired Rate of Return
(L.O. 3)

Frank Marini, controller of the Akron Corporation, is developing his company's minimum desired rate of return for the year. This measure will be used as an acceptance-rejection standard in capital expenditure decision analyses during the coming year. As in the past this rate will be based on the company's weighted average cost of capital. Capital mix and respective costs (after tax) for the previous twelve months were as follows:

	Percentage of Total Financing	Cost of Capital (Percent)
Debt financing	40	12
Preferred stock	10	14
Common stock	30	8
Retained earnings	20	12

The company will soon convert one-fourth of its debt financing into common stock. Changes in the cost of capital are anticipated only in debt financing, where the rate is expected to decrease to 10 percent.

Several capital expenditure proposals have been submitted for consideration for the current year. Those projects and their projected rates of return are as follows: Project A, 13 percent; Project B, 10 percent; Capital Equipment C, 12 percent; Project D, 9 percent; Capital Equipment E, 8 percent; and Project F, 14 percent.

Required

1. Compute the weighted average cost of capital for the previous year.
2. Using the anticipated adjustments to capital cost and mix, compute the weighted average cost of capital for the current year.
3. Identify the proposed capital expenditures that should be implemented on the basis of the minimum desired rate of return calculated in **2** above.

Problem 26A-3. Capital Expenditure Decision: Present-value Method
(L.O. 7, 8)

The Twelfth of Leo is a famous restaurant in the New Orleans French Quarter. "Bouillabaisse Kathryn" is the specialty of the house. Management is considering the purchase of a machine that would prepare all ingredients, mix them automatically, and cook the dish to the restaurant's rigid specifications. The machine will function for an estimated twelve years, and the purchase price, including installation, is $186,000. Estimated salvage value is $6,000. This labor-saving device is expected to increase cash flows by an average of $30,000 per year during its life. For purposes of capital expenditure decisions, the restaurant uses a 12 percent minimum desired rate of return.

Required

1. Using the present-value method to evaluate this capital expenditure, determine whether the company should purchase the machine. Support your answer.
2. If management had decided on a minimum desired rate of return of 14 percent, should the machine be purchased? Show all computations to support your answers.
3. Assuming straight-line depreciation, a 34 percent tax rate, and an after-tax minimum desired rate of return of 7 percent, should the company purchase the machine? Show your computations.

Problem 26A-4. Capital Expenditure Decision: Comprehensive (L.O. 5, 7, 8)

Quality work and timely output are the bench marks on which Spoto Photo, Inc., was organized. Now a nationally franchised company, there are more than 100 Spoto Photo outlets scattered throughout the eastern and midwestern states. Part of the franchise agreement promises a centralized photo developing process with overnight delivery to the outlets.

Because of the tremendous increase in demand for the photo processing, Mr. Angelo, the corporation's president, is considering the purchase of a new, deluxe processing machine. At a cost of $380,000, the photo processing machine will function for an estimated five years and should have a $40,000 salvage value at the end of that period. Mr. Angelo has specified that he expects all capital expenditures to produce a 20 percent before-tax minimum rate of return. The investment should be recouped in three years or less. All fixed assets are depreciated using the straight-line method. The forecasted increase in operating results because of the new machine are as follows:

Cash Flow Estimates

	Cash Revenues	Cash Expenses
Year 1	$210,000	$ 90,000
Year 2	225,000	100,000
Year 3	240,000	110,000
Year 4	200,000	90,000
Year 5	160,000	60,000

Required

1. Ignoring income taxes, analyze the purchase of the machine and decide if the company should purchase it. Use the following evaluation approaches in your analysis: (a) the accounting rate-of-return method; (b) the payback period method; and (c) the present-value method.
2. Rework **1** above, assuming a 34 percent tax rate and after-tax guidelines of a 10 percent minimum desired rate of return and a four-year payback period. Does the decision change when after-tax information is used?

Problem 26A-5. Even Versus Uneven Cash Flows (L.O. 7, 8)

Villa Park Entertainment, Ltd., operates a tour and sightseeing business in Southern California. Their trademark is the use of trolley buses. Each vehicle has its own identity and is specially made for the company. Bentley, the name of the oldest bus, was purchased fifteen years ago and has five years of its estimated life remaining. The company paid $35,000 for Bentley, whose current market value is $20,000. Bentley is expected to generate an average annual net income of $22,000 before taxes for the remainder of its useful life.

Management wants to replace Bentley with a modern-looking vehicle called Keymo. Keymo has a purchase price of $120,000 and a useful life of twenty years. Net income before taxes is projected to be

Years	Annual Net Income
1–5	$45,000
6–10	50,000
11–20	60,000

Assume that (1) all cash flows occur at year end; (2) the company uses a straight-line depreciation method; (3) the vehicles' salvage value equals 10 percent of their purchase price; (4) the minimum desired after-tax rate of return is 16 percent; and (5) the company is in the 34 percent income tax bracket.

Required

1. Compute the net present value of the future cash flows from Bentley.
2. What is the net present value of cash flows that would result if Keymo were purchased?
3. Should the company keep Bentley or purchase Keymo?

Problem Set B

Problem 26B-1. Accounting Rate-of-Return and Payback Period Methods (L.O. 5a, 5b)

The Senator Company is expanding its production facilities to include a new product line, a sporty automobile tire rim. Because of a new type of machine, tire rims can be produced with little labor cost. The controller has advised management about two machines that could do the job. The details about each machine are presented below.

	Benson Machine	Krause Machine
Estimated annual increase in revenue	$382,010	$379,250
Purchase price	390,000	410,000
Salvage value	39,000	41,000
Traceable annual costs		
Materials	175,400	160,800
Direct labor	21,200	36,900
Electrical power	4,980	4,980
Factory supervision	15,750	15,750
Factory supplies	25,150	23,750
Other factory overhead	31,320	40,250
Estimated useful life in years	8	12

The company uses the straight-line depreciation method and is in the 34 percent tax bracket. Their minimum desired after-tax rate of return is 16 percent. The maximum payback period is five years.

Required

1. From the information given, compute the change in the company's net income after taxes arising from each alternative.
2. For each machine compute the projected accounting rate of return.
3. Compute the payback period for each machine.
4. From the information generated in **2** and **3** above, which machine should be purchased? Why?

Problem 26B-2. Minimum Desired Rate of Return (L.O. 3)

Capital investment analysis is the main function of Marilyn Hunt, special assistant to the controller of UCF Manufacturing Company. During the previous twelve-month period, the company's capital mix and respective costs (after tax) were as follows:

	Percentage of Total Financing	Cost of Capital (Percent)
Debt financing	30	5
Preferred stock	20	8
Common stock	40	12
Retained earnings	10	12

Plans for the current year call for a 10 percent shift in total financing, from common stock financing to debt financing. Also, the after-tax cost of debt is expected to increase to 6 percent, although the cost of the other types of financing will remain the same.

Ms. Hunt has already analyzed several proposed capital expenditures. She expects the return on investment for each capital expenditure to be as follows: 7.5 percent on Project A; 8.5 percent on Equipment Item B; 15.0 percent on Product Line C; 6.9 percent on Project D; 9.0 percent on Product Line E; 11.9 percent on Equipment Item F; and 8.0 percent on Project G.

Required

1. Compute the weighted average cost of capital for the previous year.
2. Using the expected adjustments to cost and capital mix, compute the weighted average cost of capital for the current year.
3. Identify the proposed capital expenditures that should be implemented based on the minimum desired rate of return calculated in **2** above.

Problem 26B-3. Capital Expenditure Decision: Present-value Method (L.O. 7, 8)

Management at North Dallas Plastics has been looking at a proposal to purchase a new plastic injection-style molding machine. With the new machine the company would not have to buy small plastic parts to use in production. The estimated life of the machine is fifteen years. The purchase price, including all set-up charges, is $185,000. Salvage value is estimated to be $5,000. The net addition to the company's cash inflow due to savings from making the plastic parts within the company is estimated to be $31,000 a year. Management has decided on a minimum desired before-tax rate of return of 14 percent.

Required

1. Using the present-value method to evaluate this capital expenditure, determine whether the company should purchase the machine. Support your answer.
2. If management had decided on a minimum desired rate of return of 16 percent, should the machine be purchased? Show all computations to support your answers.
3. Assuming straight-line depreciation, a 34 percent tax rate, and an after-tax minimum desired rate of return of 8 percent, should the company purchase the machine? Show your computations.

Problem 26B-4. Capital Expenditure Decision: Comprehensive
(L.O. 5, 7, 8)

The Duncan Manufacturing Company, based in Kissimmee, Florida, is one of the fastest-growing companies in its industry. According to Mr. James, the company's production vice president, keeping up with technological change is what makes the company a leader in the industry.

Mr. James thinks a new machine introduced recently would fill an important need of the company. The machine has an expected useful life of four years, a purchase price of $125,000, and a salvage value of $20,000. The company controller's estimated operating results, using the new machine, are summarized below. The company uses straight-line depreciation for all machinery. Mr. James uses a 12 percent minimum desired rate of return and a three-year payback period for capital expenditure evaluation purposes (before-tax decision guidelines).

Cash Flow Estimates

	Cash Revenues	Cash Expenses	Net Cash Inflow
Year 1	$195,000	$150,000	$45,000
Year 2	195,000	155,000	40,000
Year 3	195,000	160,000	35,000
Year 4	195,000	170,000	25,000

Required

1. Ignoring income taxes, analyze the purchase of the machine. Decide if the company should purchase it. Use the following evaluation approaches in your analysis: (a) the accounting rate-of-return method; (b) the payback period method; and (c) the present-value method.
2. Rework **1** above, assuming a 34 percent tax rate and after-tax guidelines of an 8 percent minimum desired rate of return and a 3.5-year payback period. Does the decision change when after-tax information is used?

Problem 26B-5. Even Versus Uneven Cash Flows
(L.O. 7, 8)

Pappas and Kollias, Inc., own and operate a group of apartment buildings. Management wants to sell one of its older four-family buildings and buy a new structure. The old building, which was purchased twenty-five years ago for $80,000, has a forty-year life. The current market value is $60,000. Annual net income before taxes on the old building is expected to average $15,000 for the remainder of its life.

The new building being considered will cost $450,000. It has a useful life of twenty-five years. Net income before taxes is expected to be as follows:

Years	Annual Net Income
1–10	$40,000
11–15	30,000
16–25	20,000

Assume that (1) all cash flows occur at year end; (2) the company uses a straight-line depreciation method; (3) the buildings will have a salvage value equal to 10 percent of their purchase price; (4) the minimum desired rate of return is 14 percent; and (5) the company is in the 34 percent tax bracket.

Required

1. Compute the net present value of future cash flows from the old building.
2. What will be the net present value of cash flows if the new building is purchased.
3. Should the company keep the old building or purchase the new one?

Management Decision Case

McCall Hotel Syndicate
(L.O. 7, 8)

The McCall Hotel Syndicate owns four resort hotels in southern Wisconsin and in Missouri. Because their St. Charles, Missouri, operation (Hotel 3) has been booming over the past three years, management has decided to add a new wing, which will increase capacity by 30 percent.

A construction firm has bid on the proposed new wing. The building would have a 20-year life with no salvage value. The company uses straight-line depreciation.

Deluxe accommodations are highlighted in this contractor's proposal. The new wing would cost $30,000,000 to construct, with the following estimates of cash flows:

	Increase in Cash Inflows from Room Rentals	Increase in Cash Operating Expenses
Years 1–7	$27,900,000	$20,400,000
Year 8	30,000,000	22,000,000
Year 9	32,100,000	23,600,000
Years 10–20	34,200,000	25,200,000

Capital investment projects must generate a 12 percent after-tax minimum desired rate of return to qualify for consideration. Assume a 34 percent tax rate.

Required

Evaluate the proposal from the contractor, using present-value analysis. Make a recommendation to management.

CALDWELL NEEDLES ANDERSON

PART EIGHT ANALYSES OF ACCOUNTING INFORMATION

Because business organizations are so complex today, special reports are needed to present important information about their activities. In order to understand and evaluate financial statements, it is necessary to learn how to analyze them. Part Eight deals with these important special reports and with the analysis of financial statements.

Chapter 27 presents the statement of cash flows, which explains the major financing and investing activities of a business. It also presents this statement using both the direct and indirect approaches.

Chapter 28 explains the objectives and techniques of financial statement analysis from the standpoint of the financial analyst.

CHAPTER 27 THE STATEMENT OF CASH FLOWS

LEARNING OBJECTIVES

1. Define cash and cash equivalents and describe the statement of cash flows.
2. State the principal purposes and uses of the statement of cash flows.
3. Identify the principal components of the classifications of cash flows and state the significance of noncash investing and financing transactions.
4. Determine cash flows from operating activities using the (a) direct and (b) indirect methods.
5. Determine cash flows from (a) investing activities and (b) financing activities.
6. Prepare a statement of cash flows using the (a) direct and (b) indirect methods.
7. Interpret the statement of cash flows.
8. Prepare a work sheet for the statement of cash flows.

Earlier in this book you studied the balance sheet, the income statement, and the statement of stockholders' equity. In this chapter, you will learn to prepare a fourth major financial statement: the statement of cash flows. After studying this chapter, you should be able to meet the learning objectives listed on the left.

Each financial statement is useful in specific ways. The balance sheet shows, at a point in time, how management has invested a company's resources in assets, and how these assets are financed by liabilities and owners' equity. The income statement reports how much net income a company earned during the accounting period. The statement of stockholders' equity shows changes in the status of the ownership of a business during the accounting period including the cumulative income retained in the business.

These financial statements are useful and important, but there are important questions that they do not answer. For instance, did a company's operations generate enough cash to pay its dividends? If a company lost money during the year, does it still generate enough cash to pay its liabilities? What new financing and investing activities did the company engage in during the year? In what new assets did the company invest this year? If liabilities were reduced, how were they reduced? Or, if liabilities increased during the year, where were the proceeds invested? Did the company issue common stock during the year, and, if so, what was done with the proceeds?

Why can these questions not be answered by the income statement, balance sheet, or the statement of stockholders' equity? First, because the income statement is prepared on an accrual basis, the effect of operating activities on the cash or liquidity position of the business is not shown. Second, because the balance sheet is a static financial statement, the financing and investing activities that caused changes from one year to the next are not presented. Third, the statement of stockholders' equity discloses only transactions that affect stockholders' equity. To correlate this information, another major financial statement is necessary. Until recently, this need was met by the statement of changes in financial position. This statement, which could be prepared in two ways based on different definitions of funds, showed the sources of funds received by the business and the use of those funds in the business. Historically, the most common way of preparing the statement was to define funds as working capital (current assets minus current liabilities) and to show the sources and uses of working capital. Another way, which has rapidly become more popular, defines funds as cash and shows the sources and uses of cash. Figure 27-1 shows the

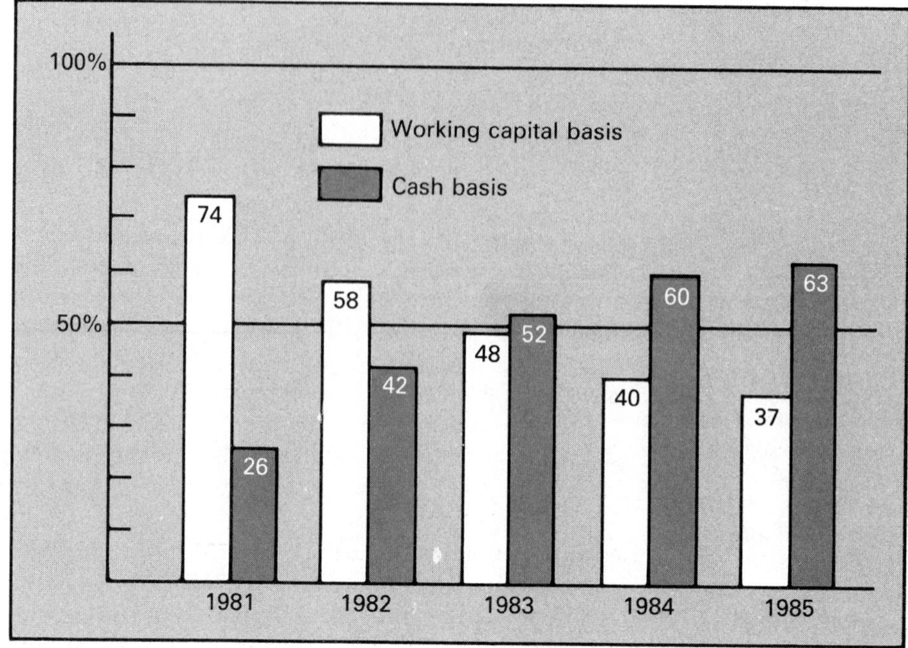

Figure 27-1. Use of Working Capital and Cash Flow Bases by 600 Large Companies
Source: American Institute of Certified Public Accountants, *Accounting Trends and Techniques,* (New York, AICPA, 1986), p. 364.

change in popularity from 1981 to 1985 from the working capital approach to the cash approach. In 1987, it is estimated that 75 percent of the companies follow the cash approach. Because of the lack of a single definition of funds and the existence of various formats for the statement used, reporting practices by businesses have varied greatly.

To remedy the confusion and lack of comparability that results from these different approaches, the Financial Accounting Standards Board adopted in November 1987 a new statement called the statement of cash flows.[1] This statement is in accord with the FASB's long-held position that a primary objective of financial statements is providing information to investors and creditors on a business's cash flows.[2] This new statement replaces the statement of changes in financial position and is prepared using a uniform format. The statement of cash flows is required every time a company prepares an income statement. The effective date of the requirement is for fiscal years ending after July 15, 1988.

The Statement of Cash Flows

The **statement of cash flows** shows the effects on cash of the operating, investing, and financing activities of a company for an accounting period. It will explain the net increase (or decrease) in cash during the accounting

1. *Statement of Financial Accounting Standards No. 95,* "Statement of Cash Flows," (Stamford, Conn.: Financial Accounting Standards Board, 1987).
2. *Statement of Financial Accounting Concepts No. 1,* "Objectives of Financial Reporting for Business Enterprises," (Stamford, Conn.: Financial Accounting Standards Board, 1978), par. 37–39.

OBJECTIVE 1
Define cash and cash equivalents and describe the statement of cash flows

period. For purposes of preparing this statement, **cash** is defined to include both cash and cash equivalents. **Cash equivalents** are short-term highly liquid investments including money market accounts, commercial paper, and U.S. treasury bills. A company maintains cash equivalents as a vehicle for earning interest while it is temporarily not needed for operations. Suppose, for example, that a company has $1,000,000 that it will not need for thirty days. To earn a return on this sum, the company may place the cash in an account that earns interest (money market accounts); it may loan the cash to another corporation by purchasing that corporation's short-term note (commercial paper); or it might purchase a short-term obligation of the U.S. government (treasury bill). In this context, short-term is defined as ninety days or less. Since cash and cash equivalents are considered the same, transfers between the cash account and cash equivalents are not treated as cash receipts or cash payments.

Cash equivalents should not be confused with short-term investments or marketable securities, which are not combined with the cash account on the statement of cash flows. Purchases of marketable securities are treated as cash outflows and sales of marketable securities are treated as cash inflows on the statement of cash flows. In this chapter, cash will be assumed to include cash and cash equivalents.

Purpose of the Statement of Cash Flows

OBJECTIVE 2
State the principal purposes and uses of the statement of cash flows

The primary purpose of the statement is to provide information about a company's cash receipts and cash payments during an accounting period. A secondary purpose is to provide information about a company's investing and financing activities during the accounting period. Some of the information on these activities may be inferred by examining the other financial statements, but it is on the statement of cash flows that all the transactions affecting cash are summarized.

Internal and External Uses of the Statement of Cash Flows

The statement of cash flows is useful internally to management and externally to investors and creditors. Management may use the statement of cash flows to assess the liquidity of the business, to determine dividend policy, and to evaluate the effects of major policy decisions involving investments and financing. In other words, management will use the statement of cash flows for such decisions as determining whether or not short-term financing is necessary to pay its current liabilities, to determine whether to raise or lower its dividends, and to plan its investing and financing needs.

Investors and creditors will find the statement useful in assessing the company's

1. Ability to generate positive future cash flows.
2. Ability to pay its liabilities.
3. Ability to pay dividends.
4. Need for additional financing.

In addition, the statement will explain the differences between the net income on the income statement and the net cash flows generated from operations. It will show both cash and noncash effects of investing and financing activities during the accounting period.

Classification of Cash Flows

OBJECTIVE 3 Identify the principal components of the classifications of cash flows and state the significance of noncash investing and financing transactions

The statement of cash flows classifies cash receipts and cash payments into the categories of operating, investing, and financing activities. The components of these activities are illustrated in Figure 27-2 and are summarized below:

1. **Operating activities** include the cash effects of transactions and other events that enter into the determination of net income. Included in this category as cash inflows are cash receipts received from customers for goods and services, and interest and dividends received on loans and investments. Included as cash outflows are cash payments for wages, goods and services, interest, and taxes applied to employees, suppliers, government bodies, and others.
2. **Investing activities** include the acquiring and selling of long-term assets, the acquiring and selling of marketable securities other than cash equivalents, and the making and collecting of loans. Cash inflows include the cash received from selling long-term assets and marketable securities and from collecting loans. Cash outflows include the cash expended for purchases of long-term assets and marketable securities and the cash loaned to borrowers.
3. **Financing activities** include (1) obtaining or returning resources from or to owners and providing them with a return on their investment and (2) obtaining resources from creditors and repaying the amounts borrowed or otherwise settling the obligation. Cash inflows include the proceeds from issues of stocks and from short-term and long-term borrowing. Cash outflows include the repayments of loans and payments to owners, including cash dividends. Treasury stock transactions are also considered financing activities. Repayment of accounts payable or accrued liabilities are not considered repayments of loans under financing activities but are classified as cash outflows under operating activities.

A company will occasionally engage in significant **noncash investing and financing transactions** such as the exchange of a long-term asset for a long-term liability or the settlement of a debt by issuing capital stock. For instance, a company might issue a long-term mortgage for the purchase of land and building, or it might convert long-term bonds into common stock. These transactions represent significant investing and financing activities, but they would not be reflected on the statement of cash flows because they do not involve either cash inflows or cash outflows. However, since one purpose of the statement of cash flows is to show investing and financing activities and since transactions like these will have future effects on cash flows, the FASB has determined that they should be disclosed in a separate schedule to the statement of cash flows. In this way, the reader of the statement will have a complete picture of the investing and financing activities.

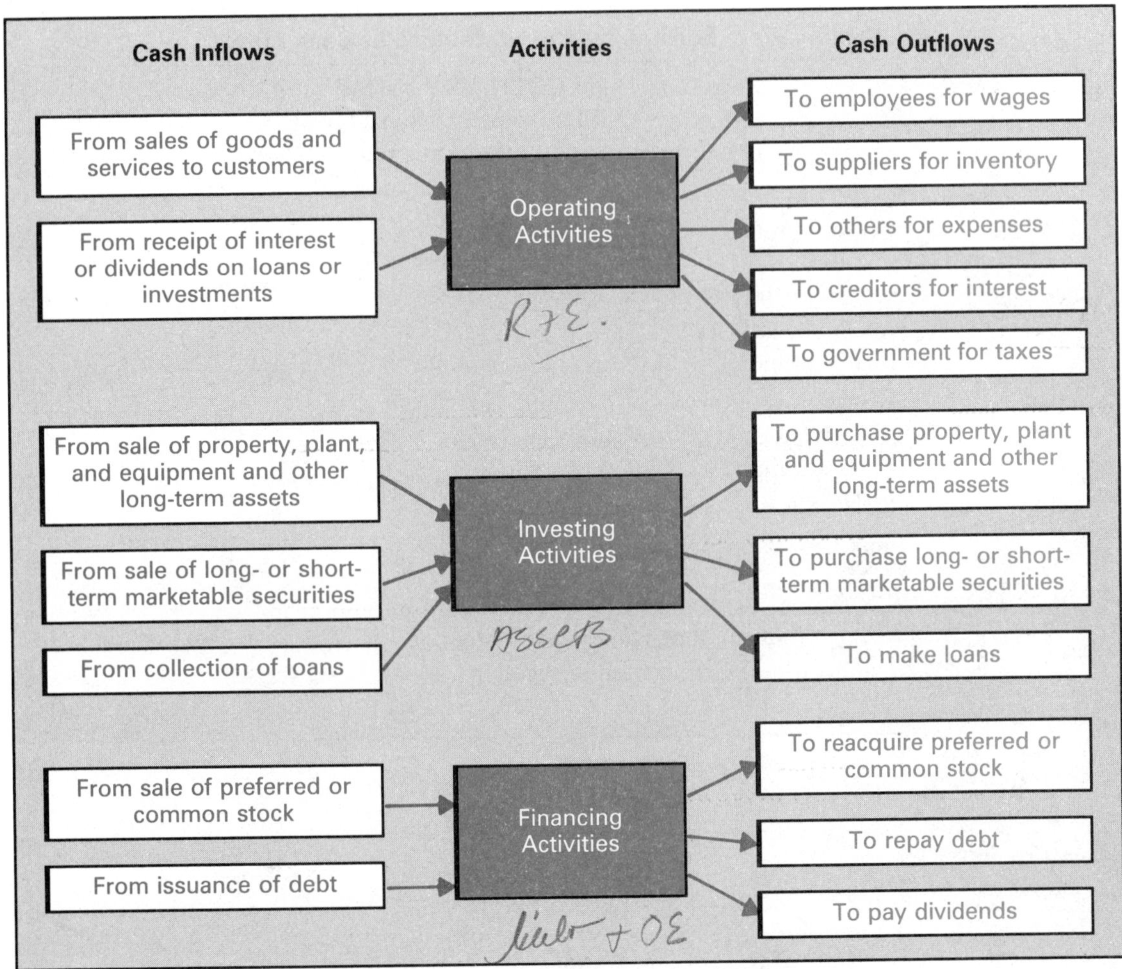

Figure 27-2. Classification of Cash Inflows and Cash Outflows

Format of the Statement of Cash Flows

The general format of the statement of cash flows, shown in Exhibit 27-1, is divided into three categories corresponding to the three activities discussed above. The cash flows from operating activities is followed by cash flows from investing activities and cash flows from financing activities. The individual inflows and outflows from investing and financing activities are shown separately in their respective categories. For instance, cash inflows from sale of property, plant, and equipment are shown separately from the cash outflows for the purchase of property, plant, and equipment. Similarly, cash inflows from borrowing are shown separately from cash outflows to retire loans. A list of noncash transactions appears in the schedule at the bottom of the statement.

Exhibit 27-1. Format for the Statement of Cash Flows

COMPANY NAME
Statement of Cash Flows
Period Covered

Cash Flows from Operating Activities		
(list of individual inflows and outflows)	XXX	
Net Cash Flows from Operating Activities		XXX
Cash Flows from Investing Activities		
(list of individual inflows and outflows)	XXX	
Net Cash Flows from Investing Activities		XXX
Cash Flows from Financing Activities		
(list of individual inflows and outflows)	XXX	
Net Cash Flows from Financing Activities		XXX
Net Increase (Decrease) in Cash		XX

Schedule of Noncash Investing and Financing Transactions

(List of Individual Transactions)	XXX

Preparing the Statement of Cash Flows

To demonstrate the preparation of the statement of cash flows, an example will be worked step-by-step. The data for this example are presented in Exhibits 27-2 and 27-3 and consist of the balance sheets for December 31, 19x1 and 19x2 and the 19x2 income statement for Ryan Corporation with additional data about transactions affecting noncurrent accounts during 19x2. Since the changes in the balance sheet accounts will be used in analyzing the various accounts, these changes are entered in Exhibit 27-2. For each individual account, an indication is made as to whether the change is an increase or decrease.

There are four steps in preparing the statement of cash flows:

1. Determining cash flows from operating activities.
2. Determining cash flows from investing activities.
3. Determining cash flows from financing activities.
4. Presenting the information obtained in the first three steps in the form of the statement of cash flows.

Exhibit 27-2. Balance Sheet with Changes in Accounts Indicated for Ryan Corporation

Ryan Corporation
Balance Sheet
December 31, 19x1 and 19x2

	19x2	19x1	Change	Increase or Decrease
Assets				
Current Assets				
Cash	$ 46,000	$ 15,000	$ 31,000	Increase
Accounts Receivable (net)	47,000	55,000	(8,000)	Decrease
Inventory	144,000	110,000	34,000	Increase
Prepaid Expenses	1,000	5,000	(4,000)	Decrease
Total Current Assets	$238,000	$185,000	$ 53,000	
Investments	$115,000	$127,000	$ (12,000)	Decrease
Plant Assets				
Plant Assets	$715,000	$505,000	$210,000	Increase
Accumulated Depreciation	(103,000)	(68,000)	(35,000)	Increase
Total Plant Assets	$612,000	$437,000	$175,000	
Total Assets	$965,000	$749,000	$216,000	
Liabilities				
Current Liabilities				
Accounts Payable	$ 50,000	$ 43,000	$ 7,000	Increase
Accrued Liabilities	12,000	9,000	3,000	Increase
Income Taxes Payable	3,000	5,000	(2,000)	Decrease
Total Current Liabilities	$ 65,000	$ 57,000	$ 8,000	
Long-Term Liabilities				
Bonds Payable	$295,000	$245,000	$ 50,000	Increase
Total Liabilities	$360,000	$302,000	$ 58,000	
Stockholders' Equity				
Common Stock, $5 par value	$276,000	$200,000	$ 76,000	Increase
Paid-in Capital in Excess of Par Value	189,000	115,000	74,000	Increase
Retained Earnings	140,000	132,000	8,000	Increase
Total Stockholders' Equity	$605,000	$447,000	$158,000	
Total Liabilities and Stockholders' Equity	$965,000	$749,000	$216,000	

Exhibit 27-3. Income Statement and Other Information on Noncurrent Accounts for Ryan Corporation

Ryan Corporation
Income Statement
For the Year Ended December 31, 19x2

Sales		$698,000
Cost of Goods Sold		520,000
Gross Margin		$178,000
Operating Expenses (Including Depreciation Expense of $37,000)		147,000
Operating Income		$ 31,000
Other Income (Expenses)		
Interest Expense	$(23,000)	
Interest Income	6,000	
Gain on Sale of Investments	12,000	
Loss on Sale of Plant Assets	(3,000)	(8,000)
Income Before Taxes		$ 23,000
Income Taxes		7,000
Net Income		$ 16,000

Other transactions affecting noncurrent accounts during 19x2:

1. Purchased investments in the amount of $78,000.
2. Sold investments for $102,000. These investments cost $90,000.
3. Purchased plant assets in the amount of $120,000.
4. Sold plant assets that cost $10,000 with accumulated depreciation of $2,000 for $5,000.
5. Issued $100,000 of bonds at face value in a noncash exchange for plant assets.
6. Repaid $50,000 of bonds at face value at maturity.
7. Issued 15,200 shares of $5 par value common stock for $150,000.
8. Paid cash dividends in the amount of $8,000.

Determining Cash Flows From Operating Activities

The income statement indicates the success or failure of a business in earning an income from its operating activities, but it does not reflect the inflow and outflow of cash from operating activities. The reason for this is that the income statement is prepared on an accrual basis. Revenues are recorded even though the cash for them may not have been received, and expenses are incurred and recorded even though cash may not yet have been expended for them. As a result, to arrive at cash flows from operations, one must convert the figures on the income statement from an accrual basis to a cash basis by adjusting the earned revenues to cash received from sales and incurred expenses to cash expended, as shown in Figure 27-3.

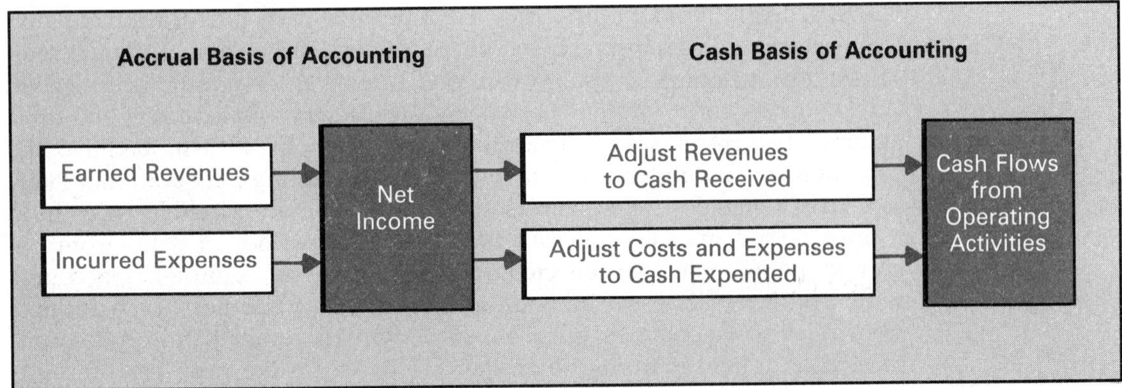

Figure 27-3. Relationship of Accrual and Cash Bases of Accounting

OBJECTIVE 4(a) Determine cash flows from operating activities using the direct method

There are two methods of converting the income statement from an accrual basis to a cash basis: the direct method and the indirect method. The **direct method** is accomplished by adjusting each item in the income statement in turn from the accrual basis to the cash basis. The result is a statement that begins with cash receipts from sales and then deducts cash payments for purchases, operating expenses, interest payments, and income taxes, to arrive at net cash flows from operating activities, as follows:

Cash Flows from Operating Activities		
Cash Receipts from		
Sales	xxx	
Interest and Dividends Received	xxx	xxx
Cash Payments for		
Purchases	xxx	
Operating Expenses	xxx	
Interest Payments	xxx	
Income Taxes	xxx	xxx
Net Cash Flows from Operating Activities		xxx

OBJECTIVE 4(b) Determine cash flows from operating activities using the indirect method

The **indirect method**, on the other hand, does not adjust each item in the income statement individually but begins with net income and lists all the adjustments necessary to convert net income to cash flow from operations, as follows:

Net Income		xxx
Adjustments to Reconcile Net Income to Net Cash Provided by Operating Activities (list of individual items)	xxx	xxx
Net Cash Flows from Operating Activities		xxx

Both approaches produce the same result and the FASB accepts both methods. However, the FASB recommends that the direct method be used. In the paragraphs that follow, the direct method will be used to illustrate the conversion of the income statement for Ryan Corporation to a cash basis and the process will be summarized using the indirect method.

Cash Receipts from Sales. Sales are a positive cash flow for a company. Cash sales are direct increases in the cash flows of the company, but credit sales are not because they are recorded originally as accounts receivable. When they are collected, they become inflows of cash. One cannot, however, assume that credit sales are automatically inflows of cash, because the collections of accounts receivable in any one accounting period are not likely to equal credit sales. Receivables may prove to be uncollectible, sales from a prior period may be collected in the current period, or sales from the current period may be collected next period. For example, if accounts receivable increases from one accounting period to the next, cash receipts from sales will not be as great as sales. On the other hand, if accounts receivable decreases from one accounting period to the next, cash receipts from sales will exceed sales. The relationships among sales, changes in accounts receivable, and cash receipts from sales are reflected in the following transaction.

$$\text{Cash Receipts from Sales} = \text{Sales} \begin{cases} + \text{ decrease in accounts receivable} \\ \text{or} \\ - \text{ increase in accounts receivable} \end{cases}$$

Refer to the balance sheet and income statement for Ryan Corporation in Exhibits 27-2 and 27-3. Note that sales are $698,000 and accounts receivable decreased by $8,000. Thus, cash received from sales is $706,000, calculated as follows:

$706,000 = $698,000 + $8,000

Ryan Corporation collected $8,000 more from sales than it sold during the year. This relationship may be illustrated as follows:

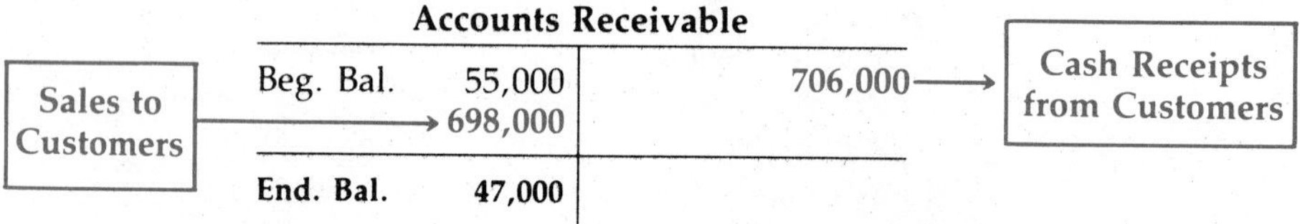

If Ryan Corporation had unearned revenues or advances from customers, an adjustment would be made for changes in these items as well.

Cash Receipts from Interest and Dividends Received. Although interest and dividends received are most closely associated with investment activity and are often called investment income, the FASB has decided to classify the cash received from these items as operating activities. To simplify the examples in this text, it is assumed that interest income equals interest received and that dividends income equals dividends received. Thus, from Exhibit 27-3, cash received from interest received for Ryan Corporation is assumed to equal $6,000, the amount of interest income.

Cash Payments for Purchases. Cost of goods sold from the income statement must be adjusted for changes in two balance sheet accounts to arrive at cash payments for purchases. First, cost of goods sold must be adjusted for changes in inventory to arrive at net purchases. Then, net purchases must be adjusted for the change in accounts payable to arrive at cash payments for purchases. If inventory has increased from one accounting period to another, net purchases will be more than cost of goods sold, and if inventory has decreased, net purchases will be less than cost of goods sold. Conversely, if accounts payable has increased, cash payments for purchases will be less than net purchases, and if accounts payable has decreased, cash payments for purchases will be more than net purchases. These relationships may be stated in equation form as follows:

$$\text{Cash Payments for Purchases} = \text{Cost of Goods Sold} \begin{cases} + \text{ Increase in Inventory} \\ \text{or} \\ - \text{ Decrease in Inventory} \end{cases} \begin{cases} + \text{ Decrease in Accounts Payable} \\ \text{or} \\ - \text{ Increase in Accounts Payable} \end{cases}$$

From Exhibits 27-2 and 27-3, cost of goods sold is \$520,000, inventory increased by \$34,000, and accounts payable increased by \$7,000. Thus, cash payments for purchases is \$547,000, calculated as follows:

$$\$547{,}000 = \$520{,}000 + \$34{,}000 - \$7{,}000$$

In this example, Ryan Corporation purchased \$34,000 more inventory than it sold and it paid out \$7,000 less in cash than it purchased. The net result is that cash payments for purchases exceeded cost of goods sold by \$27,000 (\$547,000 − \$520,000). These relationships may be visualized as follows:

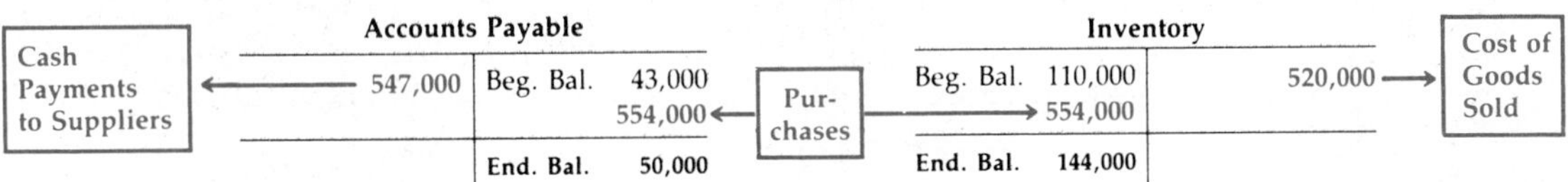

Cash Payments for Operating Expenses. Just as cost of goods sold does not represent the amount of cash paid for purchases during an accounting period, operating expenses will not match the amount of cash paid to employees, suppliers, and others for goods and services. Three adjustments must be made to operating expenses to arrive at the cash flows. The first adjustment is for changes in prepaid expenses, since in addition to arising from cash payments, operating expenses also relate to the prepaid expense accounts, such as prepaid insurance or prepaid rent. If prepaid assets increase during the accounting period, more cash will have been paid out than appears on the income statement in the form of expenses. If prepaid assets decrease, more expenses will appear on the income statement than cash spent.

The second adjustment is for changes in liabilities resulting from accrued expenses, such as wages payable and payroll taxes payable. If accrued liabilities increase during the accounting period, operating expenses on the income statement will be more than the cash spent. And if accrued liabilities decrease, operating expenses will be less than the cash spent.

The third adjustment is because certain expenses do not require a current outlay of cash, so they must be subtracted from operating expenses to arrive at cash payments for operating expenses. The most common expenses in this category are depreciation expense, amortization expense, and depletion expense. The expenditures for plant assets, intangibles, and natural resources occur when they were purchased and are classified as an investing activity at that time. Depreciation expense, amortization expense, and depletion expense are simply allocations of the costs of those original purchases to the current accounting period and do not affect cash flows in the current period. For example, Ryan Corporation recorded 19x2 depreciation expense, as follows:

Depreciation Expense	37,000	
Accumulated Depreciation		37,000
To record depreciation on plant assets		

No cash payment is made in this transaction. Thus, to the extent that operating expenses include depreciation and similar items, an adjustment is needed to reduce operating expenses to the amount of cash expended. These three adjustments are summarized in the following equation.

$$\text{Cash Payments for Operating Expenses} = \text{Operating Expenses} \left\{ \begin{array}{l} + \text{ Increase in Prepaid Expenses} \\ \text{or} \\ - \text{ Decrease in Prepaid Expenses} \end{array} \right\} \left\{ \begin{array}{l} + \text{ Decrease in Accrued Liabilities} \\ \text{or} \\ - \text{ Increase in Accrued Liabilities} \end{array} \right\} \left\{ - \text{ Depreciation and Other Noncash Expenses} \right\}$$

From Exhibits 27-2 and 27-3, operating expenses (including depreciation of $37,000) were $147,000, prepaid expenses decreased by $4,000, and accrued liabilities increased by $3,000. As a result, the cash payments for operating expenses for Ryan Corporation are $103,000, computed as follows:

$103,000 = $147,000 − $4,000 − $3,000 − $37,000

If prepaid expenses and accrued liabilities that are not related to specific operating expenses exist, they are not to be used in these computations. An example of such a case is income taxes payable, which is the accrued liability related to income taxes expense. The cash payment for income taxes is discussed in a later section.

Cash Payments for Interest. The FASB classifies cash payments for interest as operating activities in spite of the fact that some authorities argue that they should be considered financing activities because of their association with loans incurred to finance the business. The FASB feels that interest expense is a cost of operating the business. We follow the FASB position in this text. Also, for the sake of simplicity, all examples in this text assume interest payments are equal to interest expense on the income statement. Thus, from Exhibit 27-3, Ryan Corporation's interest payments are assumed to be $23,000 in 19x2.

Cash Payments for Income Taxes. The amount for income taxes expense that appears on the income statement rarely equals the amount of income taxes actually paid during the year. One reason for this difference is that the final payments for the income taxes in one year are not due until sometime in the following year. A second reason is that there may be differences between what is deducted from, or included in, income for accounting purposes and what is included or deducted for purposes of calculating income tax liability. The latter reason often results in a deferred income tax liability. Its effects on cash flows are beyond the scope of this chapter.[3] Here, we deal only with the changes that result from increases or decreases in the income taxes payable. To determine cash payments for income taxes, income taxes expense on the income statement is adjusted by the change in income taxes payable. If income taxes payable increased during the accounting period, the cash payments for taxes will be less than the expense on the income statement. If the income taxes payable decreased, the cash payments for taxes will be more than the income taxes on the income statement. In other words, the following equation is applicable.

$$\text{Cash Payments for Income Taxes} = \text{Income Taxes} \begin{cases} + \text{ Decrease in Income Taxes Payable} \\ \text{or} \\ - \text{ Increase in Income Taxes Payable} \end{cases}$$

From Exhibits 27-2 and 27-3, Ryan Corporation has income taxes on the income statement of $7,000 and a decrease of $2,000 in income taxes payable on the balance sheet. As a result, the cash payments for income taxes during 19x2 are $9,000, calculated as follows:

$$\$9{,}000 = \$7{,}000 + \$2{,}000$$

Other Income and Expenses. In computing cash flows from operations, some items classified on the income statement as other income and expenses are not considered operating items because they are more closely related to financing and investing activities than to operating activities. These items must be analyzed individually to determine their proper classification on the statement of cash flows. For instance, interest income and interest expense on Ryan Corporation's income statement have already been dealt with as operating activities. However, the effects on cash flows of gains and losses are considered with the item that gave rise to the gain or loss. The effects of gains or losses on the sale of assets are considered with investing activities, and the effects of gains or losses related to liabilities are considered with financing activities. Consequently, the effects of the gain on sale of investments and of the loss on sale of plant assets on Ryan Corporation's income statement are considered under cash flows from investing activities.

Schedule of Cash Flows From Operating Activities—Direct Method. It is now possible to prepare a schedule of cash flows from operations using the direct method and the calculations made in the preceding paragraphs. In Exhibit 27-4, Ryan Corporation had Cash Receipts from Sales and Interest Received of $712,000 and Cash Payments for Purchases, Operating Expenses, Interest Payments, and Income Taxes of $682,000 resulting in Net Cash Flows from Operating Activities of $30,000 in 19x2.

Schedule of Cash Flows from Operating Activities—Indirect Method. It is also possible to calculate net cash flows from operations using the indirect method, as shown in Exhibit 27-5. Note that the net cash flows from operating activities is the same as it was under the direct method (Exhibit 27-4). Under

3. Deferred income taxes are discussed in Chapter 14.

Exhibit 27-4. Schedule of Net Cash Flows from Operating Activities— Direct Method

Ryan Corporation
Schedule of Cash Flows from Operating Activities
For the Year Ended December 31, 19x2

Cash Flows from Operating Activities		
Cash Receipts from		
Sales	$706,000	
Interest Received	6,000	$712,000
Cash Payments for		
Purchases	$547,000	
Operating Expenses	103,000	
Interest Payments	23,000	
Income Taxes	9,000	682,000
Net Cash Flows from Operating Activities		$ 30,000

Exhibit 27-5. Schedule of Cash Flows from Operating Activities— Indirect Method

Ryan Corporation
Schedule of Cash Flows from Operating Activities
For the Year Ended December 31, 19x2

Cash Flows from Operating Activities		
Net Income		$16,000
Adjustments to Reconcile Net Income to Net Cash Provided by Operating Activities		
Depreciation	$37,000	
Gain on Sale of Investments	(12,000)	
Loss on Sale of Plant Assets	3,000	
Decrease in Accounts Receivable	8,000	
Increase in Inventory	(34,000)	
Decrease in Prepaid Expenses	4,000	
Increase in Accounts Payable	7,000	
Increase in Accrued Liabilities	3,000	
Decrease in Income Taxes Payable	(2,000)	14,000
Net Cash Flows from Operating Activities		$30,000

the indirect method, the same adjustments for the changes in current assets and current liabilities are made as were done using the direct method, except that they are all made as additions to or subtractions from net income instead of as adjustments to the individual income statement items. For instance, under the direct method above, the decrease in accounts receivable was added to sales to adjust sales from the accrual basis to the cash basis. Since sales is included in the computation of net income, the same effect is achieved by adding the decrease in accounts receivable to net income. The same logic applies to adjustments to cost of goods sold, operating expenses, and income taxes, except that the signs will be opposite for these adjustments. The following table summarizes these adjustments.

	Adjustments to Convert Net Income to Net Cash Flows from Operating Activities	
	Add to Net Income	**Deduct from Net Income**
Current Assets		
Accounts Receivable (net)	Decrease	Increase
Inventory	Decrease	Increase
Prepaid Expenses	Decrease	Increase
Current Liabilities		
Accounts Payable	Increase	Decrease
Accrued Liabilities	Increase	Decrease
Income Taxes Payable	Increase	Decrease

Net income must also be adjusted for expenses such as depreciation expense, amortization expense, depletion expense, and other income and expenses in accordance with the same logic as used in the preceding discussion. These items are to be added or deducted according to the following schedule:

	Adjustments to Convert Net Income to Net Cash Flows from Operating Activities
	Add to (Deduct from) Net Income
Depreciation Expense	Add
Amortization Expense	Add
Depletion Expense	Add
Losses	Add
Gains	Deduct

Note that these adjustments to net income are made for several reasons. Depreciation expense is added because it is a noncash expense that was deducted in the income statement to arrive at net income. Adjustments are made for gains and losses because their effects will be taken into consideration when investing and financing activities are discussed in the next section. The additions or deductions for the increases and decreases in current assets and current liabilities are included because each is necessary to adjust an income statement item from the accrual basis to the cash basis.

Determining Cash Flows from Investing Activities

OBJECTIVE 5(a) Determine cash flows from investing activities

The second step in preparation of the statement of cash flows is determining cash flows from investing activities. The procedure followed in this step is to examine individually the accounts that involve cash receipts and cash payments from investing activities. The objective in each case is to explain the change in the account balance from one year to the next.

Investing activities center around the long-term assets on the balance sheet, but also include transactions affecting short-term investments from the current asset section of the balance sheet and investment income from the income statement. From the balance sheet in Exhibit 27-2, Ryan Corporation has long-term assets of investments and plant assets, but it does not have short-term investments. From the income statement in Exhibit 27-3, it has investment income in the form of interest income and a gain on sale of investments. Also, from Exhibit 27-3, the following five items pertain to investing activities that took place during 19x2:

1. Purchased investments in the amount of $78,000.
2. Sold investments that cost $90,000 for $102,000, resulting in a gain of $12,000.
3. Purchased plant assets in the amount of $120,000.
4. Sold plant assets that cost $10,000 with accumulated depreciation of $2,000 for $5,000, resulting in a loss of $3,000.
5. Issued bonds at face value in the amount of $100,000 in a noncash exchange for plant assets.

The following paragraphs analyze the accounts related to investing activities for the purpose of determining their effects on cash flows.

Investments. The objective here is to explain the $12,000 decrease in investments (from Exhibit 27-2) by analyzing the increases and decreases in investments and determining the effects on the cash account. Purchases increase investments and sales decrease investments. Item **1** above shows purchases of $78,000 during 19x2. This transaction is recorded as follows:

Investments	78,000	
Cash		78,000
To record purchase of investments		

The effect of this transaction is a $78,000 decrease in cash flows.

Item 2 above shows a sale of investments at a gain. It is recorded as follows:

Cash	102,000	
Investments		90,000
Gain on Sale of Investments		12,000
To record sale of investments for a gain		

The effect of this transaction is a $102,000 increase in cash flows. Note that the gain on sale of investments is included in the $102,000. This is the reason it was excluded earlier from the income statement in computing cash flows from operations. If it had been left in that section, it would have been counted twice.

The $12,000 decrease in the investments account during 19x2 has now been explained, as may be seen in the T account below:

Investments			
Beg. Bal.	127,000	**Sales**	**90,000**
Purchases	**78,000**		
End. Bal.	**115,000**		

The cash flow effects from these transactions will be shown under cash flows from investing activities on the statement of cash flows as follows:

Purchase of Investments	**$ (78,000)**
Sale of Investments	**102,000**

Note that both purchases and sales are disclosed separately as cash outflows and cash inflows. They are not netted against each other into a single figure. This disclosure gives the reader of the statement a more complete view of this investing activity.

If Ryan Corporation had short-term investments or marketable securities, the analysis of cash flows would be the same as is presented in this section for the investments account.

Plant Assets. In the case of plant assets, it is necessary to explain the changes in both the asset account and the related accumulated depreciation account. From Exhibit 27-2, Plant Assets increased by $210,000 and Accumulated Depreciation increased by $35,000. Purchases increase plant assets and sales decrease plant assets. Accumulated Depreciation is increased by the amount of depreciation expense and is decreased by the removal of the accumulated depreciation associated with plant assets that are sold. There are three items listed in Exhibit 27-3 that affect plant assets. Item 3 indicates that Ryan Corporation purchased plant assets in the amount of $120,000 during 19x2. The entry to record this transaction is

Plant Assets	120,000	
Cash		**120,000**
To record purchase of plant assets		

This transaction results in a cash outflow of $120,000.

Item 4 states that Ryan Corporation sold plant assets for $5,000 that had cost $10,000 and which had accumulated depreciation of $2,000. The entry to record this transaction is

Cash	**5,000**	
Accumulated Depreciation	2,000	
Loss on Sale of Plant Assets	3,000	
Plant Assets		10,000
To record sale of plant assets at a loss		

Note in this transaction that the positive cash flow is equal to the amount of cash received, or $5,000. The loss on sale of plant assets is considered here rather than in the operating activities section, where it was deleted from the income statement when computing cash flows from operating activities. The amount of loss or gain on the sale of an asset is determined by the amount of cash received.

The disclosure of the two preceding transactions in the investing activities section of the statement of cash flows is as follows:

Purchase of Plant Assets	**$(120,000)**
Sale of Plant Assets	**5,000**

As with investment activities, cash outflows and cash inflows are not netted, but are presented separately to give full information to the statement reader.

Item 5 is a noncash exchange that affects two long-term accounts, Plant Assets and Bonds Payable. It is recorded as follows:

Plant Assets	100,000	
Bonds Payable		100,000
Issued bonds at face value for plant assets		

Although this transaction is not an inflow or outflow of cash, it is a significant transaction involving an investing activity (purchase of plant assets) and a financing activity (issue of bonds payable). Because one purpose of the statement of cash flows is to show important investing and financing activities, it is listed in a separate schedule accompanying the statement, as follows:

Schedule of Noncash Investing and Financing Transactions

Issue of Bonds Payable for Plant Assets	**$100,000**

Using these transactions and the depreciation expense for plant assets of $37,000, all the changes in the plant assets accounts are now accounted for, as shown in these T accounts:

Plant Assets

Beg. Bal.	505,000	**Sale**	**10,000**
Purchase	**120,000**		
Noncash Purchase	**100,000**		
End. Bal.	**715,000**		

Accumulated Depreciation

Sale	**2,000**	Beg. Bal.	68,000
		Dep. Exp.	37,000
		End. Bal.	**103,000**

If the balance sheet includes specific plant asset accounts such as Buildings and Equipment and their related accumulated depreciation accounts, and other long-term asset accounts, such as intangibles or natural resources, the analyses would be the same.

The changes in all the asset accounts for Ryan Corporation are now explained and the treatment of investment income has been presented. It is now possible to move to the financing activities.

Determining Cash Flows from Financing Activities

OBJECTIVE 5(b) Determine cash flows from financing activities

The third step in preparation of the statement of cash flows is determining cash flows from financing activities. The procedure followed in this step is the same as that applied to the analysis of investing activities, including related gains and/or losses except the accounts to be analyzed are the long-term liability accounts and the stockholders' equity accounts. Also to be taken into account are cash dividends from the statement of stockholders' equity. From Exhibit 27-3, the following four items from 19x2 pertain to financing activities:

5. Issued $100,000 of bonds at face value in a noncash exchange for plant assets.
6. Repaid $50,000 of bonds at face value at maturity.
7. Issued 15,200 shares of $5 par value common stock for $150,000.
8. Paid cash dividends in the amount of $8,000.

Bonds Payable. From Exhibit 27-2, Bonds Payable increased by $50,000 and is affected by Items 5 and 6 above. Item 5 was analyzed previously under plant assets and pertains to both plant assets and bonds payable. It is reported on the schedule of noncash investing and financing transactions, but must be remembered here in preparing the T account for Bonds Payable. Item 6 results in a cash outflow as can be seen in the following transaction:

	Debit	Credit
Bonds Payable	50,000	
Cash		50,000
To record repayment of bonds at face value at maturity		

This cash outflow is shown in the financing activities section of the statement of cash flows as follows:

Repayment of Bonds	$(50,000)

With knowledge of these transactions, the change in the Bonds Payable account is explained as follows:

Bonds Payable

Repayment	50,000	Beg. Bal.	245,000
		Noncash Issue	100,000
		End. Bal.	**295,000**

If Ryan Corporation had notes payable, either short-term or long-term, the same analysis would be used as presented here for bonds payable.

Common Stock. As with plant assets, related stockholders' equity accounts should be analyzed together. For example, Paid-In Capital in Excess of Par Value should be examined together with Common Stock. For Ryan Corporation, Common Stock increased by $76,000 and Paid-In Capital in Excess of Par Value increased by $74,000. These increases are explained by Item 7, which states that Ryan Corporation issued 15,200 shares of stock for $150,000. The entry to record this cash inflow is as follows:

Cash	150,000	
Common Stock		76,000
Paid-In Capital in Excess of Par Value		74,000
Issue of 15,200 shares of $5 par value common stock		

This cash inflow is shown in the cash flows from financing activities section of the statement of cash flows as follows:

Issue of Common Stock	$150,000

This transaction is all that is needed to explain the changes in these accounts during 19x2, as follows:

Common Stock

	Beg. Bal.	200,000
	Issue	76,000
	End. Bal.	**276,000**

Paid-In Capital in Excess of Par Value

	Beg. Bal.	115,000
	Issue	74,000
	End. Bal.	**189,000**

Retained Earnings. At this point in the analysis, there are several items already dealt with that affect Retained Earnings. For instance, in the case of Ryan Corporation, net income was used as part of the analysis of cash flows from operating activities. The only other item (Item 8) affecting the retained earnings of Ryan Corporation is cash dividends during 19x2 of $8,000, as reflected by the following transaction:

Retained Earnings	8,000	
Cash		8,000
To record cash dividend for 19x2		

Ryan Corporation may have declared the dividend before paying it and debited the Dividends Declared account instead of Retained Earnings, but after paying the dividend and closing the Dividends Declared account to

Retained Earnings, the effect is as shown. Cash dividends are displayed in the financing activities section of the statement of cash flows as follows:

Dividends Paid	$(8,000)

The change in the Retained Earnings account is explained as follows:

Retained Earnings			
Dividends	8,000	Beg. Bal.	132,000
		Net Income	16,000
		End. Bal.	**140,000**

Presenting the Information in the Form of the Statement of Cash Flows

OBJECTIVE 6 Prepare a statement of cash flows using the (a) direct and (b) indirect methods

At this point in the analysis, all income statement items have been analyzed, all balance sheet changes have been explained, and all additional information has been taken into account. The resulting information may now be assembled into a statement of cash flows for Ryan Corporation, as shown in Exhibit 27-6. The direct approach is used because the operating activities section contains the data from Exhibit 27-4, which shows the net cash flows from operating activities determined by the direct approach. The statement is just as easily prepared using the indirect approach with the data in Exhibit 27-5, and is presented in Exhibit 27-7. The only difference in these two statements is the approach used in the operating activities sections. The Schedule of Noncash Investing and Financing Transactions is presented below each statement.

In *Statement No. 95*, the FASB states a preference for the direct method form of the statement of cash flows but allows companies to use the indirect method form if they wish. When the direct method is used, a schedule explaining the difference between reported net income and cash flows from operating activities must be provided. An acceptable format for this schedule is the cash flows from operating activities section of the indirect method form of the statement of cash flows, as shown in Exhibits 27-5 or 27-7.

Interpretation of the Statement of Cash Flows

OBJECTIVE 7 Interpret the statement of cash flows

Now that the statement is prepared, it is important to know how to interpret and use it. What can one learn about Ryan Corporation and its management by reading its statement of cash flows?

Starting with the first section of the statement in Exhibits 27-6 or 27-7, note that Ryan Corporation generated net cash flows from operating activities of $30,000, which compares very favorably with the net income of $16,000. From Exhibit 27-7, the largest positive factor is the depreciation expense of $37,000. This is an expense that did not require a current cash outlay and is an important cause of the difference between net income and cash flows from operating activities.

Exhibit 27-6. The Statement of Cash Flows—Direct Method

Ryan Corporation
Statement of Cash Flows
For the Year Ended December 31, 19x2

Cash Flows from Operating Activities		
Cash Receipts from		
Sales	$706,000	
Interest Received	6,000	$712,000
Cash Payments for		
Purchases	$547,000	
Operating Expenses	103,000	
Interest Payments	23,000	
Income Taxes	9,000	682,000
Net Cash Flows from Operating Activities		$ 30,000
Cash Flows from Investing Activities		
Purchase of Investments	$(78,000)	
Sale of Investments	102,000	
Purchase of Plant Assets	(120,000)	
Sale of Plant Assets	5,000	
Net Cash Flows Used by Investing Activities		(91,000)
Cash Flows from Financing Activities		
Repayment of Bonds	$(50,000)	
Issue of Common Stock	150,000	
Dividends Paid	(8,000)	
Net Cash Flows from Financing Activities		92,000
Net Increase (Decrease) in Cash		$ 31,000

Schedule of Noncash Investing and Financing Transactions

Issue of Bonds Payable for Plant Assets	$100,000

The largest drain on cash in the operating activities section is the $34,000 increase in inventory. Management may want to explore ideas of reducing inventory during the next year. Other changes in current assets and current liabilities, except for the small decrease in income taxes payable, have positive effects on cash flows in this section.

Investors and creditors may want to compare net cash flows from operating activities to dividends paid in the financing activities section to determine if the company has adequate cash flows from operations to cover its payments to investors. Ryan Corporation is in good condition in this regard. Dividends paid are $8,000, compared to $30,000 in net cash flows from operating activities. The additional funds of $22,000 are available for other purposes and serve as a cushion for the payment of dividends.

Moving to the investing activities, it is apparent that the company is

Exhibit 27-7. Statement of Cash Flows—Indirect Method

Ryan Corporation
Statement of Cash Flows
For the Year Ended December 31, 19x2

Cash Flows from Operating Activities		
Net Income		$ 16,000
Adjustments to Reconcile Net Income to Net Cash Provided by Operating Activities		
Depreciation	$ 37,000	
Gain on Sale of Investments	(12,000)	
Loss on Sale of Plant Assets	3,000	
Decrease in Accounts Receivable	8,000	
Increase in Inventory	(34,000)	
Decrease in Prepaid Expenses	4,000	
Increase in Accounts Payable	7,000	
Increase in Accrued Liabilities	3,000	
Decrease in Income Taxes Payable	(2,000)	14,000
Net Cash Flows from Operating Activities		$ 30,000
Cash Flows from Investing Activities		
Purchase of Investments	$ (78,000)	
Sale of Investments	102,000	
Purchase of Plant Assets	(120,000)	
Sale of Plant Assets	5,000	
Net Cash Flows Used by Investing Activities		(91,000)
Cash Flows from Financing Activities		
Repayment of Bonds	$ (50,000)	
Issue of Common Stock	150,000	
Dividends Paid	(8,000)	
Net Cash Flows from Financing Activities		92,000
Net Increase (Decrease) in Cash		$ 31,000

Schedule of Noncash Investing and Financing Transactions

Issue of Bonds Payable for Plant Assets	$100,000

expanding because there is a net cash outflow of $91,000 in this section. The company has expanded by purchasing plant assets of $120,000. Various other investing activities have reduced the cash need to $91,000. This is not the whole story on the expansion of the business, however, because the schedule of noncash investing and financing transactions reveals that the company bought another $100,000 in plant assets by issuing bonds. In other words, total purchases of plant assets were $220,000. Part of this expansion was financed by issuing bonds in exchange for plant assets and most of the rest was financed through other financing activities.

Net cash flows of $92,000 were provided by financing activities to offset most of the $91,000 net cash flows needed from the investing activities section. The company looked to its owners for this financing by issuing common stock for $150,000, while repaying $50,000 in bonds payable. Taking into account the noncash transaction, bonds payable increased by $50,000.

In summary, Ryan Corporation has paid for its expansion with a combination of cash flows from operating activities, net sales of investment assets, issuance of common stock, and a net increase in bonds payable.

Preparing the Work Sheet

OBJECTIVE 8
Prepare a work sheet for the statement of cash flows

Previous sections illustrated the preparation of the statement of cash flows for Ryan Corporation, a relatively simple company. To assist in preparation of the statement of cash flows in more complex companies, accountants have developed a work sheet approach. The work sheet approach is a special format that allows for the systematic analysis of all the changes in the balance sheet accounts to arrive at the statement of cash flows. In this section, this procedure is demonstrated by preparing the statement of cash flows for Ryan Corporation. The work sheet approach uses the indirect approach to determining cash flows from operating activities because this approach adjusts net income for the changes in each balance sheet account instead of adjusting each item individually in the income statement.

Procedures in Preparing the Work Sheet

The work sheet for Ryan Corporation is presented in Exhibit 27-8. The work sheet has four columns labeled as follows:

Column A: Description

Column B: Account balances for the end of the prior year (19x1)

Column C: Analysis of transactions for the current year

Column D: Account balances for the end of the current year (19x2)

The following steps are followed in the preparation of the work sheet. As you read each one, refer to Exhibit 27-8.

1. Enter the account names from the balance sheet in column A. Note that all accounts with debit balances are listed first, followed by all accounts with credit balances.
2. Enter the account balances for 19x1 in column B and the account balances for 19x2 in column D. In each column, total the debits and the credits. The total debits should equal the total credits in each column. This is a check on whether or not you transferred all the accounts from the balance sheet correctly.
3. Below the data entered in Step 2, insert the captions: Cash Flows from Operating Activities; Cash Flows from Investing Activities; and Cash Flows from Financing Activities, leaving several lines of space between each one. As you do the analysis, write the results in the appropriate categories.

Exhibit 27-8. Work Sheet for the Statement of Cash Flows

Ryan Corporation
Work Sheet for Statement of Cash Flows
For the Year Ended December 31, 19x2

Description	Account Balances 12/31/x1	Analysis of Transactions: Debit	Analysis of Transactions: Credit	Account Balances 12/31/x2
Debits				
Cash	15,000	(x) 31,000		46,000
Accounts Receivable (net)	55,000		(b) 8,000	47,000
Inventory	110,000	(c) 34,000		144,000
Prepaid Expenses	5,000		(d) 4,000	1,000
Investments	127,000	(h) 78,000	(i) 90,000	115,000
Plant Assets	505,000	(j) 120,000	(k) 10,000	715,000
		(l) 100,000		
Total Debits	817,000			1,068,000
Credits				
Accumulated Depreciation	68,000	(k) 2,000	(m) 37,000	103,000
Accounts Payable	43,000		(e) 7,000	50,000
Accrued Liabilities	9,000		(f) 3,000	12,000
Income Taxes Payable	5,000	(g) 2,000		3,000
Bonds Payable	245,000	(n) 50,000	(l) 100,000	295,000
Common Stock	200,000		(o) 76,000	276,000
Paid-in Capital	115,000		(o) 74,000	189,000
Retained Earnings	132,000	(p) 8,000	(a) 16,000	140,000
Total Credits	817,000	425,000	425,000	1,068,000
Cash Flows from Operating Activities				
Net Income		(a) 16,000		
Decrease in Accounts Receivable		(b) 8,000		
Increase in Inventory			(c) 34,000	
Decrease in Prepaid Expenses		(d) 4,000		
Increase in Accounts Payable		(e) 7,000		
Increase in Accrued Liabilities		(f) 3,000		
Decrease in Income Taxes Payable			(g) 2,000	
Gain on Sale of Investments			(i) 12,000	
Loss on Sale of Plant Assets		(k) 3,000		
Depreciation Expense		(m) 37,000		
Cash Flows from Investing Activities				
Purchase of Investments			(h) 78,000	
Sale of Investments		(i) 102,000		
Purchase of Plant Assets			(j) 120,000	
Sale of Plant Assets		(k) 5,000		
Cash Flows from Financing Activities				
Repayment of Bonds			(n) 50,000	
Issue of Common Stock		(o) 150,000		
Dividends Paid			(p) 8,000	
		335,000	304,000	
Net Increase in Cash			(x) 31,000	
		335,000	335,000	

4. Analyze the changes in each balance sheet account using information from both the income statement and from other transactions as appropriate (see Exhibit 27-3) and enter the results in the debit and credit columns in column C. Identify each item with a letter. On the first line identify the change in cash with an (x). In a complex situation, these letters will reference a list of explanations on another working paper.
5. When all the changes in the balance sheet accounts have been explained, add the debit and credit columns in both the top and bottom portions of column C. The debit and credit columns in the top portion should equal each other. They should not be equal in the bottom portion. If no errors have been made, the difference in the bottom portion should equal the increase or decrease in the cash account identified with an (x) on the first line of the work sheet. Add this difference to the lesser of the two columns, and identify it as either an increase or decrease in cash. Label the change with an (x) and compare it with the change in cash on the first line of the work sheet, also labeled (x). The amounts should be equal, as they are in Exhibit 27-8, where the net increase in cash was $31,000.

After completing the work sheet, the statement of cash flows may be prepared by using the information in the lower half of the work sheet, as shown previously in Exhibit 27-7.

Analyzing the Changes in Balance Sheet Accounts

The most important step in the preparation of the work sheet is the analysis of the changes in the balances of the balance sheet accounts. Although there are a number of transactions and reclassifications in this work sheet to analyze and record, the overall procedure is systematic and not so complicated. These overall procedures are as follows:

1. Record net income
2. Account for changes in current assets and current liabilities
3. Account for changes in noncurrent accounts using the information about other transactions
4. Reclassify any other income and expense items not already dealt with. In studying the following explanations, recall that the identification letters refer to the corresponding transactions and reclassifications in the work sheet.

a. ***Net Income.*** Net income results in an increase in Retained Earnings. It is also the starting point under the indirect method for determining cash flows from operating activities. Under this method, additions and deductions are made to net income to arrive at cash flows from operating activities. Work sheet entry **a** is as follows:

(a) Cash Flows from Operations: Net Income	16,000	
Retained Earnings		16,000

b.–g. ***Changes in Current Assets and Current Liabilities.*** Entries **b** to **g** record the effects of the changes in current assets and current liabilities on cash flow. In each case, there is a debit or credit to the current asset or current liability to account for the change in the year and a corresponding debit or credit in the operating activities section of the work sheet. Recall that in the prior analysis, each item on the accrual-based income statement is adjusted for the change in the related current asset or current liability to arrive at the cash-based figure. The same reasoning applies in recording these changes in accounts as debits or credits in the operating activities section. For example, work sheet entry **b** records the decrease in Accounts Receivable as a credit (decrease) to Accounts Receivable and as a debit in the operating activities section because the decrease has a positive effect on cash flows, as follows:

	Debit	Credit
(b) Cash Flows from Operating Activities:		
Decrease in Accounts Receivable	8,000	
Accounts Receivable		8,000

Work sheet entries **c–g** reflect the effects of the changes in the other current assets and current liabilities on cash flows from operating activities. As you study these entries below, note how the effects on cash flows of each entry are automatically determined by debits or credits that reflect the changes in the balance sheet accounts.

	Debit	Credit
(c) Inventory	34,000	
Cash Flows from Operating Activities:		
Increase in Inventory		34,000
(d) Cash Flows from Operating Activities:		
Decrease in Prepaid Expenses	4,000	
Prepaid Expenses		4,000
(e) Cash Flows from Operating Activities:		
Increase in Accounts Payable	7,000	
Accounts Payable		7,000
(f) Cash Flows from Operating Activities:		
Increase in Accrued Liabilities	3,000	
Accrued Liabilities		3,000
(g) Income Taxes Payable	2,000	
Cash Flows from Operating Activities:		
Decrease in Income Taxes Payable		2,000

h.–i. ***Investments.*** Among the other transactions affecting noncurrent accounts during 19x2 (See Exhibit 27-3), two items pertain to investments. One is the purchase of $78,000 and the other is the sale at $102,000. The purchase is recorded in the work sheet as a cash flow in the investing activities section, as follows:

	Debit	Credit
(h) Investments	78,000	
Cash Flows from Investing Activities:		
Purchase of Investments		78,000

Note that instead of crediting cash, a credit entry with the appropriate designation is made in the appropriate section in the lower half of the work sheet. The sale transaction is more complicated because it involves a gain that appears on the income statement and is included in net income. The work sheet entry accounts for this gain. The entry is as follows:

(i) Cash Flows from Investing Activities: Sale of Investments	102,000	
Investments		90,000
Cash Flows from Operating Activities: Gain on Sale of Investments		12,000

This entry records the cash inflow in the investing activities section, accounts for the remaining difference in the Investments account, and removes the gain on sale of investments from its inclusion in net income.

j.–m. ***Plant Assets and Accumulated Depreciation.*** There are four transactions that affect plant assets and the related accumulated depreciation. These are the purchase of plant assets, the sale of plant assets at a loss, the noncash exchange of plant assets for bonds, and the depreciation expense for the year. Because these transactions can seem complicated, it is important to work through them systematically when preparing the work sheet. First, the purchase of plant assets for $120,000 is entered (entry **j**) in the same way the purchase of investments was entered in entry **h**. Second, the sale of plant assets is similar to the sale of investments, except a loss is involved instead of a gain and accumulated depreciation is involved, as follows:

(k) Cash Flows from Investing Activities: Sale of Plant Assets	5,000	
Cash Flows from Operating Activities: Loss on Sale of Plant Assets	3,000	
Accumulated Depreciation	2,000	
Plant Assets		10,000

The cash inflow from this transaction is $5,000. The rest of the entry is necessary to add the loss back into net income in the operating activities section of the statement since it was deducted out to arrive at net income and to record the effects on plant assets and accumulated depreciation.

The third transaction (entry **l**) is the noncash issue of bonds for the purchase of plant assets, as follows:

(l) Plant Assets	100,000	
Bonds Payable		100,000

Note that this transaction does not affect cash, but needs to be recorded because the objective is to account for all the changes in the balance sheet accounts. A note needs to be made to recall this transaction when the statement of cash flows is prepared, however, because it is listed in the schedule of noncash investing and financing transactions.

At this point the increase of $210,000 ($715,000 – $505,000) in plant assets has been explained by the two purchases less the sale ($120,000 + $100,000 – $10,000 = $210,000), but the change in Accumulated Depreciation has not been completely explained. The depreciation expense for the year needs to be entered, as follows:

(m) Cash Flows from Operating Activities:		
Depreciation Expense	37,000	
Accumulated Depreciation		37,000

The debit is to the operating activities section of the work sheet because, as explained earlier in the chapter, no current cash outflow is required for depreciation expense. The effect of this debit is to add the amount for depreciation expense back to net income. The $35,000 increase in Accumulated Depreciation has now been explained by the sale transaction and the depreciation expense (–$2,000 + $37,000 = $35,000).

n. ***Bonds Payable.*** Part of the change in Bonds Payable was explained in entry l when the noncash transaction, $100,000 issue of bonds for plant assets, was entered. All that remains is to enter the repayment as follows:

(n) Bonds Payable	50,000	
Cash Flows from Financing Activities:		
Repayment of Bonds		50,000

o. ***Common Stock and Paid-In Capital In Excess of Par Value.*** Similarly, one transaction affects both of these accounts. It is an issue of 15,200 shares of $5 par value common stock for a total of $150,000. The work sheet entry is:

(o) Cash Flows from Financing Activities:		
Issue of Common Stock	150,000	
Common Stock		76,000
Paid-in Capital in Excess of Par Value		74,000

p. ***Retained Earnings.*** Part of the change in Retained Earnings has already been recognized when net income was entered (entry **a**). The only remaining effect to be recognized is the effect of the $8,000 in cash dividends paid during the year, as follows:

(p) Retained Earnings	8,000	
Cash Flows from Financing Activities:		
Dividends Paid		8,000

x. The final step is to total the debit and credit columns in the top and bottom portions of the work sheet and enter the net change in cash at the bottom of the work sheet. The columns in the upper half equal $425,000. In the lower half, the debit column totals $335,000 and the credit column totals $304,000. The credit difference of $31,000 (entry **x**) equals the change in cash on the first line of the work sheet.

Chapter Review

Review of Learning Objectives

1. **Define cash and cash equivalents and describe the statement of cash flows.**
For purposes of preparing the statement of cash flows, cash is defined to include cash and cash equivalents. Cash equivalents are short-term (ninety days or less) highly liquid investments including money market accounts, commercial paper, and U.S. treasury bills. The statement of cash flows explains the changes in cash and cash equivalents from one accounting period to the next by showing cash outflows and cash inflows from the operating, investing, and financing activities of a company for an accounting period.

2. **State the principal purposes and uses of the statement of cash flows.**
The primary purpose of the statement of cash flows is to provide information about a company's cash receipts and cash payments during an accounting period. Its secondary purpose is to provide information about a company's investing and financing activities. It is useful to management as well as to investors and creditors in assessing the liquidity of a business, including the ability of the business to generate future cash flows and to pay its debts and dividends.

3. **Identify the principal components of the classifications of cash flows and state the significance of noncash investing and financing transactions.**
Cash flows are classified as operating activities, which include the cash effects of transactions and other events that enter into the determination of net income; investing activities, which include the acquiring and selling of long- and short-term marketable securities, property, plant, and equipment, and the making and collecting of loans excluding interest; and financing activities, which include obtaining and returning or repaying resources excluding interest to owners and creditors. Noncash investing and financing transactions are important exchanges of assets and/or liabilities that do not involve cash but nevertheless are of interest to investors and creditors in evaluating the financing and investing activities of the business.

4. **Determine cash flows from operating activities using the (a) direct and (b) indirect methods.**
The direct method of determining cash flows from operating activities is accomplished by adjusting each item in the income statement in turn from the accrual basis to the cash basis. The indirect method does not adjust each item in the income statement individually but begins with net income and lists all noncash effects to adjust net income to a cash flow basis.

5. **Determine cash flows from (a) investing activities and (b) financing activities.**
Cash flows from investing activities are determined by identifying the cash flow effects of the transactions that affect each account relevant to investing activities. These accounts include all long-term assets and short-term marketable securities. The same procedure is followed for financing activities except the accounts involved are short-term notes payable, long-term liabilities, and the owners' equity accounts. The effects of gains and losses from the income statement must also be considered with their related accounts. When the change in a balance sheet account from one accounting period to the next has been explained, all the cash flow effects should have been identified.

6. **Prepare a statement of cash flows using the (a) direct method and (b) indirect method.**
The statement of cash flows has categories for cash flows from operating activities, investing activities, and financing activities. The section on cash flows from operating activities may be prepared using either the direct or indirect method. Significant noncash transactions are included in a schedule of noncash investing and financing transactions that accompanies the statement of cash flows.

7. **Interpret the statement of cash flows.**
Interpretation of the statement of cash flows begins with the cash flows from operations to determine if it is positive and to assess the differences between net income and net cash flows from operating activities. It is usually informative to relate cash flows from operations to dividend payments in the financing section to see if the company is comfortably covering these important cash outflows. It is also useful to examine the investing activities to determine if the company is expanding, and if so, in what areas of business it is investing; and if not, in what areas it is contracting. Based on the analysis of the investing area, it is now possible to look to the financing section to evaluate how the company is financing the expansion, or if it is not expanding, how it is reducing its financing obligations. Finally, it is important to evaluate the impact of the noncash investing and financing transactions listed in the statement of cash flows information in the lower portion.

8. **Prepare a work sheet for the statement of cash flows.**
A work sheet is useful in preparing the statement of cash flows for complex companies. The basic procedures in the work sheet approach are to analyze the changes in the balance sheet accounts for the effects on cash flows in the top portion and to classify the effects according to the format of the statement of cash flows in the lower portion of the work sheet. When all the changes in the balance sheet accounts have been explained and entered on the work sheet, the change in the cash account will also be explained, and the information will be available to prepare the statement of cash flows. The work sheet lends itself to the indirect method of preparing the statement of cash flows.

Review Problem
The Statement of Cash Flows

The comparative balance sheets for the years 19x6 and 19x7 and the income statement of 19x7 for Northwest Corporation are shown below.

Northwest Corporation
Balance Sheets
December 31, 19x7, and December 31, 19x6

	19x7	19x6	Change	Increase or Decrease
Assets				
Cash	$ 115,850	$ 121,850	$ (6,000)	Decrease
Accounts Receivable (net)	296,000	314,500	(18,500)	Decrease
Inventory	322,000	301,000	21,000	Increase
Prepaid Expenses	7,800	5,800	2,000	Increase
Long-Term Investments	36,000	86,000	(50,000)	Decrease
Land	150,000	125,000	25,000	Increase
Building	462,000	462,000	—	—
Accumulated Depreciation, Building	(91,000)	(79,000)	(12,000)	Increase
Equipment	159,730	167,230	(7,500)	Decrease
Accumulated Depreciation, Equipment	(43,400)	(45,600)	2,200	Decrease
Intangible Assets	19,200	24,000	(4,800)	Decrease
Total Assets	$1,434,180	$1,482,780	$ (48,600)	
Liabilities and Stockholders' Equity				
Accounts Payable	$ 133,750	$ 233,750	$(100,000)	Decrease
Notes Payable (current)	75,700	145,700	(70,000)	Decrease
Accrued Liabilities	5,000	—	5,000	Increase
Income Taxes Payable	20,000	—	20,000	Increase
Bonds Payable	210,000	310,000	(100,000)	Decrease
Mortgage Payable	330,000	350,000	(20,000)	Decrease
Common Stock—$10 par value	360,000	300,000	60,000	Increase
Paid-in Capital in Excess of Par Value, Common	90,000	50,000	40,000	Increase
Retained Earnings	209,730	93,330	116,400	Increase
Total Liabilities and Stockholders' Equity	$1,434,180	$1,482,780	$ (48,600)	

Northwest Corporation
Income Statement
For the Year Ended December 31, 19x7

Sales		$1,650,000
Cost of Goods Sold		920,000
Gross Margin		$ 730,000
Operating Expenses (Including Depreciation Expense of $12,000 on Buildings and $23,100 on Equipment and Amortization Expense of $4,800)		470,000
Operating Income		$ 260,000
Other Income (Expense)		
Interest Expense	$(55,000)	
Dividend Income	3,400	
Gain on Sale of Investment	12,500	
Loss on Disposal of Equipment	(2,300)	(41,400)
Income Before Taxes		$ 218,600
Income Taxes		52,200
Net Income		$ 166,400

The following additional information was taken from the company's records:

a. Long-term investments that cost $70,000 were sold at a gain of $12,500; additional long-term investments were made in the amount of $20,000.
b. Five acres of land were purchased for $25,000 for a parking lot.
c. Equipment that cost $37,500 with accumulated depreciation of $25,300 was sold at a loss of $2,300; new equipment in the amount of $30,000 was purchased.
d. Notes Payable in the amount of $100,000 were repaid; an additional $30,000 was borrowed by signing notes payable.
e. Bonds Payable in the amount of $100,000 were converted into 6,000 shares of common stock.
f. Mortgage Payable was reduced by $20,000 during the year.
g. Cash dividends declared and paid were $50,000.

Required

1. Prepare a schedule of cash flows from operating activities using the (a) direct method and (b) indirect method.
2. Prepare a statement of cash flows using the direct method.

Answer to Review Problem

1. (a) Schedule of cash flows from operating activities—direct method prepared.

Northwest Corporation
Schedule of Cash Flows from Operating Activities
For the Year Ended December 31, 19x7

Cash Flows from Operating Activities		
Cash Receipts from		
Sales	$1,668,500[1]	
Dividends Received	3,400	$1,671,900
Cash Payments for		
Purchases	$1,041,000[2]	
Operating Expenses	427,100[3]	
Interest Payments	55,000	
Income Taxes	32,200[4]	1,555,300
Net Cash Flows from Operating Activities		$ 116,600

[1] $1,650,000 + $18,500 = $1,668,500
[2] $920,000 + $21,000 + $100,000 = $1,041,000
[3] $470,000 + $2,000 − $5,000 − ($12,000 + $23,100 + $4,800) = $427,100
[4] $52,200 − $20,000 = $32,200

1. (b) Schedule of cash flows from operating activities—indirect method prepared.

Northwest Corporation
Schedule of Cash Flows from Operating Activities
For the Year Ended December 31, 19x7

Net Income		$166,400
Add (or Deduct) Items Not Affecting Cash Flows from Operating Activities		
Depreciation Expense, Buildings	$ 12,000	
Depreciation Expense, Equipment	23,100	
Amortization Expense, Intangible Assets	4,800	
Gain on Sales of Investments	(12,500)	
Loss on Disposal of Equipment	2,300	
Decrease in Accounts Receivable	18,500	
Increase in Inventory	(21,000)	
Increase in Prepaid Expenses	(2,000)	
Decrease in Accounts Payable	(100,000)	
Increase in Accrued Liabilities	5,000	
Increase in Income Taxes Payable	20,000	(49,800)
Net Cash Flows from Operating Activities		$116,600

2. Statement of cash flows—direct method prepared.

Northwest Corporation
Statement of Cash Flows
For the Year Ended December 31, 19x7

Cash Flows from Operating Activities		
Cash Receipts from		
Sales	$1,668,500	
Dividends Received	3,400	$1,671,900
Cash Payments for		
Purchases	$1,041,000	
Operating Expenses	427,100	
Interest Payments	55,000	
Income Taxes	32,200	1,555,300
Net Cash Flows from Operating Activities		$ 116,600
Cash Flows from Investing Activities		
Sale of Long-Term Investments	$ 82,500	
Purchase of Long-Term Investments	(20,000)	
Purchase of Land	(25,000)	
Sales of Equipment	9,900	
Purchase of Equipment	(30,000)	
Net Cash Flows from Investing Activities		17,400
Cash Flows from Financing Activities		
Repayment of Notes Payable	$(100,000)	
Issuance of Notes Payable	30,000	
Reduction in Mortgage	(20,000)	
Dividends Paid	(50,000)	
Net Cash Flows Used by Financing Activities		(140,000)
Net Increase (Decrease) in Cash		$ (6,000)

Schedule of Noncash Investing and Financing Transactions

Conversion of Bonds Payable into Common Stock	$100,000

Chapter Assignments

Questions

1. How has the practice in the reporting of changes in financial position and of investing and reporting activities changed during the 1980s?
2. What is the term *cash* in the statement of cash flows understood to mean and include?
3. In order to earn a return on cash on hand during 19x3, Sallas Corporation transferred $45,000 from its checking account to a money market account, purchased a $25,000 treasury bill, and bought $35,000 in common stocks. How will each of these transactions affect the statement of cash flows?

4. What are the purposes of the statement of cash flows?
5. Why is the statement of cash flows needed when most of the information in it is available from comparative balance sheets and the income statement?
6. What are the three classifications of cash flows and some examples of each?
7. Why is it important to disclose certain noncash transactions? How should they be disclosed?
8. Cell-Borne Corporation has a net loss of $12,000 in 19x1 but has positive cash flows from operations of $9,000? What are some conditions that may have caused this situation?
9. What items on the income statement are not classified as operating activities? Why? Where are they classified?
10. Glen Corporation has other income and expenses: interest expense, $12,000; interest income, $3,000; dividend income, $5,000; and loss on retirement of bonds, $6,000. How do each of these items appear on or affect the statement of cash flows?
11. What are the essential differences between the direct method and the indirect method of determining cash flows from operations?
12. What are the effects of the following items on cash flows from operations: (a) an increase in accounts receivable, (b) a decrease in inventory, (c) an increase in accounts payable, (d) a decrease in wages payable, (e) depreciation expense, and (f) amortization of patents?
13. What is the proper treatment on the statement of cash flows of a transaction in which a building that cost $50,000 with accumulated depreciation of $32,000 is sold for a loss of $5,000?
14. What is the proper treatment on the statement of cash flows of (a) a transaction in which buildings and land are purchased by the issuance of a mortgage for $234,000 and (b) a conversion of $50,000 in bonds payable into 2,500 shares of $6 par value common stock?
15. Why is the work sheet approach considered to be more compatible with the indirect method as opposed to the direct method of determining cash flows from operations?
16. Assuming in each independent case only one transaction occurred, what transactions would likely cause (1) a decrease in investments and (2) an increase in common stock? How would each case be treated on the work sheet for a statement of cash flows?
17. In interpreting the statement of cash flows, what are some comparisons that can be made with cash flows from operations? For what reasons would a company have a decrease in cash flows from investing activities?

Classroom Exercises

Exercise 27-1. Classification of Cash Flow Transactions
(L.O. 3)

InterFirst Corporation engaged in the following transactions. Identify each as (1) an operating activity, (2) an investing activity, (3) a financing activity, (4) a noncash transaction, or (5) none of the above.

a. Declared and paid a cash dividend.
b. Purchased an investment.
c. Received cash from customers.
d. Paid interest.
e. Sold equipment at a loss.
f. Issued long-term bonds for plant assets.
g. Received dividends on securities held.
h. Issued common stock.
i. Declared and issued a stock dividend.
j. Repaid notes payable.
k. Paid employees for wages.
l. Purchased a 60-day treasury bill.
m. Purchased land.

Cash
Equiv

Exercise 27-2. Computing Cash Flows from Operating Activities— Direct Method (L.O. 4)

a. During 19x2, Rentral Corporation had cash sales of $34,500 and sales on credit of $123,000. During the same year, accounts receivable decreased by $18,000. Determine the cash received from customers during 19x2.
b. During 19x2, Rentral Corporation had cost of goods sold of $119,000. During the same year, merchandise inventory increased by $12,500 and accounts payable decreased by $4,300. Determine the cash payments for purchases during 19x2.
c. During 19x2, Rentral Corporation had operating expenses of $45,000 including depreciation of $15,600. Also during 19x2, related prepaid expenses decreased by $3,100 and relevant accrued expenses increased by $1,200. Determine cash payments to suppliers of goods and services during 19x2.
d. Income Taxes Expense for Rentral Corporation was $4,300 for 19x2 and Income Taxes Payable decreased by $230. Determine cash payment for income taxes during 19x2.

Exercise 27-3. Computing Cash Flows from Operating Activities— Indirect Method (L.O. 4)

During 19x1, Canton Corporation had net income of $34,000. Included on the income statement was Depreciation Expense of $2,300 and Amortization Expense of $300. During the year, accounts receivable increased by $3,400, inventories decreased by $1,900, prepaid assets decreased by $200, accounts payable increased by $5,000, and accrued liabilities decreased by $450. Determine cash flows from operating activities using the indirect method.

Exercise 27-4. Computing Cash Flows from Operating Activities— Direct Method (L.O. 4)

The income statement for the Cummings Corporation appears below.

Additional information: (a) All sales were on credit, and accounts receivable increased by $2,200 during the year. (b) All merchandise purchased was on credit. Inventories increased by $3,500, and accounts payable increased by $7,000 during the year. (c) Prepaid rent decreased by $700, accrued salaries payable increased by $500, and income taxes payable decreased by $300 during the year. Prepare a schedule of cash flows from operating activities using the direct method.

Cummings Corporation
Income Statement
For the Year Ended June 30, 19xx

Sales		$60,000
Cost of Goods Sold		30,000
Gross Margin from Sales		$30,000
Other Expenses		
Salaries Expense	$16,000	
Rent Expense	8,400	
Depreciation Expense	1,000	25,400
Income Before Income Taxes		$ 4,600
Income Taxes		1,200
Net Income		$ 3,400

Exercise 27-5. Calculating Cash Flows from Operating Activities— Indirect Method (L.O. 4)

Using the data provided in Exercise 27-4, prepare a schedule of cash flows from operating activities for Cummings Corporation using the indirect method.

Exercise 27-6. Calculating Cash Flows from Investing Activities— Investments (L.O. 5)

The T account for the Investments account for Sader Company at the end of 19x3 appears below:

Investments

Beg. Bal.	38,500	Sales	42,000
Purchases	58,000		
End. Bal.	**54,500**		

In addition, the income statement shows a loss on the sale of investments of $6,500. Compute the amounts to be shown and show how they are to appear as cash flows from investing activities on the statement of cash flows.

Exercise 27-7. Calculating Cash Flows from Investing Activities— Plant Assets (L.O. 5)

The T accounts for the Plant Assets and Accumulated Depreciation accounts for Sader Company at the end of 19x3 appear below:

Plant Assets

Beg. Bal.	65,000	Disposals	23,000
Purchases	33,600		
End. Bal.	**75,600**		

Accumulated Depreciation

Disposals	14,700	Beg. Bal.	34,500
		19x3 Depreciation	10,200
		End. Bal.	**30,000**

In addition, the income statement shows a gain on sale of plant assets of $4,400. Compute the amounts to be shown and show how they are to appear as cash flows from investing activities on the statement of cash flows.

Exercise 27-8. Calculating Cash Flows from Financing Activities (L.O. 3, 5)

All transactions involving notes payable and related accounts engaged in by Sader Company during 19x3 are as follows:

Cash	12,000	
Notes Payable		12,000
Bank loan		
Patent	20,000	
Notes Payable		20,000
Purchase of patent by issuing note payable		
Notes Payable	5,000	
Interest Expense	500	
Cash		5,500
Repayment of note payable at maturity		

Determine the amounts and how these transactions are to be shown in the statement of cash flows for 19x3.

Exercise 27-9. Preparing the Statement of Cash Flows
(L.O. 6)

Tsin Corporation's comparative balance sheets on June 30, 19x1 and 19x2, and the 19x2 income statement appear below.

	19x2	19x1
Assets		
Cash	$ 69,900	$ 12,500
Accounts Receivable (net)	21,000	26,000
Inventory	43,400	48,400
Prepaid Expenses	3,200	2,600
Furniture	55,000	60,000
Accumulated Depreciation, Furniture	(9,000)	(5,000)
Total Assets	$183,500	$144,500
Liabilities and Stockholders' Equity		
Accounts Payable	$ 13,000	$ 14,000
Income Taxes Payable	1,200	1,800
Notes Payable (long-term)	37,000	35,000
Common Stock—$5 par value	115,000	90,000
Retained Earnings	17,300	3,700
Total Liabilities and Stockholders' Equity	$183,500	$144,500

Income Statement
For the Year Ended June 30, 19x2

Sales	$234,000
Cost of Goods Sold	156,000
Gross Margin	78,000
Operating Expenses	45,000
Operating Income	33,000
Interest Expense	2,800
Income Before Income Taxes	30,200
Income Taxes	12,300
Net Income	$ 17,900

Additional information: (a) issued $22,000 note payable for purchase of furniture; (b) sold furniture that cost $27,000 with accumulated depreciation of $15,300 at carrying value; (c) depreciation on the furniture during the year, $19,300; (d) repaid a note in the amount of $20,000; issued $25,000 of common stock at par value; (e) dividends declared and paid, $4,300.

Without using a work sheet, prepare a statement of cash flows for 19x2 using the direct method of determining cash flow.

Exercise 27-10. Preparing a Work Sheet for the Statement of Cash Flows
(L.O. 8)

Using the information in Exercise 9, prepare a work sheet for the statement of cash flows for Tsin Corporation for 19x2. From the work sheet, prepare a statement of cash flows using the indirect method.

Interpreting Accounting Information

Airborne Express, Inc.[4]
(L.O. 7)

Airborne Express is an air express transportation company, providing next day, morning delivery of small packages and documents throughout the United States. Airborne Express is one of three major participants, along with Federal Express and United Parcel Service, in the air express industry. The letter to the stockholders from the 1986 annual report states, "Airborne Express enjoyed a very satisfying year in 1986, in that we made consistent progress toward accomplishing our major objectives: reducing average unit cost, enhancing our market position, and as a result improving earnings." It goes on to state, "We continue to operate in a highly volatile environment, in which many of our competitors faced with little or no growth scenarios engage in drastic price cutting practices in an effort to establish their niche in the industry." Airborne's 1986 Statement of Changes in Financial Position is presented in the format of the new statement of cash flows on the next page. (Note that although Airborne's statement of changes in financial position was prepared before the requirement for the new statement of cash flows, it is very similar in format to the new statement.

Required

1. What are the primary causes of the difference between net earnings and net funds (cash) provided by operations in 1986?
2. Does Airborne Express generate enough net cash flows from operating activities to satisfy dividends and provide additional funds for expansion?
3. Has Airborne Express been an expanding company over the last three years? If so, what are the primary means of financing the expansion?

4. Exerpt from 1986 annual report used by permission of Airborne Express, P.O. Box 662, Seattle, Washington 98111.

Consolidated Statements of Changes in Financial Position
Airborne Freight Corporation and Subsidiaries

Year Ended December 31	1986	1985	1984
		(In thousands)	
Cash, at January 1	$ 3,321	$ 1,222	$ 2,212
Funds Provided by Operations:			
Net earnings	$ 13,215	$ 8,169	$ 10,829
Depreciation and amortization	26,270	19,100	15,889
Deferred taxes	4,297	2,747	5,333
Total Funds Provided by Operations	$ 43,782	$ 30,016	$ 32,051
Changes in working capital that provided (used) funds:			
Receivables	(2,353)	(13,748)	(5,913)
Inventories and prepaid expenses	(2,881)	(1,879)	(2,903)
Accounts payable	10,366	4,577	5,269
Accrued expenses, salaries and taxes payable	(5,517)	8,872	696
Current portion of long-term debt	2,449	402	271
Net Funds Provided by Operations	$ 45,846	$ 28,240	$ 29,471
Dividends Paid	$ (3,512)	$ (3,494)	$ (3,461)
Investments:			
Additions to property and equipment, net	$(75,862)	$(52,523)	$(31,853)
Additions to equipment under capital leases	(10,957)	—	—
Decrease (increase) in restricted construction funds	10,328	3,837	(13,674)
Increase in other assets	(1,548)	(1,704)	(791)
Funds Used For Investing Activities	$(78,039)	$(50,390)	$(46,318)
Financing:			
Proceeds from issuance of subordinated debt	$ 50,000	$ —	$ —
Increase in long-term capital lease obligations	7,276	—	—
Increase (decrease) in long-term debt, net	(22,227)	27,277	18,704
Proceeds from issuance of common stock	467	466	614
Funds Provided by Financing Activities	$ 35,516	$ 27,743	$ 19,318
Increase (Decrease) In Cash	$ (189)	$ 2,099	$ (990)
Cash, at December 31	$ 3,132	$ 3,321	$ 1,222

See notes to consolidated financial statements.

Problem Set A

Problem 27A-1. Classification of Transactions (L.O. 3)

Analyze the transactions presented in the schedule below, and place an X in the appropriate columns to indicate the classification of the transaction and its effect on cash flows using the direct method.

Transactions	Cash Flows Classification				Effect on Cash		
	Operating Activity	Investing Activity	Financing Activity	Noncash Transactions	Increase	Decrease	No Effect
a. Incurred a net loss.							
b. Declared and issued a stock dividend.							
c. Paid a cash dividend.							
d. Collected accounts receivable.							
e. Purchased inventory with cash.							
f. Retired long-term debt with cash.							
g. Sale of investment for a loss.							
h. Issued stock for equipment.							
i. Purchased a one-year insurance policy for cash.							
j. Purchased treasury stock with cash.							
k. Retired a fully depreciated truck (no gain or loss).							
l. Paid interest on note.							
m. Received dividend on investment.							
n. Sale of treasury stock.							
o. Paid income taxes.							
p. Transferred cash to money market account.							
q. Purchased land and building with a mortgage.							

Problem 27A-2. Cash Flows from Operating Activities (L.O. 4)

The income statement for Sandberg Clothing Store is shown below:

Sandberg Clothing Store
Income Statement
For the Year Ended June 30, 19xx

Sales		$2,400,000
Cost of Goods Sold		
Beginning Inventory	$ 620,000	
Purchases (net)	1,520,000	
Goods Available for Sale	2,140,000	
Ending Inventory	700,000	
Cost of Goods Sold		1,440,000
Gross Margin from Sales		960,000
Operating Expenses		
Sales and Administrative Salaries Expense	556,000	
Other Sales and Administrative Expenses	312,000	
Total Operating Expenses		868,000
Income Before Income Taxes		92,000
Income Taxes		23,000
Net Income		$ 69,000

Additional information: (a) Other sales and administrative expenses include depreciation expense of $52,000 and amortization expense of $18,000. (b) At the end of the year, accrued liabilities for salaries were $12,000 less than the previous year, and prepaid expenses were $20,000 more than last year. (c) During the year, accounts receivable (net) increased by $144,000, accounts payable increased by $114,000, and income taxes payable decreased by $7,200.

Required

1. Prepare a schedule of cash flows from operating activities using the direct method.
2. Prepare a schedule of cash flows from operating activities using the indirect method.

Problem 27A-3. Cash Flows from Operating Activities (L.O. 4)

The income statement of Thompson Greeting Card Company is on the next page:

Relevant accounts from the balance sheet for December 31, 19x1 and 19x2 are as follows:

	19x1	**19x2**
Accounts Receivable (net)	$23,670	$18,530
Inventory	34,990	39,640
Prepaid Expenses	8,900	2,400
Accounts Payable	22,700	34,940
Accrued Liabilities	8,830	4,690
Income Taxes Payable	17,600	4,750

Thompson Greeting Card Company
Income Statement
For the Year Ended December 31, 19x2

Sales		$456,000
Cost of Goods Sold		286,700
Gross Margin From Sales		$169,300
Operating Expenses (including Depreciation Expense of $21,430)		87,400
Operating Income		$ 81,900
Other Income (Expenses)		
Interest Expense	$(8,400)	
Interest Income	4,300	
Loss on Sale of Investments	(5,800)	(9,900)
Income Before Income Taxes		$ 72,000
Income Taxes		18,500
Net Income		$ 53,500

Required

1. Prepare a schedule of cash flows from operating activities using the direct method.
2. Prepare a schedule of cash flows from operating activities using the indirect method.

Problem 27A-4. The Statement of Cash Flows—Direct Method
(L.O. 6, 7)

Sanchez Corporation's comparative balance sheets as of June 30, 19x6 and 19x7 and its 19x7 income statement appear below and on the next page.

	19x7	19x6
Assets		
Cash	$167,000	$ 20,000
Accounts Receivable (net)	100,000	120,000
Finished Goods Inventory	180,000	220,000
Prepaid Expenses	600	1,000
Property, Plant, and Equipment	628,000	552,000
Accumulated Depreciation, Property, Plant, and Equipment	(183,000)	(140,000)
Total Assets	$892,600	$773,000
Liabilities and Stockholders' Equity		
Accounts Payable	$ 64,000	$ 42,000
Notes Payable (due in 90 days)	30,000	80,000
Income Taxes Payable	26,000	18,000
Mortgage Payable	360,000	280,000
Common Stock—$5 par value	200,000	200,000
Retained Earnings	212,600	153,000
Total Liabilities and Stockholders' Equity	$892,600	$773,000

Income Statement
For the Year Ended June 30, 19x7

Sales		$1,040,900
Cost of Goods Sold		656,300
Gross Margin from Sales		$ 384,600
Operating Expenses (including Depreciation Expense of $60,000)		189,200
Income from Operations		$ 195,400
Other Income (Expenses)		
Loss on Disposal of Equipment	$ (4,000)	
Interest Expense	(37,600)	(41,600)
Income Before Income Taxes		$ 153,800
Income Taxes		34,200
Net Income		$ 119,600

Additional Information about 19x7: (a) equipment assets that cost $24,000 with accumulated depreciation of $17,000 were sold at a loss of $4,000; (b) land and building were purchased in the amount of $100,000 through an increase of $100,000 in the mortgage payable; (c) a $20,000 payment was made on the mortgage; (d) the notes were repaid, but the company borrowed an additional $30,000 through the issuance of a new note payable; (e) a $60,000 cash dividend was declared and paid.

Required

1. Prepare a statement of cash flows using the direct method and a supporting schedule of noncash investing and financing transactions. (Do not use a work sheet.)
2. What are the primary reasons for Sanchez Corporation's large increase in cash from 19x6 to 19x7?

Problem 27A-5. The Work Sheet and the Statement of Cash Flows—Indirect Method (L.O. 6, 8)

Use the information for Sanchez Corporation in Problem 27A-4.

Required

1. Prepare a work sheet for gathering information for the preparation of the statement of cash flows.
2. From the information on the work sheet, prepare a statement of cash flows using the indirect method and a supporting schedule of noncash investing and financing transactions.

Problem 27A-6. The Work Sheet and the Statement of Cash Flows—Indirect Method (L.O. 6, 7, 8)

The balance sheets for Sullivan Ceramics, Inc. for December 31, 19x2 and 19x3 appear on the next page:

Required

1. Prepare a work sheet for the statement of cash flows for Sullivan Ceramics.
2. Prepare a statement of cash flows from the information in the work sheet using the indirect method and a supporting schedule of noncash investing and financing transactions.
3. Why did Sullivan Ceramics have a decrease in cash in a year when they had a net income of $48,000? Discuss and interpret.

	19x3	19x2
Assets		
Cash	$ 138,800	$ 152,800
Accounts Receivable (net)	369,400	379,400
Inventory	480,000	400,000
Prepaid Expenses	7,400	13,400
Long-Term Investments	220,000	220,000
Land	180,600	160,600
Building	600,000	460,000
Accumulated Depreciation, Building	(120,000)	(80,000)
Equipment	240,000	240,000
Accumulated Depreciation, Equipment	(58,000)	(28,000)
Intangible Assets	10,000	20,000
Total Assets	$2,068,200	$1,938,200
Liabilities and Stockholders' Equity		
Accounts Payable	$ 235,400	$ 330,400
Notes Payable (current)	20,000	80,000
Accrued Liabilities	5,400	10,400
Mortgage Payable	540,000	400,000
Bonds Payable	500,000	380,000
Common Stock	600,000	600,000
Paid-In Capital in Excess of Par Value	40,000	40,000
Retained Earnings	127,400	97,400
Total Liabilities and Stockholders' Equity	$2,068,200	$1,938,200

Additional information about Sullivan's operations during 19x3: (a) net income, $48,000; (b) building and equipment depreciation expense amounts were $40,000 and $30,000, respectively; (c) intangible assets were amortized in the amount of $10,000; (d) investments in the amounts of $58,000 were purchased; (e) investments were sold for $75,000, on which a gain of $17,000 was made; (f) the company issued $120,000 in long-term bonds at face value; (g) a small warehouse building with the accompanying land was purchased through the issue of a $160,000 mortgage; (h) the company paid $20,000 to reduce mortgage payable during 19x7; (i) the company borrowed funds in the amount of $30,000 by issuing notes payable and repaid notes payable in the amount of $90,000; (j) cash dividends in the amount of $18,000 were declared and paid.

Problem Set B

Problem 27B-1. Classification of Transactions
(L.O. 3)

Analyze the transactions in the schedule on the next page, and place an X in the appropriate columns to indicate the classification of the transaction and its effect on cash flows using the direct method.

Transaction	Cash Flows Classification				Effect on Cash		
	Operating Activity	Investing Activity	Financing Activity	Noncash Transactions	Increase	Decrease	No Effect
a. Recorded net income.							
b. Declared and paid cash dividend.							
c. Issued stock for cash.							
d. Retired long-term debt by issuing stock.							
e. Paid accounts payable.							
f. Purchased inventory.							
g. Purchased a one-year insurance policy.							
h. Purchased a long-term investment with cash.							
i. Sold marketable securities at a gain.							
j. Sold a machine for a loss.							
k. Retired fully depreciated equipment.							
l. Paid interest on debt.							
m. Purchased marketable securities.							
n. Received dividend income.							
o. Received cash on account.							
p. Converted bonds to common stock.							
q. Purchased short-term treasury bill.							

Problem 27B-2. Cash Flows from Operating Activities (L.O. 4)

The income statement for Perelli Food Corporation is shown below:

Perelli Food Corporation
Income Statement
For the Year Ended December 31, 19xx

Sales		$520,000
Cost of Goods Sold		
Beginning Inventory	$220,000	
Purchases (net)	400,000	
Goods Available for Sale	$620,000	
Ending Inventory	250,000	
Cost of Goods Sold		370,000
Gross Margin from Sales		$150,000
Selling and Administrative Expenses		
Selling and Administrative Salaries Expense	50,000	
Other Selling and Administrative Expenses	11,500	
Depreciation Expense	18,000	
Amortization Expense (Intangible Assets)	1,500	81,000
Income Before Income Taxes		$ 69,000
Income Taxes		17,500
Net Income		$ 51,500

Additional information: (a) accounts receivable (net) increased by $18,000, and accounts payable decreased by $26,000 during the year. (b) accrued salaries payable at the end of the year were $7,000 more than last year; (c) the expired amount of prepaid insurance for the year is $500 and equals the decrease in the Prepaid Insurance account; (d) income taxes payable decreased by $5,400 from last year.

Required

1. Prepare a schedule of cash flows from operating activities using the direct method.
2. Prepare a schedule of cash flows from operating activities using the indirect method.

Problem 27B-3. Cash Flows from Operating Activities (L.O. 4)

The income statement of Johnson Electronics, Inc. appears on the next page:

Relevant accounts from the balance sheet for February 28, 19x2 and 19x3 are as follows:

	19x2	19x3
Accounts Receivable (net)	$ 48,920	$65,490
Inventory	102,560	98,760
Prepaid Expenses	5,490	10,450
Accounts Payable	55,690	42,380
Accrued Liabilities	8,790	3,560
Income Taxes Payable	13,800	24,630

Johnson Electronics, Inc.
Income Statement
For the Year Ended February 28, 19x3

Sales		$928,000
Cost of Goods Sold		643,500
Gross Margin from Sales		$284,500
Operating Expenses (including Depreciation Expense of $21,430)		176,900
Operating Income		$107,600
Other Income (Expenses)		
Interest Expense	$(27,800)	
Dividend Income	14,200	
Loss on Sale of Investments	(12,100)	(25,700)
Income Before Income Taxes		$ 81,900
Income Taxes		21,500
Net Income		$ 60,400

Required

1. Prepare a schedule of cash flows from operating activities using the direct method.
2. Prepare a schedule of cash flows from operating activities using the indirect method.

Problem 27B-4. The Statement of Cash Flows—Direct Method (L.O. 6, 7)

Glenview Corporation's comparative balance sheets as of December 31, 19x1 and 19x2 and its 19x2 income statement appear below.

	19x2	19x1
Assets		
Cash	$ 82,400	$ 25,000
Accounts Receivable (net)	82,600	100,000
Merchandise Inventory	175,000	225,000
Prepaid Rent	1,000	1,500
Furniture and Fixtures	74,000	72,000
Accumulated Depreciation, Furniture and Fixtures	(21,000)	(12,000)
Total Assets	$394,000	$411,500
Liabilities and Stockholders' Equity		
Accounts Payable	$ 71,700	$100,200
Notes Payable (long-term)	20,000	10,000
Bonds Payable	50,000	100,000
Income Taxes Payable	700	2,200
Common Stock—$10 par value	120,000	100,000
Paid-in Capital in Excess of Par Value	90,720	60,720
Retained Earnings	40,880	38,380
Total Liabilities and Stockholders' Equity	$394,000	$411,500

Income Statement For the Year Ended December 31, 19x2		
Sales		$804,500
Cost of Goods Sold		563,900
Gross Margin from Sales		$240,600
Operating Expenses (including Depreciation Expense of $23,400)		224,700
Income from Operations		$ 15,900
Other Income (Expenses)		
Gain on Disposal of Furniture and Fixtures	$ 3,500	
Interest Expense	(11,600)	(8,100)
Income Before Income Taxes		$ 7,800
Income Taxes		2,300
Net Income		$ 5,500

Additional information about 19x2: (a) furniture and fixures that cost $17,800 with accumulated depreciation of $14,400 were sold at a gain of $3,500; (b) furniture and fixtures were purchased in the amount of $19,800; (c) a $10,000 note payable was paid and $20,000 was borrowed on a new note; (d) bonds payable in the amount of $50,000 were converted into 2,000 shares of common stock; (e) $3,000 in cash dividends were declared and paid.

Required

1. Prepare a statement of cash flows using the direct method and a supporting schedule of noncash investing and financing transactions. (Do not use a work sheet.)
2. What are the primary reasons for Glenview Corporation's large increase in cash from 19x1 to 19x2 in spite of a low net income?

Problem 27B-5. The Work Sheet and the Statement of Cash Flows—Indirect Method (L.O. 6, 8)

Use the information for Glenview Corporation in Problem 27B-4.

Required

1. Prepare a work sheet for gathering information for the preparation of the statement of cash flows.
2. From the information on the work sheet, prepare a statement of cash flows using the indirect approach and a supporting schedule of noncash investing and financing transactions.

Problem 27B-6. The Work Sheet and the Statement of Cash Flows—Indirect Method (L.O. 6, 7, 8)

The balance sheets for Finnegan Fabrics, Inc. for December 31, 19x2 and 19x3 appear on the next page:

Required

1. Prepare a work sheet for the statement of cash flows for Finnegan Fabrics.
2. Prepare a statement of cash flows from the information in the work sheet using the indirect method.
3. Why did Finnegan Fabrics have an increase in cash in a year when they had a net loss of $28,000? Discuss and interpret.

	19x3	19x2
Assets		
Cash	$ 38,560	$ 27,360
Accounts Receivable (net)	102,430	75,430
Inventory	112,890	137,890
Prepaid Expenses	—	20,000
Land	25,000	—
Building	137,000	—
Accumulated Depreciation, Building	(15,000)	—
Equipment	33,000	34,000
Accumulated Depreciation, Equipment	(14,500)	(24,000)
Patents	4,000	6,000
Total Assets	$423,380	$276,680
Liabilities and Stockholders' Equity		
Accounts Payable	$ 10,750	$ 36,750
Notes Payable	10,000	—
Accrued Liabilities (current)	—	12,300
Mortgage Payable	162,000	—
Common Stock	180,000	150,000
Paid-in Capital in Excess of par Value	57,200	37,200
Retained Earnings	3,430	40,430
Total Liabilities and Stockholders' Equity	$423,380	$276,680

Additional information about Finnegan's operations during 19x3: (a) net loss, $28,000; (b) building and equipment depreciation expense amounts, $15,000 and $3,000, respectively; (c) equipment that cost $13,500 with accumulated depreciation of $12,500 was sold for a gain of $5,300; (d) equipment purchases, $12,500; (e) patent amortization, $3,000; purchase of patent, $1,000; (f) borrowed funds by issuing notes payable, $25,000; repaid notes payable, $15,000; (g) land and building were purchased for $162,000 by signing a mortgage for the total cost; (h) issued 3,000 shares of $10 par value common stock for a total of $50,000; (i) cash dividend, $9,000.

Decision Case

Adams Print Gallery
(L.O. 6, 7)

Bernadette Adams, President of Adams Print Gallery, Inc., is examining the income statement presented on the next page, which has just been handed to her by her accountant, Jason Rosenberg, CPA.

Required

1. To what statement is Mr. Rosenberg referring? From the information given, prepare the additional statement using the direct method.
2. Explain why Ms. Adams has a cash problem in spite of profitable operations.

Adams Print Gallery, Inc.
Income Statement
For the Year Ended December 31, 19x2

Sales	$432,000
Cost of Goods Sold	254,000
Gross Margin	178,000
Operating Expenses (including Depreciation Expense of $10,000)	102,000
Operating Income	76,000
Interest Expense	12,000
Income Before Taxes	64,000
Income Taxes	14,000
Net Income	$ 50,000

After looking at the statement, Ms. Adams said to Mr. Rosenberg, "Jason, the statement seems to be well done, but what I need to know is why I don't have enough cash to pay my bills this month. You show that I have earned $50,000 in 19x2, but I only have $2,000 in the bank. I know I bought a building on a mortgage and paid a cash dividend of $24,000, but what else is going on?" Mr. Rosenberg replied, "To answer your question, Bernadette, we have to look at comparative balance sheets and prepare another type of statement. Here, take a look at these balance sheets." The statements handed to Ms. Adams are shown below.

Adams Print Gallery, Inc.
Balance Sheet
December 31, 19x1 and 19x2

	19x2	19x1
Assets		
Cash	$ 2,000	$ 20,000
Accounts Receivable (net)	89,000	73,000
Inventory	120,000	90,000
Prepaid Expenses	5,000	7,000
Building	200,000	—
Accumulated Depreciation	(10,000)	—
Total Assets	$406,000	$190,000
Liabilities and Stockholders' Equity		
Accounts Payable	$ 37,000	$48,000
Income Taxes Payable	3,000	2,000
Mortgage Payable	200,000	—
Common Stock	100,000	100,000
Retained Earnings	66,000	40,000
Total Liabilities and Stockholders' Equity	$406,000	$190,000

CHAPTER 28 FINANCIAL STATEMENT ANALYSIS

LEARNING OBJECTIVES

1. Describe and discuss the objectives of financial statement analysis.
2. Describe and discuss the standards for financial statement analysis.
3. State the sources of information for financial statement analysis.
4. Identify the issues related to the evaluation of the quality of a company's earnings.
5. Apply horizontal analysis, trend analysis, and vertical analysis to financial statements.
6. Apply ratio analysis to financial statements in the study of an enterprise's liquidity, profitability, long-term solvency, and market tests.

This chapter presents a number of techniques intended to aid in decision making by highlighting important relationships in the financial statements. This is called financial statement analysis. After studying this chapter, you should be able to meet the learning objectives listed on the left.

Effective decision making calls for the ability to sort out relevant information from a great many facts and to make adjustments for changing conditions. Very often, financial statements in a company's annual report run ten or more pages, including footnotes and other necessary disclosures. If these statements are to be useful in making decisions, decision makers must be able to find information that shows important relationships and helps them make comparisons from year to year and from company to company. The many techniques that together are called **financial statement analysis** accomplish this goal.

Objectives of Financial Statement Analysis

Users of financial statements fall into two broad categories: internal and external. Management is the main internal user. The tools of financial analysis are, of course, useful in management's operation of the business. However, because those who run the company have inside information on operations, other techniques are available to them. Since these techniques are covered in managerial accounting courses, the main focus here is on the external use of financial analysis.

Creditors make loans in the form of trade accounts, notes, or bonds, on which they receive interest. They expect a loan to be repaid according to its terms. Investors buy capital stock, from which they hope to receive dividends and an increase in value. Both groups face risks. The creditor faces the risk that the debtor will fail to pay back the loan. The investor faces the risk that dividends will be reduced or not paid or that the market price of the stock will drop. In each case, the goal is to achieve a return that makes up for the risk taken. In general, the greater the risk taken, the greater the return required as compensation.

external users

Any one loan or any one investment can turn out badly. As a result, most creditors and investors put their funds into a **portfolio**, or group of loans or investments. The portfolio allows them to

OBJECTIVE 1
Describe and discuss the objectives of financial statement analysis

average both the return and the risk. Nevertheless, the portfolio is made up of a number of loans or stocks, on which individual decisions must be made. It is in making these individual decisions that financial statement analysis is most useful. Creditors and investors use financial statement analysis in two general ways. (1) They use it to judge past performance and current position. (2) They use it to judge future potential and the risk connected with the potential.

Assessment of Past Performance and Current Position

Past performance is often a good indicator of future performance. Therefore, an investor or creditor is interested in the trend of past sales, expenses, net income, cash flow, and return on investment. These trends offer a means for judging management's past performance and are a possible indicator of future performance. In addition, an analysis of current position will tell where the business stands today. For example, it will tell what assets the business owns and what liabilities must be paid. It will tell what the cash position is, how much debt the company has in relation to equity, and how reasonable the inventories and receivables are. Knowing a company's past performance and current position is often important in achieving the second general objective of financial analysis.

Assessment of Future Potential and Related Risk

The past and present information is useful only to the extent that it has bearing on future decisions. An investor judges the potential earning ability of a company because that ability will affect the value of the investment (market price of the company's stock) and the amount of dividends the company will pay. A creditor judges the potential debt-paying ability of the company. The potentials of some companies are easier to predict than others, and so there is less risk associated with them. The riskiness of the investment or loan depends on how easy it is to predict future profitability or liquidity. If an investor can predict with confidence that a company's earnings per share will be between \$2.50 and \$2.60 next year, the investment is less risky than if the earnings per share are expected to fall between \$2.00 and \$3.00. For example, the potential associated with an investment in an established and stable electric utility, or a loan to it, is relatively easy to predict on the basis of the company's past performance and current position. The potential associated with a small minicomputer manufacturer, on the other hand, may be much harder to predict. For this reason, the investment or loan to the electric utility is less risky than the investment or loan to the small computer company. Often, in return for taking the greater risk, the investor in the minicomputer company will demand a higher expected return (increase in market price plus dividends) than the investor in the utility company. Also, a creditor of the minicomputer company will need a higher interest rate and possibly more assurance of repayment (a secured loan, for instance) than a creditor to the utility company. The higher interest rate is payment to the creditor for assuming a higher risk.

Standards for Financial Statement Analysis

OBJECTIVE 2
Describe and discuss the standards for financial statement analysis

In using financial statement analysis, decision makers must judge whether the relationships they have found are favorable or unfavorable. Three standards of comparison often used are (1) rule-of-thumb measurements, (2) past performance of the company, and (3) industry norms.

Rule-of-Thumb Measures

Many financial analysts and lenders use "ideal" or rule-of-thumb measures for key financial ratios. For example, it has long been thought that a current ratio (current assets divided by current liabilities) of 2:1 is acceptable. The credit-rating firm of Dun & Bradstreet, in its *Key Business Ratios,* offers these guidelines:

Current debt to tangible net worth. Ordinarily, a business begins to pile up trouble when this relationship exceeds 80%.

Inventory to net working capital. Ordinarily, this relationship should not exceed 80%.

Although such measures may suggest areas that need further investigation, there is no proof they are the best for any company. A company with a larger than 2:1 current ratio may have a poor credit policy (resulting in accounts receivable being too large), too much or out-of-date inventory, or poor cash management. Another company may have a less than 2:1 ratio resulting from excellent management in these three areas. Thus, rule-of-thumb measurements must be used with great care.

Past Performance of the Company

An improvement over the rule-of-thumb method is the comparison of financial measures or ratios of the same company over a period of time. This standard will at least give the analyst some basis for judging whether the measure or ratio is getting better or worse. It may also be helpful in showing possible future trends. However, since trends do reverse at times, such projections must be made with care. Another disadvantage is that the past may not be a good measure of adequacy. In other words, it may not be enough to meet present needs. For example, even if return on total investment improved from 3 percent last year to 4 percent this year, the 4 percent return may not be adequate.

Industry Norms

One way of making up for the limitations of using past performance as a standard is to use industry norms. This standard will tell how the company being analyzed compares with other companies in the same industry. For example, suppose that other companies in the same industry as the company in the paragraph above have an average rate of return on total investment of 8 percent. In such a case the 3 and 4 percent returns are probably not adequate. Industry norms can also be used to judge trends. Suppose that because of a downward turn in the economy, a company's profit margin dropped from 12 to 10 percent. A finding that other companies in the same industry had an average drop in profit margin from 12 to 4 percent would indicate that the company being analyzed did relatively well.

There are three limitations to using industry norms as standards. First, although two companies seem to be in the same industry, they may not be strictly comparable. Consider two companies said to be in the oil industry. The main business of one may be marketing oil products it buys from other producers through service stations. The other, an international company, may discover, produce, refine, and market its own oil products. The operations of these companies cannot be compared.

Second, most large companies today operate in more than one industry. Some of these **diversified companies**, or **conglomerates**, operate in many unrelated industries. The individual segments of a diversified company generally have different rates of profitability and degrees of risk. In using the consolidated financial statements of these companies for financial analysis, it is often impossible to use industry norms as standards. There are simply no other companies that are closely enough related. One partial solution to this problem is a requirement by the Financial Accounting Standards Board in *Statement No. 14*. This requirement states that diversified companies must report revenues, income from operations, and identifiable assets for each of their operating segments. Depending on specific criteria, segment information may be reported for operations in different industries, in foreign markets, or to major customers.[1] An example of reporting for industry segments is given in Exhibit 28-1, which comes from Eastman Kodak's annual report. It is interesting to compare the two reported segments, imaging and chemicals. In 1985, imaging sales were about 3.6 times chemical sales ($8,531 million versus $2,348 million). But they produced only about 2.1 times as much earnings from operations ($378 million versus $183 million).

Third, companies in the same industry with similar operations use different accounting procedures. That is, inventories may be valued by using different methods, or different depreciation methods may be used for assets that are alike. Even so, if little information is available about a company's prior performance, industry norms probably offer the best available standards for judging a company's current performance. They should be used with care.

Sources of Information

The external analyst is often limited to publicly available information about a company. The major sources of information about publicly held corporations are published reports, SEC reports, business periodicals, and credit and investment advisory services.

1. *Statement of Financial Accounting Standards No. 14*, "Financial Reporting for Segments of a Business Enterprise" (Stamford, Conn.: Financial Accounting Standards Board, 1976).

Exhibit 28-1. Segment Information

	1985	1984	1983
Sales, including intersegment sales*			
Imaging	$ 8,531	$ 8,380	$ 8,097
Chemicals	2,348	2,464	2,285
Intersegment sales			
Imaging	(12)	(12)	(9)
Chemicals	(236)	(232)	(203)
Sales to unaffiliated customers	$10,631	$10,600	$10,170
Earnings from operations			
Imaging	$ 378	$ 1,266	$ 813
Chemicals	183	281	214
Earnings from operations	$ 561	$ 1,547	$ 1,027
Interest and other income (charges)			
Imaging	(1)	63	22
Chemicals	14	—	1
Corporate	139	128	87
Interest expense	(183)	(114)	(117)
Earnings before income taxes	$ 530	$ 1,624	$ 1,020
Assets			
Imaging	$ 9,387	$ 7,926	$ 7,555
Chemicals	2,136	2,054	2,124
Corporate (cash and marketable securities)	734	918	1,470
Intersegment receivables	(115)	(120)	(221)
Total assets at year end	$12,142	$10,778	$10,928
Depreciation expense			
Imaging	$ 655	$ 587	$ 540
Chemicals	176	171	112
Total depreciation expense	$ 831	$ 758	$ 652
Capital expenditures			
Imaging	$ 1,244	$ 818	$ 710
Chemicals	251	152	179
Total capital expenditures	$ 1,495	$ 970	$ 889

* The products of each segment are manufactured and marketed in the U.S. and in other parts of the world. The Imaging segment includes film, paper, equipment, and other related products. The Chemical segment includes fibers, plastics, industrial and other chemicals. Sales between segments are made on a basis intended to reflect the market value of the products.

All information from Eastman Kodak reports reprinted by permission.

Published Reports

OBJECTIVE 3
State the sources of information for financial statement analysis

The annual report of a publicly held corporation is an important source of financial information. The major parts of this annual report are (1) management's analysis of the past year's operations, (2) the financial statements, (3) the notes to the statements, including the principal accounting procedures used by the company, (4) the auditor's report, and (5) a summary of operations for a five- or ten-year period. Also, most publicly held companies publish **interim financial statements** each quarter. These reports present limited information in the form of condensed financial statements, which may be subject to a limited review or a full audit by the independent auditor. The interim statements are watched closely by the financial community for early signs of important changes in a company's earnings trend.[2]

SEC Reports

Publicly held corporations must file annual reports, quarterly reports, and current reports with the Securities and Exchange Commission (SEC). All such reports are available to the public at a small charge. The SEC calls for a standard form for the annual report (Form 10-K). This report is fuller than the published annual report. Form 10-K is, for this reason, a valuable source of information. It is available, free of charge, to stockholders of the company. The quarterly report (Form 10-Q) presents important facts about interim financial performance. The current report (Form 8-K) must be filed within fifteen days of the date of certain major events. It is often the first indicator of important changes that may affect the company's financial performance in the future.

Business Periodicals and Credit and Investment Advisory Services

Financial analysts must keep up with current events in the financial world. Probably the best source of financial news is the *Wall Street Journal,* which is published daily and is the most complete financial newspaper in the United States. Some helpful magazines, published every week or every two weeks, are *Forbes, Barron's, Fortune,* and the *Commercial and Financial Chronicle.* For further details about the financial history of companies, the publications of such services as Moody's Investors Service and Standard & Poor's Industrial Surveys are useful. Data on industry norms, average ratios and relationships, and credit ratings are available from such agencies as Dun & Bradstreet Corp. Dun & Bradstreet offers, among other useful services, an annual analysis using 14 ratios of 125 industry groups classified as retailing, wholesaling,

2. Accounting Principles Board, *Opinion No. 28,* "Interim Financial Reporting" (New York: American Institute of Certified Public Accountants, 1973); and *Statement of Financial Accounting Standards No. 3,* "Reporting Accounting Change in Interim Financial Statements" (Stamford, Conn.: Financial Accounting Standards Board, 1974).

manufacturing, and construction in its *Key Business Ratios*. Another important source of industry data is the *Annual Statement Studies*, published by Robert Morris Associates, which presents many facts and ratios for 223 different industries. Also, a number of private services are available to the analyst for a yearly fee.

Evaluating a Company's Quality of Earnings

OBJECTIVE 4
Identify the issues related to the evaluation of the quality of a company's earnings

It is clear from the preceding sections that the current and expected earnings of a company play an important role in the analysis of a company's prospects. In fact, a recent survey of 2,000 members of the Financial Analysis Federation indicated that the two most important economic indicators in evaluating common stocks were expected changes in earnings per share and expected return on equity.[3] Net income is an important component of both measures. Because of the importance of net income or the "bottom line" in measures of a company's prospects, interest in evaluating the quality of the net income figure, or the *quality of earnings*, has become an important topic. The quality of a company's earnings may be affected by (1) the accounting methods and estimates the company's management chooses and/or (2) the nature of nonoperating items in the income statement.

Choice of Accounting Methods and Estimates

There are two aspects to the choice of accounting methods that affect the quality of earnings. First, some accounting methods are by nature more conservative than others because they tend to produce a lower net income in the current period. Second, there is considerable latitude in the choice of the estimated useful life over which assets are written off or in the amount of estimated residual value. In general, an accounting method, an estimated useful life, and/or residual value that results in lower current earnings is considered to produce a better quality of earnings.

In earlier chapters, various acceptable alternative methods were used in the application of the matching rule. These methods are based on allocation procedures, which in turn are based on certain assumptions. Here are some of these procedures:

1. For estimating uncollectible accounts expense: percentage of net sales method and accounts receivable aging method
2. For pricing the ending inventory: average cost method; first-in, first-out (FIFO); and last-in, first-out (LIFO)
3. For estimating depreciation expense: straight-line method, production method, sum-of-the-years'-digits method, and declining-balance method
4. For estimating depletion expense: production (extraction) method
5. For estimating amortization of intangibles: straight-line method

3. Cited in *The Week in Review* (Deloitte Haskins & Sells), February 28, 1985.

All of these procedures attempt to allocate the costs of assets to the periods in which those costs contribute to the production of revenue. They are based on a determination of the benefits to the current period (expenses) versus the benefits to future periods (assets). They are estimates, and the period or periods benefited cannot be demonstrated conclusively. They are also subjective, because in practice it is hard to justify one method of estimation over another. For this reason, it is important for the accountant as well as the financial statement user to understand the possible effects of different accounting procedures on net income and financial position. For example, suppose that two companies have similar operations but that one uses FIFO for inventory pricing and the straight-line (SL) method for computing depreciation and the other uses LIFO for inventory pricing and the sum-of-the-years'-digits (SYD) method for computing depreciation. The income statements of the two companies might appear as follows:

	FIFO and SL Company	LIFO and SYD Company
Sales	$500,000	$500,000
Goods Available for Sale	$300,000	$300,000
Less Ending Inventory	60,000	50,000
Cost of Goods Sold	$240,000	$250,000
Gross Margin	$260,000	$250,000
Less: Depreciation Expense	$ 40,000	$ 70,000
Other Expenses	170,000	170,000
Total Operating Expenses	$210,000	$240,000
Net Income	$ 50,000	$ 10,000

This fivefold difference in income stems only from the difference in method. Differences in the estimated lives and residual values of the plant assets could cause an even greater difference. In practice, of course, differences in net income occur for many reasons, but the user must be aware of the differences that can occur as a result of the methods chosen by management.

The existence of these alternatives could cause problems in the interpretation of financial statements were it not for the conventions of full disclosure and consistency, described in Appendix B. Full disclosure requires that management explain the significant accounting policies used in preparing the financial statements in a note to the statements. Consistency requires that the same accounting procedure be followed from year to year. If a change in procedure is made, the nature of the change and its monetary effect must be explained in a note.

Nature of Nonoperating Earnings

As seen in Chapter 13, the corporate income statement consists of several components. The top of the statement presents earnings from current ongoing operations called income from operations. The lower part of the statement can contain such nonoperating items as discontinued operations, extraordinary gains and losses, and effects of accounting changes. These items may drastically affect the bottom line, or net income, of the company. For example, Eastman Kodak (see Exhibit 28-3) had an unusual charge of $563 million in 1985 that related primarily to the discontinuing of its instant camera line and the loss of a patent suit with Polaroid. This loss had a detrimental effect on reported Net Earnings in 1985 and the loss of this business may adversely affect future years' earnings.

These nonoperating items should be taken into consideration when interpreting a company's earnings. For example, in 1983, U.S. Steel made an apparent turnaround by reporting first quarter earnings of $1.35 a share versus a deficit of $1.31 a year earlier. However, the "improved" earnings included a gain from sales of assets of $.45 per share and sale of tax benefits on newly acquired assets of $.40 per share, as well as other items totaling $.61 per share. These items total $1.46, an amount greater than the reported earnings for the year.[4] The opposite effect can also occur. For the first six months of 1984, Texas Instruments reported a loss of $112 million compared with a profit of $64.5 million the previous year. The loss was caused by write-offs of $58 million for nonoperating losses, $83 million for inventory, and $37 million for increased reserves for rebates, price protection for retailers, and returned inventory.[5] In reality this large write-off was a positive step on Texas Instruments' part because getting out of the low-profit home computer business meant TI's future cash flows would not be drained by the unprofitable home computer operations.

For practical reasons, the trends and ratios in the sections that follow use the net income component and other components as if they are comparable from year to year and from company to company. However, the astute analyst will always look beyond the ratios to the quality of the components in making interpretations.

Tools and Techniques of Financial Analysis

Few numbers by themselves mean very much. It is their relationship to other numbers or their change from one period to another that is important. The tools of financial analysis are intended to show relationships and changes. Among the more widely used of these techniques are horizontal analysis, trend analysis, vertical analysis, and ratio analysis.

4. Dan Dorfman, "Three Well-Known Stocks with Earnings of Dubious Quality," *Chicago Tribune* (June 28, 1984), p. 11.
5. "Loss at Texas Instruments Hits $119.2 Million," *The Wall Street Journal* (November 14, 1984).

Horizontal Analysis

OBJECTIVE 5
Apply horizontal analysis, trend analysis, and vertical analysis to financial statements

Generally accepted accounting principles call for presenting comparative financial statements that give the current year's and past year's financial information. A common starting point for studying such statements is **horizontal analysis**, which involves the computation of dollar amount changes and percentage changes from the previous to the current year. The percentage change must be figured to show how the size of the change relates to the size of the amounts involved. A change of $1 million in sales is not so drastic as a change of $1 million in net income, because sales is a larger amount than net income. Exhibits 28-2 and 28-3 (next two pages) present the comparative balance sheet and income statement, respectively, for Eastman Kodak, with the dollar and percentage changes shown. The percentage change is computed as follows:

$$\text{percentage change} = 100\left(\frac{\text{amount of change}}{\text{previous year amount}}\right)$$

The **base year** in any set of data is always the first year being studied. For example, from 1984 to 1985, Eastman Kodak's current assets increased by $546 million, from $5,131 million to $5,677 million, or by 10.6 percent, computed as follows:

$$\text{percentage increase} = 100\left(\frac{\$546\text{ million}}{\$5{,}131\text{ million}}\right) = 10.6\%$$

Care must be taken in the analysis of percentage change. For example, in analyzing the changes in the components of total assets in Exhibit 28-2, one might view the 14.4 percent increase in receivables as being offset by the 16.1 percent decrease in cash. In dollar amount, though, receivables increased by almost ten times as much as cash decreased ($296 million versus $31 million). Dollar amounts and percentage increases must be considered together. On the liability side of the balance sheet, both long-term bonds and accounts payable are up substantially (by 141.6 percent and 63.5 percent).

In the income statement (Exhibit 28-3), the most important changes from 1984 to 1985 show a 0.3 percent growth in sales compared to a 5.0 percent increase in costs and expenses. When the dollar amounts of these changes are combined, they result in a 27.3 percent decrease in earnings from operations. In addition, net earnings were adversely affected by an unusual change in 1985. Other income and expenses were also down. Overall net earnings were down 64.0 percent after a 71.8 percent decrease in income taxes.

Trend Analysis

A variation of horizontal analysis is **trend analysis**, in which percentage changes are calculated for several successive years instead of between two years. Trend analysis is important because, with its long-run view, it may point to basic changes in the nature of the business. Besides comparative financial statements, most companies give out a summary of operations and data on other key indicators for five or more years.

Exhibit 28-2. Comparative Balance Sheet with Horizontal Analysis

Eastman Kodak
Consolidated Balance Sheet
December 29, 1985, and December 30, 1984

	(In millions)		Increase (Decrease)	
	1985	1984	Amount	Percentage
Assets				
Current Assets				
Cash	$ 161	$ 192	$ (31)	(16.1)
Marketable securities	652	819	(167)	(20.4)
Receivables	2,346	2,050	296	14.4
Inventories	1,940	1,758	182	10.4
Prepaid expense and deferred charges	578	312	266	85.3
Total Current Assets	$ 5,677	$ 5,131	$ 546	10.6
Properties				
Land, buildings, machinery, and equipment less accumulated depreciation of $5,386 and $4,801	5,977	5,389	588	10.9
Long-term receivables and other noncurrent assets	488	258	230	89.1
Total Assets	$12,142	$10,778	$1,364	12.7
Liabilities				
Liabilities				
Current Liabilities				
Payables	$ 2,989	$ 1,828	$1,161	63.5
Taxes payable	156	268	(112)	(41.8)
Dividends payable	180	210	(30)	(14.3)
Total current liabilities	$ 3,325	$ 2,306	$1,019	44.2
Long-term Liabilities				
Long-term bonds	988	409	579	141.6
Other long-term liabilities	219	203	16	7.9
Deferred income tax liabilities	1,048	723	325	45.0
Total Liabilities	$5,580	$ 3,641	$1,939	53.3
Ownership				
Common stock (par value)	$ 621	$ 414	$ 207	50.0
Additional paid-in capital	312	520	(208)	(40.0)
Retained earnings	6,710	6,931	(221)	3.2
Treasury stock at cost	(1,081)	(728)	(353)	48.5
Total Ownership	$ 6,562	$ 7,137	$(575)	(8.1)
Total Liabilities and Ownership	$12,142	$10,778	$1,364	12.7

Exhibit 28-3. Comparative Income Statement with Horizontal Analysis

Eastman Kodak
Consolidated Statement of Earnings
For Years Ended December 29, 1985, and December 30, 1984

	(In millions)		Increase (Decrease)	
	1985	1984	Amount	Percentage
Sales	$10,631	$10,600	$ 31	0.3
Costs and Expenses				
Cost of goods sold	7,129	6,887	242	3.5
Selling and administrative expenses	2,378	2,166	212	9.8
Total costs and expenses	9,507	9,053	454	5.0
Earnings from Operations	1,124	1,547	(423)	(27.3)
Unusual charges	(563)	—	(563)	NA
Other income and expenses including interest expense of $183 and $114	(31)	77	(108)	(140.3)
Earnings Before Income Taxes	530	1,624	(1,094)	(67.4)
Provision for income taxes	198	701	(503)	(71.8)
Net Earnings	$ 332	$ 923	$ (591)	(64.0)
Average number of common shares outstanding*	227.3	242.6	(15.3)	(6.3)
Net Earnings per Share*	$ 1.46	$ 3.80	(2.34)	(61.6)

* Per share data and average number of common shares outstanding for 1984 have been restated to reflect the 3-for-2 stock split in 1985.

Selected items from Eastman Kodak's summary of operations together with trend analysis are presented in Exhibit 28-4. Trend analysis uses an **index number** to show changes in related items over a period of time. For index numbers, one year, the base year, is equal to 100 percent. Other years are measured in relation to that amount. For example, the 1985 index of 102.8 for sales was figured as follows:

$$\text{index} = 100\left(\frac{\text{index year amount}}{\text{base year amount}}\right) = \left(\frac{\$10,631}{\$10,337}\right) = 102.8$$

An index number of 102.8 means that 1985 sales are 102.8 percent or 1.028 times 1981 sales. A study of the trend analysis in Exhibit 28-4 shows that sales grew more rapidly than net earnings over the five-year period. Sales had an index of 102.8 in 1985 versus 26.8 for net earnings. Income per common share closely paralleled net earnings (28.6 in 1985

Exhibit 28-4. Trend Analysis

Eastman Kodak Summary of Operations Selected Data (Sales and Net Earnings in Millions)					
	1985	1984	1983	1982	1981
Sales	$10,631	$10,600	$10,170	$10,815	$10,337
Net Earnings	332	923	565	1,162	1,239
Per Common Share*					
Income*	1.46	3.80	2.28	4.75	5.11
Dividends*	2.43	2.40	2.37	2.37	2.33
Trend Analysis					
Sales	102.8	102.5	98.4	104.6	100.0
Net Earnings	26.8	74.5	45.6	93.8	100.0
Per Common Share					
Income	28.6	74.4	44.6	93.0	100.0
Dividends	104.3	103.0	101.7	101.7	100.0

* Per share data prior to 1985 restated to reflect 3-for-2 stock split in 1985.

versus 26.8), while dividends per share followed sales more closely (104.3 in 1985 versus 102.8). Apparently, the company felt it was important to keep up an increasing level of dividends in spite of the decrease in net earnings from 1981 to 1985. Also, note that the trend analysis places the large increase in net earnings from 1983 to 1984 in perspective with the higher level of earnings in 1981 and 1982.

Vertical Analysis

Vertical analysis uses percentages to show the relationship of the different parts to the total in a single statement. Vertical analysis sets a total figure in the statement equal to 100 percent and computes the percentage of each component of that figure. (This figure would be total assets or total liabilities and stockholders' equity in the case of the balance sheet, and revenues or sales in the case of the income statement.) The resulting statement of percentages is called a **common-size statement**. Common-size balance sheets and income statements for Eastman Kodak are shown in Exhibits 28-5 and 28-6 (next two pages). Generally, current assets and current liabilities are given only in total, because ratios are used to analyze their components very carefully. Vertical analysis is useful for comparing the importance of certain components in the operation of the business. It is also useful for pointing out important changes in the components from one year to the next when comparative common-size statements are presented. For Eastman Kodak, the composition of assets in Exhibit 28-5 changed. Slightly fewer assets were in properties (49.2 percent versus 50.0 percent) and current assets (46.8 percent versus 47.6 percent) in 1985 as opposed to 1984. However, more assets were in long-term receivables and other noncurrent assets. Also, the part of total liabilities made up of current liabilities went up from 21.4 percent to 27.4 percent. Similarly, long-term bonds increased from 3.8 percent to 8.1 percent. These two changes contributed to a much higher percentage of the company financed by total liabilities in 1985 than in 1984 (45.9 percent versus 33.8 percent). The common-size income statement (Exhibit 28-6) shows the importance of the increase in costs and expenses from 85.4 to 89.4 percent of sales. This increase was the major cause of the decrease in earnings from operations from 14.6 to 10.6 percent of sales. The unusual charges were

Exhibit 28-5. Common-Size Balance Sheet

Eastman Kodak
Common-Size Balance Sheet
December 29, 1985, and December 30, 1984

	1985	1984
Assets		
Current Assets	46.8%	47.6%
Properties (less Accumulated Depreciation)	49.2	50.0
Long-Term Receivables and Other Noncurrent Assets	4.0	2.4
Total Assets	100.0%	100.0%
Liabilities		
Current Liabilities	27.4%	21.4%
Long-Term Bonds	8.1	3.8
Other Long-Term Liabilities	1.8	1.9
Deferred Income Tax Liabilities	8.6	6.7
Total Liabilities	45.9%	33.8%
Ownership		
Common Stock	5.1%	3.8%
Additional Paid-In Capital	2.6	4.8
Retained Earnings	55.3	64.3
Treasury Stock at Cost	(8.9)	(6.7)
Total Ownership	54.1%	66.2%
Total Liabilities and Ownership	100.0%	100.0%

5.3 percent of sales, further decreasing earnings before income taxes. The favorable change in income taxes is shown by the decrease in the provision for income taxes from 6.6 percent to 1.9 percent of sales.

Common-size statements are often used to make comparisons between companies. They allow an analyst to compare the operating and financing characteristics of two companies of different sizes in the same industry. For example, the analyst may want to compare Eastman Kodak to other companies in terms of the percentage of total assets financed by debt or the percentage of general administrative and selling expenses to sales and revenues. Common-size statements would show these relationships.

Ratio Analysis

Ratio analysis is an important means of stating the relationship between two numbers. To be useful, a ratio must represent a meaningful relationship, but use of ratios cannot take the place of studying the underlying data. Ratios are guides or short cuts that are useful in evaluating the financial position and operations of a company and in comparing them to previous years or to other companies. The primary purpose of ratios is to point out areas for further investigation. They should be used in connection with a general understanding of the company and its environment.

Ratios may be stated in several ways. For example, the ratio of net income of $100,000 to sales of $1,000,000 may be stated as (1) net income

Exhibit 28-6. Common-Size Income Statement

Eastman Kodak
Common-Size Statement of Earnings
For Years Ended December 29, 1985, and December 30, 1984

	1985	1984
Sales	100.0%	100.0%
Costs and Expenses		
Cost of Goods Sold	67.0	65.0
Selling and Administrative Expenses	22.4	20.4
Total Costs and Expenses	89.4%	85.4%
Earnings from Operations	10.6%	14.6%
Unusual Charges	5.3	—
Other Income and Expenses	(.3)	.7
Earnings Before Income Taxes	5.0%	15.3%
Provision for Income Taxes	1.9	6.6
Net Earnings	3.1%	8.7%

is 1/10 or 10 percent of sales; (2) the ratio of sales to net income is 10 to 1 (10:1) or 10 times net income, or (3) for every dollar of sales, the company has an average net income of 10 cents.

Survey of Commonly Used Ratios

OBJECTIVE 6
Apply ratio analysis to financial statements in the study of an enterprise's liquidity, profitability, long-term solvency, and market tests

In the following sections, ratio analysis is applied to four objectives; the evaluation of (1) liquidity, (2) profitability, (3) long-term solvency, and (4) market strength. We address each objective in an introductory way. Then we expand the evaluation to bring in ratios related to these objectives. Data for the analyses come from the financial statements of Eastman Kodak presented in Exhibits 28-2 and 28-3. Other data are presented as needed.

Evaluating Liquidity

The aim of liquidity is for a company to have enough funds on hand to pay bills when they are due and to meet unexpected needs for cash. The ratios that relate to this goal all have to do with working capital or some part of it, because it is out of working capital that debts are paid as they mature. Some common ratios connected with evaluating liquidity are the current ratio, the quick ratio, receivable turnover, and inventory turnover.

Current Ratio. The **current ratio** expresses the relationship of current assets to current liabilities. It is widely used as a broad indicator of a company's liquidity and short-term debt-paying ability. The ratio for Eastman Kodak for 1985 and 1984 is figured as follows:

Current Ratio	**1985**	**1984**
$\dfrac{\text{current assets}}{\text{current liabilities}}$	$\dfrac{\$5{,}677}{\$3{,}325} = 1.71$	$\dfrac{\$5{,}131}{\$2{,}306} = 2.23$

The current ratio for Eastman Kodak shows a major decrease from 1984 to 1985.

Quick Ratio. One of the current ratio's faults is that it does not take into account the make-up of current assets. They may appear to be large enough, but they may not have the proper balance. Clearly, a dollar of cash or even accounts receivable is more readily available to meet obligations than is a dollar of most kinds of inventory. The **quick ratio** is designed to overcome this problem by measuring short-term liquidity. That is, it measures the relationship of the more liquid current assets (cash, marketable securities or short-term investments, and receivables) to current liabilities. This ratio for Eastman Kodak for 1985 and 1984 is figured as follows:

Quick Ratio	1985	1984
$\dfrac{\text{cash + marketable securities + receivables}}{\text{current liabilities}}$	$\dfrac{\$161 + \$652 + \$2,346}{\$3,325}$	$\dfrac{\$192 + \$819 + \$2,050}{\$2,306}$
	$= \dfrac{\$3,159}{\$3,325} = 0.95$	$= \dfrac{\$3,061}{\$2,306} = 1.33$

This ratio shows a major decrease from 1984 to 1985.

Receivable Turnover. The ability of a company to collect for credit sales in a timely way affects the company's liquidity. The **receivable turnover** ratio measures the relative size of a company's accounts receivable and the success of its credit and collection policies. This ratio shows how many times, on average, the receivables were turned into cash during the period. Turnover ratios usually consist of one balance sheet account and one income statement account. The receivable turnover is computed by dividing sales by average accounts receivable. Theoretically, the numerator should be credit sales, but the amount of credit sales is rarely made available in public reports. So we will use total sales. Further, in this ratio and others where an average is required, we will take the beginning and ending balances and divide by 2. If we had internal financial data, it would be better to use monthly balances to find the average, because the balances of receivables, inventories, and other accounts can vary widely during the year. In fact, many companies choose a fiscal year that begins and ends at a low period of the business cycle when inventories and receivables may be at the lowest levels of the year. Using a 1983 accounts receivable ending balance of $1,779 million, Eastman Kodak's receivable turnover is computed as follows:

Receivable Turnover	1985	1984
$\dfrac{\text{sales}}{\text{average accounts receivable}}$	$\dfrac{\$10,631}{(\$2,346 + \$2,050)\frac{1}{2}}$	$\dfrac{\$10,600}{(\$2,050 + \$1,779)\frac{1}{2}}$
	$= \dfrac{\$10,631}{\$2,198} = 4.84$ times	$= \dfrac{\$10,600}{\$1,914.5} = 5.54$ times

When the previous year's balance is not available for computing the average, it is common practice to use the ending balance for the current year.

Within reasonable ranges, the higher the turnover ratio the better. With a higher turnover the company is turning receivables into cash at a faster pace. The speed at which receivables are turned over depends on the company's credit terms. Since a company's credit terms are usually stated in days, such as 2/10, n/30, it is helpful to convert the receivable turnover to **average days' sales uncollected.** This conversion is made by dividing the length of the accounting period (usually 365 days) by the receivable turnover (as computed above) as follows:

Average Days' Sales Uncollected	1985	1984
$\frac{\text{days in year}}{\text{receivable turnover}}$	$\frac{365 \text{ days}}{4.84} = 75.41$ days	$\frac{365 \text{ days}}{5.54} = 65.88$ days

In the case of Eastman Kodak, both the receivable turnover and the average days' sales uncollected worsened from 1984 to 1985. The average accounts receivable was turned over about 4.8 times during 1985, down from 5.5 times in 1984. This means Eastman Kodak had to wait on average about 75 days to receive payment for credit sales, up 10 days from 1984.

Inventory Turnover. Inventory is two steps removed from cash (sale and collection). **Inventory turnover** measures the relative size of inventory and affects the amount of cash available to pay maturing debts. Of course, inventory should be maintained at the best level to support production and sales. In general, however, a smaller, faster-moving inventory means that the company has less cash tied up in inventory. It also means that there is less chance for the inventory to become spoiled or out of date. A build-up in inventory may mean that a recession or some other factor is preventing sales from keeping pace with purchasing and production. Using a 1983 ending inventory balance of $1,710 million, inventory turnover for 1985 and 1984 at Eastman Kodak is computed as follows:

Inventory Turnover	1985	1984
$\frac{\text{cost of goods sold}}{\text{average inventory}}$	$\frac{\$7{,}129}{(\$1{,}940 + \$1{,}758)\frac{1}{2}}$	$\frac{\$6{,}887}{(\$1{,}758 + \$1{,}710)\frac{1}{2}}$
	$= \frac{\$7{,}129}{\$1{,}849} = \frac{3.86}{\text{times}}$	$= \frac{\$6{,}887}{\$1{,}734} = \frac{3.97}{\text{times}}$

Consistent with receivable turnover, there was a decline in inventory turnover from 1984 to 1985, due primarily to an increase in the size of average inventory.

Evaluating Profitability

A company's long-run survival depends on its being able to earn a satisfactory income. Investors become and remain stockholders for only one reason. They believe that the dividends and capital gains they will receive will be greater than the returns on other investments of about the same risk. An evaluation of a company's past earning power may give the investor a better understanding for decision making. Also, a company's ability to earn an income usually affects its liquidity position. For this reason, evaluating profitability is important to both investors and creditors. In judging the profitability of Eastman Kodak, five ratios will be presented: profit margin, asset turnover, return on assets, return on equity, and earnings per share.

Profit Margin. The **profit margin** ratio measures the percentage of each revenue dollar that results in net income. It is computed for Eastman Kodak as follows:

Profit Margin[6]	**1985**	**1984**
$\frac{\text{net income}}{\text{sales}}$	$\frac{\$332}{\$10{,}631} = 3.1\%$	$\frac{\$923}{\$10{,}600} = 8.7\%$

The ratio confirms what was clear from the common-size income statement (Exhibit 28-6): that the profit margin decreased from 1984 (8.7 percent) to 1985 (3.1 percent). The analysis of the common-size income statement showed that this decline was due to an increase in costs and expenses as a percentage of total sales as well as unusual charges reducing net income.

Asset Turnover. **Asset turnover** is a measure of how efficiently assets are used to produce sales. It shows how many dollars in sales are produced by each dollar invested in assets. In other words, it tells how many times in the period assets were "turned over" in sales. The higher the asset turnover, the more concentrated is the use of assets. Using the data for Eastman Kodak from Exhibits 28-2 and 28-3 and 1983 total assets of $10,928 million, the asset turnovers for 1985 and 1984 are as follows:

Asset Turnover	**1985**	**1984**
$\frac{\text{sales}}{\text{average total assets}}$	$\frac{\$10{,}631}{(\$12{,}142 + \$10{,}778)\frac{1}{2}}$	$\frac{\$10{,}600}{(\$10{,}778 + \$10{,}928)\frac{1}{2}}$
	$= \frac{\$10{,}631}{\$11{,}460} = .93$ times	$= \frac{\$10{,}600}{\$10{,}853} = .98$ times

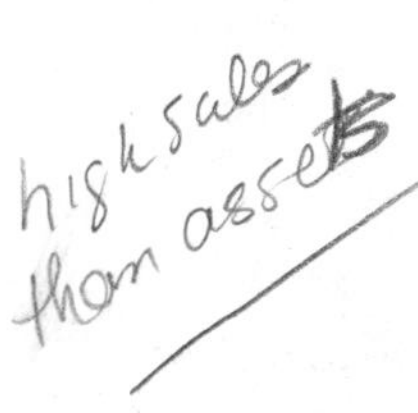

Compared to other industries, Eastman Kodak needs a large investment in assets for each dollar of sales. A retailer may have an asset turnover of between 4.0 and 6.0. In the case of Eastman Kodak, however, the turnover was only .98 in 1984 and .93 in 1985. This fact means that Eastman Kodak makes sales of a little less than one dollar for each dollar of assets. Or to put it another way, a dollar invested puts less than a dollar into sales.

Return on Assets. The best overall measure of the earning power or profitability of a company is **return on assets,** which measures the amount earned on each dollar of assets invested. The return on assets for 1985 and 1984 for Eastman Kodak is as follows:

Return on Assets[7]	**1985**	**1984**
$\frac{\text{net income}}{\text{average total assets}}$	$\frac{\$332}{\$11{,}460} = 2.9\%$	$\frac{\$923}{\$10{,}853} = 8.5\%$

6. In comparing companies in an industry, some analysts use net income before income taxes as the numerator to eliminate the effect of differing tax rates among the individual firms.
7. Some authorities would add interest expense to net income in the numerator because they view interest expense as a cost of acquiring capital, not a cost of operations.

Eastman Kodak's return on assets decreased from 8.5 percent in 1984 to 2.9 percent in 1985, an unfavorable change.

One reason why return on assets is a good measure of profitability is that it combines the effects of profit margin and asset turnover. The 1985 and 1984 results for Eastman Kodak can be analyzed as follows:

	Profit Margin		Asset Turnover		Return on Assets
Ratios:	$\frac{\text{net income}}{\text{sales}}$	×	$\frac{\text{sales}}{\text{average total assets}}$	=	$\frac{\text{net income}}{\text{average total assets}}$
1985	3.1%	×	.93	=	2.9%
1984	8.7%	×	.98	=	8.5%

From this analysis, it is clear that the decrease in return on assets in 1985 can be attributed to the decrease in profit margin.

Return on Equity. An important measure of profitability from the stockholders' standpoint is **return on equity**. This ratio measures how much was earned for each dollar invested by owners. For Eastman Kodak, this ratio for 1985 and 1984 is figured as follows (1983 owners' equity equals $7,520 million):

Return on Equity	1985	1984
$\frac{\text{net income}}{\text{average owners' equity}}$	$\frac{\$332}{(\$6{,}562 + \$7{,}137)\frac{1}{2}}$	$\frac{\$923}{(\$7{,}137 + \$7{,}520)\frac{1}{2}}$
	$= \frac{\$332}{\$6{,}849.5} = 4.8\%$	$= \frac{\$923}{\$7{,}328.5} = 12.6\%$

As might be expected from the analysis of other profitability ratios above, this ratio also went down from 1984 to 1985.

A natural question is, Why is there a difference between return on assets and return on equity? The answer lies in the company's use of **leverage**, or debt financing. A company that has interest-bearing debt is said to be leveraged. If the company earns more with its borrowed funds than it must pay in interest for those funds, then the difference is available to increase the return on equity. Leverage may work against the company as well. Thus an unfavorable situation occurs when the return on assets is less than the rate of interest paid on borrowed funds. Because of Eastman Kodak's leverage, the decrease in return on assets from 1984 to 1985 of 8.5 to 2.9 percent resulted in a larger decrease in return on equity of 12.6 to 4.8 for the same two years. (The debt to equity ratio is presented later in this chapter.)

Earnings per Share. One of the most widely quoted measures of profitability is earnings per share of common stock. Exhibit 28-4 shows that the net earnings per share for Eastman Kodak declined from $3.80 to $1.46, reflecting the decrease in net income from 1984 to 1985. These disclosures must be made in financial statements; calculations of this kind were presented in Chapter 13.

Evaluating Long-Term Solvency

Long-term solvency has to do with a company's ability to survive over many years. The aim of long-term solvency analysis is to point out early that a company is on the road to bankruptcy. Studies have shown that accounting ratios can show as much as five years in advance that a company may fail.[8] Declining profitability and liquidity ratios are key signs of possible business failure. Two other ratios that analysts often consider as indicators of long-term solvency are the debt to equity ratio and the interest coverage ratio.

Debt to Equity Ratio. The existence of increasing amounts of debt in a company's capital structure is thought to be risky. The company has a legal obligation to make interest payments on time and to pay the principal at the maturity date. And this obligation holds no matter what the level of the company's earnings is. If the payments are not made, the company may be forced into bankruptcy. In contrast, dividends and other distributions to equity holders are made only when the board of directors declares them. The **debt to equity ratio** shows the relationship of the company's assets provided by creditors to the amount provided by stockholders and measures the extent to which the company is leveraged. The larger the debt to equity ratio, the more fixed obligations the company has and so the riskier the situation. It is computed as follows:

Debt to Equity Ratio	1985	1984
$\frac{\text{total liabilities}}{\text{owners' equity}}$	$\frac{\$5,580}{\$6,562} = .85$	$\frac{\$3,641}{\$7,137} = .51$

From 1984 to 1985, the debt to equity ratio for Eastman Kodak went up from .51 to .85. This finding agrees with the analysis of the common-size balance sheet (Exhibit 28-5), which shows that the total debt of the company increased as a percentage of total assets in 1985.

Interest Coverage Ratio. One question that usually arises at this point is, If debt is bad, why have any? The answer is that, as with many ratios, it is a matter of balance. In spite of its riskiness, debt is a flexible means of financing certain business operations. Also, because it usually carries a fixed interest charge, it limits the cost of financing and presents a situation where leverage can be used to advantage. Thus if the company is able to earn a return on the assets greater than the cost of the interest, the company makes an overall profit.[9] However, the company runs the

8. William H. Beaver, "Alternative Accounting Measures as Indicators of Failure," *Accounting Review* (January 1968); and Edward Altman, "Financial Ratios, Discriminant Analysis and the Prediction of Corporate Bankruptcy," *Journal of Finance* (September 1968).
9. In addition, there are advantages to being a debtor in periods of inflation because the debt, which is fixed in dollar amount, may be repaid with cheaper dollars.

risk of not earning a return on assets equal to the interest cost of financing those assets, thereby incurring an overall loss. One measure of the degree of protection creditors have from a default on interest payments is the **interest coverage ratio**, computed as follows:

Interest Coverage Ratio	**1985**	**1984**
$\dfrac{\text{net income before taxes + interest expense}}{\text{interest expense}}$	$\dfrac{\$530 + \$183}{\$183}$	$\dfrac{\$1{,}624 + \$114}{\$114}$
	= 3.90 times	= 15.25 times

Interest coverage worsened in 1985; the interest payments are protected by a ratio of only 3.90 times.

Market Test Ratios

The market price of a company's shares of stock is of interest to the analyst because it represents what investors as a whole think of a company at a point in time. Market price is the price at which people are willing to buy and sell the stock. It provides information about how investors view the potential return and risk connected with owning the company's stock. This information cannot be obtained simply by considering the market price of the stock by itself. Companies have different numbers of outstanding shares and different amounts of underlying earnings and dividends. Thus the market price must be related to the earnings per share, dividends per share, and prices of other companies' shares to get the necessary information. This analysis is done through the price/earnings ratio, the dividends yield, and market risk.

Price/Earnings Ratio. The **price/earnings (P/E) ratio** measures the ratio of the current market price of the stock to the earnings per share. Assuming a current market price of \$60 and using the 1985 earnings per share for Eastman Kodak of \$1.46 from Exhibit 28-4, we can compute the price/earnings ratio as follows:

$$\frac{\text{market price per share}}{\text{earnings per share}} = \frac{\$60}{\$1.46} = 41.1 \text{ times}$$

This ratio changes from day to day and from quarter to quarter as market price and earnings change. It tells how much the investing public as a whole is willing to pay for \$1 of Eastman Kodak's earnings per share. At this time, Eastman Kodak's P/E ratio is 41.1 times the underlying earnings for that share of stock. This is an abnormally high ratio due to the unusual charge that reduces earnings per share in 1985. Investors are expecting the company's earnings to bounce back.

This ratio is very useful and widely applied because it allows companies to be compared. When a company's P/E ratio is higher than the P/E ratios for other companies, it *usually* means that investors feel that the company's earnings are going to grow at a faster rate than those of the other companies. On the other hand, a lower P/E ratio *usually* means a more negative assessment by investors. To compare two well-known companies, the market was less favorable toward General Motors (7.0 times earnings per share) than it was toward IBM (14.0 times earnings per share) in 1986.

Dividends Yield. The **dividends yield** is a measure of the current return to an investor in the stock. It is found by dividing the current annual dividend by the current market price of the stock. Assuming the same \$60 per share and using the 1985 dividends of \$2.43 per share for Eastman Kodak from Exhibit 28-4, we can compute the dividends yield as follows:

$$\frac{\text{dividends per share}}{\text{market price per share}} = \frac{\$2.43}{\$60} = 4.1\%$$

Thus an investor who owns Eastman Kodak stock at \$60 had a return from dividends in 1985 of 4.1 percent. The dividends yield is only one part of the investor's total return from investing in Eastman Kodak. The investor must add or subtract from the dividends yield the percentage change (either up or down) in the market value of the stock. Since the company earned only \$1.46 per share in 1985, it must increase its earnings to continue paying a dividend of \$2.

Market Risk. It was pointed out earlier that besides assessing the potential return from an investment, the investor must also judge the risk associated with the investment. Many factors may be brought into assessing risk—the nature of the business, the quality of the business, the track record of the company, and so forth. One measure of risk that has gained increased attention among analysts in recent years is market risk. **Market risk** is the volatility of (or changes up and down in) the price of a stock in relation to the volatility of the prices of other stocks. The computation of market risk is complex, because it uses computers and sophisticated statistical techniques such as regression analysis. The idea, however, is simple. Consider the following data about the changes in the prices of the stocks of Company A and Company B and the average change in price of all stocks in the market:

Average Percentage Change in Price of All Stock	Percentage Change in Price of Company A's Stock	Percentage Change in Price of Company B's Stock
+10	+15	+5
−10	−15	−5

In this example, when the average price of all stocks went up by 10 percent, Company A's price increased 15 percent and Company B's increased only 5 percent. When the average price of all stocks went down by 10 percent, Company A's price decreased 15 percent and Company B's decreased only 5 percent. Thus, relative to all stocks, Company A's stock is more volatile than Company B's stock. If the prices of stocks go down, the risk of loss is greater in the case of Company A than in the case of Company B. If the market goes up, however, the potential for gain is greater in the case of Company A than in the case for Company B.

Market risk can be approximated by dividing the percentage change in price of the particular stock by the average percentage change in the price of all stocks, as follows:

$$\text{Company A} \quad \frac{\text{specific change}}{\text{average change}} = \frac{15}{10} = 1.5$$

$$\text{Company B} \quad \frac{\text{specific change}}{\text{average change}} = \frac{5}{10} = .5$$

These measures mean that an investor can generally expect the value of an investment in Company A to increase or decrease 1.5 times as much as the average increase or decrease in the price of all stocks. An investment in Company B can be expected to increase or decrease only .5 times as much as the price of all stocks.

Analysts call this measure of market risk **beta** (β), after the mathematical symbol used in the formula for calculating the relationships of the stock prices. The actual betas used by analysts are based on several years of data and are continually updated. These calculations require the use of computers and are usually obtained from investment services.

The market risk or beta for U.S. Steel in a recent year was 1.01. This means that, other things being equal, a person who invests in the stock of U.S. Steel can expect its volatility or risk to be about the same as the stock market as a whole (which has a beta of 1.0). This makes sense when one considers that U.S. Steel is a mature company and the largest steel producer, with output closely related to the ups and downs in the economy as a whole.

If the investor's objective is to assume less risk than that of the market as a whole, other companies in the steel industry can be considered. The second largest steel company is Bethlehem Steel, but it can be eliminated because its beta of 1.25 makes it riskier than U.S. Steel. National Steel, the third largest steel processor, has been more stable over the years than its competitors, with a beta of only .75. It is a less risky stock in that there is less potential for loss in a "down" market, but there is also less potential for gain in an "up" market. The beta for National Steel is very low and compares favorably with that of a major utility such as American Telephone and Telegraph, which has a beta of .65.

Typically, growth stocks and speculative stocks are riskier than stocks in the market as a whole. Tandy Corporation (Radio Shack), a good example of a growth company, has had a beta of 1.45. It has rewarded investors' patience over the years but has been much more volatile and thus riskier than the average stock that would have a beta of 1.00.

Investment decisions are not made on the basis of market risk alone, of course. First, other risk factors such as those indicated by the other ratios and analyses discussed in this chapter as well as by the industry, national, and world economic outlooks must be considered. Second, the expected return must be considered. Further, most investors try to own a portfolio of stocks whose average beta corresponds to the degree of risk they are willing to assume in relation to the average expected return of their portfolio.

Chapter Review

Review of Learning Objectives

1. **Describe and discuss the objectives of financial statement analysis.**
Creditors and investors use financial statement analysis to judge the past performance and current position of a company. In this way they also judge its future potential and the risk associated with this potential. Creditors use the information gained from analysis to help them make loans that will be repaid with interest. Investors use the information to help them make investments that provide a return that is worth the risk.

2. **Describe and discuss the standards for financial statement analysis.**
Three commonly used standards for financial statement analysis are rule-of-thumb measures, past performance of the company, and industry norms. Rule-of-thumb measures are weak because of the lack of evidence that they can be applied widely. The past performance of a company can offer a guideline for measuring improvement but is not helpful in judging performance relative to other companies. Although the use of industry norms overcomes this last problem, its disadvantage is that firms are not always comparable, even in the same industry.

3. **State the sources of information for financial statement analysis.**
The major sources of information about publicly held corporations are published reports such as annual reports and interim financial statements, SEC reports, business periodicals, and credit and investment advisory services.

4. **Identify the issues related to evaluating the quality of a company's earnings.**
Current and prospective net income is an important component in many ratios used to evaluate a company. The user should recognize that the quality of reported net income can be influenced by the choices made by the company's management. First, management has control over accounting methods and estimates used in computing net income. Second, discontinued operations, extraordinary gains or losses, or accounting changes may affect net income positively or negatively.

5. **Apply horizontal analysis, trend analysis, and vertical analysis to financial statements.**
Horizontal analysis involves the computation of dollar amount changes and percentage changes from year to year. Trend analysis is an extension of horizontal analysis in that percentage changes are calculated for several years. The changes are usually computed by setting a base year equal to 100 and calculating the measures for subsequent years as a percentage of that base year. Vertical analysis uses percentages to show the relationship of the component parts to the total in a single statement. The resulting statements in percentages are called common-size statements.

6. **Apply ratio analysis to financial statements in the study of an enterprise's liquidity, profitability, long-term solvency, and market tests.**
The following table summarizes the basic information on ratio analysis.

Ratio	Components	Use or Meaning
Liquidity Ratios		
Current ratio	$\frac{\text{current assets}}{\text{current liabilities}}$	Measure of short-term debt-paying ability
Quick ratio	$\frac{\text{cash + short-term investments + receivables}}{\text{current liabilities}}$	Measure of short-term liquidity
Receivable turnover	$\frac{\text{sales}}{\text{average accounts receivable}}$	Measure of relative size of accounts receivable balance and effectiveness of credit policies.
Average days' sales uncollected	$\frac{\text{days in year}}{\text{receivable turnover}}$	Measure of time it takes to collect an average receivable
Inventory turnover	$\frac{\text{cost of goods sold}}{\text{average inventory}}$	Measure of relative size of inventory
Profitability Ratios		
Profit margin	$\frac{\text{net income}}{\text{sales}}$	Income produced by each dollar of sales
Asset turnover	$\frac{\text{sales}}{\text{average total assets}}$	Measure of how efficiently assets are used to produce sales
Return on assets	$\frac{\text{net income}}{\text{average total assets}}$	Overall measure of earning power or profitability of all assets employed in the business
Return on equity	$\frac{\text{net income}}{\text{average owners' equity}}$	Profitability of owners' investment
Earnings per share	$\frac{\text{net income}}{\text{outstanding shares}}$	Means of placing earnings on a common basis for comparisons
Long-Term Solvency Ratios		
Debt to equity	$\frac{\text{total liabilities}}{\text{owners' equity}}$	Measure of relationship of debt financing to equity financing
Interest coverage	$\frac{\text{net income before taxes + interest expense}}{\text{interest expense}}$	Measure of protection of creditors from a default on interest payments
Market Test Ratios		
Price/earnings (P/E)	$\frac{\text{market price per share}}{\text{earnings per share}}$	Measure of amount the market will pay for a dollar of earnings

Ratio	Components	Use or Meaning
Dividends yield	$\frac{\text{dividends per share}}{\text{market price per share}}$	Measure of current return to investor
Market risk	$\frac{\text{specific change in market price}}{\text{average change in market price}}$	Measure of volatility of the market price of a stock in relation to that of other stocks

Review Problem
Comparative Analysis of Two Companies

Maggie Washington is considering an investment in one of two fast-food restaurant chains because she believes the trend toward eating out more often will continue. Her choices have been narrowed to Quik Burger and Big Steak, whose balance sheets and income statements follow.

Balance Sheets
(in thousands)

	Quik Burger	Big Steak
Assets		
Cash	$ 2,000	$ 4,500
Accounts Receivable (net)	2,000	6,500
Inventory	2,000	5,000
Property, Plant, and Equipment (net)	20,000	35,000
Other Assets	4,000	5,000
Total Assets	$30,000	$56,000
Liabilities and Stockholders' Equity		
Accounts Payable	$ 2,500	$ 3,000
Notes Payable	1,500	4,000
Bonds Payable	10,000	30,000
Common Stock ($1 par value)	1,000	3,000
Paid-in Capital in Excess of Par Value, Common	9,000	9,000
Retained Earnings	6,000	7,000
Total Liabilities and Stockholders' Equity	$30,000	$56,000

Income Statements
(in thousands)

	Quik Burger	Big Steak
Sales	$53,000	$86,000
Cost of Goods Sold (including restaurant operating expense)	37,000	61,000
Gross Margin from Sales	$16,000	$25,000
General Operating Expenses		
Selling Expenses	$ 7,000	$10,000
Administrative Expenses	4,000	5,000
Interest Expense	1,400	3,200
Income Taxes Expense	1,800	3,400
Total Operating Expenses	$14,200	$21,600
Net Income	$ 1,800	$ 3,400

In addition, dividends paid were $500,000 for Quik Burger and $600,000 for Big Steak. The market prices of the stock were $30 and $20, respectively. And the betas were 1.00 and 1.15. Information pertaining to prior years is not readily available to Maggie. Assume that all Notes Payable are current liabilities, that all Bonds Payable are long-term liabilities and income tax rate at 50%.

Required

Conduct a comprehensive ratio analysis of each company and compare the results. This analysis should be done in the following steps:

1. Prepare an analysis of liquidity.
2. Prepare an analysis of profitability.
3. Prepare an analysis of long-term solvency.
4. Prepare an analysis of market tests.
5. Compare the analysis of each company by inserting the ratio calculations from the preceding four steps in a table with the following columns: *Ratio Name, Quik Burger, Big Steak,* and *Company with More Favorable Ratio.* Indicate in the last column the company that apparently had the more favorable ratio in each case. (If ratios are within .1 of each other, consider them neutral.)
6. In what ways would having prior years' information aid this analysis?

Answer to Review Problem*

Ratio Name	Quik Burger	Big Steak
1. Liquidity analysis		
a. Current ratio	$\frac{\$2{,}000 + \$2{,}000 + \$2{,}000}{\$2{,}500 + \$1{,}500} = \frac{\$6{,}000}{\$4{,}000} = 1.5$	$\frac{\$4{,}500 + \$6{,}500 + \$5{,}000}{\$3{,}000 + \$4{,}000} = \frac{\$16{,}000}{\$7{,}000} = 2.3$

* All items in thousands, except for per share amounts.

Ratio Name	Quik Burger	Big Steak
b. Quick ratio	$\frac{\$2{,}000 + \$2{,}000}{\$2{,}500 + \$1{,}500} = \frac{\$4{,}000}{\$4{,}000} = 1.0$	$\frac{\$4{,}500 + \$6{,}500}{\$3{,}000 + \$4{,}000} = \frac{\$11{,}000}{\$7{,}000} = 1.6$
c. Receivable turnover	$\frac{\$53{,}000}{\$2{,}000} = 26.5$ times	$\frac{\$86{,}000}{\$6{,}500} = 13.2$ times
d. Average days' sales uncollected	$\frac{365}{26.5} = 13.8$ days	$\frac{365}{13.2} = 27.7$ days
e. Inventory turnover	$\frac{\$37{,}000}{\$2{,}000} = 18.5$ times	$\frac{\$61{,}000}{\$5{,}000} = 12.2$ times
2. Profitability analysis		
a. Profit margin	$\frac{\$1{,}800}{\$53{,}000} = 3.4\%$	$\frac{\$3{,}400}{\$86{,}000} = 4.0\%$
b. Asset turnover	$\frac{\$53{,}000}{\$30{,}000} = 1.8$ times	$\frac{\$86{,}000}{\$56{,}000} = 1.5$ times
c. Return on assets	$\frac{\$1{,}800}{\$30{,}000} = 6.0\%$	$\frac{\$3{,}400}{\$56{,}000} = 6.1\%$
d. Return on equity	$\frac{\$1{,}800}{\$1{,}000 + \$9{,}000 + \$6{,}000} = \frac{\$1{,}800}{\$16{,}000} = 11.3\%$	$\frac{\$3{,}400}{\$3{,}000 + \$9{,}000 + \$7{,}000} = \frac{\$3{,}400}{\$19{,}000} = 17.9\%$
e. Earnings per share	$\frac{\$1{,}800}{1{,}000 \text{ shares}} = \$1.80$	$\frac{\$3{,}400}{3{,}000 \text{ shares}} = \$1.13$
3. Long-term solvency		
a. Debt to equity	$\frac{\$2{,}500 + \$1{,}500 + \$10{,}000}{\$1{,}000 + \$9{,}000 + \$6{,}000} = \frac{\$14{,}000}{\$16{,}000} = .9$	$\frac{\$3{,}000 + \$4{,}000 + \$30{,}000}{\$3{,}000 + \$9{,}000 + \$7{,}000} = \frac{\$37{,}000}{\$19{,}000} = 1.9$
b. Interest coverage	$\frac{\$1{,}800 + \$1{,}800 + \$1{,}400}{\$1{,}400} = \frac{\$5{,}000}{\$1{,}400} = 3.6$ times	$\frac{\$3{,}400 + \$3{,}400 + \$3{,}200}{\$3{,}200} = \frac{\$10{,}000}{\$3{,}200} = 3.1$ times
4. Market test analysis		
a. Price/earnings ratio	$\frac{\$30}{\$1.80} = 16.7$ times	$\frac{\$20}{\$1.13} = 17.7$ times
b. Dividends yield	$\frac{\$500 \div 1{,}000}{\$30} = 1.7\%$	$\frac{\$600 \div 3{,}000}{\$20} = 1.0\%$
c. Market risk	1.00	1.15

5. Comparative analysis

Ratio Name	Quik Burger	Big Steak	Company with More Favorable Ratio*
1. Liquidity analysis			
a. Current ratio	1.5	2.3	Big Steak
b. Quick ratio	1.0	1.6	Big Steak
c. Receivable turnover	26.5 times	13.2 times	Quik Burger
d. Average days' sales uncollected	13.8 days	27.7 days	Quik Burger
e. Inventory turnover	18.5 times	12.2 times	Quik Burger
2. Profitability analysis			
a. Profit margin	3.4%	4.0%	Big Steak
b. Asset turnover	1.8 times	1.5 times	Quik Burger
c. Return on assets	6.0%	6.1%	Indeterminate
d. Return on equity	11.3%	17.9%	Big Steak
e. Earnings per share	$1.80	$1.13	Noncomparable†
3. Long-term solvency			
a. Debt to equity	.9	1.9	Quik Burger
b. Interest coverage	3.6 times	3.1 times	Quik Burger
4. Market test analysis			
a. Price/earnings ratio	16.7 times	17.7 times	Big Steak
b. Dividends yield	1.7%	1.0%	Quik Burger
c. Market risk	1.00	1.15	Quik Burger is less risky

* This analysis indicates the company with the apparently more favorable or unfavorable ratio. Class discussion may focus on conditions under which different conclusions may be drawn.
† Earnings per share is noncomparable because of the considerable difference in the number of common stockholders of the two firms. If information for prior years were available, it would be helpful in determining the earnings trend of each company.

6. Usefulness of prior years' information

The availability of prior years' information would be helpful in two ways. First, turnover and return ratios could be based on average amounts. Second, a trend analysis could be performed for each company.

Chapter Assignments

Questions

1. What differences and similarities exist in the objectives of investors and creditors in using financial statement analysis?
2. What role does risk play in making loans and investments?
3. What standards are commonly used to evaluate ratios, and what are their relative merits?
4. Where may an investor look to find information about a company in which he or she is thinking of investing?
5. What is the basis of the following statement? "Accounting income is a useless measurement because it is based on so many arbitrary decisions." Is it true?

6. Why would an investor want to do both horizontal and trend analyses of a company's financial statements?
7. What is the difference between horizontal and vertical analysis?
8. What does the following sentence mean: "Based on 1967 equaling 100, net income increased from 240 in 1983 to 260 in 1984"?
9. What is the purpose of ratio analysis?
10. Why would a financial analyst compare the ratios of Steelco, a steel company, to the ratios of other companies in the steel industry? What might cause such a comparison to be invalid?
11. In a period of high interest rates, why are receivable and inventory turnovers especially important?
12. The following statements were made on page 35 of the November 6, 1978, issue of *Fortune* magazine: "Supermarket executives are beginning to look back with some nostalgia on the days when the standard profit margin was 1 percent of sales. Last year the industry overall margin came to a thin 0.72 percent." How could a supermarket earn a satisfactory return on assets with such a small profit margin?
13. Circo Company has a return on assets of 12 percent and a debt to equity ratio of .5. Would you expect return on equity to be more or less than 12 percent?
14. Under what circumstances would a current ratio of 3:1 be good? Under what circumstances would it be bad?
15. Company A and Company B both have net incomes of $1,000,000. Is it possible to say that these companies are equally successful? Why or why not?
16. The market price of Company J's stock is the same as Company Q's stock. How might one determine whether investors are equally confident about the future of these companies?
17. Why is it riskier to own a stock whose market price is more changeable than the market price of other stocks? Why may it be beneficial to own such a stock?
18. "By almost any standard, Chicago-based Helene Curtis rates as one of America's worst-managed personal care companies. In recent years its return on equity has hovered between 10% and 13%, well below the industry average of 18% to 19%. Net profit margins of 2% to 3% are half that of competitors. . . . As a result, while leading names like Revlon and Avon are trading at three and four times book value, Curtis' trades at less than two-thirds book value."[10] Considering that many companies are happy with a return on equity (owners' investment) of 10% and 13%, why is this analysis so critical of Curtis's performance? Assuming that Curtis could double its profit margin, what other information would you need to project the resulting return on owners' investment? Why does the writer feel that it is obvious that Revlon's and Avon's stocks are trading for more than Curtis's?

Classroom Exercises

Exercise 28-1. Trend Analysis (L.O. 5)

Prepare a trend analysis of the data on the next page using 19x1 as a base year, and tell whether the situation shown by the trends is favorable or unfavorable. (Round your answers to one decimal point.)

10. *Forbes,* November 13, 1978, p. 154.

	19x5	19x4	19x3	19x2	19x1
Sales	$12,760	$11,990	$12,100	$11,440	$11,000
Cost of Goods Sold	8,610	7,700	7,770	7,350	7,000
General and Administrative Expenses	2,640	2,592	2,544	2,448	2,400
Operating Income	1,510	1,698	1,786	1,642	1,600

Exercise 28-2. Vertical Analysis (L.O. 5)

Express the comparative income statements below as common-size statements, and comment on the changes from 19x1 to 19x2. (Round computations to one decimal point.)

Kravitz Company
Comparative Income Statement
For the Years Ended December 31, 19x2 and 19x1

	19x2	19x1
Sales	$212,000	$184,000
Cost of Goods Sold	127,200	119,600
Gross Margin from Sales	84,800	64,400
Selling Expenses	53,000	36,800
General Expenses	25,440	18,400
Total Operating Expenses	78,440	55,200
Net Operating Income	$ 6,360	$ 9,200

Exercise 28-3. Liquidity Analysis (L.O. 6)

Partial comparative balance sheet and income statement information for Harmon Company appear below.

	19x2	19x1
Cash	$ 3,400	$ 2,600
Marketable Securities	1,800	4,300
Accounts Receivable (net)	11,200	8,900
Inventory	13,600	12,400
Total Current Assets	$30,000	$28,200
Current Liabilities	$10,000	$ 7,050
Sales	$80,640	$55,180
Cost of Goods Sold	54,400	50,840
Gross Margin from Sales	$26,240	$ 4,340

In addition, the year-end balance of accounts receivable and inventories were $8,100 and $12,800, respectively, in 19x0. Compute the current ratio, quick ratio, receivable turnover, average days' sales uncollected, and inventory turnover for each year. Comment on the change in liquidity position from 19x1 to 19x2. (Round computations to one decimal point.)

Exercise 28-4. Horizontal Analysis (L.O. 5)

Compute amount and percentage changes for the balance sheet below, and comment on the changes from 19x1 to 19x2. (Round the percentage changes to one decimal point.)

Kravitz Company
Comparative Balance Sheets
December 31, 19x2 and 19x2

	19x2	19x1
Assets		
Current Assets	$ 18,600	$ 12,800
Property, Plant, and Equipment (net)	109,464	97,200
Total Assets	$128,064	$110,000
Liabilities and Stockholders' Equity		
Current Liabilities	$ 11,200	$ 3,200
Long-Term Liabilities	35,000	40,000
Stockholders' Equity	81,864	66,800
Total Liabilities and Stockholders' Equity	$128,064	$110,000

Exercise 28-5. Profitability Analysis (L.O. 6)

At year-end, Ortiz Company had total assets of $320,000 in 19x0, $340,000 in 19x1, and $380,000 in 19x2 and a debt to equity ratio of .67 in all three years. In 19x1, the company made a net income of $38,556 on revenues of $612,000. In 19x2, the company made a net income of $49,476 on revenues of $798,000. Compute the profit margin, asset turnover, return on assets, and return on equity for 19x1 and 19x2. Comment on the apparent cause of the increase or decrease in profitability. (Round the percentages and other ratios to one decimal point.)

Exercise 28-6. Long-Term Solvency and Market Test Ratios (L.O. 6)

An investor is considering investments in the long-term bonds and common stock of Companies S and T. Both companies operate in the same industry, but Company S has a beta of 1.0 and Company T has a beta of 1.2. In addition, both companies pay a dividend per share of $2, and the yield of both companies' long-term bonds is 10 percent. Other data for the two companies are presented on the next page.

	Company S	Company T
Total Assets	$1,200,000	$540,000
Total Liabilities	540,000	297,000
Net Income Before Taxes	144,000	64,800
Interest Expense	48,600	26,730
Earnings per Share	1.60	2.50
Market Price on Common Stock	20	23¾

Compute debt to equity ratios, interest coverage ratios, price/earnings (P/E) ratios, and dividend yield ratios, and comment on the results. (Round computations to one decimal point.)

Exercise 28-7. Effect of Alternative Accounting Methods (L.O. 4)

At the end of its first year of operations, a company could calculate its ending merchandise inventory, according to three different methods, as follows: FIFO, $62,500; weighted average, $60,000; LIFO, $58,000. If the weighted-average method is used, the net income for the year would be $28,000.

1. Determine the net income if the FIFO method is used.
2. Determine the net income if the LIFO method is used.
3. Which method is most conservative?
4. Will the consistency convention be violated if the LIFO method is chosen?
5. Does the full-disclosure convention require disclosure of the inventory method selected by management in the financial statements?

Exercise 28-8. Preparation of Statements from Ratios and Incomplete Data (L.O. 6)

Presented below and on the next page are the income statement and balance sheet of Schlegel Corporation with most of the amounts missing.

Schlegel Corporation
Income Statement
For the Year Ended December 31, 19x1
(in thousands of dollars)

Sales		$9,000
Cost of Goods Sold		?
Gross Margin from Sales		?
Operating Expenses		
Selling Expenses	$?	
Administrative Expenses	117	
Interest Expense	81	
Income Taxes Expense	310	
Total Operating Expenses		?
Net Income		$?

Schlegel Corporation
Balance Sheet
December 31, 19x1
(in thousands of dollars)

Assets		
Cash	$?	
Accounts Receivable (net)	?	
Inventories	?	
Total Current Assets		?
Property, Plant, and Equipment (net)		2,700
Total Assets		$?
Liabilities and Stockholders' Equity		
Current Liabilities	$?	
Bond Payable, 9% interest	?	
Total Liabilities		$?
Common Stock—$10 par value	$1,500	
Paid-in Capital in Excess of Par Value, Common	1,300	
Retained Earnings	2,000	
Total Stockholders' Equity		$4,800
Total Liabilities and Stockholders' Equity		$?

Additional information: (a) the only interest expense is on long-term debt; (b) the debt to equity ratio is .5; (c) the current ratio is 3:1, and the quick ratio is 2:1; (d) the receivable turnover is 4.5, and the inventory turnover is 4.0; (e) the return on assets is 10 percent; (f) all ratios are based on the current year's information.

Complete the financial statements using the information presented. Show supporting computations.

Interpreting Accounting Information

28-1. Ford Motor Company I (L.O. 6)

Standard & Poor's Corporation (S & P) offers wide financial information services to investors. One of its services is rating the quality of bond issues of U.S. corporations. Its top bond rating is AAA, followed by AA, A, BBB, BB, B, and so forth. The lowest rating of C is reserved for companies that are in or near bankruptcy. *Business Week* reported on February 2, 1981, that S & P had downgraded the bond rating for Ford Motor Company, a leading U.S. automobile maker, from AAA to AA. The cause of the downgrading was a deterioration of Ford's financial strength as indicated by certain ratios considered important by S & P. These ratios, S & P's guidelines, and Ford's performance are summarized in the table on the next page:

Ratio	S & P Guideline for AAA Rating	Ford's Performance 1978	1979	1980
Interest Coverage	15 times	15.3 times	6.5 times	Loss
Pretax Return on Assets	15% to 20%	13.4%	6.6%	Loss
Debt to Equity	50%	34%	37.8%	63.4%
Cash Flow as a Percentage of Total Debt*	100%	152.6%	118.5%	91%
Short-Term Debt as a Percentage of Total Debt	25%	43.1%	48.3%	52.5%

* Cash flow includes net income plus noncash charges to earnings.

Required

1. Identify the objective (profitability, liquidity, long-term solvency) measured by each of the S & P ratios. Why is each ratio important to the rating of Ford's long-term bonds?
2. In the *Business Week* article, several actions were suggested for Ford to take to regain its previous status. Tell which of the ratios each of the following actions would improve: (a) "cutting operating costs"; (b) "scrapping at least part of its massive spending plans over the next several years"; (c) "eliminate cash dividends to stockholders"; (d) "sale of profitable nonautomobile-related operations such as its steelmaker, aerospace company, and electronic concerns."

28-2. Ford Motor Company II (L.O. 6)

By 1983 S & P had dropped the rating on Ford's bond issues to BBB. Selected data for the years ended December 31, 1982 and 1983, from Ford Motor Company's 1983 annual report appear below (in millions):

	1982	1983
Balance Sheet Data		
Short-Term Debt	$10,424.0	$10,315.9
Long-Term Debt	2,353.3	2,712.9
Stockholders' Equity	6,077.5	7,545.3
Total Assets	21,961.7	23,868.9
Income Statement Data		
Income (Loss) Before Income Taxes	(407.9)	2,166.3
Interest Expense	745.5	567.2
Statement of Changes in Financial Position		
Funds (Cash Basis) Provided by Operations	2,632.0	5,001.5

Required

1. Compute for 1982 and 1983 the same ratios that were used by S & P in Interpreting Accounting Information 28-1.
2. If you were S & P, would you raise the rating on Ford's long-term bonds in 1984? Why or why not?

Problem Set A

Problem 28A-1. Analyzing the Effects of Transactions on Ratios
(L.O. 6)

Sabo Corporation engaged in the transactions listed in the first column of the table below. Opposite each transaction is a ratio and space to indicate the effect of each transaction on the ratio.

Required

Place an X in the appropriate column, showing whether the transaction increased, decreased, or had no effect on the indicated ratio.

Transaction	Ratio	Effect: Increase	Effect: Decrease	Effect: None
a. Sold merchandise on account.	Current ratio			
b. Sold merchandise on account.	Inventory turnover			
c. Collected on accounts receivable.	Quick ratio			
d. Wrote off an uncollectible account.	Receivable turnover			
e. Paid on accounts payable.	Current ratio			
f. Declared a cash dividend.	Return on equity			
g. Incurred advertising expense.	Profit margin			
h. Issued stock dividend.	Debt to equity			
i. Issued bond payable.	Asset turnover			
j. Accrued interest expense.	Current ratio			
k. Paid previously declared cash dividend.	Dividends yield			
l. Purchased treasury stock.	Return on assets			

Problem 28A-2. Horizontal and Vertical Analysis
(L.O. 5)

The condensed comparative income statement and comparative balance sheet of Kuo Corporation follow. All figures are given in thousands of dollars.

Comparative income statement:

	19x2	19x1
Sales	$1,625,600	$1,573,200
Cost of Goods Sold	1,044,400	1,004,200
Gross Margin from Sales	$ 581,200	$ 569,000
Operating Expenses		
Sales Expenses	$ 238,400	$ 259,000
Administrative Expenses	223,600	211,600
Interest Expense	32,800	19,600
Income Taxes Expense	31,200	28,400
Total Operating Expenses	$ 526,000	$ 518,600
Net Income	$ 55,200	$ 50,400

Comparative balance sheet:

	19x2	19x1
Assets		
Cash	$ 40,600	$ 20,400
Accounts Receivable (net)	117,800	114,600
Inventory	287,400	297,400
Property, Plant, and Equipment (net)	375,000	360,000
Total Assets	$820,800	$792,400
Liabilities and Stockholders' Equity		
Accounts Payable	$133,800	$238,600
Notes Payable	100,000	200,000
Bonds Payable	200,000	—
Common Stock—$5 par value	200,000	200,000
Retained Earnings	187,000	153,800
Total Liabilities and Stockholders' Equity	$820,800	$792,400

Required

(Round percentages to one decimal point.)

1. Prepare a schedule, showing amount and percentage changes from 19x1 to 19x2 for the corporate income statement and balance sheet.
2. Prepare a common-size income statement and balance sheet for 19x1 and 19x2.
3. Comment on the results found in **1** and **2** by identifying favorable and unfavorable changes in components and composition.

Problem 28A-3. Ratio Analysis (L.O. 6)

Additional data for Kuo Corporation in 19x1 and 19x2 appear below. This information should be used along with the data in Problem 28A-2.

	19x2	19x1
Dividends Paid	$22,000,000	$17,200,000
Number of Common Shares	40,000,000	40,000,000
Market Price per Share	$9.00	$15.00
Beta	1.40	1.25

Balances of selected accounts at the end of 19x0 are Accounts Receivable (net), $103,400,000; Inventory, $273,600,000; Total Assets, $732,800,000; and Stockholders' Equity, $320,600,000. All of Kuo's Notes Payable are current liabilities; all the Bonds Payable are long-term liabilities.

Required

1. Conduct a liquidity analysis by calculating for each year the: (a) current ratio, (b) quick ratio, (c) receivable turnover, (d) average days' sales uncollected, and (e) inventory turnover. Indicate whether each ratio had a favorable (F) or unfavorable (U) change from 19x1 to 19x2.
2. Conduct a profitability analysis by calculating for each year the: (a) profit margin, (b) asset turnover, (c) return on assets, (d) return on equity, and (e) earnings per share. Indicate whether each ratio had a favorable (F) or unfavorable (U) change from 19x1 to 19x2.
3. Conduct a long-term solvency analysis by calculating for each year the: (a) debt to equity ratio, and (b) interest coverage ratio. Indicate whether each ratio had a favorable (F) or unfavorable (U) change from 19x1 to 19x2.
4. Conduct a market test analysis by calculating for each year the: (a) price/earnings ratio, (b) dividends yield, and (c) market risk. Note the market beta measures, and indicate whether each ratio had a favorable (F) or unfavorable (U) change from 19x1 to 19x2.

(Round percentages and ratios to one decimal point, and consider changes of .1 or less to be neutral.)

Problem 28A-4. Effect of Alternative Accounting Methods
(L.O. 4, 6)

Burnett Company began operations this year. At the beginning of the year, the company purchased plant assets of $330,000, with an estimated useful life of ten years and no salvage value.

During the year, the company had sales of $600,000, salary expense of $100,000, and other expenses of $40,000, excluding depreciation. In addition, the company purchased inventory as follows:

January 15	400 units at $200	$ 80,000
March 20	200 units at $204	40,800
June 15	800 units at $208	166,400
September 18	600 units at $206	123,600
December 9	300 units at $210	63,000
Total	2,300 units	$473,800

At the end of the year, a physical inventory disclosed 500 units still on hand. The managers of Burnett Company know they have a choice of accounting methods but are unsure how the methods will affect net income. They have heard of FIFO and LIFO for inventory methods and straight-line and sum-of-the-years'-digits for depreciation methods.

Required

1. Prepare two income statements for Burnett Company: one using FIFO basis and straight-line method; the other using LIFO basis and sum-of-the-years'-digits method.
2. Prepare a schedule, accounting for the difference in the two net income figures obtained in **1.**
3. What effect does the choice of accounting methods have on Burnett's inventory turnover? What conclusions can you draw?

4. What effect does the choice of accounting methods have on Burnett's return on assets? Use year-end balances to compute ratios. Assume the only other asset in addition to plant assets and inventory is cash of $40,000. Is your evaluation of Burnett's profitability affected by the choice of accounting methods?

Problem 28A-5. Comprehensive Ratio Analysis of Two Companies (L.O. 6)

Felipe Cardenas is considering an investment in the common stock of a chain of retail department stores. He has narrowed his choice to two retail companies, Bing Corporation and Sadecki Corporation, whose balance sheets and income statements are presented below and on the following page.

	Bing Corporation	Sadecki Corporation
Assets		
Cash	$ 80,000	$ 192,400
Marketable Securities (at cost)	203,400	84,600
Accounts Receivable (net)	552,800	985,400
Inventory	629,800	1,253,400
Prepaid Expenses	54,400	114,000
Property, Plant, and Equipment (net)	2,913,600	6,552,000
Intangibles and Other Assets	553,200	144,800
Total Assets	$4,987,200	$9,326,600
Liabilities and Stockholders' Equity		
Accounts Payable	$ 344,000	$ 572,600
Notes Payable	150,000	400,000
Accrued Liabilities	50,200	73,400
Bonds Payable	2,000,000	2,000,000
Common Stock—$10 par value	1,000,000	600,000
Paid-In Capital in Excess of Par Value, Common	609,800	3,568,600
Retained Earnings	833,200	2,112,000
Total Liabilities and Stockholders' Equity	$4,987,200	$9,326,600

During the year, Bing Corporation paid a total of $50,000 in dividends. The market price per share of its stock is currently $30. In comparison, Sadecki Corporation paid a total of $114,000 in dividends during the year, and the current market price of its stock is $38 per share. An investment service indicated the beta associated with Bing's stock is 1.20 and that associated with Sadecki's stock is .95. Information for prior years is not readily available. Assume all Notes Payable are current liabilities and all Bonds Payable are long-term liabilities.

	Bing Corporation	Sadecki Corporation
Sales	$12,560,000	$25,210,000
Cost of Goods Sold	6,142,000	14,834,000
Gross Margin from Sales	6,418,000	10,376,000
Operating Expenses		
Sales Expense	4,822,600	7,108,200
Administrative Expense	986,000	2,434,000
Interest Expense	194,000	228,000
Income Taxes Expense	200,000	300,000
Total Operating Expenses	6,202,600	10,070,200
Net Income	$ 215,400	$ 305,800

Required

Conduct a comprehensive ratio analysis of each company, using the available information, and compare the results. (Round percentages and ratios to one decimal point, and consider changes of .1 or less to be neutral.) This analysis should be done in the following steps:

1. Prepare an analysis of liquidity by calculating for each company the: (a) current ratio, (b) quick ratio, (c) receivable turnover, (d) average days' sales uncollected, and (e) inventory turnover.
2. Prepare an analysis of profitability by calculating for each company the: (a) profit margin, (b) asset turnover, (c) return on assets, (d) return on equity, and (e) earnings per share.
3. Prepare an analysis of long-term solvency by calculating for each company the: (a) debt to equity ratio, and (b) interest coverage ratio.
4. Prepare an analysis of market tests by calculating for each company the: (a) price/earnings ratio, (b) dividends yield, and (c) market risk.
5. Compare the analysis of each company by inserting the ratio calculations from **1** through **4** in a table with the following column heads: *Ratio Name, Bing Corporation, Sadecki Corporation,* and *Company with More Favorable Ratio.* Indicate in the right-hand column which company had the more favorable ratio in each case.
6. In what ways could the analysis be improved if prior years' information were available?

Problem Set B

Problem 28B-1. Analyzing the Effects of Transactions on Ratios (L.O. 6)

Brock Corporation engaged in the transactions listed in the first column of the table below. Opposite each transaction is a ratio and spaces to mark the effect of each transaction on the ratio.

Transaction	Ratio	Effect		
		Increase	Decrease	None
a. Issued common stock for cash.	Asset turnover			
b. Declared cash dividend.	Current ratio			
c. Sold treasury stock.	Return on equity			
d. Borrowed cash by issuing a note payable.	Debt to equity			
e. Paid salary expense.	Inventory turnover			
f. Purchased merchandise for cash.	Current ratio			
g. Sold equipment for cash.	Receivable turnover			
h. Sold merchandise on account.	Quick ratio			
i. Paid current portion of long-term debt.	Return on assets			
j. Gave a sales discount.	Profit margin			
k. Purchased marketable securities for cash.	Quick ratio			
l. Declared a 5% stock dividend.	Current ratio			

Required

Place an X in the appropriate column to show whether the transaction increased, decreased, or had no effect on the indicated ratio.

Problem 28B-2. Horizontal and Vertical Analysis (L.O. 5)

The condensed comparative statements of Jamali Corporation appear as shown on the next page.

Required

(Round all ratios and percentages to one decimal point.)

1. Prepare a schedule showing amount and percentage changes from 19x1 to 19x2 for the comparative income statement and balance sheet.
2. Prepare a common-size income statement and balance sheet for 19x1 and 19x2.
3. Comment on the results found in **1** and **2** by identifying favorable and unfavorable changes in components and composition.

Jamali Corporation
Comparative Income Statement
For the Years Ended December 31, 19x2 and 19x1

	19x2	19x1
Sales	$791,200	$742,600
Cost of Goods Sold	454,100	396,200
Gross Margin from Sales	337,100	346,400
Operating Expenses		
Selling Expenses	130,100	104,600
Administrative Expenses	140,300	115,500
Interest Expense	25,000	20,000
Income Taxes Expense	14,000	35,000
Total Operating Expenses	309,400	275,100
Net Income	$ 27,700	$ 71,300

Jamali Corporation
Comparative Balance Sheet
December 31, 19x2 and 19x1

	19x2	19x1
Assets		
Cash	$ 31,100	$ 27,200
Accounts Receivable (net)	72,500	42,700
Inventory	122,600	107,800
Property, Plant, and Equipment	577,700	507,500
Total Assets	$803,900	$685,200
Liabilities and Stockholders' Equity		
Accounts Payable	$104,700	$ 72,300
Notes Payable	50,000	50,000
Bonds Payable	200,000	110,000
Common Stock—$10 par value	300,000	300,000
Retained Earnings	149,200	152,900
Total Liabilities and Stockholders' Equity	$803,900	$685,200

Problem 28B-3. Ratio Analysis (L.O. 6)

Additional data for Jamali Corporation in 19x1 and 19x2 appear below. These data should be used in conjunction with the data in Problem 28B-2.

	19x2	19x1
Dividends Paid	$31,400	$35,000
Number of Common Shares	30,000	30,000
Market Price per Share	40	60
Beta	1.00	.90

Balances of selected accounts for 19x0 are Accounts Receivable (net), $52,700; Inventory, $99,400; Total Assets, $647,800; and Stockholders' Equity, $376,600. All of Jamali's Notes Payable are current liabilities; all the Bonds Payable are long-term liabilities.

Required

1. Prepare a liquidity analysis by calculating for 19x1 and 19x2 the (a) current ratio, (b) quick ratio, (c) receivable turnover, (d) average days' sales uncollected, and (e) inventory turnover. Indicate whether each ratio improved or not from 19x1 to 19x2 by using an F for favorable or U for unfavorable.
2. Prepare a profitability analysis by calculating for each year the (a) profit margin, (b) asset turnover, (c) return on assets, (d) return on equity, and (e) earnings per share. Indicate whether each ratio had a favorable (F) or unfavorable (U) change from 19x1 to 19x2.
3. Prepare a long-term solvency analysis by calculating for each year the (a) debt to equity ratio and (b) interest coverage ratio. Indicate whether each ratio had a favorable (F) or unfavorable (U) change from 19x1 to 19x2.
4. Conduct a market test analysis by calculating for each year the (a) price/earnings ratio, (b) dividends yield, and (c) market risk. Note the market risk measure, and indicate whether each ratio had a favorable (F) or unfavorable (U) change from 19x1 to 19x2.

Note: Round all answers to one decimal point, and consider changes of .1 or less to be neutral.

Problem 28B-4. Effect of Alternative Accounting Methods (L.O. 4, 6)

Owen Company began operations by purchasing $200,000 in equipment that has an estimated useful life of nine years and an estimated residual value of $20,000.

During the year, the company purchased inventory as follows:

January	2,000 units at $25	$ 50,000
March	4,000 units at $24	96,000
May	1,000 units at $27	27,000
July	5,000 units at $27	135,000
September	6,000 units at $28	168,000
November	2,000 units at $29	58,000
December	3,000 units at $28	84,000
Totals	23,000 units	$618,000

The company sold 19,000 units for a total of $880,000 and incurred salary expenses of $170,000 and expenses other than depreciation of $120,000.

Owen's management is anxious to present its income statement most fairly in its first year of operation and realizes that there are alternative accounting methods available for accounting for inventory and equipment. Management wants to determine the effect of various alternatives on this year's income. Two sets of alternatives are required.

Required

1. Prepare two income statements for Owen Company: one using FIFO basis for inventory and straight-line method for depreciation; the other using LIFO basis for inventory and sum-of-the-years'-digits method for depreciation.
2. Prepare a schedule accounting for the difference in the two net income figures obtained in **1.**
3. What effect does the choice of accounting methods have on Owen's inventory turnover? What conclusion can you draw?
4. What effect does the choice of accounting methods have on Owen's return on assets? Use year-end balances to compute ratios, assuming the only other asset in addition to plant assets and inventory is cash of $30,000. Is your evaluation of Owen's profitability affected by the choice of accounting methods?

Problem 28B-5. Comprehensive Ratio Analysis of Two Companies
(L.O. 6)

Geraldine Ming has decided to invest some of her savings in common stock. She feels that the chemical industry has good growth prospects and has narrowed her choice to two companies in that industry. As a final step in making the choice, she decided to make a comprehensive ratio analysis of two companies, Berland and Schmidt. Balance sheet and income statement data for the two companies appear below and on the next page.

During the year, Berland paid a total of $140,000 in dividends, and the current market price per share of its stock is $20. Schmidt paid a total of $600,000 in dividends during the year, and the current market price per share of its stock is $9. An investment service reports that the beta associated with Berland's stock is 1.05 and that associated with Schmidt's is .8. Information pertaining to prior years is not readily available. Assume that all Notes Payable are current liabilities and that all Bonds Payable are long-term liabilities.

	Berland	Schmidt
Assets		
Cash	$ 126,100	$ 514,300
Marketable Securities (at cost)	117,500	1,200,000
Accounts Receivable (net)	456,700	2,600,000
Inventories	1,880,000	4,956,000
Prepaid Expenses	72,600	156,600
Property, Plant, and Equipment (net)	5,342,200	19,356,000
Intangibles and Other Assets	217,000	580,000
Total Assets	$8,212,100	$29,362,900

	Berland	Schmidt
Liabilities and Stockholders' Equity		
Accounts Payable	$ 517,400	$ 2,342,000
Notes Payable	1,000,000	2,000,000
Income Taxes Payable	85,200	117,900
Bonds Payable	2,000,000	15,000,000
Common Stock—$1 par value	350,000	1,000,000
Paid-in Capital in Excess of Par Value, Common	1,747,300	5,433,300
Retained Earnings	2,512,200	3,469,700
Total Liabilities and Stockholders' Equity	$8,212,100	$29,362,900

	Berland	Schmidt
Sales	$9,486,200	$27,287,300
Cost of Goods Sold	5,812,200	$18,372,400
Gross Margin from Sales	3,674,000	8,914,900
Operating Expenses		
Selling Expense	1,194,000	1,955,700
Administrative Expense	1,217,400	4,126,000
Interest Expense	270,000	1,360,000
Income Taxes Expense	450,000	600,000
Total Operating Expenses	3,131,400	8,041,700
Net Income	$ 542,600	$ 873,200

Required

Conduct a comprehensive ratio analysis of each company using the current end-of-year data. Compare the results. (Round all ratios and percentages to one decimal point.) This analysis should be done in the following steps:

1. Prepare an analysis of liquidity by calculating for each company the (a) current ratio, (b) quick ratio, (c) receivable turnover, (d) average days' sales uncollected, and (e) inventory turnover.
2. Prepare an analysis of profitability by calculating for each company the (a) profit margin, (b) asset turnover, (c) return on assets, (d) return on equity, and (e) earnings per share.
3. Prepare an analysis of long-term solvency by calculating for each company the (a) debt to equity ratio and (b) interest coverage ratio.
4. Prepare an analysis of market tests by calculating for each company the (a) price/earnings ratio, (b) dividends yield, and (c) market risk.

5. Compare the analysis of each company by inserting the ratio calculations from **1** through **4** in a table with the column heads *Ratio Name; Berland; Schmidt; Company with More Favorable Ratio.* In the right-hand column of the table indicate which company had the more favorable ratio in each case. (If the ratios are within .1 of each other, consider them neutral.)
6. How could the analysis be improved if prior years' data were available?

Decision Case

Tedtronics Corporation
(L.O. 4)

Ted Lazzerini retired at the beginning of 19x1 as president and principal stockholder in Tedtronics Corporation, a successful producer of word-processing equipment. As an incentive to the new management, Ted supported the board of directors' new executive compensation plan, which provides cash bonuses to key executives for the years in which the company's earnings per share exceed the current dividends per share of $2.00, plus a $.20 per share increase in dividends for each future year. Thus for management to receive the bonuses, the company must earn per share income of $2.00 the first year, $2.20 the second, $2.40 the third, and so forth. Since Ted owns 500,000 of the 1,000,000 common shares outstanding, the dividend income will provide for his retirement years. He is also protected against inflation by the regular increase in dividends.

Earnings and dividends per share for the first three years of operation under the new management were as follows:

	19x3	19x2	19x1
Earnings per share	$2.50	$2.50	$2.50
Dividends per share	2.40	2.20	2.00

During this time management earned bonuses totaling more than $1,000,000 under the compensation plan. Ted, who had taken no active part on the board of directors, began to worry about the unchanging level of earnings and decided to study the company's annual report more carefully. The notes to the annual report revealed the following information:

a. Management changed from using the LIFO inventory method to the FIFO method in 19x1. The effect of this change was to decrease cost of goods sold by $200,000 in 19x1, $300,000 in 19x2, and $400,000 in 19x3.
b. Management changed from using the double-declining-balance accelerated depreciation method to the straight-line method in 19x2. The effect of this change was to decrease depreciation by $400,000 in 19x2 and by $500,000 in 19x3.
c. In 19x3, management increased the estimated useful life of intangible assets from five to ten years. The effect of this change was to decrease amortization expense by $100,000 in 19x3.

Required

1. Compute earnings per share for each year according to the accounting methods in use at the beginning of 19x1.
2. Have the executives earned their bonuses? What serious effect has the compensation package apparently had on the net assets of Tedtronics? How could Ted have protected himself from what has happened?

APPENDIX A SPECIAL-PURPOSE JOURNALS

LEARNING OBJECTIVES

1. Explain the objectives and uses of special-purpose journals.
2. Construct and use a sales journal.
3. Construct and use a purchases journal.
4. Construct and use a cash receipts journal.
5. Construct and use a cash payments journal and other special-purpose journals.

Large companies, faced with hundreds or thousands of transactions every week and perhaps every day, must have an efficient and economical way of recording transactions in the journal and posting entries to the ledger. The easiest and most usual way to do this is to group the company's typical transactions into common categories and use an input device, called a **special-purpose journal,** for each category. The special-purpose journals add no new theory to accounting. They are simply aids to record keeping. After completing this appendix you should be able to meet the learning objectives listed on the left.

Types of Special-Purpose Journals

Most business transactions, usually 90 to 95 percent, fall into one of four categories. Each kind of transaction may be recorded in a special-purpose journal as shown below.

Transaction	Special-Purpose Journal	Posting Abbreviation
Sales of merchandise on credit	Sales journal	S
Purchases on credit	Purchases journal	P
Receipts of cash	Cash receipts journal	CR
Disbursements of cash	Cash payments journal	CP

The general journal is used for recording transactions that do not fall into any of the special categories. For example, purchase returns, sales returns, and adjusting and closing entries are recorded in the general journal. (When transactions are posted from the general journal to the ledger accounts, the posting abbreviation used is J.) It is important to note that use of these four journals greatly reduces the amount of detailed recording work. In addition a division of labor can be gained if each journal is assigned to a different employee. This division of labor is very important in establishing good internal control, as shown in Chapter 6.

Sales Journal

Special-purpose journals are designed to record particular kinds of transactions. Thus all transactions in a special-purpose journal result in debits and credits to the same accounts. The **sales journal,** for example, is designed to handle all credit sales, and only credit sales.

OBJECTIVE 2
Construct and use a sales journal.

Exhibit A-1 illustrates a typical sales journal. Six sales transactions involving five people are recorded in this sales journal. As each sale takes place, several copies of the sales invoice are made. The accounting department of the seller uses one copy to make the entry in the sales journal. From the invoices are copied the date, the customer's name, the invoice number, the amount of the sale, and possibly the credit terms. These data correspond to the columns of the sales journal. If the seller commonly offers different credit terms to different customers, one more column showing the terms can be used. In this case, we assume that each customer has received the same credit terms.

Note the following time-saving features of the sales journal:

1. Only one line is needed to record each transaction. Each entry consists of a debit to each customer in Accounts Receivable. The corresponding credit to Sales is understood.
2. Account names do not have to be written out, because account names occurring most frequently are used as column headings. Thus entry in a column has the effect of debiting or crediting the account.
3. No explanations are necessary, because the function of the special-purpose journal is to record one type of transaction. Only credit sales can be recorded in the sales journal. Sales for cash must be recorded in the cash receipts journal, which is described later in this chapter.
4. Only one amount—the total credit sales for the month—needs to be posted. It is posted twice: once as a debit to Accounts Receivable and once as a credit to Sales. Instead of the six sales entries in the example, there might be hundreds of actual sales transactions in a more realistic situation. Thus one can see the saving in posting time.

Controlling Accounts and Subsidiary Ledgers. Every entry in the sales journal represents a debit to a customer's account in Accounts Receivable. In previous chapters, all such transactions have been posted to Accounts Receivable. However, this single Accounts Receivable entry does not readily tell how much each customer bought and paid for or how much each customer owes. In practice, almost all companies that sell to customers on credit keep an individual accounts receivable record for each customer. If the company has 6,000 credit customers, there are 6,000 accounts receivable. To include all these accounts in the ledger with the other assets, liabilities, and owner's equity accounts would make it very bulky. Consequently, most companies take the individual customers' accounts out of the general ledger, which contains the financial statement accounts, and place them in a separate ledger called a **subsidiary ledger**. The customers' accounts are filed alphabetically in this accounts receivable ledger or numerically if account numbers are used.

When a company puts its individual customers' accounts in an accounts receivable ledger, there is still a need for an Accounts Receivable account in the general ledger to maintain its balance. This Accounts Receivable account in the general ledger is said to control the subsidiary ledger and is called a **controlling** or **control account**. It is a controlling account in the sense that its balance should equal the total of the individual account balances in the subsidiary ledger. This is true because in transactions involving accounts

Exhibit A-1. Sales Journal and Related Ledger Accounts

Sales Journal — Page 1

Date		Account Debited	Invoice Number	Post. Ref.	Debit/Credit Accounts Receivable/ Sales
July	1	Peter Clark	721	✓	750
	5	Georgetta Jones	722	✓	500
	8	Eugene Cumberland	723	✓	335
	12	Maxwell Hertz	724	✓	1,165
	18	Peter Clark	725	✓	1,225
	25	Michael Powers	726	✓	975
					4,950
					(114/411)

Post total at end of month.

Accounts Receivable — 114

Date		Post. Ref.	Debit	Credit	Balance Debit	Balance Credit
July	31	S1	4,950		4,950	

Sales — 411

Date		Post. Ref.	Debit	Credit	Balance Debit	Balance Credit
July	31	S1		4,950		4,950

receivable, such as credit sales, there must be postings to the individual customer accounts every day and to the controlling account in the general ledger in total each month. If a wrong amount has been posted, the sum of all customer account balances in the receivable subsidiary accounts ledger will not equal the balance of the Accounts Receivable controlling account in the general ledger. When these amounts do not match, the accountant knows that there is an error and can find and correct it.

The concept of controlling accounts is shown in Exhibit A-2, where boxes are used for the accounts receivable ledger and the general ledger. The principle involved is that the single controlling account in the general ledger takes the place of all the individual accounts in the subsidiary ledger. The trial balance can be prepared using only the general ledger accounts.

Most companies, as you will see, use an accounts payable subsidiary ledger as well. It is also possible to use a subsidiary ledger for almost any account in the general ledger where management wants a specific account for individual items, such as Merchandise Inventory, Notes Receivable, Temporary Investments, and Equipment.

Summary of the Sales Journal Procedure. Observe from Exhibit A-2 that the procedures for using a sales journal are as follows:

Exhibit A-2. Relationship of Sales Journal, General Ledger, and Accounts Receivable Ledger and the Posting Procedure

Sales Journal — Page 1

Date		Account Debited	Invoice Number	Post. Ref.	Debit/Credit Accounts Receivable/ Sales
July	1	Peter Clark	721	✓	750
	5	Georgetta Jones	722	✓	500
	8	Eugene Cumberland	723	✓	335
	12	Maxwell Hertz	724	✓	1,165
	18	Peter Clark	725	✓	1,225
	25	Michael Powers	726	✓	975
					4,950
					(114/411)

Post individual amounts daily to subsidiary ledger accounts.

Post total at end of month to general ledger accounts.

Accounts Receivable Ledger

Peter Clark

Date		Post Ref.	Debit	Credit	Balance
July	1	S1	750		750
	18	S1	1,225		1,975

Eugene Cumberland

Date		Post. Ref.	Debit	Credit	Balance
July	8	S1	335		335

Continue posting to Maxwell Hertz, Georgetta Jones, and Michael Powers.

General Ledger

Accounts Receivable — 114

Date		Post. Ref.	Debit	Credit	Balance Debit	Balance Credit
July	31	S1	4,950		4,950	

Sales — 411

Date		Post. Ref.	Debit	Credit	Balance Debit	Balance Credit
July	31	S1		4,950		4,950

1. Enter each sales invoice in the sales journal on a single line, recording date, customer's name, invoice number, and amount.
2. At the end of each day, post each individual sale to the customer's account in the accounts receivable ledger. As each sale is posted, place a check mark in the Post. Ref. (posting reference) column to indicate that it has been posted. In the Post. Ref. column of each customer account, place an S1 (representing Sales Journal—page 1) to indicate the source of the entry.

3. At the end of the month, sum the Debit/Credit column to determine the total credit sales, and post the total to the general ledger accounts (debit Accounts Receivable and credit Sales). Place the numbers of the accounts debited and credited beneath the total in the sales journal to indicate that this step has been completed, and place an S1 in the Post. Ref. column of each account to indicate the source of the entry.
4. Verify the accuracy of the posting by adding the account balances of the accounts receivable ledger and by matching the total with the Accounts Receivable controlling account balance in the general ledger. This step can be accomplished by listing the accounts in a schedule of accounts receivable, as shown in Exhibit A-3.

Sales Taxes. Other columns, such as a column for credit terms, can be added to the sales journal. The nature of the company's business will determine whether they are needed.

Many cities and states require retailers to collect a sales tax from their customers and periodically remit the total amount of the tax to the state or city. In this case, an additional column is needed in the sales journal to record the necessary credit to Sales Taxes Payable. The required entry is illustrated in Exhibit A-4. The procedure for posting to the ledger is exactly the same as previously described except that the total of the Sales Taxes Payable column must be posted as a credit to the Sales Taxes Payable account at the end of the month.

Most companies also make cash sales. Cash sales are usually recorded in a column of the cash receipts journal. This procedure is discussed later in the chapter.

Purchases Journal

OBJECTIVE 3
Construct and use a purchases journal

The techniques associated with the sales journal are very similar to those of the purchases journal. The **purchases journal** is used to record all purchases on credit and may take the form of either a single-column journal or a multicolumn journal. In the single-column journal, shown in Exhibit A-5,

Exhibit A-3. Schedule of Accounts Receivable

Mitchell's Used Car Sales
Schedule of Accounts Receivable
July 31, 19xx

Peter Clark	$1,975
Eugene Cumberland	335
Maxwell Hertz	1,165
Georgetta Jones	500
Michael Powers	975
Total Accounts Receivable	$4,950

Exhibit A-4. Section of a Sales Journal with a Column for Sales Taxes

Sales Journal							Page 7
					Debit	Credits	
Date		Account Debited	Invoice Number	Post. Ref.	Accounts Receivable	Sales Taxes Payable	Sales
Sept.	1	Ralph P. Hake	727	✓	206	6	200

only credit purchases of merchandise for resale to customers are recorded. This kind of transaction is recorded with a debit to Purchases and a credit to Accounts Payable. When the single-column purchases journal is used, credit purchases of things other than merchandise are recorded in the general journal. Also, cash purchases are not recorded in the purchases journal but in the cash payments journal, which is explained later.

As with Accounts Receivable, the Accounts Payable account in the general ledger is used by most companies as a controlling account. So that the company will know how much it owes each supplier, it keeps a separate account for each supplier in an accounts payable subsidiary ledger. The ideas and techniques described above for the accounts receivable subsidiary ledger and general ledger account apply also to the accounts payable subsidiary ledger and general ledger account. Thus the total of the separate accounts in the accounts payable subsidiary ledger will equal the balance of the Accounts Payable controlling account in the general ledger. The reason is that the total of the individual credit purchases posted to the separate accounts each day is equal to the total credit purchases posted to the controlling account each month.

The steps for using a purchases journal, as shown in Exhibit A-5, are as follows:

1. Enter each purchase invoice in the purchases journal on a single line, recording date, supplier's name, invoice date, terms if given, and amount.
2. At the end of each day, post each individual purchase to the supplier's account in the accounts payable subsidiary ledger. As each purchase is posted, place a check in the Post. Ref. column of the purchases journal to show that it has been posted. Also place a P1 (representing Purchases Journal—page 1) in the Post. Ref. column of each supplier's account to show the source of the entry.
3. At the end of the month, sum the credit purchases, and post the amount in the general ledger accounts (Accounts Payable and Purchases). Place the numbers of the accounts debited and credited beneath the total in the purchases journal to show that this step has been carried out.

Exhibit A-5. Relationship of Single-Column Purchases Journal to the General Ledger and the Accounts Payable Ledger

Purchases Journal — Page 1

Date		Account Credited	Date of Invoice	Terms	Post. Ref.	Debit/Credit Purchases/ Accounts Payable
July	1	Jones Chevrolet	7/1	2/10, n/30	✓	2,500
	2	Marshall Ford	7/1	2/15, n/30	✓	300
	3	Dealer Sales	7/3	n/30	✓	700
	12	Thomas Auto	7/11	n/30	✓	1,400
	17	Dealer Sales	7/17	2/10, n/30	✓	3,200
	19	Thomas Auto	7/17	n/30	✓	1,100
						9,200
						(511/212)

Post individual amounts daily.

Post total at end of month.

Accounts Payable Ledger

Dealer Sales

Date		Post. Ref.	Debit	Credit	Balance
July	3	P1		700	700
	17	P1		3,200	3,900

Jones Chevrolet

Date		Post. Ref.	Debit	Credit	Balance
July	1	P1		2,500	2,500

Continue posting to Marshall Ford and Thomas Auto.

General Ledger

Accounts Payable — 212

Date		Post. Ref.	Debit	Credit	Balance Debit	Balance Credit
July	31	P1		9,200		9,200

Purchases — 511

Date		Post. Ref.	Debit	Credit	Balance Debit	Balance Credit
July	31	P1	9,200		9,200	

4. Check the accuracy of the posting by adding the balances of the accounts payable ledger accounts and matching the total with the Accounts Payable controlling account balance in the general ledger. This step may be carried out by preparing a schedule of accounts payable.

The single-column purchases journal may be expanded to record credit purchases of things other than merchandise by adding a separate column for other debit accounts that are often used. For example, the multicolumn purchases journal in Exhibit A-6 has columns for Freight In, Store Supplies, Office Supplies, and Other. Here the total credits to Accounts Payable ($9,437) equal the total debits to Purchases, Freight In, Store Supplies, and Office Supplies ($9,200 + $50 + $145 + $42 = $9,437). As in the procedure already described, the individual transactions in the Accounts Payable column are posted daily to the accounts payable subsidiary ledger, and the totals of each column in the journal are posted monthly to the correct general ledger accounts. Some credit purchases call for a debit to an account that has no special column (that is, no place to record the debit) in the purchases journal. These transactions are recorded in the Other Accounts column with an indication of the account to which the debit is to be made.

Cash Receipts Journal

OBJECTIVE 4
Construct and use a cash receipts journal

All transactions involving receipts of cash are recorded in the **cash receipts journal.** Examples of such transactions are cash from cash sales, cash from credit customers in payment of their accounts, and cash from other sources. To be most efficient, the cash receipts journal must be multicolumn. Several columns are necessary because, though all cash receipts are alike in that they require a debit to Cash, they are different in that they require a variety of credit entries. Thus you should be alert to several important differences between the cash receipts journal and the journals previously presented. Among these differences are an Other Accounts column, use of account numbers in the Post. Ref. column, and daily posting of the credits to Other Accounts.

Exhibit A-6. A Multicolumn Purchases Journal

Purchases Journal — Page 1

					Credit	Debits						
										Other Accounts		
Date	Account Credited	Date of Invoice	Terms	Post. Ref.	Accounts Payable	Purchases	Freight In	Store Supplies	Office Supplies	Account	Post. Ref.	Amount
July 1	Jones Chevrolet	7/1	2/10, n/30	✓	2,500	2,500						
2	Marshall Ford	7/1	2/15, n/30	✓	300	300						
2	Shelby Car Delivery	7/2	n/30	✓	50		50					
3	Dealer Sales	7/3	n/30	✓	700	700						
12	Thomas Auto	7/11	n/30	✓	1,400	1,400						
17	Dealer Sales	7/17	2/10, n/30	✓	3,200	3,200						
19	Thomas Auto	7/17	n/30	✓	1,100	1,100						
25	Osborne Supply	7/21	n/10th	✓	187			145	42			
					9,437	9,200	50	145	42			
					(212)	(511)	(514)	(132)	(133)			

The cash receipts journal illustrated in Exhibit A-7 is based on the following selected transactions for July:

July 1 Henry Mitchell invested $20,000 in a used-car business.
5 Sold a used car for $1,200 cash.
8 Collected $500 from Georgetta Jones, less 2 percent sales discount.
13 Sold a used car for $1,400 cash.
16 Collected $750 from Peter Clark.
19 Sold a used car for $1,000 cash.
20 Sold some equipment not used in the business for $500 cash.
24 Signed a note at the bank for a loan of $5,000.
26 Sold a used car for $1,600 cash.
28 Collected $600 from Peter Clark, less 2 percent sales discount.

The cash receipts journal, as illustrated in Exhibit A-7, has three debit columns and three credit columns. The three debit columns record Cash Sales Discounts, and Other Accounts.

1. *Cash* Each entry must have an amount in this column because each transaction must be a receipt of cash.
2. *Sales Discounts* The company in the illustration allows a 2 percent discount for prompt payment. Therefore, it is useful to have a column for sales discounts. Note that in the transactions of July 8 and 28, the debits to Cash and Sales Discounts equal the credit to Accounts Receivable.
3. *Other Accounts* The Other Accounts column is sometimes called Sundry Accounts and is used in the case of transactions that involve a debit to Cash and a debit to some other account besides Sales Discounts.

The credit columns are the following:

1. *Accounts Receivable* This column is used to record collections on account from customers. The customer's name is written in the space entitled Account Credited so that the payment can be entered in his or her account in the accounts receivable ledger.
2. *Sales* This column is used to record all cash sales during the month. Retail firms that normally use cash registers would make an entry at the end of each day for the total sales from each cash register for that day. The debit, of course, is in the Cash Debit column.
3. *Other Accounts* This column is used for the credit portion of any entry that is neither a cash collection from accounts receivable nor a cash sale. The name of the account to be credited is indicated in the Account Credited column. For example, the transactions of July 1, 20, and 24 involved credits to accounts other than Accounts Receivable or Sales. If a company finds that it is consistently crediting a certain account in the Other Accounts column, it may be appropriate to add another credit column to the cash receipts journal for that particular account.

The posting of the cash receipts journal, as illustrated in Exhibit A-7 can be summarized as:

1. Post the Accounts Receivable column daily to each individual account in the accounts receivable subsidiary ledger. A check mark in the Post. Ref.

Exhibit A-7. Relationship of the Cash Receipts Journal to the General Ledger and the Accounts Receivable Ledger

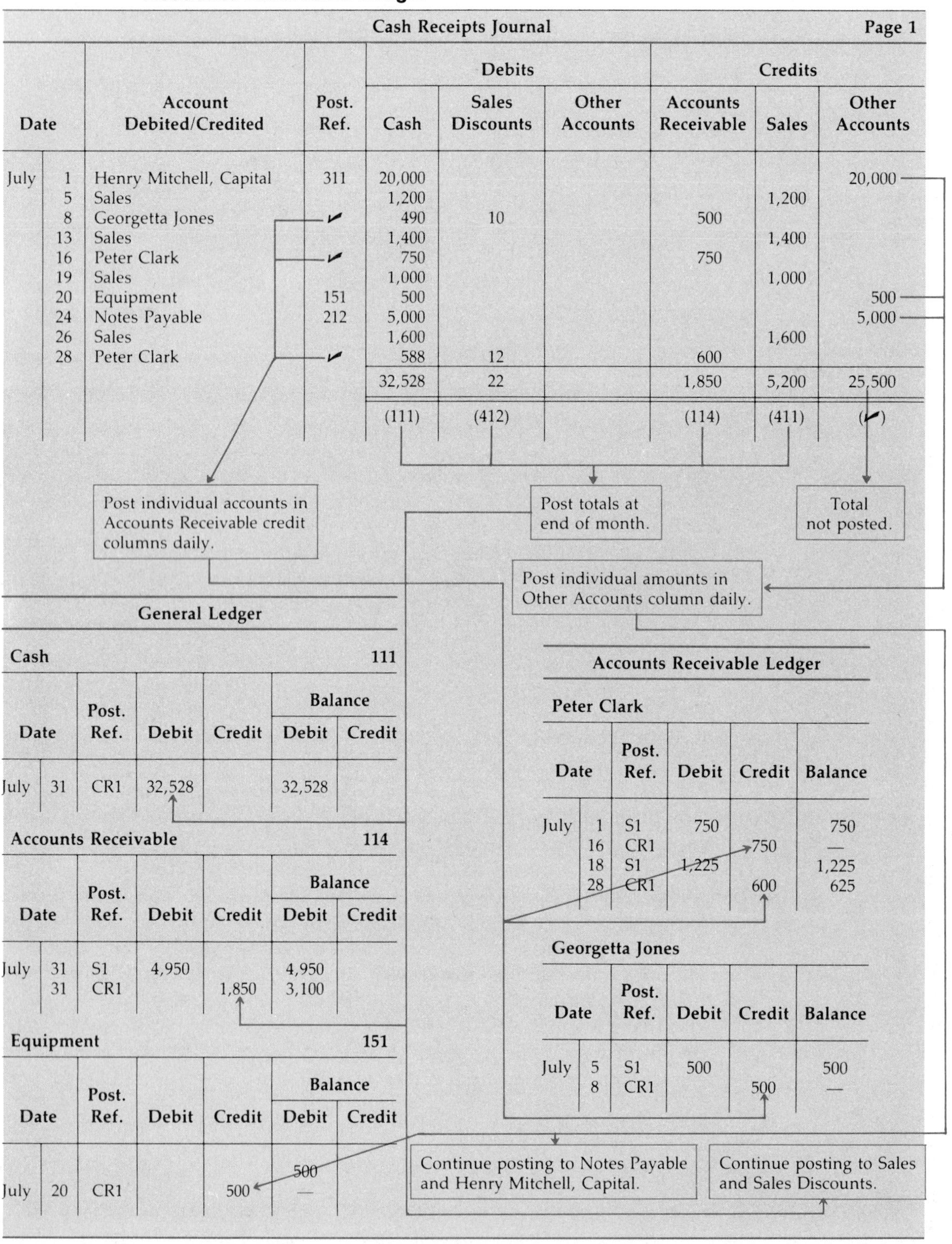

Cash Receipts Journal — Page 1

Date		Account Debited/Credited	Post. Ref.	Debits: Cash	Debits: Sales Discounts	Debits: Other Accounts	Credits: Accounts Receivable	Credits: Sales	Credits: Other Accounts
July	1	Henry Mitchell, Capital	311	20,000					20,000
	5	Sales		1,200				1,200	
	8	Georgetta Jones	✓	490	10		500		
	13	Sales		1,400				1,400	
	16	Peter Clark	✓	750			750		
	19	Sales		1,000				1,000	
	20	Equipment	151	500					500
	24	Notes Payable	212	5,000					5,000
	26	Sales		1,600				1,600	
	28	Peter Clark	✓	588	12		600		
				32,528	22		1,850	5,200	25,500
				(111)	(412)		(114)	(411)	(✓)

General Ledger

Cash — 111

Date		Post. Ref.	Debit	Credit	Balance: Debit	Balance: Credit
July	31	CR1	32,528		32,528	

Accounts Receivable — 114

Date		Post. Ref.	Debit	Credit	Balance: Debit	Balance: Credit
July	31	S1	4,950		4,950	
	31	CR1		1,850	3,100	

Equipment — 151

Date		Post. Ref.	Debit	Credit	Balance: Debit	Balance: Credit
					500	
July	20	CR1		500	—	

Accounts Receivable Ledger

Peter Clark

Date		Post. Ref.	Debit	Credit	Balance
July	1	S1	750		750
	16	CR1		750	—
	18	S1	1,225		1,225
	28	CR1		600	625

Georgetta Jones

Date		Post. Ref.	Debit	Credit	Balance
July	5	S1	500		500
	8	CR1		500	—

column of the cash receipts journal indicates that the amount has been posted, and a CR1 (representing Cash Receipts Journal—page 1) in the Post. Ref. column of each account indicates the source of the entry.

2. Post the debits/credits in the Other Accounts columns daily or at convenient short intervals during the month to the general ledger accounts. Write the account number in the Post. Ref. column as the individual items are posted to indicate that the posting has been done, and write CR1 in the Post. Ref. column of each account to indicate the source of the entry.
3. At the end of the month, total the columns. The sum of the debit column totals must equal the sum of the credit column totals, as follows:

Debit Column Totals		**Credit Column Totals**	
Cash	$32,528	Accounts Receivable	$ 1,850
Sales Discounts	22	Sales	5,200
Other Accounts	0	Other Accounts	25,500
Total Debits	$32,550	Total Credits	$32,550

This step is called crossfooting—a procedure we encountered earlier.

4. Post the column totals as follows:
   a. Cash debit column—posted as a debit to the Cash account.
   b. Sales Discounts debit column—posted as a debit to the Sales Discounts account.
   c. Accounts Receivable credit column—posted as a credit to the Accounts Receivable controlling account.
   d. Sales credit column—posted as a credit to the Sales account.
   e. The account numbers are written below each column as they are posted to indicate that this step has been completed. A CR1 is written in the Post. Ref. column of each account to indicate the source of the entry.
   f. Note that the Other Accounts column totals are not posted by total because each entry was posted separately. The individual accounts were posted in step 2 above. Accountants place a check mark at the bottom of the column to show that it is not posted.

Cash Payments Journal

OBJECTIVE 5
Construct and use a cash payments journal and other special-purpose journals

All transactions involving payments of cash are recorded in the **cash payments journal** (also called the cash disbursements journal). Examples of such transactions are cash purchases, payments of obligations resulting from earlier purchases on credit, and other cash payments. As with the cash receipts journal, the cash payments journal must be multicolumn and is similar in design to the cash receipts journal.

The cash payments journal illustrated in Exhibit A-8 is based on the following selected transactions of Mitchell's Used Car Sales for July:

July 2 Purchased merchandise (a used car) from Sondra Tidmore for cash, $400.

Exhibit A-8. Cash Payments Journal

Cash Payments Journal — Page 1

Date		Ck. No.	Payee	Account Credited/Debited	Post. Ref.	Credits: Cash	Credits: Purchases Discounts	Credits: Other Accounts	Debits: Accounts Payable	Debits: Other Accounts
July	2	101	Sondra Tidmore	Purchases	511	400				400
	6	102	*Daily Journal*	Advertising	612	200				200
	8	103	Siviglia Agency	Rent Expense	631	250				250
	11	104	Jones Chevrolet		✓	2,450	50		2,500	
	16	105	Charles Kuntz	Salary Expense	611	600				600
	17	106	Marshall Ford		✓	294	6		300	
	24	107	Grabow & Co.	Prepaid Insurance	119	480				480
	27	108	Dealer Sales		✓	3,136	64		3,200	
	30	109	A & B Equipment Company	Office Equipment	144					400
				Service Equipment	146	900				500
	31	110	Burns Real Estate	Notes Payable/Land	212/141	5,000		10,000		15,000
						13,710	120	10,000	6,000	17,830
						(111)	(512)	(✓)	(211)	(✓)

Post individual amounts in Other Accounts column daily.

Post individual amounts in Accounts Payable column daily.

Post totals at end of month.

Totals not posted.

General Ledger

Cash — 111

Date		Post. Ref.	Debit	Credit	Balance Debit	Balance Credit
July	31	CR1	32,528		32,528	
	31	CP1		13,710	18,818	

Prepaid Insurance — 119

Date		Post. Ref.	Debit	Credit	Balance Debit	Balance Credit
July	24	CP1	480		480	

Continue posting to Land, Office Equipment, Service Equipment, Notes Payable, Purchases, Salary Expenses, Advertising, and Rent Expense.

Continue posting to Purchases Discounts and Accounts Payable.

Accounts Payable Ledger

Jones Chevrolet

Date		Post. Ref.	Debit	Credit	Balance
July	1	P1		2,500	2,500
	11	CP1	2,500		—

Marshall Ford

Date		Post. Ref.	Debit	Credit	Balance
July	2	P1		300	300
	17	CP1	300		—

Dealer Sales

Date		Post. Ref.	Debit	Credit	Balance
July	3	P1		700	700
	17	P1		3,200	3,900
	27	CP1	3,200		700

6 Paid for newspaper advertising in the *Daily Journal,* $200.
8 Paid one month's land and building rent to Siviglia Agency, $250.
11 Paid Jones Chevrolet for July 1 invoice (previously recorded in purchases journal in Exhibit A-5), $2,500, less 2 percent purchase discount earned for payment in ten days or less.
16 Paid Charles Kuntz, a salesperson, his salary, $600.
17 Paid Marshall Ford invoice of July 2 (previously recorded in purchases journal in Exhibit A-5), $300, less 2 percent discount earned for payment in fifteen days or less.
24 Paid Grabow & Company for two-year insurance policy, $480.
27 Paid Dealer Sales invoice of July 17 (previously recorded in purchases journal in Exhibit A-5), $3,200, less 2 percent purchase discount earned for payment in ten days or less.
30 Purchased office equipment for $400 and service equipment for $500 from A & B Equipment Company. Issued one check for the total cost.
31 Purchased land for $15,000. Issued check for $5,000 and note payable for $10,000.

The cash payments journal, as illustrated in Exhibit A-8, has three credit columns and two debit columns. The credit columns are as follows:

1. *Cash* Each entry must have an amount in this column because each transaction must involve a payment of cash.
2. *Purchases Discounts* When purchases discounts are taken, they are recorded in this column.
3. *Other Accounts* This column is used to record credits other than Cash or Purchases Discounts. Note that the July 31 transaction shows a purchase of Land for $15,000 by issuing a check for $5,000 and a Note Payable for $10,000.

The debit columns are as follows:

1. *Accounts Payable* This column total is used to record payments to suppliers that have extended credit to the company. The supplier's name is written in the space entitled Payee so that the payment can be entered in his or her account in the accounts payable ledger.
2. *Other Accounts* Cash can be expended for many reasons. Thus an Other Accounts or Sundry Accounts column is needed in the cash payments journal. The title of the account to be debited is written in the Other Accounts Debit column, and the amount is entered in the amount column. If a company finds that a particular account occurs often in the Other Accounts column, it may be desirable to add another debit column to the cash payments journal.

The posting of the cash payments journal, as illustrated in Exhibit A-8, can be summarized as follows:

1. The Accounts Payable column should be posted daily to each individual account in the accounts payable subsidiary ledger. A check mark is placed in the Post. Ref. column to indicate that the posting is accomplished.
2. The debits/credits in the Other Accounts debit/credits columns should be posted daily or at convenient short intervals during the month to the general ledger. The account number is written in the Post. Ref. column

as the individual items are posted to indicate that the posting has been completed and a CP1 (representing Cash Payments Journal—page 1) is written in the Post. Ref. column of each account.

3. At the end of the month, the columns are totaled and crossfooted. That is, the sum of the credit columns totals must equal the sum of the debit column totals, as follows:

Credit Column Totals		Debit Column Totals	
Cash	$13,710	Accounts Payable	$ 6,000
Purchases Discounts	120	Other Accounts	17,830
Other Accounts	10,000	Total Debits	$23,830
Total Credits	$23,830		

4. The column totals for Cash, Purchases Discounts, and Accounts Payable are posted at the end of the month to their respective accounts in the general ledger. The account numbers are written below each column as they are posted to indicate that this step has been completed, and a CP1 is written in the Post. Ref. column of each account. A check mark is placed under the total of the Other Accounts columns to indicate that it is not posted.

General Journal

Transactions that do not involve sales, purchases, cash receipts, or cash payments should be recorded in the general journal. Usually there are only a few such transactions. The two examples that follow are compound entries that do not fit in a special-purpose journal: a return of merchandise, and an allowance from a supplier for credit. Adjusting and closing entries are also recorded in the general journal.

July 25 Returned one of the two used cars purchased on credit from Thomas Auto for $1,400 on July 12.

26 Agreed to give Maxwell Hertz a $35 allowance on his account because a tire blew out on the car he purchased.

These entries are shown in Exhibit A-9. The entries on July 25 and 26 include a debit or a credit to a controlling account (Accounts Payable or Accounts Receivable). The name of the customer or supplier is also given here. When such a debit or credit is made to a controlling account in the general journal, the entry must be posted twice: once in the controlling account and once in the individual account in the subsidiary ledger. This procedure keeps the subsidiary ledger equal to the controlling account. Note that the July 26 transaction is posted by a debit to Sales Returns and Allowances in the general ledger (shown by the account number 413), by a credit to the Accounts Receivable controlling account in the general ledger (shown by the account number 114), and by a credit to the Maxwell Hertz account in the accounts receivable subsidiary ledger (shown by the check mark).

Exhibit A-9. Transactions Recorded in the General Journal

General Journal					Page 1
Date		Description	Post. Ref.	Debit	Credit
July	25	Accounts Payable, Thomas Auto	212/✓	700	
		Purchases Returns and Allowances	513		700
		Returned used car for credit; invoice date: 7/11			
	26	Sales Returns and Allowances	413	35	
		Accounts Receivable, Maxwell Hertz	114/✓		35
		Allowance given because of faulty tire			

Flexibility of Special-Purpose Journals

The functions of special-purpose journals are to reduce and simplify the work in accounting and to allow for the division of labor. These journals should be designed to fit the business in which they are used. As noted earlier, if certain accounts show up often in the Other Accounts column of a journal, it may be wise to add a column for those accounts when a new page of a special-purpose journal is prepared.

Also, if certain transactions appear over and over again in the general journal, it may be a good idea to set up a new special-purpose journal. For example, if Mitchell Used Car Sales finds that it must often give allowances to customers, it may want to set up a sales returns and allowances journal. Sometimes, a purchases returns and allowances journal may be in order. In short, special-purpose journals should be designed to take care of the kinds of transactions a company commonly encounters.

Questions

1. How do special-purpose journals save time in entering and posting transactions?
2. Long Transit had 1,700 sales on credit during the current month.
   a. If the company uses a two-column general journal to record sales, how many times will the word *Sales* be written?
   b. How many postings to the Sales account will have to be made?

   c. If the company uses a sales journal, how many times will the word *Sales* be written?
   d. How many postings to the Sales account will have to be made?
3. What is the purpose of the Accounts Receivable controlling account? What is its relationship to the accounts receivable subsidiary ledger?
4. Why are the cash receipts journal and cash payments journal crossfooted? When is this step performed?
5. A company has the following numbers of accounts with balances: 18 asset accounts, including the Accounts Receivable account but not the individual customer accounts; 200 customer accounts; 8 liability accounts, including the Accounts Payable account but not the individual creditor accounts; 100 creditor accounts; 35 owner's equity accounts, including income statement accounts. The total is 361 accounts. How many accounts in total would appear in the general ledger?

Exercises

Exercise A-1. Matching Transactions to Special-Purpose Journals (L.O. 1)

A company uses a one-column sales journal, a one-column purchases journal, a cash receipts journal, a cash payments journal, and a general journal.

Indicate in which journal each of the following transactions would be recorded: (1) sold merchandise on credit; (2) sold merchandise for cash; (3) gave a customer credit for merchandise purchased on credit and returned; (4) paid a creditor; (5) paid office salaries; (6) customer paid for merchandise previously purchased on credit; (7) recorded adjusting and closing entries; (8) purchased merchandise on credit; (9) purchased sales department supplies on credit; (10) purchased office equipment for cash; (11) returned merchandise purchased on credit; (12) paid taxes.

Exercise A-2. Characteristics of Special-Purpose Journals (L.O. 1)

Trout Corporation uses a sales journal, a single-column purchases journal, a cash receipts journal, a cash payments journal, and a general journal.

1. In which journal would you expect to find the fewest transactions recorded?
2. At the end of the accounting period, to which account or accounts should the total of the purchases journal be posted as a debit and/or credit?
3. At the end of the accounting period, to which account or accounts should the total of the sales journal be posted as a debit and/or credit?
4. What two subsidiary ledgers would probably be associated with the journals listed above? From which journals would postings normally be made to each of the two subsidiary ledgers?
5. In which of the journals are adjusting and closing entries made?

Exercise A-3. Identifying the Content of a Special-Purpose Journal (L.O. 4)

Shown at the top of the following page is a page from a special journal.

1. What kind of journal is this?
2. Give an explanation for each of the following transactions: (a) August 27, (b) August 28, (c) August 29, and (d) August 30.
3. Explain the following: (a) the numbers under the bottom lines, (b) the checks entered in the Post. Ref. column, (c) the numbers 115 and 715 in the Post. Ref. column, and (d) the check below the Other Accounts column.

Date		Account Credited	Post. Ref.	Debits		Credits		
				Cash	Sales Discounts	Other Accounts	Accounts Receivable	Sales
		Balance Forward		39,799	787	26,100	10,204	4,282
Aug.	27	Quincy James	✓	490	10		500	
	28	Notes Receivable	115			1,000		
		Interest Earned	715	1,120		120		
	29	Cash Sale		960				960
	30	Ruth Chones	✓	200			200	
				42,569	797	27,220	10,904	5,242
				(111)	(412)	(✓)	(114)	(411)

Exercise A-4. Finding Errors in Special-Purpose Journals
(L.O. 3)

A company records purchases in a one-column purchases journal and records purchases returns in its general journal. During the past month an accounting clerk made each of the errors described below. Explain how each error might be discovered.

1. Correctly recorded an $86 purchase in the purchases journal but posted it to the creditor's account as a $68 purchase.
2. Made an addition error in totaling the Amount column of the purchases journal.
3. Posted a purchases return recorded in the general journal to the Purchases Returns and Allowances account and to the Accounts Payable account but did not post it to the creditor's account.
4. Made an error in determining the balance of a creditor's account.
5. Posted a purchases return to the Accounts Payable account but did not post to the Purchases Returns and Allowances account.

Exercise A-5. Posting from a Sales Journal
(L.O. 2)

Ferraro Corporation began business on September 1. The company maintained a sales journal, which appeared at the end of the month as shown below.

Sales Journal — **Page 1**

Date		Account Debited	Invoice Number	Post. Ref.	Amount
Sept.	4	Barbara Dunston	1001		172
	10	Louise Moriarty	1002		317
	15	Ron Wallach	1003		214
	17	Barbara Dunston	1004		97
	25	Bill Ong	1005		433
					1,233

1. On a sheet of paper, open general ledger accounts for Accounts Receivable (account number 112) and Sales (account number 411) and an accounts receivable subsidiary ledger with an account for each customer. Make the appropriate postings from the sales journal. State the posting references that you would place in the sales journal on page A-17.
2. Prove the accounts receivable subsidiary ledger by preparing a schedule of accounts receivable.

Exercise A-6. Multicolumn Purchases Journal
(L.O. 3)

Pascual Company uses a multicolumn purchases journal similar to the one illustrated in Exhibit A-6. During the month of October, Pascual made the following purchases:

Oct. 1 Purchased merchandise from Sanchez Company on account for $2,700, invoice dated October 1, terms 2/10, n/30.
2 Received freight bill dated Oct. 1 from Gem Freight for above merchandise, $175, terms n/30.
23 Purchased supplies from La Russo, Inc., for $120; allocated one-half each to store and office; invoice dated Oct. 20, terms n/30.
27 Purchased merchandise from Washington Company on account for $987; total included freight in of $87; invoice dated Oct. 25, terms n/30, FOB shipping point.
30 Purchased office supplies from La Russo, Inc., $48, invoice dated October 30, terms n/30.
31 Purchased a one-year insurance policy from Haller Agency, $240, terms n/30.

1. Draw a multicolumn purchases journal similar to the one in Exhibit A-6.
2. Enter the above transactions in the purchases journal. Then foot and crossfoot the columns.

Problems

Problem A-1. Identification of Transactions
(L.O. 1)

Bullock Company uses a general journal, purchases journal, sales journal, cash receipts journal, and cash payments journal similar to those illustrated in the text. On September 30, the A. Huan account in the accounts receivable subsidiary ledger appeared as follows:

A. Huan

Date		Item	Post. Ref.	Debit	Credit	Balance
Aug.	31		S4	754		754
Sept.	4		J7		64	690
	10		CR5		200	490
	15		S6	228		718

On September 30, the account of Gomez Company in the accounts payable subsidiary ledger appeared as follows:

Gomez Company

Date		Item	Post. Ref.	Debit	Credit	Balance
Sept.	16		P7		1,964	1,964
	21		J9	212		1,752
	28		CP8	1,752		—

Required

1. Write an explanation of each entry affecting the A. Huan account receivable including the journal from which the entry was posted.
2. Write an explanation of each entry affecting the Gomez Company account payable including the journal from which the entry was posted.

Problem A-2. Cash Receipts and Cash Payments Journals
(L.O. 4, 5)

The items below detail all cash transactions by Truman Company for the month of July. The company uses multicolumn cash receipts and cash payments journals similar to those illustrated in the chapter.

July 1 The owner, Barbara Truman, invested $60,000 cash and $14,000 in equipment in the business.
2 Paid July rent to Marx Agency, $500, with check no. 75.
3 Cash sales, $1,600.
6 Purchased store equipment, for $5,000, from Kasko Company, with check no. 76.
7 Purchased merchandise for cash, $6,500, from Lanier Company, with check no. 77.
8 Paid Blank Company invoice, $1,800, less 2 percent, with check no. 78.
9 Paid advertising bill, $350, to WCOL, with check no. 79.
10 Cash sales, $3,910.
12 Received $800 on account from D. Penn.
13 Purchased used truck for cash, $3,520, from Ackley Company, with check no. 80.
19 Received $4,180 from Lacey Company, in settlement of a $4,000 note plus interest.
20 Received $1,078 ($1,100 less $22 cash discount) from Roberto Arlt.
21 Paid Truman $2,000 from business for personal use by issuing check no. 81.
23 Paid Linger Company invoice, $2,500, less 2 percent discount, with check no. 82.
26 Paid Barber Company for freight on merchandise received, $60, with check no. 83.
27 Cash sales, $4,800.
28 Paid A. Pruden for monthly salary, $1,400 with check no. 84.
31 Purchased land from R. Franklin for $20,000, paying $5,000 with check no. 85 and signing a note payable for $15,000.

Required

1. Enter the preceding transactions in the cash receipts and cash payments journals.
2. Foot and rule the journals.

Problem A-3. Purchases and General Journals
(L.O. 3, 5)

The following items represent the credit transactions for Swedlow Company during the month of August. The company uses a multicolumn purchases journal and a general journal similar to those illustrated in the text.

Aug. 2 Purchased merchandise from Gibbs Company, $1,200.
5 Purchased van from Rose Company, $7,000.
8 Purchased office supplies from Escalera Company, $400.
12 Purchased filing cabinets from Escalera Company, $550.
14 Purchased merchandise, $1,400, and store supplies, $200, from Hornsby Company.
17 Purchased store supplies from Gibbs Company, $100, and office supplies from Cuyler Company, $50.
20 Purchased merchandise from Hornsby Company, $1,472.
24 Purchased merchandise from Gibbs Company, $2,452; the $2,452 invoice total included shipping charges, $232.
26 Purchased office supplies from Escalera Company, $150.
30 Purchased merchandise from Hornsby Company, $290.
31 Returned defective merchandise purchased from Hornsby Company on August 20 for full credit, $432.

Required

1. Enter the preceding transactions in the purchases journal and the general journal. Assume that all terms are n/30 and that invoice dates are the same as the transaction dates.
2. Foot and rule the purchases journal.
3. Open the following general ledger accounts: Store Supplies (116); Office Supplies (117); Trucks (142); Office Equipment (144); Accounts Payable (211); Purchases (611); Purchases Returns and Allowances (612); and Freight In (613). Open accounts payable subsidiary ledger accounts as needed. Post from the journals to the ledger accounts.

Problem A-4. Comprehensive Use of Special-Purpose Journals
(L.O. 2, 3, 4, 5)

Shiflett Refrigerating Company completed the following transactions:

May 1 Received merchandise from Jenner Company, $2,500, invoice dated April 29, terms 2/10, n/30, FOB shipping point.
2 Issued check no. 230 to Pang Agency for May rent, $2,000.
3 Received merchandise from Oberlin Manufacturing, $5,400, invoice dated May 1, terms 2/10, n/30, FOB shipping point.
5 Issued check no. 231 to Felsenthal Company for repairs, $560.
6 Received $400 credit memorandum pertaining to May 3 shipment from Oberlin Manufacturing for unsatisfactory merchandise returned to Oberlin Manufacturing.
7 Issued check no. 232 to Lopez Company for freight charges on May 1 and May 3 shipments, $184.
8 Sold merchandise to M. Krantz, $1,000, terms 1/10, n/30, invoice no. 725.

9 Issued check no. 233 to Jenner Company in full payment less discount.
10 Sold merchandise to L. Charles for $1,250, terms 1/10, n/30, invoice no. 726.
11 Issued check no. 234 to Oberlin Manufacturing for balance of account less discount.
12 Purchased advertising on credit from WBNS, $450, terms n/20.
14 Issued credit memorandum to L. Charles for $50 for merchandise returned.
15 Cash sales for first half of the month, $9,670. (To shorten these problems, cash sales are recorded only twice a month instead of daily, as they would be in actual practice.)
16 Sold merchandise to R. Guerrero, $700, terms 1/10, n/30, invoice no. 727.
17 Received check from M. Krantz for May 8 purchase less discount.
19 Received check from L. Charles for balance of account less discount.
20 Received merchandise from Jenner Company, $2,800, invoice dated May 19, terms 2/10, n/30, FOB shipping point.
21 Received freight bill from Ming Company, $570, terms n/5.
22 Issued check no. 235 for advertising purchase of May 12.
23 Received merchandise from Oberlin Manufacturing, $3,600, invoice dated May 22, terms 2/10, n/30, FOB shipping point.
24 Issued check no. 236 for freight charge of May 21.
26 Sold merchandise to M. Krantz, $800, terms 1/10, n/30, invoice no. 728.
27 Received credit memorandum from Oberlin Manufacturing for defective merchandise received May 23, $300.
28 Issued check no. 237 to Benjamin Company for purchase of office equipment, $350.
29 Issued check no. 238 to Jenner Company for one-half of May 20 purchase less discount.
30 Received check in full from R. Guerrero, discount not allowed.
31 Cash sales for the last-half of month, $11,560.
31 Issued check no. 239, payable to Payroll Account for monthly sales salaries, $4,300.

Required

1. Prepare a sales journal, a purchases journal, a cash receipts journal, a cash payments journal, and a general journal similar to the ones illustrated in this chapter. Use one as the page number for each journal.
2. Open the following general ledger accounts: Cash (111); Accounts Receivable (112); Office Equipment (141); Accounts Payable (211); Sales (411); Sales Discounts (412); Sales Returns and Allowances (413); Purchases (511); Purchases Discounts (512); Purchases Returns and Allowances (513); Freight In (514); Sales Salaries Expense (521); Advertising Expense (522); Rent Expense (531); and Repairs Expense (532).
3. Open the following accounts receivable subsidiary ledger accounts: M. Krantz, L. Charles, and R. Guerrero.
4. Open the following accounts payable subsidiary ledger accounts: Oberlin Manufacturing, WBNS, Jenner Company, and Ming Company.
5. Enter the transactions in the journals and post as appropriate.
6. Foot the journals and make end-of-month postings.
7. Prepare a trial balance of the general ledger and prove the control balances of Accounts Receivable and Accounts Payable by preparing schedules of accounts receivable and accounts payable.

APPENDIX B FINANCIAL ACCOUNTING CONCEPTS

LEARNING OBJECTIVES

1. State the objectives of financial reporting.
2. State the qualitative characteristics of accounting information and describe their interrelationships.
3. Define and describe the use of the conventions of comparability and consistency, materiality, conservatism, full disclosure, and cost-benefit.

Financial reporting has both internal and external aspects. Internal management has an interest in the resources, debts, and earnings of the business and in changes in these items. Management is responsible for informing those outside of the company's financial position and performance. Financial statements, which are often audited by independent accountants, are the most important means of communicating accounting information to external users. This appendix looks at the objectives, form, and evaluation of financial statements in external reporting. After studying this appendix, you should be able to meet the learning objectives on the left.

Since those outside the business who have a financial interest in it have no access to the accounting records, they must depend on what is presented to them. For them to understand and interpret these external financial reports, certain rules and standards must be followed in preparing the financial statements. This appendix begins by describing the objectives of financial information. It then discusses some qualities that accounting information ought to have and some conventions helpful in interpreting it.

Objectives of Financial Information[1]

The United States has a highly developed exchange economy. In such an economy, most goods and services are exchanged for money or claims to money instead of being used or bartered by their producers. Most business is carried on through investor-owned companies called corporations, including many large ones that buy, sell, and get financing in U.S. and world markets.

By issuing stocks and bonds that are traded in the market, businesses can raise capital for production and marketing activities through financial institutions, small groups, and the public at large. Investors are

1. The discussion in this section is based on *Statement of Financial Accounting Concepts No. 1,* "Objectives of Financial Reporting by Business Enterprises" (Stamford, Conn.: Financial Accounting Standards Board, 1978), pars. 6–16 and 28–40.

OBJECTIVE 1
State the objectives of financial reporting

interested mainly in returns from dividends and in the market prices of their investments, rather than in managing a company's business. Creditors want to know if a business can repay a loan according to the loan terms. Thus, investors and creditors both need to know if a company can generate favorable cash flows. Financial statements are important to both groups in making this judgment. They offer valuable information that helps investors and creditors judge a company's ability to pay dividends and pay back debts with interest. In this way, they help the market put scarce resources to work in companies that can use them most efficiently.

The needs of users and the general business environment described above are the basis for the Financial Accounting Standards Board's three objectives of financial reporting:[2]

1. *To furnish information useful in making investment and credit decisions* Financial reporting should offer information that is useful to present and potential investors and creditors as well as to others in making rational investment and credit decisions. The reports should be in a form that makes sense to those who have some understanding of business and are willing to study the information carefully.
2. *To provide information useful in assessing cash flow prospects* Financial reporting should supply information to help present and potential investors and creditors and others judge the amounts, timing, and risk of expected cash receipts from dividends or interest and the proceeds from the sale, redemption, or maturity of stocks or loans.
3. *To provide information about business resources, claims to those resources, and changes in them* Financial reporting should give information about the business resources of a company, the obligations to transfer resources to other units and to owner's equity, and the effects of transactions that change its resources and claims to those resources.

General-purpose external financial statements are the most important way of periodically presenting the information that has been gathered and processed in the accounting system to investors, creditors, and other interested parties outside the business. For this reason, these statements—the balance sheet, the income statement, the statement of owner's equity, and the statement of changes in financial position—are the most important output of the accounting system. These financial statements are called "general purpose" because of their use for a wide audience. They are "external" because the users are outside the business. As there may be some differences between managers, who must prepare the statements, and the investors or creditors, who invest in or lend money to the businesses, these statements are often audited by accountants outside the company to increase confidence in their reliability.

2. The discussion in this section is based on *Statements of Financial Accounting Concepts No. 1*, "Objectives of Financial Reporting by Business Enterprises" (Stamford, Conn.: Financial Accounting Standards Board, 1978), pars. 32–54.

Qualitative Characteristics of Accounting Information[3]

It is easy for a student in the first accounting course to get the idea that accounting is 100 percent accurate. This idea is reinforced by the fact that all the problems in this book and other introductory books can be solved. The numbers all add up, what is supposed to equal something else does, and so forth. Accounting seems very much like mathematics in its perfection. In this course, the basics of accounting are presented in a simple form at first to promote better understanding. In practice, however, accounting information is neither simple nor perfect and rarely satisfies all criteria. The FASB emphasizes this fact in the following statement:

> The information provided by financial reporting often results from approximate, rather than exact, measures. The measures commonly involve numerous estimates, classifications, summarizations, judgments and allocations. The outcome of economic activity in a dynamic economy is uncertain and results from combinations of many factors. Thus, despite the aura of precision that may seem to surround financial reporting in general and financial statements in particular, with few exceptions the measures are approximations, which may be based on rules and conventions, rather than exact amounts.[4]

Understandability

OBJECTIVE 2
State the qualitative characteristics of accounting information and describe their interrelationships

The goal of accounting information—to provide the basic data that different users need to make informed decisions—is an ideal. The gap between the ideal and the actual provides much of the interest and controversy in accounting. It is also a major reason why the burden for interpreting and using the information properly falls partly on the decision maker. The decision maker not only must judge what information to use and how to use it but also must understand it. The **understandability** of the information, however, depends on both the decision maker and the accountant. The accountant presents information that is believed to be generally useful, but the decision maker must interpret the information and use it in making the decision. To aid in understanding this process of interpretation, the FASB has described the qualitative characteristics of accounting information. **Qualitative characteristics** are the standards for judging the information that accountants give to decision makers. They are shown in Figure B-1.

The Usefulness of Accounting Information

If accounting information is to be useful, it must have two major qualitative characteristics: relevance and reliability.

3. The discussion in this section is based on *Statement of Financial Accounting Concepts No. 2*, "Qualitative Characteristics of Accounting Information" (Stamford, Conn.: Financial Accounting Standards Board, 1980). Copyright by Financial Accounting Standards Board, High Ridge Park, Stamford, CT 06905, USA. Reprinted with permission. Copies of the complete document are available from the FASB.
4. *Statement of Financial Accounting Concepts No. 1*, par. 20.

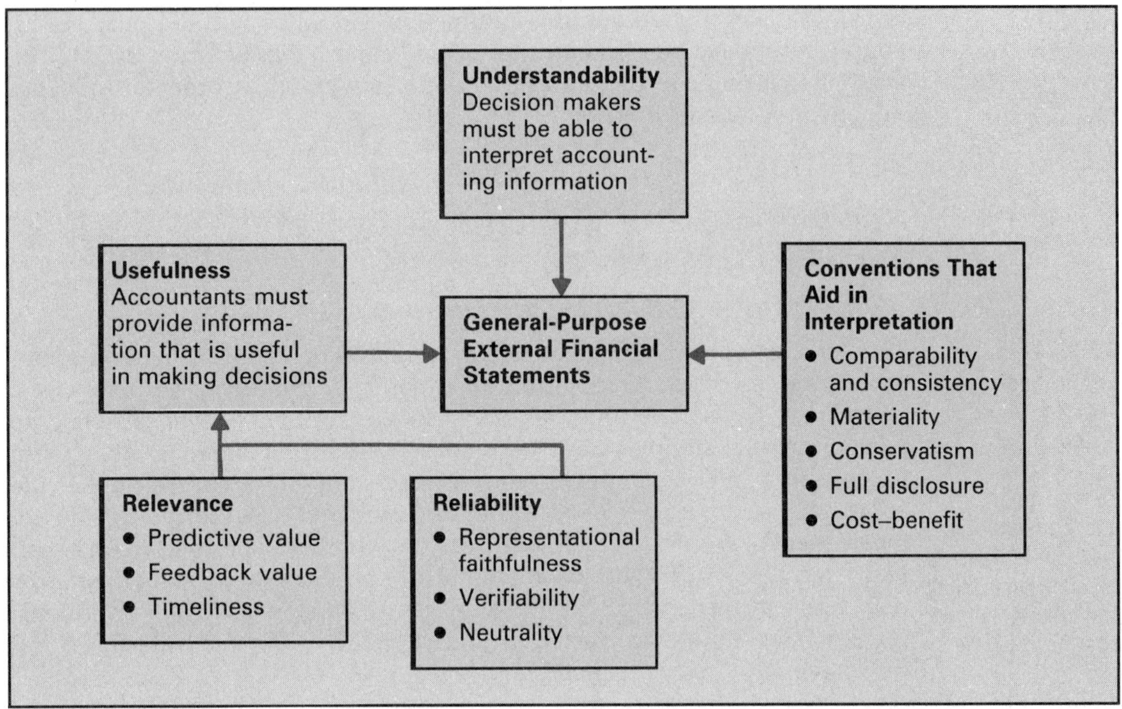

Figure B-1. The Qualitative Characteristics of Accounting Information

Relevance. **Relevance** means that the information is able to make a difference to the outcome of a decision. Information can influence a decision if it has predictive value and feedback value and if it is timely. **Predictive value** means that the information is useful to the decision maker in making a prediction, not that it is itself a prediction. To have **feedback value,** the information must tell something about the accuracy of earlier expectations. **Timeliness** means having the accounting information arrive in time for the user to make a decision. If the information is not ready when needed, it has no value for future action and is not relevant.

Reliability. To be useful, information must be reliable as well as relevant. **Reliability** is related to representational faithfulness, verifiability, and neutrality. **Representational faithfulness** has to do with how well the information agrees with what it is meant to represent. Accounting information is supposed to give a clear picture of the economic resources and obligations of a business and the events affecting those resources and obligations. **Verifiability** deals with the credibility of accounting information and means that the information can be confirmed or duplicated by independent parties using the same ways of measuring. **Neutrality** means that in carrying out generally accepted accounting principles, the main concern should be the relevance and reliability of the accounting information, not the effect that carrying out the principles may have on a particular interest. Neutrality does not mean that accounting information should be without purpose. It simply means that business activity must be reported as faithfully as possible, without coloring the picture that is being presented in order to influence anyone in a certain direction.

Conventions to Aid Interpretation of Financial Information

OBJECTIVE 3
Define and describe the use of the conventions of comparability and consistency, materiality, conservatism, full disclosure, and cost-benefit

To a large extent, financial statements are based on estimates and on rather arbitrary rules of recognition and allocation. In this book we point out a number of flaws that financial statements may have. One is failing to recognize the changing value of the dollar. Another is treating intangibles, like research and development costs, as assets only if purchased outside the company, but not if developed within the company. These problems do not mean that financial statements are useless; they are, of course, essential. However, the people who use them must know how to interpret them. To help users in this interpretation, accountants depend on five conventions: (1) comparability and consistency, (2) materiality, (3) conservatism, (4) full disclosure, and (5) cost-benefit.

Comparability and Consistency

Adding to the usefulness of accounting information is the characteristic of comparability. Information about a company is more useful if it can be compared with similar facts about the same company over several time periods or about another company for the same time period. **Comparability** means that the information is presented in such a way that the decision maker can recognize similarities, differences, and trends between different companies or between different periods' operations for the same company. Consistent use of accounting measures and procedures is important in achieving comparability. The **consistency** convention requires that a particular accounting procedure, once adopted, will not be changed from one period to another unless the user is informed of the change. Thus, without a statement to the contrary, users of financial statements may assume that there have been no arbitrary changes in methods that may affect interpretation of the statements.

If management decides that a certain procedure is not appropriate and should be changed, generally accepted accounting principles require that the fact of the change and its dollar effect be described in the notes to the financial statements:

> The nature of and justification for a change in accounting principle and its effect on income should be disclosed in the financial statements of the period in which the change is made. The justification for the change should explain clearly why the newly adopted accounting principle is preferable.[5]

5. Accounting Principles Board, *Opinion No. 20,* "Accounting Changes" (New York: American Institute of Certified Public Accountants, 1971), par. 17.

For example, during the current year, a company might report that it had changed its method of accounting for inventories because management felt the new method reflected actual cost flows more realistically.

Materiality

The term **materiality** refers to the relative importance of an item or event. If an item or event is material, it is likely to be relevant to the user of the financial statements. The accountant is often faced with many small items or events that make little difference to users no matter how they are handled. For example, in Chapter 10 it is suggested that it is more practical to account for small tools on an inventory basis than to depreciate them. Also, small capital expenditures of less than $100 or $500 may be charged as expense rather than recorded as equipment and depreciated.

In general, an item is material if there is a reasonable expectation that knowing about it would influence the decisions of users of financial statements. The materiality of an item depends on the nature of the item as well as the amount of the item. For example, in a multimillion-dollar company, a mistake in recording an item of $5,000 may not be important, but discovering a $5,000 bribe or theft may be very significant. Also, a great many small errors together may result in a material amount. Accountants must judge the materiality of many things, and the users of financial statements must depend on their judgment.

Conservatism

Accountants try to base their decisions on logic and evidence that will lead to the fairest report of what really happened. In judging and estimating, however, accountants are often faced with uncertainties or doubts. In these cases, they look to the convention of **conservatism**. This convention means that when accountants face major uncertainties as to which accounting procedure to use, they are generally careful to choose the one that will be least likely to overstate assets and income.

One of the most common applications of the conservatism convention is the use of the lower-of-cost-or-market method in accounting for short-term investments, described in Chapter 7, and for inventories, presented in Chapter 8. Under this method, if the market value is greater than cost, the more conservative cost figure is used. If the market value is less than cost, then the more conservative market value is used.

Conservatism can be a useful tool in doubtful cases, but the abuse of this convention will certainly lead to incorrect and misleading financial statements. Suppose that someone incorrectly applied the conservatism convention by charging a long-term asset to expense in the period of purchase. In this case, income and assets for the current period would be understated, and income of future periods would be overstated. For this reason, accountants depend on the conservatism convention only as a last resort.

Full Disclosure

The convention of **full disclosure** requires that financial statements and their footnotes present all information relevant to the user's understanding of the case. In other words, accounting information should offer any explanation that is needed to keep it from being misleading. Such explanations in the notes are considered an integral part of the financial statements. For instance, as noted in the section on consistency on page B-5, a change from one accounting procedure to another should be reported. In general, the form of the financial statements, as described later in this appendix, may affect their usefulness in making certain decisions. Also, certain items are considered essential to financial statement readers, such as the amount of depreciation expense and income taxes expense on the income statement and the amount of the accumulated depreciation accounts on the balance sheet.

Other examples of disclosures required by the Financial Accounting Standards Board and other official bodies are the accounting procedures used in preparing the statements, important changes in accounting estimates, important events taking place after the date of the statements, and assets and income of the major divisions of a company. However, there is a point where the statements become so cluttered that they impede rather than aid understanding. Beyond required disclosures, the application of the full-disclosure convention is based not on definite standards, but on the judgment of management and the accountants who prepare the statements.

The principle of full disclosure has also been influenced by users of accounting information in recent years. To protect the investor, independent auditors, the stock exchanges, and the SEC have all made many more demands for disclosure by publicly owned companies. The SEC has been pushing especially hard for the enforcement of full disclosure. So today more and better information about corporations is available to the public than ever before.

Cost-Benefit

The **cost-benefit** convention underlies all the qualitative characteristics and conventions. It holds that the benefits to be gained from providing new accounting information should be greater than the costs of providing it. Of course, certain minimum levels of relevance and reliability must be reached for accounting information to be useful. Beyond these minimum levels, however, it is up to the FASB and the SEC, which require the information, and the accountant, who provides the information, to judge the costs and benefits in each case. Most of the costs of providing information fall at first on the preparers, though the benefits are reaped by both preparers and users. Finally, both the costs and the benefits are passed on to society in the form of prices and social benefits from more efficient allocation of resources. The costs and benefits of a particular requirement for an accounting disclosure are both direct and indirect, immediate and deferred. For example, it is hard to judge the final costs and benefits of a far-reaching and costly regulation. The FASB, for instance, allows companies to make a supplemental disclosure of the effects of changes in current costs on their financial statements. Cost-benefit is a question faced by all regulators, including the FASB and the SEC. Even though there are no definitive ways of measuring costs and benefits, much of the accountant's work deals with these concepts.

Questions

1. What are the three objectives of financial reporting?
2. What are the qualitative characteristics of accounting information, what is their significance, and how are they interrelated?
3. What are the accounting conventions, and how does each aid in the interpretation of financial information?
4. What are some of the differences between the income statement for a sole proprietorship and that for a corporation?

Exercises

Exercise B-1. Accounting Concepts and Conventions (L.O. 3)

Each of the statements below violates a convention in accounting. In each case, state which of the following concepts or conventions is illustrated: consistency, materiality, conservatism, full disclosure, or cost-benefit.

1. A series of reports that are time-consuming and expensive to prepare are presented to the board of directors each month even though the reports are never used.
2. A company changes from one method of accounting for depreciation to another.
3. The same company does not indicate in the financial statements that the method of depreciation was changed, nor does it specify the effect of the change on net income.
4. A new office building next to the factory is debited to the Factory account because it represents a fairly small dollar amount in relation to the factory.
5. The asset account for a pickup truck still used in the business is written down to salvage value even though the carrying value under conventional depreciation methods is higher.

Problems

Problem B-1. Accounting Conventions (L.O. 3)

In each case below, an accounting convention may have been violated.

1. After careful study, Rahal Company, which has offices in forty states, has determined that, in the future, the depreciation of its office furniture should be changed. The new method is adopted for the current year, and the change is noted in the financial statements.
2. Pressley Corporation has in the past recorded operating expenses in general accounts for each classification, such as Salaries Expense, Depreciation Expense, and Utility Expense. Management has determined that in spite of the additional record-keeping costs, the company's income statement should break down each operating expense into its selling expense and administrative expense components.
3. Meng, the auditor of Ono Corporation, discovered that an official of the company may have authorized the payment of a $1,000 bribe to a local official. Management argued that, because the item was so small in relation to the

size of the company ($1,000,000 in sales), the illegal payment should not be disclosed.

4. Murray's Book Store built a small addition to the main building to house a new computer games division. Because of uncertainty about whether the computer games division would succeed or not, a conservative approach was taken by recording the addition as expense.
5. Since its origin ten years ago, Bonilla Company has used the same generally accepted inventory method. Because there has been no change in the inventory method, the company does not declare in its financial statements what inventory method it uses.

Required

In each case, state the convention that is applicable, explain briefly whether or not the treatment is in accord with the convention and generally accepted accounting principles, and explain why.

Problem B-2. Accounting Conventions
(L.O. 3)

In each case below, accounting conventions may have been violated.

1. Pearsall Manufacturing Company uses the cost method for computing the balance sheet amount of inventory unless the market value of the inventory is less than the cost, in which case the market value is used. At the end of the current year, the market value is $77,000 and the cost is $80,000. Pearsall uses the $77,000 figure to compute net income because management feels that the more cautious approach is to use the market figure.
2. Turpin Company has annual sales of $5,000,000. It follows the practice of charging any items costing less than $100 to expense in the year purchased. During the current year, it purchased several chairs at different times for the executive conference rooms at $97 each, including freight. Although the chairs were expected to last for at least ten years, the chairs were charged to expense in accordance with company policy.
3. Cardenas Company closed its books on December 31, 19x8, before preparing its annual report. On December 30, 19x8, a fire had destroyed one of the company's two factories. Although the company had fire insurance and would not suffer a loss on the building, a significant decrease in sales in 19x9 was expected because of the fire. The fire damage was not reported in the 19x8 financial statements because the operations for that year were not affected by the fire.
4. Blasingame Drug Company spends a substantial portion of its profits on research and development. The company has been reporting its $2,500,000 expenditure for research and development as a lump sum, but management recently decided to begin classifying the expenditures by project even though the record-keeping costs will increase.
5. During the current year, Hoak Company changed from one generally accepted method of accounting for inventories to another method.

Required

In each case, state the convention that is applicable, and explain briefly whether or not the treatment is in accord with the convention and generally accepted accounting principles.

APPENDIX C THE USE OF FUTURE VALUE AND PRESENT VALUE IN ACCOUNTING

LEARNING OBJECTIVES

1. Distinguish simple interest from compound interest.
2. Use compound interest tables to compute (a) the future value of a single invested sum at compound interest, and (b) the future value of an ordinary annuity.
3. Use present value tables to compute (a) the present value of a single sum due in the future, and (b) the present value of an ordinary annuity.
4. Apply the concept of present value to some simple accounting situations.

Interest is an important cost to the debtor and an important revenue to the creditor. Because interest is a cost associated with time, and "time is money," it is also an important consideration in any business decision. For example, an individual who holds $100 for one year without putting that $100 in a savings account has forgone the interest that could have been earned. Thus there is a cost associated with holding this money equal to the interest that could have been earned. Similarly, a business person who accepts a noninterest-bearing note instead of cash for the sale of merchandise is forgoing the interest that could have been earned on that money. These examples illustrate the point that the timing of the receipt and payment of cash must be considered in making business decisions. After studying this appendix, you should be able to meet the learning objectives listed on the left.

Simple Interest and Compound Interest

Interest is the cost associated with the use of money for a specific period of time. **Simple interest** is the interest cost, for one or more periods, if we assume that the amount on which the interest is computed stays the same from period to period. **Compound interest** is the interest cost, for two or more periods, if we assume that after each period the interest of that period is added to the amount on which interest is computed in future periods. In other words, compound interest is interest earned on a principal sum that is increased at the end of each period by the interest of that period.

Example: Simple Interest. Joe Sanchez accepts an 8 percent, $30,000 note due in 90 days. How much will he receive in total at that time? Remember the formula for calculating simple interest, which was presented in Chapter 8, on notes receivable:

$$\begin{aligned} \text{interest} &= \text{principal} \times \text{rate} \times \text{time} \\ \text{interest} &= \$30{,}000 \times 8/100 \times 90/360 \\ \text{interest} &= \$600 \end{aligned}$$

The total that Sanchez will receive is computed as follows:

$$\begin{aligned} \text{total} &= \text{principal} + \text{interest} \\ \text{total} &= \$30{,}000 + \$600 \\ \text{total} &= \$30{,}600 \end{aligned}$$

OBJECTIVE 1
Distinguish simple interest from compound interest

Example: Compound Interest. Ann Clary deposits $5,000 in a savings account that pays 6 percent interest. She expects to leave the principal and accumulated interest in the account for three years. How much in total will be in her account at the end of three years? Assume that the interest is paid at the end of the year and is added to the principal at that time and that this total in turn earns interest. The amount at the end of three years can be figured as follows:

(1) Year	(2) Principal Amount at Beginning of Year	(3) Annual Amount of Interest (col. 2 × .06)	(4) Accumulated Amount at End of Year (col. 2 + col. 3)
1	$5,000.00	$300.00	$5,300.00
2	5,300.00	318.00	5,618.00
3	5,618.00	337.08	5,955.08

At the end of three years, Clary will have $5,955.08 in her savings account. Note that the annual amount of interest increases each year by the interest rate times the interest of the previous year. For example, between year 1 and year 2, the interest increased by $18 ($318 − $300), which exactly equals .06 times $300.

Future Value of a Single Sum Invested at Compound Interest

OBJECTIVE 2a
Use compound interest tables to compute the future value of a single invested sum at compound interest

Another way to ask the question in the example of compound interest above is, What is the future value of a single sum ($5,000) at compound interest (6 percent) for three years? **Future value** is the amount an investment will be worth at a future date if invested at compound interest. A businessperson often wants to know future value, but the method of finding future value above takes too much time. Imagine how long the calculation would take if the example were ten years, not three. Fortunately, there are tables that make problems involving compound interest much quicker to solve. Table C-1, showing the future value of $1 after a given number of time periods, is an example. It is actually part of a larger table, D-1, in Appendix D. Suppose we want to solve the problem of Clary's savings account above. We simply look down the 6 percent column in Table C-1 until we reach period 3 and find the factor 1.191. This factor when multiplied by $1 gives the future value of that $1 at compound interest of 6 percent for three periods (years in this case). Thus we solve the problem:

$$\begin{array}{ccc} \text{principal} \times \text{factor} & = & \text{future value} \\ \$5{,}000 \times 1.191 & = & \$5{,}955 \end{array}$$

Except for a rounding error of $.08, the answer is exactly the same. Another example will illustrate this simple technique again.

Example: Future Value of a Single Invested Sum at Compound Interest. Ed Bates invests $3,000, which he believes will return 5 percent interest

Table C-1. Future Value of $1 After a Given Number of Time Periods

Periods	1%	2%	3%	4%	5%	6%	7%	8%	9%	10%	12%	14%	15%
1	1.010	1.020	1.030	1.040	1.050	1.060	1.070	1.080	1.090	1.100	1.120	1.140	1.150
2	1.020	1.040	1.061	1.082	1.103	1.124	1.145	1.166	1.188	1.210	1.254	1.300	1.323
3	1.030	1.061	1.093	1.125	1.158	1.191	1.225	1.260	1.295	1.331	1.405	1.482	1.521
4	1.041	1.082	1.126	1.170	1.216	1.262	1.311	1.360	1.412	1.464	1.574	1.689	1.749
5	1.051	1.104	1.159	1.217	1.276	1.338	1.403	1.469	1.539	1.611	1.762	1.925	2.011
6	1.062	1.126	1.194	1.265	1.340	1.419	1.501	1.587	1.677	1.772	1.974	2.195	2.313
7	1.072	1.149	1.230	1.316	1.407	1.504	1.606	1.714	1.828	1.949	2.211	2.502	2.660
8	1.083	1.172	1.267	1.369	1.477	1.594	1.718	1.851	1.993	2.144	2.476	2.853	3.059
9	1.094	1.195	1.305	1.423	1.551	1.689	1.838	1.999	2.172	2.358	2.773	3.252	3.518
10	1.105	1.219	1.344	1.480	1.629	1.791	1.967	2.159	2.367	2.594	3.106	3.707	4.046

Source: Henry R. Anderson and Mitchell H. Raiborn, *Basic Cost Accounting Concepts* (Boston: Houghton Mifflin, 1977), excerpt from Table 1, p. 552. Reprinted by permission.

compounded over a five-year period. How much will Bates have at the end of five years? From Table C-1, the factor for period 5 of the 5 percent column is 1.276. Therefore, we calculate as follows:

$$\text{principal} \times \text{factor} = \text{future value}$$
$$\$3{,}000 \times 1.276 = \$3{,}828$$

Bates will have $3,828 at the end of five years.

Future Value of an Ordinary Annuity

OBJECTIVE 2b Use compound interest tables to compute the future value of an ordinary annuity

Another common problem involves an **ordinary annuity,** which is a series of equal payments made at the end of equal intervals of time, with compound interest on these payments.

Example: Future Value of an Ordinary Annuity. Assume that Ben Katz deposits $200 at the end of each of the next three years in a savings account that pays 5 percent interest. How much money will he have in his account at the end of the next three years? One way of computing the amount is shown in the following table:

(1) Year	(2) Beginning Balance	(3) Interest Earned (5% × col. 2)	(4) Periodic Payment	(5) Accumulated at End of Period (col. 2 + col. 3 + col. 4)
1	$ —	$ —	$200	$200.00
2	200.00	10.00	200	410.00
3	410.00	20.50	200	630.50

Katz would have $630.50 in his account at the end of three years, made up of $600 in periodic payments and $30.50 in interest.

This calculation can also be simplified by using Table C-2. We look down the 5 percent column until we reach period 3 and find the factor 3.153. This factor when multiplied by $1 gives the future value of a series of three $1 payments (years in this case) at compound interest of 5 percent. Thus we solve the problem:

$$\text{periodic payment} \times \text{factor} = \text{future value}$$
$$\$200 \times 3.153 = \$630.60$$

Except for a rounding error of $0.10, this result is the same as the one above.

Present Value

OBJECTIVE 3a Use present value tables to compute the present value of a single sum due in the future

Suppose that you had the choice of receiving $100 today or one year from today. Without even thinking about it, you would choose to receive the $100 today. Why? You know that if you have the $100 today, you can put it in a savings account to earn interest and will have more than $100 a year from today. Therefore, we can say that an amount to be received in the future (future value) is not worth as much today as an amount to be received today (present value) because of the cost associated with the passage of time. In fact, present value and future value are closely related. **Present value** is the amount that must be invested now at a given rate of interest to produce a given future value.

Example: Present Value. Sue Dapper needs $1,000 one year from now. How much should she invest today to achieve that goal if the interest rate is 5 percent? From earlier examples, the following equation may be established:

$$\begin{aligned}
\text{present value} \times (1.0 + \text{interest rate}) &= \text{future value} \\
\text{present value} \times 1.05 &= \$1,000 \\
\text{present value} &= \$1,000 \div 1.05 \\
\text{present value} &= \$952.38
\end{aligned}$$

Thus to achieve a future value of $1,000, a present value of $952.38 must be invested. Interest of 5 percent on $952.38 for one year equals $47.62, and these two amounts added together equal $1,000.

Present Value of a Single Sum Due in the Future

When more than one time period is involved, the calculation of present value is more complicated. Consider the following example.

Example: Present Value of a Single Sum in the Future. Don Riley wants to be sure of having $4,000 at the end of three years. How much must he invest today in a 5 percent savings account to achieve this goal? Adapting the above equation, we compute the present value of $4,000 at compound interest of 5 percent for three years in the future.

Table C-2. Future Value of $1 Paid in Each Period for a Given Number of Time Periods

Periods	1%	2%	3%	4%	5%	6%	7%	8%	9%	10%	12%	14%	15%
1	1.000	1.000	1.000	1.000	1.000	1.000	1.000	1.000	1.000	1.000	1.000	1.000	1.000
2	2.010	2.020	2.030	2.040	2.050	2.060	2.070	2.080	2.090	2.100	2.120	2.140	2.150
3	3.030	3.060	3.091	3.122	3.153	3.184	3.215	3.246	2.278	3.310	3.374	3.440	3.473
4	4.060	4.122	4.184	4.246	4.310	4.375	4.440	4.506	4.573	4.641	4.779	4.921	4.993
5	5.101	5.204	5.309	5.416	5.526	5.637	5.751	5.867	5.985	6.105	6.353	6.610	6.742
6	6.152	6.308	6.468	6.633	6.802	6.975	7.153	7.336	7.523	7.716	8.115	8.536	8.754
7	7.214	7.434	7.662	7.898	8.142	8.394	8.654	8.923	9.200	9.487	10.09	10.73	11.07
8	8.286	8.583	8.892	9.214	9.549	9.897	10.26	10.64	11.03	11.44	12.30	13.23	13.73
9	9.369	9.755	10.16	10.58	11.03	11.49	11.98	12.49	13.02	13.58	14.78	16.09	16.79
10	10.46	10.95	11.46	12.01	12.58	13.18	13.82	14.49	15.19	15.94	17.55	19.34	20.30

Source: Henry R. Anderson and Mitchell H. Raiborn, *Basic Cost Accounting Concepts* (Boston: Houghton Mifflin, 1977), excerpt from Table 2, p. 553. Reprinted by permission.

Year	Amount at End of Year		Divide by		Present Value at Beginning of Year
3	$4,000.00	÷	1.05	=	$3,809.52
2	3,809.52	÷	1.05	=	3,628.12
1	3,628.12	÷	1.05	=	3,455.35

Riley must invest a present value of $3,455.35 to achieve a future value of $4,000 in three years.

This calculation is again made much easier by using the appropriate table. In Table C-3, we look down the 5 percent column until we reach period 3 and find the factor 0.864. This factor when multiplied by $1 gives the present value of that $1 to be received three years from now at 5 percent interest. Thus we solve the problem:

$$\begin{array}{ccc} \text{future value} \times \text{factor} & = & \text{present value} \\ \$4{,}000 \times 0.864 & = & \$3{,}456 \end{array}$$

Except for a rounding error of $0.65, this result is the same as the one above.

Present Value of an Ordinary Annuity

OBJECTIVE 3b Use present value tables to compute the present value of an ordinary annuity

It is often necessary to find the present value of a series of receipts or payments. When we calculate the present value of equal amounts equally spaced over a period of time, we are computing the present value of an ordinary annuity.

Example: Present Value of an Ordinary Annuity. Assume that Kathy Foster has sold a piece of property and is to receive $15,000 in three equal

Table C-3. Present Value of $1 to Be Received at the End of a Given Number of Time Periods

Periods	1%	2%	3%	4%	5%	6%	7%	8%	9%	10%
1	0.990	0.980	0.971	0.962	0.952	0.943	0.935	0.926	0.917	0.909
2	0.980	0.961	0.943	0.925	0.907	0.890	0.873	0.857	0.842	0.826
3	0.971	0.942	0.915	0.889	0.864	0.840	0.816	0.794	0.772	0.751
4	0.961	0.924	0.888	0.855	0.823	0.792	0.763	0.735	0.708	0.683
5	0.951	0.906	0.883	0.822	0.784	0.747	0.713	0.681	0.650	0.621
6	0.942	0.888	0.837	0.790	0.746	0.705	0.666	0.630	0.596	0.564
7	0.933	0.871	0.813	0.760	0.711	0.665	0.623	0.583	0.547	0.513
8	0.923	0.853	0.789	0.731	0.677	0.627	0.582	0.540	0.502	0.467
9	0.914	0.837	0.766	0.703	0.645	0.592	0.544	0.500	0.460	0.424
10	0.905	0.820	0.744	0.676	0.614	0.558	0.508	0.463	0.422	0.386

Source: Henry R. Anderson and Mitchell H. Raiborn, *Basic Cost Accounting Concepts* (Boston: Houghton Mifflin, 1977), excerpt from Table 3, p. 554. Reprinted by permission.

annual payments of $5,000, beginning one year from today. What is the present value of this sale, assuming a current interest rate of 5 percent? This present value may be computed by calculating a separate present value for each of the three payments (using Table C-3) and summing the results, as shown below.

Future Receipts (Annuity)				Present Value Factor at 5 percent (from Table A-3)		Present Value
Year 1	Year 2	Year 3				
$5,000			×	0.952	=	$ 4,760
	$5,000		×	0.907	=	4,535
		$5,000	×	0.864	=	4,320
Total Present Value						$13,615

The present value of this sale is $13,615. Thus there is an implied interest cost (given the 5 percent rate) of $1,385 associated with the payment plan that allows the purchaser to pay in three installments.

We can make this calculation by using Table C-4. We look down the 5 percent column until we reach period 3 and find factor 2.723. This factor when multiplied by $1 gives the present value of a series of three $1 payments (spaced one year apart) at compound interest of 5 percent. Thus we solve the problem:

periodic payment × factor = present value
$5,000 × 2.723 = $13,615

This result is the same as the one computed above.

Table C-4. Present Value of $1 Received Each Period for a Given Number of Time Periods

Periods	1%	2%	3%	4%	5%	6%	7%	8%	9%	10%
1	0.990	0.980	0.971	0.962	0.952	0.943	0.935	0.926	0.917	0.909
2	1.970	1.942	1.913	1.886	1.859	1.833	1.808	1.783	1.759	1.736
3	2.941	2.884	2.829	2.775	2.723	2.673	2.624	2.577	2.531	2.487
4	3.902	3.808	3.717	3.630	3.546	3.465	3.387	3.312	3.240	3.170
5	4.853	4.713	4.580	4.452	4.329	4.212	4.100	3.993	3.890	3.791
6	5.795	5.601	5.417	5.242	5.076	4.917	4.767	4.623	4.486	4.355
7	6.728	6.472	6.230	6.002	5.786	5.582	5.389	5.206	5.033	4.868
8	7.652	7.325	7.020	6.733	6.463	6.210	5.971	5.747	5.535	5.335
9	8.566	8.162	7.786	7.435	7.108	6.802	6.515	6.247	5.995	5.759
10	9.471	8.983	8.530	8.111	7.722	7.360	7.024	6.710	6.418	6.145

Source: Henry R. Anderson and Mitchell H. Raiborn, *Basic Cost Accounting Concepts* (Boston: Houghton Mifflin, 1977), excerpt from Table 4, p. 556. Reprinted by permission.

Time Periods

In all the examples above and in most other cases, the compounding period is one year, and the interest rate is stated on an annual basis. However, in each of the four tables the left-hand column refers, not to years, but to periods. This wording is used because there are compounding periods of less than one year. Savings accounts that record interest quarterly and bonds that pay interest semiannually are cases in point. To use the tables in such cases, it is necessary to (1) divide the annual interest rate by the number of periods in the year, and (2) multiply the number of periods in one year by the number of years.

Example: Time Periods. Assume that a $6,000 note is to be paid in two years and carries an annual interest rate of 8 percent. Compute the maturity (future) value of the note, assuming that the compounding period is semiannual. Before using the table, it is necessary to compute the interest rate that applies to the compounding period and the number of periods. First, the interest rate to use is 4 percent (8% annual rate ÷ 2 periods per year). Second, the number of compounding periods is 4 (2 periods per year × 2 years). From Table C-1, therefore, the maturity value of the note may be computed as follows:

principal × factor = future value
$6,000 × 1.170 = $7,020

The note will be worth $7,020 in two years.

This procedure for determining the interest rate and the number of periods when the compounding period is less than one year may be used with all the tables.

Applications of Present Value to Accounting

The concept of present value is used widely in accounting. Here, the purpose is to show its usefulness in some simple applications. In-depth study of present value is left up to more advanced courses.

Imputing Interest on Noninterest-Bearing Notes

OBJECTIVE 4 Apply the concept of present value to some simple accounting situations

Clearly there is no such thing as an interest-free debt, regardless of whether the interest rate is explicitly stated. The Accounting Principles Board has declared that when a long-term note does not explicitly state an interest rate (or if the interest rate is unreasonably low), a rate based on the normal interest cost of the company in question should be assigned, or imputed.[1] The next example applies this principle.

Example: Imputing Interest on Noninterest-Bearing Notes. On January 1, 19x8, Gato purchases merchandise from Haines by making an $8,000 noninterest-bearing note due in two years. Gato can borrow money from the bank at 9 percent interest. Gato pays the note in full after two years. Prepare journal entries to record these transactions.

Note that the $8,000 note represents partly a payment for merchandise and partly a payment of interest for two years. In recording the purchase and sale, it is necessary to use Table C-3 to determine the present value of the note. The calculation follows.

future value	×	present value factor (9%, 2 years)	=	present value
$8,000	×	0.842	=	$6,736

The imputed interest cost is $1,264 ($8,000 − $6,736). The entries necessary to record the purchase in the Gato records and the sale in the Haines records are shown below.

Gato Journal

Purchases	6,736	
Discount on Notes Payable[2]	1,264	
Notes Payable		8,000

Haines Journal

Notes Receivable	8,000	
Discount on Notes Receivable		1,264
Sales		6,736

On December 31, 19x8, the adjustments to recognize the interest expenses and interest earned will be:

Gato Journal

Interest Expense	606.24	
Discount on Notes Payable		606.24

Haines Journal

Discount on Notes Receivable	606.24	
Interest Earned		606.24

1. Accounting Principles Board, *Opinion No. 21,* "Interest on Receivables and Payables" (New York: American Institute of Certified Public Accountants, June 1, 1982), par. 13.
2. Under APB, *Opinion No. 21,* notes payable and receivable are to be shown net of any discount or premium. This example shows the face value of the notes and the discount separately for purposes of instructional clarity.

The interest is found by multiplying the original purchase by the interest for one year ($6,736 × .09 = $606.24). When payment is made on December 31, 19x9, the following entries will be made in the respective journals:

Gato Journal			Haines Journal		
Interest Expense	657.76		Discount on Notes Receivable	657.76	
Notes Payable	8,000.00		Cash	8,000.00	
Discount on Notes Payable		657.76	Interest Earned		657.76
Cash		8,000.00	Notes Receivable		8,000.00

The interest entries represent the remaining interest to be expensed or realized ($1,264 − $606.24 = $657.76). This amount approximates (because of rounding errors in the table) the interest for one year on the purchases plus last year's interest [($6,736 + $606.24) × .09 = $660.80].

Valuing an Asset

An asset is recorded because it will provide future benefits to the company that owns it. This future benefit is the basis for the definition of an asset. Usually, the purchase price of the asset represents the present value of these future benefits. It is possible to evaluate a proposed purchase price of an asset by comparing that price with the present value of the asset to the company.

Example: Valuing an Asset. Sam Hurst is thinking of buying a new labor-saving machine that will reduce his annual labor cost by $700 per year. The machine will last eight years. The interest rate that Hurst assumes for making managerial decisions is 10 percent. What is the maximum amount (present value) that Hurst should pay for the machine?

The present value of the machine to Hurst is equal to the present value of an ordinary annuity of $700 per year for eight years at compound interest of 10 percent. From Table C-4, we compute the value as follows:

periodic savings × factor = present value
$700 × 5.335 = $3,734.50

Hurst should not pay more than $3,734.50 for the new machine.

Other Accounting Applications

There are many other applications of present value to accounting. Examples of its application to bond valuation, finding the amount of mortgage payments, and accounting for leases are presented in Chapter 14. Others are the recording of pension obligations; the determination of premium and discount on debt; accounting for depreciation of plant, property, and equipment; analysis of the purchase price of a business; evaluation of capital expenditure decisions; and generally any problem where time is a factor.

Exercises

Tables D-1 to D-4 in Appendix D may be used to solve these exercises.

Exercise C-1. Future Value Calculations (L.O. 2)

Naber receives a one-year note that carries a 12 percent annual interest rate on $1,500 for the sale of a used car.

Compute the maturity value under each of the following assumptions: (1) The interest is simple interest. (2) The interest is compounded semiannually. (3) The interest is compounded quarterly. (4) The interest is compounded monthly.

Exercise C-2. Future Value Calculations (L.O. 2)

Find the future value of (1) a single payment of $10,000 at 7 percent for ten years, (2) ten annual payments of $1,000 at 7 percent, (3) a single payment of $3,000 at 9 percent for seven years, and (4) seven annual payments of $3,000 at 9 percent.

Exercise C-3. Present Value Calculations (L.O. 3)

Find the present value of (1) a single payment of $12,000 at 6 percent for twelve years, (2) twelve annual payments of $1,000 at 6 percent, (3) a single payment of $2,500 at 9 percent for five years, and (4) five annual payments of $2,500 at 9 percent.

Exercise C-4. Future Value Calculations (L.O. 2)

Assume that $20,000 is invested today. Compute the amount that would accumulate at the end of seven years when the interest is (1) 8 percent annual interest compounded annually, (2) 8 percent annual interest compounded semi-annually, and (3) 8 percent annual interest compounded quarterly.

Exercise C-5. Future Value Calculations (L.O. 2)

Calculate the accumulation of periodic payments of $500 for four years, assuming (1) 10 percent annual interest compounded annually, (2) 10 percent annual interest compounded semiannually, (3) 4 percent annual interest compounded annually, and (4) 16 percent annual interest compounded quarterly.

Exercise C-6. Future Value Applications (L.O. 2)

a. Two parents have $10,000 to invest for their child's college tuition, which they estimate will cost $20,000 when the child enters college twelve years from now.

   Calculate the approximate rate of annual interest that the investment must earn to reach the $20,000 goal in twelve years. (Hint: Make a calculation; then use Table D-1.)

b. Bill Roister is saving to purchase a summer home that will cost about $32,000. He has $20,000 now, on which he can earn 7 percent annual interest.

   Calculate the approximate length of time he will have to wait to purchase the summer home. (Hint: Make a calculation; then use Table D-1.)

Exercise C-7. Working Backward from a Future Value (L.O. 2)

May Marquez has a debt of $45,000 due in four years. She wants to save money to pay it off by making annual deposits in an investment account that earns 8 percent annual interest.

Calculate the amount she must deposit each year to reach her goal. (Hint: Use Table D-2; then make a calculation.)

Exercise C-8. Present Value of a Lump-Sum Contract (L.O. 3)

A contract calls for a lump-sum payment of $30,000. Find the present value of the contract, assuming that (1) the payment is due in five years, and the current interest rate is 9 percent; (2) the payment is due in ten years, and the current interest rate is 9 percent; (3) the payment is due in five years, and the current interest rate is 5 percent; and (4) the payment is due in ten years, and the current interest rate is 5 percent.

Exercise C-9. Present Value of an Annuity Contract (L.O. 3)

A contract calls for annual payments of $600. Find the present value of the contract, assuming that (1) the number of payments is seven, and the current interest rate is 6 percent; (2) the number of payments is fourteen, and the current interest rate is 6 percent; (3) the number of payments is seven, and the current interest rate is 8 percent; and (4) the number of payments is fourteen, and the current interest rate is 8 percent.

Exercise C-10. Noninterest-Bearing Note (L.O. 4)

On January 1, 19x8, Olson purchases a machine from Carter by signing a two-year, noninterest-bearing $16,000 note. Olson currently pays 12 percent interest to borrow money at the bank.

Prepare journal entries in Olson's and Carter's records to (1) record the purchase and the note, (2) adjust the accounts after one year, and (3) record payment of the note after two years (on December 31, 19x9).

Exercise C-11. Valuing an Asset for the Purpose of Making a Purchasing Decision (L.O. 4)

Kubo owns a service station and has the opportunity to purchase a car wash machine for $15,000. After carefully studying projected costs and revenues, Kubo estimates that the car wash will produce a net cash flow of $2,600 annually and will last for eight years. Kubo feels that an interest rate of 14 percent is adequate for his business.

Calculate the present value of the machine to Kubo. Does the purchase appear to be a correct business decision?

Exercise C-12. Determining an Advance Payment (L.O. 3)

Ellen Saber is contemplating paying five years' rent in advance. Her annual rent is $4,800. Calculate the single sum that would have to be paid now for the advance rent, if we assume compound interest of 8 percent.

APPENDIX D COMPOUND INTEREST AND PRESENT VALUE TABLES

Table D-1. Future Value of $1 After a Given Number of Time Periods

Periods	1%	2%	3%	4%	5%	6%	7%	8%	9%	10%	12%	14%	15%
1	1.010	1.020	0.030	1.040	1.050	1.060	1.070	1.080	1.090	1.100	1.120	1.140	1.150
2	1.020	1.040	1.061	1.082	1.103	1.124	1.145	1.166	1.188	1.210	1.254	1.300	1.323
3	1.030	1.061	1.093	1.125	1.158	1.191	1.225	1.260	1.295	1.331	1.405	1.482	1.521
4	1.041	1.082	1.126	1.170	1.216	1.262	1.311	1.360	1.412	1.464	1.574	1.689	1.749
5	1.051	1.104	1.159	1.217	1.276	1.338	1.403	1.469	1.539	1.611	1.762	1.925	2.011
6	1.062	1.126	1.194	1.265	1.340	1.419	1.501	1.587	1.677	1.772	1.974	2.195	2.313
7	1.072	1.149	1.230	1.316	1.407	1.504	1.606	1.714	1.828	1.949	2.211	2.502	2.660
8	1.083	1.172	1.267	1.369	1.477	1.594	1.718	1.851	1.993	2.144	2.476	2.853	3.059
9	1.094	1.195	1.305	1.423	1.551	1.689	1.838	1.999	2.172	2.358	2.773	3.252	3.518
10	1.105	1.219	1.344	1.480	1.629	1.791	1.967	2.159	2.367	2.594	3.106	3.707	4.046
11	1.116	1.243	1.384	1.539	1.710	1.898	2.105	2.332	2.580	2.853	3.479	4.226	4.652
12	1.127	1.268	1.426	1.601	1.796	2.012	2.252	2.518	2.813	3.138	3.896	4.818	5.350
13	1.138	1.294	1.469	1.665	1.886	2.133	2.410	2.720	3.066	3.452	4.363	5.492	6.153
14	1.149	1.319	1.513	1.732	1.980	2.261	2.579	2.937	3.342	3.798	4.887	6.261	7.076
15	1.161	1.346	1.558	1.801	2.079	2.397	2.759	3.172	3.642	4.177	5.474	7.138	8.137
16	1.173	1.373	1.605	1.873	2.183	2.540	2.952	3.426	3.970	4.595	6.130	8.137	9.358
17	1.184	1.400	1.653	1.948	2.292	2.693	3.159	3.700	4.328	5.054	6.866	9.276	10.76
18	1.196	1.428	1.702	2.026	2.407	2.854	3.380	3.996	4.717	5.560	7.690	10.58	12.38
19	1.208	1.457	1.754	2.107	2.527	3.026	3.617	4.316	5.142	6.116	8.613	12.06	14.23
20	1.220	1.486	1.806	2.191	2.653	3.207	3.870	4.661	5.604	6.728	9.646	13.74	16.37
21	1.232	1.516	1.860	2.279	2.786	3.400	4.141	5.034	6.109	7.400	10.80	15.67	18.82
22	1.245	1.546	1.916	2.370	2.925	3.604	4.430	5.437	6.659	8.140	12.10	17.86	21.64
23	1.257	1.577	1.974	2.465	3.072	3.820	4.741	5.871	7.258	8.954	13.55	20.36	24.89
24	1.270	1.608	2.033	2.563	3.225	4.049	5.072	6.341	7.911	9.850	15.18	23.21	28.63
25	1.282	1.641	2.094	2.666	3.386	4.292	5.427	6.848	8.623	10.83	17.00	26.46	32.92
26	1.295	1.673	2.157	2.772	3.556	4.549	5.807	7.396	9.399	11.92	19.04	30.17	37.86
27	1.308	1.707	2.221	2.883	3.733	4.822	6.214	7.988	10.25	13.11	21.32	34.39	43.54
28	1.321	1.741	2.288	2.999	3.920	5.112	6.649	8.627	11.17	14.42	23.88	39.20	50.07
29	1.335	1.776	2.357	3.119	4.116	5.418	7.114	9.317	12.17	15.86	26.75	44.69	57.58
30	1.348	1.811	2.427	3.243	4.322	5.743	7.612	10.06	13.27	17.45	29.96	50.95	66.21
40	1.489	2.208	3.262	4.801	7.040	10.29	14.97	21.72	31.41	45.26	93.05	188.9	267.9
50	1.645	2.692	4.384	7.107	11.47	18.42	29.46	46.90	74.36	117.4	289.0	700.2	1,084

Source: All tables in Appendix D are from Henry R. Anderson and Mitchell H. Raiborn, *Basic Cost Accounting Concepts* (Boston: Houghton Mifflin, 1977), pp. 552–557. Reprinted by permission.

Table D-1 provides the multipliers necessary to find the future value of a *single* cash deposit made at the *beginning* of year 1. Three factors must be known before the future value can be figured: (1) time period in years, (2) stated annual rate of interest to be earned, and (3) dollar amount invested or deposited.

Example. Find the future value of $5,000 deposited now that will earn 9 percent interest compounded annually for five years. From Table D-1, the

Table D-2. Future Value of $1 Paid in Each Period for a Given Number of Time Periods

Periods	1%	2%	3%	4%	5%	6%	7%	8%	9%	10%	12%	14%	15%
1	1.000	1.000	1.000	1.000	1.000	1.000	1.000	1.000	1.000	1.000	1.000	1.000	1.000
2	2.010	2.020	2.030	2.040	2.050	2.060	2.070	2.080	2.090	2.100	2.120	2.140	2.150
3	3.030	3.060	3.091	3.122	3.153	3.184	3.215	3.246	3.278	3.310	3.374	3.440	3.473
4	4.060	4.122	4.184	4.246	4.310	4.375	4.440	4.506	4.573	4.641	4.779	4.921	4.993
5	5.101	5.204	5.309	5.416	5.526	5.637	5.751	5.867	5.985	6.105	6.353	6.610	6.742
6	6.152	6.308	6.468	6.633	6.802	6.975	7.153	7.336	7.523	7.716	8.115	8.536	8.754
7	7.214	7.434	7.662	7.898	8.142	8.394	8.654	8.923	9.200	9.487	10.09	10.73	11.07
8	8.286	8.583	8.892	9.214	9.549	9.897	10.26	10.64	11.03	11.44	12.30	13.23	13.73
9	9.369	9.755	10.16	10.58	11.03	11.49	11.98	12.49	13.02	13.58	14.78	16.09	16.79
10	10.46	10.95	11.46	12.01	12.58	13.18	13.82	14.49	15.19	15.94	17.55	19.34	20.30
11	11.57	12.17	12.81	13.49	14.21	14.97	15.78	16.65	17.56	18.53	20.65	23.04	24.35
12	12.68	13.41	14.19	15.03	15.92	16.87	17.89	18.98	20.14	21.38	24.13	27.27	29.00
13	13.81	14.68	15.62	16.63	17.71	18.88	20.14	21.50	22.95	24.52	28.03	32.09	34.35
14	14.95	15.97	17.09	18.29	19.60	21.02	22.55	24.21	26.02	27.98	32.39	37.58	40.50
15	16.10	17.29	18.60	20.02	21.58	23.28	25.13	27.15	29.36	31.77	37.28	43.84	47.58
16	17.26	18.64	20.16	21.82	23.66	25.67	27.89	30.32	33.00	35.95	42.75	50.98	55.72
17	18.43	20.01	21.76	23.70	25.84	28.21	30.84	33.75	36.97	40.54	48.88	59.12	65.08
18	19.61	21.41	23.41	25.65	28.13	30.91	34.00	37.45	41.30	45.60	55.75	68.39	75.84
19	20.81	22.84	25.12	27.67	30.54	33.76	37.38	41.45	46.02	51.16	63.44	78.97	88.21
20	22.02	24.30	26.87	29.78	33.07	36.79	41.00	45.76	51.16	57.28	72.05	91.02	102.4
21	23.24	25.78	28.68	31.97	35.72	39.99	44.87	50.42	56.76	64.00	81.70	104.8	118.8
22	24.47	27.30	30.54	34.25	38.51	43.39	49.01	55.46	62.87	71.40	92.50	120.4	137.6
23	25.72	28.85	32.45	36.62	41.43	47.00	53.44	60.89	69.53	79.54	104.6	138.3	159.3
24	26.97	30.42	34.43	39.08	44.50	50.82	58.18	66.76	76.79	88.50	118.2	158.7	184.2
25	28.24	32.03	36.46	41.65	47.73	54.86	63.25	73.11	84.70	98.35	133.3	181.9	212.8
26	29.53	33.67	38.55	44.31	51.11	59.16	68.68	79.95	93.32	109.2	150.3	208.3	245.7
27	30.82	35.34	40.71	47.08	54.67	63.71	74.48	87.35	102.7	121.1	169.4	238.5	283.6
28	32.13	37.05	42.93	49.97	58.40	68.53	80.70	95.34	113.0	134.2	190.7	272.9	327.1
29	33.45	38.79	45.22	52.97	62.32	73.64	87.35	104.0	124.1	148.6	214.6	312.1	377.2
30	34.78	40.57	47.58	56.08	66.44	79.06	94.46	113.3	136.3	164.5	241.3	356.8	434.7
40	48.89	60.40	75.40	95.03	120.8	154.8	199.6	259.1	337.9	442.6	767.1	1,342	1,779
50	64.46	84.58	112.8	152.7	209.3	290.3	406.5	573.8	815.1	1,164	2,400	4,995	7,218

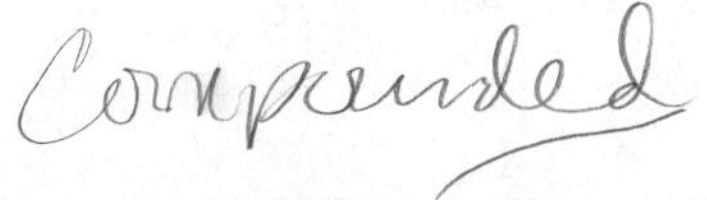

Table D-3. Present Value of $1 to Be Received at the End of a Given Number of Time Periods

Periods	1%	2%	3%	4%	5%	6%	7%	8%	9%	10%	12%
1	0.990	0.980	0.971	0.962	0.952	0.943	0.935	0.926	0.917	0.909	0.893
2	0.980	0.961	0.943	0.925	0.907	0.890	0.873	0.857	0.842	0.826	0.797
3	0.971	0.942	0.915	0.889	0.864	0.840	0.816	0.794	0.772	0.751	0.712
4	0.961	0.924	0.888	0.855	0.823	0.792	0.763	0.735	0.708	0.683	0.636
5	0.951	0.906	0.863	0.822	0.784	0.747	0.713	0.681	0.650	0.621	0.567
6	0.942	0.888	0.837	0.790	0.746	0.705	0.666	0.630	0.596	0.564	0.507
7	0.933	0.871	0.813	0.760	0.711	0.665	0.623	0.583	0.547	0.513	0.452
8	0.923	0.853	0.789	0.731	0.677	0.627	0.582	0.540	0.502	0.467	0.404
9	0.914	0.837	0.766	0.703	0.645	0.592	0.544	0.500	0.460	0.424	0.361
10	0.905	0.820	0.744	0.676	0.614	0.558	0.508	0.463	0.422	0.386	0.322
11	0.896	0.804	0.722	0.650	0.585	0.527	0.475	0.429	0.388	0.350	0.287
12	0.887	0.788	0.701	0.625	0.557	0.497	0.444	0.397	0.356	0.319	0.257
13	0.879	0.773	0.681	0.601	0.530	0.469	0.415	0.368	0.326	0.290	0.229
14	0.870	0.758	0.661	0.577	0.505	0.442	0.388	0.340	0.299	0.263	0.205
15	0.861	0.743	0.642	0.555	0.481	0.417	0.362	0.315	0.275	0.239	0.183
16	0.853	0.728	0.623	0.534	0.458	0.394	0.339	0.292	0.252	0.218	0.163
17	0.844	0.714	0.605	0.513	0.436	0.371	0.317	0.270	0.231	0.198	0.146
18	0.836	0.700	0.587	0.494	0.416	0.350	0.296	0.250	0.212	0.180	0.130
19	0.828	0.686	0.570	0.475	0.396	0.331	0.277	0.232	0.194	0.164	0.116
20	0.820	0.673	0.554	0.456	0.377	0.312	0.258	0.215	0.178	0.149	0.104
21	0.811	0.660	0.538	0.439	0.359	0.294	0.242	0.199	0.164	0.135	0.093
22	0.803	0.647	0.522	0.422	0.342	0.278	0.226	0.184	0.150	0.123	0.083
23	0.795	0.634	0.507	0.406	0.326	0.262	0.211	0.170	0.138	0.112	0.074
24	0.788	0.622	0.492	0.390	0.310	0.247	0.197	0.158	0.126	0.102	0.066
25	0.780	0.610	0.478	0.375	0.295	0.233	0.184	0.146	0.116	0.092	0.059
26	0.772	0.598	0.464	0.361	0.281	0.220	0.172	0.135	0.106	0.084	0.053
27	0.764	0.586	0.450	0.347	0.268	0.207	0.161	0.125	0.098	0.076	0.047
28	0.757	0.574	0.437	0.333	0.255	0.196	0.150	0.116	0.090	0.069	0.042
29	0.749	0.563	0.424	0.321	0.243	0.185	0.141	0.107	0.082	0.063	0.037
30	0.742	0.552	0.412	0.308	0.231	0.174	0.131	0.099	0.075	0.057	0.033
40	0.672	0.453	0.307	0.208	0.142	0.097	0.067	0.046	0.032	0.022	0.011
50	0.608	0.372	0.228	0.141	0.087	0.054	0.034	0.021	0.013	0.009	0.003

necessary multiplier for five years at 9 percent is 1.539, and the answer is:

$$\$5{,}000(1.539) = \underline{\underline{\$7{,}695}}$$

Situations requiring the use of Table D-2 are similar to those requiring Table D-1 except that Table D-2 is used to find the future value of a *series* of *equal* annual deposits.

Single Payment. discounted

Table D-3. (*continued*)

14%	15%	16%	18%	20%	25%	30%	35%	40%	45%	50%	Periods
0.877	0.870	0.862	0.847	0.833	0.800	0.769	0.741	0.714	0.690	0.667	1
0.769	0.756	0.743	0.718	0.694	0.640	0.592	0.549	0.510	0.476	0.444	2
0.675	0.658	0.641	0.609	0.579	0.512	0.455	0.406	0.364	0.328	0.296	3
0.592	0.572	0.552	0.516	0.482	0.410	0.350	0.301	0.260	0.226	0.198	4
0.519	0.497	0.476	0.437	0.402	0.320	0.269	0.223	0.186	0.156	0.132	5
0.456	0.432	0.410	0.370	0.335	0.262	0.207	0.165	0.133	0.108	0.088	6
0.400	0.376	0.354	0.314	0.279	0.210	0.159	0.122	0.095	0.074	0.059	7
0.351	0.327	0.305	0.266	0.233	0.168	0.123	0.091	0.068	0.051	0.039	8
0.300	0.284	0.263	0.225	0.194	0.134	0.094	0.067	0.048	0.035	0.026	9
0.270	0.247	0.227	0.191	0.162	0.107	0.073	0.050	0.035	0.024	0.017	10
0.237	0.215	0.195	0.162	0.135	0.086	0.056	0.037	0.025	0.017	0.012	11
0.208	0.187	0.168	0.137	0.112	0.069	0.043	0.027	0.018	0.012	0.008	12
0.182	0.163	0.145	0.116	0.093	0.055	0.033	0.020	0.013	0.008	0.005	13
0.160	0.141	0.125	0.099	0.078	0.044	0.025	0.015	0.009	0.006	0.003	14
0.140	0.123	0.108	0.084	0.065	0.035	0.020	0.011	0.006	0.004	0.002	15
0.123	0.107	0.093	0.071	0.054	0.028	0.015	0.008	0.005	0.003	0.002	16
0.108	0.093	0.080	0.060	0.045	0.023	0.012	0.006	0.003	0.002	0.001	17
0.095	0.081	0.069	0.051	0.038	0.018	0.009	0.005	0.002	0.001	0.001	18
0.083	0.070	0.060	0.043	0.031	0.014	0.007	0.003	0.002	0.001		19
0.073	0.061	0.051	0.037	0.026	0.012	0.005	0.002	0.001	0.001		20
0.064	0.053	0.044	0.031	0.022	0.009	0.004	0.002	0.001			21
0.056	0.046	0.038	0.026	0.018	0.007	0.003	0.001	0.001			22
0.049	0.040	0.033	0.022	0.015	0.006	0.002	0.001				23
0.043	0.035	0.028	0.019	0.013	0.005	0.002	0.001				24
0.038	0.030	0.024	0.016	0.010	0.004	0.001	0.001				25
0.033	0.026	0.021	0.014	0.009	0.003	0.001					26
0.029	0.023	0.018	0.011	0.007	0.002	0.001					27
0.026	0.020	0.016	0.010	0.006	0.002	0.001					28
0.022	0.017	0.014	0.008	0.005	0.002						29
0.020	0.015	0.012	0.007	0.004	0.001						30
0.005	0.004	0.003	0.001	0.001							40
0.001	0.001	0.001									50

Example. What will be the future value at the end of thirty years if $1,000 is deposited each year on January 1, assuming 12 percent interest compounded annually? The required multiplier from Table D-2 is 241.3, and the answer is:

$$\$1{,}000(241.3) = \underline{\underline{\$241{,}300}}$$

Table D-4. Present Value of $1 Received Each Period for a Given Number of Time Periods

Periods	1%	2%	3%	4%	5%	6%	7%	8%	9%	10%	12%
1	0.990	0.980	0.971	0.962	0.952	0.943	0.935	0.926	0.917	0.909	0.893
2	1.970	1.942	1.913	1.886	1.859	1.833	1.808	1.783	1.759	1.736	1.690
3	2.941	2.884	2.829	2.775	2.723	2.673	2.624	2.577	2.531	2.487	2.402
4	3.902	3.808	3.717	3.630	3.546	3.465	3.387	3.312	3.240	3.170	3.037
5	4.853	4.713	4.580	4.452	4.329	4.212	4.100	3.993	3.890	3.791	3.605
6	5.795	5.601	5.417	5.242	5.076	4.917	4.767	4.623	4.486	4.355	4.111
7	6.728	6.472	6.230	6.002	5.786	5.582	5.389	5.206	5.033	4.868	4.564
8	7.652	7.325	7.020	6.733	6.463	6.210	5.971	5.747	5.535	5.335	4.968
9	8.566	8.162	7.786	7.435	7.108	6.802	6.515	6.247	5.995	5.759	5.328
10	9.471	8.983	8.530	8.111	7.722	7.360	7.024	6.710	6.418	6.145	5.650
11	10.368	9.787	9.253	8.760	8.306	7.887	7.499	7.139	6.805	6.495	5.938
12	11.255	10.575	9.954	9.385	8.863	8.384	7.943	7.536	7.161	6.814	6.194
13	12.134	11.348	10.635	9.986	9.394	8.853	8.358	7.904	7.487	7.103	6.424
14	13.004	12.106	11.296	10.563	9.899	9.295	8.745	8.244	7.786	7.367	6.628
15	13.865	12.849	11.938	11.118	10.380	9.712	9.108	8.559	8.061	7.606	6.811
16	14.718	13.578	12.561	11.652	10.838	10.106	9.447	8.851	8.313	7.824	6.974
17	15.562	14.292	13.166	12.166	11.274	10.477	9.763	9.122	8.544	8.022	7.102
18	16.398	14.992	13.754	12.659	11.690	10.828	10.059	9.372	8.756	8.201	7.250
19	17.226	15.678	14.324	13.134	12.085	11.158	10.336	9.604	8.950	8.365	7.366
20	18.046	16.351	14.878	13.590	12.462	11.470	10.594	9.818	9.129	8.514	7.469
21	18.857	17.011	15.415	14.029	12.821	11.764	10.836	10.017	9.292	8.649	7.562
22	19.660	17.658	15.937	14.451	13.163	12.042	11.061	10.201	9.442	8.772	7.645
23	20.456	18.292	16.444	14.857	13.489	12.303	11.272	10.371	9.580	8.883	7.718
24	21.243	18.914	16.936	15.247	13.799	12.550	11.469	10.529	9.707	8.985	7.784
25	22.023	19.523	17.413	15.622	14.094	12.783	11.654	10.675	9.823	9.077	7.843
26	22.795	20.121	17.877	15.983	14.375	13.003	11.826	10.810	9.929	9.161	7.896
27	23.560	20.707	18.327	16.330	14.643	13.211	11.987	10.935	10.027	9.237	7.943
28	24.316	21.281	18.764	16.663	14.898	13.406	12.137	11.051	10.116	9.307	7.984
29	25.066	21.844	19.189	16.984	15.141	13.591	12.278	11.158	10.198	9.370	8.022
30	25.808	22.396	19.600	17.292	15.373	13.765	12.409	11.258	10.274	9.427	8.055
40	32.835	27.355	23.115	19.793	17.159	15.046	13.332	11.925	10.757	9.779	8.244
50	39.196	31.424	25.730	21.482	18.256	15.762	13.801	12.234	10.962	9.915	8.305

Table D-3 is used to find the value today of a *single* amount of cash to be received sometime in the future. To use Table D-3, you must first know: (1) time period in years until funds will be received, (2) annual rate of interest, and (3) dollar amount to be received at end of time period.

Example. What is the present value of $30,000 to be received twenty-five years from now, assuming a 14 percent interest rate? From Table D-3, the required multiplier is 0.038, and the answer is:

$$\$30{,}000(0.038) = \underline{\underline{\$1{,}140}}$$

Table D-4. *(continued)*

14%	15%	16%	18%	20%	25%	30%	35%	40%	45%	50%	Periods
0.877	0.870	0.862	0.847	0.833	0.800	0.769	0.741	0.714	0.690	0.667	1
1.647	1.626	1.605	1.566	1.528	1.440	1.361	1.289	1.224	1.165	1.111	2
2.322	2.283	2.246	2.174	2.106	1.952	1.816	1.696	1.589	1.493	1.407	3
2.914	2.855	2.798	2.690	2.589	2.362	2.166	1.997	1.849	1.720	1.605	4
3.433	3.352	3.274	3.127	2.991	2.689	2.436	2.220	2.035	1.876	1.737	5
3.889	3.784	3.685	3.498	3.326	2.951	2.643	2.385	2.168	1.983	1.824	6
4.288	4.160	4.039	3.812	3.605	3.161	2.802	2.508	2.263	2.057	1.883	8
4.639	4.487	4.344	4.078	3.837	3.329	2.925	2.598	2.331	2.109	1.922	8
4.946	4.772	4.607	4.303	4.031	3.463	3.019	2.665	2.379	2.144	1.948	9
5.216	5.019	4.833	4.494	4.192	3.571	3.092	2.715	2.414	2.168	1.965	10
5.453	5.234	5.029	4.656	4.327	3.656	3.147	2.752	2.438	2.185	1.977	11
5.660	5.421	5.197	4.793	4.439	3.725	3.190	2.779	2.456	2.197	1.985	12
5.842	5.583	5.342	4.910	4.533	3.780	3.223	2.799	2.469	2.204	1.990	13
6.002	5.724	5.468	5.008	4.611	3.824	3.249	2.814	2.478	2.210	1.993	14
6.142	5.847	5.575	5.092	4.675	3.859	3.268	2.825	2.484	2.214	1.995	15
6.265	5.954	5.669	5.162	4.730	3.887	3.283	2.834	2.489	2.216	1.997	16
6.373	6.047	5.749	5.222	4.775	3.910	3.295	2.840	2.492	2.218	1.998	17
6.467	6.128	5.818	5.273	4.812	3.928	3.304	2.844	2.494	2.219	1.999	18
6.550	6.198	5.877	5.316	4.844	3.942	3.311	2.848	2.496	2.220	1.999	19
6.623	6.259	5.929	5.353	4.870	3.954	3.316	2.850	2.497	2.221	1.999	20
6.687	6.312	5.973	5.384	4.891	3.963	3.320	2.852	2.498	2.221	2.000	21
6.743	6.359	6.011	5.410	4.909	3.970	3.323	2.853	2.498	2.222	2.000	22
6.792	6.399	6.044	5.432	4.925	3.976	3.325	2.854	2.499	2.222	2.000	23
6.835	6.434	6.073	5.451	4.937	3.981	3.327	2.855	2.499	2.222	2.000	24
6.873	6.464	6.097	5.467	4.948	3.985	3.329	2.856	2.499	2.222	2.000	25
6.906	6.491	6.118	5.480	4.956	3.988	3.330	2.856	2.500	2.222	2.000	26
6.935	6.514	6.136	5.492	4.964	3.990	3.331	2.856	2.500	2.222	2.000	27
6.961	6.534	6.152	5.502	4.970	3.992	3.331	2.857	2.500	2.222	2.000	28
6.983	6.551	6.166	5.510	4.975	3.994	3.332	2.857	2.500	2.222	2.000	29
7.003	6.566	6.177	5.517	4.979	3.995	3.332	2.857	2.500	2.222	2.000	30
7.105	6.642	6.234	5.548	4.997	3.999	3.333	2.857	2.500	2.222	2.000	40
7.133	6.661	6.246	5.554	4.999	4.000	3.333	2.857	2.500	2.222	2.000	50

Table D-4 is used to find the present value of a *series* of *equal* annual cash flows.

Example. Arthur Howard won a contest on January 1, 1985, in which the prize was $30,000, payable in fifteen annual installments of $2,000 every December 31, beginning in 1985. Assuming a 9 percent interest rate, what is the present value of Mr. Howard's prize on January 1, 1985? From Table D-4, the required multiplier is 8.061, and the answer is:

$$\$2{,}000(8.061) = \underline{\underline{\$16{,}122}}$$

Table D-4 applies to *ordinary annuities,* in which the first cash flow occurs one time period beyond the date for which present value is to be computed. An *annuity due* is a series of equal cash flows for N time periods, but the first payment occurs immediately. The present value of the first payment equals the face value of the cash flow; Table D-4 then is used to measure the present value of $N - 1$ remaining cash flows.

Example. Find the present value on January 1, 1985, of twenty lease payments; each payment of $10,000 is due on January 1, beginning in 1985. Assume an interest rate of 8 percent:

$$\begin{aligned} \text{present value} &= \text{immediate payment} + \left\{\begin{array}{l}\text{present value of 19} \\ \text{subsequent payments of 8\%}\end{array}\right. \\ &= \$10{,}000 + [10{,}000(9.604)] \\ &= \underline{\underline{\$106{,}040}} \end{aligned}$$

APPENDIX E INTERNATIONAL ACCOUNTING

LEARNING OBJECTIVES

1. Define exchange rate and state its significance
2. Record transactions that are affected by changes in foreign exchange rates

Money is the basic unit by which accountants measure business transactions and present financial information. Chapter 1 noted that accountants generally assume that the monetary unit, the dollar in the United States, is a stable measuring unit. Most of the accounting methods presented so far have adhered to this assumption. This appendix is devoted to an important case where the stability of the monetary unit is not assumed, that is, the changing rates at which the dollar can be exchanged for foreign currencies, or international accounting. After studying this appendix, you should be able to meet the learning objectives listed on the left.

As businesses grow, it is natural for them to look for new sources of supply and new markets in other countries. Today, it is common for businesses, called **multinational** or **transnational** corporations, to operate in more than one country, and many of them operate throughout the world.[1] Table E-1 shows the extent of foreign business for a few multinational corporations. IBM, for example, has operations in eighty countries and receives about half of its sales and income from outside the United States. Nestlé, the giant Swiss chocolate and food products company, operates in fifteen countries and receives 98 percent of its sales from outside Switzerland. The economies of such industrial countries as the United States, Japan, Great Britain, West Germany, and France have given rise to large worldwide corporations. In addition, sophisticated investors no longer restrict their investment activities to their domestic securities markets. Many Americans invest in foreign securities markets, and non-Americans invest heavily in the stock market in the United States.

OBJECTIVE 1
Define exchange rate and state its significance

Such transactions have two major effects on accounting. First, most sales or purchases of goods and services in other countries involve different currencies. Thus, one currency needs to be translated into another, using exchange rates. An **exchange rate** is the value of one currency in terms of another. For example, an English person purchasing goods from a U.S. company and paying in U.S. dollars must exchange British pounds for U.S. dollars before making payment. In effect, the currencies are goods that can be bought and sold. Table E-2 illustrates the exchange rates of several currencies in terms of

1. At the time this appendix was written, exchange rates were fluctuating rapidly. Thus, the examples, exercises, and problems in this book use exchange rates in the general range for the countries involved.

Table E-1. Extent of Foreign Business for Selected Companies

Company	Country	Total Revenue (Millions)	Foreign Revenue as % of Total
Exxon	U.S.A.	$86,673	68.1
Mitsubishi	Japan	70,520	64.0
General Motors	U.S.A.	96,372	16.8
British Petroleum	Britain	53,131	81.0
International Business Machines (IBM)	U.S.A.	50,056	43.0
Volkswagenwerk	Germany	17,935	51.5
Bank America	U.S.A.	13,390	38.4
Nestlé	Switzerland	17,184	98.1
Procter & Gamble	U.S.A.	13,552	26.7
Xerox	U.S.A.	11,736	27.2

Source: Forbes, July 28, 1986, pp. 176, 183, and 207–208. Used by permission.

dollars. It shows the exchange rate for British pounds as $1.49 per pound on a particular date. Like the price of any good or service, these prices change daily according to supply and demand for the currencies. For example, less than three years earlier the exchange rate for British pounds was $2.00, and last year it was $1.20. Accounting for these price changes in recording foreign transactions is the subject of the next section.

Accounting for Transactions in Foreign Currencies

OBJECTIVE 2
Record transactions that are affected by changes in foreign exchange rates

Among the first activities of an expanding company in the international market are the buying and selling of goods and services. For example, a maker of precision tools may try to expand by selling its product to foreign customers. Or it might try to lower its product cost by buying a less expensive part from a source in another country. Up to this point in the text, all transactions were recorded in dollars, and it was assumed that the dollar is a uniform measure in the same way that inches and centimeters are. In the international marketplace, a transaction may take place in Japanese yen, British pounds, or some other currency. The values of these currencies rise and fall daily in relation to the dollar.

Foreign Sales. When a domestic company sells merchandise abroad, it may bill either in its own country's currency or in the foreign currency. If the billing and the subsequent payment are both in the domestic currency, no accounting problem arises. For example, assume that the precision toolmaker sells $150,000 worth of tools to a British company and bills the British company in dollars. The entry to record the sale and payment is very familiar:

Date of sale:		
Accounts Receivable, British company	150,000	
Sales		150,000
Date of payment		
Cash	150,000	
Accounts Receivable, British company		150,000

However, if the U.S. company bills the British company in British pounds and accepts payment in pounds, the U.S. company may incur an exchange gain or loss. An exchange gain or loss will occur if the exchange rate of dollars to pounds changes between the date of sale and the date of payment. For example, assume that the sale of $150,000 above was billed as £100,000, reflecting an exchange rate of 1.50 (that is, $1.50 per pound) on the sale date. Now assume that by the date of payment, the exchange rate had fallen to 1.45. The entries to record the transactions are shown below.

Date of sale:		
Accounts Receivable, British company	150,000	
Sales		150,000
£100,000 × $1.50 = $150,000		
Date of payment:		
Cash	145,000	
Exchange Gain or Loss	5,000	
Accounts Receivable, British company		150,000
£100,000 × $1.45 = $145,000		

The U.S. company has incurred an exchange loss of $5,000 because it agreed to accept a fixed number of British pounds in payment, and before the payment was made, the value of each pound went down in value. Had the value of the pound in relation to the dollar increased in value, the U.S. company would have made an exchange gain.

Foreign Purchases. Purchases are the opposite of sales. So the same logic applies to them except that the relation of exchange gains and losses to the

Table E-2. Partial Listing of Foreign Exchange Rates

Country	Prices in $ U.S.	Country	Prices in $ U.S.
Britain (pound)	1.49	Japan (yen)	.0065
Canada (dollar)	.72	Mexico (peso)	.003
France (franc)	.14	West Germany (mark)	.45
Italy (lira)	.0006		

Source: The Wall Street Journal (June 6, 1986). Used by permission.

changes in exchange rates is reversed. For example, assume that the above maker of precision tools purchases $15,000 of a certain part from a Japanese supplier. If the purchase and subsequent payment are made in U.S. dollars, no accounting problem arises.

Date of purchase:		
Purchases	15,000	
Accounts Payable, Japanese company		15,000
Date of payment:		
Accounts Payable, Japanese company	15,000	
Cash		15,000

However, the Japanese company may bill the U.S. company in yen and be paid in yen. If so, the U.S. company will incur an exchange gain or loss if the exchange rate changes between the dates of purchase and payment. For example, assume that the transaction above is in yen and the exchange rates of the dates of purchase and payment are $.0060 and $.0055 per yen, respectively. The entries follow.

Date of purchase:		
Purchases	15,000	
Accounts Payable, Japanese company		15,000
Y2,500,000 × $.006 = $15,000		
Date of payment:		
Accounts Payable, Japanese company	15,000	
Exchange Gain or Loss		1,250
Cash		13,750
Y2,500,000 × $.0055 = $13,750		

In this case, the U.S. company received an exchange gain of $1,250 because it had agreed to pay a fixed Y2,500,000 and, between the dates of purchase and payment, the exchange value of the yen in relation to the dollar decreased.

Realized Versus Unrealized Exchange Gain or Loss. The preceding illustration dealt with completed transactions (in the sense that payment was completed), and the exchange gain or loss was recognized on the date of payment in each case. If financial statements are prepared between the sale or purchase and the subsequent receipt or payment, there will be unrealized gains or losses if the exchange rates have changed. The Financial Accounting Standards Board, in its *Statement No. 52,* requires that exchange gains and losses "shall be included in determining net income for the period in which the exchange rate changes,"[2] including interim (quarterly) periods and whether or not the transaction is complete.

This ruling has caused much debate. Critics charge that it gives too much influence to temporary exchange rate changes, leading to random changes in earnings that hide long-run trends. Others feel the use of current exchange

2. *Statement of Financial Accounting Standards No. 52,* "Foreign Currency Translation" (Stamford, Conn.: Financial Accounting Standards Board, 1981), par. 15.

rates on the balance sheet date to value receivables and payables is a major step toward economic reality (current values).

To show these effects, we will assume the following facts about the preceding case, in which a U.S. company buys parts from a Japanese supplier:

	Date	Exchange Rate ($ per Yen)
Date of purchase	Dec. 1	.0060
Balance sheet date	Dec. 31	.0051
Date of payment	Feb. 1	.0055

The only difference is that the transaction has not been completed by the balance sheet date and the exchange rate was $.0051 per yen on that date. The facts and entries can be shown below.

	Dec. 1	Dec. 31	Feb. 1
Purchase recorded in U.S. dollars (billed as Y2,500,000)	$15,000	$15,000	$15,000
Dollars to be paid to equal Y2,500,000	15,000	12,750	13,750
Unrealized gain (or loss)	—	$ 2,250	
Realized gain (or loss)			$ 1,250

Dec. 1	Purchases	15,000	
	Accounts Payable, Japanese company		15,000
Dec. 31	Accounts Payable, Japanese company	2,250	
	Exchange Gain or Loss		2,250
Feb. 1	Accounts Payable, Japanese company	12,750	
	Exchange Gain or Loss	1,000	
	Cash		13,750

In this case, the original sale was billed in yen by the Japanese company. Following the rules of *Statement No. 52*, an exchange gain of $2,250 is recorded on December 31, and an exchange loss of $1,000 is recorded on February 1. Even though the net effect of these large up-and-down changes is the net exchange gain of $1,250 over the whole transaction, the effect on each year may be important.

Questions

1. What does it mean to say that the exchange rate of a French franc in terms of the U.S. dollar is .15? If a bottle of French perfume costs 200 francs, how much will it cost in dollars?
2. If an American firm does business with a German firm and all their transactions take place in German marks, which firm may incur an exchange gain or loss and why?

Exercises

Exercise E-1. Recording International Transactions: Fluctuating Exchange Rate (L.O. 2)

U.S. Corporation purchased a special-purpose machine from German Corporation on credit for 30,000 DM (marks). At the date of purchase, the exchange rate was $.39 per mark. On the date of payment, which was made in marks, the value of the mark had increased to $.41.

Prepare journal entries to record the purchase and payment in the U.S. Corporation's accounting records.

Exercise E-2. Recording International Transactions (L.O. 2)

U.S. Corporation made a sale on account to British Company on November 15 in the amount of £200,000. Payment was to be made in British pounds on February 15. U.S. Corporation's fiscal year is the same as the calendar year. The British pound was worth $1.20 on November 15, $1.08 on December 31, and $1.28 on February 15.

Prepare journal entries on U.S. Corporation's books to record the sale, year-end adjustment, and collection.

Problems

Problem E-1. Recording International Transactions (L.O. 2)

Shore Company, whose year end is June 30, engaged in the following international transactions:

May 15 Purchased goods from a Japanese firm for $110,000; terms n/10 in U.S. dollars (yen = $.0040).
17 Sold goods to a German company for $140,000; terms n/30 in marks (mark = $.35).
21 Purchased goods from a Mexican company for $120,000; terms n/30 in pesos (peso = $.004).
25 Paid for the goods purchased on May 15 (yen = $.0045).
31 Sold goods to an Italian firm for $200,000; terms n/60 in lira (lira = $.0005).
June 5 Sold goods to a British firm for $56,000; terms n/10 in U.S. dollars (pound = $1.30).
7 Purchased goods from a Japanese firm for $162,000; terms n/30 in yen (yen = $.0045).
15 Received payment for the sale made on June 5 (pound = $1.40).
16 Received payment for the sale made on May 17 (mark = $.40).
17 Purchased goods from a French firm for $66,000; terms n/30 in U.S. dollars (franc = $.11).
20 Paid for the goods purchased on May 21 (peso = $.003).
22 Sold goods to a British firm for $84,000; terms n/30 in pounds (pound = $1.40).
30 Made year-end adjustment for incomplete foreign exchange transactions (franc = $.12; peso = $.003; mark = $.40; lira = $.0003; pound = $1.30; yen = $.0050).
July 7 Paid for the goods purchased on June 7 (yen = $.0045).
19 Paid for the goods purchased on June 17 (franc = $.10).
22 Received payment for the goods sold on June 22 (pound = $1.20).
30 Received payment for the goods sold on May 31 (lira = $.0004).

Required

Prepare general journal entries for the above transactions.

Problem E-2. Recording International Transactions
(L.O. 2)

Hiu Import/Export Company, whose year end is December 31, engaged in the following transactions (exchange rates in parentheses):

Oct. 14 Sold goods to a Mexican firm for $20,000; terms n/30 in U.S. dollars (peso = $.004).
26 Purchased goods from a Japanese firm for $40,000; terms n/20 in yen (yen = $.0040).
Nov. 4 Sold goods to a British firm for $39,000; terms n/30 in pounds (pound = $1.30).
14 Received payment in full for October 14 sale (peso = $.003).
15 Paid for the goods purchased on October 26 (yen = $.0044).
23 Purchased goods from an Italian firm for $28,000; terms n/10 in U.S. dollars (lira = $.0005).
30 Purchased goods from a Japanese firm for $35,200; terms n/60 in yen (yen = $.0044).
Dec. 2 Paid for the goods purchased on November 23 (lira = $.0004).
3 Received payment in full for goods sold on November 4 (pound = $1.20).
8 Sold goods to a French firm for $66,000; terms n/30 in francs (franc = $.11).
17 Purchased goods from a Mexican firm for $37,000; terms n/30 in U.S. dollars (peso = $.004).
18 Sold goods to a German firm for $90,000; terms n/30 in marks (mark = $.30).
31 Made year-end adjusting entries for incomplete foreign exchange transactions (franc = $.09; peso = $.003; pound = $1.10; mark = $.35; lira = $.0004; yen = $.0050).
Jan. 7 Received payment for goods sold on December 8 (franc = $.10).
16 Paid for goods purchased on December 17 (peso = $.002).
17 Received payment for goods sold on December 18 (mark = $.40).
28 Paid for goods purchased on November 30 (yen = $.0045).

Required

Prepare general journal entries for the above transactions.

APPENDIX F OVERVIEW OF INCOME TAXES FOR INDIVIDUALS

LEARNING OBJECTIVES

1. Explain and differentiate some basic concepts related to income taxes and accounting.
2. Identify the major components used in determining the income tax liability of individuals.

The United States Congress first passed a permanent income tax law in 1913, after the Sixteenth Amendment to the Constitution gave legality to such a tax. Its original goal was to provide revenue for the U.S. government, and today the income tax is still a major source of revenue. Of course, most states and many cities also have an income tax. Because these tax laws are in many cases much like those in the federal tax system, the discussion in this appendix is limited to the federal income tax. After studying this appendix, you should be able to meet the learning objectives listed on the left.

Although it is still an important purpose of the federal income tax laws to produce revenue, Congress has also used its taxing power as an instrument of economic policy. Among the economic goals proposed by Congress are a fairer distribution of income, stimulation of economic growth, full employment, encouragement of exploration for oil and minerals, control of inflation, and a variety of social changes.

All three branches of the federal government have a part in the federal income tax system. The Internal Revenue Service (IRS), which is an agency of the Treasury Department, administers the system. The income tax law is based on over fifty revenue acts and other related laws that have been passed by Congress since 1913. Also, the IRS issues regulations that interpret the law. It is the federal court system, however, that must uphold these important regulations and that has final authority for interpreting the law.

The income tax has had important effects on both individuals and businesses. In 1913, an individual who earned $30,000 paid only $300 or $400 in income taxes. Under the Tax Reform Act of 1986, an individual who earns the same amount may pay as much as $5,000 or more, and corporations may pay as much as one-third of their income in taxes. Clearly, the income tax is an important cost of doing business today.

Some Basic Concepts Related to Federal Income Taxes

To understand the nature of federal income taxes, it is important to distinguish between taxable income and accounting income, between tax planning and tax evasion, between cash basis and accrual basis, and among classifications of taxpayers.

Taxable Income and Accounting Income

OBJECTIVE 1
Explain and differentiate some basic concepts related to income taxes and accounting.

The government assesses income taxes on **taxable income**, which usually is gross income less various exemptions and deductions specified by the law and the IRS regulations. Taxable income is generally found by referring to information in the accounting records. However, it is very unlikely that taxable income and accounting income for an entity will be the same, because they have different purposes. The government levies income taxes to obtain revenue from taxpayers and to carry out economic policies totally unrelated to the measurement of economic income, which is the purpose of accounting.

Tax Planning and Tax Evasion

The arrangement of a taxpayer's affairs in such a way as to incur the smallest legal tax is called **tax planning**. For almost every business decision, alternative courses of action are available that will affect taxable income in different ways. For example, the taxpayer may lease or buy a truck, may use LIFO, FIFO, or average cost to account for inventories, or may time an expenditure to be accounted for in one accounting period or another. Once the taxpayer chooses and acts upon an alternative, however, the IRS will usually treat this alternative as the final one for income tax determination. Therefore, in tax planning it is important to consider tax-saving alternatives before putting decisions into effect.

It is the natural goal of any taxable entity to pay as small a tax as possible; both the tax law and the IRS hold that no entity should pay more than is legally required. The best way to accomplish this goal is by careful tax planning. It is, however, illegal to evade paying taxes by concealing actual tax liabilities. This is called **tax evasion**.

Cash Basis and Accrual Basis

In general, taxpayers may use either the cash basis or the accrual basis to arrive at their taxable income. Most individuals use the **cash basis**—the reporting of items of revenue and expense when they are received or paid—because it is the simplest method. Employers usually report their employees' income on a cash basis, and companies that pay dividends and interest on a cash basis must also report them in this way.

Professional and other service enterprises such as those of accountants, attorneys, physicians, travel agents, and insurance agents also typically use the cash basis in determining taxable income. One advantage of this method is that fees charged to clients or customers are not considered to be earned until payment is received. Thus it is possible to defer the taxes on these revenues until the tax year in which they are received. Similarly, expenses such as rent, utilities, and salaries are recorded when they are paid. Thus a business can work at tax planning by carefully timing its expenditures. Still, this method does not apply to expenditures for buildings and equipment used for business purposes. Such items are treated in accordance with the accelerated cost recovery system discussed in Chapter 10.

Businesses that engage in production or trading of inventories must use the **accrual basis** of accounting rather than the cash basis. In other words, they must report revenues from sales in the period in which they sold the goods, regardless of when they received the cash. And they must record purchases in the year of purchase rather than in the year of payment. They must follow the usual accounting for beginning and ending inventories in determining cost of goods sold. However, the tax laws do not require a strict accrual method in the accounting sense for manufacturing and merchandising concerns. Various modified cash and accrual bases are possible as long as they yield reasonable and consistent results from year to year.

Classifications of Taxpayers

The federal tax law recognizes four classes of taxpayers: individuals, corporations, estates, and trusts. Members of each class must file tax returns and pay taxes on taxable income. This appendix discusses only individuals. Taxation of corporations is covered in Chapter 13. Taxation of estates and trusts is left for a more advanced course.

Although they are business entities for accounting purposes, sole proprietorships and partnerships are not taxable entities. Instead, a proprietor must include the business income on an individual income tax return. Similarly, each partner in a business must include his or her share of the partnership income on an individual return. Each partnership, however, must file an information return showing the results of the partnership's operations and how each partner's share of the income was determined.

In contrast, corporations are taxable entities that must file tax returns and are taxed directly on their earnings. If, after paying its income tax, the corporation distributes some of its earnings to its stockholders, the stockholders must report the dividend income as part of their gross income. This rule has led to the claim that corporate income is subject to **double taxation**—once when it is earned by the company and once when it is paid to the owners of the company's stock.

Income Tax for Individuals

OBJECTIVE 2
Identify the major components used in determining the income tax liability of individuals.

It is important to study income tax for individuals for several reasons. First, most persons who earn taxable income must file a tax return. Second, all persons who operate proprietorships or partnerships must report the income from their businesses on their individual tax returns. Third, many of the same tax terms are used for both individuals and corporations.

The Internal Revenue Code establishes the method of calculating taxable income for individuals. The starting place for figuring taxable income is finding gross income. The next step is to find the amount of adjusted gross income by subtracting deductions from gross income. Under this heading are the expenses of running a business or profession and certain other specified expenses. Then, from adjusted gross income one subtracts a second kind of deduction, called deductions from adjusted gross income, to arrive at taxable income. Under this second heading come (1) certain business and personal expenses and (2) allowances known as exemptions. These procedures can be outlined as follows:

Gross income	$xxx	
Less deductions from gross income	xxx	
Adjusted gross income		$xxx
Less deductions from adjusted gross income:		
a. Itemized or standard deduction	$xxx	
b. Exemptions	xxx	xxx
Taxable income		$xxx

Gross Income

The Internal Revenue Code defines **gross income** as income from all sources, less allowable exclusions. Under this heading are wages, salaries, bonuses, fees, tips, interest, dividends, pensions, and annuities. Rents, royalties, alimony, prizes, profits or shares of profits from business, and gains on sale of property or stocks are also included. Income from illegal sources also must be reported as gross income.

Deductions from Gross Income

The calculation of **adjusted gross income** is important to the individual because it serves as the basis for certain personal deductions in figuring taxable income. These **deductions from gross income** are meant to give people a fairer base than gross income. For example, some people may have a high gross income but may have had many business expenditures to gain that gross income. So it is fair to let them deduct the amount spent in earning the gross income.

Deductions from Adjusted Gross Income

Deductions from adjusted gross income fall under two headings: (1) the standard deduction or itemized deductions, and (2) exemptions. The **standard deduction** is an amount allowed every taxpayer for personal and business expenses. The amounts allowable to taxpayers according to their filing statuses is shown in Table F-1. If the taxpayer's actual itemized allowable deductions exceed the standard deduction, the taxpayer may deduct the expenses as itemized deductions. Allowable itemized deductions for this purpose include medical and dental expenses, taxes, charitable contributions, casualty losses, employee business expenses not reimbursed by employers, and other miscellaneous expenses such as union and professional dues, all subject to certain limitations.

Besides the standard deduction and itemized deductions, the taxpayer is allowed another kind of deduction, called an **exemption**. For each exemption,

Table F-1. Amounts Allowed as Standard Deductions

Filing Status	1987	1988
Married filing jointly, and surviving spouses	$3,760	$5,000
Heads of households	2,540	4,400
Single individuals	2,540	3,000
Married individuals filing separately	1,880	2,500

the taxpayer may deduct $1,900 ($1,950 in 1988, $2,000 in 1989) from adjusted gross income. A taxpayer is allowed one exemption for himself or herself, and one for each dependent. To qualify as a dependent, a person must be (1) closely related to the taxpayer or have lived in the taxpayer's house for the whole year, (2) must have received over half of his or her support during the year from the taxpayer, (3) must not file a joint return with his or her spouse, if married, (4) must have a limited amount of gross income, and (5) must be a U.S. citizen or a resident of the United States, Canada, or Mexico. If a husband and wife file a joint return, they may combine their exemptions. Elderly and blind taxpayers are no longer allowed additional exemptions for age or blindness, as they were before 1987, but they are allowed increased standard deductions.

Computing Tax Liability

In general, the income tax is a **progressive tax**, which means that the rate becomes larger as the amount of taxable income becomes larger. In other words, the higher a person's taxable income, the larger the proportion of it that goes to pay taxes.[1] Different rate schedules apply to single taxpayers, married taxpayers who file joint returns, married taxpayers who file separate returns, and single taxpayers who qualify as heads of households. Taxpayers can calculate their **tax liability** by referring to the tax rate schedules in Exhibit F-1.[2] By looking at these schedules, one can easily see the progressive nature of the tax. It is clear from Exhibit F-1 that the marginal tax rate (that is, the rate of taxation on each *additional* dollar of taxable income) can go as high as 38.5 percent. Subject to further amendments of the Internal Revenue Code, the highest marginal rate in 1988 and following years will be 28 percent (33 percent, including surtax for certain individuals).

1. In contrast to a progressive tax rate, a **regressive tax** rate becomes less as one's income rises. An example of a regressive tax is the social security (FICA) tax, which is levied on incomes only up to a certain amount. A **proportional tax** is one in which the rate is the same percentage regardless of income. Examples are most sales taxes and the income taxes of some states, such as Illinois.
2. The Internal Revenue Service provides tax tables in which the tax liabilities for specific taxable incomes for taxpayers in each filing status are calculated for taxpayers' convenience.

Exhibit F-1. Tax Rates in 1987 and Following Years

Tax Rate Structure for 1987

For taxable years beginning in 1987, five-bracket rate schedules are provided, as shown in the table below.

	Taxable Income Brackets		
Tax Rate	Married, Filing Joint Returns	Heads of Household	Single Individuals
11 percent	0–$3,000	0–$2,500	0–$1,800
15 percent	$ 3,000–28,000	$ 2,500–23,000	$ 1,800–16,800
28 percent	28,000–45,000	23,000–38,000	16,800–27,000
35 percent	45,000–90,000	38,000–80,000	27,000–54,000
38.5 percent	Over $90,000	Over $80,000	Over $54,000

For married individuals filing separate returns, the taxable income bracket amounts for 1987 begin at one-half the amounts for joint returns. The bracket amounts for surviving spouses are the same as those for married individuals filing joint returns.

Tax Rate Structure in 1988 and Following Years

The tax rate structure for 1988 and following years consists of two brackets and tax rates—15 and 28 percent—beginning at zero taxable income.

Filing Status	Tax Rate	Brackets
Married Individuals Filing Jointly and Surviving Spouses	15%	0–$29,750
	28%	Over $29,750
Heads of Household	15%	0–$23,900
	28%	Over $23,900
Single Individuals	15%	0–$17,850
	28%	Over $17,850

Note: For married individuals filing separate returns, the 28 percent bracket begins at $14,875, i.e., one-half the taxable income amount for joint returns. For certain taxpayers, a 5 percent surcharge is applicable, which would bring the maximum tax rate to 33 percent.

Beginning in 1989, the taxable income amounts at which the 28 percent rate starts will be adjusted for inflation.

Capital Gains and Losses

The income tax law accorded capital gains special treatment from 1922 through 1987. Beginning in 1988, the special treatment for net capital gains has been eliminated. Nevertheless, certain limitations have been retained for taxpayers who suffer capital losses. Assets subject to these rules, called

capital assets, usually include stocks, bonds, and other investment property. Under certain circumstances, business buildings, equipment, and land are included. Capital assets usually do not include trade receivables, inventories, and other properties created by the taxpayer, such as literary or artistic works.

One effective means of tax planning is to arrange transactions involving capital assets to reduce or defer taxes. If a taxpayer sells stock at a gain near the end of the year, the gain is taxable during that year. By waiting until just after the first day of the next year, a taxpayer can defer the tax on the gain for an entire year.

Net Capital Gain. Net capital gains are taxed at an optional, preferential rate of 28 percent in 1987. After 1987, net capital gains are taxed at the same rate as other income of the taxpayer.

Net Capital Loss. Can a taxpayer reduce taxes by selling stock or other investments that have declined in value at a loss? In other words, can a taxpayer deduct such losses from other income, such as salary income, and thereby reduce the tax on the other income? When a taxpayer's transactions involving capital assets for a year result in a *net* capital loss, the amount of the loss that may be deducted from other income is limited. Capital losses can be offset against capital gains. Other income, however, can only be reduced by a maximum of $3,000 in any one year. Any excess *net* capital loss over the $3,000 must be carried forward to be deducted in future years.

Credit Against the Tax Liability

Tax credits are subtractions from the computed tax liability and should not be confused with deductions that are subtracted from income to determine gross income. Since tax credits reduce tax liability dollar for dollar, they are more beneficial to taxpayers than equal dollar amounts of deductions from taxable income. Tax credits are allowed to the elderly, for dependent care expenses, for income taxes paid in foreign countries, and for jobs provided to members of certain groups.

Withholding and Estimated Tax

For most individuals the tax year ends on December 31, and their return is due three and one-half months later, on April 15. If they are wage earners or salaried employees, their employer is required to withhold an estimated income tax from their pay during the year and remit it to the Internal Revenue Service. The employer reports this withholding to the employee on form W-2 on or before January 31 for the preceding year (see Chapter 9 for a discussion of payroll procedures). Taxpayers who have income beyond a certain amount that is not subject to withholding must report a Declaration of Estimated Tax and pay an **estimated tax**, less any amount expected to be withheld, in four installments during the year. When taxpayers prepare their tax returns, they deduct the amount of estimated tax withheld and the amount paid in installments from the total tax liability to find the amount they must pay when they file the tax return.

Questions

1. What is the difference between tax planning and tax evasion?
2. What are the four classes of taxpayers?
3. J. Vickery's sole proprietorship had a net income of $37,500 during the taxable year. During the same year, Vickery withdrew $24,000 from the business. What income must Vickery report on his individual tax return?
4. Which of the two methods of accounting, cash or accrual, is more commonly used by individual taxpayers?
5. Why is it sometimes claimed that corporate income is subject to double taxation?
6. If a friend of yours turned down the opportunity to earn an additional $500 of taxable income because it would put him or her in a higher tax bracket, would you consider this action rational? Why?

Exercise F-1

Computation of Tax Liability

From Exhibit F-1, figure the 1987 and 1988 income tax for each of the following: (1) single individual with taxable income of $12,500, (2) single individual with taxable income of $59,000, (3) married couple filing jointly with taxable income of $11,250, (4) married couple filing jointly with taxable income of $59,000. Assume that none of these taxpayers have income tax credits to apply against the amounts due.

GLOSSARY

Absorption costing: an approach to product costing that assigns a representative portion of *all* manufacturing costs to individual products. (17)

Accelerated cost recovery system (ACRS): requires that a cost recovery allowance be computed on the unadjusted cost of the property being recovered. (10)

Accelerated methods: methods of depreciation that allocate relatively large amounts of the depreciable cost of the asset to earlier years and reduced amounts to later years. (10)

Account: the basic storage unit for data in accounting systems; consists of one for each asset, liability, component of owner's equity, revenue, and expense. (1)

Accountant's report (or auditor's report): a report by an independent public accountant that accompanies the financial statements and contains the accountant's opinion regarding the fairness of presentation of the financial statements.

Account balance: the difference in total dollars between the total debit footing and the total credit footing of an account. (2)

Accounting: an information system that measures, processes, and communicates financial information about an identifiable economic entity to permit users of the system to make informed judgments and decisions. (1)

Accounting cycle: all steps in the accounting process including analyzing and recording transactions, posting entries, adjusting and closing the accounts, and preparing financial statements; accounting system. (4)

Accounting equation, see Balance sheet equation

Accounting period problem: the difficulty of assigning revenues and expenses to short periods of time such as months or years; related to the periodicity assumption. (3)

Accounting rate of return method: a method used to measure the estimated performance of a capital investment that yields an accounting rate of return computed by dividing the project's average after-tax net income by the average cost of the investment over its estimated life. (26)

Accounting system, see Accounting cycle

Accounts receivable: short-term liquid assets that arise from sales on credit to customers at either the wholesale or the retail level. (7)

Accounts receivable aging method: a method of estimating uncollectible accounts expense based on the assumption that the probability of collecting accounts receivable at the end of the period will depend on the length of time individual accounts are past due. (7)

Accrual: the recognition of an expense or revenue that has arisen but has not yet been recorded. (3)

Accrual accounting: all the techniques developed by accountants to apply the matching rule. (3)

Accrual basis: the reporting of revenues from sales in the period in which they are sold, regardless of when the cash is received, and the reporting of expenses in the period of purchase, regardless of when payment is made. (Appendix F)

Accrued expense: an expense that has been incurred but is not recognized in the accounts, necessitating an adjusting entry; unrecorded expense. (3)

Accrued revenue: a revenue for which the service has been performed or the goods have been delivered but that has not been recorded in the accounts; unrecorded revenue. (3)

Accumulated depreciation: a contra-asset account used to accumulate the total past depreciation on a specific long-lived asset. (3)

Activity accounting, see Responsibility accounting

Addition: an expenditure resulting from an expansion of an existing plant asset. (10)

Adjusted gross income: gross income minus deductions from gross income. (Appendix F)

Adjusted trial balance: a trial balance prepared after all adjusting entries have been reflected in the accounts. (3)
Adjusting entry: entry made to apply accrual accounting to transactions that span more than one accounting period. (3)
Aging of accounts receivable: the process of listing each customer in accounts receivable according to the due date of the account. (7)
All financial resources (concept of funds): the concept of funds used in preparation of the statement of changes in financial position when exchange transactions are considered as both a source and a use of working capital.
Allowance for uncollectible accounts: a contra accounts receivable account in which appears the estimated total of the as yet unidentified accounts receivable that will not be collected. (7)
American Institute of Certified Public Accountants (AICPA): the professional association of CPAs. (1)
Amortization: the periodic allocation of the cost of an intangible asset over its useful life. (10)
Annual report: a corporation's yearly financial report to its stockholders, sent as part of management's responsibility to report to the owners of the company; also filed with the SEC.
Appropriated retained earnings: a restriction of retained earnings that indicates that a portion of a company's assets are to be used for purposes other that paying dividends. (13)
Articles of incorporation: a contract between the state and the incorporators forming the corporation. (12)
Asset: an economic resource owned by a business that is expected to benefit future operations. (1)
Asset turnover: a ratio that measures how efficiently assets are used to produce sales. (28)
Audit committee: in the organization of a corporation, a committee with several outside directors which ensures that the board of directors will be objective in judging management's performance. (12)
Audit trail: the sequence of written approval by key individuals supporting an expenditure in a voucher system. (6)
Auditing: the principal and most distinctive function of a certified public accountant; the process of examining and testing the financial statements of a company in order to render an independent professional opinion as to the fairness of their presentation; also called the attest function. (1)
Auditor's report, see Accountant's report
Authorized stock: the maximum number of shares a corporation may issue without changing its charter with the state. (12)
Average cost of capital: a minimum desired rate of return on capital expenditures computed by finding the average of the cost of debt, cost of preferred stock, cost of equity capital, and cost of retained earnings. (26)
Average-cost method: an inventory costing method under which each item of goods sold and of inventory is assigned a cost equal to the average cost of all goods purchased. (8)
Average days' sales uncollected: a ratio that measures how many days it takes before the average receivable is collected. (28)
Avoidable costs: a cost that will be eliminated if a particular product, service, or corporate segment is discontinued. (25)

Balance sheet: a financial statement that shows the financial position of a business at a particular date. (1)
Balance sheet equation: algebraic expression of financial position; assets = liabilities + owner's equity; also called the accounting equation. (1)
Bank reconciliation: the process of accounting for the differences between the balance appearing on the bank statement and the balance of cash according to the depositor's records. (6)
Bank statement: a monthly statement of the transactions related to a particular bank account. (6)
Base year: the first year to be considered in any set of data. (28)
Basic standards: standards that are seldom revised or updated to reflect current operating costs and price level changes. (22)
Batch processing: a type of computer system design in which separate computer jobs such as purchasing, inventory control, payroll, production scheduling, and so forth are processed individually but in a carefully coordinated way.
Beginning inventory: merchandise on hand for sale to customers at the beginning of the accounting period. (5)
Beta: the measure of market risk. (28)
Betterment: an expenditure resulting from an improvement to but not an enlargement of an existing plant asset. (10)
Bond: a security, usually long-term, representing money borrowed by a corporation from the investing public. (14)

Bond certificate: the evidence of a company's debt to the bondholder. (14)
Bond indenture: a supplementary agreement to a bond issue that defines the rights, privileges, and limitations of bondholders. (14)
Bonding: investigating an employee and insuring the company against any theft by that individual. (6)
Bond issue: the total number of bonds that are issued at one time. (14)
Bond sinking fund: a fund established by the segregation of assets over the life of the bond issue to satisfy investors that money will be available to pay the bondholders at maturity. (14)
Bonus: in partnership accounting, an amount that accrues to the original partners when a new partner pays more to the partnership than the interest received or that accrues to the new partner when the amount paid to the partnership is less than the interest received. (11)
Bookkeeping: the means by which transactions are recorded and records are kept; a process of accounting. (1)
Book value: total assets of a company less total liabilities; owners' equity. (13, 26)
Break-even point: that point in financial analysis at which total revenue equals total cost incurred and at which a company begins to generate a profit. (19)
Budgetary control: the total process of (1) developing plans for a company's anticipated operations and (2) controlling operations to aid in accomplishing those plans. (21)
Business transaction: an economic event that affects the financial position of a business entity. (1)

Callable bonds: bonds that a corporation has the option of buying back and retiring at a given price, usually above face value, before maturity. (14)
Callable preferred stock: preferred stock that may be redeemed and retired by the corporation at its option. (12)
Capital assets: certain types of assets that qualify for special treatment when gains and losses result from transactions involving the assets. (Appendix F)
Capital budgeting: the combined process of identifying a facility need, analyzing alternative courses of action to satisfy that need, preparing the reports for management, selecting the best alternative, and rationing available capital expenditure funds among competing resource needs. (26)
Capital expenditure: an expenditure for the purchase or expansion of plant assets. (10)
Capital expenditure decision: the decision to determine when and how much money to spend on capital facilities for the company. (26)
Capital lease: long-term lease that is in effect an installment purchase of assets; recorded by entering on the books an asset and a corresponding liability at the present value of the lease payments; each lease payment is partly a repayment of debt and partly an interest payment on the debt. (14)
Carrying value: the unexpired portion of the cost of an asset; sometimes called book value. (10)
Cash basis of accounting: a basis of accounting under which revenues and expenses are accounted for on a cash received and cash paid basis. (3, Appendix F)
Cash budget, see Cash Flow Forecast.
Cash disbursements journal, see Cash payments journal
Cash equivalents: short-term, highly liquid investments, including money market accounts, commercial paper, and U.S. treasury bills. (27)
Cash flow forecast: a forecast or budget that shows the firm's projected ending cash balance and the cash position for each month of the year so that periods of high or low cash availability can be anticipated; also called a cash budget. (21)
Cash flow statement: a financial statement that shows a company's sources and uses of cash during an accounting period.
Cash payments journal: a multicolumn special-purpose journal in which disbursements of cash are recorded; also called cash disbursements journal. (A)
Cash receipts journal: a multicolumn special-purchase journal in which transactions involving receipts of cash are recorded. (A)
Cash short or over: an account used to record small shortages or overages that result from the handling of cash. (6)
Certified management accountant (CMA): management accountants who have met stringent licensing requirements. (1)
Certified public accountant (CPA): public accountants who have met stringent licensing requirements. (1)

Chart of accounts: a numbering scheme that assigns a unique number to each account to facilitate finding the account in the ledger. (2)
Check: a negotiable instrument used to pay for goods and services. (6)
Check authorization: a document prepared by the accounting department authorizing the payment of the invoice; supported by a purchase order, invoice, and receiving report. (6)
Check register: a special-purpose journal used in a voucher system to record each expenditure made by check. (6)
Classification problem: the difficulty of assigning all the transactions in which a business engages to the appropriate account or accounts. (2)
Classified financial statements: financial statements divided into useful subcategories. (5)
Clearing entries, see Closing entries
Closely held corporation: a corporation whose stock is owned by a few individuals and whose securities are not publicly traded.
Closing entries: journal entries made at the end of the accounting period that set the stage for the next accounting period by closing the expense and revenue accounts of the balances and transferring the net amount to the owner's capital account or retained earnings; clearing entries. (4)
Common-size statement: a statement in which all components of the statement are shown as a percentage of a total in the statement; results from applying vertical analysis. (28)
Common stock: the stock representing the most basic rights to ownership of a corporation. (12)
Common stock equivalents: convertible securities that, at the time of issuance, have a value that is closely related to their conversion value, that is, the value of the stock into which they could be converted. (13)
Comparability: the qualitative characteristic of accounting information that presents information in such a way that the decision maker can recognize similarities, differences, and trends over time and/or make comparisons with other companies. (B)
Comparative financial statements: financial statements in which data for two or more years are presented in adjacent columnar form.
Compatibility principle: a principle of systems design that holds that the design of a system must be in harmony with organizational and human factors of a business.
Compensating balance: a minimum account that a bank requires a company to keep in its bank account as part of a credit-granting arrangement. (7)
Complex capital structure: a capital structure with additional securities (convertible stocks and bonds) that can be converted into common stock. (13)
Compound entry: a journal entry that has more than one debit and/or credit entry. (2)
Compound interest: the interest cost for two or more periods, if one assumes that after each period the interest of that period is added to the amount on which interest is computed in future periods. (Appendix C)
Comprehensive income: the change in equity (net assets) of an entity during a period from transactions and other events and circumstances from nonowner sources except those changes resulting from investments by owners and distributions to withdrawals by owners.
Computer: an electronic tool for the rapid collection, organization, and communication of large amounts of information. (1)
Computer operator: the person who runs the computer.
Condensed financial statements: presents only the major categories of the financial statement. (5)
Conglomerate: a company that operates in more than one industry; a diversified company. (28)
Conservatism: an accounting convention that means when accountants are faced with major uncertainties as to which alternative accounting procedure to apply, they tend to exercise caution and choose the procedure that is least likely to overstate assets or income. (B)
Consignment: goods placed on the premises of one company (the consignee) by the owner of the goods (the consignor) but not included in physical inventory, because title to the goods remains with the owner until the goods are sold. (8)
Consistency: an accounting convention that requires that a particular accounting procedure, once adopted, will not be changed from period to period. (B)
Consolidated financial statements: the combined financial statements of a parent company and its subsidiaries.
Constant dollar accounting: the restatement of historical cost statements for general price level changes with the result that all amounts are

stated in dollars of uniform general purchasing power.

Contingent liability: a potential liability that can develop into a real liability if a possible subsequent event occurs. (7, 9)

Continuity problem: the difficulty associated with the indefinite life of business enterprises; related to the going concern assumption. (3)

Contra account: an account whose balance is subtracted from an associated account in the financial statements. (3)

Contributed or paid-in capital: that part of owners' equity representing the amounts of assets invested by stockholders. (12)

Contribution margin: the excess of revenues over all variable costs related to a particular sales volume. (19)

Control: the process of seeing that plans are carried out. (1)

Control (of parent over subsidiary): in connection with long-term investments, the ability of the investing company to determine the operating and financial policies of the investee company.

Controllable costs and revenues: those costs that result from a particular manager's actions and decision and over which he or she has full control. (20)

Controllable overhead variance: the difference between actual overhead costs incurred and factory overhead budgeted for the level of production achieved. (23)

Controlling (or control) account: an account in the general ledger that summarizes the total balance of a group of related accounts in a subsidiary ledger. (A, 17)

Control principle: a principle of systems design that holds an accounting system must provide all the features of internal control needed to safeguard assets and ensure the reliability of data.

Conversion costs: the combined total of direct labor and factory overhead costs incurred by a production department or other work center. (18)

Convertible bonds: bonds that may be exchanged for other securities of the corporation, usually common stock. (14)

Convertible preferred stock: stock that can be converted into common stock. Bonds may also have this feature. (12)

Corporation: a body of persons granted a charter legally recognizing them as a separate entity having its own rights, privileges, and liabilities distinct from those of its members. (1, 12)

Cost: exchange price associated with a business transaction at the point of recognition; original cost; historical cost. (2)

Cost allocation (assignment): the process of assigning a specific cost or pool of costs to a specific cost objective or cost objectives. (19)

Cost behavior: the manner in which costs respond to changes in activity or volume. (19)

Cost-benefit principle: a principle of systems design that holds that the value or benefits from a system and its information output must be equal to or greater than its cost. (A, B)

Cost center: any organizational segment or area of activity for which there is a reason to accumulate costs. (19)

Cost expense center: An organizational unit with a manager who is responsible for its actions and costs. (20)

Cost flow: the association of costs with their assumed flow within the operations of a company. (8)

Cost method: a method of accounting for long-term investments when the investor has neither significant influence nor control of the investee; the investor records the investment at cost and recognizes dividends as income when they are received.

Cost objective: the destination of an assigned cost. (19)

Cost of debt: the ratio of loan charges to net proceeds of the loan. After-tax considerations and present value of interest charges should be acknowledged in the computation. (26)

Cost of equity capital: the rate of return to the investor that maintains the stock's value in the marketplace. (26)

Cost of goods manufactured: a term used in the statement of costs of goods manufactured that represents the total manufacturing costs attached to units of product completed during an accounting period. (16)

Cost of goods sold: item on income statement that is computed by subtracting the merchandise inventory at the end of the year from the goods available for sale; deducted from revenue to give gross profit. (5)

Cost of preferred stock: the stated dividend rate of the individual stock issue. (26)

Cost of retained earnings: the opportunity cost or dividends foregone by the stockholder. (26)

Cost-plus transfer price: the sum of costs in-

curred by the producing division plus an agreed on profit percentage. (24)
Cost principle: a principle of systems design that defines cost as the value of an item at the time it was brought into or taken out of the business entity. (A)
Cost summary schedule: a process costing schedule in which total manufacturing costs accumulated during the period are distributed to units completed and transferred out of the department of the units in ending Work in Process Inventory. (18)
Cost-volume-profit (C-V-P) analysis: an analysis based on the relationships among operating cost, sales volume and revenue, and target net income; used as a planning device to predict one of the factors when the other two are known. (19)
Coupon bonds: bonds whose owners are not registered with the issuing corporation but that have interest coupons attached. (14)
Credit: the right side of an account. (2)
Crossfooting: horizontal addition and subtraction of rows in adjacent columns. (4)
Cumulative preferred stock: preferred stock on which unpaid dividends accumulate over time and must be satisfied in any given year before a dividend may be paid to common stockholders. (12)
Current assets: cash or other assets that are reasonably expected to be realized in cash or sold during a normal operating cycle of a business or within one year if the operating cycle is shorter than one year. (5)
Current liabilities: obligations due to be paid within the normal operating cycle of the business or within a year, whichever is longer. (5, 9)
Current ratio: a measure of liquidity; current assets divided by current liabilities. (28)
Current value accounting: a method of accounting that would recognize the effects of specific price changes in the financial statements.
Currently attainable standards: standard costs that are updated periodically to reflect changes in operating conditions and current price levels for direct materials, direct labor, and factory overhead costs. (22)

Data processing: the means by which the accounting system collects data, organizes them into meaningful forms, and issues the resulting information to users.
Debenture bonds, see Unsecured bonds
Debit: the left side of an account. (2)
Debt to equity ratio: a ratio that measures the relationship of assets provided by creditors to the amount provided by stockholders. (28)
Decentralization: a system of management in which operating managers are free to make business decisions within their own departments, as long as they fit into the framework of strategic policies established by top management for the entire company. (20)
Decision model: a symbolic or numerical representation of the variables and parameters affecting a decision. (25)
Declining-balance method: an accelerated method of depreciation. (10)
Deductions from gross income: certain personal deductions allowed in computing taxable income. (Appendix F)
Deferral: the postponement of the recognition of an expense already paid or of a revenue already received. (3)
Deferred income taxes: the difference between the Income Taxes Expense and the current Income Taxes Payable accounts. (13)
Deferred revenues: obligations for goods or services that the company must deliver in return for an advance payment from a customer. (9) (see also Unearned revenues)
Deficit: a debit balance in the Retained Earnings account. (13)
Definitely determinable liability: a liability that is determined by contract or statute and can be measured precisely. (9)
Deflation: a decrease in the general price level.
Depletion: the proportional allocation of the cost of a natural resource to the units removed; the exhaustion of a natural resource through mining, cutting, pumping, or otherwise using up the resource. (10)
Deposits in transit: deposits mailed or taken to the bank but not received by the bank in time to be recorded before preparation of the monthly statement. (6)
Deposit ticket: a document used to make a deposit in a bank. (6)
Depreciable cost: the cost of an asset less its residual value. (10)
Depreciation (depreciation expense): the periodic allocation of the cost of a tangible long-lived asset over its estimated useful life. (3, 10)
Direct charge-off method: a method of accounting for uncollectible accounts by debiting ex-

penses directly when bad debts are discovered instead of using the allowance method; a method that is unacceptable because it violates the matching rule. (7)

Direct cost: a manufacturing cost that is traceable to a specific product or cost objective. (16)

Direct labor: all labor costs for specific work performed on products that are conveniently and economically traceable to end products. (16)

Direct labor efficiency variance: the difference between actual hours worked and standard hours allowed for the good units produced, multiplied by the standard labor rate. (22)

Direct labor rate standards: the hourly labor cost per function or job classification that is expected to exist during the next accounting period. (22)

Direct labor rate variance: the difference between the actual labor rate paid and the standard labor rate, multiplied by the actual hours worked. (22)

Direct labor time standard: an hourly expression of the time it takes for each department, machine, or process to complete production on one unit or one batch of output; based on current time and motion studies of workers and machines and past employee/machine performances. (22)

Direct materials: materials that become an integral part of the finished product and are conveniently and economically traceable to specific units of productive output. (16)

Direct materials price standard: a carefully derived estimate or projected amount of what a particular type of material will cost when purchased during the next accounting period. (22)

Direct materials price variance: the difference between the actual price paid for materials and the standard price, multiplied by the actual quantity purchased. (22)

Direct materials quantity standard: an expression of forecasted or expected quantity usage that is influenced by product engineering specifications, quality of materials used, and productivity of the machines being used, and the quality and experience of the machine operators and set-up people. (22)

Direct materials quantity variance: the difference between the actual quantity of materials used and the standard quantity that should have been used, multiplied by the standard price. (22)

Direct method: method of preparing the statement of cash flows by adjusting each item in the income statement in turn from the accrual basis to the cash basis. The result is a statement that begins with cash receipts from sales and then deducts cash payments for purchases, operating expenses, and income taxes, to arrive at net cash flows from operating activities. (27)

Discontinued operations: segments of a business that are no longer part of the ongoing operations of the company. (13)

Discount: *verb:* to take out the interest on a promissory note in advance; *noun:* the amount of the interest deducted. (7, 14)

Discounted cash flow: the process of discounting future cash flows back to the present using an anticipated discount rate. (26)

Dishonored note: a promissory note that the maker cannot or will not pay at the maturity date. (7)

Disposal value, see Residual value

Diversified company, see Conglomerate

Dividend: a distribution of assets of a corporation to its stockholders. (12, 13)

Dividends in arrears: the accumulated unpaid dividends on cumulative preferred stock from prior years. (12)

Dividends yield: a ratio that measures the current return to an investor in a stock. (28)

Double-declining balance method: an accelerated method of depreciation, related to the declining-balance method, under which the fixed rate used in the method is double the straight-line rate; this rate is the maximum allowable for income tax purposes. (10)

Double-entry system: a system of recording business transactions requiring that each transaction have equal debit and credit totals, thereby maintaining a balance within the accounts taken as a whole. (2)

Double taxation: a term referring to the fact that earnings of a corporation are taxed twice, both as the net income of the corporation and as the dividends distributed to the stockholders. (12, Appendix F)

Duration of note: length of time in days between the making of a promissory note and its maturity date. (7)

Early extinguishment of debt: the extraordinary gain that occurs when a company purchases its bonds on the open market and retires them, rather than waiting to pay them off at face value. (28)

Earnings per (common) share: item on corporate income statements that shows the net income earned on each share of common stock; net income divided by the weighted average number of common shares and common share equivalents outstanding; also called net income per share. (13)
Effective interest method: a method of determining the interest and amortization of bond discount or premium for each interest period that requires the application of a constant interest rate to the carrying value of the bonds at the beginning of the period. (14)
Eliminations: adjustments that appear on work sheets in the preparation of consolidated financial statements that are intended to reflect the financial position and operations from the standpoint of a single entity.
Employee earnings record: a record of earnings and withholdings for a single employee. (9)
Ending inventory: merchandise on hand for sale to customers at the end of the accounting period. (5)
Equity: the residual interest in the assets of an entity that remains after deducting its liabilities. (1)
Equity method: a method of accounting for long-term investments under which the investor records the initial investment at cost and records its proportionately owned share of subsequent earnings and dividends of the investee as increases or decreases, respectively, in the investment account.
Equivalent units: a measure of productive output of units for a period of time, expressed in terms of fully completed or equivalent whole units produced; partially completed units are restated in terms of equivalent whole units; also called equivalent production. (18)
Estimated liability: a definite obligation of the firm, the exact amount of which cannot be determined until a later date. (9)
Estimated tax: an amount paid in advance by a taxpayer in anticipation of income not subject to withholding. (Appendix F)
Estimated useful life: the total number of service units expected from a long-term asset. (10)
Evaluation: the process of scrutinizing the entire decision system for the purpose of improving it. (1)
Excess capacity: machinery and equipment purchased in excess of needs so that extra capacity is available on a stand-by basis during peak usage periods or when other machinery is down for repair. (19)
Exchange rate: the value of one currency in terms of another. (E)
Exchange transaction: when used in connection with the statement of changes in financial position, an exchange of a long-term asset for a long-term liability.
Ex-dividend: stock sold after the date of record set for distribution of a dividend; right to the dividend does not transfer with the sale. (12)
Exemption: a type of deduction from adjusted gross income based on personal characteristics and number of dependents. (Appendix F)
Expenditure: a payment or incurrence of an obligation to make a future payment for an asset or service rendered. (10)
Expenses: the costs of the goods and services used up in the process of obtaining revenue; expired cost. (1)
Extraordinary items: events or transactions that are distinguished by their unusual nature and the infrequency of their occurrence. (13)
Extraordinary repairs: repairs that affect the estimated residual value or estimated useful life of an asset. (10)

Factory (manufacturing) overhead: a diverse collection of production-related costs that are not practically or conveniently traceable to end products and must be assigned by some allocation method. (16)
Favorable standard cost variance: a variance occurring when actual costs are less than standard costs. (22, 23)
Feedback value: usefulness of information to the decision maker in assessing the accuracy of earlier predictions. (B)
Financial accounting: accounting information reported to and used by those outside the organization. (1)
Financial Accounting Standards Board (FASB): body that has responsibility for developing and issuing rules on accounting practice; issues Statements of Financial Accounting Standards. (1)
Financial position: the collection of resources belonging to a company and the sources of these resources or claims on them at a particular point in time; shown by a balance sheet. (1)
Financial statement analysis: the collective term used for the techniques that show significant relationships in financial statements and that

facilitate comparisons from period to period and among companies. (28)

Financial statements: the means by which accountants communicate to information users; financial reports. (1)

Finished goods inventory: an inventory account unique to the manufacturing or production area to which the costs assigned to all completed products are transferred. The balance at period-end represents all manufacturing costs assigned to goods completed but not sold as of that date. (16)

First-in, first-out (FIFO) method: an inventory costing method under which the cost of the first items purchased are assigned to the first items sold and the costs of the last items purchased are assigned to the items remaining in inventory. (8)

Fiscal year: any twelve-month accounting period used by a company. (3)

Fixed assets: another name, no longer in wide use, for long-term nonmonetary assets. (10)

Fixed cost: a cost that remains constant in total within a relevant range of volume or activity. (19)

Fixed manufacturing costs: production-related costs that remain relatively constant in amount during the accounting period and vary little in relation to increases or decreases in production. (16)

Flexibility principle: a principle of systems design that holds that the accounting system should be sufficiently flexible to accommodate growth in the volume of transactions and organizational changes in the business. (A)

Flexible budget: a summary of anticipated costs prepared for a range of different activity levels and geared to changes in the level of productive output. (22, 23)

FOB destination: term relating to transportation charges meaning that the supplier bears the transportation costs to the destination. (5)

FOB shipping point: term relating to transportation charges meaning that the buyer bears the transportation costs from the point of origin. (5)

Footing: a memorandum total of a column of numbers; to foot, to total a column of numbers. (2)

Freight in: transportation charges on merchandise purchased for resale; transportation in. (5)

Full costing: a method of accounting for oil and gas development and exploration under which the costs associated with both successful and unsuccessful explorations are capitalized and depleted over the useful life of the producing resources. (10)

Full disclosure: an accounting convention requiring that financial statements and their accompanying footnotes contain all information relevant to the user's understanding of the situation. (B)

Fully diluted earnings per share: net income applicable to common stock divided by the sum of the weighted-average common stock and common stock equivalents and other potentially dilutive securities. (13) See also Earnings per common share.

Functional currency: currency of the country where the subsidiary carries on most of its business. (E)

Funds: equivalent to working capital when used in connection with the statement of changes in financial position.

Future value: the amount that an investment will be worth at a future date if invested at compound interest. (Appendix C)

General journal: the simplest and most flexible type of journal. (2)

Generally Accepted Accounting Principles (GAAP): the conventions, rules, and procedures necessary to define accepted accounting practice at a particular time. (1)

General price level: a price level that reflects the price changes of a group of goods or services.

General-purpose external financial statements: means by which the information accumulated and processed in the financial accounting system is periodically communicated to those persons, especially investors and creditors, who use it outside the enterprise. (B)

Going concern: the assumption that unless there is evidence to the contrary the business will continue to operate for an indefinite period. (3)

Goods available for sale: the sum of merchandise inventory at the beginning of a period plus net purchases during the period. (5)

Goods flow: the actual physical movement of inventory goods in the operations of a company. (8)

Goodwill: the excess of the cost of a group of assets (usually a business) over the market value of the assets individually. (10)

Government Accounting Standards Board (GASB): issues accounting standards for state and local governments. (1)

Gross income: income from all sources, less allowable exclusions. (Appendix F)
Gross margin: difference between revenue from sales and costs of goods sold; also called gross margin from sales. (5)
Gross margin pricing: an approach to price determination in which the projected price equals total production cost per unit times the total production cost per unit plus a markup percentage. The markup percentage is computed by dividing total selling, general, and administrative expenses plus the desired profit by total production cost. (24)
Gross method: system of recording purchases initially at the gross purchase price; does not allow for discounts lost, only discounts taken. (12)
Gross payroll: a measure of the total wages or salary earned by an employee before any deductions are subtracted. This amount is also used to determine total manufacturing labor costs. (16)
Gross profit method: used to estimate the value of inventory; assumes that the ratio of gross margin for a business is relatively stable from year to year. (8)
Gross sales: total sales for cash and on credit for a given accounting period. (5)
Group depreciation: the grouping of items of similar plant assets together for purposes of calculating depreciation. (10)

Hardware: all the equipment needed for the operation of a computer data processing system.
Horizontal analysis: the computation of dollar amount changes and percentage changes from year to year. (28)

Ideal standards: perfection standards that allow minimum materials, labor time, and cost constraints for manufacturing a particular product or creating a service. (22)
Imprest system: a petty cash system in which a petty cash fund is established at a fixed amount of cash and is periodically reimbursed for the exact amount necessary to bring it back to the fixed amount. (6)
Income averaging: a formula that allows taxpayers whose income fluctuates widely to average their income over five years. (Appendix F)
Income from operations: the excess of gross profit from sales over operating expenses. (5)
Income statement: a financial statement that shows the amount of income earned by a business over an accounting period. (1)
Income summary: a nominal account used during the closing process in which are summarized all revenues and expenses before the net amount is transferred to the capital account or retained earnings. (4)
Income tax allocation: an accounting method designed to accrue income taxes on the basis of accounting income whenever there are differences in accounting and taxable income. (13)
Income tax expense, see Provision for income taxes
Incremental analysis: a decision analysis format that highlights only relevant decision information or the differences between costs and revenues under two or more alternative courses of action. (25)
Index number: a number constructed by setting the base year equal to 100 percent and calculating other years in relation to the base year. (28)
Indirect cost: a manufacturing cost that is not traceable to a specific product or cost objective and must be assigned by some allocation method. (16)
Indirect labor: labor costs for production-related activities that cannot be associated with, or are not conveniently and economically traceable to, end products and must be assigned by some allocation method. (16)
Indirect materials: less significant materials and other production supplies that cannot be conveniently or economically assigned to specific products and must be assigned by some allocation method. (16)
Indirect method: method of preparing the statement of cash flows by beginning with the net income and listing all the adjustments necessary to convert net income to cash flow from operations. (27)
Inflation: an increase in the general price level.
Installment accounts receivable: accounts receivable that are payable in periodic payments. (7)
Intangible assets: long-term assets that have no physical substance but have a value based on rights or privileges accruing to the owner. (5, 10)
Interest: the cost associated with the use of money for a specific period of time. (9, Appendix C)

Interest coverage ratio: a ratio that measures the protection of creditors from a default on interest payments. (28)
Interest earned: payment by a bank of interest earned on a company's average balance which is reported by the bank on the bank statement. (6)
Interim financial statements: financial statements prepared on a condensed basis for an accounting period of less than one year. (28)
Internal accounting controls: the controls employed primarily to protect assets and ensure the accuracy and reliability of the accounting records. (6)
Internal administrative controls: controls established to ensure operational efficiency and adherence to managerial policies; related to the decision processes leading to management's authorization of transactions. (6)
Internal control: the plan of organization and all of the coordinate methods and measures adopted within a business to safeguard its assets, check the accuracy and reliability of its accounting data, promote operational efficiency, and encourage adherence to prescribed managerial policies. (6)
Internal Revenue Service (IRS): federal agency that interprets and enforces the U.S. tax laws governing the assessment and collection of revenue for operating the government. (1)
Inventory cost: cost recorded upon purchase of inventory; includes invoice price less cash discounts plus freight and transportation in and applicable insurance, taxes, and tariffs. (8)
Inventory turnover: a ratio that measures the relative size of inventory. (28)
Investment center: an organizational unit with a manager who is responsible for its actions, incuding costs, revenues, and resulting profit. In addition, the manager must be evaluated on the effective use of assets employed to generate those profits. (20)
Investments: assets, generally of a long-term nature, that are not used in the normal operation of a business and that management does not intend to convert to cash within the next year. (5)
Invoice: a document prepared by a supplier requesting payment for goods or services provided. (6)
Issued stock: shares of stock sold or otherwise transferred to the stockholders. (12)
Item-by-item method: a method of applying the lower-of-cost-or-market rule to inventory pricing. (8)

Job card: a labor card supplementing the time card, on which each employee's time on a specific job is recorded; used to support an employee's daily time recorded on the time card and to assign labor costs to specific jobs or batches of products. (17)
Job order: a customer order for a specific number of specially designed, made-to-order products. (17)
Job order cost card: a document maintained for each job or work order in process, upon which all costs of that job are recorded and accumulated as the job order is being worked on. These cards make up the subsidiary ledger of the Work in Process Inventory Control account. (17)
Job order cost accounting system: a product costing system used in the manufacturing of unique or special-order products in which direct materials, direct labor, and manufacturing overhead costs are assigned to specific job orders or batches of products. (17)
Joint cost: a cost that collectively applies or relates to several products or cost objectives and can be assigned to those cost objectives only by means of arbitrary cost allocation; also called common cost. (19)
Journal: a chronological record of all transactions; place where transactions are first recorded. (2)
Journal entry: a separate entry in the journal, that records a single transaction. (2)
Journalizing: the process of recording transactions in a journal. (2)

Last-in, first-out (LIFO) method: an inventory costing method under which the costs of the last items purchased are assigned to the first items sold and the cost of the inventory is composed of the cost of items from the oldest purchases. (8)
Ledger: a book or file of all of a company's accounts, arranged as in the chart of accounts. (2)
Ledger account form: a form of the account that has four columns, one for debit entries, one for credit entries, and two columns (debit and credit) for showing the balance of the account; used in the general ledger. (2)

Legal capital: the minimum amount that can be reported as contributed capital; usually equal to par value or stated value. (12)
Leverage: the use of debt financing. (28)
Liability: a debt of the business; an amount owed or an obligation to perform a service to creditors, employees, government bodies, or others; a claim against assets. (1, 9)
Limited life: the characteristic of a partnership shown when certain events such as the admission, withdrawal, or death of a partner can terminate the partnership. (11)
Liquidating dividend: a dividend that exceeds retained earnings. (13)
Liquidation: the process of ending a business; entails selling assets, paying liabilities, and distributing any remaining assets to the partners. (11)
Liquidity: the position of having enough funds on hand to pay a company's bills when they are due and provide for unanticipated needs for cash. (1)
Long-term liabilities: debts of a business that fall due more than one year ahead, beyond the normal operating cycle, or are to be paid out of noncurrent assets. (5, 9)
Long-term nonmonetary assets: assets that (1) have a useful life of more than one year, (2) are acquired for use in the operation of the business, and (3) are not intended for resale to customers; fixed assets. (8, 10)
Lower-of-cost-or-market (LCM) rule: a method of inventory pricing under which the inventory is priced at cost or market, whichever is lower. (8)

Major category method: a method of applying the lower-of-cost-or-market method to inventory pricing. (8)
Make-or-buy decision: a decision commonly faced by management as to whether to make the item, product, or component or to purchase it from outside sources. (25)
Management: the group of people in a business with overall responsibility for achieving the company's goals. (1)
Management accounting: the aspect of accounting that consists of specific information gathering and reporting concepts and accounting procedures that, when applied to a company's financial and production data, will satisfy internal management's needs for product costing information, data used for planning and control of operations, and special reports and analyses used to support management's decisions. (1, 15)
Management advisory services: consulting services offered by public accountants. (1)
Management by exception: a review process whereby management locates and analyzes only the areas of unusually good or bad performance. (23)
Management information system: the interconnected subsystems that provide the information necessary to operate a business. (1)
Manual data processing: a system of data processing in which recording, posting, and other bookkeeping procedures are done by hand.
Manufacturing cost flow: the defined or structured flow of direct materials, direct labor, and manufacturing overhead costs from their incurrence through the inventory accounts and finally to the Cost of Goods Sold account. (16)
Marginal cost: the change in total cost caused by a one unit change in output. (24)
Marginal revenue: the change in total revenue caused by a one unit change in output. (24)
Marginal tax rates: the tax rate that applies to the last increment of taxable income. (Appendix C)
Market: in inventory valuation, the current replacement cost of inventory. (8)
Marketable securities: investment in securities which are readily marketable; short-term investments. (7)
Market risk: the volatility or fluctuation of the price of a stock in relation to the volatility or fluctuation of the prices of other stocks. (28)
Market transfer price: a transfer price that is heavily influenced by prices external to a division or company. (24)
Market value: the price investors are willing to pay for a share of stock on the open market. (13)
Master budget: an integrated set of departmental or functional period budgets that have been consolidated into forecasted financial statements for the entire company. (21)
Matching rule: the rule of accounting that revenue must be assigned to the accounting period in which the goods were sold or the services performed, and expenses must be assigned to the accounting period in which they were used to produce revenue; the rule underlying accrual accounting. (3)
Materiality: an accounting convention that refers to the relative importance of an item. (B)

Materials inventory: an inventory account made up of the balances of materials and supplies on hand at a given time; also called the stores and materials inventory control account. (16)
Materials requisition: a document that must be completed and approved before raw materials are issued to production. This form is essential to the control of raw materials and contains such information as the types and quantities of raw materials and supplies needed and the supervisor's approval signature. (16)
Maturity date: the due date of a promissory note. (7)
Maturity value: the total proceeds of a promissory note including principal and interest at the maturity date. (7)
Merchandise inventory: goods on hand and available for sale to customers. (5)
Minority interest: the percentage of ownership attributable to minority stockholders times the net assets of the subsidiary, an amount which appears in the stockholders' equity section of a consolidated balance sheet.
Miscellaneous charges and credits: bank charges for services such as collection and payment of promissory notes, stopping payment on checks, and printing checks. (6)
Mixed cost: a cost category that results when more than one type of cost is charged to the same general ledger account. The Repairs and Maintenance account is an example of a mixed cost account. (19)
Monetary assets: consists of cash and other assets representing the right to receive a specific amount of cash. (8)
Money measure: a concept in accounting that requires that business transactions be measured in terms of money. (1)
Mortgage: a type of long-term debt secured by real property that is paid in equal monthly installments. (14)
Multinational corporations: corporations that do business or operate in more than one country; also, transnational corporation. (E)
Multistep form: form of the income statement that arrives at net income in steps. (5)
Mutual agency: the authority of partners to act as agents of the partnership within the scope of normal operations of the business. (11)

Natural resources: long-term assets purchased for the physical substance that can be taken from them and used up rather than for the value of their location. (10)
Negotiated transfer price: a transfer price that is bargained for by the managers of the buying and selling divisions. (24)
Net assets: the total of assets remaining after deducting liabilities; sometimes equated with owner's equity. (1)
Net capital gain: the excess of net long-term capital gain over any net short-term capital loss. (13, Appendix F)
Net income: the net increase in owner's equity resulting from the profit seeking operations of a company; net income = revenue − expenses. (1)
Net income per share, see Earnings per common share
Net long-term capital gain (or loss): the combined total of all gains and losses on long-term capital assets during a tax year. (13, Appendix F)
Net loss: the net decrease in owner's equity resulting from the profit seeking operations of a company; equals revenue minus expenses. (1)
Net method: recording purchases initially at the net price; allows a business to identify discounts lost, as well as discounts taken. (5)
Net of taxes: the effect of applicable taxes (usually income taxes) considered when determining the overall effect of an item on the financial statements. (13)
Net payroll: the amount paid to the employee (cash or check) after all payroll deductions have been subtracted from gross wages. (16)
Net purchases: under the periodic inventory method, gross purchases less purchases discounts, purchases returns and allowances, plus freight charges on the purchases. (5)
Net realizable value (NRV): the established selling price of an item in the ordinary course of business less reasonable selling costs.
Net sales: gross proceeds from sales of merchandise less sales returns and allowances and sales discounts. (5)
Net short-term capital gain (or loss): the combined total of all gains and losses on short-term assets during a tax year. (13, Appendix F)
Neutrality: carrying out generally accepted accounting principles as faithfully as possible, the main concern being relevance and reliability of the accounting information rather than the effect on a particular interest. (B)

Nominal accounts: temporary accounts showing the accumulation of revenue and expenses only for an accounting period; at the end of the accounting period, these account balances are transferred to owner's equity. (3)
Noncash expense: an expense—such as depreciation—that reduces net income and income tax expense, but for which there is no cash outflow in the period in which the expense is recognized. (26)
Noncumulative preferred stock: preferred stock on which the dividend may lapse and does not have to be paid if not paid within a given year. (12)
Nonmonetary assets: assets that represent unexpired costs that will become expenses in future accounting periods. (8)
No-par stock: capital stock that does not have a par value. (12)
Normal balance: the balance one would expect an account to have; the usual balance of an account. (2)
Normal capacity: the average annual level of operating capacity that is required to satisfy anticipated sales demand; adjusted to reflect seasonal business factors and operating cycles. (19, 23)
Notes to the financial statements: a section of a corporate annual report that contains notes that aid the user in interpreting some of the items in the financial statements. (5)
Notice of protest: a sworn statement that a promissory note was presented to the maker for payment and the maker refused to pay. (7)
NSF (nonsufficient funds) check: a check that is not paid when the depositor's bank presents it for payment to the maker's bank. (6)

Obsolescence: the process of becoming out of date; a contributor, together with physical deterioration, to the limited useful life of tangible assets. (10)
On-line processing: a type of computer system design in which input devices and random-access storage files are tied directly to the computer, enabling transactions to be entered into the records as they occur and data to be retrieved as needed.
Operating expenses: expenses other than cost of goods sold incurred in the operation of a business; especially selling and administrative expenses. (5)
Operating lease: periodic payment for the right to use an asset or assets, recorded in a manner similar to the way in which rent expense payments are recorded. A short-term cancelable lease for which the risks of ownership lie with the lessor. (14)
Opinion section (of accountant's report): the portion of the report that tells the results of the accountant's audit of the financial statements.
Ordinary annuity: a series of equal payments made at the end of equal intervals of time, with compound interest on these payments. (Appendix C)
Ordinary repairs: expenditures, usually of a recurring nature, that are necessary to maintain an asset in good operating condition.
Organization costs: the costs of forming a corporation. (12)
Other revenues and expenses: any revenues and expenses unrelated to normal business operations such as revenues from investments (dividends and interest from stocks, bonds, and savings accounts), interest earned on credit or from notes extended to customers, and interest expense and other expenses that result from borrowing money or from credit being extended to the company. (5)
Outstanding stock: the shares of a corporation's stock held by stockholders. (12)
Overapplied factory overhead, see underapplied factory overhead.
Overhead efficiency variance: the difference between actual direct labor hours worked and standard labor hours allowed, multiplied by the standard variable overhead rate. (23)
Overhead spending variance: the difference between the actual overhead costs incurred and the amount that should have been spent, based on actual hours worked or other productive input measures. (23)
Overhead volume variance: the difference between the factory overhead budgeted for the level of production achieved and the overhead applied to production using the standard overhead rate. (23)
Owner's equity: the resources invested by the owner of the business; assets − liabilities = owner's equity; also called residual equity. (1)
Owner's investments: assets that the owner puts into the business. (1)
Owner's withdrawals: assets that the owner takes out of the business. (1)

Parameters: in a management decision model, uncontrollable factors and operating constraints and limitations. (25)
Parent company: a company that owns a controlling interest in another company.
Participative budgeting: all levels of supervisory and data input personnel take part in the budgeting process in a meaningful, active way. (21)
Partners' equity: the owners' equity section of the balance sheet in a partnership. (11)
Partnership: an association of two or more persons to carry on as co-owners a business for profit. (1, 11)
Partnership agreement: the contractual relationship between partners that identifies the details of the partnership; agreement should clarify such things as name of the business, duties of partners, partner investments, profit and loss ratios, and procedures for admission and withdrawal of partners. (11)
Par value: the amount printed on each share of stock, which must be recorded in the capital stock accounts; used in determining the legal capital of a corporation. (12)
Payback method: a method used to evaluate a capital expenditure proposal that focuses on the cash flow of the project and determines the payback period or the time required to recoup the original investment through cash flow from the item or project. (26)
Payroll register: a detailed listing of a firm's total payroll, prepared each payday. (9)
Pension fund: contributions from both employer and employee out of which benefits to retirees are paid. (14)
Pension plan: a contract between a company and its employees wherein the company agrees to pay benefits after retirement. (14)
Percentage of net sales method: a method of estimating uncollectible accounts expense based on the assumption that a certain percentage of total net sales will not be collectible. (7)
Performance evaluation: the application of financial management techniques so actual results can be compared with expectations and performance judged. (20)
Period budget: a forecast of annual operating results for a segment or functional area of a company that represents a quantitative expression of planned activities. (21)
Period costs (expenses): expired costs of an accounting period that represent dollars attached to resources used or consumed during the period; any cost or expense item on an income statement. (16)
Periodic inventory method: a method of accounting for inventory under which the cost of goods sold is determined by adding the net cost of purchases to beginning inventory and subtracting the ending inventory. (5, 8, 16)
Periodicity: the assumption that the measurement of net income for any period less than the life of the business is necessarily tentative, but nevertheless a useful approximation. (3)
Perpetual inventory method: a method of accounting for inventory under which the sales and purchases of individual items of inventory are recorded continuously, therefore allowing cost of goods sold to be determined without taking a physical inventory. (5, 8, 22)
Petty cash fund: a small fund established by a company to make small payments of cash. (6)
Petty cash system, see Imprest system
Petty cash voucher: a document that supports each payment made out of a petty cash fund. (6)
Physical deterioration: one of two major factors causing tangible assets to have a limited useful life. (10) (see also Obsolescence)
Physical inventory, see Taking a physical inventory
Physical volume method: an approach to the problem of allocating joint production costs to specific products that is based on or uses some measure of physical volume (units, pounds, liters, grams, etc.) as the basis for joint cost allocation. (19)
Planning: the process of formulating a course of action. (1)
Portfolio: a group of loans or investments designed to average the return and risks of a creditor or investor. (28)
Post-closing trial balance: a trial balance prepared after all adjusting and closing entries have been posted and just before the next period as a final check on the balance of the ledger. (4)
Posting: the process of transferring journal entry information from the journal to the ledger. (2)
Potentially dilutive securities: the potential to dilute earnings per share, as held by stock options and convertible preferred stocks or bonds. (13)
Practical capacity: theoretical capacity reduced by normal and anticipated work stoppages. (19)
Predetermined overhead rate: an overhead cost factor that is used to assign manufacturing (factory) overhead costs (all indirect manufac-

turing costs) to specific units, jobs, or cost objectives. (17)

Predictive value: usefulness of information to the decision maker in making a prediction, not that it is itself a prediction; a qualitative characteristic of accounting information. (B)

Preferred stock: a type of stock that has some preference over common stock, usually including dividends. (12)

Premium: the amount by which the issue price of a stock or bond exceeds the face value. (14)

Prepaid expenses: expenses paid in advance that do not expire during the current accounting period; an asset account. (3)

Present value: the amount that must be invested now at a given rate of interest to produce a given future value. (Appendix C)

Present value method: a discounted cash flow approach to measure the estimated performance of a capital investment. The value of all future cash flows discounted back to the present (present value) must exceed the initial investment if a positive decision is to be made. (26)

Price/earnings (P/E) ratio: a ratio that measures the relationship of the current market price of a stock to the earnings per share. (28)

Price index: a series of numbers, one for each period, that represents an average price for a group of goods and services, relative to the average price of the same group of goods and services at a beginning date.

Primary earnings per share: net income applicable to common stock divided by the sum of the weighted-average common shares and common stock equivalents. (16) See also Earnings per (common) share.

Prior period adjustments: events or transactions that relate to an earlier accounting period but were not determinable in the earlier period. (13)

Proceeds from discounting: the amount received by the borrower when a promissory note is discounted; proceeds = maturity value − discount. (7)

Process cost accounting system: a product costing system used by companies that produce a large number of similar products or have a continuous production flow where manufacturing costs are accumulated by department or process rather than by batches of products. (17)

Product cost: costs identified as being either direct materials, direct labor, or manufacturing overhead, traceable or assignable to products; they become part of a product's unit manufacturing cost, and are in inventories at period end. (16)

Production method: a method of depreciation that bases the depreciation charge for a period of time solely on the amount of use of the asset during the period of time. (10)

Profit: imprecise term for the earnings of a business enterprise. (3)

Profitability: the ability of a business to earn a satisfactory level of profits and to attract investor capital. (1)

Profit center: an organizational unit with a manager who is responsible for its actions, including costs, revenues, and resulting profit. (20)

Profit margin: a measure of profitability; the percentage of each sales dollar that results in net income; net income divided by sales. (28)

Profit margin pricing: an approach to price determination in which the projected price equals total costs per unit times the total costs per unit plus a markup percentage. The markup percentage is computed by dividing the desired profit by total costs and expenses. (24)

Program: the means by which a computer is instructed; consists of a sequence of instructions that, when carried out, will produce a desired result.

Programmer: the person who writes the programs that instruct the computer based on the specifications of the systems analyst.

Progressive tax: a tax based on a rate structure that increases the rate of tax as the amount of taxable income becomes larger. (Appendix F)

Promissory note: an unconditional promise to pay a definite sum of money on demand or at a future date. (7)

Property, plant, and equipment: tangible assets of a long-term nature used in the continuing operation of the business. (5)

Proportional tax: method of taxation in which the rate holds to the same percentage, regardless of income. (Appendix F)

Protest fee: the charge made by a bank for preparing and mailing a notice of protest. (7)

Proxy: a legal document, signed by the stockholder, giving another party the authority to vote his or her shares. (12)

Public accounting: the field of accounting that offers services in auditing, taxes, and management advising to the public for a fee. (1)

Publicly held corporation: a corporation registered with the Securities and Exchange Commission; its securities are traded publicly.

Purchase method: a method of preparing consolidated financial statements.
Purchase order: a document prepared by the accounting department authorizing a supplier to ship specified goods or provide specified services. (6, 16)
Purchase requisition (request): a document, used to begin the raw materials purchasing function, that originates in the production department and identifies the items to be purchased, states the quantities required, and must be approved by a qualified manager or supervisor. (6, 16)
Purchases: an account used under the periodic inventory system in which the cost of all merchandise bought for resale is recorded. (5)
Purchases discounts: allowances made for prompt payment for merchandise purchased for resale; a contra purchases account. (5)
Purchases journal: a type of special-purchase journal in which are recorded credit purchases of merchandise (if it is a single-column journal) or credit purchases in general (if it is a multi-column journal). (A)
Purchases returns and allowances: account used to accumulate cash refunds and other allowances made by suppliers on merchandise originally purchased for resale; a contra purchases account. (5)
Purchasing power: the ability of a dollar at a point in time to purchase goods or services. (21)
Purchasing power gains and losses: gains and losses that occur as a result of holding monetary items during periods of inflation or deflation.

Qualitative characteristics: criteria for judging the information accountants provide to decision makers; the primary criteria are relevance and reliability. (6) See also Standards of quality.
Quick ratio: a ratio that measures the relationship of the more liquid current assets (cash, marketable securities, and accounts receivable) to current liabilities. (28)

Ratio analysis: a means of stating a meaningful relationship between two numbers. (28)
Real accounts: balance sheet accounts; accounts whose balances can extend past the end of an accounting period. (3)
Receivable turnover: a ratio that measures the relative size of accounts receivable. (28)
Receiving report: a document prepared when ordered goods are received, the data of which are matched with the descriptions and quantities listed on the purchase order to verify that the goods ordered were actually received. (6, 16)
Recognition problem: the difficulty of deciding when a business transaction occurs; usually determined to be the point in a sale when title is transferred. (2)
Registered bonds: bonds for which the name and address of the bond owner are recorded with the issuing company. (14)
Regressive tax: method of taxation in which the rate decreases as one's income rises. (Appendix F)
Relative sales value method: an approach to the problem of allocating joint production costs to specific products that is based on or uses the product's revenue-producing ability (sales value) as the basis for joint cost allocation. (19)
Relevance: standard of quality requiring that accounting information bear directly on the economic decision for which it is to be used; one of the primary qualitative characteristics of accounting information. (B)
Relevant decision information: future cost, revenue, or resource usage data used in decision analyses that differ among the decision's alternative courses of action. (25)
Relevant range: a range of productive activity that represents the potential volume levels within which actual operations are likely to occur. (19)
Reliability: standard of quality requiring that accounting information be faithful to the original data and that it be verifiable; one of the primary qualitative characteristics of accounting information. (B) See also Representational faithfulness and Verifiability.
Replacement cost: an entry value that represents the cost to buy (or replace), in the normal course of business, new assets of equivalent operating or productive capacity.
Reporting currency: currency in which the consolidated financial statements involving foreign subsidiaries are presented.
Representational faithfulness: the agreement of information with what it is supposed to represent. (B)
Residual equity: the common stock of a corporation. (12)
Residual value: the estimated net scrap, sal-

vage, or trade-in value of a tangible asset at the estimated date of disposal; also called salvage value or disposal value. (10)

Responsibility accounting system: an accounting system that personalizes accounting reports by classifying and reporting cost and revenue information according to defined responsibility areas of specific managers or management positions; also called activity accounting or profitability accounting. (20)

Responsibility center: an organizational unit identified in a responsibility accounting system whose manager is responsible for its actions: examples include a cost/expense center, a profit center, and an investment center. (20)

Retail method: a method of estimating inventory at cost in a retail enterprise. (8)

Retained earnings: the stockholders' equity that has arisen from retaining assets from earnings in the business; the accumulated earnings of a corporation from its inception minus any losses, dividends, or transfers to contributed capital. (13)

Return on assets: a measure of profitability that shows how efficiently a company is using all its assets; net income divided by total assets. (28)

Return on assets pricing: an approach to price determination in which a profit factor is added to the total cost and expenses per unit to arrive at the objective price. The profit factor is computed by multiplying the desired rate of return by total costs of assets employed and dividing this product by anticipated units to be produced. (24)

Return on equity: a measure of profitability related to the amount earned by a business in relation to the owners' investment in the business; net income divided by owners' equity. (28)

Return on investment: a performance indicator for divisions that relates properly measured operating income to average assets employed during a period. (20)

Revenue: a measure of the asset values received from customers during a specific period of time; equals the price of goods sold and services rendered during that time. (1)

Revenue expenditure: an expenditure necessary to maintain and operate plant and equipment; charged to expense because the benefits from the expenditure will be used up in the current period. (10)

Revenue recognition: the process of determining when a sale takes place; a technique of accrual accounting. (3)

Revenues from sales: revenues arising from sales of goods by the merchandising company. (5)

Reversing entries: optional general journal entries made on the first day of an accounting period that are the exact reverse of adjusting entries made in the previous period. (4)

Salaries: compensation to employees who are paid at a monthly or yearly rate. (9)

Sales discounts: discounts given to customers for early payment for sales made on credit; a contra sales account. (5)

Sales journal: a type of special-purpose journal used to record credit sales. (A)

Sales mix analysis: an analysis to determine the most profitable combination of product sales when a company produces more than one product. (25)

Sales returns and allowances: account used to accumulate amount of cash refund granted to customers or other allowances related to prior sales; a contra sales account. (5)

Salvage value, see Residual value

Schedule of equivalent production: a process costing schedule in which equivalent production is computed for the period for both materials and conversion costs. (18)

Scope section (of accountant's report): the portion of the accountant's report that tells the extent of the accountant's audit of the financial statements.

Secured bonds: bonds that give the bondholders a pledge of certain assets of the company as a guarantee of repayment. (14)

Securities and Exchange Commission (SEC): an agency of the federal government that has the legal power to set and enforce accounting practices for firms reporting to it. (1)

Semivariable cost: a cost that possesses both variable and fixed cost behavior characteristics in that part of the cost is fixed and part varies with the volume of output. (19)

Separate entity: a concept in accounting that requires a business to be treated as separate from its creditors, customers, and owners. (1)

Serial bonds: a bond issue with several different maturity dates. (14)

Share of stock: a unit of ownership in a corporation. (12)

Short-term investments (marketable securities): investments intended to be held only until needed to pay a current obligation. (7)

Short-term liquid assets: assets such as cash, temporary investments, accounts receivable, and notes receivable that derive their usefulness from their relative availability for the payment of current obligations; these assets are not used in the productive functions of the enterprise. (7)

Short-term nonmonetary assets: current assets such as inventory, supplies, and prepaid expenses. (8)

Significant influence (of investor over investee company): ability of an investor to affect operating and financial policies of an investee company, even though the investor holds less than 50 percent of the voting stock of the investee.

Simple capital structure: a capital structure with no other securities (either stocks or bonds) that can be converted into common stock. (13)

Simple interest: the interest cost for one or more periods, if one assumes that the amount on which the interest is computed stays the same from period to period. (Appendix C)

Single-step form: form of the income statement that arrives at net income in a single step. (5)

Software: comprises the programs, instructions, and routines that make possible the use of computer hardware.

Sole proprietorship: a business formed by one person. (1)

Source documents: written evidence supporting and detailing transactions.

Source of working capital: a transaction that results in net increase in working capital.

Special order decision: a type of decision faced by management in which a customer wishes to purchase a large number of similar or identical products at prices below those listed in brochures or advertisements. If capacity exists to produce the order while not disturbing the regular production process, the company can consider the order; also called special product order decision. (25)

Special-purpose journal: an input device in an accounting system that is used to record a single type of transaction. (A)

Specific-identification method: an inventory costing method under which the actual cost of specific items is used for determining cost of goods sold. (8)

Specific price level: a price level that reflects the price changes of a specific commodity or item.

Split-off point: a particular point in a manufacturing process where a joint product splits or divides and two or more separate products emerge. (19)

Standard costs: realistically predetermined costs for direct materials, direct labor, and factory overhead that are usually expressed as a cost per unit of finished product. (22)

Standard direct labor cost: a standard cost computed by multiplying the direct labor time standard by the direct labor rate standard. (22)

Standard direct materials cost: a standard cost computed by multiplying the direct materials price standard by the direct materials quantity standard. (22)

Standard factory overhead cost: a standard cost computed by multiplying the standard variable overhead rate and the standard fixed overhead rate by the appropriate application base. (22)

Standard fixed overhead rate: an overhead application rate computed by dividing the total budgeted fixed overhead costs by the normal capacity for the period. (22)

Standard variable overhead rate: an overhead application rate computed by dividing the total budgeted variable overhead costs by the application base being used by the company. (22)

Stated value: a value assigned by the board of directors to no-par stock. (12)

Statement of cash flows: shows the effects on cash of the operating, investing, and financing activities of a company for an accounting period. It will explain the net increase (or decrease) in cash during the accounting period. (27)

Statement of cost of goods manufactured: formal statement summarizing the flow of all manufacturing costs incurred during a period; yields the dollar amount of costs of products completed and transferred to Finished Goods Inventory in that period. (16)

Statement of owner's equity: a financial statement that shows the changes in the owner's capital account during the year. (1)

Statement of retained earnings: a statement summarizing the changes in retained earnings during an accounting period. (13)

Statement of stockholders' equity: summary of changes in components of the stockholders' equity section of the balance sheet. (13)

Stock certificate: a document issued to a

stockholder in a corporation indicating the number of shares of stock owned by the stockholder. (12)
Stock dividend: a proportional distribution of shares of a corporation's stock to the corporation's stockholders. (13)
Stockholders' equity: the owners' equity section of a corporation's balance sheet. (12)
Stock option plan: an agreement to issue stock to some or all employees according to terms set in the plan. (12)
Stock split: an increase in the number of outstanding shares of stock accompanied by a proportionate reduction in the par or stated value. (13)
Stock subscription: an issuance of stock where the investor agrees to pay for the stock on some future date or in installments at an agreed price. (12)
Straight-line method: a method of depreciation that assumes that depreciation is dependent on the passage of time and that allocates an equal amount of depreciation to each period of time; the method of amortizing bond discount that makes the amortization equal for each interest period. (10, 14)
Subsidiary: a company whose stock is more than 50 percent owned by another company.
Subsidiary ledger: a ledger separate from the general ledger; contains a group of related accounts the total of whose balances equals the balance of a controlling account in the general ledger. (A)
Successful efforts accounting: a method of accounting for oil and gas development and exploration costs under which the costs of successful exploration are capitalized and depleted over the useful life of the producing resources and the costs of unsuccessful explorations are expensed immediately. (10)
Summary of significant accounting policies: section of a corporate annual report that discloses which generally accepted accounting principles the company has followed in preparing the financial statements. (B)
Sum-of-the-years'-digits method: an accelerated method of depreciation. (10)
Supporting service function: an operating unit or department not directly involved in production but needed for the overall operation of the company. (19)
System design: a phase of system installation whose purpose is to formulate the new system or changes in the existing system.
System implementation: a phase of system installation whose purpose is to put in operating order a new system or change in an existing system.
System investigation: a phase of system installation whose purpose is to determine the requirements of a new system or to evaluate an existing system.
Systems analyst: the person who, in a computer system, carries out the functions of systems investigation and systems design.

T account: a form of an account which has a physical resemblance to the letter T; used to analyze transactions. (2)
Taking a physical inventory: the act of making a physical count of all merchandise on hand at the end of an accounting period. (5)
Tangible assets: long-term assets that have physical substance. (10)
Taxable income: the amount on which income taxes are assessed. (Appendix F)
Tax credits: deductions from the computed tax liability. (13, Appendix F)
Tax evasion: the illegal concealment of actual tax liabilities. (Appendix F)
Tax liability: the amount of tax that must be paid based on taxable income and the applicable tax table. (Appendix F)
Tax planning: the arrangement of a taxpayer's affairs in such a way as to incur the smallest legal tax. (Appendix F)
Tax services: services offered by public accountants in tax planning, compliance, and reporting. (1)
Term bonds: bonds of a bond issue that all mature at the same time. (14)
Theoretical capacity: the maximum productive output of a department or a company if all machinery and equipment were operated at optimum speed without any interruptions in production for a given time period; also called ideal capacity. (19)
Time card: a basic time record document of an employee upon which either the supervisor or a time clock records the daily starting and finishing times of the person. (16)
Time and materials pricing: an approach to price determination for a service-oriented business in which actual parts and labor costs are

used as the basis for computing the projected price. In addition to actual materials and labor cost, a factor including profit and overhead costs is multiplied by the actual materials and labor costs so as to include overhead and profit in the price. (24)

Timeliness: the qualitative characteristic of accounting information that reaches the user in time to help in making a decision. (B)

Total inventory method: a method of applying the lower-of-cost-or-market method to inventory pricing. (8)

Total manufacturing costs: a term used in the statement of cost of goods manufactured that represents the total of direct materials used, direct labor, and manufacturing overhead costs incurred and charged to production during an accounting period. (16)

Total overhead variance: the difference between actual overhead costs incurred and overhead costs applied to good units produced. (23)

Traceable fixed cost: fixed costs that are directly identified with a segment's operations and are assignable to a product or a segment without proration or allocation. (25)

Trade credit: credit to customers at either the wholesale or the retail level. (7)

Trade discounts: a price quoted below the catalogue or list price; a device to avoid frequent reprinting costs. (5)

Transfer price: the price at which goods and services are exchanged among company divisions. (24)

Transferred-in cost: costs transferred from a previous department or process in a process costing system. When accounting for costs and units transferred-in, treat them as you would materials added at the beginning of the process. (24)

Translation adjustments: changes in the financial statement due wholly to the exchange rate fluctuations.

Translation gains or losses: the effects of changes in the exchange rates as reported on the income statement.

Transportation in, see Freight in

Treasury stock: capital stock of a company, either common or preferred, that has been issued and reacquired by the issuing company but has not been reissued or retired. (13)

Trend analysis: the calculation of percentage changes for several successive years; a variation of horizontal analysis. (28)

Trial balance: a listing of accounts in the general ledger with their debit or credit balances in respective columns and a totaling of the columns; used to test the equality of debit and credit balances in the ledger. (2)

2/10, n/30: credit terms enabling the debtor to take a 2 percent discount if the invoice is paid within ten days after the invoice date; otherwise, the debtor must pay the full amount within thirty days. (5)

Uncollectible accounts: accounts receivable from customers who cannot or will not pay. (7)

Underapplied or overapplied factory overhead: the difference resulting when the amount of factory overhead costs applied to products during an accounting period is more or less than the actual amount of factory overhead costs incurred in that period. (17)

Understandability: the qualitative characteristic of accounting information that is presented in a form and in terms that its user can understand. (B)

Unearned revenue: a revenue received in advance for which the goods will not be delivered or the services performed during the current accounting period; a liability account. (3)

Unfavorable standard cost variance: a variance occurring when actual costs are greater than standard costs. (22, 23)

Unit cost: the amount of manufacturing costs incurred in the completion or production of one unit of product; usually computed by dividing total production costs for a job or period of time by the respective number of units produced. (17)

Unit cost analysis schedule: a process costing statement used to (1) accumulate all costs charged to the Work in Process Inventory account of each department or production process, and (2) compute cost per equivalent unit for materials and conversion costs. (18)

Unlimited liability: each partner has a personal liability for all debts of the partnership. (11)

Unsecured bonds: bonds issued on the general credit of a company; debenture bonds. (14)

Use of working capital: a transaction that results in a net decrease in working capital.

Valuation problem: the difficulty of assigning a value to a business transaction; in general, determined to be original, or historical, cost. (2)

Variable cost: a cost that changes in total in direct proportion to productive output or any other volume measure. (19)
Variable costing: an approach to product costing in which only variable manufacturing costs are assigned to products for product costing and inventory valuation purposes; also called direct costing. (25)
Variable cost pricing: an approach to price determination in which the projected price equals the variable production cost per unit times the variable production cost per unit plus a markup percentage. The markup percentage is computed by dividing the sum of the desired profit; total fixed production costs; and total selling, general, and administrative expenses by total variable production cost. (24)
Variable manufacturing costs: types of manufacturing costs that increase or decrease in direct proportion to the number of units produced. (16)
Variables: in a management decision model, factors controlled by management. (25)
Variance analysis: the process of computing the amount of, and isolating the causes of, differences between actual costs and standard costs. (22)
Verifiability: the qualitative characteristic of accounting information that can be confirmed or duplicated by independent parties using the same measurement techniques. (B)
Vertical analysis: the calculation of percentages to show the relationship of the component parts of a financial statement to the total in the statement. (28)
Voucher: a written authorization prepared for each expenditure in a voucher system. (6)
Voucher check: a check specifically designed for use in a voucher system. (6)
Voucher register: a special-purpose journal in which vouchers are recorded after they have been properly approved. (6)
Voucher system: any system providing documentary evidence of and written authorization for business transactions, usually associated with expenditures. (6)

Wages: compensation for employees at an hourly rate or on a piecework basis. (9)
Wasting assets: another term for natural resources. (10)
Working capital: the amount by which total current assets exceed total current liabilities
Working papers: documents prepared and used by the accountant that aid in organizing the accountant's work and provide evidence to support the basis of the financial statements. (4)
Work in process inventory: an inventory account unique to the manufacturing or production area to which all manufacturing costs incurred and assigned to products are charged. The balance at period-end represents all costs assigned to goods partially completed at that particular time. (16)
Work sheet: a type of working paper that is used as a preliminary step and aid to the preparation of financial statements. (4)

Zero bracket amount: an amount of gross income equal to the amount on which no income tax liability would result. (Appendix F)
Zero coupon bonds: bonds with no periodic interest payment, but simply a promise to pay a fixed amount at the maturity date. (14)

INDEX

Note: Boldface indicates a key term and the page where it is defined.